Frommer's

# POSTCARDS

## FROM

# SOUTHEAST ASIA

*Wat Benchamabophit (The Marble Wat), Bangkok, Thailand—one of the most beautiful of the city's royal temples. See chapter 5. © Paul Chesley/Tony Stone Images.*

*Barong dancer, Bali—an example of the integration of religion, mythology, music, dance, and art in everyday Balinese life. See chapter 10. © Cliff Hollenbeck Photography.*

*Pura Ulu Danau Temple, Lake Bratan, Bali—one of the most photographed temples on the island. See chapter 10. © John Elk III Photography.*

*Bangli Temple, Bali, Indonesia. See chapter 10. © Andrea Pistolesi Photography.*

*Sri Mariamman Temple nestled among the high-rises of modern Singapore. The oldest Hindu temple on the island, it's located in the Chinatown section, near Marina Bay. See chapter 8. © Robert Holmes Photography.*

*Hong Kong's Central District, as seen from Victoria Peak. See chapter 4. © John Elk III Photography.*

*Petaling Street, the center of the Chinatown district, Kuala Lumpur, Malaysia. See chapter 9. © Stuart Dee/The Image Bank.*

*Boating through Aberdeen Harbor, Hong Kong. Once a fishing village, Aberdeen is still known for its hundreds of sampans and junks, plus a couple of huge floating restaurants. See chapter 4. © Dave G. Houser Photography.*

*Wat Mahathat, a large temple complex in Sukhothai, first capital of Thailand. See chapter 5. © Dave G. Houser Photography.*

*Sri Mariamman Hindu Temple, Georgetown, Penang, Malaysia. Sri Mariamman is a Hindu goddess worshipped for her powers to cure disease. See chapter 9. © John Elk III Photography.*

*The Holy See of Cao Daism in Tay Ninh, Vietnam. Unique to Vietnam, Cao Dai draws its beliefs from a variety of world religions. Onlookers can watch the noon processional service from a balcony overhead. See chapter 6. © John Elk III Photography.*

*On the water near Pattaya, one of Thailand's most raucous resort areas. See chapter 5. © R. Steedman/The Stock Market.*

*Phuket, Southern Thailand's finest resort destination. See chapter 5. © Markham Johnson/ Robert Holmes Photography.*

*A local trimaran plies a lagoon off Miniloc Island in Palawan Province, the Philippines' last frontier. See chapter 11. © John Callahan/Tony Stone Images.*

*Wat Aham, one of the 33 historic Buddhist temples in Luang Prabang, Laos, a UNESCO World Heritage Site. See chapter 7. © Thomas Renaut/Tony Stone Images.*

*Local fisherman in Dalat, Vietnam. See chapter 6. © Robert Van Der Hilst/Tony Stone Images.*

*Entrance to Nghia An Hoi Quan Pagoda in Cholon, Ho Chi Minh City's Chinese district, Vietnam. See chapter 6. © John Elk III Photography.*

*Villa Escudero, Luzon, Philippines. Set amidst a pastoral grove of coconut palms, verdant fields, and mountains, the villa brings you back to the days of colonial plantation life. See chapter 11. © Robert Holmes Photography.*

*Orangutan, Sepilok, Malaysian Borneo. See chapter 9. © Joseph Van Os/The Image Bank.*

*Ifugao tribal couple, Banaue, Philippines. According to tribal mythology, the Ifugao ("eaters of rice") were descended from the deity Kabunyan. Their rice terraces were built as a tribute to the heavens in thanks for the sustaining food, and rise like stairways to Kabunyan's domain. See chapter 11. © Robert Holmes Photography.*

*Visitors enjoying an elephant ride at Maesa Elephant Camp in the mountains just north of Chiang Mai, Thailand. See chapter 5. © Dave G. Houser Photography.*

*World War II ruins at Corregidor Island, Philippines. A 1945 battle here ended with Americans retaking the island from the Japanese. See chapter 11. © Robert Holmes Photography.*

*Visitors near the mouth of the underground river at St. Paul's Subterranean National Park, Palawan, Philippines. Once inside, you travel 1.5 kilometers past stalagmites and stalactites. See chapter 11. © Robert Holmes Photography.*

Ifugao tribal couple, Banaue, Philippines. According to tribal mythology, the Ifugao ("eaters of rice") were descended from the deity Kabunyan. Their rice terraces were built as a tribute to the heavens in thanks for the sustaining food, and rise like stairways to Kabunyan's domain. See chapter 11. © Robert Holmes Photography.

Visitors enjoying an elephant ride at Maesa Elephant Camp in the mountains just north of Chiang Mai, Thailand. See chapter 5. © Dave G. Houser Photography.

*The king of the Philippine road, the ubiquitous jeepney. Your Philippines experience will not be complete without squeezing into or on top of one. See chapter 11. © Robert Holmes Photography.*

*Snorkler at El Nido, Miniloc Island, Palawan, Phillipines. See chapter 11. © Robert Holmes Photography.*

# Frommer's®

1st
Edition

# Southeast
# Asia

by Jennifer Eveland, Michelle Fama,
Mary Herczog, Stacy Lu, Beth Reiber,
and Jon Siskin

MACMILLAN • USA

## MACMILLAN TRAVEL

A Macmillan General Reference USA, Inc.
1633 Broadway
New York, NY 10019

Find us online at **www.frommers.com**

ISBN 0-02-862776-8
ISSN 1098-9455

Editors: David Gibbs, Matt Hannafin, Stacy Lu, Kelly Regan
Production Editor: Mark Enochs
Photo Editor: Richard Fox
Design by Michele Laseau
Digital Cartography by Roberta Stockwell and Gail Accardi
Page creation by John Bitter, Natalie Evans, and Dave Pruett
Front cover photo: Rics terraces, Bali.
Back cover photo: Marble Mountain, central Vietnam.

## SPECIAL SALES

Bulk purchases (10+ copies) of Frommer's and selected Macmillan travel guides are
available to corporations, organizations, mail-order catalogs, institutions, and charities at
special discounts, and can be customized to suit individual needs. For more information
write to Special Sales, Macmillan General Reference, 1633 Broadway, New York, NY
10019.

Manufactured in the United States of America

# Contents

# List of Maps

## ABOUT THE AUTHORS

**Jennifer Eveland** (Thailand, Malaysia, and Singapore) was a child when she and her family first moved to Singapore, and after returning to the United States, she was drawn again and again to the magic of Singapore, East Asia, and Southeast Asia. She is the author of *Frommer's Singapore & Malaysia* and *Frommer's Thailand,* 4$^{th}$ Edition (available February 2000), and currently lives in Bangkok, Thailand.

**Michelle Fama** (The Philippines) lived and traveled throughout East Africa, Egypt, and South America before coming aboard as the author of the Philippines chapter in this guide. She has been a producer at abcnews.com in New York and is currently a writer/producer for gorp.com, one of the leading outdoor recreation/adventure travel sites on the Web.

**Mary Herczog** (Bali and Lombok) lives in Los Angeles and works in the film industry when she isn't traveling and writing for Frommer's. Her other books include *Frommer's Las Vegas, Frommer's New Orleans,* and contributions to *Frommer's Los Angeles.* She hopes this list will soon include more exotic foreign destinations, though Bali—where she spent lots of time in the temples and so felt only marginally guilty when she did goof off on a beach—was a pretty good start.

**Stacy Lu** (Vietnam, Laos, and Cambodia) loves writing as a career, in part because it justifies her travel addiction: In 1998 she visited eleven countries, using the Netherlands and China as home bases. Her work has appeared in *The New York Times, Forbes Digital,* and *Travel Holiday.* She lives, for now, in Tarrytown, New York, and is a producer at abcnews.com.

**Beth Reiber** (Hong Kong) worked for several years in Germany as a freelance travel writer for major U.S. newspapers and in Tokyo as the editor of *Far East Traveler.* Now a freelancer again and residing in Lawrence, Kansas, with her husband and two young children, she is the author of *Frommer's Hong Kong, Frommer's Japan,* and *Frommer's Tokyo,* and is a contributor to *Frommer's Europe from $50 a Day.*

**Jonathan Siskin** (intro and planning chapters) is a peripatetic writer/broadcaster whose travels have taken him to more than 100 countries on all seven continents. His articles on leisure and business travel have appeared in newspapers and magazines from coast to coast and his radio reports have been heard worldwide over the Armed Forces Radio Network. While spending a year living in Australia, he took his first trip to Southeast Asia and continues to return to this incomparable part of the world as often as he can.

## ACKNOWLEDGMENTS

**Jennifer Eveland:** Thanks to Tania Goh at the Singapore Tourism Board; Azizah Aziz at the Malaysia Tourism Board in New York, and Cindy Lim at MTB in Kuala Lumpur; Nat Boonthanakit at the Tourism Authority of Thailand in New York; John Bozman, Kyle McCarthy, and John Levy for their work on previous editions of *Frommer's Thailand;* and all of the good people I met through my travels to research this work. With very special thanks to Andrew Chan in KL and BSB, Greg Duffell in BKK, Joy Cantarella and Tatiana Reis in NYC, Michele "The Hudak" Hudak for her deep insights into Burmese bark baths, and my family for their tireless source of support and inspiration. Finally, I wish to thank Matt Hannafin for blessing my life with this groovy job.

**Michelle Fama:** For their support, I'd like to thank the good people at the Holiday Inn–Manila, my sis Gina, Dave Morinelli, Mike at Red Coral Diving School in Boracay and "Bar 956," especially Devin Teal. A million thanks to Gregg Geller and Kelly Regan for giving me this opportunity. Finally, I wish to thank my family, especially Joanne Galbier for being a steady homebase. And, as always, gratitude to Jason Shipman for being my biggest cheerleader.

**Stacy Lu:** Boundless thanks to editor Kelly Regan for her help and concern, to Suzanne Kelleher for being my fairy godmother, to Barry "Dad" Hurchalla for editing and the use of his office, and to my marvelous husband, Henry Lu, for everything else.

**Mary Herczog:** Extra special thanks to Steve Hochman (for Bali music sections and superb travel companionship) and Melina Caruso. Thanks to Matt Hannafin and Derk Richardson, and to Joe Rhode for the Bali art section.

**Jon Siskin:** I am deeply grateful to photographer Lydia Maruszko who first opened my eyes to the pleasures of travel to distant lands. I'd also like to thank James Ruggia, Ken Fish, and Robert Philips, whose knowledge and insights proved invaluable in completing the introductory section of the book; and a special thanks to editor Matt Hannafin.

Special thanks to David Dannert for his invaluable research assistance.

## AN INVITATION TO THE READER

In researching this book, we discovered many wonderful places—hotels, restaurants, shops, and more. We're sure you'll find others. Please tell us about them, so we can share the information with your fellow travelers in upcoming editions. If you were disappointed with a recommendation, we'd love to know that, too. Please write to:

*Frommer's Southeast Asia, 1st Edition*
Macmillan Travel
1633 Broadway
New York, NY 10019

## AN ADDITIONAL NOTE

Please be advised that travel information is subject to change at any time—and this is especially true of prices. We therefore suggest that you write or call ahead for confirmation when making your travel plans. The authors, editors, and publisher cannot be held responsible for the experiences of readers while traveling. Your safety is important to us, however, so we encourage you to stay alert and be aware of your surroundings. Keep a close eye on cameras, purses, and wallets, all favorite targets of thieves and pickpockets.

## WHAT THE SYMBOLS MEAN

**✪ Frommer's Favorites**

Our favorite places and experiences—outstanding for quality, value, or both.
The following abbreviations are used for credit cards:

| | | | |
|---|---|---|---|
| AE | American Express | ER | enRoute |
| CB | Carte Blanche | JCB | Japan Credit Bank |
| DC | Diners Club | MC | MasterCard |
| DISC | Discover | V | Visa |

## FIND FROMMER'S ONLINE

Arthur Frommer's Budget Travel Online (www.frommers.com) offers more than 6,000 pages of up-to-the-minute travel information—including the latest bargains and candid, personal articles updated daily by Arthur Frommer himself. No other Web site offers such comprehensive and timely coverage of the world of travel.

# The Best of Southeast Asia

*By Jennifer Eveland, Michelle Fama, Mary Herczog, Stacy Lu,*
*and Beth Reiber*

To the Western visitor, Southeast Asia is an assault on the senses, an immersion into a way of life utterly unlike that to which we're accustomed. From bustling cities like Hong Kong, Singapore, and Kuala Lumpur to tiny fishing villages in Vietnam and the Philippines, from the jungles of Malaysian Borneo to the deluxe resorts of Bali, from the temples of Luang Prabang in Laos to the bacchanal of Patpong in Thailand, Southeast Asia offers a glimpse of the extraordinary, an explosion of colors, sounds, smells, textures, and *life* that will send you home with a wider vision of the human experience. In this chapter, we'll share our picks of the region's unrivaled highlights.

## 1 The Most Unforgettable Travel Experiences

- **Riding the Star Ferry (Hong Kong).** To reacquaint myself with the city, one of the first things I do on each return trip is hop aboard the Star Ferry for one of the most dramatic—and cheapest—5-minute boat rides in the world. Hong Kong's harbor is one of the world's busiest, and beyond it rises one of earth's most breathtaking skylines. See chapter 4.
- **Gazing upon Hong Kong from Victoria Peak (Hong Kong).** You don't know Hong Kong until you've seen it from here. Take the tram to Victoria Peak, famous for its views of Central, the harbor, and Kowloon beyond, followed by a 1-hour circular hike and a meal with a view. Don't miss the nighttime view, one of the most spectacular and romantic in the world. See chapter 4.
- **Making merit (Thailand).** In Thailand, Buddhist monks do not earn income, but survive on gifts of food and necessary items given by devoted Buddhists in the community. The monk in his gold-colored robes who walks from house to house each morning is not begging for food, but is offering an opportunity for the giver to receive merit. In contributing to the monk's survival, the giver of food and gifts is supporting the *sangha*, the monkhood, and therefore becomes closer to Buddhist ideals. I once had the opportunity to make merit at a small temple. The captain of the boat I was aboard escorted me to the abbot, to whom I presented a bucket filled with all-purpose items, following the customs the captain taught me. In return I was blessed with a prayer, and a

# Southeast Asia

deeper view of the ways in which the Thai people respect their religion. If you are interested in making merit this way, talk to your hotel's concierge. You may be able to join kitchen staff as they head to a nearby monastery in the early morning. See chapter 5.

- **Staying in a village stilt house (Vietnam).** It's as much due to a lack of tourist facilities as to personal choice, but traveling to the northern hills and far south of Vietnam, you may find yourself bunked in a local house, many traditionally built on stilts that sit out over water or mountain. This will be a supremely unique experience; staying in stilts provides the best chance of really seeing how the villagers live. See chapter 6.

- **Participating in a Baci ceremony (Laos).** The Baci is a touching Lao ceremony used to say welcome or farewell and to honor achievements. Participants sit in a circle and receive group blessings, after which there is traditional dancing and *lao lao,* rice wine. It's a chance for the ultra-friendly Lao people to express their hospitality to you, their honored guest. See chapter 7.

- **Sipping a Singapore Sling in the Long Bar (Raffles Hotel, Singapore).** Ahhhh, the Long Bar. Home of the Singapore Sling. I like to come in the afternoons, before the tourist rush. Sheltered by long timber shutters that close out the tropical sun, the air cooled by lazy punkahs (small fans that wave gently back and forth above), you can sit back in old rattan chairs and have your saronged waitress serve you sticky alcoholic creations while you toss back a few dainty crab cakes. Life can be so decadent. OK, so the punkahs are electric, and, come to think of it, the place is air-conditioned (not to mention that it costs a small fortune), but it's fun to image the days when Somerset Maugham, Rudyard Kipling, or Charlie Chaplin would be sitting at the bar sipping Slings and spinning exotic tales of their world travels. Drink up, my friend; it's a lovely high. See chapter 8.

- **Walking the streets of Georgetown (Penang, Malaysia).** Evidence of former British colonization and early Chinese, Indian, and Arab immigration is apparent in many major cities in Malaysia, but Penang has a special charm. In some ways the city still operates the way it did half a century ago. The shophouses are filled with small businesses—bicycle repair shops, hardware stores, Chinese medicine halls, coffee shops. From upstairs windows you can still see laundry hanging on bamboo poles. Life hums in these streets, and for anyone who has witnessed the homogenization of Singapore, or the modernization of Kuala Lumpur, Penang is a charming reminder of what life may have been like in these old outposts. See chapter 9.

- **Observing open-air public cremations (Bali).** As Hindus believe that cremation is the only way a soul can be freed of its earthly body and travel to its next incarnation (or to enlightenment), cremations are joyous occasions, full of floats and fanfare that can resemble a Mardi Gras parade. Complicated towers hold the body, carried aloft by cheering men. At the burning ground, the body is placed in a receptacle resembling a winged lion, a bull, or some other fabulous creature, and set on fire. It's beautiful and awesome, a marvelous show of pageantry and faith, and yet a natural part of everyday life. See chapter 10.

- **Sharing an Ifugao tradition (Batad, Philippines).** Make the strenuous hike to the village of Batad, where you can watch the Ifugao people cultivating and maintaining their magnificent rice terraces. You will walk along the terraces and down many (I mean many) stairs and finally be among the villagers. Most likely you'll be invited inside a traditional Nipa Hut. Ask to taste the rice wine and you will not only get a glass and a course on how they make it, but will be shown many hunting treasures like boar and monkey skulls as well as a most touching heirloom: grandpa's bones in a bag. It's a traditional practice among the Ifugao people to keep the bones of their ancestors. See chapter 11.

- **Sunset at El Nido (Palawan, Philippines).** "Have you ever seen heaven?" a local boy asked me while I was lounging on the beach. Before I could reply, he simply pointed to the horizon and left. Filipinos pride themselves on having beautiful, heavenly sunsets and no matter how many times they see it, they always stop to admire it. I was looking out over the calm South China Sea. Falling coconuts and the distinctive drawling croak of the monitor lizard were the only sounds I heard. The breeze was a whisper and everything else natural seemed to settle back in awe of the sky's portrait. See chapter 11.

## 2 The Best Small Towns & Villages

- **Chiang Saen (Thailand).** Crumbling 11th-century temples and a splendid museum take you back to the birthplace of the Lanna Kingdom, one of Thailand's wealthiest and most influential. The neighboring Golden Triangle, notorious trade point for the international opium industry, snaps you back to modern realities. See chapter 5.

- **Hoi An (Vietnam).** The small size of Hoi An belies its importance to Vietnam; it was once a major trading port, with canals leading right up to merchants' quarters for easy delivery of goods. The canals are now peaceful streets, but not much else has changed. Almost every building in central Hoi An is a historic Vietnamese-, Japanese-, and Chinese-influenced residence or meeting hall. It's a captivating, friendly spot on the Perfume River. See chapter 6.

- **Kuala Terengganu (Malaysia).** The capital of Malaysian handicrafts has yet to be plotted on any standard tourist itinerary. Explore the city's cottage industries and experience a more orthodox side of Malaysian Islam in this quiet cultural gem. See chapter 9.

- **Ubud (Bali).** The teeming center of Bali, bursting with art and greenery and some of the best food on the island. Even though it's dependent on tourism and far from a typical Bali village, you still get a sense of a real town, with real life going on around you. Ubud is the richest region in Bali for art production and, as it's centrally located, is the perfect base for exploring the rest of the island. See chapter 10.

- **Sagada (Northern Luzon, Philippines).** Green hills, cliff-side hiking trails, Saturday markets, and life untouched by the hand of tourism mark this intriguing, small, quaint, and beautiful village in Mountain Province, home to the colorful Ifugao people. See chapter 11.

## 3 The Best Beaches

- **Chaweng Beach (Ko Samui, Thailand).** Chaweng is total fun in the sun. The beach itself is gorgeous, with bungalows nestled in the trees just beyond the sand. Behind the beach lies a small town full of life, from wonderful Thai and seafood eateries to shopping to wild nightlife options. See chapter 5.

- **Phan Thiet (Vietnam).** Phan Thiet is the latest paradise to be discovered in Vietnam. Right now it's developed enough to be comfortable without being overrun. Imagine a white sand beach near a small fishing village, only 3 miles from Saigon, with a lovely resort that costs only a little more than US$60 a night. Put a new golf course designed by Nick Faldo nearby and you've got Phan Thiet. See chapter 6.

- **Nha Trang (Vietnam).** What makes Nha Trang so much fun is the very Vietnamese resort flavor that surrounds it, including masseuses and manicurists wandering along the sands peddling their services, and inexpensive, delicious, and abundant seafood. The coast also faces gorgeous outlying islands, to which there are all manner of available boat trips: snorkeling, diving, and just plain drinking. See chapter 6.

- **Juara Bay (Tioman Island, Malaysia).** This beach is what they meant when they coined the word "isolated." Be prepared to live like Robinson Crusoe—in tiny huts with cold-water showers, many with no electricity at all. But, oh, the beach! A wide crescent of palm-lined sand hugging the clearest blue water, and with very few other people in sight. See chapter 9.

- **Lombok (Indonesia).** The pure white sand beaches of Lombok, with clear aquablue water lapping against them, are sometimes so private you can have one all to yourself. And it's just a short hop from neighboring Bali. See chapter 10.

- **Boracay (Philippines).** Despite the criticism that it's become overrun with tourism, Boracay's talcum-white sand beaches still remain enchanting and postcard perfect. The calm, clear waters are just right for snorkeling, diving, or just relaxing. Life couldn't get much better than simultaneously getting a one-hour back massage for $3 and a manicure for $1. Her name was Sinead and her red vest said "Massage 63." These numbered back healers comb the white beaches until shortly after dark, so don't worry, they'll find you. After rubbing coconut oil all over you, their magic hands will have you feeling better than the tin man after a lube job. See chapter 11.

## 4 The Best Outdoor Adventures

- **Phang-nga Bay (Thailand).** From the island of Phuket, sea canoe operators guide visitors through the caves hidden deep inside the craggy island-rocks of Phang-nga Bay. Outside, the islands thrust up to the sky, their jagged edges laced with scattered trees. Lie flat in your canoe to slip through the small cave openings, inside which you'll find magnificent chambers believed to have once hidden pirate operations. See chapter 5.

- **Sea kayaking in Halong Bay (Vietnam).** The more than 3,000 arresting limestone karst formations rising out of Halong Bay's peaceful blue-green waters provide a natural obstacle course for paddling. Moving among them, you'll pass in and among intriguing grottos and caverns. Nights are spent camping out in natural parks or on the deck of a mother ship. See chapter 6.

- **Caving in Vang Vien (Laos).** There are countless caves and caverns hidden in the magnificent mountains surrounding Vang Vieng, a small village along the Nam Song River. Some of them are well known and some are barely on the map. Either way, exploring them and the small town below is truly an adventure. See chapter 7.

- **Tioman Island or Redang Marine Park (Malaysia).** If you scuba dive or would like to learn how, the waters here are packed with exciting corals and creatures accessible through experienced dive operators. Snorkeling trips are also common, and reveal the magic of the sea to those who wish to stay closer to the surface. See chapter 9.

- **Scuba diving and snorkeling in Taman Negara (Malaysia).** With suitable options for all budgets and levels of comfort and desired adventure, Malaysia's largest national park opens the wonders of primary rain forest and the creatures who dwell in it to everyone. From the canopy, walk high atop the forest to night watches for nocturnal life, this adventure is as stunning as it is informative. See chapter 9.
- **Hiking Gunung Agung (Bali).** Bali's highest mountain/volcano, Gunung Agung (9,888 ft. or 3,014m high), is utterly sacred to the Balinese, who believe it to be the center of the world. Climbing it is a serious trek that absolutely calls for a guide and proper supplies. Most hotels can arrange for it, but you will have to start out in the middle of the night or very early in the morning to make the top by sunrise. See chapter 10.
- **Riding an elephant at the Elephant Safari Park (Pesanggaran, Bali).** Take a jostling, swaying trip through the jungle, then be sure to do the optional elephant bath. This entails mounting an elephant bareback, arms about a guide's waist, and riding along as the animal slowly walks into a deep pool of (clean) river water. At the handler's command the elephant rears up and plunges in to its knees, submerging you up to your chin. Maybe the most fun I had in Bali. See chapter 10.
- **Experiencing underwater Philippines (Palawan, Philippines).** In El Nido, all I could hear was the rhythmic hissing of packaged air being sucked into my lungs and bubbles being exhaled. I felt no weight, only freedom and extreme curiosity. For the non-diver, the experience of the first introductory dive is amazing. And for seasoned scuba divers, you already understand the privilege and beauty of visiting the foreign living room of the coral reefs. Bat fish, puffer fish, angel fish, lion fish, moray eels, turtles, and, yes, sharks—all are represented here in the Philippines, considered one of the best diving destinations in the world. See chapter 11.
- **Swimming with whale sharks (Luzon, Philippines).** In Donsol Lake, near the town of Legazpi in Southern Luzon, await the world's largest fish. You have an unforgettable opportunity to get up close and personal with these gentle giants as you snorkel above them and beside them. Be careful not to get too close to their huge mouths! See chapter 11.
- **Trekking Mount Pinatubo (Philippines).** The lunar-looking Lahar, the gritty sand and ash that Pinatubo spewed into the atmosphere when it erupted in 1991, makes you feel like you are on the moon or in some sci-fi flick. The 5-hour hike through the lahar fields and hot sulfuric ravines is well worth the wet shoes and intense heat. Below the crater rim is a hot but gorgeous aquamarine lake. Take a swim in its buoyant waters and watch the smoke escaping from the earth's crevices. Beware of quicksand. See chapter 11.

## 5 The Most Intriguing Temples, Shrines, Palaces & Archaeological Sites

- **The Giant Buddha (Hong Kong).** Laze on the open aft-deck during the hour-long ferry ride to Lantau island (and enjoy great views of the harbor and skyline along the way), followed by a ride over lush hills to see the world's largest, seated, outdoor bronze Buddha, located at the Po Lin Monastery. Complete your pilgrimage with a vegetarian meal at the monastery. See chapter 4.

- **The Grand Palace & Wat Phra Kaeo (Bangkok, Thailand).** These two places are number-one on every travel itinerary to Bangkok, and rightly so. The palace is indeed grand, with mixtures of traditional Thai and European Victorian architecture. Wat Phra Kaeo, the royal temple that houses Thailand's revered and mysterious Emerald Buddha, is a small city in itself, with a dozen or more picturesque outer buildings and monuments that devour rolls of film. See chapter 5.
- **Ayutthaya (Thailand).** Before Bangkok, there was Ayutthaya. This was the thriving capital of Siam that the first Europeans saw when they visited Amazing Thailand. A rich and powerful kingdom of over a million inhabitants, the monarchy supported the arts, especially literature, and as the city grew, international trade was encouraged. All that remains are brick remnants of a grand palace and many temples that were sacked during the Burmese invasion. It's best to hire a guide who can walk you through and point out the significance of each site. See chapter 5.
- **Emperor Jade Pagoda (Saigon, Vietnam).** The Emperor Jade, a classical Chinese temple, looks like the movie set of what an exotic pagoda should look like. Filled with smoky incense and bowing worshippers, it's chockablock with fantastic carved figurines depicting heaven, hell, and everything in between. See chapter 6.
- **Tomb of Khai Dinh (Hue, Vietnam).** Khai Dinh was an egotistic, eccentric emperor, which was bad for the people of Vietnam but great for the tomb he left behind. A gaudy mix of gothic, baroque, and classical Chinese architecture, the exterior is remarkable, and the stunning interior is completely covered with intricate glass and ceramic mosaic work. See chapter 6.
- **Wat Xieng Thong (Luang Prabang, Laos).** The glittering Xieng Thong, built in 1560, sits grandly on a peninsula jutting out into the Mekong River. The facades of two of its buildings are covered with glittering glass mosaics; another building contains an ornate chariot with the heads of seven dragons and the remains of a king. There are also about a dozen English-speaking monks roaming the premises, all excellent conversationalists. See chapter 7.
- **Plain of Jars (Xieng Kuong, Laos).** How did hundreds of huge stone urns, one almost 10 feet tall, come to be placed on a few meadows in northern Laos? No one really knows. The most likely explanation is that the urns were made by prehistoric folk in the area about 2,000 years ago, to be used as sarcophagi. See chapter 7.
- **Thian Hock Keng (Singapore).** One of Singapore's oldest Chinese temples, it is a fascinating testimony to Chinese Buddhism combined with traditional Confucian beliefs and natural Taoist principles. Equally fascinating is the modern world that carries on just outside the old temple's doors. See chapter 8.
- **Jame Mosque (Kuala Lumpur, Malaysia).** Built at the central point of the city, this is one of the oldest mosques in Kuala Lumpur. It is the heart of Malay Islam, as evidenced by the Muslim shops, eateries, and daily activities carrying on in the streets surrounding it. See chapter 9.
- **Jalan Tokong (Malacca, Malaysia).** This street, in the historical heart of the city, has a Malay mosque, a Chinese temple, and a Hindu temple living peacefully side-by-side—the perfect example of how the many foreign religions that came to Southeast Asia shaped its communities and learned to coexist in harmony. See chapter 9.
- **Gunung Kawi (Bali).** Gunung Kawi is a shrine consisting of monolithic fauxtombs, the origin and purpose of which remain unknown—a fact that only adds to their power and mystery. An outstanding, awe-inducing sight. See chapter 10.

## 6 The Best Museums

- **National Museum (Bangkok, Thailand).** From pre-history to recent events, this museum—the former palace of the brother of King Rama I—answers many questions about Thai history and culture through the ages. Inside buildings that are themselves works of fine Thai design, you'll find Buddha images, ancient arts, royal paraphernalia, and fine arts. Rama's sister also lived here, and her house is decorated in the same style as it was in the late 1700s. See chapter 5.
- **Vietnam History Museum (Saigon, Vietnam).** This museum does an all-round good job of presenting Vietnam's (particularly South Vietnam's) culture and history. From prehistoric objects to imperial housewares and exhibits on ethnic minorities, you'll be able to easily take in the show thanks to the extensive English explanations. See chapter 6.
- **The Cham Museum (Danang, Vietnam).** This open-air colonial structure houses the largest collection of Cham sculpture in the world. Not only are relics of this ancient Hindu-inspired culture rare, but the religious artwork itself—more than 300 pieces of sandstone—is voluptuous, captivating, and intense. See chapter 6.
- **Images of Singapore (Sentosa Island, Singapore).** No one has done a better job than this museum in chronicling for the public the horrors of the Pacific Theatre and Japanese Occupation in Southeast Asia. Video and audio displays take you on a chronological journey through Singapore's World War II experience. The grand finale is the Surrender Chambers, life-sized wax dioramas of the fateful events. Oh yeah, and there's also dioramas depicting historical figures throughout Singapore's early development, as well as depictions of traditional cultural festivals. See chapter 8.

## 7 The Best Festivals & Celebrations

- **Chinese New Year (Hong Kong and Singapore).** If you're in Southeast Asia around the end of January, beginning of February, hop up to Hong Kong or down to Singapore for the festivities. It's a 3-day party, with parades (complete with dragons and stilt-walkers) and fireworks. See chapters 4 and 8.
- **Songkran (Thailand).** Every year from the 13th to the 15th of April, Thais welcome the New Year (according to their calendar), and since Songkran falls in the middle of the hottest season in an already hot country, how do you think people celebrate? Every Thai heads out into the streets with water guns and buckets of ice water (sometimes laced with talcum powder, just to add to the mess), and spends the next three days soaking each other, and *you*. Foreigners are especially favorite targets. Don't get mad, arm thyself: Water bazookas are on sale everywhere. Have a ball! See chapter 5.
- **Mid-Autumn Festival (Vietnam).** This lunar celebration, usually taking place in late September or early October, has the stuff of all great holidays: color, pageantry, and adorable children, who dance and parade through towns carrying paper lanterns they've made themselves.
- **That Luang Festival (Vientiane, Laos).** Thousands of Buddhist followers from all over the country, and even a few neighboring countries, converge on the spectacular That Luang temple in Vientiane. There are alms-giving ceremonies and flower processions, and then the whole affair dissolves into a carnival that stretches over several days. See chapter 7.

- **Thaipusam (Singapore and Malaysia).** Around the end of January, beginning of February, Hindus celebrate Thaipusam. Men give thanks for prayers answered by carrying kavadis, huge steel racks attached to their bodies with skewers piercing the skin. Cheeks are pierced and fruits are hung from the skin using sharp hooks. A parade of devotees carry these things in a deep trance—and the next day they wake up virtually unharmed. See chapters 8 and 9.
- **Masskara Festival (Bacolod City, Philippines).** Bring your beads, masks, and pig-catching and pole-climbing skills for this event, held every October 6–19 in Bacolod City, Negros Island. You'll be dancing in the streets all in the name of lifting the spirits. Locals and tourists come from all over for this festival. It's the Filipino version of Mardi Gras or Carnival.

## 8  The Biggest Cultural No-Nos

- **Photographing a villager without permission in Vietnam.** There's nothing a visitor wants more than to take away indelible images of the colorful, rustic lifestyles of the Vietnamese ethnic minorities. However, many rural people are superstitious about photographs or may resent the intrusion of privacy. Ask first. See chapter 6, plus "Etiquette Tips" in chapter 2.
- **Losing your temper in Laos or Thailand:** The Lao and Thai people enjoy a Buddhist sensibility in their daily life, approaching even unfortunate events with calm cheerfulness. They would be shocked and dismayed at anger or ill temper, and raising your voice won't achieve any purpose whatsoever. No matter how frustrated you become, keep it under wraps, or the people around you will see to it you never get where you need to go. See chapters 7 and 5, plus "Etiquette Tips" in chapter 2.
- **Looking (or being) poor in Singapore.** You probably won't run into too many cultural faux pas in cosmopolitan Singapore, but in Singapore, poverty is the pits. Bring your smartest clothes and your coolest attitude if you want to impress the locals here. See chapter 8, plus "Etiquette Tips" in chapter 2.
- **Using your left hand for anything in Bali, Lombok, Singapore, or Malaysia.** Particularly avoid using it to touch people. (It's used for more hygienic matters only.) Touching children's heads as well—with left hand *or* right—will make you unpopular, as the head is the holiest part of the body. See chapters 10, 8, and 9, plus "Etiquette Tips" in chapter 2.
- **Hanging clothes to dry in Bali.** Or otherwise out in public (off hotel balconies and chairs and the like). See chapter 10, plus "Etiquette Tips" in chapter 2.
- **Showing too much skin (regional).** Except perhaps in Hong Kong and Singapore and in heavily touristed areas, modest Southeast Asians accept beachwear at the beach, revealing vacation clothing at resorts, and sexy attire at discos. Everywhere else, dress with respect for the locals and their traditions. See "Etiquette Tips" in chapter 2.
- **Wearing shorts or short skirts to a temple or mosque (regional).** It'll get you tossed out. See "Etiquette Tips" in chapter 2.

## 9  The Best Resorts & Luxury Hotels

- **The Peninsula Hotel (Hong Kong).** Hong Kong's most famous hotel exudes elegance, from its Rolls-Royce fleet to the white-gloved doormen that stand at attention outside the palatial, gilded lobby. Rooms in the 32-story tower sport unparalleled views of Victoria Harbour, and even jaded travelers are likely to be impressed with the sheer breadth of amenities offered here. See chapter 4.

- **Island Shangri-La Hong Kong (Hong Kong).** Viennese chandeliers, Oriental carpets, and more than 500 paintings and artwork adorn this, the tallest hotel on Hong Kong Island. The 17-story atrium features a marvelous 16-story-high Chinese painting, believed to be the largest landscape painting in the world. Spacious, impeccable rooms face either the Peak or Victoria Harbour—both stunning views. See chapter 4.

- **The Oriental Hotel (Bangkok, Thailand).** The original address in Thailand, The Oriental has seen modernization detract from its charms of yesterday, but there's still ambience all around. See chapter 5.

- **The Amanpuri (Phuket, Thailand).** A seductive bungalow resort in exquisite Thai style that will thrill even the most discerning guests. See chapter 5.

- **The Regent (Chiang Mai, Thailand).** Luxurious Thai-style suites, excellent restaurants, a multitude of activities, and the most amazing swimming pool you've ever seen await you. Don't forget to meet their resident water buffalo family—they work the resort's private rice paddies. See chapter 5.

- **Ana Mandara Beachside Resort (Nha Trang, Vietnam).** The details are perfect in this small-scale resort, from the incense burning in the open longhouse-style lobby to the small signs identifying tropical fish in the lobby's pond. Each stylish room has the air of a secluded hut with its own veranda, many overlooking the palm-lined coast. Both the food and the staff's smiles are perfect. See chapter 6.

- **Raffles Hotel (Singapore).** For Old World opulence, Raffles is second to none. A pure fantasy of the days when tigers still lurked around the perimeters. See chapter 8.

- **Four Seasons Hotel (Singapore).** Elegance and warmth combine to make this place a good bet. Consider a regular room here before you book a suite elsewhere. See chapter 8.

- **The Regent (Kuala Lumpur, Malaysia).** For my money, the Regent offers the smartest decor, best service, and best selection of facilities in the whole city. See chapter 9.

- **The Aryani Resort (Kuala Terengganu, Malaysia).** An exotic retreat, Aryani combines local Terengganu flavors with all the pampering you'd want from a getaway resort. See chapter 9.

- **Shangri-La's Rasa Sayang Resort (Penang, Malaysia).** The oldest resort on the beach has claimed the best stretch of sand and snuggled the most imaginatively modern yet traditionally designed resort in gardens just beyond. See chapter 9.

- **The Four Seasons (Jimbaran, Bali).** With its individual bungalows and plunge pools overlooking the blue blue sea and its famous Four Seasons pampering, The Four Seasons Jimbaran is one of the great hotels in the world. See chapter 10.

- **Amandari (Ubud, Bali).** Its individual bungalows overlooking a deep green gorge, the Amandari offers another sybaritic Bali experience. If you can afford it (or the Four Seasons Jimbaran), do. Even if you can't, do. See chapter 10.

- **Amanpulo (North of Palawan, Philippines).** There is none finer in all of the Philippines than this exclusive resort, situated on its own private island north of Palawan. A peaceful oasis for rich, famous, and powerful people who want to be pampered with private Jacuzzis, private beaches, personal service, and your very own personal motorized cart to tote you around the beautiful surroundings. See chapter 11.

## 10   The Best Hotel Bargains

- **Bossotel Inn (Bangkok, Thailand).** Located in a prime spot, close to the Chao Phraya River, the Bossotel is the perfect budget answer to the Shangri-La and Orientals that dominate accommodations along the river. See chapter 5.
- **River Ping Palace (Chiang Mai, Thailand).** If you're going to travel on a budget, do it with style—and style is what River Ping Palace has wrapped up in its old Thai-style teak mansion buildings. See chapter 5.
- **Delta Caravelle Hotel (Saigon, Vietnam).** The Caravelle is exemplary of the many bargains to be had in Saigon. Just renovated, it features plush, comfortable rooms in a huge downtown hotel with all the amenities, including a deluxe gym and spa and the hippest bar in Saigon. All this for $89 per double room and $160 a suite, including breakfast. See chapter 6.
- **Anou Hotel (Vientiane, Laos).** The Anou is clean, bright, and friendly, and in a fantastic downtown location. The big rooms, going for US$25 to US$35, feature real wood floors and comfortable beds, and the suites are huge. This is the kind of hotel that makes Southeast Asia such a marvelous budget destination. See chapter 7.
- **RELC (Singapore).** For a safe and simple place to call home in Singapore, RELC can't be beat. One wonders how they keep costs so low when their location is so good. See chapter 8.
- **Traders Hotel (Singapore).** Value-for-money is the name of the game, with all sorts of promotional packages, self-service launderettes, vending machines, and a checkout lounge just a few of the offerings that make this the most convenient hotel in the city. See chapter 8.
- **Stanford Hotel (Kuala Lumpur, Malaysia).** No-frills never looked so good. Stamford looks like a scaled-down four-star hotel, so you won't feel like you're going budget. See chapter 9.
- **Heeren House (Malacca, Malaysia).** Bargain or no bargain, this boutique hotel in the heart of the old city is *the* place to stay in Malacca if you want to really get a feel of the local atmosphere. See chapter 9.
- **Telang Usan Hotel (Kuching, Malaysia).** An informal place, Telang Usan is homey and quaint, and within walking distance of many major attractions in Kuching. See chapter 9.
- **The homestay/losmen of Bali.** These small-time accommodations will give you a large, comfortable (though no-frills) room or bungalow with a big, often fancy breakfast for about US$5 a night for two. See chapter 10.
- **Dolarog Beach Resort (El Nido, Palawan, Philippines).** The peaceful huts are situated on their own private island and will give you that same "away from it all feel" that the exclusive resorts guarantee—but for only around $30 a night! See chapter 11.

## 11   The Best Local Dining Experiences

- **Dining on dim sum (Hong Kong).** Nothing conveys a sense of Chinese life more vividly than a visit to a crowded, lively Cantonese restaurant where trolleys of dim sum in bamboo steamers are wheeled from customer to customer during breakfast and lunch. Simply peer into the passing bamboo baskets and choose what appears the most tempting. A great way to start the day. See chapter 4.
- **Taking high tea at the Peninsula (Hong Kong).** The British rulers may be gone, but their legacy lives on in the afternoon tea, complete with finger

sandwiches and scones. Virtually all upper-class hotels offer afternoon tea, but none can compare with the experience offered in the lobby of Hong Kong's most venerable hotel, long a favored people-watching spot. Come for afternoon tea, listen to classical music, and gaze away. See chapter 4.

- **Street food (Bangkok, Thailand).** On every street, down every alley, you'll find someone setting up a cart with an umbrella. Noodles, salads, and satay are favorites, and some hawkers set up tables and stools on the sidewalk for you to take a load off. Thai cafe life! See chapter 5.
- **Pho (Vietnam).** Don't leave the country without sampling one if not many bowls of this delicate noodle soup, made with vermicelli-thin rice noodles, chicken *(ga)* or beef *(bo)*, and several fresh accompaniments, according to the chef's whim: basil, mint, chili peppers, bean sprouts. There are regional variations to boot. See chapter 6.
- **Kua Lao (Vientiane, Laos).** Kua Lao is traditional Lao cuisine in a like setting, including music. Situated in a restored colonial, with a series of dining rooms, it is the premier Lao restaurant in the country. The extensive menu goes on for pages. There is an entire page of vegetarian entrees, and another entire page of something you don't see often: traditional Lao desserts. See chapter 7.
- **Hawker centers (Singapore).** Think of them as shopping malls for food—great food! For local cuisine, who needs a menu with pictures when you can walk around and select anything you want as it's prepared before your eyes. See chapter 8.
- **Gurney Drive (Penang, Malaysia).** Penang is King for offering a variety of Asian cuisine, from Chinese to Malay to Indian and everything else in between. Visiting this large hawker center by the sea is like taking "Intro to Penang 101." See chapter 9.
- **Satri's Warung (Bali).** With 24 hours' advance notice, Satri's will cook you a smoked duck or—our favorite (we dream of it all the time)—banana chicken feast, a whole bird, plus three plates of salad or fabulous vegetables, rice, and fruit for dessert, for about $7 for two. See chapter 10.
- **What's inside pot no. 1? (Philippines).** In many of the Philippines' towns on almost all its islands, the best food can be found not at the five-star resorts but on the counter in front of a family's home. As you stroll along the street you'll notice four or five silver pots lined up in a row. Feel free to have a peek and ask the cook what's inside—maybe pork adobo, chicken curry, pig knuckles. Pull up a chair, choose your pot, and experience true Filipino cuisine. See chapter 11.

## 12 The Best Markets

- **Stanley (Hong Kong).** Stall after stall of casualwear, silk clothing, bathing suits, tennis shoes, accessories, and souvenirs and crafts imported from China make this a shopper's paradise. After a day of bargaining, I like to recuperate in one of Stanley's trendy yet casual restaurants. See chapter 4.
- **Temple Street Night Market (Hong Kong).** Highlights include shopping for casual clothing, music, toys, and accessories; enjoying a meal at a *dai pai dong* (roadside food stall); watching amateur street musicians; and having your fortune told. See chapter 4.
- **Chatuchak Weekend Market (Bangkok, Thailand).** Words cannot describe it. It's so big, I'm thinking of selling homing devices to people who are afraid they'll get lost inside. Don't buy a thing until you spend at least a half day wandering down the endless aisles eyeballing the multitude of merchandise available. See chapter 5.

- **Night Bazaar (Chiang Mai, Thailand).** Most of those gorgeous handicrafts you find all over Thailand are made in the north, and at Chiang Mai's sprawling Night Bazaar you'll find the widest selection, best quality, and best prices. See chapter 5.
- **Hoi An Central Market (Hoi An, Vietnam).** On the banks of the busy Perfume River lies this entire city block of narrow, roofed aisles. Produce of every description is for sale inside—handicrafts, household items, and services such as facials and massages—and on the outskirts, an entire warehouse is devoted to silk and silk tailoring. See chapter 6.
- **Morning Market (Vientiane, Laos).** Laos's famous market is three huge buildings with traditional tiered roofs. Silver handicrafts, fabrics, jewelry, electronics, books, and much, much more occupy each building's several floors. The aisles are wide and made for wandering and poking through the wares, and the proprietors are friendly, gentle bargainers. See chapter 7.
- **Arab Street (Singapore).** Sure, Singapore is a shopper's paradise, but it needs more places like Arab Street, where small shops lining the street sell everything from textiles to handicrafts. Bargaining is welcome. See chapter 8.
- **Central Market (Kuala Lumpur, Malaysia).** One-stop shopping for all the rich arts and handicrafts Malaysia produces—and it's air-conditioned, too. See chapter 9.

## 13  The Best Shopping Bargains

- **Custom-tailored clothes (Hong Kong).** Nothing beats the thrill of having something custom-made to fit you perfectly. If this is your dream, make a trek to a tailor one of your first priorities, so that you'll have time for several fittings. See chapter 4.
- **Hill tribe handicrafts (Night Bazaar, Chiang Mai, Thailand).** From unusual silver designs to colorful embroidery, you'll fill your birthday and holiday shopping list in about an hour, and it'll cost you a fraction of your budget. See chapter 5.
- **Antiques (Thailand).** Before you head out on vacation, visit some Oriental Galleries in your home country and take a look at the prices of the items you like. Once you're here you'll be amazed at how little these things really cost. Most places will be glad to pack and ship purchases for you, and you'll still come out ahead. See chapter 5.
- **Tailored silk suits (Thailand and Hanoi, Hoi An, and Saigon, Vietnam).** For a fraction of what you'd pay at home, you can have a lined silk (or wool) suit tailored in a day or less, including a fitting or two. Bring pictures of your favorite designer outfits for a clever copy, and an empty suitcase or two for the trip home. See chapter 6.
- **Silver or lacquer handicrafts (Vietnam).** You'll find amazingly good workmanship and prices throughout the country, particularly for lacquerware. You can bargain like a demon, but be careful to ensure that the silver is genuine. See chapter 6.
- **Hand-woven textiles (Laos).** The Laos hand-weave textured fabrics, piece by piece, on primitive wooden looms. Such painstaking work costs more than a few dollars, but ranging from sophisticated silk to gaily colored ethnic prints, the designs are pure art and uniquely Laotian. See chapter 7.
- **Silver filigree jewelry (Malaysia).** This fine silver is worked into detailed filigree jewelry designs to make brooches, necklaces, bracelets, and other fine jewelry. See chapter 9.

- **Pewter (Malaysia).** Malaysia is the home of Selangor Pewter, one of the largest pewter manufacturers in the world. Their many showrooms have all sorts of items to choose from. See chapter 9.
- **Fabric and wood carvings (Bali).** Even though as a tourist you may spend more than a local, just about anything you buy in Bali (but especially, fabric and wood carvings, particularly those you commission) is dirt cheap, particularly when you see how much the same item goes for back home. See chapter 10.

## 14  The Hottest Nightlife Spots

- **Patpong (Bangkok, Thailand).** Yes, *that* Patpong. If go-go bars and sex shows aren't your style, you'll still find plenty to do. After you're finished shopping in the huge night market, there are plenty of restaurants, pubs, and discos that cater to folks who prefer more traditional nightlife. See chapter 5.
- **Saigon (Vietnam).** From the tawdry Apocalypse Now bar to rooftop garden scenes like Saigon-Saigon and cool jazz spots like Q-Bar, Saigon is famous for its rollicking nightlife. Most evenings begin with an elegant French or Vietnamese dinner at amazingly reasonable prices and then move on to incessant bar-hopping in the city's compact downtown, mingling with trendy locals and fun-loving expats. See chapter 6.
- **Singapore (The Whole City).** Nightlife is becoming increasingly sophisticated in Singapore, where locals have more money for recreation and fun. Take the time to choose the place that suits your personality. Jazz club? Techno disco? Cocktail lounge? Wine bar? Good old pub? They have it all. See chapter 8.
- **Bangsar (near Kuala Lumpur, Malaysia).** Folks in Kuala Lumpur know to go to Bangsar for nighttime excitement. A couple blocks of concentrated restaurants, cafes, discos, pubs, and wine bars will tickle any fancy. Good people-watching, too. See chapter 9.
- **Kuta Beach (Bali).** The Tijuana or Tangiers of Bali, Kuta is one big nightlife spot. Drink till you drop. See chapter 10.
- **Makati (Manila, Philippines).** Bring your trendiest outfit and shoes for some of the most jet-setting watering holes in Southeast Asia. The Giraffe, Venezia, Zu, and Euphoria are a few names to throw around. For a more bohemian experience, check out the spots in Malate like Verve Room or Hobbit House. See chapter 11.

# 2

# Introducing Southeast Asia

*By Jon Siskin*

Though the nations that comprise Southeast Asia each boast their own individual history, topography, and vibrant national personality, certain currents of history, language, and culture run throughout the region. In this section, we'll give a short intro to these elements of regional identity.

## 1 The Region Today

As we enter the 21st century, Southeast Asia is looking toward a prosperous future as countries throughout the region strive to build up their tourism infrastructure and augment their appeal as destinations. Despite the economic problems of the last two years, many of the region's governments have developed infrastructures that have encouraged global investors to construct world-class hotels and facilities that satisfy discerning travelers. Political stability remains a key factor in the outlook for the future as the most successful countries will be those that can maintain a strong, progressive central government able to maximize the economic benefits that accrue through a thriving tourism industry.

As the economic giants of Southeast Asia, with the highest standard of living, **Singapore** and **Hong Kong** lead the pack in terms of the quality and quantity of tourism facilities. **Thailand** and **Malaysia** have also devoted huge amounts of investment capital to hotel construction, airport development, and road and railway improvements that have spurred the growth of travel throughout these countries.

As Indonesia's most popular destination, **Bali** continues to capitalize on a winning formula for attracting tourists that combines rich cultural offerings with world-class resorts. Meanwhile, the **Philippines** and **Vietnam** have made substantial progress in upgrading their tourism infrastructure. Although they still have a long way to go, the lesser developed countries of **Burma, Cambodia,** and **Laos** are gradually warming up to tourism as they emerge from long periods of isolation from the rest of the world. (Some more than others: Of the three, only Laos is covered extensively in this guide. Burma and Cambodia are covered in chapter 12, "Difficult Destinations.") The estrangement of these countries from mass tourism is a blessing in disguise for travelers, as it has helped preserve one of the most unspoiled and esoteric regions left on earth. Endowed with magnificent scenic beauty and unique cultures, these countries reward visitors who don't mind going a bit off the beaten path with a fascinating and profound travel experience—but maintaining political, economic, and social stability will be critical if these countries are to succeed in developing their infrastructures and reaping the monetary rewards from increased tourism.

In this section, we'll give you a little bit of background on each country's history and some words on the state of its tourism infrastructure today. See the individual country chapters for more on both subjects.

## HONG KONG

Few cities can rival Hong Kong when it comes to palatial hotels, sophisticated dining, shopping facilities, live performances, cultural events, and other tourist pleasures. Sometimes referred to as "New York with chopsticks," Hong Kong moves at a break-neck pace day and night and shows no signs of slowing down anytime soon.

Of course, it didn't start out this way. Hong Kong was once a lair for pirates and remained an inconspicuous dot on the map prior to the arrival of the British, who moved in and claimed it as a British colony in 1841, then officially took possession of it in 1842, under terms of the **Treaty of Nanking** at the end the first Opium War. In 1860, the British took possession of Kowloon following the second Opium War, and in 1898 the New Territories—stretching north of Kowloon all the way to the Chinese border—were added to the colony under terms of a 99-year lease, and in that 99 years Britain turned Hong Kong into a major center of business and trade. It wasn't until 1984 that the U.K. agreed to return Hong Kong to China, under the condition that China would preserve Hong Kong's free-enterprise system until at least the year 2047.

From outward appearances, little seems changed here since China took control of Hong Kong in 1997, as it has demonstrated its ability to adapt to changing circumstances and continues to enjoy a high degree of autonomy. Under the terms of the Joint Declaration determining the future of Hong Kong, China must provide for the continuation of its capitalist economy and lifestyle for 50 years as Hong Kong makes the transition into its new status as a Special Administrative Region (SAR) of China.

Unlike Singapore (see below), Hong Kong retains much of its original Oriental flair, from its Chinese-embellished architecture to its ubiquitous noodle parlors and picturesque tea rooms. However, Western influence is undeniable. All indications are that Hong Kong will continue to be one of the world's most popular destinations, providing an ideal introduction to Southeast Asia.

## THAILAND

Long known as "The Land of Smiles," Thailand has a Buddhist spirit that's reflected in the warm, gracious, and helpful attitude extended to tourists. The Thais' happy-go-lucky, optimistic outlook enables them to accept foreigners as well as get along with each other with a minimum of conflict.

Thailand's written history dates from the 13th century, when a group of native tribes founded the independent kingdom of Sukhothai in northern Siam (Thailand was known as Siam until 1939). The most important ruler of this era was King Ramkamhaeng, who reigned for 40 years (beginning in 1275), during which time he established Buddhism as the national religion, created the Thai alphabet, and introduced a uniform system of currency. Unfortunately, none of the three succeeding kings would match Ramkamhaeng's achievements and Sukhothai grew increasingly vulnerable to attacks by the Burmese, who eventually forced the Thais to flee in 1350. A new capital of Siam was established at Ayutthaya (40 miles north of Bangkok), where it would remain for more than 400 years, during which time Ayutthaya expanded by annexing portions of Laos, Cambodia, Malaysia, and Singapore. By the 16th century, Ayutthaya was receiving traders from Japan, France, Holland, Spain, and England and reached the height of power and influence in the 17th century, when it was considered the most important capital in Southeast Asia. During the 1700s, however, the kingdom began to weaken and it finally met its end in 1767 at the hands of the Burmese. Soon after, the Thais established a new capital at Thonburi across the Chao Phraya River from modern day **Bangkok** and succeeded in driving out the Burmese. Following Taksin to power was one of his generals, who proclaimed himself King Rama I and moved the capital across the river to Bangkok in 1782.

Throughout the 19th and 20th centuries and into the 21st, Thailand has been ruled by a series of monarchs. It is the only Southeast Asian country that avoided colonization by the Europeans, and was left relatively unscathed during World War II after offering little resistance and quickly capitulating to the Japanese. While in the post-war era it has experienced student riots and occasional periods of political unrest, Thailand today remains one of the most stable countries in the region.

Thais are as devoted to their religion (95% of the population is Buddhist) as they are to their king, who serves as both head of state and head of the armed forces. Thailand is the only Asian country with a constitutional monarchy, and its legislative power is vested in a parliament consisting of a 161-member Senate and 347-member House of Representatives.

Today, Thailand's tourism industry is booming, creating a situation that has both its pros and its cons. These are epitomized by what has happened in **Bangkok,** which, in its rush toward modernization, has built up an inventory of more than 70,000 hotel rooms while creating one of the most polluted and congested cities in Asia. Nevertheless, it remains a fascinating place to explore, with more than 400 Buddhist temples and monasteries within city limits

While development has now slowed in Bangkok due to the Southeast Asian economic crisis (see chapter 3 for an examination of the crisis and its effects), other parts of the country have come on strong, including **Phuket** and **Koh Samui** in the south and **Chiang Mai** in the north. Tourism has been aided by the government's encouragement of foreign investment, which has been spearheaded by the Japanese and the Americans.

## VIETNAM

The history of Vietnam reveals a pattern of violent confrontations and clashes between dynasties and kingdoms seeking to expand their territory and influence. Vietnam initially came under the dominance of China's Han Dynasty, which invaded and conquered the area around the Red River Delta in the second century B.C. and would maintain a presence here for more than a 1,000 years until they were finally forced out in A.D. 938. It wasn't until the French arrived in the 1850s that Vietnam would again be ruled by a foreign power. The next 100 years saw colonialism give way to war, first with the French, then with the Americans. Today, with war wounds steadily healing, Vietnam has begun to re-emerge in the world community.

While its political system is still dominated by the Communist Party, the Vietnamese government has demonstrated flexibility and encouraged initiative in its relationships with other countries, liberalizing foreign investment laws and relaxing visa regulations.

Among the most promising tourist-related developments to take place during the 1990s was the construction of quality hotels in major cities such as **Hanoi** and **Ho Chi Minh City** (Saigon). In terms of air travel, often maligned Vietnam Airlines has taken a turn for the better by overhauling its aging fleet with the purchase of new Boeing jet aircraft.

# LAOS

One of Southeast Asia's least explored and least inhabited countries, Laos's tourism infrastructure is still in its youthful stages following years of recovery from its horrific suffering during the Vietnam War. Still little-visited, it is a fantastically unique and exotic place.

The nation's history reveals a constant struggle between internal and external factions. Laos did not become a unified nation until the 14th century, and prior to that it was under the control of the Khmers of Cambodia and the Sukothai Kingdom of Thailand. The first Lao kingdom, known as Lan Xang ("land of a million elephants"), was established in 1379 in the town of **Luang Prabang,** and over the next 2 centuries expanded into a regional power. Eventually the kingdom weakened due to repeated incursions from Burma and Vietnam and was dissolved in 1574 when it split into two factions. Laos later fell under Thai domination with the sacking of **Vientiane** in 1778. The French assumed control in 1887 and remained until Laos declared its independence in 1953. In the ensuing years, Laos became embroiled in a civil war between communist and non-communist forces and was a major target for bombing during the Vietnam War by U.S. B-52s seeking to stop the flow of supplies along the **Ho Chi Minh Trail,** which extended from Laos into Vietnam.

Laos began steadily moving to a market economy in the 1990s, and Japan and the United States chipped in with aid packages of their own. But the country still maintains a one-party system, along with tight information and social control. It continues to follow political structures laid out by the Vietnamese, and to be influenced economically by Thailand. At peace for the first time in centuries, Laos became a member of ASEAN (Association of Southeast Asian Nations) in 1997. Hopefully, the country will continue to carve out its own identity in Southeast Asia.

# SINGAPORE

It's been less than 200 years since Singapore was a nondescript backwater on the southern tip of the Malay Peninsula. Originally a haven for pirates who hid out here between raids on ships en route to and from China, Singapore had little contact with the outside world prior to the arrival in 1819 of Sir Stamford Raffles, an official with the British East India Trading Company. Raffles' arrival would turn everything around. Today, immaculate and efficient as a Swiss watch, squeaky-clean, sanitized Singapore boasts a low crime rate, an English-speaking population, and a policy of religious tolerance for its mix of Buddhists, Hindus, Muslims, and Christians. Much of the success of this tiny nation—just one-third the size of Rhode Island—is attributed to the efforts of its first prime minister, **Lee Kuan Yew,** who presided over Singapore's transformation into an Asian tiger by pursuing a policy of free trade with government control. However, some visitors who recall the early Singapore condemn the rush to modernization, during which many of the island's original buildings were torn down and replaced by futuristic skyscrapers and high-rise hotels. The Westernization of Singapore also has affected traditional customs, although religious values remain strong.

Today Singapore is the number-one shopping center in the tropics with its collection of gleaming, air-conditioned shopping malls on Orchard Road, located conveniently close to some of the finest hotels in Southeast Asia. Refusing to rest on its laurels, Singapore continues to add to its impressive list of attractions as it moves toward implementing its ambitious Tourism 21 plan for the 21st century.

## MALAYSIA

Due to its strategic location on the major trade route between India and China, Malaysia's early history was dominated by the occupation of its territory by a succession of southeast Asian empires. In 1403, the Palembang prince Parameswara (also known as Iskander Shah) established the coastal town of **Malacca,** which over the next 300 years developed into the wealthiest Southeast Asian trading post and naval port. Among the traders it attracted were Arabs, whose religion eventually spread throughout the Malay peninsula. Malacca would later fall under the control of the Portuguese, the Dutch, and eventually the British, who established their control in 1786, the same year they claimed **Penang,** sealing their control of the Malay Peninsula for the next century and a half—control that didn't end until 1957, when Britain finally granted Malaysia its independence.

Malaysia's economic prospects have been on the rise since the 1970s due to a stable political system that has spurred its growth into one of the most developed nations in Southeast Asia. Recent economic setbacks are likely to be overcome by a country that has already proven to be one of the strongest and most resilient in the region. The government is headed by a prime minister and a cabinet and there is also a constitutional monarch who is selected for a rotating 5-year term from among Malaysia's nine traditional kings.

Another point in Malaysia's favor is its policy of tolerance toward the melting pot of religious and ethnic groups who have worked together in harmony for generations. The Malays, who make up most of the population, are Muslims, while Buddhism, Hinduism, and Christianity are practiced by those of Chinese, Indian, and Eurasian descent.

The strength of the domestic economy has been buoyed by a steady rise in tourism to destinations on both the Malay Peninsula and in Sabah and Sarawak (Eastern Malaysia's two states are located on the northern portion of Borneo). Major destinations with solid infrastructures include the capital, **Kuala Lumpur;** historic **Malacca;** the beach resorts of **Penang, Langkawi,** and **Kuantan;** and the hill town resorts in the **Cameron and Genting Highlands.** Meanwhile, **Sabah** is in the midst of a 10-year development that will add 10 hotels, two 18-hole golf courses, and theme parks. The recent opening of Kuala Lumpur's new international airport coupled with the construction of quality international chain hotels (Shangri-La, Pan Pacific, Hilton, Marriott) bode well for the future.

## BALI

Much of Balinese history is recorded in legends and preserved in its religion and its people's adherence to the traditions of their ancestors. Despite the fact that the Dutch began colonizing the rest of Indonesia in the early 1600s, Bali remained relatively ignored until 1906, after which it functioned as part of the Dutch East Indies until the end of the Japanese occupation during World War II. Indonesia declared its independence in August 1945, and after years of fighting finally forced the Dutch out in 1949.

While Islam is the dominant religion throughout most of Indonesia, Bali remains the only Indonesian island where Hinduism still thrives (Hindus make up just 2% of Indonesia's population of 195 million, while 90% are Muslims). Infused with animistic beliefs, Balinese Hinduism has taken a unique form that differs from the Hinduism originally introduced to Bali by Indian settlers in the 13th century.

As with many of the peoples of Southeast Asia, the Balinese peoples' religion affects every aspect of daily life, including cultural activities and performances for tourists.

# The Indonesian Crisis

As we began preparations and research for this book, Indonesia entered a period of turmoil, with riots and protests against three decades of military rule eventually forcing out longtime president Suharto. Serious rioting occurred in Jakarta in May and November, 1998, and sporadic and unpredictable violence occurred elsewhere in the country. Throughout the crisis, Bali remained the only major Indonesian tourist destination largely unaffected by the turmoil.

At this writing, both the U.S. State Department and the British Foreign and Commonwealth Office warn that Indonesia's political and economic situation is likely to remain unsettled through 1999, as the results of parliamentary elections become known and a new president is selected. Following that, we cannot predict, and have thus opted to exclude the unstable areas of Indonesia from coverage in this guide, limiting ourselves to the islands of Bali and Lombok, which have stayed clear of unrest.

To monitor government warnings on travel in Indonesia, see the U.S. State Department's Web site at **http://travel.state.gov/travel_warnings.html** and the British Foreign and Commonwealth Office's site at **www.fco.hov.uk**.

Dance performances featuring themes from Hindu folklore are performed regularly in hotels as well as at some of the thousands of villages temples and shrines dedicated to Hindu deities.

Bali's most developed infrastructure is concentrated in its popular beach resorts such as **Kuta Beach, Sanur Beach,** and **Nusa Dua Beach,** all of which feature every imaginable accommodation, from inexpensive guest houses to upscale hotels. Fortunately, not all of this exquisite island has been overrun by tourists. Those who want to avoid the hordes should head for the countryside or up into the mountains where there are unspoiled villages that have changed little over time. **Ubud** is the island's leading cultural center.

## THE PHILIPPINES

Malays from Indonesia are believed to have been among the first settlers of the islands now comprising the Philippines, arriving here around the third century B.C. and becoming the ancestors from which the country's present population is largely descended. By the 10th century, the Philippines had become a mecca for Chinese, Arab, and Indian traders, and in 1521 the explorer Ferdinand Magellan brought the first Europeans. Following this, the Filipinos would experience more than 300 years of Spanish colonial rule, beginning with the first permanent Spanish settlement in 1565 on the island of Cebu.

Along with naming the country in honor Spain's King Philip II and spreading Christianity throughout the islands, the Spanish imposed many elements of their culture on the Filipinos, from architecture to education to cuisine. Catholicism today remains especially strong in the northern two-thirds of the islands, where the Spanish exerted their greatest efforts (over 80% of the population in this area are Catholics). Today the Philippines is the only predominantly Christian nation in Southeast Asia.

The Spanish maintained control of the Philippines until 1898, when they were ousted by the Americans during the **Spanish American War,** during which a U.S. squadron destroyed the Spanish fleet in Manila Bay and then occupied Manila. Instead of pulling out, the U.S. decided to purchase the islands from Spain for $20 million and to remain here indefinitely. It would take another 50 years of U.S. occupation before the Philippines would become an independent nation in 1946.

Since then, the Philippines' history has been plagued by political instability and corruption. Democracy suffered a severe setback during the 20-year (1965–85) reign of **Ferdinand Marcos,** whose declaration of martial law from 1968 to 1981 allowed him to suspend the Philippine Congress, impose stringent press censorship, and neutralize all political dissent. Democratic elections were not restored until 1986, when Corazon Aquino emerged victorious and Marcos fled the country. While uncertainty still lingers in regard to the Philippines' political future, for now stability has been restored and democratic elections are held every 6 years (a president can serve only one 6-year term).

Tourism remains one of the Philippines' most important sources of revenue and there is a solid infrastructure in place on the two major islands of **Luzon** and **Mindanao.** The Philippines has long been aware of the importance of tourism, as it was the first Southeast Asian country to have its own convention and visitors bureau and was also the first to open a convention center.

The capital of **Manila** now has over 13,000 quality hotel rooms, while the ancient city of **Cebu** has also added to its hotel inventory. Another plus for travel to these islands are the Filipinos themselves, a happy, spirited people with a well-deserved reputation for hospitality.

## CAMBODIA & BURMA

Both Cambodia and Burma (Myanmar) are endowed with magnificent scenic beauty and unique cultures, and offer fascinating and profound travel experiences to visitors. Unfortunately, the progressive approach to world relations and tourism shown by neighboring Vietnam has not yet been emulated by these countries' governments, whose policies still reflect disarray, repression, and an inability to deal constructively with internal and external problems. After being closed to tourism for years due to a series of wars and the actions of repressive governments, these countries are showing some signs of encouraging more visitors by upgrading the quality of their infrastructure. New hotels have been built in Rangoon and Mandalay in Burma and there is also some new hotel construction in Phnom Penh and near Angkor Wat in Cambodia. Disarray continues, in Burma, however, to the point where our author found entry into the country virtually blocked in late 1998, following the expulsion of a group of Americans for pro-democracy activities.

Because of the everyday instability of these two countries, we've underplayed their coverage in this guide. See chapter 12 for information on group travel, which is your safest and most sensible travel option here.

## 2 A Southeast Asian Cultural Primer

A vast diversity of ethnic groups people Southeast Asia. Whether living in modern cities or remote hills, each group has its own special cultural practices which are often influenced by religion. With so much mingling and mixing of peoples occurring throughout Southeast Asian history, it should come as no surprise that the region's cornucopia of cultures have intertwined and adopted various elements, beliefs, and practices from each other.

## THE CULTURAL MAKEUP OF SOUTHEAST ASIA
### HONG KONG & SINGAPORE

The similarities in economic growth and the pursuit of free enterprise shared by Hong Kong and Singapore extend to the ethnic makeup of their populations. Ninety-eight

# Buddha & Buddhism

Buddhism is the primary religion of Thailand, Laos, Vietnam, Burma, and Cambodia, and is practiced to a lesser extent in the other Southeast Asian nations. It is a religion without a God, mystical in the sense that it strives for the intuitive realization of the oneness of the universe. It requires that individuals work out their own salvation as commanded by the Buddha himself, to "look within, thou art the Buddha," and in his final words, to "work out your own salvation with diligence." Buddhism has one aim only: to abolish suffering. It proposes to do this one step at a time, by each person ridding him or herself of the causes of suffering, which are desire, malice, and delusion.

Other aspects of the philosophy include the law of **karma,** whereby every action has effects and the energy of past action, good or evil, continues forever and is "reborn." Merit can be gained by entering the monkhood (and most males do so for a few days or months), helping in the construction of a monastery or a stupa, contributing to education, giving alms, or performing any act of kindness, no matter how small. When the monks go daily with their begging bowls from house to house, they are giving the people an opportunity to make merit; similarly, the people selling caged birds, which people purchase and free, are allowing people to gain merit by freeing the birds.

Buddha himself was a great Indian sage, born **Siddhartha Gautama** in the sixth century B.C. A prince, he spent his boyhood carefully sheltered from the outside world, and when he finally left the palace walls he encountered an old man, a sick man, and a corpse. He concluded that all is suffering and, resolving to search for relief from that suffering, he went into the forest and lived there for many years as a solitary ascetic, ultimately achieving enlightenment and nirvana (escape from the cycle of reincarnation) while sitting under a sacred fig tree.

Upon his death, two schools arose. The oldest and probably closest to the original is **Theravada** (Doctrine of the Elders), sometimes referred to less correctly as Hinayana (the Small Vehicle), which prevails in Sri Lanka, Burma, Laos, Thailand, and Cambodia. The other school is **Mahayana** (the Large Vehicle), which is practiced in China, Korea, Vietnam, and Japan.

Buddha images are honored and revered in the Eastern tradition; they are not idols of worship but images that in their physical form radiate spirituality and convey the essence of Buddhist teachings—serenity, enlightenment, purity of mind, purity of tongue, and purity of action. Similar energy is believed to inhabit the miniature Buddhas that are worn as talismans to protect against evil spirits.

percent of Hong Kong's 6.3 million residents are **Chinese,** with a remainder consisting of **Indians, Filipinos, Americans,** and **British,** while approximately 80% of Singapore's population of 2.8 million are Chinese, with **Malays** (15%) and **Indians** (5%) making up the rest.

Although Western culture has had a strong impact on both Hong Kong (fact: five of the world's 10 busiest McDonalds are located here) and Singapore, both still preserve their connections to many aspects of Chinese culture passed down from their ancestors. In Hong Kong, fortune-telling, astrology, superstition, and ancestor worship still play a role in the daily life of a people whose religions may include elements of Buddhist, Tao, and Christian beliefs. In the morning, you may see men and women practicing the ancient art of Tai Chi in the shadow of a skyscraper, while in the

# Understanding Feng Shui

Have you ever noticed how some homes seem to give off terrific vibes the moment you enter the front door while others leave you feeling disturbed and wanting to get out fast? The Chinese believe *feng shui* (pronounced fung *shway* and meaning "wind and water") has a lot to do with these positive and negative feelings.

The earliest recorded record of feng shui dates from the Han dynasty (202 B.C.–A.D. 220) and the practice is still widely and highly regarded in Asia today. In essence, the idea of feng shui revolves around the way physical surroundings relate to the invisible flow of *chi* (natural energy), which must move smoothly throughout the home or business in order for life to play itself out beneficially. Walls, doors, windows, or furnishings can throw off this flow through their color, balance, placement, or proportion—even by their points on the compass. Your bed, for example, placed on the wrong wall or facing the wrong way, could encourage chi to rush into a room and out again, taking wealth and health with it. If your bed is situated directly under an exposed beam, you might as well make a standing appointment with the chiropractor, 'cause that's some *baaad* feng shui.

In Singapore and Hong Kong, particularly (as both have large Chinese populations), company presidents regularly call upon feng shui masters to rearrange their office furniture, and the master is usually the first person called in on new construction jobs to assess the building plans for their adherence to good feng shui practices. It's not uncommon to hear stories about buildings being partially torn down late in the construction process, simply because a master hadn't examined the plans earlier and, when finally consulted, had deemed that the structure did not promote good feng shui. The extra cost is considered a valid investment—after all, what's a few dollars saved now if bad feng shui will later cause the business to fail? For the average homeowner who doesn't want to consult a feng shui master (or can't afford to), a plethora of books is available to advise on creating successful living spaces.

For every life situation there's a feng shui solution. And don't worry what people will think when they see those four purple candles in the corner of your living room or the pair of wooden flutes dangling from an exposed beam. Let 'em laugh—you'll be grinning all the way to the bank.

—Jennifer Eveland

evening, outside a temple, you might encounter a fortune-teller interpreting someone's future. In Singapore, its ethnic legacy lives on in the preserved neighborhoods of Chinatown, Little India, and Arab Street.

Whether it's entertainment, cuisine, or the arts, the Chinese influence in both Singapore and Hong Kong is unmistakable. Among the most popular cultural pursuits are puppet plays which tell the story of Chinese dynasties and Chinese Opera (*wayung*), which is performed in the more modern Cantonese style as well as the classic Beijing style.

While the majority of Hong Kong's 30,000 restaurants serve Cantonese-style Chinese food, there is also a good selection of establishments serving Shanghai, Beijing, Hangzhou, Szechuan, and many other varieties of Chinese cooking. Cantonese cuisine also dominates the Singapore restaurant scene; however, many Singapore natives are descended from the Fukien Province in China and prefer Hokkien style, which features fresh seafood dishes and stews. Both countries can satisfy virtually every taste for ethnic food, including Thai, Indian, Malay, Indonesian, Vietnamese, and Burmese.

**English** is spoken widely in both Hong Kong and Singapore, as Hong Kong's two official languages are Chinese (Cantonese) and English, while in Singapore the schools are required to educate children in their mother tongue and English.

## THAILAND

Thailand's population is 75% **Thai,** 10 to 15% **Chinese,** and a mix of **Malay, Indian, Persian, Khmer,** and **Lao.** While the Thais have their own distinct language, **English** is generally the second language and is the preferred language of international trade and tourism.

Thai culture is best reflected in music, dance, and architecture. The hundreds of **Buddhist temples** *(wats)* located in the big cities and the countryside feature steeply sloping Thai roofs brilliantly adorned with glazed tiles. The interiors of these temples usually contain a Thai-style *chedi* (pagoda and stupa) consisting of a bell-shaped dome tapering into a spire. Classical **Thai music,** which is played by a woodwind and percussion band of between 5 and 20 players, produces a sound that is an amalgam of Indian, Chinese, Burmese, Malay, and Khmer musical traditions. Classical **Thai dance** borrows heavily from Indian temple dancing and is usually performed either by an all-male ensemble dressed in masks or by women dancing both male and female roles.

## VIETNAM, LAOS, CAMBODIA & BURMA

Together the countries of Vietnam, Cambodia, Laos, and Burma make up one of the most ethnically diverse regions of Southeast Asia. Outside of the cities, little **English** is spoken in any of these countries except by tour guides and others who have frequent contact with Western visitors. Much of the architecture and art in Cambodia, Laos, and Burma is influenced by Buddhism and includes some of the world's most renowned temples along with exquisitely sculpted Buddha images. The temple complexes of Angkor Wat in Cambodia and Bagan in Burma are among the architectural wonders of the ancient world, while the finest temples in Laos are found in the ancient capital of Luang Prabang.

**VIETNAM**    In Vietnam, the ethnic Vietnamese are a fusion of **Viet, Thai, Indonesian,** and **Chinese** who first settled here between 200 B.C. and A.D. 200. While Vietnam has no official religion, several religions have significantly impacted Vietnamese culture, including Buddhism, Confucianism, Taoism, and Animism. Animism, which is the oldest religious practice in Vietnam and many other Southeast Asian countries, is centered around belief in a spirit world.

**LAOS**    In Laos, approximately half the population are ethnic **Lao** who are descendants of the original inhabitants who migrated here from China, Thailand, and India.

**CAMBODIA**    The population of Cambodia is made up primarily of ethnic **Khmers** who have lived here since around the second century A.D. and whose religion and culture have been influenced by interaction with Indians, Javanese, Thais, Vietnamese, and Chinese.

**BURMA**    The Burmese people are descended from three ethnic groups: the **Mons,** a Buddhist people originally from Cambodia; the **Burmans,** who migrated south from China and Tibet; and the **Shans** from Thailand.

## MALAYSIA

Malaysia's population consists primarily of ethnic **Malaysians** (50%), while **Chinese-Malaysians** (33%), many of whom immigrated from China in the 1800s to work in the tin mines, are also well represented. The third largest group is the **Indian-Malaysians,** who were brought over to work the rubber plantations in the early 20th century.

Malay is the national language but **English** is also widely spoken in business transactions and the travel industry. A variety of Chinese dialects, Tamil, Portuguese, and Arabic are also spoken.

**Malaysian music,** which shows influences from Cambodia, India, and the Middle East, features the use of several distinctive instruments, including a three-stringed spike fiddle and an oboe known as a *serunai*. **Malay dances,** which focus on precise movements of the arms and hands, come in many popular forms including court dances and seasonal dances. Malay **shadow plays,** a mix of theater and puppetry, are similar to the shadow plays performed throughout Southeast Asia. Among the favorite Malaysian recreational pastimes are kite flying, using ornately decorated paper kites, and top spinning. (The traditional Malay top, called a *gasing,* can be a real work of art, generally wide and flat with a polished wood center and a smooth steel lip around the edge. Malays take their top spinning *very* seriously.)

## BALI

No country in Southeast Asia has a more ethnically diverse population than Indonesia, with more than 350 ethnic groups with their own languages and cultures scattered among the 6,000 inhabited islands of this vast archipelago of more than 14,000 islands.

Of all the islands, Bali stands out for its especially rich cultural life, which is inextricably linked with its Hindu beliefs. In Bali life doesn't imitate art, life *is* art, as virtually everyone is involved in some sort of daily artistic endeavor, whether it's painting, dancing, or playing a musical instrument. Flower offerings to the gods are a common sight and the Balinese are forever paying homage to Hindu deities at more than 20,000 temples and during the 60 annual festivals on the island.

The majority of the island's population is native Balinese, there are quite a few people from other parts of Indonesia, and they are there for work opportunities. English is widely spoken in the touristed parts of Bali, which means just about everywhere you go someone will speak enough English to help you out.

### THE PHILIPPINES

The Philippines, where **English** is one of three official languages along with Spanish and the Filipino dialect Tagalog, stands out from the rest of Southeast Asia as the only predominantly Christian country in the region. Islam is also practiced, with the Muslim population concentrated on the Philippines' second largest island, Mindanao.

Filipinos are primarily of **Malay** ancestry, with mixtures of **Spanish, Chinese,** and other groups. Altogether, several hundred languages and dialects are spoken in the islands.

## ETIQUETTE TIPS

"Different countries, different customs," as Sean Connery said to Michael Caine in *The Man Who Would Be King.* And while each country covered in this book will prove that rule by having their own twists on etiquette, some general pointers will allow you to go though your days of traveling without inadvertently offending your hosts. (For etiquette tips on individual countries, see the country chapters.)

## GREETINGS, GESTURES & SOCIAL INTERACTION

In these modern times, the **common Western handshake** has become extremely prevalent throughout Southeast Asia, but it is by no means universal. There are a plethora of traditional greetings, so when greeting someone—especially an older man and even more especially a woman, of any age—it's safest to wait for a gesture, then follow suit. In Muslim culture, for instance, it is not acceptable for men and women not related by blood or marriage to touch. (See individual country chapters for the various traditional greetings.)

In interpersonal relations in strongly Buddhist areas (Laos, Vietnam, and Thailand) it helps to **take a gentle approach to human relationships.** A person showing violence or ill temper would be regarded with surprise and disapproval. A gentle approach will take you farther.

A delicate matter that's best to get out of the way immediately: In countries with significant Muslim and Hindu cultures (Malaysia, Singapore, Indonesia, Bali) **only use your right hand in social interaction.** Traditionally, the left hand is used only for personal hygiene. Not only should you eat with your right hand and give and receive all gifts with your right hand, but you should make sure all gestures, especially **pointing** (and even more especially, pointing in temples and mosques), are made with your right hand. In all the countries discussed in this book, it's also considered more polite to point with your knuckle (with your hand facing palm down) than with your finger.

In all the countries covered in this guide, ladies seated on the floor should never sit with their legs crossed in front of them—instead, always tuck your legs to the side. Men may sit with legs crossed. Both men and women should also be careful **not to show the bottoms of their feet,** which are considered the lowliest, most unclean part of the body. If you cross your legs while on the floor or in a chair, don't point your soles toward other people. Also be careful not to use your foot to point or gesture. **Shoes should be removed** when entering a temple or private home. And don't ever step over someone's body or legs.

On a similar note, in Buddhist and Hindu cultures the head is considered the most sacred part of the body; therefore, **do not casually touch another person's head**—and this includes patting children on the head.

## DRESSING FOR CULTURAL SUCCESS

The basic rule is **dress modestly.** Except perhaps on the grounds of resorts and in heavily touristed areas such as Bali's Kuta and Thailand's Pattaya, foreigners displaying navels, chests, or shoulders or wearing short shorts or short skirts will attract stares. While shorts and bathing suits are accepted on the beach, you should avoid parading around in them elsewhere, no matter how hot it is.

## TEMPLE & MOSQUE ETIQUETTE

Many of Southeast Asia's greatest and most remarkable sights are its places of worship, usually Buddhist wats, Hindu temples, and Islamic mosques (masjids). When visiting these places, more so than at any other time, it's important to observe certain rules of decorum.

When visiting the **mosques,** be sure to dress appropriately. Neither men nor women will be admitted wearing shorts. For the ladies, please do not wear short skirts or sleeveless, backless, or low-cut tops. Both men and women are required to leave their shoes outside. Also remember: Never enter the mosque's main prayer hall. This area is reserved for Muslims only. No cameras or video cameras are allowed, and

# Getting in Touch with Your Inner Haggler

In the smaller shops and at street vendors throughout Southeast Asia, you'll find that prices are never marked, and it will be expected that you bargain. The most important thing to remember when bargaining is to keep a friendly, good-natured banter between you and the seller. It's all in a day's work for him. Before you start out, it's always good to have at least some idea how much your purchase is worth, to give you a base point for negotiation. Shop around, ask questions. A simple "How much?" is the place to start, to which they'll reply with their top price. Never accept the first price! Try a smile and ask "Is that your best price?" Sometimes they'll ask what your paying price is. Knock the price down about 30%—they'll look shocked, but it's a starting point for bidding. Just remember to smile and be friendly, and you should be able to negotiate something you both like. Caveat: If it's a larger, more expensive item, don't get into serious bargaining unless you're serious about buying. If the shopkeeper agrees on what you say you're willing to pay, it's generally considered rude to not make the purchase. If no agreement is made, however, you can always say thank you and walk away.

See individual country chapters for more on shopping.

remember to turn off cellular phones and pagers. Friday is the Sabbath day, and you should not plan on going to the mosques between 11am and 2pm on this day.

Visitors are welcome to walk around and explore most **temples** and **wats.** As in the mosques, remember to dress appropriately—some temples may refuse to admit you if you're showing too much skin—and to leave your shoes outside. Photography is permitted in most temples, though some, such as Wat Phra Kaeo in Thailand, prohibit it. Never climb on a Buddha image, and if you sit down, never point your feet in the direction of the Buddha. Also, women should never touch a monk, try to shake his hand, or even give something to one directly (the monk will provide a cloth for you to lay the item upon, and he will collect it). Monks are not permitted to touch women, or even to speak directly to them anywhere but inside a temple or wat.

# Planning a Trip to Southeast Asia

**3**

*By Jon Siskin*
("Money" section by Jon Siskin and Jennifer Eveland)

The country chapters in this guide provide specific information on traveling to and getting around in all of Southeast Asia's individual countries, but in this chapter we'll give you some region-wide tips and info that will help you plan your trip.

## 1 Passport & Visa Requirements at a Glance

Most countries covered in this guide require that citizens of the U.S., U.K., Canada, Australia, and New Zealand have only a **passport** for entry; Vietnam, Laos, Cambodia, and Burma (Myanmar) require citizens of these countries to have **visas.** See individual country chapters for more specific information.

**BALI**  Visitors from the U.S., Australia, most of Europe, New Zealand, and Canada do not need visas. They will be given a stamp that allows them to stay for 60 days, provided they are entering the country through an officially designated gateway: Ngurah Rai Airport or the seaports of Padang Bai and Benoa. If you want to stay longer than 60 days, you must get a tourist or business visa before coming to Indonesia. Tourist visas are valid only for 4 weeks and can not be extended, while business visas can be extended for 6 months at Indonesian immigration offices.

**BURMA (MYANMAR)**  Myanmar consulates issue visas for stays of up to four weeks. Be warned: They may refuse your application if they suspect you represent a media firm or a pro-democracy or human rights organization. Look like a tourist.

**CAMBODIA**  All visitors are required to carry a passport and visa. A one-month visa can be had at the Phnom Penh or Siem Reap airports for US$20. Bring two passport photos for your application.

**HONG KONG**  A valid passport is the only document most tourists, including Americans, need to enter Hong Kong. Americans can stay up to 1 month without a visa. Australians, New Zealanders, Canadians, and other British Commonwealth citizens can stay 3 months without a visa, while citizens of the United Kingdom can stay for 6 months without a visa.

### Inoculations

None of the countries in this guide require you to have any inoculations or vaccinations for entry unless you are coming from or passing through areas infected with yellow fever. See the individual country chapters for details.

**LAOS**   Residents of every Western country need a passport and visa to visit Laos. Although the official time limit is 15 days, most people get 30 days for just asking. Five-day transit visas are also available. Contrary to rumor, you do not need to book an organized tour to obtain a visa, so don't believe any travel agents who tell you so. Further, as you travel from province to province, even to a major city like Luang Prabang, you must check in with the immigration authorities upon both entry and exit. See chapter 7, Laos, for information on obtaining your visa.

**MALAYSIA**   To enter Malaysia you must have a valid passport. Citizens of the United States do not need visas for tourism and business visits. Citizens of Canada, Australia, New Zealand, and the U.K. do not require a visa for tourism or business visits not exceeding 1 month.

**THE PHILIPPINES**   For stays of up to 21 days, only a passport and a return or continuing ticket are required. If you wish to stay longer than 21 days, you can obtain a 59-day visa from a Philippine embassy or consulate in your country.

**SINGAPORE**   To enter Singapore you'll need a valid passport. Visas are not necessary for citizens of the United States, Canada, the United Kingdom, Australia, and New Zealand. Upon entry, visitors from these countries will be issued a 30-day pass for a social visit only.

**THAILAND**   All visitors to Thailand must carry a valid passport with proof of onward passage (either a return or through ticket). Visas are not required for stays of up to 30 days for citizens of the U.S., Australia, Canada, Ireland, New Zealand, or the U.K.

**VIETNAM**   Residents of the U.S., Canada, Australia, New Zealand, and the United Kingdom need both a passport and a valid visa to enter Vietnam. A tourist visa usually lasts for 30 days and costs US$50, although some people are inexplicably able to get longer visas upon request. Multiple-entry business visas are available that are valid for up to 3 months, but you must have a sponsoring agency in Vietnam and it can take much longer to process. For short business trips, it's less complicated simply to enter as a tourist.

## PASSPORT INFORMATION FOR FIRST-TIMERS & RENEWERS

If you've never had a passport before, see the information below for application procedures. Passport applications are downloadable from the Internet sites listed below.

**UNITED STATES**   If you're applying for a first-time passport, you need to do it in person at one of 13 passport offices throughout the U.S.; a federal, state, or probate court; or a major post office (though not all post offices accept applications; call the number below to find the ones that do). You need to present a certified birth certificate as proof of citizenship, and it's wise to bring along your driver's license, state or military ID, and social security card as well. You also need two identical passport-sized photos (2 in. by 2 in.), taken at any corner photo shop (not one of the strip photos, however, from a photo-vending machine).

For people over 15, a passport is valid for 10 years and costs US$60 (US$45 plus a US$15 handling fee); for those 15 and under, it's valid for 5 years and costs US$40.

### Travel Tip: Safeguard Your Passport

Safeguard your passport—it's the only official way for you to prove you are who you say you are. Keep it in an inconspicuous, inaccessible place like a money belt. If you lose it, visit the nearest consulate of your native country as soon as possible for a replacement.

If you're over 15 and have a valid passport that was issued within the past 12 years, you can renew it by mail and bypass the US$15 handling fee. Allow plenty of time before your trip to apply; processing normally takes 3 weeks but can take onger during busy periods (especially spring). For general information, call the **National Passport Agency** (☎ 202/647-0518). To find your regional passport office, call the **National Passport Information Center** (☎ 900/225-5674; http://travel.state.gov).

**CANADA**    You can pick up a passport application at one of 28 regional passport offices or most travel agencies. The passport is valid for 5 years and costs US$60. Children under 16 may be included on a parent's passport but need their own to travel unaccompanied by the parent. Applications, which must be accompanied by two identical passport-sized photographs and proof of Canadian citizenship, are available at travel agencies throughout Canada or from the central **Passport Office, Department of Foreign Affairs and International Trade,** Ottawa, Ont. K1A 0G3 (☎ 800/567-6868; www.dfait-maeci.gc.ca/passport). Processing takes 5 to 10 days if you apply in person, or about 3 weeks by mail.

**THE UNITED KINGDOM**    To pick up an application for a regular 10-year passport, visit your nearest passport office, major post office, or travel agency. You can also contact the London Passport Office at ☎ 0171/271-3000 or search its Web site at www.open.gov.uk/ukpass/ukpass.htm. Passports are £21 for adults and £11 for children under 16.

**IRELAND**    You can apply for a 10-year passport, costing IR£45, at the Passport Office, Setanta Centre, Molesworth Street, Dublin 2 (☎ 01/671-1633; www.irlgov.ie/iveagh/foreignaffairs/services). Those under age 18 and over 65 must apply for a IR£10 3-year passport. You can also apply at 1A South Mall, Cork (☎ 021/272-525) or over the counter at most main post offices.

**AUSTRALIA**    Apply at your local post office or passport office or search the government Web site at www.dfat.gov.au/passports/. Passports for adults are A$126 and for those under 18 A$63.

**NEW ZEALAND**    You can pick up a passport application at any travel agency or Link Centre. For more info, contact the Passport Office, P.O. Box 805, Wellington (☎ 0800/225-050). Passports for adults are NZ$80 and for those under 16 NZ$40.

## 2 Money

At the risk of sounding blasé about international economic turmoil, there's one fact that's hard to ignore: The recent Southeast Asian financial crisis has created travel bargains galore. This might be the best time in years to travel in the region.

In this section we'll introduce you to the region's post-crisis economic outlook and its currencies, fill you in on where your money will go furthest, and discuss taxes and exchange.

## THE SOUTHEAST ASIAN FINANCIAL CRISIS

After three decades of stellar economic growth, the East Asian Economic Miracle crashed and burned in mid-1997. On July 2 of that year, Thailand's economy became the first to raise the alarm when it floated its currency, a move that caused the baht to devalue 20% in the week to follow. On its tail, the Malaysian ringgit, Indonesian rupiah, and Philippine peso soon suffered similar fates.

The world watched as the economic scene unfolded, revealing a Southeast Asian legacy of suspicious government ties to industry, massive overseas borrowing, overbuilt property markets, and lax bank lending practices. The booming economies had been susceptible to the seduction of cheap and plentiful foreign money and the whim of currency speculation. Borrowers that once carried too much debt became hopeless in the face of plummeting local currency values. Loans defaulted, businesses closed, unemployment rose. Nations that once took pride in over 8% annual GDP growth rates stared down the barrel of growth rates below 1%. While leaders paddled to stay afloat, economists had a field day.

The International Monetary Fund came to town with promises of bailouts and expert advice. **Thailand** took US$17 million of IMF money, and **Indonesia** over US$40 million. While Thailand now expects a slow but steady recovery, IMF policies have more or less failed Indonesia, and the country remains Asia's basket case. The only nation to thumb its nose at the IMF has been **Malaysia,** whose unconventional reform policies have met with both harsh criticism and anticipatory curiosity. Now, as nations pump cash into failing banks (some with loan default predictions as high as 50%) and eye the volatile economies of Japan and China with furrowed brow, everybody is holding their breath.

### EFFECTS OF THE CRISIS ON TOURISM

As a result of the crisis, **Southeast Asian tourism** has taken a brutal beating. With the exception of Thailand, which launched the highly successful "Amazing Thailand: Amazing Value" campaign in the nick of time, every country has reported decreases in tourist traffic—decreases that hit government coffers and private enterprise hard.

So, if no one else is going to Southeast Asia why should you?

First of all, the most obvious reason is that **your foreign currency goes a lot farther than it used to.** To use Thailand as an example, in June 1997, U.S. $1 dollar got you around 25 Thai baht; in January 1998, that same buck got you 55 baht. While these days it's hovering around 37 baht to the dollar, it's still a bargain. You'll find similar favorable currency rates elsewhere in the region (see the currency conversion chart in this chapter). The Malaysian ringgit is artificially pegged to the U.S. dollar at about 3.80, but that's still much higher than the 2.50 ringgit you'd have gotten before the crisis. Indonesia wins the prize. The pre-crisis rupiah was about 2,430 to the dollar. Today a dollar goes for about 8,850. The Singapore dollar has been discounted by about 30 (Singapore) cents to its current rate of 1.65 Sing to the U.S. dollar. Likewise in the Philippines, whereas the U.S. dollar was once worth 26.37 pesos, it's now hovering around a steady 40.

Beyond saving on your in-country spending, though, **you'll also spend less money getting to Southeast Asia than ever before.** According to the Association of Asia-Pacific Airlines, the number of passengers its members carried fell almost 9% in the past year. Southeast Asian airlines are not only cutting back on routes and staff to meet operating costs, but are offering great discounts to fill seats. Just after the crisis hit, Malaysian Airlines advertised a round-trip ticket to Kuala Lumpur from New York/New Jersey's Newark International Airport for only US$700. While the price has now risen, you're sure to find good deals around if you look into local airlines. In many

## Where Your Money Goes Furthest

While you will definitely get a lot of bang for your buck wherever you go in Southeast Asia, exactly how much bang will be determined to some extent by which countries you visit. Among the most affordable at press time are **Thailand, Malaysia,** and **Bali,** though bargains can even be found in Singapore and Hong Kong.

---

cases, **package tour** rates have also been substantially reduced, and **domestic travel**—for instance, Malaysia Airlines or Thai Airlines hops within each country—is similarly greatly discounted, mainly because so few of the locals are planning holidays.

What's more, travel agents, transportation companies, and hotels are banding together to cook up all sorts of packages to lure you here. Refer to each country's "When to Go" section for off-peak travel seasons for even better deals.

**International luxury hotels** have adopted several strategies for weathering the crisis—among them quoting rates in U.S. dollars as opposed to local currency, a policy that prevents them from losing their shirts amid unpredictable currency values. In some instances, however, room rates have been lowered. Four-star and three-star hotels, as well as guest houses, have almost all discounted standard room rates. A word of advice: Never accept the first offer. Competition is fierce, so always ask for a discount rate, package deal, long-term stay rate, off-peak rate—anything you can think of. Then ask them to throw in free breakfast.

**Retail sales** have become a big problem for Southeast Asian economies. The locals have really tightened their belts, causing shop owners to panic. Singapore, that infamous shop-a-holic fantasy, has seen many businesses close from the strain. Interestingly, what's hit them the hardest is the decline of notoriously spend-crazy Japanese tourists and Indonesian fat cats who'd blow their wads on luxury items to hide it from the tax man. As a result, you'll see all kinds of sales, enticing offers, and great deals. People want to make a sale. The down side of this is that many shops have closed. For that matter, so have many restaurants and nightspots.

The bottom line is, if you've ever dreamed of experiencing Southeast Asia, there is no better time to do it than right now. Get it while the gettin's good. Tourism boards are inventing new ways to attract you to their shores even as you read this (hell, the Singapore Tourism Board would make the sewer system an attraction if it thought it could get a dime out of it). Still in all, and respecting the fact that the people of these countries face difficult economic times ahead, you are most welcome to come visit—and help them out by spending a little cash. Everybody wins.

## CARRYING MONEY & GETTING THE BEST EXCHANGE RATES

It used to be that travelers depended on traveler's checks when making a trip, but that was before the days of credit cards and easy cash access through ATMs. We learned recently that an ATM has been installed in Antarctica, and if that doesn't say something about how easy it is to get access to your money in the world today, I don't know what does.

That said, Southeast Asia still has many areas where you will not find ATMs and where, except in large hotels, you'll even have a hard time using credit cards. For this reason, we recommend using a combination of traveler's checks, credit cards, and cash when traveling to this part of the world.

**TRAVELER'S CHECKS**   Traveler's checks have long been the most popular way to carry money since they are replaceable if lost or stolen and are also widely accepted at exchange bureaus in major airports as well as at most banks, hotels, and other establishments such as restaurants and shops that deal frequently with tourists. Of these, I recommend exchanging them at banks and currency exchange booths controlled by banks rather than at airports and hotels, which typically charge the highest commissions.

You can get traveler's checks at almost any bank. **American Express** offers denominations of US$10, US$20, US$50, US$100, US$500, and US$1,000. You'll pay a service charge ranging from 1 to 4%. You can also get American Express traveler's checks over the phone by calling ☎ **800/221-7282;** by using this number, Amex gold and platinum cardholders are exempt from the 1% fee. AAA members can obtain checks without a fee at most AAA offices.

**Visa** offers traveler's checks at Citibank locations nationwide, as well as several other banks. The service charge ranges between 1.5 and 2%; checks come in denominations of US$20, US$50, US$100, US$500, and US$1,000. **MasterCard** (☎ **800/223-9920**) and **Thomas Cook** (☎ **800/223-7373** in the U.S. and Canada; www.thomas-cook.com) also offer traveler's checks. Call for a location near you.

If you opt to carry traveler's checks, be sure to keep a record of their serial numbers, separately from the checks of course, so you're ensured a refund in an emergency.

**AUTOMATED TELLER MACHINES (ATMs)**    ATMs, which are commonplace in Hong Kong, Singapore, Kuala Lumpur, Bangkok, and other frequently touristed cities, are another means of obtaining local currency. Use of an ATM gives you the best bank rate of the day and exceeds the rates offered by change bureaus and hotels. However, once you leave the major cities you will rarely find an ATM. (Before departing for Southeast Asia you should check with your bank to make sure that foreign ATM machines will accept your bank card.) See individual country chapters for more information on ATM availability.

**CREDIT CARDS**    Credit cards are invaluable when traveling. They are a safe way to carry money and provide a convenient record of all your expenses. Major credit cards, including American Express, Visa, and MasterCard, are widely accepted in Southeast Asia hotels, restaurants, and shops. Some banks may also be willing to give you a cash advance against your card (though you'll start paying hefty interest on the advance the moment you receive the cash, and you won't receive frequent-flyer miles on an airline credit card). At most banks, you don't even need to go to a teller; you can get a cash advance at the ATM if you know your PIN number. If you've forgotten your PIN number or didn't even know you had one, call the phone number on the back of your credit card and ask the bank to send it to you. It usually takes 5 to 7 business days, though some banks will provide the number over the phone if you tell them your mother's maiden name or pass some other security clearance.

Almost every credit card company has an emergency 800-number that you can call to report **lost or stolen cards.** They may be able to wire you a cash advance off your credit card immediately, and in many places, they can deliver an emergency credit card in a day or two. The issuing bank's 800-number is usually on the back of the credit card—though of course that won't help you much if the card was stolen. The toll-free information directory will provide the number if you dial ☎ **800/555-1212.** Citicorp Visa's U.S. emergency number is ☎ **800/336-8472.** American Express cardholders and traveler's check holders should call ☎ **800/221-7282** for all money emergencies. MasterCard holders should call ☎ **800/307-7309.**

**EXCHANGING CURRENCY**    When arriving at an airport, it's a good idea to change only a small amount into local currency (enough to get from the airport to the hotel) since you will get a better exchange rate at a bank or ATM. If you're carrying most of your money as traveler's checks, change only as many checks into the local currency as you will need so that you don't end up with an excessive amount when departing the country.

The best exchange rates often are available through local money changers that, depending on the country, may or may not have government approval. For example, in Singapore and Malaysia money changers operating out of booths in shopping centers and small shops offer the best rates.

## THE PREVALENCE OF THE U.S. DOLLAR

Because of the devaluation of most of Southeast Asia's currencies during the recent financial crisis, we're faced with a situation where many businesses—particularly hotels and larger restaurants and stores—prefer doing business in U.S. dollars to dealing in their official national currency. This practice has become so prevalent that the writers researching this book found that these establishments actually quoted their official prices in dollars, foregoing even a pretext of dealing in their national currency.

As unfortunate as this is may be for national economic pride, it does make things somewhat easier for the traveler. Comparing prices from country to country is easier, and carrying and exchanging cash—both in-country and between countries—is also easier: For the most part, you won't have to cart around sacks full, for example, of Vietnamese dong, which are exchanged at the rate of approximately 13,000 or 14,000 to the dollar. If you prefer to do most of your business in dollars, even smaller vendors will usually take them in the big cities, but in the rural areas the local currency will usually be preferred.

In this book, we've listed **hotel, restaurant, and attraction rates** in whatever form the establishments quoted them—in U.S. dollars (designated as US$) where those were quoted, and in local currencies (with U.S. dollar equivalents) where those were used.

Note that with the exception of the Singapore dollar, Malaysian ringgit, and Hong Kong dollar (which have remained stable), all other Southeast Asian national currencies are in an extreme state of flux, so before you budget your trip based on rates we give in this book, be sure to check the currency's current status. CNN's Web site has a convenient **currency converter** at **www.cnn.com/travel/currency.**

## WORKING WITH THE LOCAL CURRENCY

You will have to rely primarily on local currency when traveling in the countryside and/or visiting towns and villages situated off the main tourist routes where neither traveler's checks or credit cards are accepted. No matter where you travel, its always a good idea to have some U.S. dollars handy, preferably in small bills, which may help ease you through any unforeseen emergencies. The U.S. dollar has long been the most readily accepted foreign currency throughout Southeast Asia.

Below we've listed the currencies of all countries in this guide, with their denominations. See the chart on page 36 for comparisons of these currencies to U.S., Australian, Canadian, and New Zealand dollars, and to British pounds.

**BURMA (MYANMAR)**    The main unit of currency is the **kyat** (pronounced chat) which is made up of 100 **pyas.** Kyats come in notes with denominations of 1, 5, and 10. There are also 1 kyat coins and coins of 1, 5, 10, 25, and 50 pyas. The exchange rate is stable at approximately 6.25 kyat to the dollar. It is illegal to carry Burmese currency out of the country, so be sure to exchange whatever you have remaining when you leave the country.

**CAMBODIA**    The monetary unit is the **Riel,** which is available in 50, 100, 200, 500, 1,000, 5,000, 10,000, 20,000, and 50,000 riel notes. Cambodia's volatile exchange rate typically fluctuates from 2,5000 to 3,750 riels to US $1. It's a good idea to bring a supply of U.S. dollars since the dollar is considered Cambodia's second currency and is accepted by many hotels, guest houses, and restaurants (in fact, some establishments prefer dollars to local currency—see discussion above).

## Southeast Asian Currency Conversions

| | U.S. $1 | Aust. $1 | Can. $1 | NZ $1 | British £1 |
|---|---|---|---|---|---|
| Cambodian riel | 3,770 | 2,337 | 2,475 | 1,985 | 6,065 |
| Hong Kong dollar | 7.80 | 4.85 | 5.10 | 4.10 | 12.55 |
| Indonesian rupiah | 8,850 | 5,485 | 5,805 | 4,665 | 14,240 |
| Laotian kip | 4,160 | 2,580 | 2,730 | 2,190 | 6,695 |
| Malaysian ringgit | 3.80 | 2.35 | 2.50 | 2 | 6.10 |
| Myanmar kyat | 6.25 | 3.80 | 4.10 | 3.30 | 10.05 |
| Philippines peso | 40.25 | 24.95 | 26.40 | 21.20 | 64.75 |
| Singapore dollar | 1.65 | 1 | 1.10 | .85 | 2.65 |
| Thai baht | 37 | 22.95 | 24.25 | 19.50 | 59.55 |
| Vietnam dong | 13,850 | 8,590 | 9,085 | 7,300 | 22,285 |

**HONG KONG**   Hong Kong **dollar (HK$)** notes come in different colors. There are denominations of HK$10 (green), HK$50 (blue), HK$100 (red), HK$500 (yellow), and HK$1,000 (orange). There are also HK$1, HK$2, and HK$5 coins plus 10, 20, and 50¢ coins. The exchange rate is approximately HK$7.80 to US$1.

**INDONESIA (BALI)**   The **rupiah (Rp)** is the main currency, with bills of Rp100, Rp500, Rp1,000, Rp5,000, Rp10,000, Rp20,000, and Rp50,000 and coins in denominations of 25, 50, 100, and 500. Indonesia's currency was hit hard in 1998 and 1999, leading to exchange rates that fluctuated wildly— from a pre-crisis rate of approximately Rp2,300 to US$1, the rupiah plunged to Rp14,700 to US$1 in July 1998 and at press time was hovering around Rp8,850 to US$1.

**LAOS**   The primary unit of currency is the **kip,** which comes in denominations of 1, 10, 20, 50, 100, and 500, 1,000, 2,000, and 5,000. The exchange rate is approximately 4,200 kip to US$1. As in Cambodia, many tourist establishments prefer payment in U.S. dollars. In many areas of Laos, both U.S. dollars and Thai baht are preferred over the local currency

**MALAYSIA**   The **ringgit,** which is also referred to as the Malaysian dollar, is the unit of currency and prices are marked RM. One ringgit equals 100 sen, and notes come in RM1, RM2, RM5, RM10, RM20, RM50, RM100, RM500 and RM1,000. Coins come in denominations of 1, 2, 5, 10, and 50 sen. The value of the ringgit was stabilized throughout the SE Asian financial crisis at RM3.8 to US$1.

**PHILIPPINES**   The Philippines **peso,** which is divided into 100 **centavos,** is available in 2, 5, 10, 20, 50, and 100 peso bills, as well as 1, 5, 10, 25 and 50 centavo and 1 and 5 peso coins. The exchange rate is approximately 40 pesos to US$1.

**SINGAPORE**   The **Singapore dollar** (commonly referred to as the "Sing" dollar) is the unit of currency, with notes issued in denominations of S$1, S$2, S$5, S$10, S$20, S$50, S$100, S$500, and S$1,000; coins come in denominations of 1, 5, 10, 20 and 50¢ and the gold-colored S$1. The exchange rate is approximately S$1.65 to US$1.

**THAILAND**   The Thai **baht,** which is made up of 100 **satangs,** comes in colored notes of 10baht (brown), 20baht (green), 100baht (red), and 500baht (purple). Coins come in denominations of 1 baht and 5 baht and also 25 and 50 satangs. The exchange rate is approximately 37baht to US$1.

**VIETNAM**    The main unit of Vietnamese currency is the **dong,** which comes in denominations of 200, 500, 1,000, 2,000, 5,000, 10,000, 20,000 and 50,000 notes. There are no coins. While it is officially against the law to accept U.S. currency, many tourism facilities in the cities take dollars. However, in the countryside and well away from major cities only dong are accepted. The exchange rate is approximately 14,000 VND to US$1.

## TIPPING & TAXES

While tipping is always a matter of individual discretion, it is not expected by most hotels and restaurants throughout Southeast Asia, which add a 10 to 15% service charge to the bill. The only places where tipping is expected are in major upscale hotels, restaurants, and bars that cater to Western tourists. You should also tip personal guides a small amount of currency or give them a small gift.

**Airport departure taxes,** which vary in amounts from country to country (see the individual country chapters for rates), are commonplace and must be paid in local currency (though some countries accept U.S. dollars) prior to leaving on an international flight.

## 3  When to Go

Whenever and wherever you travel in Southeast Asia, you are likely to encounter hot and humid weather. All of Southeast Asia lies within the tropics, and the countries closest to the equator—Singapore, Malaysia, Indonesia, the Philippines, and southern Thailand—have the hottest annual temperatures. Vietnam, Laos, Cambodia, Burma, and the rest of Thailand located 10 to 20 degrees above the equator also have high humidity but slightly "cooler" temperatures.

Rather than spring, summer, winter, and fall, there are typically **two main seasons** in southeast Asia: dry and wet (the latter typically known as "monsoon" season). For example, **Vietnam, Cambodia, Laos,** and **Burma** all share a similar year-round climate, with rainy season from May and September and only light, infrequent periods of rain the rest of the year. The dry months of October through March are also the most pleasant time to visit **Hong Kong,** while the most rain usually falls between July and September, during typhoon season.

**Singapore, Malaysia,** and **the Philippines** are hot and humid year-round, with annual average maximum and minimum daily temperatures of 90° and 72° and year-round humidity above 90%. Temperatures are considerably cooler in the hill country of Malaysia's Cameron and Genting Highlands, where average daytime temperature is 72 and 56 at night. The Highlands also have more annual rainfall than the lowland areas of Malaysia, including Kuala Lumpur and Penang.

Most major cities are located at or near sea level, where average daytime temperatures are in the 80- to 90° range year-round. The best way to escape the heat and humidity is to head for the hills and mountains in the higher altitude regions of Thailand, Malaysia, Vietnam, Burma, Laos, and the Philippines.

## HOLIDAYS, CELEBRATIONS & FESTIVALS

Some of the holidays celebrated in Southeast Asia may affect your vacation plans, either positively (because you'll get to see the destination at its most festive, as for instance during Chinese New Year) or adversely (because some businesses and attractions may be closed on national holidays). See the individual country chapters for listings of the major holidays celebrated in each country.

# Ringing in the New Year, Chinese-Style

Chinese New Year, a 15-day celebration of the new year according to the Lunar Calendar, is the most important festival of the Chinese culture and, owing to the large Chinese population spread across Southeast Asia, is a huge occasion throughout the region. It was originally called *chun jie* or Spring Festival, to celebrate the passing of winter and spring's promise of a fertile and prosperous growing season. In modern times, it is still seen as a chance to put the past behind and start afresh, with new hopes for prosperity, health, and luck. During the celebration, homes and businesses display large red banners with the characters *gong xi fa cai,* which mean "Wishing you great prosperity." Stores generally mark up prices dramatically just before the New Year to cash in on the opportunity. Outside of homes, the Chinese hang the character *fu,* which means "luck." The *fu* is usually hung upside down because in Chinese the words for "luck upside down" sound similar to the words for "luck arrives." Red, symbolizing luck and prosperity, is predominant in banners and is the color of the *hong bao,* packets of money given to children and single young adults by parents and married friends. Money is given in even dollar amounts (as even numbers are considered auspicious) and should be opened in private. Oranges and tangerines are given as gifts (also in even numbers), symbolizing gold and luck, both in their colors and in Chinese puns. Also important are noisy firecrackers, which are believed to ward off evil spirits and also serve (through their noise) as a sign of life.

New Year's Day, the first day of celebration, generally falls somewhere between January 21 and February 19. In preparation, the Chinese pay off old debts, since debt is believed to lead to bad luck in the coming year if not taken care of, and clean their homes from tip to toe, sweeping the floors in a symbolic clearing away of old misfortunes. All cleaning is done before New Year's Eve, because New Year's day is auspicious, and to sweep on this day would be to sweep *away* good luck. (So hide your broom.) New Year's Eve is the night of the reunion feast, where family members gather and invite the spirits of deceased ancestors to gather for a meal, the centerpiece of which is a large fish to symbolize unity.

New Year's is a time for rejoicing with family and friends, praying to ancestors, and going to the parades, which usually feature dragon dances, stiltwalkers, and floats. While the first and second days are spent visiting friends and family, the third is considered unlucky for visiting, and most people return to work.

The final day of the celebration, the 15th day, is the **Lantern Festival,** which coincides with the first full moon of the new year. Paper lanterns are hung in doorways, a romantic backdrop for this day that the Chinese consider auspicious for lovers.

—Jennifer Eveland

## PACKING TIPS

Depending on where you travel in Southeast Asia, you'll experience a range of temperatures, though mostly what you'll feel is year-round **tropical heat.** Some northern hill areas of Laos, Thailand, and Vietnam can dip into the 40s (°F) during the cool season (November through February), though even during this period temperatures in the southern parts of the countries will remain in the 70s and 80s.

**Lightweight clothing** in natural fibers (or breathable travel gear) is essential in the tropical heat, as are a hat and a pair of sunglasses. For sightseeing, the most comfortable clothing will be lightweight cotton long pants and shorts. T-shirts tend to be on the heavy side, but may be practical for packing. Except at resorts and the beach, avoid wearing shorts in Vietnam, Laos, and more conservative areas of Malaysia, and remember that neither men nor women should enter temples and mosques wearing shorts or sleeveless tank tops (women are also requested not to enter wearing miniskirts or sleeveless, backless, or low-cut tops; also, in Malaysia, women are required to cover their arms, legs, and heads in order to enter a mosque, so you'll want to carry a light scarf). Bring a raincoat or poncho just in case, and a **light sweater** for cooler temperatures; even in places like Singapore and the Philippines, which are hot all year round, you'll use the sweater indoors, to combat sometimes overly frigid air conditioning.

A pair of rugged open **sport sandals** is also a must, and a pair of rubber flip-flops come in handy in hotel rooms with tile or wood floors, and for use in public showers. Bring **shoes** that fit loosely. If you come from colder climates, your feet will swell from the heat, as well as from being on them all day while you're taking in the sights. Don't even trust your favorite pair: If they're a snug fit, they'll turn into your worst enemies before long. Pack wool socks if you plan to hike. They're breathable, repel moisture, and are better at preventing blisters than cotton socks.

**Film** is easy to get in all of these countries, and is usually much cheaper than in the West (the exceptions being Singapore and Hong Kong, where it costs about the same). If you're thinking of **renting a bike** along the way, bringing your own helmet isn't a bad idea. Most **toiletries**, even Western brands, are easily available at pharmacies and stores in the big cities. A pair of your own **plastic chopsticks** or a small cutlery set may also come in handy.

Particularly if you're traveling outside of the big cities, you should carry your own **mini-medical kit,** including a mild anti-diarrheal like Pepto-Bismol and something stronger like Imodium, plus cold medicine, a mosquito repellent containing DEET, sunscreen (including some for your lips), feminine hygiene products (if you're a female), sanitary hand wipes, a pain reliever and fever reducer, and a powdered replenishment formula if you're stricken with bad diarrhea. You may want to bring Cipro (ciprofloxicin), an antibiotic that kills diarrhea-causing bacteria; check with your doctor. If you are taking **prescription medication,** make sure to bring enough to last your entire trip, and carry your doctor's prescription with you. Bring a spare pare of glasses or contact lenses as well.

## 4 Getting There

Bangkok, Singapore, and Hong Kong receive the most international flights and offer the most extensive network of connecting flights to other cities and destinations throughout Southeast Asia. See the appendix for airline phone and Web site information, and see the individual country chapters for more specific and detailed travel information.

### TO HONG KONG
The following carriers fly to Hong Kong's Chek Lap Kok Airport.

**FROM THE U.S.**   United, Northwest, Cathay Pacific, China Airlines, Singapore Airlines, Thai Airways, and Hong Kong Dragon Airlines.

**FROM CANADA**   Cathay Pacific, Canadian Airlines International, Air Canada, Singapore Airlines, and China Airlines.

**FROM THE U.K.**   Cathay Pacific, British Airways, Virgin Atlantic Airways, Singapore Airlines, China Airlines, and Hong Kong Dragon Airlines.

**FROM AUSTRALIA**   Cathay Pacific, Qantas, Ansett Australian Airlines, Singapore Airlines, and Hong Kong Dragon Airlines.

**FROM NEW ZEALAND**   Air New Zealand and Cathay Pacific.

## TO SINGAPORE

The following carriers fly to Singapore's Changi Airport.

**FROM THE U.S.**   Singapore Airlines has the most weekly flights from the U.S. to Changi International Airport. United and Northwest are the only U.S. airlines offering flights to Singapore.

**FROM CANADA**   Singapore Airlines provides service from Canada, along with Canadian Airlines International.

**FROM THE U.K.**   You can fly to Singapore via Singapore Airlines, British Airways, and Qantas Airways.

**FROM AUSTRALIA**   Singapore Air, Qantas, Ansett Australian Airlines, British Airways, and Royal Dutch Airlines all provide service to Singapore.

**FROM NEW ZEALAND**   Singapore Airlines and Air New Zealand offer New Zealand-Singapore flights.

## TO BANGKOK

The following international airlines provide service to Bangkok's Don Muang International Airport.

**FROM THE U.S.**   Service is provided by the national carrier, Thai Airways, as well as United, Northwest, Cathay Pacific, All Nippon Airways, Asiana Airlines, Japan Air Lines, China Airlines, Eva Airlines, Korean Air, Malaysia Air Lines, and Singapore Air Lines.

**FROM THE U.K.**   Airlines with flights from the U.K. to Bangkok include Thai Airways, British Airways, and Singapore Airlines.

**FROM CANADA**   Canadian Airlines International flies to Bangkok from Vancouver via Hong Kong four days a week.

**FROM AUSTRALIA**   Service is provided by Qantas, Thai Airways, Singapore Airlines, and British Airways.

## FLYING FOR LESS: TIPS FOR GETTING THE BEST AIRFARES

Passengers within the same airplane cabin are rarely paying the same fare for their seats. Business travelers who need to purchase tickets at the last minute, change their itinerary at a moment's notice, or get home before the weekend pay the premium rate, known as the full fare. Passengers who can book their ticket long in advance, who don't mind staying over Saturday night, or who are willing to travel on a Tuesday, Wednesday, or Thursday after 7pm, will pay a fraction of the full fare. Here are a few other easy ways to save.

1. **Keep tabs on airline discounts.** Periodically, airlines lower prices on their most popular routes. Check your newspaper for advertised discounts or call the airlines directly and ask if any **promotional rates** or special fares are available. You'll almost never see a sale during the peak summer vacation months of July and August, or during the Thanksgiving or Christmas seasons; but in periods of

low-volume travel, you should pay no more than US$400 for a cross-country flight. If your schedule is flexible, ask if you can secure a cheaper fare by staying an extra day or by flying midweek. (Many airlines won't volunteer this information.) If you already hold a ticket when a sale breaks, it may even pay to exchange your ticket, which usually incurs a US$50 to US$75 charge.

Note, however, that the lowest-priced fares are often nonrefundable, require advance purchase of 1 to 3 weeks and a certain length of stay, and carry penalties for changing dates of travel.

2. **Consolidators, also known as bucket shops, are a good place to find low fares.** Consolidators buy seats in bulk from the airlines and then sell them back to the public at prices below even the airlines' discounted rates. Their small boxed ads usually run in the Sunday travel section of your newspaper, at the bottom of the page. Before you pay, however, ask for a confirmation number from the consolidator and then call the airline itself to confirm your seat. Be prepared to book your ticket with a different consolidator—there are many to choose from—if the airline can't confirm your reservation. Also be aware that bucket shop tickets are usually non-refundable or rigged with stiff cancellation penalties, often as high as 50% to 75% of the ticket price.

   **Council Travel** (☎ 800/226-8624; www.counciltravel.com) and **STA Travel** (☎ 800/781-4040; www.sta.travel.com) cater especially to young travelers, but their bargain basement prices are available to people of all ages. **Travel Bargains** (☎ 800/AIR-FARE; www.1800airfare.com) was formerly owned by TWA but now offers the deepest discounts on many other airlines, with a 4-day advance purchase. Other reliable consolidators include **1-800-FLY-CHEAP** (www.1800flycheap.com); **TFI Tours International** (☎ 800-745-8000 or 212/736-1140), which serves as a clearinghouse for unused seats; or "rebaters" such as **Travel Avenue** (☎ 800/333-3335 or 312/876-1116) and the **Smart Traveller** (☎ 800/448-3338 in the U.S. or 305/448-3338), which rebate part of their commissions to you.

3. **Search the Internet for cheap fares.** See the "Cyber Deals for Net Surfers" section below for tips.

4. **Book a seat on a charter flight.** Discounted fares have pared the number available, but they can still be found. Most charter operators advertise and sell their seats through travel agents, thus making these local professionals your best source of information for available flights. Before deciding to take a charter flight, however, check the restrictions on the ticket: You may be asked to purchase a tour package, to pay in advance, to be amenable if the day of departure is changed, to pay a service charge, to fly on an airline you're not familiar with (this usually is not the case), and to pay harsh penalties if you cancel—but to be understanding if the charter doesn't fill up and is canceled up to 10 days before departure. Summer charters fill up more quickly than others and are almost sure to fly, but if you decide on a charter flight, seriously consider cancellation and baggage insurance.

5. **Look into courier flights.** Companies that hire couriers use your luggage allowance for their business baggage; in return, you get a deeply discounted ticket. Flights are often offered at the last minute, and you may have to arrange a pretrip interview to make sure you're right for the job. **Now Voyager,** open Monday to Friday from 10am to 5:30pm and Saturday from noon to 4:30pm (☎ 212/431-1616), flies from New York. Now Voyager also offers noncourier discounted fares, so call the company even if you don't want to fly as a courier.

6. **Join a travel club** such as **Moment's Notice** (☎ 718/234-6295) or **Sears Discount Travel Club** (☎ 800/433-9383, or 800/255-1487 to join), which supply unsold tickets at discounted prices. You pay an annual membership fee to get the club's hotline number. Of course, you're limited to what's available, so you have to be flexible.

## CYBER DEALS FOR NET SURFERS

It's possible to get some great deals on airfare, hotels, and car rentals via the Internet. Grab your mouse and surf before you take off—you could save a bundle on your trip. The Web sites highlighted below are worth checking out, especially since all services are free. Always check the lowest published fare, however, before you shop for flights on-line.

**Arthur Frommer's Budget Travel** (www.frommers.com)   Home of the Encyclopedia of Travel and *Arthur Frommer's Budget Travel* magazine and daily newsletter, this site offers detailed information on 200 cities and islands around the world, and up-to-the-minute ways to save dramatically on flights, hotels, car reservations, and cruises. Book an entire vacation on-line and research your destination before you leave. Consult the message board to set up "hospitality exchanges" in other countries, to talk with other travelers who have visited a hotel you're considering, or to direct travel questions to Arthur Frommer himself. The newsletter is updated daily to keep you abreast of the latest breaking ways to save, to publicize new hot spots and best buys, and to present veteran readers with fresh, ever-changing approaches to travel.

**Microsoft Expedia** (www.expedia.com)   The best part of this multi-purpose travel site is the "Fare Tracker": You fill out a form on the screen indicating that you're interested in cheap flights from your nearest airport to up to three destinations, and, once a week, they'll e-mail you the best airfare deals. The site's "Travel Agent" will steer you to bargains on hotels and car rentals, and with the help of hotel and airline seat pinpointers, you can book everything right on-line. This site is even useful once you're booked. Before you depart, log on to Expedia for maps and up-to-date travel information, including weather reports and foreign exchange rates.

**Travelocity** (www.travelocity.com)   This is one of the best travel sites out there, especially for finding cheap airfare. In addition to its "Personal Fare Watcher," which notifies you via e-mail of the lowest airfares for up to five different destinations, Travelocity will track the three lowest fares for any routes on any dates in minutes. You can book a flight right then and there, and if you need a rental car or hotel, Travelocity will find you the best deal via the SABRE computer reservations system (a huge travel agent database). Click on "Last Minute Deals" for the latest travel bargains, including a link to "H.O.T. Coupons" (www.hotcoupons.com), where you can print out electronic coupons for travel in the U.S. and Canada.

**The Trip** (www.thetrip.com)   This site is really geared toward the business traveler, but vacationers-to-be can also use The Trip's exceptionally powerful fare-finding engine, which will e-mail you every week with the best city-to-city airfare deals for as many as 10 routes. The Trip uses the Internet Travel Network, another reputable travel agent database, to book hotels and restaurants.

**E-Savers Programs**   Several major airlines offer a free e-mail service known as E-Savers, via which they'll send you their best bargain airfares on a regular basis. Here's how it works: Once a week (usually Wednesday), or whenever a sale fare comes up, subscribers receive a list of discounted flights to and from various destinations, both international and domestic. Here's the catch: These fares are usually only available if you leave the very next Saturday (or sometimes Friday night) and return on the following Monday or Tuesday. It's really a service for the spontaneously inclined and travelers looking for a quick getaway. But the fares are cheap, so it's worth taking a look. If you have a preference for certain airlines (in other words, the ones you fly most frequently), sign up with them first. See the appendix for a listing of airline Web sites.

One caveat: You'll get frequent-flier miles if you purchase one of these fares, but you can't use miles to buy the ticket.

**Smarter Living** (www.smarterliving.com)   If the thought of all that surfing and comparison shopping gives you a headache, then head right for Smarter Living. Sign up for their newsletter service, and every week you'll get a customized e-mail summarizing the discount fares available from your departure city. Smarter Living tracks more than 15 different airlines, so it's a worthwhile time-saver.

## 5 Getting Around Between Countries

While flying in Southeast Asia may at times be a hassle and strain your patience, it is the preferred and often only way to travel between countries, as train travel is extremely limited and travel by road is not recommended. Only if you have a high threshold for frustration, discomfort, and delay should you consider traveling by road or rail. With the exception of Thailand, Malaysia, and in and around Singapore and Hong Kong, roads are in appalling condition throughout much of Southeast Asia and, when coupled with heavy traffic in countries like Vietnam, vehicles typically move at an agonizingly slow pace. On the other hand, in countries with a decent network of highways (like Malaysia and Thailand), drivers often travel at breakneck speeds and accidents are not uncommon.

See individual country chapters for tips on getting around within each country.

### BY PLANE

Depending on your specific itinerary, you may fly on international carriers including Singapore Airlines, Malaysia Airlines, Thai Airways, Cathay Pacific, or Garuda (Indonesia), as well as various domestic carriers including Pelangi (Malaysia) Myanma (Burma), Lao Aviation (Laos), and Vietnam Airlines.

**From Singapore,** some of the most heavily serviced inter-Asia air routes include Singapore-Bangkok, Singapore-Hong Kong, Singapore-Manila and Singapore-Denpasar (Bali); there is also frequent service from Bangkok-Singapore, Bangkok-Hong Kong, Bangkok-Manila, and Bangkok-Yangon(Rangoon).

**Hong Kong** has the most flights to Vietnam (Hanoi and Ho Chi Minh City) and the Philippines (Manila).

Some of the most popular domestic routes include the following city pairs: Bangkok to Phuket and Bangkok to Chiang Mai, Thailand; Kuala Lumpur to Penang, Malaysia; Hanoi to Ho Chi Minh City, Vietnam; Yangon to Bagan and Bagan to Mandalay, Burma; Phnom Penh to Siem Reap (near Angkor Wat), Cambodia. There is also now a direct flight from Bangkok to Siem Reap.

### BY TRAIN

With a few exceptions, trains that operate throughout Southeast Asia are poorly maintained, overcrowded, and slow. The most popular rail route—and the only one with interconnecting service between countries in all of Southeast Asia—runs from Singapore to Bangkok (and vice versa) through the heart of the Malaysian peninsula, with

---

### International Driver's Licenses

Of the countries covered in this volume, only the Philippines permits foreign visitors to drive using only a driver's license from their home country. To drive in all others (excluding Vietnam, where foreign visitors aren't permitted to drive at all), you'll have to obtain an international driver's license; U.S. citizens can obtain an international permit from the Automobile Association of America (AAA).

---

stops along the way at the cities of Johor Bahru, Malacca, Kuala Lumpur, and Butterworth (for Penang). It takes 6 hours from Singapore to Kuala Lumpur and another 35 hours from KL to Bangkok. You can board the train at the Singapore Rail Station in Tanjong Pagar, at the Kuala Lumpur Central Railway Station on Jalan Hishamuddin, and in Bangkok at the Hualamphong Railway Station on Rama Road.

Upscale travelers with unlimited budgets can travel on one of the world's foremost luxury trains, the **Eastern & Oriental express,** which covers the distance between Singapore and Bangkok in 42 hours. Eastern and Oriental Express also operates a deluxe **river cruiser** in Burma, the 126-passenger *Road to Mandalay,* which travels between Bagan and Mandalay. For information and reservations for both the Great South Pacific Express and the *Road to Mandalay,* contact Orient-Express Hotels, 1155 Avenue of the Americas, New York, NY 10036 (☎ **800/524-2420;** www.orient-expresshotels.com/oeh).

## 6 Package Tours & Escorted Tours

Before you start your search for the lowest airfare, you may want to consider booking your flight as part of a travel package such as an escorted tour or a package tour. What you lose in adventure, you'll gain in time and money saved when you book accommodations, and maybe even food and entertainment, along with your flight.

### ESCORTED TOURS

Packaged travel may not be the option for you if you like to navigate strange places at whim. If you like to plan your coordinates in advance, however, many package options will enable you to do just that—and save you money in the process.

Some people love escorted tours. They let you relax and take in the sights while a bus driver fights traffic for you; they spell out your costs up front; and they take you to the maximum number of sights in the minimum amount of time with the least amount of hassle. If you do choose an escorted tour, you should ask a few simple questions before you buy:

1. **What is the cancellation policy?** Do they require a deposit? Can they cancel the trip if they don't get enough people? Do you get a refund if they cancel? If you cancel? How late can you cancel if you are unable to go? When do you pay in full?
2. **How busy is the schedule?** How much sightseeing do they plan each day? Do they allow ample time for relaxing by the pool, shopping, or wandering?
3. **What is the size of the group?** The smaller the group, the more flexible the itinerary, and the less time you'll spend waiting for the rest of your group. Tour operators may be evasive about this, because they may not know the exact size of the group until everybody has made their reservations; but they should be able to give you a rough estimate. Some tours have a minimum group size and may cancel the tour if they don't book enough people.

4. **What is included in the price?** Don't assume anything. You may have to pay for transportation to and from the airport. A box lunch may be included in an excursion, but drinks might cost extra. Beer might be included, but wine might not. Can you opt out of certain activities, or does the group leave at a certain time every day, with no exceptions? Are all your meals planned in advance? Can you choose your entree at dinner, or does everybody get the same chicken cutlet?

## PACKAGE TOURS

Package tours are not the same thing as escorted tours. They are simply a way to buy airfare and accommodations at the same time. For popular destinations like Bali and Thailand, they are a smart way to go, because they save you a lot of money. In many cases, a package that includes airfare, hotel, and transportation to and from the airport will cost you less than just the hotel alone would have, had you booked it yourself. That's because packages are sold in bulk to tour operators, who then resell them to the public at a cost that drastically undercuts standard rates.

Packages, however, vary widely. Some offer a better class of hotels than others. Some offer the same hotels for lower prices. Some offer flights on scheduled airlines, while others book charters. In some packages, your choice of accommodations and travel days may be limited. Some packages let you choose between escorted vacations and independent vacations; others will allow you to add on just a few excursions or escorted day trips (also at lower prices than you could locate on your own) without booking an entirely escorted tour. Each destination usually has one or two packagers that are usually cheaper than the rest because they buy in even greater bulk. If you spend the time to shop around, you will save in the long run.

### FINDING A PACKAGE DEAL

The best place to start your search is the travel section of your local Sunday newspaper. Also check the ads in the back of national travel magazines like *Travel & Leisure, National Geographic Traveler,* and *Condé Nast Traveler.* One of the biggest packagers in the Northeast, **Liberty Travel,** usually boasts a full-page ad in Sunday papers. You won't get much in the way of service, but you will get a good deal. Check your local directory for one of its many local branches nationwide, or visit the Liberty Web site at www.libertytravel.com. **American Express Vacations** (☎ **800/241-1700;** www.leisureweb.com) is another option. Check out its **Last Minute Travel Bargains** site, offered in conjunction with **Continental Airlines,** (www6.americanexpress.com/travel/lastminutetravel/default.asp), with deeply discounted vacation packages and reduced airline fares that differ from the E-savers bargains that Continental e-mails weekly to subscribers. **Northwest Airlines** offers a similar service. Posted on Northwest's Web site every Wednesday, its **Cyber Saver Bargain Alerts** offer special hotel rates, package deals, and discounted airline fares.

Another good resource is the airlines themselves, which often package their flights together with accommodations. Fly-by-night packagers are uncommon, but they do exist; when you buy your package through the airline, however, you can be pretty sure that the company will still be in business when your departure date arrives.

The biggest hotel chains and resorts also offer package deals. If you already know where you want to stay, call the resort itself and ask if they can offer land/air packages.

## TOUR OPERATORS SPECIALIZING IN SOUTHEAST ASIA

Whether you want to ride an elephant through the jungle, trek among indigenous people, shake hands with an orangutan, swim beneath a waterfall, snorkel in a clear

## Travel Insurance for Escorted Tours

If you choose an escorted tour, think strongly about purchasing travel insurance from an independent agency, especially if the tour operator asks you to pay up front. See the section on insurance later in this chapter for more info.

blue lagoon, lounge on a white sand beach, or wander through exotic markets, there's a Southeast Asia tour packager for you, offering a wide range of travel options using the finest and most reliable travel services available in the region

Among the most experienced and knowledgeable tour operators specializing in Southeast Asia are **Absolute Asia** and **East Quest.** Both companies offer a diverse blend of cultural and adventure travel programs and will customize tours and design itineraries to suit each individual's particular interest. Anyone traveling with Absolute Asia has three options: follow the itinerary as is, combine it with another itinerary, or design their own trip.

All tour operators offer escorted package tours for groups and can also customize packages for independent travelers. See individual country chapters for additional tour operators specializing in each country.

**Absolute Asia.** 180 Varick Street, 16th floor, New York, NY 10014. ☎ **800/736-8187;** www.absoluteasia.com.

Absolute Asia offers an array of innovative itineraries that make up its "Exotic Journeys" program, highlighted by its Discover Indochina tour, an 18-day program that covers the top sites and attractions of Vietnam, Cambodia, and Laos. Other popular programs are a 16-day itinerary including Vietnam, Singapore, and Bali and a 22-day Thailand and Burma trip. For those who have less time to spend, Absolute Asia offers packages in individual countries ranging from 3 days/2 nights to 8 days/7 nights.

The company also arranges tours featuring treks through jungles and rain forests and offers the opportunity to visit with indigenous tribes such as the Iban people of Sarawak (East Malaysia) who have given up their headhunting ways and are nowadays better known for their elaborate tattoos and colorful weaving. For those especially interested in the arts, Absolute Asia can arrange for private visits to art galleries and meetings with some of Indochina's finest contemporary artists.

**East Quest.** One Union Square West, Suite 606, New York, NY 10013 ☎ **800/638-3449;** www.eastquest1@aol.com.

East Quest's Indochina programs featuring Vietnam, Laos, and Cambodia range from 5 to 18 days. Among the choices are a 15-day Indochina Explorer tour focusing on Vietnam and Cambodia, while its Laos Explorer spends 15 days in a comprehensive tour of northern and southern Laos. On all its tours, East Quest uses a variety of lodgings, from deluxe villas and luxury hotels to simple bungalows or local inns, and matches travelers with the accommodations that best satisfy their taste and budget.

Among East Quest's special interest programs are dive packages to Thailand, Malaysia, Bali, and the Philippines, which can be tied in with longer tours. Included in these packages are 2 or 3 days of diving with unlimited shore dives, two boat dives per day, tanks, backpacks, weight belts and weights, and full board accommodations. There are also East Quest spa packages available to Bali and Thailand.

**Backroads.** 801 Cedar Street, Berkeley, CA  94710-1800 ☎ **800/462-2848.**

For those who want to explore Southeast Asia by bicycle, cycling and hiking specialist Backroads has a 10-day Bali tour and a 12-day Thailand Golden Triangle tour.

**Explore Worldwide.** Head office in the U.K.: Frederick Street, Aldershot Hants GU11 1LQ, fax 01252 343170; in Canada call Explore Worldwide's Canada representative, Trek Holidays, at ☎ 800/661-7265; in the U.S., contact Adventure Center, 1311 63rd Street, Suite 200, Emeryville, CA 94608, ☎ 800/227-8747; in Australia, call Adventure World at ☎ 1-800/221-931.

London-based tour operator Explore Worldwide is another company offering adventure and cultural tours to Southeast Asia that include jungle exploration and trekking expeditions. For example, there are tours to Thailand, Vietnam, Laos, and Cambodia that include trekking to hill tribes in the region of the Golden Triangle. There is also a Laos-Cambodia itinerary highlighted by a visit to Angkor Wat and a riverboat excursion along the Mekong River. Another tour features visits to Thailand's forests, beaches, and tropical islands.

**Abercrombie & Kent.** 1520 Kensington Rd., Suite 212, Oakbrook, IL 60523-2141. ☎ **800/323-7308;** www.abercrombiekent.com.

Well-known luxury tour operator Abercrombie & Kent's Southeast Asia programs are highlighted by two comprehensive itineraries. Its "Images of Indochina" tour visits Hong Kong, Vietnam, Cambodia, Laos, and Thailand, while "Four Pagodas" visits the same countries with the addition of Burma. These tours also include stays at the finest hotels in Southeast Asia, such as the Oriental in Bangkok and the Mandarin Oriental in Hong Kong.

**Asian Pacific Adventures.** 826 S. Sierra Bonita Ave., Los Angeles, CA 90036-4704. ☎ **213/935-3156.**

Among Asian Pacific Adventures' tours is a 25-day "Best of Indochina," which visits Laos, Vietnam, and Cambodia; a 15-day "Best of Vietnam"; and a 19-day "Rainforests of North Vietnam." It also offers a 15-day Bali tour entitled "Bali: Through an Artist's Eye," which includes visits with wood carvers, weavers, and basket makers.

## 7  Health & Insurance

### GENERAL AVAILABILITY OF HEALTH CARE FACILITIES

The best hospitals and health care facilities are located in the large cities and major tourist centers of countries which have the greatest number of Western tourists—i.e., Singapore, Hong Kong, Malaysia (Kuala Lumpur), Thailand (Bangkok), and the Philippines (Manila). In rural areas of these countries and throughout the lesser developed countries of Vietnam, Cambodia, Laos, and Burma, there are limited health-care facilities, as hospitals are few and far between, and generally of poor quality. Even in heavily touristed Bali, you're better off evacuating to one of the more developed countries if faced with a serious medical situation.

### COMMON DISEASES

Among Southeast Asia's tropical diseases carried by mosquitoes are **malaria, dengue fever,** and **Japanese encephalitis.** Larium, a common malaria prophylactic, can cause reactions, and DEET, the active ingredient in most effective mosquito repellents, can have other adverse health effects, particularly with children, so check with your physician if you're worried about using either. Hepatitis A may be contracted from water or food, while cholera epidemics sometimes occur in remote areas. Bilharzia, schistosomiasis, and giardia are parasitic diseases that can be contracted from swimming or drinking from stagnant or untreated water in lakes or streams.

Anyone contemplating sexual activity should be aware that HIV is rampant in many Southeast Asian countries, along with other STDs such as gonorrhea, syphilis, herpes, and hepatitis B.

The **International Association for Medical Assistance to Travelers (IAMAT)** (☎ **716/754-4883** or 416/652-0137; www.sentex.net/~iamat) offers tips on travel and health concerns in the countries you'll be visiting, and lists local English-speaking doctors. The United States **Centers for Disease Control and Prevention** (☎ **404/ 332-4559;** www.cdc.gov) provides up-to-date information on necessary vaccines and health hazards by region or country (by mail, their booklet is US$20; on the Internet, it's free). The **U.S. State Department's 24 hour travel advisory** (☎ 202/647-5225; Web site http://travel.state.gov/travel_warnings.html) also lists the latest information on diseases affecting a particular country.

## DEALING WITH THE HEAT & HUMIDITY

Limit your exposure to the sun, especially during the first few days of your trip and, thereafter, from 11am to 2pm. Use a sunscreen with a high protection factor and apply it liberally. Remember that children need more protection than adults do. Always make sure to drink plenty of bottled water (at least eight glasses a day), which is the best defense against heat exhaustion and the more serious, life-threatening heatstroke. Also, remember that coffee, tea, soft drinks, and alcoholic beverages should not be substituted for water, as they are diuretics that dehydrate the body. In extremely hot and humid weather, try to stay out of the midday heat and confine most of your daytime traveling to early morning and late afternoon. If you ever feel weak, fatigued, dizzy, or disoriented, get out of the sun immediately and go to a shady, cool place. To prevent sunburn, always wear a hat and apply sunscreen to all exposed areas of skin.

## DIETARY PRECAUTIONS

Unless you intend to confine your travels to the big cities and dine only at restaurants that serve Western-style food, you will likely be eating many foods that you don't normally consume. This may lead initially to upset stomachs and/or diarrhea, which usually lasts just a few days as your body adapts to the change in cuisine. Except for Singapore, where tap water is safe to drink, **always drink bottled water** (never use tap water for drinking or even brushing teeth). It's also recommended to peel all fruits and vegetables and avoid raw shellfish and seafood. Also, beware of ice unless it is made from purified water. (Any suspicious water can be purified by boiling or treating with iodine). If you're a vegetarian, you will find that Southeast Asia is a great place to travel, as vegetarian dishes abound throughout the region. In terms of hygiene, restaurants are generally preferred to street stalls. Be sure to carry diarrhea medication as well as any prescription medications you may need. It's also a good idea to carry your own set of plastic chopsticks or a small cutlery set, just in case you suspect the cleanliness of those that are presented to you at a restaurant.

## WHAT TO DO IF YOU GET SICK AWAY FROM HOME

It can be hard to find a doctor you can trust when you're in an unfamiliar place, and in some countries covered in this guide, medical care is simply not up to Western standards. Try to take proper precautions the week before you depart, to avoid falling ill while you're away from home. Amid the last-minute frenzy that often precedes a vacation break, make an extra effort to eat and sleep well—especially if you feel an illness coming on.

If you worry about getting sick away from home, you may want to consider **medical travel insurance** (see the section on insurance, below). In most cases, however, your existing health plan will provide all the coverage you need. Be sure to carry your identification card in your wallet.

If you suffer from a chronic illness, consult your doctor before your departure. For conditions like epilepsy, diabetes, or heart problems, wear a **Medic Alert Identification Tag** (☎ **800/825-3785;** www.commedicalert.org), which will immediately alert doctors to your condition and give them access to your records through Medic Alert's 24-hour hotline. Membership is US$35, plus a US$15 annual fee.

Pack prescription medications in your carry-on luggage. Carry written prescriptions in generic, not brand-name form, and dispense all prescription medications from their original labeled vials. Also bring along copies of your prescriptions in case you lose your pills or run out.

If you wear contact lenses, pack an extra pair in case you lose one.

The **International Association for Medical Assistance to Travelers (IAMAT)** and the **U.S. Centers for Disease Control and Prevention** (see above for contact info) list English-speaking doctors in the countries you'll be visiting. Also note that when you're abroad, any local consulate can provide a list of area doctors who speak English. If you do get sick, you may want to ask the concierge at your hotel to recommend a local doctor—even his or her own.

## INSURANCE

There are three kinds of travel insurance: trip cancellation, medical, and lost luggage coverage. **Trip cancellation insurance** is a good idea if you have paid a large portion of your vacation expenses up front. The other two types of insurance, however, don't make sense for most travelers. Rule number one: Check your existing policies before you buy any additional coverage.

Your existing health insurance should cover you if you get sick while on vacation (though if you belong to an HMO, you should check to see whether you are fully covered when away from home). If you need hospital treatment, most health insurance plans and HMOs will cover out-of-country hospital visits and procedures, at least to some extent. However, most make you pay the bills up front at the time of care, and you'll get a refund after you've returned and filed all the paperwork. Members of **Blue Cross/Blue Shield** can now use their cards at select hospitals in most major cities worldwide (☎ **800/810-BLUE** or www.bluecares.com/blue/bluecard/wwn for a list of hospitals). For independent travel health-insurance providers, see below. Your homeowner's insurance should cover stolen luggage. The airlines are responsible for US$1,250 on domestic flights if they lose your luggage; if you plan to carry anything more valuable than that, keep it in your carry-on bag.

The differences between travel assistance and insurance are often blurred, but in general the former offers on-the-spot assistance and 24-hour hotlines (mostly oriented toward medical problems), while the latter reimburses you for travel problems (medical, travel, or otherwise) after you have filed the paperwork. The coverage you should consider will depend on how much protection is already contained in your existing health insurance or other policies. Some credit- and charge-card companies may insure you against travel accidents if you buy plane, train, or bus tickets with their cards. Before purchasing additional insurance, read your policies and agreements over carefully. Make sure your policy covers **emergency evacuation,** since medical care in some Southeast Asian countries (Vietnam and Laos, for instance), is still substandard. Also check that your insurance covers motorbike riding if there's any chance you'll choose that method of getting around. Call your insurers or credit/charge-card companies if you have any questions.

Some credit cards (American Express and certain gold and platinum Visas and MasterCards, for example) offer automatic flight insurance against death or dismemberment in case of an airplane crash.

If you do require additional insurance, try one of the companies listed below. But don't pay for more than you need. For example, if you need only trip cancellation insurance, don't purchase coverage for lost or stolen property. Trip cancellation insurance costs approximately 6 to 8% of the total value of your vacation.

Among the reputable issuers of travel insurance are:

- **Access America,** 6600 W. Broad St., Richmond, VA 23230 (☎ 800/284-8300)
- **Travel Guard International,** 1145 Clark St., Stevens Point, WI 54481 (☎ 800/826-1300)
- **Travel Insured International, Inc.,** P.O. Box 280568, East Hartford, CT 06128 (☎ 800/243-3174)
- **Columbus Travel Insurance,** 279 High St., Croydon CR0 1QH (☎ 0171/375-0011 in London; www2.columbusdirect.com/columbusdirect)
- **International SOS Assistance,** P.O. Box 11568, Philadelphia PA 11916 (☎ 800/523-8930 or 215/244-1500), strictly an assistance company
- **Travelex Insurance Services,** P.O. Box 9408, Garden City, NY 11530-9408 (☎ 800/228-9792).

Companies specializing in accident and medical care include:

- **MEDEX International,** P.O. Box 5375, Timonium, MD 21094-5375 (☎ 888/MEDEX-00 or 410/453-6300; fax 410/453-6301; www. medexassist.com)
- **Travel Assistance International** (Worldwide Assistance Services, Inc.), 1133 15th St. NW, Suite 400, Washington, DC 20005 (☎ 800/821-2828 or 202/828-5894; fax 202/828-5896)
- **The Divers Alert Network** (DAN) (☎ 800/446-2671 or 919/684-2948) insures scuba divers.

## 8 Tips for Travelers with Special Needs

### TIPS FOR TRAVELERS WITH DISABILITIES

Except for the modern, upscale international hotels, most buildings in Southeast Asia are not wheelchair-accessible or user-friendly when it comes to handling the special needs of disabled travelers. That said, a disability shouldn't stop anyone from traveling. There are more resources out there than ever before that can help you get around the obstacles. *A World of Options,* a 658-page book of resources for disabled travelers, covers everything from biking trips to scuba outfitters. It costs US$35 (US$30 for members) and is available from **Mobility International USA,** P.O. Box 10767, Eugene, OR, 97440 (☎ **541/343-1284,** voice and TDD; www.miusa.org). Annual membership for Mobility International is US$35, which includes their quarterly newsletter, *Over the Rainbow.* In addition, **Twin Peaks Press,** P.O. Box 129, Vancouver, WA 98666 (☎ **360/694-2462**), publishes travel-related books for people with disabilities.

**The Moss Rehab Hospital** (☎ 215/456-9600) has been providing friendly and helpful phone advice and referrals to disabled travelers for years through its **Travel Information Service** (☎ 215/456-9603; www.mossresourcenet.org).

You can join **The Society for the Advancement of Travel for the Handicapped** (SATH), 347 Fifth Ave. Suite 610, New York, NY 10016 (☎ 212/447-7284; fax 212-725-8253; www.sath.org) for US$45 annually, US$30 for seniors and students, to gain access to their vast network of connections in the travel industry. They provide information sheets on travel destinations, and referrals to tour operators that specialize in traveling with disabilities. Their quarterly magazine, *Open World for Disability and*

*Mature Travel,* is full of good information and resources. A year's subscription is US$13 (US$21 outside the US).

Travelers with disabilities may also want to consider joining a tour that caters specifically to them. One of the best operators is **Flying Wheels Travel,** 143 West Bridge (P.O. Box 382), Owatonna, MN 55060 (☎ **800/535-6790**). They offer various escorted tours and cruises, with an emphasis on sports, as well as private tours in minivans with lifts. Other reputable specialized tour operators include **Access Adventures** (☎ **716/889-9096**), which offers sports-related vacations; **Accessible Journeys** (☎ **800/TINGLES** or 610/521-0339), for slow walkers and wheelchair travelers; **The Guided Tour,** Inc. (☎ **215/782-1370**); **Wilderness Inquiry** (☎ **800/728-0719** or 612/379-3858); and **Directions Unlimited** (☎ **800/533-5343**).

You can obtain a copy of *Air Transportation of Handicapped Persons* by writing to Free Advisory Circular No. AC12032, Distribution Unit, U.S. Department of Transportation, Publications Division, M-4332, Washington, DC 20590.

Vision-impaired travelers should contact the **American Foundation for the Blind,** 11 Penn Plaza, Suite 300, New York, NY 10001 (☎ **800/232-5463**), for information on traveling with seeing-eye dogs.

## TIPS FOR GAY & LESBIAN TRAVELERS

Most Southeast Asian countries are extremely conservative and not used to dealing with public displays of affection between straight couples, much less gay or lesbian couples. To avoid offending local sensibilities, it's best to be discreet and not flaunt one's sexual preferences in public.

**The International Gay & Lesbian Travel Association** (IGLTA) (☎ **800/ 448-8550** or 954/776-2626; fax 954/776-3303; www.iglta.org), links travelers with the appropriate gay-friendly service organization or tour specialist. With around 1,200 members, it offers quarterly newsletters, marketing mailings, and a membership directory that's updated quarterly. Membership often includes gay or lesbian businesses but is open to individuals for US$150 yearly, plus a US$100 administration fee for new members. Members are kept informed of gay and gay-friendly hoteliers, tour operators, and airline and cruise-line representatives. Contact the IGLTA for a list of its member agencies, who will be tied into IGLTA's information resources.

General gay and lesbian travel agencies include **Family Abroad** (☎ **800/999-5500** or 212/459-1800; gay and lesbian); **Above and Beyond Tours** (☎ **800/397-2681;** mainly gay men); and **Yellowbrick Road** (☎ 800/642-2488; gay and lesbian).

There are also two good, biannual English-language gay guidebooks, both focused on gay men but including information for lesbians as well. You can get the *Spartacus International Gay Guide* or *Odysseus* from most gay and lesbian book stores, or order them from Giovanni's Room (☎ **215/923-2960**), or A Different Light Bookstore (☎ **800/343-4002** or 212/989-4850). Both lesbians and gays might want to pick up a copy of *Gay Travel A to Z* (US$16). **The Ferrari Guides** (www.q-net.com) is yet another very good series of gay and lesbian guidebooks.

*Out and About,* 8 W. 19th St. no. 401, New York, NY 10011 (☎ **800/929-2268** or 212/645-6922), offers guidebooks and a monthly newsletter packed with good information on the global gay and lesbian scene. A year's subscription to the newsletter costs US$49. *Our World,* 1104 North Nova Rd., Suite 251, Daytona Beach, FL 32117 (☎ **904/441-5367**), is a slicker monthly magazine promoting and highlighting travel bargains and opportunities. Annual subscription rates are US$35 in the U.S., US$45 outside the US.

## TIPS FOR SENIORS

Asking for discounts can sometimes be problematic if your ticket seller's or restaurateur's English isn't up to par, but you can ask (you'll find discounts particularly in Singapore and Hong Kong). Be sure to mention the fact that you're a senior citizen when you first make your travel reservations. For example, many hotels offer seniors discounts.

Members of the **American Association of Retired Persons (AARP)**, 601 E St. NW, Washington, DC 20049 (☎ **800/424-3410** or 202/434-2277), get discounts not only on hotels but on airfares and car rentals, too. AARP offers members a wide range of special benefits, including *Modern Maturity* magazine and a monthly newsletter.

**The National Council of Senior Citizens**, 8403 Colesville Rd., Suite 1200, Silver Spring, MD 20910 (☎ **301/578-8800**), a nonprofit organization, offers a newsletter 6 times a year (partly devoted to travel tips) and discounts on hotels and auto rentals; annual dues are US$13 per person or couple.

**Mature Outlook,** P.O. Box 9390, Des Moines, IA 50306 (☎ **800/336-6330**), began as a travel organization for people over 50, though it now caters to people of all ages. Members receive discounts on hotels and receive a bimonthly magazine. Annual membership is US$19.95, which entitles members to discounts and, often, free coupons for discounted merchandise from Sears.

**Golden Companions,** P.O. Box 5249, Reno, NV 89513 (☎ **702/324-2227**), helps travelers 45-plus find compatible companions through a personal voice-mail service. Contact them for more information.

*The Mature Traveler,* a monthly 12-page newsletter on senior citizen travel, is a valuable resource. It is available by subscription (US$30 a year) from GEM Publishing Group, Box 50400, Reno, NV 89513-0400. Another helpful publication is *101 Tips for the Mature Traveler,* available from Grand Circle Travel, 347 Congress St., Suite 3A, Boston, MA 02210 (☎ **800/221-2610** or 617/350-7500; fax 617/346-6700).

**Grand Circle Travel,** 347 Congress St., Suite 3A, Boston, MA 02210 (☎ **800/221-2610** or 617/350-7500), is one of the hundreds of travel agencies specializing in vacations for seniors. Many of these packages, however, are of the tour-bus variety, with free trips thrown in for those who organize groups of 10 or more. Seniors seeking more independent travel should probably consult a regular travel agent. **SAGA International Holidays,** 222 Berkeley St., Boston, MA 02116 (☎ **800/343-0273**), offers inclusive tours and cruises for those 50 and older. SAGA also sponsors the more substantial "Road Scholar Tours" (☎ **800/621-2151**), which are fun-loving but with an educational bent.

If you want something more than the average vacation or guided tour, try **Elderhostel** (☎ **877/426-8056;** www.elderhostel.org) or the University of New Hampshire's **Interhostel** (☎ **800/733-9753**), both variations on the same theme: educational travel for senior citizens. On these escorted tours, the days are packed with seminars, lectures, and field trips, and the sightseeing is all led by academic experts. **Elderhostel,** 75 Federal St., Boston, MA 02110-1941 (☎ **877/426-8056;** www. elderhostel.org), arranges study programs for those aged 55 and over (and a spouse or companion of any age) in 78 countries around the world, including Asia. Most courses last about 3 weeks and many include airfare, accommodations in student dormitories or modest inns, meals, and tuition. Write or call for a free catalog, which lists upcoming courses and destinations. **Interhostel** takes travelers 50 and over (with companions over 40), and offers 2- and 3-week trips. The courses in both these programs are ungraded, involve no homework, and often focus on the liberal arts. They're not luxury vacations, but they're fun and fulfilling.

## TIPS FOR FAMILIES WITH CHILDREN

Several books on the market offer tips to help you travel with kids. Most concentrate on the U.S., but two, *Family Travel* (Lanier Publishing International) and *How to Take Great Trips with Your Kids* (The Harvard Common Press), are full of good general advice that can apply to travel anywhere. Another reliable tome, with a world-wide focus, is *Adventuring with Children* (Foghorn Press).

*Family Travel Times* is published 6 times a year by TWYCH (Travel with Your Children; ☎ 888/822-4388 or 212/477-5524), and includes a weekly call-in service for subscribers. Subscriptions are US$40 a year for quarterly editions. A free publication list and a sample issue are available by calling or sending a request to the above address.

## TIPS FOR WOMEN TRAVELERS

Women travelling together or alone will find touring this region particularly pleasant and easy (as evidenced by the fact that all but one of the destination chapters of this book were written by women). The Buddhist and Islamic codes of conduct and ethics followed by many mean that you will be treated with respect and courtesy. While you may not find many local women dining or touring alone, as a visitor, your behavior will be accepted. You will rarely, if ever, be approached or hassled by strangers. At the same time, you can feel free to start a conversation with a stranger without fear of mis-interpretation. Note that if you are travelling with a man, public displays of affection are not welcome, and it's you, the female, who will be scorned. Also, you will have to take even more care than your male counterpart to dress modestly, meaning no cleavage- or midriff-baring tops, mini-skirts, or short shorts. Otherwise, you risk offending people on the grounds of either religious or local moral standards.

All this said, it's still not advisable to take risks that you wouldn't normally take at home. Don't hitchhike, accept rides, or walk around late at night, particularly in dimly lit areas or in unfamiliar places. Be acutely aware of purse or jewelry snatchers in large cities. When meeting strangers in nightclubs, for example, buy your own drinks and keep an eye on them.

## TIPS FOR SINGLE TRAVELERS

Many people prefer traveling alone save for the relatively steep cost of booking a single room, which usually comes to well over half the price of a double. **Travel Companion** (☎ 516/454-0880) is one of the oldest roommate finders for single travelers. Register with them and find a trustworthy travel mate who will split the cost of the room with you.

Several tour organizers cater to solo travelers as well. **Experience Plus** (☎ 800/685-4565; fax 907/484-8489) offers an interesting selection of single-only trips. **Travel Buddies** (☎ 800/998-9099 or 604/533-2483) runs single-friendly tours with no singles supplement. **The Single Gourmet Club** (133 E. 58th St., New York, NY 10022; ☎ 212/980-8788; fax 212/980-3138) is an international social, dining, and travel club for singles, with offices in 21 cities in the USA and Canada, and one in London.

You may also want to research the **Outdoor Singles Network** (P.O. Box 781, Haines, AK 99827). An established quarterly newsletter (since 1989) for outdoor-loving singles, ages 19 to 90, the network will help you find a travel companion, pen-pal, or soulmate within its pages. A 1-year subscription costs US$45, and your own personal ad is printed free in the next issue. Current issues are US$15. Write for free information or check out the group's Web site at www.kcd.com/bearstar/osn.html.

# 4 Hong Kong

*by Beth Reiber*

**V**iewed from Victoria Peak, Hong Kong surely rates as one of the most stunning cities in Southeast Asia, if not the world. In the foreground rise the skyscrapers of Hong Kong Island, numerous, dense, and astonishingly tall. Beyond that is Victoria Harbour, with its incredibly busy traffic of everything from the historic Star Ferry to cruise liners, cargo ships, and fishing vessels. On the other side is Kowloon Peninsula, growing larger seemingly by the minute with ambitious land reclamation projects, housing estates, and ever-higher buildings, all against a dramatic backdrop of gently rounded mountains.

If this is your first stop in Asia, Hong Kong will seem excitingly exotic, with its profusion of neon Chinese signs, roasted ducks hanging in the windows of restaurants, colorful street markets, herb medicinal shops, fortune-tellers, and crush of people, 98% of whom are Chinese.

If you're arriving from elsewhere in Asia, however, Hong Kong may seem welcomingly familiar, with its first-class hotels, restaurants serving everything from California-style pizzas to French haute cuisine, easy-to-navigate transportation system, English language street signs, and gigantic shopping malls.

Hong Kong's unique blend of exotic and familiar, East and West, is due of course to its 156 years as a British colony—from 1842, when Britain acquired Hong Kong Island as a spoil of the first Opium War, to its 1997 handover to the Chinese. As a Special Administrative Region (SAR), Hong Kong has been guaranteed its capitalist lifestyle and social system for 50 years, and for the casual observer, little seems changed. English is still an official language, the Hong Kong dollar remains legal tender, and entry formalities are largely the same. Although Hong Kong is pricier than most other Asian destinations, the Asian financial crisis has made it more affordable than ever, with reduced hotel rates and competitive restaurant prices.

Shopping remains Hong Kong's chief draw, whether it's bargain-hunting at one of its many streetside markets or browsing upscale boutiques at air-conditioned malls. Dearer to my heart is the justifiably celebrated dining: Hong Kong boasts what is arguably the greatest concentration of Chinese restaurants in the world, along with top-notch restaurants serving cuisines from around the globe. The city has also revved up its sightseeing attractions, offering museums, parks, temples, and other amusements. If all you want to do is lie on a beach or get away from it all, you can do that, too. And Macau, with its fascinating blend of Portuguese and Chinese cultures, is just an hour's boat ride away.

# 1 Getting to Know Hong Kong

## THE LAY OF THE LAND

Hong Kong, covering 404 square miles (652 sq km), can be divided into four distinct parts: **Hong Kong Island** with the Central District, the Western District, Wan Chai, and Causeway Bay, and with such major attractions as Hong Kong Park, Victoria Peak, Stanley Market, Ocean Park, and the Zoological and Botanical Gardens; **Kowloon Peninsula** with Tsim Sha Tsui and its many hotels, restaurants, museums, and shops at its tip, as well as the Yau Ma Tei and Mong Kok districts; the **New Territories,** which stretch north from Kowloon all the way to the Chinese border and now house approximately half of Hong Kong's people, primarily in huge public-housing estates in satellite towns; and **235 outlying islands,** most of them barren and uninhabited.

## HONG KONG NEIGHBORHOODS & CITY LAYOUT

**CENTRAL DISTRICT**    This is where the story of Hong Kong all began, when a small port and community were established on the north end of the island by the British in the 1840s. Today, Central serves as Hong Kong's nerve center for banking, business, and administration, and boasts some of Hong Kong's most innovative architecture, a handful of exclusive hotels, high-end shopping centers, and bars and restaurants catering mostly to Hong Kong's white-collar workers.

**LAN KWAI FONG**    Named after an L-shaped street in Central, this is Hong Kong's most well-known nightlife and entertainment district, occupying not only Lan Kwai Fong but overflowing onto neighboring streets like D'Aguilar and Wyndham.

**MID-LEVELS**    Located halfway up Victoria Peak, the Mid-Levels is a popular residential area with its swank apartments, views of Central, lush vegetation, and slightly cooler temperatures. Serving white-collar workers who commute down to Central every day is the Hillside Escalator Link, the world's longest people-mover.

**SOHO**    This new dining and nightlife district, flanking the Hillside Escalator Link that connects Central with the Mid-Levels, is popular with Mid-Levels residents and those seeking a quieter, saner alternative to the crowds of Lan Kwai Fong. Dubbed SoHo for the region "south of Hollywood Road," it has since blossomed into an ever-growing neighborhood of cafe-bars and small, intimate restaurants specializing in ethnic and innovative cuisine.

**WESTERN DISTRICT**    West of the Central District, the Western District is one of the oldest, most traditional areas on Hong Kong Island, a fascinating neighborhood of shops selling herbs, ginseng, dried seafood, and other Chinese products. It's also famous for Hollywood Road, long popular for its many antiques and curio shops, and Man Mo Temple, one of Hong Kong's oldest temples.

**WAN CHAI**    Few places in Hong Kong have changed as dramatically or noticeably as Wan Chai, located east of Central. Once notorious for its sleazy bars, easy women, tattoo parlors, and sailors on leave, Wan Chai has become respectable (and almost unrecognizable) with new, mostly business-style hotels, more high-rises, the Hong Kong Arts Centre, the Academy for Performing Arts, and the Hong Kong Convention and Exhibition Centre.

**CAUSEWAY BAY**    Just east of Wan Chai, Causeway Bay is a popular shopping destination, with its Japanese department stores and clothing, shoe, and accessory

# Hong Kong Region

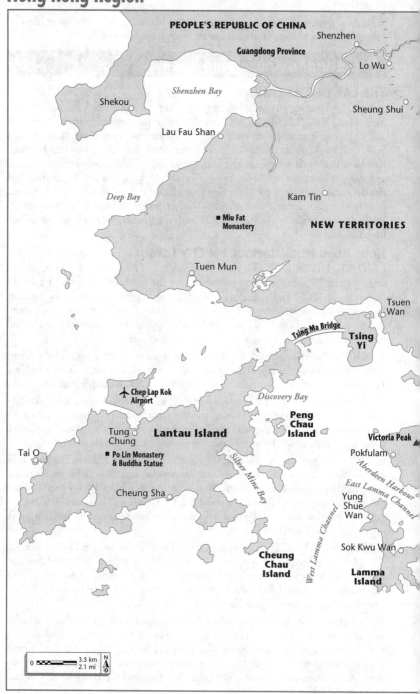

PEOPLE'S REPUBLIC OF CHINA

Shenzhen

Guangdong Province

Lo Wu

Shenzhen Bay

Shekou

Sheung Shui

Lau Fau Shan

Deep Bay

Kam Tin

■ Miu Fat
Monastery

NEW TERRITORIES

Tuen Mun

Tsuen
Wan

Tsing Ma Bridge

Tsing
Yi

✈ Chep Lap Kok
Airport

Discovery Bay

Peng
Chau
Island

Victoria Peak ▲

Tung
Chung

Lantau Island

Pokfulam

Aberdeen Harbour

Tai O

■ Po Lin Monastery
& Buddha Statue

Silver Mine Bay

East Lamma Channel

Yung
Shue
Wan

Cheung Sha

West Lamma Channel

Sok Kwu Wan

Cheung
Chau
Island

Lamma
Island

0 ▰▰▰▰ 3.5 km
      2.1 mi

N

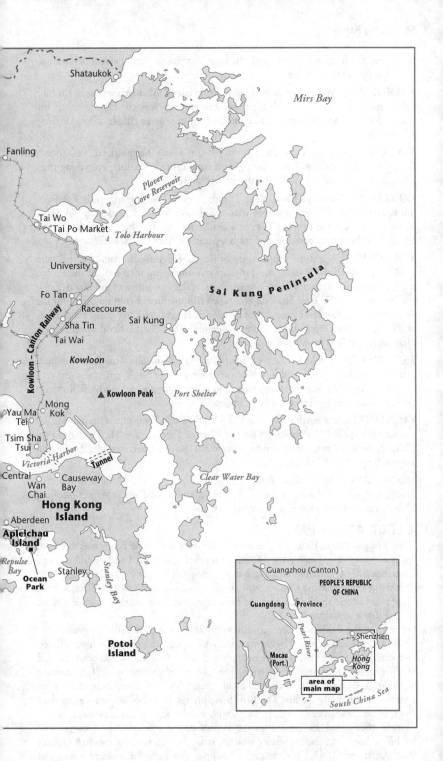

Shataukok

*Mirs Bay*

Fanling

*Plover
Cove Reservoir*

Tai Wo
Tai Po Market

*Tolo Harbour*

University

Fo Tan

Racecourse

Sha Tin

Sai Kung

**S a i   K u n g   P e n i n s u l a**

Tai Wai

*Kowloon*

**Kowloon – Canton Railway**

▲ Kowloon Peak

*Port Shelter*

Mong
Kok

Yau Ma
Tei

Tsim Sha
Tsui

*Victoria Harbor*

**Tunnel**

Central

Wan
Chai

Causeway
Bay

*Clear Water Bay*

**Hong Kong
Island**

Aberdeen

**Apleichau
Island**

*Repulse
Bay*

**Ocean
Park**

Stanley

*Stanley Bay*

**Potoi
Island**

Guangzhou (Canton)

**PEOPLE'S REPUBLIC
OF CHINA**

**Guangdong**   **Province**

*Pearl River*

**Macau
(Port.)**

Shenzhen

*Hong
Kong*

**area of
main map**

*South China Sea*

boutiques. On its eastern perimeter is the large Victoria Park and beyond that the colorful Aw Boon Haw Gardens.

**ABERDEEN**   On the south side of Hong Kong Island, Aberdeen was once a fishing village but is now studded with high-rises and housing projects. However, it is still known for its hundreds of sampans, junks, boat people, and a couple of huge floating restaurants.

**STANLEY**   Located on the quiet south side of Hong Kong Island, this former fishing village is home to Hong Kong's most famous market, selling everything from silk suits to name-brand shoes, casualwear, and souvenirs.

**KOWLOON**   North of Hong Kong Island, across Victoria Harbour, is Kowloon, 4.8 square miles (7.74 sq km) that were ceded to Britain "in perpetuity" in 1860. Kowloon includes the districts Tsim Sha Tsui, Tsim Sha Tsui East, Yau Ma Tei, and Mong Kok. Boundary Street in the north separates it from the New Territories.

**TSIM SHA TSUI**   At the southern tip of Kowloon Peninsula, Tsim Sha Tsui (also spelled "Tsimshatsui") is where most tourists stay and spend their money, since it has the greatest concentration of hotels, restaurants, and shops (some of my friends call it the "tourist ghetto"). Tsim Sha Tsui boasts several museums, a cultural center for the performing arts, Kowloon Park, one of the world's largest shopping malls, a nice selection of international restaurants, a jumping nightlife, and Nathan Road, appropriately nicknamed the "golden mile of shopping."

**TSIM SHA TSUI EAST**   East of Tsim Sha Tsui, Tsim Sha Tsui East was built entirely on reclaimed land and is home to several expensive hotels, entertainment centers, shopping and restaurant complexes, and on its eastern edge, the KCR Kowloon Station, with train service to the New Territories and China.

**YAU MA TEI**   Just north of Tsim Sha Tsui on Kowloon Peninsula is the Yau Ma Tei district (also spelled "Yaumatei"). Like the Western District, Yau Ma Tei is also very Chinese, with an interesting produce market, a jade market, and the fascinating Temple Street Night Market.

**MONG KOK**   On Kowloon Peninsula north of Yau Ma Tei, Mong Kok is a residential and industrial area, home of the Bird Market, the Ladies' Market on Tung Choi Street, and countless shops catering to Chinese.

## A LOOK AT THE PAST

Hong Kong's modern history begins a mere 160 years ago, under conditions that were less than honorable. During the 1800s, tea was being imported to England in huge quantities from China, the only place it was grown. The British tried to engage the Chinese in trade, but the Chinese were not interested in anything but silver bullion. They also forbade the British to enter their kingdom, with the exception of a small trading depot in Canton.

But then the British hit upon a commodity that proved irresistible: **opium.** Produced in India and exported by the East India Company, this powerful drug enslaved everyone from poor peasants to the nobility, and before long China was being drained of silver traded to support a drug habit. The Chinese emperor, fearful of the damage being wreaked on society and alarmed by his country's loss of silver, declared a ban on opium imports in the 1830s. The British simply ignored the ban, smuggling their illegal cargo up the Pearl River. In 1839, with opium now India's largest export, the Chinese confiscated and destroyed the British opium stockpiles in Canton. The British declared war, and eventually won the struggle. As a result of this first **Opium War,** waged until 1842, China was forced to open new ports for trade, to agree to an

# Recommended Books & Films

Even though it is now dated, one of my favorite books about Hong Kong is Jan Morris's **Hong Kong** (Random House, 1988), which traces the evolution of the British colony from its birth during the Opium Wars to the late 1980s. This book gives a unique perspective on the workings of the colony and imparts an astonishing wealth of information, making it fascinating armchair reading. Another intimate view of the city is **Hong Kong: Borrowed Place, Borrowed Time** (Praeger, 1968) by Richard Hughes, a foreign correspondent who lived in Hong Kong for several decades and was said to have been the inspiration for several characters in John Le Carré's novels.

Fictional accounts that depict the character of Hong Kong are Richard Mason's **The World of Suzie Wong** (World Pub., 1957) and Han Suyin's **A Many-Splendored Thing** (Little Brown, 1952), an autobiographical account of life in Hong Kong shortly after the Chinese revolution in the late 1940s and early 1950s. James Clavell's **Tai-Pan** (Atheneum, 1966) is a novel about Hong Kong's beginnings; **Noble House** (Delacorte Press, 1981) is its sequel. John Le Carré's **The Honourable Schoolboy** (G. K. Hall, 1977) details the activities of George Smiley, acting head of the British Secret Service in Hong Kong. I also recommend **Hong Kong Collage** (Oxford University Press, 1998), edited by Martha P.Y. Cheung, which presents essays, short stories and other contemporary works by Chinese writers, most born in Hong Kong and presenting a dynamic view of their native land.

Novels that have been made into movies include **A Many-Splendored Thing, The World of Suzie Wong, Tai-Pan,** and **Noble House.** Otherwise, two contemporary films by Chinese directors include **Summer Snow,** directed by Ann Hui, a 1995 box-office smash about a Hong Kong family coping with an elderly father suffering from Alzheimer's who comes to live with them, and **Made in Hong Kong,** directed by Chan Kwo and chosen as the best film in the 1998 Hong Kong Academy Awards. Finally, **Chinese Box,** directed by Hong Kong-born and -raised Wayne Wang, presents an unparalleled view of Hong Kong during the last six months of the handover, with actual street scenes shot in Hong Kong during the same period and complete with CNN footage, all as a backdrop to the romantic interludes of a British journalist played by Jeremy Irons and his love interest, beautiful Gong Li.

exorbitant cash indemnity for the loss of the destroyed opium, and to cede Hong Kong Island in perpetuity to the British in a treaty China never recognized. Not only was this **Treaty of Nanking** demoralizing to the Chinese, it also ensured that their country would remain open to the curse of opium.

When the British took control of Hong Kong Island in 1842, some 7,000 Chinese lived in its farming and fishing communities, and Britain's prospects for developing a thriving port did not look rosy. Although it had a deep and protected harbor, no one, including the Chinese, was much interested in the island itself, and many in the British government considered its acquisition an embarrassing mistake. What's more, no sooner had the island been settled than a typhoon tore through the settlement. Repairs were demolished only 5 days later by another tropical storm. Fever and fire followed, and the weather grew so oppressive and humid that the colony seemed to be enveloped in a giant steam bath.

Yet as the number of headstones in the hillside cemetery multiplied, so did the number of the living. By 1846, the population had reached an astonishing 24,000. By the turn of the century the number had swelled to 300,000. British families lived along the waterfront and called it **Victoria** (now the Central District), slowly moving up toward the cooler temperatures of Victoria Peak. The Chinese, barred from living in the Peak and other European neighborhoods, stayed in a shantytown farther west, now called the **Western District.** A typical Hong Kong dwelling consisted of four Chinese families and their animals in one room. Conditions were so appalling that when the bubonic plague struck in 1894 it raged for almost 30 years, claiming more than 20,000 lives.

Most of the newcomers to Hong Kong were mainland Chinese, who arrived with the shirts on their backs and nothing to lose. Every turmoil that sent a shudder through China—famine, flood, or civil war—flung a new wave of farmers, merchants, peasants, coolies, and entrepreneurs into Hong Kong. Everyone's dream was to make a fortune; it was just a matter of timing and good *joss* (luck). The Chinese philosophy of hard work and good fortune found fertile ground in the laissez-faire atmosphere of the colony.

Hong Kong's growth in this century has been no less astonishing in terms of both trade and population. In 1911 the overthrow of the Manchu dynasty in China sent a flood of refugees into Hong Kong, followed in 1938 by an additional 500,000 immigrants. Another mass influx of Chinese refugees arrived after the fall of Shanghai to the Communists in 1950. From this last wave of immigrants, including many Shanghai industrialists, emerged the beginnings of Hong Kong's now-famous textile industry.

As a British colony, Hong Kong was administered by a governor appointed by the queen. There were no free elections, and the Legislative Council, Hong Kong's main governing body, was also appointed. As 1997 drew nearer, marking the end of the 99-year lease on the New Territories, it soon became clear that China had no intention of renewing the lease or renegotiating a treaty it had never recognized in the first place. Finally, after more than 20 rounds of talks and meetings, Britain's Prime Minister Margaret Thatcher signed the Sino-British Joint Declaration of 1984, agreeing to transfer all of Hong Kong to Chinese Communist rule on June 30, 1997. For its part, China declared Hong Kong a **"Special Administrative Region,"** granting it special privileges under a "one country, two systems" policy that guaranteed Hong Kong's capitalist lifestyle and social system for at least 50 years after 1997. As such, Hong Kong would remain largely self-governing, and its people would retain rights to their property, freedom of speech, and ability to travel freely in and out of Hong Kong. Throughout the negotiations, residents of Hong Kong were never consulted about their future.

Then came the events of June 1989 in Beijing's **Tiananmen Square,** in which hundreds of students and demonstrators were ordered shot by Chinese authorities in a brutal move to quash the pro-democracy movement. China's response to the rebellion sent shock waves through Hong Kong and led to rounds of angry protest. Those who could, emigrated, primarily to Australia, Canada, and the United States; at its height, more than 1,000 people were emigrating each week. The vast majority of Hong Kong Chinese remained, however, confident or at least hopeful that China realized it had more to gain by keeping Hong Kong as it was.

Today, foremost in every visitor's mind is, "How much has Hong Kong changed since the handover?" Actually, not much. Entry formalities for Americans and most other nationalities remain unchanged. English remains an official language, and the English names of buildings, streets, and attractions remain the same. The Hong Kong dollar, pegged to the U.S. dollar, remains legal tender, and in most hotels, restaurants, and shops that cater to tourists, it's business as usual.

But there are subtle differences. The British population dropped more than 10 percent in the first 6 months after the handover, and bars, restaurants, and other establishments that have long catered to the expat community have closed down. Meanwhile, the **Asian economic crisis** has brought an influx of new expatriates looking for work, most notably Filipinos. And although border regulations between Hong Kong and China have remained unchanged, the SAR has been deluged with a new flood of mainlanders—an estimated 50,000 a year.

Changes in Hong Kong occur at a dizzying pace: relatively new buildings are torn down to make way for even newer, shinier skyscrapers; whole neighborhoods are obliterated in the name of progress; reclaimed land is taken from an ever-shrinking harbor; and traditional villages are replaced with satellite towns. Hong Kong's city skyline has surged upward and outward so dramatically since my first visit in 1983, it sometimes seems like decades rather than a year or two must have elapsed each time I see it anew. Change is commonplace, and yet it's hard not to lament the loss of familiar things that suddenly vanish; it's harder still not to brood over what's likely to come. But Hong Kong, founded by the narcotics trade and created to make money, has always been like this. There are strikingly few monuments or statues to the city's past. Even the city's original settlement long ago lost most of its colonial-age buildings.

But don't worry. If this is your first trip to Hong Kong, you're much more likely to notice its Chinese aspects than its Western elements. Ducks hanging by their necks in restaurant windows, bamboo scaffolding, herb medicinal shops, streetside markets, Chinese characters on huge neon signs, wooden fishing boats, shrines to the kitchen god, fortune-tellers, temples, laundry fluttering from bamboo poles, dim sum trolleys, and the clicking of mahjongg tiles all conspire to create an atmosphere overwhelmingly Chinese.

## HONG KONG'S PEOPLE & CULTURE

With a population of approximately 6.6 million, Hong Kong is overwhelmingly Chinese—some 98% of its residents are Chinese, more than half of them born in Hong Kong. But the Chinese themselves are a diverse people and they hail from different parts of the country. Most are **Cantonese,** from southern China, the area just beyond Hong Kong's border—hence, Cantonese is one of the official languages of the city. Other Chinese include the **Hakka,** traditionally farmers, whose women are easily recognizable by their hats with a black fringe, and the **Tanka,** the majority of Hong Kong's boat population. Hong Kong's many Chinese restaurants specializing in Cantonese, Szechuan, Chiu Chow, Pekingese, Shanghainese, and other regional foods are testaments to the city's diversity.

Hong Kong is one of the most densely populated areas in the world, at about half the size of Rhode Island, with a total land area of slightly more than 400 square miles (645 sq km). The best place to appreciate this is atop Victoria Peak, where you can feast your eyes on Hong Kong's famous harbor, and as far as the eye can see, mile upon mile of high-rise apartments. If Hong Kong were a vast plain, it would be as ugly as Tokyo. But it's saved by undulating mountain peaks, which cover virtually all of Hong Kong and provide a dramatic background to its cityscape and coastal areas.

Most public housing is in the New Territories, in a forest of high-rises that leaves foreign visitors aghast. Each apartment building is approximately 30 stories tall, containing about 1,000 apartments and 3,000 to 4,000 residents. Seven or eight apartment buildings comprise an estate, which is like a small town with its own name, shopping center, recreational and sports facilities, playgrounds, schools, and social services. Each apartment is indescribably small by Western standards—approximately 250 square feet (76 square meters), with a single window. It consists of a combination living room/bedroom, a kitchen nook, and bathroom, and is typically shared by a couple with one or two children. According to government figures, every household in Hong Kong has at least one television; many have one for each member of the household, even if the house consists only one or two rooms. But as cramped, unimaginative, and sterile as these housing projects may seem, they're a vast improvement over the way much of the population used to live. They also account for most of Hong Kong's construction growth in the past two decades, especially in the New Territories.

## CULTURAL LIFE

Much of Hong Kong's drama is played in its streets, whether it's amateur Chinese opera singers at the famous Temple Street Night Market, a fortune-teller who has set up a chair and table at the side of the road or in front of a Taoist temple, or a sidewalk calligrapher who will write letters for those who can't. Virtually everything the Chinese consider vital still thrives in Hong Kong, including ancient religious beliefs, superstitions, wedding customs, and festivals.

Of the various Chinese performing arts, **Chinese opera** is the most popular and widely loved. Dating back to the Mongol period, it has always appealed to both the ruling class and the masses. Virtue, corruption, violence, and lust are common themes, and performances feature elaborate costumes and makeup, haunting atonal orchestrations, and crashing cymbals. The actor-singers train for years to achieve the high-pitched and shrill falsettos that characterize Chinese opera, and the costumes signify specific stage personalities. Yellow is reserved for emperors, while purple is the color worn by barbarians. Unlike Western performances, Chinese operas are noisy affairs, with families coming and going during long performances, chatting with friends, and eating.

## 2  Planning a Trip to Hong Kong

### VISITOR INFORMATION

Though the information stocked by the Hong Kong Tourist Association offices abroad are sometimes not as up-to-date or as thorough as that available in Hong Kong itself or through the Internet (**www.hkta.org/usa** for U.S. residents or **www.hkta.org/worldwide** for residents of all other countries), it's worth contacting a local HKTA office before leaving home for general information and a map.

### IN THE U.S.

**New York:** 590 Fifth Ave., 5th floor, New York, NY 10036-4706 (☎ **212/869-5008** or 212/869-5009; fax 212/730-2605; e-mail hktanyc@hkta.org). **Chicago:** 401 North Michigan Ave., Suite 1640, Chicago, IL 60611 (☎ **312/329-1828;** e-mail hktachi@hkta.org); **Los Angeles:** 10940 Wilshire Blvd., Suite 1220, Los Angeles, CA 90024-3915 (☎ **310/208-4582;** fax 310/208-4582; e-mail hktalax@hkta.org).

### IN THE U.K.

London: 125 Pall Mall, 4th and 5th floors, London SW1Y 5EA (☎ **0171/930-4775;** fax 0171/9304777; e-mail hktalon@hkta.org).

### IN CANADA

**Toronto:** Hong Kong Trade Center, 3rd floor, 9 Temperance St., Toronto ON M5H 1Y6 (☎ **416/366-2389;** fax 416/366-1098; e-mail hktayyz@hkta.org).

## IN AUSTRALIA

**Sydney:** Level 4, 80 Druit St., Sydney, NSW 2000 (☎ **02/9283 3083;** fax 02/247-8812; e-mail hktasyd@hkta.org).

## IN NEW ZEALAND

**Auckland:** P.O. Box 2120, Auckland (☎ **09/572-2707;** fax 09/575-2620; e-mail hkta@iconz.co.nz).

## IN HONG KONG

The **HKTA** has an office at the **Hong Kong International Airport** (☎ **852/2181 0000**), in the arrivals hall, just past Customs. It's open daily from 6am to midnight and is an excellent source for tourist information and should be quite literally one of your first stops upon arrival. In town, there are two HKTA offices conveniently located on both sides of the harbor. In Kowloon, there's an office in Tsim Sha Tsui right in the Star Ferry concourse, open Monday through Friday from 8am to 6pm and Saturday, Sunday, and public holidays from 9am to 5pm. On Hong Kong Island, you'll find the HKTA office near the Star Ferry concourse in the Central District, in the basement, Shop 8, of the Jardine House (that's the tall building with round windows next to the Star Ferry). It's open Monday through Friday from 9am to 6pm and Saturday from 9am to 1pm.

Additionally, look for more than 100 **TouristInfo PowerPhones** placed throughout Hong Kong, including HKTA offices, Mass Transit Railway (MTR) subway stations, and the International Airport. Functioning both as telephones and as interactive tourist-information centers, they provide 24-hour, touch-screen access to such varied topics as sightseeing, shopping, entertainment, transport, hotels, and flight departures, as well as colorful maps, full-motion videos, and details about HKTA's sightseeing tours and other services—all free of charge.

Finally, if you have a question about Hong Kong, you can also call the **HKTA Visitor Hotline** (☎ 852/2807 6177), available Monday through Friday from 8am to 6pm, and on Saturday, Sunday, and public holidays from 9am to 5pm. After hours, a telephone-answering device will take your call and a member of HKTA will contact you. If you're traveling with a laptop and modem, you can surf HKTA's Web site at www.htka.org.

The HKTA publishes a large assortment of excellent literature about Hong Kong, free of charge. "The Official Hong Kong Guide," published monthly, is a booklet available at HKTA offices and in guest rooms of most upper- and middle-range hotels. It contains practical information, including a short description of Chinese foods, shopping tips, a rundown of organized sight-seeing tours, an overview of Hong Kong's major attractions, and a listing of festivals, events, and exhibits being held that month.

For sightseeing, the most important booklet is the free *Official Sightseeing Guide.* Not only does it list every attraction in Hong Kong along with a short description, but it also tells the open hours, cost, and how to reach the site by public transportation. Two other nifty booklets are the *Official Dining and Entertainment Guide* highlighting Hong Kong's various cuisines, complete with descriptions of major dishes; and *The Official Shopping Guide,* which gives practical advice on shopping and lists all HKTA member stores.

You can also get a free map of Hong Kong from HKTA, as well as brochures outlining each of HKTA's organized tours, invaluable leaflets showing major bus routes throughout Hong Kong, and current ferry timetables to the outlying islands.

To find out what's going on in theater, music, and the arts during your stay, be sure to pick up HKTA'S free *Hong Kong Diary,* a weekly leaflet, and *Hong Kong Now,* a weekly tabloid. *HK Magazine,* a weekly distributed free at restaurants, bars, and other outlets around town and aimed at a young readership, lists what's going on at the city's theaters and other venues, including Hong Kong's alternative scene. In addition, "Hong Kong Life," published as a supplement to the *Hong Kong Standard* newspaper on Sunday, describes what's going on in Hong Kong the coming week. The *South China Morning Post* carries its entertainment section on Friday.

## ENTRY REQUIREMENTS

A valid passport is the only document most tourists, including Americans, need to enter Hong Kong. Americans can stay up to one month without a visa. Australians, New Zealanders, Canadians, and other British Commonwealth citizens can stay three-months without a visa, while citizens of the United Kingdom can stay for six months without a visa.

## CUSTOMS REGULATIONS

Visitors are allowed to bring in, duty free, 1 liter of alcohol and 200 cigarettes (or 50 cigars or 250 grams of tobacco). There are no restrictions on currencies brought into or taken out of Hong Kong.

## MONEY

The basic unit of currency is the **Hong Kong dollar,** which is divided into 100 **cents.** Three banks, the Hongkong and Shanghai Banking Corporation, the Standard Chartered Bank, and the Bank of China, all issue their own colorful notes, in denominations of HK$10 (which is being phased out), HK$20, HK$50, HK$100, HK$500, and HK$1,000. Coins are minted in bronze for 10¢, 20¢, and 50¢ pieces, in silver for HK$1, HK$2, and HK$5, and in nickel and bronze for HK$10.

Throughout Hong Kong you'll see the dollar sign ("$"), which of course refers to Hong Kong dollars, not U.S. dollars. To avoid confusion, this guide identifies Hong Kong dollars with the symbol "HK$" (followed in parentheses by the U.S. dollar conversion).

**CURRENCY EXCHANGE & RATES**    Since 1983, the Hong Kong dollar has been pegged to the U.S. dollar at a rate of approximately HK$7.80 to each US$1. However, when exchanging money at banks, hotels, and currency exchange offices, you'll receive less than the official conversion rate, generally from 7.73 (at a bank) to 7.33 (at a hotel). For the sake of convenience, all conversions in this chapter are based on HK$7.70 to $1 U.S. (or HK$1 = 13¢), then rounded off. For British readers, the exchange rate is approximately HK$12.85 to £1 (or HK$1 = 6 pence).

**ATM machines** are found throughout Hong Kong, including at MTR subway stations and in banks.

Banks offer the best exchange rate, though rates can vary. Some offer a good rate but charge a commission; others may not charge commission but have lower rates. Most charge a commission on **traveler's checks** (unless, of course, you're cashing American Express checks at an American Express office), but the exchange rate is better for traveler's checks than cash. **Banking hours** are generally Monday through Friday from 9am to 4:30pm and Saturday from 9am to 12:30pm, though some banks stop their transactions an hour before closing time.

Hotels give a slightly less favorable exchange rate but are open nights and weekends. Money changers are found in tourist areas, especially along Nathan Road in Tsim Sha Tsui. Avoid them if you can, since they often charge a commission or a "changing fee," or give a much lower rate.

There are also 24-hour money-changing machines in Hong Kong, called **Ea$yxchange,** which accept the British pound, U.S., Canadian, and Australian

## Departure Tax

Note that when you're leaving Hong Kong, the departure tax for Hong Kong is HK$50 (US$6.50) for both adults and children.

dollars, and other currencies for exchange into Hong Kong dollars. You'll find them at several Wing Lung Banks around town, including 4 Carnarvon Rd. in Tsim Sha Tsui; 636 Nathan Rd., in Mong Kok; and Shop 101, Convention Plaza, 1 Harbour Rd., Wan Chai.

## WHEN TO GO

**PEAK SEASON**    Hong Kong's peak tourist season used to be in the spring and fall, but now tourists are flocking to the territory year-round. No matter when you go, therefore, make hotel reservations in advance, particularly if you're arriving during the Chinese New Year or one of the festivals described below.

**CLIMATE**    Because of its subtropical location, Hong Kong's weather is generally mild in winter and uncomfortably hot and humid in summer, with an average annual rainfall of 89 inches. The most pleasant time of year is late September to early December, when skies are clear and sunny, temperatures are in the 70s, and the humidity drops to 70%. January and February are the coldest months, with temperatures often in the 50s. In spring (March to May), the temperature can range between 60°F and 80°F and the humidity rises to about 84%, with fog and rain fairly common. That means there may not be much of a view from the cloud-enveloped Victoria Peak.

By summer, temperatures are often in the 90s, humidity can be 90% or more, and there's little or no relief even at night. This is when Hong Kong receives the most rain; it's also typhoon season. However, Hong Kong has a very good warning system, so there's no need to worry about the physical dangers of a tropical storm. The worst that can happen is that you may have to stay in your hotel room for a day or more, or that your plane may be delayed or diverted. It has never happened to me, but it happened to a friend of mine—she was glad she was staying at the Regent instead of Chungking Mansion, since she was confined to her hotel for an entire weekend.

**PUBLIC HOLIDAYS**    Hong Kong has 17 public holidays a year, including some of the festivals described below. The majority are Chinese and therefore are celebrated according to the lunar calendar. Two (Labor Day and Buddha's Birthday) were new in 1999, and in 2000 two holidays left over from British colonial days will be dropped, though at press time it had not been decided which. At any rate, since many shops and restaurants remain open except during the Chinese New Year, the holidays should not cause any inconvenience to visitors. Banks, however, do close.

**Public holidays** are: New Year's Day (January 1), Chinese New Year (mid-February), Ching Ming Festival (early April), Easter (Good Friday, Saturday, Easter Sunday, and Easter Monday), Labor Day (May 1), Buddha's Birthday (May), Tuen Ng Festival (Dragon Boat Festival, June), Sino-Japanese War Victory Day (August 16), day following the Mid-Autumn Festival (September), National Day (October 1), the day after National Day (October 2), Chung Yeung Festival (late October), Christmas Day (December 25), and the first weekday after Christmas.

## HEALTH CONCERNS

No shots or inoculations are required for entry to Hong Kong from the United States, but you will need proof of a vaccination against cholera if you have been in an infected area during the 14 days preceding your arrival. Check with your travel agent or call the Hong Kong Tourist Authority if you are traveling elsewhere in Asia before reaching Hong Kong.

If you need a prescription from a Hong Kong doctor filled, there are plenty of drugstores in the territory. They will not, however, fill prescriptions from elsewhere.

Generally, you're safe eating anywhere in Hong Kong, even at roadside food stalls. Stay clear of local oysters, however, and remember that many restaurants outside the major hotels and tourist areas include MSG in their dishes as a matter of course. See "Dining" for more information.

## GETTING THERE
### BY PLANE

Hong Kong's outdated Kai Tak airport was retired in 1998, replaced with the much larger **Hong Kong International Airport** (☎ 852/2181 0000), situated about 15 miles from Hong Kong's central business district. In the arrivals hall, just past Customs, visitors can pick up English-language maps and sightseeing brochures and get directions to their hotel at the **Hong Kong Tourist Association (HKTA),** open daily from 6am to midnight. Also in the arrivals hall are the **Hong Kong Hotel Association,** open daily from 6am to 1am, where you can book a room in one of some 60 member hotels free of charge, and the **Macau Government Tourist Office,** open daily from 9am to 10:30pm.

Airlines that fly nonstop between North America and Hong Kong include **Canadian Airlines International** (☎ 800/665-1177), with daily flights from Vancouver; **Cathay Pacific Airways** (☎ 800/233-2742), with daily service from Los Angeles, Vancouver, and Toronto; **Northwest Airlines** (☎ 800/225-2525), with service three times a week from Minneapolis; **Singapore Airlines** (☎ 800/742-3333), with daily service from San Francisco; and United Airlines (☎ 800/241-6522), with daily service from San Francisco, Los Angeles, and Chicago. **Japan Airlines** (☎ 800/525-3663), **Korean Air** (☎ 800/438-5000), and **Philippines Airlines** (☎ 800/435-9725) all fly to Hong Kong from the U.S., but make other stops en route.

### Getting Into the City from the Airport

The quickest, most efficient way to get to downtown Hong Kong is via the sleek **Airport Express Line.** Trains run every 4 to 8 minutes between 6am and 1am and take 18 minutes to reach Kowloon Station (off Jordan Street at the old Jordan Ferry Pier and near hotels in Tsim Sha Tsui and Yau Ma Tei) and 23 minutes to reach Hong Kong Station in the Central District at Exchange Square on Hong Kong Island. Fares are HK$90 (US$11.70) to Kowloon and HK$100 (US$13) to Central. Both Kowloon and Hong Kong stations are served by the Mass Transit Railway (MTR) subway system and by taxi service. In addition, more than 15 high-end hotels provide free shuttle service from Hong Kong or Kowloon Station.

There are also express airport buses to major downtown areas. Most important for tourists are Airbus A21, which travels through Mong Kok, Yau Ma Tei, Jordan, and Tsim Sha Tsui; and Airbus A11, which travels through Central, Wan Chai, and Causeway Bay. Buses depart every 10 to 12 minutes and require exact fares ranging from HK$33 (US$4.30) for Kowloon to HK$40 (US$5.20) for Causeway Bay.

The easiest way to travel from the international airport, of course, is to simply jump in a taxi, which is quite cheap in Hong Kong but expensive for the long haul from the airport. Depending on traffic and your final destination, a taxi to Tsim Sha Tsui costs approximately HK$350 (US$45.50), while a taxi to Central District will cost about HK$380 (US$49.40). There's also an extra luggage charge of HK$5 (US65¢) per piece of baggage.

# GETTING AROUND

Each mode of public transportation—bus, ferry, tram, and train/subway—has its own fare system and requires a new ticket each time you transfer from one mode of transportation to the other. However, if you're going to be in Hong Kong more than a couple days and will be traveling extensively on the subway, consider purchasing the **Octopus,** which allows users to hop on and off trains, subways, and some buses and ferries without having to purchase tickets each time or fumble for exact change. Sold at all MTR subway stations and some ferry piers, this electronic smart card costs HK$150 (US$19.50), including a HK$50 (US$6.50) refundable deposit.

Otherwise, transportation on buses and trams requires the exact fare, making it imperative to have a lot of loose change with you wherever you go.

**BY SUBWAY**   Hong Kong's **Mass Transit Railway (MTR)** is modern, easy to use, and much faster than the older modes of transportation. Built to transport commuters from the New Territories and linking Kowloon with Hong Kong Island, the MTR consists of four color-coded lines. Single-ticket, one-way fares range from HK$4 to HK$20 (US50¢–US$2.60), depending on the distance. Plastic credit-card size tickets are inserted into slots at entry turnstiles. *Be sure to save your ticket until the end of your journey,* when you will again insert it into the turnstile (only this time you won't get it back). The MTR operates daily from 6am to 1am. Note that there are no public restrooms at MTR stations. For general inquiries, call the MTR Hotline at ☎ **852/2881 8888.**

**BY TRAIN**   The **Kowloon-Canton Railway (KCR)** is useful for traveling north from Kowloon to the New Territories. You can board the train at the KCR Kowloon Railway Station in Hung Hom (near Tsim Sha Tsui East) or at Kowloon Tong station, also a subway stop. The KCR offers express through-trains to Guangzhou, Shanghai, and Beijing, as well as local commuter service for towns in the New Territories. Sheung Shui is the last stop if you don't have a visa for China. Departing every 3 to 10 minutes daily from approximately 5:35am to midnight, the commuter train from Kowloon to Sheung Shui takes only a half hour and costs HK$9 (US$1.15) for ordinary (second) class and HK$18 (US$2.35) for first class one-way. If you're curious about the New Territories, its scenery, and satellite towns, this is a fast, cheap, and painless way to see it.

**BY BUS**   Hong Kong buses are a delight—especially the British-style double-deckers—and are good for traveling to places where subways don't go, such as to the southern part of Hong Kong Island. The HKTA has individual leaflets for Hong Kong Island, Kowloon, and the New Territories that show bus routes to major tourist spots, indicating where you can catch the bus and its frequency, the fare, and where to get off.

Major bus terminals include Exchange Square in the Central District, Admiralty Station, and Tsim Sha Tsui in front of the Star Ferry concourse. Depending on the route, buses run from about 6am to midnight, with fares ranging from HK$1.20 to HK$34.20 (US15¢–US$4.45). Unless you have an Octopus card, good on some buses (see above), *you must have the exact fare,* which you deposit into a box as you get on. Drivers often don't speak English, so you may want to have someone at your hotel write down your destination in Chinese.

**BY TRAM**   Tramlines, found only along the north end of Hong Kong Island, are a great, nostalgic way to travel through the Western District, Central, Wan Chai, and Causeway Bay. Established in 1904, these old, narrow, double-decker affairs clank their way from Kennedy Town in the west to Shau Kei Wan in the east, with one branch making a detour to Happy Valley. Enter the trams from the back and try to get a seat on the top deck. Regardless of how far you go, you pay the exact fare of HK$1.60 (US20¢) into a little tin box next to the bus driver as you exit. Trams run daily from 6am to 1am.

**BY STAR FERRY**　A 5-minute trip across Victoria Harbour on one of the white-and-green ferries of the Star Ferry Company, in operation since 1898, is one of the most celebrated rides in the world and one of Hong Kong's top attractions. It costs only HK$1.70 (US22¢) for ordinary (second) class; if you really want to splurge, it's HK$2.20 (US28¢) for first class on the upper deck. Ferries ply the waters between Central and Tsim Sha Tsui daily from 6:30am to 11:30pm, with departures every 3 to 5 minutes, except for early in the morning or late at night, when they leave every 10 minutes. Don't miss it.

**BY OTHER FERRIES**　Besides the Star Ferry, there are other ferries crossing the harbor between Kowloon and Hong Kong Island, including ferries between Central and Hung Hom, hoverferries between Central and Tsim Sha Tsui East, and ferries between Tsim Sha Tsui and Wan Chai.

There's also a large fleet serving the outlying islands, with most ferries departing from piers west of the Star Ferry terminus in Central. The latest schedules and fares are available from the Hong Kong Tourist Association (HKTA) or by calling the Hong Kong Ferry Company Ltd. (HKF) (☎ **852/2542 3081** or 852/2542 3082).

**BY TAXI**　As a rule, taxi drivers in Hong Kong are strictly controlled and fairly honest. Taxis free to pick up passengers display a red FOR HIRE flag in the windshield during the day and a lighted TAXI sign on the roof at night. Fares start at HK$14.50 (US$1.90) for the first 1.24 miles (2km), then are HK$1.30 (US17¢) for each 275 yards (200m). Luggage costs an extra HK$5 (US65¢) per piece, and taxis ordered by phone add a HK$5 (US65¢) surcharge. Trips through tunnels cost extra: HK$20 (US$2.60) for the Cross-Harbour Tunnel, HK$30 (US$3.90) for the Eastern Harbour Crossing, HK$45 (US$5.85) for the Western Harbour Tunnel, and HK$5 (US65¢) for the Aberdeen Tunnel.

Taxis in the New Territories charge HK$12.50 (US$1.60) at flag-drop. They cover only the New Territories and are not allowed to transport you back into Kowloon.

**BY MAXICABS & MINIBUSES**　These small buses are the poor person's taxis; although they are quite useful for the locals, they're a bit confusing for tourists. There are two types of vehicles: the green-and-yellow ones, called **maxicabs,** which follow fixed routes, charge fixed rates ranging from HK$1.50 to HK$18 (US20¢–US$2.35) depending on the distance, and require the exact fare as you enter; and the red-and-yellow **minibuses,** which have no fixed route and will stop when you hail them. Fares for these range from HK$2 to HK$7 (US25¢–US90¢), depending on the distance, but are often higher on rainy days, race days, or cross-harbor trips. You pay as you exit; just yell when you want to get off.

**BY CAR**　Rental cars are not advisable in Hong Kong and hardly anyone uses them, even businesspeople. Nothing is so far away that you can't get there easily, quickly, and cheaply by taxi or public transport, and parking is at a premium. If you're unconvinced, Avis, Budget, and Hertz have branches here, along with a couple of dozen local firms. A valid driver's license is required, and remember, traffic flows on the left-hand side of the street.

**BY RICKSHAW**　Rickshaws hit the streets of Hong Kong in the 1870s and were once the most common form of transport in the colony. Now they're almost a thing of the past—no new licenses are being issued. A few ancient-looking men hang around the Star Ferry terminal in the Central District, but I've never once seen them hauling a customer. Instead, they make money by charging HK$50 (US$6.50) for tourists who want to take their picture. If you do want to take a ride, they'll charge up to HK$100 (US$13) to take you around the block, by far the most expensive form of transportation in Hong Kong. Be sure to negotiate the price first.

## Fast Facts: Hong Kong

**American Express**   American Express offices are located in the Henley Building, 5 Queen's Rd. Central, in the Central District, and just off Nathan Road at 25 Kimberley Rd. in Tsim Sha Tsui. For information, call ☎ **852/2732 7327.** Both offices are open Monday through Friday from 9am to 5pm and Saturday from 9am to 12:30pm.

**Business Hours**   Although opening hours can vary among banks, banking hours are generally Monday through Friday from 9am to 4:30pm and Saturday from 9am to 12:30pm. Keep in mind, however, that some banks stop their transactions an hour before closing time.

Most business offices are open Monday through Friday from 9am to 5pm, with lunch hour from 1 to 2pm; Saturday business hours are generally 9am to 1pm.

Most shops are open 7 days a week. Shops in the Central District are generally open from 10am to 6pm; in Causeway Bay and Wan Chai, from 10am to 9:30pm; in Tsim Sha Tsui, from 10am to 9 or 10pm (and some even later than that); and in Tsim Sha Tsui East, from 10am to 7:30pm. As for bars, most stay open until at least 2am; some stay open until the crack of dawn.

**Crime**   See "Safety," below.

**Doctors & Dentists**   Most first-class hotels have in-house doctors or can refer you to a doctor or dentist. Otherwise, call the U.S. consulate for more information. If it's an emergency, dial 999 or contact one of the recommendations under "Hospitals," below.

**Drug Laws**   Penalties for possession, use, and trafficking in illegal drugs are strict, and convicted offenders can expect lengthy jail sentences and fines. Just say no.

**Electricity**   The electricity used in Hong Kong is 220 volts, alternating current (AC), 50 cycles (in the U.S. it's 110 volts and 60 cycles). Most hotels have adapters to fit shavers of different plugs and voltages, but for other gadgets you'll need transformers and plug adapters (Hong Kong outlets take plugs with three rectangular prongs).

**Embassies & Consulates**   Since visa, passport, and other departments may have limited open hours, you should telephone for exact opening hours. **United States:** 26 Garden Rd., Central District (☎ **852/2523 9011**). **Canada:** 12th Floor of Tower One, Exchange Square, 8 Connaught Place, Central District (☎ **852/2810 4321**). **U.K.,** 1 Supreme Court Rd., Central District (☎ **852/2901 3000**). **Australia,** 23rd and 24th floors, Harbour Centre, 25 Harbour Rd., Wan Chai, on Hong Kong Island (☎ **852/2827 8881**). **New Zealand,** Room 2705, Jardine House, Connaught Place, Central District (☎ **852/2525 5044**).

**Emergencies**   All emergency calls are free—just dial **999** for police, fire, or ambulance.

**Hospitals**   The following hospitals can help you around the clock: Queen Mary Hospital, 102 Pokfulam Rd., Hong Kong Island (☎ **852/2855 4111**); Hong

# Telephone Dialing Info at a Glance

- **To place a call from your home country to Hong Kong,** dial the international access code (011 in the U.S., 0011 in Australia, 0170 in New Zealand, 00 in the U.K.), plus the country code (**852**), plus the phone number (for example, 011-852-0000 0000).

- **To place a call within Hong Kong,** simply dial the local number (local calls are free).

- **To place a direct international call from Hong Kong,** dial the international access code (**001**) plus the country code, the area or city code, and the number (for example, 001-01-212/000-0000).

- **To reach the international operator,** dial **10013.**

- **To call AT&T direct,** call ☎ 800/96 1111; for MCI call ☎ 800/961121; and for Sprint call ☎ 800/96-1877.

- **International country codes** are as follows: Australia 61, Burma 95, Cambodia 855, Canada 1, Indonesia 62, Laos 856, Malaysia 60, New Zealand 64, the Phillipines 63, Singapore 65, Thailand 66, U.K. 44, U.S. 1, Vietnam 84.

Kong Adventist Hospital, 40 Stubbs Rd., Hong Kong Island (☎ **852/2574 6211**); and Queen Elizabeth Hospital, 30 Gascoigne Rd., Kowloon (☎ **852/2958 8888**).

**Languages**    English and Cantonese are the two official languages. Most residents of Hong Kong speak Cantonese, and English is generally only understood in hotels and tourist shops.

**Liquor Laws**    The drinking age in Hong Kong is 18. The hours for bars vary according to the district, though those around Lan Kwai Fong and Tsim Sha Tsui stay open the longest, often till dawn.

**Police**    You can reach the police for an emergency by dialing ☎ **999,** the same number as for a fire or an ambulance. There's a crime hotline (☎ **852/2527 7177**), a 24-hour service that also handles complaints against taxis.

**Post Offices/Mail**    Most hotels have stamps and can mail your letters for you. Otherwise, major post offices are open Monday through Friday from 8am to 6pm and Saturday from 8am to 2pm. The main post office is on Hong Kong Island at 2 Connaught Place, in the Central District near the Star Ferry concourse. On the Kowloon side, post offices are located at 405 Nathan Rd., between the Jordan and Yau Ma Tei MTR subway stations; and at 10 Middle Rd., 1 block north of Salisbury Road in Tsim Sha Tsui. Airmail letters up to 20 grams and postcards cost HK$3.10 (US40¢) to the United States or Europe. Mailboxes are a bright orange-red. For general inquiries, call ☎ **852/2921 2222.**

If you don't know where you'll be staying in Hong Kong, you can still receive mail at two locations. Have it sent to you "Post Restante" at the General Post Office, 2 Connaught Place, Central District, Hong Kong Island, which is located near the Star Ferry terminus; or at the Kowloon Central Post Office, 405 Nathan Rd., Yau Ma Tei (between Yau Ma Tei and Jordan MTR station). Both will hold mail for 2 months; when you come to collect it, be sure to bring along your passport for identification.

**Safety**   Hong Kong is relatively safe for the visitor, especially if you use common sense and stick to such well-traveled nighttime areas as Tsim Sha Tsui or Causeway Bay. The main thing you must guard against is pickpockets, who often work in groups to pick men's pockets or slit open a woman's purse, quickly taking the valuables and then relaying them on to accomplices who disappear in the crowd. You should also be on guard on crowded public conveyances such as the MTR. To be on the safe side, keep your valuables in your hotel's safety-deposit box and carry your passport or large amounts of money in a moneybelt.

**Taxes**   Hotels will add a 10% service charge and a 3% government tax to your bill. Restaurants and bars will automatically add a 10% service charge, but there is no tax. There's an airport departure tax of HK$50 (US$6.50) for adults and children older than 12. If you're taking the boat to Macau, you must pay a Hong Kong departure tax of HK$19 (US$2.45), which is already included in the price of your boat ticket.

**Telephone & Fax**   Local calls made from homes, offices, shops, and restaurants are free, so don't feel shy about asking to use the phone. From public phone booths, a local call costs HK$1 (US13¢) for each 5 minutes; from hotel rooms, about HK$3 to HK$5 (US40¢–US65¢). For directory assistance, dial ☎ 1081 for local numbers, 10013 for international inquiries.

Most hotels will handle faxes and overseas calls and offer direct dialing. Otherwise, long-distance calls can be made from specially marked International Dialing Direct (IDD) public phones. The cheapest and most convenient method for making international calls is with a PhoneCard, which comes in denominations ranging from HK$50 to HK$300 (US$6.50 to US$39) and is available at Star Ferry piers, HKTA information offices, and machines located beside telephones. You can also charge your telephone call to a major credit card by using one of about 100 credit-card phones in major shopping locations.

As this book goes to press, the cost of a direct-dial call to the United States, made by dialing 001-1-area code-telephone number, is HK$6.80 (US90¢) per minute. Otherwise, you can make a collect call from any public or private phone by dialing 10010. You can also make cashless international calls from any telephone in Hong Kong by using Home Direct, which gives you immediate and direct access to an operator in the country you're calling. For information on dial access numbers for Home Direct, phone locations, places where phonecards can be purchased and operated, time zones, or other matters pertaining to international calls, call 10013.

**Time Zone**   Hong Kong is 13 hours ahead of New York, 14 hours ahead of Chicago, and 16 hours ahead of Los Angeles. Hong Kong does not observe daylight saving time, so subtract 1 hour from the above times in summer.

**Tipping**   Even though restaurants and bars will automatically add a 10% service charge to your bill, you're still expected to leave small change for the waiter. A general rule of thumb is to leave 5%, but in most Chinese restaurants where meals are usually inexpensive it's acceptable to leave change up to HK$5 (US65¢). In the finest restaurants you should leave 10%.

You're also expected to tip taxi drivers, bellhops, barbers, and beauticians. For taxi drivers, simply round up your bill to the nearest HK$1 or add a HK$1 (US15¢) tip. Tip people who cut your hair 5% or 10%, and give bellhops HK$10 to HK$20 (US$1.30–US$2.60), depending on the number of your bags. If you use a public restroom with an attendant, you may be expected to leave a small gratuity—HK$2 (US25¢) should be enough. In addition, chambermaids and room attendants are usually given about 2% of the room charge.

**Toilets** The best places to track down public facilities in Hong Kong are in its many hotels. Fast food restaurants and shopping malls are another good bet. There may be an attendant on hand who will expect a small tip of about HK$2 (U.S. 25¢). Note that there are no public facilities at any of the MTR subway stations.

**Water** It's perfectly safe to drink Hong Kong's water, but visitors prone to upset stomachs should stick to bottled water, which is widely available. In summer, it's wise to carry bottled water with you.

# 3 Accommodations

The good news is that many hotels, in the wake of the Asian financial crisis and a decrease in tourism since the 1997 handover, have begun offering promotional packages or even reducing their rates. The bad news is that rates are still high compared to those of most Southeast Asian destinations, and inexpensive hotels are few and far between. The rates listed below are the hotels' official, or "rack" rates, and you should probably be able to do better. Be sure to ask whether any promotional fares are being offered when you make your reservation. Remember too that rates can vary significantly within a hotel, depending on views and height: rooms on the highest floors facing famous Victoria Harbour are understandably the most expensive.

Although the greatest concentration of hotels is on the Kowloon side, Hong Kong is so compact and easily traversed by public transportation that location is not the issue it is in larger, sprawling metropolises. Hong Kong's top hotels are among the best in the world, many with sweeping views of Victoria Harbour and offering superb service and amenities, including so-called "executive floors" catering mostly to business travelers with such added luxuries as express check-in, private lounge, complimentary breakfast and cocktails, and often in-room fax machines and other perks. Moderate hotels comprise the majority of hotels in Hong Kong. They have rather small rooms compared to their American counterparts, cater largely to tour groups, and usually offer such in-room amenities as hair dryers, room safes, cable or satellite TV with in-house pay movies, and tea- and coffee-making facilities, as well as a tour desk and no-smoking rooms. Inexpensive hotels are in short supply and offer just the basics of bathroom, air conditioning, televisions, and telephones.

**TAXES & SERVICE CHARGES** Keep in mind that prices given in this book are for room rates only—a 10% service charge and 3% government tax will be added to your bill.

# KOWLOON
## VERY EXPENSIVE
✪ **The Peninsula Hotel.** Salisbury Rd., Tsim Sha Tsui, Kowloon, Hong Kong. ☎ **852/2366 6251** or 800/262-9467 in the U.S. Fax 852/2722 4170. www.peninsula.com. E-mail: pen@peninsula.com. 300 units. A/C MINIBAR TV TEL. HK$2,900–HK$4,600 (US$377–US$598) single or double; from HK$5,200 (US$656) suite. AE, DC, MC, V. MTR: Tsim Sha Tsui.

This is Hong Kong's most famous hotel, the place to stay if you are an incurable romantic, have a penchant for the historical, and can afford its high prices. Built in 1928, it exudes elegance, from its white-gloved doormen to one of the largest fleets of Rolls-Royces in the world. Priding itself on service, it maintains one of the highest

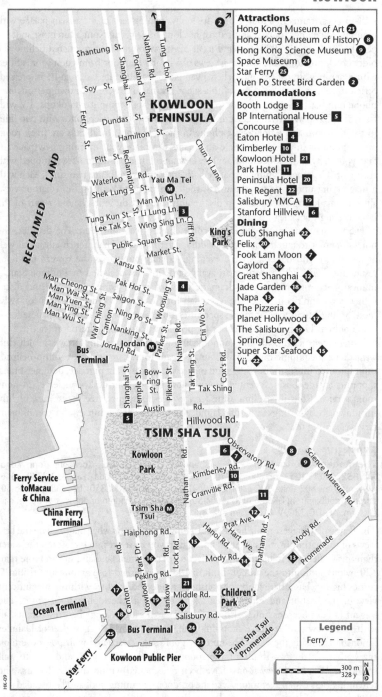

**Attractions**
Hong Kong Museum of Art 23
Hong Kong Museum of History 8
Hong Kong Science Museum 9
Space Museum 24
Star Ferry 25
Yuen Po Street Bird Garden 2

**Accommodations**
Booth Lodge 3
BP International House 5
Concourse 1
Eaton Hotel 4
Kimberley 10
Kowloon Hotel 21
Park Hotel 11
Peninsula Hotel 20
The Regent 22
Salisbury YMCA 19
Stanford Hillview 6

**Dining**
Club Shanghai 22
Felix 20
Fook Lam Moon 7
Gaylord 16
Great Shanghai 12
Jade Garden 18
Napa 13
The Pizzeria 21
Planet Hollywood 17
The Salisbury 19
Spring Deer 14
Super Star Seafood 15
Yü 22

**Legend**
Ferry – – – –

0        300 m
         328 y

staff-to-guest ratios in Hong Kong. Its lobby, reminiscent of a Parisian palace with high gilded ceilings, pillars, and palms, has long been Hong Kong's foremost spot for people-watching. In 1993, a magnificent 32-story tower was constructed behind the older hotel, providing breathtaking views of Victoria Harbour from guest rooms fitted with amenities almost beyond belief. Even jaded travelers are likely to be impressed. Spacious rooms are all equipped with a silent fax machine with your own personalized phone number (messages are sent to your room via fax); computer hookups; TV with laser-disc/CD player (free CDs and movies available); three telephones with two lines in the bedroom and a hands-free phone in the bathroom (local calls are free); room safe; and a box in the closet where attendants can place your morning newspaper or take your dirty shoes for complimentary cleaning. Huge bathrooms are equipped with their own TV, mood lighting, separate bath and shower stall, and two sinks, each with a magnifying mirror. It may be worth the extra money to spring for a harbor view, since rooms facing the back are a disappointment and those in the older part of the hotel are slightly claustrophobic.

Every restaurant in the Peninsula comes highly recommended. For decades, the hotel's premier restaurant has been Gaddi's, offering traditional French cuisine as well as live music and dancing in the evening. Equally popular is the tower's top-floor restaurant, Felix, which features an avant-garde interior designed by Philippe Starck, innovative continental cuisine, dramatic views of Hong Kong, and a bar and disco. Other good choices include The Verandah for Continental cuisine, Chesa for Swiss food, Spring Moon for Cantonese specialties, and Imasa for traditional Japanese food. The Lobby is Hong Kong's best spot for people watching and afternoon tea.

Hotel amenities include free indoor swimming pool with sun terrace, health club with exercise equipment, Jacuzzis, saunas, steam rooms, solariums, rooftop helipad, soundproofed music room with grand piano where guests can practice, designer-brand shopping arcade, business center, beauty salon, barber, tour desk, concierge, 24-hour room service, Rolls-Royce limousine service, free newspaper, free shoeshines, nightly turndown, baby-sitting, same-day laundry service, in-house nurse, and complimentary welcoming tea.

## EXPENSIVE

**The Regent Hong Kong.** 18 Salisbury Rd., Tsim Sha Tsui, Kowloon, Hong Kong. ☎ **852/2721 1211** or 800/545-4000 in the U.S. and Canada. Fax 852/2739 4546. www.rih.com. 602 units. A/C MINIBAR TV TEL. HK$2,600–HK$4,350 (US$338–US$565.50) single or double; from HK$4,650 (US$604.50) junior suite. Children under 15 stay free in parents' rm. AE, DC, MC, V. MTR: Tsim Sha Tsui.

The Peninsula's biggest rival, The Regent Hong Kong boasts what may well be the best views of the harbor from Tsim Sha Tsui. In fact, you can't get much closer to the water than this—the hotel is located on a projection of reclaimed land and sits on more than 120 pylons sunk into the harbor. Built in 1980 of polished rose granite and rising 17 stories high, it has a bare lobby of polished granite and marble, with the magnificent view of the harbor and Hong Kong Island serving as the lobby's focal point. The Regent (a Four Seasons hotel) also provides some of Hong Kong's best restaurants, all with great views, an exclusive shopping mall, and the world's largest fleet of Daimler limousines, outside the U.K. The outdoor pool's sun terrace and whirlpools overlook the harbor, as do two-thirds of the rooms, with floor-to-ceiling and wall-to-wall windows. All harbor-view rooms have been redecorated within the last 2 years. The remaining (less expensive) rooms face the outdoor swimming pool and landscaped sun terrace; some of these are actually larger than the harbor-view rooms. All rooms feature such updated facilities as dataports for personal computers and the convenience of free bottled water; some of the more expensive rooms even have in-room fax machines. But unlike most deluxe hotels, there are no designated executive floors, the underlying concept being that all rooms should offer the same degree of efficient and personalized service. There's a butler for every six rooms, on call 24 hours a day. A notable feature of the Regent is its spacious bathrooms, each fitted in Italian marble with a sunken bathtub and separate shower unit.

Other facilities include business center, health spa, upscale shopping arcade, beauty salon, concierge, 24-hour room service, house doctor, baby-sitting, free newspaper, nightly turndown, limousine service, same-day laundry service, complimentary welcoming tea, and minibars in suites (mini refrigerators in rooms).

The **Plume** is one of Hong Kong's finest French restaurants, while **Yü** is the city's trendiest seafood restaurant. **Lai Ching Heen** is an elegant Cantonese restaurant, but for fun entertainment, there's **Club Shanghai,** decorated like a 1930s Shanghai nightclub and offering dim sum dinners.

## MODERATE

**BP International House.** 8 Austin Rd., Tsim Sha Tsui, Kowloon, Hong Kong. ☎ **852/2376 1111** or 800/223-5652 in the U.S. and Canada. Fax 852/2376 1333. www.hwtour.com/bpi. E-mail: bpi-rs@megahotels.com.hk. 535 units. A/C TV TEL. HK$1,600–HK$2,200 (US$208–US$286) single or double, HK$2,300–HK$2,500 (US$299–US$325) Corporate Room. Children under 13 stay free in parents' rm. AE, DC, MC, V. MTR: Jordan.

This is one of the newest moderately priced lodgings in Tsim Sha Tsui, built in 1993 and rising 25 stories above the north end of Kowloon Park. The word "House" is slightly misleading, since it is actually a hotel, modern with a spacious marbled lobby and catering mainly to tour groups and budget-conscious business travelers. In addition to a Chinese restaurant and coffee shop, there are vending machines that dispense beverages on each floor and a token-operated laundry (though laundry and dry-cleaning services are available). Within the same building is a full-line health club (for an extra fee), and the indoor and outdoor public swimming pools in Kowloon Park are just a stone's throw away. The guest rooms, located on the 14th through 25th floors, are clean, pleasant, and modern, with satellite TV. Although the hotel is located inland, the best and priciest rooms offer great views of the distant harbor. (With height limitations in Kowloon now removed due to the relocation of the airport, however, you can expect taller buildings to eclipse those views.) Business travelers usually opt for one of the Corporate Rooms on the top three floors, which provide such extras as minibars, room safes, and hair dryers. There are also very simple "Family Rooms" equipped with bunk beds that sleep four for HK$1,640 (US$213).

✿ **Eaton Hotel.** 380 Nathan Rd., Yau Ma Tei, Kowloon, Hong Kong. ☎ **852/2782 1818.** Fax 852/2782 5563. www.hotelbook.com/hotel/14206. E-mail: ehhk04@asiaonline.net. 464 units. A/C MINIBAR TV TEL. HK$1,350 (US$175) single; HK$1,550–HK$2,700 (US$201–US$351) double. Corporate discounts available. AE, DC, MC, V. MTR: Jordan.

This accommodation has more class and more facilities than most others in its price range, making it one of my top picks. A handsome, 21-story hotel located above a shopping complex not far from the night market on Temple Street, it features one of the longest hotel escalators I've ever seen, which takes guests straight up to the fourth-floor lobby. The lobby lounge is bright and cheerful, with a four-story glass-enclosed atrium that overlooks a garden terrace with a water cascade, where you can sit outside with drinks in nice weather. The guest rooms are small but come with such comforts as feather duvet, tea- and coffee-making facilities, hair dryer, pay movies, safe, voice mail, and dataports. Rooms on the top floors and in a new addition are more expensive, with fax machines and fancier decor, including some innovatively designed rooms with views of a distant harbor. Otherwise, the best views are of Nathan Road. Facilities include a very good Cantonese restaurant, coffee shop, cozy bar with a "colonial" atmosphere and terrace seating, nice but small rooftop pool with sunning terrace, fitness room, and business center. Services include complimentary newspaper, room service (7am to 2am), baby-sitting, and same-day laundry service.

**Hotel Concourse.** 22 Lai Chi Kok Rd., Mong Kok, Kowloon, Hong Kong. ☎ **852/2397 6683.** Fax 852/2381 3768. www.hkstar.com/concourse. E-mail: info@hotelconcourse.com. hk. 430 units. A/C MINIBAR TV TEL. HK$1,280–HK$2,080 (US$166–US$270) single or double; from HK$2,800 (US$364) suite. Children under 13 stay free in parents' rm. AE, DC, MC, V. MTR: Prince Edward.

This hotel with a friendly staff is at the northern end of Kowloon Peninsula, in an area known as Mong Kok. Since not many tourists venture this far north, the area has more local flavor than Tsim Sha Tsui. Affiliated with China Travel Service (the official Chinese travel agency), the hotel is popular with mainland Chinese, including many tour groups. For that reason, the lobby can be quite noisy and busy (like the rest of Hong Kong). The hotel is simple, reminiscent of business hotels in Japan, and offers clean, functional rooms, the most expensive of which are deluxe corner rooms, larger and brighter with large desks and fax machines. If you are just looking for an inexpensive room without such extras as swimming pool, business center, or shops, this may be the place for you. There are several restaurants, including a casual Western one, a Cantonese restaurant renowned for its dim sum, and Hong Kong's only hotel Korean restaurant. Guest services include a free newspaper, same-day laundry service, room service (7am to 1am), baby-sitting, and a house doctor.

**Kimberley Hotel.** 28 Kimberley Rd., Tsim Sha Tsui, Kowloon, Hong Kong. ☎ **852/2723 3888.** Fax 852/2723 1318. www.kimberley.com.hk. E-mail: kh-rsvn@kimberley.com.hk. 546 units. A/C MINIBAR TV TEL. HK$1,550–HK$2,050 (US$201–US$266) single; HK$1,650–HK$2,150 (US$215–US$279) double; from HK$2,450 (US$318) suite. AE, DC, MC, V. MTR: Tsim Sha Tsui.

Opened in 1991, the 20-story Kimberley is on the northern edge of Tsim Sha Tsui, about a 15-minute walk from the Star Ferry. It caters to both the tourist and business trade, including many Japanese. Guest rooms, constructed with V-shaped windows that let in more sunlight and allow for more panoramic—though unscenic—views, are equipped with hair dryers, very firm beds, phone in the bathroom, and tea- and coffee-making facilities. The most expensive rooms are on higher floors and are larger, but even these are rather small. Facilities include two restaurants serving Japanese and Chinese food, coffee shop offering lunch and dinner buffets, cocktail lounge, shopping arcade, business center, sauna (extra fee charged), fitness room, putting green, and golf cage. Services include free newspaper, room service (6am to midnight), same-day laundry service, house doctor, and baby-sitting.

✪ **Kowloon Hotel.** 19–21 Nathan Rd., Tsim Sha Tsui, Kowloon, Hong Kong. ☎ **852/2369 8698** or 800/262-9467 in the U.S. Fax 852/2739 9811. E-mail: khh@ peninsula.com. 736 units. A/C MINIBAR TV TEL. HK$1,500–HK$2,550 (US$195–US$331) single; HK$1,600–HK$2,650 (US$208–US$344) double; from HK$3,700 (US$481) suite. AE, DC, MC, V. MTR: Tsim Sha Tsui.

If you like high-tech, this is the place for you. The Kowloon is a modern, glass-walled structure with a great location just behind The Peninsula. (Both hotels are under the same management.) The Star Ferry is just a few minutes' walk away. Although rooms are minuscule, with no views from their V-shaped bay windows, the hotel offers the most technically advanced rooms in its price category. Every room boasts an interactive telecenter (a multi-system TV offering satellite programming and linked to a central computer), which doubles as a word-processor, interfaces with an in-room fax machine (each with its own private number and serving also as a printer), gives access to the Internet (guests receive personal e-mail addresses), and provides such information as up-to-the-minute flight details, incoming messages, hotel bills, and video games. Guests can also retrieve voice mail messages electronically from outside the hotel. Other room features include tea- and coffee-making facilities, room safe, and hair dryer. The hotel lobby has a computerized street directory for consulates, points of interest, and other addresses, which you can print out in both English and Chinese, for yourself and your taxi driver. Facilities include a business center, shopping arcade, and four restaurants, including a very good pizzeria and a restaurant specializing in international buffets. Services include free newspaper, limousine service, baby-sitting, same-day laundry service, and room service (from 6:30am to 2am).

**Park Hotel.** 61–65 Chatham Rd. S., Tsim Sha Tsui, Kowloon, Hong Kong. ☎ **852/2366 1371.** Fax 852/2739 7259. E-mail: park2@chevalier.net. 423 units. A/C MINIBAR TV TEL. HK$1,600–HK$2,100 (US$208–US$273) single; HK$1,700–HK$2,200 (US$221–US$286) double; from HK$2,600 (US$338) suite. One child under 12 can stay free in parents' rm. AE, DC, MC, V. MTR: Tsim Sha Tsui.

Built in 1961 and kept up-to-date with renovations, the clean and comfortable Park has long been one of the best-known medium-priced hotels in Kowloon. You can't go wrong staying here. Especially popular with Australians and Asians, this hotel probably has the largest rooms in its price range, a plus if you're tired of cramped quarters. The best rooms are those on the upper floors of the 16-floor property; the lower floors can be noisy, especially rooms facing the street. Facilities include Western and Cantonese restaurants, a coffee shop, bar, shopping arcade, and beauty salon. Services include 24-hour medical service, 24-hour room service, baby-sitting, same-day laundry service, and limousine service. The location on the border between Tsim Sha Tsui and Tsim Sha Tsui East, across from the Science Museum, is not as convenient as that of many other hotels in this category, though it is within walking distance of the MTR (about 5 minutes) and hoverferry service to Central (about 8 minutes).

✪ **Stanford Hillview Hotel.** 13–17 Observatory Rd., Tsim Sha Tsui, Kowloon, Hong Kong. ☎ **852/2722 7822** or 800/44-UTELL in the U.S. Fax 852/2723 3718. E-mail: sfhvhkg@ netvigator.com. 163 units. A/C MINIBAR TV TEL. HK$1,300–HK$1,900 (US$169–US$247) single or double. AE, DC, MC, V. MTR: Tsim Sha Tsui.

This small, intimate hotel, built in 1991, is in the heart of Tsim Sha Tsui and yet is a world away, located on top of a hill in the shade of huge banyan trees, and next to the Observatory, with its colonial building and greenery. The lobby is quiet and subdued (quite a contrast to most Hong Kong hotels) and the staff is friendly and accommodating. The hotel has a business center, as well as a restaurant offering international buffets and à la carte menus of Western and Asian dishes. Rooms were all renovated and fitted with dataports in 1998. The most expensive rooms are on higher floors; ask for one facing the Observatory. Room service is available from 6:30am to 11:30pm, and there's also same-day laundry service and baby-sitting. All in all, a very civilized place.

## INEXPENSIVE

✪ **Booth Lodge.** 11 Wing Sing Lane, Yau Ma Tei, Kowloon, Hong Kong. ☎ **852/2771 9266.** Fax 852/2385 1140. 53 units. A/C MINIBAR TV TEL. HK$620–HK$1,200 (US$81–US$156) single or double. AE, MC, V. MTR: Yau Ma Tei.

About a 30-minute walk to the Star Ferry but close to the Jade Market and the Temple Street Night Market, and only a 2-minute walk from the MTR station, Booth Lodge is just off Nathan Road on the seventh floor of the Salvation Army building. Recently renovated, it has a comfortable lobby and an adjacent coffee shop offering à la carte dining and very reasonably priced lunch and dinner buffets with Chinese, Japanese, and Western selections. Best is the restaurant's outdoor brick terrace overlooking a wooded hillside, where buffet barbecues are held Friday and Saturday evenings. Rooms, all twins or doubles and either standard rooms or larger deluxe rooms, are clean and equipped with hair dryers. Some that face Nathan Road have views of a harbor in the distance, though those facing the wooded hillside are quieter. There's laundry service, as well as a tour desk and gift shop.

✪ **The Salisbury YMCA.** Salisbury Rd., Tsim Sha Tsui, Kowloon, Hong Kong. ☎ **852/2369 2211.** Fax 852/2739 9315. www.ymcahk.org.hk. E-mail: room@ymcahk.org.hk. 380 units. A/C. HK$880 (US$114) single; HK$1,030–HK$1,270 (US$134–US$165) double; from HK$1,720 (US$224) suite. Dormitory bed HK$190 (US$25). AE, DC, MC, V. MTR: Tsim Sha Tsui.

For decades the overwhelming number-one choice among inexpensive accommodations in Hong Kong has been the YMCA on Salisbury Road, which has the good fortune of being right next to The Peninsula Hotel on the waterfront, just a 2-minute walk from both the Star Ferry and subway station. Although the Salisbury may seem expensive for a YMCA, the location and facilities are worth the price; here you have Tsim Sha Tsui's cheapest rooms with harbor views. Modern and spacious, the Salisbury YMCA welcomes families as well as individual men and women, with 19 single rooms (none with harbor view) and more than 280 double rooms (the most expensive of which have great harbor views), as well as suites (with and without harbor views). Although simple in decor, rooms are on a par with those at more expensive hotels, with such in-room amenities as telephones, satellite TVs with complimentary in-house movies, stocked refrigerators, tea- and coffee-making facilities, safes, and hair dryers. For budget travelers, there are 14 dormitory-style rooms, each with two bunk beds, individual reading lights, private bathroom, and lockers, available only to visitors staying in Hong Kong fewer than 10 days (write or fax for reservations; walk-ins are also accepted). There are three food and beverage outlets, including the **Salisbury Restaurant,** which serves buffet meals. A sports facility boasts two indoor swimming pools (free for YMCA guests, and including a children's pool) and a fitness gym, two squash courts, and indoor climbing wall (fee charged). Laundry service is available.

## CENTRAL DISTRICT
### EXPENSIVE

✪ **Island Shangri-La Hong Kong.** Pacific Place, 88 Queensway, Central, Hong Kong. ☎ **852/2877 3838** or 800/942-5050 in the U.S. and Canada. Fax 852/2521 8742. www.shangri-la.com. 565 units. A/C MINIBAR TV TEL. HK$2,300–HK$3,650 (US$299–US$474.50) single; HK$2,500–HK$3,850 (US$325–US$500.50) double; from HK$5,300 (US$689) suite. Children under 19 stay free in parents' rm. AE, DC, MC, V. MTR: Admiralty.

Hong Kong Island's tallest hotel (measured from sea level) offers the ultimate in extravagance and luxury, rivaling the grand hotels in Paris or London. More than 700 Viennese chandeliers, lush Tai Ping carpets, artistic flower arrangements, and more than 500 paintings and artwork adorn the hotel. The 17-story atrium, which stretches from the 39th to the 56th floor, features a marvelous 16-story-high Chinese painting, believed to be the largest landscape painting in the world. Also in the atrium is a private lounge open only to hotel guests and a two-story old world–style library, fitted with leather armchairs and classic lamps and stocked with reference materials, special-interest books, videotapes, and compact discs. The hotel is enhanced by the connecting Pacific Place shopping center, with its many options in dining; and Hong Kong Park is across the street. Rooms, among the largest in Hong Kong and the largest on Hong Kong Island, face either the Peak or Victoria Harbour and feature

# Tips for the Business Traveler in Hong Kong

- **Bring plenty of business cards.** They are exchanged constantly, and you'll be highly suspect without them (if you run out, hotel business centers can arrange to have new ones printed within 24 hours). When presenting your card, hold it out with both hands, turned so that the receiver can read it. Chinese names are written with the family name first, followed by the given name and then the middle name.

- **Use formal names for addressing business associates,** unless told to do otherwise. You'll find that many Hong Kong Chinese used to dealing with foreigners have adopted a Western first name.

- **Shaking hands is appropriate** for greetings and introductions.

- **Business attire**—a suit and tie for men—is worn throughout the year, even in summer.

- **Entertainment** is an integral part of conducting business in Hong Kong, whether it's a meal in which the host orders the food and serves his or her guests, an evening at the race tracks, or a round of golf.

- **If an invitation is extended, it is understood that the host will treat.** Do not insist on paying; this will only embarrass your host. Accept graciously, and promise to pick up the tab next time around.

marble-topped desks, dataports and dual phone lines to accommodate personal computers, a hands-free phone, Chinese lacquerware TV cabinets and movies on demand, silk bedspreads, a safe, free bottled water, and oversize bathrooms equipped with two sinks, separate tub and shower areas (in the harbor-view rooms only), bidet, bath scales, and even jewelry boxes. Fresh flowers and teddy bears placed on pillows during nightly turndown are nice touches. Guests paying rack rates receive such additional services as free laundry and dry cleaning throughout their stay, complimentary breakfast, free local telephone calls, and a late 6pm check out.

**Petrus** is the hotel's signature restaurant, occupying a prime spot on the top floor and serving French cuisine with a view. Next door is **Cyrano,** a lounge offering jazz entertainment every night and stunning views of the harbor. The **Lobster Bar** is *the* place to go for meals featuring the sea's best crustacean, but for casual dining with a breezy Californian atmosphere, highly recommended is the **Island Café,** specializing in buffets.

Facilities and services include outdoor heated swimming pool, Jacuzzi, sauna, steam bath, health club, 24-hour business center, drugstore, barbershop, beauty salon, shopping arcade, concierge, free newspaper, 24-hour room service, same-day laundry service, welcoming tea, limousine service, baby-sitting, medical clinic, and free shuttle service to Central.

## CAUSEWAY BAY/WAN CHAI
### VERY EXPENSIVE

**Grand Hyatt Hong Kong.** 1 Harbour Rd., Wan Chai, Hong Kong. ☎ **852/2588 1234** or 800/233-1234 in the U.S. and Canada. Fax 852/2802 0677. www.hyatt.com. 572 units. A/C MINIBAR TV TEL. HK$3,200–HK$3,800 (US$416–US$494) single; HK$3,450–HK$4,050 (US$448.50–US$526.50) double; HK$3,950–HK$4,250 (US$513.50–US$552.50) Regency Club executive floor double; from HK$5,500 (US$715) suite. Children under 12 stay free in parents' rm (maximum: 3 persons per rm). AE, DC, MC, V. MTR: Wan Chai.

# Central District

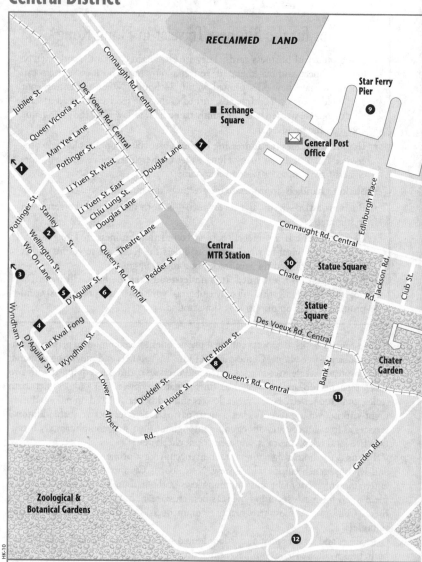

RECLAIMED LAND

Star Ferry Pier 9

Exchange Square

General Post Office

Edinburgh Place

Connaught Rd. Central

Des Voeux Rd. Central

Jubilee St.

Queen Victoria St.

Man Yee Lane

Pottinger St.

Li Yuen St. West

Li Yuen St. East

Chiu Lung St.

Douglas Lane

Douglas Lane

7

Pottinger St.

Stanley St.

Wellington St.

Wo On Lane

Theatre Lane

Queen's Rd. Central

Pedder St.

Connaught Rd. Central

Central MTR Station

Chater

10

Statue Square

Jackson Rd.

Club St.

2

3

5

6

Statue Square

Bank St.

Chater Garden

D'Aguilar St.

Lan Kwai Fong

Wyndham St.

Wyndham St.

Des Voeux Rd. Central

4

D'Aguilar St.

Lower

Albert

Rd.

Duddell St.

Ice House St.

Ice House St.

8

Queen's Rd. Central

11

Garden Rd.

Zoological & Botanical Gardens

12

HK-10

## Attractions

Hong Kong Museum of
Medical Science 3
Man Mo Temple 3
Peak Tram Terminal 12
Star Ferry 9
Tsui Museum of Art 11

## Accommodations

Empire Hotel 17
Grand Hyatt 19
Harbour View International 19
Island Shangri-La 15
The Park Lane 19

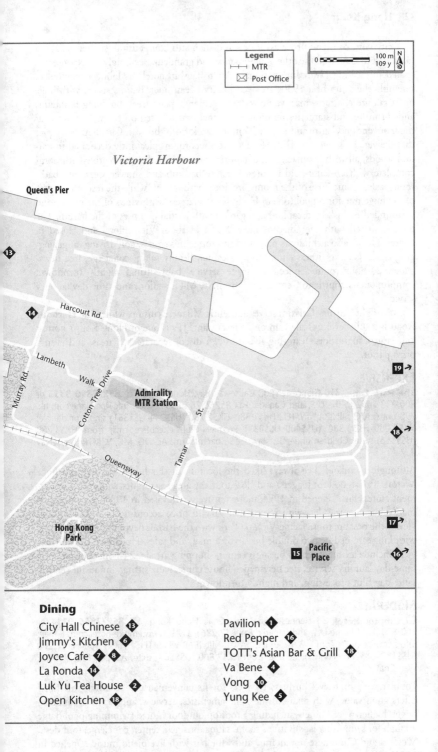

## Dining

City Hall Chinese 13
Jimmy's Kitchen 6
Joyce Cafe 7 8
La Ronda 14
Luk Yu Tea House 2
Open Kitchen 18

Pavilion 1
Red Pepper 16
TOTT's Asian Bar & Grill 18
Va Bene 4
Vong 10
Yung Kee 5

In a city with so many first-class hotels and such stiff competition, sooner or later a hotel had to exceed all the others in opulence and grandeur. Seemingly no expense was spared in creating Hyatt International's Asian flagship hotel. Its lobby, decorated to resemble the salon of a 1930s art deco luxury ocean liner, flaunts space, with huge black granite columns, massive flower arrangements, palm trees, bubbling fountains, and furniture and statuettes reminiscent of that era. Located on the waterfront near the Convention Centre and only a 5-minute walk from the Wan Chai Star Ferry pier that delivers passengers to Tsim Sha Tsui, it offers rooms pleasantly decorated in natural woods, all with fax machines, dataports, voice mail, safes and marble bathrooms complete with 18-karat-gold fixtures, separate bathtub and shower areas, and bathroom scales. Some 70% of the rooms provide a harbor view, while the rest offer a view of the huge free-form pool (one of Hong Kong's largest, with views of the harbor and surrounded by lush landscaping) and garden with partial glimpses of the harbor. The pool is shared with the adjacent New World Harbour View Hotel and closed in winter. There's also a children's pool, two rooftop tennis courts, golf driving range, jogging track, Jacuzzi, fitness club, business center, beauty salon, concierge, free newspaper, 24-hour room service, limousine service, baby-sitting, nightly turndown, complimentary shuttle to Central and Admiralty MTR station, and same-day laundry service.

The bright and airy **Grissini** serves authentic Milanese cuisine, while **One Harbour Road** is a split-level upscale Cantonese restaurant. **JJ's** is one of Hong Kong's hottest and largest nightspots, featuring live music, a disco, separate bar areas, and even a pizza parlor.

## EXPENSIVE

**The Park Lane.** 310 Gloucester Rd., Causeway Bay, Hong Kong. ☎ **852/2890 3355** or 800/233-5652 in the U.S. and Canada. Fax 852/2576 7853. E-mail: info@parklane.com.hk. 798 units. A/C MINIBAR TV TEL. HK$1,880–HK$2,780 (US$244–US$361) single or double; HK$3,080–HK$3,380 (US$400–US$439) Premier Club executive rms; from HK$4,280 (US$556) suite. Children under 12 stay free in parents' rm. AE, DC, MC, V. MTR: Causeway Bay.

Although it's inland, I've always liked the location of this hotel—across from huge Victoria Park (good for joggers) and close to many area restaurants, shops, and department stores. First opened in 1974 and extensively renovated in 1994, it attracts primarily business travelers with rooms that vary in price according to floor level and view—the best are those facing Victoria Park with the harbor beyond. All rooms come with king-size bed or two double beds, voice mail, and safes. Hotel facilities and services include a fitness center, business center, shopping arcade, 24-hour room service, same-day laundry service, free newspaper, house clinic, baby-sitting, limousine service, same-day film processing, and nightly turndown.

## MODERATE

✪ **Empire Hotel.** 33 Hennessy Rd., Wan Chai, Hong Kong. ☎ **852/2866 9111** or 800/830-6144 in the U.S. and Canada. Fax 852/2861 3121. www.empire-hotel.com. E-mail: info@empire-hotel.com. 376 units. A/C MINIBAR TV TEL. HK$1,400–HK$2,200 (US$182–US$286) single or double; from HK$2,800 (US$364) suite. AE, DC, MC, V. MTR: Wan Chai.

Popular with mid-level business travelers for its convenience to Central, this hotel offers good value, with many of the same amenities, services, and facilities found in larger, higher-priced hotels, including a rooftop outdoor heated swimming pool (large enough for swimming laps), fitness room, sauna, business center, concierge, tour desk, Western and Cantonese restaurants, and wine bar with live piano music. Opened in 1991, it's nicely situated in the heart of Wan Chai, with room rates based on the size of the room (none provides a view of the harbor). Comfortable and pleasant, rooms are equipped with a safe, tea- and coffee-making facilities, hair dryer, fax machine, and other amenities, including the Data View Information System, which allows guests to receive messages on their television sets, check flight schedules, play video games, and view the hotel services directory. There are also in-house pay movies and satellite programs. Services include a free newspaper, room service (6:30am to midnight), same-day laundry service, free weekday shuttle service to Admiralty and Causeway Bay, limousine service, medical and dental services, and baby-sitting.

### INEXPENSIVE

✪ **Harbour View International House.** 4 Harbour Rd., Wan Chai, Hong Kong. ☎ **852/2802 0111.** Fax 852/2802 9063. 320 units, all with bathroom. A/C MINIBAR TV TEL. HK$1,150–HK$1,650 (US$149.50–US$214.50) single or double. Children under 12 stay free in parents' rm. AE, DC, MC, V. MTR: Wan Chai.

Opened in 1986, this YMCA occupies a prime spot on the Wan Chai waterfront, next to the Hong Kong Arts Centre and not far from the convention center. Rooms, all twins or doubles, are simple but functional. Facilities and services include a coffee shop, one restaurant with a view of the harbor serving Chinese and Western food, room service (7am to 11:30pm), and laundry service. Best of all, more than half the rooms have V-shaped windows that face the harbor—one of the least expensive views in Hong Kong. Rooms that face inland are even cheaper.

## 4 Dining

Dining is one of *the* things to do in Hong Kong. Not only is the food excellent, but the range of culinary possibilities is staggering, with more than 8,000 restaurants to choose from. In an attempt to attract dwindling numbers of tourists, restaurants have modified their meals and lowered prices. Ethnic and health-conscious restaurants have exploded onto the scene, offering varied cuisine for good value. Best of all, fewer tourists means fewer crowds. You may be able to get a seat in your favorite restaurant even without a reservation.

Chinese restaurants specialize in regional cuisines, offering Cantonese, Pekingese, Shanghainese, Szechuan, and other regional fare (refer to the Hong Kong Tourist Association's free booklet, *The Official Dining & Entertainment Guide,* for a rundown of regional dishes). Of these, Cantonese restaurants are most numerous and usually offer dim sum as well. Eaten for breakfast, lunch, and with afternoon tea, dim sum consists mostly of finely chopped foods wrapped in thin dough and then steamed, fried, boiled, or braised. Served from trolleys wheeled through the restaurant or chosen from a menu, dim sum is an experience not to be missed, as much for the atmosphere as for the food.

Hong Kong also abounds in excellent Western restaurants, from French to Italian to Californian. Good bargains are fixed-price lunches and buffets, especially those offering international cuisines. Avoid dining from 1 to 2pm on weekdays, the traditional lunch hour for office workers, and keep in mind that closing hours are strictly observed, with the last orders usually taken at least 30 minutes beforehand.

You can expect to spend more than HK$300 (US$39) for dinner per person, excluding drinks, for **expensive** restaurants, HK$150 to HK$300 (US$19.50–US$39) for **moderate** restaurants, and less than HK$150 (US$19.50) for **inexpensive** restaurants. In addition, a 10% service charge will be added to your bill.

### CUISINE

**CANTONESE FOOD**   The majority of Chinese restaurants in Hong Kong are Cantonese; this is not surprising since most Hong Kong Chinese are originally from

Canton Province (now called Guangdong). It's also the most common style of Chinese cooking around the world and probably the one with which you're most familiar. Among Chinese, Cantonese cuisine is considered the finest, and many Chinese emperors employed Cantonese chefs in their kitchens.

Since the Cantonese eat so much seafood, your best choice in a Cantonese restaurant is fish. Among the recommended choices are garoupa (a local fish), pomfret, red mullet, sole, abalone, and sea cucumber. Shark's-fin soup is an expensive delicacy. Other Cantonese specialties include roast goose, duck, and pigeon; pan-fried lemon chicken; and stir-fried minced quail and bamboo shoots rolled in lettuce and eaten with the fingers.

Another popular Cantonese dish is dim sum, eaten for breakfast and lunch and with afternoon tea; in Hong Kong it is especially popular for Sunday family outings. It consists primarily of finely chopped meat, seafood, and vegetables wrapped in thin dough and then either steamed, fried, boiled, or braised. Dim sum can range from steamed dumplings to meatballs, fried spring rolls, and spareribs.

Many Cantonese restaurants offer dim sum from about 7:30am until 4pm, traditionally served from trolleys wheeled between the tables but nowadays just as often available from a written menu. The trolleys are piled high with steaming bamboo baskets, so ask the server to let you peek inside. If you like what you see, simply nod your head. A serving of dim sum usually consists of two to four pieces on a plate and averages about HK$20 to HK$35 (US$2.60 to US$4.55) per plate. Your bill is calculated at the end of the meal by the number of plates on your table or by a card stamped each time you order a dish. But it's more than just the price that draws me to traditional dim sum restaurants—they are noisy, chaotic, and the perfect place to read a newspaper or gossip. No one should go to Hong Kong without visiting a dim sum restaurant at least once.

For a light snack or late-night meal, try congee, which is a rice porridge popular for breakfast and usually topped with a meat, fish, or vegetable. Many of Hong Kong's countless, cheapest restaurants specialize in congee, as well as noodles in soup, the most famous of which is probably wun tun meen, noodle soup with shrimp dumplings.

**PEKINGESE FOOD**  Many Pekingese dishes originated in the imperial courts of the emperors and empresses and were served at elaborate banquets. This theatrical flamboyance is still evident today in the making of Pekingese noodles and the smashing of the clay around "beggar's chicken." Because of its northern source, the food of Peking (or Beijing) tends to be rather hearty, and richer than Cantonese food. Liberal amounts of peppers, garlic, ginger, leeks, and coriander are used. Noodles and dumplings are more common than rice, and roasting is the preferred method of cooking.

Most famous among Peking-style dishes is Peking (or Beijing) duck, but unfortunately a minimum of six persons is usually required for this elaborate dish. The most prized part is the crisp skin, which comes from air-drying the bird and then coating it with a mixture of syrup and soy sauce before roasting. It's served by wrapping the crisp skin and meat in thin pancakes together with spring onion, radish, and sweet plum sauce.

Another popular dish prepared with fanfare is beggar's chicken: a whole chicken is stuffed with mushrooms, pickled Chinese cabbage, herbs, and onions, wrapped in lotus leaves, sealed in clay, and then baked all day. The guest of honor usually breaks open the hard clay with a mallet, revealing a tender feast more fit for a king than a beggar.

For do-it-yourself dining, try the Mongolian hot pot, where diners gather around a common pot in a scene reminiscent of campfires on the Mongolian steppes. One version calls for wafer-thin slices of meat, usually mutton, to be dipped in a clear stock and then eaten with a spicy sauce. Another variety calls for a sizzling griddle, over which thin-sliced meat, cabbage, bean sprouts, onions, and other vegetables are barbecued in a matter of seconds.

**SHANGHAINESE FOOD**    A big, bustling city, Shanghai does not technically have a cuisine of its own. Rather, it incorporates the food of several surrounding regions and cities, making it the most diverse cuisine in China. Because of the cold winters in Shanghai, its food is heavier, richer, sweeter, and oilier than Cantonese or Pekingese food. Because the hot summers can spoil food quickly, specialties include pickled or preserved vegetables, fish, shrimp, and mushrooms. Some dishes are heavy on the garlic, and portions tend to be enormous. The dishes are often stewed, braised, or fried.

The most popular Shanghainese delicacy in Hong Kong is freshwater hairy crab, flown in from Shanghai in autumn, steamed, and eaten with the hands. Other Shanghainese dishes include "yellow fish" (braised eel with huge chunks of garlic) and "drunken chicken" (chicken marinated in Chinese wine). As for the famous hundred-year-old egg, it's actually only several months old, with a limey, pickled-ginger taste. Breads, noodles, and dumplings are favored instead of rice.

**SZECHUAN FOOD**    This is my favorite Chinese cuisine—the spiciest, hottest, and with the most fiery style of cooking. The culprit is the Szechuan chili, fried to increase its potency. Seasoning also includes chili-bean paste, peppercorns, garlic, ginger, coriander, and other spices. Foods are simmered and smoked rather than stir-fried. The most famous Szechuan dish is smoked duck; it's seasoned with peppercorns, ginger, cinnamon, orange peel, and coriander; marinated in rice wine; then steamed; and then smoked over a charcoal fire of camphor wood and tea leaves.

Other specialties include pan-fried prawns in spicy sauce, sour-and-peppery soup, sautéed diced chicken in chili-bean sauce, and dry-fried spicy string beans. Most Szechuan menus indicate which dishes are hot.

**CHIU CHOW FOOD**    In the 1980s Szechuan restaurants were opening in droves, but these days Chiu Chow restaurants are the latest trend. The name refers to the people, dialect, and food of the Swatow area in southeastern Canton. Chiu Chow chefs pride themselves on their talents for vegetable carvings—those incredible birds, flowers, and other adornments that are a part of every Chiu Chow banquet.

Influenced by Cantonese cooking, Chiu Chow food is rich in protein, light, and tasty; sauces are liberally applied. A meal begins with a cup of kwun yum tea, popularly called Iron Buddha and probably the world's strongest and most bitter tea. It's supposed to cleanse the system and stimulate the taste buds. Drink some of this stuff and you'll be humming for hours.

Two very expensive Chiu Chow delicacies are shark's fin and birds' nests. Other favorites include steamed lobster, deep-fried shrimp balls, sautéed slices of whelk, fried goose blood, goose doused in soy sauce, stuffed eel wrapped in pickled cabbage, and crispy fried chuenjew leaves, which literally melt in the mouth.

# KOWLOON
## EXPENSIVE

**Club Shanghai.** In The Regent Hotel, Salisbury Rd., Tsim Sha Tsui. ☎ **852/2721 1211,** ext. 2242. Reservations required. Fixed-price dinner HK$330 (US$42.90). AE, DC, MC, V. Mon–Thurs 6pm–2am, Fri–Sat 6pm–3am. SHANGHAINESE.

A romanticized version of 1930s Shanghai is the theme of this hotel nightclub, with its dim red lights, stuffed armchairs draped with lace antimacassars, potted palms, fringed lampshades, decorative opium pipes, and waitresses wearing high-collared slit dresses, all against a backdrop of harbor views. As the only Hong Kong establishment offering dim sum for dinner, its fixed-priced "Wok & Roll" meal features dim sum served from trolleys, Asian appetizers, soup, and choice of main course, served with Shanghainese vegetable rice or Shanghainese noodles. A duet provides soft entertainment until 9pm, followed by a band playing dance music.

✪ **Felix.** In the Peninsula Hotel, Salisbury Rd., Tsim Sha Tsui. ☎ **852/2366 6251**, ext. 3188. Reservations required. Main courses HK$190–HK$270 (US$24.70–US$32.45); fixed-price meals HK$500–HK$700 (US$65–US$91). AE, DC, MC, V. Daily 6pm–2am (last order 10:30pm). MTR: Tsim Sha Tsui. PACIFIC RIM/EAST-MEETS-WEST.

Located on the top floor of the Peninsula's new tower, this strikingly avant-garde restaurant comes as something of a shock in the otherwise staid and traditionally conservative hotel. But what else can you expect from a restaurant designed by Philippe Starck, who was given free rein to create one of Hong Kong's most unusual settings. Your first hint that Felix is not your ordinary dining experience begins with the elevator's wavy walls, which suggest a voyage to the world beyond. The wave pattern continues inside the restaurant—a huge aluminum wavy wall and two glass facades curve seductively to reveal stunning views of the city. Off to the sides of the high-ceilinged dining area, done mostly in mahogany, are two eye-catching zinc cylinders, which vaguely resemble gigantic snails and contain cocoon-cozy bars and what may be one of the world's tiniest discos, complete with a heat-sensitive floor that illuminates dancers' movements. Be sure to check out the rest room for the thrill of its slightly exhibitionist setting. The dining area itself is rather—what can I say—stark, with various styles of tables in marble, glass, and wood, all devoid of such "superfluous" decorations as table linen or flowers. The chair backs, also designed by Starck, are embellished with portraits of himself and his friends, but such details may be overlooked when the restaurant is full. Indeed, even the view tends to take second place in this self-conscious, people-watching setting. The food, featuring Pacific Rim ingredients brought together in East-meets-West combinations, is quite good but also secondary to the setting. Dishes have ranged from a ginger-marinated sea bass on wasabi potatoes with Asian mustard to a hibachi filet of steak on spinach and mixed mushrooms with a red wine sauce and fig jam.

✪ **Fook Lam Moon.** 53–59 Kimberley Rd., Tsim Sha Tsui. ☎ **852/2366 0286**. Main courses HK$90–HK$190 (US$11.70–US$24.70); dim sum HK$28–HK$50 (US$3.65–US$6.50). AE, DC, MC, V. Daily 11:30am–11:30pm. MTR: Tsim Sha Tsui. CANTONESE.

Upon entering this restaurant (look for the shrine to the kitchen god at the entrance), you immediately feel as if you've stepped back a couple of decades to a Hong Kong that has all but vanished. Considered by some Hong Kong old-timers to be the best Cantonese restaurant in the world, Fook Lam Moon specializes in exotic dishes, including shark's fin, bird's nest, and abalone, served in a variety of ways, as well as more down-to-earth dishes such as fried crispy chicken and pan-fried lobster bars. Shark's fin, however, is the obvious number-one choice, with 19 different renditions listed on the menu. If you feel like splurging, prices for half a bowl of shark's fin begin at HK$250 (US$32.50). If you aren't careful, you could end up spending a small fortune (count on at least HK$1,000/US$130 per person for the exotic dishes), but whatever you order it's apt to be memorable. You can also come for dim sum, served daily until 3pm.

There's another branch in Wan Chai at 35–45 Johnston Rd. (☎ 852/2866 0663; MTR: Wan Chai), with the same hours.

**Napa.** In the Kowloon Shangri-La Hotel, 64 Mody Rd., Tsim Sha Tsui East. ☎ **852/2721 2111,** ext. 8060. Pizza and pasta HK$115–HK$128 (US$14.95–US$16.65); main courses HK$180–HK$240 (US$23.40–US$31.20); fixed-price lunch HK$120–HK$180 (US$15.60–US$23.40); fixed-price dinner HK$408 (US$53.05). AE, DC, MC, V. Daily noon–3pm and 6:30pm–midnight. MTR: Tsim Sha Tsui. CALIFORNIAN.

Located on the top floor of the Kowloon Shangri-La Hotel and boasting great harbor views, this smart-looking restaurant is so upbeat it could make an optimist of even the most travel-weary diner. Crisply decorated with light-colored woods, modern art, and art deco–style fixtures (check out the naughty lamps in the bay windows), it offers what may well be the best Caesar salad in town, served in a Parmesan basket with sour dough croutons. Another good starter is the fiery roasted tomato soup with poblano peppers and crispy tortilla strips. Follow it with the double bone lamb chops with a sun-dried tomato crust or tuna from the mesquite grill. For lighter appetites, there's also a limited selection of pastas and pizza. Live jazz accompanies diners every evening except Sunday.

**Yü.** In The Regent Hotel, Salisbury Rd., Tsim Sha Tsui. ☎ **852/2721 1211,** ext. 2340. Reservations necessary (request a window seat). Main courses HK$200–HK$380 (US$26–US$49.40). AE, DC, MC, V. Daily 6–11pm. MTR: Tsim Sha Tsui. SEAFOOD.

There's no mistaking what this restaurant serves—it's all right there in front of you, swimming blissfully in a 40-foot "bubble wall," unaware that its days are numbered. On the other side of the restaurant spreads Victoria Harbour. Located in the swank Regent Hotel but trendily low-key, Yü offers a nice concept—fresh seafood for cautious diners reluctant to tempt fate by ordering locally caught fish in the cheaper, noisier, and more colorful seaside restaurants favored by Hong Kong Chinese. Of course, you pay a mountain more to eat here, but from the looks of things there are plenty of takers. All the seafood, including a variety of grouper, trout, and other fish, lobsters, crabs, prawns, abalone, mussels, and oysters, are kept alive in tanks until the moment they're ordered. Colorful cards of fish are presented to diners to show the day's catch, which can be prepared according to the diner's wishes. However, many diners stick to the imported oysters or begin their meal with the seafood platter—fresh seafood laid on a mountain of ice, including oysters, shrimp, prawns, mussels, and lobster, served with different sauces. Another good choice is the lobster bisque or seafood basket, a variety of bamboo-steamed seafood. Sautéed lobster with black beans and fine noodles is the restaurant's signature dish.

## MODERATE

✪ **Gaylord.** 23–25 Ashley Rd., Tsim Sha Tsui. ☎ **852/2376 1001.** Main courses HK$60–HK$180 (US$7.80–US$23.40); lunch buffet HK$88 (US$11.45). AE, DC, MC, V. Daily 11:30am–3pm and 6–11pm. MTR: Tsim Sha Tsui. INDIAN.

This long-established, first-floor restaurant in the heart of Tsim Sha Tsui is classy and comfortable, with private booths and overstuffed sofas. Singers perform in the evenings. It's popular for its authentic North Indian classics, including tandoori, lamb curry cooked in North Indian spices and herbs, chicken cooked in hot fiery vindaloo curry, prawns cooked with green pepper and spices, and fish with potatoes and tomatoes. There are a dozen vegetarian dishes, and the lunchtime buffet, served every day except Sundays and public holidays until 2:30pm, is a winner.

✪ **Great Shanghai.** 26 Prat Ave., Tsim Sha Tsui. ☎ **852/2366 8158.** Main courses HK$75–HK$200 (US$9.75–US$26). AE, DC, MC, V. Daily 11am–3pm and 6:30–11pm. MTR: Tsim Sha Tsui. SHANGHAINESE.

Established in 1958, this well-known spot in Tsim Sha Tsui is a big old-fashioned dining hall. It's about as close as you can get to food the way Mom used to cook, assuming, of course, you're from Shanghai. In addition to its bright lights, white table-cloths, and army of waiters in green shirts, Great Shanghai has a gigantic menu with more than 300 items, most in the HK$85–HK$140 (US$11.05–US$18.20) range. Since the area of Shanghai has no cuisine of its own, it has borrowed heavily from neighboring provinces, including Szechuan. Try the Shanghainese dumplings, prawns in chili sauce, vegetarian imitation goose, diced chicken with cashews, cold chicken in wine sauce, Szechuan soup, or Peking duck (sliced meat and crispy skin rolled in thin pancakes). The house specialty is beggar's chicken for HK$260 (US$33.80), which is a whole chicken stuffed with herbs, mushrooms, and other ingredients, wrapped in lotus leaves, sealed in clay, and baked all day. It's available only at night (call in your order by mid-afternoon). My own particular favorite is braised shredded eel, but all eel dishes here are good. I've also left the ordering entirely up to the waiter and ended up with a good, well-rounded sampling of Shanghainese food.

**Jade Garden Restaurant.** Star House (4th floor), 3 Salisbury Rd., Tsim Sha Tsui. ☎ **852/2730 6888.** Main courses HK$68–HK$130 (US$8.85–US$16.90); dim sum HK$15–HK$37 (US$1.95–US$4.80). AE, DC, MC, V. Mon–Sat 10am–3pm and 5:30–11:30pm; Sun and holidays 8am–11:30pm. MTR: Tsim Sha Tsui. CANTONESE.

Jade Garden is part of a wildly successful chain of restaurants owned by the Maxim's Group (other establishments in the group include Sichuan Garden, Shanghai Garden, Peking Garden, and Chiu Chow Garden, the latter two with branches in Star House). Jade Garden is geared toward the Chinese-food novice. If you don't know much about Chinese food but feel you should try it, Jade Garden may be for you. As in most Cantonese restaurants, lunch, available daily until 3pm, is dim sum served from trolleys pushed through the aisles. If you'd rather order from the menu or come for dinner, you might consider drunken shrimp in soup, pan-fried stuffed bean curd, fried prawns with lemon peel and orange, or, if you feel like splurging, barbecued Peking duck.

Jade Garden has another branch in Tsim Sha Tsui at 25–31 Carnarvon Rd. (☎ 852/2369 8311), open daily from 7:30am to midnight. On the Hong Kong side, there are Jade Garden restaurants in the Swire House at 11 Chater Rd. (☎ 852/2526 3031; MTR: Central), open Monday to Saturday from 11:30am to midnight and Sunday from 10am to midnight; in the Jardine House at 1 Connaught Place (☎ 852/2524 5098; MTR: Central), open daily from 11am to 3pm and 5:30 to 11:30pm; and in Causeway Bay at 500 Hennessy Rd. (☎ 852/2895 2200; MTR: Causeway Bay), open daily from 8am to midnight.

**✪ The Pizzeria.** In the Kowloon Hotel, 19–21 Nathan Rd., Tsim Sha Tsui. ☎ **852/2369 8698,** ext. 3322. Pasta and pizza HK$98–HK$148 (US$12.75–US$19.25); main courses HK$138–HK$198 (US$17.95–US$25.75); lunch buffet HK$148 (US$19.25); fixed-price dinner HK$298–HK$328 (US$38.75–US$42.65). AE, DC, MC, V. Daily noon–3pm and 6–11pm. MTR: Tsim Sha Tsui. ITALIAN.

Located on the second floor of the Kowloon Hotel (just behind The Peninsula), this casual and bustling dining hall with large windows is one of my favorite places in Tsim Sha Tsui for a relaxed meal at reasonable prices, especially when I want great pizza or pasta and don't feel like getting dressed up. Despite its name, the restaurant specializes in pasta, with an à la carte menu that changes often but has included such mouthwatering choices as lobster lasagne enriched with fresh spinach and mushrooms, tortellini with mushrooms and truffles in an herb-cream sauce, and ink noodles in a lobster tarragon sauce. There are eight different kinds of pizza, and main courses have included grilled prawns with thyme olive oil in a bed of spinach and saffron risotto, and roasted spring chicken with pancetta, rosemary gravy and pesto polenta. Save room for dessert—they're all delicious.

**Planet Hollywood.** 3 Canton Rd., Tsim Sha Tsui. ☎ **852/2377 7888.** Main courses HK$78–HK$198 (US$10.15–US$25.75). AE, DC, MC, V. Daily 11:30am–2am. MTR: Tsim Sha Tsui. AMERICAN.

The escalator ride up to this establishment and the music that accompanies it is like the entrance to a theme park, and that theme is Hollywood. Glitzy and festive, it makes the Hard Rock Cafe down the street seem downright provincial. If you're star crazy, this is the place for you; you can gawk at such movie memorabilia as the doll Chuckie from *Child's Play*, the car used by Bruce Lee in the *Green Hornet* TV series, and Sharon Stone's ice pick from *Basic Instinct.* When I ate lunch there, Jackie Chan was holding a press conference about his latest film. Large screens show Hollywood hits. The menu includes everything from blackened shrimp and buffalo wings to sandwiches, burgers, pastas, pizzas, fajitas, steak, ribs, and fish and chips, as well as some local dishes such as spring rolls, pot stickers, Hainanese chicken rice, sweet-and-sour prawns, and wok-fried beef in oyster sauce. On weekdays, a fixed-price lunch is available until 4pm for HK$89 (US$11.55).

✪ **Spring Deer Restaurant.** 42 Mody Rd., Tsim Sha Tsui. ☎ **852/2723 3673.** Small dishes HK$50–HK$90 (US$6.50–US$11.70). AE, MC, V. Daily noon–2:30pm and 6–11pm. MTR: Tsim Sha Tsui. PEKINGESE.

An old favorite in Hong Kong, this long-established restaurant offers excellent Pekingese food at reasonable prices. It's cheerful and very accessible to foreigners, but don't expect anything fancy. In fact, your tablecloth may have holes in it, but it will be clean—and the place is usually packed with groups of loyal fans. This is one of the best places to come if you want to try its specialty—honey-glazed Peking duck, which costs HK$280 (US$36.40). Since you'll probably have to wait 40 minutes for the duck if you order it during peak time (7:30 to 9:30pm), it's best to arrive either before or after the rush. Chicken dishes are also well liked, including the deep-fried chicken in soy sauce, and the handmade noodles are excellent. Most dishes come in small, medium, and large sizes; small is suitable for two people. Remember, you'll want to order one dish each, plus a third to share. Unfortunately, since Spring Deer is crowded with groups, the lone diner is apt to be neglected in the shuffle; it's best to come here only if there are at least two of you.

## INEXPENSIVE

**The Salisbury.** In the Salisbury YMCA, 41 Salisbury Rd., Tsim Sha Tsui. ☎ **852/2369 2211**, ext. 1026. Lunch buffet HK$98 (US$12.75); dinner buffet HK$218 (US$28.35). AE, DC, MC, V. Mon–Sat noon–2:30pm, daily 6:30–9:30pm. MTR: Tsim Sha Tsui. INTERNATIONAL.

One of the cheapest places for a filling meal in Tsim Sha Tsui is the YMCA's main restaurant, a bright and cheerful dining hall located on the fourth floor of the south tower. Best are the buffets: the lunch buffet includes a roast beef wagon, as well as other meat dishes, soups, salads, and desserts, while the dinner buffet includes many more entrees plus unlimited soda or beer.

**Super Star Seafood Restaurant.** 91–93 Nathan Rd., Tsim Sha Tsui. ☎ **852/2366 0878.** Main courses HK$75–HK$200 (US$9.75–US$26); fixed-price menu HK$260–HK$300 (US$33.80–US$39); dim sum HK$19–HK$23 (US$2.45–US$3). AE, DC, MC, V. Daily 7am–midnight. MTR: Tsim Sha Tsui. CANTONESE SEAFOOD.

Walk past the tanks filled with fish, lobsters, and crabs, up to this lively Cantonese restaurant on the first floor, very popular with local Chinese. As its name implies, the restaurant specializes in seafood; recommended are the deep-fried stuffed crab claws, sliced sole with spice and chili, baked lobster with minced spinach, and fish in season.

I like it most, however, for the dim sum, served until 5pm daily in a typical Chinese setting. There's no English menu, so you'll just have to choose from the offerings of the various trolleys as they're wheeled past your table.

# CENTRAL DISTRICT
## EXPENSIVE

**La Ronda.** In the Furama Kempinski Hotel (30th floor), 1 Connaught Rd., Central. ☎ **852/2848 7422.** Reservations required at dinner. Lunch buffet HK$240 (US$31.20); dinner buffet HK$380 (US$49.40). AE, DC, MC, V. Daily noon–2:30pm; Sun–Thurs 6:30–10:30pm, Fri–Sat 5:30–10:30pm. MTR: Tsim Sha Tsui. INTERNATIONAL.

A revolving, 30th-floor restaurant with stunning views! The buffets are quite a spread too, offering salads, desserts, appetizers, and international cuisine ranging from sushi and roast beef to curries and Chinese and Western dishes. The food, while mediocre, is more than compensated for by the view. You can save money by coming for lunch, which is cheaper, or for an early dinner on weekends. On Friday and Saturday nights and evenings before public holidays, there are two seatings. From 5:30 to 7:30pm there's the Sunset Buffet, which costs only HK$280 (US$36.40); thereafter the price rises to the usual HK$380 (US$49.40). There's live entertainment nightly, and on Friday and Saturday nights from 9:30pm there's dancing for an additional HK$100 (US$13), including two drinks.

✪ **Petrus.** In the Island Shangri-La (56th floor), Pacific Place, Supreme Court Road, Central. ☎ **852/2877 3838.** Reservations recommended. Jacket required. Main courses HK$305–HK$405 (US$39.65–US$52.65); fixed-price lunch HK$298–HK$365 (US$38.75–US$47.45); fixed-price dinner HK$650–HK$740 (US$84.50–US$96.20). AE, DC, MC, V. Mon–Sat noon–2:30pm, daily 7–10:30pm. MTR: Admiralty. FRENCH.

Simply put, the views from this 56th-floor restaurant are breathtaking, probably the best of any hotel restaurant on the Hong Kong side. The only place with a better view is atop Victoria Peak. If you can bear to take your eyes off the windows, you'll find the restaurant decorated like a French castle, with the obligatory crystal chandeliers, black marble and gilded columns, statues, thick draperies, impressionist paintings, murals gracing dome-shaped ceilings, and classical music playing softly in the background. The cuisine emphasizes contemporary French creations, with a menu that changes often but has included such intriguing combinations as pan-fried sea bass with lobster gravy and gratinated Australian rack of lamb in a walnut crust. Foie gras is a specialty, available in several variations. As expected, the wine list is among the best in Hong Kong. In any case, with the impressive blend of great views, refined ambiance, and excellent cuisine, this restaurant is a top choice for a splurge, romantic dinner, or special celebration.

✪ **Va Bene.** 58–62 D'Aguilar St., Central. ☎ **852/2845 5577.** Reservations required. Pasta HK$178–HK$188 (US$23.15–US$24.45); main courses HK$188–HK$258 (US$24.45–US$33.55); fixed-price lunch HK$168 (US$21.85). AE, DC, MC, V. Mon–Fri noon–3pm and daily 7pm–midnight (last order 10:30pm). MTR: Central. ITALIAN.

This upscale restaurant, in the middle of Central's Lan Kwai Fong nightlife district, strives for the simplicity of a rustic Italian villa with its sponged, mustard-hued walls, sky-blue ceiling, and rows of terra-cotta pots serving as the main decorations. With consistently excellent food and under the exuberant and watchful eye of maitre'd and co-owner Pino Piano, Va Bene is extremely popular with Hong Kong's well-heeled expat community, making it a lively and boisterous—though cramped—spot for a meal. Perhaps you'll want to start with carpaccio (wafer-thin beef tenderloin served with white mushrooms and shavings of Parmesan), artichokes cooked in olive oil and garlic, or the capellini primavera or linguine with clams. As a main course, you can choose from a number of veal, beef, and seafood offerings, including veal scaloppine, pan-roasted salmon served with sautéed red and yellow peppers, or the oven-poached sea bass served with braised potatoes, pine nuts, and black olives. Good Italian wines, great desserts, and attentive service round out the evening; expect to spend about HK$500 (US$65) per person.

**Vong.** In the Mandarin Oriental Hotel (25th floor), 5 Connaught Rd., Central. ☎ **852/2825 4028.** Reservations required. Main courses HK$200–HK$330 (US$26–US$42.90); fixed-price lunch HK$320 (US$57.15). AE, DC, MC, V. Daily noon–3pm and 6–midnight. MTR: Central. FRANCO-ASIAN.

Chef Jean-Georges Vongerichten, who made a name for himself with several well-known New York restaurants, set Hong Kong abuzz when he opened much-talked-about Vong on the 25th floor of the Mandarin Oriental Hotel. Matching Petrus for its spectacular views of the harbor, this chic, black-and-gold-decorated venue serves what may well be the best interpretation of East-meets-West Franco-Asian cuisine in the eastern hemisphere, with exquisite combinations that set taste buds buzzing with excitement. Appetizers range from shrimp satay dipped in a fresh oyster sauce to sautéed foie gras with ginger and mango. Main courses are all tempting—perhaps you'll choose the spiny lobster with Thai herbs, the steamed sea bass in cardamon sauce with savoy cabbage and watercress, or the chicken marinated in lemongrass with sweet rice steamed in banana leaf. If choosing only one dish causes anguish, order the Tasting Menu for HK$488 (US$63.45) per person (as long as the whole table is willing to go along). The only complaint is that Vong is so popular and busy, its noise level and activity approaches that of an outdoor market, making it a good place for people watching but not for a romantic tete-a-tete.

## MODERATE

**Jimmy's Kitchen.** 1 Wyndham St., Central. ☎ **852/2526 5293.** Main courses HK$125–HK$204 (US$16.25–US$26.50). AE, DC, MC, V. Daily noon–11pm. MTR: Central. CONTINENTAL.

This restaurant opened in 1928, a replica of a similar, American-owned restaurant in Shanghai. Now one of Hong Kong's oldest Western restaurants, Jimmy's Kitchen had several homes before moving in the 1960s to its present site. Some of its waiters are descendants from the original staff. The atmosphere reminds me of an American steakhouse, with white tablecloths, dark-wood paneling, and elevator music, but it's a favorite with older foreigners living in Hong Kong and serves dependably good, unpretentious European food. The daily specials are written on a blackboard, and an extensive à la carte menu offers seafood, steaks, salads, soups, chicken, Indian curries, and hearty German fare. A good old standby.

There's a branch at 29 Ashley Rd. in Tsim Sha Tsui (☎ **852/2376 0327**), open daily from noon to 11pm (MTR: Tsim Sha Tsui).

**Joyce Cafe.** The Galleria, 9 Queen's Rd. Central, Central. ☎ **852/2810 1335.** Main courses HK$100–HK$190 (US$13–US$24.70). AE, DC, MC, V. Mon–Sat 10am–7pm, Sun 11am–6pm. MTR: Central. INTERNATIONAL/VEGETARIAN.

Located in the fashion-conscious Galleria shopping complex, this is *the* cafe for beautiful people, who stay that way apparently by dining on the light and healthy food for which the trendy establishment is famous. Pastas, salads, and sandwiches are its mainstay, though by no means are they ordinary. Pastas, for example, range from penne with sun-dried tomatoes, aubergines, and olives tossed in sweet basil, tomato, and fresh ricotta sauce to Shanghai vegetable wontons, made with eight different kinds of vegetables. The spinach salad is among the best in town, and there's also a Japanese lunch box, available vegetarian or with fish. There are enough fruit and vegetable juices to make you sprout leaves. Who knows, after a few meals here, we might actually be able to fit into some of the designer clothing sold nearby.

✪ **Luk Yu Tea House.** 24–26 Stanley St., Central. ☎ **852/2523 5464.** Main courses HK$100–HK$220 (US$13–US$28.60); dim sum HK$25–HK$55 (US$3.25–US$7.15). No credit cards. Daily 7am–10pm. MTR: Central. CANTONESE.

Luk Yu, first opened in 1933, is the most famous teahouse remaining in Hong Kong. In fact, unless you have a time machine, you won't get any closer to old Hong Kong than at this wonderful Cantonese restaurant, with its ceiling fans, spittoons, individual wooden booths for couples, marble tabletops, wood paneling, and stained-glass windows. It's one of the best places to try a selection of Chinese teas, including bo lai, jasmine, lung ching (a green tea), and sui sin (narcissus or daffodil). But Luk Yu is most famous for its dim sum, served daily from 7am to 5:30pm. The problem for foreigners is that the place is always packed with regulars with their own reserved seats, and the staff is sometimes surly to newcomers. And if you come after 11am, dim sum is no longer served by trolley but from an English menu with pictures but no prices, which could end up being quite expensive unless you ask before ordering. If you want to come during the day (certainly when Luk Yu is most colorful), try to bring along a Chinese friend. Otherwise, consider coming for dinner when it's not nearly so hectic and there's an English menu listing more than 200 items, including all the Cantonese favorites.

**Pavilion.** 3 Tun Wo Lane, Central. ☎ **852/2869 7768.** Main courses HK$175–HK$185 (US$22.75–US$24.05); fixed-price lunch HK$130 (US$16.90). AE, DC, MC, V. Mon–Sat noon–2:30pm and 7–10pm (last order). MTR: Central. CONTINENTAL.

Although not south of Hollywood Road (from which SoHo derives its name), Pavilion is very much a part of the new SoHo dining and nightlife scene and may well qualify as the best restaurant in the area. You'll find it off Cochrane, at the end of a short alley on the other side of a plastic (!) hedge. The restaurant, which adjoins the Petticoat Lane bar and a tapas bar under the same ownership, is not much larger than a walk-in closet; on the wall is a quote by M.F.K. Fisher that proclaims provocatively "Almost everyone has something secret he likes to eat." If you're claustrophobic, try to get a seat alfresco in the romantic courtyard. The changing menu is limited to about three pastas and five entrees, but they're always right on. Examples of past dishes include roasted red duck Thai style with sweet potato, mango compote and braised rice; rack of lamb crusted with lemon garlic and mint, polenta and wilted greens; and grilled salmon filet with potatoes, asparagus, and sauce mousseline.

✪ **Yung Kee.** 32–40 Wellington St., Central. ☎ **852/2522 1624.** Main courses HK$65–HK$150 (US$8.45–US$19.50); dim sum HK$11–HK$24 (US$1.45–US$3.10). AE, DC, MC, V. Daily 11am–11:30pm. MTR: Central. CANTONESE.

Yung Kee started out in 1941 as a small shop selling roast goose, which it did so well that it soon expanded into a very successful Cantonese enterprise. Through the years it has won numerous food awards and is the only restaurant in Hong Kong ever to be included in *Fortune* magazine's top 15 restaurants of the world. Its specialty is still roast goose with plum sauce, cooked to perfection with tender meat on the inside and crispy skin on the outside and available only for dinner for HK$380 (US$49.40). Other specialties include roasted suckling pig or duck, cold steamed chicken, barbecued pork, bean curd with prawns, any of the fresh seafood, and hundred-year-old eggs (which are included with each meal). Dining is on one of the upper three floors, but if all you want is a bowl of congee or some other rice dish, join the office workers who pour in for a quick meal on the informal ground floor. Dim sum, available from an English menu, is served daily until 5pm.

## INEXPENSIVE

**City Hall Chinese Restaurant.** City Hall (2nd floor), Low Block, Central. ☎ **852/2521 1303.** Reservations recommended, especially at lunch. Main courses HK$70–HK$160 (US$9.10–US$20.80); dim sum HK$17–HK$38 (US$2.20–US$4.95). AE, V. Mon–Fri 10am–3pm and 5:30–11:30pm, Sat 10am–11:30pm, Sun and holidays 8am–11:30pm. MTR: Central. CANTONESE.

Decorated in Chinese red, this large restaurant on the second floor of city hall offers a view of the harbor and is so popular at lunchtime that you'll probably have to wait if you haven't made a reservation. The clientele is almost exclusively Chinese, and the food includes the usual shark's-fin, bird's-nest, abalone, pigeon, duck, vegetable, beef, and seafood dishes. The food is fast but average; better, in my opinion, is the dim sum, served from trolleys until 3pm (ask for the dim sum menu in English). Lunchtime fare also includes various noodle and rice dishes, all priced less than HK$100 (US$13).

# CAUSEWAY BAY/WAN CHAI

## EXPENSIVE

**TOTT'S Asian Grill & Bar.** In the Excelsior Hotel, 281 Gloucester Rd., Causeway Bay. ☎ 852/2837 6786. Reservations recommended for dinner (request a window seat). Main courses HK$108–HK$288 (US$14.05–US$37.44); fixed-price lunch HK$128–HK$188 (US$16.65–US$24.45). AE, DC, MC, V. Mon–Sat noon–2:30pm; daily 6:30–11pm. MTR: Causeway Bay. ASIAN/EAST-MEETS-WEST.

This flashy restaurant seems to suffer from an identity crisis: gigantic Chinese paint brushes at the entrance; a blood-red interior with zebra-striped chairs. I don't know whether I'm in Africa or China until I look at the fabulous view from the restaurant's 34th-floor perch. This is Hong Kong at its most eclectic and funky, and though the setting seems contrived, the restaurant itself is relaxed, fun, and highly recommended for its innovative and varied fusion cuisine. Come early for a drink at the bar (happy hour is 5 to 8pm); or retire there after dinner for live music and dancing nightly except Sunday. There's also an outdoor terrace where you can take your drinks with you to enjoy the view. A glass-enclosed kitchen reveals food being prepared in woks, over charcoal grills, and in tandoori and wood-burning pizza ovens. The menu is surprisingly diverse in cuisine and prices, allowing diners to eat modestly priced dishes like duck pizza with portobello mushrooms, roasted bell pepper, and mozzarella cheese; or go all out on roasted baby rack of lamb glazed by ginger, carrot, and turmeric with marsala potatoes. It's also a good choice for those who want dining and entertainment all at the same place.

## MODERATE

✪ **Red Pepper.** 7 Lan Fong Rd., Causeway Bay. ☎ 852/2576 8046. Reservations recommended, especially at dinner. Small dishes HK$80–HK$125 (US$10.40–US$16.25). AE, DC, MC, V. Daily 11:30–11:30pm (last order). MTR: Causeway Bay. SZECHUAN.

Open since 1970, the Red Pepper has a large following among the colony's expatriates, many of whom seem to come so often that they know everyone in the place. It's a very relaxing, small restaurant, with a rather quaint decor of Chinese lanterns and carved dragons in the ceiling. Specialties include fried prawns with chili sauce on a sizzling platter, sour-pepper soup, smoked duck marinated with oranges, and shredded chicken with hot garlic sauce and dry-fried string beans. Most dishes are available in two sizes, with the small dishes suitable for two people.

## INEXPENSIVE

✪  **Open Kitchen.** Hong Kong Arts Centre (6th floor), 2 Harbour Rd., Wan Chai. ☎ **852/2827 2923.** Main courses HK$68–HK$88 (US$8.85–US$11.45). AE, MC, V. Daily 8am–11pm. MTR: Wan Chai. INTERNATIONAL.

This self-serve cafeteria, bright with natural lighting, gets my vote as the best place in Wan Chai for an inexpensive and quick meal. Not only does it offer a good selection of food at very reasonable prices, but it also boasts a view of the harbor and even has a tiny outdoor terrace. True to its name, chefs working in an open kitchen prepare everything from lamb chops, grilled steak, and tandoori chicken to sea bass and spring chicken. There are four or five kinds of pasta, along with choices of sauce. Lighter fare includes a salad bar, soups, sandwiches, sushi, quiche, and desserts. You can also come just for a drink, but the minimum charge per person is HK$20 (US$2.60).

# AROUND HONG KONG ISLAND
## VICTORIA PEAK

**Cafe Deco.** Peak Galleria, Victoria Peak. ☎ **852/2849 5111.** Reservations required (request window seat with view). Pizzas and pastas HK$78–HK$125 (US$10.15–US$16.25); main courses HK$95–HK$168 (US$12.35–US$21.85); fixed-price lunch, Mon–Fri only, HK$158 (US$20.55). AE, DC, MC, V. Daily 10am–11pm (last order). Peak tram. INTERNATIONAL.

No expense was spared, it seems, in designing this chic, airy restaurant with its wood inlaid floor, authentic art deco trimmings (many imported from the United States and Europe), and open kitchen serving cuisines of China, Japan, Thailand, India, Italy, and Mexico. Ever since it opened in 1994, a nattily dressed crowd has been clamoring to get in. In the evening (except Sunday), diners are treated to live jazz. All this is secondary, however, to the restaurant's real attraction—the best view of Hong Kong in town. The view alone is reason enough to dine here, though some of it has been stolen with the completion of the Peak Tower's viewing platform. To assure a ringside window seat, be sure to make reservations for the second floor at least two weeks in advance, emphasizing that you don't want your view obstructed by the Peak Tower. The food, designed to appeal to visitors from around the world, is as trendy as the restaurant, with an eclectic mix of international dishes and ingredients, including tandoori kebabs and dishes, Asian noodles, grilled steaks and chops, oysters, sushi, pizzas, create-your-own pastas, soups, sandwiches, salads, and desserts. Some of the entrees fall short of expectations; the pizzas, however, are great and may be the best items on the menu. The salads are generous enough for two to share.

**Marché Mövenpick.** Peak Tower (levels 6 & 7), 128 Peak Rd., Victoria Peak. ☎ **852/2849 2000.** Main courses HK$58–HK$75 (US$7.55–US$9.75). AE, DC, MC, V. Daily 11am–11pm. Peak tram. INTERNATIONAL.

This Swiss chain has been very successful in Europe with its "marketplace" concept in self-service dining, and with the international crowds that visit the Peak, my guess is that it will do quite well here, too. For one thing, its location in the newly completed Peak Tower affords great views over Hong Kong. The food is reasonably priced and varied enough to please even fickle palates, the staff is efficient and friendly, and there's even a children's corner, with a small slide, toys, crayons, and other diversions, making it a good place for families. Upon entering, you'll be given a card, which is stamped each time you add a dish to your tray. There are various counters offering different foods, including salads, pizza, pasta, vegetables, sushi, Chinese dishes, and entrees ranging from grilled pork chops and roasted spring chicken to king prawns and sole. You can take as much or as little as you wish—if you're coming for drinks, try to hit the daily 4–7pm happy hour.

## STANLEY

✪ **Stanley's French Restaurant.** 86–88 Stanley Main St., Stanley. ☎ **852/2813 8873.** Reservations required. Main courses HK$165–HK$220 (US$22.45–US$28.60); fixed-price lunch HK$95–HK$165 (US$12.35–US$21.45). AE, DC, MC, V. Daily noon–3pm; tea 3–5pm; dinner 7–10:30pm. Bus: nos. 6, 6A, or 260. FRENCH.

Whatever you save by bargain-shopping at Stanley Market may well go toward a meal at Stanley's Restaurant, and I can't think of a better place to spend it. This is an absolutely charming spot, refined, cozy, and romantic, tucked away in a corner of the market, beside Stanley Beach. There are several floors of dining, all in small rooms that look as if they're part of someone's home. There are flowers on the tables, pictures on the walls, and even an upstairs outdoor patio (my favorite place to dine). Although the menu changes often, for starters you might try Caesar salad, considered a house specialty, or the lobster and spinach bisque with sherry. Examples of past dishes include sautéed Tasmanian scallops and calamari in lemon-garlic butter, soya-flavored filet of black cod, and prime beef sirloin with Cajun spices on gratinated spinach and crisp potatoes. There are also daily specials, written on a blackboard that will be brought to your table.

## ABERDEEN

**Jumbo Floating Restaurant.** Aberdeen Harbour, Hong Kong Island. ☎ **852/2553 9111.** Main courses HK$80–HK$400 (US$10.40–US$52); dim sum HK$20–HK$26 (US$2.60–US$3.40). Table charge HK$8 (US$1.05) per person. AE, DC, MC, V. Mon–Sat 11am–11pm; Sun 8am–11pm. Bus: no. 70 from Central to Aberdeen, then the restaurant's private boat. CANTONESE.

No doubt you've heard about Hong Kong's floating restaurants. Although often included in organized nighttime tours, they're no longer touted by the tourist office as a must-see—there are simply too many other restaurants that are more authentic, more affordable, and have better food. If you're set on the idea, the Jumbo Floating Restaurant, which claims to be the largest floating restaurant in the world, is your best bet. Simply take the bus to Aberdeen and then board one of the restaurant's free shuttle boats, with departures every few minutes. As for the restaurant, it has more reds, golds, and dragon motifs than you've ever seen in one place. Dishes include everything from noodles and rice combinations to fresh lobster, scallops, grouper balls, and fresh seafood (prawns are a particular favorite). Dim sum is served from trolleys until 4pm—certainly the least expensive way to enjoy the floating restaurant experience.

## 5 Attractions

Every visitor to Hong Kong should eat dim sum in a typical Cantonese restaurant, ride the Star Ferry across Victoria Harbour, and, if the weather is clear, take the Peak Tram for the glorious views from Victoria Peak. If you have more time, I also recommend the Hong Kong Museum of Art for its collection of Chinese antiquities, Stanley Market for its inexpensive fashions and souvenirs, an excursion via ferry to one of the outlying islands, joining one of the Hong Kong Tourist Association's special-interest organized tours, and a stroll through the Temple Street Night Market.

## ✪ VICTORIA PEAK

At 1,308 feet (399m), Victoria Peak is Hong Kong Island's allest mountain and offers spectacular views; if possible, go on a clear day. Since the peak is typically cooler than the sweltering city below, it has always been one of Hong Kong's most exclusive places to live. More than a century ago, the rich reached the peak via a grueling 3-hour trip in sedan chairs, transported to the top by coolies. In 1888 the **peak tram** began operating, cutting the journey to a mere 8 minutes.

The easiest way to reach the Peak Tram Station, located in Central on Garden Road, is to take one of the free, open-top shuttle buses that operate between the tram terminal and the Star Ferry in Central, with departures every 20 minutes from 9am to 7pm Monday to Friday and from 9am to 8pm Saturday and Sunday. Otherwise, the tram terminal is about a 12-minute walk from the Star Ferry. Trams depart from Peak Tram Station every 10 to 15 minutes between 7am and midnight. One-way tickets cost HK$18 (US$2.35) for adults, HK$6 (US80¢) for senior citizens, and HK$5(US65¢) for children. Round-trip tickets cost HK$28 (US$3.65), HK$12 (US$1.55), and HK$8 (US$1.05), respectively.

Upon reaching the Peak, you'll find yourself at the very modern **Peak Tower,** designed by British architect Terry Farrell and looking for all the world like a Chinese cooking wok. Head straight for the viewing terrace on Level 5, where you have one of the world's most breathtaking views, with the skyscrapers of Central, the boats plying Victoria Harbour, Kowloon, and the many hills of the New Territories undulating in the background.

Of the three attractions located in Peak Tower, most well known is **Ripley's Believe It or Not! Odditorium,** Level 3 (☎ **852/2849 0698**). It contains oddities (and replicas of oddities) collected by Robert L. Ripley on visits to 198 countries over 55 years, including a shrunken head from Ecuador, torture devices from around the world, a two-headed calf, and models of the world's tallest and fattest men. Be forewarned that some of the items are purely grotesque, or, at best, out of date in a more politically correct world. It's open daily from 9am to 10pm and costs HK$60 (US$7.80) for adults and HK$40 (US$5.20) for senior citizens and children.

**Peak Explorer,** Level 6 (☎ **852/2849 0866**), is a 36-seat motion-simulator theater that features changing, 8-minute fast-paced films and seats that move, jerk, roll, and rock in accordance to the action on the screen. Best for young children is **Rise of the Dragon,** Level 2 (☎ **852/2849 0866**). It begins with a mazelike walk though a street meant to depict old Wan Chai in the 1920s, followed by a 7-minute ride aboard the Dragon Train past five tableaux depicting scenes from Hong Kong's history, including a typhoon, pirates aboard a ship, and a New Year's festival. Both are open daily from 9am to 10pm and admission for either is HK$40 (US$5.20) for adults and HK$30 (US$3.90) for children.

But the best thing to do atop Victoria Peak, in my opinion, is to take an hour-long circular hike on Lugard Road and Harlech Road, located just a stone's throw from the Peak Tower. Mainly a footpath overhung with banyan trees and passing lush vegetation alternating with secluded mansions, the road snakes along the side of the cliff, offering great views of Central District below, the harbor, Kowloon, and then Aberdeen and the outlying islands on the other side. This is one of the best walks in Hong Kong; at night, it offers one of world's most romantic views. Don't miss it.

## MUSEUMS

Keep in mind that municipal museums are closed December 25 and 26, January 1, and the first three days of the Chinese New Year (traditionally around the end of January/beginning of February). Private museums are usually closed additionally on bank holidays.

✪ **Hong Kong Museum of Art.** Hong Kong Cultural Centre Complex, 10 Salisbury Rd., Tsim Sha Tsui. ☎ **852/2734 2167.** Admission HK$10 (US$1.30) adults, HK$5 (US65¢)

children, students, and senior citizens. Free admission Wed. Tues–Sat 10am–6pm, Sun and holidays 1–6pm. MTR: Tsim Sha Tsui.

If you visit only one museum in Hong Kong, this should be it. Located on the Tsim Sha Tsui waterfront just a 2-minute walk from the Star Ferry terminus, this museum has a vast collection of Chinese antiquities and fine art, including ceramics, bronzes, jade, cloisonné, lacquerware, bamboo carvings, women's costumes (look for the fist-sized shoes for bound feet), and textiles, as well as paintings, wallhangings, scrolls, and calligraphy dating from the 16th century to the present. The works are arranged in five permanent galleries on three floors of exhibit space, plus two galleries devoted to changing exhibits. The Historical Pictures Gallery is especially insightful, with 1,000 works in oils, watercolors, pencil drawings, and prints that provide a visual account of life in Hong Kong, Macau, and Guangzhou (Canton) in the late 18th and 19th centuries. Another gallery displays contemporary Hong Kong works by local artists. A bonus is the beautiful backdrop of Victoria Harbor.

**Hong Kong Museum of History.** 100 Chatham Rd. South, Tsim Sha Tsui. ☎ **852/2724 9042.** Admission HK$10 adults (US$1.30), HK$5 (US65¢) children and senior citizens. Free admission Wed. Tues–Sat 10am–6pm, Sun and holidays 1–6pm. MTR: Tsim Sha Tsui (take the A1 exit for Kowloon Park).

This museum outlines 3,000 years of Hong Kong's history, from its beginnings as a Neolithic settlement and its development as a fishing village to its transformation into a modern metropolis. Through displays that include replicas of fishing boats, furniture, clothing, and items from daily life, the museum introduces Hong Kong's ethnic groups and their traditional means of livelihood, customs, and beliefs, including the Tanka boat people, the Five Great Clans who built walled communities in the New Territories, and the Hakka, primarily rice farmers. My favorite part is a re-created old Hong Kong street, complete with a reconstructed Chinese herbal medicine shop that was located in Central until 1980. There are also 19th- and early 20th-century photographs, poignantly showing how much Hong Kong has changed through the decades.

**Hong Kong Museum of Medical Sciences.** 2 Caine Lane, Mid-Levels, Hong Kong Island. ☎ **852/2549 5123.** Admission HK$10 (US$1.30) adults, HK$5 (US65¢) children and senior citizens. Tues–Sat 10am–5pm, Sun and holidays 1–5pm. MTR: Central; then bus no. 26 from Des Voeux Rd. in front of Hongkong Bank headquarters to Man Mo Temple; walk up Ladder St. to Caine Lane.

This unique museum, located in the Edwardian-style former Pathological Institute founded 100 years ago to combat the colony's most horrific outbreak of bubonic plague, charts the historical development of medical science in Hong Kong. Several rooms remain almost exactly as they were, including an autopsy room and a laboratory filled with old equipment, while others serve as exhibition rooms devoted to such areas as the development of dentistry and radiology (note the X-ray of the bound foot). But what makes the museum particularly fascinating is its comparison of traditional Chinese and Western medicines—it's the only medical museum in the world to do so—and its funding of research into Chinese medicine. Included are displays on acupuncture and Chinese herbs.

**Hong Kong Science Museum.** 2 Science Museum Rd., Tsim Sha Tsui East. ☎ **852/2732 3232.** Admission HK$25 (US$3.25) adults, HK$12.50 (US$1.60) children, students, and senior citizens. Free admission Wed. Tues–Fri 1–9pm, Sat–Sun 10am–9pm. MTR: Tsim Sha Tsui.

The mysteries of science and technology come to life with plenty of hands-on exhibits sure to appeal to children and adults alike. More than 500 exhibits cover four floors,

# Chinese Medicine

For most minor ailments, the Chinese are more likely to pay a visit to their neighborhood medicine store than see a doctor. Most traditional medicine stores cater solely to the practice of Chinese herbal medicine, with some cures dating back 2,000 years. The medicinal stock, however, includes much more than roots and plants—take a look inside one of Hong Kong's many medicinal shops and you'll find a bewildering array of jars and drawers containing everything from ginseng and deer's horn to fossilized bones and animal teeth. Deer's horn is said to be effective against fever; bones, teeth, and seashells are used as tranquilizers and cures for insomnia. In prescribing treatment, herbalists take into account the patient's overall mental and physical well-being, in the belief that disease and illness are caused not by viruses but by an imbalance in bodily forces. In contrast to Western medicine, treatment is often preventive rather than remedial. Visitors particularly interested in traditional Chinese medicine will want to visit the newly established **Hong Kong Museum of Medical Sciences** (see "Attractions," below).

Acupuncture is also alive and well in Hong Kong. With a history that goes back 4,000 years, acupuncture is based on 365 pressure points, which in turn act upon bodily organs. The slender stainless steel needles used vary in length from half an inch to 10 inches. Most acupuncturists also use moxa (dried mugwort)—a slow-burning herb that applies gentle heat.

with sections devoted to the life sciences; light, sound and motion; virtual reality; meteorology and geography; electricity and magnetism; computers and robotics; construction; and transportation and communication. One area is specially designed for children between the ages of 3 and 7.

**Hong Kong Space Museum.** Hong Kong Cultural Centre Complex, 10 Salisbury Rd., Tsim Sha Tsui. ☎ **852/2734 2722.** Admission to Exhibition Halls HK$10 (US$1.30) adults, HK$5 (US65¢) children, students, and senior citizens, free admission on Wed; Space Theatre HK$32 (US$4.15) adults, HK$16 (US$2.10) children, students, and senior citizens. Tues–Fri 1–9pm, Sat–Sun and holidays 10am–9pm. MTR: Tsim Sha Tsui.

Located opposite The Peninsula Hotel on the Tsim Sha Tsui waterfront, the Space Museum is easy to spot with its white-domed planetarium. It consists of two parts: exhibition halls and the Space Theatre. The Hall of Space Science explores humankind's journey to space, with exhibits on ancient astronomical history, manned space flights, and future space programs. There are also several interactive rides and exhibits, including a ride on a virtual paraglider (a harness that holds occupants aloft with the same approximate gravity they'd experience walking on the moon) and a multi-axis chair developed for astronaut training to give the sensation of tumbling through space. The Hall of Astronomy presents information on the solar system and solar science. Space Theatre, one of the largest planetariums in the world, with a 75-foot domed roof, presents both Omnimax screenings and Sky shows with a Zeiss star projector that can project up to about 9,000 stars. Forty-minute to hour-long shows range from celestial phenomena like the Milky Way to such wonders of the world as the Great Barrier Reef. Call for show schedules.

**Tsui Museum of Art.** Henley Building (4th floor), 5 Queen's Rd. Central, Central. ☎ **852/2868 2688.** Admission HK$30 (US$3.90) adults, HK$15 (US$1.95) children, students, and senior citizens. Mon–Fri 10am–6pm, Sat 10am–2pm. Closed public holidays. MTR: Central (take the Chater Garden exit).

This privately owned collection of some 3,000 Chinese antiquities includes bronzes, bamboo, wood and ivory carvings, jade carvings, enameled ware, glass, and furniture, which are displayed on a rotating basis in a couple small rooms. Its most prominent exhibit, however, is of Chinese ceramics, spanning 5,000 years from the Neolithic period to the Qing dynasty. Look for the museum's most prized possessions—a Ming dynasty blue-and-white porcelain dish with a bird perched on a lychee branch, and a doughnut-shaped blue-and-white porcelain container, one of only three such pieces in the world and used to store the jade belt or necklace of a major official.

## TEMPLES

For information on Po Lin Monastery and its adjacent Giant Tian Tan Buddha, refer to the section on "Outlying Islands," below.

**Man Mo Temple.** Hollywood Rd. and Ladder St., Western District, Hong Kong Island. ☎ **852/2803 2916.** Free admission. Daily 8am–6pm. Bus: no. 26 from Des Voeux Rd. Central (in front of the Hongkong Bank headquarters) to the second stop on Hollywood Rd., across from the temple.

Hong Kong Island's oldest and most important temple was built in the 1840s and is named after its two principal deities: Man, the god of literature, who is dressed in red and holds a calligraphy brush; and Mo, the god of war, wearing a green robe and holding a sword. Ironically, Mo finds patronage from both the police force (shrines in his honor can be found in all Hong Kong police stations) and triad secret societies. Two ornately carved sedan chairs in the temple were once used during festivals to carry the statues of the gods around the neighborhood. But what makes the temple particularly memorable are the giant incense coils hanging from the ceiling, imparting a fragrant, smoky haze. They are purchased by patrons seeking fulfillment of their wishes, such as good health or a successful business deal, and burn for as long as 3 weeks.

**Wong Tai Sin.** Wong Tai Sin Estate, Kowloon. Temple daily 7am–5:30pm; gardens Tues–Sun 9am–4pm. Free admission to temple, though donations of about HK$1 (US13¢) are expected at the temple's entrance and for Nine Dragon Wall Garden; admission to Good Wish Garden HK$2 (US26¢) extra. MTR: Wong Tai Sin and then a 3-minute walk (follow the signs).

Located six subway stops northeast of Yau Ma Tei in the far north end of Kowloon Peninsula, Wong Tai Sin is Hong Kong's most popular Taoist temple. Although the temple itself dates only from 1973, it adheres to traditional Chinese architectural principles with its red pillars, two-tiered golden roof, blue friezes, yellow latticework, and multicolored carvings. What makes the temple popular, however, is that everyone who comes here is seeking information about their fortune—from advice about business or horse racing to determining which day is most auspicious for a wedding. Most worshippers make use of a bamboo container holding numbered sticks. After lighting a joss stick and kneeling before the main altar, the worshipper gently shakes the container until one of the sticks falls out. The number corresponds to a certain fortune, which is then interpreted by a soothsayer at the temple. You can wander around the temple grounds, on which can be found halls dedicated to the Buddhist Goddess of Mercy and Confucius; the Nine Dragon Garden, a Chinese garden with a pond, waterfall, and a replica of the famous Nine Dragons mural (the original is in Beijing's Imperial Palace); the Good Wish Garden, a replica of the Yi He Garden in Beijing with circular, square, octagonal, and fan-shaped pavilions, ponds, an artificial waterfall, and rocks and concrete fashioned to resemble animals; and a clinic with both Western medical services and traditional Chinese herbal treatments.

# PARKS & GARDENS
## Aw Boon Haw Gardens.

Formerly known as Tiger Balm Gardens, the Aw Boon Haw Gardens, Tai Hang Road, Causeway Bay, are probably the most bizarre gardens you'll ever see. They were created in 1935 by Chinese millionaire and philanthropist Aw Boon Haw, who made his fortune with a cure-all ointment called Tiger Balm. The 7½-acre gardens feature grottoes and colorfully painted statues from Chinese mythology, some of which are rather grotesque, especially those depicting unfortunate souls being tortured in hell. The message here is quite clear: behave yourself, or else! Because the gardens are so colorful, you can get some great photographs to show the folks back home. They are open daily from 9:30am to 4pm and admission is free. To reach them, take bus no. 11 from the Central Ferry Piers bus terminal.

## Hong Kong Park.

Opened in 1991, Hong Kong Park, Supreme Court Road and Cotton Tree Drive, Central, features a dancing fountain at its entrance; Southeast Asia's largest greenhouse, with more than 2,000 rare plant species; an aviary housing 500 exotic birds in a tropical rainforest setting with an elevated walkway; various gardens; a children's playground; and a viewing platform. The most famous building on the park grounds is the Flagstaff House Museum of Tea Ware (☎ 852/2869 0690), the oldest colonial building in Hong Kong. Built in 1844 in Greek Revival style for the commander of the British forces, it now displays some 500 pieces of tea ware ranging from earthenware to porcelain, primarily of Chinese origin and dating from the seventh century to the present day. (Don't miss the museum shop, which sells beautifully crafted teapots and tea.) Finally, since the marriage registry is located at the edge of the park, the gardens are also a favorite place for wedding photographs, especially on weekends and auspicious days of the Chinese calendar. The park is open daily from 7am to 11pm, while the Flagstaff House Museum of Tea Ware is open Tuesday through Sunday from 10am to 5pm. Admission to both is free. To reach the park, take the MTR to Admiralty Station, then follow the signs through Pacific Place.

## Kowloon Park.

Occupying the site of an old military encampment first established in the 1860s, Kowloon Park, Nathan Road, is Tsim Sha Tsui's largest recreational and sports facility, boasting an indoor heated Olympic-size swimming pool, three outdoor leisure pools linked by a series of waterfalls, an open-air sculpture garden featuring works by local and overseas sculptors, a Chinese garden, a fitness trail, an aviary, a maze formed by hedges, a children's playground, and a bird lake with flamingos and other waterfowl. The Hong Kong Museum of History (described above) is also here. Not far from the Tsim Sha Tsui MTR station, the park is open daily from 6am to midnight, with free admission.

## Yuen Po Street Bird Garden.

Songbirds are favorite pets in Chinese households; perhaps you've noticed wooden bird cages hanging outside shops or from apartment balconies, or perhaps you've even seen someone taking his bird for an outing in its cage. To see more of these prized birds, which are valued not for their plumage but for their singing talents, visit the fascinating Yuen Po Bird Garden, Prince Edward Road West, Mong Kok, which consists of a series of Chinese-style gateways and courtyards lined with stalls selling songbirds, beautifully crafted wood and bamboo cages, live crickets and mealy worms, and tiny porcelain food bowls. Nothing, it seems, is too expensive for these tiny creatures. This garden is very Chinese and a lot of fun to visit; young children love it. Take the MTR to Prince Edward Road station and walk 10 minutes west on Prince Edward Road West, turning left at the railway overhead onto Yuen Po Street. Admission is free and it's open daily from 7am to 8pm.

**Zoological and Botanical Gardens.**

Established in 1864, the Zoological and Botanical Gardens, Upper Albert Road, Central, are spread on the slope of Victoria Peak, making it a popular respite for Hong Kong residents; if you're tired of Central and its traffic, this is a pleasant place to regain your perspective. Arrive early, around 7am, to see Chinese residents going through the slow motions of *tai chi chuan* (shadowboxing), a disciplined physical routine of more than 200 individual movements, designed to exercise every muscle of the body and bring a sense of peace and balance to its practitioners. In the gardens themselves, which retain some of their Victorian charm, flowers are almost always in bloom, from azaleas in the spring to wisteria and bauhinea in the summer and fall. Plants in the botanical gardens include Burmese rosewood trees, Indian rubber trees, camphor trees, and the Hong Kong orchid. The small zoo houses jaguars, monkeys, leopards, and kangaroos, and there's an aviary with about 900 birds representing 280 species, including Palawan peacocks, birds of paradise from Papua New Guinea, cranes, and Mandarin ducks. The botanical garden is open daily from 6am to 10pm; the zoo is open daily from 6am to 7pm. Admission is free. Take the MTR to Central and then walk 15 minutes up Garden Road; or take bus nos. 3B or 12 from the Jardine House on Connaught Road Central, getting off at the Caritas Centre and following the uphill path.

# AMUSEMENT PARKS

✪ **Ocean Park.** Aberdeen, Hong Kong Island. ☎ **852/2552 0291** or 2873 8577. Admission HK$140 (US$18.20) adults, HK$70 (US$9.41) children ages 3–11. 1 adult may bring 1 child into the park free. Daily 10am–6pm. Bus: Ocean Park Citybus from the Admiralty MTR station.

If you're a kid or a kid at heart, you'll love Ocean Park, a combination marine park and amusement center, complete with a replica of an old Chinese village called the Middle Kingdom. Situated along a dramatic rocky coastline on the island's southern shore, the park is divided into three areas, connected by a spectacular 8-minute cable-car ride and an escalator. Because of the wide range of attractions, Ocean Park is interesting for children and senior citizens alike, as well as everyone in between.

Among the many attractions are Kids' World, with its kiddie rides, playgrounds, and shows geared toward children; thrill rides that include a roller coaster and Ferris wheel; a 100-seat theater with hydraulically actuated seats that move in time to the fast-paced action on the screen; Butterfly House, with 1,000 free-flying butterflies; Golden Pagoda, set in a lush garden, with more varieties of goldfish than you ever imagined possible; an artificial wave cove that is home to sea lions; a shark aquarium, viewed from an underwater tunnel; and an Ocean Theatre with shows by talented dolphins, sea lions, and a killer whale. My favorite attraction is Atoll Reef, one of the world's largest aquariums, with 4,000 fish of 400 different species viewed from an observation passageway which circles the aquarium on four levels.

**Middle Kingdom** is a re-creation of a small village from China's past, with full-size temples, shrines, pavilions, pagodas, street scenes, and public squares. Be sure to stop by the Exhibition Hall, which briefly describes China's history through 13 imperial dynasties, a span of 4,000 years, along with explanations on such subjects as the Great Wall, the principles of feng shui, the Chinese writing system, and foot binding. There are also several little shops selling a variety of Chinese products, including a tea shop, and a palm reader, as well as performances by Chinese acrobats and magicians. To do Ocean Park justice, plan on spending a minimum of 4 hours here.

**Water World.** Aberdeen, Hong Kong Island. ☎ **852/2552 0291** or 2873 8577. Admission HK$65 (US$8.45) adults, HK$33 (US$4.30) children; after 5pm HK$44 (US$5.70) adults, HK$22 (US$2.85) children. July–Aug daily 9am–9pm; June and Sept 1–13 daily 10am–6pm; mid-Sept to end of Sept Sat–Sun 10am–6pm. Bus: Ocean Park Citybus from Admiralty MTR station.

Located next to Ocean Park and under the same management, Water World is a good place to cool off on a hot summer's day. It contains several pools with various slides and diving platforms, a winding "river" you can float down, a rapids ride, and even a pool with a sandy beach and waves. Don't forget your bathing suit.

## HORSE RACING

If you're here anytime from September through mid-June, join the rest of Hong Kong at the horse races. Introduced by the British more than 150 years ago, horse racing is by far the most popular sporting event in Hong Kong, due largely to the fact that, aside from the local lottery, racing is the only legal form of gambling in Hong Kong. Winnings are tax free.

There are two tracks—**Happy Valley** on Hong Kong Island, which you can reach by taking the tram to Happy Valley or the MTR to Causeway Bay; and **Sha Tin** in the New Territories, reached by taking the KCR railway to Racecourse Station. Races are held Wednesday evenings, most Saturday afternoons, and some Sunday afternoons. The lowest admission price is HK$10 (US$1.30), which is for the general public and is standing room only. If you want to watch from the more exclusive club members' enclosure, are at least 18 years old, and have been in Hong Kong fewer than 21 days, you can purchase a temporary member's badge for HK$50 (US$6.50), available on a first-come, first-served basis by showing your passport at either the Badge Enquiry Office at the main entrance to the members' private enclosure (at either track) or at the off-course betting center near the Star Ferry concourse in Central.

You can also see the races by joining the "Come Horse Racing" tour, sponsored by the Hong Kong Tourist Association and including transportation, lunch or dinner, entry to the members' enclosure, and even hints on betting. Tours cost HK$530 (US$68.90) and are limited to individuals 18 years of age and older who have been in Hong Kong fewer than 21 days.

## OUTLYING ISLANDS

An excursion to an outlying island provides not only an opportunity to experience rural Hong Kong, but also the chance to view Hong Kong's skyline and harbor by ferry, and very cheaply at that. I recommend either Lantau, famous for its giant outdoor Buddha and monastery serving vegetarian meals, or Cheung Chau, popular with families for its unhurried, small-village atmosphere and beach. Both islands are reached in about an hour via ferries that depart approximately hourly from the Outlying Ferry Piers, located less than a 5-minute walk west of the Star Ferry in the Central District. (For information on ferry schedules and prices, drop by the HKTA for a free timetable.) On weekdays and before noon on Saturday, tickets cost HK$9.20 to HK$9.70 (US$1.20–US$1.25) for ordinary class and HK$17 (US$2.20) for deluxe. On Saturday afternoon and Sunday, prices rise to HK$12.50 to HK$17 (US$1.60–US$2.20) for ordinary class and HK$32 (US$4.15) for a deluxe ticket, but try to avoid weekends, when ferries are crowded with day-trippers. I highly recommend deluxe class, since this upper-deck ticket entitles you to sit on an open deck out back, a great place to sip coffee or beer when the weather is nice and watch the harbor float past. In addition, deluxe cabins are the only ones that are air-conditioned.

## LANTAU

Hong Kong's largest island and twice the size of Hong Kong Island, Lantau has a population of only 45,000. As home of Hong Kong's new international airport, however, that is expected to grow to more than 200,000 by the year 2111, with most new residents concentrated in a new satellite town called Tung Chung.

Luckily, more than half of the mountainous and lush island remains preserved in county parks. After taking the ferry from Central to Silvermine Bay (called *Mui Wo* in Chinese), you'll see some of this wonderful countryside on the 40-minute bus ride to the **Giant Tian Tan Buddha,** the largest, seated outdoor bronze Buddha in the world, and the nearby **Po Lin Monastery.** Both are situated on the plateau of Ngong Ping at an elevation of 2,460 feet (750m). The Giant Buddha, more than 100 feet (30m) tall and weighing 250 tons, is reached via 268 steps and offers great views of the surrounding countryside. Admission to the viewing platform is free and is open daily from 10am to 6pm.

Before ascending the stairs to the Buddha, however, stop by the ticket counter at the bottom of the steps to purchase a meal ticket for Po Lin Monastery, famous for its vegetarian meals (☎ **852/2985 5248** or 852/2985 5113). Your ticket will be for a specific time, at an assigned table. Two different meals of soup, vegetarian dishes, and rice are available: the ordinary, HK$60 (US$7.80) meal is served in an unadorned, non-air-conditioned dining hall, and the procedure is rather unceremonious, with huge dishes of vegetables, rice, and soup brought to communal tables covered with plastic tablecloths. Grab a Styrofoam bowl and chopsticks and help yourself. Packed with families, the dining hall here is certainly colorful. The HK$100 (US$13) "Deluxe" meal is served in a new hall void of character, but it's air-conditioned, meals are served on china plates, and the food is a notch above the cheaper meal. Both, however, are good and are available daily from noon to 4pm. No credit cards are accepted.

Be sure to explore the grounds of the colorful monastery, established near the turn of the century by reclusive Buddhist monks. Its ornate main temple houses three magnificent bronze statues of Buddha, representing the past, present, and future, and boasts a brightly painted vermilion interior with dragons and other Chinese mythical figures on the ceiling.

## CHEUNG CHUA

If you have only a few hours to spare and don't want to worry about catching buses and finding your way around, Cheung Chau is your best bet. It's a tiny island (only 1 square mile) with more than 25,000 people living in a thriving fishing village. There are no cars on the island, making it a delightful place for walking around and exploring. The island is especially popular with Chinese families for its rental bicycles and beach, but my favorite thing to do here is to walk the tiny, narrow lanes of Cheung Chau village.

Inhabited for at least 2,500 years by fisherfolk, Cheung Chau still supports a sizable population of fishing families, and fishing remains the island's main industry. Inhabited junks are moored in the harbor, and the waterfront where the ferry lands, known as the **Praya,** buzzes with activity as vendors sell fish, lobster, and vegetables. The village itself is a fascinating warren of narrow alleyways, food stalls, open markets, and shops selling everything from medicinal herbs to toys.

The best thing to do is simply explore. About a 3-minute walk from the ferry pier is **Pak Tai Temple,** near a playground on Pak She Fourth Street. Built in 1783, it's dedicated to the "Supreme Emperor of the Dark Heaven," long worshipped as a Taoist god of the sea. As you roam the village, you'll pass open-fronted shops selling incense, paper funeral objects such as cars (cremated with the deceased to accompany him or her to the next life), medicinal herbs, jade, rattan, vegetables, rice, and—a reflection of the island's increasing tourist trade—sun hats, sunglasses, and beach toys. You'll also pass people's homes; their living rooms hold the family altar and open onto the street. This is the traditional Chinese home, with the family business and communal rooms on the ground floor and the bedrooms up above. On the other side of the island (directly opposite from the ferry pier and less than a 10-minute walk away), is **Tung Wan Beach,** the most popular beach on the island.

## ORGANIZED TOURS

**BOAT TOURS**    One of the most popular cruises is a 1-hour trip aboard a **Star Ferry,** with boats departing from the Star Ferry piers in both Central and Tsim Sha Tsui seven times daily between 11am and 9pm. Tickets, which include complimentary drinks, cost HK$150 (US$19.50) for adults and HK$100 (US$13) for children and can be booked at the Star Ferry terminals. Otherwise, **Watertours** (☎ **852/2739 3302** or 852/2367 1970), Hong Kong's largest tour operator of boat and junk cruises, offers everything from 2-hour cruises to more than a dozen longer boat trips, including Chinese junk cruises to Aberdeen, sunset and evening cruises, and trips to Cheung Chau and Lantau. You can pick up a Watertours pamphlet at HKTA offices and in many hotels.

**HKTA TOURS**    Special-interest tours offered by the Hong Kong Tourist Association are highly recommended. My favorite is the 4-½ -hour **Family Insight Tour,** which provides insight into daily life in Hong Kong with a visits to a family in their housing-estate apartment, a children's day-care center or nursing home, a market selling household goods, and the Wong Tai Sin Temple, Hong Kong's most popular Taoist temple. Other tours include the **"Land Between" Tour,** which takes visitors through the vast New Territories with stops at a Buddhist monastery, a traditional rural market, a bird sanctuary, and a fishing village; the **Heritage Tour,** which covers historic Chinese architecture in the New Territories, including a walled village (now a museum) and an ornate mansion; the **Feng Shui Tour,** which explores the Chinese principles of establishing harmony with nature in the construction of new buildings; and the **"Come Horse Racing" Tour.** For more information on these and other tours, drop by any HKTA office.

## 6 Shopping

Shopping has always been one of the main reasons people come to Hong Kong, and at first glance the city does seem to be one huge department store. Good buys include products from the People's Republic of China (porcelain, jade, cloisonné, silk handicrafts and clothing, hand-embroidery, jewelry, and artwork), Chinese antiques, clothing, shoes, jewelry, furniture, carpets, leather goods, luggage, handbags, briefcases, Chinese herbs, watches, toys, and eyeglasses. As for electronic goods and cameras, they are not the bargains they once were, though good deals can be found in recently discontinued models, such as last year's Sony Discman. Hong Kong is a duty-free port, so there is no sales tax.

Tsim Sha Tsui boasts the greatest concentration of shops in Hong Kong, particularly along Nathan Road. Be sure to explore its side streets, especially Mody Road for shops specializing in washable silk and casual clothing and Granville Road for luggage shops and export overruns. One of the largest malls in the world stretches along Canton Road.

For upscale shopping, Central is where you'll find international designer labels, in boutiques located in the Landmark, Prince's Building, and The Galleria. Causeway Bay caters more to the local market, with lower prices, small shops selling everything from shoes and clothing to Chinese herbs, several Japanese department stores, and a large shopping complex called Times Square.

Antique and curio lovers usually head for Hollywood Road and Cat Street on Hong Kong Island, where everything from snuff bottles to jade carvings is for sale. Finally, one of my favorite places to shop is Stanley Market on the southern end of Hong Kong Island, where vendors sell silk clothing and business and casual wear, as well as Chinese crafts and products.

Because shopping is such big business in Hong Kong, most stores are open 7 days a week, closing only for 2 or 3 days during the Chinese New Year. Most stores open at 10am, and remain open until 6pm in Central, 9pm in Tsim Sha Tsui, and 9:30pm in Causeway Bay. Street markets are open every day.

**WARNING**   Hong Kong is a buyer-beware market. To be on the safe side, try to make major purchases at HKTA member stores, which display the HKTA logo (a round circle with a red Chinese junk in the middle) on their storefronts. About 750 member stores are listed in *The Official Shopping Guide,* available free at HKTA offices. Still, it's always a good idea to obtain a receipt from the shopkeeper with a description of your purchase, including the brand name, model number, serial number, and price for electronic and photographic equipment; for jewelry and gold watches, there should be a description of the precious stones and the metal content. If you're making a purchase using a credit card, you should also ask for the customer's copy of the credit-card slip.

## SHOPPING A TO Z
### ANTIQUES

Several of the Chinese-product stores, listed below under "Chinese Crafts & Products," stock antiques, especially porcelain. You can also find antiques and collectibles in Harbour City, a megamall in Tsim Sha Tsui, particularly along the so-called "Silk Road" on level 3 of the Hongkong Hotel Arcade. Many hotel shopping arcades have at least a few shops specializing in antiques. Otherwise, the most famous area for antiques and chinoiserie is around **Hollywood Road** and **Cat Street,** both above the Central District on Hong Kong Island. Hollywood Road twists along for a little more than half a mile, with shops selling porcelain, clay figurines, silver, and rosewood and blackwood furniture, as well as fakes and curios. Near the western end is Upper Lascar Row, popularly known as Cat Street, where sidewalk vendors sell snuff bottles, curios, and odds and ends. Other buys include original and reproduction Qing and Ming dynasty Chinese furniture, original prints, scrolls, and archaeological items.

**Cat Street Galleries.** 38 Lok Ku Rd., Central. ☎ **852/2543 1609.** MTR: Central. Bus: no. 26 (from Des Voeux Rd. Central in front of the Hongkong Bank) to the second stop on Hollywood Rd.

Cat Street Galleries, on Cat Street, houses several individually owned booths of arts and crafts and expensive antiques from the various dynasties. It's open Monday through Saturday from 11am to 5:30pm.

**Charlotte Horstmann and Gerald Godfrey.** Shop 104, Ocean Terminal, Harbour City, 3 Canton Rd., Tsim Sha Tsui. ☎ **852/2735 7167.** Mon–Sat 9:30am–6pm. MTR: Tsim Sha Tsui.

This small shop, located in the Ocean Terminal shopping mall on Canton Road, is an emporium of expensive, top-quality Asian antiques. Since the shop itself is rather small, be sure to make an appointment to see the adjoining 10,000-square-foot warehouse. Its stock varies, but Chinese art and jade are well represented; antiques from Indonesia, Thailand, Cambodia, India, and Korea are usually also available. It's open Monday through Saturday from 9:30am to 6pm.

**China Art.** 15 Upper Lascar Row, Central. ☎ **852/2542 0982.** MTR: Central. Bus: no. 26 (from Des Voeux Rd. Central in front of the Hongkong Bank) to the second stop on Hollywood Rd.

Located on Upper Lascar Row (popularly known as Cat Street), this family-owned shop is one of Hong Kong's best for antique Chinese furniture, including chairs, tables, and wardrobes, mostly from the Ming dynasty (1368–1644). It's open Monday through Saturday from 9am to 6pm.

**True Arts & Curios.** 89 Hollywood Rd., Central. ☎ **852/2559 1485.** Mon–Sat 10:30am–6:30pm, Sun 2:30–6:30pm. MTR: Central.

This tiny shop is so packed with antiques and curios that there's barely room for customers. You'll find snuff bottles, porcelain, antique silver, earrings, hair pins, and children's shoes (impractical but darling, with curled toes). But the true finds here are some 2,000 intricate wood carvings, pried from the doors and windows of dismantled temples and homes. You'll find them hanging from the ceiling and in bins, many of them dusty and grimy from years of neglect. The best ones are carved from a single piece of wood, masterpieces in workmanship and available at modest prices. Open Monday through Saturday from 10:30am to 6:30pm and Sunday from 2:30 to 6:30pm.

## CHINESE CRAFTS & PRODUCTS

In addition to the shops listed here which specialize in traditional and contemporary arts, crafts, souvenirs, and gift items from China, there are several souvenir shops at Stanley Market that carry lacquered boxes, china, embroidered tablecloths, figurines, and other Chinese imports.

✪ **Chinese Arts and Crafts Ltd.** Shop 230, Pacific Place, 88 Queensway, Central. ☎ **852/2523 3933.** MTR: Admiralty.

In business for more than 30 years, this is the best upscale shop for Chinese arts and crafts and is one of the safest places to purchase jade. You can also buy silk dresses and blouses, arts and crafts, antiques, jewelry, watches, carpets, cloisonné, furs, Chinese herbs and medicine, rosewood furniture, chinaware, Chinese teas, and embroidered tablecloths or pillowcases—in short, virtually all the upmarket items China produces. It's a great place for gifts in all price ranges. This shop, located at Pacific Place, is open daily from 10:30am to 7pm.

Other branches include: Star House, 3 Salisbury Rd., Tsim Sha Tsui (☎ **852/2735 4061;** MTR: Tsim Sha Tsui), open daily from 10am to 9:30pm; and in the China Resources Building, 26 Harbour Rd., Wan Chai (☎ **852/2827 6667;** MTR: Wan Chai), open daily 10am to 6:30pm.

✪ **Shanghai Tang.** Pedder Building, 12 Pedder St., Central. ☎ **852/2525 7333.** MTR: Central.

Step back into Shanghai of the 1930s at this upscale, two-level store with its gleaming wooden and tiled floors, raised cashier cubicles, ceiling fans, and helpful clerks wearing classical Chinese jackets. This is Chinese chic at its best, with neatly stacked rows of traditional Chinese clothing ranging from cheongsams and silk pajamas to padded jackets, caps, and shoes—all in bright, contemporary colors and styles. If you're looking for a lime-green Mao jacket, this is the place for you. You'll also find funky accessories and home furnishings, from Mao-emblazoned watches to '30s-style alarm clock remakes and fuchsia-colored serving trays. Open Monday through Saturday from 10am to 8pm and Sunday from noon to 6pm.

## DEPARTMENT STORES

**Lane Crawford Ltd.** Lane Crawford House, 70 Queen's Rd. Central, Central. ☎ **852/2526 6121.** MTR: Central.

This locally owned upscale department store, with large clothing departments for the whole family, has branches on both sides of the harbor and is similar to established chain stores in England and the United States. The main store is open daily from 10am to 7:30pm. Other branches can be found at: Pacific Place, 88 Queensway, Central (☎ **852/2845 1838;** MTR: Admiralty); Times Square, 1 Matheson St., Causeway Bay (☎ **852/2118 3638;** MTR: Causeway Bay); and Shop 100, Ocean Terminal, Harbour City, 3 Canton Rd., Tsim Sha Tsui (☎ **852/2730 2393;** MTR: Tsim Sha Tsui).

**Matsuzakaya.** 2–20 Paterson St., Causeway Bay. ☎ **852/2890 6622.** MTR: Causeway Bay.

This department store, first established in Japan more than 300 years ago, carries women's, men's, and children's clothing, shoes, handbags, cosmetics, housewares, porcelain, glassware, toys, and cookware. It also features boutiques by Fendi, Bally, Cartier, Nina Ricci, Rosenthal, Wedgwood, Noritake, and Swarovski. It's open daily from 10:30am to 10pm.

**Mitsukoshi.** 500 Hennessy Rd., Causeway Bay. ☎ **852/2576 5222.** MTR: Causeway Bay.

Mitsukoshi is another long-established department store; it first opened as a kimono shop in Japan in the 1600s and is still one of Japan's most exclusive stores. Today it houses the boutiques of well-known designers of shoes, accessories, and clothing—with high prices to match. It also carries lingerie, cosmetics, and household goods. Open daily from 10:30am to 10pm.

**Seibu.** Pacific Place, 88 Queensway, Central. ☎ **852/2868 0111.** MTR: Admiralty.

One of the largest department store chains in Japan (its Tokyo store is the third-largest department store in the world), this was Seibu's first store to open outside Japan. An upscale, sophisticated department store targeting Hong Kong's affluent yuppie population, it is the epitome of chic, from its art deco Italian furnishings to fashions from the world's top design houses. More than 65% of its merchandise is European, and 25% is from Japan. The Loft department carries well-designed housewares and gifts, while Seed is the place to go for the latest fashions. Junko Shimada, Kenzo, and Paul Smith have boutiques here. The food department is especially good, stocking many imported items that are not available elsewhere in Hong Kong. Open Sunday through Thursday from 10:30am to 8pm and Friday and Saturday from 10:30am to 9pm.

**Wing On.** 211 Des Voeux Rd., Central. ☎ **852/2852 1888.** MTR: Sheung Wan.

Founded in Shanghai almost a century ago and one of Hong Kong's oldest department stores, this main shop offers a wide selection of clothing, jewelry, accessories, and household items. It's open Monday through Friday from 10am to 7pm and Saturday and Sunday from 10am to 6:30pm. Other branches can be found at: 26 Des Voeux Rd. Central, Central (☎ **852/2524 7171;** MTR: Central); and Wing On Plaza, 62 Mody Rd., Tsim Sha Tsui East (☎ **852/2723 2211;** MTR: Tsim Sha Tsui).

## FASHION

Hong Kong has been a center for the fashion industry ever since the influx of Shanghainese tailors fleeing the 1949 communist revolution in China. If you're looking for international designer brands and money is no object, the **Landmark,** located on Des

Voeux Road Central, Central, is an ultrachic shopping complex, with boutiques for Gucci, Tiffany, Polo/Ralph Lauren, Missoni, DKNY, Versace, Sonia Rykiel, Aigner, Louis Vuitton, Lanvin, and Paloma Picasso. **The Peninsula Hotel** and **The Regent Hotel,** both in Tsim Sha Tsui, have shopping arcades filled with designer names.

For trendier designs catering to an upwardly-mobile younger crowd, check **The Galleria,** 9 Queen's Rd. Central, which has boutiques for Issey Miyake's Plantation, Katharine Hamnett, and Thierry Mugler, among many other smart shops. In addition, check out the **Joyce Boutique** chain, the first fashion house in Hong Kong, established in the 1970s by Joyce Ma to satisfy Hong Kong women's cravings for European designs. Today her stores carry clothing by Issey Miyake, Jean-Paul Gaultier, Yohji Yamamoto, Rei Kawakubo (Comme des Garcons), Vivienne Westwood, and others on the cutting edge of fashion. You'll find Joyce shops at 16 Queen's Rd. Central, Central District (☎ **852/2810 1120;** MTR: Central) and 23 Nathan Rd. in Tsim Sha Tsui (☎ **2367 8128;** MTR: Tsim Sha Tsui).

For a wider range in prices, the department stores listed above are best for one-stop shopping for the entire family, as are Hong Kong's many malls and shopping centers. Otherwise, small, family-owned shops abound in both Tsim Sha Tsui and Stanley Market, offering casualwear, washable silk outfits, and other clothing at very affordable prices. Cheaper still are factory outlets and street markets (see below).

**FACTORY OUTLETS**    Savvy shoppers head for Hong Kong's factory outlets to take advantage of excess stock, overruns, and quality-control rejects. Because these items have been made for the export market, the sizes are Western. Bargains include clothes made of silk (the latest craze is "washable silk"), cashmere, cotton, linen, knitwear, and wool. Most outlets are located on Kowloon Peninsula in an area known as **Hung Hom,** clustered in a large group of warehouse buildings called **Kaiser Estates** on Man Yuen Street. Another good place for outlets is the **Pedder Building,** 12 Pedder St., Central. For a list of factory outlets along with their addresses, telephone numbers, and types of clothing, pick up the free pamphlet, *Factory Outlets,* available at HKTA offices. Most outlets are open from 9 or 10am to 6pm Monday through Friday; some are open Saturday and Sunday as well.

## MARKETS

**STANLEY**    Stanley Market is probably the most popular and best-known market in Hong Kong. Located on the southern coast of Hong Kong Island, it's a great place to buy inexpensive clothing, especially sportswear, bathing suits, cashmere sweaters, casual clothing, silk blouses and dresses, and linen suits. Men's, women's, and children's clothing is available. Although prices are not the bargain they once were, I buy more of my clothes here than anywhere else in Hong Kong, especially when it comes to cheap, fun fashions. The inventory changes continuously—one year it seems everyone is selling jeans; the next year it's linen suits or washable silk. In recent years, souvenir shops selling crafts and products from China have also gained popularity.

To reach Stanley, take bus nos. 6 or 260 from Central's Exchange Square bus terminal near the Star Ferry. The bus ride to Stanley takes approximately 30 minutes. From Kowloon, take bus no. 973 from Mody Road in Tsim Sha Tsui East or from Canton Road in Tsim Sha Tsui. Shops are open daily from 9 or 10am to 6pm.

**LI YUEN STREET EAST & WEST**    These two streets are parallel pedestrian lanes in the heart of the Central District, very narrow and often congested with human traffic. Their stalls are packed with handbags, clothes, scarves, sweaters, toys, baby clothes, watches, makeup, umbrellas, knickknacks, and even brassieres. Don't neglect the open-fronted shops behind the stalls. These two streets are located just a couple of minutes' walk from the Central MTR station or the Star Ferry, between Des Voeux Road Central and Queen's Road Central. Vendors are open daily from 10am to 7pm.

**JADE MARKET**   Jade, believed by the Chinese to hold mystical powers and to protect its wearer, is available in all sizes, colors, and prices at the Jade Market, located on Kansu Street in two temporary structures in the Yau Ma Tei District of Kowloon. Unless you know your jade, you won't want to make any expensive purchases here, but it's great for bangles, pendants, earrings, and inexpensive gifts, as well as inexpensive freshwater pearls from China. It's open daily from 10am to about 3pm and is located near the Jordan MTR station.

**LADIES' MARKET**   Stretching along Tung Choi Street (between Argyle and Dundas Streets) in Mong Kok, Kowloon, Ladies' Market specializes in inexpensive women's and children's fashions, shoes, socks, hosiery, jewelry, sunglasses, watches, handbags, and other accessories. Some men's clothing is also sold. Although many of the products are geared more toward local tastes and sizes, an increase in tourism has brought more fashionable clothing and t-shirts, and you may find a few bargains here. In any case, the atmosphere is fun and festive, with plenty of *dai pai dong* food stalls in the evening to feed hungry shoppers. The nearest MTR station is Mong Kok. Vendors are open daily from about noon to 10:30pm.

**TEMPLE STREET NIGHT MARKET**   Temple Street in the Yau Ma Tei District of Kowloon is a night market that opens up when the sun goes down. It offers t-shirts, jeans, menswear, watches, lighters, pens, sunglasses, jewelry, cassette tapes and CDs, electronic gadgets, alarm clocks, luggage, and imitation designer watches. Bargain aggressively, and check the products carefully to make sure they're not faulty or poorly made. The night market is great entertainment, a must during your visit to Hong Kong, and is at its liveliest daily from about 8 to 11pm. It's located near the Jordan MTR station.

## MEGAMALLS & SHOPPING CENTERS
**Harbour City.** Canton Rd., Tsim Sha Tsui. MTR: Tsim Sha Tsui.

This is the largest of the megamalls in Hong Kong, and probably the largest in Asia. Conveniently located right next to the dock that disgorges passengers from cruise liners and just to the east of the Star Ferry, it encompasses Ocean Terminal, Ocean Galleries, Ocean City, the Hongkong Hotel arcade, and Gateway I and II, all interconnected by air-conditioned walkways and stretching more than a half mile along Canton Road. Altogether there are more than 600 outlets selling clothing, accessories, jewelry, cosmetics, antiques, electronic goods, furniture, housewares, toys, Asian arts and crafts, and much more. There's enough to keep you occupied for the rest of your life, but this is an especially good place on a rainy or humid day when you'd rather be inside than out. Shops include Lane Crawford, Marks & Spencer, Aiger, DKNY, Esprit, Jean-Paul Gaultier, Plantation, Salvatore Ferragamo, Bally, Luis Vuitton, Gold Pfeil, Timberland, and Toys "Я" Us. Some shops are closed on Sunday but otherwise the hours are from about 10 or 11am to 8pm.

**Pacific Place.** 88 Queensway, Central.

Pacific Place is the largest and most ambitious commercial project to hit Central; in fact, it has shifted the city center toward the east. Besides three hotels, Pacific Place has a mall with 200 retail outlets and three major department stores (Marks & Spencer, Lane Crawford, and Seibu). Shops include the Body Shop, Gucci, Cartier, Cerruti

1881 Homme, Hermès, Hugo Boss, Kenneth Cole, Dunhill, and Chinese Arts and Crafts. Most are open daily from about 10:30am to 8pm.

## 7  Hong Kong After Dark

Hong Kong's nightlife is concentrated in Tsim Sha Tsui, in Central's entertainment areas of Lan Kwai Fong and SoHo, and Wan Chai. If you're watching your Hong Kong dollars, take advantage of "happy hour," when many bars offer two drinks for the price of one or drinks at reduced prices. Furthermore, many pubs, bars, and lounges offer free live entertainment, from jazz to Filipino combos, which you can enjoy simply for the price of a beer. Remember, however, that a 10% service charge will be added to your bill.

To find out what's going on, pick up *Hong Kong Diary* or *Hong Kong Now,* both available free at HKTA offices. *HK Magazine,* a weekly distributed free at restaurants, bars, and other outlets, is aimed at a young readership with its revues of plays, concerts, and events in Hong Kong's alternative scene. Finally, the *Hong Kong Standard* publishes its entertainment section on Sunday, while the *South China Morning Post* carries an entertainment section on Friday.

## PERFORMING ARTS

To obtain tickets for the Hong Kong Philharmonic Orchestra, Hong Kong Chinese Orchestra, Chinese opera, and other performances and events, call the **Urban Council Ticketing Office (URBTIX)** at ☎ **852/2734 9009,** or drop by outlets located at the Hong Kong Cultural Centre, 10 Salisbury Rd. in Tsim Sha Tsui or City Hall, Low Block, 7 Edinburgh Place in Central, both open daily from 10am to 9:30pm.

### Chinese Opera.

Chinese opera predates the first Western opera by about 600 years, though it wasn't until the 13th and 14th centuries that performances began to develop a structured operatic form, along with distinct regional styles. Most popular in Hong Kong are Peking-style opera, with its spectacular costumes, elaborate makeup, and feats of acrobatics and swordsmanship; and the less flamboyant but more readily understood Cantonese-style opera. Plots usually dramatize legends and historical events and extol such virtues as loyalty, filial piety, and righteousness. Accompanied by seven or eight musicians, the performers sing in shrill, high-pitched falsetto, a sound Westerners may not initially appreciate.

For visitors, the easiest way to see a Chinese opera is during a festival, such as the Hong Kong Arts Festival, held from about mid-February through early March each year. Otherwise, Cantonese opera is performed fairly regularly at Town Halls in the New Territories, as well as in City Hall in Central, but tickets, generally ranging from HK$90 to HK$200 (US$11.70–US$26), usually sell out well in advance. Contact HKTA for an updated schedule.

### Hong Kong Chinese Orchestra.

Established in 1977, the Hong Kong Chinese Orchestra is the world's largest professional Chinese-instrument orchestra, with 85 musicians performing both new and traditional works using traditional and modern Chinese instruments and combining them with Western orchestrations. Performances are held at the Hong Kong Cultural Centre, 10 Salisbury Rd., Tsim Sha Tsui (☎ 852/2734 2010), and at City Hall, Edinburgh Place, Central District (☎ 852/2921 2840), with tickets ranging from HK$55 to HK$105 (US$7.15–US$13.65).

# Only in Hong Kong

For a memorable evening in Hong Kong, consider taking a **cruise of Victoria Harbour.** The Aberdeen & Harbour Night Cruise, offered by Watertours, includes a sunset cruise on a traditional-style Chinese junk with unlimited drinks, dinner aboard a floating restaurant in Aberdeen, and a stop at a scenic overlook midway up Victoria Peak. There are also 1-hour cruises aboard the famous Star Ferry. For more information, contact HKTA.

Hong Kong is also great for unhurried, **evening strolls.** One of the most beautiful and romantic sights in the world must be that afforded from **Victoria Peak** at night. To enjoy it at its fullest, follow the circular path along Lugard Road and Harlech Road, from which you'll be rewarded with great views of glittering Hong Kong. Popular with both lovers and joggers, the path is lit at night and leads past expensive villas and primeval-looking jungles. Definitely the best stroll in Hong Kong, it takes about an hour.

On the other side of the harbor, there's a promenade along the **Tsim Sha Tsui waterfront,** popular among young Chinese couples. It stretches from the Star Ferry terminus all the way through Tsim Sha Tsui East, with very romantic views of a lit-up Hong Kong Island across the choppy waters.

If you're in Hong Kong anytime from September through May on a Wednesday evening, you can go to the **horse races in Happy Valley** or **Sha Tin.** Although you can go on your own for as little as HK$10 (US$1.30), you can also take an organized trip to the races offered by the Hong Kong Tourist Association. Otherwise, if you're looking for colorful atmosphere, head for the **Temple Street Night Market,** near the Jordan MTR station in Kowloon. Extending for several blocks, it has stalls offering clothing, accessories, watches, and much more, as well as *dai pai dong* (roadside food stalls) specializing in seafood, including clams, shrimp, mussels, and crab. But the most wonderful part of the market is its northern end, near the Tin Hau temple, where you'll find palm readers and fortune-tellers, some of whom speak English, as well as street musicians and singers performing mostly Cantonese opera. Get there before 9pm to see the musicians. Otherwise, the night market is in full swing from about 8 to 11pm daily.

**Hong Kong Philharmonic Orchestra.**

The Hong Kong Cultural Centre, 10 Salisbury Rd. in Tsim Sha Tsui (☎ **852/2734 2010**) is home of the Hong Kong Philharmonic, founded in 1975 and performing regularly from September to June and at other scheduled events throughout the year. Its conductor is David Atherton; guest conductors and soloists appear during the concert season. In addition to Western classical pieces, its repertoire is enriched by works commissioned from Chinese composers. Tickets range from HK$65 to HK$270 (US$8.45–US$35.10); HK$50 (US$6.50) for students.

# DANCE CLUBS/DISCOS

**Club 97.** 9 Lan Kwai Fong, Central. ☎ **852/2810 9333.** No cover Sun–Wed, HK$97 (US$12.60) Thurs–Sat. MTR: Central.

This small, cavelike disco, decorated in funky "Moroccan" style with black-and-white tiles, mirrors, and tiny lights reminiscent of stars, is fun and usually crowded to capacity. In fact, it's so small that it sometimes feels like a private party—even more so because it's officially a members-only disco. However, nonmembers are allowed in if the place isn't too crowded; plan for a weeknight. It's easy to strike up a conversation with your neighbors here, since they are generally a mixture of expatriates and Chinese. The Tea Dance, a gay happy hour, takes place on the first Sunday of the month with half-price drinks, and again every Friday from 6 to 10pm. All in all, a very retro-hip joint. Hours are Monday to Thursday 9pm to 4am, Friday 6pm to 6am, Saturday 10pm to 6am, and Sunday 10pm to 2am.

**Hard Rock Cafe.** 100 Canton Rd., Tsim Sha Tsui. ☎ **852/2377 8118.** Cover (including 2 drinks) Thurs–Sat HK$150 (US$19.50); women get in free Thurs–Fri; no cover Sun–Wed. MTR: Tsim Sha Tsui.

This well-known tribute to rock 'n' roll clears away the tables on its upper floor after 10:30pm Thursday through Saturday, when it throws a dance party and rocks to the sound of a DJ. From Sunday through Wednesday beginning at 10pm, a live band plays. The restaurant opens daily at 11:30am for burgers and other American fare.

**JJ's.** In the Grand Hyatt Hotel, 1 Harbour Rd., Wan Chai. ☎ **852/2588 1234,** ext. 7323. Cover HK$100 (US$13) Mon–Thurs (including 1 drink), HK$200 (US$26) Fri–Sat (including 2 drinks). No cover before 8:30pm. MTR: Wan Chai.

This upscale, glitzy entertainment complex was the first in Hong Kong to offer several diversions under one roof, making it a good choice for those who like to move from one scene to the next without actually having to go anywhere. Decorated in a style that is part Victorian and part whimsical, giving it an eccentric and playful ambience, it consists of a main bar, a disco with house tracks and laser lights, a restaurant serving pizza and sandwiches, and a room with live music featuring jazz or rhythm-and-blues. Sundays feature a New Orleans–inspired buffet spread and Dixieland jazz for HK$275 (US$35.75) per person from noon to 3pm; from 3:30 to 6:30pm, a tea dance with a big band playing music of the 1940s and a tea buffet, costing HK$125 (US$16.25) per person; from 7 to 10pm, a fixed-price meal enjoyed to the strains of Latin jazz and costing HK$225 (US$29.25) per person. JJ's is open Monday through Thursday from 5:30pm to 2am, Friday from 5:30pm to 3am, Saturday from 6pm to 4am, and Sunday from noon to 10pm. Happy hour is Monday through Friday from 5:30 to 8:30pm.

**Propaganda.** 1 Hollywood Rd., Central. ☎ **852/2868 1316.** Cover (including 1 drink) Thurs HK$80 (US$10.40), Fri HK$110 (US$14.30), Sat HK$160 (US$20.80). No cover Mon–Wed or after 3:30am Fri–Sat; reduced cover before 10:30pm Thurs–Sat. MTR: Central.

Hong Kong's most popular gay disco, Propaganda is located in the SoHo nightlife district, with a discreet entrance in a back alley. The crowd is 95% gay, but everyone is welcome. Come late if you want to see this alternative hot spot at its most crowded, but remember that before 10:30pm admission is free Monday through Thursday and reduced Friday and Saturday. Open Monday through Thursday from 9pm to 3:30am and Friday and Saturday from 9pm to 6am.

# THE BAR SCENE
## KOWLOON

**Chasers.** 2–3 Knutsford Terrace, Tsim Sha Tsui. ☎ **852/2367 9487.** MTR: Tsim Sha Tsui.

One of several bars lining the narrow, alleylike Knutsford Terrace, which parallels Kimberley Road to the north, this is among the most popular, filled with a mixed clientele that includes both the young and the not-so-young, foreign and Chinese. It features a house Filipino band Tuesday through Sunday from 9pm, playing rock, jazz, rhythm-and-blues, and everything in between, free of charge. Open Monday from 4pm to 4am, Tuesday through Sunday from 2pm to 6am.

**Delaney's.** 3–7 Prat Ave., Tsim Sha Tsui. ☎ **852/2301 3980.** MTR: Tsim Sha Tsui.

This very successful, upmarket Irish pub is decorated in Old-World style with plank flooring and wine-merchant decor behind the long bar. Its convivial atmosphere gets an extra boost from live Irish bands playing free of charge 3 nights a week (at last check, Tuesday, Thursday and Saturday). Major soccer and rugby events are shown on a big screen. An à la carte menu lists Irish stew, beef and Guinness pie, corned beef and cabbage, and other national favorites. Hours are daily from 8:30am to 2:30am. There's another Delaney's in Wan Chai at 18 Luard Rd. (☎ **852/2804 2880**).

**MadDogs.** 32 Nathan Rd., Tsim Sha Tsui. ☎ **852/2301 2222.** MTR: Tsim Sha Tsui.

Located beneath the Imperial Hotel, this basement establishment is the Kowloon version of a long-established and popular English-style pub near the Lan Kwai Fong district in Central. Opened in 1990, it looks as though it has been here forever and attracts mainly tourists staying in the many neighboring hotels. Happy hour is from 5 to 10pm daily, and there's a DJ after 8pm and sometimes live music, but never a cover charge. It's open Sunday through Thursday from 8am to 2am and Friday and Saturday from 8am to 4am, making it a good place to come if you want beer for breakfast.

The Central branch, 1 D'Aguilar St. (☎ **852/2810 1000**), is often packed, especially during happy hour daily from 4 to 10pm. On weekends there's a DJ. It's open Monday through Thursday from 11am to 2am, Friday and Saturday from 11am to 3am, and Sunday from 10am to 2am.

**Ned Kelly's Last Stand.** 11A Ashley Rd., Tsim Sha Tsui. ☎ **852/2376 0562.** MTR: Tsim Sha Tsui.

This is a lively Aussie saloon, attracting a largely middle-aged crowd with free live Dixieland jazz or swing Monday through Saturday from 9pm to 2am. It serves Australian chow and pub grub, and happy hour is from 4 to 9pm. Open daily from 11:30am to 2am.

## CENTRAL DISTRICT

**Bull and Bear.** Hutchinson House, 10 Harcourt Rd., Central. ☎ **852/2525 7436.** MTR: Central.

The huge, sprawling Bull and Bear was at the forefront of Hong Kong's English-pub craze, opening back in 1974. Notorious from the beginning, it can get pretty rowdy on weekend nights; one British expatriate described it as a "meat market." It attracts mainly business types at lunch with its steak-and-kidney pie, salads, sandwiches, and daily specials. Happy hour is daily from 5 to 9pm. Open Monday through Saturday from 8am to midnight and Sunday from noon to midnight.

**California.** 24–26 Lan Kwai Fong St., Central. ☎ **852/2521 1345.** Disco cover charge Fri–Sat HK$100 (US$13). MTR: Central.

Located in Central's nightlife district, this chic bar was once the place to see and be seen—the haunt of the young nouveaux riche. Newer establishments have since encroached upon California's exalted position, but it remains a respected and sophisticated restaurant/bar. You might consider starting your night on the town here with dinner and drinks—the restaurant is popular for its hamburgers (the house specialty), pizza, pasta, and sandwiches. Happy hour is 5 to 8pm. On Friday and Saturday nights from 11pm to 4am, it becomes a happening disco, with DJs playing the latest hits. It's open Monday through Thursday from noon to midnight, Friday and Saturday from noon to 4am, and Sunday from 6 to 11pm.

**Dublin Jack.** 37 Cochrane St., Central. ☎ **852/2543 0081**). MTR: Central.

With its bright red exterior, it's easy to spot this Irish pub next to the Hillside Escalator Link in Central's SoHo entertainment district. But packed with expats on their way home to the Mid-Levels after a day's work in Central, it's hard to elbow your way in through the door. Happy hour is from 3 to 8pm daily; the bar is open daily from noon to 2am.

## CAUSEWAY BAY/WAN CHAI

**BB's.** 114–120 Lockhart Rd., Wan Chai. ☎ **852/2529 7702.** MTR: Wan Chai.

This popular, cool, and sophisticated Wan Chai bar offers free live music several times a week from 8:30 to 11:30pm, including jazz on Sunday and rhythm-and-blues on Monday. A DJ spins tunes on Thursday, Friday, and Saturday nights. It's open from 11am to 3am daily, with happy hour from 4 to 9pm.

**Joe Bananas.** 23 Luard Rd., Wan Chai. ☎ **852/2529 1811.** Cover HK$100 (US$13) Fri–Sat after 10pm, including 1 drink. MTR: Wan Chai.

Under the same management as MadDogs, this combination bar/restaurant/disco has long been one of the most popular and hippest hangouts in Wan Chai. Called "JB's" by the locals, and decorated like an American diner with its jukebox, posters, and music memorabilia, it offers dancing every evening after 10pm. A cover is charged on weekends. Open Monday through Saturday from 11am to 5am and Sunday from 5pm to 5am; happy hour daily from 5 to 10pm.

# 8  A Side Trip to Macau

Macau was established as a Portuguese colony in 1557, centuries before the British acquired Hong Kong. Just 40 miles (65km) west of Hong Kong, across the Pearl River Estuary, Macau is a small and unpretentious provincial town, only 8.6 square miles (14 sq km) in area and reminding old-timers of what Hong Kong used to look like 40 years ago. But with its unique mixture of Portuguese and Chinese cultures, Macau feels different from Hong Kong, different from China, different from anywhere else. Maybe it's the jumble of Chinese signs and stores mixed in with pastel-colored colonial-style buildings, the temples alongside Catholic churches, the flair of Portugal blended with the practicality of the Chinese. There are beaches, churches, fortresses, temples, gardens, museums, and fascinating neighborhoods to explore, as well as casinos and restaurants serving wonderful Macanese cuisine.

On December 20, 1999, the international spotlight will turn on Macau as Portugal's 400 years of rule come to an end and Macau becomes a Special Administrative Region of China. Like Hong Kong, Macau will be permitted to have its own internal government and economic system for another 50 years after the Chinese assume control.

## ENTRY REQUIREMENTS

Americans, Canadians, Australians, Irish, British, and New Zealanders need only **passports**—no visas—for stays up to 20 days. Macau's official currency is the **pataca** (ptc), pegged to the Hong Kong dollar at a rate of $103.20 patacas to HK$100 (or 8 patacas for each US$1). However, because Hong Kong dollars are readily accepted everywhere in Macau at a rate of HK$1 to 1 ptc, even on buses and for taxis (though you are likely to receive change in patacas), it's not worth the hassle to exchange money for short stays. Hotel rates are generally quoted only in Hong Kong dollars, and unused patacas *cannot* be used in Hong Kong. Like the Hong Kong dollar, the

# Macau

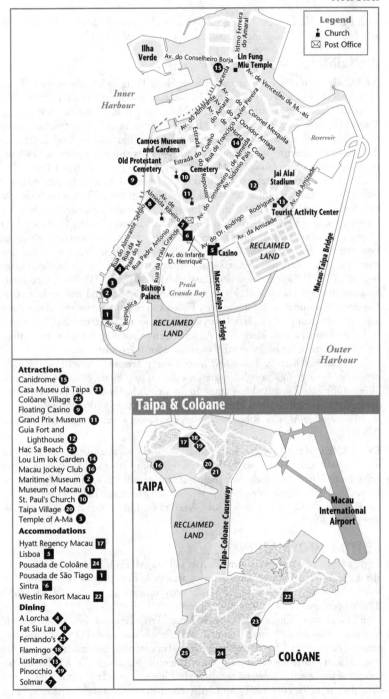

**Legend**
- ✝ Church
- ✉ Post Office

Ilha Verde

Inner Harbour

Av. do Conselheiro Borja

Istmo Ferreira do Amaral

Lin Fung Miu Temple

Av. de Venceslau de Morais

Camoes Museum and Gardens

Old Protestant Cemetery

Estrada do Coelho

Rua de Francisco Xavier Pereira

Av. do Coronel Mesquita

Reservoir

Cemetery

Jai Alai Stadium

Tourist Activity Center

RECLAIMED LAND

Bishop's Palace

Praia Grande Bay

Casino

RECLAIMED LAND

Macau-Taipa Bridge

Outer Harbour

## Attractions
Canidrome 15
Casa Museu da Taipa 21
Colôane Village 25
Floating Casino 9
Grand Prix Museum 11
Guia Fort and Lighthouse 12
Hac Sa Beach 23
Lou Lim Iok Garden 14
Macau Jockey Club 16
Maritime Museum 2
Museum of Macau 11
St. Paul's Church 10
Taipa Village 20
Temple of A-Ma 3

## Accommodations
Hyatt Regency Macau 17
Lisboa 5
Pousada de Colôane 24
Pousada de São Tiago 1
Sintra 6
Westin Resort Macau 22

## Dining
A Lorcha 4
Fat Siu Lau 8
Fernando's 23
Flamingo 18
Lusitano 13
Pinocchio 19
Solmar 7

## Taipa & Colôane

TAIPA

RECLAIMED LAND

Taipa-Coloane Causeway

Macau International Airport

COLÔANE

pataca is identified by the "$" sign, sometimes also written "M$" or "MOP$." To avoid confusion, I have identified patacas by the shortened "ptcs."

## ARRIVING

**BY BOAT**    Macau is easily accessible from Hong Kong by boat, with most departures from the **Macau Ferry Terminal,** located just west of the Central District in the Shun Tak Centre, 200 Connaught Rd., on Hong Kong Island. Situated above Sheung Wan MTR station, the terminal houses booking offices for all forms of transportation to Macau, as well as the Macau Government Tourist Office (Room 336, on the same floor as boats departing for Macau). Limited service is also available from Kowloon, from the newer China Hong Kong Terminal on Canton Road, Tsim Sha Tsui.

The fastest, most convenient way to travel to Macau is via a 55-minute ride on a **jetfoil,** with departures from the Macau Ferry Terminal every 15 minutes from 7am to 5:30pm and every 30 to 60 minutes throughout the night. One-way fares Monday through Friday are HK$144 (US$18.70) for first class and HK$130 (US$16.90) for economy class; weekend and night fares cost slightly more. **Turbocats,** which depart from the Macau Ferry Terminal approximately every half hour between 7:30am and 8pm and then hourly to 11pm, take approximately 1 hour to reach Macau. Tickets cost HK$239 (US$31.05) for first class and HK$137 (US$17.80) for economy Monday through Friday, with higher fares charged for weekend and night service. Departure taxes are included in the fares. Tickets can be purchased at the Macau Ferry Terminal or at any MTR Travel Service Centre found at several MTR stations, including Tsim Sha Tsui, Mong Kok, Admiralty, and Causeway Bay. Note that jetfoils have limited space for baggage, while turbocats allow more carry-ons.

In Macau, you'll arrive at the new **Macau Ferry Terminal,** located on the main peninsula. After going through Customs, be sure to stop by the Macau Government Tourist Office for a map and brochures. In the arrivals hall is also a counter for hotels operating free shuttle buses. Otherwise, city buses 3, 3A, and 10 travel from the terminal to Avenida Almeida Ribeiro, the main downtown street. The fare is $2.30 ptcs (US30¢).

**BY PLANE**    Macau's International Airport, located on Taipa Island and connected to the mainland by bridge, serves flights mainly from China and a few other Asian cities. Several first-class hotels offer complimentary transfer on request. Otherwise, an airport bus, AP1, travels from the airport to the ferry terminal, Lisboa Hotel, and the Border Gate; the fare is $6 ptcs (US80¢). A taxi to the Lisboa costs approximately $40 ptcs (US$5.20).

## VISITOR INFORMATION

There are two **Macau Government Tourist Offices** (MGTO) in Hong Kong—in the arrivals lobby of the International Airport, open daily from 9am to 10:30pm, and in room 336 on the third floor of the Macau Ferry Terminal in Central (☎ **852/2857 2287**), open daily from 9:30am to 5:45pm.

In Macau, you'll find a MGTO at the Macau Ferry Terminal, located just outside Customs and open daily from 9am to 10pm; there is also a MGTO at Macau International Airport, open for all incoming flights. For complete information, stop by the main Macau Government Tourist Office, Largo do Senado, 9 (☎ **853/315 566**), located in the center of town on the main plaza just off Avenida Almeida Ribeiro and open daily from 9am to 6pm. Other tourist information offices are located at St. Paul's Church, open daily from 9am to 6pm, and at **Guia Fort and Lighthouse,** open daily from 9am to 5:30pm. The tourist hotline in Macau is ☎ **853/3971 120.** Be sure to pick up a free map of the city, brochures on everything from churches to fortresses, and the tourist tabloid *Macau Travel Talk.*

Finally, you can also obtain information on Macau by visiting its Web site at **www.macau.tourism.gov.mo;** its e-mail address is promgto@macau.ctm.net.

## GETTING AROUND

Macau comprises a small peninsula and two small islands—Taipa and Colôane, linked to the mainland by bridges and a causeway. The peninsula, surrounded by an Inner and an Outer Harbour, is where you'll find the city of Macau, as well as the ferry terminal and most of its hotels, shops, and attractions. Macau's main road is Avenida Almeida Ribeiro; about halfway down its length is the attractive Largo do Senado, or Senate Square, Macau's main plaza.

Because the peninsula is only 2½ miles in length and a mile at its greatest width, you can walk most everywhere. If you get tired, jump into one of the licensed metered **taxis,** all painted black and beige and quite inexpensive. The charge is $9 ptcs (US$1.15) at flag-drop for the first 1.5 kilometers (0.9 miles), then $1 ptc (US13¢) for each subsequent 250 meters (825 feet). There's a surcharge of $5 ptcs (US65¢) if you go to Taipa and $10 ptcs (US$1.30) to Colôane. There is no surcharge, however, for the return journey to Macau.

**Public buses** run daily from 7am to midnight, with fares costing $2.30 ptcs (US30¢) for travel within the peninsula, $3 ptcs (US40¢) for travel to Taipa, and $4.50 ptcs (US60¢) for travel to Colôane. Buses heading for Taipa and Colôane Islands make a stop in front of the Hotel Lisboa, located on the peninsula near the Macau-Taipa Bridge. If you wish to head to the ferry terminal, look for one of a dozen buses that say "Jetfoil." The MGTO has a free map with bus routes.

There are also **pedicabs,** tricycles with seating for two passengers. Once the most common form of transportation in Macau, increased traffic and rising affluence have rendered them almost obsolete. Today pedicab drivers vie mostly for the tourist dollar, charging about $100 ptcs (US$13) for an hour of sight-seeing. Be sure to settle on the fare, the route, and the length of the journey before climbing in.

Finally, if you want to drive around on your own, you can see Macau by **Moke,** a small, Jeep-like vehicle. However, because traffic on the peninsula is so congested, I recommend hiring a Moke only for exploring the islands. Mokes rent for $480 ptcs (US$62.40) per 24 hours Monday through Friday and $500 ptcs (US$65) per 24 hours on Saturday, Sunday, and holidays, and are available from **Happy Mokes,** with a location at the Macau Ferry Terminal, level 1, counter 1025 (☎ **853/726868**). Drivers must be at least 21 years old and must have held a driver's license for at least 2 years. Contact the Macau tourist office for more information. *Note: Driving in Macau is on the left.*

## ACCOMMODATIONS

In addition to the rates given below (quoted in Hong Kong dollars), there is a 10% hotel service charge and a 5% government tax. If you plan on visiting Macau in late November, when the Grand Prix is held, you should book well in advance.

### VERY EXPENSIVE

✪ **Westin Resort Macau.** 1918 Estrada de Hac Sa, Colôane Island, Macau. ☎ **800/228-3000** in the U.S. and Canada, 853/871111 or 852/2803 2333 for reservations in Hong Kong. Fax 853/871122. www.westin.com. E-mail: Macau@westin.com. 208 units. A/C MINIBAR TV TEL. HK$2,000–HK$2,250 (US$260–US$292.50) single or double; from HK$5,000 (US$650) suite. Children under 19 stay free in parents' rm. AE, DC, MC, V. Free shuttle bus from ferry terminal, airport, and Hotel Lisboa.

Opened in 1993, this is Macau's most stunning luxury resort hotel, complete with landscaped grounds, an outdoor swimming pool, an indoor pool, tennis courts, health club, and Macau's first golf course. Located just a stone's throw from Hac Sa Beach on Colôane Island, it's a bit far from the center of town (about a 15-minute ride from the ferry pier on the hotel's complimentary shuttle bus, with departures every 30 minutes), but its isolation makes it perfect for those wishing to get away from it all. The hotel, Mediterranean in design and atmosphere, is spacious and airy, with a red terracotta tile roof and a comfortable lounge off the lobby which takes advantage of its idyllic setting by providing lots of windows that overlook the sea and by offering live music 6 nights a week. To assure tranquillity, there's a separate check-in counter for tour groups. For families, there's the Westin Kids Club, which provides children ages infant through 12 with appropriate amenities and activities, a child-care center, and wading pool. Constructed in tiers to harmonize with the hillside overlooking Hac Sa Beach, all of the hotel's large rooms face the South China Sea and feature a huge 270-square-foot private terrace, room safe, satellite TV with in-house movies, computer hookups, tea- and coffee-making facility, shaving/makeup mirror, and separate areas for showering and bathing. The room rates are based on altitude, with the highest floors (fifth through eighth) costing more.

Facilities and services also include two squash courts, lawn bowling, jogging lanes, sauna, massage, child-care center (HK$30 [US$3.90] per hour), games room, table tennis, lobby kiosk, gift shop, 24-hour room service, same-day laundry service, baby-sitting, and complimentary shuttle bus.

There are five restaurants and bars, including a Cantonese restaurant with an outdoor terrace overlooking the sea, a coffee shop offering both Portuguese and Macanese food, a Japanese restaurant, and a hotel bar with outdoor seating.

## EXPENSIVE

✪ **Hyatt Regency Macau.** Estrada Almirante Marquês Esparteiro, Taipa Island, Macau. ☎ **800/233-1234** in the U.S. and Canada, 853/831234 or 852/2956 1234 for reservations in Hong Kong. Fax 853/830195. www.hyatt.com. 326 units. A/C MINIBAR TV TEL. HK$1,280–HK$1,680 (US$166–US$218) single or double; HK$1,880 (US$244) Regency Club; from HK$3,280 (US$426) suite. 2 children under 18 stay free in parents' rm. AE, DC, MC, V. Free shuttle bus from ferry terminal and airport, or bus no. 28A from the ferry terminal.

If you're looking for a resort getaway with a tropical atmosphere, extensive recreational facilities for the entire family, great restaurants, and comfortable rooms, the Hyatt is a top choice. Located on Taipa Island with free shuttle service to the peninsula, the hotel adjoins the Taipa Island Resort, a sprawling, 3-acre complex set amidst lush greenery with an outdoor heated pool open year-round, four flood-lit tennis courts, two squash courts, fitness rooms, and more. It's also a good choice for families with its wading pool, playground, and wonderful child-care center (open Sunday through Friday from 10:30am to 7:30pm and free for up to 4 hours for hotel guests) For children aged 5 to 12, there's Camp Hyatt, with fun activities offered weekends and holidays. The guest rooms, recently refurbished with black rattan furnishings and Asian artwork, offer all the usual amenities, including satellite TV with pay in-house movies, room safe, and a voice-mail system. The least expensive rooms face inland toward new apartment construction, while the best rooms offer views of the Outer Harbour and Macau's rapidly changing skyline.

Other facilities and services include multi-purpose course for volleyball, basketball, and badminton; aerobics class; sauna; steam room; Jacuzzi; massage; hair salon; games room with table tennis and pool tables; business center; free shuttle to the ferry, airport, Hotel Lisboa, and Grand Prix Museum; same-day laundry service; 24-hour

# In case you want to see the world.

**At American Express, we're here to make your journey a smooth one. So we have over 1,700 travel service locations in over 130 countries ready to help. What else would you expect from the world's largest travel agency?**

do more

**Travel**

Call 1 800 AXP-3429 or visit
www.americanexpress.com/travel

# In case you want to be welcomed there.

We're here to see that you're always welcomed at establishments everywhere. That's why millions of people carry the American Express® Card – for peace of mind, confidence, and security, around the world or just around the corner.

do more

Cards

# In case you're running low.

We're here to help with more than 190,000 Express Cash locations around the world. In order to enroll, just call American Express at 1 800 CASH-NOW before you start your vacation.

do more

**Express Cash**

# And in case you'd rather be safe than sorry.

We're here with American Express® Travelers Cheques. They're the safe way to carry money on your vacation, because if they're ever lost or stolen you can get a refund, practically anywhere or anytime. To find the nearest place to buy Travelers Cheques, call 1 800 495-1153. Another way we help you do more.

do more

**Travelers Cheques**

room service; free newspaper; in-house nurse and doctor on call 24 hours; and baby-sitting. In short, you could easily unwind here for days.

The **Chinese** is a hip Cantonese restaurant specializing in country-style cooking, while the **Flamingo** is a Macanese restaurant with a tropical hot-pink setting, terrace seating, and views of a small lake. There's also a restaurant serving lunch and dinner buffets, a cocktail lounge with live entertainment, and a 24-hour casino. If you feel like exploring or dining on local cuisine, the quaint Taipa Village is only a 15-minute walk away.

✪ **Pousada de Saño Tiago.** Avenida da República, Fortaleza de Saño Tiago da Barra, Macau. ☎ **853/378111,** or 852/2739 1216 for reservations in Hong Kong. Fax 853/552170. 24 units. A/C MINIBAR TV TEL. HK$1,380–HK$1,680 (US$179–US$218) single or double; from HK$1,880 (US$244) suite. AE, CB, DC, MC, V. Free shuttle bus or taxi from ferry and airport.

Built around the ruins of the Portuguese Fortress da Barra, which dates from 1629, this delightful small inn on the tip of the peninsula is guaranteed to charm even the most jaded of travelers. The entrance is dramatic—a flight of stone stairs leading through a cavelike tunnel that was once part of the fort, with water trickling in small rivulets on one side of the stairs. Once inside, guests are treated to the hospitality of a Portuguese inn, with bedroom furniture imported from Portugal and stone, brick, and Portuguese blue tile throughout. The outdoor swimming pool is a great place to while away the afternoon, and most of the rooms, all of which face the sea, have balconies. Unfortunately, the hotel is currently plagued by nearby land reclamation, which will accommodate a new and wider road. Still, this place is a true find, perfect for a romantic getaway. The Maritime Museum and A-Ma Temple are within easy walking distance; you can also walk to the city center in about a half hour.

Amenities include baby-sitting, same-day laundry and dry-cleaning service, medical and dental service, free newspaper, parcel and postal service, room service (7am to 11:30pm), complimentary shuttle to and from the ferry pier on request. Cafe Da Barra, with an elegant, drawing-room ambiance, is open for dinner with a mix of classic Portuguese and Continental cuisine. Os Gatos, which offers dining on either a tree-shaded outdoor patio with glimpses of the sea or in a glass-enclosed air-conditioned room, serves specialties from Macau, Portugal, and the Mediterranean region.

## MODERATE

**Hotel Lisboa.** Avenida da Amizade, Macau. ☎ **853/577666,** or 852/2546 6944 for reservations in Hong Kong; 800/821-0900 in the U.S. and Canada. Fax 853/567193. www.macau.ctm.net/~lisboa. E-mail: lisboa@macau.ctm.net. 928 units. A/C TV TEL. HK$900–HK$1,600 (US$117–US$208) single or double; from HK$1,900 (US$247) suite. Children under 13 stay free in parents' rm. AE, DC, MC, V. Free shuttle bus or bus nos. 28A, 28B, or 28C from the ferry terminal.

The Lisboa is in a class by itself. Built in 1969, it's a Chinese version of Las Vegas—huge, flashy, and with a bewildering array of facilities that make it almost a city within a city. I always get lost in this hotel. Located near one of the bridges to Taipa island, it also has great feng shui, which may explain why its casino is one of the most popular in Macau. You certainly can't get much closer to the action than the Lisboa; it is very popular among the Hong Kong Chinese and tour groups from China and Taiwan, making its lobby rather noisy and crowded. Its casino, one of the largest, never closes, and there are a bewildering number of restaurants, shops, and nighttime diversions, including the Crazy Paris Show, a revue of scantily clad European women. Other facilities include an outdoor swimming pool, fitness center, children's playground, large shopping arcade, electronic games room, beauty salon, and barber shop. One advantage to staying here is that buses to the outlying islands and other parts of Macau stop at the front door. As for the rooms, they're located in an older wing, a newer wing, and a tower completed in 1993 which offers the best—and most expensive—harbor views, including rooms with traditional Chinese architecture and furniture. Otherwise, rooms seem rather old-fashioned in color schemes of green, pink, or orange, but they do boast cable and satellite TV with 18 channels and pay movies. In short, this is the place to be if you want to be in the thick of it. I suspect some guests check in and never leave the premises. Guests enjoy 24-hour room service, same-day laundry service, house doctor, money-exchange banks, complimentary shuttle service, free newspaper on request, and baby-sitting.

**Pousada de Colôane.** Cheoc Van Beach, Colôane Island, Macau. ☎ **853/882143** or 853/882144. Fax 853/882251. 22 units. A/C MINIBAR TV TEL. HK$680–HK$750 (US$88–US$97.50) single or double. Weekday (Mon–Thurs) discount available. AE, MC, V. Bus: nos. 21A, 25, or 26 from Lisboa Hotel (tell the bus driver you want to get off at the hotel).

This small, family-owned property, perched on a hill above Cheoc Van Beach with views of the sea, is a good place for couples and families in search of a reasonably priced isolated retreat. More than 30 years old and a bit worn and shabby in spots, it's nevertheless a relaxing place, with modestly furnished rooms, all of which have large balconies and face the sea and beach. There is a small outdoor swimming pool, a children's playground, an outdoor terrace where you can have drinks, and a Portuguese restaurant.

**SINTRA.** Avenida de D. Joaño IV, Macau. ☎ **800/821-0900** in the U.S. and Canada, 853/710111 or 852/2546 6944 for reservations in Hong Kong. Fax 853/567769. www.macau.ctm.net/~sintra. E-mail: bcsintra@macau.ctm.net. 240 units. A/C TV TEL. HK$680–HK$960 (US$88–US$125) single or double; from HK$1,480 (US$192) suite. Children under 13 stay free in parents' rm. AE, DC, MC, V. Free shuttle bus or bus nos. 3A or 10 from the ferry terminal.

This moderately priced hotel, under the same management as Hotel Lisboa, enjoys a prime location in the heart of Macau, within easy walking distance of Avenida de Almeida Ribeiro (Macau's main street). Originally built in 1975 but completely overhauled in the mid-1990s, it looks spanking new. The higher-priced rooms are larger and occupy higher floors, some with partial views of the harbor, but many rooms will probably lose their view once the nearby land-reclamation project is finished. The hotel's one restaurant (open 24 hours) serves Western and Chinese food, including dim sum breakfasts and buffet lunches, and there's a business center, a shopping center, sauna (for men only), 24-hour room service, and same-day laundry service.

## DINING

As a former trading center for spices and a melting pot for Portuguese and Chinese cultures, it's little wonder that Macau developed its own very fine Macanese cuisine. One of the most popular dishes is African chicken, grilled or baked with chilies and piri-piri peppers. Other favorites include Portuguese chicken (baked with potatoes, tomatoes, olive oil, curry, coconut, saffron, and black olives), bacalhau (codfish), Macau sole, caldeirada (seafood stew), spicy giant shrimp, baked quail and pigeon, curried crab, Portuguese sausage, and feijoada (a Brazilian stew of pork, black beans, cabbage, and spicy sausage). And don't forget Portuguese wine, inexpensive and a great bargain.

Restaurants will add a 10% service charge to your bill.

## EXPENSIVE

**O Flamingo.** In the Hyatt Regency Hotel, Taipa Island. ☎ **853/831234.** Reservations recommended Sat–Sun. Main courses HK$68–HK$105 (US$8.85–US$13.65); fixed-price lunch HK$78 (US$10.15). AE, DC, MC, V. Daily noon–3pm and 7–11pm. Bus: nos. 11, 21, 21A, 28A, or 33. MACANESE/PORTUGUESE.

If I had time for only one memorable meal in Macau, this would be a serious contender. Decorated in hot pink, the restaurant has a great Mediterranean ambience, with ceiling fans, swaying palms, and a terrace overlooking lush landscaping and a duck pond. An air-conditioned enclosure was recently added for lightweights unaccustomed to alfresco dining, but for me the real pleasure of coming here is the terrace. The bread is homemade, and the specialties are a unique blend of Portuguese, Chinese, African, Indian and Malay spices, resulting in delicious Macanese fare as well as traditional Portuguese dishes. Try the spicy king prawns with chili sauce, curried crab, African chicken with chili-coconut sauce, grilled sardines, codfish, or Macanese fried rice with chorizo, shrimp, chicken and vegetables. A strolling three-man band sets the mood.

**Lusitano.** Centro de Actividades Turisticas Macau, Rua de Luis Gonzaga Gomes. ☎ **853/705993.** Reservations recommended. Main courses HK$95–HK$130 (US$12.35–US$16.90); fixed-price meal HK$98 (US$12.75); weekend dinner buffet HK$150 (US$19.50). AE, DC, MC, V. Bus: nos. 3, 3A, 10, 10A, 12, 23, 28A, 28B, 28C, 32, or AP1. PORTUGUESE.

Opened in 1998 in the Tourist Activity Center, which also contains the Wine and Grand Prix museums and is located about a 10-minute walk from the ferry terminal, this huge restaurant has an ambitious goal—to serve authentic Portuguese cuisine to the accompaniment of floor shows featuring Portuguese folk songs and dance. With 500 seats, it has a distinct ballroom/convention center atmosphere, a clear indication it hopes to survive on the tourist market, but it's also good, family-style entertainment, the only place of its kind in Macau. The menu is good, too, spicy and salty just as Portuguese food should be, with plenty of regional Portuguese wines to wash it all down. The fish is flown fresh from Portugal, and specialties include monkfish with rice, grilled sea bass, bacalhau, Portuguese steak, and lamb in sparkling red wine sauce. Friday and Saturday nights feature a buffet, with about 10 choices of entrees.

## MODERATE

**A Lorcha.** Rua do Almirante Sergio, 289. ☎ **853/313193.** Reservations recommended for lunch. Main courses HK$52–HK$78 (US$6.75–US$10.15). AE, MC, V. Wed–Mon 12:30–3:30pm and 7–11pm. Bus: nos. 1, 1A, 2, 5, 6, 7, 8, 9, 10, 10A, 11, 18, 21, 21A, or 28B. PORTUGUESE.

Just a stone's throw from the Maritime Museum and A-Ma Temple, this is your best bet if you find yourself hungering for Portuguese food in the area. Look for its whitewashed walls, an architectural feature repeated inside the tiny restaurant with its low, arched ceiling. Casual yet often filled with business people, it offers stewed broad beans Portuguese-style, codfish in a cream sauce, fried shrimp, clams prepared in garlic and olive oil, and other traditional dishes. Its name, by the way, refers to a type of Portuguese boat, appropriate for a colony founded by seafaring explorers.

**Fat Siu Lau.** Rua da Felicidade, 64. ☎ **853/573585** or 853/573580. Main courses HK$45–HK$135 (US$5.85–US$17.55). No credit cards. Daily 11am–midnight. Bus: nos. 3, 3A, 6, 7, 10, 11, 19, 21, or 21A. MACANESE.

This is Macau's oldest restaurant (dating from 1903), and though trendier restaurants have stolen the spotlight, it remains a good standby. The three floors of dining have been renovated in upbeat modern art deco, but the exterior matches all the other storefronts on the handsome renovated street—whitewashed walls and red shutters and doors. Macanese specialties include roast pigeon marinated according to a 90-year-old secret recipe; spicy African chicken; curried crab; grouper stewed with tomatoes, bell pepper, onion, and potatoes; and grilled king prawns.

**Fernando's.** Praia de Hac Sa, 9, Colôane. ☎ **853/882264** or 853/882531. Main courses HK$60–HK$130 (US$7.80–US$16.90). No credit cards. Daily noon–9:30pm. Bus: nos. 21A, 25, or 26A. PORTUGUESE.

For years Fernando's was just another shack on Hac Sa Beach, hardly distinguishable from the others (it's the one closest to the beach, below the vines). But then a brick pavilion was added out back, complete with ceiling fans and an adjacent open-air bar, and now everyone knows the place. The strictly Portuguese menu includes a wide range of seafood, feijoada, veal, chicken, pork ribs, suckling pig, and salads. The bread comes from the restaurant's own bakery, and the vegetables are grown on the restaurant's own garden plot across the border in China. Only Portuguese wine is served. Very informal, and not for those who demand pristine conditions—there is no air conditioning, not even in the kitchen.

**Pinocchio.** Rua do Sol, Taipa Village, Taipa Island. ☎ **853/827128** or 853/827328. Main courses HK$48–HK$118 (US$6.25–US$15.35). MC, V. Daily 12:30–10pm. Bus: nos. 11, 22, 28A, 33, or AP1. PORTUGUESE/MACANESE.

Taipa Island's first Western restaurant is still going strong, though some who have known it since its early days claim the entire atmosphere changed when a roof was added to the original roofless two-story brick warehouse. Specialties include curried crab, king prawns, charcoal-grilled sardines, fried codfish cakes, grilled spareribs, roast veal, roast quail, and Portuguese-style cooked fish. The wine list is extensive.

**Solmar.** Avenida da Praia Grande, 8–10. ☎ **853/574391.** Main courses HK$66–HK$85 (US$8.60–US$11.05). No credit cards. Daily 11am–11:30pm. Bus: nos. 3, 3A or 10. PORTUGUESE.

Everyone comes to this typical, informal Portuguese cafe/restaurant, one of Macau's old-timers, to socialize and gossip. Although specializing in seafood and African chicken, the menu also lists Macau sole, curried crab, Portuguese vegetable soup, prawns in hot sauce, and of course, Portuguese wines.

## ATTRACTIONS

✪ **St. Paul's Church.** Rua de Saño Paulo. ☎ **853/358444.** Free admission. Grounds open daily 24 hrs.; museum daily 9am–5pm. Bus: no. 10 to Largo do Senado square (off Avenida Almeida Ribeiro), then follow the wavy, tiled sidewalk leading uphill to the northeast for about 10 mins.

The most famous structure in Macau is the ruin of St. Paul's Church. Crowning the top of a hill in the center of the city and approached by a grand sweep of stairs, only its ornate facade and some excavated sites remain. It was designed by an Italian Jesuit and built in the early 1600s with the help of Japanese Christians who had fled persecution in Nagasaki. In 1835 the church caught fire during a typhoon and burned to the ground, leaving only its now-famous facade. The facade is adorned with carvings and statues depicting Christianity in Asia, resulting in a rather intriguing mix of images that includes a Virgin Mary flanked by a peony (representing China) and a chrysanthemum (representing Japan), and a Chinese dragon, Portuguese ship, and demon. Beyond the facade is the excavated crypt, where glass-fronted cases hold the bones of 17th-century Christian martyrs from Japan and Vietnam. Here, too, is the tomb of Father Allesandro Valignano, who founded the church and helped introduce

Christianity in Japan. Next to the crypt is the underground Museum of Sacred Art, which contains religious works of art produced in Macau from the 17th to the 20th centuries, including 17th-century oil paintings by exiled Japanese Christian artists, crucifixes of filigree silver, and carved wooden saints.

⭐ **Museum of Macau.** Citadel of Saño Paulo do Monte (St. Paul Monte Fortress). Admission $15 ptcs (US$1.95) adults, $8 ptcs (US$1.05) senior citizens and children. Tues–Sun 10am–6pm. Located next to St. Paul's Church.

A must-see, this very ambitious project provides an excellent overview of Macau's history, local traditions, and arts and crafts. It's located beside St. Paul's Church in the bowels of ancient Monte Fortress (which was destroyed by the same fire that gutted St. Paul's). Displays, arranged chronologically, commence with the beginnings of Macau and the arrival of Portuguese traders and Jesuit missionaries. Particularly interesting is the room comparing Chinese and European civilizations at the time of their encounter in the 16th century, including descriptions of their different writing systems, philosophies, and religions. Other displays deal with the daily life and traditions of old Macau, including festivals, wedding ceremonies, and industries ranging from fishing to fireworks factories. Displays include paintings and photographs of Macau through the centuries, traditional games and toys, an explanation of Macanese cuisine and architecture, and a re-created Macau street.

⭐ **Maritime Museum.** Rua de S. Tiago da Barra. ☎ **853/595481** or 853/595483. Admission HK$10 (US$1.30) adults, HK$5 (US65¢) children, free for senior citizens and children under 10. Sun, half price. Wed–Mon 10am–5:30pm. Bus: nos. 1, 1A, 2, 5, 6, 7, 8, 9, 10, 10A, 11, 18, 21, 21A, or 28B.

Macau's oldest museum, ideally situated on the waterfront of the Inner Harbour where visitors can observe barges and other boats passing by, does an excellent job tracing the history of Macau's lifelong relationship with the sea. It's located at the tip of the peninsula, across from the Temple of A-Ma, in approximately the same spot where the Portuguese first landed. The museum begins with dioramas depicting the legend of A-Ma, protectress of seafarers and Macau's namesake, and continues with models of various boats, including trawlers, Chinese junks, Portuguese sailing boats, and even modern jetfoils. There are also life-size original boats on display, ranging from the sampan to an ornate festival boat. Various fishing methods are detailed, from trawling and gill netting to purse seining, as well as various voyages of discovery around the world. There is also a small aquarium, as well as a simulator which for $15 ptcs (US$1.95) extra allows two passengers to explore a reef. Best of all, the museum operates 30-minute boat tours aboard a restored fishing junk, with sailings at 10:30am, 11:30am, 3:30pm, and 4pm daily except Tuesday and the first Sunday of the month. Cost of the trip is $10 ptcs (US$1.30) for adults and $5 ptcs (US65¢) for children. Senior citizens and children younger than 10 sail free.

**Temple of A-Ma.** Rua de S. Tiago da Barra. Free admission. Daily 8am–5pm. Bus: nos. 1, 1A, 2, 5, 6, 7, 8, 9, 10, 10A, 11, 18, 21, 21A, or 28B.

Macau's oldest temple is situated at the bottom of Barra Hill at the entrance to the Inner Harbour, across from the Maritime Museum. With parts of it dating back more than 600 years, it is dedicated to A-Ma, goddess of seafarers. According to legend, a poor village girl seeking free passage was finally taken aboard a small fishing boat, the only boat to survive a subsequent typhoon. When the craft landed, the young girl revealed herself to be A-Ma, and the fishermen repaid their gratitude by building this temple on the spot where they came ashore. At any rate, the temple was already here when the Portuguese arrived, and they named their city A-Ma-Gao (Bay of A-Ma) after it. The temple contains images of A-Ma and stone carvings of the Chinese fishing boat that carried her to Macau. The temple has good feng shui, spreading along the steep slope of Barra Hill with views of the Inner Harbour, with several shrines set in the rocky hillside and linked by winding paths through moon gates.

**Lou Lim Iok Garden.** Estrada de Adolfo Loureiro. Admission $1 ptc (US13¢). Daily from dawn to dusk. Bus: nos. 5, 9, 12, 22, or 28C.

Macau's most flamboyant Chinese garden was built in the 19th century by a wealthy Chinese merchant and modeled after the famous gardens in Soochow. Tiny, with narrow winding paths, bamboo groves, a nine-turn zigzag bridge (believed to deter evil spirits), and ponds filled with carp, it's a nice escape from the city. If possible, come in the morning, when the garden is filled with Chinese doing tai chi chuan exercises, musicians practicing traditional Chinese music, and bird lovers strolling their birds in ornate wooden cages.

## TAIPA & COLÒANE ISLANDS

Closest to the mainland, **Taipa** has exploded with new construction in recent years, but it's still worth seeing **Taipa Village,** a small, traditional community with narrow lanes and two-story colonial buildings painted in yellows, blues, and greens. Village life remains in full view here, with children playing, women sorting the day's vegetables on towels in the street, and workers carrying produce and goods in baskets balanced from poles on their shoulders. There are a number of fine, inexpensive restaurants here, making dining reason enough to come. For sightseeing, don't miss the **Casa Museu da Taipa (Taipa House Museum),** on Avenida da Praia (☎ 853/827088). The home of a Macanese family in the early 1900s, it combines both European and Chinese designs, filled with period furniture, paintings, and personal artifacts reflective of a dual heritage and the fact that most entertaining in this outpost was done at home. It's open Tuesday through Sunday from 9:30am to 1pm and 3 to 5:30pm. Admission is free. Bus nos. 11, 22, 28A, 33, and AP1 all go to Taipa Village.

Farther away and connected to Taipa via causeway, **Colôane** is less developed than Taipa. It's known for its **beaches,** particularly Cheoc Van and Hac Sa, both with lifeguards. To reach them, take bus nos. 21A, 25 or 26A. Farther along the coast is the laid-back, quaint community of **Colôane Village,** with its sweet **Chapel of St. Francis Xavier,** built in 1928 and dedicated to Asia's most important and well-known Catholic missionary.

For more information on Taipa and Colôane, pick up a free pamphlet from the Macau tourist office called *Macau, Outlying Islands.*

## GAMBLING

The most sophisticated of Macau's 11 casinos are located in hotels—the **Mandarin Oriental, Hyatt Regency, Kingsway Hotel, Holiday Inn,** and **Hotel Lisboa,** all open 24 hours. Among those catering primarily to Chinese, none is more interesting than the ornately decorated **Floating Macau Palace Casino,** moored in the Inner Harbour at Rua das Lorchas (near Avenida Almeida Ribeiro). Open 24 hours, it's worth strolling through for a look at Chinese gambling.

Other popular forms of gambling in Macau include horse racing most Saturdays and Sundays and some Wednesday evenings from September to June at the **Macau Jockey Club** on Taipa Island (☎ 853/821188 or 8631317); and greyhound races, held on Tuesdays, Thursdays and either Saturday or Sunday at 8pm at the open-air **Canidrome,** Avenida General Castelo Branco, located near the border gate with China (☎ 853/574413). Call for more information or stop by the Macau Government Tourist Office.

## SHOPPING

A duty-free port, Macau has long been famous for its jewelry stores, especially those offering gold jewelry along Avenida do Infante D. Henrique and Avenida de Almeida Ribeiro. Portuguese wines are another good bargain, as are Chinese antiques and leather garments. In recent years, a number of fashionable clothing boutiques have also opened in the center of town, but more colorful are the clothing stalls near Largo do Senado square, many of which sell overruns and seconds from Macau's garment factories.

# 5 Thailand

*By Jennifer Eveland*

In 1998 the Tourism Authority of Thailand kicked off a new tourism campaign called "Amazing Thailand." They could not have chosen a better adjective. Amazing are the clear blue waters that lap at sandy palm-lined shores on Thailand's coasts and islands. Amazing are the country's thousands of ornate and historic temples that house serene Buddha images amidst the sweet smell of jasmine. Amazing are the Thai people, their warm smiles welcoming visitors to enjoy their world. Every experience is a thrill, from a sampling of the renowned spicy Thai cuisine to shopping adventures in sprawling bazaars to the sexy shows that entice guests to experience "sanuk," fun Thai-style, for there is no better place in Southeast Asia to experience both the exotic and the pleasurable. Thailand invites the world to experience the allure of the Orient, while providing endless opportunities for the relaxation and good times that holiday travelers seek. Thailand is truly amazing.

The world has caught on to Thailand's magic. The country for years has enjoyed some of the highest tourism rates in the region, and even amidst the economic crisis that has almost every Southeast Asian nation scurrying for decreasing tourism dollars, Thailand has managed to increase its tourism traffic. Indeed the collapse of the Thai baht in July 1997 accounts for much of this increase, as the currency stretches a long way to make a fantastic vacation even more enjoyable.

One benefit of the developed tourism industry is the accessibility of the country to outsiders. While venturing into the unknown, you will rarely feel uneasy. Regional and local transportation, Western-style accommodations, and locals well-versed in rudimentary English allow foreigners to roam with relative ease and comfort. And despite often incomprehensible cultural differences, widespread travel has increased the ease with which the Thai people greet outsiders and allow for foreign tastes and manners.

## 1 Getting to Know Thailand

### THE LAY OF THE LAND

In the center of Southeast Asia, Thailand is located roughly equidistant from China and India, sharing cultural affinities with both. It borders Burma (Myanmar) to the north and west, Laos to the northeast, Cambodia (Kampuchea) to the east, and Malaysia to the south. Thailand's southwestern coast stretches along the Andaman Sea, and its southern and southeastern coastlines border the Gulf of Thailand (still often called the Gulf of Siam).

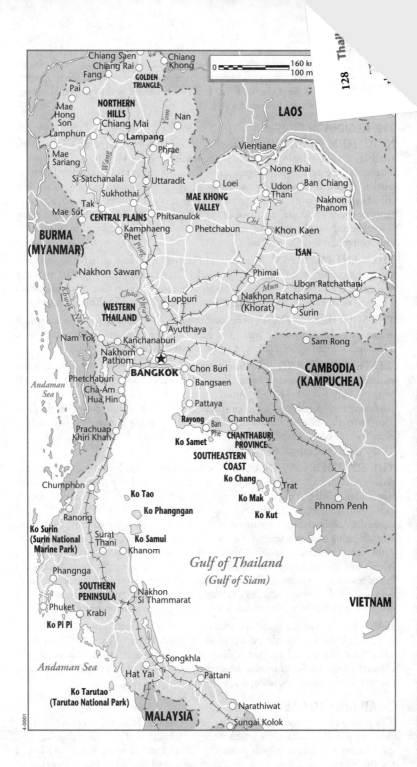

Chiang Saen
Chiang Rai
Chiang Khong
Fang
**GOLDEN TRIANGLE**
Pai
**NORTHERN HILLS**
Mae Hong Son
Chiang Mai
Nan
**LAOS**
Lamphun
**Lampang**
Phrae
Mae Sariang
Vientiane
Nong Khai
Si Satchanalai
Uttaradit
Loei
Udon Thani
Ban Chiang
Sukhothai
**MAE KHONG VALLEY**
Nakhon Phanom
Tak
**CENTRAL PLAINS**
Phitsanulok
Mae Sot
Kamphaeng Phet
Phetchabun
Khon Kaen
**BURMA (MYANMAR)**
**ISAN**
Nakhon Sawan
Phimai
Ubon Ratchathani
Lopburi
Nakhon Ratchasima (Khorat)
Surin
**WESTERN THAILAND**
Ayutthaya
Nam Tok
Kanchanaburi
Sam Rong
Nakhon Pathom
**CAMBODIA (KAMPUCHEA)**
**BANGKOK**
Chon Buri
Bangsaen
*Andaman Sea*
Phetchaburi
Chà-Am
Hua Hin
Pattaya
**Rayong**
Ban Phe
Chanthaburi
Ko Samet
**CHANTHABURI PROVINCE**
**SOUTHEASTERN COAST**
Ko Chang
Chumphon
Ko Tao
**Ko Mak**
Trat
Ranong
Ko Phangngan
**Ko Kut**
Phnom Penh
**Ko Surin (Surin National Marine Park)**
Surat Thani
Ko Samui
Phangnga
Khanom
**SOUTHERN PENINSULA**
Nakhon Si Thammarat
*Gulf of Thailand (Gulf of Siam)*
Phuket
Krabi
**VIETNAM**
**Ko Pi Pi**
*Andaman Sea*
Songkhla
Hat Yai
Pattani
**Ko Tarutao (Tarutao National Park)**
Narathiwat
**MALAYSIA**
Sungai Kolok

0    160 km
     100 mi

...hailand covers approximately 180,000 square miles (289,668 square km)—about ...e size of France. The country, which the Thais often compare in shape to the pro-file of an elephant's head, facing right, is divided into six major geographic zones, within which there are 73 provinces.

## THE REGIONS IN BRIEF

**NORTHERN THAILAND**   Northern Thailand (the forehead of the elephant) is a relatively cool mountainous region at the foothills of the Himalayas. Like most of Thailand, the cool hills in the north are well suited for farming, particularly for straw-berries, asparagus, peaches, litchis, and other fruits. At higher elevations many hill-tribe farmers cultivate opium poppies, a crop that is rarely profitable (and ruinous to farmers who become addicted) though the agricultural program advanced by the king is introducing more productive crops. The cities in the north covered in this chapter are Chiang Mai and Chiang Rai.

**THE CENTRAL PLAIN**   The Central Plain is an extremely fertile region, pro-viding the country and the world with much of its abundant rice crop. The main city of the area is Phitsanulok, northeast of which are the impressive remains of Sukhothai, Thailand's first capital. To the south is Lopburi, an ancient Mon-Khmer settlement.

**THE SOUTHEAST COAST**   The southeast coast is lined with seaside resorts, such as Pattaya and the islands Ko Samet and Ko Chang. Farther east, in the mountains, is Thailand's greatest concentration of sapphire and ruby mines.

**WESTERN THAILAND**   On the opposite side of the country, west of Bangkok, are mountains and valleys carved by the Kwai River, made infamous during World War II by the "Death Railway," built by Allied prisoners of war who worked and lived under horrifying conditions, and a bridge (made famous by the film *Bridge on the River Kwai*) over the river near Kanchanaburi. Just to the north of Bangkok (which is in every way the center of the country, along the Chao Phraya River banks) is Ayutthaya, Thailand's second capital after Sukhothai.

**THE SOUTHERN PENINSULA**   The long, narrow Southern Peninsula (the ele-phant's trunk), extends south to the Malaysian border, with the Andaman Sea on the west and the Gulf of Thailand on the east. The eastern coastline along the gulf extends more than 1,125 miles (1,802km); the western shoreline runs 445 miles (716km) along the Andaman Sea. This region is the most tropical in the country, with heavy rainfall during monsoon seasons. The northeast monsoon, roughly from November to April, brings clear weather and calm seas to the west coast; the southwest monsoon, March to October, brings similar conditions to the east coast. There are glamorous beach resorts here (people visit them even during the rainy season; it doesn't rain all day), such as the western islands of Phuket and nearby Ko Phi Phi. Ko Samui, off the east coast, is a bit more relaxed and not yet as expensive as the former two.

**ISAN**   Finally, Isan, the broad and relatively infertile northeast plateau (the ear of the elephant), is the least developed region in Thailand, bordered by the Mekong River (*Mae Nam Khong* in Thai). Isan is dusty in the cool winter and muddy during the summer monsoon. Fewer tourists make their way to Isan than any other part of the country, so I've opted not to cover it in this chapter.

## THAILAND TODAY

Today, under a pyramid of king, nation, and religion, Thais enjoy greater freedom than any people in Asia and continue to tenaciously hold their nation together. The government is a constitutional monarchy (though the constitution is still biased toward military rule), with King Bhumibol Adulyadej the head of state and chief of staff of the armed forces. The country's political structure remains relatively flexible, yet many Thais feel that despite constant changes in leadership as political parties form new alliances and old political figures are recycled, the government remains more or less the same mixture in a different cup.

The nation's most pressing concern at the time of writing, and most likely for years to come, is recovery from the **economic crisis** and the politicians who stall the legislative process to protect their own business interests. Reform proposals for debt restructuring that are desperately needed to jump start the economy have been stonewalled in parliament by politicians who are linked to many failed businesses. Media reporting of political activities is wide open, especially in comparison to most of Thailand's ASEAN neighbors, and the press here can't seem to resist any story involving accusations of corruption in politics. In international relations, at the time of writing, Thailand's main concerns involved its immediate neighbors Cambodia and Myanmar. Refugees crossing over both borders have squeezed Thailand's resources, and pressure from the West to stop drug trafficking from Myanmar have put Thailand in the middle of some heated regional and global situations (though none of these should effect law-abiding visitors to the country in any way).

## A LOOK AT THE PAST

While the origin of the Thai people is debated, the history of the country is very much a source of national pride. Thailand is the only Asian country never to have been occupied by a Western power. In fact, the country has never been completely overrun by any foreign power since national consolidation during the Sukhothai period in the 13th century—the Japanese exercised control during World War II but never fully occupied the territory. Independence, and the determination to maintain it, explains much about the development of the Thai nation.

The most significant cultures to contribute to Thailand's early development were the **Mon** and **Khmer,** both groups migrating from southern China during the first century BC. The Mon concentrated along the Chao Phraya River valley while the Khmer ultimately settled in Thailand's northeastern section in or near what is now Cambodia. Each group, through art, language, religion, architecture, and politics, influenced later Thai culture. During the height of the Mon Empire (6th to 11th centuries), the first Tibeto-Burman people settled in the northern hills. These people were the original hill-tribe dwellers, roaming throughout the northern part of Indochina for centuries.

During the Mon period, inhabitants of the Nanchao Kingdom in southern China banded together to live as a common Thai people. Oppressive Chinese economic policies forced the Thais to migrate south to the Indochinese peninsula. They established small, independent states in the north, developed a trade network with Chinese merchants from Yunnan Province, and introduced improved methods of irrigation and rice cultivation.

By the 13th century the Mon Empire was in decline from increasing Khmer domination. But it was the imminent assault by Kublai Khan in Burma that moved the Thai states to form three great kingdoms: Lanna Thai, Phayao, and Sukhothai.

**Lanna Thai** ("A Million Thai Ricefields") was founded by King Mengrai, who conquered the dissolving Mon kingdom and built a new capital at Chiang Mai ("New City") in 1296.

At this time Khmer kings in Angkor controlled much of Thailand. In 1238 two local headmen combined forces to expel a Khmer division—a victory that led to the founding of the **Kingdom of Sukhothai** ("Dawn of Happiness" in Pali). The zenith of the Sukhothai period was reached during the reign of its third ruler, King

Ramkamhaeng (1275–1317). After expelling the Khmer forces, the remaining independent Thai kingdoms made alliances with Sukhothai, which led to a unified Thai state. Ramkamhaeng is credited with creating the Thai alphabet from Mon and Khmer models derived from southern India, establishing Theravada Buddhism as the dominant religion, and expanding trade and diplomacy throughout all of Asia.

After Ramkamhaeng, the nation's economic and military status diminished, and power shifted farther south to Ayutthaya, 240 miles (400km) south of Sukhothai in the Chao Phraya valley. In 1350 the prince of U Thong built the city and declared himself King Ramathibodi. He drove the Khmers farther south and the other Thai kingdoms were reduced to vassal states. The **Ayutthaya** period changed the Thai attitude toward the monarchy. The king would now be considered the divinely appointed "Lord of Life," the supreme religious leader and protector of the Buddhist faith. King Ramathibodi and those kings who followed him lived in opulence, dignity, and distance. Citizens were required to prostrate themselves before him and forbidden to touch him.

Europeans entered the scene in the early 1500s when King Ramathibodi II (1491–1529) granted the **Portuguese** permission to live and trade in Ayutthaya in return for arms, ammunition, and instruction in the manufacture of cannons and muskets. Portuguese mercenaries even fought in campaigns against Chiang Mai.

Meanwhile the Burmese were getting restless. In 1569 its army sacked Ayutthaya and took the Crown Prince Naresuan back to Burma as a hostage. In an event famous in Thai history, Naresuan used knowledge gained during his captivity to mount a successful guerrilla insurgency against the Burmese. The Burmese made several attempts to reconquer the Thai kingdoms, and during one battle Naresuan engaged the crown prince of Burma in hand-to-hand combat on elephants and killed him. When his father died in 1590, the prince ascended the throne as King Naresuan the Great.

Naresuan's brother and successor, King Ekatosarot, sought to develop his nation economically and in 1608 allowed the **Dutch** to open their first trading station in Ayutthaya. Soon after a group of English merchants arrived with a letter from King James I and were given land for the construction of a factory. At its height in the 17th century, the city's population was greater than that of contemporary London, and it was increasingly cosmopolitan, attracting citizens from as far away as England, Holland, France, Spain, Portugal, Japan, China, and Persia.

In 1760, King Alaungpaya of Burma led an unsuccessful invasion of Thailand, during which he was apparently killed by one of his own cannons. In 1767, Alaungpaya's son Hsinbyushin led a second Burmese invasion. After a 14-month siege Ayutthaya fell, thousands of its citizens were slaughtered, and the city was plundered and burned and 4 centuries of Thai culture very nearly obliterated. Much of the royal family and 90,000 captives were also taken back to Burma as part of the spoils. One young general, Phya Taksin, however, broke through the Burmese line and escaped to Chanthaburi, on the southeast coast. He assembled a new army and navy and 7 months later returned to Ayutthaya to drive out the Burmese occupation forces. He established his new capital at Thonburi, opposite present day Bangkok, and proclaimed himself King Taksin.

For the next 15 years, Taksin successfully fought the Burmese and reformed the country's political and social system, but he later suffered from extreme mental illness, including paranoia. Two able generals waiting in the wings, the brothers Chao Phya Chakri and Chao Phya Sarasih, quietly orchestrated a revolt in 1782, and King Taksin was forced to abdicate and retire to a monastery. General Chakri was crowned King Rama I, first of the present dynasty.

Rama I relocated the capital across the Chao Phraya River to **Bangkok** ("Village of Wild Plums"), which was more spacious, less swampy, and more easily defended. For

# Wats 101

The wat, or Buddhist temple/monastery, is the defining architectural structure in Thailand. Bangkok alone has over 400, with thousands more spread out across the land. As it's a safe bet, then, that you'll be coming across more than a few, I thought we'd bone up on our wat phraseology.

With their Chinese wooden building techniques and polychromatic schemes and their Japanese-influenced carved flowing lines, the **Sukhothai-era Thai wats** (13th and 14th centuries) represented the first "pure" Thai Buddhist style, and it was during this time that the mainstays of Thai wat architecture were created. They include (in order of artistic importance): the *phra chedi* (stupa), *bot, wihaan, phra prang, mondop,* and *prasat.*

The dome-shaped **phra chedi**—usually called simply *chedi* and better known in the West as stupa—is the most venerated structure and an elaboration of the basic mound. Originally it enshrined relics of the Buddha—later of holy men and kings. A stupa consists of a dome (tumulus), constructed atop a round base (drum) and surmounted by a cubical chair representing the seated Buddha, over which is the *chatra* (umbrella) in one or several (usually nine) tiers.

The **bot** (*ubosoth* or *uposatha*) is where the *bhikku* (monks) meditate and all ceremonies are performed. It consists of either one large nave or one nave with lateral aisles built on a rectangular plan where the Buddha image is enshrined. At the end of each ridge of the roof are graceful finials, called *chofa,* (meaning "sky tassel"), which are reminiscent of animal horns but are thought to represent celestial geese or the Garuda (a mythological monster ridden by the god Shiva). The triangular gables are adorned with gilded wooden ornamentation and glass mosaics.

The **wihaan** (*vihara* or *viharn*) is a replica of the bot that is used to keep Buddha images.

The **phra prang,** which originated with the corner tower of the Khmer temple, is a new form of Thai stupa, elliptical in shape and also housing images of the Buddha.

The **mondop** may be made of wood or brick. On a square-pillared base the pyramidal roof is formed by a series of receding stories, enriched with the same decoration tapering off in a pinnacle. It may serve to enshrine some holy object or it may serve as a kind of library and storeroom for religious ceremonial objects, as it does at Wat Phra Kaeo in Bangkok.

The **prasat** ("castle") is a direct descendant of the Khmer temple, with its round-topped spire and Greek-cross layout. At the center is a square sanctuary with a domed *sikhara* and four porchlike antechambers that project from the main building, giving the whole a steplike contour. The *prasat* serves either as the royal throne hall or as a shrine for some venerated objects, such as the *prasat* of Wat Phra Kaeo in Bangkok, which enshrines the statues of the kings of the present dynasty.

the next 27 years he laid the groundwork for a city that was to surpass the grandeur of Ayutthaya, began a new administrative and economic order, and built up the armed forces. By the 18th century, Thailand reopened its doors to the outside world. Christian missionaries from England and America brought Thailand modern Western medicine, education, and agriculture.

King Mongkut (Rama IV, the king of *The King and I,* who ruled 1851–68) and his son, King Chulalongkorn (Rama V, 1868–1910), were the architects of Thailand's emergence during the 19th century into the modern world. They abolished slavery, established a modern technological infrastructure, reformed civil laws, signed trade treaties with most global powers of the time, and built a strong army. King Mongkut was the first Thai King to learn English and to study Western methods of government and diplomacy. Unfortunately, in *The King and I* he was depicted as little more than a temperamental buffoon, a picture that was far from the truth and offensive to the Thai people, who to this day hold their kings in very high esteem.

Despite their love of the king, in 1932, following rising unrest among the military, government officials, and a growing merchant class, the people held an uprising that transferred much of the king's power to a new democratic, parliamentary form of government.

The country's attempts to establish a firm political base were set back by Japanese occupation during World War II, which began in the Pacific on December 8, 1941.

For the next half-century, the government was led by a series of military field marshals and generals (brought to power through coups), with short intervening periods of civilian control. There has been strife. Thailand managed to stay out of direct involvement in the Vietnam War, but suffered the burden of refugees crossing the border. In response, Thailand was mainly responsible for forming the **Association of Southeast Asian Nations (ASEAN).** The U.S. also pumped billions into the Thai economy, widening the gap between rich and poor. Communism began to seep into the minds of those struggling as well as to liberal-minded students and intellectuals, which prompted harsh military rule and political repression, including the killing of 69 student protestors by the armed forces in 1973.

Thanks to two able premiers in succession, the 1980s were years of political stability and double-digit economic growth. However, a military coup in February 1991—the 10th successful one this century—led by General Suchinda Kraprayoon ushered in another repressive regime. His successor, Banharn Silpa-archa, leader of the Chart Thai Party, was brought down in 1996 following accusations that he accepted bribes. In addition, two prominent members of his party were also accused by the U.S. of involvement in the drug trade. General Chavalit Yongjaiyudh followed Banharn, and it was under his administration that the economic crisis hit Thailand in July 1997. While his government sat on their hands in indecision over how to proceed, connections between public officials and bad financial institutions became more apparent and international investors lost confidence in Thailand. While in August 1997, Thailand accepted $17 billion in bailouts from the International Monetary Fund, political in-fighting stalled the government's action until November, when Chuan Leekpai was elected into office, once again, to try to straighten things out.

## THAILAND'S PEOPLE & CULTURE

The Thais are a true melting pot of many people and cultures. They descended from ancient and more recent immigrants from southern China who for centuries absorbed Mon, Khmer, Laotian, Persian, Indian, and Malay people and influences. Today, the people of modern Thailand cannot credit their ethnic identity as anything other than Thai. The hill tribe peoples of the north are descended from Tibeto-Burman people who migrated down the Himalayas to the hills of northern Indochina.

### RELIGION

Thai culture cannot be fully appreciated without some understanding of **Buddhism,** which is followed by 90% of the population. Although Buddhism first came to Thailand in the third century B.C., when missionaries were sent from India, it was not until the 14th century that the *sangha* (monastic order) was established. The king entered the order, thus beginning the close connection between the royal house and the *sangha* that continues to this day. (For more information, see the section on Buddha and Buddhism in chapter 2.)

Other religions and philosophies are also followed in Thailand, including Islam, Christianity, Hinduism, and Sikhism. Sunni Islam is followed by more than two million Thais, mostly in the south. Even after centuries of evangelism, there are only a quarter of a million Christians living in the country.

## ETIQUETTE

Disrespect for the royal family and religious figures, sites, and objects will cause great offense. While photography is permitted in temples (except for Wat Phra Kaeo), never climb on a Buddha image, and if you sit down, never point your feet in the direction of the Buddha. Women should never touch a monk or give something to one directly. A monk will provide a cloth for you to lay the item upon, and he will collect it.

Thais consider the feet the lowest part of the body, so pointing your feet at someone is considered offensive. Shoes should be removed when entering a temple or private home. And don't ever step over someone's body or legs. Alternately, the head, as the highest part of the body, should never be touched, not even in jest.

Perhaps the most important advice I can give is this: In public never show anger, temper or frustration. The Thai people consider such public displays a sign of a less developed, primitive being. While banging your fist on the counter may get you better service back home, in Thailand you'll be promptly ignored. You'll catch more bees with honey.

A lovely Thai greeting is the *wai:* Place your palms together, raise the tips of your fingers to your chin, and make a subtle bow from the waist while bending your knees slightly. A *wai* is initiated by the person of lower social status. In general, you should not *wai* to children and to someone providing a service to you.

Address a Thai person by his or her first name preceded by "Khun," such as Khun Tawee. Don't be surprised if you are solely addressed by your first name—such as Mr. John or Ms. Mary. Thais have surnames, but rarely use them.

Even though this is a tropical country and you've probably come in search of the ultimate beach experience, it is offensive to the Thais to see tourists go shirtless or even to wear shorts, except at the beach. It is particularly inappropriate for men or women to wear shorts in temples.

## THAI CUISINE: FROM TIGER PRAWNS TO PAD THAI

Enjoying exquisite food is one of the true joys of traveling in Thailand. If you aren't familiar with Thai cooking, imagine the best of Chinese food ingredients and preparation combined with the sophistication of Indian spicing and topped off with red and green chilies. The styles of cooking available in Bangkok run the gamut from mild northern khan toke to extremely spicy southern curries. Basic ingredients include a cornucopia of shellfish, fresh fruits, and vegetables—asparagus, tamarind, bean sprouts, carrots, mushrooms of all kinds, various kinds of spinach, and bamboo shoots, combined with pungent spices such as basil, lemongrass, mint, chili, garlic, and coriander. Thai cooking also uses coconut milk, curry paste, peanuts, and a large variety of noodles and rice.

Among the dishes you'll find throughout the country are: tom yum goong, a Thai hot-and-sour shrimp soup; satay, charcoal-broiled chicken, beef, or pork strips skewered on a bamboo stick and dipped in a peanut-coconut curry sauce; spring rolls, similar to egg rolls but with a thinner crust and usually containing only vegetables; larb, a spicy chicken or ground-beef concoction with mint-and-lime flavoring; salads, most with a dressing of onion, chili pepper, lime juice, and fish sauce; pad thai ("Thai noodles"), rice noodles usually served with large shrimp, eggs, peanuts, fresh bean sprouts, lime, and a delicious sauce; khao soi, a northern curried soup served at small food stalls; a wide range of curries, flavored with coriander, chili, garlic, and fish sauce or coconut milk; spicy tod man pla, one of many fish dishes; sticky rice, served in the north and made from glutinous rice, prepared with vegetables and wrapped in a banana leaf; and Thai fried rice, a simple rice dish made with whatever the kitchen has on hand. "American fried rice" usually means fried rice topped by an easy-over egg and sometimes accompanied by fried chicken.

A word of caution: Thai palates relish incredibly spicy food, normally much more fiery than is tolerated in even the most piquant Western cuisines. Protect your own palate by saying "Mai phet, farang," meaning "not spicy, foreigner."

Traditionally, Thai menus don't offer fancy desserts, but the local fruit is luscious enough. Familiar fruits are pineapple (served with salt to heighten its flavor), mangoes, bananas, guava, papaya, coconut, and watermelon, as well as the latest rage, apples grown in the royal orchards. Less familiar possibilities are durian, in season during June and July, which is a Thai favorite, but an acquired taste, as it smells like rotten onions; mangosteen, a purplish, hard-skinned fruit with delicate, whitish-pink segments that melt in the mouth, available April to September; jackfruit, which is large, yellow-brown with a thick, thorned skin that envelops tangy-flavored flesh, available year-round; longan, a small, brown-skinned fruit with very sweet white flesh available July to October; tamarind, a spicy little fruit in a pod that you can eat fresh or candied; rambutan, which is small, red, and hairy, with transparent sweet flesh clustered round a woody seed, available May to July; and pomelo, similar to a grapefruit, but less juicy, available October to December. Some of these fruits are served as salads—the raw green papaya, for example, can be quite good.

## LANGUAGE

Thai is derived principally from Mon, Khmer, Chinese, Pali, Sanskrit, and, increasingly, English. It is a tonal language, with distinctions based on inflection—low, mid, high, rising, or falling tone—rather than stress, and can elude most speakers of Western languages. One interesting aspect of the language that can be confusing to first-time visitors is that the polite words roughly corresponding to our sir and ma'am are not determined by the gender of the person addressed but by the gender of the speaker; females say *ka,* and males say *krap.*

**English** is spoken in the major cities at most hotels, restaurants, and shops, and is the second language of the professional class, as well as the international business language.

Unfortunately there is no universal transliteration system, so you will see the usual **Thai greeting** written in Roman letters as *sawatdee, sawaddi, sawasdee, sawusdi,* and so forth. Some consistency has been imposed in transliterating place names. For example, you will still see the Laotian capital written Wiang Chan as well as Vientienne or Viantiane, and the word *Ratcha* ("Royal"), as in Ratchadamnoen, can be rendered *Raja, Radja,* and *Raj.* Sometimes you'll see Ko Samet as Koh Samed, or the ancient city of Ayutthaya spelled Ayudhya, but for most destinations, the spelling has been more or less standardized as presented in this chapter.

**Central Thai** is the official written and spoken language of the country, and most Thais understand it, but there are three other major dialects: **Northeastern-Thai,** spoken in Isan, and closely related to Lao; **Northern Thai,** spoken in the northwest, from Tak Province to the Burmese border; and **Southern Thai,** spoken from Chumphon Province south to the Malaysian border. The hill tribes in the North have their own distinct languages, most related to Burmese or Tibetan.

## USEFUL THAI PHRASES

| | |
|---|---|
| Hello | sa-wa-dee-krup (males); sa-wa-dee-ka (females) |
| How are you? | sa-bai-dee-rue |
| I am fine | sa-bai-dee |
| Excuse me | kor-tod-krup (males); kor-tod-ka (females) |
| I understand | kao-jai |
| I don't understand | mai-kao-jai |
| Do you speak English? | khun-pood-pa-sa-ang-rid-dai-mai |
| Not spicy please | kor-mai-ped |
| Thank you | kop-koon-krup (male); kop-koon-ka (female) |
| How much? | tao-rai |
| That's expensive | paeng |
| Discount | lod-ra-ka |
| Where is the toilet? | hong-nam-yoo-hee-nai |
| Stop here | yood-tee-nee |

# 2 Planning a Trip to Thailand

## VISITOR INFORMATION & TOURS

A major source of free and excellent information is the **Tourism Authority of Thailand (TAT),** with offices throughout the country and abroad. Consult the TAT on travel plans, hotels, transportation options, and current schedules for festivals and holidays. The TAT also has excellent regional and city maps at their information offices. Once in the country, you'll also find good, privately produced maps—usually free— available at most hotels and many businesses. At most bookstores, you can find colorful maps of major shopping areas in Bangkok and Chiang Mai by Nancy Chandler, famous artist and shopaholic.

### IN THE U.S.

**Los Angeles:** 3440 Wilshire Blvd., Suite 1100, Los Angeles, CA 90010 (☎ **213/382-2353,** fax 213/389-7544). **Chicago:** 303 East Wacker Dr., Suite 400, Chicago, IL 60601 (☎ **312/819-3990,** fax 312/565-0359). **New York:** 5 World Trade Center, Suite 3443, New York, NY 10048 (☎ **212/432-0433,** fax 212/912-0920). While there is no TAT office in **Canada,** you can contact a U.S. representative, and they'll be happy to mail or fax information to you.

### IN AUSTRALIA

**Sydney:** Level 2, National Australia Bank House, 255 George St., Sydney 2000, N.S.W. (☎ **02/247-7549,** fax 02/251-2465). Like Canada, **New Zealand** has no TAT representative of its own, but the office in Sydney can forward information upon request.

### IN THE U.K.

**London:** 49 Albemarle St., London WIX 3FE (☎ **071/499-7679,** fax 071/629-5519).

### WEB SITES

Internet users can obtain information from
   • **www.cs.ait.ac.th/tat/index.html** (Sawadee Thailand, the TAT's virtual travel information center)
   • **www.mahidol.ac.th/Thailand/Thailand-main.html** (Welcome to Thailand, for cultural, geographic, historical, and economic information)

## ENTRY REQUIREMENTS

All visitors to Thailand must carry a valid **passport** with **proof of onward passage** (either a return or through ticket). Visa applications are not required if you are staying up to 30 days and are a national of 41 designated countries, including Australia, Canada, Ireland, New Zealand, the U.K., and the U.S. New Zealanders may stay up to 3 months. Visa extensions may be obtained at the nearest immigration office and cost 500 baht (US$13.51). Visitors who overstay their visa will be fined 200 baht (US$5.40) for each extra day.

**No inoculations or vaccinations are required** unless you are coming from or passing through areas infected with yellow fever. Malaria infections do occur in the areas to the southeast of Bangkok, but the rest of the country is malaria-free. Dengue fever, also contracted through mosquito bites, is a threat in Thailand as it is everywhere in Southeast Asia.

## CUSTOMS REGULATIONS

Tourists are allowed to enter the country with 1 liter of alcohol and 200 cigarettes (or 250 grams of cigars or smoking tobacco) per adult, duty free. There are no restrictions on the import of foreign currencies or traveler's checks, but you cannot export foreign currency in excess of $10,000 unless declared to Customs upon arrival.

## MONEY

The Thai unit of currency is the **baht** (written B, as in "100B") divided into 100 **satang,** though you'll rarely see a satang coin. Copper-colored coins represent 25 and 50 satang; silver-colored coins are 1B, 2B, 5B, and 10B. Bank notes come in denominations of 10B (brown), 20B (green), 50B (blue), 100B (red), 500B (purple), and 1,000B (khaki).

At this writing, the Thai baht was trading at a rate of approximately 37 to one U.S. dollar.

Most major banks in Bangkok now have **automated teller machines,** and ATMs are increasingly common in major tourist spots. The largest banks in Thailand are **Bangkok Bank, Thai Farmers Bank,** and **Bank of Ayudhya,** all of which accept cash cards on the Cirrus/Mastercard or PLUS/Visa networks.

Traveler's checks are negotiable in most banks, hotels, restaurants, and tourist-oriented shops, but you'll receive a better rate by cashing them at commercial banks.

Nearly all international hotels and larger businesses accept **major credit cards,** but few accept personal checks. Despite protests from credit-card companies, many establishments add a 3% to 5% surcharge for payment by credit card, but this can be refunded if you report it. Use discretion in using your card and in questionable establishments. Don't let your card out of your sight, even for a moment, and be sure to keep all receipts. I've found mysterious charges for gemstones on my cards, and reporting the problem is a hassle once you get home.

In smaller towns and more remote places, cash only is the name of the game.

## WHEN TO GO

**PEAK SEASON**    Because Thailand is in the center of two distinct monsoon seasons, peak seasons will differ from destination to destination. For example, the peak season for Ko Samui in the Gulf of Thailand is from mid-December to mid-January. From January through April, Ko Samui has great weather, but it turns hot until October, when the rainy season arrives. November is the height of the rainy season, with extreme rains.

Conversely, Phuket's weather is best between September and March, with November through March being the height of visitor traffic. April welcomes the monsoon, which lasts until August. During this time you'll find great discounts on accommodations and some activities.

For individual destinations peak seasons have been explained in the section text.

**CLIMATE**   Thailand has two distinct climate zones: The humid south is tropical, and the humid north is a tropical savanna.

For Bangkok and areas in the north and east, there are three distinct seasons. The hot season lasts from March to May, with scorching temperatures averaging in the upper 90s Fahrenheit (mid-30s Celsius), lots of bright sunshine, and very little rain. The rainy season begins in early June and continues until late October; the average temperature is 84° F (29°C) with 90% humidity. During the rainy season, a daily (or evening) shower is probable, and sometimes torrential, but will never last more than a few hours. The cool season, from November through February, has more comfortable temperatures from the high 70s to low 80s F (26°C). In the north during this season, day temperatures can be as low as 60°F (16°C) in Chiang Mai and 41°F (5°C) in the hills.

The southern half of the country, particularly the southern Malay Peninsula, has intermittent showers year-round, and daily ones during the monsoon (temperatures average in the low 80s [30°C]). On the western coast, including Phuket, the best weather occurs between November and April, while the east coast and Ko Samui are best from March to October. However, Thailand's monsoon isn't as imposing as in other Asian countries—you can actually travel around the country in some comfort.

**PUBLIC HOLIDAYS**   Many holidays are based on the Thai lunar calendar; check with TAT for the current year's schedule and for holidays and festivals specific to certain regions.

The national holidays as well as New Year's Eve (December 31) and New Year's Day (January 1) are: Makha Puja (February full moon), Chakri Day (April 6), Songkran (Thai New Year, April 12–14); Coronation Day (May 5), Visakha Puja (May full moon), Asalha Puja (July full moon), Her Majesty the Queen's Birthday (August 12), Chulalongkorn Day (October 23), His Majesty the King's Birthday (December 5), and Constitution Day (December 10).

## HEALTH CONCERNS

You probably won't develop any health problems in Thailand; however, malaria, Japanese encephalitis, typhoid, and hepatitis A are endemic to some rural parts of Thailand, and some prophylaxis may be in order. The Royal Thai Consulate recommends a **malaria pill** if you are going to be hiking. The best advice, however, is to avoid bites altogether. Insect repellant is a necessity, even in urban Bangkok, and can be found at pharmacies and convenience stores all over the country. Get one with DEET.

Above all, to avoid food and water-borne ailments, **do not drink the tap water,** even in Bangkok where the Municipal Authority purifies it. Bottled water in local and international brands is available everywhere for little money. And look out for ice cubes; make sure they're from boiled water. Avoid fresh dairy products, including ice cream. Don't eat unpeeled fruit or uncooked vegetables, except at the larger hotels and restaurants. I'll frequently eat street food, which is some of the best eating around, but I stick to places where I can see the food being prepared (to be sure it wasn't sitting under a warm lamp for hours), and I check out all the ingredients they use for freshness.

# The Thai Sex Industry & AIDS

Every day you're in Thailand, in any part of the country, you will see foreigners enjoying the company of Thai women and men. Although prostitution is illegal, it's as much a part of the tourism industry as superb hotels and stunning beaches. The estimated 800,000 Thai-born **commercial sex workers (CSWs)** outnumber schoolteachers by at least 30%, and the numbers are increasing as the economic crisis forces many unemployed workers to find other sources of income. Government statistics estimate **as many as 400,000 CSWs carry the AIDS virus,** about half of the CSW population. Despite government campaigns to educate Thais about the epidemic, some 50,000 Thais died of AIDS-related illnesses in 1997. Nearly 900,000 are thought to be infected, and that number is expected to double in the next decade. I'll spare you a secondary school hygiene lecture, just saying this: Prostitutes confess that too many of their clients refuse to wear condoms during sexual intercourse. Be smart. Durex and other popular brands are sold at pharmacies and convenience stores.

Western embassies report numerous cases of tourists drugged in their hotel rooms by a lady of the evening, waking 2 days later to find all their valuables gone. Stick to women who are employed by dance clubs and business establishments that you will be able to find the next day if need be. The **Tourist Police** (in Bangkok ☎ 1699) take this stuff very seriously and should be consulted if you have any trouble.

Don't swim in freshwater streams or pools (other than chlorinated hotel pools), as they are frequently contaminated with sewage. Avoid the ocean near the outlets of sewage pipes and freshwater streams, because of contaminated water (especially around Pattaya) and the poisonous sea snakes that inhabit these areas.

When you're out and about, make sure you pace yourself. The heat and humidity are dangerous as well as uncomfortable. Drink lots of liquid to avoid dehydration. Diarrhea is to be expected in the adjustment to a new cuisine and climate, but should last no longer than 48 hours. Seek medical attention if it does last longer.

## GETTING THERE
### BY PLANE

Bangkok International Airport (Don Muang) is a major hub in Southeast Asia, with flights to all the major cities in the region, as well as the rest of the world. You'll have to pay a 500B (US$13.50) departure tax for all international departures.

**FROM NORTH AMERICA**　**Thai Airways International** (☎ 800/426-5204) in conjunction with United Airlines flies daily to Bangkok from Los Angeles. **United Airlines** (☎ 800/241-6522; www.ual.com) and **Northwest Airlines** (☎ 800/447-4747; www.nwa.com) can connect pretty much any airport in North America to Bangkok via daily flights. **Canadian Airlines International** (☎ 800/665-1177) flies to Bangkok from Vancouver via Hong Kong 4 days a week.

**FROM AUSTRALIA**　**Thai Airways** (☎ 1800/651-960) services Bangkok from Sydney daily and from Brisbane, Melbourne, and Perth three times a week. From Perth, two of the flights stop in Phuket before flying on to Bangkok. **Qantas** (☎ 131211; www.quantas.com) has, in addition to dailies from Sydney, direct flights to Bangkok from Brisbane and Melbourne three times a week. **British Airways**

(☎ **322/223-3123** Brisbane or 425-7711 Perth; www.british-airways.com) flies daily from Sydney.

**FROM THE U.K.**   Daily, nonstop flights from London to Bangkok are offered by **British Airways** (☎ **0345/222111** local call from anywhere within the U.K.; www.british-airways.com).

## BY TRAIN

Thailand is accessible via train from Singapore and peninsular Malaysia. Malaysia's Keretapi Tanah Melayu Berhad (KTM) begins in Singapore (☎ **65/222-5165**), stopping in Kuala Lumpur (☎ **03/273-8000**) and Butterworth, Penang (☎ **04/323-7962**) before heading for Thailand, where it joins service with the **State Railway of Thailand.** Bangkok's Hua Lamphong Railway Station is centrally located on Krung Kassem Road (☎ **02/223-7010** or **02/223-7020**). Taxis, tuk-tuks, and public buses are just outside the station.

The *Eastern & Oriental Express,* sister to the Venice-Simplon Orient Express, runs once a week between Singapore and Bangkok in exquisite luxury, with occasional departures between Bangkok and Chiang Mai. For international reservations, from the U.S. and Canada call ☎ **800/524-2420,** from Australia ☎ **3/9699-9766,** from New Zealand ☎ **9/379-3708,** and from the U.K. ☎ **171/805-5100.** From Singapore, Malaysia, and Thailand, contact E&O in Singapore at ☎ **65/392-3500.**

## BY BUS

There is limited private bus transportation between major cities in peninsular Malaysia and Hat Yai in southern Thailand.

# GETTING AROUND

Transportation within Thailand is accessible, efficient, and inexpensive. If your time is short, fly. But if you have the time to take in the countryside, travel by bus, train, or private car.

## BY PLANE

Bangkok is the hub for all domestic flights, which depart from and arrive at **Bangkok International Airport** (Don Muang) (☎ **02/535-2081** for domestic flights only). Most domestic flights are on **Thai Airways,** part of Thai Airways International, Lan Luang Road, Bangkok (☎ **02/280-0070**), with Bangkok as its hub. Flights connect Bangkok and 25 domestic cities, including Chiang Mai, Chiang Rai, and Phuket. There are also connecting flights between many cities.

**Bangkok Airways,** 140 Sukhumvit Rd. (☎ **02/253-4014**), flies to Phuket and Ko Samui from Bangkok daily, and between Phuket and Ko Samui. There are also daily flights between Bangkok, Sukhothai, and Chiang Mai. The new **Angel Airlines** (☎ **02/953-2260**) serves Bangkok and Singapore, and domestically Bangkok, Chiang Mai, and Phuket.

## BY TRAIN

Excellent, comfortable train service runs through much of the country with a full range of service available. The **State Railway of Thailand** (☎ **02/223-7010** or **02/223-7020**) organizes routes along four separate lines, all starting and ending in Bangkok. The Southern Line stops at Kanchanaburi, the River Kwai Bridge, Hua Hin, and Surat Thani (Ko Samui stop), with international service continuing to Butterworth (Penang, Malaysia), from where you can connect to trains to Kuala Lumpur and Singapore. Express Trains depart Bangkok five times daily. The Northern Line stops at Don Muang, Bang Pa-In, Ayutthaya, Lopburi, Phitsanulok, Lampang, Lamphum, and Chiang Mai, with express departures three times daily.

There are three categories of trains (in order of speed and comfort): express, rapid, and ordinary. In most cases, only rapid and express trains have sleeping berths; express trains also offer first-class compartments. On top of the standard fares, the supplementary charges are 60B (US$1.62) for express service, 40B (US$1.08) for rapid, and 120B (US$3.24) for air-conditioned 2nd- and 3rd-class coach. The first-class, air-conditioned, double-cabin sleeping berth surcharge is 520B (US$14.05). The second-class surcharge for an air-conditioned berth is 270B (US$7.29) for a lower berth.

The State Railway of Thailand also offers a **rail pass** for unlimited trips up to 20 days. The price including supplementary charges is 2,000B (US$54.05), not including them is 1,100B (US$29.70). The rail pass can't be used for first class travel.

## BY BUS

Thailand has a very efficient and inexpensive bus system, highly recommended for budget travelers and short-haul trips. Options abound, but the major choices are public or private, air-conditioned or non-air-conditioned. Most travelers use the private, air-conditioned buses. Ideally, buses are best for short excursions; expect to pay a minimum of 50B (US$1.35) for a one-way ticket. Longer-haul buses are an excellent value, but their slowness and lack of comfort can be a real liability.

There are three main bus terminals in Bangkok, each servicing a different part of the country. Buses to and from the southern peninsula originate at the Southern Bus Terminal (☎ **02/435-1199**) on Charan Sanitwong Road, across the river at the Bangkok Noi Station. Buses to the east coast arrive and depart from the Eastern Bus Terminal (☎ **02/390-1230**) on Sukhumvit Road opposite Soi 63 (Ekamai Road). Buses to all the northern areas are at the Northern Bus Terminal (☎ **02/272-5761**) on Phahonytin Road near the Chatuchak Weekend Market.

## BY CAR

**Renting a car** is almost too easy in Thailand. I don't recommend driving yourself in Bangkok because the traffic patterns are very confusing and jams are entirely frustrating. Outside the city, it's a good option, though Thai drivers are quite reckless. One caution: In many places, should you have an accident you will most likely be held responsible, regardless of actual fault. Many times the person believed most able to pay is the person who ultimately foots the bill.

Among the many car-rental agencies, **Avis** (☎ **800/331-1212** in the U.S., or 02/255-5300 in Bangkok, 2/12 Wireless Rd., Bangkok) and **Hertz** (☎ **800/654-3131** in the U.S., or 02/382-0293 in Bangkok, 420 Sukhumvit 71 Rd., Bangkok) have offices around the country, at Bangkok International Airport and via representatives in Bangkok and other major destinations. Average costs run between 1,500B (US$40.55) per day for a Honda Civic to 9,000B (US$243.25) per day for a Mercedes E230 or Volvo 960. Cars can also be rented with a driver, which will cost extra depending on where you wish to go.

Thailand drives on the left side of the road at a maximum speed limit of 60kmph inside a city and 80kmph outside.

## TIPS ON ACCOMMODATIONS

Thailand has all kinds of accommodations, from world-renowned luxury hotels and resorts to great backpacker hotels and bungalows. Some pricier places have recently taken to quoting rates in U.S. dollars as opposed to Thai baht as a buffer against fluctuating currency values. In places like Phuket and Ko Samui, you have a rainy season which brings with it special rates that can be between 30 and 50% off the rack rates.

Other places, such as Hua Hin and Cha-Am, impose peak-season surcharges. The prices listed in this book are rack rates quoted at the time of publishing, and are subject to change. However, be prepared to negotiate with reservations agents—these places almost always have special discounts, packages, or free service add-ons for extra value.

## TIPS ON DINING

While Bangkok and the major tourist areas have a wide variety of quality international restaurants, of course you have a wide range of Thai food options as well, from fine dining to local coffee shop fare to street food. As for street food, be cautious: Check out the stall to see that it's clean and ingredients are fresh. If it passes your muster, the food's probably OK to eat. In smaller towns, your only options will be Thai food, with some Chinese and Western selections on the menu. Most places expect to use less spice for foreigners, but you can always remind the waiter. (Conversely, make sure you ask for spicy if you want the chilis, since some places will automatically turn down the heat when they see you coming.)

## TIPS ON SHOPPING

In shopping malls and boutiques, where prices are almost always marked, you will be expected to pay full rate for any item. However, in markets and smaller shops, bargaining is the name of the game. Keep it nice and sporting and you should be fine. If you spend a long time negotiating or suggest a price that is accepted, then you may be considered rude if you walk away without finishing the sale. In rural areas such as the north, where some local people derive a large percentage of their income from handicrafts sales, I refrain from ferocious bargaining—the kind lady selling the silver bangle can probably do more with the extra 10 cents than I can. Keep in mind, however, that in high-traffic tourist areas, prices are always inflated. A major annoyance is the horrible 3% charge shops try to tack onto credit card purchases. There have been times when I've talked the shopowner into not charging me, but then there have been times when I've walked out of the store without making the purchase. They're not supposed to charge you extra, but of course nobody is really enforcing it.

# Fast Facts: Thailand

**American Express**    Sea Tours Co Ltd, Suite Nos. 88–92, 8th Floor, Payatai Plaza Rajthavee, Bangkok (☎ **02/216-5783**).

**Business Hours**    Government offices (including branch post offices) are open Monday to Friday 8:30am to 4:30pm, with a lunch break between noon and 1pm. Businesses are generally open 8am to 5pm. Shops often stay open from 8am until 7pm or later, 7 days a week. Department stores are generally open 10am to 7pm.

**Doctors**    In Bangkok and major tourist destinations you'll find hospitals and clinics with English-speaking staff, all of whom are well trained. Often these clinics are stocked with better equipment than places back home, and care is of high standard quality. Consultation is usually as low as 300B (US$8.11) per visit.

**Drug Laws**    While illegal narcotics are more readily available in Thailand, and drug laws don't include the death penalty like neighboring Malaysia and Singapore, many tourists make the mistake of misreading Thailand's drug policy. Consumption or possession of marijuana, hallucinogenic mushrooms, LSD, opium, or opiate relatives are very much illegal, and carry penalties of 1 to 10 years jail time plus 10,000B to 500,000B (US$270–US$13,513) in fines, and you can expect to receive persona non grata status after you've served your time. Each year about 1,000 tourists are prosecuted for drug crimes.

**Electricity**    All outlets—except in some luxury hotels—are 220 volts, 50 cycles, AC. Outlets are two prong, flat or round.

**Embassies**    In Bangkok: United States, 120 Wireless Rd. (☎ 02/205-4000); Australia, 37 South Sathorn (☎ 02/287-3970); U.K., 1031 Witthayu Rd. (☎ 02/253-0191); Canada, 138 Silom Rd. (☎ 02/237-4125); New Zealand, 93 Wireless Rd. (☎ 02/254-3865); Vietnam, 83/1 Wireless Rd. (☎ 02/251-7201); Lao People's Democratic Republic, 193 South Sathorn Rd. (☎ 02/287-3964); Myanmar, 132 North Sathorn Rd. (☎ 02/233-2237).

**Emergencies**    Throughout the country, the emergency number is **191** for police or medical assistance, or **1699** for the Tourist Police. Don't expect many English speakers at these numbers outside the major tourist areas.

**Hospitals**    In Bangkok, the private Bumrungrad Hospital, 33 Sukhumvit 3 Rd., Nana Nua (☎ 02/667-2999), and Bangkok Nursing Home, 9 Convent Rd. between Silom and Sathorn roads (☎ 2/233-2610), deliver quality care with an English-speaking staff. Consultation visits cost about B300 (U$8). For major emergencies, you'll need your passport and a deposit of no more than B20,000 (US$540) before you're admitted. Credit cards are accepted.

In Pattaya, the Pattaya International Hospital is on Beach Road Soi 4 (☎ 038/428-3745). The Phuket International Hospital is at 44 Chalermprakiat Ror 9 Rd. in Phuket town (☎ 076/249-400). In Chiang Mai, McCormick Hospital, Kaew Narawat Road (☎ 053/241-107), is your better bet for English-speaking staff.

**Internet/E-mail**    Service is available almost everywhere in the country, with Internet cafes popping up even at beach areas. Usage rates vary from about 2B (US5¢) per minute to 300B (US$8.10) per hour.

**Language**    Central Thai is the official written and spoken language of the country, and most Thais understand it, even if their main language is one of the three other major dialects: Northeastern Thai, Northern Thai, and Southern Thai. English is spoken in the major cities at most hotels, restaurants, and shops, and is the second language of the professional class, as well as the language used for international business.

**Liquor Laws**    Thailand does have liquor laws, but you'll be hard pressed to see them enforced. The law that prohibits sale of alcoholic beverages to children under 18 years of age is never enforced. It seems public drunken behavior is almost compulsory in the tourist party zones in Bangkok, Pattaya, Ko Samui, Phuket, Chiang Mai, and anywhere else you see a bar. Like everywhere else in the world, fines are imposed for those found driving while under the influence of alcohol.

**Newspapers & Magazines**    There are three domestic English-language dailies, the *Bangkok Post,* the *Nation,* and the less available *Thailand Times.* Most major international magazines are widely available in bookstores and newsstands.

**Police**    In Bangkok, the extremely helpful Tourist Police can be reached at 1699. See individual city chapters for local numbers.

**Post Offices/Mail**    You can use "poste restante" as an address anywhere in the country; this way, you can have mail sent to you addressed care of "Poste

Restante, GPO, [Name of City]". You'll have to pay a minimal fee (a few baht) when you pick up your mail. Airmail postcards to the U.S., Australia, Canada, the U.K., and New Zealand cost 12B (US30¢) for a small sized card; first-class letters cost 19B (US50¢) per 5 grams.

**Safety**    For the average tourist, your only danger may be from pickpockets or those who would take your things on overnight train or bus trips. Keep your belongings close at hand. Almost all hotels have safes, whether in guest rooms or at the lobby.

If anything bad or suspicious happens to you, make sure you talk to the Tourist Police immediately. These guys have the power to be very helpful, and take complaints seriously: they've been known to lock everyone inside a bar until a "lost" wallet is recovered.

Last word: Don't gamble. Thai card games are set up to take your money.

**Telephone & Fax**    Major hotels in Bangkok, Pattaya, Phuket, Chiang Mai, and the provincial capitals have international direct dial and long-distance service, and in-house fax transmission. Hotels levy a surcharge on local and long-distance calls, which can add up to 50% in some cases. Credit card or collect calls are a much better value, but most hotels also add a hefty service charge for them to your bill.

Most major post offices, usually open 7am to 11pm, have special booths for overseas calls, as well as fax and telex services. There are Overseas Telegraph and Telephone offices (also called OCO or Overseas Call Office) open 7 days a week and 24 hours a day throughout the country for long-distance international calls and telex and fax services. Local calls can be made from any red public pay telephone. Calls cost 1B (US2¢) for 3 minutes, with additional 1B coins needed after hearing multiple beeps on the line. Blue public phones are for long-distance calls within Thailand, and use coins. Card phones can be found in most airports, in many public buildings, and in larger shopping centers. Cards can be purchased in several denominations at Telephone Organization of Thailand offices.

**Time Zone**    Bangkok and all of Thailand are 7 hours later than GMT (Greenwich Mean Time). During winter months, this means that Bangkok is exactly 7 hours ahead of London, 12 hours ahead of New York, 15 hours ahead of Los Angeles, and 2 hours behind Sydney. Daylight saving time will add 1 hour to these figures.

**Tipping**    If a service charge is not added to your restaurant check, a 10% to 15% tip is appropriate. In small noodle shops, a 10B (US25¢) tip may be given if the service is particularly good. Airport or hotel porters expect tips of 20B (US55¢) per bag. Tipping taxi drivers is not expected.

**Toilets**    By and large, rest rooms are readily available in the major areas of the country at hotels and restaurants, but expect to pay around 5B (US15¢) for usage in public areas like bus and train stations. You also may encounter "squatters," ceramic bowls mounted at floor level. Keep your balance and bring your own toilet paper.

**Touts**    People will offer to take you to shops (usually jewelry shops) with "special bargains." Tuk-tuk drivers are particularly suspect. These guys are all seeking commissions from the shop owners, and you'll never get the bargains promised, and the jewelry is always fake.

**Water**    Don't drink the tap water, even in major hotels. Most hotels provide bottled water in or near the minibar or in the bathroom; use it for brushing your

# Telephone Dialing Info at a Glance

- **To place a call from your home country to Thailand,** dial the international access code (011 in the U.S., 0011 in Australia, 0170 in New Zealand, 00 in the U.K.), plus the country code (**66**), plus the Thailand area code (Bangkok 2, Pattaya 38, Hua Hin 32, Surat Thani and Ko Samui 77, Phuket 76, Chiang Mai and Chiang Rai 53), followed by the six- or seven-digit phone number (for example, from the U.S. to Bangkok, you'd dial 011+66+2+000-0000).

- **To place a call within Thailand,** you must use area codes if calling between states. Note that for calls within the country, area codes are all preceded by a zero (i.e., Bangkok 02, Pattaya 038, Hua Hin 032, Surat Thani and Ko Samui 077, Phuket 076, Chiang Mai and Chiang Rai 053).

- **To place a direct international call from Thailand,** dial the international access code (001), plus the country code of the place you are dialing, plus the area code, plus the residential number of the other party.

- **To reach the international operator,** dial 100.

- **International country codes** are as follows: Australia 61, Burma 95, Cambodia 855, Canada 1, Hong Kong 852, Indonesia 62, Laos 856, Malaysia 60, New Zealand 64, the Philippines 63, Singapore 65, U.K. 44, U.S. 1, Vietnam 84.

teeth as well as for drinking. Bottled water in convenience shops costs under 10B (US25¢). Most restaurants serve bottled or boiled water and ice made from boiled water, but always ask to be sure.

## 3 Bangkok

From the moment you arrive, Bangkok will grip your senses. Streets throb with traffic. The world's most opulent hotels cohabitate with squat buildings gray from smog. On every corner, street vendors fill the air with savory smells, and stalls packed with souvenirs, handicrafts, and cheap buys seem to clog every sidewalk. In the mornings, business people rush to work with cellular phones pressed to their ears while monks draped in saffron robes glide peacefully in search of breakfast offerings. In the evenings, if the fiery and delicious Thai cuisine isn't racy enough, there's a nightlife unrivaled by any other city on the planet. Bangkok will suck you in with promises of a most exotic vacation, and will never fail to deliver.

Vintage 19th-century photographs of Bangkok show vivid images of life on the Chao Phraya River, bustling with vessels ranging from the humblest rowboat to elaborate royal barges. Built along the banks of the broad, S-shaped river, the city spread inland through a network of klongs (canals) that rivaled the intricacy—though never the elegance—of Venice.

As Bangkok became more densely populated and developed, more and more of the klongs were filled in to create broad thoroughfares. Cars, buses, motorcycles, and tuk-tuks (motorized three-wheeler rickshaws) followed, and today, the resultant rush-hour traffic jams are so horrendous (commuters spend, on average, 40 working days per year waiting in traffic!) that the best way to travel around the city is, once again, via the river.

"Old Bangkok," called the **Historic District** here and nestled next to the Chao Phraya River, contains most of the city's historical sights such as the Grand Palace and most of the city's original wats (temples with resident monks). Following the river south, you'll run into the narrow lanes of Bangkok's **Chinatown.** Further down, a few of Bangkok's best hotels, including the famous Oriental Hotel, have made their mark on the city. Inland from the river, Bangkok's **central business district** is situated on Sathorn, Silom, and Surawongse roads, beginning at Charoen Krung Road (sometimes still referred to by its old name, New Road) leading all the way to Rama IV Road. Connecting from here is **Wireless Road,** where many of the larger foreign embassies have built huge compounds. Bangkok's **main shopping thoroughfare,** on Rama I Road, between Payathai and Ratchadamri roads, sports huge modern shopping complexes like the World Trade Center and Siam Square. Follow Rama I east and you'll run into Sukhumvit Road. While Sukhumvit isn't in the hub of the tourist area, it has a large concentration of expatriate residences, which makes for all sorts of good international restaurants, inexpensive shopping, and nightlife.

Get to know the Thai word *soi,* meaning lane. Main thoroughfares in the city have individual names, with many of the smaller side streets numbered in sequence for identification purposes. For example, Sukhumvit Soi 5 is the home of the Amari Boulevard Hotel, while Sukhumvit Soi 8, a few minutes' walk east and across the street, is where you'll find Le Banyan restaurant. Once upon a time each little soi had an individual name—yikes! Some are still known today, such as Nana Tua, Sukhumvit Soi 4, and its sister Nana Nua, Sukhumvit 3.

## VISITOR INFORMATION

The TAT's main office is at 4 Ratchadamnoen Nok Ave. (☎ **02/281-0422**), with another temporary office at 372 Bamrung Muang Rd. (☎ **02/226-0060**).

## GETTING THERE

Because most people enter Thailand via Bangkok, specific information on travel to Bangkok is covered in the country's "Getting There" section earlier in this chapter.

**BY AIR**    Most travelers arrive at Bangkok International Airport (Don Muang), which has domestic (☎ **02/535-2081**) and international (☎ **02/535-1111**) terminals. The airport has conveniences such as currency exchange offices, restaurants, post offices, hotel reservations counters, duty free shopping, and emergency medical service. **To get to central Bangkok,** limousines can be booked at the Arrival Hall starting from 650B (US$17.55). Just outside of the Arrivals Hall you'll be able to catch a cab for less: the metered fare plus 50B (US$1.35) airport pickup surcharge.

**BY TRAIN**    Passengers arriving by train will arrive at the Hua Lamphong Railway Station (☎ **02/223-7010** or **02/223-7020**) on Krung Kassem Road in central Bangkok. There never fails to be a line of taxis and tuk-tuks waiting outside.

**BY BUS**    If you're arriving from the southern parts of Thailand, or from Malaysia, you'll come into the Southern Bus Terminal(☎ **02/435-1199**) on Charan Sanitwong Road, across the river near the Bangkok Noi Station. From east coast destinations, you'll arrive at the Eastern Bus Terminal (☎ **02/390-1230**) on Sukhumvit Road opposite Soi 63 - Ekamai Road. From northern areas of the country you'll be dropped at the Northern Bus Terminal (☎ **02/272-5761**) on Phahonyothin Road near the Chatuchak Weekend Market. Metered taxis are either waiting at these terminals, or are easy enough to flag down.

## GETTING AROUND

Prepare yourself for traffic jams and pollution. Bangkok's notorious motor vehicle problem still remains a major issue, despite all sorts of ideas to lessen the load. The best one is the overhead rail system, which darkens major thoroughfares all over town but isn't expected to open until the year 2000, at least. While taxis are your best bet, try to get around by boat to some of the sights, such as the Grand Palace, Wat Po, and the National Museum, for peace of mind as well as the fascinating river scenery.

**BY TAXI**   Unless you venture to the outer residential neighborhoods, you're never at a loss for a taxi in Bangkok. Metered taxis can be flagged down from sidewalks, and will swing by hotels and shopping malls looking for fares. The meter starts at 35B (US95¢) for the first 2 kilometers, and increases by about 5B (US15¢) per kilometer thereafter (increases will depend on how fast traffic is moving). Basically, for most trips around town you won't spend more than 100B (US$2.70). Tipping is not expected, but many will fumble for change in search of one. While you may encounter cabbies who try to negotiate a fare up front, insist they use the meter. A useful tip: many drivers come from Isan in the northeast of the country, and have terrible English. It's always a good idea to have the concierge or desk clerk at your hotel write your destination for you in Thai before you venture out.

**BY TUK-TUK**   These are crazy little vehicles: three-wheeled scooters with an open cart, complete with flashing lights, metallic ornamentation, bright colors, and rumbling motors. Drivers will negotiate the fare before you set out; make sure you bargain. The fun part is that these guys are kamikazes, zipping through traffic as you grip the bars for support. The not so fun part is when you're stuck in traffic with exhaust fumes smoking all around you. Use them for short trips, and never during rush hour.

**BY CAR & DRIVER**   A great option for sightseeing in comfort is to hire a car and driver for a day or half-day. The larger hotels can arrange these for you, but a cheaper alternative is to contact a local travel agent or car rental company. Try **Avis** (☎ **800/331-1212** in the U.S., or **02/255-5300** in Bangkok, 2/12 Wireless Rd., Bangkok) or **Hertz** (☎ **800/654-3131** in the U.S., or **02/382-0293** in Bangkok, 420 Sukhumvit 71 Rd., Bangkok). **World Travel Service Ltd.,** 1053 Charoen Krung Rd., 10500 Bangkok (☎ **02/233-5900**), can also provide an English-speaking tour guide and can help arrange a suitable itinerary.

**BY BOAT**   Once upon a time Bangkok was a city of waterways, not unlike Venice. While today most *klongs,* or canals, have been paved over for motor vehicle traffic, some remain, and the mighty Chao Phraya River is still considered the lifeline of the city. Today, the most common form of transportation around the city is by taxi, but if you can take a trip somewhere via the river or a klong, you'll experience a wonderful side to the city; a tranquil ride through neighborhoods, past temples and the Grand Palace. It is highly recommended.

The **Chao Phraya Express Company** (☎ **02/222-5330**) will shuttle you between the many piers on either side of the river (almost all maps indicate the location of the piers), the most common ones being the piers at the Oriental Hotel, the River City shopping mall (Wat Muang Khae Ferry Pier), and the Grand Palace (Tha Chang Ferry Pier).

The cost depends on how far you go. It is usually between 5B and 10B (US15¢–US25¢). Look for the Chao Phraya Express logo on the side of the boat.

At the ferry piers you can also charter a private long-tail boat to take you through the klongs in Bangkok and on the Thonburi side of the river. For only 300B (US$8.11) an hour, the trip is incredibly fun, passing riverside houses and shops and seeing how the locals live.

**BY MOTORCYCLE TAXI**   If tuk-tuk drivers aren't kamikaze enough, you always have motorcycle taxis. Distinguished by their colored vests, these guys are great for getting you where you want to go in a jiffy, even if traffic is bumper to bumper. Just hop on the back. They'll weave you through, so be careful not to knock your knees on the sides of buses. At about 5B to 40B (US15¢–US$1.10) for a short trip, they're a bargain.

**BY BUS**   Bangkok has an extensive and dependable system of city buses. Maps are available at bookstores and magazine stands marked with the more popular routes. A trip on an air-conditioned bus will set you back only 6B (US15¢). Beware of pick-pockets and purse slashers if it gets crowded.

**ON FOOT**   Bangkok's heat, humidity, and air pollution prohibit walking long dis-tances. Besides, half the sidewalks seem to be in a state of perpetual ruin. If you're walking around a limited area, you'll be fine. Walking around Old Bangkok, the area near the Grand Palace, and many of the city's wats is not too difficult, as long as you start in the morning while it's still cool.

# Fast Facts: Bangkok

**Banks/Currency Exchange**   Banks with money changers and ATMs are easy to find in the areas around hotels and shopping malls. Bangkok Bank, Thai Farmers Bank, and Bank of Ayudhya are Thailand's three biggest banks, and they will accept debit and cash advance cards on the MasterCard/Cirrus and Visa/PLUS networks.

**Internet/E-mail**   Centrally located Internet cafes include Byte in @ Cup (4th Floor, Siam Discovery Center, ☎ 02/658-0433), Cyberia Internet Café (654–8 Sukhumvit Rd. at Soi 24, ☎ 02/259-3356), and The Café (9/25 Suriwongse Rd. next to Jim Thompson's Silk, ☎ 02/233-7794). Rates vary from 200B–300B (US$5.40–US$8.10) per hour.

**Police**   The Tourist Police can be reached at 1699.

**Post Office/Mail**   The General Post Office (☎ 02/233-1050) is on Charoen Krung Road between the Oriental Hotel and the Sheraton Royal Orchid Hotel.

**Telephone**   Bangkok's city code is 2.

## ACCOMMODATIONS

Because of the currency fluctuation in Thailand and the rest of the region, many luxury hotels have chosen to quote room rates in U.S. dollars.

### ALONG THE RIVER
**Very Expensive**

✪ **The Oriental, Bangkok.** 48 Oriental Ave. (on the riverfront off Charoen Krung Rd.), Bangkok 10500. In the U.S. and Canada ☎ **800/526-6566,** from Australia 800/653-328, from the U.K. 171/537-2988, or 02/236-0400 in Bangkok. Fax 02/236-1937. www.mandarin-oriental.com. 396 units. A/C MINIBAR TV TEL. US$260–$270 double; from US$320 suite. AE, DC, EURO, MC, V.

The Oriental has long been in the pantheon of the world's best hotels. Its history goes back to the 1860s when the original hotel, no longer standing, was established by two Danish sea captains soon after King Mongkut (Rama IV) reopened Siam to world trade. The hotel has withstood occupation by Japanese and American troops and played host to a long roster of Thai and international dignitaries and celebrities, most famously writers such as Joseph Conrad, Somerset Maugham, Noel Coward, Graham Greene, John Le Carré, and James Michener. Jim Thompson, of Thai silk trade fame, even served briefly as the hotel's proprietor. New buildings have been added—the first

# Bangkok Accommodations & Dining

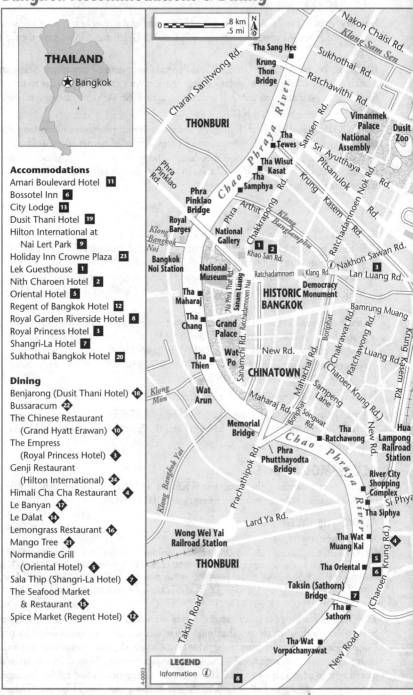

**Accommodations**
Amari Boulevard Hotel **11**
Bossotel Inn **6**
City Lodge **13**
Dusit Thani Hotel **19**
Hilton International at
  Nai Lert Park **9**
Holiday Inn Crowne Plaza **23**
Lek Guesthouse **1**
Nith Charoen Hotel **2**
Oriental Hotel **5**
Regent of Bangkok Hotel **12**
Royal Garden Riverside Hotel **8**
Royal Princess Hotel **3**
Shangri-La Hotel **7**
Sukhothai Bangkok Hotel **20**

**Dining**
Benjarong (Dusit Thani Hotel) **18**
Bussaracum **22**
The Chinese Restaurant
  (Grand Hyatt Erawan) **10**
The Empress
  (Royal Princess Hotel) **3**
Genji Restaurant
  (Hilton International) **24**
Himali Cha Cha Restaurant **4**
Le Banyan **17**
Le Dalat **14**
Lemongrass Restaurant **16**
Mango Tree **21**
Normandie Grill
  (Oriental Hotel) **5**
Sala Thip (Shangri-La Hotel) **7**
The Seafood Market
  & Restaurant **15**
Spice Market (Regent Hotel) **12**

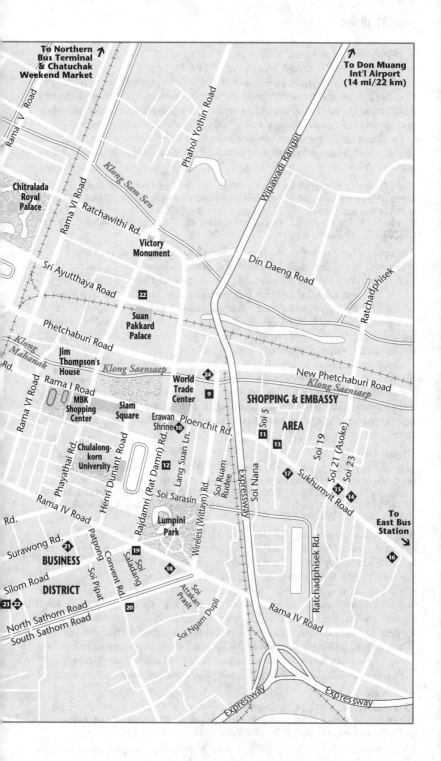

in 1876, the larger and more modern pair in 1958 and 1976—so that today it's more modern than colonial, though it retains considerable charm.

In addition to the usual amenities found at other top hotels, there is the Thai Cooking School; the dreamy Oriental spa with full massage and beauty treatments; the *Oriental Queen I* and *II* to run you up the Chao Phraya; the haute couture shopping arcade; and restaurants with a wide range of quality options.

Facilities include two small outdoor swimming pools, fitness center, tennis and squash courts, beauty salon, and tour boat for daily excursions to Ayutthaya and the Summer Palace.

**The Shangri-La Hotel.** 89 Soi Wat Suan Phlu, New Rd. (adjacent to Sathorn Bridge, with access off Charoen Krung Rd. at south end of Silom Rd.), Bangkok 10500. ☎ **800/942-5050** from the U.S. and Canada, 800/222448 from Australia, 0800/442179 from New Zealand, or 02/236-7777. Fax 02/236-8579. www.shangri-la.com. 868 units. A/C MINIBAR TV TEL. US$200–$280 double; suites from US$340. AE, DC, MC, V.

The opulent but thoroughly modern Shangri-La, on the banks of the Chao Phraya, boasts acres of polished marble, a jungle of tropical plants and flowers, and two towers with breathtaking views of the river. All guest rooms have a view of the river, are decorated with lush carpeting and teak furniture, and have marble baths. The views are terrific from the higher floor deluxe rooms, and most have either a balcony or a small sitting room, making them closer to junior suites and a particularly good value for on-the-river upscale accommodations. For such an enormous place, the level of service and facilities is surprisingly good.

The super-luxurious Krung Thep Wing adds another 17-story, river-view tower to the grounds, as well as a riverside swimming pool and a restaurant and breakfast lounge. Guests register in their spacious rooms, surrounded by colorful Thai paintings and glistening Thai silk. Amenities that include two outdoor swimming pools, a fitness center, tennis courts, and squash courts make this city hotel more like a getaway spot.

### Expensive

**Marriott Royal Garden Riverside Hotel.** 257/1-3 Charoen Nakhorn Rd.(on the Thonburi (east) side of the Chao Phraya River, north of the Krung Thep Bridge, 15 min. by boat from River City), Thonburi, Bangkok 10600. In the U.S. and Canada ☎ **800/344-1212,** from the U.K. 0800/951-000, or 02/476-0021. Fax 02/476-1120. 420 units. A/C MINIBAR TV TEL. US$125–US$145 double; US$175–US$225 suite. AE, DC, MC, V.

This luxuriously sprawling complex on the banks of the Chao Phraya is across the river and a few miles downstream from the heart of Bangkok. As you board the hotel's long-tail boat and make the short trip down river, you will feel the crazy city release you from its grip. Once at the hotel, you'll think you're at a resort, with the three wings of the hotel surrounding a large landscaped pool area with lily ponds and fountains, and a wonderful spa for a uniquely calming Bangkok experience. Marriott Royal Garden also has tennis courts and a shopping arcade. Rooms are comfortable and modern, tastefully decorated in light tones and fully equipped with all the amenities. When it's time for dinner, there are Trader Vic's Polynesian Restaurant and a Benihana Japanese-American Steakhouse, to name just a couple of your dining options.

Boats go to and from River City shopping mall every half-hour.

### Moderate

✪ **Bossotel Inn.** 55/12-14 Soi Charoen Krung 42/1 (off Charoen Krung Rd., on Soi 42, toward the Shangri-La Hotel), Bangrak, Bangkok 10500. ☎ **02/630-6120.** Fax 02/237-3225. 46 units. A/C MINIBAR TV TEL. 800B (US$21.60) double. AE, MC, V.

It's not on the water and there isn't a view to speak of, but the spiffy, renovated new wing of the Bossotel, in particular, warrants consideration.

# Go halfway around the world.

# Sound like you're halfway around the block.

**Global connection with the AT&T Network**

## AT&T
### direct service

Calling home from far away? With the world's most powerful network, **AT&T Direct** Service connects you clear and fast, plus gives you the option of an English-speaking operator. All you need is your AT&T Calling Card or credit card.* Sounds good, especially from the middle of nowhere. FOR A LIST OF **AT&T ACCESS NUMBERS**, TAKE THE ATTACHED WALLET GUIDE.

# For Travelers who want more than the Official Line

Macmillan Publishing USA

## Also Available:

- The Unofficial Guide to Branson
- The Unofficial Guide to California with Kids
- The Unofficial Guide to Chicago
- The Unofficial Guide to Cruises
- The Unofficial Disney Companion
- The Unofficial Guide to Disneyland
- The Unofficial Guide to the Great Smoky & Blue Ridge Region
- The Unofficial Guide to Miami & the Keys
- Mini-Mickey: The Pocket-Sized Unofficial Guide to Walt Disney World
- The Unofficial Guide to New Orleans
- The Unofficial Guide to New York City
- The Unofficial Guide to San Francisco
- The Unofficial Guide to Skiing in the West
- The Unofficial Guide to Washington, D.C.

Many of the guests are either long-term visitors or repeat offenders, because, quite frankly, Bossotel delivers large, clean rooms in a fantastic location without draining your wallet. While rooms are very basic, the furniture and decor don't clash (believe me, that's impressive for a budget hotel in these parts). While the lobby coffee shop stops room delivery service at around 10:30pm, the continental and local food has improved greatly over the past year, as has the service. They also have HBO and CNN in the guest rooms, as well as laundry service and a small business center. Check out the traditional Thai massage on the 2nd floor—hotel guests can get a very good 2-hour massage for only 240B (US$6.40). Unbelievable.

## HISTORIC BANGKOK

### Expensive

✪ **Royal Princess Hotel.** 269 Larn Luang Rd.(east of Wat Saket), Bangkok 10100. ☎ **02/281-3088.** Fax 02/280-1314. 170 units. A/C MINIBAR TV TEL. 3,600B (US$97.30) double; 11,000B (US$297.30) suite. AE, DC, MC, V.

This first-class hotel near the Grand Palace in the Ratanakosin Island area more than lives up to the high standards of the Thai-owned Dusit Thani Hotels and Resorts family. Completed in 1989, its proximity to government offices brings a steady flow of official visitors, but it's also great for travelers interested in the sights of old Bangkok.

Public spaces are wall-to-wall marble, and bustle with activity, yet the scale is intimate. Guest rooms are very tastefully furnished and bright. While higher-priced deluxe rooms have balconies overlooking the tropically landscaped pool, the superior rooms of the same style look out over the neighborhood. It's a 10-minute taxi ride to either the Grand Palace or Vimanmek Palace, and though the area lacks a diversity of dining, the authentic flavor of this old neighborhood more than compensates.

### Inexpensive

Bangkok has a small area that is well-known and well-used by budget travelers and backpackers. **Khao San Road,** a 10- to 15-minute walk from the National Museum, is lined on both sides with guesthouses, cafes, Internet cafes, and souvenir stands. The place crawls with travelers, so you'll probably find a more authentic Bangkok experience elsewhere. Still, it's cheap and convenient. Reservations are rarely taken seriously. Just show up and shop around—front office folks are glad to show you a room or two. Good ones to try are the dependable **Lek Guesthouse,** 125–127 Khao San Rd. (☎ **02/282-4927**), at 200B (US$5.40) per night; and the quiet and clean **Nith Charoen Hotel,** 183 Khao San Rd. (☎ **02/281-5201**), at 300B (US$8.10) per night. Neither place accepts credit cards.

## THE BUSINESS DISTRICT

### Very Expensive

**The Dusit Thani.** Rama IV Rd. (at corner of Silom and Rama IV rds. opposite Lumpini Park), Bangkok 10500. ☎ **02/236-0450.** Fax 02/236-6400. www.dusit.com. 520 units. A/C MINIBAR TV TEL. 5,000B–6,300B (US$200–US$252) double; 9,200B (US$368) Landmark Deluxe. Extra bed 1,200B (US$48). AE, DC, MC, V.

"The Dusit" continues to be a favorite meeting place for locals, the expatriate community, and visiting celebrities, as after 28 years of operation, it retains its reputation as one of Bangkok's premier hotels. The lobby, while grand, is not the same marble and mirror disaster as some of the newer hotels in Asia. Splashing lobby fountains, exotic flower displays, and a poolside waterfall cascading through dense foliage make it a welcome retreat at the end of a day's sightseeing. Unfortunately, the old gal could stand some renovations; some of the guest rooms look a little too well worn. Superior rooms in the Executive Wing are newly redone (1996), and far fresher.

The small outdoor swimming pool is in the center of the hotel—maybe a little cramped and exposed. While the fitness center is also small, workout equipment is state of the art, and equipped with sauna, steam bath and massage.

**The Sukhothai.** 13/3 Sathorn Tai Rd.(south of Lumpini Park, near intersection of Rama IV and Wireless rds.), Bangkok 10120. In the U.S. and Canada ☎ **800/637-7200,** from Australia 1800/655-147, from New Zealand 0800/442-519, from the U.K. 0800/962-115, or 02/287-0222. Fax 02/287-4980. 222 units. A/C MINIBAR TV TEL. US$220–US$264 double; US$320–US$1,800 suite. AE, DC, MC, V.

The sleek new Sukhothai, a property of the prestigious Beaufort Group from Singapore, brings unexpected luxury to a noisy, busy locale better known for the neighboring low-budget YWCA and YMCA hostels. Inside the Sukhothai's five white pavilions, visitors find a welcome, if studied, serenity. Designers have successfully combined contemporary minimalist values with traditional Thai beauty, dressing broad, colonnaded public spaces with antique sculptures and celadon ceramics; and highlighting geometric black-tiled lotus ponds with redbrick stupas. The scheme is equally successful in the guest rooms, where generous usage of rich Thai silks, teak panels, live plants, and small antique treasures warm the modern decor. Though elegant design is the Sukhothai's most obvious attribute, guests commend its excellent service and assured sense of privacy.

The outdoor swimming pool is one of the largest in Bangkok, but surprisingly, there's not much to write home about, as the surroundings are scant on landscaping. There's a small, up-to-date fitness center with sauna, spa and massage, two squash courts, one tennis court, and a Guerlain beauty salon.

### Expensive

✪ **Hilton International Bangkok at Nai Lert Park.** 2 Wireless Rd. (between Ploenchit Rd. and New Phetchaburi Rd.), Bangkok 10330. In the U.S. ☎ **800/HILTONS,** from Australia 800/222-255, from New Zealand 0800/448-002, or 02/253-0123. Fax 02/253-6509. 343 units. A/C MINIBAR TV TEL. US$180–US$193 double; US$366–US$1,166 suite. AE, DC, MC, V.

Set in lushly landscaped Nai Lert Park, near the British and American embassies, this tropical paradise is something of a mixed blessing—you will sleep far from the madding crowds, but you may find the taxi ride to the river or tourist sights a minor nuisance (though the adventurous will ride the convenient klong boat to the Grand Palace Area). However, after a long day of business or sightseeing, returning to the peaceful tranquillity of the Hilton has the very comfortable feeling of returning home. The airy atrium lobby, with its classic teak pavilion and open garden views, ranks as one of the great public spaces in Bangkok. And the gorgeous free form pool in landscaped gardens is a total resort experience. The spacious guest rooms all have bougainvillea-draped balconies; the most preferred (and expensive) rooms overlook the pool. Facilities include a fitness center with tennis and squash courts and a high-end shopping arcade.

**Holiday Inn Crowne Plaza.** 981 Silom Rd. (1 block northeast of Charoen Krung Rd.), Bangkok 10500. In the U.S. and Canada ☎ **800/465-4329,** from Australia 800/553-888, from New Zealand 0800/442-888, from the U.K. 0800/897121, or 02/238-4300. Fax 02/238-5289. 726 rooms. A/C MINIBAR TV TEL. 5,300B–6,500B (US$143–US$175) double; 8,000B–40,000B (US$216–US$1,081) suite. AE, DC, MC, V.

Crowne Plaza, Holiday Inn's upmarket chain of hotels, provides high quality service and a level of luxury unexpected by those familiar with standard Holiday Inn accommodations in the U.S. This is the top choice for families traveling to Bangkok; while there is an 500B (US$13.50) charge for an extra bed, there's no charge for children under 19 years of age accompanying parents. Their very comfortable guest rooms are lovely, with masculine striped fabrics offsetting floral prints for a soft and homelike appeal. Rooms in the Plaza Tower are an especially good value, though smaller than those in the Crowne Tower, with high ceilings that give a spacious feel and oversized porthole windows, framed by heavy drapery, overlooking the city. The location is very convenient, near the expressway, a short walk from the river (and the Shangri-La and Oriental), in the middle of the gem-trade district. The huge lobby seating areas are always humming with travelers who are either resting from a day's adventure, or waiting to begin a new one. There's a small fitness center equipped with a sauna. Outdoor tennis courts are lighted for evening play. The outdoor swimming pool is under a sun shield, with a separate deck for sun worshippers.

## THE SHOPPING/EMBASSY AREA
### Very Expensive
**The Regent.** 155 Ratchadamri Rd. (south of Rama I Rd.), Bangkok 10330. In the U.S. ☎ **800/545-4000,** from Australia 800/022-800, from New Zealand 0800/440-800, from the U.K. 0800/282-245, or 02/251-6127. Fax 02/253-9195. 400 units. A/C MINIBAR TV TEL. US$240 double; US$320–US$620 suite. AE, DC, MC, V.

The Regent is a modern palace. From your first entrance into the massive lobby you'll be captivated by the grand staircase, huge and gorgeous Thai murals and gold sun bursts on the vaulted ceiling. The impeccable service begins at the front desk, where guests are greeted, then escorted to their room to complete their check-in and enjoy the waiting fruit basket and box of chocolates. An air of luxury pervades each room, put forth by the traditional style Thai murals, handsome color schemes, and a plush carpeted dressing area off the tiled bath. The more expensive rooms have a view of the Royal Bangkok Sport Club and race track. Cabana rooms and suites face the large pool and terrace area which is filled with palms and lotus pools. Coming soon: The Regent has big plans for in-room Internet service through the television. The Regent has one of the finest hotel spas in Bangkok. The secluded Clinique La Prairie guides guests through individually tailored beauty programs and treatments.

### Expensive
**Amari Boulevard Hotel.** 2 Soi 5, Sukhumvit Rd. (north of Sukhumvit Rd., on Soi 5), Bangkok 10110. ☎ **02/255-2930.** Fax 02/255-2950. A/C MINIBAR TV TEL. US$150 double; US$2,700 suite. AE, DC, EURO, MC, V.

The Sukhumvit Road area doesn't provide the best street access to the sights in old Bangkok, but who needs street access when there's a perfectly good klong nearby? All you need do is hop a water taxi and take a fascinating trip through Bangkok's old "back alleys" to the Chao Phraya. Besides, many people choose to stay in the Sukhumvit Road area to be close to major shopping malls and plentiful food and entertainment options. Amari Boulevard offers two kinds of rooms. The newer Krung Thep Wing has spacious rooms with terrific city views, while the original wing has attractive balconied rooms that are a better value. When rooms are discounted 40% to 60% in the low season, this hotel is a very good value. Facilities include a rooftop swimming pool and a well-equipped fitness center.

### Inexpensive
**City Lodge.** Soi 9, Sukhumvit Rd. (corner of Sukhumvit and Soi 9), Bangkok 10110. ☎ **02/253-7705.** Fax 02/255-4667. 28 units. A/C MINIBAR TV TEL. 1,000B (US$27) double; 1,500B (US$40)suite. MC, V.

Budget watchers will appreciate the two small, spiffy City Lodges. Both the newer lodge on Soi 9, and its nearby cousin, the older, 35-room City Lodge on Soi 19 (☎ **02/254-4783,** fax 02/255-7340), provide clean, compact rooms with simple, modern decor. Each has a pleasant coffee shop (facing the bustle on Sukhumvit Road at Soi 9; serving Italian fare on Soi 19), a small but friendly staff, and privileges at the rooftop swimming pool at the more deluxe Amari Boulevard Hotel on Soi 5. All three belong to the Amari Hotels and Resorts Group. No frills here, but still a lot of comfort for your money.

# DINING

Chances are your hotel will have at least one or two options for in-house dining—some hotels boasting four or five different options. In fact, some of Bangkok's best dining is in its hotels, and I've included some of the better choices in this chapter. Usually the more authentic dining experience is out around town—from noodle hawkers on the sidewalks to traditional Thai dishes served in beautiful local settings. Bangkok also has some fine international dining establishments with guest chefs from Europe and America.

## ALONG THE RIVER

### Very Expensive

**Normandie Grill.** The Oriental, 48 Oriental Ave. ☎ **02/236-0400.** Reservations required. Main courses 600B–1,600B (US$16.40–US$43.25); set dinner 3,500B (US$94.60). AE, DC, MC, V. Daily noon–2pm and 7–11pm. Off Charoen Krung Rd., overlooking the river. FRENCH.

The ultra-elegant Normandie, atop the renowned Oriental Hotel, with panoramic views of Thonburi and the Chao Phraya River, is the apex in formal dining in Thailand, both in price and quality. The room glistens in gold and silver, from place settings to chandeliers and the warm tones of golden silks. Some of the highest rated master chefs from France have made guest appearances at Normandie, adding their own unique touches to the menu. The set menu begins with pan-fried goose liver, followed with a pan-fried turbot with potato and leek in a parsley sauce. The beef filet main course, in a red wine sauce, is a stroll through heaven. The set also includes cheese, coffee, and a sinful dessert. Reservations are a must, as the dining room is relatively small, and a jacket and tie are required.

### Moderate

**Sala Thip.** The Shangri-La Hotel, 89 Soi Wat Suan Plu (overlooking Chao Phraya River, near Sathorn Bridge). ☎ **02/236-7777.** Reservations recommended. Main courses 200B–450B (US$5.40–US$12.15). AE, DC, MC, V. Mon–Sat 6–10:30pm; high-season Sun buffet dinner 6–10:30pm. THAI.

Sala Thip, on the river terrace of the Shangri-La Hotel, is arguably Bangkok's most romantic Thai restaurant. Classical music and traditional cuisine are superbly presented under one of two aged, carved teak pavilions perched over a lotus pond or at outdoor tables overlooking the river. (For those who crave a less humid environment, grab a table in one of the air-conditioned dining rooms.) Although the food may not inspire aficionados, it is skillfully prepared and nicely served. Set menus help the uninitiated with ordering. They include numerous courses such as Thai spring rolls, pomelo salad with chicken, spicy seafood soup, snapper with chili sauce, and your choice of Thai curries.

### Inexpensive

**Himali Cha Cha Restaurant.** 1229/11 Charoen Krung Rd. (on a side street off New Rd., corner of Surawong). ☎ **02/235-1569.** Main courses 75B–250B (US$2.05–US$6.75). AE, DC, MC, V. Daily 11am–3:30pm and 6–11:30pm. INDIAN.

Cha Cha, Himali's graying chef and proprietor, was on Lord Mountbatten's staff in India. He then cooked for the diplomatic corps in Laos before coming to Bangkok to open this restaurant in 1980. You'll find him in attendance at the cash register nightly. House specialties include a mutton barbecue, chicken tikka, and chicken masala. The

Indian thali plates are great, especially for lunch. Two people can taste this sampling of seven dishes with bread and rice for 475B ($19) for the vegetarian thali and 625B ($25) with meat.

## HISTORIC DISTRICT NEAR THE GRAND PALACE
### Expensive

✪ **The Empress.** Royal Princess Hotel, 269 Larn Luang Rd. ☎ **02/281-3088.** Reservations recommended. Main courses 120B–1,600B (US$3.25–US$43.25). AE, DC, MC, V. Daily 11:30am–2:30pm and 6–10pm. West of Krung Kasem Rd. CHINESE.

This elegant hotel restaurant specializes in dim sum and gourmet Cantonese cuisine, without MSG. The high-style mint and jade green padded banquettes are jammed at lunch with government officials, upscale tourists, and local businesspeople, all savoring a selection from the 20 or so dim sum choices. The fresh steamed, fried, and boiled morsels (mostly seafood) provide an inexpensive midday break. Cantonese main course specialties include a tart abalone salad, whole steamed fish, and bird's-nest soup. Even the lesser priced fare is delicious and artfully presented. Try the tender tea leaf smoked duck, steamed bean curd stuffed with minced prawns, and sautéed seasonal vegetables with crabmeat sauce. And how can you resist a dish called Escaping Eunuch? This soup is packed with chunks of sea cucumber, abalone, shark's fin, dried scallops, black chicken, and mushrooms—delicious.

## BUSINESS DISTRICT
### Expensive

**Benjarong.** The Dusit Thani, Rama IV Rd. (corner of Silom Rd.) ☎ **02/236-0450,** ext. 2699. Reservations recommended. Main courses 180B–600B (US$4.85–US$16.20). AE, MC, V. Daily 11:30am–2pm and 6:30–10pm. Closed for lunch Saturday and Sunday. THAI.

You'll want to get dressed up for this elegant dining room, named for the exquisite five-color pottery once reserved exclusively for the use of royalty. Benjarong prides itself on offering the five basic flavors of Thai cuisine (salty, bitter, hot, sweet, and sour) in traditional "royal" dishes. While their à la carte menu is extensive, the most popular dishes are the sweet red curry crab claws and the exotic grilled fish with black beans in banana leaves.

✪ **Spice Market.** The Regent, 155 Ratchadamri Rd. (south of Rama I Rd.). ☎ **02/ 251-6127.** Reservations recommended. Main courses 150B–600B (US$4.05–$16.20). AE, DC, MC, V. Daily 11:30am–2:30pm and 6:30–11pm. THAI.

Many contend that the Spice Market is the city's finest pure Thai restaurant. The theatrical decor reflects the name: burlap spice sacks, ceramic pots, and glass jars set in dark-wood cabinets around the dining area playfully re-create the mercantile feel of a traditional Thai shop house. The food is artfully presented, authentically spiced, and extraordinarily delicious. House specialties include nam prik ong, crispy rice cakes with minced pork dip; nua phad bai kapraow, fried beef with chili and fresh basil; and siew ngap, red curry with roasted duck in coconut milk. The menu's "chili rating" guarantees that spices are tempered to your palate.

### Moderate

**Bussaracum.** 139 Sathiwon Building, Pan Rd. off Silom Rd. ☎ **02/226-6312.** Reservations recommended. Main courses 110B–280B (US$2.95–US$7.55). AE, DC, MC, V. Daily 11:30am–2pm and 5:30–10:30pm. THAI.

This is a traditional favorite for Thais hosting foreigners because of the fine food and the classical royal decor.

At this tranquil, teak-paneled sanctuary with linen tablecloths, the menu changes monthly. Their rhoom (minced pork and shrimp in egg-net wrapping) was the favorite appetizer of King Rama II. The saengwa (cold shrimp salad served in a squash gourd) is an unusual dish that complements their noteworthy tom yam soup and gaeng kari gai hang (special chicken curry). Allow the helpful staff to make suggestions, and finish the meal with bauloy sarm see, a dessert of taro and pumpkin in coconut milk.

### Inexpensive

**The Mango Tree.** 37 Soi Anumarn Ratchathon (off west end of Surawong Rd., across from Tawana Ramada Hotel). ☎ **02/236-2820.** Reservations recommended. Main courses 190B–350B (US$5.15–US$9.45). AE, DC, MC, V. Daily 10am–2pm and 6–10pm. THAI.

Reader John D. Connelly of Chicago brought this excellent classical Thai restaurant to our attention. A lovely 80-year-old Siamese house with its own tropical garden, it offers a quiet retreat from the hectic business district. Live traditional music and classical Thai decorative touches fill the house with charm, and the attentive staff serves well-prepared dishes from all regions of the country. I am particularly fond of their green chicken curry, which is mild, and their crispy spring rolls.

## THE SHOPPING/EMBASSY AREA

### Expensive

**The Chinese Restaurant.** Grand Hyatt Erawan, 494 Ratchadamri Rd. (corner of Ploenchit Rd.). ☎ **02/254-1234.** Reservations recommended. Main courses 150B–900B (US$4.05–US$24.30). AE, DC, MC, V. Daily 11:30am–2:30pm and 6:30–11pm. CHINESE.

Style and substance are harmoniously blended in this ultra-elegant gourmet Cantonese restaurant. We recommend their exceptionally light dim sum, including some imaginative vegetable and seafood combinations wrapped in seaweed, instead of the typical rice flour pastry. Their shark's fin, the highlight of any respectable Chinese restaurant, is very good. Overall, a delightful gastronomic experience in a high-style Shanghai deco-inspired dining room.

✪ **Genji Restaurant.** Hilton International, 2 Wireless Rd. (in Nai Lert Park, north of Ploenchit Rd.) ☎ **02/253-0123.** Reservations recommended; required for a tatami room. Main courses 100B–1,200B (US$2.70–US$32.45); set dinners 850B–2,000B (US$22.95–US$54.05). AE, DC, MC, V. Daily noon–2:30pm and 6:30–10:30pm. JAPANESE.

One of the best Japanese restaurants in Bangkok is located in a great hotel that caters to a large Japanese clientele. If you go to Genji for lunch you'll likely discover a room full of Japanese businesspeople, a good sign for sushi eaters. Lunch served from the set menu is not only delicious but also an excellent value. At dinner there are both set menus and an enormous selection of à la carte dishes such as excellent sushi, sashimi (1,800B or US$48.65 for fish imported from Japan, and 350B or US$9.45 for the local selections), and makizushi, as well as rich hot-pot concoctions, a variety of fish and seafood, and Kobe beef.

✪ **Le Banyan.** 59 Soi 8, Sukhumvit Rd. (1 block south of Sukhumvit Rd.). ☎ **02/252-5556.** Fax 02/253-4560. Reservations recommended. Main courses 450B–600B (US$12.15–US$16.20). AE, MC, V. Mon–Sat 6:30–10pm. FRENCH.

In the same league as the top hotel French restaurants, this local favorite serves fine classic French cuisine with Thai touches. A spreading banyan tree on the edge of the gardenlike grounds, on a quiet Sukhumvit soi, inspires the name. Dining rooms are warmly furnished, with sisal matting and white clapboard walls adorned with Thai carvings, old photos, and prints of early Bangkok.

The most popular house special is the sensational pressed duck, its juices mixed with goose liver, shallots, and port. Also excellent are the foie gras and filet of beef. All are served with seasonal vegetables and can be enjoyed with a reasonably priced wine.

## Moderate

**Lemongrass Restaurant.** 5/1 Sukhumvit Soi 24. ☎ **02/258-8637.** Reservations required for dinner. Main courses 120B–550B (US$3.25–US$14.85); set menus 500B–1,500B (US$13.50–US$40.55). AE, DC, MC, V. Daily 11am–2pm and 6–11pm. THAI.

Nouvelle Thai cuisine, somewhat tailored to the Western tastes of its predominantly expatriate customers, is the specialty of this pleasant restaurant in an old Thai mansion handsomely converted and furnished with antiques. There are occasional complaints about small portions and slow service, but most of the waiters speak some English and will help guide you through the menu, which contains a full spectrum of Thai cuisine, including fiery southern dishes.

We recommend the kai yang pak panang (chicken grilled on a stick with a rich sauce), tom yang kung (a spicy sweet-and-sour prawn soup with ginger shoots), chili-stuffed pork, Burmese-style pork curry, and of course the tender and juicy lemongrass chicken.

**The Seafood Market & Restaurant.** 388 Sukhumvit Rd.(corner of Soi 21). ☎ **02/258-0218.** Reservations recommended for large parties. Main courses approximately 250B–650B (US$6.75–US$17.55). AE, DC, MC, V. Daily 11am–midnight. SEAFOOD.

The Seafood Restaurant is a cross between the consummate tourist restaurant and an American-style supermarket: high ceilings, long, cool fluorescent lighting, shopping carts, and checkout lines. Their three-story neon marquee proudly boasts, "If it swims, we have it!" Below it, the open-air kitchen appears reckless and wild, outdoing even Benihana. Inside, you walk to the rear to choose your fish, fresh vegetables or fruit (from a vast array, all sold by the pound), and to select from the imported wine and liquor choices. Food consultants (not waiters) will tell you how your fish selection is best cooked (either grilled, steamed, or fried, with or without Thai seasoning). Though its spices are distinctly Thai, the Seafood Restaurant will please those who prefer fresh foods and don't mind paying a premium for them.

## Inexpensive

✪ **Le Dalat.** 47/1 Soi 23, Sukhumvit Rd. (about a half mile north of Sukhumvit Rd.) ☎ **02/258-4192.** Reservations recommended at dinner. Main courses 120B–160B (US$3.25–US$4.30). AE, DC, MC, V. Daily 11am–2:30pm and 6–10pm. VIETNAMESE/FRENCH.

We appreciate Le Dalat both for its fine food and its lovely garden setting. The restaurant is casual, understatedly elegant, with excellent food prepared by Vietnamese-trained Thai chefs. We recommend the bi guon (spring rolls with herbs and pork), chao tom (pounded shrimp laced with ground sugarcane in a basket of fresh noodles), and cha ra (fresh filet of grilled fish). In nice weather, you'll enjoy dining in the gracefully landscaped outdoor garden.

## ATTRACTIONS

When Rama I established Bangkok as the new capital city in the 1780s, he built a new palace and royal temple on the banks of the Chao Phraya River. The city sprang up around the palace and spread outward from this point as population and wealth grew. Today this area contains most of Bangkok's major historical sites, including a great number of **wats**, or Buddhist temples, that were built during the last 200 years. The city's attractions may seem like wat after wat, but they are each very unique in character, employing different architectural elements, cultural influences, and histories of their own. If you're short on time, the most interesting and easily accessible wats to catch are Wat Phra Kaeo, the royal wat that houses the Emerald Buddha at the Grand Palace, and Wat Po, home of the reclining Buddha.

# Bangkok Attractions

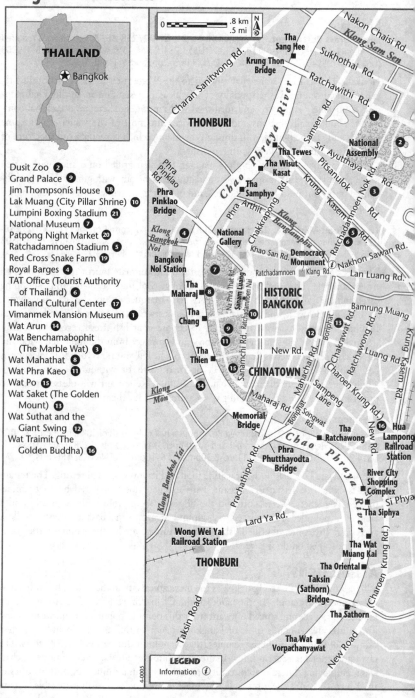

THAILAND

★ Bangkok

Dusit Zoo ②
Grand Palace ⑨
Jim Thompson's House ⑱
Lak Muang (City Pillar Shrine) ⑩
Lumpini Boxing Stadium ㉑
National Museum ⑦
Patpong Night Market ⑳
Ratchadamnoen Stadium ⑤
Red Cross Snake Farm ⑲
Royal Barges ④
TAT Office (Tourist Authority
   of Thailand) ⑥
Thailand Cultural Center ⑰
Vimanmek Mansion Museum ①
Wat Arun ⑭
Wat Benchamabophit
   (The Marble Wat) ③
Wat Mahathat ⑧
Wat Phra Kaeo ⑪
Wat Po ⑮
Wat Saket (The Golden
   Mount) ⑬
Wat Suthat and the
   Giant Swing ⑫
Wat Traimit (The
   Golden Buddha) ⑯

0 ⸺ .8 km
     .5 mi

N

THONBURI

Nakon Chaisi Rd.
Klong Sam Sen
Sukhothai Rd.
Ratchawithi Rd.
Samsen Rd.
Sri Ayutthaya Rd.
Pitsanulok Rd.
Krung Kasem Rd.
Ratchadamnoen Nok Rd.

Tha Sang Hee
Krung Thon Bridge

National Assembly ①
Dusit Zoo ②
Wat Benchamabophit ③

Chao Phraya River

Charan Sanitwong Rd.

Phra Pinklao Rd.

Tha Tewes
Tha Wisut Kasat
Tha Samphya

Phra Pinklao Bridge

Phra Arthit
Chakkrapong Rd.
Klong Banglamphu

National Gallery

Khao San Rd.
Ratchadamnoen Klang Rd.
Nakhon Sawan Rd.
Lan Luang Rd.

Democracy Monument ⑥

Klong Bangkok Noi

Royal Barges ④

Bangkok Noi Station

National Museum ⑦

Tha Maharaj

Wat Mahathat ⑧

Sanam Luang
Na Phra That Rd.
Ratchadamnoen Nai

HISTORIC BANGKOK

Bamrung Muang

Lak Muang ⑩

Tha Chang

Grand Palace ⑨
Wat Phra Kaeo ⑪

Wat Suthat ⑫
Wat Saket ⑬

Boriphat
Chakrawat Rd.
Ratchawong Rd.
Luang Rd

Krung Kasem Rd.

Tha Thien

New Rd.

Wat Po ⑮

Sanamchi Rd.
Mahachai Rd.

CHINATOWN

Charoen Krung Rd.

Klong Mon

Wat Arun ⑭

Maharaj Rd.

Sampeng Lane
Songwat Rd.
Boriphat

Tha Ratchawong

Wat Traimit ⑯

Hua Lampong Railroad Station

Klong Bangkok Yai

Memorial Bridge

Chao Phraya River

Phra Phutthayodta Bridge

Prachathipok Rd.

River City Shopping Complex

Si Phya
Tha Siphya

Lard Ya Rd.

Wong Wei Yai Railroad Station

THONBURI

Tha Wat Muang Kai
Tha Oriental

Taksin (Sathorn) Bridge

Taksin Road

Tha Sathorn

(Charoen Krung Rd.)

New Road

Tha Wat Vorpachanyawat

LEGEND
Information ⓘ

4-0005

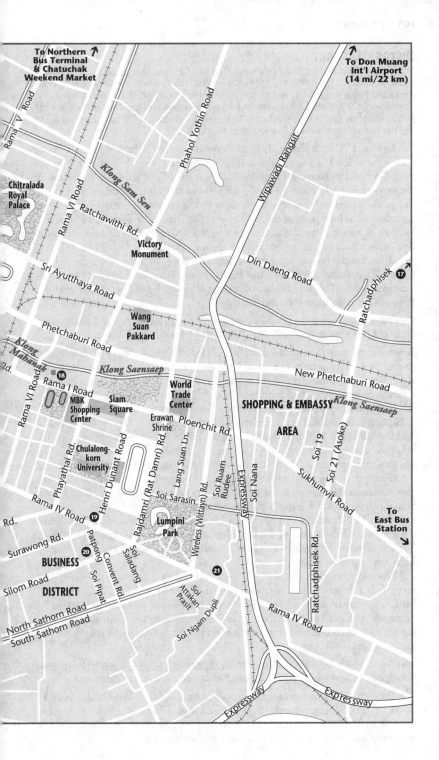

To Northern
Bus Terminal
& Chatuchak
Weekend Market

To Don Muang
Int'l Airport
(14 mi/22 km)

Rama V Road

Phahol Yothin Road

Wipawadi Rangsit

Chitralada
Royal
Palace

Rama VI Road

Klong Sam Sen

Ratchawithi Rd.

Victory
Monument

Din Daeng Road

Ratchadphisek

17

Sri Ayutthaya Road

Phetchaburi Road

Wang
Suan
Pakkard

Klong
Mahanak

Rd.

Klong Saensep

New Phetchaburi Road

Rama VI Road

Rama I Road

18

MBK
Shopping
Center

Siam
Square

World
Trade
Center

SHOPPING & EMBASSY

Klong Saensep

Erawan
Shrine

Ploenchit Rd.

AREA

Soi 19

Soi 21 (Asoke)

Phayathai Rd.

Chulalong-
korn
University

Henri Dunant Road

Rajdamri (Rat Damri) Rd.

Lang Suan Ln.

Soi Ruam
Rudee

Expressway

Soi Nana

Sukhumvit Road

Rama IV Road

19

Soi Sarasin

Lumpini
Park

Wireless (Wittayu) Rd.

21

To
East Bus
Station

Surawong Rd.

Patpong

20

Soi
Saladang

Convent Rd.

Ratchadphisek Rd.

BUSINESS

Silom Road

DISTRICT

Soi Pipat

Soi
Attakan
Prasit

North Sathorn Road

South Sathorn Road

Soi Ngam Dupli

Rama IV Road

Expressway

Expressway

## HISTORIC DISTRICT

**The Grand Palace.** Near the river on Na Phra Lan Rd. near Sanam Luang. ☎ **02/222-0094.** Admission 125B (US$3.40). Price includes Wat Phra Kaeo and the Coin Pavilion inside the Grand Palace grounds, as well as admission to the Vimanmek Palace (near the National Assembly). Daily 8:30am–11:30am and 1–3:30pm; most individual buildings are closed to the public except on special days proclaimed by the king. Take the Chao Phraya Express Boat to the Tha Chang Pier, then walk first east, then south.

The Grand Palace is almost always the first stop on any sightseeing agenda. Rama I built the oldest buildings in the square-mile complex when he moved the capital from Thonburi to Bangkok in the 1780s. It was the official residence and offices of the kings until 1946, when the royal family moved to Chitralada Palace. These days, the palace is used only for royal ceremonies and as the royal guesthouse for visiting dignitaries. The focal point of the compound is the Chakri Maha Prasad, an intriguing mixture of Victorian architecture topped with a Thai temple-style roof that today houses the ashes of royal family members. To the left, the Amarinda Vinichai Hall is the venue for the highest royal ceremonies, including coronations. To the right of Chakri Maha Prasad stands the Dusit Hall, a perfect example of Thai architecture in the highest order. The Grand Palace compound also has a Royal Decorations and Coin Pavilion—its main draw is air-conditioning.

**Wat Phra Kaeo.** In the Grand Palace complex. ☎ **02/222-0094.** Admission included in the Grand Palace fee of 125B (US$3.40). Daily 8:30–11:30am and 1–3:30pm.

When Rama I built the Grand Palace, he included this temple, the royal temple most revered by the Thai people. The famed "emerald" Buddha, a 2-foot tall northern Thai style image made from green jasper, sits atop a towering gold altar. The statue dons a different costume for each of the three seasons in Thailand, changed by the king himself, who climbs up to the image as it can be lowered for no one.

Historians believe that artists created the statue in the 14th century. The emerald Buddha hid inside a plaster Buddha image until 1434, when movers accidentally dropped it, setting it free. The king at Chiang Mai demanded it be brought to his city, but three attempts failed. Each time the elephant transporting the image stopped at the same spot in Lampang, so the king gave in to the will of the spirits and built a *chedi* (a sacred monument) for it there. 32 years later, King Tiloka of Chiang Mai brought the image to Chiang Mai. The emerald Buddha stayed in the Wat Chedi Luang until 1552, when a later King from Luang Prabang carted it off to Laos. When the king moved the capital of Laos to Vientiane, the image followed him. Rama I finally recaptured the statue in a successful invasion of Laos, and placed it in Wat Phra Kaeo, where it remains today.

The wat compound is a small city in itself, including a library with stunning Ayutthaya style mother-of-pearl inlay doors, a reliquary like a golden bell–shaped Sri Lankan style chedi, a *wihaan* (hall) bejeweled with chipped porcelain mosaics, and a miniature model of Angkor Wat, the sprawling temple complex at the ancient Khmer capital, with its corn-shaped chedis. Murals on the surrounding walls tell the story of the *Ramayana*.

**Wat Po.** Maharat Rd., near the river. ☎ **02/222-0933.** Admission 20B (US55¢). Daily 8am–5pm; massages offered until 6pm. About a half mile south of the Grand Palace.

Wat Po (Wat Phra Chetuphon), the Temple of the Reclining Buddha, was built by Rama I in the 16th century and is the oldest and largest Buddhist temple in Bangkok. Considered Thailand's first public university, the temple's many monuments and artworks explain principles of religion, science, and literature.

Most people go straight to the enormous Reclining Buddha in the northern section. It's more than 140 feet (46m) long and 50 feet (16m) high, and was built during the mid-19th-century reign of Rama III. The statue is brick, covered with layers of plaster and always-flaking gold leaf; the feet are inlaid with mother-of-pearl illustrations of 108 auspicious *laksanas* ("characteristics") of the Buddha. Behind the Buddha, a line of 108 bronze bowls, each representing a previous incarnation of the Lord, awaits visitors to drop coins (acquired nearby for a 20B donation) for luck.

Outside, the grounds contain 91 *chedis* (stupas or sacred mounds), four *wihaans* (halls), and a *bot* (the central shrine in a Buddhist temple). The Traditional Medical Practitioners Association Center teaches traditional Thai massage and medicine. Stop in for a massage (only 200B, US$5.41, per hour), or ask about their 7- to 10-day massage courses.

**Wat Mahathat (Temple of the Great Relic).** Na Phra That Rd. ☎ **02/221-5999.** Free admission. Daily 9am–5pm. Na Prathat Rd., near Sanam Luang Park, between the Grand Palace and the National Museum.

Built to house a relic of the Buddha, Wat Mahathat is one of Bangkok's oldest shrines and the headquarters for Thailand's largest monastic order. Also the home of the Mahachulalongkorn Buddhist University, the most important center for the study of Buddhism and meditation, Wat Mahathat offers some programs in English.

Adjacent to it, between Maharat Road and the river, is the city's biggest amulet market, where a fantastic array of religious amulets, charms, talismans, and traditional medicine is sold. Each Sunday hundreds of worshippers squat on the ground studying tiny images of the Buddha with magnifying glasses, hoping to find one that will bring good fortune or ward off evil.

**The National Museum.** Na Phra That Rd. ☎ **02/224-1333.** Admission 20B (US55¢). Wed–Sun 9am–4pm. Free English-language tours: Buddhism Culture, Wed 9:30am; art, culture, religion, Thurs 9:30am; call the museum or check a newspaper for more details and current schedule. About a half mile north of Grand Palace.

The National Museum, a short (15-min.) walk north of the Grand Palace and the Temple of the Emerald Buddha, is the country's central treasury of art and archaeology. It was originally the palace that the brother of Rama I built as part of the Grand Palace complex in 1782. Rama V converted the palace into a museum in 1884. Today it is the largest museum in Southeast Asia.

To see the entire collection, plan on at least 3 hours. If you're rushed, go straight to the Red House, a traditional 18th-century Thai building that was originally the living quarters of Princess Sri Sudarak, sister of King Rama I. It's furnished in period style, with many pieces originally owned by the princess.

Another essential stop is the Phuttaisawan (Buddhaisawan) Chapel, built in 1787 to house the Phra Phut Sihing, one of Thailand's most revered Buddha images, brought here from its original home in Chiang Mai. The main building of the royal palace contains gold jewelry, some from the royal collections, and Thai ceramics, including many pieces in the five-color bencharong style. The Old Transportation Room contains ivory carvings, elephant chairs, and royal palanquins. There are also rooms of royal emblems and insignia, stone carvings, wood carvings, costumes, textiles, musical instruments, and Buddhist religious artifacts. Fine art and sculpture are found in the newer galleries at the rear of the museum compound.

**Lak Muang (City Pillar Shrine).** Sanam Chai Rd. Free admission. Mon–Fri 8:30am–4:30pm. About a quarter mile northeast of the Grand Palace on the southeast corner of Sanam Luang.

The "City Pillar," northeast of the Grand Palace complex, is said to be inhabited by the spirit that protects Bangkok. Rama I erected a wooden pillar—probably following the Hindu custom of installing a *lingam* (phallus), a symbol of Shiva—to mark the heart of his new city. Locals come in supplication and with offerings for the guardian deity.

**Vimanmek Mansion Museum.** 193/2 Ratchavitee Rd., Dusit Palace grounds. ☎ 02/281-8166. Admission 50B (US$1.35); free if you already have a 125B ticket to the Grand Palace and Wat Phra Kaeo. Daily 9:30am–4pm. Opposite the Dusit Zoo, north of the National Assembly Building.

Built in 1901 by King Chulalongkorn the Great (Rama V) as the Celestial Residence, this large, beautiful, golden teakwood mansion was restored in 1982 for Bangkok's bicentennial and reopened by Queen Sirikit as a private museum with a collection of the royal family's memorabilia. An intriguing and informative hour-long tour takes you through a series of apartments and rooms (81 in all) in what is said to be the largest teak building in the world. The original Abhisek Dusit Throne Hall houses a display of Thai handicrafts, and nine other buildings north of the mansion display photographs, clocks, fabrics, royal carriages, and other regalia. Classical Thai and folk dance and martial art demonstrations are given daily at 10:30am and 2pm.

**Wat Benchamabophit (the Marble Wat).** Si Ayutthaya Rd. ☎ 02/281-2501. Admission 10B (US25¢). Daily 8am–5pm. South of the Assembly Building near Chitralada Palace.

Wat Benchamabophit, which tourists call the Marble Wat because of the white Carrara marble of which it's constructed, is an early 20th-century temple designed by Prince Narai, the half brother of Rama V. It's the most modern and one of the most beautiful of Bangkok's royal wats. Many smaller buildings nearby reflect a melding of European materials and designs with traditional Thai religious architecture. Walk inside the compound, beyond the main bot, to view the many Buddhas that represent various regional styles. During the early mornings, monks chant in the main chapel, sometimes humming so intensely that it seems as if the temple is going to lift off.

**Wat Saket (The Golden Mount).** Ratchadamnoen Klang and Boripihat rds. Entrance to wat is free; admission to the chedi, open 9am–5pm, 10B (US25¢).

Wat Saket is easily recognized by its golden chedi atop a fortresslike hill near the pier for Bangkok's east-west klong ferry. The wat was restored by King Rama I, and 30,000 bodies were brought here during a plague in the reign of Rama II. Rama V built the golden chedi to house a relic of Buddha, said to be from India or Nepal, given to him by the British. The concrete walls were added during World War II to keep the structure from collapsing.

The Golden Mount, a short but breathtaking climb that's best made in the morning, is most interesting for its vista of old Rattanakosin and the rooftops of Bangkok. Every late October to mid-November (for 9 days around the full moon), Wat Sakhet hosts Bangkok's most important temple fair, when the Golden Mount is wrapped with red cloth and a carnival erupts around it, with food and trinket stalls, theatrical performances, freak shows, animal circuses, and other monkey business.

**Wat Suthat and The Giant Swing.** Sao Chingcha Sq. ☎ 02/222-0280. Admission 10B (US25¢). Daily 9am–5pm. Near the intersection of Bamrung Muang Rd. and Ti Thong Rd.

The temple is among the oldest and largest in Bangkok, and Somerset Maugham declared its roofline the most beautiful. It was begun by Rama I and finished by Rama III; Rama II carved the panels for the wihaan's doors. It houses a beautiful 14th-century Phra Buddha Shakyamuni that was brought from Sukhothai, and the ashes of King Rama VIII, Ananda Mahidol, brother of the current king, are contained in its base. The wall paintings for which it is known were done during Rama III's reign.

The huge teak arch—also carved by Rama II—in front is all that remains of an orig-inal giant swing, which was used until 1932 to celebrate and thank Shiva for a boun-tiful rice harvest and to ask for the god's blessing on the next. The minister of rice, accompanied by hundreds of Brahman court astrologers, would lead a parade around the city walls to the temple precinct. Teams of men would ride the swing on arcs as high as 82 feet in the air, trying to grab a bag of silver coins with their teeth. Due to injuries and deaths, the dangerous swing ceremony has been discontinued.

**Dusit Zoo.** Rama V and Ratchawithi rds. ☎ **02/281-2000.** Admission 20B (US55¢). Daily 8am–6pm.

The Dusit (also called Khao Din) Zoo is in a lovely park between the Chitralada Royal Palace and the National Assembly. Besides admiring the many indigenous Asian ani-mals (including royal white elephants), you can rent paddleboats on the pond. Chil-dren can ride the elephants while their parents rest and snack at one of the zoo's cafes under broad shade trees.

**Red Cross Snake Farm (Pasteur Institute).** 1871 Rama IV Rd. (☎ **02/252-0161,** ext. 40). Admission 70B (US$1.90). Daily 8:30am–3:30pm. At the corner of Rama IV Rd. and Henry Dunant.

Established in 1923 by the Red Cross to provide inoculations against tropical diseases (which it still does), the institute has since risen in popularity because of its impressive collection of live poisonous snakes. There are slide shows as well as snake-handling and venom-milking demonstrations weekdays at 10:30am and 2pm and on weekends and holidays at 10:30am.

## SHOPPING/EMBASSY AREA

**Jim Thompson's House.** Soi Kasemsan 2. ☎ **02/215-0122.** Admission 100B (US$2.70). Mon–Sat 9am–5pm. On a small soi off Rama I Rd., opposite the National Stadium.

Jim Thompson was a New York architect who served in the OSS (Office of Strategic Services, now the CIA) in Thailand during World War II and afterward settled in Bangkok. Almost single-handedly he revived Thailand's silk industry, employing Thai Muslims as skilled silk weavers and building up a thriving industry. After expanding his sales to international markets, Mr. Thompson mysteriously disappeared in 1967 while vacationing in the Cameron Highlands in Malaysia. Despite extensive investi-gation, his disappearance has never been resolved.

His Thai house is composed of six linked teak and theng (harder than teak) wood houses from central Thailand that were rebuilt according to Thai architectural princi-ples, but with Western additions (such as a staircase and window screens). In some rooms the floor is made of Italian marble, but the wall panels are pegged teak. Volun-teers guide you through rooms filled with Thompson's splendid collection of Khmer sculpture, Chinese porcelain, Burmese carving (especially a 17th-century teak Buddha), and antique Thai scroll paintings.

## BUSINESS DISTRICT

**Wat Traimit (The Golden Buddha).** Traimit Rd. Admission 10B (US25¢). Daily 9am–5pm. West of Hua Lampong Station, just west of the intersection of Krung Kasem and Rama IV rds.; walk southwest on Traimit Rd. and look for a school on the right with a playground. The wat is up a flight of stairs overlooking the school.

Wat Traimit, which is thought to date from the 13th century, would hardly rate a second glance if not for its astonishing Buddha, which is nearly 10 feet high, weighs over 5 tons, and is believed to be cast of solid gold during the Sukhothai period. It was discovered by accident in 1957 when an old stucco Buddha was being moved from a storeroom by a crane, which dropped it and shattered the plaster shell, revealing the

---

**Travel Tip: Pick Up a Market Map**

I recommend you purchase Nancy Chandler's Map of Bangkok, alias "The Market Map and Much More." Ms. Chandler is Thailand's most famous shopper, and her colorful artistic skills make Bangkok's most important markets jump off the page.

---

shining gold beneath. This powerful image has such a bright, reflective surface that its edges seem to disappear, and it is truly dazzling.

## THONBURI

**Wat Arun (Temple of Dawn).** West bank of the Chao Phraya, opposite Tha Thien Pier. ☎ 02/465-5640. Admission 10B (US25¢). Daily 8am–5:30pm. Take a water taxi from Tha Tien Pier (near Wat Po) or cross the Phra Pinklao Bridge and follow the river south on Arun Amarin Rd.

The 260-foot-high (86m), Khmer-inspired tower rises majestically from the banks of the Chao Phraya, across from Wat Po. This religious complex served as the royal chapel during King Taksin's reign (1809–24), when Thonburi was the capital of Thailand.

The original tower was only 50 feet (16m) high, but was expanded during the rule of Rama III (1824–51) to its current height. The exterior is decorated with flower and decorative motifs made of colorful ceramic shards donated to the monastery by local people, at the request of Rama III. At the base of the complex are Chinese stone statues, once used as ballast in trading ships, gifts from Chinese merchants. Wat Arun is a sight to behold shimmering in the sunrise, but truly the best time to visit is in late afternoon for the sunset.

**The Royal Barges.** On Klong Bangkok Noi, north of the Phra Pinklao Bridge, Thonburi. ☎ 02/424-0004. Admission 10B (US25¢). Daily 8:30am–4:30pm. Take a taxi over the Phra Pinklao Bridge or take a ferry to Tha Rot Fai ("Railway Landing"), walk west along the street parallel to and between the tracks and the klong until you come to a bridge over the klong, cross the bridge and follow the wooden walkway.

If you've hired a long-tail boat on the Chao Phraya, stop by this unique museum housing the royal barges. These elaborately decorated sailing vessels, the largest over 50 yards long and rowed by up to 60 men, are used by the royal family on state occasions or for high religious ceremonies. The king's barge, the *Suphanahong,* is decorated with red-and-gold carvings of fearsome mythological beasts, like the Garuda or the dragon on the bow and stern.

## SHOPPING

Don't even think about leaving Bangkok with money left over. With a huge assortment of **Thai silks,** tailors on every block, classical artwork and antiques, hill-tribe handicrafts, fine silver, beautiful gemstones, porcelain, and reptile skin products, shopping is your destiny in Thailand. I haven't even started describing all the **street bazaars** where you can find cheap batik clothing, knock-off watches, jeans and designer shirts, and all sorts of souvenirs. A friend of mine likes to pack a "goodie bag" when she comes to Thailand, an empty bag that she fills throughout her stay. Inevitably it's overflowing by day three. Whatever your travel budget, set aside a large chunk of it for the many items you just won't resist.

The main shopping mall drag is Rama I Road between Ratchadamri and Phyathai Roads, where you'll find the **World Trade Center,** with department stores Isetan and Zen Central; **Gaysorn Plaza** for haute couture; **Siam Center** for trendy styles; and **Mah Boon Krong,** a huge local mall filled with bargains. **Siam Square,** also on Rama

I Road just across from Siam Center, sprawls through alleys filled with food, small vendors with bargains, hip boutiques, and Bangkok's Hard Rock Café. Just north of here on Phetburi Road is **Phanthip Plaza,** Bangkok's computer mall. For antiques go to **River City,** off Charoen Krung Road overlooking the Chao Phraya River, which is just packed with reputable dealers selling everything Thai, Khmer, Chinese, and otherwise.

When you're ready for the real Bangkok shopping experience, head on down to **Chinatown. Thieves' Market,** at Chakkarat and Charoen Krung roads, is a maze of new, and some old, finds. Off Pahurat Road is the **Pahurat Cloth Market,** with fabrics from all over the region. **The Old Siam** shopping mall on Triphet Road has some great handicraft places. For a longer shopping trip, there's **Sampeng Lane,** stretching for blocks and blocks; this narrow alley is lined with wholesalers with everything from paper supplies and beads and lace to batik sarongs and religious supplies.

Everyone will tell you the ultimate shopping experience is at the **Chatuchak Weekend Market**—and they are so right! Chatuchak is crazy shopping. Located about 30 minutes north of central Bangkok near the airport, it's block after block of small stalls packed with clothing, leather goods, accessories, cheap jewelry, textiles, handicrafts, souvenirs, antiques, household items, tools and mechanical wares, pottery, live pets (from fish to fighting cocks), plants, fresh and dried foods, and other sundries. Start early, at around 9am, and give yourself at least the whole morning. Food vendors and drink stands will help you rest and cool off.

**Night markets** are also a thrill in Bangkok. The most famous one is at **Patpong,** which goes up at around 6 or 7pm nightly and carries on till around 3am or so. It promises all sorts of souvenirs, crafts, and knock-off deals, but make sure you bargain well. Also, if you're in the **Sukhumvit** area, there's an afternoon and evening bazaar every day beginning at Sukhumvit Soi 1 and running down farther than you can walk.

Special areas with high concentrations of shops are along **Silom Road,** where you'll find many many **tailors** and **gem dealers;** and along Charoen Krung Road between the Shangri-La and Royal Orchid Sheraton Hotels for **antiques and art dealers.**

## BANGKOK AFTER DARK

Bangkok is probably the only city in the world that gets hotter after the sun goes down. You can cool off with a drink at a beer pub or cocktail lounge, or heat things up with a night at the discos. You needn't be too worried about your safety in most of the city, as Bangkok is fairly safe for tourists, save for the occasional pickpocket. Taxis and tuk-tuks are on hand through the night and early morning.

For local entertainment, nothing beats **Thai boxing.** Each night of the week, young men pummel each other with whatever part of their bodies they can—feet, knees, shoulders—you name it, while a small percussion and woodwind band whistle out traditional melodies. Almost as exciting are the mad gamblers in the house, who display an intricate manner of hand signals during each bout. On Mondays, Wednesdays, Thursdays, and Sundays, events are staged at **Ratchadamnoen Stadium** (Ratchadamnoen Nok Avenue, ☎ 02/281-4205). On Tuesdays, Fridays, and Saturdays go to **Lumphini Stadium** (Rama IV Road, ☎ 02/251-4303). Although the program starts at 6pm, don't arrive until 9pm or so; they save the big names for last. Tickets are 1,000B (US$27.05) ringside seating, 440B (US$11.90) standing, and 220B (US$5.95) for standing in the cage at the back.

### THE BAR & CLUB SCENE

If a nice cocktail is in order, the **Shangri-La Hotel Lobby Lounge** (89 Soi Wat Suan Phlu, New Rd., ☎ 02/236-7777) has live performances Monday through Saturday of light pop and soft sounds. In the Sukhumvit Road area, **The Landmark** Hotel

---

**Travel Tip: Where to Find Nightlife Listings**

Keep your eyes peeled for the hip Bangkok *METRO Magazine* and *Time Out Bangkok,* which carry great listings on restaurants, pubs, and local happenings around town.

---

Piano Bar (138 Sukhumvit Rd., ☎ 02/254-0404) has live piano favorites daily except Sundays. Another swell lobby bar is at **The Dusit Thani** (Rama VI Road, ☎ 02/236-0450) for live jazz and light pop daily, including Sundays. For the best cigar lounge in town, **Private Cellar** (Pavilion Y, Royal City Avenue, New Phetchburi Road, ☎ 02/203-0926) is tops in terms of selection, class, and price.

There are quite a few bars around town that cater to a wide array of tastes. The quintessential Irish pub in town is **Delaney's** (Convent Road, Silom, ☎ 02/266-7160), famous for Irish eats, televised sports, and Guinness draught. **O'Reilly's** (corner of Thaniya Street and Silom Road, ☎ 02/632-7515), a newer place on the scene, serves up drinks in a relaxed, easy-to-talk-in Irish pub style. For micro-brewery fans, **Paulaner Brauhaus** (Sukhumvit Soi 24, ☎ 02/261-0238), Bangkok's original, brews its own light and dark libations.

For a little music with your fun, the **Hard Rock Café** (Siam Square Soi 1, ☎ 02/251-0792) has live rock and pop (and great burgers). **Riva's** (Sheraton Grande Sukhumvit Hotel, ☎ 02/653-0333) has excellent live performances of funky beats that'll make your hips sway. Those who prefer something a little jazzier might want to check out the Oriental Hotel's **Bamboo Bar** (Oriental Lane off Charoen Krung Road, ☎ 02/236-1937).

If music makes you move, the best discos are **Concept CM²** (Novotel Siam, Siam Square Soi 6, ☎ 02/255-6888), **Narcissus** (112 Sukhumvit Soi 23, ☎ 02/258-2549), and **Taurus** (Sukhumvit Soi 26 beside Four Wings Hotel, ☎ 02/261-3991). All are trendy, happening places with hip music and even hipper clientele. Dress to impress.

**Cabaret shows** are quite a hit with tourists in Thailand, and you'll find shows in almost all the major tourist areas. Choreographed lip-sync numbers are oftentimes hilarious, and the costumes and sets would turn RuPaul's pancake green. In Bangkok, the two biggest are **Calypso** (Basement, Asia Hotel, Phayathai Road, ☎ 02/261-6355) and **Mambo** (Washington Theater, Sukhumvit Soi 22, ☎ 02/259-5128).

## THE SEX SHOWS

Last but not least, the nightlife Bangkok is most famous for: the racy go-go bars and sex shows. They are centered around three areas in the city, Patpong, Nana Complex, and Soi Cowboy. The largest and most famous of the three, **Patpong,** (located between Silom and Surawong roads), boasts four streets of clubs with discos and bars, eateries, go-go clubs, gay bars, karaoke clubs, massage parlors, seedy hotels, and the famous sex shows, which to be honest are more bizarre than sexy. There's also a huge outdoor night bazaar. Patpong is full of touts trying to lure you into their sex show, but be careful. Some places charge steep covers and all sorts of additional unexplained charges may appear on your check, and you may not be allowed to leave without paying. Remember those **Tourist Police** (☎ 1699), who have a police box on Surawong Road, if you have problems. To prevent being ripped off, go to either **Fire Cat** (for shows) or **King's Castle** (fun for guessing which ladies are in fact girls, or *katoey* boy-girls). While seedy, both are reputable. **Nana Complex** (Sukhumvit Soi 21 and Soi 23), is a virtual mini-mall-a-go-go, with three stories of go-go bars to choose from.

Finally, **Soi Cowboy** (running parallel to Sukhumvit Soi, between Soi and Soi 23), originally made famous during the Vietnam War, has fallen into sleepier times since Nana and Patpong took over. Clubs here are small and a little more laid back these days.

All of the clubs will allow patrons to bring a dancer out of the club after paying a bar penalty. While prostitution in Thailand is technically illegal, the law is almost never enforced. Furthermore, it is *recommended* for safety reasons that gentlemen who are going to seek paid female companionship request the company of bar dancers. For special safety precautions regarding the sex industry in Bangkok, see the "The Thai Sex Industry & AIDS" under "Health Concerns."

## DAY TRIPS FROM BANGKOK

When planning your travel itinerary, set aside a couple days for trips just outside of Bangkok. An early morning jaunt to the **floating market,** a maze of waterways teeming with waterfront shops and long-tail boat commerce, is usually tops on any sightseeing list. The famous **River Kwai** day trip can be touching for those who remember World War II and are moved by historical accounts of the war. **Ayutthaya,** the Kingdom of Siam's second capital (before Bangkok), is a historical site that's commonly visited as a day trip, combined with a visit to the Summer Palace at Bang Pa-in.

The most common way to get to any of these sites is to book a day trip through a **tour operator.** World Travel (☎ 02/233-5900) is the most well-established and reputable operator, and can put together a tour to accommodate anything you want to do.

### FLOATING MARKET AT DAMNOEN

The Floating Market at Damnoen Saduak, Ratchaburi, is about 2 hours south of Bangkok. At a real floating market, food vendors sell their goods from small boats to local folk in other boats or in klong-side homes. There are some floating markets in Bangkok that have become so commercialized and touristy, they're beyond the point of interest. Some will tout this market as more "authentic" than that in Bangkok. It's certainly as precise a duplicate as you could imagine; it's fine for photographers, and you'll enjoy it as long as you resist the urge to buy anything. Goods are sold at this pressurized souvenir supermarket at up to five or six times their normal Bangkok prices!

There are many tour operators that take groups down. **World Travel** (☎ 02/233-5900) offers daily trips to the floating market combined with Kanchanaburi (see below). The full-day tour costs 1,320B (US$35.70) per person.

To do it on your own, take a ferry from the River City Pier (*Pearl of Siam,* ☎ 02/292-1649) between the hours of 7am and 10am (boats leave every 30 minutes) at a cost of around 300B (US$8.10) per person.

### KANCHANABURI

Kanchanaburi, 79 miles (128km) west of Bangkok, stands at the junction where two tributaries—the Kwai Noi and the Kwai Yai—meet to form the Mae Khlong River. For most visitors, the town is indelibly marked by its famous bridge spanning the Kwai River. A visit to this site is, for some, an emotional pilgrimage to honor the suffering and heroism of those who perished (and the few who survived) under their brutal Japanese overseers. As moving as the story is, many find the actual site a good bit less inspiring and would recommend it only for those who are really passionate about this chapter of World War II history.

The city, near the bridge, is surrounded by some spectacular scenery, particularly to the north and west of town. Mountains rise in misty haze along the river; waterfalls abound as the jungle stretches away. You'll drive past fields of tapioca, tobacco, sugarcane, tamarind, mango, papaya, banana, and palm trees.

Before going to see the bridge itself, stop at the **JEATH** (Japanese, English, American, Australian, Thai, and Holland—the nationalities that built the railway) **War Museum,** open daily 8:30am–5pm; admission 25B (US70¢), adjacent to Wat Chaichumpol in town. Constructed of thatch and bamboo to resemble prisoners' barracks, it provides a sobering display of the suffering of the war prisoners who built the bridge and the railroad. The museum is filled with photographs, personal mementos, and newspaper accounts of the POW's lives, recording the tortures the Japanese inflicted upon them—malnutrition, disease, and despair.

You can also stop by the **Kanchanaburi War Cemetery,** on Saeng Chuto Road in town, near the railroad station, where every stone tells a story of a lost life. Many of the 6,982 graves are those of young men who died in their 20s and 30s far from home. Another cemetery, a few miles out of town, contains close to 2,000 graves. Another 1,750 POWs lie buried at the **Chon-Kai War Cemetery,** once the site of a POW camp, and now a tranquil place on the banks of the Kwai Noi about 1.2 miles (2km) south of town.

The **Bridge over the River Kwai** is about 2½ miles (4½ km) north of the town center. The steel bridge was brought from Java and assembled by POWs. It was bombed several times and rebuilt after the war, but the curved spans are the originals. You can walk across it, looking toward the mountains of Myanmar as you go. For some it's a nerve-racking experience, as rickety railroad ties laid on an open grid allow you to see the water below. If you visit during the River Kwai Bridge Week (usually the end of November or the beginning of December), you can also see a sound and light spectacle.

The Japanese originally calculated that it would take 5 to 6 years to complete the 264-mile (425-km) track, but they reduced that figure to 18 months for the POWs. It was finished in a year. Some 16,000 Allied prisoners, mostly British, Australian, and American, died building it. Even more brutal was the fate of another 100,000 Burmese, Chinese, Indians, Indonesians, Malays, and Thais who were also killed under forced labor and buried in unmarked graves where they dropped.

A day trip to Kanchanburi is usually combined with a stop at the Damnoen Floating Market. To arrange a trip, call World Travel (see above), who offer excellent daily trips for 1,320B (US$35.70) per person.

## AYUTTHAYA & BANG PA-IN
### Ayutthaya

Ayutthaya, 47 miles (76km) northwest of Bangkok, is one of Thailand's great historical highlights. From its establishment in 1350 by King U-Thong (Ramathibodi I) until its fall to the Burmese in 1767, Ayutthaya was Thailand's capital and home to 33 kings of various dynasties. At its zenith and until the mid-18th century, Ayutthaya was a vast, majestic city with three palaces and 400 splendid temples on an island threaded with 35 miles of canals—a city that mightily impressed European visitors. Traces of two major foreign settlements can still be seen. Religious objects, coins, porcelain, clay pipes, and skeletons of the Portuguese (who arrived in 1511) are displayed at the settlement's memorial building.

There is something hauntingly sad about Ayutthaya. In 1767, after a 15-month siege, it was destroyed by the Burmese; today every temple testifies to the hatred that drives humans to rampant and wanton destruction. Here stands a row of headless

# Ayutthaya Attractions

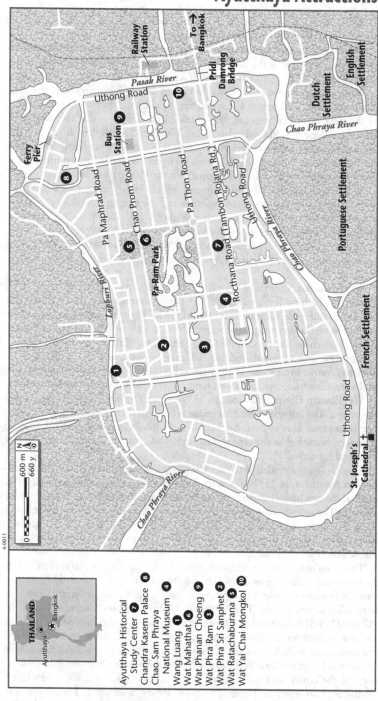

N
0        600 m
0        660 y

4-0011

Railway Station

To → Bangkok

Pasak River

Pridi Damrong Bridge

Uthong Road

**10**

**9**

Bus Station

Dutch Settlement

English Settlement

Chao Phraya River

Ferry Pier

**8**

Pa Maphrad Road

Chao Prom Road

Pa Thon Road

Lopburi River

Pa-Ram Park

**5**

**6**

Rocthana Road (Tambon Rojana Rd.)

**7**

Uthong Road

Chao Phraya River

Portuguese Settlement

**4**

**2**

**3**

**1**

Uthong Road

French Settlement

Chao Phraya River

St. Joseph's Cathedral

THAILAND

Ayutthaya ● ★ Bangkok

Ayutthaya Historical Study Center **7**
Chandra Kasem Palace **8**
Chao Sam Phraya National Museum **4**
Wang Luang **1**
Wat Mahathat **6**
Wat Phanan Choeng **9**
Wat Phra Ram **3**
Wat Phra Sri Sanphet **2**
Wat Ratachaburana **5**
Wat Yai Chai Mongkol **10**

169

Buddhas, there a head lies caught in the roots of a tree. Some temples are still being rescued from the jungle, and more are undergoing careful excavation.

The fascinating architecture of Ayutthaya mixes many elements: Khmer influence in the design of many of the ancient wats; buildings reminiscent of the Sukhothai era; and similarities to Bangkok's Wat Arun, built to emulate the grand Ayutthaya style.

**Wang Luang,** the old royal palace, located in the northwestern end of the ancient city overlooking the Lopburi River, was destroyed by the Burmese. The foundations of the three main buildings can still be made out, and the size of the compound is impressive. Near the old royal palace stands **Wat Phra Sri Sanphet,** originally built in 1448 as the king's private chapel (the equivalent of the Wat Phra Kaeo, Temple of the Emerald Buddha, in Bangkok) and renovated in the 16th and 17th centuries. The 55-foot bronze standing Buddha was originally cast in 1500 during the reign of the ninth king, Ramathipodi, and covered with gold. In 1767, the Burmese tried to melt the gold, causing a fire that destroyed the image and the temple; the one you see today is a replica. Nearby are three Sri Lankan-style chedis, built during the 15th century to enshrine the ashes of three Ayutthaya kings.

To the east of the royal palace, the prang of **Wat Phra Ram** soars into the sky. Originally built in 1369 by King Ramesuen (second king of Ayutthaya), the complex is in ruins.

**Wat Mahathat,** in front of the palace, dates from 1384, during the reign of King Borom Ratchathirat I. Across stands **Wat Ratachaburana,** built in 1424; its prangs and chedis still retain some of their original stucco. In the two crypts, excavators have found bronze Buddha images and votive tablets, as well as golden objects and jewelry, many of which are displayed in the Chao Sam Phraya Museum (see below). There are also murals, rows of seated Buddhas, standing disciples, and *Jataka* (tales from the Buddha's former lives) scenes in the four niches, as well as a frieze of heavenly beings and some Chinese scenes. Both wats remain severely damaged despite restoration.

**Wat Phanan Choeng** was built in 1324, 26 years before King U-Thong founded Ayutthaya. The impressive Buddha image is 62 feet (20.6m) high and more than 45 feet (15m) from knee to knee. Adjacent to it is a small Chinese temple, a memorial to a princess betrothed to the king of Thailand, who committed suicide when he failed to attend her arrival.

King U-Thong founded **Wat Yai Chai Mongkol,** a few minutes' walk southeast of ancient Ayutthaya, in 1357. (Cross the Pridi Damrong Bridge and the railroad, turn right at the first major intersection, pass through the commercial area, and find it on the left.) The recently restored white reclining Buddha near the entrance was built by King Naresuan. The massive pagoda was also built by King Naresuan to celebrate his defeat of the Burmese at Suphanburi in 1593 by killing their crown prince in a single-handed combat on elephants.

There's no better place to submerge yourself in history than in this ancient city, and its three main exhibit centers, two of which are branches of the national museum, will provide excellent overviews of Ayutthaya, and in-depth examination of Siamese history, religion, and culture. **The Ayutthaya Historical Study Center** (Rochana Rd.; ☎ 035/245-5124; admission 100B/US$2.70; daily 9am–4:30pm) serves as an educational resource for students, scholars, and the public. The center presents displays of the ancient city including models of the palace and the port, as well as a fine selection of historical objects. **Chao Sam Phraya National Museum** (Rochana Rd., 1½ blocks west of the center near the junction of Sri Sanphet Rd.; admission 30B/US80¢; Wed–Sun 9am–4pm) is Thailand's second largest museum. It houses impressive antique bronze Buddha images, carved panels, religious objects, and other local artifacts. **Chandra Kasem Palace** (northeast part of old city; admission 30B/US80¢; Wed–Sun 9am–4pm), the other branch of the National Museum, was built in 1577 by King Maha Thamaraja (the 17th Ayutthaya monarch) for his son, who became King Naresuan. It was destroyed but later restored by King Mongkut, who stayed there whenever he visited Ayutthaya. On display are exquisite gold artifacts, jewelry, carvings, Buddhas, and domestic and religious objects from the 13th through 17th centuries.

## Bang Pa-In

Only 38 miles (61km) north of Bangkok, this royal palace is usually combined with Ayutthaya in a 1-day tour. Much of it isn't open to the public, but it's still a nice stroll through gardens to admire the architecture. The 17th-century temple and palace were originally built by Ayutthaya's King Prasat Thong. They were abandoned when Bangkok became the capital until King Mongkut began returning occasionally in the mid-19th century. His son King Chulalongkorn constructed the **royal palace** as it is seen today. Admission to the palace is 40B (US$1.10). It's open daily 8:30am to 3pm.

The Bang Pa-In architectural style mixes Thai with strong European influences. The building in the middle of the lake is the **Phra Thinang Aisawan Thippa-At,** an excellent example of classic Thai style. Behind it, in gaudy Versailles style, are the former **king's apartments,** which today serve as a hall for state ceremonies. The **Phra Thinang Wehat Chamrun,** also noteworthy, is a Chinese-style building (open to the public) where court members usually lived during the rainy and cool seasons. Also worth visiting is the **Phra Thinang Withun Thatsuna,** an observatory on a small island that affords a fine view of the countryside.

If you have time, cross the river on what seems like the oldest cable car in the world to the Gothic-style **Wat Nivet Thamaprawat** (built during King Chulalongkorn's reign), south of the palace grounds.

## Getting to Ayutthaya & Bang Pa-In

The most popular way to see Ayutthaya and Bang Pa-In is by **bus and boat tour—** either a bus there and boat trip back, or vice versa. It's really worth getting on the boat tour, as the Chao Phraya River allows a relevant perspective of both Ayutthaya and Bangkok, punctuating the importance of the river to the development of these cities. The *Oriental Queen,* a luxurious cruise boat operated by the Oriental Hotel (☎ 02/236-0400), leaves the Oriental Pier every day at 8am. Buses meet the boat in Ayutthaya for tours of the city ruins and the lovely Bang Pa-In Summer Palace. At 5pm, the buses leave for the 2-hour return trip to Bangkok. You can also travel up by bus and return by boat. Cost is 1,900B (US$51.35) per person, including lunch, tour, and full transportation.

✪ If you really want to turn your trip to Ayutthaya into an adventure, travel aboard the *Manohra Song.* This authentic 60-year old rice barge was rebuilt from its solid teak hull to meet international yacht-class standards. Four state rooms, with en suite bathrooms, are lavished in warm teak and mahogany, Thai silks and regional arts and sculpture. The ship's crew serves cocktails, snacks, and delicious Thai meals on deck, which is luxuriously designed with both European and Thai touches, with a forward sundeck lounge area. The overnight trip includes a stop at Wat Bang Na, where ship's staff will accompany you to make merit to the abbot, if you so desire. The trip, inclusive of all meals, tours, and transfers, runs between US$339 and $387 per person, double occupancy, depending on the season. For reservations telephone the *Manohra Song* Cruises Booking Office at ☎ 02/476-0021; fax 02/476-1805.

For bus tours at about 1,430B (US$38.65) per person, as well as bus and boat operations at 1,900B (US$51.35), contact **World Travel** (☎ **02/233-5900**).

## 4 The East Coast

Thailand's beaches, along the Gulf of Thailand (also known as the Gulf of Siam), are world-renowned for their clean white sand, palm groves, and warm water. Today, most areas are served by a sophisticated tourism infrastructure and indulgent accommodations. Although no sandy crescent is protected from the hotel developer's hand, there are still areas that are relatively quiet.

**Pattaya,** the oldest and most decadent of Thailand's southern resorts, lures people seeking a break from the big city because of its proximity to Bangkok ($2\frac{1}{2}$ hours by bus). It has suffered from what used to be its once positive image as the sex playground of Southeast Asia; AIDS, environmental pollution, and bad foreign publicity have contributed to a considerable drop in tourism. The local government has been cleaning up Pattaya Bay and enacting strict new waste management guidelines, and although the situation has improved somewhat, there's still far more work to be done.

**Ko Samet** is the star of Rayong Province: a small island (somewhat protected as a national park) whose primitive bungalows create a very different feel from Pattaya's swinging hotels. It's easily reached by a 45-minute ferry ride from the tiny port of Ban Phe ($4\frac{1}{2}$ hours from Bangkok by bus); though isolated, it often gets crowded due to its popularity with foreign low-budget tourists and Thais, especially during holidays.

## 5 Pattaya

You'll hear Pattaya, 91 miles (147km) east of Bangkok, called anything from "Asia's premier resort" to "one big open-air brothel"—its legacy as Thailand's R&R capital for Vietnam-weary American troops. It does indeed have several hundred beer bars, discos with scantily-clad Thai teens, massage parlors, and transvestite clubs all jammed together along a beachfront strip. But it has another more elegant and sophisticated side in its big international resorts, retreats set in sprawling, manicured seaside gardens. It remains a popular destination with tour groups and independent travelers, mostly male but plenty of families too, and is still the favored weekend destination among Bangkok residents. For those who desire a more tranquil beach environment, we recommend heading south to Hua Hin.

### VISITOR INFORMATION

The staff at the **TAT office** in Pattaya gives incredibly helpful information. Visit their office at 382/1 Mu 10 Beach Rd., ☎ **038/427-6677.**

### GETTING THERE

**BY AIR**   Bangkok Airways (in Bangkok ☎ **02/229-3456;** in Pattaya ☎ **038/411-965;** in Koh Samui ☎ **077/425-012**) has direct flights to U-Tapao, 19 miles (30km) south of Pattaya, from both Bangkok and Koh Samui. The number for **U-Tapao Airport** information is ☎ **038/245-595.** Taxis are not on standby at the airport, but many of the larger hotels can arrange pickup if you book in advance.

**BY TRAIN**   From Bangkok's Hua Lumphong Railway Station (☎ **02/223-7010** or 02/223-7020), the State Railway of Thailand operates a daily train to the Pattaya Railway Station off Siam Country Club Road (☎ **038/429-285**). Fare is 31B (US85¢) one-way.

**BY BUS**   The most common and practical form of transportation to Pattaya is the bus. Buses depart from Bangkok's Eastern Bus Terminal (on Sukhumvit Road opposite Soi 63 - Ekamai Road; ☎ **02/390-1230**) every half-hour beginning from 5am until 11pm daily. For air-conditioned coach, the fare is 77B (US$2.10). The bus

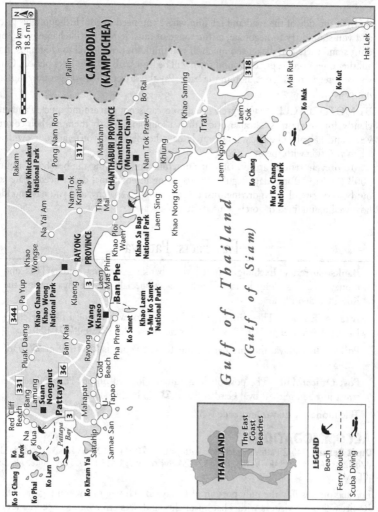

station in Pattaya for air-conditioned buses to and from Bangkok is on North Pattaya Road. From there, catch a songtao to your destination (see getting around below).

Thai Airways operates the **Thai Limousine Service** with departures from Bangkok International Airport (Don Muang). Coaches leave three times daily and cost 200B (US$5.40) per person. For information call ☎ **02/973-3191**. In Pattaya call ☎ **038/ 423-140**.

**BY PRIVATE CAR**    Taxis to Pattaya can be arranged at the taxi counters of Bangkok International Airport for 1,200B (US$32.43), or from Bangkok can be booked through **World Travel Service Ltd.,** 1053 Charoen Krung Rd., 10500 Bangkok (☎ **02/233-5900**) for the same price.

## GETTING AROUND

**BY SONGTAO (or Baht Bus)**    Outside of Bangkok, these pickup trucks provide the most convenient form of public transportation, for locals and tourists alike. Open air, but covered with a cap, they're outfitted with two long benches in the back. Flag one down at the side of the road and tell him where you need to go. He'll quote his price, and you should try to negotiate, as the songtaos outside hotels will charge more, but don't stand there and dicker too much. If you think his price is still too high, just find another one. Average prices around town will be from 20B (US55¢) per person. Once you've agreed on the price, hop in the back. Pay the driver when you get out. Tips are not expected.

**BY MOTORCYCLE** Motorcycle taxi drivers can scoot you around quickly and efficiently, for (sometimes) cheaper prices than a songtao. Identify them by their colored vests, and bargain like crazy. They rarely have helmets, and you're at your own risk when you ride with them.

**Motorcycle rentals** are available at numerous outlets along the beach for around 500B (US$13.50) per day. Regulations requiring international driver licenses are lax, but be very careful when driving. Insurance coverage is sketchy, and you have no idea how well maintained or sorely abused these bikes are.

## Fast Facts: Pattaya

**Banks/Currency Exchange** You'll find banking facilities with ATMs and money changers along Pattaya Beach Road, especially in the area around the Royal Garden Plaza.

**Internet/E-mail** There are little Internet centers everywhere. I like the classy Pattaya K@fe Net at 219/59-60 Soi Yamato Beach Rd. (☎ 038/421-050).

**Police** In Pattaya, the number for the Tourist Police is ☎ 1699 or ☎ 038/429-371.

**Post Office/Mail** The post office is suitably located on Soi Post Office, the street just before the Royal Garden Plaza (☎ 038/429341).

**Telephone** Pattaya's area code is 38.

## ACCOMMODATIONS

**Dusit Resort.** 240/2 Pattaya Beach Rd., Pattaya City. ☎ **038/425-611.** Fax 038/428-239. 474 units. A/C MINIBAR TV TEL. US$132–US$264 double; US$308–US$972 suite. AE, DC, JCB, MC, V.

Located on possibly the only portion of Pattaya Beach safe for swimming, the Dusit Resort welcomes visitors with Thai hospitality and Western comfort. Sea themes are delightful in the guest rooms. If you request the sea-view rooms, the cooling blues and greens of the decor blend superbly with the view of the bay from the balcony. The less expensive garden view rooms offer value for money, and the views of the resort's lush landscaping are still quite lovely.

You'll want for nothing, given Dusit's two large beautiful outdoor pools, three lighted tennis courts, squash courts, games room, water-sports center, fitness center, snooker and billiards room, plus a wonderful traditional Thai massage spa staffed with graduates from the Wat Po School of Traditional Thai Massage in Bangkok.

**Flipper Lodge Hotel.** 520/1 Soi 8, Pattaya Beach Rd., Pattaya City. ☎ **038/426-401.** Fax 038/410-255. 126 units. A/C MINIBAR TV TEL. 860B–900B (US$23–US$24) double. AE, MC, V.

A very popular choice for budget travelers, Flipper has an excellent location in the center of Pattaya Beach Road, clean respectable rooms, good service, and great views (make sure you request with booking). The coffee shop has great local and Western fare, but the two pools aren't anything to write home about. The only other facility

# Pattaya

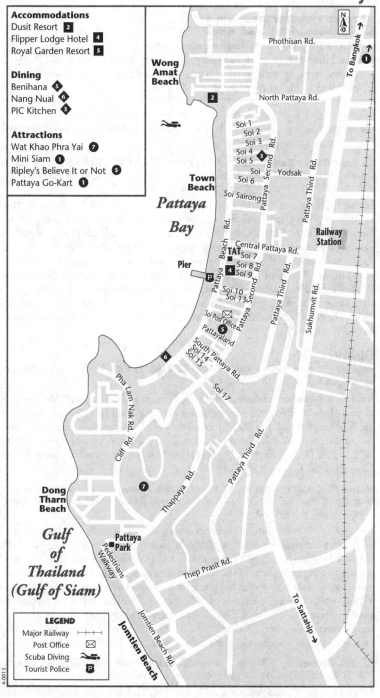

**Accommodations**
Dusit Resort **2**
Flipper Lodge Hotel **4**
Royal Garden Resort **5**

**Dining**
Benihana **5**
Nang Nual **6**
PIC Kitchen **3**

**Attractions**
Wat Khao Phra Yai **7**
Mini Siam **1**
Ripley's Believe It or Not **5**
Pattaya Go-Kart **1**

Phothisan Rd.

To Bangkok
**1**

Wong Amat Beach

North Pattaya Rd.

**2**

Soi 1
Soi 2
Soi 3
Soi 4
Soi 5
Soi
Soi 6

Pattaya Second Rd.

Yodsak

**3**

Pattaya Third Rd.

Soi Sairong

**Railway Station**

Pattaya Bay

*Pattaya Bay*

**Town Beach**

Central Pattaya Rd.

**TAT**
Soi 7
Soi 8
Soi 9

**Pier**

Beach Rd.

Pattaya Rd.

**4**

**P**

Soi 10
Soi 13

Pattaya Second Rd.

Pattaya Third Rd.

Sukhumvit Rd.

Soi Post Office

Pattayaland

**5**

South Pattaya Rd.
Soi 14
Soi 15

**6**

Soi 17

Pha Lam Nak Rd.

Cliff Rd.

Thappaya Rd.

Pattaya Third Rd.

**7**

**Dong Tharn Beach**

*Gulf of Thailand (Gulf of Siam)*

**Pattaya Park**

Pedestrians Walkway

Thep Prasit Rd.

To Sattahip

Jomtien Beach Rd.

**Jomtien Beach**

## LEGEND
Major Railway  ├─┼─┼─┤
Post Office  ✉
Scuba Diving  🤿
Tourist Police  **P**

4-0013

175

> ### Magazines for Visitor Info
>
> Keep an eye peeled for a couple magazines, available both in Pattaya and sometimes around Bangkok. *Explore Pattaya & The East Coast* and *What's On Pattaya* are updated regularly with current features and good tourist information. You'll also easily find a wide variety of maps.

the Flipper boasts is a snooker table. The Flipper is a good pick for long-term stays, as they'll lower rates to attractive lows.

✪ **Royal Garden Resort.** 218 Beach Rd., Pattaya City. ☎ **800/344-1212** in the U.S. and Canada, 0800/951-000 from the U.K., or 038/412-120. Fax 038/429-926. 300 units. US$95–US$140 double; US$195–US$640 suite. AE, DC, JCB, MC, V.

Smack in the center of Pattaya Beach (you really can't get a better location), Royal Garden surprises guests with its large courtyard garden and landscaped pool area. You'd hardly know Pattaya City was just beyond the walls. With its helpful staff and handsome accommodations, this resort makes for a great retreat. Spacious balconied rooms have views of the gardens or the sea, and have many creature comforts not found in other hotels, including an in-house video-on-demand service. The adjoining Royal Garden Plaza makes your dining and entertainment options even more attractive. The pool is the largest in Pattaya, while the fitness center is modern and well-equipped. There's also tennis, and the resort can arrange any water-sports activity you so desire.

# DINING

**Benihana.** 2nd Level, Royal Garden Plaza. ☎ **038/425-029.** Reservations not necessary. AE, DC, JCB, MC, V. JAPANESE-AMERICAN.

Most of our American readers are thinking, "Benihana? In Thailand?" Well, for those of you who've sampled tom yam gung and paad thai until it's coming out your ears, you'll be happy to visit this place. It has all the fun of Benihana's original restaurants—fantastic teppanyaki grill displays performed by chefs who have as much humor as skill, and the food is just great. The beef is like butter. Come here for a good time and a lot of laughs. You won't be disappointed.

**Nuang Nual.** South Pattaya Rd. ☎ **038/428-708.** Reservations not necessary, except for large groups. 70B–350B (US$1.90–US$9.45); seafood sold at market value. Daily 10am to 11pm. AE, MC, V. SEAFOOD

At night, when South Pattaya Road becomes a pedestrian mall, take a walk past the noisy open-air watering holes and colorful souvenir shops to Nuang Nual. The entrance is as brightly lit as a supermarket, and looks like one too, with rows upon rows of all sorts of creatures of the sea in tanks or on ice in coolers. The maitre d' will escort you to your table on the huge outdoor patio overlooking the bay, and hand you a menu which is more or less a book. Choose your creature, and they'll prepare it to your specifications: Thai style, Chinese, or Western. On my last visit, the squid dish I had was incredibly tender. They also have meats and vegetable dishes, as well as soups and fried rice and noodles. Get there early so you can get a table with a good view.

✪ **PIC Kitchen.** Soi 5 Pattaya 2nd Rd. ☎ **038/428-374.** Reservations not necessary. 75B–320B (US$2–US$8.65). Daily 8am–noon. AE, DC, MC, V. THAI.

Named for the Pattaya International Clinic PIC Hospital next door (don't worry, they're unrelated) PIC Kitchen is highly recommended for its wonderful atmosphere. Small Thai teak pavilions, both air-conditioned and open-air, have seating areas on the floor, Thai style, or at romantic tables. Delicious and affordable Thai cuisine is served à la carte or in lunch and dinner sets. The spring rolls and deep fried crab claws are mouthwatering. Other dishes come pan-fried, steamed, or charcoal grilled, with spice added to taste. At night, groove to a live jazz band from 7pm to 1am.

# ATTRACTIONS
## PATTAYA BEACH

This 2½-mile (4km) strip may seem harmless to the naked eye, but be warned, the rumors you've heard are true. It's very, very polluted. Rapid growth of the tourism sector was not accompanied by growth of pubic facilities works, and for years waste has been disposed of improperly, ironically destroying the very attraction drawing tourists here in the first place. As if raw sewage isn't enough, the beach attracts many varieties of poisonous sea snakes.

Water activities still reign in the area, but for swimming you should either stick to the very north of Pattaya Beach near the Dusit Resort, or head a little south to Jomtien Beach. Another option is to take a day trip to one of the islands in the Gulf of Thailand.

To get to Jomtien Beach, grab a songtao on Beach Road or Pattaya 2nd Road for around 50B (US$1.35). Swimming is centered around the northern section of the beach, while the southern parts are for other water sports such as catamaran sailing, parasailing, waterskiing, and windsurfing. You'll find a lot of places on the beach that rent equipment and even provide lessons, for prices that are always rising and falling, depending on tourist traffic. Expect to pay as little as 150B (US$4.05) per hour for windsurfing equipment, and up to 1,500B (US$40.55) per hour for a jet ski. Parasailing is around 500B (US$13.50) per flight.

Day trips to Ko Lan (Coral Island) or nearby Ko Pai are best if you want cleaner and less crowded beaches. Ko Lan, 4.8 miles (7.7km) west of Pattaya, has beaches with eateries, overnight accommodations, water sports and other facilities. On weekends it gets very crowded, so you may want to try Ko Pai, which is beautiful, but has no facilities at all. The local ferryboat to Ko Lan costs 20B (US55¢) per person and takes 45 minutes. The last ferry back is at 5pm. For a speedboat hire expect to pay 800B to 2,000B (US$21.60–US$54) per day. Once at the island, you can take a motorcycle taxi to the various beaches for between 20B and 50B (US55¢–US$1.35). The easiest way to arrange the boat trip is through the **TAT office** (☎ 038/427-6677). You will also need to see them for arrangements to Ko Pai.

It seems dive operators in Pattaya are easier to find than ATMs. Scuba diving sites around Ko Lan, Ko Sak, Ko Krok, and the more secluded Ko Rin, while a little abused and not the best diving in Thailand, still reveal beautiful life beneath the sea. I recommend the good people at **Dolphin Diving Center** (183/31 Moo 10, Soi Post Office; ☎ 038/427-185), who take small groups out for two dives daily—total cost including equipment, two tanks, transport, a hot meal and a divemaster guide is 2,800B (US$75.70). Overnight dives can also be arranged.

When your skin is charred, your head is water-logged, and you want a change of pace from all that beach living, Pattaya has a few worthwhile activities, both fun and cultural. On the culture side of life, there's **Wat Khao Phra Yai** on Big Buddha Hill (Pratumnak Road between South Pattaya and Jomtien). This 32.5-foot (10.8m) gold colored stucco Buddha, believed to be the protector of the city, peers out into the sea. The view of the bay is quite nice from the wat as well. Pattaya also has a **Mini Siam** theme park (387 Sukhumvit Rd. near North Pattaya Road, ☎ 038/421-628), with replicas of major Thai attractions like the Temple of the Emerald Buddha and the Bridge over the River Kwai and, strangely, some European monuments as well. They're open daily from 7am to 10pm, and charge 200B (US$5.40) for adults and 100B (US$2.70) for children.

For something completely unusual, the **Ripley's Believe It or Not** showcase (3rd Floor, Royal Garden Plaza, 218 Beach Rd.; ☎ **038/710-294;** open 10am to midnight daily; admission 150B or US$4.05) is hilarious, with unusual exhibits and odd facts from around the globe. Just next door is the Ripley's Motion Master simulator ride. Both are highly recommended if you're traveling with your children.

The **Pattaya Elephant Village** (see the Elephant Desk at Tropicana Hotel, Beach Road; ☎ **038/423-031**) stages elephant shows daily at 2:30pm. You can also arrange for a little jungle trekking on elephant back. If that's not quite your speed, check out **Pattaya Go-Kart** (Sukhumvit Road next to Mini Siam; ☎ **038/422-044**) with a 400-meter track that is also suitable for children. Rates run between 100B to 200B (US$2.70–US$5.40) per 10 minutes, depending on the power of your kart.

## PATTAYA AFTER DARK

Given Pattaya's origins as a retreat for American GIs on R&R, it doesn't take a lot of imagination to envision the main attractions here: beer and women. **Pattaya Beach Road,** especially South Pattaya Beach, which at night becomes the pedestrian mall "Pattayaland," is lined with open air bars, go-go clubs, and massage parlors, with gay bars centered around Pattayaland Sois 1–3.

For cleaner fun, there are some lively bars and discos in the city. **Hopf Brew House** (219 Beach Rd.; ☎ **038/710-650**) brews its own beer served by the glass, goblet, or ampolla, to the beat of a live band. For discos, the largest is **Palladium** (Pattaya 2nd Road; ☎ **038/242-933**), a gigantic club with the largest dance floor you've ever seen pulsating with pop and dance beats and a great light show. The smaller **Disco Duck** (Little Duck Pattaya Resort Hotel, Central Pattaya Road; ☎ **038/428-101**) has a fun atmosphere, catering to middle-class Thai folks from Bangkok, with live bands, videos, and light shows.

Pattaya's most beautiful *katoeys* (transsexuals) don sequinned gowns and feather boas to strut their stuff for packed houses nightly. At **Alcazar** (78/14 Pattaya 2nd Rd., opposite Soi 5; ☎ **038-410505**) the shows are at times hilarious. If you've seen a cabaret show elsewhere in Thailand, you may be disappointed to see familiar acts, which are standard in almost every show.

## 6 Ko Samet

Ko Samet is 137 miles (220km) east of Bangkok via Highway 3, or 115 miles (185km) via Highway 3 and the Pattaya bypass. Ban Phe, the mainland port that operates ferries to and from Ko Samet, is 22 miles (35km) east of Rayong city, along Sukhumvit Highway. As you turn south toward the Gulf of Thailand, you'll pass through a bustling village to the seaside main street, dominated by the large pier and its colorful fishing boats destined for Ko Samet.

**Ko Samet** (also called Ko Kaeo Phitsadan) first became popular with Thais from the poetry of Sunthon Phu, a venerated 19th-century author and Rayong native who set his best-known epic on this "tropical island paradise." Fortunately, despite its appeal to Thais and foreigners, a shortage of potable water kept rampant commerce and tourism at bay for many years. In 1981, Samet became part of the six-island **Khao Laem Ya—Samet National Park,** a designation meant to preserve its relatively undeveloped status. Since then, small-scale construction has boomed, and there are more than 50 licensed bungalow hotels with nearly 2,500 rooms on the 3.6-mile (6km) long island. In 1990, a TAT-sponsored effort to close the national park to overnight visitors met with such fierce resistance that 4 days later Samet was reopened for business as

# Ko Samet

usual. Until inadequate water supplies, waste treatment, and garbage disposal are dealt with, the TAT is encouraging visitors to go to the still lovely Samet for day trips only, but that rarely happens.

The small island's northern half is triangular, with a long tail leading to the south that looks somewhat like a kite. Most of the beaches are on the east coast of the tail; although Ko Samet is only about six-tenths of a mile (1km) wide, it has a rocky spine and there are few paths that connect the two coasts.

Passengers alight from the ferry at **Na Dan,** the island's main port. It's a 10-minute walk south past the **health center** and school to **Hat Sai Kaeo** (Diamond Beach, on the northeast cape), the island's most developed and crowded beach, which is linked by a dirt path to 10 other small beach developments. Most day-trippers take the regular ferry and then catch one of the songtaos that meet the boats and travel inland as far as Wong Duan. You can also catch a ride with one of the individual resort ferries or hike the shoreline path between beaches.

The more developed beaches are Hat Sai Kaeo, Ao Pai, and Vong Deuan. Most of the other beaches offer facilities that barely afford human survival. The three most developed beaches are also the most expensive, mostly because everything, including water, must be imported from the mainland. And while these beaches can get pretty busy on weekends during peak season, especially Hat Sai Kaeo, which probably should be avoided either way, they are still quite relaxing. The atmosphere here is very laid back. However, even the high-end accommodations are basic. Expect a quaint bungalow with a small deck in the front and a concrete latrine in the back, with a cold water shower only. Your first day at Ko Samet will be a little shocking if you've never

**Ko Samet Survival Gear**

Some tips: Arm yourself with **mosquito repellent.** A **flashlight** is also a good idea, for finding your way after dark, and in the smaller bungalows which turn off electricity in the late evening. You might want to bring along a **towel.** Vong Deuan resort has towels, but few of the smaller places do. **A good sarong** is the ultimate— beach blanket, towel, wrap, bed sheet, sun shield. I never leave home without at least two.

roughed it before. Your second day will be filled with relaxation and fun. By the third day, you'll never want to leave. If you stay for a fourth, you'll be redecorating your bungalow.

## GETTING THERE

**BY BUS**    Buses leave Bangkok every hour between 7am and 9pm for the 3½-hour journey, departing from the Eastern Bus Terminal (☎ 02/390-1230) on Sukhumvit Road opposite Soi 63 (Ekamai Road). The one-way trip to Ban Phe, the town where you catch the ferry to Ko Samet, costs 108B (US$2.90).

**BY PRIVATE BUS**    Many Bangkok travel agencies operate their own buses to Ban Phe—it's the easiest way to go. **S. T. Travel** has a minibus leaving from its office at 102 Rambutri Rd. (at Khao San Road), Banglamphu, daily at 8am. Trip time is 3½ hours; cost is 200B (US$5.40) one-way. Call them in Bangkok (☎ 02/281-3662) or in Ban Phe (☎ 038/651-461) for schedule information and reservations.

Several buses a day leave from Pattaya to Ban Phe. Trip time: 1 hour; 300B (US$8.10) round-trip. Contact **Malibu Travel Service** (Soi Post Office; ☎ 038/423-180).

**BY TAXI**    Malibu Travel Service in Pattaya will arrange a private car to take you to Ban Phe for 900B (US$24.30) one-way. Call them at the number above for details and booking.

**FERRIES TO KO SAMET**    During the high season, from November to April, ferries leave Ban Phe pier for the main port, Na Dan, every half hour. Trip time: 40 minutes, cost 40B ($1.10). The first boat departs at 9:30am and the last at 5pm. Several other agents in Ban Phe sell passage on their own boats to Wang Duen beach; departures are at least a few times daily. One-way fare is 50B (US$1.35). Contact Malibu Travel's Ban Phe office at ☎ 038/651-292.

From the ferry landing on Samet, you must catch a water taxi to the other beaches. Cost is from between 20B to 60B (US55¢–US$1.60) per person, depending on your destination. You can also take a songtao to other beaches for between 10B and 50B (US25¢–US$1.35). There is one road on Samet connecting the main town, Samet Village, halfway down the eastern shore of the island to Vong Deuan. Beyond that are footpaths.

One note about water taxis and songtaos. They don't like to make the trip if you're only one or two passengers, in which circumstances premiums are charged. A water taxi could soak you for up to 300B (US$8.10), and a songtao could run you into the ground for 400 (US$10.80), especially if they know you have no other choice. Now's a good time to remember your Thai etiquette, and refrain from blowing your top; otherwise, you're walking.

The Thai government charges a parks admission fee of 50B (US$1.35) per entry to the island. To be quite honest, I never paid, nor did I ever see anyone collecting this fee from tourists.

# Fast Facts: Ko Samet

**Banks/Currency Exchange**   Ko Samet is pretty much a cash-operation only. While there are no ATMs, there is a money changing service at the post office.

**Post Office/Mail**   The post office is at the Naga Bar along the main road in Ao Pai. (See how laid back this place is? The post office is at a *bar*.)

**Provisions**   In Na Dan, also called Samet Village, as well as Vong Duean, there are some small provision shops by the main ferry landing.

**Telephone**   The same bar that houses the post office has an international phone and fax service.

## ACCOMMODATIONS

The two best beaches on Ko Samet are Ao Pai and Vong Deuan beach. Ao Pai is smaller, with bungalows set in the jungle, just a hop from the beach. It's quiet and you'll feel more privacy. The best of the bungalows here are the **Ao Pai Huts** (☎ 01/353-2644), along the main dirt road about 10 minutes' ride (20B) from the main jetty. These simple bungalows are tidy and well constructed, with clean bathrooms and space to put your baggage. During the busy season rates are 500B (US$13.50) with air-conditioning, and 300B (US$8.10) without. During off-peak season rates run 300B and 150B (US$8.10 and $4.05), respectively. Rates apply for both single and double occupancy.

Vong Deuan beach offers the best and largest variety of accommodations, but it gets a greater volume of traffic. Still, the sandy cove is quite large, and the mood here tends to be more active and fun. **Vong Deuan Resort** (☎ 01/446-1944; Bangkok contact 02/392-4390) has bungalows that are more modern and come with a few amenities—like towels. Bungalows with air-conditioning run from 1,100B to 1,200B (US$30–US$32), without from 800B to 900B (US$22–US$24). On Vong Deuan Beach, you can also try **Malibu Garden Resort** (Ban Phe ☎ 038/651-057 or Pattaya 038/710-676), possibly the most posh of the resorts on Ko Samet—it has hot water and TVs, but you will sacrifice the Robinson Crusoe appeal of the island. Air-conditioned bungalows cost between 1,400B and 2,200B (US$38–US$56). Bungalows with fans only are from 800B to 1,700B (US$22–US$46).

## DINING

You people will just have to forage for nuts and berries.

Just kidding. All of the bungalows offer some sort of eating experience, mostly bland local food and beer, with some Western breakfast offerings. In the evenings a few places entice dinner guests with video screenings of recently released movies, which are always popular. In Ao Pai, Naga Bar on the main road is quiet, with a fairly decent menu, a beer selection, and a bakery that has surprisingly wonderful fresh goods in the mornings. In Vong Deuan, places like **Nice & Easy, Oasis, Baywatch,** and **Seahorse** serve dinner, and get pretty lively later on. You can expect most dishes in these places to cost you 60B to 100B (US$1.60–US$2.70).

## SPORTS & OUTDOOR ACTIVITIES

**Windsurfing** is particularly popular with weekenders from Bangkok. The island's best is said to be north of Hat Sai Kaeo (Diamond Beach), around the cape that bulges out of Samet's east side. The rocky north coast is even more challenging, with strong currents and sometimes erratic winds caused by the deep channel between the island and the mainland. Windsurfers are available at most guesthouses for 100B to 175B

(US$2.70–US$4.75) per hour, without instruction. Hat Sai Kaeo also has jet skis for rent at about 1,200B (US$32.45) per hour.

You can book any of the speedboats at the beaches for round-island tours at about 300B (US$8.10) per person, and for snorkeling on the rocky uninhabited western side of the island, which is said to be the best for underwater life. They'll be happy to do a morning drop and afternoon fetch for 300B.

## 7  The Southern Peninsula

Thailand's slim Malay Peninsula extends 777 miles (1,250km) south from Bangkok to the Malaysia border at Sungai Kolok. Just as the beach resort of Phuket in the Andaman Sea dominates the list of west coast pleasures, so **Ko Samui,** a more laid-back and traditional Thai resort island in the Gulf of Thailand (also known as the Gulf of Siam), dominates the east.

The first significant tourist destination is only 150 miles (240km) south of Bangkok, the beach resort of **Hua Hin.** The once-elegant retreat of royalty is blossoming with a flashy nouveau grandeur designed to appeal to Bangkok's elite. Well-priced luxury resorts and family-oriented cabana hotels provide a getaway for tourists, too.

Following the quiet coast road to Surat Thani, you arrive at the ferries for increasingly popular Ko Samui, a coconut-studded isle that's sure to please the most demanding tropical-paradise seeker.

## 8  Hua Hin

Hua Hin is 140 miles (240km) south of Bangkok and 138 miles (223km) north of Chumphon. Developed in the 1920s, Hua Hin was actually Thailand's first beach resort, initially favored exclusively by the royal family (they still use the *Klai Kangwon* or "Far from Worries" Palace in the summer) and the upper crust of Bangkok society. In the 1940s and 1950s, and especially prior to the development of Pattaya in the mid-1960s, Hua Hin (and its sister resort of Cha-Am) changed dramatically as it became the most popular destination for middle-class Thai families commuting from Bangkok. Although its popularity declined with the ascendance of Phuket, Ko Samui, and Pattaya, recent renewal of the resorts here, with newly built grand hotels and luxurious high-rise condos, has created tourist interest in the area. If you're planning a visit, try to avoid the period from November to February, Hua Hin's rainy and windy season.

### VISITOR INFORMATION

There is a **Tourist Information Service Center** (☎ 032/511-047) at the corner of Damnoenkasem and Phetchkasem roads. A good publication to pick up here is the *Hua Hin Observer,* with a good map and local promotions listings.

### GETTING THERE

**BY TRAIN**   Twelve trains leave daily from Bangkok. Trip time: 3½ hours special express, 4½ hours rapid; 229B (US$6.20) for air-conditioned special express, continuing south to Surat Thani. For train information, call Hua Lamphong Railway Station at ☎ 02/223-7010 or **02/223-7020.** The Hua Hin Railway Station (☎ 032/ **511-073**) is at the head of Damnoenkasem Road, which leads through the center of town straight to the beach. Songtaos wait for alighting passengers. Trips to nearby resorts are from 40B (US$1.10). Many resorts can arrange pickup for you when you make your reservation.

Thung Wua Laem

↑ **Hua Hin & Cha Am**

Chumphon

BURMA (MYANMAR)

41

○ Ranong

Lang Suan

**RANONG PROVINCE**

○ Ko Tao

**Mu Ko Ang Thong National Park**

**Ko Phangan**

**Ko Ta Luang**

**Ko Samui**

Chaiya ○

Surat Thani ○

401

○ Phanom

**No Dog Island (Ko Taen)**

○ Sichon

*Gulf of Thailand*
*(Gulf of Siam)*

401

○ Tha Sala

Phrasaeng ○

4009

41

Nakhon Si Thammarat ○

Thung Yai ○

401

○ Hua Sai

Klong Thom ○

403

41

4

○ Huai Yot

Phatthalung ○

**Ko Lanta Yai**

Trang ○

**TRANG PROVINCE**

**Ko Li Bong**

○ Sathing Pra

*Andaman Sea*

Songkhla

○ Thung Wa

○ Hat Yai

Route 4

**Ko Tarutao**

Pattani ●

Narathiwat ○

○ Yala

**YALA PROVINCE**

Tak Bai ●

**MALAYSIA**

Sungai Kolok ○

**THAILAND**

★ Bangkok

**The Southeast Coast**

### LEGEND

Airport ✈

Beach ☂

Ferry Route - - - -

Scuba Diving 🤿

0    60 km
    37 mi

N

**BY BUS**   Buses depart every hour from 4am to 10:20pm daily from Bangkok's Southern Bus Terminal (☎ **02/435-1199**). The trip takes 3 hours and fare is 97B (US$2.60). The bus terminal in Hua-Hin is on Srasong Road. For information, dial ☎ **032/511-654**.

## GETTING AROUND

Damnoenkasem Road, cutting through the center of town, runs from the Railway Station straight to the beach, intercepted by Phetchasem Road, following parallel to the beach. You'll find most of life's necessities along these two roads—banks, tourist information, post office, tour operators, restaurants, and bars. Down Damnoenkasem toward the beach, bordered by Poolsuk and Naretdamri Roads, an area of guesthouses, cafes, and shops jump-starts the otherwise quiet town.

Hua Hin is small and can be walked, although many visitors try an outing by *samlor,* a human-powered pedicab. Shorter trips can be as cheap as 20B (US55¢), with long trips up to 100B (US$2.70). Be prepared to negotiate. Songtaos, pickup truck taxis, can be waved by the side of the road, and can also be booked for half-day and full-day excursions. Trips around town and to resorts are about 50B (US$1.35). Full day booking is about 800B (US$21.60)

# Fast Facts: Hua Hin

**Banks/Currency Exchange**    You'll find your major banks along Petchkasem Road for ATMs and money exchange.

**Internet/E-mail**    The Internet has been slow to come to Hua Hin. The first and only place to provide service is the All Nations Guesthouse at 10–10 Dechanuchit Rd. (☎ 032/512-747). Don't expect a fast connection or much privacy.

**Police**    Tourist Police can be reached at ☎ 032/515/995.

**Post Office/Mail**    The post office (☎ 032/511-063) is on Damnoenkasem Road near where it intersects with Petchkasem.

**Telephone**    Hua Hin's area code is 32.

## ACCOMMODATIONS

**All Nations Guesthouse.** 10–10/1 Deachanuchit Rd., P.O. Box 56, Hua Hin 77110. ☎ **032/512747.** 18 units. 200B (US$5.40) with fan; 600B (US$16.20) with air-conditioning. No credit cards.

In the middle of the guesthouse and nightlife alleys of town, All Nations is a central meeting point for travelers and expats, who have a beer in the bar-lobby, watch a football game, share travel stories and tips, and use the only Internet cafe for miles. It's the favorite place for budget travelers, due to its friendly carefree charm. All rooms have a small balcony, but none have private bathroom. If they're full, they'll direct you to another nearby guesthouse.

✪ **Hotel Sofitel Central.** 1 Damnoenkasem Rd., Hua Hin, 77110. ☎ **800/221-4542** in the U.S. and Canada, 800/642-244 from Australia, 0800/444-422 from New Zealand, 181/283-4500 in the U.K., or 032/512-021. Fax 032/511014. 214 units. A/C MINIBAR TV TEL. 5,100B–6,600B (US$138–US$178) double; 11,650B–32,200B (US$315–US$870) suite. Peak season supplement charge Dec 20–Jan 10: 1,300B (US$35.15). AE, DC, MC, V.

The Sofitel Central, once known as the Railway Hotel, was the place to stay in the 1920s. With the revival of Hua Hin as a tourist destination and the renewed interest in this architectural gem in the mid-1980s (it served as the French Embassy in the film *The Killing Fields),* this restored and rebuilt hotel is not only a wonderful place to stay but a must-see stop on any tour of the area. If for no other reason, go to see the well-landscaped grounds, which include a 60-year-old eccentric topiary garden, an orchid and butterfly farm, wide lawns, flowering trees, and elegantly planned shrubbery. Suites are spacious and have fans and marble baths, teak floors, and sitting rooms with chandeliers. The high-ceilinged superior rooms are done with the same quality and taste as the suites. Villas, with 42 bedrooms tucked into one- and two-unit seaside bungalows, were built in the 1950s, and have an authentically casual and rustic feel.

The Villa Wing has a Thai restaurant with once-weekly classical dance performances. Sofitel's three gorgeous outdoor pools, tennis courts, and billiards room can keep you busy once you've taken in the sights, or you can try one of the their daily craft and language lessons. They'll also arrange water sports and golf upon request. The Villa Wing also has its own small pool, beach access, and small playground.

**Royal Garden Resort.** 107/1 Petchkasem Beach Rd., Hua Hin 77110. ☎ **800/344-1212** in the U.S. and Canada, ☎ 0800/951-000 from the U.K., or ☎ 032/511-881. Fax 032/512-422. 220 units. A/C MINIBAR TV TEL. US$120–US$180 double; US$280–US$400 suite. Peak season supplemental charges Dec 20–Jan 10: US$40 per night. AE, DC, JCB, MC, V.

The extremely well-outfitted and maintained Royal Garden Resort is best suited for those in search of beach and sports activities. Singles and families are here throughout the year, lured principally by the ponds, pools, boats, golf, tennis, and other racket sports, as well as by the pet elephant and the junglelike grounds leading out to the calm sea. Top it off with a children's playground and a fitness center, and you have the perfect equation for a family vacation. The hotel is relatively convenient, with complimentary shuttle service into town and to its sister establishment, the more traditional Thai-style Royal Garden Village (see below). Deluxe rooms are the best choice—large, amenity filled, and facing the sea.

The hotel has facilities for tennis and golf, plus boat rentals, a fitness center, and a children's playground.

✪ **Royal Garden Village.** 43/1 Petchkasem Beach Rd., Hua Hin 77110. ☎ **800/344-1212** in the U.S. and Canada, 0800/951-000 from the U.K., or 032/520-250. Fax 032/520-259. 162 units. A/C MINIBAR TV TEL. US$137–US$163 double; US$170 beach terrace; US$392 suite. Peak season supplemental charges Dec 20–Jan 10: US$40 per night. AE, DC, JCB, MC, V.

A series of elegantly designed Thai-style pavilions make up the structure of the lobby and the public facilities at this "village" away from the town center, off the main road. A lovely Kaliga tapestry hangs prominently in the open-air sala-style lobby, which is tastefully decorated with ornately carved teak wooden lanterns, warm wood floors, and furniture with rose-colored cushions. A series of teak pavilions each houses 12 guest rooms. Consistent with the lobby, rooms are furnished in Thai style with teak-and-rattan furniture. Superior rooms have a garden view and deluxe rooms overlook the sand and sea. For a few dollars more, the beach terrace rooms have large patios, perfect for requesting a fun (or romantic) barbecue set up by the staff.

The list of recreation facilities goes on forever, from the large free-form pool, to lighted tennis courts, lawn games, sailing, parasailing, windsurfing, waterskiing, motorcycle and bicycle rentals, and more.

## DINING
**Itsara**. 7 Napkehard St., Hua Hin. ☎ 032/530-574. Reservations recommended for Saturday dinner. Main courses 60B–290B (US$1.60–US$7.85). MC, V. Mon–Fri 10am–noon; Sat and Sun 2pm–noon. Seaside, a 40B–70B (US$1.10–US$1.90) samlor ride north from the town center. THAI.

Formerly called Ban Tuppee Kaow, Itsara is a two-story greenhouse built in the 1920s and not especially well maintained, though it is atmospheric. By the sea, the terrace seating is the best in the house, with views of the beach. During weekend lunches it's especially quiet and peaceful. Specialties include a sizzling hot plate of noodles with prawn, squid, pork, and vegetables. A large variety of fresh seafood and meats are prepared steamed or deep fried, and can be served with either salt, chili, or red curry paste. Beer, Mekhong whiskey, and soft drinks are available.

**Meekaruna Seafood.** 26/1 Naratdamri Rd., Hua Hin. ☎ **032/511-932.** Reservations not necessary. Main courses 120B–500B (US$3.25–US$13.50). AE, DC, MC, V. Daily 10am–10pm. Near the fishing pier. SEAFOOD.

This small family-run restaurant serves fresh fish in a dining pavilion across the street or outdoors at tables overlooking the main fishing pier in Hua Hin. The menu is in English (with photographs), and you'll find the lack of hype—compared to the other fish places with their flashy entrances and hustling touts—refreshing. Among the many good dishes are steamed pomfret with plum sauce, charcoal-grilled shrimp, and the fried vegetable combination with seafood. Wear bug repellent!

**Palm Seafood Pavilion.** Hotel Sofitel Central, 1 Damnoenkasem Rd. ☎ **032/512021.** Reservations recommended. Main courses 150B–600B (US$4.05–US$16.20); seafood buffet 650B (US$17.55) per person. AE, DC, MC, V. Daily noon–2:30pm and 6–10:30pm. CONTINENTAL.

This plant-filled crystal pavilion offers a very romantic dining experience. Attentive but discreet service, beautiful table settings and linen, soothing classical music, and excellent, elegantly prepared food all contribute in pleasing harmony. Seafood lovers should try the salmon consommé with tiny mushroom ravioli, fresh barracuda with fruit curry sauce, or steamed cottonfish served with creamed spinach. The dessert menu is an eyeful of sweet goodies. Be sure to call ahead, as they frequently book private barbecues and parties.

## SPORTS & OUTDOOR ACTIVITIES

Most people come here to sit on an evergreen-lined beach or revel in the luxury of an august resort complex, but there are a few other diversions that might appeal to you.

Hua Hin has become a golfing haven, and there are now 11 courses in the area. Reservations are suggested and necessary most weekends. **Royal Hua Hin Golf Course** (Damnoenkasem Road near the Hua Hin Railway Station, ☎ **032/512-475,** in Bangkok 02/241-1360), Thailand's first championship golf course, opened in 1924 and was recently upgraded. It features topiary figures along its fairways and is open daily 6am to 6pm; greens fees are 800B (US$21.60) for weekdays and 1,200B (US$32.45) for weekends. **Springfield Royal Country Club** (193 Huay-Sai Nua, Petchkasem Road, Cha-Am, ☎ **032/471303,** in Bangkok 02/231-2244) was cleverly designed by Jack Nicklaus in 1993, and has a beautiful valley setting. Greens fees are 1,200B (US$32.45) weekdays and 1,800B (US$48.65) weekends.

Water-sports enthusiasts should note that hotel owners are discouraging guests from renting jet skis because of safety and pollution concerns. There have been a number of accidents with both boat drivers and swimmers (who are inadvertently run over by inexperienced drivers). Scooters not only spew fumes and excess fuel into the water, but many tourists have also been ripped off in gasoline or "lost or damaged" parts schemes involving credit-card deposits. Another pollution source is the ubiquitous ponies for hire that schlepp up and down the beach; keep in mind that other people swim and laze on the same stretch of sand)! Jet ski rentals start at 500B (US$13.50) per hour.

## SHOPPING

If you walk down Damnoenkasem to the beach you'll pass the Hua Hin Bazaar, an outdoor market packed with local handicrafts. If you've been spending a lot of time in Bangkok and the north, you'll notice how the crafts here reflect the southern, ocean-inspired culture. Everything you can imagine is made of seashells.

At night the 2-block long night market on Dechanuchit Road west of Phetchkasem Road packs in hawkers with sweet foods, cheap clothes, and all sorts of fun trinkets. After shopping, check out the back streets between Phetchkasem Road and the beach for all sorts of nightspots, from relaxed pubs and rowdy discos to racy go-go bars. Thai boxing is sometimes held at the Thai Boxing Garden on Poolsuk Road. Talk to the Tourist Information Center or check the local paper for details.

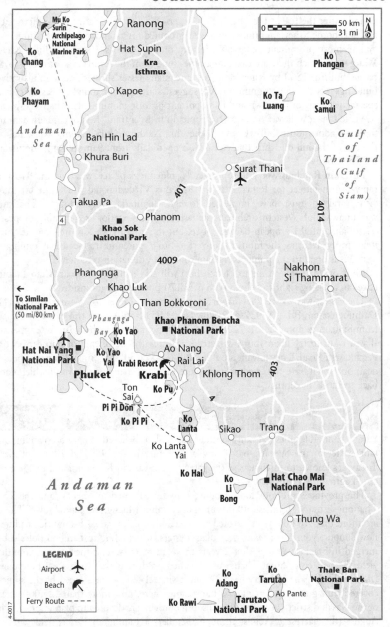

0    50 km
31 mi

**Mu Ko Surin Archipelago National Marine Park**

Ranong

Hat Supin

**Ko Chang**

**Kra Isthmus**

**Ko Phangan**

Kapoe

**Ko Phayam**

*Andaman Sea*

Ko Ta Luang

**Ko Samui**

Ban Hin Lad

Khura Buri

Surat Thani

*Gulf of Thailand (Gulf of Siam)*

401

4014

Takua Pa

4

Phanom

**Khao Sok National Park**

4009

Nakhon Si Thammarat

Phangnga

Khao Luk

Than Bokkoroni

← To Similan National Park (50 mi/80 km)

*Phangnga Bay*

**Ko Yao Noi**

**Khao Phanom Bencha National Park**

**Hat Nai Yang National Park**

**Ko Yao Yai**

Ao Nang

Rai Lai

**Krabi Resort**

**Phuket**

**Krabi**

Khlong Thom

403

Ton Sai

**Ko Pu**

Pi Pi Don

**Ko Pi Pi**

**Ko Lanta**

Sikao

Trang

Ko Lanta Yai

**Ko Hai**

Ko Li Bong

**Hat Chao Mai National Park**

*Andaman Sea*

Thung Wa

**LEGEND**

✈ Airport

⛱ Beach

--- Ferry Route

Ko Adang

Ko Tarutao

**Thale Ban National Park**

Ko Rawi

**Tarutao National Park**

Ao Pante

4-0017

## A SIDE TRIP TO PHETCHABURI

Hua Hin makes for a great fun-in-the-sun holiday, but after you're tired of the beach and want to take in some of Thailand's cultural wonders, the ancient city of **Phetchaburi** is close at hand. Best seen by day trips (Phetchaburi has little to offer in terms of tourist facilities), the city is very easy to visit from Hua Hin.

One of the country's oldest towns, Phetchaburi quite possibly dates from the same period as Ayutthaya, as it is thought to have been first settled during the Dvaravati period. After the rise of the Thai nation, it served as an important royal military city and was home to several princes who were groomed for ascendance to the throne.

The most prominent geographic feature of the town is a series of hills. **Khao Wang**—on which there are two monasteries (one from the Ayutthaya period), a royal palace built in 1860 by King Mongkut, and many lesser shrines and administrative buildings—is the most significant. We suggest starting your tour here, as there is a spectacular view of the town and its important historic monuments. Khao Wang can be visited via a walkway or, as most people do it, by a tram. It is open daily 8am to 5:30pm; admission is 30B (US80¢). The Phra Nakhon Khiri National Museum, at the top of the hill on Khiri Rataya Road, is open daily from 9am to 4pm; admission is 25B (US70¢).

**Phraram Ratchaniwet,** a European-style golden teak palace, was built in 1916 as a rainy-season retreat for Rama V. In 1918, Rama VI designated it a venue for state visits, and it must have impressed foreign dignitaries who thought Thailand was unaware of Western architectural fashion. The exterior is a jumble of post-Victorian/central European baroque style, but the interior is exquisite—and exquisitely empty, awaiting the funds to convert it into a museum. It's located in a military base but is open to the public daily 8am to 4pm. A donation is requested.

Most organized day trips to Phetchaburi will also include a stop at **Khao Luang cave,** an amazing sight to behold with over 170 Buddha images inside.

The easiest way to see Phetchaburi is through a tour operator. **Western Tours** (11 Damnoenkasem Rd., ☎ **032/512-560,** fax 032/512-560) has a trip every Thursday from 8:30am to 3pm. Cost is 700B (US$18.90) per person, inclusive of refreshments. If you want to try it on your own, strike a deal with one of the songtao drivers on Petchkasem Road. They'll want around 800B (US$21.60). It's probably not the better deal, but you'll have the freedom to explore the city's many wats, two of which date back to the 17th century.

## 9 Surat Thani

Surat Thani, 400 miles (644km) south of Bangkok, is believed to have been an important center of the Sumatra-based Srivijaya Empire in the 9th and 10th centuries. Today, it's known to foreigners as the gateway to beautiful Ko Samui and to Thais as a rich agricultural province.

The province's precious food product is oysters, farmed in Ka Dae and the Tha Thanong Estuary 18 miles (30km) south of Amphur Muang, the capital town. There are more than 16,000 acres devoted to aquaculture in the area. Fallow rice paddies now support young *hoi takram,* or tilam oysters, which cling to bamboo poles submerged in brackish water. After 2 years they can be harvested; the summer months yield the best crop. Surat Thani's other famed product is the Rong Rian rambutan (*ngor* in Thai). The industry has blossomed since 1926, when a breed of the spine-covered fruit grown in Penang was transplanted here; now more than 125,000 acres of the Nasan district, 24 miles (40km) south of town, are devoted to plantations. Each August (the harvest is August through October) a Rambutan Fair is held, with a parade of fruit-covered floats and performances by trained monkeys.

The city is built up along the south shore of the Tapi River. Talad Mai Road, 2 blocks south of the river, is the city's main street, with the TAT office at its west end, and the bus station and central market at its east end. Frequent minitrucks, or songtao taxis, ply Talad Mai; prices are based on distance but rarely exceed 25B (US70¢), if you bargain.

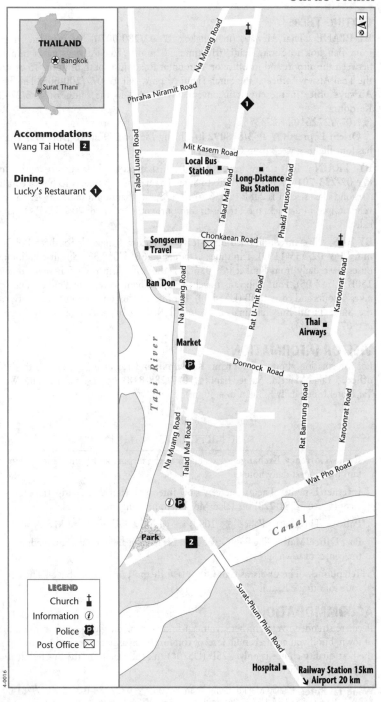

THAILAND

★ Bangkok

● Surat Thani

**Accommodations**
Wang Tai Hotel **2**

**Dining**
Lucky's Restaurant **1**

Na Muang Road

Phraha Niramit Road

Talad Luang Road

Mit Kasem Road

Local Bus Station

Talad Mai Road

Long-Distance Bus Station

Phakdi Anusorm Road

Chonkaean Road

Songserm Travel

Ban Don

Na Muang Road

Rat U-Thit Road

Karoonrat Road

Thai Airways

Market

Donnock Road

Rat Bamrung Road

Karoonrat Road

Na Muang Road

Talad Mai Road

Wat Pho Road

Canal

Park

**2**

Surat-Phum Phim Road

*Tapi River*

**LEGEND**
Church ✝
Information ⓘ
Police 🅿
Post Office ✉

Hospital ■

Railway Station 15km
↘ Airport 20 km

4-0016

189

## GETTING THERE

**BY PLANE** **Thai Airways** (in Bangkok ☎ **02/280-0070**) has two daily flights from Bangkok to Surat Thani (trip time: 70 min.). Thai Airways has a minibus between the airport and its office on Karoonrat Road, just south of town. To contact the Thai Airways office at the Surat Thani Airport, call ☎ **077/200-605.** The **Thai Airways** office in the city is inconveniently located in the southeast at 3/27–38 Karoonrat Rd. (☎ **077/272610** or 273355).

Orient Express (☎ **053/818092** in Chiang Mai or 079/200071 in Surat Thani) has four flights a week from Chiang Mai.

**BY TRAIN** Ten trains leave daily from Bangkok's Hua Lampong station (☎ **02/223-7010** or 02/223-7020) to Surat Thani. The trip time is 13 hours; cost for a second-class sleeper is 248B (US$6.70). The Surat Thani train station is very inconvenient, but mini-trucks meet trains to transport you to town for 20B (US55¢) shared ride.

**BY BUS** Five air-conditioned buses leave daily from Bangkok's Southern Bus Terminal (☎ **02/435-1199**). Trip time: 11 hours; 346B (US$9.35). Six air-conditioned buses leave daily from Phuket (☎ 076/211-480). The trip takes 5 hours and costs 150B (US$4.05). Four minivans travel to Surat Thani daily from Phuket. The trip takes 4 hours and costs 160B (US$4.30). For information on buses out of the city, call the Surat Thani Bus Terminal, on Kaset II Road a block east of the main road (☎ **077/272341**).

## VISITOR INFORMATION

For information about Surat Thani, Ko Samui, and Ko Phangan, contact the **TAT office,** 5 Talad Mai Rd., Surat Thani (☎ **077/288-818**), up the street from the Wang Tai Hotel (open daily 8:30am to 4:30pm).

# Fast Facts: Surat Thani

**Banks/Currency Exchange** Exchanges at the airport and train station maintain the longest daily hours.

**Internet/E-mail** There's one very slow Internet terminal at Pantip Travel Services (☎ 077/281-223) on Talad Moi Road, near the bus terminal.

**Police** The Tourist Police (☎ 1699) are with the TAT on Talad Mai Road.

**Post Office/Mail** The Post Office is on Na Muang and Chonkasean roads near the center of town.

**Telephone** The Overseas Call Office is at the post office (see above). The city code for Surat Thani is **77.**

## ACCOMMODATIONS

If you're stranded overnight here, you can find convenient guesthouses in the center of town, but if you need a certain level of comfort (such as hot water and private bath), the best quality choice is only a 25B (US70¢) tuk-tuk ride from the bus terminal or ferry company offices.

**Wang Tai Hotel.** 1 Talad Mai Rd., Surat Thani 84000. ☎ **077/283-020.** Fax 077/281-007. 850B–1,000B (US$22.95–US$27.05) double. AE, MC, V. South side of town near TAT.

This newish hotel tower offers the most comfortable quarters in Surat Thani. The on-premises Thong Restaurant serves acceptable Thai food and breakfast buffets, while at the quick and easy Coffee Corner you can grab your brew and a fresh pastry while you run to your ferry.

## DINING

There are some small restaurants in the center of town, where you can try locally farmed fresh oysters. In the north end of town you can find **Lucky's Restaurant** at 452/84-85 Talad Mai Rd. (☎ **077/273-267**). The open-air dining room and an air-conditioned hall are busy and loud, both filled with locals enjoying the inexpensive, well-cooked food. The tom yam klung, a shrimp soup with straw mushrooms, makes a good starter before their superb fried oyster omelet.

## ATTRACTIONS

Most people who get to know Surat Thani do so because they've got nothing to do while they wait for the ferry to Ko Samui or the train to Bangkok. The town is small and quiet, with little to do. If you do have some time, I recommend a trip out to see the **Monkey Training College,** 24 Moo 4 Tambon Thungkong (☎ **077/227-351**), open daily 9am to 6pm. For 300B (US$8.10) you can see how Mr. Somphon Saekhow, trainer for some 40 years (and a quirky showman), teaches his monkeys to climb coconut tress and harvest the nuts. While there are monkey shows on Ko Samui and Phuket, this school is the real deal—no silly costumes and horrid living conditions. Flag down an empty songtao and ask the driver if he'll take you there and back—he'll get to see the show for free.

## 10  Ko Samui

The island of Ko Samui lies 52 miles (84km) off Thailand's east coast in the Gulf of Thailand, near the mainland commercial town of Surat Thani, which is itself 400 miles (644km) south of Bangkok. Since the 1850s, Ko Samui has been visited by Chinese merchants sailing from Hainan Island in the South China Sea to trade coconuts and cotton, the island's two most profitable products.

You'll hear Ko Samui compared to Phuket all the time. While Phuket enjoys international fame (or notoriety, depending on your point of view) as a gorgeous beach resort haven, Ko Samui attracts those who want to avoid the hype and settle for more down-to-earth relaxation. Ko Samui's gorgeous beaches were once far less crowded than today, and simple bungalow accommodations and eateries made for a more authentic Southeast Asian island experience. As Ko Samui's reputation as the "alternative Thai island" grew, so did the number of visitors landing on its shores. Increasing demand inspired the opening of an international airport in 1988 that now services more than 20 packed daily flights. In recent years big resorts are getting in on the action, opening up huge accommodations à la Phuket. While they provide more comforts and facilities, they lack the carefree Ko Samui charm that drew travelers here in the first place.

Ko Samui is still in some places an idyllic tropical retreat with little traffic, clean warm water, fine sand beaches, and simple bungalows, some of them very atmospheric and comfortable at the same time. Though it is the country's third-largest island, with a total area of 90 square miles (150 sq km), Ko Samui's entire coastline can be toured by car or motorcycle in about 2½ hours. The island is hilly, densely forested, and rimmed with coconut palm plantations. The Ko Samui airport is in the northeast corner of the island. The hydrofoils, car ferry, and express boats arrive on the west coast, in or near (depending on the boat) Nathon. With few exceptions, the island's paved roads follow the coastline.

Most of Samui's fine beaches are on the north and east coasts. The long east coast stretch between Chaweng and Lamai beaches is the most popular destination for vis-

## What's On in Ko Samui

Ko Samui has an enormous amount of independently produced literature for visitors. Good magazines to keep your eye peeled for are *Accommodation Samui,* with detailed hotel, restaurant, and other listings; *What's on Samui,* for adverts and articles about things to do on the island; and *Samui Guide,* with practical tour and transport specifics. There are at least a half-dozen map guides. I like the free map provided by Bangkok Airways, with major beaches highlighted. The small Tourist Information Center (☎ 077/420-504) in Nathon, on the waterfront street to the left of the piers, also has some useful information.

itors and, consequently, where you'll find the greatest concentration of hotels, bungalows, restaurants, and night life. The south coast is home to the island's small fishing fleet, dating back to the era of the China trade. The west coast has a few sandy strips, but the busy boat traffic lessens its surfside appeal.

The high season on Ko Samui is from mid-December to mid-January. January to April has the best weather, before it gets hot. October through mid-December are the wettest months, with November bringing extreme rains and fierce winds that make the east side of the island rough for swimming. Some years, the island's west side is buffeted by summer monsoons from the mainland.

## GETTING THERE

Getting to Ko Samui is simple. Direct flights from Bangkok, Phuket, Pattaya, and even Singapore make visiting the island a snap. In addition, there are several bus and train options to Surat Thani (the nearest mainland town to the various piers); a hydrofoil from a canal in south Surat Thani; and express ferries from Thathon, another port 3 miles (5km) south of Surat Thani.

**BY PLANE**   Eighteen flights depart daily from Bangkok on **Bangkok Airways** (☎ 02/253-4014), generally one every 40 minutes between the hours of 7:20am and 7:50pm. A daily flight from Phuket (Bangkok Airways Pattaya office ☎ 073/225-033) and another daily from the U-Tapao airport near Pattaya (Bangkok Airways Pattaya office ☎ 038/411-965) connect the major beach destinations, with additional Bangkok Airways flights connecting the northern cities through Bangkok. From Singapore, Bangkok Airways flies direct each day (Singapore office ☎ 65/546-8982).

Ko Samui Airport is a great little airport—open-air pavilions with thatch roofs surrounded by gardens and palms. You'll really feel like you've landed in paradise. For airport information call ☎ 077/425-012. For Bangkok Airways reservations at Ko Samui airport call ☎ 077/425-012. If you're staying at a larger resort, airport minivan shuttles can be arranged when you book your room. If not, just out at the main road you'll find songtaos, pickup truck taxis that can take you to the beach you're staying at. If there are many of you, trips can be as low as 40B each (US$1.10), depending on how far you're going. For one or two people going a longer distance, they may try to up the price to 60B or 80B (US$1.60–US$2.15). If you depart Ko Samui via the airport, there's an additional 150B (US$4.05) airport tax that's usually added to your ticket charge.

**BY TRAIN TO SURAT THANI**   Ten trains leave daily from Bangkok's Hua Lampong station (☎ 02/223-7010 or 02/223-7020) to Surat Thani. The trip takes 13 hours; a second-class sleeper costs 519B (US$14), a second-class seat 248B (US$6.70). One train departs daily from Butterworth Station in Penang, Malaysia, for Surat Thani (in Butterworth call ☎ 04/323-7962).

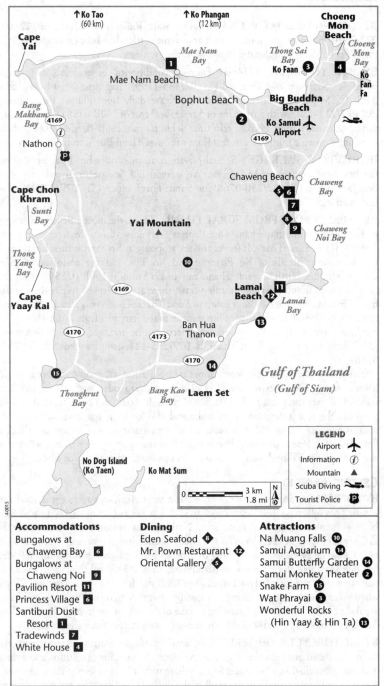

# Ko Samui

↑ Ko Tao
(60 km)

↑ Ko Phangan
(12 km)

Choeng Mon Beach

Cape Yai

*Mae Nam Bay*

**1**

*Thong Sai Bay*
Ko Faan  **3**

**4**  Choeng Mon Bay

Ko Fan Fa

Mae Nam Beach

Bophut Beach

**2**

*Bang Makham Bay*

4169

ⓘ

Nathon

🅿

Big Buddha Beach

Ko Samui Airport ✈

4169

Chaweng Beach

*Chaweng Bay*

**5 6**
**7**

**8**
**9**

Cape Chon Khram

*Sunti Bay*

**Yai Mountain** ▲

*Chaweng Noi Bay*

**10**

*Thong Yang Bay*

4169

Cape Yaay Kai

Lamai Beach  **11**
**12**

*Lamai Bay*

4170

4173

Ban Hua Thanon

**13**

4170

**14**

**15**

*Thongkrut Bay*

*Bang Kao Bay*  Laem Set

**Gulf of Thailand**
*(Gulf of Siam)*

No Dog Island (Ko Taen)

Ko Mat Sum

0   3 km
    1.8 mi

N

**LEGEND**

Airport ✈
Information ⓘ
Mountain ▲
Scuba Diving ≋
Tourist Police 🅿

40015

**Accommodations**
Bungalows at Chaweng Bay **6**
Bungalows at Chaweng Noi **9**
Pavilion Resort **11**
Princess Village **6**
Santiburi Dusit Resort **1**
Tradewinds **7**
White House **4**

**Dining**
Eden Seafood **8**
Mr. Pown Restaurant **12**
Oriental Gallery **5**

**Attractions**
Na Muang Falls **10**
Samui Aquarium **14**
Samui Butterfly Garden **14**
Samui Monkey Theater **2**
Snake Farm **15**
Wat Phrayai **3**
Wonderful Rocks (Hin Yaay & Hin Ta) **13**

**BY TRAIN/BUS/BOAT PACKAGE**  The **State Railway of Thailand** (☎ 02/223-7010) simplifies the journey with an overnight train-bus-boat excursion package for 778B (US$21) that departs Bangkok in the evenings.

**BY BUS TO SURAT THANI**  Four air-conditioned buses leave daily from Bangkok's Southern Bus Terminal (☎ 02/435-1199). Trip time is 10 hours; cost, 346B (US$9.35). Six air-conditioned buses leave daily from Phuket Bus terminal (☎ 077/211-480), with a trip time of 5 hours and cost of 150B (US$4.05). Six minivans depart daily from Phuket; trip time 4 hours, cost 160B (US$4.30). The boat companies provide minibus transfers from the Surat Thani Bus Terminal to the piers.

**BY BUS/BOAT PACKAGE**  Several private companies offer bus-boat service, but the buses can sometimes be inferior. We recommend **Songserm Travel;** call their Bangkok office (☎ 02/250-0768) or Surat Thani office (☎ 077/272928) for information.

**BY EXPRESS BOAT FROM SURAT THANI**  This is the most efficient way to get to Ko Samui from Surat Thani. One Express Ferry leaves from the ferry pier at the Tapee River in Surat Thani. It leaves at 8am, stopping at Ko Samui, then heading off for the nearby islands of Ko Phangan and Ko Tao, and the mainland port of Chumphon, just north of Surat Thani. Fare to Ko Samui is 150B (US$4.05) for the 2½-hour trip. If you miss the morning boat, there are four speed ferries that depart from Thathon, about a half hour south of Surat Thani. The ferry is also 2½ hours and costs 150B (US$4.05), inclusive of bus transfer to the ferry pier from Surat Thani. The last boat leaves at 4pm. Passage on either ferry can be arranged through **Songserm** (30/2 Bangkung Muang, Surat Thani ☎ 077/285-124, or in Bangkok, ☎ 02/250-0768).

You probably won't have to worry about transportation once you reach Nathon, Ko Samui's ferry pier. Touts on the ferry offer very cheap rides, some as low as 20B (US55¢) if they can get a packed truckload from the boat (and be warned, they'll tie people to the roof if they can get an additional 20B for it). If you have no accommodations booking, many will even make a few stops along the way so you can check a few places out before deciding. If you don't find transport to your liking, when you reach the pier you'll find many songtaos, pickups outfitted with bench seats.

## Getting Around

**BY SONGTAO**  Songtaos are the easiest and most efficient way to get around the island. They advertise their destinations to such beaches as Lamai, Chaweng, and Mai Nam with colorfully painted signs. From Nathon most go north and clockwise as far as Chaweng; some head south as far as Lamai; an interchange is necessary at a pavilion near Chaweng Noi for those wishing to proceed further in either direction. You can hail one anywhere along the round-island road. To visit a site off the beaten track (or one other than that painted on a truck's sign), ask the driver to make a detour. Check when your songtao stops running. It's usually around sundown, but some will hang around outside the discos in Chaweng to take night owls home to other beaches. The cost is 20B to 40B (US55¢–US$1.10) one-way, with steeper fares after hours.

**BY MOTORCYCLE OR JEEP**  Ko Samui's roads are narrow, winding, poorly maintained, and not lighted at night. In the island's first decade of tourism, more than 350 foreigners died in vehicle accidents. Still, renting a bike or jeep is the easiest way around if you want to get out to see all of the different beaches. Use extreme caution, and wear a helmet when on a moped or motorcycle. Your defensive driving skills will be required to navigate around slow motorcycles at the side of the road and the occasional wandering dog.

Hertz operates out of the Ko Samui Airport (☎ 077/245-598), out of Chaweng (☎ 077/230-500), and at Le Meridien 15 minutes south of the Nathon Pier (☎ 077/243-019). Daily charges run from 1,610B (US$43.50) for a jeep, 1,850B (US$50) for a Toyota Corolla, and up to 4,370B (US$118.10) for a Volvo. At the beach towns every one of the many tour operators will rent you a Suzuki Samurai for 700B to 900B (US$18.90–US$24.32) a day. These guys are real lax about the whole business of international driver licenses. You don't even necessarily have to prove you can drive, just show your passport and pay the man. Sound scary? You should see their insurance policies.

Many other places along the beaches will rent you a motorcycle—anything from a scooter for 150B (US$4.05) a day to a chopper for 700B to 900B (US$18.90–US$24.30) a day. Insist they provide a helmet.

## Fast Facts: Ko Samui

**Banks/Currency Exchange**    The major banks are in Nathon, along Tawerat-phakdee Road, running parallel to the waterfront road. Money-changing facilities are available at each beach.

**Internet/E-mail**    For Internet service on Chaweng head for the Go Internet Café opposite the Central Samui Beach Resort (☎ 077/230-535). The best Internet and business services overall are at Sawadee Internet Service (131 Moo 4, T. Maret Lamai, Lamai Beach ☎ 077/231-176).

**Police**    For tourist police emergencies dial 1699.

**Post Office/Mail**    The main post office (☎ 077/421-013) is near the Tourist Information Center by the waterfront, but you probably won't want to hike all the way back to the main pier to post a letter. Any hotel or bungalow will handle it for you.

**Telephone**    There are pay telephones, both coin and card, and in the main villages at Chaweng and Lamai beaches you can find overseas calling offices to call home and send or receive faxes. The area code is 077.

## EXPLORING THE ISLAND

I defy you to find a Thai tourist spot without the requisite **snake farm.** Samui's is at the far southwest corner of the island on 4170 Road (☎ 077/423-247), with daily shows at 11am and 2pm. A 200B (US$5.40) adult admission and 120B (US$3.25) for children buys you a 1-hour guided tour. For something a little more tranquil, visit the **Butterfly Garden** (☎ 077/424-020), off the 4170 Road near Laem Din on the southeast corner. It's open daily 9am to 5pm; admission for adults is 120B (US$3.25), for children 60B (US$1.60). Near the Butterfly Garden, at the Samui Orchid Resort, is the **Samui Aquarium** (☎ 077/424-017) with sealife in huge aquariums lining a 40-foot (120m) passageway. It's open daily 9am to 5pm; admission is 250B (US$6.75) adults; 150B (US$4.05) children.

Along Samui's main roads, you'll find little hand-painted signs along the lines of "Monkey Work Coconut." These home-grown tourist spots show off monkey skills involved in the local coconut industry. The proper **Samui Monkey Theater** (☎ 077/245-140) is just south of Bophut village on 4169 Road. Shows are at 10:30am, 2pm, and 4pm daily. Admission is 150B (US$4.05) for adults and 50B (US$1.35) for children.

Every night on Samui your dinner will be interrupted by a roaming pickup truck with a crackling PA system blaring out incomprehensible Thai. These guys advertise local **Thai boxing bouts** and, every once in a while, **buffalo fights.** Grab one of their flyers for times and locations.

Ko Samui's famed **Wonderful Rocks**—the most important of which are the sexually suggestive **Hin Yaay & Hin Ta** (Grandmother and Grandfather Stones)—are located at the far southern end of Lamai Beach. To get to them, walk about an hour south of Chaweng Beach, or take any mini-truck to Lamai Beach and get off at Paradise Bungalows.

The gold-tiled **Wat Phrayai** (Big Buddha), more than 80 feet (26.6m) tall, sits atop Ko Faan (Barking Deer Island), a small islet connected to the shore by a dirt causeway almost 1,000 feet (330m) long. Though of little historic value, it's an imposing presence on the northeast coast and is one of Samui's primary landmarks. It's open all day; a 20B (US55¢) contribution is recommended. It's easy to reach; just hop on any songtao going to Big Buddha Beach. You can't miss it.

The main island road forks at Ban Hua Thanon. At the village of Ban Thurian, the road climbs north past **Na Muang Falls,** a pleasant waterfall once visited by many kings of the Chakri dynasty. After the rainy season ends in December, it reaches a height of almost 100 feet (33m) and a width of about 66 feet (22m). Na Muang is a steamy 3-mile (5km) walk from the coast road and makes for a nice bathing and picnic stop. Feel free to trek to the falls on the back of an elephant. Na Muang Trekking (☎ **077/230-247**) will take you for a half-hour trip, or longer.

## SPORTS & OUTDOOR ACTIVITIES

Local aquanauts agree that the best **scuba diving** is off Ko Tao, a small island north of Ko Phangan and Ko Samui. Since conditions vary with the seasons, the cluster of tiny islands south of Samui or Mu Ko Angthong National Park are often better destinations. Follow the advice of a local dive shop. **Easy Divers,** in operation for 10 years, has locations in Chaweng (on the beach road next to Silver Sand Resort, ☎ **077/230-548**) and Lamai (main road between Sand Sea Resort and Lamai Resort, ☎ **077/231-190**). They offer all sorts of PADI courses, daily dive tours to 13 different sites, international safety standard boats, good equipment, and complete insurance packages. Day dives cost 2,400B to 3,145B (US$64.86–US$85) depending on the itinerary, which changes daily.

Some of the best **snorkeling** off Ko Samui is found off the north end of Chaweng Beach. Several shops along Chaweng Beach rent snorkeling gear for about 150B (US$4.05) per day. Blue Stars Sea Kayaking (at the Gallery Lafayette next to the Green Mango in Chaweng, ☎ **077/230-497**) takes people kayaking and snorkeling to the Marine National Park. For **catamaran sailing,** check out Tradewinds Resort in Chaweng (☎ **077/230-602**). A 3-hour course is 2,500B (US$67.55) while straight rentals are 800B (US$21.60) per hour. At Lamai and Chaweng, you'll see many jet skis for rent, but by in large, people are trying to cut back on the activity due to environmental hazards and numerous accidents involving inexperienced drivers and unsuspecting snorkelers.

Fishermen should talk to **Camel Fishing Game** (in Lamai, across from Bauhaus Pub, ☎ **077/424-523;** 1,500B [US$40.55] for a full day) about daily trips with all equipment and lunch provided.

Other types of sporting activities, some that you'd never expect, are also scattered around the island. Take a break from the beach for go-karts at **Samui Go-Karts** (☎ **077/425-097**) on 4169 (Samui's main road) about 1.6 miles (1km) west of Bophut village. They're open 9am to 9pm daily; cost is 300B to 500B (US$8.10–US$13.50) for 10 minutes. The **Samui Shooting Range,** on 4169 between Bophut and Chaweng (☎ **077/425-370**), has all-age target practice with instructors. Hours:

daily 10am to 6pm; prices range from 350B (US$9.45) for 10 shots from a .22 caliber pistol to 700B (US$18.90) for 10 from a shotgun.

## RESORTS & BUNGALOWS ON KO SAMUI

Every habitable cove on Ko Samui has at least one bungalow complex and snack cafe, but each community has a different personality. Chaweng, and Chaweng Noi (north), are the most popular beaches, with plentiful accommodations, restaurants, nightlife, shopping, and conveniences. At the time this was written they were paving the beach road, and the place was ankle deep in mud and potholes, almost impossible to navigate but hopping nevertheless. The next popular beach is Lamai. It's a little shorter than Chaweng, but has some good and less expensive options for bungalows and restaurants. I've concentrated on these two areas, as they have the most activity, but I've also included a few quiet and atmospheric resorts on other parts of the island. You may wish to stay at one of these places and commute to your fun.

For bungalow accommodation, double and single occupancy carry the same flat price. Many places offer additional beds for a small daily fee.

### CHAWENG & CHAWENG NOI BAYS

Other than Lamai Beach, the two Chawengs (the main and south ["noi"] parts) are the most popular destinations on Ko Samui, and generally draw a more upscale, clean-cut crowd (see Lamai Bay, below). Nowadays there are a few families and an increasing number of European retirees scattered among the predominantly young travelers. Chaweng, the north or main bay, was the first to be developed and is crowded at its north end with simple, budget bungalows with cafes that turn into scenes of active nightlife; Chaweng Noi is more peaceful day or night. Our hotel and restaurant selections in each area are within a half-hour's walk of one another. The fine sand beach extends for about 3½ miles (5.83km) and is an ideal place to swim, windsurf, jog, or just sunbathe.

The main island circle road is 0.3 to 1.8 miles inland from the beach, but there's a one-lane paved road closer to the beach with a number of supermarkets, restaurants, clubs, travel agents, photo shops, money exchanges, and the Tourist Police. Just inland from the rocky point that divides the two bays are a cluster of shops behind the First Bungalow. Here you'll find an inexpensive laundry, a postcard and souvenir shop, a motorbike rental shop (300B [US$8.10] per day), and the Chaweng Library, a commercial book exchange where books in eight languages can be rented for 15B to 30B (US40¢–US80¢) until you've read them, with a 100B (US$2.70) deposit, open daily 9am to 6pm.

#### Accommodations in Chaweng

✪ **The Princess Village.** 101/1 Moo 3 (center of Chaweng Beach, Ko Samui 84320, Surat Thani. ☎ **077/422-216.** Fax 077/422-382. 12 units. A/C MINIBAR. 3,630B (US$98.10) garden view; 4,240B (US$114.60) beach view. AE, MC, V.

If you've wondered what sleeping in Jim Thompson's House or the Suan Pakkard Palace—both in Bangkok—might be like, try the regal Princess Village. Traditional teak houses from Ayutthaya have been restored and placed around a lushly planted garden. Several have sea views and each is on stilts above its own lotus pond; use-worn stairs lead up to a large veranda with roll-down bamboo screens.

Inside, you'll find a grand teak bed covered in embroidered silk or cotton and antique furniture and artwork worthy of the Ramas. Small, carved dressing tables and spacious bathrooms contain painted ceramics, silverware, a porcelain dish, a large khlong jar for water storage, or other Thai details amid the modern conveniences. Traditional shuttered windows on all sides have no screens, but lacy mosquito netting and a ceiling fan, combined with sea breezes, create Thai-style ventilation. The view from the terrace cafe on the beach creates a wonderful setting for an afternoon beer.

**Tradewinds.** 17/14 Moo 3, Chaweng Beach, Ko Samui 84320, Surat Thani. ☎ 077/230-602. Fax 077/231-247. 20 units. A/C MINIBAR. Dec 20–Jan 10 2,500B–3,000B (US$65–US$81); Jan 10–June 1 and August 2,000B–2,500B (US$54–US$65); other months 1,500B–2,000B (US$40–US$54). AE, MC, V.

In the center of Chaweng, Tradewinds has one of the best locations of the beach's accommodations. Step out the front door and you're in the center of the fun: restaurants, clubs, shopping. Meanwhile, the other side of the resort opens out to Chaweng's long, lovely beach. From the higher-priced bungalows you can step right off your front porch into the sand. The other bungalows are placed in shady secluded gardens, not far from the beach. All are modern and fully furnished with large beds and rattan furnishings. Spotless and bright, they're perfect for travelers who want the intimate feeling of a bungalow village but don't want to sacrifice modern conveniences. If you don't want to go out for a meal, the superb Thai restaurant (with Western selections as well) is romantically situated on the beach.

Tradewinds is home to Samui's catamaran sailing center, and also arranges daily snorkeling, trekking, and kayaking trips.

### Dining in Chaweng

**Eden Seafood.** 49/1 Moo 3 (south end of Beach Rd.; call Eden for free pickup from hotel), Chaweng Beach. ☎ **077/422-375.** Reservations not necessary. Main courses 100B–250B (US$2.70–US$6.75). AE, MC, V. Daily 4pm–midnight. SEAFOOD.

From this pleasant group of thatch pavilions—some overlooking a winding creek from several different levels—diners can choose from the freshest pomfret, red or white snapper, lobster, tiger prawns, mussels, or catch of the day (priced per kilogram), or select from the à la carte menu. Fish is steamed, fried with sweet-and-sour sauce, grilled, or poached with garlic and peppers. Don't forget the oysters, fresh from the famed farms of Surat Thani. The live music, a guy with a Casio accompanying Thai women warbling ballads, adds a spacey but admittedly enjoyable touch. The gracious staff proudly presents an extensive drink list, which includes very sweet, Thai-produced red and Australian house wines for 80B a glass.

**The Oriental Gallery.** 39/1 Moo 3, Chaweng Beach. ☎ **077/422-200.** Reservations not necessary. Daily 2pm–11:30pm. THAI.

Opened in 1991, the Oriental Gallery combines a fine arts and antiques gallery with a swanky little cafe. Gorgeous treasures fill the dining area, both indoors and in the small outdoor patio garden. You'll almost be too busy admiring the pieces to look at the menu, which features some appetizing Thai soups, noodle dishes, and more. The selections are prepared and presented with similar good taste, and are not too spicy for tender foreign tongues. The friendly and knowledgeable gallery owners are around to chat about Thai antiques and art, and to explain any pieces that catch your eye.

## LAMAI BAY

The long sand beach on Lamai Bay is comparable to Chaweng's (see "Chaweng & Chaweng Noi Bays," above), but the clientele is decidedly rowdier and more colorful, if not always younger. Though there are many bungalows, few are above the most primitive of standards, and they tend to attract backpackers. I've only listed one resort here, because it's the only place that's comfortable enough for me to recommend. However, there's lots of new construction, most of it in the budget category, and a range of cafes, bars, discos, tourist services, and bungalows make Lamai the cheapest resort on the island.

The north end of the beach strip is known as Coral Cove, a rocky area where bungalows are built up on the hillside. South of it, along the inland lagoon where fishermen moor their boats, there's a paved service road and beach access lane, both between the shoreline and the main island circle road. Public mini-trucks cruise the inner service road and will deliver you to the "back door" of most of the beach-front bungalows. Lamai Noi is the quieter south end of the beach, somewhat removed from the fray by its autonomous network of inland service roads.

## Accommodations in Lamai

**The Pavilion Resort.** 124/24 Moo 3 (north end of Lamai Beach), Lamai Beach, Ko Samui 84310, Surat Thani. ☎ **077/424-420,** or in Bangkok 02/635-6935. Fax 077/424-029. 50 units. A/C MINIBAR. Peak season Dec 21–April 30 and July 16–August 31: 3,600B (US$97) double in hotel wing; 4,200B–5,200B (US$113–US$140) cottage. Other times 3,200B (US$86); and 3,600B–4,400B (US$97–US$118), respectively. AE, DC, MC, V.

One of Lamai's newer facilities, this resort has attached rooms in a hotel block and Polynesian-style octagonal bungalows, all scattered throughout the beachfront grounds (there are limited sea views). It is possibly the most deluxe accommodation you'll find on Lamai. Hotel rooms are nicely appointed, each with its own safe, and have good-sized patios for sunbathing. The larger bungalows have a campy primitive feel, as well as the comfort of a private bath and hot water. The pool and dining pavilion are right on the surf—combined with ground-floor hotel rooms, it makes for comfortable, easy access resort for the disabled. The proximity to Lamai's nightlife is a plus for most guests, while the beachside swimming pool and Jacuzzi, with cafe dining and bar, provide a very quiet escape from the goings-on in the rest of Lamai.

## Dining in Lamai

**Mr. Pown Restaurant.** 124/137 Moo 3, Lamai Beach. ☎ **01/970-7758.** Reservations not necessary. 120B and up (US$3.25); seafood sold at market value. AE, MC, V. SEAFOOD.

Of all the seafood places along the main drag in Lamai, Mr. Pown is the nicest. Fresh seafood is carefully laid on ice in front of the entrance, so you can choose your own toothy fish or local lobster. The restaurant is patio-style, and tables near the front railing are great fun for people-watching. The menu is an extensive list of seafood of all kinds prepared in many Chinese, Thai, and Western styles. There's also an assortment of accompanying Chinese and Thai soup, vegetable, and meat dishes. The lobster is delicious but expensive.

## ACCOMMODATIONS OUTSIDE CHAWENG & LAMAI

✪ **Santiburi Dusit Resort.** 12/12 Moo 1, Mae Nam Beach, Ko Samui 84330, Surat Thani. ☎ **077/425-031.** Fax 077/425-040. 73 units. A/C MINIBAR TV TEL. 8,500B–9,000B (US$229–US$243) single or double; 10,500B–19,500B (US$284–US$527) suite. AE, DC, MC, V.

A quiet getaway, this tranquil resort—the name means peaceful town—is a village of palatial pavilions informally arrayed around the largest swimming pool on the island (an oval more than 150 feet, or 50 meters, long). A small river winds through its lush tropical gardens to the long, clean beach. Modeled after a mountain retreat built by King Rama IV more than a century ago and strongly influenced by Western neoclassical architecture, yet distinctly Thai, it evokes that earlier era without neglecting modern comfort and convenience. Guests are welcomed by the sounds of splashing water and a relaxed but attentive staff in a cool, intimate lobby that opens onto the spacious 23-acre compound. Rooms are large, lush, and inviting, with the special warmth of natural teak, traditionally styled furniture, hand-woven fabrics, and other distinctive Asian touches; the bathrooms are especially large. Three dining establishments, one Thai, one East-meets-West, and a poolside cafe, mean you don't have to trek to the nearest beach for variety. Dusit will arrange any water sports you'd like. There are also tennis courts, a squash court, and a fitness center.

**The White House.** Cheng Mon Beach, Ko Samui 84140, Surat Thani. ☎ **077/422382.** Fax 077/425233. 40 units. A/C MINIBAR. 2,650B–3,400B (US$72–US$92) single or double. AE, MC, V.

This new resort in the graceful Ayutthaya style, built around a central garden with a lotus pond and swimming pool, is dripping with atmosphere. The lobby—almost a museum—is impeccably decorated with original Thai artwork and images. Spacious and elegant rooms with tea and coffee service flank a central walkway that's lined with orchids and other attractive plants in large pots. Down by the beach there's a pool with a bar and an especially graceful teak *sala*. The resort's quality Swiss management team, with proven success on Ko Samui, assures a pleasant stay. White House, in the northeastern part of the island, is far from the action of Chaweng and Lamai, but there are jeep and motorbike rentals available.

## KO SAMUI AFTER DARK

The beaches of Chaweng and Lamai have the island's widest variety of nightlife.

Chaweng's hot spot seems to be centered around The **Reggae Pub,** with a nightly band that keeps the crowd moving (it gets especially crowded on weekends), pool tables, snack bar, and outside video theater. Around Reggae Pub and along Chaweng's beach road are open-air bars with names like Doors Pub, Blues Brothers, and Black Cat, each with its own personality that shifts with the demands of clientele. The **Green Mango,** near the north end of the strip, is a popular Euro-pop disco with an okay Thai food cafe and more Thai (thatch/bamboo/palm frond) decor.

Lamai is the place for more raucous nightlife. On Lamai Beach Road, parallel to the beach, beginning just south of the Weekender Resort and continuing for about half a mile south, is a strip of Thai, continental, pizza, and seafood restaurants, all open-air, all pretty cheap, plus lots of bars and discos. Opportunities to meet young Thai women abound.

At the **Lamai Night Plaza,** opposite Soi Noy in the middle of this strip, a dozen or so open-air bars cluster back-to-back in a compound of Pattaya-style flesh and booze vendors. Several bars also show videos. Warning: The girls make a commission off what you drink, so watch out or you'll end up buying everyone a round; guard your wallet, avoid the drug trade (heavily policed on this island), and be wary of accepting drinks (often drugged) from a stranger. Finally, the large, well advertised **Bauhaus Pub** sounded like fun, but turned out to be a bunch of bored guys sitting around watching football.

## SIDE TRIPS FROM KO SAMUI

A lot of people on Samui will chat up the surrounding islands in the Gulf of Thailand for all sorts of reasons: some good, some bad, and some purely misguided. Ko Phangan, Ko Tao, and the islands of Mu Ko Ang Thong National Marine Park are smaller than Samui, and less developed, that's for sure, but not always as idyllic as you might hope for.

Ko Phangan is the biggest myth going. While the beaches are stunning, the cheap bungalow accommodations, restaurants, and bars that have sprung up have no proper facilities to handle the waste and garbage they produce. Much of it gets washed up on the beach or just floats around in the water. Most of the people who venture out to the island are backpacking twenty-somethings, rowdy party-seekers, budget travelers seeking adventure, and hippies who've seen better days. Zen meditation workshops, vegetarian food, and drugs take center stage.

Any stories you hear about the **Haad Rin Full Moon Parties** are true. On the full moon of each month anywhere from 5,000 to 8,000 folks head for Haad Rin on the southwestern peninsula, the most popular spot on the island. Beachfront bars invite international DJs to spin all kinds of music from dusk until dawn (the party gets into full force somewhere between 9pm and midnight and carries on until the sun comes up). The main attraction is drugs: marijuana, hallucinogenic mushrooms, LSD, Ecstasy, and "Speed Punch." If that's your scene, hop aboard one of the boats that leave the pier at Big Buddha beach. They cart partyers out all day and evening until 1am. Don't even think about finding accommodations for the night unless you arrive at least a few days, maybe more, in advance. Otherwise, do like so many others and pass out on the beach. Look after your belongings and don't leave valuables in your bungalow. A word of caution: the police are hip to the Full Mooners, and come around in plain clothes. Jail time is a reality and fines are huge. Rave at your own risk.

Scuba enthusiasts will tell you about Ko Tao. Live coral reefs and stunning sea life are fabulous at this highly rated dive site. Any of the many dive operators on Ko Samui are glad to take you out for a day trip, PADI open water course, overnight dive package (in bungalows on the west and south coasts), or night dive. The downside of Ko Tao is scuba traffic, which can take some of the fun out of it during high season.

**Mu Ko Angthon National Marine Park** is some 40 islands, mostly beautiful limestone rock towers that have been sectioned off for preservation. The National Park headquarters is on **Ko Wua Ta Lap** (Sleeping Cow Island), where there are dormitory accommodations and camping facilities for overnighters. To request a permit to visit and details about your stay, contact the national parks head office in Bangkok at ☎ **02/579-0529.** A good day trip into the park is via a kayak and snorkeling tour from Ko Samui. See above for booking details.

## 11  Phuket

No other Thai destination has changed so rapidly as Phuket, yet it remains Thailand's finest resort destination. At its best, this island in the Andaman Sea, 534 miles (862km) south of Bangkok and 178 miles (287km) southwest of Surat Thani, is almost idyllic. It has long sandy beaches (some with dunes), warm water, excellent snorkeling and scuba diving off Ko Similan, ideal windsurfing conditions, mountains, and the best seafood in all of Thailand.

During the past decade the Thai government has granted economic incentives to encourage developers to shape the island into an international-class resort. Hotels—some of them enormous—are taking over every beach where once only a scattering of modest bungalows stood. As groups pour in from Singapore, Hong Kong, Germany, and Italy, backpackers head off to nearby Ko Pi Pi, or Ko Samui on the Gulf.

Some of the resorts are disarmingly attractive and elegant. The "Miami Beach" strip of concrete and steel is rarely seen on Phuket (although Patong Beach has sunk below the level of the most honky-tonk beachside resort we've ever encountered). In its place are serene bays framed by tastefully designed retreats that are modeled after hillside villas or luxury bungalows. It's nearly impossible to find a totally secluded beach, but there are a number of very attractive and comfortable facilities with a high level of service, not a bad trade-off for those in search of all the luxuries. If you're traveling with a family, want to be pampered, or are looking for action, Phuket might be the place for you.

The season on Phuket extends from September to March, with the 4 months between November and March being prime time. The monsoon strikes from April to August; during the period from late June through August, the so-called promotional season, many hotels and other establishments and services offer discounts up to 50%.

During the monsoon season few people come to Phuket due to the perception that it rains all day and night, every day. It doesn't, and we think that for the more flexible it's an ideal time to make a visit.

Phuket is Thailand's largest island, its terrain vast and varied. Wide, grassy plains give way to lush forests that are dense with mangroves, rubber, and palm trees.

The name "Phuket" is derived from the Malay "Bukit," meaning mountain, and hills dominate much of the island, spilling their craggy rocks on the gentle beach coves below. From most high points you can see a number of nearby islands and islets, among them, hourglass-shaped Ko Pi Pi, off the southern shore. In parts of the interior, open-pit mining for tin and other metals has scarred the land.

If you arrive by car or coach, you cross over to Phuket from the mainland at the northern tip of the island via the Sarasin Bridge. A few miles east of the inland road is the Khao Phra Thaeo Wildlife Park, notable for Ton Sai falls, a lovely spot for a cool break on a blistering day. The park is home to a variety of birds and other fauna, as well as diverse flora, including a variety of palm that is unique to the island. The road continues south to the middle of the island and the largest town, Phuket.

In the southeastern quarter, Phuket is the island's commercial and transportation nexus. Most, if not all, local buses go to Phuket town (usually called simply "Phuket"). Because inland Phuket is often very hot and noisy with buzzing motorcycles and cars, most tourists usually head for the shore, where the blazing sun, fine white sand, and refreshing sea encourage a longer stay than planned.

Phuket's most attractive beaches are on the west coast, extending from Nai Harn, on the southern tip, to Bang Tao, about 19 miles (30km) north. Most bungalows and new resorts are in between, along the Kata, Kata Noi, Karon, Karon Noi, Patong, and Surin corridor. A coastal road linking most of these beaches has been completed. For now, travel between some of the beaches north of Patong requires a detour to the interior, although some stretches are navigable with four-wheel-drive vehicles.

In the northern and inland sections of the island, peasants still use basic tools and water buffalo to work the fields. In contrast, road crews tear up agricultural lanes along the perimeter of these centuries-old farms to create wide, modern thoroughfares for the tourist trade.

This section is largely dedicated to activities on the western coast of the island, mainly the Karon and Patong beaches where most people spend their time. However, many fine resorts are outside of these areas, so they're included as well.

## GETTING THERE

**BY PLANE    Thai Airways** (☎ 02/280-0070 in Bangkok) flies 10 times daily from Bangkok (trip time: 1 hour; 2,400B [US$65]); and once daily from Surat Thani (trip time: 45 minutes; 600B [US$16]). **Thai Airways'** office in Phuket is at 78 Ranong Rd., Phuket town (☎ 076/211-195 domestic; ☎ 076/212-499 international).

**Bangkok Airways** (☎ 02/253-4014 in Bangkok; ☎ 077/425-012 in Ko Samui) connects Phuket with Ko Samui once daily. Bangkok Airways office in Phuket is at 158/2-3 Yaowarat Rd., Phuket town (☎ 076/225-033, or ☎ 076/327-114 at Phuket Airport).

Phuket is also serviced by Singapore Airlines and Malaysian Airlines.

The attractive, modern Phuket International Airport is located on the north end of the island. There are banks, money-changing facilities, car rental agents (see "Getting Around" later in this section) and a post office. The Phuket Tourist Business Association booth can help you make hotel arrangements if you haven't booked a room.

Many resorts will fetch you from the airport upon request for a fee, usually steep. The airport limousine counter, operated by **Tour Royale** (☎ 076/341-214), offers many options for getting to your hotel from the airport. The cheapest way is the

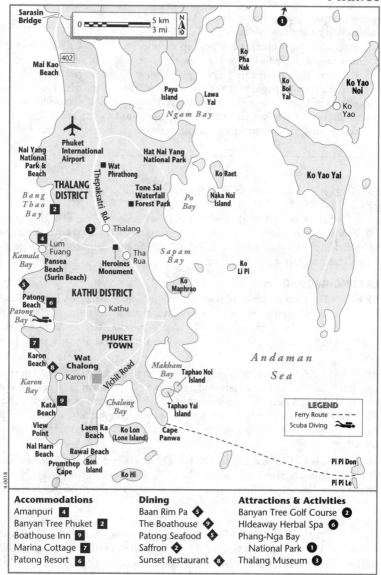

**Accommodations**
Amanpuri **4**
Banyan Tree Phuket **2**
Boathouse Inn **9**
Marina Cottage **7**
Patong Resort **6**

**Dining**
Baan Rim Pa **5**
The Boathouse **9**
Patong Seafood **5**
Saffron **2**
Sunset Restaurant **8**

**Attractions & Activities**
Banyan Tree Golf Course **2**
HIdeaway Herbal Spa **6**
Phang-Nga Bay
   National Park **1**
Thalang Museum **3**

minibus which operates every hour on the hour from 9am to 11pm daily. Stopping in Patong, Kata, Karon, and Phuket, it costs from 80B to 180B (US$2.15–US$4.85), depending on how far you're going. Taxi service from the airport, also arranged at the limousine counter, will cost from between 360B (US$9.75) to Phuket town to 540B (US$14.60) to Kata beach. The VIP Volvo transfer will set you back between 480B and 750B (US$12.95–US$20.25).

**BY BUS** Four air-conditioned buses leave daily from Bangkok's Southern Bus Terminal (☎ 02/435-1199, on Charan Sanitwong Road). Trip time is 14 hours or 457B

| What's On in Phuket |
| --- |

Some great local publications to pick up include the free *Phuket Food-Shopping-Entertainment*, packed with hotel and restaurant write-ups and ads for many of the island's activities. The monthly ultra-glossy *Greater Phuket Magazine* provides in-depth articles and photo essays about the island and its people. The Tourism Authority of Thailand is on the ball in Phuket, though you have to travel all the way into Phuket town to see them at 73–75 Phuket Road (☎ **076/211-036**). The people behind the counter know everything there is to know about travel in the area.

(US$12.35). Six buses leave daily from Surat Thani. Trip time is 6 hours; cost is 90B–200B (US$2.45–US$5.40).

The **intercity** bus terminal is at the city Park Complex on Phangnga Road (☎ **076/211-480**), east of Phuket town, a 10-minute walk to the center; a tuk-tuk to or from the center should cost you 20B (US55¢). For information on how to get to the beaches, see "Getting Around," below.

## GETTING AROUND

**BY BUS**   The **local** bus terminal is in front of the Central Market on Ranong Road in Phuket town. Fares to the most popular destinations range from 15B to 25B (US40¢–US70¢). Buses are typically scheduled to operate every 15 to 30 minutes from 6am to 5pm, but usually run whenever there is a full load of passengers or produce.

**BY TUK-TUK**   Within Phuket town, tuk-tuks (motorized three-wheeled vehicles) cost 20B (US55¢), more or less, depending on your ability to bargain. They can also be hired for longer distances, but if economy is your aim, you'd probably do better joining the locals in a songtao. For an idea of fares, expect to pay from 120B (US$3.25) in between neighboring beaches, and up to 300B (US$8.10) from town to the airport.

**BY SONG TAO**   Mini-truck taxis, with benches in a covered bed, run to most of the beaches from an informal station near the small park north of the TAT office in Phuket town. Regular service ends about 5pm, and you will have to bargain to charter a ride.

**BY CAR**   Avis has quite a few counters on Phuket. At the airport, they can be reached at ☎ **076/351-243.** They also have counters at the Amanpuri and Banyantree Resort, both reviewed in this section. A Suzuki Caribbean is 1,800B (US$48.65) per day while a Volvo is 9,000B (US$243.25), with all kinds of other vehicles in between.

Inexpensive Suzuki Caribbeans can be found at almost all travel agents at the beach areas for 700B to 900B (US$18.90–US$24.30) per day. World Rent a Car (opposite the airport, ☎ **076/205-359**) can greet you at the airport or deliver a car to your resort.

## Fast Facts: Phuket

**American Express**   The American Express agent in Phuket is Sea Tours (☎ 076/218-417), 95/4 Phuket Rd., Phuket town, 1 block south of the TAT. They're open Mon–Fri 8:30am–5pm, Sat 8:30am to noon. For lost or stolen traveler's checks or cards, the 24-hour number in Bangkok is 02/273-0022.

**Banks/Currency Exchange**    Banks are located in Phuket town, with many larger branches on Ranong and Rasada roads. There are bank offices at the airport, as well as branches of major Thai banks at Kata, Karon, and Patong beaches. Money changers are also around, especially in major shopping areas on each beach.

**Internet/E-mail**    Service is fairly easy to find at all the beaches. My favorite is Pizzadelic, a combination pizzeria, bar, and Internet cafe at 93/3 Taveewongse Rd. in Patong (☎ 076/341-545). They have fairly reliable service, plus you can have a beer while you e-mail. At Karon, try the Karon Beach Internet Center at 36/31 Patak Rd. (☎ 076/286-086); and in Phuket town go to The Tavern, 64/3–4 Rasada Rd., Soi Shopping Center (☎ 076/223-569).

**Police**    The emergency number for the Tourist Police is 1699. For Marine Police call (☎ 076/342-518).

**Post Office/Mail**    The General Post Office in Phuket town (☎ 076/211020) is at the corner of Thalang Road and Montri Road. In Karon there's a small post office on the north end of Karon Beach Road between My Friendship Hotel and South Sea Resort. In Patong the post office is on Thaveewongse Road (the main beach road) in the center of the strip near the Banthai Hotel.

## ACCOMMODATIONS
### KATA & KARON BEACH

These are among the island's most attractive beaches, about 12 miles (20km) southwest of Phuket town and several miles north of Nai Harn. By day, the beaches are beginning to resemble Saint-Tropez, with rows of rented beach chairs and umbrellas lining the fine white sand, at times packed and even hectic in the high season.

The two beaches are separated by a rocky promontory but are quite similar, in both ambiance and development. A few primitive bungalows and an occasional hotel behemoth interrupt the long coastline.

✪ **The Boathouse Phuket.** 114 Patak Rd., Kata Beach, Phuket 83100. ☎ **076/330-015.** Fax 076/330-561. 36 units. A/C MINIBAR TV TEL. 6,800B double (US$184); 13,000B (US$351) suite. Peak-season supplement 1,800B (US$48.65) (Dec 23–Feb 28). AE, DC, MC, V.

With its own beach at the quieter south end of Kata Beach, this small inn is a favorite. All the comfortable, attractive rooms face the sea, each with a terrace overlooking the huge Jacuzzi pool in the courtyard. The small beachside pool has massage and therapy facilities nearby. Nothing about the hotel calls attention to itself; it's the well-trained, friendly, attentive staff that makes it special. The Boathouse also offers discount theme packages: Health Holidays, inclusive of massage and herbal steam treatments; and a Thai Cooking Class weekend getaway. The hotel's high-style Thai and continental restaurant serves some of the best food on the island and boasts one of the best wine "cellars" in Thailand.

**Marina Cottage.** 120 Patak Rd. (on bluff at south end of Karon Beach Rd.), Kata Karon Beach, Phuket 83000. ☎ **076/330-625.** Fax 076/330-516. 104 units. A/C MINIBAR TV TEL. 3,200B (US$86) double bungalow; 2,000B (US$54) double fan-cooled bungalow. MC, V.

These simple Thai cottages, tucked in the woods above the cusp of Kata and Karon beaches, are connected with a network of passageways and sky bridges through palm trees and forest. They are better equipped and more accommodating than most bungalows along these beaches, and each has its own balcony. All are a hike down to the rocky shore; rates vary according to the view. Some rooms have air-conditioning. A pleasant restaurant cottage serves good, inexpensive Thai food, and has a nice view of the sunset.

The Marina Cottage is home to **Marina Divers** (☎ 076/381625), a PADI International Diving School, which conducts classes, rents equipment, and leads expeditions around the island reefs.

## PATONG BEACH

Patong has a proliferation of hotels and guesthouses, and yes, the night life scene includes go-go girls and massage parlors. Unfortunately, Patong has now strayed far into the realm of the tacky and become a kind of soul brother to Pattaya (or Tijuana, Mexico, for that matter). Despite pollution controls and water treatment, the beach is not terribly clean, and there's often a funky smell. Even with this warning, many people love it and flock to the place for its nightlife. Patong is hardly a virgin island paradise (as many people probably think based on glitzy hotel brochures), but it can be fun for those seeking a heady dose of after-dark activities.

**Patong Resort.** 208 Ratchutit Rd., Patong Beach, Phuket ☎ **076/340-551.** Fax 076/340-189. 325 units. A/C MINIBAR TV TEL. 1,826B double (US$49); 4,800B (US$130) suite. AE, MC, V.

Possibly the best hotel to recommend on Patong, the Patong Resort towers above the skyline, providing rooms on upper floors with aerial views of the beach and its activities below. It is at the same time in the center of town yet set back a bit off the main drag, so you can remove yourself if Patong gets to be a bit much. While Patong can be a seedy camp, this resort is respectable—I ate breakfast in the coffee shop with plenty of families. Guest rooms are quiet but lack the Thai touches or pastel beach decor standard in almost all the local resorts. The courtyard pool is large, but not very secluded. Patong Resort also has a fitness center.

## ACCOMMODATIONS OUTSIDE KATA, KARON & PATONG

✪ **Amanpuri.** Pansea Beach, Phuket 83110. ☎ **076/324-333.** Fax 076/324100. 43 units. A/C MINIBAR TEL. AE, DC, MC, V. North end of cove.

The discreet and sublime Amanpuri is the Phuket address for visiting celebrities, from Hollywood and elsewhere. Small wonder, as it's the most elegant and secluded resort in Thailand and quite possibly all of Southeast Asia, for that matter. The lobby is an open-air pavilion with a standing Buddha, a lovely swimming pool, and stairs leading to the beach. Superior Pavilion Suites are freestanding houses creeping up the dense coconut palm grounds from the main building. Each is masterfully designed in a traditional Thai style, with teak and tile floors, sliding teak doors, exquisite built-ins, and well-chosen accents, including antiques. Private *salas* (covered patios) are perfect for romantic dining or secluded sunbathing. For special mood setting, check under the bathroom sinks for heavenly incense and burners. Less expensive suites are available inland from the resort, across the road. Two restaurants, the Restaurant Amanpuri and the Terrace, serve Western cuisine (including imported rarities that are hard to find in Thailand) and great Thai dishes. For excitement, they have their own yacht fleet, water-sports equipment and instruction, swimming pool, tennis and squash courts, fitness center, sauna, and private beach. For quiet times, there's a library with books, videos, and CDs (stereo systems are standard in each room).

✪ **Banyan Tree Phuket.** 33 Moo 4, Srisoonthorn Rd., Cherngtalay District, Amphur Talang, Phuket 83110. ☎ **800/525-4800** in the U.S. and Canada, 1800/251-958 in Australia, 0800/964-470 in the U.K., or 076/324-374. Fax 076/324-375. 86 units. A/C MINIBAR TV TEL. April–Oct: garden villa US$300; Jacuzzi villa US$390; pool villa US$520; 2-bedroom pool villa US$1,000. Oct–March: garden villa US$400; Jacuzzi villa US$510; pool villa US$700; 2-bedroom pool villa US$1,280. AE, DC, MC, V. North end of beach.

Banyan Tree is part of Laguna Phuket, a sprawling resort consortium that includes four other resorts and an 18-hole golf course, all connected by ferries. Far from the crowds of rowdy Patong and Karon beaches, Banyan Tree is a famous hideaway for honeymooners and people who just want to relax. Private villas with walled courtyards (many with private pool or Jacuzzi) are spacious and grand, lushly styled in teakwood with an outdoor bath and a platform bed under large Thai murals depicting the *Ramakien,* the story of the *Ramayana.* The resort can arrange private barbecues at your villa, and massage under each villa's *sala,* an outdoor Thai-style pavilion. The reception area is a large open *sala* with lovely lotus pools. Within the main building are the resort's five main restaurants for a choice of Thai, Mediterranean, Southeast Asian, and other international cuisine.

The Banyan Tree Spa wins awards every year. A small village in itself, the spa provides a wide range of beauty and health treatments in relaxing rooms, plus Jacuzzi, sauna, steam, hair styling, fitness pavilion (with daily meditation lessons), separate spa pool, and a cafe serving delicious light and healthy dishes.

Banyan Tree's main pool is one of the most amazing I've ever seen: a free-form lagoon, landscaped with greenery and rock formations, with a water canal whose currents gently pull you through the passage. In addition to the Banyan Tree Phuket Golf Club, there are three outdoor tennis courts, sailing, windsurfing, and canoeing. The resort can arrange pretty much any activity, both inside and outside the resort. For added options, Banyan Tree guests have signing privileges at the sister resorts of the Laguna consortium.

# DINING
## IN PATONG

**Baan Rim Pa.** Kalim Beach Rd., north end of Patong Beach. ☎ **076/340-789.** Reservations necessary. Entrees 250B–1,200B (US$6.75–US$32.40). AE, DC, MC, V. Open daily noon–2:30pm and 6–10pm. THAI.

In a beautiful Thai-style teak house, Baan Rim Pa has dining in the romantic indoor setting or with a gorgeous view of the bay from outdoor terraces. This restaurant is one of the most popular on the island, for locals who wish to entertain as well as for visitors, so be sure to reserve your table early. Thai cuisine features seafood, with a variety of other meat and vegetable dishes including a rich duck curry and a sweet honey chicken dish. The seafood basket is a fantastic assortment of prawns, mussels, squid, and crab.

**Patong Seafood Restaurant.** Patong Beach Rd., Patong Beach. ☎ **076/340-247.** Reservations not necessary. 80B–250B (US$2.15–US$6.75); seafood at market price. AE, DC, MC, V. Open daily 7am–11pm. SEAFOOD.

Take an evening stroll on the lively Patong Beach strip and you'll find quite a few open-air seafood restaurants displaying their catches of the day at their entrances, laid out on chipped ice. The best choice of them all is the casual Patong Seafood, for the freshest and the best selection of seafood, including several types of local fish, lobster, squid (very tender), prawn, and crab. The menu has a fantastic assortment of preparation styles, with photos of popular Thai noodles and Chinese stir-fry dishes. Service is quick and efficient. The place fills up quickly, so it's best to arrive here early.

## IN KARON

**Sunset Restaurant.** 102/6 Patak Rd., Karon Beach. ☎ **076/396-465.** Reservations not necessary. Entrees 80B–180B (US$2.15–US$4.85); seafood at market price. AE, DC, MC, V. Open daily 8am–11pm. SEAFOOD

While Patak Road, running perpendicular to the main beach road, doesn't really have a view of the sunset, this restaurant is notable for its fine seafood, prepared in both local and Western styles. Their lobster thermidor and Western-style steamed fish are fresh and scrumptious, as are their mixed seafood platters. Thai dishes are either spicy or tempered upon request, depending on your preference. Simple tables have neat batik cloths, which is about the only nice touch in the decor. Nevertheless, it's a favorite spot for foreigners living in Phuket, and one of the best places in this part of the island.

## In Kata

**The Boathouse.** The Boathouse Inn, 114 Patak Rd. ☎ **076/330-557.** Reservations accepted. 200B (US$5.40) and up, seafood sold at market price. AE, DC, MC, V. Open daily 7:30am–11pm. THAI/INTERNATIONAL.

So legendary is the Thai and Western cuisine at the Boathouse that the inn where it resides offers popular holiday packages for visitors who wish to come and take cooking lessons from its chef. Inside the restaurant, a large bar and separate dining area have nautical touches. Cuisine is nouvelle, combining the best of East and West and the best ingredients in satisfying portions. If you're in the mood for the works, the Phuket lobster is one of the most expensive dishes on the menu but is worth every baht. The Boathouse also has an excellent selection of international wines. Bon appetit.

## Dining Outside Patong, Kata & Karon

**Saffron.** Banyan Tree Phuket, 33 Moo 4, Srisoonthorn Rd., Cherngtalay, Amphur Talang. ☎ **076/324-374.** Reservations accepted. Entree 300B–600B (US$8.10–US$16.20). Open daily 6:30–10:30pm. AE, DC, MC, V. THAI.

Saffron is a small place, but it's full of charm provided by unique antiques lit by the subtle glow of dripping candles. The specialty dishes here are the various styles of Thai curries, which the restaurant showcases with a curry buffet dinner every Friday night for 690B (US$18.65) per person. Staff is attentive and friendly, and will recommend dishes for you if you can't decide. There's also a good selection of international wines available.

# SPORTS, OUTDOOR ACTIVITIES & ATTRACTIONS

Phuket's picturesque beaches, clear waters, and surrounding islands are a paradise for vacationers who want tropical island splendor. You can spend days, if not weeks, taking advantage of all the scuba, fishing, kayaking, snorkeling, and other water activities around. You wouldn't expect to find sports like bungee jumping or go-kart racing here, but they're surprisingly popular. Eco-tours into the island's jungle interior reveal waterfalls and rapids (which can be toured via raft), while trips to nearby islands for trekking, snorkeling, or just relaxing on the beach remove you from Phuket's tourism mayhem. But if it's tourism mayhem you want, there are plenty of elephant treks, a snake farm, and an assortment of small local museums and parks to see.

The island's more than 45 **scuba** operators are testimony to the beautiful attractions that lie deep in the Andaman Sea. Sites at nearby coral walls, caves, and wrecks can be explored in full-day, overnight or long-term excursions. All operators advertise full PADI courses, Divemaster courses, and 1-day introductory lessons. The best recommendations all point to **Fantasea Divers,** the oldest and most reputable firm. Their main office is at Patong Beach at 219 Ratchautit Rd. (☎ **076/340-088;** fax 076/340-309), but they have other branches along Thaveewongse Road (the main beach road) in Patong. Another well-regarded firm is **Dive Asia,** with a location in Kata beach (121/10 Moo 4, Patak Road; ☎ **076/396-199**) and Karon beach (36/10 Moo 1, Patak Road; ☎ **076/330-589;** fax 076/284-033). Your average day trip consists of a morning and afternoon dive, with lunch provided in between. Expect to pay from 2,500B to 3,000B (US$67.45–US$81.10) depending on your dive itinerary. Equipment rentals are 800B (US$21.60) extra.

For a very unique water adventure, try a **sea kayak** trip to Phang-nga Bay National Park, a 1½-hour drive north of Phuket (3 hours by boat) off Thailand's mainland.

Between 5 and 10 million years ago, limestone thrusted above the water's surface, creating over 120 small islands. These craggy rock formations (the famous scenery for the James Bond classic, *The Man With the Golden Gun)* look like they were taken straight from a Chinese scroll painting. Sea kayaks are perfect for inching your way into the many breathtaking caves and chambers that hide inside the jagged cliffs. Price including lunch and transfers is 2,500B (US$67.45) for adults, 1,250B (US$33.80) for children. Contact Andaman Sea Kayak (☎ **076/235-353**).

Sportspeople will appreciate **big game fishing** for marlin, sailfish, and wahoo organized through Aloha Tours. Aloha has many different kinds of boats to choose from, and will provide professional equipment. A full day can set you back 1,900B (US$51.30). Call ☎ **076/381-215** or fax 076/381-592 for bookings.

Meanwhile, back on terra firma, it wouldn't be an Asian resort without **golf.** The best course on Phuket is the Banyan Tree (34 Moo 4, Srisoonthorn Road, at the Laguna Resort Complex on Bang Tao Bay, ☎ **076/324-350**), a par-71 championship course with many water features. Guests of the Banyan Tree Resort pay 1,900B (US$51.35) greens fees, while others pay 2,400B (US$64.85) weekdays and weekends. The Blue Canyon Country Club (165 Moo 1, Thepkasattri Road, near the airport, ☎ 076/327-440) is a 72-par championship course that boasts memorable holes. An older course, the Phuket Country Club (80/1 Vichitsongkram Rd., west of Phuket town, ☎ **076/321-038**), has beautiful greens and fairways, plus a giant lake. Greens fees are 2,420B (US$65.40) any day of the week.

Eco-tourism seems to be the buzzword in Phuket, with every other tour operator finding a new way to fit "eco-" into its title. Some tourist agents' idea of environmentally friendly tourism includes rides on buffalo carts and trips to see monkey shows. While there's no way to completely circumvent tourism's impact on the environment, there are legitimate operators who offer adventure trips and make attempts to minimize damage. They'll make arrangements for **treks** either by foot or jeep into the jungle parts of the island, **mountain biking** tours, **elephant treks,** and **water rafting.** The Tourism Authority recommends Green Asia Travel (☎ **076/236-156**) and Phuket Safari Travel (☎ **076/340-906**).

A romantic and charming way to see Phuket's jungles and beaches is on horseback. Phuket Riding Club (☎ **076/288-213**) and Phuket Laguna Riding Club (☎ **076/324-099**) welcome riders of all ages and experience levels and can provide instruction for beginners and children. The jungle tour can be done in an hour for 500B (US$13.50), while the beach tour takes about 2 hours.

Jungle Bungy Jump (open daily 9am to 6pm) has to be the wackiest thing I've seen on Phuket. If you have the nerve to jump out more than 166 feet (50 meters) over the water, call their "Bungy Hotline" at ☎ **076/321-351.** For 1,400B (US$37.85), you get insurance coverage and a certificate that says you actually did it. Another fast-paced activity is at Phuket Go-Kart (☎ **076/321-949;** open 9am to 5pm daily; 370B–450B [US$10–$12.15] per 10 minutes), 0.60 mile (1km) south from the Kathu Police Station. If your pulse isn't racing yet, **jungle warfare** with Paintball Asia (behind the Phuket Shooting Range, ☎ **076/381-667**) might do the trick. It's open 9am to 6pm every day. The cost is 500B (US$13.50) per person including equipment.

When you're ready to take in a little culture, the first place to stop is the **Thalang National Museum** toward the eastern side of the island off Route 4027 (☎ 076/311-426). It's open daily from 9am to 4pm; admission is 30B (US80¢). There you can learn about Phuket before the coming of the tourist.

**The Hideaway Herbal Aromatic Spa** (47/4 Soi Nanai, Patong, ☎ **077/340-591**) is the perfect cure for jet lag, stress, or a rainy day. A tiny compound of open-air thatch salas are tucked into a hillside, where the relaxed and informal staff prepares baths and performs traditional Thai massage and aromatic herbal face, foot, and hair treatments using age-old Thai beauty treatments. Their signature skin care products will make your body feel like silk. For those used to the usual generic spa routine, this home-grown place is a welcome retreat, and surprisingly affordable, too. You can have the works for what it costs for a single treatment at a resort spa.

## SHOPPING

Although Patong beach is a virtual bazaar by night, shopping is not a recommended activity in Phuket. Thailand's best shopping for quality antiques and handicrafts is found in Chiang Mai and Bangkok. Most of what you're going to find here are seashell souvenirs and batik beach wear. All of the handicrafts you do find have been shipped in from up north. If you're heading that way, shop at the source for better selection and value, for prices in Phuket are grossly inflated. A shop owner tried to sell me a batik wrap skirt for 380B (US$10.25)—exactly like the one I bought in Pattaya for 120B (US$3.25)!

## PHUKET AFTER HOURS

Nightlife in Phuket begins and ends in **Patong Beach.** In the evenings, Thaveewong Road (the main road along the beachfront) and the small lanes that lead inland from it turn into a bustling bazaar, with souvenir and handicraft stalls, seafood restaurants, and every storefront well lit and ready for business. Tossed in between these spots are **open-air watering holes,** looking like odd tiki huts set up with an outdoor bar and stools and a few small tables. Most of these places are patronized by visitors stopping for a beer or two, or male travelers looking to meet one of the Thai ladies that hang around the bar.

Toward the north end of the beach, **Soi Bangla** has the largest concentration of bars, turning into a slightly seedier area where the famous go-go bars and sex shows of Bangkok's Patpong have been translated into a smaller scale for visitors to Phuket.

For a really fun disco, **Banana Pub,** 94 Thaweewong Rd. (☎ **076/340-301**), is always happening, throbbing with good dance music and the sometimes wacky revelry of the party people inside. If dancing is not your thing, the people-watching is still fantastic. Another reputable disco is the **Shark Club,** Bangla Road (☎ **076/340-525**), where you'll find a better mix of foreigners and locals.

Phuket also has a resident cabaret troupe at **Simon Cabaret,** 100/6-8 Moo 4, Patong Karon Road (☎ **076/342-011**), between Patong and Karon Beaches. It's a featured spot on every planned tour agenda, so be prepared for busloads. However, I still think the cabaret makes for a fun and interesting visit—many of the tourists who attend are Asians, and the show mainly caters to them, with lip-sync performances that in turn make all the Koreans laugh, the Japanese laugh, and the Chinese laugh. It can be a lot of fun. In between the comedy are dance numbers with pretty impressive sets, costumes, and naturally, transsexuals.

## 12  An Introduction to Northern Thailand

The southern regions of Thailand may be a vacation paradise of beaches and blue waters, but when many Thais think of a holiday, they head for the northern hills, where the air is cooler and the atmosphere more culturally stimulating. The historic cities of **Chiang Mai, Chiang Rai,** and the small but interesting **Golden Triangle** (Chiang Saen), a former cowboy town for the opium trade, are a welcome change for visitors who want to experience Thailand's beauty beyond the beaches.

Northern Thailand is comprised of 15 provinces, many of them sharing borders with Burma (Myanmar) to the north and west and Laos to the northeast. This verdant, mountainous terrain, which includes Thailand's largest mountain, Doi

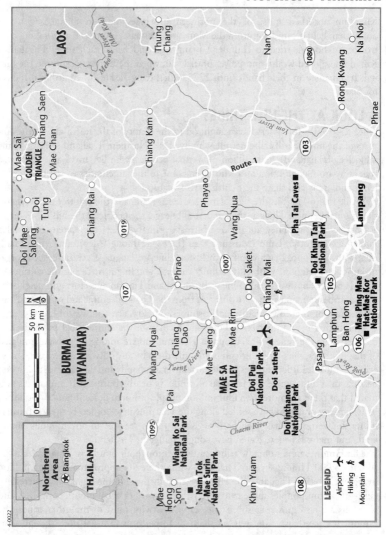

Inthanon, at 8,408 feet (2,563m), supports nomadic farming and teak logging at high altitudes and systematic agriculture in the valleys. Traditionally, opium poppies were the main cash crop for the people here, but government efforts have largely replaced their cultivation with rice, tobacco, soybeans, corn, and sugarcane.

## A SHORT REGIONAL HISTORY

The tribal people of the north migrated primarily from Laos, southwestern China, Burma, and Tibet beginning in the sixth century A.D. By the 11th century, Thai (also spelled Tai) people began to move from Southern China, inhabiting the northern hills and building the Lanna Kingdom, one of Thailand's most powerful. King Mengrai, a brilliant leader who united the Thai tribes, established the first Lanna capital at Chiang Rai in 1262 A.D. It was about this time that Kublai Khan invaded Burma. For added protection, King Mengrai forged ties with the Sukhothai Kingdom to the south, and in 1296 moved his capital to Chiang Mai. For the next century, the Lanna

Kingdom absorbed most of the northern provinces, and in alliance with the Sukhothai, held off invasion from the Mons and Khmers. Ayutthaya, after taking control of Sukhothai, tried to conquer Chiang Mai and failed each time. The Lanna Kingdom enjoyed wealth and power until 1556, when the Burmese captured the capital. It remained in their hands until 1775, when King Taskin (of Ayutthaya) took it for Siam.

## A LOOK AT THE HILL TRIBES

Since the 1970s, foreigners have caught on to the beauty of the north and to the cultures of the unique **hill tribe people** who live here. Northern Thailand is home to the majority of Thailand's half-million plus tribal peoples, who live in villages that are a trek away from civilization and who often come to the larger cities to sell their excellent handicrafts and share their culture with visitors.

While many Thais in the central and southern regions of the country acknowledge the original Chinese Thais as their ancestral lineage, the people of the hill tribes retain a separate identity. They are divided into six primary tribes: the Karen, Akha (also known as the Kaw), Lahu (Mussur), Lisu (Lisaw), Hmong (Meo), and Mien (Yao), each with subgroups that are linked by history, lineage, language, costume, social organization, and religion. With close ethnic, cultural, and linguistic ties to the cultures of their Laotian, Southwestern Chinese, Burmese, and Tibetan ancestors and neighbors, the hill tribes remain to this day different from the Thais of central and southern Thailand, retaining their own traditional costumes, religion, art, and way of life.

Numbering over a quarter-million—almost half of the entire tribal population—the **Karen** are the largest tribal group in Thailand and are among the most assimilated of the hill tribes, making it difficult to identify them by any outward appearance; however, the most traditional tribespeople wear silver armbands and don a beaded sash and headband, and the single women wear all white. In nearby Burma (Myanmar), it's estimated that there are more than four million people of Karen descent (and of Buddhist belief), many of whom have settled along the Thai-Burmese border. For years, Burma's military government has been battling Karen rebels seeking an autonomous homeland, and many Burmese Karen have sought refuge in Thailand.

The **Hmong** are a nomadic tribe scattered throughout Southeast Asia and China. About 65,000 Hmong live in Thailand, while there are approximately four million living in China. In Thailand, the Hmong generally dwell in the highlands, where they cultivate opium poppies more extensively than any other tribal group; corn, rice, and soybeans are also grown as subsistence crops. As with most of the other tribes, the Hmong are pantheistic and rely on shamans to perform spiritual rites, though their elite is staunchly Catholic. Like the Chinese, with whom they resided for so many centuries, Hmong are skilled entrepreneurs, and many are beginning to move down from the hills to pursue a less rigorous and more profitable life in other occupations.

The **Lahu** people, of whom about 40,000 abide in Thailand, are a fractured group with a great many subdivisions, and if any tribe reflects the difficulties of maintaining a singular cultural identity in the tumult of migration, it's the Lahu. Consider Lahu religion: Originally animist, they adopted the worship of a deity called G'ui sha (possibly Tibetan in origin), borrowed the practice of merit-making from Buddhism (Indian or Chinese), and ultimately incorporated Christian (British/Burmese) theology into their belief system. In addition, they practice a kind of Lahu voodoo as well as follow a messianic tradition. The Lahu are skilled musicians, their bamboo and gourd flutes being the most common instruments sold in the Night Market in Chiang Mai. They welcome strangers more than any other tribe in Thailand.

There are now estimated to be 33,000 **Mien** living in Thailand, concentrated in Chiang Rai, Phayao, Lampang, and Nan provinces. Even more than the Hmong, the

Mien are closely connected to their origins in southern China. They incorporated the Han (Chinese) spoken and written language into their own, and many Mien legends, history books, and religious tracts are recorded in Chinese. The Mien people also assimilated ancestor worship and a form of Taoism into their theology, in addition to celebrating their New Year on the same date (relying on the same calendar system) as the Chinese. Mien farmers practice slash-and-burn agriculture but do not rely on opium poppies; instead they cultivate dry rice and corn. The women produce rather elaborate and elegant embroidery, which often adorns their clothing. Their silver work is intricate and highly prized even by other tribes, particularly the Hmong.

The **Lisu** are one of the smaller ethnic minorities in northern Thailand, representing less than 5% of all hill-tribe people. They arrived in Chiang Rai Province in the 1920s, migrating from nearby Burma, occupying high ground and growing opium poppies as well as other subsistence crops. Like their Chinese cousins (many have intermarried), the Lisu people are reputed to be extremely competitive and hard-working. Even their clothing is brash, with brightly colored tunics embellished with hundreds of silver beads and trinkets. The Lisu are achievers who live well-structured lives. Their rituals rely on complicated procedures that demand much from the participants. Everything from birth to courtship to marriage to death is ruled by an orthodox tradition, much borrowed from the Chinese.

Of all the tradition-bound tribes, the **Akha,** accounting for only 3% of all minorities living in Thailand, have probably maintained the most profound connection with their past. At great events in one's life, the full name (often more than 50 generations of titles) of an Akha is proclaimed, with each name symbolic of a lineage dating back more than a thousand years. All aspects of life are governed by the Akha Way, an all-encompassing system of myth, ritual, plant cultivation, courtship and marriage, birth, death, dress, and healing. They are widely spread throughout southern China, Laos, Vietnam, and Burma (Myanmar), the first Akha migrating from Burma to Thailand in the beginning of the 20th century. They are "shifting" cultivators, depending on subsistence crops, planted in rotation, and raising domestic animals for their livelihood. The clothing of the Akha is among the most attractive of all the hill tribes: Simple black jackets with skillful embroidery are the everyday attire for both men and women.

## WEATHER

There are three distinct seasons in the North. The **hot season** (March through May) is dry with temperatures up to 86°F (30°C); the **rainy season** (June through October) is cooler, with the heaviest daily rainfall in September; and the **cool season** (November through February) is brisk, with daytime temperatures as low as 59°F (21°C) in Chiang Mai town and 41°F (5°C) in the hills. November to May is the best time for trekking, with February, March, and April (when southern Thailand gets extremely hot) usually being the least crowded months.

## 13 Chiang Mai

The largest and most well known city in the north, Chiang Mai is the primary gateway to the hills and people who live there. The city itself is a treasure trove of small but magnificent temples and, without argument, the epitome of shopping for Thai and hill tribe arts and handicrafts. If you can be seduced away from the city limits, you'll find cottage industries, hill tribe villages, and natural wonders.

Chiang Mai begins at the **"Old City,"** a square fortress surrounded by a moat, and some remains of its original massive walls. Several of the original gates have been restored and serve as useful reference points. Within the Old City are three of the area's most important wats (temples): Wat Chedi Luang, Wat Phra Singh, and Wat Chiang Man.

Most of the major streets radiate from the Old City and fan out in all directions. The **main business and shopping area** is the half-mile stretch between the east side of the Old City and the Ping River. Here you'll find Chiang Mai's **Night Market,** many shops, hotels, and restaurants.

## GETTING THERE

**BY AIR**  **Thai Airways** (☎ 02/280-0070), **Bangkok Airways** (☎ 02/253-4014), and **Angel Airlines** (☎ 02/953-2260) all service Chiang Mai, running 15 flights daily from Bangkok between them. They each have ticketing offices in Chiang Mai. Thai Airways is at 240 Prapokklao Rd. (☎ 053/210-210); Bangkok Airways (☎ 053/281-519) and Angel Airlines (☎ 053/270-222, extension 2281) are at the Chiang Mai Airport. For general airport information, dial ☎ 270-222.

The Chiang Mai Airport is also connected to many international cities in Southeast Asia. There are daily flights to and from Yangon and Mandalay in Myanmar provided by Air Mandalay (in Chiang Mai ☎ 053/818-049). A daily flight **from Vientiane,** Laos, via Lao Aviation (in Vientiane ☎ 021/212-051; in Chiang Mai ☎ 053/418-258), another daily **from Kuala Lumpur** in Malaysia via Malaysian Airlines (in Kuala Lumpur ☎ 603/764-3000; ☎ 053/276-766), and three flights **from Singapore** aboard Silk Air (in Singapore ☎ 65/221-2221; in Chiang Mai ☎ 053/276-459) attest to the easy access of this northern destination.

**Taxis** wait outside the airport, and can be booked at the ground transportation counter for about 150B (US$4.05). Thai Airways also offers a shuttle, which is less direct but costs about half the price.

**BY TRAIN**  From Bangkok's Hua Lampong Railway Station (☎ 02/223-7010 or 02/223-7020), seven daily trains make the 11- to 15-hour trip to Chiang Mai, Sprinter trains being the fastest, Rapid being the slowest. Sleeper berths are highly recommended, and should be booked in advance. Expect to pay 593B (US$16.05) for first-class, 281B (US$7.60) for second-class, and 121B (US$3.25) for third-class passage.

The **Chiang Mai Depot** is on Charoenmuang Road, east of the Old City crossing the Ping River (☎ 053/247-462 for same day booking and ☎ 053/242-094 advance booking). Tuk-tuks hang around for travelers as they arrive. The short trip to town is only around 40B or 50B (US$1.10–US$1.35).

**BY BUS**  Travel by bus from Bangkok only takes 9 hours, but then again, buses aren't the most comfortable way to travel, so it may feel like it takes longer. From Bangkok's **Northern Bus Terminal** (☎ 02/272-5761), first-class air-conditioned buses leave hourly from 6am to 8pm for a cost of 369B. The **Arcade Bus Station** in Chiang Mai is on Kaew Nawaratt Road (☎ 053/247-462), to the northeast of the Old City. There are minibus services to take you the short trip from the station to town.

## GETTING AROUND

**BY TAXI**  Good luck finding one, as they don't cruise the streets, sticking to regular fares from the airport. Major hotels and travel agencies can provide car and limo services, but at a premium. A good bit of advice if you arrive by plane: Check out your taxi driver. Many of these guys speak English well enough and are familiar with the city and its attractions. I even met one who had a neatly bound portfolio of letters written by travelers who recommended his excellent services. These guys can be hired by the hour or day and will take you anywhere you want to go. Negotiate like a crazy person.

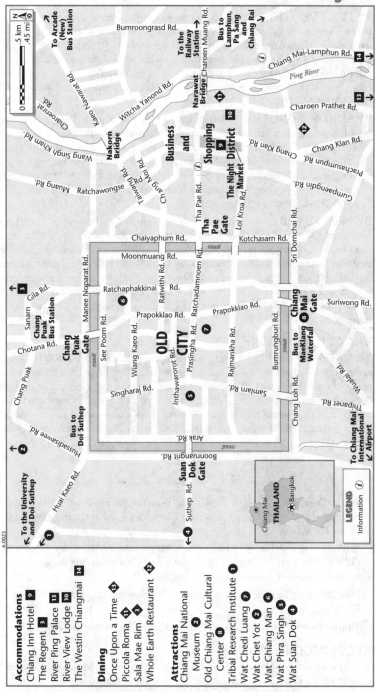

**BY TUK-TUK**   This can be a convenient way to get around if you're a firm nego-tiator. They can be flagged down pretty much everywhere. By the way, the guys who hang around outside major hotels will always quote you top dollar. Walk up the street a bit and flag down another one and you'll get a far better deal. And be careful of the tuk-tuk drivers who try to take you shopping or to places you don't want to go. They'll hustle you if they can. Most trips around town are expensive, from 40B to 100B (US$1.10–US$2.70).

**BY SEELOR (SONGTAO)**   Most of the locals get around by these pickup truck mini-buses, and they are the most recommended form of transportation for trips around the city. These red trucks can be flagged down if they're going in your general direction. Tell the driver where you're going (you may want to get someone at your hotel to write it in Thai for you), and if he can fit it in with the rest of the passengers' routes, you're on. Pay him when you reach your destination—anywhere from 10B to 20B (US25¢–US55¢), a real bargain.

**BY PRIVATE CAR**   Cars can be rented through Budget Rent-a-Car (189/17–19 Wualai Rd., ☎ 053/202-871) or Hertz (90 Sridonchai Rd., ☎ 053/279-474). Suzuki Caribbeans start at 1,500B (US$40.55) per day, with Toyotas, Volvos, and Mercedes climbing up the price scale to about 9,000B (US$243.25) per day. Weekly discounts are available, as are chauffeured cars. Drivers will require an international driver license, and good insurance coverage will be provided. Though it's expensive, hiring a car and driver is a good idea if you don't want to deal with reckless Thai drivers or con-fusing road maps.

### Visitor Information

The **TAT office** is at 105/1 Chiang Mai-Lamphun Rd. (☎ **053/248-604**). It's not exactly centrally located, but it's only a hop over the Ping River from the main busi-ness and shopping district. The staff here is excellent, and they have terrific resources. A few free and informative travel publications are distributed in hotels and major tourist areas. *Welcome to Chiang Mai & Chiang Rai, Guidelines,* and *Chiang Mai* con-tain city maps, articles about local culture and events, advertisements, and classified listings.

## Fast Facts: Chiang Mai

**Banks/Currency Exchange**   You'll find branches for every major bank (with ATMs and money-changing services) on Changklan Road in the area around the Night Market.

**Internet/E-mail**   For good Internet service, the businesslike Assign Internet 2 (☎ 053/818-911) in Chiang Mai Pavilion, 145 Changklan Rd. near the Night Bazaar, is the most central.

**Post Office**   The main Post Office is at 402 Charoenmuang Rd. (☎ 053/241-070).

**Tourist Police**   Tourist Police in Chiang Mai can be reached at ☎ 053/1155.

## ACCOMMODATIONS

The largest number of hotels is concentrated in the business and shopping district to the east of the Old City, and staying in these hotels is very convenient for reaching most attractions, restaurants, and night spots. In addition, some smaller and very charming hotels sit on the banks of the Ping River. These tend to reflect more local character, and can be very relaxing.

## VERY EXPENSIVE

**Chiang Inn Hotel.** 100 Chang Klan Rd., Chiang Mai 50100. ☎ **053/270-070.** Fax 053/27499. 170 rms. A/C MINIBAR TV TEL. 1,815B double; 6,000B–9,000B (US$162.15–US$243.25) suite. AE, DC, MC, V. 2 blocks south of Tha Pae Rd., 2 blocks west of river, just north of Night Market.

The recently renovated Chiang Inn is right across the street from the Chiang Inn Plaza, an arcade of Western chain joints like Burger King and Dunkin Donuts, but it's set back from the lively street and quieter at night than you'd expect. The compact, teak-paneled lobby has a homey yet elegant feel and is almost always crowded with Europeans. Spacious rooms are clean but are decorated in a bland fashion that's not much in keeping with the price of the facility. Still, for location, the Chiang Inn is tops. There's also a large pool with a sun deck, tennis courts, a business center, and a small shopping arcade (although you'll be hard pressed to find better shopping than just outside the hotel at the night market). Be warned, the Chiang Inn is a favorite hangout for tuk-tuk drivers who try to charge visitors an arm and a leg and take them to places they don't wish to visit.

✪ **The Regent.** Mae Rim–Samoeng Old Rd., Mae Rim, Chiang Mai 50180. ☎ **800/545-4000** in the U.S. and Canada, 800/022-800 in Australia, 0800/440-800 in New Zealand, 0800/282-245 in the UK, or 053/298181. Fax 053/298190. 67 suites. A/C MINIBAR TV TEL. US$320–US$410 pavilion suites; US$900–US$2,000 residence suites. AE, DC, MC, V. 20 minutes north of city off Chiangmai–Maerim Rd.

Northern Thailand's finest resort is well isolated from the bustle of the city on 20 acres of landscaped grounds in the Mae Rim Valley. The beautiful central garden includes two small lakes, lily ponds, and terraced rice paddies (which are maintained by the resort); and two-story Lanna-style pavilions are clustered informally around it. Spacious suites are understatedly elegant with polished teak floors and vaulted ceilings, decorated with traditional Thai fabrics and art, each with an adjoining private *sala* (open-air pavilion). Bathrooms are particularly large and luxurious, with two vanities and a big sunken tub and separate shower, overlooking a secluded garden.

The pool is a spectacle. As you stand at the head, the false edge at the opposite end seems to drop off into the paddy fields below and rise into the mountains beyond. At night, torches are lit in the fields, providing a mysterious aura to the views from the resort's restaurants. This luxury retreat spares no detail for your vacation enjoyment, with a modern fitness studio, luxurious spa with massage and sauna, two lighted tennis courts with full-time pro, and mountain bikes with maps of the surrounding countryside. If you're worried about being far from Chiang Mai, the resort provides regular shuttles to and from the main business and shopping district. On a whimsical note, Regent is the only resort in the world to boast its own resident family of water buffalo, and they are the most pampered and prissy beasts you've ever seen.

**The Westin Chiangmai.** 318/1 Chiangmai–Lamphun Rd., Chiang Mai 50007. ☎ **053/275300.** Fax 053/275299. 528 units. A/C MINIBAR TV TEL. 5,200B–7,200 (US$140.55–US$194.60) double; 12,500B (US$337.85) suite. AE, DC, MC, V. South of center, across Mengrai Bridge on east bank of river.

Chiang Mai's newest and best high-rise hotel is isolated across the river just south of town. The attractive lobby is both spacious and welcoming, and the staff is friendly and well-trained. The rooms are large and plush, with subdued colors and attractive teak furnishings, each with a view. While the location of the Westin isn't as prime as those of other city hotels, the tour desk and complimentary shuttle to and from the airport make it a bit more convenient. However, if working out is important, be aware that Westin has one of the few decent fitness centers in Chiang Mai. Other facilities include an outdoor swimming pool and beauty salon.

## EXPENSIVE

✪ **River View Lodge.** 25 Charoen Prathet Rd., Soi 2, Chiang Mai 50100. ☎ **053/271109.** Fax 053/279019. 36 units. A/C TEL. 1,450B–1,800B (US$39.20–US$48.65) single or double. MC, V. On river 2 blocks south of Thae Pae Rd.

Veteran shopper and mapmaker Nancy Chandler stays here when in Chiang Mai, and for good reason. First of all, River View's location on the river makes for a peaceful retreat, and yet it's only a short walk to the city's main business and shopping district. Second, the atmosphere is fabulous, from the antiques (all for sale) scattered throughout the hotel's public spaces to the quaint, shady garden that separates the small swimming pool from the open-sided cafe restaurant. Large guest rooms have fresh terra-cotta tile floors with sparse but well-maintained furnishings and no-fuss decor. Bathrooms have shower stalls only, and some of the rooms have wall-to-wall carpeting that doesn't feel as cooling as the tiled rooms. Rates vary depending on the view, and many rooms have balconies.

## MODERATE

✪ **River Ping Palace.** 385/2 Charoen Prathet Rd., Chiang Mai 50100. ☎ **053/274932.** Fax 053/273675. 11 units. A/C MINIBAR. 600B–900B (US$16.20–US$24.30) double; 1,400B (US$37.85) suite. AE, MC, V. On the river, a 20-minute walk south of the Night Market, between Monfort College and the Mengrai Bridge.

If you really want a taste of old Thailand, check into the River Ping Palace for a night. This old, lovingly restored compound of once-private teak houses has been converted into a guesthouse, dressed in four-poster beds with romantic mosquito netting, antique cabinets, rattan armchairs, Victorian brass wall sconces, framed historical photos, and unique accessories. The upstairs lanai overlooking the river is especially wonderful for enjoying lazy afternoon cocktails. The only complaint is that the facility is not exactly modern—it's difficult fitting so many functioning bathrooms into the old dame, so you must sacrifice a little convenience, especially during rainstorms when the roof gets leaky in spots. The management fights a never-ending battle to keep up with maintenance. At time of writing, the suite room, located in its own teak house, was under renovation. Still, in all, it's ambiance and authenticity in one wild package. Its restaurant, Once Upon a Time, serves excellent northern cuisine, and is reviewed later in this section.

# DINING
## EXPENSIVE

**Piccola Roma.** 3/2–3 Charoen Prathet Rd. ☎ **053/271256.** Reservations recommended at dinner. Main dishes 160B–400B (US$4.30–US$10.80). AE. Daily 11am–2pm and 5–11pm. Near river, south of Nawarat Bridge. ITALIAN.

Locals praise this taverna as the best of the city's many Italian restaurants. The northern Italian setting and cuisine are as memorable as your host, executive chef Angelo Faro. Make sure to ask him about his daily recommendations, which depend upon his latest fresh finds at the markets. If you're lucky enough to select a dish that is prepared at your table, there's no extra charge for the entertainment. A good regularly featured menu item is the black linguine in inky squid sauce. A small selection of wines is available to accompany your meal.

**Sala Mae Rim.** Mae Rim–Samoeng Old Rd., Mae Rim, Chiang Mai. ☎ **053/298181.** Reservations recommended. Entree 150B–300B (US$4.05–US$8.10). Open daily noon–2:30pm and 6–10:30pm. DC, JCB, MC, V. NORTHERN THAI.

Unless you're staying at The Regent, Sala Mae Rim is just slightly out of the way, but for amazingly delicious northern Thai cuisine amidst a fairy tale setting—on a terrace overlooking the resort's rice paddy fields, and with a view of the distant mountains if you come for an early cocktail—it's second to none. After sunset, blazing torches illuminate the fields below. The menu is northern Thai, which features less spicy dishes than the fiery southern Thai tradition. Kaow soi kai, a famous dish in Chiang Mai, is a savory and satisfying noodle dish with chicken in a rich curry gravy. You'll think you're in heaven. Also excellent are sai oua (spicy pork sausage, which is also a Chiang Mai classic) and thom sam (fresh sea bass with tamarind and coriander). An excellent selection of international wines is available.

## MODERATE

✪ **Once Upon a Time.** 385/2 Charoen Prathet Rd. ☎ **053/274932.** Reservations recommended. Main courses 80B–200B (US$2.15–US$5.40). AE, MC, V. Daily 4:30pm–midnight. Lunch is served during festivals or by request. West side of river, just north on Mengrai Bridge. THAI.

If you want the best Thai food, served in the most beautiful compound of restored teak houses, there's no better choice. The two-story teak dining pavilion shares a tranquil garden with the charming River Ping Palace guesthouse (reviewed above). Downstairs serves specialties such as hohmok, an array of seafood souffles made with prawn, mussels, or fish and coconut milk; mildly spiced grilled duck in a coconut-milk curry; pla chon, fresh river fish served with dipping sauces; and delicious and distinctive gai yang (barbecue chicken). Upstairs, under the peaked roof, diners can sit on cushions in the khan toke style and sample the same specials or an array of northern Thai dishes, including pork curry and piquant chili pastes.

**Whole Earth Restaurant.** 88 Sri Dornchai Rd. ☎ **053/282463.** Reservations recommended. Main courses 60B–250B (US$1.60–US$6.75). No credit cards. Daily 11am–10pm. 2 blocks west of river, off Chang Klan Rd. VEGETARIAN/ASIAN.

If you're looking for Asian food in the typically California/health food/Western vein, head for this New Age place in a traditional Lanna Thai pavilion. The extensive menu is prepared by a gifted Pakistani chef and is part vegetarian, part Thai, and part Indian. The old pavilion has an indoor air-conditioned non-smoking section and a long open-air verandah set for dining with a view of the gardens (they'll bring a fan to your table upon request). In a good location, near to the main shopping and business areas, Whole Earth gets busy at lunch and dinner, so try to call ahead if you can.

## DINING WITH A CULTURAL SHOW

**Old Chiang Mai Cultural Center.** 185/3 Wualai Rd. ☎ **053/275-097.** Reservations required. Set dinner and show TK. Nightly shows at 7 and 10pm. THAI. Efficient hotel pickup and return can be arranged by the center.

I don't know about you, but I like to avoid the really touristy activities—and usually the planned "dinner and traditional show" is one of the most dreaded things on my itinerary. But, to be honest, the Cultural Center does an honorable job. Yes, you must face the busloads of tourists, but the show is quite fun, with traditional Thai dancing (including male sword dances, which are pretty neat) that are wonderfully entertaining. Despite their busy workload, waiters and waitresses still stop to check on you from time to time, and while the food is only palatable, they never let your bowls become empty. Afterwards, a display of tribal costumes and dances is presented in an outdoor pavilion. Even if it's not your style, consider checking it out—you just might have a good time.

## ATTRACTIONS

After Bangkok, Chiang Mai has the greatest concentration of exquisitely crafted wats (temples) in the country—more than 700 of them. Assuming you aren't planning a wat-by-wat tour, you can see all the principal sights in one day if you start early in the morning, particularly if you travel by tuk-tuk.

**Wat Chedi Luang.** Prapokklao Rd., south of Ratchadamnoen Rd. Suggested contribution 20B (US55¢. Open daily 6am–5pm.

Because it's near the Tha Par Gate, most visitors begin their sightseeing at Wat Chedi Luang, where there are two wats of interest. This complex, which briefly housed the Emerald Buddha (now at Bangkok's Wat Phra Kaeo), dates from 1411, when the original chedi was built by King Saen Muang Ma. The already massive edifice was expanded to 280 feet (85m) in height by the mid-1400s, only to be ruined by a severe earthquake in 1545, just 11 years before Chiang Mai fell to the Burmese. A Buddha still graces its exterior.

The remarkable *nagas* (serpents) guarding the stairway entrance to the typical northern viharn (the large hall where Buddha images are housed) are exceptionally ornate and ferocious. Next to the tall gum tree on the left is a shrine honoring Sao Inthakhin, also referred to as the City Pillar. It is believed that the upkeep of this wat is directly related to the well-being of Chiang Mai.

Wat Phan Tao, also on the grounds, has a wooden viharn and bot (the temple where the main Buddha is enshrined), a reclining Buddha, and fine carving on the eaves and door.

**Wat Phra Singh.** Samlarn Rd. and Ratchadamnoen Rd. Suggested contribution 20B (US55¢. Open daily 6am–5pm.

This compound was built during the zenith of Chiang Mai's power (its chedi was built in 1345) and is one of the more venerated shrines in the city. The beautiful 14th-century library to the right of the compound contains delicate manuscripts on mulberry bark, while the vihaarn, the building that contains Buddha images, houses a northern-style Buddha that is renowned throughout the region for its beauty. The building's walls are covered in elaborate murals that tell stories from Buddhist tradition and illustrate scenes from daily life in Chiang Mai's past glory.

**Wat Chiang Man.** Wiang Kaeo and Ratchaphakkinai rds., in the Old City near the northern Chang Puak Gate. Suggested contribution 20B (55¢). Open daily 6am–5pm.

Thought to be Chiang Mai's oldest wat, this was built during the 14th century by King Mengrai, the founder of Chiang Mai, on the spot where he first camped. It's believed to have been a royal temple. Like many of the wats in Chiang Mai, this complex reflects many architectural styles. Some of the structures are pure Lanna, with black wood carvings reflecting the northern style and the skills of northern craftsmen. Others show influences from as far away as Sri Lanka; notice the typical row of elephant supports. Wat Chiang Man is most famous for its two Buddhas: Phra Sritang Khamani (a miniature crystal image also known as the White Emerald Buddha) and the marble Phra Sri-la Buddha. Unfortunately, the wihaan that safeguards these religious sculptures is almost always closed.

**Wat Suan Dok.** Suthep Rd. From the Old City, take the Suan Dok Gate and continue 1 mile west. Suggested contribution 20B US55¢. Open daily 6am–5pm.

I like this complex less for its architecture (the buildings, though monumental, are undistinguished) than for its contemplative spirit and pleasant surroundings. The temple was built amid the pleasure gardens of the 14th-century Lanna Thai monarch King Ku Na. Unlike most of Chiang Mai's other wats (more tourist sights than working temples and schools), Wat Suan Dok houses quite a few monks who seem to have isolated themselves from the distractions of the outside world. Among the main attractions in the complex are the bot, with a very impressive Chiang Saen Buddha (one of the largest bronzes in the north) dating from 1504 and some garish murals; the chedi, built to hold a relic of the Buddha; and a royal cemetery with some splendid shrines.

**Wat Chet Yot.** Superhighway near the Chiang Mai National Museum, north of the intersection of Nimanhemin and Huai Kaeo rds., about half a mile, on the left. Suggested contribution 20B (US55¢). Open daily 6am–5pm.

Wat Chet Yot (also called Wat Maha Photharam) is one of the central city's most elegant sites. The chedi was built during the reign of King Tilokkarat in the late 15th century (his remains are in one of the smaller chedis), and in 1477 the World Sangkayana convened here to revise the doctrines of the Buddha. The unusual design of the main seven-peaked rectangular chedi was copied from the Maha Bodhi Temple in Bodh Gaya, India, where the Buddha first achieved enlightenment. The temple also has architectural elements of Burmese, Chinese Yuan, and Ming influence. The extraordinary proportions; the angelic, levitating devata figures carved into the base of the chedi; and the juxtaposition of the other buildings make Wat Chet Yot (Seven Spires) a masterpiece. The Lanna-style Buddha hidden in the center was sculpted in the mid–15th century; a door inside the niche containing the Buddha leads to the roof, on which rests the Phra Kaen Chan (Sandalwood Buddha). There is a nice vista from up top, but only men are allowed to ascend the stairs.

**Chiang Mai National Museum.** Superhighway, just north of the seven-spired Wat Chet Yot. ☎ **053/221-308.** Admission free. Open Wed–Sun 9am–4pm, closed holidays.

This modern complex houses the province's fine collection of Lanna Thai art. Woodwork, stonework, and the many religious images garnered from local wats, all well labeled, help to chronicle the distinct achievements of the Lanna Kingdom from the 14th to 18th centuries. These works reveal how Burmese religious art grew more influential over the years of occupation. Knowledge of both cultures will serve you well while touring the north. Note the display of weapons that were used to combat the Burmese.

**Tribal Research Institute.** Chiang Mai University, 4km (2.4 miles) west of the Old City, off Huai Kaeo Rd. ☎ **053/221-332.** Free admission. Open Mon–Fri 8:30am–noon and 1–4:30pm.

If you plan to go trekking or have any interest in the hill-tribe people, visit this facility. The institute conducts research, publishes excellent books and brochures, coordinates trekking groups, and runs a small, informative museum devoted to the ethnographic legacy of the northern tribal groups. There's an informative library next door.

## OUTSIDE THE CITY
**Wat Phra That.** Suggested contribution 20B (US55¢). Open daily 7am–5pm; come early or late to avoid the crowds.

The jewel of Chiang Mai, Wat Phra That glistens in the sun on the slopes of Doi Suthep mountain. One of four royal wats in the north, at 3,250 feet (1,000m), it occupies an extraordinary site with a cool refreshing climate, expansive views over the city, the mountain's idyllic forests, waterfalls, and flowers.

In the 14th century, during the installation of a relic of the Buddha in Wat Suan Dok (in the Old City), the holy object split in two, with one part equaling the original's size. A new wat was needed to honor the miracle. King Ku Na placed the new relic on a sacred white elephant and let it wander freely through the hills. The elephant climbed to the top of Doi Suthep, trumpeted three times, made three counterclockwise circles, and knelt down, choosing the site for Wat Phra That.

The original chedi was built to a height of 26½ feet. Other structures were raised to bring greater honor to the Buddha and various patrons. The most remarkable is the steep 290-step *naga* staircase, added in 1557, leading up to the wat—one of the most dramatic approaches to a temple in all of Thailand. To shorten the 5-hour climb, the winding road was constructed in 1935 by thousands of volunteers under the direction of a local monk.

**Doi Inthanon National Park.** Admission 10B (US25¢). Open daily sunrise to sunset. Camping is allowed in the park, but you must check with the TAT or the national park office to obtain permits, schedule information, and regulations.

Thailand's tallest mountain (at 8,408 feet/2,563m), Doi Inthanon is 29 miles (47km) south of Chiang Mai. It crowns a 360-square-mile (581 sq km) national park filled with impressive waterfalls and wild orchids. Doi Inthanon Road climbs 30 miles (48km) to the summit. Along the way is the 100-foot-high Mae Klang Falls, a popular picnic spot with food stands. Nearby Pakan Na Falls is less crowded because it requires a bit of climbing along a path to reach. At the top of the mountain, there's a fine view and two more falls, Wachirathan and Siriphum, both worth exploring.

## TREKKING FROM CHIANG MAI

Trekking from Chiang Mai has been a tourist activity only since the mid-1970s, but it's become so popular that dozens of agencies sell 2-night/3-day expeditions led by "fluent, multilingual tribal leaders." Even the unfit, the elderly, or the disabled who might never have contemplated a traditional trek, entailing daily 9-mile (15km) hikes and sleeping on the floor of tribal chief's huts, can now enjoy day treks of rafting, riding on elephant back, or driving by jeep to see the northern hill tribes.

Because of their popularity and easy access, most trekking routes within a close range of Chiang Mai return to the same tribal villages, which then grow to depend on trek revenue. Villagers don traditional costumes, perform music, dance, produce crafts, and offer the obligatory opium pipe to better-paying Western guests. But if you're willing to pay more, and walk a little farther over more rigorous trails to the unusual places, you can still get back into some lesser-known territory.

The TAT publishes a list of companies that operate out of Chiang Mai, but I found their information on currently operating tour companies to be totally outdated. Companies go into and out of business regularly and favorite guides move to new agencies, so it takes some effort to find a trek that suits your needs. Most companies are concentrated along Tha Pae and Moon Muang roads near the Old City. It's best to allow a day just for research, but if you're pressed for time, contact the TAT and explain your specific needs to them. They often know the schedules and rates of the larger trekking outfits and can make suggestions. In addition, your trekking options will be limited if you are travelling in a smaller group of, say, two people, as many operators don't like to go through all the effort unless you are prepared to pay a premium.

Two of the most reputable trekking companies are **Singha Travel,** 277 Tha Pae Rd. (☎ **053/282-579,** fax 053/279-260); and **Chiang Mai Tribal Tour,** 204 Tha Pae Rd. (☎ **053/270-159**).

The standard beginner's trek is usually 2 nights, 3 days, with about 3 hours of not-too-strenuous walking each day. Most companies offer this type of trek north toward the Golden Triangle, northwest toward Mae Hong Son, or southwest toward Mae Sariang. Some negotiating for the price of a trek is in order. Visit a few of the Tha Pae Road or Moon Muang Road agencies, determine the price range of the trip you want to join, and offer about 30% less. Many trekking companies arrange custom trips, even on short notice, with a corresponding increase in price. For a 3-day/2-night trek, expect to pay about 1,200B (US$32.45) per person. If you plan a longer trek (up to 5 days and beyond), start your budgeting at 1,800B (US$48.65) per person.

## BIKE TOURING

**Green Pedal Tour,** 2 Rajwithi Rd. (☎ **053/418-403,** fax 053/418-404) offers a range of back-road bicycle excursions for those with the energy to transport themselves with their own power. While bike tours are a fantastic way to take in the countryside and get a closer, and unique, view of Chiang Mai's daily life, they are recommended only for those who are fit. Chiang Mai's heat and hilly terrain will make you miserable if you have doubts. A full day tour, including bike rental, lunch, and beverages, costs from 1,100B (US$29.75) per person.

## SHOPPING
While traveling through the many regions of Thailand you're sure to find Thai arts and handicrafts in abundance in shops and at souvenir stalls. Most of the truly creative and unique items are made in the north part of the country, and if Chiang Mai is on your itinerary, your best bet is to delay any purchases until you've arrived here. Not only will you find the best selection of jewelry, embroidery, silks, pottery, carved wood, and religious artifacts, but you'll probably buy them at a much more reasonable price as well.

The centerpiece of Chiang Mai shopping is the famous **Night Bazaar.** In the late afternoon merchants set up their tents on the sidewalks along Chang Klan Road beginning at the intersection of Loi Kroa Road. Until about 11pm nightly the street and the alleys beyond become a maze of good excuses to blow your vacation cash.

The **Anusarn Market,** located just southwest of the Night Bazaar, closes an hour earlier, but has less tourist traffic and more bargains.

Dedicated shoppers will have to devote at least half a day to shopping along the Chiang Mai–Sankamphaeng Road (Route 1006). It runs due east out of Chiang Mai, and after several kilometers becomes lined with shops, showrooms, and factories extending another 5.4 miles (9km). Here you'll find Chiang Mai Tusnaporn, 9/9 Ban Nong Khong, Sankamphaeng Rd. (☎ 053/338-006), for woodwork and furniture; Chiang Mai Silverware, 62/10–11 Sankamphaeng Rd. (☎ 053/246-037) for bronze and silver; Shinawatra, 145/1–2 Sankamphaeng Rd. (☎ 053/338-053) for silk; Bo Sang Umbrella Center, 111/2 Bo Sang–Sankamphaeng Rd. (☎ 053/338-324) for Thai arts and crafts; and Baan Celadon, Sankamphaeng Rd., 5½ km (☎ 053/338-288) for ceramics, to name just a few temptations. Most are open daily from 8am to 6pm. If you hire a car for a half day, you can take your time, stopping at each place to peruse.

## CHIANG MAI AFTER DARK
Most folks will head out to the Night Bazaar for an evening full of shopping adventure, and if you get tired along the way, duck into one of the back alleys, which are lined with tiny bars. Take your time to check them out, as each has a personality of its own.

Most discos and lounges are located in major hotels, and many will feature live music, whether it's a quiet piano bar or a rock pub featuring a Philippino band. The Crystal Cave Disco at the Empress Hotel on Chang Klan Road (☎ 053/270-240) is particularly popular, as is the live jazz and pop in the Empress's lobby bar. The Caribbean feel is nice at The Terrace at the Surawongse Zenith Hotel, 110 Chang Klan Rd. (☎ 053/270-051). I recommend picking up a copy of *Welcome to Chiang Mai & Chiang Rai* magazine at your hotel for listings of events that are happening while you're in town.

## 14   Chiang Rai

Chiang Rai (485 miles/780km NE of Bangkok; 112 miles/180km NE of Chiang Mai) is Thailand's northernmost province; the mighty Mae Kok River (known to most readers as the Mekong of Vietnam fame) shares borders with Laos to the east and

Burma to the west. The scenic Mae Kok River, which supports many hill-tribe villages along its banks, flows right through the provincial capital of Chiang Rai.

Chiang Rai is 1,885 feet (575m) above sea level in a fertile valley, and its cool refreshing climate, tree-lined riverbank, small Night Market, and easy-to-get-around layout lures travelers weary of traffic congestion and pollution in Chiang Mai.

It's a small city, with most services grouped around the main north-south street, Phahonyothin Road, until it turns right (east) at the Clock Tower, after which it's called Ratanaket. There are three noteworthy landmarks: the small **clock tower** in the city's center; the **statue of King Mengrai** (the city's founder) at the northeast corner of the city, on the superhighway to Mae Chan; and the **Mae Kok River** at the north edge of town. Singhakai Road is the main artery on the north side of town, parallel to the river. The bus station is on Prasopsuk Road, one block east of Phahonyothin Road, near the Wiang Inn Hotel. The Night Market is on Phahonyothin Road near the bus station.

## GETTING THERE

**BY PLANE**    **Thai Airways** has three direct 85-minute flights daily from Bangkok to Chiang Rai (in Bangkok, ☎ 02/280-0070); and two 40-minute flights daily from Chiang Mai (in Chiang Mai ☎ 053/210-210).

The new **Chiang Rai International Airport** (call Thai Airways for airport and flight information, ☎ 053/793-084) is about 10km (6.2 miles) north of town. Taxis hover outside and charge from 60B (US$1.60) for a lift to town.

**BY BUS**    The 4-hour bus journey can be made from Chiang Mai's **Arcade Bus Station** (☎ 053/242-664), with departures every 30 to 45 minutes from 6am to 5:30pm daily. Fares are anywhere between 57B and 102B (US$1.55–US$2.75), depending on the comfort you desire. Make sure you take the 4-hour bus—there's an older route that still operates and takes about 6 hours. The **Kohn Song Bus Station** in Chiang Rai (☎ 053/711-369) is on Prasopsuk Road off the main Phahonyothin Road in the center of town.

If you plan to travel by bus from Bangkok, depart from the **Northern Bus Terminal** (☎ 02/272-5761) on Phahonyothin Road near the Chatuchak Weekend Market. The trip is an uncomfortable 12 hours and costs 412B (US$11.15). Four buses leave daily.

**BY CAR**    The fast and not particularly scenic route from Bangkok is Highway 1 North, direct to Chiang Rai. A slow, scenic approach on blacktop mountain roads is Route 107 north from Chiang Mai to Fang, then Route 109 east to Highway 1.

## VISITOR INFORMATION

The **TAT** office (☎ 053/717-434) is located at 448/16 Singhakai Rd., near Wat Phra Singh on the north side of town, and the Tourist Police are next door. The monthly *Welcome to Chiang Mai and Chiang Rai* is distributed free by most hotels.

## GETTING AROUND

**BY TRISHAW OR TUK-TUK**    You'll probably find walking the best method of transport. However, there are *samlors* (bicycle trishaws) parked outside the Night Market and on the banks of the Mae Kok River; they don't budge for less than 20B for short local trips. During the day there are tuk-tuks, which charge 35B to 100B (US95¢–US$2.70) for in-town trips.

**BY BUS**    Frequent local buses are the easiest and cheapest way to get to nearby cities. All leave from the **bus station** (☎ 053/711-369) on Prasopsuk Road near the Wiang Inn Hotel.

**BY MOTORCYCLE**　A dependable local company for rentals is **Soon Motorcycle,** 197/2 Trirath Rd. (☎ 053/714-068). Daily rates run about 450B (US$12.15) for a 250cc motorcycle, 150B (US$4.05) for a 100cc moped, including a helmet.

**BY CAR**　**Avis** (☎ 053/793-048) has a branch at the airport, where self-drive vehicles rent from 1,800B (US$48.65) for a Jeep to 2,000B (US$54.05) for a sedan, and cars with driver cost 3,200B (US$86.50) per day, including insurance and 200km (120 miles) free. At **P.D. Tour & Car Rental Services,** Phahonyothin Road opposite the Wangcome Hotel (☎ 053/712-829, fax 053/719-041), a jeep goes for about 950B (US$25.70) per day and a sedan for 1,200B (US$32.45), not including gas.

## Fast Facts: Chiang Rai

**Banks/Currency Exchange**　Some Thai banks have branches on Thanalai Road off Rattanakhet Road in the north of town, not far from the TAT office, and on Phahonyothin Road.

**Internet/E-mail**　The only reliable (well, almost reliable) Internet service is provided by Chiang Rai Internet & E-mail Service and Training Center (611 Phahonyothin Rd. opposite the Golden Triangle Inn, ☎ 718-675).

**Post Office/Mail**　The post office is on Utrakit Road 2 blocks north of the clock tower, also near the TAT.

**Tourist Police**　The Tourist Police are located on Singhakai Road, near Wat Phra Singh on the north side of town, next door to the TAT office.

## ACCOMMODATIONS
### VERY EXPENSIVE

**Dusit Island Resort Hotel.** 1129 Kraisorasit Rd., Amphur Muang 57000, Chiang Rai. ☎ 053/715-777. Fax 053/715801. 271 units. A/C MINIBAR TV TEL. 4,840B double (US$130.80); from 7,250B (US$195.95) suite. AE, DC, MC, V. Over bridge at northwest corner of town.

Chiang Rai's best resort hotel occupies a large delta island in the Mae Kok River. It's sure to please those looking for international luxury and resort comforts, though at the expense of local flavor and homeyness. The dramatic lobby is a soaring space of teak, marble, and glass, as grand as any in Thailand, with panoramic views of the Mae Kok. Rooms are luxuriously appointed in pastel cottons and teak trim, but have thin walls that let in noise form adjacent rooms. The Dusit Island's manicured grounds, outdoor pool, tennis courts, fitness center, and billiards room create a resort ambience, but that shouldn't dissuade you from exploring the town.

### EXPENSIVE

**Wiang Inn.** 893 Phahonyothin Rd., Amphur Muang 57000, Chiang Rai. ☎ 053/711-533. Fax 053/711-877. 256 units. A/C MINIBAR TV TEL. 1,883B–2,354B (US$50.90–US$63.60); from 4,700B (US$127.05) suite. AE, DC, MC, V. Center of town, south of bus station.

Wiang Inn offers full amenities, a helpful staff, several dining venues, a large pool, a reputable tour desk, and a convenient location, around the corner from the bus station and opposite the Night Market. Large rooms are trimmed in dark teak, with pale teak furniture and Thai artwork, including Lanna murals over the beds and ceramic vase table lamps. It's very well maintained, despite the steady stream of tour groups— which make an early booking advisable. Facilities are limited to a small pool and a massage center, but it is the best choice for a centrally located place to stay.

## DINING

**Golden Triangle International Cafe.** 590 Phahonyothin Rd. ☎ **053/711-399.** Entrees 80B–250B (US$2.15–US$6.75). Open 8am–10:30pm daily. V, MC. THAI.

This place has the homey feel of a tavern and some old town touches to the decor, but the best reason to eat here is the menu, which is almost like a short book explaining Thai dinner menus, the various dishes that make up a meal, and the ingredients and preparation of each. The "choose your own noodle" dishes give you the chance to experiment with various tastes, and are prepared in quick and tasty fashion. A small selection of wines is available.

**T. Hut.** Phahonyothin Rd. ☎ **053/712162.** Main courses 50B–65B (US$1.35–US$1.75). Daily 5pm–midnight. MC, V. 300m south of Satharn Payabarn Rd., near gas station. THAI.

For delicious, authentically northern cuisine, try this restaurant in a contemporary Thai house, with peaked roofs, stucco walls, and a large garden surrounding a spirit house. The gentle staff speaks little English but will understand mai pet ("not spicy"). Yam moo yaw is a favorite Chiang Rai ham that's especially good combined with their salad kai, green mango and chicken salad. Nua Yan T. Hut, their special, is very spicy grilled beef.

## ATTRACTIONS
### EXPLORING CHIANG RAI'S WATS
**Wat Phra Kaeo.** On Trairat Rd. on the northwest side of town, just north of Ruang Nakhon Rd.

Phra Kaeo is the best known of the northern wats because it once housed the Emerald Buddha now at Bangkok's royal Wat Phra Kaeo. Near its Lanna-style chapel is the chedi, which (according to legend) was struck by lightning in 1436 to reveal the precious green jasper Buddha. There is now a green jade replica of the image on display.

**Wat Phra Singh.** 2 blocks east of Wat Phra Kaeo.

The restored wat is thought to date from the 15th century. Inside is a replica of the Phra Singh Buddha, a highly revered Theravada Buddhist image; the original was removed to Chiang Mai's Wat Phra Singh.

**Wat Doi Tong (Phra That Chomtong).** Atop a hill above the northwest side of town, up a steep staircase off Kaisornrasit Rd.

This Burmese-style wat offers an overview of the town and a panorama of the Mae Kok valley. It's said that King Mengrai himself chose the site for his new Lan Na capital from this very hill. The circle of columns at the top of the hill surrounds the new *lak muang* (city pillar), built to commemorate the 725th anniversary of the city and King Bhumibol's 60th birthday. It is often criticized for its failure to represent local style. (You can see the old wooden *lak muang* in the wihaan of the wat.)

## VISITING THE HILL TRIBES
Most of the hill-tribe villages within close range of Chiang Rai have become somewhat assimilated by the routine visits of group tours. If your time is too limited for a trek, several in-town travel agencies offer day trips to the countryside. Prices are based on a two-person minimum and decline as more people sign up; rates include transportation and a guide.

**Far-East North Tours,** 873/8 Phahonyothin Rd. (☎ 053/713625), has a half-day trip by long-tail boat to a Karen village, then a short elephant ride and short walk to a Lahu village for 1,100B (US$29.75) per person. The **Chiang Mai Travel Center,** 893 Paholyothin Rd. (☎ 053/714799), has a more exotic day drive east along the Mae Khong to Chiang Khong, to visit Kamu, Hmong, and Mien villages, stopping on the return in Chiang Saen, for 1,800B (US$48.65) per person.

## LONG-TAIL BOAT TRIPS ON THE MAE KOK RIVER

The Mae Kok is one of Chiang Rai's best assets. Though shallow and silted much of the year, it's still the most picturesque avenue for sightseeing in the region. Travelers may enjoy hopping on the **Thaton long-tail boat taxi service** (the local water-taxis) that leaves the Chiang Rai pier each morning at 10am. Although it stops at a Karen tribal village en route, you'll only stay at each stop for a moment—the fun is in the ride itself.

For about 300B (US$8.10) per half hour, you'll be able to **charter** your own noisy long-tail boat (from the pier off the river road opposite the Dusit Island Resort) to sightsee in the area. Most local travel agents arrange this, chartering boats to the Karen village, continuing to the elephant parking lot where these delightful creatures await their charges, then returning to Chiang Rai by minivan.

## SHOPPING

The recent influx of tourists has made Chiang Rai a magnet for hill-tribe clothing and handicraft products. You'll find many boutiques in the Night Market (see "Chiang Rai After Dark," below), as well as some fine shops scattered around the city. Most are open daily from 8:30am to 10pm and accept credit cards. There's much less available than in Chiang Mai, but prices are reasonable.

**Chiang Rai Handicrafts Center,** 273 Moo 5, Phahonyothin Rd. (☎ **053/713-355**), is the largest of the hill-tribe shops, with a huge selection of well-finished merchandise, an adjoining factory, and a good reputation for air-mail shipping.

## CHIANG RAI AFTER DARK

Most visitors stroll through the Night Market and shop for souvenirs. It's really a miniversion of the more famous market in Chiang Mai. Shops clustered along Phahonyothin Road near the Wiang Inn, and around the two lanes leading off it to the Wangcome Hotel, stay open till 10pm.

There's a small and rather tawdry nightlife district west and south of the Clock Tower along Punyodyana Road, a private lane with clubs named **Lobo, La Cantina, My Way, Mars Bar,** and **Butterfly.** Just around the corner to the south, near the Wangcome Hotel, you'll also find **Chiangrai Karoaki** and **Regency,** where you might get a turn at the mike.

## 15 Chiang Saen & the Golden Triangle

The small village of Chiang Saen (581 miles/935km NE of Bangkok; 148 miles/239km NE of Chiang Mai) has the sleepy, rural charm of Burma's ancient capital of Pagan. The single lane road from Chiang Rai (37 miles/59km) follows the small Mae Nam Chan River past coconut groves and rice paddies guarded by water buffalo. Little Chiang Saen, the birthplace of expansionary King Mengrai, was abandoned for the new Lanna Thai capitals of Chiang Rai, then Chiang Mai, in the 13th century. With the Mae Khong River and the Laos border hemming in its growth, modern developers went elsewhere. Today, the slow rural pace, decaying regal wats, crumbling fort walls, and overgrown moat contribute greatly to its appeal. After visiting the excellent museum and local sites, most travelers head west along the Mae Khong to the Golden Triangle, the north's prime attraction.

### GETTING THERE

**BY BUS**    Four buses travel to Chiang Saen daily from Chiang Mai via Chiang Rai, the 5-hour trip costing between 73B and 130B, depending on the level of comfort. Forty buses a day from Chiang Rai make the hour-long trip for about 45B.

**BY CAR**   Take the superhighway Route 110 north from Chiang Rai to Mae Chan, then Route 1016 northeast to Chiang Saen.

## VISITOR INFORMATION

There is no TAT, but the staff at the few guesthouses speak some English and try to be helpful.

## GETTING AROUND

Route 1016 is the village's main street, which intersects after 550 yards (500m) with the Mae Khong River. Along the river road, there are a few guesthouses to the west, and an active produce, souvenir, and clothing market to the east. There's so little traffic it's a pleasure to walk; all of the in-town sights are within 15 minutes' walk of each other and are impossible to miss.

**BY PEDICAB**   Pedicab drivers hover by the bus stop on the main street in town to take you to the Golden Triangle for 60B one-way.

**BY SONGTAO**   *Songtao* (truck taxis) can be found on the main street across from the market; rides cost only 10B. You can also flag these guys down between Chiang Saen and Golden Triangle when you see them.

**BY LONG-TAIL BOAT**   Long-tail boat captains offer Golden Triangle tours for about 300B per boat (seating eight) one-way. Many people enjoy the half-hour cruise, take a walk around the village of Sob Ruak after they've seen the Golden Triangle, and then continue on by bus.

## Fast Facts: Chiang Saen & the Golden Triangle

**Everything You Need**   Siam Commercial Bank, the bus stop, post office, and police station, and the Chiang Saen National Museum are all on main street. There is a currency exchange booth at the Golden Triangle.

## ACCOMMODATIONS & DINING

**Le Meridien Baan Boran Hotel.** Golden Triangle, Chiang Saen 57150, Chiang Rai. ☎ **800/225-5843** in the U.S. and Canada, 1800/622-240 in Australia, 0800/454-040 in New Zealand, 0800/404-040 in the UK, or ☎ 053/716-678. Fax 053/716-702. 110 units. A/C MINIBAR TV TEL. US$100–US$140 double; US$250 suite. AE, DC, MC, V. Above river, 7.5 miles (12km) northwest of Chiang Saen.

In stunning contrast to most new hotels, this one is a triumph of ethnic design. You'll never question whether you're in the scenic hill-tribe region because the Le Meridien Baan Boran's elegance and style depend on locally produced geometric and figurative weavings, carved teak panels, and pervasive views of the juncture of the Ruak and Mae Khong rivers. On a hilltop just 1.2 miles (2km) west of the infamous Golden Triangle, the balconied rooms have splendid views. This oasis of comfort has attached rooms that are so spacious and private you'll feel like you're in your own bungalow. Tiled foyers lead to large bathrooms and bedrooms furnished in teak and traditionally patterned fabrics. The **Yuan Lue Lau** is a lovely, casual dining pavilion with river views. Thai and continental set menus or main courses, snacks, and breakfast are served. Frequent barbecues and buffets are held on a lower, river-view terrace.

## ATTRACTIONS

Allow at least half a day to see all of Chiang Saen's historical sights before exploring the Golden Triangle. To help with orientation, make the museum your first stop.

**Chiang Saen National Museum.** Admission 20B (US55¢). Open Wed to Sun 9am to 4pm, closed holidays.

The museum houses a small but very fine collection of the region's historic and ethnographic products, including large bronze and stone Buddhas dating from the 15th to 17th centuries, pottery from Sukhothai-era kiln sites, and handicrafts and cultural items of local hill tribes.

**Wat Pa Sak.**

The best preserved of the town's wats, Pa Sak is set in a landscaped historical park that contains a large, square-based stupa and six smaller chedis and temples. The park preserves what's left of the compound's 1,000 teak trees. The wat is said to have been constructed in 1295 by King Saen Phu to house relics of the Buddha, though some historians believe its ornate combination of Sukhothai and Pagan styles dates it later. The area's oldest wat is still an active Buddhist monastery.

**Wat Phra Chedi Luang.**

Rising from a cluster of wooden dorms, Wat Phra Chedi Luang (or Jadeeloung) has a huge brick chedi that dominates the main street. The wat complex was established in 1331 under the reign of King Saen Phu and was rebuilt in 1515 by King Muang Kaeo. The old brick foundations, now supporting a very large seated plaster Buddha flanked by smaller ones, are all that remain.

**Wat Mung Muang.**

Mung Muang is the 15th-century square-based stupa seen next to the post office. Above the bell-shaped chedi are four small stupas. Across the street, you can see the bell-shaped chedi from **Wat Phra Bouj.** which is rumored to have been built by the prince of Chiang Saen in 1346, though historians believe it's of the same period as Mung Muang.

# THE GOLDEN TRIANGLE

The infamous Golden Triangle (7.5 miles/12km northwest of Chiang Saen) is a delta-shaped sandbar in the middle of the river where the Mae Khong and Mae Ruak rivers join, separating Thailand, Myanmar, and Laos. It disappears and reappears depending on seasonal water flow and can be reached via one of the noisy long-tail boats that hang around, charging 300B (US$8.10) per half-hour river tour. The area's appeal as a vantage point over forbidden territories is quickly diminishing as there is now a legal crossing into Laos from nearby Chiang Khong.

Nonetheless, a "look" at the home of ethnic hill tribes and their legendary opium trade is still fascinating. Each February, after the dry-season harvest, mule caravans transport poppy crops from the mountains to heroin factories in the Golden Triangle. Despite years of DEA-financed campaigns, the annual yield is still nearly 4,000 tons—accounting for about half of the heroin sold in the United States. The appeal of this geopolitical phenomenon has created **Sob Ruak,** an entire village of thatch souvenir stalls, cheap river-view soda and noodle shops, and very primitive guesthouses. The **Opium House Museum** (open daily from 9am to 5pm, admission free) is small but informative, laying out the process of poppy cultivation and describing the drug's use through paraphernalia and dioramas.

Golden Triangle doesn't take too long to see, so I recommend a relaxing afternoon beer at **Jang's Place,** a small local establishment just across from the sandbar. Be warned: You may get so comfortable you'll never leave. Don't worry, though, they'll send out for food.

# 6 Vietnam

*By Stacy Lu*

Per square inch, Vietnam has as much to offer a traveler as any country in the world, packing at least seven distinct national identities into a relatively small total area. The country has over 2,000 years of its own history to boast, and while occupation by the Chinese, French, and Americans has left its brutal imprints on the Vietnamese story, it has also left a rich cultural smorgasbord. Chinese and French food, language, and architecture have been assimilated smoothly into Vietnamese culture and exist as attractive embellishments to an already fascinating nation.

An ancient Confucian university, a Zen monastery, a Buddhist temple built in the Hindu style, a Vietnamese puppet show, French country chalets and gourmet restaurants—you'll find them all in Vietnam. The Kingdom of Cham, an Indian- and Khmer-influenced nation, also made what is present-day Vietnam its home from the 2nd through 18th centuries, leaving a stunning legacy of art in its temples and sculpture.

Ethnic Vietnam can be seen by visiting some of the country's more than 54 minority groups, usually living in rural, mountainous areas. Their distinct clothing, language, and customs present another side of the country entirely.

Then there is the land of natural beauty. From tall mountains and craggy limestone formations to dense jungles, river deltas, and pristine beaches, Vietnam's ecological treasures alone are worth a trip. Adventure and outdoor travel outfitters have discovered the country of late, and many travelers come to trek, bicycle, and paddle their way through the country. On the other side of the spectrum, luxurious Vietnam is available in the form of five-star hotels and idyllic seaside resorts.

Wartime Vietnam is here, too. In fact, if you want to see the country's past in terms of its wars, you can easily do so. American veterans and history buffs of all nationalities visit former bases and battle sites. The Vietnamese, though, would rather put their turbulent history behind them. This sentiment is almost a public policy. You'll hear people repeating it like a mantra, and you'll find few even willing to talk about the wars on a casual basis.

Rather, the Vietnamese are going forward to establish their country as a unified whole, a unique entity in the world, a strong nation at peace at last. From the smallest northern village to frantic Saigon in the south, all seem to be rushing to develop infrastructure as quickly as possible, to make money and embrace foreign investment and tourism.

# Vietnam

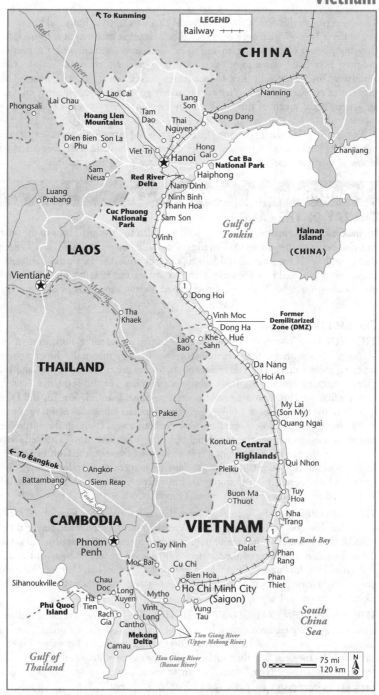

**LEGEND**
Railway +++

To Kunming

CHINA

Red River

Phongsali

Lai Chau
Lao Cai
Lang Son
Nanning

Hoang Lien Mountains
Tam Dao
Thai Nguyen
Dong Dang

Dien Bien Phu
Son La
Viet Tri
Hong Gai
Cat Ba National Park

Sam Neua
Hanoi
Red River Delta
Haiphong

Zhanjiang

Luang Prabang

Nam Dinh
Ninh Binh
Thanh Hoa
Cuc Phuong National Park
Sam Son

LAOS

Vinh

*Gulf of Tonkin*

Hainan Island
(CHINA)

Vientiane

Mekong

① Dong Hoi

Tha Khaek

Vinh Moc
Dong Ha
Hué
Former Demilitarized Zone (DMZ)

Lao Bao
Khe Sahn

THAILAND

Da Nang
Hoi An

Pakse

My Lai (Son My)
Quang Ngai

Kontum
Central Highlands

To Bangkok

Pleiku

Qui Nhon

Angkor
Siem Reap

Battambang

Buon Ma Thuot

Tuy Hoa

*Tonle Sap*

CAMBODIA

VIETNAM

Nha Trang

Phnom Penh

Tay Ninh

Dalat

Cam Ranh Bay

Moc Bai
Cu Chi

① Phan Rang

Sihanoukville

Chau Doc
Long Xuyen
Mytho
Bien Hoa
Phan Thiet

Phu Quoc Island

Ha Tien
Vinh Long
Ho Chi Minh City (Saigon)

Rach Gia
Cantho
Vung Tau

*South China Sea*

Mekong Delta

*Tien Giang River (Upper Mekong River)*

Camau

*Hau Giang River (Bassac River)*

*Gulf of Thailand*

0 ▬▬ 75 mi
120 km

N

231

Thanks in part to this policy, the country truly has developed in leaps and bounds. If you've never been to Vietnam before, you'll be amazed at how easy it is to navigate. Everybody seems to speak English and to be somehow connected with the tourism industry. Everybody wants to sell you something, too, but that can work to your advantage: You'll have your pick of tour guides, ticket agents, and chauffeurs. That may not be necessary, though; Vietnam's relatively good roadways and newly efficient air system make much of this small country within very easy reach of the casual traveler.

A final word: Go now. The region's financial crises led many of Vietnam's expats and much of its business travel business to flee the scene. Hotel and restaurant prices are as low as they'll ever be, and many tour operators are giving big discounts.

# 1  Getting to Know Vietnam

## THE LAY OF THE LAND
Vietnam is an S-shaped peninsula that borders China to the north, Laos to the west, and Cambodia to the southwest. Covering about 128,000 square miles, it is roughly the size of Italy. It has a varied and lush topography with two deltas, tropical forests, craggy mountains and rock formations, and a coastline that stretches for 2,025 miles, much of it white sand beaches. Vietnam can also claim thousands of islands off its coast.

### THE REGIONS IN BRIEF
**THE NORTH**    The northern highlands, occupying the entire northwest tip of Vietnam, are known for their scenic beauty, with craggy mountains hovering over sweeping green valleys. The inhabitants of the region are ethnic minorities and hill tribes, scratching out a living from subsistence farming and still somewhat isolated from civilization. Popular tourism destinations are **Sapa, Lao Cai, Son La,** and **Dien Bien Phu,** the former French military garrison. Vietnam's tallest mountain, Fansipan, 10,312 feet (3,143m), hovers over Sapa near the border with China in the northwest, part of the mountain range the French dubbed "The Tonkinese Alps." The **Red River Delta** lies to the east of the highlands. It is a triangular shape off the **Gulf of Tonkin,** an extension of the South China Sea. In the Gulf is spectacular **Halong Bay,** 3,000 limestone formations jutting up from still blue waters. South of the highlands but still in the northern region is **Hanoi,** Vietnam's capital city.

**THE CENTRAL COAST**    To the east is the central coastline, location of major cities **Hué, Hoi An,** and **Danang.** Hué is Vietnam's former capital and imperial city from 1802 to 1945. Hoi An, a major trading port in the mid–16th century, still shows the architectural influences of the Chinese and Japanese traders who passed through and settled here, leaving buildings that are still perfectly preserved. Danang, Vietnam's fourth-largest city, is a port town whose major attractions include the museum of Cham antiquities and nearby China Beach.

**THE SOUTH CENTRAL COAST & HIGHLANDS**    The central highlands area is a temperate, hilly region occupied by many of Vietnam's ethnic minorities. Travelers are most likely to visit historical **Dalat,** a resort town nestled in the Lang Bien Plateau, established by the French at the turn of the century as a recreation and convalescence center. On the coast is **Nha Trang,** Vietnam's pre-eminent sea resort.

**THE MEKONG DELTA**    Farthest south, the Mekong Delta is a flat land formed by soil deposits from the Mekong River. Its climate is tropical, characterized by heat, high rainfall, and humidity. The Delta's sinuous waterways drift past fertile land used for cultivating rice, fruit trees, and sugar cane. The lower delta is untamed swampland.

The region shows the influences of ancient Funan and Khmer cultures, and the scars as well from war misery, particularly in battles with neighboring Cambodia. **Saigon (Ho Chi Minh City),** Vietnam's largest cosmopolitan area, lies just past its northern peripheries.

## VIETNAM TODAY

As a destination, Vietnam is impressive for the sheer variety of what it can offer. A history of more than 1,000 years has developed a rich and varied culture, heavily spiced with remnants of other occupants like the Chinese, French, and Cham, a Hindu culture that has largely disappeared. Vietnam's 54 ethnic groups, many of them hill tribes living in remote villages, also make it ethnically one of the most diverse in Southeast Asia. The land's topography, with grandiose mountains, lush tropical forests, and beaches of plush sand, is perfect for trekking, paddling, biking, and every water sport you can name. Its major cities, Hanoi and Saigon, are exciting and cosmopolitan, and have countless cultural and historical attractions, as well as accommodations from budget to ultra-deluxe. As a rapidly developing nation, Vietnam is inexpensive and yet comfortable enough to appeal to travelers of all tastes.

## A LOOK AT THE PAST

Vietnam began in the Red River Valley, around the time of the third century B.C., as a small kingdom of Viet tribes called Au Lac. The tiny kingdom was quickly absorbed into the Chinese Qin dynasty in 221 B.C., but as that dynasty crumpled became part of a new land called Nam Viet, ruled by a Chinese commander. In 111 B.C., it was back to China again, this time as part of the Han empire. It was to remain part of greater China for the next thousand years or so. The Chinese form of writing was adopted (to be replaced by a Roman alphabet in the 17th century), Confucianism was installed as the leading ideology, and Chinese statesmen became the local rulers. Few effectively challenged Chinese rule, with the exception of two nobleman's daughters, the Trung sisters, who led a successful but short-lived revolt in A.D. 39.

In 939, the Chinese were finally thrown off and the Vietnamese were left to determine their own destiny under a succession of dynasties. The kingdom flourished and strengthened, enough for the Vietnamese to repel the intrusion of Mongol invaders under Kublai Khan from the north in the mid–13th century, and armies from the kingdom of Champa from Danang and the east. Gathering strength, Vietnam gradually absorbed the Cham empire and continued to move south, encroaching upon Khmer land, taking the Mekong Delta and almost extinguishing the Khmer as well. There followed a brief period of Chinese dominance in the early 1400s, but the biggest risk to the country's stability was to come from the inside.

Torn between rival factions in court, the country split along north-south lines in 1545; the north following the Le dynasty; the south, the Nguyen. The country was reunited under emperor Gia Long in 1802, but by the 1850s the French, already settled and on the prowl in Indochina, launched an offensive that resulted in the Vietnamese accepting protectorate status 3 decades later.

Although the French contributed greatly to Vietnamese infrastructure, the proud people bridled under colonial rule. In 1930, revolutionary **Ho Chi Minh** found fertile ground to establish a nationalist movement. As in China, World War II and occupation by the Japanese in 1940 helped fuel the movement by creating chaos and nationalist fervor, and upon the retreat of the Japanese, Ho Chi Minh declared Vietnam an independent nation in August 1945.

The French did not agree, however, and the two sides fought bitterly until 1954. The French, having lost a decisive battle at Dien Bien Phu, agreed to a cease-fire at the Geneva Convention that year. The two sides determined that the country would be split along north and south at the Seventeenth Parallel, with the Viet Minh (League for the Independence of Vietnam) having control of the north and the French supporters having control of the south. Elections were to be held in 2 years to determine who would lead a new, unified Vietnam.

Mainly because of resistance from an American-supported regime in the south, led by Ngo Dinh Diem, the elections were never held. The communists continued to gain power and Diem was assassinated, putting the southern regime in peril. Finally, in 1965, American president Lyndon Johnson dispatched the first American combat troops to Danang to prop up the south. The Soviet Union and China weighed in with assistance to the north. The rest is history. After a decade of heavy fighting that took 58,000 American and as many as four million Vietnamese lives, the communists took Saigon on April 30, 1975. In 1976, north and south were officially reunited. Rather than enjoying the newfound peace, Vietnam invaded Cambodia after border skirmishes in 1978. China, friend of Cambodia, then invaded Vietnam in 1979.

In the mid 1980s, Vietnam began moving toward *doi moi*, a free-market policy, to save itself from bankruptcy. To further ingratiate itself with the international community, it withdrew its army from Cambodia in 1989, and as the 1990s began, the country began opening to the world. It further reorganized its economy toward a market-oriented model, sought diplomatic relations, and in 1991 signed a peace agreement with Cambodia. In 1994, America capitulated and lifted its long-standing trade embargo against Vietnam, and the two countries established diplomatic relations in 1995. Vietnam also joined ASEAN (Association of Southeast Asian Nations).

Today, Vietnam is flourishing. It has become the world's third largest rice exporter. Its per capita income increases steadily each year, though pockets of extreme poverty still remain in rural areas. Foreign investment, at least until the recent regional economic crises, was booming. And tourists are increasingly discovering its pleasures.

For historical background during French occupation, read Graham Greene's *The Quiet American;* for history on the American War, Neil Sheehan's *A Bright Shining Lie* is considered the standard bearer; Michael Herr's *Dispatches* is another view. A few movies to whet your appetite: *Indochine,* a 1992 film with Catherine Deneuve set during the time of the communist revolution; *The Scent of Green Papaya,* 1994, story of an elite Vietnamese family and their servant girl; and *Cyclo,* 1995, about youth gangs in present-day Vietnam.

## VIETNAMESE CULTURE

Vietnam has a cultural landscape as varied and colorful as its topography. The Viet ethnic group is well in the majority, comprising about 88% of the population, but there are 53 other minority ethnic groups, many of whom are hill tribes living in villages largely untouched by modern civilization.

Though Vietnam has rushed into modernization over the past several years, the economy is still largely agrarian, with farmers, fishermen, and forestry workers accounting for 73% of the workforce and most of the population still residing in small villages. The Vietnamese have a strong sense of family and of community, and are accustomed to close human contact and far-reaching interrelationships. This may be one of the reasons why, despite centuries of occupation by foreigners, Vietnamese cultural traditions have survived. Moreover, outsiders are still welcomed. Americans, in fact, will get a wide smile and thumbs-up, although the reception is notably better in the south than in the north. As a Saigon taxi driver put it, "America number one! America and Vietnam, we just had a little problem." A classic understatement.

## CUISINE

Each region has its specialties, but the hallmarks of Vietnamese food are light, fresh ingredients, heavy on the rice, pork, and fish, with fresh garnishes such as mint, coriander, fish sauce, and chili pepper. Two of the local dishes you're most likely to encounter are pho, a noodle soup in a clear broth, and bun cha, fresh rice noodles with barbecued pork in sauce. Chinese-influenced dishes can be found, including hot pot, a cook-your-own group activity where fresh vegetables and chunks of meat and fowl are dipped into boiling broth and then consumed. The French have left their mark as well. Along with excellent restaurants, you'll find espresso and crusty French bread on every street corner.

## THE ARTS

Ancient, distinctive Vietnamese art forms remain today, like **water puppetry,** where wooden hand puppets actually dance across water, and *cheo,* traditional **folk opera.** There is an emerging interest in fine arts, with countless galleries in almost every major Vietnamese city, and an emphasis on traditional techniques such as lacquer and silk painting and wood blocking. **Vietnamese music,** using string and woodwind instruments, bamboo xylophones, and metal gongs, is delicate, distinctive, and appealing. **Literature** has existed since the forming of the nation in folklore, proverbs, and idioms singular to each village and ethnic group and passed down from century to century. Many of the old tales have been translated and printed in books that you can easily find in a foreign-language bookstore.

## RELIGION

About 70% of all Vietnamese are **Buddhists,** mainly Mahayana, 10% are **Catholics,** and the rest **Confucianists, animists** (believing in gods of nature), or followers of the unique Vietnamese religion **Cao Daism,** an interesting combination of the major world faiths. **Islam** and **Protestantism** also have small pockets of believers. While we're on the topic of -isms, it's hard for the casual observer to see any observance to **communism** at all, other than the prevalence of state-owned entities.

## ETIQUETTE

Although the Vietnamese are generally tolerant of foreign ways, they dress very modestly. Foreigners displaying navels, chests, or shoulders or wearing hot pants will attract stares. Butt thongs and nude beach bathing are out of the question. Some temples flatout refuse to admit persons in shorts, and some smaller towns like Hoi An post signs asking tourists to dress "appropriately," which means you may have a run-in with the police if you don't.

Unfortunately, one unfortunate by-product of the relative newness of tourism in Vietnam is an eagerness to separate you from your money. This so-called communist state is in fact relentlessly capitalist. The child hawkers, "tour guides," and cyclo drivers can be extraordinarily persistent, following you for blocks, grabbing your arm, and hounding you at temples and open-air restaurants. Even if you don't want to be rude, avoiding eye contact and saying nothing is the best way to extricate yourself. It can be wearying, and hopefully the whole scene will calm down soon.

## LANGUAGE

The ancient Vietnamese language, though not complex structurally, is tonal and therefore difficult for many Westerners to master. In its earliest written form, *nom,* it was based on the Chinese pictographic writing forms, but in the 17th century a French scholar developed a Roman alphabet for it. Today, most city dwellers seem to speak at least a little English or French. They will be eager to practice with you, especially if you are alone, although few people speak well enough for you to get close with them.

## USEFUL VIETNAMESE WORDS & PHRASES

| English | Vietnamese | Pronounced |
|---|---|---|
| Hello | *xin chao* | seen chow |
| Good bye | *tam biet* | tam bee-*et* |
| Yes | *vang* | vahng |
| No | *khong* | kawng |
| Thank you | *cam on* | cahm un |
| You are welcome | *khong co gi* | kawng koe gee |
| Excuse me | *xin loi* | seen loy |
| Where is | *o dau* | er dow |
| Turn right | *re phai* | ray fie |
| Turn left | *re trai* | ray chrai |
| Toilet | *nha ve sinh* | nya vay shin |
| Hotel | *khach san* | kak san |
| Restaurant | *nha hang* | nya hahng |
| Potable water | *nuoc khoang* | nook kwang |
| I don't understand | *toi khong hieu* | toy kawng hew |
| How much? | *bao nhieu* | baugh nyew |
| When? | *luc nao* | look now |
| I need a doctor | *toi can bac si* | toy cahn back see |
| Hospital | *benh vien* | ben vee-in |
| Antibiotic | *thuoc khang sinh* | dook kahng shin |

### Numbers

Numbers over 10 are constructed by simply saying 10 (*muoi*) plus the smaller number (i.e., *muoi mot* for 11, *muoi hai* for 12). The same pattern of contruction holds for larger numbers.

| 1 | *mot* | mot |
|---|---|---|
| 2 | *hai* | hi |
| 3 | *ba* | ba |
| 4 | *bon* | bawn |
| 5 | *nam* | nahm |
| 6 | *sau* | sow (rhymes with "how") |
| 7 | *bay* | buy |
| 8 | *tam* | tahm |
| 9 | *chin* | cheen |
| 10 | *muoi* | moo-i |
| 11 | *muoi mot* | moo-i mot |
| 20 | *hai muoi* | hi moo-i |
| 100 | *mot tram* | mot chram |
| 1000 | *mot ngan* | mot nyan |

### Days of the Week

| Monday | *thu hai* | doo hi |
|---|---|---|
| Tuesday | *thu ba* | doo ba |
| Wednesday | *thu tu* | doo too |
| Thursday | *thu nam* | doo nahm |

| Friday | *thu sau* | doo sow |
|---|---|---|
| Saturday | *thu bay* | doo by |
| Sunday | *chu nhat* | choo nyat |
| Today | *hom nay* | hawm ny |

**Emergencies**

| Help! | *Cuu voi!* | ku voy |
|---|---|---|
| Police! | *Canh sat!* | cahn saht |
| Stop! | *Ngung lai!* | nyoong lie |

## 2  Planning a Trip to Vietnam

### VISITOR INFORMATION

Vietnam's national tourism administration is a government agency rather than a font of information, although it does have a fairly good Web site at **www. vietnamtourism.com.** It operates mainly through its state-owned tourism agencies, **Saigontourist** and **Hanoitourist.** Neither agency offers particularly good bargains, so shop around before you actually book something. Two state-owned tourism groups—**Vietnamtourism,** 2974 Monticello Dr., Falls Church, VA 22042 (☎ **703/641-7738;** fax 703/641-7739; e-mail representative Doug Reese at dreese@erols.com), and **Saigontourist,** 6606 Antoine Dr., Houston, TX 77091-1297 (☎ 800/349-4932 or 713/683-3708; fax 713/957-2076; e-mail info@indochina.com)—have offices in the U.S. They provide comprehensive services including tours and bookings.

### WEB SITES

- **www.vietnamembassy-usa.org** (the Vietnam Embassy in the U.S.)
- **www.destinationvietnam.com** (a colorful on-line magazine with excellent travel articles on dining and destinations)
- **http://asiatravel.com/vietinfo.html** (general information)
- **www.delphi.com/vietnamweb/** (general information)

### TOUR OPERATORS
#### IN NORTH AMERICA

- **Abercrombie & Kent,** 1520 Kensington Rd., Oak Brook, IL 60523-2141 (☎ **800/323-7308** or 708/954-2944; www.abercrombiekent.com). Upscale and excellent.
- **Absolute Asia,** 180 Varick St., New York, NY 10014 (☎ **800/736-8187** or 212/627-1950; fax 212/627-4090).
- **Mountain Travel-Sobek,** 6420 Fairmount Ave., El Cerrito, CA 94530. (☎ **888/ 687-6235** or 510/527-8100; fax 510-525-7710; e-mail: info@mtsobek.com).
- **Adventures Abroad,** 2148-20800 Westminster Hwy., Richmond, BC, Canada V6V 2W3. (☎ **800/665-3998** or 604/303-1099. www.adventures-abroad.com; e-mail: adabroad@infoserve.net).
- **Asia Transpacific Journeys,** 3055 Center Green Dr., Boulder, CO 80301 (☎ **800/642-2742** or 303/443-1633; fax 303/443-7078; www.southeastasia. com; e-mail: info@southeastasia.com). ATJ specializes in small group and custom tours.
- **Latitudes, Expeditions East,** 870 Market St., Suite 482, San Francisco, CA 94102 (☎ **800/580-4883** or 415/398-0458; fax 415/680-1522; e-mail: info@weblatitudes.com).

## IN AUSTRALIA/NEW ZEALAND

- **Intrepid Small Group Adventures,** P.O. Box 2781, Fitzroy, D.C. Victoria, Australia (☎ 3/9743-2626; fax 3/9419-4426; e-mail: info@intrepidtravel.com.au).
- **ActiveTravel,** P.O. Box 5779, Dunedin, New Zealand (☎ 800/326-2283 New Zealand only or 3/477-8045; fax 03/477-8802; e-mail: irene@activeco.co.nz).
- **Mountain Travel-Sobek,** Australian Sales Office (☎ 02/9264-5710; fax 02/9267-3074; e-mail: adventure@africatravel.com.au).

## IN THE U.K.

- **Mountain Travel-Sobek,** European Sales Office (☎ 49/444-8901; fax 49/446-5526; e-mail: sales@mtsobekeu.com).

## FAR-FLUNG & ADVENTURE TRAVEL

To really see Vietnam's natural beauty, you should hike it, bike it, or kayak it. Adventure travel and ecotourism are increasingly popular here, particularly cross-country biking tours. Given Vietnam's size and relatively flat terrain along the coast, it's easier than you might think. You can also look up some of these agents to cover some of the more challenging and out-of-the-way destinations, such as the seldom-explored northwest, the central highlands, or the innermost regions of the Mekong Delta.

### In the United States & Canada

- **Asian Pacific Adventures.** 826 South Sierra Bonita Ave., Los Angeles, CA 90036-4704 (☎ 800/825-1680 or 323/935-3156; fax 323/935-2691). Offers biking tours through Vietnam.
- **The Global Spectrum.** 1901 Pennsylvania Ave. NW, Washington, DC 20006 (☎ 800/419-4446 or 202/293-2065; fax 202/296-0815; e-mail: gspectrum@idsonline.com). Group tours; also specializes in tours for veterans.
- **Worldwide Adventures,** 36 Finch Ave. W., Toronto, Ontario, Canada M2N 2G9 (☎ 800/387-1483; www.worldwidequest.com).
- **Butterfield & Robinson,** 70 Bond St., Toronto, Ontario, Canada M5B 1X3 (☎ 800/678-1147 or 416/864-1354; fax 416/864-0541; www. butterfield.com; e-mail: info@butterfield.com). Deluxe biking tours for all physical levels.
- **World Expeditions,** 78 George St., Ottawa, Ontario, Canada K1N 5W1 (☎ 613/ 241-2700; fax 613/241-4189; e-mail info@worldexpeditions.com). Hiking, biking, trekking, and camping. Gets rave reviews.

### In the U.K.

- **Imaginative Traveller,** 14 Barley Mow Passage, Chiswick, London W4 4PH (☎ 181/742-8612). Organizes motorcycle tours.

### In Vietnam

- **Buffalo Tours,** 11 Hang Muoi, Hanoi, Vietnam (☎ 04/828-0702; fax 04/826-9370; e-mail: Buffalo@netnam.org.vn). Specializes in hiking and trekking tours to the northeast; also offers a Halong Bay kayaking trip.
- **Phuong Nam Co,** 6 Ho Tung Mao St., Dalat, Vietnam (☎ 063/822-781; fax 063/822-138). Camping, trekking, hunting, jeep tours, or canoeing in the central highlands region. Two-day packages, including cooks and guides, start at US$50.

## ENTRY REQUIREMENTS

Residents of the U.S., Canada, Australia, New Zealand, and the United Kingdom need both passports and a valid visa to enter Vietnam. A tourist visa usually lasts for

# "They finally realize the war is over":
## Tours for American Vets

Vietnam tourists today comprise those from all walks of life, but a goodly percent of them are, surprisingly, American **Vietnam veterans.** It's not unusual to run across groups or individuals as you make your way across the country, some simply seeing how the story ended or others on more somber missions, such as staging memorial services.

There are even tour operators specializing in veteran return visits. One such group is the Global Spectrum in Washington, D.C. Richard Schonberger, himself a veteran of the 101st Airborne Division, arranges group and private tours for about 250 veterans a year for Global. He says veterans account for about 15% of the company's annual Vietnam business.

Itineraries are often tailored to a division's history, though there are few remaining bunkers or barbed wire to see. Most groups visit general operating areas. An itinerary might include starting out in Saigon with an excursion to the Cu Chi tunnels, going down to the Mekong Delta, then heading up to Qui Nhon and to the Central Highlands and Pleiku, then on to Danang, China Beach, Hué, and of course, the De-militarized Zone (DMZ), also known as the 17th Parallel.

But why would a veteran want to return to Vietnam, scene of terror and destruction?

"One of the things we found is that most vets didn't get a taste of real Vietnamese culture, and most want to experience that the second time around," Schonberger says. Further, "Probably the most uniform reaction of veterans is a feeling of closure and healing." he says. "When you can cross the Ben Hai River at the DMZ and actually walk from north to south, that's when you really know the war is over."

For more information, contact **The Global Spectrum,** 1901 Pennsylvania Ave. NW, Washington, DC 20006 (☎ **800/419-4446** or 202/293-2065); or **Nine Dragons Tours,** Glendale Center Mall, 6101 North Keystone Ave., Indianapolis, IN 46220-2485 (☎ **800/909-9050** or 317/726-1501).

30 days and costs US$50, although some people are inexplicably able to get longer visas upon request. It will take a week to 10 days to process, and must be submitted with your passport, the application, and two passport photos. You will receive a copy of the application, which must be submitted to the immigration officials checking your passport when you leave the country. Once inside Vietnam, you can **extend your**

### Travel Tip

Please note that except for the very newest international hotels, special accommodations for **travelers with disabilities** are almost nonexistent in Vietnam. Going with a tour agent that is aware of your disability and can arrange transportation (like mini-buses) accordingly is probably the best way to go. **Accessible Journeys,** 35 W. Sellers Ave., Ridley Park, PA 19078 (☎ **800/846-4537** or 610/521-0339), provides tours for travelers with wheelchairs or walkers.

# Vietnam for the Business Traveler

Even with the current regional economic crises, Vietnam is still as much a business destination as a tourist spot, thanks to a loosening of economic restrictions in the mid-1980s. Major cities like Hanoi and Saigon have a plethora of new business hotels with every facility and service a businessperson could wish for. Even plugging in and hooking up your computer—the last item every hotel seems to think of—is relatively easy. However, the closest **Internet dialup number,** unless you sign up with one of the few Vietnamese ISPs, will probably be in Thailand.

Outside of the two metropolitan centers, services and communications become more difficult, although you shouldn't have any problem with basics like electricity and international telephone capabilities. Internet access is available at post offices, too, as is express mail, and most hotels can assist you with travel arrangements.

The Vietnamese themselves are hardworking and eager to do business at every level of society, though processes can be hampered by arcane government regulations. Establishing and maintaining personal, face-to-face relationships is critical to accomplishing even the simplest procedure. If you have too many stumbling blocks, you haven't found the right Vietnamese partner. A few points to remember:

- **Punctuality.** While appointments may not be made as quickly and as often as you might like, they are kept when set.

- **Dining.** Dining is part of establishing a good business relationship in Vietnam, and you should budget a goodly amount of time and money for wining and dining potential business allies. If you initiated the business transaction, you should pick up the tab; the Vietnamese may wish to treat you to a celebratory dinner after negotiations are completed.

- **Communications.** Vietnamese are loath to commit themselves. Even when they do, written contracts are often not followed as closely as a Western business partner would expect. Subtle hints will be given to alert you to the true nature of a success or failure, so pay attention carefully.

- **Power Structures.** Business is conducted formally, with strict attention to hierarchy. No one likes to lose face, particularly those at the top, so it will be difficult getting Vietnamese to admit to any mistakes or weaknesses.

- **Negotiating.** There is a good deal of reluctance to get down to brass tacks when it comes to money in Vietnam. Terms will come at the very end of negotiations and probably carry conditions—which means, however, that you are free to set your own. Be patient.

For more information, look to *Vietnam: The No BS Business Guide,* edited by Thomas M. F. Timberman, and *Passport Vietnam: Your Pocket Guide to Vietnamese Business, Customs & Etiquette* by Jeffrey Curry & "Jim" Chinh Nguyen.; or contact the American Chamber of Commerce in Hanoi, c/o The Press Club, 59A Ly Thai To St., Hanoi (☎ 04/934-2790; fax 04/934-2787). There is an excellent, informative Web site from the Center for Trade with Vietnam at www.freeyellow.com/members4/vietrading/. The Vietnam Business Journal online can be found at www.viam.com.

---

**Travel Tip**

When exchanging currency, the bigger the bill you change, the better your rate.

---

**visa** twice, each time for 30 days, according to Saigontourist, which, along with many travel agencies and state-owned hotels, is empowered to extend your visa. If someone gives you trouble about extending your visa, stick to your guns and ask around. Multiple-entry business visas are available that are valid for up to 3 months, but you must have a sponsoring agency in Vietnam and it can take much longer to process. For short business trips, it's less complicated simply to enter as a tourist.

If you are flying in, you will automatically be assigned either Hanoi or Saigon as entry points. If you plan to enter the country overland, you must specify your points of entry and departure and stick to them. Check your visa to make sure it's correct when you get it. If you change your plans once you're in the country, you can change the points of exit through a travel agency. Otherwise, you can face fines of up to US$40 when you try to leave.

### VIETNAMESE EMBASSY LOCATIONS

**In the U.S.:** Vietnam Embassy, Office of Passport Services, 1233 20th St. NW, Suite 400, Washington, DC 20036 (☎ **202/647-0518;** fax 202/861-1297).

**In Canada:** Vietnam Embassy, Passport Office, 226 Maclaren St., Ottawa, Ontario, Canada, K2P OL9 (☎ **613/236-0772;** fax 613/236-2704).

**In Australia:** Vietnam Embassy, 6 Timbarra Crescent, O'Malley, Canberra, ACT 2606 (☎ **2/6286-6059**).

**In the U.K.:** Vietnam Embassy, 12–14 Victoria Rd., London W8-5RD, U.K. (☎ **0171/1912;** fax 0171/937-6108).

## CUSTOMS REGULATIONS

The first and most important thing to remember is not to lose your entry/exit slip, the blue piece of paper that will be clipped to your passport upon arrival. If you do, you may be fined. When you enter the country, declare your electronic goods and any expensive jewelry, and keep the form you're given. It will help ensure a smooth departure. You must declare cash in excess of US$7,000 or the equivalent. You can also import 200 cigarettes, 2 liters of alcohol, and perfume and jewelry for personal use. Antiques cannot be exported, although the laws are vague and irregularly enforced. If you're buying a reproduction, have the shop state as much on your receipt, just in case.

## MONEY

The official currency of Vietnam is the **dong** (VND), which comes in denominations of 50,000, 10,000, 5,000, 1,000, 500, and 200.

**CURRENCY EXCHANGE & RATES**   At the time I did my research, the exchange rate was 13,850 Vietnamese VND to one U.S. dollar. The U.S. dollar is used as an informal second currency, and most things more than a few dollars are quoted as such. I've listed prices in this guide as they are quoted. Every hotel, no matter how small, will gladly change money for you, and they should offer the going bank rate. Jewelry stores can change money, too. You may squeeze an extra 150 VND or so to the dollar from the black market. Changers usually loiter outside banks or post offices. Count the money you're given carefully, and be alert to counterfeits. The bigger the bill you

## What Things Cost in Vietnam

|  | U.S. $ | Can. $ | Aust. $ | N.Z. $ | U.K. £ |
|---|---|---|---|---|---|
| Taxi from the airport to city center, Hanoi | $14 | $21.30 | $22.50 | $26.46 | £8.70 |
| Local telephone call | 10¢ | 15¢ | 16¢ | 19¢ | 6p |
| Double room at a very expensive hotel | $180 | $274 | $290 | $340 | £112 |
| Double room at an expensive hotel | $90 | $137 | $145 | $170 | £56 |
| Double room at a moderate hotel | $50 | $76 | $80 | $94 | £31 |
| Double room at an inexpensive hotel | $30 | $46 | $48 | $56 | £19 |
| Dinner for one, expensive, w/o wine | $17 | $26 | $27 | $32 | £11 |
| Dinner for one, moderate, w/o wine | $8 | $12 | $13 | $15 | £5 |
| Dinner for one, inexpensive, w/o wine | $3 | $4.50 | $4.80 | $5.70 | £1.85 |
| Glass of local beer | $1.10 | $1.70 | $1.75 | $2.10 | 70p |
| Coca-Cola | 60¢ | 90¢ | $1 | $1.15 | 35p |
| Cup of Vietnamese coffee at a local cafe | 50¢ | 75¢ | 80¢ | 95¢ | 30p |
| Roll of 36-exposure color film | $2 | $3 | $3.20 | $3.80 | £1.25 |
| Admission to national historical museum | 70¢ | $1.10 | $1.15 | $1.30 | 45p |

change, the better your rate. Don't accept torn or very grubby bills, as you may have a problem reusing them. It may make more sense to pay in U.S. dollars whenever possible, unless you get a very good exchange rate on the black market. Businesses quoting in dollars use a rule of thumb of 14,000, higher than the official exchange rate.

Banks in any city I've mentioned can cash **traveler's checks** for you, in U.S., Canadian, and Australian dollars or pounds sterling, although U.S. dollars get the best rate. Vendors usually don't like to accept traveler's checks, however. Hanoi and Saigon each have a few **Automated Teller Machines (ATMs)** that dispense cash in dong and dollars.

As a general rule, **credit cards** are accepted only at major hotels, restaurants, tour guide operators, and some shops in Hanoi and Saigon, though they're increasingly accepted outside these two major cities. Any Vietcombank branch, as well as big foreign banks, will handle **credit card cash withdrawals.**

**LOST/STOLEN CREDIT CARDS & TRAVELER'S CHECKS**   To report lost or stolen cards or traveler's checks, call the nearest branch of Vietcombank. Otherwise, you can go to a post office to place a collect call to the card's international toll-free collect number for cash and card replacement. The international numbers are as follows:

| **Travel Tip** |
|---|

**Film** is cheap in Vietnam at about US$2 per roll, and the quality of developing services is good. If your **camera** breaks down, though, have it fixed at home. Disposables are available.

---

**American Express,** ☎ 336/393-1111; **Visa,** ☎ 757/677-4701; **MasterCard,** ☎ 904/448-8661. Note that foreigners aren't permitted to make collect calls, so you'll have to get a Vietnamese to assist you. Or you can use **AT&T,** whose access number in Vietnam is ☎ 12010288.

## WHEN TO GO

**PEAK SEASON**    The peak seasons vary from region to region, according to the weather. See individual city/town sections for more information.

**CLIMATE**    Vietnam's climate varies greatly from north to south. The north has four distinct seasons, with a chilly but not freezing winter from November to April. Summers are warm and wet. Dalat, in the central highlands, has a temperate climate year-round. The south (which means Nha Trang on down) has hot, humid weather throughout the year, with temperatures peaking March through May into the 90s. In addition, the south has a monsoon season from April to mid-November, followed by a "dry" season.

If, like many people, you're planning to do a south-north or north-south sweep, you may want to avoid both the monsoons and heat in the south by going sometime between November and February. If you're planning a beach vacation, however, keep in mind that the surf on the south central coast (China Beach, Nha Trang) is too rough for water sports from October through March.

**PUBLIC HOLIDAYS**    Public holidays are New Year's Day (January 1), Tet/Lunar New Year (early to mid-February; state holiday lasts 4 days), Saigon Liberation Day (April 30), International Labour Day (May 1), National Day (September 2). Government offices and tourist attractions will be closed.

While **Tet** (the lunar new year, in mid-February) is Vietnam's biggest holiday, it's very much a family-oriented time. Much of the country will close down, including stores, restaurants, and museums, and accommodations may be difficult to find.

## HEALTH CONCERNS

Health considerations should comprise a major part of your Vietnam trip planning, even if you're only going for a few weeks. You'll need to cover all the bases to protect yourself from tropical weather and illnesses, and will need to get special vaccinations if rural areas are on your itinerary. You should begin your vaccinations as necessary at least weeks prior to your trip, to give them time to take effect. If you follow the guidelines here and those of your doctor, however, there's no reason you can't have a safe and healthy trip.

### DIETARY PRECAUTIONS

First, you'll want to avoid contaminated food and water, which can bring on a host of ills: bacillary and amoebic dysentery, giardia (another nasty intestinal disease), typhoid, and cholera, to name a few. Take note: **There is no public potable water in Vietnam.** Drink only bottled or boiled water, without ice except in very upscale places that assure you in writing that they make their own ice from clean water. Wash your hands often with soap, particularly before eating, and eat fruit only if you have peeled it yourself. **Try to avoid uncooked food.** This is difficult with Vietnamese cuisine, which uses fresh condiments; and of course you'll want to try the fresh fruit milk shakes, ice cream, and so forth. So use your best judgement. Find the cleanest small restaurants (tip: look at the floors) and carry your own pair of plastic or disposable chopsticks or eating utensils for the inevitable moment a restaurant gives you a pair of used wooden ones. Cleaning glasses and bowls with handy wipes in a downscale place doesn't hurt, either.

If despite all your precautions you still fall ill with diarrhea or stomach problems—as happened to your hapless guidebook writer—stick to easily digested foods until it clears up. Any Vietnamese will tell you to eat rice porridge and bananas and drink lots of weak green tea, which is sound advice. Yogurt (packaged only—avoid the fresh on-the-street stuff) can also help replenish necessary bacteria you may lose. You should also dose yourself with a rehydration solution to replace lost salt in the body. Bring some with you. In a pinch, you can purchase it at pharmacies in Vietnam. Once you feel like branching out, try a bowl of *pho ga,* noodle soup with shredded chicken. Should your symptoms persist for more than a few weeks, seek medical attention, and if you become ill after returning home, tell your doctor about your travels.

## VACCINATIONS
The following vaccinations are important for Vietnam: Hepatitis A or immune glob-ulin (IG), Hepatitis B, typhoid, and Japanese encephalitis if you plan to visit rural areas during the rainy season or stay longer than 4 weeks, and rabies if you're planning to go to rural areas where you might be exposed to wild animals. You should also con-sider booster doses for tetanus-diphtheria, measles, and polio.

**Malaria** is not a problem in the cities, but if you're going rural you should take an oral prophylaxis. Most Vietnamese mosquitoes are chloroquine-resistant, so meflo-quine, also known as Larium, is commonly prescribed. It can have side effects, including dizziness and nausea. Before taking Larium, tell your doctor if you are preg-nant or planning on becoming pregnant. The best prevention is to wear clothing that fully covers your limbs, and to use an insect repellant that contains at least 30% DEET (diethylmethyltoluamide) for adults and 6 to 10% for children. Some people have allergic reactions to DEET, so test it at home before you leave.

## GETTING THERE
### BY PLANE
There is a myriad of air routes into Vietnam. You can fly almost any carrier that goes into Bangkok, Hong Kong, Kuala Lumpur, or Tokyo and get a regional carrier from there. If you're not picky about your choice of carrier or connection destination, there are great bargains to be had on the heels of the region's economic crises.

**FROM THE U.S.    Cathay Pacific** (☎ 800/233-2742) flies to Vietnam via Hong Kong for excellent fares, although if you connect in Hong Kong there are countless deals out there. **Vietnam Airlines** (☎ 852/2810-6680 in Hong Kong) flies to Hanoi and Saigon from Hong Kong, and may soon be flying from Los Angeles to both

---

**Travel Tips**

**Dress codes** in Vietnam are casual except for the most formal of big city restaurants, so pack with this in mind. Keep it light, too, as you'll end up carrying your own goods more than once or twice along the way.

Hanoi and Saigon. **China Airlines** (☎ 800/227-5118) flies from Los Angeles via Taipei to Saigon. **Thai Airways International** (☎ 800/426-5204, but good luck getting through) flies from Los Angeles to Saigon via Bangkok.

**FROM CANADA**   **Cathay Pacific** (☎ 800/233-2742) flies to both Hanoi and Saigon from Vancouver or Toronto via Hong Kong.

**FROM AUSTRALIA**   **Vietnam Airlines** (☎ 2/92523303) flies directly from Sydney or Melbourne to Hanoi or Saigon. From Melbourne, you can fly into Saigon via **Qantas** (☎ 13/1211**), Ansett Australia** (☎ 13/1300), **Lauda Air** (☎ 800/642-438), or **Malaysian Airlines** (☎ 13/2677).

**FROM NEW ZEALAND**   From Auckland, **United Airlines** (☎ 9/379-2800)**, Qantas** (☎ 0800/808767 or 9/3578900), and **Lauda Air** (☎ 29/241-4277 in Sydney) connect in Sydney and Kuala Lumpur before heading on to Saigon.

**FROM FRANCE & THE U.K.**   From Paris, the most convenient route, both **Air France** (☎ 181/742-6600) and **Vietnam Airlines** (☎ 1/4454-3922 in Paris) fly to Hanoi and Saigon. From London, **Thai Airways** (☎ 171/499-9113) flies to Saigon via a connecting flight in Bangkok. To Hanoi, you can fly **KLM Royal Dutch Airlines** (☎ 099/075-0900) among others, to Hong Kong, and **Cathay Pacific** (☎ 171/747-8888) from there.

## GETTING AROUND
It is almost ridiculously easy to get around Vietnam. First, it seems like everybody is in the tourist business. A passerby on the street could probably book you a tour, if you asked. Along with established government-run and private tour agencies, hotels and cafes provide booking services. They all feed into a few big contractors, like tributaries into a river, so prices for the same services can vary. There hasn't been much of a problem with fraud yet, but do stick with the well-established agencies, tourist cafes, or hotels.

### BY PLANE
**Vietnam Airlines** is the only domestic airline carrier in the country, but prices are reasonable and the service good. Seats are usually easy to come by. Purchasing tickets is again very easy; many major hotels have V.A. agents in the lobby.

### BY TRAIN
Vietnam's major rail network runs from Hanoi to Saigon and back, with stops along the way including coastal towns like Hué, Danang, and Nha Trang. The **Reunification Express** is ironically the non-express train; there is an express route as well. To give you an idea of timing, from Hanoi all the way to Saigon is 34 hours on the express train; from Hanoi to Hué about 14 on an overnight express. It's an interesting way to get around, although not much cheaper than flying. Make sure you get "soft sleeper" seats. Air conditioning will cost you about US$13 per ticket but may be most welcome, depending on when you're there. Hotels and tour agencies will gladly arrange tickets for you.

### BY BUS/MINIVAN
Public buses are generally crowded and breakdowns are common, so try to restrict use to major cities, if at all. Most tour agencies run minibuses for excursions and from town to town. Both the **Kim Café** and **Sinh Café,** with branches in Hanoi and Saigon, run ultra-convenient open-end bus tickets one-way from north to south or vice versa, stopping at Hué, Hoi An, Danang, Nha Trang, and Dalat along the way, for US$36. You can pick up this route at any stop along the way.

Vietnamese do like to smoke. Only top-end restaurants serving Western cuisine are likely to have a **nonsmoking section.** Some major hotels do; inquire when making a booking.

## BY CAR

For all practical purposes, it is possible to rent a car in Vietnam only if it comes with a driver. However, it is a good way to see things outside of a city, or to take a 1-day city tour of major sights. Any major hotel or tour agency can assist you. For distances of longer than a few hours' drive, stick to minivans for safety, unless you have a very trustworthy driver and a heavy-duty vehicle.

## TIPS ON ACCOMMODATIONS

A recent building boom followed by the regional currency crisis has brought hotel prices crashing down here. Always ask for seasonal reductions or promotional rates; discounts can be as high as 50% of the rack rate. While this means that deluxe hotels now have mid-range prices, the level of cleanliness and amenities is so high that you can stay in lower range hotels, pay very little, and still come away smiling. A 20% Value Added Tax (VAT) was instituted in January 1999, but expect differences in how hotels follow the policy. Inquire carefully. You need only book far ahead for the most popular hotels; see individual cities and towns for details.

## TIPS ON DINING

Many of the world's finest culinary traditions are represented in Vietnam, including French, Chinese, Japanese, and, of course, Vietnamese. Explore all of your options, particularly in the French arena, as you won't find lower prices anywhere. This should not, however, preclude you from dipping into **street stalls.** They offer fantastic local delicacies like bun bo (cold rice noodles with fried beef), banh khoi (crispy thin rice-based crepes filled with chopped meat and shrimp), and chao (rice porridge with garnishes of meat, egg, or chilies). Note that many upscale places levy a 10% government tax plus a 5% service charge, or may be adding the new 20% VAT.

## TIPS ON SHOPPING

Bring an empty suitcase. Vietnam offers fabulous bargains on **silk,** both as fabric and made-to-order clothing, as well as **lacquerware, silver,** and **fine art.** Hanoi is probably best for most buys, particularly paintings; save the lacquerware and home furnishings for Saigon. Further, the goods are meant to be bargained for, except for those in the most upscale shops.

# Fast Facts: Vietnam

**American Express**   There are no American Express offices in Vietnam.

**Business Hours**   Vendors and restaurants tend to be all-day operations, opening at about 8am and closing at 9 or 10pm. Government offices, including banks and travel agencies, are usually open from 8 to 11:30am and 1 to 4pm.

**Crime**   Violent crime isn't common in Vietnam, but petty thievery, especially against tourists, is a risk. Pickpocketing is rampant, and Ho Chi Minh City

## Stressed? Try Pig Brain

According to *The Guide,* a supplement to the *Vietnam Economic Times,* there are still a few folk remedies alive and well in Vietnam, most of them of Chinese origin. Old folks should eat "black chicken," a baby chicken stewed with special herbs, to build strength and increase longevity. Although the color can be off-putting, I have eaten this chicken and can verify that it is absolutely succulent and may have shaved a few months off my age. The same chicken should be eaten with lotus seeds to cure insomnia. Bull sinew stew is reserved for men only, and if it has something from a bull you can guess its purpose. Bull penis stew is just about for the same thing, except it also helps calm the nerves, as do pig heart and brain. Women about to give birth should eat pork stewed with lotus seeds and black beans. That probably doesn't mean women about to give imminent birth.

(HCMC) has a special brand of drive-by purse-snatching via motorbike. Don't wear flashy jewelry or leave valuables in your hotel room, especially in smaller hotels. There are small-time rackets perpetrated against tourists by taxi and cyclo drivers, usually in the form of a dispute on the agreed-upon price after you arrive at your destination. Or the driver doesn't seem to have change. Simply agree on a price by writing it down first.

**Doctors & Dentists**   Vietnamese health care is not yet up to Western standards. However, there are competent medical clinics in Hanoi and Saigon (see Fast Facts in individual sections) with international, English-speaking doctors. The same clinics have dentists. If your problem is serious, it is best to get to either one of these cities as quickly as possible. The clinics can arrange emergency evacuation. If the problem is minor, ask your hotel to help you contact a Vietnamese doctor. He or she will probably speak some English, and pharmacies throughout the country are surprisingly well stocked. Check the products carefully for authenticity and expiration dates. The Vietnamese are big believers in prescription drugs, although there are still some folk remedies around.

**Drug Laws**   Possessing drugs can mean a jail sentence, and selling them or possessing quantities in excess of 300 grams means a death sentence. Don't take chances.

**Electricity**   Vietnam's electricity carries 220 volts, so if you're coming from the U.S., bring a converter or adapter for electronics. Plugs are either the two-round-prong or three-flat-prong variety. If you're toting a laptop, bring a surge protector. Big hotels will have all these implements.

**Embassies**   Embassies are located in Hanoi at the following addresses: **United States,** 7 Lang Ha St., Ba Dinh District (☎ **04/843-1500;** fax 04/843-1510); **Canada,** Hung Vuong St., Ba Dinh District (☎ **04/823-5500;** fax 04/823-5333); **Australia,** Van Phuc Quarter, Ba Dinh District (☎ **04/831-7755;** fax 04/831-7711); **New Zealand,** 32 Hang Bai St., Hoan Kiem District (☎ **04/824-2481;** fax 04/826-5760); **United Kingdom,** 31 Hai Ba Trung St., 4th Floor, Hoan Kiem District (☎ **04/825-2510;** fax 04/826-5762).

**Emergencies**   Nationwide emergency numbers are as follows: For police, dial 113; fire, 114; and ambulance, 115. Operators speak only Vietnamese.

**Hospitals**    In Hanoi, the **Vietnam International Hospital** (Benh Vien Quoc Te Viet Nam), Phuong Mai Road, Dong Da (☎ **04/574-0740;** fax 04/869-8443), is an Australian joint venture and has first-class care at reasonable prices for 24 hours. Major credit cards are accepted. In Hué, if you have an emergency, go to **Hué General Hospital,** 16 Le Loi St. (☎ **054/822-325**). Take a translator. In Danang, in an emergency, try the small medical clinic at the **Furama Danang,** which is open Tuesday to Saturday 8am to 9pm; Monday and Sunday 8am to 5pm. Or go to **Hospital C** (Benh Vien C), 35 Hai Phong St. (☎ **0511/822-480**); you'll need a translator.

**Internet/E-mail**    There are a surprising number of Internet cafes in cities throughout Vietnam, and most of the larger hotels offer access, even for nonguests. Rates vary from 600 to 7,000 VND (US25¢–US$2) per minute, with the bigger cost of course coming from the hotels. If you have a dial-up number in a nearby country, it should not be too difficult to hook up your computer in an upscale hotel, as most phones use U.S. RJ11 phone plugs. Some may be hard-wired to the wall, especially in small towns, so ask at check-in if this is critical.

   If your computer breaks down, Hanoi and Saigon in particular have PC service centers (see individual chapters).

**Language**    Vietnamese is the official language of Vietnam. Older residents speak and understand French. While English is widely spoken among those in the service industry in Hanoi and Saigon, it is harder to find in other tourist destinations. Off the beaten track, arm yourself with as many Vietnamese words you can muster (see "Useful Vietnamese Words & Phrases," earlier in this chapter) and a dictionary.

**Liquor Laws**    There are virtually no liquor laws in Vietnam as far as age limits and when or where you can buy the stuff. You should avoid drunk motorbike driving, though, just as you would at home.

**Police**    You won't find a helpful cop on every street corner—just the opposite. Count on them only in cases of dire emergency, and learn a few words of Vietnamese to help you along. Moreover, police here can sometimes be part of the problem. Especially in the south, you and your car/motorbike driver might, for instance, be stopped for a minor traffic infraction and "fined." If the amount isn't too large, cooperate. Little gifts of foreign cigarettes won't hurt, either. While it's a shame to perpetuate the practice, you don't want to spend a hunk of your vacation in a police station.

**Post Offices/Mail**    A regular airmail letter will take about 10 days to reach North America, 7 to reach Europe, and 4 to reach Australia or New Zealand. Mailing things from Vietnam is expensive. A letter costs 11,000 VND (US80¢) to North America, 7,000 VND (US50¢) to Europe, and 9,000 VND (US65¢) to Australia/New Zealand; and postcards, respectively, 8,000 VND (US55¢), 7,000 VND (US50¢), and 6,000 VND (US45¢). Express mail services such as Fed-Ex and DHL are easily available and are usually located in or around every city's main post office.

**Safety**    Vietnam is considered a safe place to visit, but take heed of the following: First, the chaotic bike, motorbike, and car traffic can literally be deadly, so be cautious when crossing the street; maintaining a steady pace helps. In a taxi, belt up if possible, and lock your door. Second, women should play it safe and avoid going out alone late at night. Third, and most important: Beware of unexploded mines when hiking or exploring, especially through old war zones such as

# Telephone Dialing Info at a Glance

- **To place a call from your home country to Vietnam:** Dial the international access code (011 in the U.S., 0011 in Australia, 0170 in New Zealand, or 00 in the U.K.), plus the country code (84), the city code (4 for Hanoi, 8 for Ho Chi Minh City, 54 for Hué, 511 for Danang, 510 for Hoi An, 63 for Dalat, 58 for Nha Trang) and the phone number (for example, 011 + 84 + 4 + 000-0000).

- **To place a call within Vietnam:** First dial "0" before the city code. Note that not all phone numbers have 7 digits, and establishments may have several different numbers, one for each line.

- **To place a direct international call from Vietnam:** Most hotels offer International Direct Dialing, but with exorbitant surcharges of 10 to 25%. Faxes often have high minimum charges. To place a call, dial the international access code (00) plus the country code, the area or city code, and the number (for example, to call the U.S., you'd dial 00 + 01 + 000/000-0000).

  It is far cheaper to place a call from a post office: to the U.S. and Canada, US$3.80 for minute and US28¢ for each additional minute; to Australia and New Zealand, US$3.70 and US27¢; to the United Kingdom, US$4.10 and US31¢. Prices are slightly cheaper in the evenings (past 7pm) and on holidays. Faxes cost a flat US$5.70 for the first page, and US$4.20 for each additional page.

- **International country codes** are as follows: Australia 61, Burma 95, Cambodia 855, Canada 1, Hong Kong 852, Indonesia 62, Laos 856, Malaysia 60, New Zealand 64, the Phillipines 63, Singapore 65, Thailand 66, U.K. 44, U.S. 1.

the DMZ or My Son. Don't stray off an established path, and don't touch anything.

**Taxes**   A 20% V.A.T. tax was instituted for hotels and restaurants in January of 1999, but expect variances in how it's followed. Upscale establishments may add the full 20%, and some may even tack on an additional 5% service charge. Others may absorb the tax in their prices, and still others will ignore it entirely. Inquire before booking or eating.

**Telephone & Fax**   Most hotels offer International Direct Dialing, but with exorbitant surcharges of 10 to 25%. It is far cheaper to place a call from a post office. There are plenty of phone booths. They accept phonecards (local and international) that can be purchased at any post office or phone company branch. A local call costs 1,500 VND (US10¢). See "Telephone Dialing Info at a Glance" box in this section for more specific information.

**Time Zone**   Vietnam is 7 hours ahead of Greenwich Mean Time, in the same zone as Bangkok. It is 12 hours ahead of the U.S. and 3 hours behind Sydney.

**Tipping**   Tipping is common in Hanoi and in Saigon. In a top-end hotel, feel free to tip bellhops anywhere from 5,000 VND to US$1, and to leave a few dollars for chambermaids. Most upscale restaurants throughout the country now add a service surcharge of 5 to 10%. If they don't, and/or if the service is good, you may want to leave another 5%. Taxi drivers will be pleased if you round up the bill (again, mainly in the big cities). Use your discretion for tour guides and others who have been particularly helpful. Contrary to rumor, boxes of cigarettes as tips don't go over well. The recipient will say regretfully, "I don't smoke," when what he really means is "Show me the money." Exceptions to this are chauffeurs or minibus drivers.

**Toilets**   Public toilets (*cau tieu*) are nonexistent in Vietnam outside of tourist attractions, but you'll be welcome in hotels and restaurants. Except for newer hotels and restaurants, squat-style toilets prevail. You'll often see a tub of water with a bowl next to the toilet. Throw some water in the bowl to flush. Finally, bring your own paper and antiseptic hand wipes—just in case.

**Water**   Water is not potable in Vietnam. Outside of top-end hotels and restaurants, drink only beverages without ice, unless the establishment promises on the menu that it manufactures its own ice from clean water. Bottled mineral water, particularly the reputable "La Vie" and "A&B" brands, is everywhere. Counterfeits are a problem, so make sure you're buying the real thing, with an unbroken seal. A sure sign is typos. "La Vile" water speaks for itself.

## 3 Hanoi

Vietnam's capital, Hanoi ranks among the world's most attractive and interesting cities. It was first the capital of Vietnam in A.D. 1010, and though the nation's capital moved to Hué under the Nguyen dynasty in 1802, the city continued to flourish after the French took control in 1888. In 1954, after the French departed, Hanoi was declared Vietnam's capital once again. The remnants of over 1,000 years of history are still visible here, with that of the past few hundred years marvelously preserved.

Hanoi has a reputation, doubtless accrued from the American war years, as a dour northern political outpost. While the city is certainly smaller, slower, and far less developed than chaotic Saigon, its placid air gives it a gracious, almost regal flavor. It is set amidst dozens of lakes of various sizes, around which you can usually find a cafe, a pagoda or two, and absorbing vignettes of street life.

Among Hanoi's sightseeing highlights are the **Ho Chi Minh mausoleum and museum,** the **National Art museum,** the grisly **Hoa Lo prison** (also known to Americans as the infamous Hanoi Hilton), and the **Old Quarter,** whose ancient winding streets are named after the individual trades practiced there. Hanoi is also Vietnam's cultural center. The galleries, puppetry, music, and dance performances are worth staying at least a few days to take in. You may also want to use the city as a base for excursions to Halong Bay and Cat Ba island, to Cuc Phuong nature reserve, or north to Sapa.

### GETTING THERE
**BY PLANE**   Hanoi is one of Vietnam's major international gateways, the other being Saigon. For details, see the country's "Getting There" earlier in this chapter. Most hotels will send **shuttles** to pick you up at the airport; for about US$15, they're a good way to go.

**BY TRAIN**   If you're coming from the south, an express train from Hué takes about 14 hours and costs US$64 for a soft-berth compartment with A/C. The train station is at 180 Le Duan St., Hoan Kiem District.

### GETTING AROUND
Hanoi is divided into districts. You will most likely spend most of your time in the Hoan Kiem (downtown) and Ba Dinh (west of town) districts, with perhaps a few

forays into Dong Da (southwest) and Hai Ba Trung (south). Most addresses include a district name. If they don't, ask. You'll want to plan your travels accordingly, as getting from district to district can be time-consuming and expensive.

**BY BUS**   Hanoi has only **buses** in the way of public transport, and they are extremely crowded and using them can be difficult if you don't speak Vietnamese.

**BY TAXI**   Taxis can be hailed off the street, at hotels, and at major attractions. The meter should read 14,000 VND (about US$1) to start, and 4,000 to 5,000 VND for every kilometer after. You can also call for a cab. There are two companies: **Hanoi Taxi** (☎ 04/853-5252), and **52 Taxi** (☎ 04/852-5252). Make sure the cabbie turns on the meter, and that you're given the right change. If the driver doesn't seem to have change, tell him or her you'll wait until it's obtained.

**BY CAR**   Renting a car is convenient. You can book one with driver for about US$30 a day. If an upscale hotel quotes you more, call a **tourist cafe** (combination eateries and travel agents) or the dependable **Galaxy Hotel.**

**BY MOTORBIKE**   If you're feeling especially brave, you can rent your own motorbike. Most tourist cafes and mid- to low-range hotels offer them, as do the numerous street corner entrepreneurs. The price should be about 70,000 VND (US$5) per day. Ask for a helmet. You'll be offered rides constantly as well. Be my guest! It always seems to cost US$1.

**BY CYCLO**   Cyclos are two-seated carts powered by a man on a foot-pedal bike riding behind you. You can flag them down anywhere, particularly near hotels and tourist attractions. Unfortunately, cyclos are a dying breed. Being trundled along among whizzing motorcycles isn't very comfortable, and is definitely unsafe at night. It's nice for touring the Old Quarter, however, with its narrow streets. Bargain with the driver before setting out. You can pay as low as 10,000 VND (US70¢) for a short haul, 15,000 VND (US$1.10) for a longer haul. You can also hire by the hour for about US$2.

**BY BICYCLE**   Another option is to rent a bicycle for the day for about US$1 from a hotel or tourist cafe. Again, it's an easily available method but one best used during the day. Bring your own helmet from home.

## VISITOR INFORMATION & TOURS

Most tour companies are based in Saigon; however, many have branches in Hanoi. Operators can usually assist with local tours as well as country-wide services.

- **Ann's Tours.** 26 Yet Kieu, Hoan Kiem District, Hanoi, ☎/fax **04/822-0018.** Ask for the manager, Mr. Hoan. They offer private deluxe tours to Halong Bay and elsewhere.
- **Vidotour**. 28 Hoa Ma St., Hai Ba Trung District, ☎ **04/821-5682.** Fax 04/972-1107. Upscale and professional. Mr. Vu Huy is extremely helpful and speaks fantastic English. Get him as a guide if you can.
- **Hanoitourist**. 1 Ba Trieu St., ☎ **04/824-2330** or 04/826-5244, fax 04/825-6418. Hanoitourism is the city's largest state-run agency. They are not particularly helpful, so shop around first.
- **Hanoi Toserco.** 8 To Hien Thanh St., ☎ **04/976-2076,** fax 04/822-6055. Another state-run agency, but small enough to be helpful. They also sell open-end bus tickets from Hanoi to Saigon.

### Tourist Cafes

A good option for tours and transport for 1 or 2-day excursions to sites like Halong Bay is to visit one of Hanoi's "tourist cafes," which are small eateries and travel agents

# Hanoi Accommodations & Dining

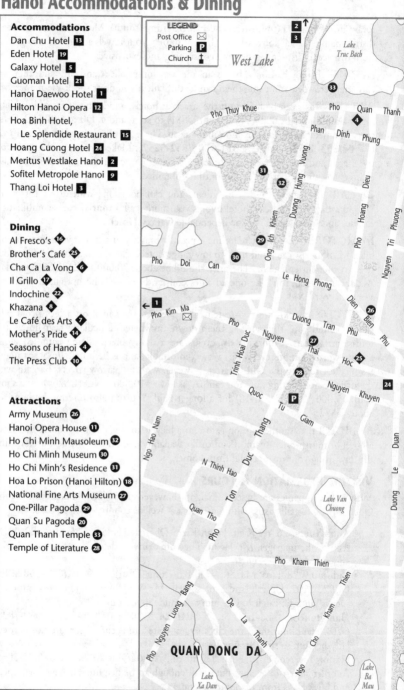

**Accommodations**
Dan Chu Hotel **13**
Eden Hotel **19**
Galaxy Hotel **5**
Guoman Hotel **21**
Hanoi Daewoo Hotel **1**
Hilton Hanoi Opera **12**
Hoa Binh Hotel,
   Le Splendide Restaurant **15**
Hoang Cuong Hotel **24**
Meritus Westlake Hanoi **2**
Sofitel Metropole Hanoi **9**
Thang Loi Hotel **3**

**Dining**
Al Fresco's **16**
Brother's Café **25**
Cha Ca La Vong **6**
Il Grillo **17**
Indochine **22**
Khazana **8**
Le Café des Arts **7**
Mother's Pride **14**
Seasons of Hanoi **4**
The Press Club **10**

**Attractions**
Army Museum **26**
Hanoi Opera House **11**
Ho Chi Minh Mausoleum **32**
Ho Chi Minh Museum **30**
Ho Chi Minh's Residence **31**
Hoa Lo Prison (Hanoi Hilton) **18**
National Fine Arts Museum **27**
One-Pillar Pagoda **29**
Quan Su Pagoda **20**
Quan Thanh Temple **33**
Temple of Literature **28**

LEGEND
Post Office ✉
Parking **P**
Church ✝

West Lake

Lake
Truc Bach

Pho    Quan    Thanh

Pho Thuy Khue

Phan   Dinh   Phung

Duong Hung Vuong

Pho   Hoang

Dieu

Nguyen Tri Phuong

Ong Ich Khiem

Pho   Doi   Can

Le Hong Phong

Dien   Bien

Phu

Pho Kim Ma

Pho

Nguyen

Duong   Tran   Phu

Trinh Hoai Duc

Thai

Hoc

Nguyen   Khuyen

Quoc

Tu   Giam

Ngo Hao Nam

N Thinh Hao

Le   Duan

Duong

Ton   Duc   Thang

Lake Van
Chuong

Quan Tho

Pho

Pho Nguyen Luong Bang

De   La   Thanh

QUAN DONG DA

Pho   Kham   Thien

Kham   Thien

Ngo   Cho

Lake
Xa Dan

Lake
Ba
Mau

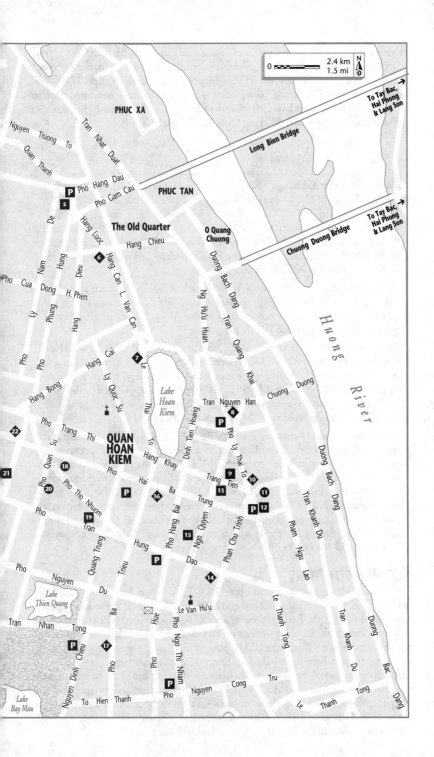

0    2.4 km
     1.5 mi

N

**PHUC XA**

Nguyen  Truong  To

Quan  Thanh

Tran  Nhat  Duat

To Tay Bac,
Hai Phong
& Lang Son

**Long Bien Bridge**

Pho Hang Dau

Pho Gam Cau

**P**
5

**PHUC TAN**

De

Hang Luoc

Hung

Dieu

H. Phen

Hang

Hang Can

L. Van Can

**The Old Quarter**

Hang  Chieu

**O Quang Chuong**

Duong Bach Dang

Chuong Duong Bridge

To Tay Bac,
Hai Phong
& Lang Son

Pho  Cua  Dong

Nam

Ly

Phung

Ng Huu Huan

Tran  Quang  Khai

*Huong*

Pho

Pho

Hang Bong

Hang Cai

Ly Quoc Su

**7**

Le

Thai

*Lake
Hoan
Kiem*

Tran  Nguyen  Han

Chuong    Duong

*River*

**22**

Pho  Trang  Thi

Su

Quan

**QUAN
HOAN
KIEM**

To

Hang  Khay

Dinh Tien Hoang

Pho Ly Thai To

**P**
8

**21**

**18**

Pho

Hai

Ba

Trang  Tien

**9**

**10**

Duong  Bach  Dang

Pho Tho Nhuom

**20**

**P**

**16**

Trung

**13**

**11**

**P**  **12**

Tran  Khanh  Du

Pho

**19**

Tran

Hung

Pho Hang Bai

Ngo Quyen

**15**

Dao

Phan Chu Trinh

Pham  Ngu  Lao

**P**

Pho

Nguyen

Du

Quang Trung

Trieu

Ba

**14**

*Lake
Thien Quang*

Hue

Le Van Hu'u

Le  Thanh  Tong

Tran  Nhan

Tong

Pho Ngo Thi Nham

Tran  Khanh  Du

**P**

**17**

Pho

Nguyen Dinh Chieu

To  Hien  Thanh

**P**

Nguyen    Cong

Tru

Le

Thanh

Tong

Duong

Bac

Dang

*Lake
Bay Mau*

253

all rolled into one. Mini-trip prices to Halong Bay and Cat Ba Island range from US$18 to US$45, but the lodging provided is quite basic. You'll see them everywhere, but a good bet is the **Queen Café**, 65 Hang Bac St., Hoan Kiem District (☎ **04/826-0860**). Ask for Mr. Quang and use my name—Stacy Lu. You can't go wrong. Another favorite is the **Green Bamboo Café,** 42 Nha Chung St. (☎ **04/826-8752**). Another option: **Real Darling Café,** 33 Hang Quat St. (☎ **04/826-9386**).

## Fast Facts: Hanoi

**Banks/Currency Exchange**   Major banks in Hanoi include: Australia New Zealand Bank (ANZ), 14 Le Thai To St., ☎ 04/825-8190, fax 04/825-8189. Bank of America, 27 Ly Thuong Kiet St., ☎ 04/824-9316, fax 04/824-9322. Citibank, 17 Ngo Quyen St., ☎ 04/825-1950, fax 04-824-3960. Standard Chartered Bank, 49 Hai Ba Trung St., 8th Floor, ☎ 04/825-8970, fax 04/825-8880. Vietcom Bank, 78 Nguyen Du St., ☎ 04/826-8035, fax 04/822-8039. ATMs are located at ANZ Bank and Citibank.

**Internet/E-mail**   The Emotion CyberNet Café at 60 Tho Nhuom and 52 Ly Thuong Kiet (☎ 04/934-1066; e-mail: Emotion@FPT.VN), across from the Hanoi Hilton, sells snacks and Internet access. Many hotels provide access as well, at fees from US10¢ to US50¢ per minute.

**Post Office/Mail**   The General Post Office is located at 6 Dinh Le St., Hoan Kiem District (☎ 04/825-7036). It's open daily 6:30am to 10pm. You can also send faxes or telexes and make international phone calls. Express mail services— FedEx (☎ 04/825-3797) and UPS (☎ 04/824-6483)—are located in the same building as the post office but have their own storefronts. Airborne Express is on the other side of the building at 1 Le Thach (☎ 04/241-514).

**Telephone**   The city code for Hanoi is 04. Most hotels provide international direct dialing, although none allow you to access an international operator or AT&T, whose Vietnam access code is 12010288. To do that, you will have to go to the General Post Office (above). There are public phone booths throughout the city for local calls, which cost 1,500 VND (US10¢). In fact, I've never seen so many public phones. To use them, you'll need to purchase a phone card at a post office. Small stores also often have a phone for public use. You may want to skirt the issue entirely by renting a mobile phone at VinaPhone, 51–53 Nguyen Thai Hoc, (☎ 04/842-9889).

## ACCOMMODATIONS

From historic charm to ultra-efficient business hotel to budget hole-in-the-wall, you'll find what you want in Hanoi. The top-end hotels tend to be a bit sterile and business-oriented—I felt like the lone sundress in a sea of suits—but they offer every facility a holiday-maker could wish for. Amenities and cleanliness levels are high across the board: Virtually every hotel over US$10 a night will have a phone, air conditioning, in-room safes, and hair dryers. Children under 12 usually stay free.

Ask for discounts! The Southeast Asia economic crisis hit Vietnam hard, and is expected to impact the region for a while. Occupancy has declined precipitously, and every manager mentioned rate cuts, many of up to 50%. Shown here are listed high-season (Feb–Oct) rates. Use them as guidelines only. Prices do not include a government VAT (Value Added Tax) of 20% except where noted.

## VERY EXPENSIVE

**Hanoi Daewoo Hotel.** 360 Kim Ma St., Ba Dinh District. ☎ **04/831-5000.** Fax 04/831-5010. E-mail Hotel@daewoohn.com.vn. 411 units. A/C MINIBAR TV TEL. US$199–US$249 double; US$319–US$349 and astronomically way up for suites; US$269–US$359 executive floor rooms. Discounts off these rates can go as high as 60%. AE, DC, JCB, MC, V.

The 3-year-old high-rise Daewoo is the kind of hotel that makes you open your mouth and say "aaaaah." Marble, marble everywhere, sumptuous fabrics, palm trees. Everything is done large—the hotel lobby, the bars, the rooms with king beds, the 262-foot (80m-long), curving pool. It's almost too large; I felt as if I was rattling around at times. The plush rooms are decorated with an Asian flavor, and over 1,000 interesting modern paintings from Vietnamese artists grace the halls. Thick, soft linens are blissful. Bathrooms are surprisingly small in the lower-end rooms but quite well appointed, with hair dryers *et al.* There are three non-smoking floors, and a very efficient Business Center—perhaps the best in Hanoi—with Internet access. Elsewhere, the young staff has a slightly stunned air, as if they simply woke up one morning to find themselves working in a big, fancy hotel.

Facilities and services include executive lounge, conference rooms, medical clinic, baby-sitting, wheelchair access, delicatessen, minimart, stationery shop, fitness center with saunas and Jacuzzis, sun terrace, aerobics studio, driving range, massage, pro shop, the amazing lagoon-style swimming pool, and wading pool. There's a lobby lounge and a pool bar. The nightclub (Club Q) has five karaoke rooms. For dining, Edo (Japanese) and La Paix (Continental fare) are among the best restaurants in Hanoi. Both are formal, expensive, excellent power lunch spots with private rooms. Café Promenade features Asian and European buffets. Silk Road offers Chinese (Cantonese) food.

**Hilton Hanoi Opera.** Hilton Hanoi Opera, 1 Le Thanh Tong St., Hoan Kiem, Hanoi, Vietnam. ☎ **800/774-1500** or 04/933-0500. Fax: 04/933-0530. 269 units. US$210–230 double; US$250 executive.

While this hotel opened after we went to press, the repro colonial exterior was stunning, next to the splendid Opera building. Further, it's brand new, and it's a Hilton. Provided the staff is up to snuff, it should provide a good experience. Amenities are business center with Internet services; conference, banquet and meeting rooms; swimming pool; health club with sauna, Jacuzzi, and massage; car rentals; florist; gift shop; and newsstand. There's an upscale Chinese restaurant, brasserie, cafe, bar, lobby lounge, and pool bar.

✪ **Sofitel Metropole Hanoi.** 15 Ngo Quyen St., Hanoi, Vietnam. ☎ **800/221-4542** or 04/826-6919. Fax: 04/826-6920. E-mail: Sofmet@netnam.org.vn. 244 units. A/C MINIBAR TV TEL. Doubles US$259–US$299; from US$279 and up for suites. AE, DC, JCB, MC, V.

The Metropole is one of the world's treasures: truly elegant and with a long past and a list of past guests that reads like Who's Who of the 20th century. In fact, there's a history book being written solely about this place. Built in 1900, the hotel had a major renovation in 1992 and added a second building in 1994. Medium-sized rooms in the original building have wooden floors, cane furniture, and high ceilings, historic yet not really luxe. Sizable modern bathrooms, but little touches like wood-frame mirrors, fresh flowers, and toiletries in hand-painted ceramics are just right. The staff couldn't be nicer or more efficient. The pool is small but the Bamboo lounge alongside is roomy and comfortable. The health club with sauna and massage is superb and actually has a great street view. The downtown location can't be beat, and there's a nice mix of tourists and businesspeople here. Push for a room in the Old Wing; the newer is already showing signs of wear and is far less fetching, with more modern, less historic decor, although the rooms are slightly larger. If you must stay there, ask for a room with a pool view.

Amenities include business center with Internet access, mini-mart, 24-hour room service, laundry and dry-cleaning services, special handicapped-access rooms, baby-sitting upon request, boutique, and minimart/bakery. There are two restaurants. Le Beaulieu is the best in Hanoi for classic French fare. It is relatively formal but offers fantastic value dinner buffets on occasion. Among the three bars, the Met Pub is one of Hanoi's places to be seen, have a beer, and listen to live jazz on Wednesday, Friday, and Saturday.

## EXPENSIVE

**Galaxy Hotel.** 1 Phan Dinh Phung St., Hanoi. ☎ **04/828-2888.** Fax 04/828-2466. 60 units. A/C MINIBAR TV TEL. US$109–US$129 double; US$149–US$180 suite. Full breakfast included. AE, DC, JCB, MC, V.

The Galaxy is king of the tour group hotels, but don't let that stop you. If you elect to stay here, it will quickly become a home away from home. A recently renovated blah 1918 building, it's located right on the edge of the Old Quarter. Good-sized rooms are spotless and very comfortable, although the fuzzy TV reception drove me nuts and the pillows were merely little wads of cotton in a case. There is room service, sort of. Prepare to pantomime. Laundry and transportation services are also available. There is an Asian restaurant on the premises and a nice little bar with current Western magazines. Beware: Travelers have reported cut-off phone service and closed front desks in the middle of the night. Yet the incredibly nice staff tries very, very hard and always remembers your name. The breakfast (included in the price) is good, and even has pancakes and sausage.

**Guoman Hotel.** 83A Ly Thuong Kiet St., Hanoi, Vietnam. ☎ **04/822-2800.** Fax 04/822-2822. 149 units. A/C MINIBAR TV TEL. US$95 double. Extra bed US$10. AE, JCB, MC, V.

This is your Basic Good Hotel, and with the price I have to say that it's a bit of a steal if you're looking for comfort and service. Only a year and a half old, right now the Guoman caters to the business crowd, but with its central location and nice amenities, it's a great choice for all. Its size and attitude, in fact, says "chain" more than "business." Rooms are big, carpeted, and very nicely if blandly furnished, and they still have that brand-new feeling. They are very well-equipped, with coffeemakers, safes, and even a power outlet and phone jack for laptops—truly a rarity in Vietnam. Other highlights: comfy just-right firm beds, fat pillows, and big spic-and-span marble and tile bathrooms. There are three non-smoking floors—another rarity in Vietnam. A pleasant on-premises restaurant, the Café Paradise, offers a US$8.50 buffet lunch. The fitness club with sauna and Jacuzzi has nice equipment but unfortunately is small and suffers badly from puckered-rug syndrome. A 1-hour massage costs just US$10. The staff is first-rate and speaks English well. There are also a business center, 24-hour room service, and laundry service.

**Meritus Westlake Hanoi.** 1 Thanh Nien Rd., Ba Dinh District. ☎ 04/823-8888. Fax 04/829-3888. www.meritus-hotels.com. E-mail sales-mktg.mwh@meritus-hotels.com. 322 units. A/C MINIBAR TV TEL. US$180 double; US$210–US$320 and way up for suites; US$88 double and US$118 suite off-season. AE, JCB, MC, V.

This hotel was launched in September of 1998. It's an extremely nice business hotel. Ask for a room with a view of West Lake. You'll find standard upscale pastel and crème hotel decor, with slightly cramped nonsuite rooms, although all have every gizmo you could wish for, including coffeemakers. The beds have very firm mattresses, and the bathrooms have a separate shower. The health club and spa are fabulous, really out-standing, with sauna, steam room, Jacuzzi, and aerobics studio. They are run by friendly American expat Krista Leavitt. Ask her for insider tips on what's hot in Hanoi. Other amenities are a business center, swimming pool with retractable roof, baby-sitting, 24-hour room service, laundry service, and doctor on call. For dining you have a choice of two restaurants; one, the Chinese Peach Pavillion, serves very good dim sum, lounge, pool cafe.

## MODERATE

**Dan Chu Hotel.** 29 Trang Tien St., Hanoi, Vietnam. ☎ **04/825-4937** or 825-3323. Fax 04/826-6786. 41 units. A/C MINIBAR TV TEL. US$65–US$105 double; US$129 suites; man-agement mentioned discounts of 20–30%. Extra person US$15. Includes breakfast. AE, DC, JCB, MC, V.

This is an old hotel with a funky but pleasant feeling, right in the heart of the down-town district. Big, atmospheric, high-ceiling rooms are spotless and have carved wood furniture, the all-too-common ugly polyester bedspreads, and clean but spare bathrooms with hair dryers. There are laundry services, car rental, massage and sauna, and a restaurant and very good gift shop on the premises. Satellite TV and in-room safes, too. The deluxe rooms have historic wood shutters and a single long balcony that overlooks the active street scene below. It's an interesting view with very noisy side-effects.

**Eden Hotel.** 78 Tho Nhuom St., Hanoi. ☎ **04/824-5273** or 04/825-2711. Fax 04/824-5619. 22 units. US$49–US$79 double; US$99 suite. Breakfast and fruit basket included. AE, DC, JCB, MC, V.

The floors of the Eden Hotel wind in varied levels around its outdoor garden atrium. The somewhat dark, attractive rooms are carpeted, and feature traditional Asian carved-wood furniture and fresh flowers—a nice touch. The standard and deluxe rooms are small, and I mean small, although the suite does have two rooms and a big bathroom. It must be mentioned here that the mattresses are foam, but they are extremely sturdy and comfortable. Bathrooms are basic and spotless, without bathtubs except in the suites. On the premises are The Pear Tree, a popular bar with billiards, and a small continental restaurant. It's a very casual but nice place. A friendly staff, even if they are all teenagers. The Eden is often full with budget travelers, so book early.

**Hoa Binh Hotel.** 27 Ly Thuong Kiet St., Hoan Kiem District, Hanoi, Vietnam. ☎ **04/825-3315** or 825-3692. Fax 04/826-9818. E-mail kshoabinh@bdvn.vnmail.vnd.net. 100 units. A/C MINIBAR TV TEL. US$45 double; US$125 deluxe. AE, DC, JCB, MC, V.

The Hoa Binh is a good, atmospheric choice. Comfort and history meet at just the right level for Vietnam, and you are reminded every minute that you are in Hanoi. Built in 1926, the attractive colonial has a colonnaded lobby with winding wooden stairs and sizable rooms with original light fixtures, molded ceilings, and gloss-wood furniture. Only the hideous polyester bedspreads and drapes and spongy mattresses ruin the effect. The bathrooms are very plain and small but spotless. Hand-held showers, though. The hotel is in a prime downtown location, and the bar has a view of the city. On the ground floor (but not hotel-owned) is the excellent restaurant Le Splendide—see "Dining." Hoa Binh has good facilities: two restaurants, a sauna, mas-sage, laundry, a tailor, a barber, and karaoke.

**Thang Loi Hotel.** Yen Phu St., Hanoi, Vietnam. ☎ **04/829-0145.** Fax 04/829-3800. E-mail thangloihtl@hn.vnn.vn. 80 units. US$55–US$85 double. US$95 suite. Includes full breakfast. AE, JCB, MC, V.

It's anything but fancy—it's a low-slung group of concrete buildings—but for a truly unique hotel experience, try Thang Loi. It resembles a summer camp lodge. The hotel was a gift from Cuba, which explains the rather dour, Cold War–era exterior, but it actually protrudes on pontoons over West Lake. Most of the immaculate but plain rooms have a balcony overlooking fisher women standing in the lake, working with baskets. The spongy mattresses are a little off-putting, as is the garish decor in the suites and the puckered carpets, but rooms have hair dryers, safes, and even scales. There's an outdoor pool, tennis courts, a barbershop, and a small sauna/massage center. The staff speaks little English but they're so nice you don't care. An odd but likeable spot.

### INEXPENSIVE

**Hoang Cuong Hotel.** 15 Nguyen Thai Hoc St., Hoan Kiem District, Hanoi, Vietnam. ☎ **04/822-0060.** Fax 04/822-0195. 10 units. A/C MINIBAR TV TEL. US$15–US$30 double. AE, DC, JCB, MC, V.

This attractive little gem is one of the best among Hanoi's budget choices, and located on the same street as many of them, near the Old Quarter. Family-run, the rooms are large and carpeted, with attractive inlaid Asian furniture and very firm foam mattress beds. There are some nice details, like hair dryers, hot water thermoses, and fans in the room. The tile bathrooms are functional and spotless. There is no elevator, and room prices are based on how far you'll have to hike up the six or so flights of stairs. But you'll soon become firm friends with the very nice staff.

## DINING

It's hard to have a bad meal in Hanoi. The French influence is here in both classical and in Vietnam-influenced versions, neither to be missed, especially at these prices. Almost every ethnic food variation is well represented in the city, in fact, and you'll be hard pressed to choose among them.

Hanoi has savory specialties that must be sampled. For that, hit the streets and dine in local, small eateries. Pho, by far the most popular local dish, is noodles with slices of beef (bo) or chicken (ga), fresh bean sprouts, and condiments. Pho Bo, at 49 Bat Dan, is one of the city's best. Bun cha, a snack of rice noodles and spring rolls with fresh condiments, has made Dac Kim restaurant (at No. 1 Hang Manh, in the Old Quarter) city-renowned. Banh cuon is meat and mushroom wrapped in a fresh rice crepe. Fantastic at Banh Cuon Nong, 17 Cha Ca in the Old Quarter.

### EXPENSIVE

**Il Grillo.** 116 Ba Trieu (in the north of Hai Ba Trung District). ☎ **04/822-7720.** Reservations suggested on weekends. Main courses US$7.50–US$23. AE, JCB, MC, V. 11am–2pm, 5:30–10:30pm. CLASSIC ITALIAN.

Il Grillo is a family-run classic Italian restaurant with a very casual, intimate atmosphere, print tablecloths, hand-painted pottery, and chalkboard specials. You won't find any Vietnamese here, but it's a favorite with the expat crowd and by virtue of its size seems to ward off big tour groups. Portions are huge and good, and the service is friendly and attentive, including personal attention from the Italian owners. The ribeye steak is a house specialty and the pasta with clams and shredded carrots unique and delicious, as is the pasta with truffles. Most spectacular, however, were the fresh, bursting-with-flavor starters: bruschetta, prosciutto, salad with anchovies. Simple yet gorgeous. There's also a nice Italian wine list.

**Le Splendide.** 44 Ngo Quyen St. (Hoa Binh Hotel, Hoan Kiem District). ☎ **04/826-6087.** Reservations recommended. Main courses US$7–US$19. AE, MC, V. Daily 11am–midnight. TOULOUSIAN FRENCH.

> **Restaurant Tip**
>
> Note that many upscale restaurants in Hanoi levy a 5% service charge on top of the 10% government tax.

A huge stained-glass window, chandeliers, and a long blonde-wood bar contribute to the utter charm of this place, as does helpful manager, Antoine. The atmosphere is elegant but youthful, even though it's a favorite with lunching businessfolks and embassy staff. The menu (in English as well as French and Vietnamese) features house specialties cassoulet, confit de canard pollè, and baked tournedos topped with foie gras. Everything is impeccably prepared and presented. Classic French deserts such as crème brûlée and fondue au chocolat are a triumph, and there's a relatively long wine list. A lovely, quiet place to linger over a memorable meal, or over the live jazz on Friday nights.

**The Press Club.** 59A Ly Thai To St., Hoan Kiem District. ☎ **04/934-0888.** Reservations suggested. Main courses US$8–US$17.50. Prix fixe menu US$19.95. AE, JCB, MC, V. Noon–2pm, 6–10:30pm. Weekend brunch 11am–3pm. CONTINENTAL.

Subdued and elegant, this place states firmly, in hushed tones, "power lunch." The indoor restaurant is sizable yet private, done in dark tones of maroon and forest green with solid-looking wood furniture and detailing. There is outdoor seating on the terrace, next to a pseudo-jazz band, which imparts a more casual atmosphere. The service is impeccable. The menu is full of safe Continental standards: antipasto starters, goat cheese salad, tuna steak, smoked trout, red snapper with capers. It is cooked to perfection, however, and the deserts are outstanding. Try banana crème brûlée, or iced coffee and praline parfait with Amaretto cream.

For a more casual, inexpensive alternative or for lunch, try the downscaled **Deli** on the first floor, an expat standby and famous for its sandwiches and gourmet pizzas.

## MODERATE

**Al Fresco's.** 23L Hai Ba Trung St., Hoan Kiem District. ☎ **04/826-7782.** Main courses US$5.50–US$11. No credit cards. 9:30am–10:30pm. TEX-MEX.

Run by Australian expats, which practically guarantees a good time, Fresco's is two floors of a friendly, casual little open-air place. It has checkered tablecloths, good oldies music, and a great view on the second floor to the street below. The place serves very good Tex-Mex, pizza, chicken wings, and the like. The ribs are the house specialty, but the fajitas are simply out of this world, too. Desserts are good old standbys like brownies àla mode. There is a healthy wine list of name-brand Australian wines and some inexpensive Bulgarian and Chilean reds.

✪ **Brother's Café.** 26 Nguyen Thai Hoc. ☎ **04/722-3866.** Buffets US$5 or US$10. AE, DC, JCB, MC, V. 11am–2pm, 6:30–10:30pm. VIETNAMESE.

Newly opened, Brother's is one of the best places to eat in Hanoi. Right now the menu features a US$5 buffet for lunch, with local delicacies such as salted chicken, sweet and sour bean sprouts, shrimp, noodles, and spring rolls; a full dessert table of sweet tofu, sweet baby rice, dragon fruit, and other exotic offerings; and fresh lemon or melon juice. Dinner is US$10, and is a grilled affair: shrimp, fish, lamb, pork, and a glass of wine. Part of the restaurant is in an exquisitely decorated colonial; part of it in a dreamy garden out back. From the pressed linen napkins to tiny fresh flowers, Brother's gets every detail just right. At night, it becomes a popular bar.

**Indochine.** 16 Nam Ngu St., Hoan Kiem District. ☎ **04/824-6097.** Fax 04/824-6104. Main courses US$2–US$11. MC, V. Daily 11am–2pm, 5:30–10:30pm. VIETNAMESE.

This place has long been a favorite with the expat and tourist crowd, and is said to be "the" place to eat in Hanoi. Yet while the food was beautifully presented and very good, I found it a bit lackluster, and the staff just didn't seem to have a clue. Perhaps it was an off night, as everyone else seems to rave about the place. There certainly are some fine things on the menu, such as the crab spring rolls, flavorful chicken and banana flower salad, and grilled prawns in banana leaves. It is well worth a visit, too, for the beautiful colonial setting, with both indoor and outdoor patio seating, amazingly good prices, and live Vietnamese classical music nightly.

✪ **Khazana.** 41B Ly Thai To St., Hoan Kiem District. ☎ **04/824-1166.** Closed Sunday lunch. Reservations suggested on weekends and for groups of 4 or more. Main courses US$5–US$10. Special US$5 set lunch. MC, V. 11:30am–2pm, 6:30–10pm. NORTHERN INDIAN.

I truly think this was the best North Indian food I've ever tasted, and judging from reviews, everyone in Hanoi seems to agree. The surroundings are elegant but not very ethnic: small round tables with Western settings, a marble floor, Indian art, impeccable service. It's a favorite of the business lunch crowd. Manager Shankar Dutta explains with loving care the ingredients of each dish, if you ask, and is justly proud of Goan fish curry, tandoori gulistan (batter-fried cottage cheese), and taar korma (spiced mutton). The dishes were fresh and bursting with flavor. Even the samosas were special.

✪ **Seasons of Hanoi.** 95B Quan Thanh. ☎ **04/843-444.** Main courses 40,000–60,000 VND (US$2.90–US$4.35). MC, V. 11:30am–2pm and 6–11pm. Reservations suggested, especially for groups. VIETNAMESE.

The atmosphere is picture-perfect at Seasons: intimate, candlelit, romantic, earth-colored surroundings in a casual yet beautifully restored colonial with authentic native furniture. There are two floors. Try to sit on the first, to avoid tourists traveling in packs. The spring rolls are heaven, as are the tempura soft-shell crabs. Fish is everywhere on the menu—fried, boiled, on kebabs, and in hot pots. If you fancy it, try the sautéed eel with chili and lemongrass. That is, unless you don't decide on the fried chicken in panda leaves first. Everything comes beautifully presented, and main courses rest on flaming warming plates. A nice wine list accompanies.

### INEXPENSIVE

**Cha Ca La Vong.** 14 Cha Ca St., Hoan Kiem District (in the heart of the Old Quarter). No phone. Main course 60,000 VND (US$4.35). No credit cards. 10am–2pm, 5–11pm. VIETNAMESE.

Cha Ca only serves one dish: marinated whitefish brought to your table over a flaming stone brazier. You stir in dill and chives, cook it for a bit more, and dish it over chilled rice noodles, mint garnish, scallions, and peanuts. Delicious. Meanwhile, you're sitting

---

**Impressions**

*"The light spreads down his chest, but his lower parts are obscured by shadows. This very much gives him the appearance of a horizontal genie. His eyes are closed, his world-famous goatee unstiffened. The skin is waxen, no doubt hugely chemicalized. Above all, I am struck by the smallness of him. He really does resemble a Chinese mandarin modelled in ivory."*

—Justin Wintle, describing an embalmed Ho in *Romancing Vietnam*

on rusted folding chairs, packed in with locals and tourists. It's a very rustic affair, but it's so popular they named a street after it. Wear old clothes in case you're spattered with the colorful grease. Drinks are extra.

**Le Café des Arts.** 11b Ngo Bao Khanh, Hoan Kiem District (in the Old Quarter). ☎ **04/828-7207.** Main courses 20,000–44,000 VND (US$1.50–US$3.15). No credit cards. 9am–9pm (bar open until midnight). BISTRO FRENCH/CONTINENTAL.

After strolling round Hoan Kiem Lake, stop off its northwest end for a drink or a bite at this friendly bistro-style eatery, run by French expats and open all day. Spacious, with tiled floors and shuttered windows looking into the narrow Old Quarter street below, the cafe features casual rattan furniture and a long, inviting bar. It also doubles as an art gallery, which explains the interesting paintings hanging throughout. The Vietnamese art crowd also provides some attractive local color. Most inviting, however, is the excellent food. Ask for the special of the day, and stick to bistro standbys like the omelets or a croque madame—toasted bread and cheese sautéed in egg—and house specialty salade bressare (very fresh chicken and vegetables in a light mayonnaise sauce). There is also good house wine by the glass.

**Mother's Pride.** 6C Phan Chu Trinh, ☎ **04/826-2168.** No credit cards. Main courses 24,000–28,000 VND (US$1.75–US$2). 10am–10:30pm. WESTERN/HOME STYLE MALAYSIAN.

Cheap and good, Mother's is a great local favorite. The main attraction is simple Malay dishes served over rice. Try the chicken curry or sweet and sour prawns, done just right. The house soup is tangy with crispy fresh basil and bean sprouts. The fresh fruit juices—smoothies really—are fantastic, the apple particularly. Mother's also serves pizza, onion rings, chicken wings, and other snacks. However, there is no atmosphere to speak of and the music selection, at least when I visited, consisted of the theme song to *Titanic* played repeatedly. We didn't linger over dessert.

## SNACKS & CAFES

One of the main attractions around Hoan Kiem Lake is **Fanny,** 16 Hang Bong, which serves exquisite French-style ice cream and sorbets from 8am to 11pm. **Moca Café,** at 14–16 Nha Tho, has great coffee and desserts. **No Noodles** at 51 Luong Van Can is the favored shop for real Western sandwiches.

## ATTRACTIONS

Remember, when sightseeing, that state-owned attractions will usually close for lunch from 11:30am to 1:30pm or so. Foreigners will be charged approximately twice what Vietnamese are charged, so you'll pay 10,000 VND (US70¢) for most public attractions. Don't bother arguing.

### BA DINH DISTRICT

**West Lake.** Bordered by Thuy Khue and Thanh Nien streets.

In Hanoi, West Lake is second only to Hoan Kiem as a nerve center for the city, steeped in legend and sporting several significant pagodas. Vietnam's oldest pagoda, Tran Quoc, was built in the sixth century and is located on Cayang Island in the middle of the lake, a beautiful setting. It has a visitors' hall, two corridors, and a bell tower, and its monument was constructed by an early Zen sect. Quan Thanh Temple, by the northern gate, was built during the reign of Le Thai To King (1010–1028). It is dedicated to Huyen Thien Tran Vo, the god who reigned over Vietnam's northern regions. Renovated in the 19th century, the impressive temple has a triple gate and courtyard, and features a 12-foot bronze statue of the god. West Lake is also a hub of local activity, particularly on weekends when families go paddle-boating on it.

**Ho Chi Minh's Mausoleum.** On Ba Dinh Square, Ba Dinh District. Tues–Thurs and Sat 8am–11am. Closed Mon and Fri.

In an imposing, somber granite and concrete structure modeled on Lenin's tomb, Ho lies in state, embalmed and dressed in his favored khaki suit. He asked to be cremated, but his wish was not heeded. A respectful demeanor is required, and a dress code may be imposed, with no shorts or sleeveless shirts allowed. Note that the mausoleum is usually closed through October and November, when Ho goes to Russia for body maintenance of an undisclosed nature. The museum may be closed during this period as well.

**Ho Chi Minh's Museum.** Left of One Pillar Pagoda, near Ba Dinh Square. Ba Dinh District. Admission: 5,000 VND (US5¢). Tues–Sun 8–11:30am and 1:30–4pm.

English-language explanations help to piece together the fragments of Ho's life and cause on display here. There are personal items on display and photos and documents detailing the rise of the nation's communist revolution. Completely unique to Vietnam are the conceptual displays symbolizing freedom, reunification, and social progress through flowers, fruit, and mirrors. Have a look.

**Ho Chi Minh's Residence.** Behind the Presidential Palace. Admission: 3,000 VND (US20¢). Tues–Sun 8–11am and 1:30–4:30pm.

Ho's residence, the well-known house on stilts, is behind the Presidential Palace, a gorgeous French colonial building built in 1901 for the resident French governor. Shunning the glorious structure nearby, Ho instead chose to live here from 1958 to 1969. The simple stilt house does have its charms, facing an exquisite landscaped lake. The basement was a meeting place for the politburo; upstairs are the bedroom and a study. Behind the house is a garden of fruit trees, many of them exotics imported from other lands, including miniature rose bushes and areca trees from the Caribbean.

**One-Pillar Pagoda.** Right of Ho Chi Minh Museum, near Ba Dinh Square. Ba Dinh District.

To the right of the Ho Chi Minh Museum is the unique One Pillar Pagoda, a wooden structure built in 1049 that sits on stilts over a lake. A king of the Ly dynasty, Ly Thai Thong King, had it built after having a dream in which Bodhisattva Avalokitesvara, the Goddess of Mercy, presented him with a lotus flower. The existing pagoda is a miniature reproduction of the original, which was said to represent a lotus emerging from the water. It is certainly interesting, and a visit to pray for fertility or good health reportedly has miraculous results. You are not admitted if you're wearing shorts, however.

**Army Museum.** 28A Dien Bien Phu St. ☎ **04/823-4264.** Admission 10,000 VND (US70¢); 2,000 VND (US15¢ surcharge for cameras. Tues–Sun 8–11:30am; 1:30–4:30pm.

This building opened in 1959, and presents the Vietnamese side of the country's struggle against colonial powers. There are three buildings of odds and ends from both the French and American wars here, including evocative photos. Most interesting, though, is the actual war equipment on display, including aircraft, tanks, bombs, and big guns, some with signs indicating just how many of which enemy the piece took out. There is a tank belonging to the troop that crashed through the Presidential Palace gates on April 30, 1975, Vietnamese Liberation Day. Outside there is also a spectacular, room-sized bouquet of downed French and U.S. aircraft wreckage. Also on the grounds is Hanoi's ancient flag tower (Cot Co), constructed from 1805 to 1812. The exhibits have English translations, which makes this an easy and worthwhile visit.

# Ho Chi Minh, the Dilettante Revolutionary

Ho Chi Minh was born **Nguyen Sinh Cung** in 1890, in a humble home in Kim Lien village, Nghe An province. He attended grade school in Hué, but, beginning his life as an activist early, was expelled for inciting student arrest. In 1911, as a handsome young fellow of 21, he boarded a steamer for France to "look for a way that might help liberate Vietnam from colonization," according to the museum that bears his name in Saigon. On the ship, he worked as kitchen help. He soon moved on to London, where he worked as a pastry chef (under Escoffier, no less) at the Carlton Hotel. Returning to France after World War I, he made a living retouching photographs as he slowly became an ardent nationalist and patriot. Along the way, he became a linguist as well, mastering languages like English, Russian, French, Cantonese, and Japanese.

In 1923, Ho went to Russia to learn more about how to make a revolution, and briefly lived in China before being forced to flee to Hong Kong by Chiang Kai Shek in 1930. During this period, he hid in Thailand for a spell, posing as a Buddhist monk. Using Hong Kong as a base, he began to build a base of support in Indochina. By this time, he had become known as Ho Chi Minh, or "giver of enlightenment." The French government, unfortunately, also knew of his growing power and put a price on his head.

In 1941, Ho escaped Hong Kong by means of an elaborate death hoax, and managed at long last to re-enter Vietnam. He retreated to the northern hills and from there began, with other Vietnamese revolutionaries, to construct the revolution. While in China in 1942, he was imprisoned as a spy and there tried his hand at poetry, turning out his ***Prison Diary,*** a Vietnamese classic. Returning to Vietnam upon its emancipation from the Japanese in 1945, he proclaimed Vietnam an independent nation and himself its leader in what became known as the **August Revolution.** It wasn't until after nine years of further warfare, though, that the French finally conceded Vietnamese independence. Soon after, there were the Americans to fight.

On September 2, 1969, truly having had a world of experience, Ho Chi Minh—cabin boy, chef, monk, poet, and revolutionary—died. He became an icon to his people and is one of the outstanding figures of the 20th century.

✪ **National Fine Arts Museum.** 66 Nguyen Thai Hoc. ☎ **04/823-3084.** Admission 10,000 VND (US70¢). Tues–Sun 8–11am, 1–4pm.

The very worthwhile arts museum features Vietnamese art of the 20th century, up to the 1970s or so. While the presentations are a bit crowded and rustic, there are explanations in English, and much of the art is outstanding, though you won't really see any works of an innovative or controversial nature. Entire rooms are devoted to the Vietnamese style of lacquer and silk painting, woodblock and folk art. Techniques are explained—a nice touch. Interesting also are the modern works of wood statuary interspersed among the exhibits. Some are patriotic in nature, but many are humorous social commentaries. The top floors are devoted to prehistoric artifacts and Buddhist sculptures, some of which are huge and impressive. Don't miss the famous 11th-century Goddess of Mercy (Kouan Yin) with her thousand arms and eyes in the far left-hand room, second floor. Best of all, the museum itself is in an old colonial and, unless there's a tour group milling around, you can stroll around in relative serenity and rest on one of the many benches provided. The gift shop has some nice modern works from known artists for sale.

## DONG DA DISTRICT

**Temple of Literature and National University (Van Mieu–Quoc Tu Giam).** Quoc Tu Giam St. ☎ 04/845-2917. Admission: 10,000 VND (US70¢). Guide: 20,000 VND (US$1.45). Daily 8am–5pm.

If Vietnam has a seat of learning, this is it. There are two entities here: Van Mieu, a temple built to worship Chinese philosopher Confucius in 1070; and Quoc tu Giam, literally "Temple of the King who Distinguished Literature," an elite institute established in 1076 to teach the doctrines of Confucius and his disciples. It existed for over 700 years as a center for Confucian learning. Moreover, it is a powerful symbol for the Vietnamese, having been established after the country emerged from a period of Chinese colonialism that lasted from 179 B.C. to A.D. 938. As such, it stands for independence and a solidifying of national culture and values.

What exists today is a series of four courtyards that served as an entrance to the university. Architecturally, it is a fine example of classic Chinese with Vietnamese influences. Still present are 82 stone stelae—stone diplomas really—erected between 1484 and 1780, bearing the names and birthplaces of 1,306 doctor laureates who managed to pass the university's rigorous examinations. Beyond the final building, known as the sanctuary, the real university began. Damaged in the French war, it is currently being restored.

## HOAN KIEM DISTRICT

✪ **Hoa Lo Prison (Hanoi Hilton).** 1 Hoa Lo St., off Quan Su St. Admission: 10,000 VND (US70¢). Tues–Sun 8–11:30am and 1:30–4:30pm.

For sheer gruesome atmosphere alone, this ranks near the top of the must-see list. Constructed by the French in 1896, mainly to house political prisoners, the Vietnamese took it over in 1954. It was subsequently used to house prisoners of war. From 1964 to 1973, it was a major POW detention facility. United States senator John McCain was a particularly famous inmate, as was ambassador to Vietnam Pete Peterson and Lieutenant Everett Alvarez, officially the first American pilot to be shot down over Vietnam.

Only part of the original complex is left. The rest of the original site was razed and is ironically occupied by a tall, gleaming office complex. To the west is the guillotine room, still with its original equipment, and the female and Vietnamese political prisoners' quarters. The courtyard linking the two has parts of original tunnels once used by a hundred intrepid Vietnamese revolutionaries to escape in 1945. There are no English explanations, so try to see the prison with a guide or ask some of the folks working there for help, as a few speak English.

**Quan Su Pagoda.** 73 Quan Su St., as it intersects Tran Hung Da, Hoan Kiem District. Daily 8am–11am and 1–4pm.

Quan Su is one of the most important temples in the country. Constructed in the 15th century along with a small house for visiting Buddhist ambassadors, in 1934 it became the headquarters of the Tonkin Buddhist Association and today it is headquarters for the Vietnam Central Buddhist Congregation. It's an active pagoda and usually thronged with worshippers; the interior is dim and smoky with incense. To the rear is a school of Buddhist doctrine.

✪ **Old Quarter & Hoan Kiem Lake.** Bordered by Tran Nhat Duat and Phung Hung streets.

The Old Quarter evolved from workshop villages clustered by trades, or guilds, in the early 13th century. It's now an area of narrow, ancient, winding streets, each named

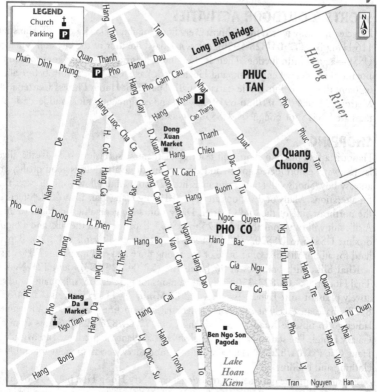

for the trade it formerly featured. Even today, streets tend to be either for silk, silver, or antiques. It's a fascinating slice of centuries-old life in Hanoi, including markets that are so pleasantly crowded the street itself narrows to a few feet. **Hoan Kiem** is considered the center of the city. It is also known as the Lake of the Recovered Sword. In the mid–15th century, the gods gave emperor Le Thai To a magical sword to defeat Chinese invaders. While the emperor was boating on the lake one day, a giant tortoise reared up and snatched the sword, returning it to its rightful owners. Stroll around the lake in the early morning or evening to savor local life among the willow trees, particularly elders playing chess or doing tai chi. In the center of the lake is the **Tortoise Pagoda**; on the northern part is **Ngoc Son pagoda,** reachable only by the Bridge of the Rising Sun and open daily from 8am to 5pm.

**Hanoi Opera House.** Intersection of Le Thanh Tong and Trang Tien sts., District 1.

This gorgeous, historic art nouveau building was built near the turn of the century. Unfortunately, to get inside you'll have to attend a performance, but that should be enjoyable as well (see "Hanoi After Dark").

## SIGHTS OUTSIDE THE CITY CENTER

**Vietnam Ethnology Museum.** Nguyen Van Huyen, 3.75 miles west of town. ☎ 04/836-0352. Admission: 10,000 VND (US70¢). Tues–Sun 8:30–11:30am and 1:30–4:30pm.

If you're interested in learning more about the 53 ethnic minorities populating Vietnam's hinterlands, stop in at this new museum. The different groups, with their history and customs, are explained via photos, videos, and displays of clothing and household and work implements. You'll need to take a taxi to get here, though.

## SPORTS & OUTDOOR ACTIVITIES

Bicycles are easily rented from almost every hotel for about US$1 a day. **TF Hanspan,** 116 Hang Bac (☎ 04/828-1996), offers a 1-day bike tour of the city and lunch for US$8—a great introduction. There is also quite a **jogging scene** in Hanoi around the Botanical Gardens, Lenin Park, and Hoan Kiem Lake. Get your run in before about 6:30am, though, before traffic starts to snarl. The **Clark Hatch Fitness Center** at the Metropolé Hotel (☎ 04/826-6919) has top-end equipment, sauna, and Jacuzzi. Day rates are US$15 for nonguests, US$5 for guests.

## SHOPPING

Hanoi is a fine place to shop, and features Vietnamese specialties such as silk, silver, lacquerware, embroidered goods, and ethnic minority crafts. Silk is good quality and an easy buy. Shops will tailor a suit in as little 24 hours, but allow yourself extra time for alterations. Many of the shops are clustered along Hang Gai, a.k.a. "Silk Street" on the northeast side of the Old Quarter. **Daily hours** are generally from 8am to 9pm. A silk suit will run from about US$25 to US$65, depending on the silk, and a blouse or shirt US$15 to US$20. Virtually every shop takes credit cards (MC, V). Bargain hard for all but the silk; offer 50% of the asking price and end up paying 70% or so.

 **Khai Silk,** with branches at 96 Hang Gai (☎ 04/825-4237) and 121 Nguyen Thai Hoc St. (☎ 04/823-3508), is justly famous for its selection, silk quality, and relatively pleasant store layout. Two sisters at **Le Minh,** 79–111 Hang Gai (☎ 04/828-8723), have an excellent selection of material and do fine work. Chic Vietnamese ladies go to upscale **Xuan,** at So 7 Hang Cot. (☎ 04/826-8987), across from the Galaxy Hotel. The staff speaks little English but has plenty of pictures. **Tan My** at 109 Hang Gai, (☎ 04/826-7081), has exquisite embroidery work, especially for children's clothing and bedding.

 For silver, antique oddities and traditional crafts, try **Hong Hoa** on 18 Ngo Quyen St., near the Metropole Hotel (☎ 04/826-8341), which has a good selection. **Giai Dieu,** on 82 Hang Gai (☎ 04/826-0222), has interesting lacquer paintings and decorative items, so stop in, as you'll probably be in the neighborhood at some point. There is also a branch at 93 Ba Trieu St. Silver jewelry, handbags, and other ornaments are sold at **80 Hang Gai St.** For fine ceramics, look to **Quang's Ceramics,** at 22 Hang Luoc St. in the Old Quarter. Unique lacquerware, including business card holders and tissue boxes, can be had at **DeltaDeco,** 12 Nha Tho St. Wood, stone, and brass lacquer reproduction sculptures of religious icons are at **KAF Traditional Sculptures and Art Accessories,** 31B Ba Trieu St. (☎ 04/822-0022).

### ART GALLERIES

Vietnam has a flourishing art scene, and Hanoi has many galleries of oil, silk, water and lacquer paintings (see above). Don't forget to bargain here, too. One of the best is **Nam Son,** at 41 Trang Tien. Others: **Thanh Mai,** 64 Hang Gai St.; **Apricot Gallery,** 40B Hang Bong St.; and **Thang Long,** 15 Hang Gai, in the Old Quarter.

## HANOI AFTER DARK

When it comes to nightlife, Hanoi is no Saigon, but there are a variety of pleasant watering holes about town and a few rowdy dance spots. Hanoi is also the best city in which to see **traditional Vietnamese arts** such as opera, theater, and water puppet shows. Invented during the Ly dynasty (1009–1225), the art of water puppetry is unique to Vietnam. The puppets are made of wood and really do dance on water. The shows feature traditional Vietnamese music and depict folklore and myth. Book for the popular puppets at least 5 hours ahead.

## THEATER & PERFORMANCE

**Municipal Water Puppet Theater,** 57B Dinh Thien Hoang St., Hoan Kiem District (☎ 04/825-5450), hosts two shows nightly at 8 and 9:15pm. Admission is US$4.

The **Hanoi Opera House (Hanoi Municipal Theatre),** 1 Trang Tien St., Hoan Kiem District (☎ 04/933-0131), hosts performances by local and international artists. The **Hanoi National Opera,** 15 Nguyen Dinh Chieu, Ba Dinh District (☎ 04/826-7361), has shows on Monday, Wednesday, and Friday at 8pm.

**Central Circus,** in Lenin Park, Hai Ba Trung District (☎ 04/822-0277), has shows at 7:45pm daily except Mondays. It's a real circus, done on a small scale, so only see it if you're desperate to entertain the kids.

Finally, **The Daewoo Hotel,** 360 Kim Ma St., Ba Dinh District (☎ 04/831-5000), often hosts visiting jazz bands.

## BARS, PUBS & DISCOS

**Apocolypse Now.** 5C Hoa Ma. ☎ **04/971-2783.**

Down and dirty. Black walls, thatched-roof bar, lights with "blood" streaks on them. Still, everybody comes, from backpackers to locals and expats, and it's all somehow great fun. Plus it's open later than practically any bar in Hanoi, until 4am or so. That's because it's definitely an "end of the night" place. Pool table, US$1 beers, no food, great music, and small dance floor.

**The Jungle Bar.** 3 Nguyen Khac Can. Hoan Kiem District. ☎ **04/826-9080.**

Three floors of fun: pool table on the first, disco with DJ on the second, and groovy salon with bamboo chairs (zebra striped cushions, natch) on the top. The second floor is very chic with curved velvet lounges and modern art. Upstairs, the two friendly bar boys proudly point out their own homemade flavored Absolut vodka, in such bizarre flavors as coffee and lemongrass. You can imagine what the US$3.50 drinks actually taste like. But you'll still wish you had someplace like this to go to at home. The place doesn't start hopping until well after 10pm.

**New Queen Bee.** 42 Lang Ha. ☎ **04/835-2612.**

The notorious Bee is a huge, loud, techno-music heaven. All the beautiful local folks are here, grinding away.

**The Verandah.** 9 Nguyen Khac Can. Hoan Kiem District. ☎ **04/825-7220.** AE, MC, V.

A joint venture between an Englishman and a Vietnamese, The Verandah has an upscale but casual colonial setting, with a red tile floor and revolving ceiling fans. It's a restaurant-cum-bar, with an interesting Asian-inspired Continental menu including pan-fried breast of duck, fried Camembert, and lamb steak. There are bar snacks with a Mexican bent and a good wine list, and even a no-smoking area. The frozen margaritas will make you mad with joy.

# EXCURSIONS FROM HANOI

## HALONG BAY

Halong Bay, a natural wonder, is 3,000 islands of varying sizes in the Gulf of Tonkin, many housing spectacular limestone grottos. It has been declared a UNESCO World Heritage Site. The bay itself is a 4-hour drive from Hanoi among often almost unbearably bad roads, and usually includes at least one overnight stay. Given the logistics, the trip is best done via an agent or with a group. When you book a tour with an overnight stay, you'll probably **cruise on a junk** for 4 to 6 hours along the bay, stopping to explore two grottos. You may pause for a swim as well. Trips can cost anywhere from US$18 to US$150 for one overnight. It depends on whether you hire a bus or a private driver, where you stay, and what you eat. The Queen Café does a fine job on the low end, and Vidotour on the higher (see "Visitor Information & Tours," earlier in this chapter).

To really get off the tourist track, also consider one of the 2- or 3-day **sea kayaking adventures** offered by Buffalo Tours or Vidotours. You can also visit Halong in 1 day via **helicopter**—a very good, if expensive, option. Ask your tour operator.

## CUC PHUONG NATIONAL PARK

Cuc Phuong, established in 1962 as Vietnam's first national park, is a lush mountain rain forest with more than 250 bird and 60 mammal species, including tigers, leopards, and the unique red-bellied squirrel. The park's many visitors—and poachers—may keep you from the kind of wildlife experience you might hope for in the brush, however. It's still the perfect setting for a good **hike,** and features goodies like a 1,000-year-old tree, a waterfall, and Con Moong Cave, where prehistoric human remains have been discovered. Cuc Phuong is a good day trip from Hanoi, and some tourist cafes offer programs for as little as US$15. It is also possible to overnight there in the park headquarters.

## HOA LU

From 968 to A.D.1010, Hoa Lu was the capital of Vietnam under the Dinh and first part of the Le dynasties. It is located in a valley surrounded by awesome limestone formations, and is known as the inland Halong Bay. It is a similarly picturesque sight, and much easier to reach. Most of what remains of the kingdom are ruins, but there are still **temples** in the valley, renovated in the 17th century. The first honors Dinh Tien Hoang and has statues of the king. The second is dedicated to Le Dai Hanh, one of Dinh's generals and the first king of the Le Dynasty, who grabbed power in 980 after Dinh was mysteriously assassinated. Hoa Lu can easily be seen on a day trip from Hanoi.

## THE FAR NORTH

The north and northwest highland regions are becoming increasingly popular destinations for hardy travelers. As well as breathtaking landscapes amidst the **Tonkinese Alps,** one of the main attractions of going farther afield is the unspoiled villages of the ethnic minority **hill tribes,** among them the Muong, Hmong, Thai, Tay, and Dao. The villagers truly haven't seen many outsiders, and visits from foreigners usually involve a lot of staring and some friendly touching on both sides. If you can make it this far, it will be a rewarding experience.

By far the easiest travel destination in the north is **Sapa,** a small market town and gathering spot for many local tribes. You can trek out to nearby villages, or simply wait for members of the various hill tribes to come to sell their wares. Their costumes alone are an eyeful: colorful embroidered tunics embellished with heavy silver ornaments. Saturday nights, there is a **"love market"**—young people get together to search for prospective mates. Fansipan, Vietnam's highest peak, stands majestic and misty nearby at 10,312 feet (3,143m).

If you go as far as Sapa on your own, it does have a four-star hotel: **Victoria Sapa Hotel,** Sapa District, Lao Cai Province ( ☎ **04/2087-1422;** fax 84/2087-1539; e-mail victoriasapa@fpt.vn).

Another relatively easy destination is **Mai Chau,** a gorgeous valley about 4 hours from Hanoi. It is the homeland of the ethnic Thai people. The road is somewhat better than the one to Sapa, and the destination not yet as developed. **Dien Bien Phu** to the far northwest is a former French commercial and military outpost, and the site of one of Vietnam's biggest military victories over the French. You can fly directly to Dien Bien Phu from Saigon for US$47 one-way.

This region is definitely one in which independent travel could prove to be extremely challenging if not well nigh impossible. The best way to take in the splendor of the natural surroundings is to do perhaps a 4- or 5-day tour, with a jeep and driver. You could tackle only one or two of the destinations in a 2-day trip. **Ann's Tours,** 26 Yet Kieu, Hoan Kiem District (☎ **04/822-0018**), offers custom-tailored, reasonable packages. Every tourist cafe offers a Sapa package, but keep in mind that low-end travel to this area will be particularly rugged. Other groups offer adventure travel in the region, including camping and hiking. **Buffalo Tours,** 11 Hang Muoi (☎ **04/828-0702**), has an excellent reputation. They offer hiking, rafting, and trekking tours. Some do involve arduous climbing and overnights in hill tribe villages without electricity and running water. Another good tour bet is **TF Hanspan,** 116 Hang Bac (☎ **04/828-1996**).

# 4  An Introduction to the Central Coast

Many of Vietnam's most significant historical sites, and some of its best beaches, are clustered along its central coast. Here you'll find **Hué,** the former Vietnamese capital, with its Imperial City and emperors' tombs. Here also is **Hoi An,** a historic tiny trading town that had its heyday in the 17th century, with more than 800 perfectly preserved classic Chinese and Vietnamese houses and temples. Formerly the seat of the Cham kingdom from the 2nd through 14th centuries, the central coast also has the greatest concentration of Cham relics and art, the highlight of which is the Cham Museum at **Danang.** And you can sample the Vietnamese **beach scene** in its youthful stages at **China Beach** and **Cua Dai.** The proximity and convenient transportation between towns means you'll be able to cover ground efficiently. Danang and Hoi An are so close, about half an hour by car, that you can easily stay in one and make day trips to the other.

## GETTING THERE
**BY PLANE**    You can fly into both Hué and Danang from Saigon or Hanoi for about US$72. Both have an airport departure tax of 20,000 VND (US$1.45). From the airport, you can take a bus into the city center for 25,000 VND (US$1.80). A taxi will cost about US$5.

**BY TRAIN**    Both Hué and Danang are stops on the north-south rail line.

**BY CAR/BUS/MINIVAN**    A tourist cafe bus or minivan trip from Hanoi to Hué will take about 14 grueling hours and cost US$11.50. Driving with a rented vehicle and driver is possible, but will probably cost several hundred dollars and isn't the safest way to travel, as road quality will be uneven.

## GETTING AROUND
**CAR/BUS/MINIVAN**    The three main coastal towns are linked by relatively good roads. You can easily rent a car or get a seat on a bus or minivan in any of the towns, in a hotel or booking agency. From Hué to Danang is about 2½ hours; from Danang to Hoi An about 40 minutes. See individual city listings for suggested prices.

# 5  Hué

Hué was once Vietnam's imperial city, the capital of the country from 1802 to 1945 under the Nguyen dynasty. Culturally and historically, it may perhaps be the most important city in the entire country. While much of it (tragically including most of Vietnam's walled citadel and imperial city) was decimated during the French and

American wars, there is still much to see. One of the most interesting sights is simply daily life on the **Perfume River,** a melange of dragon and house boats and long-tail vessels dredging for sand. You'll visit many of the attractions, including the **tombs of Nguyen dynasty emperors,** by boat. The enjoyable town has a seaside-resort sort of air, with a laid-back attitude, low-slung, colorful colonial-style buildings, and strings of lights at outdoor cafes at night. There are many local cuisine specialties to sample as well.

You may want to plan for a full-day **American war memorial excursion** to the nearby demilitarized zone (DMZ), the beginning of the Ho Chi Minh trail, and underground tunnels at Vinh Moc.

## GETTING THERE

**BY PLANE**    Flights to Hué from both Hanoi and Saigon cost US$72.

**BY TRAIN**    Trains depart daily from both Hanoi and Saigon to Hué. A trip from Hanoi to Hué takes 14 hours on an express and costs US$64 for a soft-berth compartment with A/C.

**BY CAR**    If you're coming from the south, Vietnam Tourism Danang can arrange a car from Danang to Hué for US$45. The trip takes about 2½ hours.

**BY BUS**    While public buses are definitely not recommended, many travelers choose to take an overnight private bus or minivan from Hanoi to Hué. Tickets are US$11 through one of Hanoi's tourist cafes (see "Visitor Information & Tours," earlier in this chapter), and the trip takes about 15 hours, with several rest stops.

## GETTING AROUND

Taxis are much cheaper here than in Hanoi: 6,000 VND (US45¢) starting out and 4,000 VND (US30¢) for each kilometer after. There are two companies: **ATC** (☎ **054/833-333**) and **Gili** (☎ **054/828-282**). As Hué is relatively small, renting a cyclo by the hour for US$1 to US$2 works well. Even the tiniest hotel provides motorbike rentals at 70,000 to 80,000 VND (US$5 to US$5.80) per day and bicycles for US$1.

## VISITOR INFO

There are a number of tour companies in Hué through which you can book boat trips and visits to the DMZ. Every hotel will also be able to assist you, although the tour companies will be cheaper, especially for car services.

- **The Huong Giang Company,** at 17 Le Loi St. (☎ **054/832-220** or 832-221; fax 054/821-426), organizes the usual tours to the tombs and the DMZ, although they are more flexible than most in terms of hours and transport. They are Hué's most upscale and efficient group, and also the most expensive. An all-day tour by car and boat, with guide, to the Citadel and tombs, with lunch, is US$58.
- **DMZ Tour,** 26 Le Loi St. (☎ **054/825-242** or 845-309; fax 054/845-309). Their name is their specialty. All-day tours to DMZ and Vinh Moc tunnels are US$18 per person.
- **Hué City Tourism,** 18 Le Loi St. (☎ **054/823-577**) is another option.
- **Sinh Café V,** 2 Hung Vuong St. (☎ **054/826-918**). Bus tours and tickets onward.

# Hué

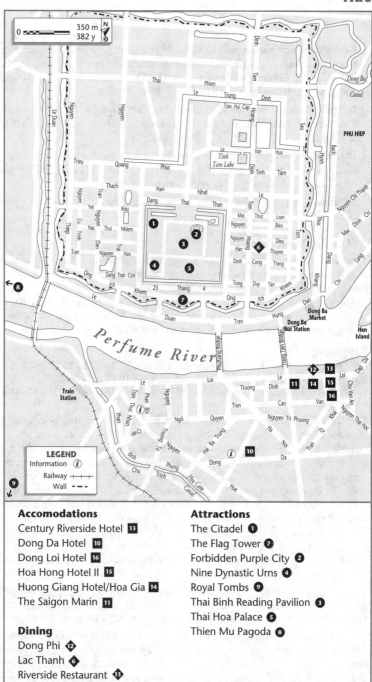

**Accomodations**

Century Riverside Hotel **13**
Dong Da Hotel **10**
Dong Loi Hotel **16**
Hoa Hong Hotel II **15**
Huong Giang Hotel/Hoa Gia **14**
The Saigon Marin **11**

**Dining**

Dong Phi **12**
Lac Thanh **6**
Riverside Restaurant **13**

**Attractions**

The Citadel **1**
The Flag Tower **7**
Forbidden Purple City **2**
Nine Dynastic Urns **4**
Royal Tombs **9**
Thai Binh Reading Pavilion **3**
Thai Hoa Palace **5**
Thien Mu Pagoda **8**

# Fast Facts: Hué

**Banks/Currency Exchange**   Most hotels change currency in Hué, but note that the rate isn't as good as in the two main cities. The two main banks are the Industrial and Commercial Bank at 2 Le Qui Don St. (☎ 054/823-275), and Vietcombank, 6 Hoang Hoa Tham St. (☎ 054/824-572).

**Internet/E-mail**   The Dong Loi Hotel, 11a Pham Ngu Lao St. (☎ 054/822-296; e-mail: interser@vnn.vn), has an Internet cafe. You can also use the services at DMZ Tour, 26 Le Loi St. (☎ 054/825-242).

**Post Office/Mail**   There are mini–post offices in the Century and Huong Giang hotels. The main post office is at 8 Hoang Hoa Tham St., and is open from 7am to 9pm. You can also place international calls there.

**Telephone**   The city code for Hué is 54. You can place IDD calls at the post office (above).

## ACCOMMODATIONS

There are three upscale hotels in Hué; the rest are budget places of varying quality, and there are some duds. Always ask to see the rooms first if it's not a hotel I recommend. Don't expect the service you might get in Saigon, except that all provide tour services and almost all include breakfast in their prices. Even though hotels insist that they accept American Express, they may refuse it when it's time to pay. As always in Vietnam, the prices are eminently flexible, so press for a discount.

### EXPENSIVE

**The Century Riverside Hotel.** 49 Le Loi, Hué, Vietnam. ☎ **800/536-7361,** 054/823-390, or 823-391. Fax 054/823-394 or 823-399. A/C MINIBAR TV TEL. 147 units. US$70–US$100 double; US$170 suites. Breakfast included. Additional 5% service charge. Extra bed US$15. AE, JCB, MC, V.

This is Hué's premier hotel, although it has close rivals. For comfort, friendliness, and location, it's quite nice. Rooms are bland chain-hotel style, smallish, clean, and comfortable, with new tile and marble bathrooms (make sure to ask for a room with recent renovations). The cheaper US$70 rooms have older carved-wood furniture. The riverview rooms are worth the extra US$10, and the pool is in a prime lounge spot by the river. The hotel also has a very nice English-speaking staff. Watch out for the hidden costs. Laundry is US$1 a piece, the exchange rate is inexplicably lower than anywhere else, and phone call costs are outrageous—even local calls are billed. Ouch! There's also sauna, massage, fitness room (only if you're desperate), 24-hour room service, laundry service, post office, and four conference rooms.

For dining, Riverside Restaurant is Hué's most upscale, serving Vietnamese and Western dishes. Terrace Café and Bar has excellent river views.

**Huong Giang Hotel.** 51 Le Loi St., Hué, Vietnam. ☎**054/822-122** or 054/823-958. Fax 054/823-102 or 823-424. 150 units. A/C MINIBAR TV TEL. US$55–US$80 double; US$170 suite; US$230 royal suite. Extra bed 35% of rm cost. Breakfast included. AE, JCB, MC, V.

This hotel is a veritable Asian wonderland, so enamored is it of heavy carved-wood and bamboo furnishings. Some might call it tacky, but it's great fun and well worth being your choice in Hué, as "imperial" is what the city's all about. The rooms are clean and comfortable in basic bamboo, and were renovated 2 years ago. Bathrooms are a disappointing dormitory style, with plastic shower curtains (mine featured a Bugs Bunny motif) and no counter space. Try to get a good deal on one of the Royal Suites, with carved-wood walls, grandiose furniture with inlaid mother-of-pearl, and a massive wood room divider—sort of a mini-pagoda right in your room. The words "emperor" and "bordello" both leap to mind. The Royal Restaurant, worth a photo for its gaudy gold-and-red-everything design alone, is for pre-arranged group dinners, where the costumed staff serves a fancy traditional dinner at a hefty price. Amenities include swimming pool, sauna, massage, tennis court, laundry service, 24-hour room service, travel and tour services, post office, currency exchange, and boutique. There are two restaurants, both very good, and the River Front Terrace Bar, the best place in Hué to have a drink and watch life on the river.

**The Saigon Marin.** 30 Le Loi St., Hué, Vietnam. ☎ **054/823-526.** Fax 054/825-155. 137 units. A/C MINIBAR TV TEL. US$60–US$100 double, US$180–US$250 suite, US$300 executive suite. US$15 extra bed. Includes breakfast, tax, and service charge. AE, JCB, MC, V.

The Marin is a completely refurbished colonial, government-run. When you first see the outside of the Marin, with its pale pink walls and columns topped by bright purple capitals, you know you are in for something special. The whole place looks like aliens landed and gave their best shot at what a restored Southeast Asian colonial should look like. The lobby isn't that big and yet has three, count 'em, *three* chandeliers. It's hard to know what to say about the rooms. They are attractive, with reproduction French colonial furniture, nice carpet, and floral drapes, but the furniture seems to be randomly placed with no thought for style or spatial relationships. The whole effect is unsettling. Yet the whole place is certainly clean, comfortable, and deluxe, by Hué standards. Nice-sized new marble bathrooms are just that, and have hair dryers. The nice-sized pool is placed in the middle courtyard and has a outdoor cafe and well-landscaped garden to the side. The staff couldn't care less.

Facilities and services include a business center, conference rooms, 24-hour room service, post office, sauna, massage, billiards, karaoke, and traditional music shows. There are two restaurants, a poolside cafe, a cafeteria, and a bar.

## MODERATE

**Hoa Hong Hotel II.** 1 Pham Ngu Lao St., Hué, Vietnam. ☎ **054/824-377** or 826-943. Fax 054/826-949. 50 units. A/C MINIBAR TV TEL. US$35–US$55 double; US$65–US$90 suite. Extra bed US$10. Includes breakfast, fax, and service charge. JCB, MC, V.

Here is yet another nice hotel bargain in Hué. Built in 1996, the rooms are very non-descript—think navy and beige, with those polyester bedspreads again. Yet they are comfortable, with good, firm beds. The bathrooms are nice-sized, with bathtubs and hair dryers, and all is spic and span. Ask for a city view rather than a noisy street-view room. The suites have authentic Asian furniture. There are two restaurants, one of which specializes in the popular "royal dinner" theme evenings, when both staff and guests dress like emperors and empresses. The lobby has a fun little bar on one end with very expensive (US$4) drinks. Tour and car rental services are available, as is round-the-clock room service. Hoa Hong II is hugely popular with tour groups, so book early.

## INEXPENSIVE

**Dong Da Hotel.** 15 Ly Thuong Kiet St., Hué, Vietnam. ☎ **054/823-071.** Fax 054/823-204. 37 units. A/C MINIBAR TV TEL. Double US$22; 2 family rooms at US$35. Includes breakfast. AE, JCB, MC, V.

Wow. What a great hotel for the price. The Dong Da is clean and friendly. Rooms have plain tile floor and basic furnishings, with nice spare furniture and Japanese screens. One could do without the fake Swiss clocks and polyurethane sofas, but the thick foam mattresses are firm and the pillows are, well, real pillows. There are even lockable drawer safes. The tile bathrooms have no separate bath or shower; it's a one-shot deal where the shower head hangs on the wall. They are spotless, however. Ask for a "standard" room, which faces a relatively quiet alley rather than the street. The family suites are two separate rooms with big double beds, and are a fantastic deal for group travel. The friendly staff will arrange bike rentals, travel, and tours. There is also a nice-looking karaoke bar and dancing hall next to the restaurant, if you fancy it.

**Dong Loi Hotel.** 11a Pham Ngu Lao St. ☎ **054/822-296** or 826-234. Fax 054/826-234. E-mail interser@vnn.vn. A/C TEL. US$15–US$35. No credit cards. Breakfast included in US$20 and up rooms.

There are plenty of inexpensive hotels in Hué, but the Dong Loi is another particularly good bargain. Family-run, it has spotless rooms with tile floors and firm beds. The attractive bathrooms are tile, and the most expensive rooms have bathtubs. Rooms priced US$20 on up have televisions. The hotel provides tour planning and laundry services, and even has an Internet cafe. The rooms facing the street give you an earful of the karaoke next store but only until 11pm. The rooms facing the back have a bonus: a free rooster wake-up call at 4am. For extra-nice treatment, show owner Mr. Le Van Dong this book and tell him I sent you.

## DINING

There are some good local dishes to sample in Hué, but relatively few spots with English menus and high-quality food. Still, the ones I found were good enough to visit more than once. Do try bun bo Hué, a noodle soup with pork, beef, and shredded green onions; and banh khoi, a thin, crispy pancake filled with ground meat and crispy vegetables.

✪ **Club Garden.** 12 Vo Thi Sau St. ☎ **054/826-327.** Main courses US$2.50–US$4. Set menus US$8–US$12. No credit cards. 7am–11pm. VIETNAMESE.

One of the best meals in Vietnam can be had at this unpretentious little restaurant. Seating is both outdoors and in. The menu's emphasis is on fish and crab, all prepared in the local style (grilled, in lemon leaves) and absolutely delicious. And note the prices! Their banh khoi, a crispy pancake stuffed with ground meat and shrimp, is the best in town. Also musts: the fried shrimp with garlic, crispy fried noodles with vegetables, and chicken cooked in lemon leaf. Dessert is fried bananas of the gods. The menu is in very good English as well as Vietnamese and French, and the family that runs the place is friendly and accommodating. Breakfast is served here as well.

**Dong Phi.** 56 Le Loi, across from the Huong Giang Hotel. ☎ **054/845-571.** Main courses 10,000–40,000 VND (US70¢–US$2.90). No credit cards. VIETNAMESE.

Seems to be open all day. Stop here if at all possible. This place was virtually empty when I visited, but it should be packed. It's your basic open-air, streetside food stop, but extremely clean and pleasant. Fantastic local fare: sautéed shrimp with garlic (albeit lots of tiny ones you have to peel yourself), pig intestine with spice (which is delicious, trust me), and first-class pho and banh khoi. It is run by an extremely friendly bunch of older ladies who only speak Vietnamese (hence my difficulty nailing down hours of business). The English menu saves the day.

**Hoa Mia Restaurant.** 51 Le Loi St., third floor, Huong Giang Hotel. ☎ **054/822-122.** Main courses 25,000–36,000 VND (US$1.80–US$2.60). AE, JCB, MC, V. 6am–10pm. VIETNAMESE/CONTINENTAL.

A most attractive restaurant, large, open, and airy, with bamboo furniture and detailing and a great view of the Perfume River. It serves excellent local cuisine. Try banh rom Hué, little triangular-shaped fried rolls stuffed with ground meat, shrimp, and vegetables; crab soup with mushroom; and grilled chicken in lemon leaves. There is even wine by the glass. Their breakfast buffet is incredible, including every kind of egg and pancake, as well as Vietnamese sweets and a table full of exotic fruit. You'll have to be patient with the slow service and unseasonal Christmas Muzak, though.

**Lac Thanh Restaurant.** 6A Dien Tien Hoang St. ☎ **054/824674.** Main courses 7,000–40,000 VND (US50¢–US$2.90). No credit cards. 7am–10pm. VIETNAMESE.

Very good eats and a lively good time to be had here. Everybody knows it, so you'll see every under-50 wayfarer you've met during your trip here. It's basically a grubby streetside place, but one that serves very nice grilled pork wrapped in rice paper, sautéed bean sprouts, grilled crab, and spareribs, among dozens of choices. Balcony seating, too. For dessert, try the local specialty ché nong, a warm congee with coconut, bananas, and nuts. The glutinous texture takes some getting used to, but definitely adds entertainment value. As you approach the restaurant, you'll be mobbed by hucksters trying to take you to the knock-off next door, which is reportedly not bad either.

**Riverside Restaurant.** 40 Le Loi, at the Century Riverside Hotel. ☎ **054/823-390.** Main courses US$3.50–US$6. AE, JCB, MC, V. Open all day. VIETNAMESE/CONTINENTAL.

This very nice, upscale restaurant has scenic views over the Perfume River as well as good food. The extensive menu includes dozens of varieties of noodles and fried rice, from spaghetti with cheese to Vietnamese rice noodles with seafood. Main dishes include sautéed shrimp with mushroom sauce over rice and grilled duck wrapped in lemon leaf.

## ATTRACTIONS

Except for the remains of its fabulous Imperial City, Hué in itself has sadly seen the worst of the French and Vietnam wars. Most of the star attractions other than the Citadel, therefore, involve half-day or day trips outside the city.

✪ **The Citadel & Imperial City.** Daily 7am–5:30pm. Admission 55,000 VND (US$4).

**The Citadel** is often used as a catch-all term for Hué's Imperial City, built by emperor Gia Long beginning in 1804 for the exclusive use of the emperor and his household, much like Beijing's Forbidden City. The city actually encompasses three walled enclosures: the Exterior Exclosure or Citadel, the Yellow Enclosure or Imperial City within that, and in the very center the Forbidden Purple City where the emperor actually lived.

Beginning at the outside looking into the main entrance at the southern gate, you'll find the **Flag Tower,** built in 1807. It is of much significance to Vietnam's military past. In 1947 it was almost destroyed during the war against the French. Rebuilt, it was a figurehead in the American War when it was defiantly occupied by the Viet Cong for 25 days during the Tet Offensive. The Palace itself was used as a field hospital for Viet Cong commandos. The Tower is in three tiers, representing the natural order of earth, human beings, and heaven.

The **Citadel** is a square, 1½-mile (2km) wall, 23 feet (7m) high and 66 feet (20m) thick,, with 10 gates. Ironically, it was constructed by a French military architect, though it failed to prevent the French from destroying the complex many years later. The main entrance to the Imperial City is the Ngo Mon, the southwest or "noon" gate. It encompasses an elegant pavilion known as the Belvedere of Five Phoenixes, constructed by Emperor Gia Long in 1823. It was used for important proclamations, such as announcements of the names of successful doctoral candidates (a list still hangs on the wall on the upper floor) and, most memorably, announcement of the abdication of the last emperor Bao Dai on August 13, 1945, to Ho Chi Minh.

The first structure you will approach is **Thai Hoa Palace.** Otherwise known as the Palace of Supreme Harmony, it was built in 1833. It was used as the throne room, a ceremonial hall where the emperor celebrated festivals and received courtiers; the original throne still stands. The Mandarins sat outside. In front are two mythical *ky lin* animals, which walk without their claws ever touching ground and which have piercing eyesight for watching the emperor, tracking all good and evil he does. Note the statues of the heron and turtle inside the palace's ornate lacquered interior, the heron representing nobility, and the turtle, the working person. Folklore has it that the two took turns saving each other's lives during a fire, symbolizing that the power of the emperor rests with his people, and vice versa.

The **Forbidden Purple City,** once the actual home of the emperor and his concubines, was almost completely razed in a fire in 1947. There are a few buildings left among the rubble, however. The new Royal Theater behind the square, a look-alike to the razed original, is under construction. The partially restored **Thai Binh Reading Pavilion,** to the left of it as you head north, is notable mostly for its beautifully landscaped surroundings, including a small lake with a Zen-like stone sculpture, and the ceramic and glass mosaic detailing on the roof and pillars, favored by flamboyant emperor Khai Dinh.

Turning around and facing south and the Noon Gate again, to your far right after a short walk you'll come to the splendid **Hung To Mieu** temple, built in 1804 to honor Gia Long's parents. To the left and south of it, newly restored, is **The Mieu Temple,** constructed in 1921–22 by emperor Minh Mang. Inside are funeral altars paying tribute to 10 of the last Nguyen dynasty emperors, omitting two who reigned only for days, with photos of each emperor and his empress(es) and various small offerings and knickknacks. The two empty glass containers to the side of each photo should contain bars of gold, probably an impractical idea today.

Across from The Mieu you'll see Hien Lam, or Glorious Pavilion, to the far right, with the **Nine Dynastic Urns** in front. Cast in 1835–37, each urn represents a Nguyen emperor, and is richly embellished with all the flora, fauna, and material goods Vietnam has to offer, mythical or otherwise.

✪ **Thien Mu Pagoda.** On the bank of the Perfume River. 8am–5pm.

Often called the symbol of Hué, Thien Mu is one of the oldest and loveliest religious structures in Vietnam. It was constructed beginning in 1601. The Phuoc Dien Tower in front was added in 1864 by emperor Thieu Tri. Each of its seven tiers are dedicated to one of the human forms taken by Buddha, or the seven steps to enlightenment—depending upon whom you ask. There are also two buildings housing a bell reportedly weighing 2 tons, and a stele inscribed with a biography of Lord Nguyen Hoang, founder of the temple.

Once past the front gate, observe the 12 huge wooden sculptures of fearsome temple "guardians"—note the real facial hair. A complex of monastic buildings lies in the center, offering glimpses of the monks' daily routines: cooking, stacking wood, whacking weeds. Stroll all the way to the rear of the complex to look at the large graveyard at the base of the Truong Son mountains, and wander through the well-kept garden of pine trees. Try not to go between the hours of 11:30am and 2pm, when the monks are at lunch, as the rear half of the complex will be closed.

**The Imperial Tombs.** Admission to each: 55,000 VND (US$4). Hours for each: 6:30am–5:30pm summer; 7am–5pm winter.

As befits its history as an Imperial City, Hué's environs are studded with tombs of past emperors. They are spread out over a distance, so the best way to see them is to hire a car for a half-day or take one of the many organized boat tours. Altogether, there were

13 kings of the Nguyen dynasty, although only seven reigned until their death. As befits an emperor, each had tombs of stature, some as large as a small town. Most tomb complexes usually consist of a courtyard, a stele (a large stone tablet with a biography of the emperor), a temple for worship, and a pond.

**Tu Duc** ruled the longest of any Nguyen dynasty emperor, from 1848 to 1883. His tomb was constructed from 1864 to 1867, and has some 50 buildings. Tu Duc was a philosopher and scholar of history and literature. His reign was unfortunate: his kingdom unsuccessfully struggled against French colonialism, he fought a coup d'etat by members of his own family, and although he had 104 wives, he left no heir. The "tomb" also served as recreation grounds for the king, having been completed 16 years prior to his death. He actually engraved his own stele, in fact. The largest in Vietnam at 20 tons, it has its own pavilion in the tomb. The highlight of the grounds is the lotus-filled lake ringed by frangipani trees, with a large pavilion in the center. The main cluster of buildings includes Hoa Khiem (Harmony Modesty) Pavilion, where the king worked, which still contains items of furniture and ornaments. Minh Khiem Duong, constructed in 1866, is said to be the country's oldest surviving theater. It's great fun to poke around in the wings. There are also pieces of original furniture lying here and there, as well as a cabinet with household objects: the Queen's slippers, ornate chests, bronze and silver books. The raised box on the wall is for the actors who played emperors; the real emperor was at the platform to the left.

✪ **Khai Dinh's** tomb, completed from 1923 to 1931, is one of the world's wonders. The emperor himself wasn't particularly revered, being overly extravagant and flamboyant (reportedly he wore a belt studded with lights that he flicked on at opportune public moments). His tomb, a gaudy mix of gothic, baroque, Hindu, and Chinese Qing dynasty architecture at the top of 127 steep steps, is a reflection of the man. Inside, the two main rooms are completely covered with fabulous, intricate glass and ceramic mosaics in designs reminiscent of Tiffany and art deco. The workmanship is astounding. The outer room's ceiling was done by a fellow who used both his feet and hands to paint, in what some say was a sly mark of disrespect for the emperor. While in most tombs the location of the emperor's actual remains are a secret, Khai Minh boldly placed his under his de facto tomb itself.

**Minh Mang,** one of the most popular Nguyen emperors and the father of last emperor Bao Dai, built a restrained, serene, classical temple, much like Hué's Imperial City, located at the confluence of two Perfume River tributaries. Stone sculptures surround a long walkway, lined with flowers, leading up to the main buildings. Much of the architecture is currently covered by scaffolding, but reconstruction work is expected to be complete in late 1999.

## EXCURSION: KHE SANH & THE DMZ

Under the Geneva Accords of 1954, an agreement struck to bring peace to Indochina after its struggle with French colonists, Vietnam was divided into North and South along the Seventeeth Parallel. The two never united. During the American War, the Seventeenth Parallel, a.k.a the DMZ, or demilitarized zone between north and south, was a tense area demarcated with barbed wire and land mines in parts, bombed and defoliated into a wasteland. The area is green with growth again and completely unremarkable except for its history and the required statue at Hien Luong Bridge, which links north and south over the Ben Hai river. Nearby are strategic sites with names you may recognize: the Rockpile, Hamburger Hill, Camp Carroll, and Khe Sanh, a former U.S. marine base that was the site of some of the war's most vicious and deadly fighting. If you take a tour of the area, you see these sites as well as the Dakrong Bridge, an official entryway into the Ho Chi Minh Trail.

# Digging In at Vinh Moc

In the mid 1960s the Americans began bombing raids of the Vinh Linh district near the DMZ, on grounds of suspected Viet Cong complicity. The more than 600 villagers, however, refused to leave their homes and literally dug in. In fact, they dug over a mile of underground tunnels over 1965–66, and then lived in them.

The tunnels are divided into various levels, the deepest about 76 feet (23m) below the surface. The complex was a fully functioning community haven, with "living rooms" for families, a conference and performance room, and an operating theater where children were delivered (you can see their pictures in the above-ground museum nearby). There are 5,670 feet (1,728m) of the tunnel left today. Seven entrances point toward the sea, where, under cover of the night, the villagers would come up for air and pass munitions along to Viet Cong boats. You'll walk through about 984 feet (300m) of the tunnels in a main artery that is 5⅓ feet high and 4 feet wide (1.62m high by 1.2m wide), going down three stages, with the clammy climate and creepy claustrophobic feeling causing perspiration to pop and hair to stand up on the back of your neck. Coming to the sea, feeling the fresh wind on your face, you'll feel relief, and also disbelief at the incredible endurance and perseverance of people who voluntarily committed themselves to enduring such conditions—who, in fact, dug themselves in.

You can see the tunnels as part of a day trip to the Demilitarized Zone (DMZ). Admission is 22,000 VND (US$1.60).

The DMZ tour office, 26 Le Loi St. (☎ 054/825-242), organizes day trips to the DMZ and Vinh Moc tunnels. Warning: The route over Highway 9 to the sites are under construction, which means narrow, very bumpy dirt roads and wooden bridges. Rethink this trip if it's a rainy day, or if you are faint of either heart or stomach.

## 6 Danang & China Beach

Danang, the fourth-largest city in Vietnam, is one of the most important sea ports in the central region. It played a prominent historical role in the American war, being the landing site for the first American troops officially sent to Vietnam. Even with the bustle of ships coming and going, poor Danang has to be one of the world's ugliest cities, and there isn't a major attraction save for the **Cham Museum.** It's a must-see, but you can catch it on the way from Hué to Hoi An. There are a few excellent-value hotels in Danang, so an option is to actually stay in the city, the biggest travel hub on the central coast, and take day trips to nearby Hoi An. China Beach, or My Khe as it's known locally, is worth a stop, having a nice light-sand coast with excellent views of the nearby Marble Mountains. The American television show was based on a U.S. military recreation base a few miles north.

### GETTING THERE

**BY PLANE**   You can fly to Danang from both Hanoi and HCMC. There is an airport tax of 20,000 VND (US$1.50) upon departure.

**BY BUS**   Many travelers take an open-end bus south from Hanoi or north from Saigon. It stops at the major coastal towns along the way. Inquire at any tourist cafe for details.

**BY CAR**    Danang is about 2½ hours by car from Hué, and the route covers the very scenic Hai Van Pass. From Hoi An, it's about half an hour. The ride makes a good day trip along with the Marble Mountains.

## VISITOR INFORMATION & TOURS

**Vietnam Tourism Danang** is located at 274 Phan Chu Trinh St. (☎ **0511/822-990;** fax 0511/822-854). They can arrange trips to the Marble Mountains and My Son, as can nearly every hotel.

## Fast Facts: Danang

**Banks/Currency Exchange**    Vietcombank is at 104 Le Loi St. (☎ 0511/ 821-955).

**Telephone**    The city code for Danang is 511.

## ACCOMMODATIONS

**Bamboo Green Hotel.** 158 Phan Chau Trinh St. ☎ **0511/822-996** or 0511/822-997. Fax 0511/822-998. E-mail Vitours@hn.vnn.vn. 42 units. A/C MINIBAR TV TEL. 42 units. US$119–US$169 double; US$169 suite. Discounts of up to 45% available during low season. All taxes, breakfast, welcome drink, and fruit included. AE, JCB, MC, V.

Operated by Vietnam Tourism, this hotel opened in 1997 and is the nicest in Danang. Rooms are large, immaculate, and well-furnished in light wood (just try to overlook the hideous poly bedspreads), and the nice-sized marble bathrooms with hair dryers look brand new, as they should. Ask for a room on the top floor for a good city view. There is a big restaurant and good tour services, sauna, and massage. The staff is friendly and snaps to.

**Furama Resort Danang.** 68 Ho Xuan Huong St., China Beach, Danang, Vietnam. ☎ **0511/847-333.** Fax 0511/847-220. E-mail furamadn@hn.vnn.vn. www.interconti. com. 200 units. A/C MINIBAR TV TEL. US$140–US$200 double; US$400 suite. AE, JCB, MC, V.

The Furama is a full-service resort, about 7 miles from Danang. It's worth staying here and spending an extra day or two simply lounging around the Viet-style low-rise buildings, enjoying the beautiful beach, landscaping, and decor. Rooms are simple yet luxe: big with solid wood floors, Vietnamese-flavored furniture, and sliding doors to balconies that overlook ocean or pool. The huge modern marble bathrooms have all the amenities. There are two gorgeous swimming pools: one a minimalist still-life and the other a faux lagoon, complete with small waterfall. Prices are determined by the view, and oceanfront units are only steps from the beach. Note that most of the water sports are available only from February through September—the surf is far too rough in other months, often even for swimming. There is an hourly shuttle bus to the city. The Furama does have some kinks to work out, though: Reservations get misplaced, the staff is perhaps a bit too laid-back, and the quality of the food is uneven.

Café Indochine offers light Vietnamese and Continental meals. The Ocean Terrace serves pizza and pastas. The Hai Van Lounge and Lagoon bar serve drinks and snacks. Amenities include well-equipped health club with sauna, massage, hair salon, medical center, business center, conference and banquet rooms, 24-hour room service, baby-sitting, game room, scuba diving, snorkeling, waterskiing, surfboard rental, tennis court, driving range, karate classes, and art gallery.

**Royal Hotel.** 17 Quang Trung St., Danang, Vietnam. ☎ **0511/823-295.** Fax 0511/827-279. 28 units. A/C MINIBAR TV TEL. US$70 double; US$120 suite. Ask about seasonal

# Who Are the Cham?

There is little written history of the Cham. What we do know is mainly via Chinese written history, a few temple stelae, and the splendid religious artwork the empire created in its prime. They were a people of Indonesian descent formed in approximately the second century A.D. in Tuong Lam, along the central coast of Vietnam, while fighting to prevent Chinese domination. They declared a new land, dubbed the Lin Yi by the Chinese, that extended from Quang Binh to present-day Danang Province. The center of the civilization for most of its existence was in Indrapura, or Tra Kieu, near present-day Danang.

The Cham belonged to the Malayo-Polynesian language family, and had their own script based on Sanskrit. They lived by rice farming, fishing, and trading pepper, cinnamon bark, ivory, and wood with neighboring nations, using Hoi An as a base. Hinduism was their dominant religion, with Buddhist influences and an infusion of Islam starting in the 14th century.

In the middle of the 10th century, internal warfare, as well as battles against both the Khmer to the south and Dai Viet to the north, began to erode the Cham kingdom. By the mid–15th century, it had been almost entirely absorbed into Vietnam. By the early 1800s, there was no longer a separate Cham nation. The Cham still exist today, however, as an ethnic minority. They have their own language and customs, and their religion is still largely based on Hinduism, though a portion of them have converted to Islam. They survive through farming and the sales of handicrafts.

discounts, which can go as high as 50%. Includes breakfast, welcome drink, and fruit basket. AE, JCB, MC, V.

Formerly the Marco Polo Hotel, this place has been a tourist standby in Danang since it was built in 1994. It's comfortable and attractive, with a floral theme rather than Asian. The small marble bathrooms are showing signs of age, but have bathtubs and hair dryers. It has three-star amenities: restaurant, tour services, business center, tennis, and nightclub. It's not as fancy, but overall it's a better bargain than the Bamboo (above).

## ATTRACTIONS

✪ **The Cham Museum.** At Tran Phu and Le Dinh Duong sts. No phone. Admission: 20,000 VND (US$1.50). Daily 7am–6pm.

The Cham Museum was established in 1936 as the Ecole Francaise d'Extreme Orient. It has the largest collection of Cham sculpture in the world, in works ranging from the 4th to 14th centuries, presented in a rough outdoor setting that suits the evocative, sensual sculptures well. The more than 300 pieces of sandstone artwork and temple decorations were largely influenced by Hindu and, later, Mahayana Buddhism. Among the cast of characters you'll see: symbols of Uroja, or "goddess mother," usually breasts or nipples; the linga, the phallic structure representing the god Shiva; the

| Danang Water Sports |

The **Furama Resort** in China Beach offers boating, snorkeling excursions, and scuba diving (in season), plus mountain bike and surfboard rentals.

holy bird Garuda; the dancing girl Kinnari; the snake god Naga; and Ganesha, child of the god Shiva, with the head of an elephant. The sculptures are arranged by period, which are in turn named after the geographic regions where the sculptures were found. Note the masterpiece Tra Kieu altar of the late seventh century, with carved scenes telling the story of the Asian epic *Ramayana*. The story is of the wedding of Princess Sita. Side one tells of Prince Rama, who broke a holy vow to obtain Sita's hand. Side two tells of ambassadors sent to King Dasaratha, Prince Rama's father, to bring him the glad tidings. Side three is the actual ceremony, and side four, the celebrations after the ceremony.

Explanations are written in English and French. There is a permanent photo exhibition of Cham relics in situ at various locations throughout Vietnam that helps put everything in context.

**The Marble Mountains.** 7 miles south of Danang and 6 miles north of Hoi An along Hwy. 1. Admission: 50,000 VND (US$3.60).

The "mountains" are actually a series of five marble and limestone formations, which the locals liken to the shape of a dragon at rest. The hills contain numerous caves, some of which have become Buddhist sanctuaries. They also served as sanctuaries for the Viet Cong during the American war. The highest mountain, Thuy Son, is climbable via steps built into the hillside. Its highlight is the Ling Ong Pagoda, a shrine within a cave. As interesting as the caves are the quarries in Non Nuoc village, at the bottom of the mountains. Fantastic animals are carved from the rock, particularly the roaring lion said to watch over the village from the peaks. Try to get a good look before you are set upon by flocks of hawkers. You can easily see the mountains as part of your trip either en route to or from Hoi An.

## AN EXCURSION TO MY SON

My Son, 44 miles outside of Danang, is one of the most important Cham temple sites, established in the late fourth century. The temples were constructed as a religious center for citizens of the Cham capital, Danang, from the 7th through 12th centuries. My Son may also have been used as a burial site for Cham kings after cremation. Originally, there were over 70 towers and monuments here, but bombing during the American war (the Viet Cong used My Son as a munitions warehouse) has sadly reduced many to rubble. Additionally, many of the smaller structures have been removed to the Cham museum in Danang. The complex has a very serene and spiritual setting, however, and what does remain is powerful and evocative. It's not hard to imagine what a wonder My Son must once have been.

Much of what remains today are structures built or renovated during the 10th century when the cult of Shiva, founder and protector of the kingdom, was predominant in the Cham court. Each group had at least the following structures: a *kalan,* or main tower, a gate tower in front of that with two entrances, a *mandapa* or meditation hall, and a repository building for offerings. Some have towers sheltering stelae with kingly epitaphs. A brick wall encircles the compound.

Architecturally, a temple complex shows Indian influences. Each is a microcosm of the world. The foundations are earth, the square bases are the temple itself, and the pointed roofs symbolize the heavens. The entrance of the main tower faces east, and surrounding smaller towers represent each continent. A trench, representing the oceans, surrounds each group. Vietnamese architecture is represented in decorative patterns and boat-shaped roofs.

Group A originally had 13 towers. A-1, the main tower, was a 69-foot-tall masterpiece before being destroyed in 1969. Group B shows influences from Indian and

Indonesian art. Note that B-6 holds a water repository for statue-washing ceremonies. Its roof is carved with an image of the god Vishnu sitting beneath a 13-headed snake god, or *naga.* Group C generally followed an earlier architectural style called Hoa Lai, which predominated from the eighth century to the beginning of the 9th. Groups G and H were the last to be built, at around the end of the 13th century.

You can make arrangements for a half-day trip to see My Son through any tourist agent in Danang, or from Hoi An.

## 7  Hoi An

If you go, Hoi An will be one of the highlights of your Vietnam visit. From the 16th to the 18th century, Hoi An was Vietnam's most important port and trading post, particularly in ceramics. Today, it is a quaint old town (844 structures have been designated historical landmarks) still showing the influences of the Chinese and Japanese traders who passed through and settled there. Moreover, it's small enough to cover easily on foot, wandering through the historic homes and temples on a quiet Saturday afternoon, perhaps stopping to lounge in an open-air cafe, or gaze at the endless oddities and exotic foods in the market, or take a **sampan ride** down the lazy river. In the afternoons when school is out, the streets are thronged with skipping children in spotless white shirts. While the city is eagerly courting tourism and your tourist dollars—meaning there's plenty of pesky vendors and hawkers—it's still relatively low-key and genuinely friendly.

### GETTING THERE

**BY PLANE OR TRAIN**   Major public transport connections go through Danang. From there, you can take a car to Hoi An for about US$12 via **Hoi An Tourist Services** (☎ **0510/861-362** or 861-445).

### GETTING AROUND

Hoi An is so small you'll memorize the map in an hour or two. Most hotels and guesthouses rent out **bicycles** for 7,000 to 10,000 VND a day, as does Hoi An Tourism (see below) to explore the outer regions of the city or Cao Dai beach. **Motorbikes** are US$3 to US$5 per day and are not difficult to drive in this tiny, calm city. **Cyclos** are here and there; 10,000 VND or so should get you anywhere within the city.

### VISITOR INFORMATION & TOURS

**Hoi An Tourist Service Company,** inside the Hoi An Hotel at 6 Tran Hung Dao Street. (☎ **0510/861-373,** fax 0510/861-636), books every type of ticket and provides tours of the city and surrounding areas, including China Beach and the Marble Mountains, and is a reliable operation. There are many tourist cafes, booking offices, and small hotels who can do the same job, but these specialize in backpacker minibus tours.

The **Hoi An Tourist Guiding Office,** 12 Phan Chu Trinh St. (☎ **0510/862-715**), offers tours of the old town and sells admission tickets. Mr. Truong Duy Tri is particularly knowledgeable and helpful. The **Sinh Café IV,** 143 Tran Phu St., at the Vinh Hung Hotel (☎ **0510/861-621**), provides bus tours and tickets to Nha Trang.

## Fast Facts: Hoi An

**Banks/Currency Exchange**   The Vietcombank branch at 4 Huong Dieu St. changes money of most major currencies and does credit card cash withdrawal transactions. Hours are Monday to Saturday 7:30am to 7pm.

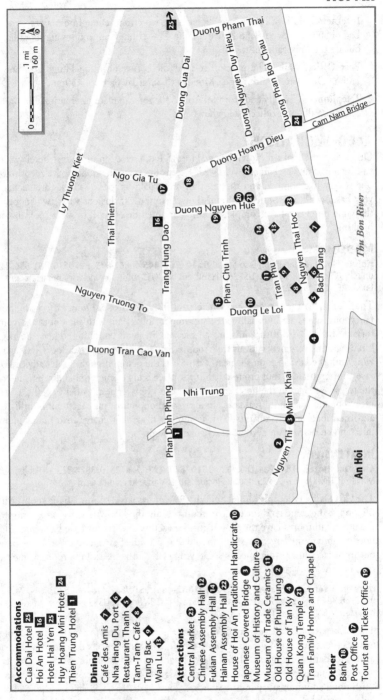

# Hoi An

Thu Bon River

An Hoi

Duong Pham Thai
Duong Cua Dai
Duong Nguyen Duy Hieu
Duong Phan Boi Chau
Cam Nam Bridge
Duong Hoang Dieu
Ly Thuong Kiet
Ngo Gia Tu
Thai Phien
Duong Nguyen Hue
Trang Hung Dao
Phan Chu Trinh
Nguyen Truong To
Nguyen Thai Hoc
Bach Dang
Tran Phu
Duong Le Loi
Duong Tran Cao Van
Nhi Trung
Phan Dinh Phung
Minh Khai
Nguyen Thi

0   .1 mi
0   160 m

**Accommodations**
Cua Dai Hotel 25
Hoi An Hotel 16
Hotel Hai Yen 25
Huy Hoang Mini Hotel 24
Thien Trung Hotel 1

**Dining**
Café des Amis 7
Nha Hang Du Port 6
Restaurant Thanh 5
Tam-Tam Café 8
Trung Bac 9
Wan Lu 13

**Attractions**
Central Market 23
Chinese Assembly Hall 12
Fukian Assembly Hall 14
Hainan Assembly Hall 22
House of Hoi An Traditional Handicraft 10
Japanese Covered Bridge 3
Museum of History and Culture 20
Museum of Trade Ceramics 11
Old House of Phun Hung 2
Old House of Tan Ky 4
Quan Kong Temple 21
Tran Family Home and Chapel 15

**Other**
Bank 18
Post Office 17
Tourist and Ticket Office 19

283

**Internet/E-mail**    There is a small, nameless storefront selling Internet access on
Le Loi Street, between Tran Phu and Phan Chu Trinh. Connections are sporadic,
but it's the only game in town.

**Post Office/Mail**    The post office is at the corner of Trang Hong Dao and
Huong Dieu streets and is open Monday to Saturday 6am to 9:30pm.

**Telephone**    The city code for Hoi An is 510. You can place international phone
calls from the post office listed above.

## ACCOMMODATIONS

Other than the Hoi An Hotel, below, Hoi An has a selection of budget hotels which
suit its toned-down character very well. Except for a few standouts we've mentioned,
one is very like another, and though they are usually spotless, facilities are generally
very basic, with all-in-one bathroom-shower combos. Inclusions vary; two rooms in
the same hotel can have completely different amenities, so ask to see a room before
booking.

### MODERATE

**Hoi An Hotel.** 6 Tran Hung Dao St. ☎ **0510/861-445** or 861-373. Fax 0510/861-636. 120
units. A/C MINIBAR TV TEL. US$36–US$60 double. US$100 suite. Includes breakfast and all
taxes. AE, JCB, MC, V.

The Hoi An is the top-end hotel here, and it's a good one. Don't expect anything
fancy, but rooms are unusually large and impeccably clean, with tile floors and comfortable beds. Basic bathrooms are all-tile and in good condition. There are three
buildings, one very new with upscale rooms: new furniture, carpeted floors. The older
wing with the US$35 rooms is nearly as nice as the newer, though, so my advice is to
save your money. It's tour group city but the place is big enough to handle 'em all, and
the tourist services in the hotel can handle your every request. Other benefits: a very
nice pool and staff, hot breakfasts, an ideal location, sauna, massage, tennis, billiards,
and traditional music concerts. This is another place that charges exorbitant phone
rates and cheats you on currency exchange, though.

### INEXPENSIVE

**Cua Dai Hotel.** 18A Cua Dai. ☎ **0510/862-231.** Fax 0510/862-232. 16 units. A/C
MINIBAR TEL. US$15–US$25 double. Includes breakfast. No credit cards.

The Cua Dai is a nice mini-hotel built in 1995. It has large, spotless, basic rooms with
tile floors; the same goes for the bathrooms. Only the US$25 rooms have bathtubs;
the other bathrooms have the shower-in-room setup. Side rooms have balconies. This
hotel is close to the larger Hai Yen, about halfway to the beach, and its breakfast patio
out front faces interesting bucolic scenery. They rent bikes. Ask for a room facing the
rear, not the noisy road.

**Hotel Hai Yen.** 22A Cua Dai St. ☎ **0510/862-445**, 0510/862-446, or 0510/861-994. Fax
0510/862-443. 31 units, 26 with A/C TEL. US$12–US$30 double. US$25 and over rms include
breakfast, MINIBAR and TV. AE, JCB, MC, V.

This is the swankiest place in Hoi An, outside of the Hoi An Hotel. About 1 year old,
it is spanking clean, and the large rooms with tile floors are nicely decorated with cane
furniture. Bathrooms are small, but clean, bright tile with bathtubs. There is a big bar
on the second floor, with a pool table. The large lobby, where breakfast is served, has
a fish pond and dramatic winding staircase. The big drawback is that it's about a half-
mile outside the town center, but bikes are rented on the premises.

**Huy Hoang Mini Hotel.** 73 Phan Boi Chau St. ☎ **0510/861-453** or 0510/862-211. 19 units, 14 with A/C. US$10–US$35 double. Includes breakfast. No credit cards.

This is another very good bargain hotel, in a new yellow-and-white faux colonial close to the Central Market. Rooms are spotless, big, and bright, with tile floors and some older carved furniture. No phones or other amenities, and only the few US$35 rooms have bathtubs. Breakfast is served in a patio in the back with views of the river. The staff is exceedingly friendly.

✪ **Thien Trung Hotel.** 63 Phan Dinh Phung St. ☎ **0510/861-720** or 0510/861-769. Doubles US$8–US$15. 20 units, 15 with A/C. US$15 rooms include breakfast. All include taxes. No credit cards.

This is one of the most attractive bargain places I've seen in Vietnam, which explains its popularity. The Thien Trung mini-hotel is 5 years old, and had a renovation 2 years ago. Rooms are grouped attractively around the garden, where breakfast is served. They have the de rigueur tile floors and plastic furniture, but are very bright, and the tile bathrooms are bigger and nicer than most, some with bathtubs. There is a small restaurant on the premises. Note that there are no telephones. The staff is eager and friendly.

## DINING

Hoi An is a feast for the stomach as well as the eyes. Local specialties include *cao lau* (rice noodles with fresh greens, rice crackers, and croutons), white rose dumplings, shrimp in clear rice dough, and fried won ton. Seafood, particularly steamed fish, is excellent and available everywhere. Fruit shakes are another common item well worth savoring, as are the pervasive banana pancakes.

✪ **Café des Amis.** 52 Bach Dang. ☎ **0510/861-616.** Set menu 40,000 VND (US$2.80). No credit cards. NOUVEAU VIETNAMESE.

This unique place is going to gain a worldwide reputation soon. It serves some of the best food in Vietnam in a nothing-special setting. There is no menu, but you choose either the seafood or vegetarian course. A series of delicious dishes such as clear soup, fried won tons with shrimp, broiled fish, stuffed calamari, or scallops on the half shell is served up by very friendly chef Mr. Kim, who was once a taster in the Vietnamese army and who travels worldwide as a guest chef. Talk to him if you can; he's an interesting fellow. Asked why he doesn't choose to raise his prices to gourmet standards as well, he says, "I am a simple man. I like many friends." The specials change daily.

**Nha Hang Du Port.** 70 Bach Dang. No phone. Main courses 10,000–25,000 VND (US70¢–US$1.80). No credit cards. 7am–11pm. VIETNAMESE.

This place is always packed, usually by French tourists, who say they're there because they read about it in a guidebook. At the risk of jumping on the bandwagon, the food is very good. The specialty is seafood: sautéed and grilled eel, frogs, fish, and crabs. There's no ambiance to speak of, however, and the riverfront setting makes you ripe prey for the seemingly countless children selling postcards and souvenirs.

**Restaurant Thanh.** 76 Bach Dang St. ☎ **0510/861-366.** Main courses 20,000–30,000 VND (US$1.50–US$2.15). No credit cards. 7am–11pm. VIETNAMESE.

There are many restaurants along the riverfront, but Thanh has a particularly poetic atmosphere, with dark wood furniture, candles, and hanging lanterns in an old Chinese house. Very romantic. A pet bird chirps along in the background. The food is simple, good, and very fresh. Their specialty is shrimp with papaya and peanut nuts, served with crisp rice crackers. Try also the steamed fish in banana leaf or the seafood hot pot. Strawberry or snake wine (wine with a bit of added snake blood) is available for accompaniment.

✪ **Tam-Tam Café.** 110 Nguyen Thai Hoc St. (on the second floor). ☎ **0510/862-212.** Main courses US$4.50–US$9. No credit cards. Open 24 hours. ITALIAN/CONTINENTAL.

Tam-Tam is one of the coolest spots in the world, let alone Hoi An. Three French expats got together to create a bar/restaurant combo in a historic setting. The decor is very local and extremely well-done, with hanging bamboo lamps, a high wooden ceiling, and fantastic wooden figurines. The dinner menu, served in a separate restaurant room with checkered table cloths, is simple—featuring generous portions of homemade pastas, steaks, and salads—but the food is delicious. The dessert menu includes flambéed crepes, sorbet, and hot chocolate. There are two barrooms. The bigger one to the left has a pool table, book swap shelf, comfortable lounge chairs, and sofas, and is *the* place to hang out in Hoi An. The extensive, expensive-but-worth-it drinks menu includes creations like the Big Bamboo, a mix of rum, pineapple, orange, lemon, and ice.

**Trung Bac.** 87 Tran Phu St. Main courses 5,000–40,000 VND (US35¢–US$2.80). No credit cards. 7am–11pm. VIETNAMESE.

Take a break while strolling along Tran Phu for this little open-air cafe. The historic building's atmosphere is nicer than those of most stalls; and the food, featuring local delights like spicy roast chicken, grilled crab, and seafood such as fried shrimp puffs on sugarcane kebabs, is also top-rate. The menu is short but has very helpful pictures. Their banana pancakes set the standard.

**Wan Lu.** 27 Tran Phu. ☎ **0510/861-212.** Main courses 5,000–30,000 VND (US35¢–US$2.15). No credit cards. 7am–11pm. VIETNAMESE.

The locals eat here. It's an open-air place and the atmosphere is a little rough, but portions are bigger and the food more authentic; the cau lao, for example, was properly served with a dish of hot chili sauce noticeably lacking in the tourist spots.

## ATTRACTIONS

Rather than having a few outstanding cultural and historical monuments, the entire town of Hoi An is a marvel. Many of its historic buildings have been refurbished and are open to the public, including family homes where you will be greeted by a friend or member of the family and taken on a tour. As well as the private houses, there are numerous halls built by Chinese tradespeople as temples and gathering spots for members of their native provinces. You can hire a guide for about 50,000 VND (US$3.60) and buy one 50,000-VND entrance ticket from a tour agency (see "Visitor Information"), which admits you to four places: one museum, one old family home, one assembly hall, and either the Japanese Bridge or Quan Cong temples.

**The Tran Family Home and Chapel.** 21 Le Loi (on the corner of Le Loi and Phan Chu Trinh sts.). Daily 8am–5pm.

In 1802, a civil service mandarin named Tran Tu Nhuc built a family home and chapel to worship his ancestors. A favorite of Viet emperor Gia Long, he was sent to China as an ambassador, and his home reflects his high status. Elegantly designed with original Chinese antiques and royal gifts such as swords, two parts of the home are open to the public: a drawing room and an ancestral chapel. The house does a splendid job of conveying all that is exotic and interesting about these people and their period. It has even been featured as a stylish layout in a fashion magazine. The drawing room has three sections of sliding doors: the left for men, the right for women, and the center, opened only at Tet and other festivals, for dead ancestors to return home. The ancestral altar in the inner room has small boxes behind it containing relics and a biography of the deceased; their pictures hang, a little spookily, to the right of the altar. A 250-year-old book with the family history resides on a table to the right of the altar. In back of the house are a row of plants, each buried with the placenta and umbilical cord of a family child, so that the child will never forget its home. As if it could.

**Chinese Assembly Hall.** 64 Tran Phu St. Daily 8am–5pm.

This hall was built in 1740 as a meeting place for all of the resident Chinese, regardless of their native province.

**Old House of Tan Ky.** 101 Nguyen Thai Hoc St. Daily 8am–5pm.

There have been either five or seven generations of Tan living here, depending on whom you speak with. Built over 200 years ago, the four small rooms are crammed with dark wood antiques. The room closest to the street is for greeting visiting merchants. Farther in is the living room, then the courtyard, and to the back, the bedroom. The first three are open to the public. A guide who will greet you at the door will hasten to explain how the house is a perfect melding of three architectural styles: ornate Chinese detailing on some curved roof beams, a Japanese peaked roof, and a simple Vietnamese cross-hatch roof support. The mosaic decorations on the wall and furniture are aged, intricate, and amazing. Take your time to look around.

**Hainan Assembly Hall.** 178 Nguyen Duy Hieu St. Daily 8am–5pm.

The Chinese merchants from Hainan Island, in the South China Sea east of Danang, built this hall. Although it is newer than most and mostly made of concrete, it is nice nevertheless, and admission is free.

**Fukian Assembly Hall.** 46 Tran Phu St. Daily 7am–6pm.

This is the grandest of the assembly halls, built in 1697 by Chinese merchants from Fukian Province. It is a showpiece of classical Chinese architecture, at least after you pass the first gate, which was added in 1975. It's loaded with animal themes: The fish in the mosaic fountain symbolizes scholarly achievement; the unicorn flanking the ascending stairs, wisdom; the dragon, power; the turtle, longevity; and the phoenix, nobility. The main temple is dedicated to Thien Hau, goddess of the sea, on the main altar. To the left of her is Thuan Phong Nhi, a goddess who can hear ships in a range of thousands of miles, and on the right, Thien Ly Nhan, who can see them. Go around the altar for a view of a fantastic detailed miniature boat. There are two altars to the rear of the temple, the one on the left honoring a god of prosperity and on the right, fertility. The goddess of fertility is often visited by local couples hoping for children. She is flanked by 12 fairies or midwives, one responsible for each of a baby's functions: smiling, sleeping, eating, and so forth.

**Quan Kong Temple.** 168 Tran Phu St. (on the corner of Nguyen Hué). Daily 8am–5pm.

This temple was built in the early 1600s to honor a famous Chin dynasty general. Highlights inside are two gargantuan 10-foot-high wooden statues flanking the main altar, one of Quan Kong's protector and one of his adopted son. They are fearsome and impressive. Reportedly the temple was a stop for merchants who came in from the nearby river to pay their respects and pray for the general's attributes of loyalty, bravery, and virtue.

**Old House of Phun Hung.** 4 Nguyen Thi Minh Khai St. Daily 8am–5pm.

This private house, constructed in 1780, is two floors of combined architectural influences. The first floor's central roof is four-sided, showing Japanese influence, and the upstairs balcony has a Chinese rounded "turtle shell" roof with carved beam supports. The house has weathered many floods. In 1964, during a particularly bad bout, its third floor served as a refuge for other town families. The upstairs is outfitted with a trapdoor for moving furniture rapidly to safety. You may be shown around by Ms. Anh, who claims to be an eighth-generation member of the family. Tour guides at every house make such claims, but unlike the other showcase residences, the family really does seem to live in this one.

**Japanese Covered Bridge.** At the western end of Tran Phu St. 8am–5pm.

The name of this bridge in Vietnamese, Lai Vien Kieu, means "Pagoda in Japan." No one is exactly sure who first built it in the early 1600s (it has since been renovated several times), but it is usually attributed to Hoi An's Japanese community. The dog flanking one end and the monkey at the other are considered to be sacred animals to the ancient Japanese, and my guide claimed the reasoning is that most Japanese emperors were born in either the Year of the Monkey or the Dog by the Asian zodiac. The small temple inside is dedicated to Tran Vo Bac De, God of the North, beloved (or cursed) by sailors, as it is he who controls the weather.

**Museum of Trade Ceramics.** 80 Tran Phu St. Daily 8am–5pm.

Located in a traditional house, this museum describes the origins of Hoi An as a trade port and displays its most prominent trade item. Objects are from the 13th through 17th centuries, and include Chinese and Thai works as well. While many of the exhibits are in fragments, the real beauty of the place is that the very thorough descriptions are in English, giving you a real sense of the town's origins and history. Furthermore, the architecture and renovations of the old house are thoroughly explained, and you're free to wander through its two floors, courtyard, and anteroom. After all the scattered explanations at the other historic houses, you'll finally get a sense of what Hoi An architecture is all about.

**Museum of History and Culture.** 7 Nguyen Hué St. Daily 8am–5pm.

Over 2,000 years of Hoi An history are briefly covered in a circa 1653 building, with exhibits of Cham relics, trade items such as ancient ceramics, and photos of local architectural details. There are English explanations, but they are scanty. If you're seeing only one museum, make it the Museum of Trade Ceramics (above). One interesting tidbit: The name "Hoi An" literally means "water convergence" and "peace."

**House of Hoi An Traditional Handicraft.** 41 Le Loi St. Daily 8am–5pm.

This is basically a silk shop with an interesting gimmick you should take a look at: On the first floor you can see both a 17th-century silk loom and a working, machine-powered cotton one. On the second, you can see where silk come from: There are trays of silkworms feeding, then a rack of worms incubating, and then a tub of hot water where the pupae's downy covering is rinsed off and then pulled, strand by strand, onto a large skein. Cool.

**Central Market.** At Nguyen Hue and Tran Phu sts.; bordered by the Thu Bon River to the south.

If you see one Vietnamese market, make it this one, by the river on the southeast side of the city. There are endless stalls of exotic foodstuffs and services, and a special big shed for silk tailoring at the east end. Walk out to the docks to see activity there, too.

## HITTING THE BEACHES

**Cua Dai beach** is an easy 20-minute bicycle ride from Hoi An through vistas of lagoons, rice paddies, and stilt houses. Simply follow Tran Hung Dao Street out of town for about 2 miles. It will turn into Cau Dai Street halfway to the beach. The small beach seems crowded with its orderly lines of deck chairs and endless child hawkers, but the surf and sand are good and the setting, gazing at the nearby **Cham Islands,** is spectacular. The tour companies offer boat excursions in-season (Mar–Sept) to the Cham Islands, a group of seven islands about 8 miles east of Hoi An. There are also boat trips on the Thu Bon River.

## SHOPPING

Hoi An is a silk extravaganza. The quality and selection are the best in the country, and you'll have more peace and quiet while fitting than in Hanoi. **Silk suits** are made to order within 24 hours for about US$20; cashmere wool is US$25. There are count-less shops. A good way to choose is by what you see out front—if there are a material and style you like, it will help with ordering. A big favorite, with top-quality work, is **Yaly,** with two branches at 18 Nguyen Hué and 27 Tran Quy Cap streets. **Minh Loan,** at 47 Hoang Dieu St., is another good choice.

Tran Phu Street is lined with **art galleries,** and the **pottery** and **carved wood** items near the market and on Tran Phu are unique and of good quality. You won't find them anywhere else, so stock up.

## 8  An Introduction to South Central Vietnam

South central Vietnam comprises the highlands, a land of rugged mountainous terrain mainly inhabited by members of Vietnam's ethnic minorities, and a stunning coastline bordered by small islands. Outside of two established resort destinations, **Dalat** and **Nha Trang,** the rest of the region is relatively unexplored by tourists. The area saw its share of fighting during the American war, though. Names like Buon Me Thot and Pleiku will undoubtedly ring a bell. Dalat, the top destination in the region, is pop-ular with both Vietnamese and foreigners. It's a former French colonial outpost nes-tled among the hills, and still retains a serene, formal air due to the overwhelming presence of historic buildings. Nha Trang, not far from Dalat but on the coast, is also one of Vietnam's most popular destinations. The atmosphere couldn't be more dif-ferent than Dalat's, however. Nha Trang is an easygoing sea town that offers little but merrymaking, which is just as welcome in its own way.

### GETTING THERE

**BY PLANE**   Both Nha Trang and Dalat are easily accessible by plane from both Hanoi and Saigon, as are Pleiku and Buon Me Thot, if you're interested in exploring the hinterlands.

**BY TRAIN**   Nha Trang is a stop on the north-south railway line.

**BY BUS/MINIVAN**   Travel between the two major cities is a 5-hour ride by bus or minivan, easily organized through a local travel agency. For details, see "Getting There" in individual town listings.

## 9  Dalat

Dalat has a unique flavor among Vietnamese towns. Founded in 1897 as a resort for French commanders weary of the Vietnamese tropics, it still has hundreds of huge colonial mansions. Some are being restored by Vietnamese nouveau riche; others are empty and decaying. Dalat's history, combined with the welcome temperate mountain climate and pastoral hillside setting, give it the feel of a European alpine resort. Which, in fact, it once was. In and around town there are also numerous pagodas to see, in serene natural settings that lend an atmosphere far different from, for example, your typical bustling Saigon temple. Dalat is also a good place in which to glimpse the influences of the Catholic Vietnamese, represented by several churches and cathedrals. Father out of town are postcard-perfect farmlands, valleys, and waterfalls. A few ethnic minorities, including the Lat and Koho, live in and around these hills, and you can visit their small villages.

Dalat is the number-one resort destination for Vietnamese couples getting married or honeymooning. If the lunar astrological signs are particularly good, it's not unusual to see ten or so wedding parties in a single day. Many of the local scenic spots, like the Valley of Love and Lake of Sighs, pander to the giddy couples. The waterfalls are swarming with vendors, costumed "bears" and "cowboys" complete with sad-looking horses and fake pistols. A carnival air prevails. Yes, it's tacky, but isn't it interesting to see how other cultures do tacky? Plus you'll get a chance to travel, lodge, and dine with Vietnamese on a holiday, a rare opportunity.

## GETTING THERE

**BY PLANE**   You can fly to Dalat from Saigon for US$33, and from Hanoi via Hué or Danang for about US$133. You can also fly from Saigon to Buon Me Thuot or Pleiku, both US$40 one-way.

**BY BUS/CAR**   Dalat is about US$15 and 6 hours by car or bus from Nha Trang and 5½ hours from Saigon. If you're coming from Saigon, contact **Dalattourist's** branch office at 21 Nguyen An Ninh, District 1 (☎ **08/823-0227**). All of the Saigon tourist cafes have a bus service to Dalat as well.

## VISITOR INFORMATION & TOURS

The main game in town is **Dalattourist** (Lamdong Tourist Company). You can access their services at **Kim Café 2,** 9 Le Dai Hanh (☎ **063/822-479** or 063/822-366; fax 063/822-479). The **Sinh Café II** is located at 9 Phu Dong Thien Vuong (☎ **063/821-952,** fax 063/822-818).

## GETTING AROUND

There are no cyclos in Dalat, and walking isn't very pleasant, given the lack of sidewalks and number of motorbikes constantly whizzing by. It's also too hilly for comfortable biking inside the city (mountain biking in the countryside is another thing entirely). An option is to **rent a car with driver** (about US$35 a day with Dalattourist), rent your own **motorbike** for US$5, or hop on the back of somebody else's. Because the sites are often outside city limits, it makes sense to take a half- or full-day tour with Dalattourist.

## Fast Facts: Dalat

**Banks/Currency Exchange**   Industrial & Commercial Bank, 46 Hoa Binh St. (☎ 063/822-364).

**Post Office/Mail**   The main office is located at 14 Tran Phu St., across from the Novotel, and is open Monday to Saturday from 6:30am to 9:30pm.

**Telephone**   The area code for Dalat is 63.

## ACCOMMODATIONS

With its status as a popular resort area for both foreigners and Vietnamese, Dalat offers some nice lodging choices. There are plenty of mini-hotels, but they're not of the quality you might find in Hanoi, for example. You'll note that no Dalat hotel has A/C; with the year-round temperate weather, none is needed.

## VERY EXPENSIVE

✪ **Sofitel Dalat Palace.** 12 Tran Phu St. ☎ **800/SOFITEL** or 063/825-444. Fax 063/825-666. E-mail sofitel@netnam2.org.vn. 43 units. MINIBAR TV TEL. US$169–US$214 double; US$319–US$414 suite. Ask about discounts and specials. AE, DC, JCB, MC, V.

A palace indeed. Built in 1922 and recently renovated, this is a gorgeous historic hotel, one of only three five-star choices in Vietnam. From the huge fireplace and mosaic floor in the lobby to the hanging tapestries, 3,000-plus oil paintings, and thick swag curtains, it's a French country chateau with Southeast Asian colonial flavor. The large rooms, with glossy original wood floors, are finished with fine fabrics and throw rugs. The bathrooms feature hand-painted tiles and antique-style raised bathtubs and fixtures. Genuine antique French clocks and working reproduction telephones complete the picture, yet nothing feels overdone. Every room has a foyer and fireplace. Lake-view rooms open to a huge shared veranda with deck chairs. The high, high ceilings and huge corridors with hanging lamps contribute to the palatial feeling.

Amenities include business center, conference rooms, 24-hour medical service, golf course, tennis courts, mountain bikes, children's playground, 24-hour room service, airport transfer, baby-sitting, delicatessen, library, and nonsmoking rooms. Le Rabelais Restaurant serves mediocre French food in an exquisite setting. Café de La Poste is good for lunch and snacks (see "Dining"). Larry's Bar is a rather touristic stone-walled pub. Have tea in Le Rabelais, or at least a drink at the bar, to gaze over the landscaped lawn and Lake Xuan Huong, and soak up the atmosphere of gracious days gone by. Service is superb. All in all, an exquisite place that should not be missed.

## EXPENSIVE

**Novotel Dalat Hotel.** 7 Tran Phu St. ☎ **800/221-4542** or 063/825-777. Fax 063/825-888. E-mail novotel@netnam2.org.vn. MINIBAR TV TEL. US$119–US$139 double; US$189 suites. Discounts and specials are common. AE, DC, JCB, MC, V.

This is the scaled-down companion hotel to the Sofitel Palace. It was renovated in 1997 from a 1932 building that was originally the Du Parc hotel, and a lovely job was done of it. The lobby has a very interesting open-face wrought-iron lift. The smallish rooms have attractive historic touches: glossy wood floors, tasteful understated wood furniture, and molded high ceilings. The bathrooms are nice-sized and efficient, spotless and apparently brand new. The Novotel shares amenities with the Palace (above).

## MODERATE

**Golf III Hotel.** 4 Nguyen Thi Minh Khai St. ☎ **063/822-316** or 826-042. Fax 063/830-396. 78 units. MINIBAR TV TEL. US$40–US$60 double; US$70–US$100 suite. AE, JCB, MC, V.

The Golf is a three-star chain hotel, Vietnamese-style (Golf I and II are cheaper versions in Dalat). The big rooms have tacky purplish upholstery and Asian carved wood detailing, and are frayed just a tiny bit around the edges, though perfectly clean. It's worth springing for a deluxe US$60 double. These rooms have parquet floors rather than carpet, and bathrooms are huge and in nice shape, many with oversized sunken tubs. This is a honeymoon hotel, after all. In fact, the constant stream of Vietnamese wedding parties in and out lends a welcome festive air to the proceedings. If that's not your thing, consider staying elsewhere. Although the hotel is near the market and not far from the golf course, it is set back from the road and the rooms are relatively quiet. There are a restaurant, bar, massage, and steam bath.

## INEXPENSIVE

**Hang Nga Guest House.** 3 Huynh Thuc Khang St. ☎ **063/822-070.** 9 units. US$29–US$60 double. MC, V.

As well as being an interesting architectural experiment, Hang Nga (see "Attractions," below) is also a guesthouse. Or guest tree, you might call it—the nine small rooms are hollowed out of huge fantasy tree trunks, and each has a theme: the bear room, ant room, bamboo room, and so forth. Statues of said animals dominate the rooms, some of which have stalactites (perfect for head-bumping) and/or small fireplaces. Furniture consists of tree trunk chairs and tables and the like, and mirrors on the ceilings (I know what you're thinking). The eagle room, which Ms. Hang says represents the U.S., is the most majestic, and has a huge mosaic concrete tub, although the bear room (Russia, natch) isn't bad either. The honeymoon suite has two floors, the upper consisting solely of a bed in a nook. You can stay here for kicks, and it will be quite memorable, but don't expect it to be very comfortable. Thin foam mattresses, small rooms, and cold cement floors are the wee price you'll pay for staying in fantasyland.

**Lavy Hotel.** 2B Lu Gia St. ☎ **063/825-465** or 826-007. Fax 063/825-466. 37 units. MINIBAR TV TEL. US$27–US$37 double; US$48 suite. AE, JCB, MC, V.

Includes breakfast and all taxes. The Lavy is nondescript in every way, but for what it offers in Dalat, it's a fantastic value. It's only 3 years old but looks 20. The rooms have smashing blue-gray carpet, bright yellow poly bedspreads, and chipped wooden furniture, and the bathrooms betray shoddy tiling. Still, all is perfectly clean and the beds are very comfortable. While it's 2 miles (4km) from the city center, there isn't a room without a view, and the peace and quiet are priceless. The standard rooms are cheaper only because they're on the upper floors and there's no elevator, so don't spend more unless you have to. The restaurant is a fantastic rooftop spot for morning coffee. Standard services like laundry, currency exchange, and tour arrangements are offered. There's even a bar and room service. What more could you want?

**Ngoc Lan Hotel.** 42 Nguyen Chi Thanh St., Dalat, Vietnam. ☎ **063/822-136** or 823-522. Fax 063/824-032. 33 units. MINIBAR TV TEL. US$20–US$45 double. Includes breakfast and tax. JCB, MC, V.

This outfit is owned by Dalattourist, and is a very comfortable 10-year-old two-star alternative not far from the market. It's your classic government-run Vietnamese hotel. Rooms are huge, with hideously mismatched plastic/wood furniture and velveteen bedspreads, but are comfortable and clean, including the beds. Bathrooms are roomy as well and a tiny bit shoddy, with aged tile, but have hair dryers. The restaurant is big and dark, and resembles your local Firehouse Lodge, right down to also doubling as a dance and wedding hall. Well, you'll only be eating breakfast there, anyway. City noise permeates all the rooms, which is inevitable for such a central location. Ask for a room with a "garden view"—they're as quiet as you can get. The sweet staff speaks little English.

# DINING

There is nothing outstanding about the dining scene in Dalat. Meals are simply prepared and heavily influenced by Chinese cuisine. The huge variety of local ingredients, particularly fruit and vegetables, makes for fresh-tasting food. Many small restaurants are located at Phan Dinh Phung Street. Most serve breakfast from about 7am and close around 10pm; none outside of a hotel accept credit cards. Do try the artichoke tea and strawberry jam, two local specialties.

Probably the best local spot is the clean, indoor, and relatively upscale **Ngoc Hai Restaurant,** at 6 Nguyen Thi Minh Khai St. (☎ **063/825-252**). Selections from the

Western end of the spectrum include roasted chicken with potatoes, Hungarian goulash, chicken pie, and fish fritters. Tasty, inexpensive food. **Café de la Poste,** in the Palace Hotel, has good sandwiches, light meals, and desserts. It's a large, airy, upscale place, perhaps more of a restaurant than a cafe. Selections are pricey for Dalat at US$2 to US$10. **Nam Do,** 6 Nguyen Thi Minh Khai St., next to Ngoc Hai Restaurant (☎ 063/824-550), serves Chinese specialties, including hot pot. The food is non-greasy and good. There are some exotics on the menu like bear claw marinated in Chinese medicine and grilled porcupine, but the restaurant was strangely all out of those. If there is a specialty in Dalat, vegetarian food might qualify. Try **Giac Duc** on 15 Phan Dinh Phung St. for a good US$3 meal. It's your basic concrete floor, plastic-furniture stall serving fresh vegetables, noodles, and various soups, along with imitation meat products, if you so desire. While the so-called beef ribs and prawns are interesting, stick to vegetable dishes like maize soup (which is baby corn, tofu, and mushrooms), dumplings, and "sauté miscellaneous": cabbage, tofu, and green vegetables. **Hoang Lan** at 118 Phan Dinh Phung is the backpacker favorite, offering basic, good, cheap Vietnamese food.

If you need a break, stop in at **Café Tung,** a dimly lit hangout with great music, on 6 Khu Hoa Binh. They serve the world's best cocoa. The owner's son, Tran Dinh Thung, would like Frommer's readers to know that he is a very eligible and friendly bachelor born in 1955, the year of the goat in the Chinese zodiac. Interested ladies, preferably born in the year of the Pig (1959) or Cat (1963), can inquire at the bar.

## ATTRACTIONS

Much of what there is to see in Dalat hinges on the outdoors: lakes, waterfalls, and dams dominate the tourist trail. Things are spread over quite some distance, so consider a tour or renting your own car or motorbike.

Remember to avoid visiting **pagodas** between 11:30am and 2pm, when nuns and monks will be having their lunch. You may disturb them and also miss a valuable opportunity for a chat. It is also correct to leave a thousand VND or two in the donation box near the altar.

**Dalat Market (Cho Da Lat).** Central Dalat.

Huge, crowded, and stuffed with produce of all varieties, this is the top stroll-through destination in Dalat.

**Huan Huong Lake.** Central Dalat.

Once a trickle originating in the Lat village, Dalat's centerpiece, Huan Huong, was created from a dam project that was finished in 1923, demolished by a storm in 1932, and reconstructed and rebuilt (with heavier stone) in 1935.

**Hang Nga Guest House and Art Gallery.** 3 Huynh Thuc Khang St. ☎ **063/22-070.** Admission: 4,000 VND (US30¢). 7am–7pm.

Otherwise known as the Crazy House, this is a Gaudi-meets-Sesame Street theme park designed by an eccentric Russian-trained architect. The garden features a tree-trunk couple arguing, a huge spider web and towering sculpted giraffe. An overhead bird-cage tunnel contraption winds throughout. Try to meet Ms. Hang Nga, of the soft voice and very heavy eyeshadow, herself. The locals call her eccentric for some reason, but she's just misunderstood. You can also stay in the guesthouse, nine small rooms hollowed out of a huge fantasy tree trunks (see "Accommodations").

**Bao Dai's Palace.** South of Xuan Huong Lake. Admission: 10,000 VND (US70¢). Open daily 7am–8pm.

Completed in 1938, this monument to bad taste provided Bao Dai, Vietnam's last emperor, a place of rest and respite with his family. Think concrete and velvet furniture. There are 26 rooms to explore, including Bao Dai's office and the bedrooms of the royal family. Deer horns from a poor animal the emperor bagged himself hang on the wall. The place has never been restored, and indeed looks veritably untouched since the emperor's ousting, which makes it all the more interesting. You can still see the grease stains on Bao Dai's hammock pillow and the ancient steam bath in which he soaked. Don't miss the etched glass map of Vietnam in the main dining room, given to Bao Dai by a group of students in 1952. The explanations are in English, and most concern Bao Dai's family. There is pathos in reading them and piecing together the mundane fate of the former royals: this prince has a "technical" job, that one is a manager for an insurance company.

**Thien Vuong Pagoda.** 2 miles southeast of town at the end of Khe Sanh St. Daily 9am–5pm.

Otherwise known as the "Chinese Pagoda," built as it was by the local Chinese population, this circa 1958 structure is unremarkable except for its serene setting among the hills of Dalat and the very friendly nuns who inhabit it. It does have three awe-inspiring sandalwood Buddhist statues that have been dated to the 16th century. Each is 13 feet (4m) high and weighs 1½ tons. Left to right, they are Dai The Chi Bo Tat, god of power; Amithaba or Sakyamuni, Buddha; and Am Bo Tat, god of mercy.

**Dalat Railway Station (Cremaillaire Railway).** Near Xuan Huong Lake, off Nguyen Trai St. Admission: 10,000 VND (US70¢). Daily 8am–5pm.

Built in 1943, the Dalat station offers an atmospheric slice of Dalat's colonial history. You can see an authentic old wood-burning steamer train on the tracks to the rear, and stroll around inside looking at the iron-grilled ticket windows, empty now. Although the steamer train no longer makes tourist runs, a newer Japanese train makes a trip to Trai Mat Street and the Linh Phuoc pagoda (below). A ride costs US$3.

**Linh Phuoc Pagoda.** At the end of Trai Mat St. Daily 8am–5pm.

Here is another example of one of Vietnam's fantasyland glass and ceramic mosaic structures. Refurbished in 1996, this modern temple features a huge golden Buddha in the main hall, and three floors of walls and ceilings painted with fanciful murals. Go to the top floor for the eye-boggling Boddhisattva room and views of the surrounding countryside. In the garden to the right, there is a 10-foot-high dragon climbing in and out of a small lake. You can get inside of it and crawl around, too.

**Su Nu Pagoda.** 72 Hoang Hoa Tham St., in the Trai Ham area. Daily 9am–5pm.

Thirty nuns live at this peaceful temple. While the structure isn't very big or impressive, the Su Nu complex is small and you are free to stroll around the temple and serene gardens, usually accompanied by a nun. If you bring an interpreter, you may be invited to have a cup of tea and discuss the way of Buddha.

**Datanla Waterfall.** On Prenn Pass 2½ miles from Dalat. Admission: 6,000 VND (US45¢). Daily 8am–5pm.

Datanla was once a major power source for the Lat people. Today, it's a mediocre fall, pretty enough after a walk through the forest but a fully fledged tourist site. See it if you're on the way to the Truc Lam Monastery (below).

✪ **Truc Lam (Bamboo Forest) Zen Monastery.** On the right side of Tuyen Lam Lake, 4 miles (6km) from Dalat. Daily 7am–5pm.

Don't call this a pagoda. There's a difference, one you can feel as soon as you ascend the hill after going past the one—count 'em, one—tiny vendor. The complex was completed in 1994 with the aim of giving new life to the Truc Lam Yen Tu Zen sect, a uniquely Vietnamese form of Zen founded by during the Tran dynasty (A.D. 1225–1400). Adherants practice self-reliance and realization through meditation. The shrine, the main building, is notable mainly for its simple structure and peaceful air, and the quarters for nuns and monks nearby are closed to the public. However, the scenery around the monastery, with views of dam-made Tuyen Lam lake and surrounding mountains, is breathtaking. The grounds themselves are furnished with a small man-made pond and mimosa trees. As Zen master Thich Thanh Tu said, "Life is but a dream."

**Valley of Love.** Phu Dong Thien Vuong St., about 2 miles north of town center. Admission: 10,000 VND (US70¢). Daily 6am–5pm.

The Valley is scenic headquarters in Dalat. You can enjoy walking amidst the rolling hills and charming lakes, all the while enjoying the antics of the Vietnamese honeymooners zipping around on motorboats and posing for pictures with local "cowboys."

**Lake of Sighs (Ho Than Tho).** Northeast of town, along Ho Xuan Huong Rd. Admission: 10,000 VND (US70¢). Daily 7am–5pm.

This lake has such romantic connotations for the Vietnamese, you would think it was created by a fairy godmother rather than French dam work. Legend has it that a 15-year-old girl named Thuy drowned herself after her boyfriend of the same age, Tam, fell in love with another. Her gravestone still exists on the side of the lake, marked with the incense and flowers left by other similarly heart-broken souls, even though the name on the headstone reads "Thao," not "Thuy." The place is crammed with honeymooners in paddleboats and motorboats.

**Prenn Falls.** At the foot of Prenn Mountain pass, 6.25 miles from Dalat. Admission: 10,000 VND (US70¢). 7am–5pm.

The Prenn falls are actually quite impressive, thundering down from a great height— and you can follow a path under them, which adds some thrill factor. The Prenn experience includes cavorting costumed bears, staged photo opportunities, and vendors selling every kind of tacky knickknack available.

## EXCURSION: THE LAT & CHICKEN VILLAGES

The name of Dalat is actually a colonial mispronunciation of the town's original name, *Dao Lach,* with *dao* meaning "water" and *Lach* referring to a minority tribe now known as Lat. The Lat still inhabit hills about 7½ miles outside the city, along with other minorities such as the Chil, Sré, and Koho peoples. If you go with a tour group, you'll probably see the inside of a Lat home and hear some traditional music from a small band of costumed performers. Afterwards, you'll share a communal pot of rice wine.

You can also visit the Koho. Their home is known as Chicken Village because of the 20-foot tall statue of said chicken. Why a chicken? Nobody knows. The Koho are very friendly, and you can walk around the rustic village and perhaps purchase samples of their outstanding hand-woven crafts. Visiting these places independently involves getting a government permit from Dalattourist for US$5, so you may as well sign up with Dalattourist for a half-day trip at US$7.

## SPORTS & OUTDOOR ACTIVITIES

Dalat is the perfect setting for **hiking** and **mountain biking.** Dalattourist offers guides and rents mountain bikes. There are a few adventure-travel outfitters in town: **Action Dalat,** 114–3 Thang 2 St. (☎ **063/829-422** or 821-833, fax 063/820-532), is a French outfit that offers overnight trekking trips to hill villages, fishing, and paragliding. **Phuong Nam Co,** at 6 Ho Tung Mao St. (☎ **063/822-781,** fax 063/822-138), offers camping, trekking, hunting, jeep tours, and canoeing in the Mount Elephant area. Two-day packages, including cooks and guides, are priced at US$50 to US$100.

Golfers can try the **Dalat Palace Golf Club's** impressive 18-hole course. One round costs Palace or Novotel guests US$65; all others pay US$85, plus a mandatory US$10 caddie fee. There is a US$50 special after 3:30pm. For reservations call ☎ 063/821-201.

## 10  Nha Trang

Nha Trang at the moment is a mid-sized town of about 200,000 people, and is Vietnam's number-one resort area. While not a particularly charming town, its surf isn't bad and the beach has a breathtaking setting, with views of the more than 20 surrounding islands. There is no shortage of good places to stay and excellent fresh seafood to eat.

Unfortunately, far from becoming a gracious hideaway, Nha Trang looks like it's on the way to becoming raucous, and it might as well just go ahead. If you accept it as such, it's a fine place at which to spend 2 or 3 days frolicking in the surf, taking a snorkeling or diving cruise to the nearby islands, or enjoying the services of one of the many massage, manicure, and depilatory practitioners roaming the beach (and even the cafes). The main drag is **Tran Phu Street,** right off the ocean. It's a wide boulevard lined with palm trees off which lie most hotels and restaurants.

Culturally, there are a few things to keep you occupied: the **Pasteur Institute** is here, offering glimpses into the life and work of one of Vietnam's most famous expats; there is the interesting **Long Son Pagoda** and the well-preserved **Po Nagar Cham Temple.**

Off-season (from October through March), the surf is far too rough for swimming and sports, and you may want to rethink stopping at Nha Trang at all.

### GETTING THERE

**BY PLANE**   Nha Trang is 1,350 km from Hanoi and 450 km from Saigon. Vietnam Airlines operates flights from Saigon for US$47, from Hanoi for US$105, from Hué for US$61, and from Danang for US$40.

**BY CAR/BUS**   If you choose to drive from Hoi An to Nha Trang, it's a 10-hour trip and will cost you about US$120 by car. An arduous 12-hour bus or minibus ride will cost only US$11. Nha Trang is also a stop on the Kim or Sinh Café's Open Tour, a one-way bus ticket from Hanoi to Saigon, or back the other way.

**BY TRAIN**   Nha Trang is a stop on Vietnam's major rail route; on an express, it's 26 hours and US$64 from Hanoi; 9 hours and US$49 from Danang; and 11½ hours and US$39 from Ho Chi Minh City. All prices are for a soft-sleeper with AC.

### GETTING AROUND

The main street in Nha Trang, Tran Phu, runs for about 2 miles (4 km), and attractions like the Po Ngar Cham towers are yet another mile out. **Taxis** are scarce, and tend to congregate around the major hotels. **Renting a bike** from your hotel for US$1 to US$2 a day is a very good option, as are **cyclos.** A cross-town trip will cost about 10,000 VND (US70¢).

# Nha Trang

0 .1 mi / 160 m
N

Duong Thang

Nguyen Binh Khiem

Nguyen Hong Son

Central Market

Duong Thang

Quang Trung

Duong Phan Chu Trinh

Pasteur

Duong

Thuong Sai

Tran Quy Cap

Thong Nhat

Hoang Van Thu

Duong Yersin

Ly Tu Trong

Duong Thai Nguyen

Duong Le Hong Phong

Duong Nguyen Trai

Duong Le Thanh Ton

Hoang Hoa Tham

Duong Tran Hung Dao

Tran Phu Street

Duong Tran Nguyen Han

Duong To Hien Thanh

Duong Nguyen Thien Thuat

Duong Hung Vuong

Nguyen Thi Minh Khai

Biet Thu

## Accommodations
Ana Mandara/Ana Pavillion 17
Bao Dai Hotel 18
Hai Yen Hotel 9
Nha Trang Lodge 11
Phu Quy 12
Post Hotel 4
Que Huong Hotel 16
Vien Dong Hotel 10

## Dining
Banana Split 7
Lac Canh 3
Little Italy 19
Ngoc Suong 15
Nha Trang Sailing Club 14
Restaurant 46 13

## Attractions
Alexandre Yersin Museum 5
Hon Chong Promontory 1
Hon Mieu Island 18
Long Son Pagoda 8
Po Ngar Cham Towers 2

## Other
Post Office 4
Vietcom Bank 6

## VISITOR INFORMATION & TOURS

You'll more than likely end up booking tickets and boat tours through your hotel in Nha Trang. If not, **Khanh Hoa Tourist** in the Vien Dong hotel at 1 Tran Hung Dao St. (☎ **058/822-753**) is an efficient organization. **Que Huong Travel Services,** at the Que Huong Hotel at 60 Tran Phu (☎ **058/825-047**), are also competent and can handle all your booking needs, although their English is scanty. For bus tickets and a tour on to Dalat, contact **Sinh Café III,** 9 Nguyen Thien Thuat, at the My A Hotel (☎ **058/827-312**). They also offer a "special tour for long-legged people." That either means a big minibus, or a lot of walking.

## Fast Facts: Nha Trang

**Currency Exchange/Banks**   Vietcombank's local branch is located at 17 Quang Trung St. (☎ 058/821-483). Hours are 7:30 to 11am and 1:30 to 4pm. It offers the usual currency and traveler's check exchange and credit card cash withdrawal services.

**Internet/E-mail**   One of the best cyber cafes in the whole country, fast and efficient, is Internet Services, at 4 Yersin St. Rates are cheap at 1,000 VND (US5¢) a minute. If you're there for a bit, the helpful staff will serve you a Coke.

**Post Office/Mail**   The main branch is at 4 Le Loi St. ☎ 058/823-866. Hours are 6:30am to 10pm Monday to Saturday. DHL express mail services and Internet access are available. There is another branch at 50 Le Thanh Ton, also with expensive Internet services at 10,000 VND (US70¢) per 10 minutes.

**Telephone**   The city code for Nha Trang is 58.

## ACCOMMODATIONS

There are many options in Nha Trang, but the scene is dominated by blah mid-end and substandard budget choices. Given the number of hotels under construction, though, that's sure to change soon.

### EXPENSIVE

✪ **Ana Mandara Beachside Resort.** Beachside, Tran Phu Boulevard. ☎ **58/829-829.** Fax 58/829-629. http://soneva-pavilion.com/ana-mandara. 68 units. A/C MINIBAR TV TEL. US$137–263 double/villa. Extra bed US$20. AE, DC, JCB, MC, V.

It's the little things that make this resort special: the native art and handiwork in the halls and rooms, the bowl with floating flowers in the bathroom, the basin of rainwater on your private veranda for rinsing sandy feet, the burning incense in the open-air lobby. This attention to detail, as well as the secluded layout of the "Vietnamese village" units, gives the whole resort a personable, small-scale feel. Each room has a rattan rising ceiling with wood beams. Rooms are good-sized, with stylish furniture and tile floors, and the bathroom has a huge window facing a private outdoor enclosure. Very special. Thirty-six units face the beach, and others face exotic-plant landscaping (the plants are labeled, of course).

Facilities and services include a business center, conference room, fitness center with private massage pavilion, tennis, jet-skiing, diving, Hobie-cat sailing, para-sailing, wind-surfing, fishing and snorkeling in season (Feb–Oct), boat tours, baby-sitting, room service, laundry, library, and free airport transportation. The lobby and swimming pool (with outdoor Jacuzzi) have spectacular ocean views, as does the splendid restaurant. Fantastic Ana Pavilion, open 24 hours, offers a diverse international menu (see "Dining"). There's also a cocktail lounge and a pool bar. The staff is super friendly, and they mean it. The prices are reasonable as well. It's a dreamscape you will hate to leave.

## MODERATE

**Bao Dai Hotel (Bao Dai's Villas).** Cau Da, Vinh Nguyen/Nha Trang, Vietnam. ☎ **058/881-049** or 881-048. Fax 058/881-471. 40 units. A/C MINIBAR TV TEL. US$25–US$80 double. Includes all taxes. No credit cards.

Next to the Ana Mandara, the Villas are the most atmospheric place to stay in Nha Trang. Built in 1923 as a seaside resort for then-emperor Bao Dai, the hotel is a cluster of plain colonial-style buildings set high on an oceanside hill. The hotel is so far out of town it's almost in another, but the peaceful atmosphere is a plus. The least expensive US$25 rooms, in two characterless new buildings, are small but nevertheless bright, spotless, and comfortable, with in-perfect-shape tile floors and bathrooms and wood furniture. If you go for the more expensive sea-view rooms, be prepared for heavy, dark carved wood and stained carpets, though their cavernous size and shuttered windows opening onto spectacular vistas make up for a lot. The bathrooms are nothing special, but are sizable and clean, with bathtubs. The hotel also organizes scuba diving and snorkeling and boat excursions to nearby Hon Mieu Island, and there is a private cove for sunbathing. The usual transport rentals are available, including an all-day car for US$35. The staff is extremely affable. Other amenities and services include laundry, room service, and a tennis court.

**Hai Yen Hotel.** 40 Tran Phu St. ☎ **058/822-828** or 058/822-974. Fax 058/821-902. 110 units. A/C MINIBAR TV TEL. US$25–US$47 double; US$63.50 suite. AE, JCB, MC, V.

The Hai Yen is owned by the Thanh Hoa tourism company, the same folks who own Vien Dong, and the two are virtually indistinguishable. It's next door, and they share recreational facilities. The Hai Yen is a bit quieter, and it has outdoor hallways and an open, airier feeling. The unfortunate blue indoor-outdoor carpeting is present, however, as are the super-basic but very clean and new bathrooms. And whoops, there's that hideous plastic furniture in the deluxe rooms on up. Plastic flowers, too. The suites have even more of same, but at least there are bathtubs. The service is rather impersonal. Try to get rooms not facing noisy Tran Phu Street. There is a big indoors restaurant.

**Nha Trang Lodge.** 42 Tran Phu St. ☎ **058/810-500** or 810-900. Fax 058/828-800. E-mail: Nt-lodge@dng.vnn.vn. 124 units. A/C MINIBAR TV TEL. US$50–US$95 double; US$145 suite. Includes breakfast. Extra bed US$20. AE, JCB, MC, V.

The 3-year-old lodge calls itself a "business hotel," and indeed it is a well-run and accommodating high-rise. Average-size rooms are chain-hotel style, with floral bedspreads and modern furniture, yet they are pleasing. For one, the carpet is nice and the furniture matches. The bathrooms are a nice size, with marble finishes. Everything is solid and comfortable, particularly the beds. There are in-room safes and big TVs, too. Spring for the US$95 ocean view if possible, with balcony, on an upper floor away from street noise. The big 24-hour Asian/Continental restaurant is clean and bright. There are also an efficient business center, conference rooms, disco/karaoke, barber, lounge with billiards, swimming pool, massage, tennis, room service, and travel services. The staff is well-trained.

**Que Huong Hotel.** 60 Tran Phu Blvd. ☎ 058/825-047 or 827-365. Fax 058/825-344. 45 units. A/C MINIBAR TV TEL. US$60 double; US$100 suite. Includes breakfast, tax, and service charge. MC, V.

This 1-year-old hotel is bright and bland. It is four floors of a squarish building across the street from the beach, but set back far enough from the road to be quiet. Ten minutes after leaving a room, you would be hard pressed to describe it, but the overall impression is favorable. Carpets, tasteful wood furnishings, and balconies come to mind. Beds are firm and comfortable. The bathrooms are weak—badly tiled and already showing signs of wear, though there are hair dryers. Suites have two bathrooms and are great for families. There are capable travel agents in the lobby. An Asian/Continental restaurant feeds the hungry hordes, and to keep them amused, there are a swimming pool, tennis court, billiards, massage, sauna, and bar disco. Que Huong also offers laundry services and a barber.

**Vien Dong Hotel.** 1 Tran Hung Dao St. ☎ **058/821-606** or 058/821-608. Fax 058/821-912. 102 units. A/C MINIBAR TV TEL. US$30–US$40 double; US$70 suite. Includes tax and service charge. AE, JCB, MC, V.

If you're on a tour, you're probably booked here. It's big and blah and impersonal, but it's a comfortable three-star with all the amenities, and having lots of people around somehow helps. Rooms have basic blue carpet and basic yellow bedspreads and simple wood furniture, and aren't especially large. Mattresses are sturdy foam. Bathrooms are clean and tidy tile, without counters and most with simple showerhead-on-wall fixtures, although they have hair dryers. "College dorm room" comes to mind. Suites have almost unbearably ugly plastic furniture and flowers, although they also have bathtubs. There are an inviting outdoor restaurant featuring nightly music, a swimming pool, a sauna, billiards, tennis, and badminton on the premises. The lobby has the best travel services in town.

## INEXPENSIVE

**Phu Quy.** 54 Hung Vuong St. ☎ **058/810-609.** 12 units, 8 with A/C. US$8–US$15 double. No credit cards.

If you're looking for your basic lowest-end accommodations, you can't go wrong here. One of many narrow mini-hotels that somehow seem to stand in groups of three in Nha Trang, the Phu Quy sports small, bright, and very clean rooms with brand-new plastic furniture. The beds are comfortable and bathrooms small, with shower-in-room facilities. There are no views to speak of, but go for the top floors to escape street noise. Of course, that means climbing lots of stairs. No amenities whatsoever, but breakfasts are good and cheap at 6,000 VND (US45¢) or so, and of course the hotel will book tickets. It is family-run, and owner Mr. Phu is as nice as they come.

**Post Hotel.** 2 Le Loi St. ☎ **058/821-252** or 058/821-250. Fax 058/824-205. 20 units. A/C MINIBAR TV TEL. US$27 double. Includes tax. MC, V.

This is a decent, unassuming budget hotel. The large rooms have old tile floors and carved wood furniture, very basic but clean. The bathrooms are large and in good condition, but only the ground floor rooms have bathtubs. The location of its attractive white colonial-style exterior is excellent; facing the ocean on a quiet stretch of Tran Phu street, it's still close to the center of town. Try for a room facing the beach. Other than Internet access, there are no services and the staff speaks little English.

# DINING
## EXPENSIVE

✪ **Ana Pavillion.** Tran Phu Blvd. (at the Ana Mandara Resort). ☎ **058/829-829.** Main courses US$11–US$17.50. Prix fixe menus US$14–US$17. AE, JCB, MC, V. ASIAN/CONTINENTAL.

The Ana Pavillion serves exquisite food in an elegant oceanfront veranda, with both indoor and outdoor seating. The food is creatively prepared and beautifully presented, and portions are healthy. Try the creamed pumpkin or taro soup with shrimp, the shredded beef and avocado salad, and the Thai-style blue crabs stir-fried in curry. For dessert, there is black sticky-rice with coconut and banana fritters, and chocolate mousse served in a fresh coconut, with coconut shavings on top. Incredible. The Pavillion also offers set dinner menus for US$14 to US$17; a fabulous value.

**Little Italy.** Tran Phu St., Huong Duong Center (just south of the Ana Mandara resort). ☎ **058/828-964.** 9am–10pm. Main courses 40,000–60,000 VND (US$2.90–US$4.35). No credit cards. CLASSIC ITALIAN.

Who knows why good Italian food is so easy to get in Vietnam? Here is yet another example. Little Italy serves up tasty pastas and salads, and the bruschetta, with good olive oil, fresh tomatoes, capers, and garlic, is to die for. The house wine, available by the glass, isn't bad, but the pizza is only so-so. Service is friendly and attentive. The casual, open-air seaside setting can also provide a good lunch experience, as guests can swim and use the restaurant's deck chairs.

## MODERATE

**Ngoc Suong.** 16 Tran Quang Khai St. ☎ **058/854-516.** Main courses 25,000– 150,000 VND (US$1.80–US$10.80). No credit cards. 10am–midnight. SEAFOOD.

Nha Trang has dozens of good seafood restaurants, but this one leads the pack. In the very pleasant thatched outdoor pavilion or the vaguely nautical, softly lit interior, fresh, simply prepared seafood is served by a competent wait staff. If you like oysters, get them grilled, small but succulent. The lyrical menu includes "crabs claws enrobed in shrimp paste," "boiled pork soak in macerated mackerel" and "crab steamed in coconut milk." There are plenty of locals here adding to the congenial atmosphere.

## INEXPENSIVE

**Banana Split.** 58 Quang Trung St. ☎ **058/829-115.** Main courses 12,000–30,000 VND (US85¢–US$2.15) No credit cards. 7am–11pm. VIETNAMESE/WESTERN.

Banana Split is the number-one roadside stall in which to meet other wanderers and have a snack, and maybe even a pedicure from the oft-visiting practitioner. It offers good pasta, spring rolls, and noodle soups, and their list of fruit shakes could well be the longest in Vietnam. The folks running the place are very friendly. Other travelers rave about the ice cream, but I still don't think it's Vietnam's strong suit. The Banana Split next door claims to be the "original," as does this one, which results in some snarling exchanges between the ladies trying to entice customers to one or the other. You probably won't notice much of a difference either way.

**Lac Canh.** 11 Hang Ca St., ☎ **058/821-391.** 7am–11pm. Main courses 15,000– 38,000 VND (US$1–US$2.75). No credit cards. CHINESE/VIETNAMESE.

There's nothing special about the Chinese-influenced Vietnamese cuisine served here, except for the specialty of the house: marinated prawns, fish, and fresh vegetables that you grill yourself on a rustic cast-iron flaming brazier. The place is packed with local and tourists. Try to sit outdoors, as the atmosphere is smoky and hygiene isn't the management's top concern. Definitely a B.Y.O.C. (bring your own chopsticks) kind of place.

> **Travel Tip**
>
> After a snack at Banana Split (see listing, above), step next store to **Lou Kim,** at 56 Quang Trung, for a 50,000-VND (US$3.60) haircut. French expat Jean-Luc has a very flamboyant, unorthodox cutting style, but the results are *trés chic.*

**Nha Trang Sailing Club.** 72–74 Tran Phu St. ☎ **058/826-528.** 7am–11pm. Bar open until 2am. Main courses 10,000–60,000 VND (US70¢–US$4.30). No credit cards. VIETNAMESE/CONTINENTAL.

Stop by this oceanside open-air bar/restaurant for a real Western breakfast, if nothing else. A good bet is their pancakes, uniquely not greasy and served with real butter. There are other Western standbys such as macaroni and cheese and hamburgers, tasty if not authentic, as well as the usual Nha Trang seafood selections. The setting, in a large hut, can't be beat. You can lounge on the beach and buy or swap a book from their well-stocked rack (have a chat with the rack's proprietor, who speaks excellent English and is an interesting fellow). The bar swings at night.

**Restaurant 46.** 46 Tran Phu St. ☎ **058/828-505.** 15,000–120,000 VND (US$1–US$8.65). No credit cards. 6am–11pm. SEAFOOD.

This is similar in form and function to Restaurant 76, Restaurant 48, and many of the other name/number places in town, but this one's outstanding, as any local will tell you. Restaurant 46 serves grilled and sautéed seafood in a very unpretentious outdoor atmosphere, with plastic chairs and tablecloths under a makeshift awning. This is great place to kick back, order a cold Coke or beer, and tackle mounds of oysters, sautéed escargot, fried abalone with mushroom, or roe crabs in tamarind sauce. There is a very long, easy-to-understand English menu.

## ATTRACTIONS

**Po Ngar Cham Towers.** 1¼ miles out of the city center on 2 Thang 4, at the end of Xom Bong Bridge. Admission: 10,000 VND (US70¢). Daily 7:30am–5pm.

This standing temple complex was built from the 8th to 13th centuries to honor goddess Yang Ino Po Ngar, mother of the kingdom. It was built over a wooden temple burned by the Javanese in 774. There were originally 10 structures; four remain. The main tower, or Po Ngar kalan, is one of the tallest Cham structures ever built. Its square tower and three-story cone roof are exemplary of Cham style. It has more remaining structural integrity than many sites, giving you a good idea of how it might have looked in all its glory. In the vestibule can be seen two pillars of carved epitaphs of Cham kings, and in the sanctuary there are two original carved doors. The statue inside is of the goddess Bharagati, a.k.a. Po Ngar, on her lotus throne. It was carved in 1050. The Po Ngar temples are still in use by local Buddhists, and the altars and smoking incense add to the intrigue of the architecture. Detracting from the whole experience are kitsch stands and endless hawkers.

Some advice: Take a taxi and perhaps see the Towers and Promontory (see below) on the same trip. A bike, cyclo, or motorbike ride along the truck-heavy road out of town is one of the most unpleasant and dangerous in all of Vietnam. If you do chance it, remember that the inner side of the street seems to be reserved for motorists going directly against the flow of traffic.

For details on Cham history, see "Who Are the Cham?" in the Danang & China Beach section.

**Hon Chong Promontory.** Nguyen Dinh Chieu St. North of the Po Ngar Towers on 2 Thang 4. Admission 10,000 VND (US70¢). Daily 8am–4pm.

The promontory offers a good view of the coastline and surrounding islands.

**Long Son Pagoda.** Thai Nguyen St. Daily 8am–5pm.

The main attraction at this circa-1930s pagoda is the huge white Buddha on the hillside behind, the symbol of Nha Trang. Around the base of the Buddha are portraits of

# Alexandre Yersin, Superman Scientist

Alexandre Yersin was a French scientist and explorer born in Switzerland in 1863, a man of monumental exploits and achievements. He sailed to Indochina as an onboard doctor and ended up settling in Vietnam, where he became the country's leading expert on tropical diseases. From 1892 to 1894, he undertook surveying tasks for the French, covering land from Nha Trang to Phnom Penh. Exploring the Central Highlands in 1893 to find the best routes for roadways, Yersin came upon the Lang Bian plateau. On the journey, he survived attacks by bandits and wild elephants with no damage greater than a spear wound and a broken fibula. Upon his return, Yersin urged the French to establish a convalescence center on the cool, green hills near Lang Bian for Frenchmen adversely affected by Vietnam's moist tropical climate. Hence Dalat was founded in 1897.

From 1898 to 1902, Yersin lived in Nha Trang, founding the Pasteur Institute there. He was also inspector general at the Dalat, Saigon, and Hanoi Pasteur Institutes. His most famous accomplishment, however, was isolating the bacteria that causes plague.

Although Vietnam's major roadways do not follow the path laid out by Yersin, you will note that many streets nevertheless bear his name. He died in 1943 and is buried in Nha Trang. A museum has been established there at the site of his former offices.

monks who immolated themselves to protest against the corrupt Diem regime. After climbing the numerous flights of stairs, you'll also be rewarded with a bird's-eye view of Nha Trang.

**Alexandre Yersin Museum.** In the Pasteur Institute, Tran Phu St. Admission: 10,000 VND (US70¢). Mon–Sat 8–11am and 2–4pm.

Here you can get an inkling of the work of one of Vietnam's greatest heroes, expat or not. Swiss doctor Yersin founded Dalat, isolated a plague-causing bacteria, and researched agricultural methods and meteorological forecasting, all to the great benefit of the Vietnamese. He founded the Institute in 1895. On display are his desk, overflowing library, and scientific instruments.

**Hon Mieu Island.** The Bao Dai Hotel (☎ 058/881-049) operates a boat trip to the island, as do the local tour operators.

The largest of the surrounding islands, Hon Mieu has a fishing village, Bai Soi, that isn't very active any longer but features many seafood restaurants. There is also an aquarium of sorts, consisting of a lake divided into three sections: one for ornamental fish, one for edible fish, and one for carnivorous varieties; there's a wharf to stand on.

## SPORTS & OUTDOOR ACTIVITIES

Diving is big in Nha Trang, in season (Mar–Sept). The **Blue Diving Club** (☎ 058/825-390, fax 058/824-214) is located at the Coconut Grove Resort opposite 40 Tran Phu St. It has day-long diving excursions including lunch for US$60 per person. They also offer PADI courses and "try dives." **Vietravel,** 80 Tran Phu St. (☎ 058/811-375), is the other major dive company, and offers a full-day program for US$50. The **Nha Trang Sailing Club** (☎ 058/826-528) also rents catamarans, jet skis, and paddleboats, and offers waterskiing and para-sailing.

You can also take a boat cruise to some of the 20 surrounding islands. **Mama Hahn's Boat Trips** offers a 9am to 5pm, US$7 boat excursion with snorkeling, a seafood or vegetarian lunch, and plenty of booze for sale. Some enjoy its Bacchanalian party-boat atmosphere—I heard New Zealanders describe it as "a piss trip"—while others might enjoy the more low-key approach of competitor **Mama Lanh.** You can book Mama Hanh at the Nha Trang Sailing Club or Banana Split Café, and Mama Lanh's at the left-side Banana Split Café (there are two; see "Dining," above).

## NHA TRANG AFTER DARK

Nha Trang has a few lively beachfront bars where tourists congregate to swap stories. Both the **Coconut Grove Resort (Cay Dua),** opposite 40 Tran Chu St., and the **Nha Trang Sailing Club** at 72–74 Tran Phu St. (see "Dining," above) have open-air bamboo hut scenes until about 1am.

## 11  Ho Chi Minh City (Saigon)

Ho Chi Minh City, or Saigon as it is once again commonly known, is a relatively young Asian city founded in the 18th century. Settled mainly by civil war refugees from north Vietnam and Chinese merchants, it quickly became a major commercial center. When the French took over a land they called Cochin China, Saigon became the capital. After the French left in 1954, Saigon remained the capital of south Vietnam until national reunification in 1975.

Saigon is still Vietnam's commercial headquarters, brash and busy, with a keen sense of its own importance. Located on the Saigon River, it's Vietnam's major port and largest city, with a population of almost five million people. True to its reputation, it is noisy, crowded, and messy. Yet Saigon is also exciting and historic, with wide downtown avenues flanked by pristine colonials. It has an attitude all its own.

Some of Saigon's tourism highlights: the **Vietnam History Museum;** the grisly **War Remnants Museum;** and Cholon, the **Chinese district,** with its pagodas and exotic stores. Dong Khoi Street—formerly fashionable Rue Catinat during the French era and Tu Do, or Freedom Street, during the American war—is still a strip of grand colonial hotels, chic shops, and cafes. The food in Saigon is some of the best Vietnam has to offer, the nightlife sparkles, and the shopping is good. The city is also a logical jumping-off point for excursions to other southerly destinations: the **Mekong Delta,** the **Cu Chi tunnels,** and **Phan Thiet beach.**

### GETTING THERE

**BY PLANE**    See the beginning of this chapter for information on international flights into Ho Chi Minh City. There is an international departure tax of US$10. Domestically, Saigon is linked by **Vietnam Airline** flights from Hanoi (US$137), Hué, Danang, Hoi An, Nha Trang, and Dalat. The departure tax is 20,000 VND (US$1.35).

**Getting into Town from the Airport:** A metered cab to the center of town will cost about VND 70,000 (US$5.05), and you should bargain with a private cab for about that amount. If the hotel you're going to offers **transport service,** book it. At US$7 to US$10, it may not be much more expensive than a taxi and may save you lots of trouble. You can also call **Airport Taxi** at ☎ **08/844-6666.** It has a set price to the city center.

**BY TRAIN**    Ho Chi Minh City is one of the two ends of Vietnam's major railway route, which runs along the coastline and stops at Hué, Danang, and Nha Trang. From Hanoi, the trip takes about 36 hours and costs US$158 for a soft berth with A/C.

---

**Scam Alert**

If you go with a taxi driver, even a metered one, from the airpport in Saigon, watch out for the **hotel bait-and-switch scam.** Drivers get commissions for leading tourists to one hotel or another, and it's common for them to insist that the hotel you're going to is full, or closed, or has some other problem, and to try to drop you elsewhere. Sit tight until you're at your intended destination. It may help for you to agree in writing where you're going before setting out.

---

**BY BUS/MINIVAN**    By bus, Saigon is about 5½ hours from Dalat, the nearest major city.

**BY CAR**    For safety reasons alone, if you're taking wheels it is better to book a minivan with a tour or group.

## GETTING AROUND

**BY BICYCLE & MOTORBIKE**    Saigon is blessed with the country's most chaotic traffic, so you might want to think twice before renting a motorbike or bicycle, which aren't as easily available as in other towns.

**BY CYCLO**    Cyclos are available for an hourly rental of about 20,000 VND (US$1.45). But they simply are not a good option in Saigon, especially outside District 1. First, drivers have an odd habit of not speaking English (or indeed, any other language) halfway through your trip and taking you to places you never asked to see, or simply driving around in circles pretending to be confused. Second, riding in a slow, open conveyance amid thousands of motorbikes and cars is unpleasant and dangerous. Third, drive-by thefts from riders is common. And this is during daytime hours! Don't even think about it at night.

**BY TAXI**    Taxis are clustered around the bigger hotels and restaurants. They cost 6,000 VND (US45¢) at flag fall and 1,000 VND (US5¢) or so for every kilometer after—far cheaper than in Hanoi. You can call **Airport Taxi** (☎ **08/844-6666**) or **Saigon Taxi** (☎ **08/822-6688**), among others.

**BY CAR**    Your most economical bet may be to simply hire a car and driver for the day from Ann's Tourist or Saigontourist (see "Visitor Information & Tours") for US$25 a day within city limits.

## VISITOR INFORMATION & TOURS

Every major tourist agency has its headquarters or a branch in Saigon. They will be able to book tours and travel throughout the city and the southern region, and usually countrywide as well.

- ✪ **Ann's Tourist Co.,** 58 Ton That Tung St., District 1 (☎ **08/833-2564;** fax 08/823-3866; e-mail anntours@yahoo.com), has a great reputation that is entirely well-deserved. It's hard to imagine a friendlier, better-run travel organization. Ann's specializes in custom tours for individuals or small groups. They can be relatively expensive, but they'll help you do virtually anything you want to in Vietnam. Ask for director Tony Nong and tell him Frommer's sent you.

- **Vidotour,** 41 Dinh Tien Hoang St., District 1 (☎ **08/829-1438,** fax 08/829-1435), is a very good upscale operation with excellent English-speaking guides.

- **Saigontourist,** 49 Le Thanh Ton St., District 1 (☎ **08/829-8914;** fax 08/822-4987; e-mail sgt.vn@bbdvn.vnd.net), is a faceless, pricey, government-run group, but they'll get you where you want to go.

# Ho Chi Minh City (Saigon)

## Accommodations
Bong Sen Hotel Annex **25**
Grand Hotel **30**
Hong Hoa Hotel **40**
Hotel Caravelle **24**
Hotel Continental **19**
Hotel Majestic **34**
Hotel Sofitel Plaza **9**
Huong Sen Hotel **27**
Kimdo Royal International
   Hotel **31**
Mondial Hotel **29**
New World Hotel Saigon **39**
Norfolk Hotel **22**
Omni Saigon Hotel **1**
Oscar Hotel **32**
Rex Hotel **23**
Saigon Prince Hotel **35**
Spring Hotel **18**

## Dining
Ancient Town **4**
BiBi **14**
Café Mogambo **15**
Camargue **16**
Cappuccino **41**
Chao Thai **13**
Lemongrass/Augustin/
   Globo Cafe **28**
Restaurant 13 **43**
Saigon Sakura **26**
Spices **36**
Yesterday Grill & Bar **3**

## Attractions
Ben Thanh Market **38**
City Hall **20**
Emperor Jade Pagoda **2**
Former U.S. Embassy **10**
General Post Office
   (Buu Dien) **8**
Ho Chi Minh Museum **37**
Museum of the Revolution **21**
Notre Dame Cathedral **7**
Reunification Palace **6**
Saigon History Museum **11**
Saigon Opera House **17**
War Remnants Museum **5**
Zoo and Botanical Gardens **12**

Thi Nghe Le Van Sy River
Thang
Dong Chinh
Ky Sau
Ly Thi
Vo Phu
Bien
Cach Chie
Dien Mang Tan
Dinh Thang
Van Tat
Cao Thi
Nguyen Anh
Vo Nguyen Nguyet
Duong Suong
Thang Le Lai
Pham Ngu Lao
Trai Bui Vien
Nguyen Nguyen Cu Trinh
Van Nguyen Dao
Cu Co Bac
Hung Co Gian
Tran Duong
Chuong River
Ben Nghe Don
Ben Ben Van

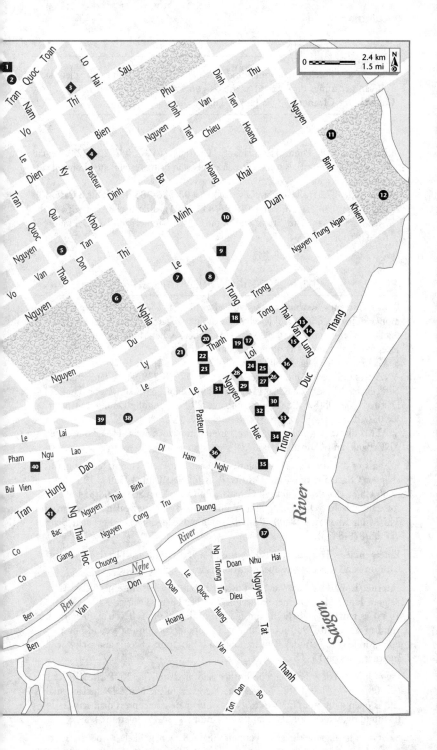

> **Travel Tip: Laundry**
>
> Almost every hotel will do your laundry, with variable results in the smaller places. You can get things dry-cleaned at the **Saigon Prince,** 63 Nguyen Hué St., or at **Capital Dry Cleaners,** 73 Ba Huyen Thanh Quan St.

- **Exotissimo,** 2 Dinh Tien Hoang, District 1 (☎ **08/825-1723;** e-mail exosgn@hcm.vnn.vn), is run by French expats who deliver careful attention and customized packages.
- **Kim Café,** 272 De Tham St., District 1 (☎ **08/836-9859**), and **Sinh Café,** 179 Pham Ngu Lao St., District 1 (☎ **08/835-5601**), offer backpacker trips to the Mekong Delta for 1 to 3 days, and to the Cu Chi Tunnels and Lao Dai Holy See for day trips.

# Fast Facts: Ho Chi Minh City

**Banks/Currency Exchange**   As with elsewhere in Vietnam, you can change money in banks, hotels, and jewelry stores. The exchange rate in Saigon is better than for many smaller cities. Note that Diner's Club cards are more readily accepted here than in any other Vietnamese city.

Major banks in Saigon: ABN Amro, 162 Pasteur, District 1, ☎ 08/822-2992. ANZ Bank, 11 Me Linh Square, District 1, ☎ 08/829-9319. Citibank, 115 Nguyen Hué Blvd., ☎ 824-2118. Hongkong Bank, 75 Pham Hong Thai St., District 1, ☎ 08/829-2288. Vietcombank, 29 Ben Chuong Duong, District 1, ☎ 08/829-7245.

ATMs dispensing dollars and dong around the clock are at Hongkong Bank, ANZ Bank, and Citibank.

**Embassies & Consulates**   For embassies, see "Fast Facts: Hanoi," earlier in this chapter. Consulates are all in District 1, as follows: United States, 51 Nguyen Dinh Chieu (☎ 08/822-9433); Canada, 203 Dong Khoi St. (☎ 08/824-2000); Australia, 5B Ton Duc Thang St. (☎ 08/829-6035); New Zealand, 41 Nguyen Thi Minh Khai St. (☎ 08/822-6907); United Kingdom, 21 Le Duan Blvd. (☎ 08/829-8433).

**Emergencies**   For police, dial 113; fire 114; and ambulance 115. Have a translator on hand if necessary; operators don't speak English.

**Internet/E-mail**   Almost every upscale hotel provides Internet services in Saigon. Hong Hoa Internet service, at 250 De Tham, District 1 (☎ 08/836-1915), is fantastic and cheap, and is open until 10:30pm. If you're downtown, you can also go to 79 Truong Dinh St. Computers are on the second floor; it's open Monday to Saturday 8am to noon and 2 to 5pm. There is also a cluster of Internet cafes on De Tham Street.

**Post Office/Mail**   The main post office is located at 2 Coq Xu Paris, District 1 (☎ 08/823-2541 or 08/823-2542). It's across from the Notre Dame cathedral and is open daily from 6:30am to 10pm. There are also express mail services in the building, which is in itself a historic landmark (see "Attractions").

**Safety**   The biggest threat to your health in Saigon is likely to be the street traffic. Cross the wildly busy streets at a slow, steady pace. Scooters think nothing

> **Handy Telephone Information**
>
> Dial **108** for information on travel, transit information, doctors and hospitals, hotels, restaurants, and entertainment, at a cost of 600 VND (US5¢) per minute. Operators speak English. There is also prerecorded information at 300 VND per minute: for health-care queries, dial ☎ 08/801-1187 (or any of the consecutive numbers up to 801-1199); flight times, ☎ 08/801-1176 to 801-1180; fairs and exhibitions, ☎ 08/801-1167; restaurants and bars, ☎ 08/801-1174; bank rates, ☎ 08/801-1186; and sexual matters (cheaper than a shrink!), ☎ 08/801-1170.

of driving up onto the sidewalk, either. Just be as aware as possible. Pickpocketing is also a big problem in Saigon, especially motorbike drive-bys. Hang on to your wallet, and don't wear flashy jewelry. Women alone should avoid wandering around in the evenings past 11pm or so. Contact your consulate or your hotel if you have a serious problem. If you insist on going to the local police, bring a translator. Also, the Saigon police tend to throw up their hands at "minor" infractions such as purse snatching or thievery.

**Telephone**   The city code for Saigon is 8. When dialing within Vietnam, the city code should be preceded by 0.

**Toilets**   There are no public toilets per se. Seek out hotels, restaurants, and tourist attractions.

## ACCOMMODATIONS

Saigon presents the best variety of hotels in Vietnam, from deluxe business and family hotels to spotless smaller options. Most of the upper-end hotels are clustered around Nguyen Hué street in District 1, as are the restaurants, shops, and bars.

Remember that prices listed here are guidelines only. Depending on occupancy, the season (low season in Saigon is March through October), and how long you're staying, you may get up to 50% off the rack rate. Cleanliness and amenities are very easy to come by. If your room doesn't have a hair dryer or hot water, for example, you need only ask.

### VERY EXPENSIVE

**New World Hotel Saigon.** 76 Le Lai St., District 1. ☎ **08/822 8888.** Fax 08/824-3694. E-mail nwhs@hcm.vnn.vn. 542 units. A/C MINIBAR TV TEL. US$140 double, US$160 executive floor; suites US$200 and up. US$160 and up rms include breakfast. AE, DC, JCB, MC, V.

This is a first-rate hotel, both for business people and families. It's big, flashy, and deluxe, and has a nice bustle about it. The impeccable, plush rooms are done in a soothing array of neutrals, and the bathrooms are sharp in black and gray marble. The fat pillows are a little mooshy and the beds a bit too firm, but you can't have everything. The place is loaded with amenities. The four executive floors with executive lounge have an impressive list of benefits: late check-out, all-day refreshments, free pressing, computer hookups, the whole bit, including free access to financial newswire info. It is well worth the US$20 more you'll pay over a standard double room. The pool has a rather noisy outdoor setting, but the large Nautilus-equipped health club is world class and the kids' play and game rooms are fantastic. Other amenities are a business center with Internet access, conference rooms, banquet and meeting facilities, tennis, and a driving range. One restaurant, Hoa Mi, is famous for its lunchtime variety of noodle soups. There are also a Chinese restaurant, overpriced coffee shop,

Saigon is divided into districts, as is Hanoi, and is very easy to navigate. Find out districts along with addresses, and try to group your travels accordingly. Most of the hotels, bars, shops, and restaurants are in District 1, easily covered on foot, while sightseeing attractions are spread among Districts 1, 3, and 5 (Cholon).

lobby and jazz lounges, and a deli shop. The staff snaps to; service is ultra-efficient. It's also one of the few places to ask straight away if you'd like a nonsmoking room.

**Omni Saigon Hotel.** 251 Nguyen Van Troi St., Phu Nhuan District (District 3). ☎ **08/844-9222;** fax 08/844-9200. E-mail omnisgn@saigonnet.vn. 248 units. A/C MINIBAR TV TEL. US$180–US$200 double; US$220–US$240 executive floor; US$250–US$300 junior suite; US$450 and up suite. Drastic discounts available; rms can be had for US$60–US$120. AE, DC, JCB, MC, V.

Once quarters for the U.S. army (some say a base for the CIA), this hotel looks like a concrete hell from the outside. Inside is another story. The lobby, with a colonial period flavor, is gorgeous and welcoming. Rooms are perfectly comfortable, lush and well-equipped with coffeemakers and safes. Incredibly good beds and linens, and formal but bland decor. The swimming pool and health club facilities (saunas and massage) are only so-so, but the food is great; the Omni is renowned around town for its Sunday brunch. The one executive floor has a small business center of its own, in-room faxes, and a particularly elegant lounge. Other amenities are conference rooms and banquet facilities, karaoke, baby-sitting, gourmet shop, and car park. The hotel puts an emphasis on nonsmoking rooms. An attached salon for men and woman is excellent. The hotel is 15 minutes from the city center in District 3, but it is also only 10 minutes from the airport, with airport transport available. The service is flawless, perhaps the best in the city. Dining is in a fine Cantonese restaurant, Japanese restaurant, pub, lobby cafe with amazing buffet meals, or pool bar.

## EXPENSIVE

✪ **Delta Caravelle Hotel.** 19 Lam Son Square, District 1. ☎ **08/823-4999.** Fax 08/824-3999. E-mail caravellehotel@bdvn.vnd.net. 335 units. A/C MINIBAR TV TEL. US$89 double; US$160 and up suite. Includes breakfast. AE, DC, JCB, MC, V.

Once the rather shabby hangout of wartime journalists, the Caravelle, which had a renovation and built a new wing in 1998, is now an extremely attractive, efficient, and well-appointed hotel. It must have good feng shui, because it simply has a nice feeling to it. It certainly offers great value for the price, and attracts a goodly number of business travelers as well as tourists. The big, new rooms are well-done and well-appointed, with plush neutral furnishings and firm beds. Coffeemakers, too. Bathrooms are sizable, in marble. The executive "signature" floors have fax machines, computer hookups, VCRs, and CD players in each room. The pool, gym, and spa are spacious and luxe (sauna, two Jacuzzies, and massage), and there's also a business center, conference rooms, banquet and meeting facilities, 24-hour room service, and indoor car park. Rooftop bar Saigon-Saigon is one of the town's hippest hangouts. There's also a Western/Vietnamese restaurant, a pool bar, and a lobby lounge.

**Hotel Sofitel Plaza Saigon.** 17 Le Duan Blvd., District 1. ☎ **08/824-1555.** Fax 08/824-1666. E-mail sofitelsgn@hcmc.netnam.vn. www.sofitel.com. 292 units. A/C MINIBAR TV TEL. Double US$88; Club US$108; US$349 and up business suite.

This hotel opened after our inspection, but if it follows the form of other Sofitel hotels in Vietnam, it's sure to have first-class atmosphere and service. Rooms are soundproofed and have outlet adapters, modem connections, and dedicated phone lines. Sounds good already. Amenities include business center, conference rooms, executive and nonsmoking floors, swimming pool, Clark Hatch fitness center, rooms for guests with disabilities, gourmet shop, laundry, 24-hour room service. Dining is in an Asian restaurant, cafe, bar, or poolside snack bar.

**Rex Hotel.** 141 Nguyen Hué Blvd., District 1. ☎ **08/829-2185** or 829-3115. Fax 08/829-6536. 207 units. A/C MINIBAR TV TEL. US$89–US$119 double; US$169–US$259 and up for suite. Off-season: US$70–US$80 double; US$95–US$135 and up for suite. Includes breakfast. AE, DC, JCB, MC, V.

The Rex has an unorthodox history. It used to be a French garage. It was expanded by this Vietnamese and then used by the United States Information Agency (and some say the CIA) from 1962 to 1970. Then, transformed in a massive renovation, it opened in 1990 as the hugely atmospheric government-run place it is today. The rooms are laden with bamboo detailing, on the ceilings, the mirrors, everywhere you look. The lampshades are big royal crowns, which is a hoot, and some of the suites have beaded curtains and Christmas lights over the bathroom mirrors. But the beds and pillows are incredible, firm but fat. In fact, they may claim the title of Best Beds in Vietnam. Each suite has a fax machine. The Rex is in a fabulous location downtown, across from a square that has a lively carnival atmosphere at night. It is also known for its rooftop bar with its panoramic Saigon view. There is a very nice staff to boot. Don't come here for the amenities, though. The small pool has a bleak view and the health club facilities (with sauna and massage) are antiquated and remind one vaguely of a prison. There are also a business center, conference hall, tailor, barber, tennis court, and three restaurants.

**Saigon Prince Hotel.** 63 Nguyen Hué Blvd., District 1. ☎ **1-800-UTELLCD** or 08/822-2999. Fax 08/824-1888. E-mail saigon-princehtl@hcm.vnn.vn. 203 units. A/C MINIBAR TV TEL. US$65–US$100 double; US$160 suite. Includes breakfast and welcome fruit basket. AE, DC, JCB, MC, V.

The four-star Saigon Prince is in a good location, at the quieter end of hotel row and near several excellent restaurants. It's run by Vietnamtourism, and is a favorite of Asian businesspeople. The beige rooms are nice-sized, tasteful, and comfortable, with plush beds, carpets, and coffeemakers, and you'll be guaranteed comfort and convenience if you stay here—however, the rooms are nondescript and already showing signs of wear. The bathrooms are smart black-and-white marble. Amenities are a business center, nightclub, health club with waterfall shower, Jacuzzi, sauna, and massage (open different hours for men and women). There's a 24-hour Western/Vietnamese restaurant, Japanese restaurant, and lobby lounge. The staff is efficient but rather impersonal. When reserving, mention this book. Also ask about current specials like The Total Business Plan: The hotel often offers free massages and a 20-minute hit at their oxygen bar. Who thinks up this stuff?

## MODERATE

**Bong Sen Hotel Annex.** 61–63 Hai Ba Trung St., District 1. ☎ **08/823-5818.** Fax 08/823-5816. E-mail bongsen2@hcm.vnn.vn. 57 units. A/C MINIBAR TV TEL. US$45–US$55 double; US$80 junior suite. Includes breakfast and tax.

This small annex to the large Saigontourist-owned Bong Sen provides many of the same amenities at a much lower price. There are room service, a concierge, babysitting, and other trappings of a major hotel. The rooms are only a bit over a year old to boot, and are bright and attractive, with light wood furniture, brand-new carpet, and blue tile bathrooms. Very chain-hotel floral. Rooms are on the small side, though, and the economy rooms have only one small window. The junior suite wasn't much bigger. Make sure you're getting the Annex, and not the main Bong Sen, which isn't as attractive nor as much of a value. When I visited, the hotel was running a stay-2-days, get-1-free special.

✪ **Grand Hotel.** 8 Dong Khoi St., District 1. ☎ **08/823-0163.** Fax 063/823-5781. 150 units. A/C MINIBAR TV TEL. US$50–US$70 double; US$120–US$294 suite. Includes breakfast, tax, and service charge. AE, JCB, MC, V.

This is it—the Real McCoy: a 1930s colonial building, done just right. It's owned by Saigontourist—fancy that! The just-reopened, renovated Grand has a serene, tasteful atmosphere. Rooms are big, with simple dark wood furniture and huge wardrobes, and without the musty smell that plagues so many Saigon hotels. The bathrooms are small, but have big counters and hair dryers. Deluxe suites, with their own kitchen, are almost too large; there are too many chairs in the kitchen to compensate for the empty space. The amenities are all here: a big, simple outdoor pool, 24-hour room service, coffeemakers upon request, a business center, a health club with sauna and massage. The quiet atmosphere very much suggests tourist rather than business, though. Don't forget to ride in the restored iron elevator and to ogle the stunning original stained glass walls on the way up and down.

**Hotel Continental.** 132–134 Dong Khoi St., District 1. ☎ **08/299201.** Fax 08/241772. 83 units. A/C MINIBAR TV TEL. US$60–US$90 double; US$100 suite. Includes breakfast, tax, and service charge.

This place is a big shame. It's not that it's so horrible, but it could be gorgeous, and it's a shambles. Built in 1890, it is the pre-eminent historic hotel in Saigon, of Somerset Maugham's *Quiet American* fame. Its last renovation was in 1980. It has a lovely colonial façade, but the lobby is overly ornate. Rooms are absolutely huge, with high ceilings. It's the red velveteen curtains and absolutely hideous bedspreads that spoil the fantasy, as do the tatty red carpets. The beds are comfortable and plush, though, as are the towels. Bathrooms are big as well, clean and with bathtubs, but are plain dorm style, without counters. The standard US$60 rooms are actually the nicest. They face the rear garden instead of the noisy street, for one, and have marble floors. The restaurant is a lovely period piece, but the hotel staff is dazed and confused.

**Hotel Majestic.** 1 Dong Khoi St., District 1. ☎ **08/822-8750** or 829-5514. Fax 08/829-5510. E-mail majestic.s.hotel@bdvn.vnd.net. 122 units. A/C MINIBAR TV TEL. US$65 double; US$85 suite; US$140 and up Majestic suite. Includes breakfast, tax, and service. AE, JCB, MC, V.

This 1925 landmark was spruced up 3 years ago. On the outside, the gorgeous colonial looks a bit like a wedding cake: pink, fancy, and bright. On the inside, things have been botched up a bit. There are the original stained-glass dome and floor mosaic in the lobby, but the concrete replica of the Ben Thanh market clock and the spindly chairs in the lobby restaurant—why, why? The rooms are big; a deluxe room, for example, can be up to 138 square feet (42 square meters). All feature original wood floors and light fixtures. The furniture is gaudy wooden and there are some interesting details—the TV is set into a red velveteen cabinet, for instance. Majestic suites have huge Jacuzzi bathtubs and posh gold fixtures. The pool is a bright spot, small but in an inner courtyard surrounded by palms and the hotel's picturesque shuttered innards. Try to get a quiet room facing it. The lobby lounge offers buffet meals throughout the day, a nice touch, with either a pianist or traditional music as live accompaniment. There's a restaurant, two bars, cafe, and lobby lounge. Amenities include the swimming pool, business center, conference rooms, banquet rooms, health club with sauna and massage, baby-sitting, florist, and airport transfer.

## Travel Tip: Minimarts & Pharmacies

There is a large store that advertises itself as "duty free," on the corners of Nguyen Hué and Le Loi streets, across from the Rex Hotel. You'll find a good selection of brand name toothpaste, face cream, sunscreen, and the like.

The best-stocked pharmacy in town is 289 **Hai Ba Trung,** District 3 (☎ **08/822-2266**), which also has a good selection of Western personal care products. It's worth the trip if you're staying in District 1. They speak some English and are open daily until 10pm. For 24-hour service, check **AEA International,** 65 Nguyen Du, District 1 (☎ **08/829-8520,** fax 08/829-8551). They're expensive, but are probably your best medical choice in Saigon. They're open 24 hours and also give medical advice over the phone and have a dental clinic.

✪ **Huong Sen Hotel.** 66–70 Dong Khoi St., District 1. ☎ **08/829-1415** or 08/829-9400. Fax 08/829-0916. 50 units. A/C MINIBAR TV TEL. US$52–US$95 double. Includes breakfast and tax. AE, DC, JCB, MC, V.

This is an outstanding hotel for the price. Conveniently located on busy Dong Khoi street, it is owned by the Vietnamese government. Rooms are big and newly renovated with simple, colorfully painted wood furniture, and floral drapes and headboards. They have nice touches like molded ceilings and marble-topped counters in the spotless bathrooms. Some have balconies. Beds are ultra-comfortable. There are a restaurant, terrace bar, sauna, massage, laundry, room service, and elevators. The staff isn't the friendliest.

**Mondial Hotel.** 109 Dong Khoi St., District 1. ☎ **08/849-6291** or 08/829-6296. Fax 08/829-6273. E-mail mondial.htl@bdvn.vnmail.vnd.net. 40 units. A/C MINIBAR TV TEL. US$50–US$75 double. Includes breakfast, tax, service charge, and welcome fruit basket.

The Mondial is a very comfortable smaller-hotel option, owned by Vietnamtourism. It is 8 years old and reportedly beginning new renovations in 1999. Rooms are mismatched everything, but are spotless and have nice comfortable beds and new carpets. Bathrooms are impeccable and small and have big marble counters. The deluxe US$65 rooms are extremely large and well-laid out, and worth the extra money. There are also rooms with one twin bed available for US$30. Bonsai trees and Romanesque statuary share space in the halls, and a traditional Vietnamese song-and-dance show is presented every night at the restaurant. Travel services are available, of course.

✪ **Norfolk Hotel.** 117 Le Thanh Ton St., District 1. ☎ **08/829-5368.** Fax 08/829-3415. E-mail norfolk@bdvn.vnd.net. 104 units. A/C MINIBAR TV TEL. US$45–US$60 double; US$90 suite. Includes breakfast. AE, DC, JCB, MC, V.

This snappy 6-year-old Australian/Vietnamese joint venture claims to have the highest occupancy rate in town. It deserves it. Rooms are bright and good sized, furnished in slightly mismatched chain-hotel style, but everything is like new, and there are even in-room safes. The beds are soft and deluxe and the TVs large. Bathrooms are small but finished with marble. Extremely efficient and friendly, the Norfolk's staff also speaks excellent English. Its restaurant is bright and upscale, featuring extensive breakfast and lunch buffets. There are also a business center, conference room, 24-hour room service, health club with sauna, and travel services. Book early.

**Oscar Hotel Saigon.** 68A Nguyen Hué Blvd., District 1. ☎ **08/829-2959.** Fax 829-2732. 108 units. A/C MINIBAR TV TEL. US$50–US$100 double. US$125–US$160 suite. AE, DC, JCB, MC, V.

The Oscar, formerly the Century Hotel, has an interesting flavor. The rooms are furnished with dark furniture, and while dimly lit are rather elegant, save for the occasional puckered carpet. Beds are the very firm brand. Baths are big, bright, and marble, very well appointed. Clientele is part business, part tourist, and the short-hall layout of the place gives rooms a secluded feel. Even though the hotel was renovated only two years ago, it has an "older hotel" feel. It also has a business center, conference room, small cafe, lobby lounge, room service, airport transfer services, a karaoke "with talented singing companions," and disco "with charming dancing partners." I know what you're thinking, but it really isn't that kind of hotel. Great location on hotel row. Its restaurant, Colours, is renowned as a good buffet and business lunch spot.

## INEXPENSIVE

✪ **Hong Hoa Hotel.** 185/28 Pham Ngu Lao St., District 1. ☎ **08/836-1915** or 836-9692. E-mail honghoa@bdvn.vnd.net. 7 units. A/C TEL. US$12–US$18 double. Includes tax and service charge. MC, V.

Bravo! This year-and-a-half-old mini-hotel covers all the bases for under US$20. Rooms are sizable and nicely furnished with real light wood furniture and tile floors. Only three of the rooms have bathtubs, but the rest have separate shower areas, and all are clean, inviting, and well-designed. The mattresses are those foam pads, but they're very comfortable and the pillows carry weight. For US$18 you can even get a TV and minibar. Downstairs is a dandy Internet center. Stay here and you'll be satisfied at how well you've beat the system.

**Kimdo Royal International Hotel.** 133 Nguyen Hué Ave., District 1. ☎ **08/822-5914** or 822-5915. Fax 08/822-5913. E-mail Kimdohotel@bdvn.vnd.net. US$30 double; US$40 junior suite; US$100 executive suite. Includes breakfast. AE, DC, JCB, MC, V.

The Kimdo is the kind of place with a wooden tree trunk clock in the lobby, pink plastic hangers and polyurethane slippers in the closet, and bedspreads of some indeterminate man-made-material. It is still immensely likeable, however, thanks to its very friendly staff, good restaurant, perfect downtown location, and absolute cleanliness. It was built nearly 100 years ago, and had a renovation in 1994. The rooms have interesting Asian carved furniture, carpets, rock-hard beds (you can request a soft one), and aged bathrooms with zero counter space. There are coffeemakers, though, and everything is spotless. Rooms are big; the junior suites simply huge. On-premises dining options include the Saigon Restaurant (which serves excellent Vietnamese cuisine), two bars, and a lobby lounge. Amenities include a business center, fitness center with sauna and massage, executive floors with private elevator, airport shuttle, travel services, room service, laundry, baby-sitting, in-room safes, and medical clinic. Direct your reservations to Mr. Phan Thanh Long, sales manager, and mention this book to get the special rates above. A great value.

✪ **Spring Hotel (Mua Xuan).** 44–46 Le Thanh Ton St., District 1. ☎ **08/829-7362.** Fax 08/822-1383. 45 units. A/C MINIBAR TV TEL. US$26–US$46 double; US$65 suite. Includes breakfast. AE, JCB, MC, V.

If you don't care about fancy amenities, look no further than this amazing place, with nicer rooms than many hotels twice the price. Said rooms are big and have comfy double and super-king-size beds, big TVs, and well-finished bathrooms with decorated tiles. The furniture is nice solid dark wood or light rattan, the floral motif isn't bad, and the carpeted floors are impeccably clean. Go as high up as you can to escape street noise, which is the hotel's one failing. On the other hand, it is centrally located, right next to the Ben Thanh market. Lowest-priced "economy" rooms have no windows. The Spring has an improbable Greco-Roman motif, with statues, colonnades, and all, but it's forgiveable, even pleasant. There are a restaurant, room service, and even a business center of sorts. The staff couldn't be nicer or more helpful.

## DINING

Saigon has the largest array of restaurants in Vietnam. Virtually every cuisine is represented, all notably. Note that most restaurants close at 10:30 to 11pm. Local specialties to sample include banh xeo, a thin rice pancake filled with shrimp, ground pork, and bean sprouts. Try it at **Banh Xia A Phu,** 10 Ba Than Hai (3/2) Blvd., District 10. Mien Ga is a delicious soup with vermicelli, chicken, mushrooms, and onions, and can be had at **140 Le Than Ton,** District 1. Lau hai san is a tangy seafood soup with mustard greens. It can be ordered at any seafood restaurant.

### EXPENSIVE

✪ **Bi Bi.** 8A/8D Thai Van Lung, District 1. ☎ **08/829-5783.** Main courses 60,000–120,000 VND (US$4.30–US$8.65). Set menu 110,000 VND (US$7.95). MC, V. 5–10:30pm. FRENCH/MEDITERRANEAN.

The food is the star at this small restaurant and art cafe, although the atmosphere has its charms as well. Bibi's cozy interior is fashioned with bright Mediterranean-style furnishings and impressionist paintings; the artwork collection changes periodically. A table near the front is devoted to drinking and card playing. The menu is an interesting mix: cannelloni and ratatouille, pastas and veal escalope. For dessert, there are perfectly done staples like apple crumble and cheese cake. Upstairs, there are a few sofas for drinking and lounging. The starters are almost as expensive as the main courses, and the short wine list comprises pricey selections, making this one of Saigon's more expensive choices if you don't choose the set menu. The food is well worth it.

**Camargue.** 16 Cao Ba Quat St, District 1. ☎ **08/824-3148.** Reservations suggested on weekend nights. Main courses 80,000–150,000 VND (US$5.75–US$10.80). AE, DC, MC, V. 5:30–11pm. FRENCH/CONTINENTAL.

Camargue is two floors of enchanting surroundings in a renovated colonial. You can choose from softly lit interior or spacious outdoor terrace seating, surrounded by palm fronds. The menu changes regularly. A sampling from our visit included warm goat cheese salad, roast pork rondalet, and venison. Camargue also seems to have given tourists the nod by adding ubiquitous, lower-priced pasta dishes. The food, alas, isn't as perfect as the surroundings, presentation, and service. Excellent, but not perfect— bland salad dressing, meat a tiny bit chewy, that sort of thing. The service is first-rate, and the bar on the first floor is as fashionable as any in the country.

### MODERATE

**Ancient Town (Pho Xua).** 211 Ter Dien Bien Phu (at the corner of Pasteur St.), District 3. ☎ **08/829-9625.** Main courses 50,000–70,000 VND (US$3.60–US$5). AE, JCB, MC, V. 5:30–10:30pm. VIETNAMESE.

Ancient Town is a relatively new spot serving traditional Vietnamese fare. The setting is upscale and perfect: cane chairs, tile floors, antiques, and an elaborately carved bar. There is live traditional music nightly except for Mondays. The food is excellent. Particularly recommended are the fish soup with dill, steamed snails with ginger, baked crab, shrimp wrapped with smoked ham, and durian ice cream to finish off.

✪ **Augustin.** 10 Nguyen Thiep. ☎ **08/829-2941.** Main courses 40,000–150,000 VND (US$2.90–US$10.80). No credit cards. Hours noon–2pm; 6–11pm. FRENCH.

Tucked into a scraggly alley off Nguyen Hué Street is Augustin, a bright, lively little French restaurant, a great favorite with French expats and tourists. The food is simple yet innovative French fare: beef pot au feu, sea bass tartare with olives. Try the seafood stew, lightly seasoned with saffron and packed with fish, clams, and shrimp. The seating is quite cozy, especially as the restaurant is always full, and the Vietnamese wait staff is exceptionally friendly, speaking both French and English. The menu is bilingual, too. A large French wine list and classic dessert menu finish off a delightful meal.

**Café Mogambo.** 20 Bis Thi Sach St., District 1. ☎ **08/825-1311.** Main courses 30,000–195,000 VND (US$2.15–US$14). MC, V. 7am–11pm. AMERICAN.

Run by American expat Mike and his Vietnamese wife Lani, Mogambo is the laid-back Yank hangout in Saigon. It's a small, dimly lit place with cane ceilings and walls and a few (gak) stuffed animals. There is a long bar with television, and a row of regulars bellied up to it. Before long, you'll be joining in the conversation and hanging out longer than you planned, too. Long diner-style banquettes that stick to your legs are one contribution to an American experience. The other is the beef; their hamburgers and steaks are the real thing, as are the sausages and meat pies. Most entrees are 70,000 VND (US$5.05) or so; it's the steaks that jack up the high end of the price range. Dessert is apple pie, of course, and a plain, hearty cup of coffee.

✪ **Chao Thai.** 16 Thai Van Lung, District 1. ☎ **08/824-1457.** Main courses 45,000–75,000 VND (US$3.25–US$5.40). Set lunch menu 80,000 VND (US$5.75). V, MC. 10:30am–2pm; 5:30–11pm. Reservations suggested only for groups of 5 or more. THAI.

The food and setting are both flawless here. The restaurant is over two floors of an elegant, roomy Thai longhouse, with wide plank wood floors, black-and-white photos of Thai temples, and some small statuary. Chao Thai is famous for its fiery papaya salad, fried catfish with basil leaves, and prawn cakes with plum sauce. The flavors are subtle and not overdone; you won't leave feeling drugged on spices or too much chili. It's a popular power lunch spot, but the atmosphere is just as warm and welcoming to walk-in tourists. The service is gracious and efficient.

**Globo Café.** 6 Nguyen Thiep, District 1. ☎ **08/822-8855.** Main courses 60,000–85,000 VND (US$4.30–US$6.15). No credit cards. 5pm–2am. CONTINENTAL.

The Globo, in an alley off hotel row, is a bar-cum-restaurant with a fun African theme: faux animal skins, drum-shaped seats at the bar. It's more subtle and sophisticated than it sounds. The dining areas are small spaces tucked at the back and on the second floor. The menu is brief but hip and excellently prepared by the resident French chef: beef filet, rib-eye steak, braised rabbit, pastas, and lasagnas. Desserts are standards like mousse, crème caramel, and lemon tart.

**Lemongrass.** 4 Nguyen Thiep St., District 1. ☎ **08/822-0496.** Main courses 48,000–78,000 VND (US$3.50–US$5.60). AE, MC, V. 11am–2pm; 4–10pm. VIETNAMESE.

Lemongrass is renowned as one of the best Vietnamese restaurants in town. You'll rub elbows with locals, expats, and tourists alike here. The atmosphere is candlelit and intimate, very Vietnamese with cane furniture and tile floors, and yet not overly formal. The long menu emphasizes seafood and seasonal specials. Particularly outstanding are the deep-fried prawn in coconut batter and the crab sautéed in salt and pepper sauce. The portions are very healthy, Asian family-style, so go with a group if at all possible and sample as many delicacies as possible.

**Saigon Sakura.** 40 Mac Thi Buoi St., District 1. ☎ **08/822-4502.** Main courses US$4–10. No credit cards. Daily 11:30am–2pm; 6:30–10pm. JAPANESE.

Saigon in general is a good place to get decent Japanese food, but this place is superlative. It's not one of your fancy theme restaurants, but Sakura is packed with Japanese visitors. Need we say more? OK, we will. The sushi is fresh and bursting with flavor, the ginger is pickled just right, the tempura is delicately prepared, and the lunch special, at US$7 to US$11 dollars for a set menu, is a great value. For that you'll get rice, beer or soft drinks, a few sushi rolls, a main course, and an array of tasty small accompaniments.

**Spices.** 132 Ham Nghi, District 1 (inside the Hai Van Nam Hotel). ☎ **08/821-1687.** Main courses 50,000–80,000 VND (US$3.60–US$5.75). No credit cards. Daily 8am–10:30pm. MALAY.

Spices is a comfortable place to enjoy some home style, inexpensive Malay cuisine. Curries are its specialty: curry Laksa is yellow noodles in curry gravy with prawns, cockles, bean curd, and vegetables. Another specialty is Hainanese chicken: chicken and rice cooked in flavored broth. Spices doesn't have much style inside, although it is spotless and somewhat formal. Its low-slung padded chairs and square tables remind you of a hotel lounge. The staff is very friendly.

**Yesterday Grill and Bar.** 142 Vo Thi Sau, District 3. ☎ **08/820-3917.** Main courses US$6–US$12. MC, V. Mon–Fri 11:30am–2pm; 5–11pm (bar is open later). Sat–Sun service starts with breakfast at 8am. TEX MEX.

Y'all got a little Tex-Mex place right here in Saigon. It's not fancy or anything, with diner seating and posters of old cars passing for decor, but the food is quite tasty. Ribs are the specialty of the house, but the grilled barbecued chicken is tender and if you're dying for a fajita, look no further. The potatoes are those memorable down-home kind, fluffy and tasting like they're made out of a box (they aren't). Grilled buffalo wings and steaks, too. Beer is served in frosted mugs, a very nice touch and just the thing after a long hot day of sightseeing. Weekend breakfast specials include omelets and pancakes.

## INEXPENSIVE

**Cappuccino.** 258 De Tham St., District 1. ☎ **08/837-1467.** Main courses 24,000–45,000 VND (US$1.75–US$3.25). No credit cards. 10am–midnight. ITALIAN.

This open-air place on De Tham Street, alias Backpacker Row II, is a good place to stop for some decent pasta, pizza, or risotto. Run by an Italian expat, it has red-and-white checkered tablecloths and smells great, but don't expect miracles for these prices. The red house wine, although good, is served chilled, the cheese isn't mozzarella, and the fresh tomatoes aren't ripe.

✪ **Restaurant 13.** 11–17 Ngo Duc Ke, District 1. ☎ **08/829-1417.** Main courses 30,000–120,000 VND (US$2.15–US$8.65). No credit cards. 6am–10pm. VIETNAMESE.

The atmosphere may be somewhat institutional in this eatery, but 13 serves excellent traditional Vietnamese food, and only that, in a clean spot without charging exorbitant prices. The place is jolly and filled with locals, tourists, and expats. Go for the seafood, anything done in coconut broth, or the sautéed squid with citronella and red pepper. The food is carefully prepared and as carefully served. In fact, the wait staff is almost too solicitous; they'll turn the pages of your menu if you let them.

## SNACKS & CAFES

While shopping on Dong Khoi, stop to savor a few moments at the **Paris Deli,** 31 Dong Khoi (☎ **08/829-7533**), a retro spot with fantastic pastries and sandwiches. **The Marine Club,** 17/A4 Le Thanh Ton, District 1 (☎ **08/829-2249**), which also has a hopping late-hours bar scene, is renowned around town for its brick-oven pizza.

# ATTRACTIONS
## ATTRACTIONS IN DISTRICT 1

**Ben Thanh Market.** At the intersection of Le Loi, Ham Nghi, Tran Hung Dao and Le Lai streets, District 1.

The clock tower over the main entrance to what was formerly known as "Les Halles Centrale" is the symbol of Saigon, and the market may as well be, too. Opened first in 1914, it's crowded, a boon for pickpockets with its narrow, one-way aisles, and loaded with people clamoring to sell you cheap goods (t-shirts, aluminum wares, silk, bamboo, and lacquer) and postcards. There are so many people calling out to you, you'll feel like you're a president at a press conference. I lasted all of 10 minutes before fleeing. The **wet market,** with its selection of meat, fish, produce, and flowers, is easier to take.

**General Post Office (Buu Dien).** 2 Coq Xu Paris, District 1. 6:30am–10pm.

A grand old colonial building. Check out the huge maps of Vietnam on either side of the main entrance and the huge portrait of Uncle Ho in the rear.

**Saigon Opera House (Ho Chi Minh Municipal Theater).** At the intersection of Le Loi and Dong Khoi sts.

This magnificent building was built at the turn of the century and renovated in the 1940s. Three stories and 1,800 seats are inside. Today, it hosts native and international opera troupes, orchestras, and ballets.

**Notre Dame Cathedral.** Near the intersection of Dong Khoi and Nguyen Du sts., District 1.

The Neo-Romanesque cathedral was constructed between 1877 and 1883 using bricks from Marseilles and stained-glass windows from Chartres. The cathedral is closed to visitors except during Sunday services, which are in Vietnamese and English.

**City Hall.** Facing Nguyen Hué Blvd.

Saigon's city hall was constructed between 1902 and 1908, a fantastic ornate example of colonial architecture unfortunately not open to the public.

**Former U.S. Embassy.** At the corner of Le Tuan and Mac Dinh Chi streets.

There is no more embassy. A high concrete and barbed-wire wall is all that's left of the building where Americans famously fled via helicopters from the incoming Viet Cong in April 1975. It looks as though some new construction is under way, however. There is a small monument to the heroism of the Vietnamese on the sidewalk in front of the site.

⭐ **History Museum.** 2 Nguyen Binh Khiem. ☎ 08/829-8146. Admission 10,000 VND (US70¢). Mon–Sat 8–11:30am and 1–4:30pm; Sun 8am–4:30pm.

If there is one must-see in Saigon, this is it. The museum, in a rambling new concrete pagodalike structure, does a good job of presenting important aspects of Vietnam's southern area in particular. There is an excellent selection of Cham sculpture and the best collection of ceramics in Vietnam. Weaponry from the 14th century onward is on display, including a yard with nothing but cannons. There is a wing dedicated to ethnic minorities of the south, including photographs, costumes, and household implements. Nguyen dynasty (1700–1945) clothing and housewares are also on display. There are archaeological artifacts from prehistoric Saigon. Its 19th and early 20th century histories are shown using photos and, curiously, a female corpse unearthed as construction teams broke ground for a recent housing project. There are even some general background explanations in English, something missing from most Vietnamese museums.

**Museum of the Revolution.** 65 Ly Tu Trong St. ☎ **08/829-9743.** Admission: 10,000 VND (US70¢). Tues–Sun 8:30–11:30am and 1:30–4:30pm.

This museum, situated in a grand historical structure built in the 1880s, is one of many in Vietnam exploring a familiar theme: the struggle of the nation against the

French and Americans. It is probably the best of its breed, with various photos, documents, models, and military artifacts detailing local activism as well as long military struggles. The signs are in Vietnamese only at the moment, which actually doesn't present much of a problem. There is a model of the Cu Chi tunnels, the underground network built by the North Vietnamese for weapons transport and living quarters during the American war. Outside are the typical but always interesting captured U.S. fighter planes, tanks, and artillery. Underneath the building is a series of tunnels leading to the **Reunification Palace,** once used by former president Ngo Dinh Diem as a hideout before his eventual capture and execution in 1962.

**Zoo and Botanical Gardens.** Nguyen Binh Khiem St. (next to the History Museum), District 1. No phone. Admission: 10,000 VND (US70¢). Daily, sunup to sundown.

Don't come here unless you have never, ever been to a zoo and are dying to go. The animals are in dismal conditions. The only creatures that look vaguely happy, in fact, are the monkeys, doubtless due to the constant handouts they get from the Vietnamese. As for the botanical gardens, where are they? There is some nice flora, but nothing's labeled, so it's hard to know what you're looking at. To be fair, it's probably best to go in the springtime, around Tet, to see the real flower season in the south.

**Reunification Palace.** 106 Nguyen Du St. Admission: 10,000 VND (US70¢). Mon–Sat 7:30–10:30am and 1–4pm; Sun 7:30am–4pm.

Designed to be the home of former President Ngo Dinh Diem, this building is most notable for its symbolic role in the fall of Saigon in April 1975, when its gates were breached by north Vietnamese tanks and the victor's flag occupied the balcony. In the former century, the French governor general lived on the site in a building called Norodom Palace, destroyed in 1962 in an assassination attempt on Diem. The current "modern" nightmare was completed in 1966, after Diem's death. Like the Bao Dai Palace in Dalat, this is a series of rather empty rooms that are nevertheless interesting because they specialize in period kitsch and haven't been gussied up a single bit. You will tour private quarters, dining rooms, entertainment lounges, and the president's office. Most interesting is the war command room with its huge maps and old communications equipment.

## OTHER DISTRICTS

✪ **Emperor Jade Pagoda (Phuoc Hai).** 73 Mai Thi Luu St., District 3. Daily 8am–5pm.

One of the most interesting pagodas in Vietnam, the Emperor Jade is filled with smoky incense and fantastic carved figurines. It was built by the Cantonese community around the turn of the century and is still buzzing with worshippers, many lounging in the front gardens. Take a moment to look at the elaborate statuary on the pagoda's roof. The dominant figure in the main hall is The Jade Emperor himself, supposedly the god of the "heavens," according to a tour guide. The emperor decides who will enter and who will be refused. He looks an awful lot like Confucius, only meaner. In an anteroom to the left you'll find Kim Hua, a goddess of fertility, and the King of Hell in another corner with his minions, who undoubtedly gets those the Jade Emperor rejects. Spooky.

✪ **War Remnants Museum.** 28 Vo Van Tan St., District 3. ☎ **08/829-0325.** Admission: 10,000 VND (US70¢). Daily 7:30–11:30am; 1–4:45pm.

This museum houses a collection of machinery, weapons of all sorts, and photos documenting both the French and American wars, although the emphasis is heavily on the latter. The museum's former name was the War Crimes Museum, which should give you some tip whose side of the story is being told here. Some of the facts, including the gory photos and relics, are undeniable and gripping, however, and it's interesting to see how the Vietnamese propaganda machine works. It is at the very least a testimony to the hellishness of war. There is an entire room devoted to biological warfare, another to weaponry, and another to worldwide demonstrations for peace (and denunciations of the U.S.). The explanations, which include English translations, are amazingly thorough for a Vietnamese museum. There's a goodly collection of well-labeled bombs, planes, and tanks in the courtyard outside. Kids will love it, but you may want to think twice before taking them inside to see things like wall-size photos of the My Lai massacre and the bottled deformed fetus supposedly damaged by Agent Orange.

**Giac Lam Pagoda.** 118 Lac Long Quan St., District 5. Daily 8am–5pm.

Giac Lam Pagoda, built in 1744, is the oldest pagoda in Saigon. The garden in the front features the ornate tombs of venerated monks, as well as a rare bodhi tree. Next to the tree is a regular feature of Vietnamese Buddhist temples, a gleaming white statue of Quan The Am Bo Tat (Avalokitesvara, the Goddess of Mercy) standing on a lotus blossom, symbol of purity. Inside the temple is a spooky funerary chamber, with photos of monks gone by, and a central chamber chock full of statues. Take a look at the outside courtyard as well.

**Ho Chi Minh Museum.** 01 Nguyen Tat Thanh St., District 4. Admission: 10,000 VND (US70¢). Daily 7:30–11:30am; 1:30–4:30pm. Closed Mon and Fri mornings.

Although not as extensive as the Ho Chi Minh Museum in Hanoi, there is enough information here in pictures, writing, mementos, and other paraphernalia to give you a good idea of Ho's life and times. More accurately, the place shows you how he is regarded by the Vietnamese: as something of a god. Why else would they put the man's sandals and suit in a museum? The placard says "the khaki suit [Ho] wore from 1954–1969." It must have been very well made. Obviously, there are explanations in English. There is also an extensive section on other revolutionary heroes. However, the museum supposes that you know something about Vietnamese history, as the displays are presented without background. Walking around the rear of the museum also affords a good opportunity to gaze at the very active port on the Saigon River.

**Cholon.** District 5. Cholon is a sizable district bordered by Hung Vuong in the north, Nguyen Van Cu to the east, the Ben Nghe Chanel to the south, and Nguyen Thi Nho to the west.

Cholon is the Chinese district of Saigon, and probably the largest Chinatown in the world. It exists in many ways as a city quite apart from Saigon. The Chinese began to settle the area in the turn of the century, and never quite assimilated with the rest of Saigon, which causes a bit of resentment among the greater Vietnamese community. You'll sense the different environment immediately, and not only because of the Chinese-language signs.

A bustling commercial center, Cholon is a fascinating maze of temples, restaurants, jade ornaments, and medicine shops. Gone, however, are the brothels and opium dens of earlier days. You can lose yourself in the narrow streets, or hit the highlights. Here is one district, by the way, where taking a cyclo by the hour makes sense to see the sites. Start at the **Binh Tay Market,** on Phan Van Khoe Street, which is even more crowded than Ben Thanh and has much the same goods, but with a Chinese flavor. There's much more produce, there are medicines, spices, and cooking utensils, and plenty of hapless ducks and chickens tied in heaps. From Binh Tay, head up to **Nguyen Trai,** the district's main artery, to see some of the major temples on or around it. Be sure to see **Quan Am,** on Lao Tu Street off Luong Nhu Hoc, for its ornate exterior. Back on Nguyen Trai, **Thien Hau pagoda** is dedicated to the Goddess of the Sea, and was popular with seafarers making thanks for their safe trip from

China to Vietnam. Finally, as you follow Nguyen Trai Street past Ly Thuong Kiet, you'll see the **Cholon Mosque,** the one indication of Cholon's small Muslim community.

## SPORTS & OUTDOOR ACTIVITIES

There are two excellent 18-hole golf courses at the Vietnam Golf and Country Club. Fees are US$50–US$80 during the week for nonmembers, depending on which course you want to play, and US$100 on Saturday and Sunday. The Clubhouse is at Long Thanh My Ward, District 9, ☎ 08/733-0126; fax 08/733-0102.

**Saigon Water Park** is a newly opened facility with the usual slides and chutes. It is at Kha Van Can, Thu Duc District (☎ **08/897-0456**).

**Tennis** enthusiasts can find courts at Lan Anh International Tennis Court, 291 Cach Mang Than Tam, District 10 (☎ **04/862-7144**).

The **pool** and well-equipped **gym and spa** at the Delta Caravelle Hotel (see "Accommodations") are available for nonguests at a day rate of US$20.

## SHOPPING

Saigon has a good selection of silk, fashion, lacquer, embroidery, and houseware. Prices are higher than elsewhere, but the selection is more sophisticated, and Saigon's cosmopolitan atmosphere makes it somewhat easier to shop (meaning shop owners aren't immediately pushing you to buy). Stores are open 7 days a week from 8am until about 7pm. Credit cards are widely accepted, save for the markets.

**Dong Khoi** is Saigon's premier shopping street. Formerly Rue Catinat, it was a veritable Rue de la Paix in colonial times. The best blocks are the last two heading toward the river. Notable shops include **Heritage,** 53 Dong Khoi, for wood carvings and other ethnic arts. **Les Epices** at 25 Dong Khoi St. sells much the same, and **Authentique Interiors,** 38 Dong Khoi, offers fantastic embroidered quilted wall hangings. **Viet Silk,** at 21 Dong Khoi, has a quality selection of ready-made clothing and can of course whip something up for you in a day.

Nearby Le Thanh Ton Street is another shopping avenue. **Nga Shop,** at 61 Le Thanh Ton, sells exquisite lacquer and wooden ware, and **Kenly Silk,** at 132 Le Thanh Ton, is a brand-name supplier with the best ready-to-wear silk garments in the business. Unique, tasteful, hand-embroidered pillows and hand-woven fabrics can be found at **MC Decoration,** 92C5 Le Thanh Ton.

Stop in at **Saigon Duty Free Shoppers,** at 102 Nguyen Hué across from the Rex Hotel, a full-size department store of bargains. You must have an international plane ticket and can pick up your goods at the airport upon departure.

### ART GALLERIES

**Xuan Gallery,** 32 Vo Van Tan, District 3 (☎ 08/829-1277), features contemporary Vietnamese painters. Also see **Gallery Saigon,** 5 Ton Duc Than St. (☎ **08/829-7102**), and **Blue Space Gallery,** 1 Le Thi Hong Gam (☎ **08/821-3695**).

### BOOKSTORES

HCMC's official "foreign language bookstore," **Xuan Thu,** is at 185 Dong Khoi St. across from the Continental Hotel (☎ **08/822-4670**). There is a good selection of classics in English and French and some foreign-language newspapers. It's open daily from 7:30am to 9pm. **Hoang Xuan Tho,** at 28 Dong Khoi, carries many major foreign-language newspapers and magazines, some good books about Vietnam, and some novels you won't find elsewhere. There are also several small bookshops on De Tham Street, some of which do swaps.

### Eyeglasses

Glasses can be made at **Friendship Optical,** 92/C1–2 Le Thanh Ton (☎ 08/823-0883). **Kiem Tan,** at 69 Pasteur behind the Rex Hotel, sells soft contact lenses.

## SAIGON AFTER DARK

When Vietnam made a fresh entree on to the world scene in the mid-1990s, Ho Chi Minh City quickly became one of the hippest party towns in the east. The mood has sobered somewhat, but it's still a fun place. Everything is clustered in District 1, so move along, as the crowd does, from spot to spot.

There is lots of **sex for sale,** as you may have heard. Gentlemen alone are likely prey. Accepting a scooter ride from a lady, by the way, is tantamount to saying "yes" to lots more.

### THE BAR SCENE

**Globo Café,** at 6 Nguyen Thiep, is a small, funky African-themed place at which to start the evening, and has live music on Fridays. The 65,000 VND (US$4.70) cocktails may discourage you from lingering, however. **Café Latin,** a swinging tapas bar at 21 Dong Du (☎ 08/822-6363), is another current hot spot. **Q-Bar,** 7 Lam Son Square (☎ 08/823-5424), is a longstanding favorite, an elegant, upscale jazz bar. Change out of your Teva's first. **Saigon-Saigon,** an open-air rooftop bar on top the Century Riverside hotel at 19 Lam Son (☎ 08/823-4999), is very chic and popular as well and has live music nightly from 10pm 'til midnight (☎ 08/824-3999). **The Gecko Bar,** at 74/1A Hai Ba Trung in District 1 (☎ 08/824-2754), is much more laid-back with music, darts, and pool table. North and not far away is the brick-walled Irish pub **O'Briens** at 74A Hai Ba Trung (☎ 08/829-3198).

### DANCING

For dancing, **Gossip** is your basic techno disco. Very hot right now, it's located in the Mercure Hotel at 79 Tran Hung Dao (☎ 08/824-2525). There is a US$8 cover charge. **Zouk** is a new, popular disco right on hotel row at 119 Nguyen Hué (☎ 08/822-4378). There is a US$3 cover. **Apocolypse Now** at 2C Thi Sach, District 1 (☎ 08/824-1463), is a still-popular HCMC landmark, and good for a short stop on your night crawl. Try to make it toward the end of the night (or early morning), when the obvious decorations, drunk tourists, and platform-shod hookers will seem more fun than sad. Watch your belongings! In a more upscale "nautical" environment, **The Marine Club** features chummy late-hour drinking bouts. Check it out at 17/A4 Le Thanh Ton, District 1 (☎ 08/829-2249).

### MUSIC & THEATER

**The Conservatory of Music,** 112 Nguyen Du St., District 1 (☎ 08/839-6646), has classical music performances, and the **Hoa Binh Theater,** 3 Thang 2, District 10, ☎ 08/865-5199), occasionally puts on shows of traditional music and dance. You can also check out the traditional music and dance entertainment put on by several of the hotels, including the **Mondial** at 109 Dong Khoi St., District 1 (☎ 08/ 849-6291).

## 12  Excursions from HCMC

### CU CHI TUNNELS

About 40 miles (65 km) northwest of Saigon lies a must-stop for most tourists. Beginning in the late 1940s, fighters against the French army dug a network of tunnels for hiding themselves and ammo. The network was expanded during the 1960s for the Viet Cong insurgents and then for use in the American war. By then, the tunnels reached all the way to the border of Cambodia, and were instrumental in Viet Cong takeover of hamlets along the way. The complex was at times home to almost 10,000 Viet Cong. Entire villages basically existed underground, with meeting rooms, kitchens, and even hospitals in the tunnels.

Today, you can crawl through a portion of the tunnels, see the secret trapdoors and booby traps for intruders. Try to see the real tunnels at **Ben Dinh,** though, and not the made-for-tourist ones at Ben Duoc. The experience is dirty and claustrophobic; at times you're crawling through the tiny, clammy openings. The tourist cafes offer day trips to the tunnels, along with the Cao Dai (see below), for about US$4.

### CAO DAI HOLY SEE (TAY NINH)

The Cao Dai religion is unique to Vietnam. It was established in 1926 by a government official named Ngo Van Chieu, who claimed spirits visited him and laid down the tenets of a new faith. Cao Daism draws its beliefs from a variety of world religions, including the works of great writers and philosophers (which makes sense to me). The religion's "saints" include Jesus Christ, Victor Hugo, Joan of Arc, Confucius, and Louis Pasteur. Its headquarters are located in a huge fantasy cathedral, constructed between 1933 and 1955 in the town of Tay Ninh. The cathedral is painted in a mosaic of colors with a blue sky ceiling, while followers in brightly colored caftans and white turbans complete the rainbow spectacle. Onlookers are invited to watch the noon processional service from a balcony overhead. (See the photo section at the beginning of this book for a photo of the Cao Dai Holy See.)

The Holy See is located at Tay Ninh, 59 miles northwest of Saigon off Highway 22. Every tourist cafe and most operators have a Cao Dai tour that also visits the tunnels of Cu Chi, with prices starting at US$4.

### PHAN THIET

The target of several new resort developers, this is currently the nicest place to go if you're looking for a **beach resort** near Saigon. It's actually a smallish fishing town on the southeastern coast, featuring peaceful light-sand beaches and sand dunes at Mue Ne, 12½ miles east of the town. The outstanding Nick Faldo–designed **Ocean Dunes Golf Course** (☎ **062/821-511**), is also a big draw.

---

### Impressions

*"The Holy See was at Taynin. A Pope and female cardinals. Prophecy by planchette. Saint Victor Hugo. Christ and Buddha looking down from the roof of the Cathedral on a Walt Disney fantasia of the East, dragons and snakes in technicolor."*

—Graham Greene, *The Quiet American*

Stay at the **Hai Duong Resort/Coco Beach,** Km 12, 5 Ham Tien, Phan Thiet (☎ **062/847-111;** fax 062/047-115; e-mail cocobeach@saigonnet.vn): US$60 double, US$140 suite. Or try the **Novotel Ocean Dunes Resort,** 1 Ton Duc Thang (☎ **062/822-393**), next to the Ocean Dunes Golf Course: US$78 double; US$98 suite. Phan Thiet is about 3 hours east of Saigon by car on Highway 1.

## THE MEKONG DELTA

I can't emphasize this enough: Don't leave without seeing ✪ **the Mekong Delta,** at least for a day. The Delta is a region of waterways formed by the Mekong, covering an area of about 37,200 miles (60,000 km). Most of it is cultivated with bright green rice paddies, fruit orchards, sugar cane fields, vegetable gardens, and traditional fish farms. There are a few cities, too, but rather than any cosmopolitan area, get out to see the outlying canals by boat, a fascinating glimpse into a way of life that has survived intact for hundreds of years. As you cruise slowly along the meandering canals, you'll see locals living right beside the water, above it in stilt houses, and in some cases, in it on houseboats. Trading is conducted from boat to boat, often in canal bends teeming with boats and their wares (hung from a tall pole as a form of advertising). The people are friendly and unaffected, and the cuisine of the upper Delta is delicious and leans heavily toward seafood.

Coming south from Saigon, the town you'll probably reach first is **My Tho,** but you should try to make it down at least as far as **Can Tho,** the Delta's largest city. It has a bustling riverfront and waterway. About 20 miles from Can Tho is **Phung Hiep,** the biggest water market in the region. The water is literally covered by the bobbing merchants.

To cope with the necessary logistics, going with a tour agent is your best bet to the Delta. **Ann's Tourist Co.,** 58 Ton That Tung St., District 1 (☎ **08/833-2564;** fax 08/823-3866; e-mail anntours@yahoo.com), has custom-made tours with six or fewer people, at reasonable prices. Their tours can include a night at a local canal stilt house—a rustic experience, to be sure, but unique. Also, once you book a trip you're guaranteed a departure, unlike at the tourist cafes. A specialty outfit direct from the Delta is **Cuu Long,** 1 Duong 1 Thang 5, Vinh Long (☎ **070/823-616;** fax 070/823-357). Their Saigon branch office: 97A Nguyen Cu Trinh, District 1 (☎ **08/830-0339**). Think twice about going to the Delta at all during the rainy season, however. Many of the roads may be washed out or the tides too high for canal travel.

# Laos 7

*By Stacy Lu*

"The Jewel of Southeast Asia." "Unforgettable." "The most perfectly preserved Southeast Asian city." Most travel literature finds it hard to describe Laos or its cities without using some kind of superlative. That is partly because the superlatives are true, and partly because Laos, landlocked and serene, is too exotic and complex to describe in a few words. Asked to do so, one can only rely on a few hard-hitting adjectives.

So what is Laos about? First, it is a nation where 60% of the people are practicing Buddhists. This fact colors every facet of life there, and is the overriding impression you'll carry away. The ornate, glittering temples on virtually every corner and the flocks of monks in colorful robes on the streets are hard to miss. So, too, is the impression that Lao people may be the friendliest on earth. Then there is the diverse population, from citified Vientiane Lao to rural hill tribes. Remains of ancient civilizations are here as well, including the odd **Plain of Jars** and **Wat Phu,** a Hindu site that may pre-date Angkor Wat. Laos also has varied enticing natural terrain to explore, from mountains in the north to jungles and tropical islands in the south.

It's a beguiling place, and one that demands you slow your pace to match its own. Strolling through a town, you may be stopped in your tracks more than once by a grand temple on the corner of a dirt road, a beautiful Lao teenager strumming her guitar, stopping to wave at you, or the toothless smile of a Lao dowager, beckoning you to come and have a peek at her new grandchild. Outside the major cities, **Vientiane** and **Luang Prabang,** travel gets tougher; but you won't hear any visitors complaining about bumpy bus rides or the lack of a four-star hotel. This is the trade-off you make for the chance to visit hill tribes living in genuinely rustic conditions, untouched by modernity.

The government says it is trying to preserve its historical and ecological treasures from massive foreign invasion, so for now the country continues to develop tourism facilities at a relatively slow pace. However, the current sketchy infrastructure is probably due as much to a lack of capital as to the government's wish to protect national heritage. One gets the sense that with an injection of tourism income, things will start to happen more quickly. After all, a big casino resort has already been built not far from the capital. Note that with the current scarcity of facilities, however, travel within Laos is relatively expensive compared with other Southeast Asian countries.

All the more reason to see Laos as soon as possible, and to savor it while you're there. If you go, you'll doubtless be rewarded with an experience brimming with history, mystique, adventure, and the friendliness of the Laotians.

## 1 Getting to Know Laos

### THE LAY OF THE LAND

Comprising 91,429 square miles, roughly the size of Great Britain or the state of Utah, Laos shares borders with China and Myanmar in the north and northwest, Cambodia in the south, Thailand in the west and Vietnam to the east. It is divided into 16 provinces. Seventy percent of its land is mountain ranges and plateaus, and with an estimated population of just over 5 million, Laos is one of the most sparsely populated countries in Asia. Natural landmarks include the Annamite mountains along the border with Vietnam, and the Mekong River, which flows from China and along Lao's border with Thailand. About 55 percent of the landscape is pristine tropical forest, sheltering such rare and wild animals as elephants, leopards, the Java mongoose, panthers, gibbons, and black bears.

### THE REGIONS IN BRIEF

**THE NORTH**   Surfaced with forests and mountains, the north is populated mainly by **nomadic hill tribes,** including the Hmong (Meo), Lu, Yao and Thai Dam. In the upper northwest, seldom explored by travelers, lie provinces Bokeo, Phangsali, and Luang Namtha, home to 39 different ethnic groups. Oudomxai Province is central north. It is a relatively unexplored area with rustic hill tribe villages and fishing towns, ideal for trekking and river tours. **Luang Prabang** Province, in the center of the region, is the major travel destination in Laos. Luang Prabang city, the first Lao capital in 1353, is a UNESCO World Heritage Site with 33 existing temples. To the southeast of Luang Prabang is Xieng Khoung, location of Lao's three highest mountains. The area is pockmarked with bomb craters, remainders of the Vietnam War. Its main attraction is the **Plain of Jars,** site of an imposing archaeological mystery, and the Hmong and Thai Dam hill tribes who live near the capital, Phonsovan. In the far northeast is Hua Phan Province.

**VIENTIANE & CENTRAL LAOS**   Vientiane is both a province and a city. It is the capital of Laos and lies along the Mekong River where it borders Thailand. A bustling town with a goodly number of historic temples for its size, it's also the most modern city in the country, with Internet cafes and high-rise hotels. Its neighboring provinces are Sayaboury to the west, and Bolkhamxay and Khammouane to the southeast.

**THE SOUTH**   Savannakhet province is the major commercial center in the tropical south, due to its proximity to Vietnam. It is also the most populated province in Laos. The city of **Savannakhet** features classic French colonial and Chinese architecture. The Boloven Plateau, on the border of Saravane and Champasack provinces, is an agricultural area with teak, tea and arabica and robusta coffee plantations, fruit orchards and cattle ranches. **Champassak,** at the confluence of the Mekong and Xe Don rivers, has been inhabited since the first century, and was once part of the Cambodian kingdom of Angkor. It is rich in culture and in ancient monuments and temples. Champasack's capital is Pakse, a former French commercial outpost. Far south of the province is the **lower Mekong delta,** also known as the "land of 4,000 islands," with its verdant landscape, flatlands, islands, and waterfalls. Sekong and Attapeu provinces are in the far southeast. They are sparsely populated, save by wild animals, and rarely see tourists. The town of Attapeu is known as "the garden village" for its tree-lined avenues.

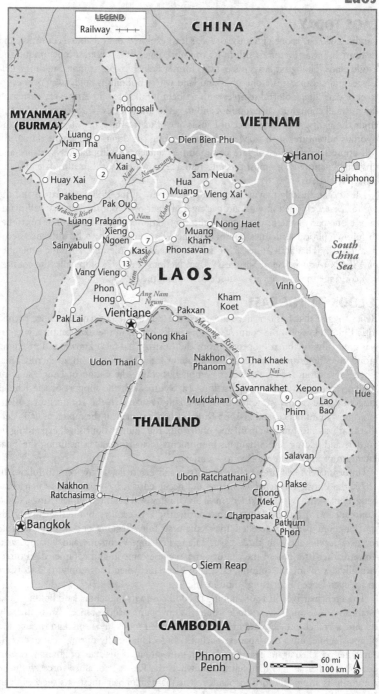

# Laos

**LEGEND**
Railway ┼┼┼┼

CHINA

MYANMAR
(BURMA)

Phongsali

VIETNAM

Luang
Nam Tha
③

Muang
Xai
②

Dien Bien Phu

Hanoi

Haiphong

Huay Xai

Pakbeng

Pak Ou

Nam Ou

Nam Senang

Sam Neua

Hua
Muang

Vieng Xai

①

Luang Prabang

Xieng
Ngoen

Nam Khan

⑥

Muang
Kham

Nong Haet

②

Sainyabuli

⑦

Phonsavan

Vinh

Kasi

⑬

LAOS

South
China
Sea

Vang Vieng

Nam Ngum

Phon
Hong

Ang Nam
Ngum

Kham
Koet

Pak Lai

Vientiane

Pakxan

Mekong River

Nong Khai

Udon Thani

Nakhon
Phanom

Tha Khaek

Se Noi

Savannakhet

Xepon

Hue

Mukdahan

⑨

Lao
Bao

Phim

THAILAND

⑬

Salavan

Ubon Ratchathani

Pakse

Nakhon
Ratchasima

Chong
Mek

Champasak

Pathum
Phon

Bangkok

Siem Reap

CAMBODIA

Phnom
Penh

0 ──── 60 mi
──── 100 km

N

## LAOS TODAY

Landlocked Laos is one of Southeast Asia's least explored and inhabited countries, and its tourism infrastructure is still in its youthful stages. It is a fantastically unique and exotic place. Though it bears traces of its former French colonists in its buildings, language, and cuisine, it is a one-of-a-kind land where Buddhism holds sway over every facet of daily life. Colorful temples with resident monks are on nearly every corner, in towns small enough to cover on foot and to get to know locals. Travelers can relax and enjoy the sights, as the slow pace of Laos is one of its treasures, or you can enjoy more rigorous adventures such as Mekong river boating, trekking, or elephant riding. All will appreciate glimpses of rare commodities: ancient, traditional ways of life and unspoiled nature. Laos's most precious resource, however, is still its ultra-friendly and attractive citizens.

Laos began steadily moving to a market economy in the 1990s, and Japan and the United States chipped in with aid packages of their own. But the country still maintains a one-party system, along with tight information and social control. It continues to follow political structures laid out by the Vietnamese, and to be influenced economically by Thailand. At peace for the first time in centuries, Laos became a member of ASEAN (Association of Southeast Asian Nations) in 1997. Hopefully, the country will continue to carve out its own identity in Southeast Asia.

## A LOOK AT THE PAST

Relics suggest that humans have inhabited the area of present-day Laos since prehistoric times. However, the country's history really begins in the sixth century, when it was gradually inhabited by people from the Austro-Thai (also known as Tai) ethnic group migrating from Angkor and the area now known as Yunnan in southern China. Their loose group of communities eventually became the nation of Lang Xang, or "million elephants," under its first king Fa Ngum, with the support of the Khmer kingdom. The capital was established in Luang Prabang. In the 16th century, Vientiane grew in influence, and in 1563 King Setthathirat made it the capital of Laos. Setthathirat was a formidable man, and under him the country flourished, expanding its borders and adding several famous monuments to its landscape, including the That Luang stupa and Wat Phra Keo in Vientiane.

Unfortunately, centuries of internal strife and external warfare were to follow. In 1575, the Burmese entered Vientiane and occupied it for 7 years, while Luang Prabang remained a separate kingdom. The country was reunited under King Nokeo Koumane in 1591 and was prosperous during the 17th century, but in the early 1700s the kingdom partially acceded to Vietnamese rule. Regions opposed to the rule seceded, leaving Laos in three parts: Luang Prabang, Vientiane, and Champasack. Towards the latter end of the century, the Siamese came in and conquered all three, virtually destroying the country, especially Vientiane, when Laos vainly tried to assert its independence under King Anou in 1827.

The French arrived in 1868, hoping to add Laos to its Indochina land holdings and establish a Mekong River trade route. With Siam's acquiescence, Laos officially became a French protectorate in 1893. France ruled indirectly, using Lao royalty as a puppet regime, until the Japanese occupied Indochina briefly during World War II. After the war, Lao again became a French protectorate. This state of affairs wasn't to last long, either, as Lao nationalists, known as the Pathet Lao, allied forces with the communists struggling for independence in Vietnam. Their quest was successful; in 1954 the French granted Lao independence.

This victory wasn't absolute, however. While the communist Pathet Lao temporarily took control of the government, a right-wing coup soon followed, reducing the Pathet Lao to a guerrilla group. Despite cease-fires and international interventions, the infighting continued for years, and eventually Laos was drawn into the Vietnam War in the mid-1960s. The Viet Cong spread its activities into northeastern and southern Laos, establishing transport routes for men and weaponry. The Americans retaliated by dropping more bombs on the country than it had used in all of World War II.

Finally, a cease-fire was declared in 1973, with the Pathet Lao dominating the consensus government. Following the communist victories in Vietnam and Cambodia in 1975, the right-wing government faction succumbed for good; the remaining royals were deposed and never heard from again, and the Pathet Lao emerged victorious. The government was established under strong influence from the Vietnamese, and the first man in power was Kaysone Phhomvihan, who is half-Vietnamese.

Not everyone was happy with the communist victory, however. Over the next 5 to 7 years, some 300,000 Laotians fled the country, many to the United States and Thailand. Pockets of rebel groups still remain today, particularly among the Hmong (Meo) hill tribes in the north.

## THE LAO PEOPLE & CULTURE

Ethnically, Laotians fall into 68 different groups, only 47 of which are fully researched and identified. All of these fit into one of three categories. The lowlanders are **Lao Loum,** the majority group, who live along the lower Mekong and in Vientiane. The **Lao Theung,** low mountain dwellers, live on mountain slopes, and the **Lao Soung** are the hill tribes or *montagnards.* Eighty percent of the population lives in villages or small hamlets, practicing subsistence farming.

The earliest **Lao religions** were animist, and most hill tribes still practice this belief, often in combination with Buddhism. But Buddhism predominates; 60 to 80% of all Laotians are practicing Theravada Buddhists. In the morning, monks walk the streets collecting food or alms, eagerly given by the Laotians, who believe it will help them in the next life. Laotians worship regularly and can often be seen making temple visits. Most young males spend at least 3 months in a wat, or monastery, usually around the time of puberty or before they marry. Impressive **religious art** and **architecture** is expressed in a singular Lao style, particularly the "standing" or "praying for rain" Buddha, upright with hands pointing straight down at the earth.

**Music and dance** are integral to the Lao character, and you'll get a taste of it during your stay. Folk or *khaen* music is played with a reed mouth organ, often accompanied by a boxed string instrument. The *lamvong* is the national folk dance, where participants dance in concentric circles. You may also witness or take part in a *baci* ceremony, a rite used as a blessing, to perform a marriage, to say welcome or farewell, or to honor achievement. Participants sit in a circle around a bouquet of flowers, or offerings of food, and join hands, saying prayers and blessings. Strings will be tied around the celebrant's wrist, and everyone partakes of a shot or two of *lao lao,* rice wine.

Laos are friendly and easygoing, but you may find it hard to make a close friend. **Language** will usually be a barrier. There is also a sense that the Lao people are just learning how to approach their foreign visitors. Solo travelers probably have the best chance of making an entree into society. While Laos suffered brutally throughout its colonial history and most horrifically during the Vietnam War, Laotians want to move on to peace and prosperity rather than dwelling on the past. It's very unlikely that an American will be approached with recrimination. But memories are still fresh: The Laotians still deal with war fallout literally and figuratively, a result of the unexploded bombs (or UXO) that litter 50% of the country.

## ETIQUETTE

The Lao are generally tolerant people, but there are a few things to keep in mind. First, upon entering a temple or wat, you must always remove your shoes. There will usually be a sign, but a good rule of thumb is to take them off before mounting the last flight of stairs. You should also take off your shoes before entering a private home, unless told otherwise.

**Dress modestly.** It's unusual to see bare Lao skin above the elbow or even above the mid-calf. Longer shorts and even sleeveless tops are permissible for foreigners of both sexes, but short shorts or skirts and bare bosoms and navels will cause stares and possibly offence, especially in a wat.

Men and women should avoid public displays of affection.

Women should never try to shake hands with or even hand something directly to a monk; monks are not permitted to touch women, or even to speak directly to them anywhere but inside a wat. (In a wat, they'll chat you up like mad.)

The **traditional greeting** is called the *nop* or *wai*. To perform this, place your hands together at chest level as if you are praying, but do not touch your body. Bow your head to your hands, and your upper body slightly. The nop is also used to say thank you and goodbye. Its use is fading in the big cities, but return the greeting if you're given it. In a business setting, a handshake is also appropriate.

The head is considered the most sacred part of the body, and the feet the lowliest. Therefore, do not casually touch another person's head, no matter how much you want to, and don't sit with your legs crossed or otherwise point your feet at something or someone. As in most cultures, pointing with the finger is also considered rude. If you are seated on the floor, men may sit with legs crossed, but women should tuck them to one side.

In interpersonal relations with the Lao, it helps to remember that many are strong Buddhists and take (or try to take) a gentle approach to human relationships. A person showing violence or ill temper would be regarded with surprise and disapproval. A gentle approach will take you farther here. For example, Lao are simply not that interested in haggling. One or two go-rounds are usually enough. Should you have a disagreement of any kind, keep your cool. Gentle persistence with a smile is the key.

Finally, it is considered polite to accept any food or drink offered and to at least taste it.

## LANGUAGE

**Lao** is the national language, but hill tribes have their own dialects. Many people in Vientiane and Luang Prabang speak **English,** and older citizens will usually be able to speak some **French. Russian** and **Chinese** are also occasionally spoken.

Lao is a tonal language closely related to Thai. While it doesn't have an official Roman alphabet, everyone takes a try at transliterating things into English. As a result, even town and street names have copious spelling irregularities, so we have chosen to list only phonetic pronunciations. Most Laotians will understand you, even without tones, and will very much appreciate your efforts to speak their language.

### USEFUL LAO WORDS AND PHRASES
#### Greetings

| | |
|---|---|
| Hello | sa bai dee |
| Good bye | laa kawn |
| Thank you | khawp chai |
| Thank you very much | khawp chai lai lai |

| You're welcome/never mind | baw pen nyahng |
| How are you? | Sa bai dee baw? |
| Yes | chow/ur |
| No | baw/baw men |
| Excuse me | khaw thoot (rhymes with "put") |

## Getting By

| Where is [noun] | [noun] yoo sai? |
| toilet | soo-um |
| hotel | hawng hem |
| telephone | toe la sap |
| taxi | tak see |
| I want to go to | khaw-ee yahk pai |
| Street | thanon (a slightly aspirated, hard "t") |
| Left | sah-ih |
| Right | kwah |
| I don't understand. | Bo kow chai. |
| How much? | Tao dai? |
| Can you make it cheaper? | Lut dai baw? |

## Numbers

| 1 | neh-ung |
| 2 | song |
| 3 | sawm |
| 4 | see |
| 5 | ha |
| 6 | hok |
| 7 | chet |
| 8 | pay-et |
| 9 | gao (rhymes with "cow") |
| 10 | seep |
| 11 | seep-et |
| 12, 13, etc. | seep + song, seep + sawm, etc. |
| 20 | sao (rhymes with "cow") |
| 1,000 | nee-ung pan |
| 10,000 | sip pan |

## Days of the Week

| Monday | wan chan |
| Tuesday | wan ahngkhan |
| Wednesday | wan pood |
| Thursday | wan pahat |
| Friday | wan sook |
| Saturday | wan sao |
| Sunday | wan atheet |

## In Case of Emergency

| Help! | Sue-wee dah! |
| Call the police! | Sue-wee un tam luat dah! |
| I need a/an ... | khaw-ee tawng kahn ... |
| doctor | maw |
| Hospital | hong maw |

**Ordering Food**

| | |
|---|---|
| coffee | kah-fey |
| black coffee | kah-fey dam |
| tea | sah |
| drinking water | nahm dee-um |
| beer | bee-yeh |
| soup | kang |
| rice noodle soup | foe |
| chicken | kie (rhymes with pie) |
| fish | pah |
| pork | moo |
| bread | kow chee |

## 2  Planning a Trip to Laos

### VISITOR INFORMATION

The Lao Tourism Authority is more of an administrative than an informative group. If you would like to write for brochures, contact: **National Tourism Authority of Lao PDR,** 08/02 Lane Xang Avenue, P.O. Box 2511, Vientiane, Lao P.D.R. (☎ 021/212-248 or 212-251; fax 021/212-769). Their travel services branch, at the same address, is **Lanatour.** Helpful on-line information can be found at the **Pacific Asian Travel Association** site, www.pata.org, and at www.laoembassy.com. **Diethelm Travel,** a tour operator in the region, publishes helpful information on www.diethelm-travel.com/laos/tours.htm. Following are a few particularly well-known Laos tour operators:

### IN NORTH AMERICA

- **Mountain Travel-Sobek,** 6420 Fairmount Ave., El Cerrito, CA 94530 (☎ **888/687-6235** or 510/527-8100; fax 510-525-7710). E-mail: info@mtsobek.com.
- **Asia Transpacific Journeys,** 3055 Center Green Dr., Boulder, CO 80301 (☎ **800/642-2742** or 303/443-1633; fax 303/443-7078). E-mail: info@southeastasia.com.
- **Adventures Abroad,** 2148-20800 Westminster Hwy., Richmond, BC, Canada V6V 2W3 (☎ **800/665-2998** or 604/303-1999). www.adventures-abroad.com. E-mail: adabroad@infoserve.net. Small-group tours.
- **World Expeditions,** 78 George St., Ottawa, Ontario, Canada K1N 5W1 (☎ **613/241-2700;** fax: (613) 241-4189). E-mail: info@worldexpeditions.com. Hiking, biking, trekking, and camping.

### IN AUSTRALIA/NEW ZEALAND

- **Intrepid Small Group Adventures,** P.O. Box 2781, Fitzroy, D.C. Victoria, Australia (☎ **3/9743-2626;** fax 3/9419-4426). www.intrepidtravel.com.au. E-mail: info@intrepidtravel.com.au.
- **Active Travel,** P.O. Box 5779, Dunedin, New Zealand (☎ **3/477-8045;** or 800/326-2283, New Zealand only; fax 03/477-8802). E-mail: irene@activeco.co.nz.
- **Mountain Travel-Sobek,** Australian Sales Office (☎ **02/9264-5710;** fax 02/9267-3047). E-mail: adventure@africatravel.com.au.

### IN THE U.K.

- **Mountain Travel-Sobek,** European Sales Office (☎ **49/444-8901;** fax 49/446-5526). E-mail: sales@mtsobekeu.com.

## Travel Insurance

Given the underdeveloped tourism industry in Laos, a policy that covers trip cancellation and loss of luggage is not a bad idea. Lao Aviation schedules can change on a dime, and even the top-end tour companies issue disclaimers about their ability to deliver on what can be quite expensive packages. Depending on the cause, you may be able to submit claims. See chapter 3 for more information on policies.

- **Regent Holidays,** Regent House, 31a High St., Shanklin, Isle of Wight, PO37 (☎ **0198/386-4212;** fax 198/386-4197).
- **Silverbird,** 4 Northfields Prospect, Putney Bridge Road, London, SW18 1PE (☎ **181/875-9191;** fax 181/875-1874).
- **British Airways Holidays,** Astral Towers, Betts Way, London Road, Crawley, RH10 2XA (☎ **129/372-3121;** fax 129/372-2624).

### IN LAOS

- **Diethelm Travel Laos.** Namphou Square, Setthathirat Road, P.O. Box 2657, Vientiane, Lao P.D.R. (☎ **021/215-920** or 213-833; fax 021/216-294). These folks are far and away the most professional group in Laos, and have a great reputation in the region. They are also the only people in Laos who satisfactorily answer overseas inquiries. Your overseas operators may be contracting through them.
- **Phattana Khetphoudoi Travel Co.** PhoneXay Road, P.O. Box 5796, Vientiane, Lao P.D.R. (☎ **021/413-888;** fax 021/413-639). Offers specialty travel, including camping, cycling, and veterans' tours.

## ENTRY REQUIREMENTS

Residents of every Western country need a passport and visa to visit Laos. Although the official time limit is 15 days, most people get 30 days for just asking. It usually costs US$50 and takes about 5 business days to process, although it will cost US$35 and take as little as a day in Bangkok. It's important to note that you have to state a date *before which* you plan to enter, rather than an entry date, and the visa will only be valid if used before that date. Once in the country, a visa can be extended for a few days to as long as a month for US$1 a day at the Immigration Office in Vientiane. Overstaying your visa will cost you a fine of US$5 a day upon exiting the country. If you live in a country without a Lao embassy (Australia and New Zealand, for example), you can obtain a visa through a tour agency or even upon arrival. You must have US$50 in cash, in U.S. dollars, and an air ticket out of the country. Five-day transit visas are also available. Contrary to rumor, you do not need to book an organized tour to obtain a visa, so don't believe any travel agents who tell you so. Furthermore, as you travel from province to province, even to a major city like Luang Prabang, you must check in with the immigration authorities upon both entry and exit.

### LAOS EMBASSY LOCATIONS

**In the U.S.:** Embassy of the Lao People's Democratic Republic, 2222 S St. NW, Washington, D.C., 20008 (☎ 202/332-6416; fax 202/332-4923).

**In Australia:** 1 Dalmain Crescent, O'Malley, Canberra, ACT 2606 (☎ 02/6286-4595; fax 02/6290-1910).

**In Thailand:** 520.502/1-3 Soi Ramkhamheng 39, Bangkapi, Bangkok 10310 (☎ 02/538-3696; fax 02/539-6678).

# Group vs. Independent Travel

You may hear rumors that you "have to" go to Laos in a group. Or perhaps the embassy, if you get your visa there, will press you to book a tour. The truth is, if you value independence and flexibility, you can certainly travel on your own. However, once you're in the country you may want to book some of your travels through an agency, especially if you go outside of Vientiane or Luang Prabang. First, getting around undeveloped Laos can be difficult and expensive (see "Getting Around," below), so if you can hook up with a minivan or tour bus, so much the better. A tour will take care of logistics for fun things like boat cruises and raft and elephant rides. Second, it's darned difficult to book hotels on your own. There will inevitably be language problems, and it will cost you a mint and take a lot of time to phone around. If you're travelling during the dry season like most people, rooms can get tight, so play it safe.

**In Vietnam:** 22 Rue Tran Bing Trong, Hanoi (☎ 04/254-576; fax 04/228-414).

## CUSTOMS REGULATIONS

You are allowed to bring to Laos 500 cigarettes, 100 cigars, or 500g of tobacco; 1 liter of alcohol; two bottles of wine; enough perfume for personal use; and unlimited amounts of money. Not that the Customs officials here do much, if any, searching. However, if you purchase silver or copper items during your stay, you may be required to pay duty upon exiting Laos, according to their weight. Antiques, particularly Buddha statues, are not allowed to leave the country.

## MONEY

The **kip** is the official Lao unit of currency, and comes in denominations of 5,000, 2,000, 1,000, 500, 100, 50, 20, 10 and 5.

**CURRENCY EXCHANGE & RATES**    At press time, the exchange rate was US$1 to 4,160 kip. Laos is very much a cash country, especially outside of Vientiane. You can change money at Wattay airport, in hotels, in banks, and on the black market, with the rate of exchange worst at hotels and best on the black market. However, U.S. dollars are accepted for major purchases, and occasionally Thai bhat as well. Change to kip for small purchases, transportation, and restaurants.

**Traveler's checks** in U.S. dollars and other major currencies are accepted in banks in Vientiane and Luang Prabang but very rarely by vendors; even the Amex travel representative won't take them. In other provinces it's best to carry cash, in kip. **Credit cards** are accepted only at major hotels or tour operators, and virtually only in Vientiane (Visa is the most widely accepted). At press time, many places in Luang Prabang were not accepting MasterCard because of an obscure bank restriction. You can make cash withdrawals on a Visa card at **Banque Pour Le Commerce Extérieur Lao** in Vientiane.

### Where to Have Your Visa Extended

For visa extensions, head for the Immigration Office in Vientiane, on Khoun Boulum Street, right off Lane Xang Avenue opposite the Morning Market. It's open Monday to Saturday, 8 to 11am and 2 to 4:30pm.

**LOST/STOLEN CREDIT CARDS & TRAVELER'S CHECKS**    To report lost or stolen Visa cards, call the **Banque pour le Commerce Extérieur Lao** in Vientiane (☎ **021/213-109**). The American Express Travel Representative in Laos is **Diethelm Travel,** Namphou Square, Setthathirat Road, Vientiane (☎ **021/215-920** or 213-833.)

Otherwise, you will have to call your vendor directly on their overseas number, as it is virtually impossible to make collect calls in Laos. The numbers are as follows: **American Express** (☎ **336/393-1111**); **Visa** (☎ **757/677-4701**); **MasterCard** (☎ **904/448-8661**). A replacement card will probably take at least 2 weeks to reach you, if at all. Your best bet is to bring several cards and spread your risk.

## WHEN TO GO

**PEAK SEASON**    High season for tourism is late November through February and the month of August.

**CLIMATE**    Laos has a topical climate, with monsoon season lasting from early May through October and a dry season from November to April. In Vientiane, average temperatures range from 71° Fahrenheit in January to 84 in April. In the northern regions, which include Xieng Khoung, it is chilly from November to February, and can approach freezing temperatures at night in mountainous areas. Beginning in mid-February, temperatures gradually climb, and April can see temperatures over 100°.

The best time to visit the south is probably November through February, to avoid the rain and heat. In the mountains of the north, May to July means still-comfortable temperatures. The monsoon season begins a bit later there as well.

**PUBLIC HOLIDAYS**    The major public holidays in Laos are: January 1 (New Year's Day), mid-April (Lunar New Year), May 1 (International Labor Day), mid-November (That Luang Festival, Vientiane), and December 2 (National Day). Businesses and government offices close for these holidays, but restaurants remain open. There are a few important festivals that you may want to catch. The **That Luang Festival** in Vientiane, during the full moon in early November (Nov 21–23, 1999; and Nov 9–11, 2000), draws the faithful countrywide and from nearby Thailand. There is a pre-dawn gathering of thousands, who join in a ceremonial offering and group prayer, and then a procession. For days afterwards, a combined trade fair and carnival offers handicrafts and flowers, games, concerts, and dance shows. Although the entire country celebrates the **Lunar New Year (Pimai Lao),** the Luang Prabang festivities include a procession, a fair, a sand-castle competition on the Mekong, a Miss New Year pageant, folk performances, and cultural shows. It's held in mid-April (Apr 14–16, 1999; and Apr 13–15, 2000). Make sure you're booked and confirmed in hotels before you go. At local temples, worshippers in brightly colored silks greet the dawn on **Buddhist Lent** (Boun Khao Phansaa) by offering gifts to the monks and pouring water into the ground as a gesture of offering to their ancestors. Lent will last 3 months (July 28, 1999). The **Vientiane Boat Race Festival** (Vientiane, Luang Prabang, and Savannakhet; Oct 11, 1999; Oct 14, 2000) is held the second weekend in October to mark the end of Buddhist Lent. Men and women compete in groups of 50, rowing long boats along the Mekong to the beating of drums. On **National Day,** the entire country celebrates a public holiday on National Day. At Vientiane, there are parades and dancing at That Luang temple (Dec 2).

## HEALTH CONCERNS

### VACCINATIONS

Start planning early, as some vaccinations are given in a series and need up to a month to take effect. Shots for hepatitis A and B are a must. You should also be vaccinated

## What Things Cost in Laos

The price of everything in Laos, particularly of transportation, is likely to change at any moment, fluctuating with exchange rates and demand. The prices here should, therefore, be used as guidelines only.

| | |
|---|---:|
| Taxi from the airport to city center, Vientiane | 3,000 kip (US70¢) |
| Local telephone call from phone booth, per minute | 45 kip (US1¢) |
| Double room at an expensive hotel | US$70 |
| Double room at a moderate hotel | US$40 |
| Double room at an inexpensive hotel | US$25 |
| Dinner for one at an expensive restaurant, without wine | US$9 |
| Dinner for one at a moderate restaurant, without wine | US$5 |
| Dinner for one at an inexpensive restaurant | US$3 |
| Glass of Beerlao, the local brand | 1,500 kip (US3¢) |
| Coca-Cola | 2,500 kip (US5¢) |
| Cup of coffee at a common coffee shop | 1,000 kip (US2¢) |
| Roll of 36-exposure color film | 15,000 kip (US$3.60) |
| Admission to national historical museum | 3,000 kip (US60¢) |

against polio and tetanus. If you plan to travel to rural areas, protect yourself against typhoid and cholera. During the rainy season, Japanese encephalitis, a mosquito-borne and possibly fatal disease, is also a risk in certain regions.

You may be prescribed an oral prophylaxis for malaria. Lao mosquitoes are resistant to chloroquine, and so you may be given mefloquine (Larium). This can have serious side effects, such as dizziness or gastrointestinal disturbances; if you're sensitive to medications, or if you're pregnant or planning to become pregnant, discuss the risks carefully with your doctor.

### HEALTH PRECAUTIONS

Advanced medical care is nonexistent outside of Vientiane, and even there it consists only of a few emergency clinics. So follow every precaution, be careful while you're there, and in case of dire emergency, get out fast.

As you may have guessed, **there is no potable water in Laos.** Don't drink tap water that hasn't been thoroughly boiled (it can carry parasites and other unwelcome additives), and don't take any drinks with ice. Bottled water is available on virtually every street corner; make sure it has an unbroken seal. You can avoid food-borne diseases by eating only thoroughly cooked, washed food, and only fruit you have peeled yourself. This can be difficult, as Lao cuisine uses many fresh ingredients and garnishes, and condiments made from dried fish that may have been stored under unsanitary conditions. Use your best judgement. Unpasteurized milk or yogurt is dangerous, as is eating fish or shellfish that hasn't been cooked properly.

The most common illness claimed by travelers to the region is diarrhea. If it or any other gastric distress befalls you, stick to easy-to-digest foods such as rice or rice porridge, weak tea, or bananas. Noodle soup is soothing as well, but skip the meat. If your symptoms last longer than 3 to 4 days, seek medical attention.

The rivers in the southern region can carry **schistosomiasis,** also known as bilharzia, a disease caused by parasitic worms. Infection occurs when your skin comes in

---

**Travel Tip: Watch Out for Unexploded Bombs**

Warning: Laos is, per square inch, the most heavily bombed country in the world to date, thanks to the Vietnam War. Certain parts of the country, in the north around the Plain of Jars, and in the south around the Ho Chi Minh Trail, are laden with unexploded bombs (or unexploded ordnances—UXO), some of which are as small as a fist. There is not much of a risk to tourists, provided you avoid wandering through the unexplored jungle in risky areas and don't pick anything up. If you're traveling with children, warn them and keep an eye on them in those areas.

---

contact with fresh water in which certain types of snails that carry the nasty schistosomes are living. Rabies is also a problem in Laos, so keep an eye on your kids and never approach an animal, wild or otherwise.

**Malaria** can be a problem outside of Vientiane. While you may be prescribed an oral prophylaxis, take some precautions to avoid getting bitten: Wear clothing that covers as much of your limbs as possible, and use an insect repellent that contains at least 30% DEET (diethylmethyltoluamide) for adults, 6 to 10% for children. Some people are allergic to DEET, so test it before you leave. Finally, bring your own kit of medical supplies (see "Packing Tips" in chapter 3).

## GETTING THERE
### BY PLANE

Chances are that you'll fly to Bangkok first if you're coming from the West. Most flights connect with Thai Airways to **Vientiane.** Flights also arrive once a week in Vientiane from Kunming, China, twice a week from Phnom Penh, once a week from Ho Chi Minh City (Lao Aviation), and once a week from Hanoi on Lao Aviation (see "Getting Around," below, for a note on safety issues). Lao Aviation and Thai Airways fly from Chiang Mai, Thailand, to **Luang Prabang** (currently once a week). Note that if you're taking this route you must already have a valid Lao visa, as you can't get one upon arrival in Luang Prabang.

**FROM THE U.S.**    From **Los Angeles,** you can fly **United Airlines** (☎ 800/241-6522), **China Airlines** (☎ 800/227-5118), **Northwest Airlines** (☎ 800/225-252), or **Japan Airlines** (☎ 800/525-3663), connecting in Tokyo or Bangkok with **Thai Airways International** (☎ 800/426-5204) to Vientiane. From **New York, Virgin Atlantic** (☎ 800/862-8621), **British Airways** (☎ 800/247-9297), and **Continental Airlines** (☎ 800/525-0280), among many others, get you to London, where you can connect for a flight to Bangkok on **Thai Airways, British Airways,** or **Qantas,** then connect with **Thai Airways** to Vientiane.

**FROM CANADA**    From **Toronto,** you will probably connect first in London via an **Air Canada** or **British Airways** flight, then go on to Bangkok. Another option is **Lufthansa,** with a connection in Frankfurt. From **Vancouver,** you can take **Canadian, United Airlines,** or **ANA,** with a connection in Tokyo, or **Alaska Airlines, Northwest** or **American Airlines,** with a stop in Los Angeles, before heading on to Bangkok.

**FROM AUSTRALIA**    From **Melbourne,** **Thai Airways** flies to Bangkok and then on to Vientiane.

**FROM NEW ZEALAND**    The easiest and cheapest path to Vientiane is a straightforward **Thai Airways** flight from Auckland, with a transfer in Bangkok.

**FROM THE U.K**  You will most likely fly **Thai Airways, British Airways,** or **Qantas** from London to Bangkok, then take a Thai Airways flight from there.

**TRANSPORTATION FROM THE AIRPORT**  You can take a jumbo, an open-air motorcycle cart, into Vientiane. The cost should be about 5,000 kip (US$1.20) to your hotel door, unless you're sharing with other folks, in which case expect to pay about 2,000 kip (US50¢).

## BY TRAIN

Trains run from Bangkok to Nong Khai, Thailand. You can then cross the Thai-Lao Friendship Bridge by shuttle bus and take a 40-minute taxi ride into Vientiane. You can also travel by train to Dong Dang, China, and cross overland to Boten in Luang Namtha. All overland checkpoints are open daily from 8:30am to 5pm. If you arrive at another time, prepare to bunk down locally.

## BY BUS

Buses depart Danang, Vietnam, to Lao Bao, crossing the border at Sepon, 156 miles east of Savannakhet. You can then take a bus to Savannakhet, but departure schedules are sketchy. You can also cross the border at Chong Mek in Thailand, and then take a taxi to Pakse. From there, you can get a bus (for 13-plus hours) or flight to Vientiane. Any one of these routes, however, will involve an arduous, adventurous trip, to put it mildly.

## BY BOAT

It is possible to travel by boat, in a sense, from Chiang Khong, Thailand. You will ride a river ferry across the Mekong to Houeixay, Laos, and then probably take a speed boat or river ferry to Luang Prabang.

## GETTING AROUND

Unlike just a few years ago, you do not need travel permits to go from province to province. The problem is that Laos's 17,110 miles of roads includes only one real highway, which gives you an idea of how tough it is to get around physically. There is no rail system. Depending on which regions you choose to visit, it makes sense to travel using a **combination of flights and overland vehicles,** such as minivans and hired cars, booked once you're in Laos. When I visited, however, some of the foreign embassies in Vietnam were issuing stern warnings about the safety of Lao Aviation. The government, in financial difficulties, let its payment and maintenance schedules lapse. As a result, many of its newer planes have been impounded, and the existing planes have dubious servicing. Lao Aviation will probably work out its problems before the country's official Visit Lao Campaign 1999, but check with your embassy before you depart. The airline does now accept Visa and traveler's checks. (Onward and upward!) If you do fly, be prepared for schedule irregularities, and make sure to confirm your flight the day before departure.

You can take **public buses** and **river barges** from town to town, but it's not recommended for long rides (how long depends on your tolerance). Realize that the bus will not be air conditioned, nor will it have shock absorbers, and if you take a barge

**Travel Tip**

Keep in mind that there is a **departure tax** of US$5 (payable in dollars or kip) when you leave Laos.

you risk spending the night on a boat deck in the open air. **Speedboats** are a faster option, though they can be more expensive and not much more comfortable.

Navigating on foot through Laos' small cities is easy. You can use **taxis** and **tuk-tuks** (covered carts behind motorbikes) in Vientiane, Luang Prabang, and Pakse, or rent **bicycles** and **motorbikes** in Vientiane and Luang Prabang. You can also rent a car, with or without a driver (you will need an international driver's license).

## TIPS ON ACCOMMODATIONS

Book your hotel early during the peak season (November through February), using travel agents and tour operators as necessary. Language difficulties can make booking outside of Vientiane almost impossible to do yourself. Don't expect discounts, either, as facilities aren't plentiful and occupancy is usually high. That said, you'll be generally happy with the standards and prices you'll encounter.

## TIPS ON DINING

You'll very much enjoy the Lao cuisine, though some accuse it of being "Thai by way of China." Try it at real restaurants whenever possible, as the street stands aren't up to those in neighboring countries. You'll also find decent food of other cuisines, including French, Thai, and Italian.

## TIPS ON SHOPPING

You'll undoubtedly leave with a few pieces of hand-woven Lao textiles, hand-crafted silver, and other lovely objects. Many things are one-of-a-kind, so if you see something you like, get it. Remember that the Laos don't particularly like bargaining, and a "no" usually means no.

# Fast Facts: Laos

**American Express**    The country's one Amex representative is Diethelm Travel, Namphou Square, Setthathirath Road, Vientiane, ☎ **021/215-920** or 213-833.

**Business Hours**    With a few exceptions, hours tend to be 8:30am to noon and 1:30 to 5pm weekdays; 8am to noon Saturdays; closed Sundays. Restaurants are open from about 11am to 2pm and 6 to 10pm daily, although many are closed for lunch on Sundays.

**Doctors & Dentists**    Medical care in Laos is primitive by Western standards. For minor problems, Vientiane has one International Medical Clinic, Mahosot Hospital, on Fa Ngum Road at the Mekong riverbank (☎ **021/214-018**). Open 24 hours. Facilities are very basic. The doctors speak French but little English. Two embassies also have clinics: The Australian Embassy Clinic is located on Nehru Street, Phonexay (☎ 021/413-603 or 413-610), open Monday, Tuesday, Thursday, Friday 8:30am to noon and 2 to 5pm; Wednesday 8:30am to noon. The Swedish Embassy Clinic is on Sok Paluang (☎ 021/315-015); hours are Monday, Tuesday, Wednesday, Friday 8am to noon and 2 to 4pm; Thursday 8am to noon. If you have a serious problem, get to Vientiane or consider emergency evacuation. Call **Lao Westcoast Helicopter Company** in Vientiane at ☎ **021/512-023** or 021/130-241.

Luang Prabang has an International Clinic on Bounkhong Road opposite the Luang Prabang provincial hospital (☎ **071/212-049**). The doctor was reportedly trained overseas, but bring a translator if you go, and cash.

If you need glasses or soft contact lenses, go to **Lao Optic,** 086/2 Mixay Arcade, Setthathirat Road (☎ **021/222-290,** 215-090 after hours). An expat doctor does the exams. They have a great selection of frames, too.

**Drug Laws**    Opium is openly grown in northeast Laos and is easily available, as is marijuana. Neither are legal, and although you may see many travelers indulging, it is highly recommended that you don't. You may face high fines or jail if you're caught.

**Electricity**    Laos runs on 220-volt electrical currents. Plugs are two-pronged, with either round or flat prongs. If you're coming from the U.S. and you must bring electrical appliances, bring your own converter. Outside of Vientiane and Luang Prabang electricity is sketchy, and there's usually none to be had after 9pm. A surge protector is a must for laptops.

**Embassies    U.S.:** Thatdam Bathrolonie Road (☎ 021/212-582 or 212-585; fax 021/212-584). **Australia:** Nehru Street, Bane Phonsay (☎ 021/413-600). The Australian embassy also assists Canada, New Zealand, and U.K. nationals. **Cambodia:** Thadeua Road, Bane Thatkhao (☎ 021/314-950 or 314-952). **Thailand:** Phonkheng Road, Bane Phonsaat (☎ 021/214-580). **Vietnam:** That Luang Road, Bane Phonsay (☎ 021/413-400).

**Emergencies**    In Vientiane, for police, dial 191; fire, 190; ambulance, 195. For medical evacuation, call **Lao Westcoast Helicopter Company** at **021/512-023** or 021/130-241.

**Internet/E-mail**    You can find Internet access at a few venues in Vientiane (see "Fast Facts: Vientiane," below). Other than that, you'll have to resign yourself to non-connectivity. Even if you have a dial-up number in nearby Vietnam or Thailand, the shortage of phone lines and the enormous expense of it all will probably stop you cold. Should your computer break down, there are several repair shops in Vientiane.

**Language**    Lao is the major language, and many people in Vientiane and Luang Prabang speak **English.** See "Language," above, for more information.

**Liquor Laws**    There are no real liquor laws in Laos, but most bars refuse to admit patrons under the age of 18. Bars usually close around midnight.

**Post Offices/Mail**    A letter or postcard should take about 10 days to reach the U.S. A letter to North America costs 2,000 kip (US50¢); to the U.K., 1,800 kip (US45¢); and to Australia and New Zealand, 1,750 kip (US40¢). Postcards are 500 kip (US10¢) less. The mail service is reportedly unreliable, however, so if you're sending something important, use an express mail service. FedEx and EMS have offices in the major cities.

**Safety**    Buddhist Laos is an extremely safe country by any standard. Violent or even petty crime is not a big risk for tourists here. Quiet Vientiane isn't much of a threat, except for the traffic—there are few lights, and because traffic isn't all that heavy it moves very, very quickly. There have been rare instances of robbery or rape in remote areas. Solo travelers should take care when going too far off the beaten track, even on a day hike. Some of the country's highways, like Route 13 near Kasi and Route 7 in the northeast, are at a very low risk for rebel and bandit attacks. Check with your consulate before doing any overland travel. Of course, petty crime does exist. Watch your belongings and don't leave valuables in your hotel rooms, particularly in smaller guest houses.

## Telephone Dialing Info at a Glance

- **To place a call from your home country to Laos,** dial the international access code (011 in the U.S., 0011 in Australia, 0170 in New Zealand, 00 in the U.K.), plus the country code (856), plus the city or area code (21 for Vientiane, 71 for Luang Prabang) and the 6-digit phone number (for example, 011 + 856 + 21/000-000).
- **To place a call within Laos,** dial the city or area code preceded by a zero, then the 6-digit number (for example, 021/000-000). A local call costs 45 kip (US1¢) a minute from a phone booth. You must use a phonecard, which you can buy at the post office, the telephone office, and mini-marts.
- **To place a direct international call from Laos,** dial the international access code (**00**) plus the country code, the area or city code, and the number (for example, 00 + 1 + 212/000-0000).
- **International country codes** are as follows: Australia 61, Burma 95, Cambodia 855, Canada 1, Hong Kong 852, Indonesia 62, Malaysia 60, New Zealand 64, the Philippines 63, Singapore 65, U.K. 44, U.S. 1, Vietnam 84.

When trekking in the north or in the south around the Ho Chi Minh Trail, even in well-visited areas such as the Plain of Jars, **beware of unexploded bombs.** Don't stray into remote areas, and don't touch anything on the ground.

**Telephone & Fax**   The international country code for Laos is 856. Published phone rates in December, considered peak season, are as follows: 1 minute to the U.S., 13,200 kip (US$3.15); to Canada 11,400 kip (US$2.75); to Australia, 4,500 kip (US$1.10); to New Zealand, 8,800 kip (US$2.10); and to the U.K., 11,400 kip (US$2.75). Most newer hotels have International Direct Dialing at surcharges of about 10%. Collect calls are impossible anywhere, and the long distance companies haven't made it to Laos yet. See the "Telephone Dialing Info at a Glance" box for more information.

**Time Zone**   Laos is 7 hours ahead of Greenwich Mean Time, in the same zone as Bangkok. That makes it 12 hours ahead of the U.S. and 3 hours behind Sydney.

**Tipping**   Tipping has arrived in Laos, particularly in Vientiane. Feel free to tip bellhops, chauffeurs, and tour guides, and to leave 5 to 10% or round up your bill in upscale restaurants. Foreign currency, especially U.S. dollars, is appreciated.

**Toilets**   You'll find toilets or *hawng nam* in hotels, restaurants, tourist attractions, and even wats. Only in the very newest hotels will you find Western-style sit-down toilets, but squat-style toilets (if they have clean floors) are actually more hygienic. Bring your own paper and sanitary hand wipes. You'll notice a bowl and a pail of water nearby for flushing. Throw two to three buckets of water into the toilet.

**Water**   There is no potable water in Laos. Drink only boiled or bottled water, which is available virtually on every street corner. Don't take ice with your drinks, especially outside of Vientiane. You may even want to consider brushing your teeth with boiled or bottled water.

## 3  Vientiane

Vientiane (vee-en-tee-*en)* has to be one of the world's most unique capitals. Like many cities in developing countries, its visage is a complex mix of old world and new. Vientiane's small scale, though, means you'll be constantly confronted by startling incongruities. For while it has a more than 1,200-year history as a cosmopolitan center, today it is still a dusty town with a population of about 250,000. Many of the residents are monks in vermilion or mustard-colored robes, attending to their business at *wats* whose peaked roofs still dominate the local skyline. The airport still uses the grab-your-bag-off-the-cart method of dispensing luggage and you can ride to town in a motorized cart. Many of the streets are unpaved. At the same time, the city has Internet cafes and advertising agencies, embassies and investment advisors. It has luxury business hotels with swimming pools and gourmet restaurants with fine wines, and the streets are crowded with big, gleaming utility vehicles.

As far as tourism goes, the city was ransacked by the Vietnamese in 1828, so it lacks some of the ancient history you can see in former capital Luang Prabang. But its temples have been beautifully reconstructed, and there are some nice colonial buildings still standing: **That Luang** is the pre-eminent temple in the country and scene of a huge festival every November; the **Patuxay victory monument** is a peculiarly Lao version of the Arc de Triomphe; the **Morning Market** has a full city block of goods to explore; and the **Mekong** glows pink at sunset. It is worth a stay of several days to take it all in and enjoy Vientiane's laid-back atmosphere while it lasts.

### VISITOR INFORMATION

For the size of the country and what you'll want to do, you actually have a good choice of agents within the country. Although Laos is heavily promoting eco-tourism, there aren't many operators who will take you off the beaten track. For assistance with that, you'll have to look for agents nearer home.

- **Diethelm Travel Laos.** Namphou Square, Setthathirat Road, P.O. Box 2657, Vientiane, Lao P.D.R. (☎ **021/215-920** or 213-833; fax 021/216-294). Monday to Friday 8am to noon, 1:30 to 5pm; Sat 8am to noon. These are the most professional folks in town and can help you arrange deluxe personalized trips or small necessities like bus tickets.
- **Sode Tour.** 114 Quai Fa Ngum. P.O. Box 70. Vientiane, Lao P.D.R. (☎ **021/215489** or 216-314l; fax 021/215-123). Experienced and reputable.
- **Inter-Lao Tourisme.** Setthathirat Road, P.O. Box 2912, Vientiane, Lao P.D.R. (☎ **021/214-232**). Moderately helpful.
- **Lao Tourism.** 08/02 Lane Xang Ave., P.O. Box 2511, Vientiane, Lao P.D.R. (☎ **021/216-671** or 212-013; fax 021/212-013). Government-owned, but offers some good rafting, trekking, and elephant-riding programs.

### GETTING THERE

Vientiane is Laos's major international airport. For information on arriving by plane or by train, see "Getting There," in "Planning a Trip to Laos," above.

### GETTING AROUND

The city lies entirely on the east side of the Mekong River (the other side is Thailand). The main streets, running parallel to each other, are Samsenthai and Setthathirat. The heart of the city is Nam Phu fountain, and many of the directions in this chapter are given in relation to it.

Central Vientiane is easily covered on foot. You can also hire a **tuk-tuk,** a covered cart behind a motorbike, or a **jumbo,** a bigger version of same. They charge about 2,000 kip (US50¢) for a full cross-town run. You should settle the price before you ride. **Motorcycles** can be rented for US$6 or so a day. **Bicycles** are available at Raintrees Bookstore and elsewhere at 5,000 kip (US$1.20) per day. You can also rent a car, to drive yourself (four-wheel drive, if you like) for US$60 a day. Call **Asia Vehicle Rental,** 08/3 Lane Xang Ave., beside Thai Farmers Bank (☎ **217-493** or 223-867). E-mail: avr@loxinfo.co.th.

## Fast Facts: Vientiane

**Banks/Currency Exchange**   Banque Pour Le Commerce Extérieur Lao is on Pangkahm Street down by the river (☎ 021/213-200). You can exchange money there in all major currencies and withdraw cash on credit cards. You can also exchange money at Banque Setthathirat, near Wat Mixay. They are open Monday to Friday 8:30am to 3:30pm.

**Internet/E-mail**   There is an Internet cafe called Planet Computers at 201 Setthathirat Rd. (☎ 021/218-972/4; e-mail: ploone@loxinfo.co.th). Costs average about 1,000 kip (US25¢) per minute (US$2 for 10 minutes) depending on how long you're on-line. The Novotel Hotel offers Internet access at a whopping US50¢ per minute, and Lao Hotel Plaza at US$2 for 10 minutes. If your laptop breaks down, you can take it to Planet, or try Microtec Computer at 169 Luang Prabang Rd. (☎ 021/213-836).

**Emergencies**   For police dial 191; fire 190; ambulance 195. For medical evacuation, call Lao Westcoast Helicopter company at ☎ 021/512-023 or 021/130-241.

**Post Office/Mail**   The General Post Office is on the corner of Thanon Khou Vieng and Lane Xang Avenue, opposite the Morning Market. Hours are Monday to Saturday 8am to noon and 1 to 5pm, closed Sundays. EMS and Fedex services are available within. There is a DHL office on Nongno Street (☎ 021/216-830 or 214-868).

**Telephone/Fax**   The central telephone office, where you can place local and IDD calls, is located on Setthathirat Road near Nam Phu Circle (Nam Phu Fountain), and is open from 8am to 10pm daily. You can also send faxes or telexes (does anybody send telexes anymore?).

## ACCOMMODATIONS

Laos is still developing its tourism industry, so hotels are not numerous. Demand is high enough and resources scarce enough that there is little incentive for renovations and service. There simply isn't that much choice, especially in Vientiane, although

### Living Without Street Addresses

You'll notice that many of the businesses in Vientiane don't seem to have street addresses. The city is so small they hardly need them. Note also that transliterations of Lao street names differ from map to map, and that "thanon" simply means street.

# Vientiane

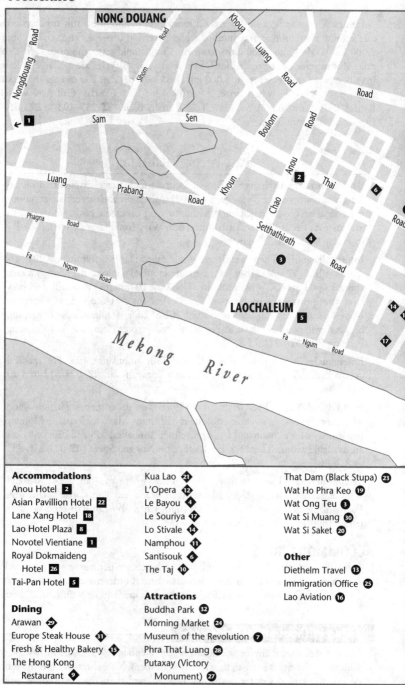

**Accommodations**
Anou Hotel **2**
Asian Pavillion Hotel **22**
Lane Xang Hotel **18**
Lao Hotel Plaza **8**
Novotel Vientiane **1**
Royal Dokmaideng
   Hotel **26**
Tai-Pan Hotel **5**

**Dining**
Arawan **29**
Europe Steak House **31**
Fresh & Healthy Bakery **15**
The Hong Kong
   Restaurant **9**

Kua Lao **21**
L'Opera **12**
Le Bayou **4**
Le Souriya **17**
Lo Stivale **14**
Namphou **11**
Santisouk **6**
The Taj **10**

**Attractions**
Buddha Park **32**
Morning Market **24**
Museum of the Revolution **7**
Phra That Luang **28**
Putaxay (Victory
   Monument) **27**

That Dam (Black Stupa) **23**
Wat Ho Phra Keo **19**
Wat Ong Teu **3**
Wat Si Muang **30**
Wat Si Saket **20**

**Other**
Diethelm Travel **13**
Immigration Office **25**
Lao Aviation **16**

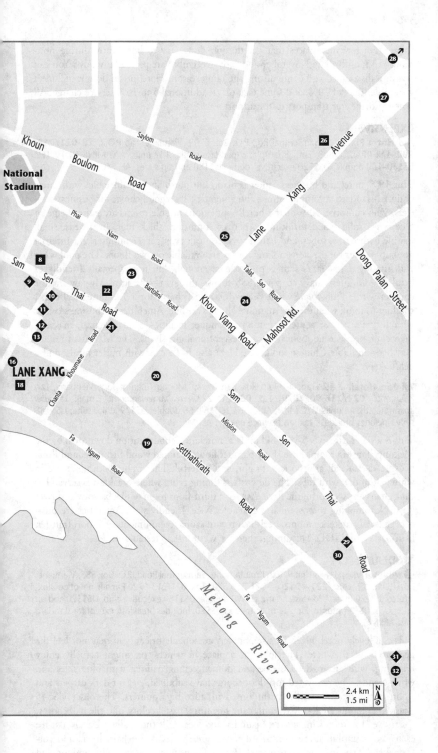

there are a few nice places that get the job done. Try to book early during non-monsoon months; late November and early December are particularly busy. You can try for a discount if you come during the rainy season. Hotel prices do not include a government tax of 10%, and some tack on an additional 5 to 10% service charge. All hotels provide free transport to the airport.

## EXPENSIVE

**Lao Hotel Plaza.** 63 Samsenthai Rd., P.O. Box 6708, Vientiane, Lao P.D.R. ☎ **021/218-800.** Fax 021/218-808. E-mail: lao-plaza@pan-laos.net.la. 142 units. A/C MINIBAR TV TEL. US$80–100 double; US$120 executive room; US$180 and up suites. AE, MC, V.

This 1997 hotel and business center is bland but plush and comfortable, with international-standard accommodations and amenities. It's a good choice for business travelers, who comprise 90% of the hotel population. Sizable rooms are either beige or blue, with solid wood furniture in perfect condition, thick rugs, firm beds, small marble bathrooms, robes, and hair dryers. You can even get a computer and Internet hookup in your room. Nonsmoking rooms are available on two floors. The pool is big and inviting. Lao Plaza's staff is professional enough, but not especially friendly or helpful. And guests have to pay US$8 to use the gym—the idea! My jaw hit the counter with a loud *thunk* when I saw a US$1.50 charge for a 3-minute local call. I shudder to think what the international charges are like. Amenities are business center with Internet access, conference rooms, banquet facilities, sauna, Jacuzzi, massage, nightclub, beer garden, bookstore, and exceptional gift shops. The May Yuan restaurant has admirable Chinese food. The Plaza also has a cafe with buffet meals, and a deli/bakery.

**Tai-Pan Hotel.** 2–12 Francois Ngin Rd., Ban Mixay, Muong Chanthabury, Vientiane, Lao P.D.R. ☎ **021/216-907/8/9.** Fax 021/216-223. www.travelao.com. E-mail: taipan@loxintfo.co.th. 44 units. A/C MINIBAR TV TEL. US$64–68 double; US$79 junior suite; US$138 suite. Includes breakfast, tax, and service charge. AE, MC, V.

This is a very attractive, 5-year-old midsize hotel, in a good location downtown by the Mekong. The big rooms have shiny parquet floors, painted wood furniture, and floral bedspreads, and all are spotless, bright, and cheerful. The sizable bathrooms are in white, clean tile, with tubs. The downstairs dining room where breakfast is served has cane chairs and a colorful tile floor. Ask for a third-floor room with a balcony and river view. Nonsmoking rooms are also available. Nice, friendly staff. Amenities are business center, conference rooms, health club with sauna, complimentary airport transfer, fruit basket, and IDD. For dining, there's a Western/Lao restaurant.

## MODERATE

✪ **Novotel Vientiane.** Unit 9, Ban Khoutarhong, Samsenthai Road, P.O. Box 585, Vientiane, Lao P.D.R. ☎ **800/221-4542** or 021/213-570. Fax 021/213-572. E-mail: novotlao@loxinfo.co.th. 220 units. US$45 standard; US$90 double; US$180 executive club; US$320 and up suite; US$800 per month, long-term. Extra bed US$20. Includes breakfast, except for standard rms. AE, MC, V.

This is a lovely hotel; given its size and very reasonable prices, you may not feel the need to look elsewhere. The lobby is a place in which you might actually enjoy lingering, with an art-deco theme and domed ceiling painted with blue skies and white clouds. The renovated top-floor rooms have subdued, elegant dark carpets and wood furniture, and marble bathrooms with nice big counters. The older US$45 "standard" rooms are less luxe, with cane furniture, pastel colors, and tile bathrooms. Executive club rooms include free laundry and local calls (normally a US50¢ flat fee each) and complimentary drinks. All rooms are spotless, with hair dryers and coffeemakers. The amiable French chef runs a fantastic restaurant, with indoor and outdoor-by-the-pool seating. His weekend brunch buffet is not to be missed; and though the daily breakfast buffet may be expensive at US$8, it's well worth it if you're hungry. The incredibly helpful staff will learn your name quickly. Facilities and services include a business center with Internet access, executive lounge, swimming pool, health club with sauna and massage, 24-hour room service, free transportation to the town center, good gift shop, bookstore, and disco.

**Royal Dokmaideng Hotel.** Lane Xang Ave., P.O. Box 3925, Vientiane, Lao P.D.R. ☎ 021/214-455. Fax 021/214-454. 40 units. A/C MINIBAR TV TEL. US$36–47 double; US$68 suite. Includes breakfast. AE, MC, V.

A very good value can be found in this clean, friendly, 5-year-old hotel, which recently reduced its rates by 50% to boost occupancy. The big rooms have attractive carpet and nice wood furnishings, with comfortable beds and plump pillows. There are nice-sized marble bathrooms, although I can't praise the moldy shower curtains or the sporadic lack of hot water. There are hair dryers, and you can get hot water thermoses upon request. The suites are huge and excellent for families. The Chinese restaurant is bright and inviting, and so is the pool. There is even a gym with a Jacuzzi and massage services (US$4.50 for an hour!). The hotel is a favorite with Chinese tour groups, which means ask for a nonsmoking room when you book, and book early to get one. Also, don't go for the standard rooms, which aren't that much cheaper at US$25 and aren't nearly as nice.

## INEXPENSIVE

✪ **Anou Hotel.** 01–03 Heng Boun St., Vientiane, Lao P.D.R. ☎ 021/213-630. Fax 021/213-632. 40 units. A/C MINIBAR TV TEL. US$25 double; US$35 suite. Includes tax and service charge. AE, V.

Here's a bargain for you. The Anou has clean, bright, good-sized rooms, some with clean beige carpet and others with hardwood floors, depending on your preference. The beds are spotless and comfortable, and the bathrooms are among the cleanest in Laos, with tile floors and walls and nice marble counters. Some of the bathrooms are shower-in-room, without bathtubs, so speak up if that matters to you. The wood furniture is in good condition. The suites are simply huge and all have wood floors, but there are only three of them. The downstairs restaurant is very inviting, and the hotel has a nice location in downtown Chinatown, surrounded by shops and restaurants.

**Asian Pavillion Hotel.** 379 Samsenthai Rd., Vientiane, Lao P.D.R. ☎ 021/213-430 or 213-431. Fax 021/213-432. 45 units. A/C MINIBAR TV TEL. US$28 double; US$35 suite. AE, JCB, MC, V.

Three years ago this place might have done just fine, but now it can rate only as a bargain hotel. The rooms are a decorator's nightmare and have ugly red carpet and slightly scuffed furniture, yet are clean. The beds are perfectly comfortable and spotless. The bathrooms are also showing signs of age, but they do have bathtubs. English speakers are at a minimum among the staff, and there are some listless-looking locals continually hanging out in the lobby watching football. The downtown location is convenient but could be noisy. There is a nice-looking restaurant and travel service on the premises. No elevators.

**Lane-Xang Hotel.** Fa Ngum Road, Vientiane, Lao P.D.R. ☎ 021/214-102. Fax 021/214-108. 109 units. A/C MINIBAR TV TEL. US$22–US$25 double; US$45–US$55 suite. Includes breakfast, tax, and service charge. AE, V.

This 40-year-old hotel, once the prize of Vientiane, is a low-end hotel today. There are tons of amenities, including two restaurants, a bar, a swimming pool, a gym with sauna and massage, elevators, and tennis courts. The rooms are nice-sized and comfortable, with new AC, clean beds, and wood floors, but they are, well, old. That means decrepit closets and peeling wallpaper. The showers have that all-too-common mold problem, too. Ask for a room with a river view. Here "single" means one bed, not one person. Do not consider a suite, whatever you do: the plastic furniture and puckered carpets are just horrendous, and the bathrooms very run down.

## DINING

French is very big in the Lao capital, and good restaurants of this ilk (along with a few serving Italian) actually outnumber those serving native Lao fare. It may sound like a pity, but the food is generally so good and so reasonably priced that you probably won't complain. There's usually a decent French wine list, or you can try lao lao, rice wine served warm, with or without herbs, snake blood, tree bark, or elephant innards. A few other local specialties to watch out for are khao poun, rice vermicelli with vegetables, meat or chilies in coconut milk; laap, minced meat, chicken or fish tossed with fresh mint leaves; or a tasty Lao-style pâté. Try sticky rice, eaten with the hands, as an accompaniment.

### EXPENSIVE

**Europe Steak House.** Tha Deua Road, Sisatanak District. ☎ **021/416-598.** Main courses US$3–US$15. Set menus US$8–US$12. V. Daily 10am–2pm and 5–11pm. STEAKHOUSE.

Steaks, steaks, steaks. If you long to sink your teeth into some fine Australian beef, try this quiet villa, surrounded by flowers in the Sisatanak suburb, a 10-minute jumbo ride from the city center. Along with steaks, there are pizzas, fish 'n' chips, spaghetti, entrecôte with rosemary potatoes, and lamb cutlet. The intimate dining room is bright and bistro-style, with linen tablecloths, flowers, and staff from nearby embassies and business folk for atmosphere. You can also sit outside on a patio surrounded by flowers, enjoying the great service and well-prepared food in healthy portions. The hamburger is one of those strange spiced-up versions, but still tasty and served with excellent crunchy fries. Another fine restaurant run by the same owners, The **Europe Restaurant** on 150 Dong Palane Thong, near the Morning Market, also serves steaks as well as an expanded menu including fish. After lunch, have a stroll and check out the nearby embassy district and its colonial mansions.

**The Hong Kong Restaurant.** 80/4 Samsenthai Rd., across from the Lao Hotel Plaza. ☎ **021/213-241.** Main courses US$5–US$13.50. No credit cards. 11:30am–2pm and 5:30–10pm. CANTONESE.

The Hong Kong (run by a bunch of folks from Beijing) is a favorite among Laos's Chinese community. The decor is standard Chinese restaurant—indoors and clean. The very fresh vegetable and soup dishes are a little under-spiced, even for Cantonese food, but the seafood specialties are good. The garlic shrimp is a must, as is the stir-fried crab with ginger. The food is surprisingly pricey, but that's probably unavoidable given the scarcity of some of the ingredients. The English menu has helpful pictures.

**L'Opera.** On the Fountain Circle. ☎ **021/215-099.** Main courses US$4.50–US$8.50. AE, V. 11:30am–2pm, 6–10pm. ITALIAN.

Real Italian. Even if you've got good Italian at home, come here for the toothsome homemade egg noodle pasta, nice Italian wine list, and fantastic authentic desserts and espresso. There is a large selection of pizzas; pizza Lao is a surprisingly good combination of tomatoes, cheese, chilies, Lao sausage, and pineapple. The ambiance is very good—a rather formal Italy meets Lao—with linen tablecloths, brick walls, and cane furniture. Very popular with expats.

**Restaurant Namphou.** On the Fountain Circle. ☎ **021/216-248.** Main courses US$4.50–US$11.50. AE, V. Daily 10:30am–3pm and 6:30–11:30pm. ASIAN/CONTINENTAL.

The ambiance couldn't be better than it is here in this intimate dining room: semi-casual native Lao yet formal enough for a business lunch. The menu is rather eclectic, a seeming combination of Thai, Lao, French, and Continental. Specialties of the house are filet mignon, a hamburger with blue cheese, and stewed deer in wine sauce. The management is extremely friendly and the service and food are excellent.

## MODERATE

✪ **Kua Lao.** 111 Samsenthai Rd. (at the intersection of Chanta Khoumane). ☎ **021/214813.** Main courses 9,800–12,800 kip (US$2.35–US$3.05). US$10 set menu. Daily 11am–2pm and 5–11:30pm. LAO.

Kua Lao is the premier Lao restaurant in the country, serving traditional Lao cuisine in a traditional setting. It's situated in a restored colonial, with a series of dining rooms. The extensive menu goes on for pages, but thankfully has English descriptions and pictures to help you out. Order one of the many specialties cooked in clay hot pots. The US$10 set menu has numerous courses and is a very good idea for sampling varied delicacies, especially if you're dining with fewer than four people. There is an entire page of vegetarian entrees, and another entire page of something you don't see often: traditional Lao desserts. The menu includes a French wine list. Music accompanies dinner. Everything is fantastic.

✪ **Le Souriya.** On Thanon Pangkham, across from Lao Aviation. ☎ **021/215-887.** Main courses US$5–US$6.50. Set lunch menu 16,000 kip (US$3.84). No credit cards. 10am–2pm and 5–10pm. FRENCH.

An intimate, candlelit spot, yet casual with open-brick walls, Le Souriya may have the finest French food in town. The food is beautifully presented and perfectly prepared, and the service is impeccable. Try the duck with peaches, pork chops with ginger and wild honey, or turkey fricassee. The set menu is a fantastic bargain. May I say again how good the food is? Not a backpacker to be found, either.

**Lo Stivale.** 44/2 Thanon Setthathirat, opposite Wat Ong Teu. ☎ **021/215-561.** Main courses US$4–US$8. AE, V. Daily 10am–10pm. MASS-MARKET ITALIAN.

In a pseudo Italian, candlelit environment, Lo Stivale features the usual pastas and meat entrees. The real highlight, though, is the pizza. Reputed to be the best in town, it certainly is fine. The pies are big, with an ultra-thin, crackerlike crust and generous fresh toppings.

## INEXPENSIVE

**Arawan.** 478 Samsenthai Rd., about 2 blocks past Wat Simuang. ☎ **021/215-373.** Main courses 9,000–30,000 kip (US$2.15–US$7.20). No credit cards. 11am–2pm and 5–10pm. RUSTIC FRENCH.

For inexpensive grilled or one-pot meals, try Arawan, perhaps for lunch after visiting Wat Simuang. The menu features all manner of meats: chicken, pork, steak (imported from New Zealand), chacroute. The food is fresh, simply prepared and very good, most entrees served with salad and French fries. There are other French specialties to be had as well: coq au vin, ragoût de mouton. Arawan has no ambiance to speak of, but the place is clean and inviting, and has an amiable French proprietor, who will be eager to chat with you if you speak some French. The menu has English translations. Most main courses go up to only about 15,000 kip (US$3.60); it's the steaks that cost the big bucks.

**Le Bayou.** Setthathirat St., across from Wat Ong Teu. ☎ **021/222-227.** Main courses US$1.50–US$4. No credit cards. Daily 11am–10pm. CONTINENTAL.

This casual place calls itself a "brasserie," but inside it has a Louisiana low-country theme, except for the French prints on the walls and the English/French menu. The menu is heavy on soups, salads, and sandwiches, which are truly unique and delicious. Try the Le Bayou sandwich, a very thin omelet, diced chicken, and melted cheese on a crispy French roll. This is definitely a lunch rather than a dinner spot. There is outdoor seating to the side.

**Santisouk.** 77/79 Nokeo Koumman St., ☎ **071/215-303.** Main courses 7,000–14,000 kip (US$1.68–US$3.36). No credit cards. 7am–11pm. LAO/FRENCH.

Santisouk specializes in large-quantity Lao specialties for little kip. The atmosphere isn't much to speak of, a rather dark institutional dining room on the bottom floor of a guest house. But at least it's indoors, and the food is tasty, particularly the fried chicken and deep fried frog with garlic. The menu isn't very descriptive, but then the food isn't very complex. Very good omelets as well.

**The Taj.** 75/4 Pangkham Rd., Nam Phu Square. ☎ **21/212-890.** Main courses 10,000–16,000 kip (US$2.40–US$3.85). Set menu 8,500–10,500 kip (US$2–US$2.50). Buffet lunch 9,500 kip (US$2.25); kids under 5 eat free. Daily 11am–2pm and 5:30–10pm. NORTH INDIAN.

The food at this Indian restaurant is terrific, especially for the price. The menu is light on unnecessary spice and heavy on the creative and flavorful, in an upscale atmosphere that is part Indian, part Continental. Try the chicken in almond sauce and the Special Taj tea, heavily flavored with ginger. Exciting and unique.

## SNACKS & CAFES

Stop at the **Healthy & Fresh Bakery** at 44/4 Ban Xieng Yeun, Setthathirat Road (two doors down from Le Santal). It's everything it says it is, and great-tasting as well. It also serves quiche and salads along with breads and sweets, and fantastic coffee. **The Scandinavian Bakery,** off Nam Phu Fountain Circle, has specialties from that region (and daily bread specials) and is always packed with travelers. A spot to stop and sample Lao food very inexpensively (as well as take in the scenery) is the **Dong Phalan night market** on Talat Nong Duoang Road, not far from the Novotel. You can graze on such Lao snacks as kebabs and spring rolls and stuff yourself for less than 10,000 kip (US$2.40) at the **Lao Hotel Plaza Beer Garden** at 63 Samsenthai Rd. There is also a string of small open-air eateries facing the Mekong River on Fa Ngum Road, between Pangkham and Nokeo Khumman streets. **PVO,** an open-air stall next to the Lao Paris Hotel on Samsenthai Road, serves outstanding Vietnamese pho (noodle soup) and spring rolls for 3,500 kip (US85¢).

## ATTRACTIONS

While Vientiane doesn't have the sheer number of wats enjoyed by Luang Prabang, they still dominate the list of must-sees here. Most sights are still within the city limits, which means you'll be able to cover them on foot, getting to know the city intimately as you go.

### Travel Tip: Photo Services in Vientiane

The best places in town to buy and develop film are the large-scale Venus Color Lab, on the corner of Samsenthai and Chanta Khumman streets, across from the Phimphone Market, or the Kodak shop in the Anou Hotel, 01–03 Heng Boun St.

⭐ **Phra That Luang.** At the end of That Luang Rd. Admission: 500 kip (US10¢). Tues–Sun 8–11am and 2–4:30pm. Closed Mon.

This is the pre-eminent temple in Lao, actually a 148-foot-tall stupa (see "What's a Wat?" on p. 352). It is not the original; the first, built in 1566 by King Setthathirat over the ruins of a 12th-century Khmer temple, was destroyed when the Siamese sacked Vientiane in 1828. It was rebuilt by the French in 1900, but the Lao people criticized it as not being true to the original. It was torn down in 1930 and remodeled to become the temple you see today. As you approach, the statue in front depicts Setthathirat. After you enter the first courtyard, look to the left to see a sacred bodhi tree, the same variety as that under which Buddha sat to achieve enlightenment. It has a tall, slim trunk and the shape of its foliage is almost perfectly round. According to the Laotians, bodhi trees only appear in sacred places. You'll never see one, for example, in someone's backyard. The stupa is built in stages. On the second level there are 30 small stupas, representing the 30 Buddhist perfections, or stages to enlightenment. That Luang is the site of one of Lao's most important temple festivals, which takes place in early November.

**Morning Market (Talaat Sao).** On Talat Sao Rd., off Lane Xang Ave. Daily 7am–5pm.

You could poke around peacefully for hours in this huge market, with its three buildings full of produce, electronics, and handicrafts of all types. Best of all, the atmosphere is very low-key. No one will follow you, shriek at you, or hassle you to buy. It's an excellent source of gifts and souvenirs.

**Wat Ho Phra Keo.** On Thanon Setthathirat, opposite Wat Sisaket. Admission 500 kip (US10¢). Tues–Sun 8:30–11:30am and 2–4:30pm.

Also built by King Setthathirat in 1566, Phra Keo was constructed to house an emerald Buddha the king took from Thailand (which the Thais took back in 1779). Today there are no monks in residence, and the wat is actually a museum of religious art, including a Khmer stone Buddha and a wooden copy of the famous Luang Prabang Buddha. In the garden, there's a transplanted jar from the Plain of Jars (see section 5, below).

**Museum of the Revolution.** Samsenthai Rd., near the Lao Plaza Hotel. Admission: 500 kip (US10¢). Mon–Fri 8–11:30am and 2–4pm, Sat 8–11:30am.

Housed in an interesting old colonial that was once used for government offices, the Museum of the Revolution has photos, artifacts, and re-creations of the Lao struggle for independence against the French and Americans. The exhibits (firearms, chairs used by national heroes and the like) are rather scanty, barely scratching the surface of such a complicated subject, but most are in English at least. Archaeological finds and maps presented on the first floor (probably because there is no other museum to house them at present) help make a visit here worthwhile. Actually, one of the most interesting exhibits is in the last room before you exit, sort of a Laos trade and commodities exhibit of produce, handiwork, and manufactured goods. Though dated, it will give you some idea of Laos's geography and commerce.

**Patuxay (Victory Monument).** At the end of Lane Xang Ave. Admission: 200 kip (US5¢). Daily 8am–5pm.

This monument was completed in 1968 and dedicated to those who fought in the war of independence against the French. Ironically, the monument is an arch modeled on the Parisian Arc de Triomphe. Its detailing is typically Lao, however, with many *kinnari* figures—half woman, half bird. It's an imposing sight, and you can climb up for a good city view.

# What's a Wat?

A **wat** is a monastery. It has several components: a **sim,** or main building, where morning and evening prayers are held; **tombs** for cremated remains of monks or local families; and perhaps a drum chapel, a schoolhouse, and monks' or nuns' lodgings. A good-sized wat will house 20 to 30 monks. A **stupa,** on the other hand, is a monument built over a holy site or relic, and they can often be found in wats.

Wats are distinguished architecturally by their roofs. Lao sims have curved, multilayered roofs, but Luang Prabang has a special style of its own, with the ceilings of the sim stretching down almost to the ground. The Buddha figure in the main sim is usually the largest in the complex. Look to the ceilings of the sim for unusual painting or decoration. In some wats you will see a 4-foot-high wooden object with a long wooden crossbeam. It looks like a scale, but it's actually used for a ceremonial washing of Buddha on feast days. Buddha sits at one end of the chute, and water is poured into the other. You may also see small towers on the grounds, actually tombs for venerated monks or local families.

Most young Lao men will spend some time in a wat, usually 3 to 6 months around the time of puberty, refining their religious knowledge. When visiting, remember to take off your shoes before entering the sim or other buildings, and female visitors should be careful not to make physical contact with a monk. A donation of 1,000 kip (US25¢) or so is appropriate.

**Wat Si Saket.** At the corner of Setthathirat and Lane Xang avenues. Admission: 500 kip (US10¢). Daily 8am–noon and 1–6pm.

Wat Si Saket, completed in 1818, is the only temple in Vientiane to survive the pillaging of the city by the Siamese in 1828, perhaps because the temple is built in traditional Thai style. It is renowned for the more than 10,000 Buddha images in the outer courtyard, of all shapes and sizes, in every possible nook and cranny. Look for Buddha characteristics that are unique to Laos: the standing or "praying for rain" Buddha; or the pose with arms up and palms facing forward, the "stop fighting" or calling for peace Buddha. The pose where Buddha points the right hand downward signifies a rejection of evil, and a calling to mother earth for wisdom and assistance. Lao Buddhas also have exaggerated nipples and square noses, to emphasize that Buddha is no longer human. The sim features a Khmer-style Buddha seated on a coiled cobra for protection.

**Wat Ong Teu.** Intersection of Setthathirat and Chou Anou roads. Daily 8am–5pm.

Wat Ong Teu is in a particularly auspicious location, surrounded by four temples: Wat Inpeng to the north, Wat Mixay to the south, Wat Haysok to the east, and Wat Chan to the west. Its name comes from its most famous inhabitant, a huge *(ongteu)* bronze Buddha. The temple, famous for its beautifully carved wooden facade, was built in the early 16th century, and rebuilt in the 19th and 20th centuries. It also serves as a national center for Buddhist studies.

**That Dam (the Black Stupa).** At the intersections of Thanons Chanta Khumman and Bartholomie.

This ancient stupa was probably constructed in the 15th century or even earlier, though it has never been dated. It is rumored to be the resting place of a mighty *naga,* or seven-headed dragon, that protected the local residents during the Thai invasion in the early 1800s.

# Where to Get a Massage

Near Wat Chan (near the intersection on Setthathirat and Chon Anon roads), Mr. Amphone, a self-proclaimed kung fu master who studied at China's Shaolin temple, gives a 1-hour **acupressure massage** for 7,000 kip (US$1.70). The price includes a five-herb steam bath: tea, lemongrass, clover, jasmine, and something untranslatable. It's an outdoor, very local experience, and the master has great hands. Inquire at the wat for directions and bring your own towel or sari. You can also head out to the **Vatnak Health Center** in the Sisatanak District (take a jumbo for the 10-minute ride), where you'll find **saunas** for 4,000 kip (US95¢), and **massages** for 10,000 kip (US$2.40) per hour (daily 4–9pm).

**Wat Si Muang.** East on Samsenthai, near where it joins Setthathirat. Daily 8am–5pm.

Wat Si Muang, another 1566 Setthathirat creation, houses the foundation pillar of the city. According to legend, a pregnant woman named Nang Si, inspired by the gods to sacrifice herself, jumped into the pit right before the stone was lowered. She has now become a sort of patron saint for the city. The temple is very popular as a result, and is the site of a colorful procession 2 days before the That Luang festival every November.

**Buddha Park.** About 15 miles southeast of town. Admission: 500 kip (US10¢), plus 500 for jumbo parking and 500 to use a camera. Daily 7:30am–5:30pm.

Buddha Park is more like a fanciful sculpture garden, full of Hindu and Buddhist statues created in the 1950s by a shamanist priest named Luang Pu. They are captivating, whether they are snarling, reposing, or saving maidens in distress (or carrying them to their doom, it's hard to tell). The huge reclining Buddha is outstanding; you can climb on its arm for a photo. There is also a big concrete dome to climb, itself filled with sculptures. The half-hour jumbo ride to get here, should you choose that route, is very dusty, but fulfilling: you get a clear view of Thailand across the Mekong.

## SPORTS & OUTDOOR ACTIVITIES

While you may not usually think of joining in on local sports activities on your vacation, the laid-back Lao seems to invite socializing. It certainly attracts interesting people. The Vientiane Hash House Harriers have a **family run** every Monday evening at 5:30pm. Information on venues can be found at the Phimphone Mini-market on the corner of Khumman and Samsenthai streets. Vientiane is small and clean enough to make this a fun experience, and a chance to meet expats. (Drinking follows.) Every Saturday at the field near the U.S. Ambassador's residence there is **softball** starting at 3:30pm. For information, call ☎ **021/413-273** (days).

## SHOPPING

Laos is famous for its hand-woven silk textiles. You can buy them in fabric, or readymade wall hangings, accessories, and clothing. Silver is everywhere, in jewelry and ornamental objects. The main shopping streets are **Samsenthai** and **Setthathirat,** around the Nam Phu fountain area. Be sure to visit **Satri Lao Silk,** at 79/4 Setthathirat, for fabrics, clothing and housewares, and **Carol Cassidy** off Setthathirat on Nokeo Khumman, who designs her own fabrics using traditional Lao motifs as a base. **Ikho 2,** off Nam Phu fountain to the east of Diethelm Travel, is also a good gift shop. To have something tailored from the extraordinary Lao fabric, go to **Kinnaly Fashion,** at 297/8 Samsenthai, or **Yani** in the Mixay Arcade, across from Wat Ong Teu. For a

## Shopping Tip: English-Language Bookstores in Vientiane

**Raintrees Bookstore** at Pangkahm Road, across from Lao Aviation, sells mostly trashy paperback novels, but when you're desperate they'll do. There are branches with better books in the Novotel and Lao Hotel Plaza hotels. You can also find foreign periodicals at the **State Books Publishing and Distribution House,** corner of Setthathirat Road and Manthatoulat Street.

broad selection of silver and gold jewelry, check the shop on the corner of Samsenthai and Pangkham roads. You can also find native handicrafts: silver, textiles, and carved wood housewares, in the **Talaat Sao morning market,** the big peaked green buildings on Lane Xang Avenue.

## VIENTIANE AFTER DARK

There are a few places around town to meet and greet other English-speakers. The **Fountain Grill,** surrounding Nam Phu fountain, is the hot spot for expats and travelers. There is also a wine bar, **Le Cave de Chateux,** on Fountain Circle. The **Lao Plaza Hotel** has a nightclub/disco and popular beer garden, and the **Novotel** has a happening disco. Be careful if you're strolling about after dark, though, as Vientiane has a goodly number of open sewers.

## EXCURSIONS FROM VIENTIANE

**Vang Vieng.** 4 hours north of Vientiane by bus.

Surrounded by mountains, limestone caves, and karst formations (underground caves and caverns formed by the movement of water), Vang Vieng is an appealing village in majestic surroundings. Travelers come here for the hiking and spelunking in the numerous surrounding caves. You may want to stay a night or two, especially to break up a long overland trip to Luang Prabang. The best place in town is the **Hotel Nam Song** (☎ 021/213-506), with clean, tile-floor, air-conditioned rooms and a magnificent view of a private lake. Double rooms are US$16 to US$25, including breakfast. Inquire at any travel agency for bus tickets to Vang Vieng. Diethelm Travel (see "Planning a Trip to Laos," above) offers rafting/trekking tours on the Nam Song River, which passes through the town.

**Lao Pako.** About 24 miles north of Vientiane on the Nam Ngum River.

Here's your chance to visit a Lao "resort," developed with ecotourism in mind. Lodging is in traditional slant-roofed longhouses, which cost from 45,000 kip (US$10.80) for a double room to 65,000 (US$15.60) for your own private bungalow. There isn't much to do except relax, trek, visit villages, and take a few rafting trips, but the experience will doubtless prove interesting. To get there, you can take a local bus for an hour or rent a vehicle. To inquire, call the resort's Vientiane office at ☎ 021/222-925 or fax 021/212-981.

## Travel Tip: Where to Find Toiletries, etc.

The **Phimphone Market** on the corners of Samsenthai and Chanta Khumman has almost every foreign toiletry you could wish for (but no mosquito repellent or feminine hygiene products). There's yogurt and ice cream, too.

# 4  Luang Prabang

We were hanging out in an open cafe by the side of a street so sleepy the only traffic was a tuk-tuk or two and a group of barefoot monks. Lounging and taking in the scenery are favorite preoccupations of many who visit Luang Prabang. My friend Bruce sighed happily after sipping the last of his pineapple banana smoothie, pushed it away and proclaimed, "This place is going to be one of the great Asian destinations in a year or two." Like Lhasa, Kathmandu, and Phuket, each of which have seen their days of glory, Luang Prabang is an enthralling place, yet it is still fragrant and untouched beneath its own exotic, protective shell—just difficult enough to reach to make it a pipe dream for most of the world. For now.

Literally meaning "great holy image," Luang Prabang has been named one of UNESCO's World Heritage Sites for its aged religious and colonial structures. The first capital of Laos, it has remained relatively untouched by war, or even the ravages of time. Thirty-three temples and wats stand in the small, gracefully laid-out town on the banks of the Mekong and Nam Khan rivers, each more beautiful than the next.

Allow yourself at least three days to sink into the city's languid rhythms. Get up at 6am to see monks strolling the streets for alms. Walk from wat to wat at 5:30pm to hear them chant their evening prayers. Finally, retire to a stilt-house—in this case, a stilt bar—to have a drink and watch the spectacular river sunsets.

## VISITOR INFORMATION & TOURS

A few companies in town provide tour services.

- **Luang Prabang Travel & Tour Co.,** 72 Phothisarat Rd. (☎ 071/212-198 or 212-379; fax 071/212-728).
- **Diethelm Travel,** Phothisarat Road, near the Villa Santi (☎ 071/212-034). Monday to Saturday 8am to noon; 2 to 5pm. Diethelm does trekking trips to the nearby Hmong Village and rafting on the Mekong.
- **Sodetour,** 105/6 Souvannabalang Road near the boat docks on the river (☎ 071/212-092). Hours Monday to Friday 8am to noon and 1:30 to 4pm, Saturday 8am to noon. Very professional outfit.

## GETTING THERE

**BY PLANE**   Lao Aviation has three daily flights from Vientiane to Luang Prabang, at 8:30am, 11am and 3:30pm, for US$55 one-way. You can also fly in from Chiang Mai, Thailand. You must have a valid Lao visa to enter.

**BY BUS/MINIVAN**   The overland route to Luang Prabang from Vientiane takes about 11 hours by public bus, depending on how many times it breaks down. However, the jaw-dropping scenery, past the mountains and limestone formations at Vang Vieng and several Hmong hill villages along the way, is well worth making the trip by land at least once. The bus costs 25,000 kip (US$6).

Unfortunately, the tour agencies have yet to provide organized minivan rides, so if you choose that mode you may be renting a vehicle on your own. One-way costs about US$140, hardly economical unless you're with a group.

**BY JEEP OR TRUCK**   Taking the mountain route by jeep or truck (it's not very safe to go by car) takes 7 hours and will cost about US$120 per day, and some rental agencies will ask you to pay for a driver's lodging as well. Do not attempt to drive yourself. It's a drive only for those who know the road well. You'll also be a sitting duck for bandit action (see below) and will probably be stopped by guards at provincial borders for your own protection. Travel agents will quote as high as US$200, but you can

## Travel Tip: Check in with Immigration

Don't forget to check in with Immigration on Thanon Wisunalat as soon as you arrive in Luang Prabang, and before departing the city. If you arrive by air, you will be checked at the airport. The bus station has immigration officials present, too. If you don't check in, you may be fined.

do better. Ask around town; you're likely to do best with a private arrangement. Somebody will know somebody with a vehicle.

**BY BOAT**   It is possible to travel by cargo boat from Vientiane to Luang Prabang, but it's a 4 or 5-day trip upriver, and you have to be willing to undertake very rough conditions: sleeping on a mat and so forth. Speedboats south from Luang Prabang to Vientiane take about 8 or 9 very noisy hours; you can charter one for about US$80.

### GETTING AROUND

Luang Prabang is easy to cover on foot, and if you get tired, tuk-tuks and jumbos cost about 1,000 kip (US25¢) a trip. For sights outside the city, jumbos usually gather next to the Central Market (Talaat Dala); prices are negotiable. You can rent motorcycles across from the Market and elsewhere for about US$7 per day. Note that the Western spelling of many street and wat names is very inconsistent, and that the same road can change names as it progresses through the city.

# Fast Facts: Luang Prabang

**Banks/Currency Exchange**   The Lane Xang Bank is at Phothisarat Road, next to the New Luang Prabang Hotel. Hours: Monday to Saturday 8:30am to 3:30am. Closed Sundays and holidays. You can exchange cash and traveler's checks in most major currencies to kip and withdraw cash using a Visa card. You can also change money at hotels and on the black market. Unlike in Vientiane, there will be no shortage of people openly offering you such services on the street, and the exchange rate will be better by 200 or 300 kip.

**Emergencies**   For police, dial ☎ 212-156; for an ambulance, ☎ 212-123.

**Post Office/Mail**   The post office is on the corner of Phothisarat and Kitsalat roads, across from Luang Prabang Travel and Tourism. Hours are Monday to Friday 8am to noon and 1 to 5pm, Saturday 8am to noon.

**Telephone**   The city code for Luang Prabang is 71. Dial a "0" first inside Laos. The telephone center in town, as it were, consists of two booths around the corner from the post office on Thanon Kitsalat. You can buy local and international cards in an office across the street.

## ACCOMMODATIONS

There are numerous places to stay in the city, most loaded with atmosphere. Don't expect any real bargains, as demand is high in the dry season. Service is, shall I say, relaxed, as befits Luang Prabang, and moldy bathrooms seem to be a common problem. Amenities like hair dryers, coffeemakers, and working televisions are rare.

### EXPENSIVE

**Phou Vao Hotel.** Phou Vao St., Luang Prabang. ☎ **071/212-194.** Fax 071/212-534. 59 units. A/C MINIBAR TV TEL. Double US$70; US$114–US$136 suite (there are 2). Additional

# Luang Prabang

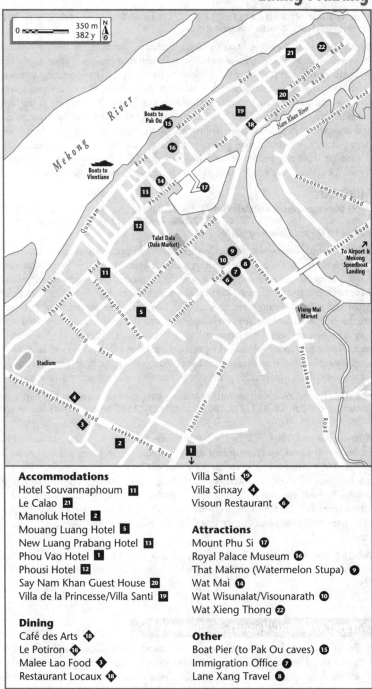

**Accommodations**
Hotel Souvannaphoum **11**
Le Calao **21**
Manoluk Hotel **2**
Mouang Luang Hotel **5**
New Luang Prabang Hotel **13**
Phou Vao Hotel **1**
Phousi Hotel **12**
Say Nam Khan Guest House **20**
Villa de la Princesse/Villa Santi **19**

**Dining**
Café des Arts **18**
Le Potiron **18**
Malee Lao Food **3**
Restaurant Locaux **18**

Villa Santi **19**
Villa Sinxay **4**
Visoun Restaurant **6**

**Attractions**
Mount Phu Si **17**
Royal Palace Museum **16**
That Makmo (Watermelon Stupa) **9**
Wat Mai **14**
Wat Wisunalat/Visounarath **10**
Wat Xieng Thong **22**

**Other**
Boat Pier (to Pak Ou caves) **15**
Immigration Office **7**
Lane Xang Travel **8**

15% surcharge Apr 13–17 and Dec 12–Jan 2. Double US$49; US$89–US$96 suite in low season (May–Sept). Includes breakfast and tax.

This is touted as the "best hotel in Luang Prabang," doubtless because it offers the most amenities and is nearly always full with French tour groups. It does have a small swimming pool, but it's rather far outside the town center. Transportation to town is available upon request; or rather when the driver is available. Rooms are smallish and recently renovated, with parquet floors and balconies that take advantage of the hotel's location on a quiet hilltop. The beds are comfortable and the wood furniture modern and attractive. There are marble bathrooms with bathtubs, but they could use some strong detergent around the grouting and they are not air-conditioned (they're doored-off from the bedrooms, which do have A/C). The staff is very young and friendly, but could use a bit of training. There's a good indoor Lao/French restaurant.

## MODERATE

**Hotel Souvannaphoum (Relais Hotel).** Phothisarath Rd., Namphou Square, P.O. Box 741, Luang Prabang, Lao P.D.R. ☎ **071/212-200.** Fax 071/212-577. 25 units. A/C. US$52 double; US$75 suite (there are 2). AE, V.

The Souvannaphoum was formerly the villa of Prince Souvannaphouma, which accounts for the beautiful, quiet setting, lobby, restaurant, and bar here. Most of the hotel is open-air and decorated with a safari lodge theme. The rooms are surprisingly basic but clean and comfortable, with nice wooden floors and marble bathrooms. The decor and amenities stop there, though. The two suites (the former royal bedrooms) are the exception, and are absolutely huge and well-decorated. You'll feel royal if you spring for one of them. Otherwise, at least ask for a room with a balcony. The staff is friendly and tries to be helpful, when you can find them. Telephone and laundry services are available, as is assistance with travel services when the Inter-Lao Tourism desk is manned, which unfortunately isn't often. The open-air restaurant is very good.

**Le Calao.** Thanon Khaem Khong (on the Mekong River, close to Wat Xieng Thuong), Luang Prabang, Lao P.D.R. ☎ **071/212-100.** 5 units. A/C. US$55 double (US$45 low season). Includes breakfast. AE, V.

A newly restored 1904 villa on the banks of the Mekong, Le Calao has arched balconies, wood floors, and an outdoor dining pavilion. Its location, size and decor are unique and picturesque. The rooms are a nice size and very comfortable, with wood furniture and tile floors, and have been well-designed to further the colonial feel of the place. The beds are firm and comfortable. Bathrooms have wood cabinetry but are otherwise rather spartan, with no bathtubs. There seems to be a staff of one. Given these factors and the lack of other amenities, the price seems expensive, even with the view.

**Monoluk Hotel.** 121/3 Phou Vao St., Luang Prabang, Laos. ☎ **071/212-250** or 071/212-509. Fax 071/212-508. 30 units. A/C MINIBAR TV TEL. US$45 double. Includes breakfast. AE, V.

---

### Travel Warning: Bandits on Highway 13

Bandits and rebels occasionally attack public and tour buses on Highway 13 from Vientiane. There have been no attacks involving tourists in the past few years, but attacks involving Lao nationals still occasionally occur. Security has improved— there are army stations in the risky areas—but check with your embassy before you go.

An interesting choice, the Manoluk. The rooms are large and have polished wood floors and ceilings, burl tables and chairs and amazingly comfortable beds. The bathrooms are similarly large, finished with tile, and clean for Luang Prabang. (They even have hair dryers.) The huge restaurant and second-floor lounge, complete with wooden deer heads, give the place the feel of a lodge. (A good feeling, it should be stressed.) The staff seems to be nonexistent, save for a person or two at the front desk watching the lobby television. Somehow, that seems to suit the laid-back, private feel of the place. There are motorcycles and bicycles for rent.

**Mouang Laung Hotel.** Bounkhong Rd., Luang Prabang, Lao P.D.R. ☎ **071/212-791.** Fax 071/212-790. 37 units. A/C MINIBAR TEL. US$45 double; US$60 suite. Includes breakfast. AE, V.

This 2-year-old hotel is styled to look like a traditional Lao building. It is quite nice, with two stories of sizable rooms with wood floors. The rooms have big balconies and hand-woven bedspreads—nice touches. The bathrooms are small but are all marble and clean. The restaurant is pleasant, as is the staff. Compared to its closest competitor, the Phou Vao, this place has fewer amenities, but it's in a much better location downtown. There is a big empty swimming pool out back, but it's rather depressing and may be dangerous for children.

✪ **Phousi Hotel.** Thanon Kitsalat (at the intersection of Kitsalat and Phothisarat roads), Luang Prabang, Lao P.D.R. ☎ **071/212193.** Fax 071/212719. 43 units. A/C MINIBAR TV TEL. US$30–40 double; US$56 family rooms. MC, V.

For all-round comfort and convenience, this is probably your best bet in Luang Prabang. The rooms are neat and clean, with nice teak furniture and floral fabrics, and spotless big tile bathrooms. The more expensive doubles have wood floors. The hotel is situated in a prime downtown spot, across from the Market. At night it glitters with strings of lights (a very nice rather than tacky effect in magical Luang Prabang), and traditional musicians serenade. The staff is accommodating and efficient. Try to book early, as it's a tour group favorite.

✪ **Villa de la Princesse (Villa Santi).** P.O. Box 681, Sakkarine St., Luang Prabang, Lao P.D.R. ☎ /fax **071/212-267.** 25 units. US$45 double; US$55 suite. V.

Formerly the residence of Lao princess Manili, this low-key villa reopened in 1992, perfectly renovated. The setting is quiet, with the rooms surrounding an inner garden. Rooms have parquet floors and teak furniture, and the tile bathrooms look brand new. Everything is spotless. A new wing was built 4 years ago, not quite as atmospheric as the old. Only four rooms have king-sized beds, so be sure to specify when you book if that's what you want. The overall charm and the convenient downtown location make this one of the top choices in Luang Prabang. There are restaurants in both the old and new wings; the one in the old wing has a slightly better atmosphere (see "Dining," below).

## INEXPENSIVE

**New Luang Prabang Hotel.** Phothisarat Rd. (next to Luang Prabang Travel), Luang Prabang, Lao P.D.R. ☎ **071/212-264.** Fax 071/212-804. 15 units. A/C MINIBAR TEL. US$30 double. Includes tax. No credit cards.

The New Luang Prabang is a 4-year-old minihotel, but it looks older. The rooms are much nicer than the faded-carpet hallways; they're clean, with nice parquet floors. Beds come in sets of two twins only, but they are comfortable and clean. Bathrooms have no separate showers or tubs; it's the all-in-one variety. The hotel is smack in the middle of the downtown area; there is no better location. The staff is very nice, but don't expect the service or facilities of a real hotel. No elevators.

**Say Nam Khan Guest House.** Ban Wat Sene (off Kingkitsalath Rd.), Luang Prabang, Lao P.D.R. ☎ **071/212-976.** 14 units. A/C. US$20–25 double. No credit cards.

This little place in a renovated colonial building on the banks of the Nam Kham River is just plain charming. The smallish rooms have comfortable beds and wood furniture. The bathrooms are clean, tile with shower-in-room. Some of the rooms have ugly red carpet, others a teak floor. There is a bar in the lobby for drinks with a river view.

## DINING

Pull up a chair. There is a great variety of inexpensive restaurants in Luang Prabang, all exemplary of the town's friendly atmosphere. What we've called "restaurant row" is easily found along the end of Phothisarat Street as it turns into Xieng Thong. It's also about the only place in town alive past 9pm.

**Café des Arts.** Xieng Thong Rd. (on "restaurant row"). No telephone. Main courses 3,800–12,500 kip (US90¢–US$3). No credit cards. 7am–11pm. FRENCH/CONTINENTAL.

The specialty here is "make your own salad" with six ingredients picked from a long list. Your trusty reviewer can vouch for the cleanliness of the fresh greens. Pasta, hamburgers, crepes, filet de boeuf and tartines round out the very appetizing menu. Breakfast is omelets galore. Open-air like all the others on restaurant row, Café des Arts has a better atmosphere than most, with real tables and chairs with linen tablecloths, and black-and-white prints on the walls.

**Le Potiron.** Xieng Thong Rd., on restaurant row. ☎ **071/212-702.** Main courses 7,900–11,000 kip (US$1.90–US$2.65). No credit cards. 5–10:30pm. FRENCH/PIZZA.

Run by a French expat, this place most closely resembles a pizza parlor with its checked tablecloths and casual atmosphere, deer and boar pâté aside. Come to think of it, the beef tongue and chocolate soufflé also add a French touch. Be my guest, but I'd still stick with the pizza. The special pie with the Luang Prabang seaweed is very tasty.

**Malee Lao Food.** Near the intersection of Phu Wao and Samsenthai. Main courses 3,500–7,000 kip (US80¢–US$1.70). Daily 10am–10pm. LAO.

Malee Lao dishes up inexpensive and delicious local cuisine in a large, casual, open-air setting crammed with backpackers. Curries predominate; try the chicken curry soup, which is actually big pieces of chicken and potato in sauce. It's best eaten sopped up by hand with sticky rice. The oolam is a Luang Prabang specialty: eggplant, meat, and mixed vegetable soup flavored with a singular bitter root. The cute kids of the household are constantly playing and running around, which adds to the very friendly atmosphere. Always crowded at dinner.

**Restaurat Locaux.** 23/6 Phothisarat Rd. Main courses 3,000–8,000 kip (US70¢–US$1.90). No credit cards. Daily 7am–11pm. LAO.

Locaux is a very casual open-air stall that serves all manner of Lao specialties. Everything is tasty, particularly the green spring rolls made with fresh vegetables. You may need to work up your nerve to order "fried Hairdo vet flour," "banana flabbier," "fried chicken + girdle + coconuts" and especially "fried sewer & sauce," but the food is much better than the English here. In a pinch, check out your neighbor's plate and ask for what he's having.

✪ **Villa Santi.** Sakkarine St., Luang Prabang (in the Villa Santi Hotel). ☎ **071/212-267.** Main courses US$2–US$5. V. Daily 7am–10pm. LAO/CONTINENTAL.

Villa Santi provides exquisite food on the upper floor of a restored colonial villa. The food is local and traditional Lao, along with some creative Asian-influenced continental: try mok pa (steamed fish cooked in banana leaves), watercress soup, and pork brochettes with lemongrass. The most exotic item on the menu is probably the wild boar pepper steak. It's more tender than you might think, and worth every penny of the US$5 it costs. Deserts are scrumptious: bananas flambéed in Cointreau, fruit salad in rum. There are more casual offerings for lunch, including hamburgers. The restaurant has indoor and outdoor balcony seating. Most evenings there will be traditional music and dancing in the courtyard below, and the restaurant is casual enough to allow you to stroll to the window for a look. Dining will be a memorable experience.

**Villa Sinxay (formerly The Luang Prabang Restaurant).** Phu Vao Rd. ☎ **071/212-587.** Main courses 4,500–9,000 kip (US$1.10–US$2.15). No credit cards. 7am–10pm. LAO/FRENCH.

Sinxay serves local specialties in a well-designed, open-air villa. It has a long reputation of serving some of the best Lao food in town. The cuisine is creative and excellent, especially for the price. Fried chicken in bamboo, stewed aulam boar (with a bitter herb unique to Luang Prabang), and laap with fish all easily passed muster. The restaurant is run by a Lao woman and her French expat husband, which explains the coq au vin on the menu. He will also proffer good French wines upon request. Traditional music some nights.

**Visoun Restaurant.** Visounnalat (also spelled Wisunalat) Rd., next to the immigration office. ☎ **071/212-268.** Main courses 3,000–10,000 kip (US70¢–US$2.40) No credit cards. Daily 7am–9pm. CHINESE.

This low-scale open-air restaurant has a very casual environment, but it serves tasty Chinese food. The menu is a bit hard to decipher, getting no more specific than "fried chicken" or "pork with long beans," but the food is fresh and good. Visoun has a very big vegetarian selection as well.

## ATTRACTIONS

**Royal Palace Museum.** Phothisarat Rd. Admission 3,000 kip (US70¢). Mon–Sat 8–11am and 1:30–4pm.

The palace, built for King Sisavang Vong from 1904 to 1909, was the royal residence until the Pathet Lao seized control of the country in 1975. The last Lao king, Sisavang Vattana, and his family were exiled to a remote region in the northern part of the country and never heard from again. Rumor has it that they perished in a prison camp, though the government has never said so. The palace remains now as a repository of treasures, rather scanty but still interesting. You can begin your tour by walking the length of the long porch; the gated, open room to your right has one of the museum's top attractions, an 83-centimeter-high golden standing Buddha that was a gift to King Fa Ngum from a Khmer king. It's the namesake of Luang Prabang, "holy image." This is only a copy, however; the real thing is in a vault of the State Bank. To your right on the inside, note the fantastic murals on the wall of the receiving room, painted in 1930. Each panel is shown to best effect as the sun hits it at different times of the day. The main throne room features lavish colored glass murals and, in a cabinet near the door, the coronation robes of the last prince. Throughout the palace are numerous *ding sun* drums, huge priceless bronze floor ornaments, some of them 1,000 years old.

Outside the palace, a large Soviet-made statue of Sisavang Vong, the first king under the Lao constitution, waves to your left. The temple on the right as you face the palace, Phra Bang, has doors created by Thid Tud, considered Laos' greatest sculptor. The temple is reportedly being renovated to house the golden standing Pra Bang Buddha.

---

**Travel Tip: Taking a Break**

The **Luang Prabang Bakery** and the **Scandinavian Bakery** are a few doors away from each other on Phothisarat Road. Both are excellent for pastries and coffee. In the evenings, check out the **Banana Fritter Man,** with a cart on the corner of Phothisarat Road in front of Luang Prabang Tourism. Watching him spin dough without catching it on his very clunky sports watch is choice entertainment in itself.

---

**Wat Mai.** Phothisarat Rd., near the Lane Xang Bank.

Wat Mai is considered one of the jewels of Luang Prabang. Its golden bas-relief facade tells the story of Phravet, one of the last avatars, or reincarnations, of the Buddha. It held the Pra Bang Buddha from 1894 until 1947. Stop by here at 5:30pm for the evening prayers, when the monks chant in harmony.

**Mount Phu Si (Phousi)**

Rising from the center of town, Phu Si has temples scattered on all sides of its slopes, and a panoramic view of the entire town from its top. **That Chomsi Stupa,** built in 1804, is its crowning glory. Taking the path to the northeast, you will pass **Wat Tham Phousi,** which has a large-bellied Buddha, Kaccayana. **Wat Phra Bat Nua,** farther down, has a yard-long footprint of the Buddha. Be prepared for the 355 steps to get there. Try to make the hike, which will take about 2 hours with sightseeing, in the early morning or late afternoon to escape the sun's burning rays.

**Wat Xieng Thong.** At the end of Thanon Xieng Thong. Admission 1,000 kip (US25¢). Daily 8am–6pm.

Xieng Thong is considered the premier wat of Luang Prabang. Built in 1560 by King Say Setthathirat, it is situated at the tip of a peninsula jutting out into the Mekong. Xieng Thong survived numerous invading armies intact, making its facade one of the oldest in the city. One of the outstanding characteristics of the complex is the several glass mosaics. Note the "tree of life" on the side of the sim. Facing the courtyard from the sim's steps, the building on the right contains the funeral chariot of King Sisavang Vong with its seven-headed *naga* (snake) decor. The chariot was carved by venerated Lao sculptor Thid Tun. There are also some artifacts inside, including ancient marionettes. Facing the sim, the building on the left, dubbed the "red chapel," has a rare statue of a reclining Buddha that dates back to the temple's construction. Its exterior is adorned with a mosaic depicting a popular folk tale.

**Wat Wisunalat/Visounarath.** At the end of Thanon Wisunalat. Admission 1,000 kip (US25¢). Daily 8am–5pm.

Wisunalat is known for its absolutely huge golden Buddha in the sim, the largest in town at easily 20 feet (6.1 meters) tall. The wat was constructed in 1512 and held the famous Pra Bang Buddha from 1513 to 1894. On the grounds facing the sim is the famous That Makmo, or watermelon stupa, a survivor since 1504. Wat Aham is a few steps away from the Wisunalat sim.

## SHOPPING

Luang Prabang features a fantastic array of the hand-woven textiles for which Laos is well known, so stock up here. In the parking lot across the street from Luang Prabang Travel, a group of Hmong women sell embroidered items, also good buys. You can buy 100% gold jewelry at good prices in and around the Morning Market, although the workmanship is crude. There are a few shops with excellent handicrafts on Phothisarat Road across from Wat Hosian.

# The Lao Massage

A Lao massage is the highlight of many a weary traveler's trip. It is characterized by long, gentle strokes along every part, and I mean every part, of your body, from the tip of each toe to the lobes of your ears. Your stomach will receive careful attention. Your buttocks will not be ignored. The upper insides of your thighs, though you may not have realized it previously, do need massaging. If you're the shy type, get a same-sex practitioner and wear underwear. The hotspot for massage in Luang Prabang is the Lao Red Cross, which offers an hour of ecstasy for 10,000 kip (US$2.40) and a steam bath for 6,000 kip (US$1.45). They are opposite Wat Visoun on Thanon Wisunalat, ☎ 071/212-303. Daily hours are 5 to 7:30pm.

## EXCURSIONS FROM LUANG PRABANG

**Pak Ou (Tam Ting) Caves.** On the banks of the Mekong, 22 miles from Luang Prabang. Admission to both caves: 2,000 kip (US50¢).

The Pak Ou caves are two crannies in the side of a mountain stuffed with thousands of old Buddha images. The site has long been sacred for the Laotians. The lower cave has over 4,000 Buddhas, ranging from 3 inches to 9 feet tall, stuck in nooks and crannies. The upper cave is actually even more interesting. Its Buddha images are placed far back into the cliff, so you'll need to bring a flashlight. The real highlight of a trip to the caves, though, is the breathtaking view of the mountains during the 2-hour boat ride. The trip will usually include a stop at Ban Xang Hai, a village specializing in jar making and rice wine distillation.

Many tour agencies charge exorbitant prices for half-day tours, as much as US$45 if you go alone. But you can simply stroll along yourself by the boat wharf, across from the Palace Museum on the river, and hire your own vessel. Mr. Pei at boat no. 112 is fair and friendly, and charges about US$5 per head.

**Kuang Si Falls.** 20 miles (36 km) south of town.

The Kuang Si falls are a spectacular sight, a huge, tiered waterfall with pristine pools below. Viewing them is a good excuse to get out of town for a bit and see the surrounding countryside, but expect the falls to be crowded with tourists and Laotians. You'll probably need to take a tuk-tuk or jumbo to go there independently, which means a two-hour ride along bumpy, dusty roads. Negotiate with the drivers across from Luang Prabang tourism; fares will be around 35,000 kip (US$6.85). You can also hire a boat (at the docks opposite the Palace Museum) to take you down the Mekong, then jump to a jumbo for a brief overland trip to the falls.

**Tad Se Falls.** 13 miles southeast of the city.

Tad Se falls are a 35-minute drive east of town by tuk-tuk or motorbike. They are on a much smaller scale than Kuang Si, but you have a good chance of a private viewing, as most tourists haven't discovered them yet. Like Kuang Si, they are many small tiered formations rather than one huge stream. A boat will charge 2,000 kip (US50¢) to take you to the falls.

**Ban Phanom Weaving Village.** About 2½ miles outside of town on Patoupakmao, past Wat Phonphao.

The Lu clan of Ban Phanom came originally from Xixuangbana in southern China, and have been weavers for hundreds of years. The village is an interesting bike ride or

---

### Travel Warning: Beware of Unexploded Ordnance

Xieng Kuong Province is one of the most heavily bombed areas on earth. UXO, or unexploded ordnance, is numerous, particularly in the form of small cluster bombs, blue or gray metal balls about the size of a fist. Don't stray into uninhabited, unexplored areas, and don't touch anything on the ground.

---

stop on the way back from one of the waterfalls, but don't expect rustic authenticity. Yes, there is an entire shed devoted to hand-weaving here, and some chickens on the loose, but the whole village has the feel of a special show for tourists. Nonetheless, it has one of the best and cheapest selections of hand-woven fabric in the whole country.

**Wat Phon Phao (Peacefulness Temple).** About 3 miles out of town, on the way to Ban Phanom. Mon–Fri 8–10am and 2–4pm.

Also known as the Golden Stupa, this temple has five floors of interesting murals depicting Buddhist tales and other temples and wats in Luang Prabang. The view of the town at the tiny upper room is worth the tuk-tuk ride from the center of town (about 5,000 kip, or US$1.20).

**Across the Mekong River.** Charter your own boat for about 10,000 kip (US$2.40) at the boat docks opposite the Royal Palace Museum.

Charter your own boat and go across to the relatively uninhabited side of the Mekong, right before it meets up with the Nam Khan. Taking a path to the east, you'll pass through a village that isn't posing for tourists. **Wat Them Xieng Mien,** which you'll come to next, has some Buddhist caves to wander through. Bring your own flashlight and inquire at the wat to enter. **Wat Chom Piet** is an abandoned wat reportedly built in the 16th century. Ask the gatekeeper there to open the doors for you. Finally, **Wat Long Khoun,** in a serene setting on the riverbank, once served as a religious retreat for Laos' royals.

## 5 Xiang Khuong & the Plain of Jars

Xiang Khouang, whose top attraction is the Plain of Jars, is relatively well developed for tourism compared to other provinces in the north. Its capital city, Phonsovan, is growing and recently added several new hotels. You can bathe in either of two hot mineral springs near the capital, Baw Hoi and Baw Yai. You may also want to see one of the nearby Hmong or Thai Dam hill tribe villages. For visitor information, contact **Inter-Lao Tourisme,** 1/5 Saysana Rd., Phonsovan (☎ 061/312-169).

### GETTING THERE

Lao Aviation flies from Vientiane to Phonsovan, capital of Xieng Khouang, at 11:30am and 1:30pm every day except Saturday; there are two flights on Sunday. Cost is US$37 one-way. Traveling by road involves several grueling days on public buses. It's not recommended.

### GETTING AROUND

Once you get to Phonsovan, your best bet is to hook up with a local tour company to get to the Plain of Jars and surrounding villages.

## ACCOMMODATIONS & DINING

The best spot in town is the **Auberge de la Plane des Jarres,** a bungalow-style complex with fireplaces owned by Sodetour. You can book at Sodetour in Vientiane

(☎ **021/213-478**), or call direct (☎ 061/212-044). There is also the new **Xieng Khouang Hotel** (☎ **061/212-049**), and there's the **Muang Phouan Hotel,** which offers very basic accommodations (☎ **061/323-046**).

If you don't care to dine at your hotel, venture to town, where you'll find noodle and snack shops on the main street.

## ATTRACTIONS

✪ The **Plain of Jars** is both a stunning sight and an archaeological mystery. Hundreds of jars of varying sizes, the largest a bit over 9 feet (2.7m) high, cover a plateau stretching across 15 miles. The origin of the jars is unknown. They have been dated to about 2,000 years, and it was originally thought that they were used for storing wine. In fact, legend has it that a mythical king, Khun Chuang, drank from the largest jar to celebrate victory over invaders. The most popular theory today, however, is that the jars were used as funerary urns. Bones, ashes, bronze ornaments, and iron tools have been recovered on the site. This theory might also explain the difference in jar sizes: the higher the person's rank, the bigger the urn. The jars were heavily damaged by American bombs during the Vietnam war, so you can only imagine what the sight must have looked like originally. The biggest jar site (there are many) is about 7 miles outside of Phonsovan. A tour will usually take you to two or three sites.

## 6  Pakse & Champasack Province

Champasack was once a capital of the pre-Angkorian kingdom of Champasack. It is the site of the ancient temple Wat Phu, second only to Cambodia's Angkor Wat in historical importance in the region.

### VISITOR INFORMATION

For visitor information, contact **Inter-Lao Tourisme,** no. 13 South Rd. (☎ **031/212-226** or 212-778), or Sodetour, Thanon Thasala Kham (☎ 031/212-122).

### GETTING THERE

**BY PLANE**   Lao Aviation flies daily from Vientiane to Pakse at 7:20am, at a cost of US$95 one-way.

**BY BUS**   You can take a private bus from Vientiane to Savannakhet for 8 hours of relative comfort, then transfer to a public bus for the rest of the trip, which should be tolerable at only 4 hours or so. You may wish to spend the night in Savannakhet to break up the trip.

### ACCOMMODATIONS & DINING

There are four main hotels in town. The **Sala Champa Hotel** is an old French villa offering doubles for US$40 (☎ **031/212-273;** fax 031/212-646). The **Champasack Palace Hotel,** a grand old place, was formerly the palace of Prince Bounome (☎ **031/212-263** or 212-778; fax 031/212-781); they charge US$44 for a double, including breakfast. Another nice colonial is the **Hotel Residence du Champa,** no. 13 Road (☎ **031/212-120** or 212-765; fax 031/212-765); it's also US$44 for a double, including breakfast. Finally, there's the **Souksamlane Hotel** on Route 13 South (☎ **031/212-002;** fax 031/212/281), a bit lower on the scale but still clean and with air conditioning, which charges US$27 for a double.

The Champasak Palace Hotel serves some of the best food in town, mainly Chinese fare. Otherwise, you can check out the few restaurants around the Pakse Hotel, near the central market.

# Defusing Death

From 1964 to 1973, Laos was on the receiving end of more than two million tons of what the military politely calls ordnance—bombs to the rest of us. Twenty-five years later, the bombs are still killing, in the form of UXO, or "unexploded ordnance," like bombs, artillery and mortar rounds, and rockets. A person who encounters a UXO has a 52% chance of dying. UXO affects the economies of 12 provinces in Laos, and estimates put the total mass of contaminated land at 50% of the country's total land mass. The most heavily contaminated areas are Xieng Khoung in the north, and east Savannakhet, Salavan, and Xekong provinces in the south. Up to 10% of the budget of any development project is used for mine and UXO clearance.

In 1995 the American government, with assistance from Canada, Australia, and Belgium, and nongovernment organizations from England, Norway, and Germany, set up a training program to help Laotians detect and defuse UXO. Students are recruited directly from the contaminated areas and trained at a site near Vientiane on de-mining techniques and how to spread community awareness. They also receive a 4-week medical course on how to assist UXO victims before being sent back to their home provinces to begin their task. De-miners work in two groups: The roving team, acting on tips or recent deaths, goes out with minesweepers, marking the site and clearing away brush; the clearing team then digs up the bomb and detonates it. Remarkably, there have been no fatalities among the 555-person staff.

The governments finished their plan of assistance in early 1999. The Lao people, trained and ready, are now single-handedly combating their small, silent, deadly enemies.

## ATTRACTIONS

**Pakse,** the capital of the province, was a turn-of-the-century French administrative post. It's noted for its hand-woven silks and cotton, which you'll find (along with much more) at the lively outdoor market.

✪ **Wat Phu.** Almost 9 miles southwest of Champasack; 28 miles from Pakse. Admission 1,000 kip (US25¢). Daily 8am–4:30pm.

This ancient temple, which dates back from the 6th to the 11th centuries, could be one of the highlights of your visit to Laos. Some say the temple's grand layout inspired Cambodia's Angkor Wat.

Wat Phu was built as a Hindu homage to the god Shiva, on a site that may have been previously used for animist worship. The complex is located on a plateau 750 miles above sea level. It is built symmetrically, with a broad causeway as the central axis. The structure immediately behind the large reservoir is recent, constructed by Lao royalty for officiating ceremonies and water games. The causeway behind this passes two pond basins, one on either side, and two worship pavilions, one for each sex. Behind these, along the steps to the next level, are, to the right, the former site of the galleries, and, to the left, the Nandi pavilion, a dedication to the bull, Shiva's traditional mount.

On the upper level is the main sanctuary, with some non-historic Buddhist statues. Originally a linga, a Shiva phallus, stood here, bathed in water from the spring behind the complex. The sanctuary was reportedly a site of human sacrifices from the pre–Wat Phu temple era. Today, during a ceremony taking place on the fourth day of the waxing moon in the sixth lunar month, a bull is ritually slaughtered by members of a nearby Mon-Khmer (an ethnic group closely related to the Khmer) tribe in honor of the founding father of Wat Phu. What you will probably see, however, is a view of the temple's surroundings, including the spring, which is considered sacred, and Lao travelers dipping themselves into the water to receive its blessings. Contact a local travel agency to make the trip by car, or better, by boat up the Mekong.

**Bolaven Plateau and Tad Lo Resort.** Bolavan is the northeast of Champasak Province; Tad Lo is 62 miles northeast of Pakse.

Bordering Champasack and Savarane provinces, the Bolaven Plateau is the site of teak, rubber, tea, and coffee plantations; cattle ranges; and rustic villages. It is home to various Mon-Khmer ethnic groups (including the Laven, for which the area is named) living in thatch huts and keeping traditions thousands of years old. You'll be able to visit their villages (some are close to the Tad Lo resort) and waterfalls of the nearby Set River, and observe local agricultural practices. Check with a tour company to get around (Sodetour are specialists in the area), or rent a car from Sousamlane Hotel in Pakse.

An excellent place to stay is the **Tad Lo Lodge,** an eco-tourism resort where you can live in simple bungalows and ride elephants. Contact Sodetour in Vientiane, ☎ **021/213-478,** or direct at 031/212-725 (in Pakse) for information and reservations.

**Don Khong Island.** 5 hours by boat from Pakse.

Don Khong is the largest of the spectacular lower Mekong islands, not far from the border with Cambodia. **Ban Khone Nua** is a small village on the island with old colonial buildings and the remains of a French railway. Sights in the area include two impressive **waterfalls,** Li Phi and Khon Phapheng. Phapheng is the biggest waterfall in Southeast Asia. By boat, you can also travel to the area known as Si Pan Don, or the Four Thousand Islands. There is one island in particular where you may be able to catch sight of the rare Irrawaddy freshwater dolphins if you're traveling January through March.

You can also overnight on the Island. The best choice is **Sala Donekhong,** with basic lodgings in a teak house at 3 Kanghong St. (☎ **031/212-077,** or book through Sodetour in Vientiane); they charge US$50 for a double.

# 8 Singapore

*By Jennifer Eveland*

**W**hen American science-fiction writer Bruce Sterling likened Singapore to Disneyland, he was, in many respects, more or less on the mark.

Compared to other Southeast Asian countries, this tiny island nation has one of the highest counts for tourist visits each year, yet many of your more intrepid travelers overlook it as a viable travel destination, believing it has become too sanitary and contemporary to boast any authentic Asian charm. Most of the old Chinese bumboats that once crowded the harbor and river have been sent away. The old godowns (warehouses) on the banks of the Singapore River have been converted into trendy river-view restaurants and bars. Even the old hawker centers and their mom-and-pop local cuisine are now regulated for cleanliness by government health authorities.

But while the intrepid traveler may be disappointed by all of this "civilization," I see something else going on, something very interesting: a distinctly Asian evolutionary transformation toward modernization.

In Singapore today you'll find stately steel and glass skyscrapers just around the corner from lanes of delicate parrot-colored pre-war shophouses, and five-star continental cuisine prepared by top international chefs just blocks from hawker stalls selling local specialties. On Orchard Road you can browse through Gucci, Louis Vuitton, and Cartier, while over at Arab Street you can bargain your heart out for fabulous hand-made regional handicrafts. At night, catch a glimpse of traditional Chinese opera on your way to the latest performance of the Singapore Symphony Orchestra. And if your international-class hotel room feels too confined, a comfortable walk through a primary rain forest is just outside the city limits.

Singaporean culture is as diverse as the cityscape, with Chinese, Malay, Indian, and European influences each adding their unique stamp on local life. Stroll through some of the neighborhoods and you'll find Chinese and Hindu temples, Muslim mosques, and Christian churches co-existing peacefully within blocks of each other. Browse through Singapore's list of public holidays to find colorful festivals celebrating the spectrum of cultures, all of which are open for everyone to enjoy. You can challenge yourself to try a different cuisine each meal, and still not have tried them all by the time you leave. With its mix of old traditions, its cosmopolitan customs, and its prism of multicultural identity, Singapore is a truly unique and unforgettable travel experience, a modern country and culture that have grown from the Singaporeans' unique heritage and vision. As a traveler, I continue to be fascinated.

## 1  Getting to Know Singapore

### THE LAY OF THE LAND

If you look at a world map, or even a map of the region, Singapore is very, very small. An island at the tip of the Malaysian peninsula, it measures a mere 351 square miles (584.8 square km). Shaped like a flat, horizontal diamond, the island is only 25 miles (42km) from east to west and 14 miles (23km) from north to south. The nation itself is actually made up of the main island of Singapore and 60 smaller islands, some of which, such as Sentosa, Kusu Island, and St. John's Island, are popular getaways.

Singapore is tropical. Its position at approximately 82 miles (137 km) north of the equator means uniform temperatures, plentiful rainfall, and high humidity. The landscape of the main island is mostly small rolling hills, while its highest peak, Bukit Timah, rises to a height of only 530 feet (163m) above sea level. Most of the island is little more than 50 feet (15m) above sea level.

### SINGAPORE NEIGHBORHOODS & CITY LAYOUT

**THE URBAN AREA**   Singapore is a city-state, which means that Singapore itself is the capital of Singapore. The urban area, centered around the Singapore River in the south of the island, contains the majority of Singapore's cultural and historical sightseeing opportunities.

In 1822, with the migration of people from around the region and the world, Sir Stamford Raffles, founder of Singapore, set about laying a Town Plan, which divided up what is today's urban area into enclaves for each of Singapore's different ethnic groups. His original demarcations survive to some extent in today's neighborhoods.

Singapore, then and now, stretches out from its heart at the Singapore River. Boat Quay, with its long rows of godowns, or warehouses, lines the waterside on the south bank. Today Boat Quay has been restored to create a strip of hip eateries and bars. Just beyond Boat Quay, residences and offices sprang up for the Chinese community of merchants and "coolie" laborers who came to work the sea trade. This area was, and still is, known as Singapore's **Chinatown.**

Farther west of Chinatown begins **Tanjong Pagar,** a district that developed later with the opening of nearby Keppel Harbour. While Chinatown and Tanjong Pagar were (and are) two distinct areas, they shared many similarities. In the daytime the streets bustled with Chinese and Indian laborers. Numerous local shops catered to their needs and to the needs of the merchant businesses, and in the streets hawkers and vendors eked out a living. At night the laborers retreated to their upstairs quarters, which were shared by up to 16 inhabitants. Or sometimes they gambled, smoked opium, or visited local cathouses. Today, as you walk the streets you can see the diversity of life that coexisted in this area. Within Chinatown there are, in addition to Chinese temples, Indian mosques and Hindu temples.

Also nearby is **Shenton Way.** Not part of the original Town Plan—in fact, built on reclaimed land—Shenton Way is home to most of the city's modern high-rises; it's Singapore's answer to Wall Street.

The other bank of the Singapore River, across from Boat Quay, is Clarke Quay. Where once the Quay was home to canneries and warehouses, today the old buildings are inhabited by shops, restaurants, and nightclubs.

# Singapore

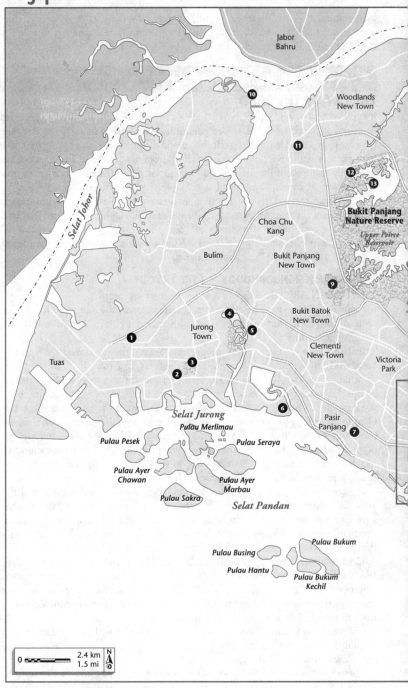

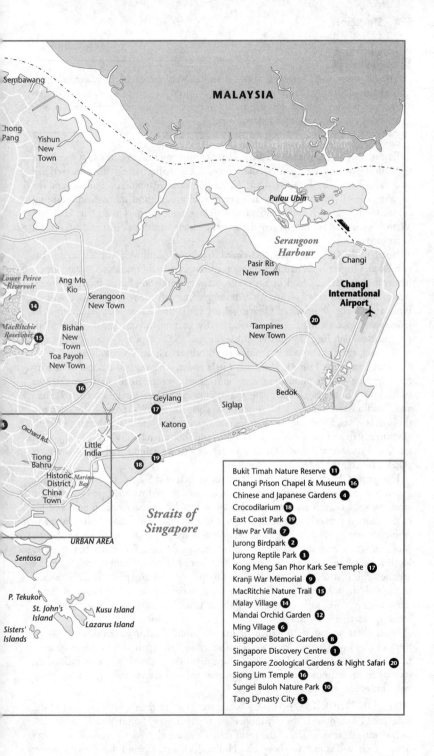

MALAYSIA

Sembawang

Chong
Pang

Yishun
New
Town

Pulau Ubin

Serangoon
Harbour

Changi

Lower Peirce
Reservoir

Ang Mo
Kio

Serangoon
New Town

Pasir Ris
New Town

Changi
International
Airport

**14**

MacRitchie
Reservoir **15**

Bishan
New
Town

Tampines
New Town

**20**

Toa Payoh
New Town

**16**

Geylang

Bedok

**3**

Orchard Rd.

**17**

Siglap

Tiong
Bahru

Little
India

Katong

**18** **19**

Historic
District
China
Town

Marina
Bay

URBAN AREA

Straits of
Singapore

Sentosa

P. Tekukor

St. John's
Island

Kusu Island

Sisters'
Islands

Lazarus Island

Bukit Timah Nature Reserve **11**

Changi Prison Chapel & Museum **16**

Chinese and Japanese Gardens **4**

Crocodilarium **18**

East Coast Park **19**

Haw Par Villa **7**

Jurong Birdpark **2**

Jurong Reptile Park **3**

Kong Meng San Phor Kark See Temple **17**

Kranji War Memorial **9**

MacRitchie Nature Trail **15**

Malay Village **14**

Mandai Orchid Garden **12**

Ming Village **6**

Singapore Botanic Gardens **8**

Singapore Discovery Centre **1**

Singapore Zoological Gardens & Night Safari **20**

Siong Lim Temple **16**

Sungei Buloh Nature Park **10**

Tang Dynasty City **5**

371

**Travel Tip**

The *Singapore Street Directory,* a book detailing every section of the island, is a great reference and easily found throughout the country. It's carried by most taxi drivers and can be very helpful if you're trying to get someplace and your driver doesn't know where it is or can't understand you.

East of Clarke Quay is the **Historic District** (also referred to as the City Centre or the Cultural or Colonial District), the heart of colonial Singapore. Raffles reserved this area in his Town Plan for the government's administrative buildings. Built around the Padang, a large field that served as a ceremonial ground and sports field, beautiful colonial buildings such as the Parliament Building, the Supreme Court, City Hall, and Victoria Concert Hall rose to give the area the stately British colonial character it still bears today.

North of the Colonial District, **Orchard Road** runs north-west where it meets Tanglin Road. Originally created for Singapore's Europeans and Eurasians, Orchard is perhaps the most famous road in Singapore, known worldwide for its shopping malls, which share both sides of the wide thoroughfare with many of Singapore's finest international-class hotels. On Orchard Road you'll find haute couture, cheap chic, jewelry and watches, luggage, electronics; the list goes on and on. And if all that shopping isn't enough fun, Orchard Road has some of the best people-watching this side of Sumatra, from glamorous international celebrities to funky local kids.

To the east of the Historic District is **Little India,** which is still a canter of activity for Singapore's Indian population. Early immigrants were originally drawn to this area to find work in the brick kilns here and to raise cattle. Street names such as Kerbau and Buffalo Road hark back to earlier days when the area was grazing land. A stroll through this neighborhood today delights travelers with coffeehouses serving up delicious northern and southern Indian delights, and shops that sell Indian clothing, silks, gold, and unique souvenirs. During Singapore's many Hindu festivals, this area is aglow with colored lights and festive activity.

**Kampong Glam** is another important ethnic enclave in Singapore. Named after the gelam tree, which was prevalent in the last century (paired with *kampong,* the Malay word for village), this area was reserved by Raffles for the Sultan of Johore and his descendents as part of the agreement signed to allow the British East India Company administrative rights over Singapore. The focal point of the community is the Sultan Mosque, whose majestic dome rises above the shophouses. But many travelers and locals alike will tell you the most exciting feature of Kampong Glam is Arab Street, an avenue dedicated to some great bargain shopping in batiks, spices, regional handicrafts, and Malay Muslim souvenirs. Because of its ties to Islam, the area also attracted many of Singapore's early Arab settlers, whose names are still associated with the area's schools, streets, and buildings.

In all, these neighborhoods span almost all of central urban Singapore, so walking from one end of Tanjong Pagar to the other end of Kampong Glam might be a bit taxing for a tourist on foot. However, because many enclaves sit just next to each other, it's easy to move from one adjacent neighborhood to another, making walking tours very convenient and relaxing.

**OUTSIDE THE URBAN AREA**   While the heart of the city centers around the Singapore River, outside the city proper are suburban neighborhoods and rural areas. In the immediate outskirts of the main urban area are the older suburban neighborhoods, such as **Katong, Geylang,** and **Holland Village.** Beyond these are the newer suburbs, called **HDB New Towns.** The HDB, or Housing Development Board, is responsible for creating large "towns" of public housing for Singapore residents. New Towns, such as **Ang Mo Kio** and **Toa Payoh,** each have their own network of supporting businesses: restaurants, schools, shops, health-care facilities, and sometimes department stores.

**NATURAL AREAS & WILDLIFE**    Before settlement by the British, the entire island of Singapore was covered with dense tropical rainforest, with mangrove swamps clinging to its shores. Today the forests and swamps cover only a small percent of land area on the main island, most of it disappearing as a result of early attempts at agriculture and later developments in shipping and urban growth. While most of Singapore's forests are categorized as secondary rain forest (having been previously cleared and grown back), there remains primary forest in the **Bukit Timah Nature Reserve,** in the center of the island. A good place to witness the life of the mangrove swamps is at **Sungei Buloh Nature Park** in the north of the island. Despite the paving over of wild areas in the past, Singapore has in recent decades initiated a serious "green" attitude toward development, including parks and gardens in city plans.

Once upon a time Singapore had a healthy population of tigers, leopards, and wild boar; however, over the years, human habits and hobbies have driven the populations down to zero. The last tiger was shot in 1932. Wildlife that remains on the island includes flying lemurs, a few species of squirrel, the long-tailed macaque, shrews, rats, snakes, lizards, toads, and tortoises. Small mousedeer and anteaters are still around, but you'll have to be lucky to see either. **Bird life** is rich, with some 326 species, 215 of which are resident and 52 of which are endangered. Many birds migrate to Singapore each year from October to March from as far north as Siberia.

Singapore's beaches are not the greatest attraction on the island. The beaches in East Coast Park and at Changi Village, while popular, have murky waters, small waves, and coarse sand streaked with seaweed. The beaches on **Sentosa Island** are much nicer. And while the seas surrounding Singapore do contain living coral reefs, heavy shipping traffic and swift currents make the water too murky to truly reveal the sea life to divers.

## A LOOK AT THE PAST

Early Singapore history remains elusive even today, as no clear accounts were ever recorded. The island was uninhabited for most of prehistory, save for a few Malay fishing settlements and hideouts for regional pirates. The most important early historical event occurred around A.D. 1400 with the arrival of **Iskander Shah,** also referred to as Parameswara. According to early Malay historical accounts, Iskander Shah was a prince from Palembang in the south of Sumatra. Following a rebellion there, he fled to Singapore, where he set up his rule and, in his coronation ceremony, alighted a lion throne to declare himself ruler of the land. It is believed Singapore inherited its modern name from *Singapura,* Sanskrit for "Lion City," in honor of Iskander Shah. A few years later Iskander was chased out of Singapore by Palembang troops and fled with his army to Malacca, up the western shore of Malaya. Although history says Iskander Shah died in Malacca, some believe the mysterious *keramat* (sacred grave) on Fort Canning Hill contains his remains.

Singapore entered the modern history books in 1819, when **Sir Stamford Raffles,** an officer with the British East India Company, selected the small island to join Penang and Malacca in the **British Malay Territories.** The British were searching for a new port to compete with the Dutch in Indonesia. Singapura was under the rule of the Sultan of Johor, ruler of southern peninsular Malaya, but Raffles negotiated a

# Urban Singapore Neighborhoods

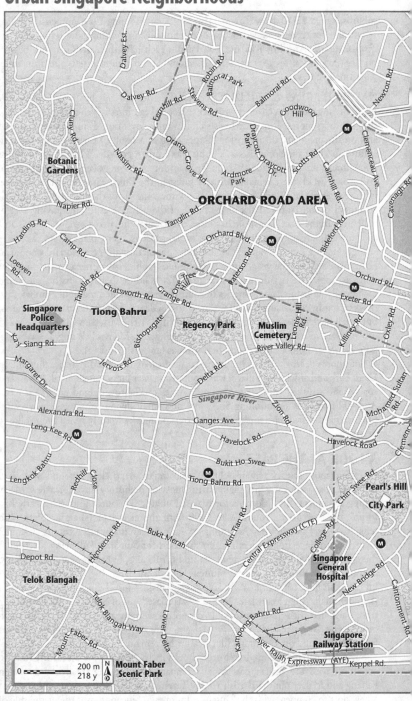

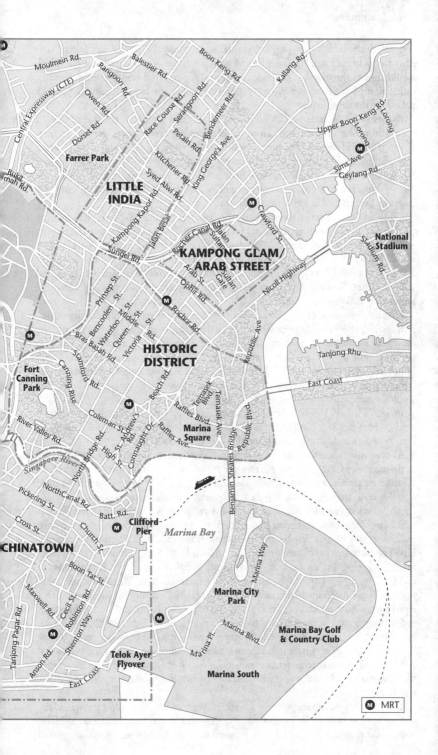

treaty with the local *temenggong* (administrator) to allow the British East India Company to set up operations. In later treaties with the sultan, it was agreed that the British would control the island in return for an annual stipend to the Sultanate, and an area called Kampong Glam (see above) was given to build the Istana Kampong Glam, a palace for the royal family.

Raffles was a dreamer and an idealist who imagined the island transformed into a successful center of trade and shipment, entertaining the business interests of merchants the world round. The eventual realization of this dream, coming at a time when other British and Dutch trading settlements weren't faring well, was attributable not merely in Singapore's ideal location between the monsoon winds that carried the sailing ships, but also due to policies originally installed by Raffles and flawlessly executed by Singapore's first governor, William Farquhar.

Trade was the name of the game, so the port was virtually tax-free, the economy absolutely laissez-faire. Merchants and traders flocked from all corners to this new port to find outlets for their wares. With the British came Indian soldiers, workers, and money lenders. Malays from the peninsula migrated to find work. Boatloads of poor and overcrowded Chinese left their homes in the southern provinces of China to find their fortunes. Wealthy Arabs and Jews set up flourishing businesses. By 1860, the population had grown to 80,792.

Despite the success of the port, it wasn't until the Industrial Revolution that Singapore would rise as a commercial center vital to the west. Two developments, the growth of steamship travel in the 1860s and the opening of the Suez Canal in 1869, cut travel time to the Orient drastically, making the world a much smaller place. Other industrial developments opened the British Malayan States to trade in valuable natural resources. Peninsular Malaya was rich in tin, and a new crop was introduced that would become equally vital: **rubber.**

In 1897, "Mad" Henry Ridley, director of Singapore's Botanic Gardens, developed a new way to tap latex from the trees and began a tireless campaign to turn failed gambier, pepper, nutmeg, and clove plantations over to rubber cultivation.

As opportunity grew, so did the population. The British colonists were the minority, as thousands of Chinese migrated from the mainland, primarily from the Fukien and Guangdong provinces, to open businesses and work in trades. Arrivals from India filled out the civil service and local police force, and provided money-lending services. Indian convicts provided the labor to build government works as well as many beautiful houses, churches, and government buildings. Intermarriage between races created pockets of subcultures that became important elements of the Singaporean community. The Eurasians capitalized on their ties to both English and Chinese communities, many becoming leaders in local government. Another group, the **Peranakans,** or Straits Chinese, grew from Chinese and Malay intermarriage. They developed a culture that is unique to the Malay cities of Penang and Malacca and to Singapore, mixing equal parts Chinese and Malay tastes to create new cuisine, couture, and architecture.

Singapore's road to progress was tragically interrupted on February 15, 1942, Chinese New Year's Day, with the fall of Singapore to invading Japanese troops during World War II. British forces in Singapore suspected the coming invasion, but lacked solid leadership and defense plans as well as support from home. The Japanese entered the Malay peninsula in the northeast and in 2 months captured cities with ease all the way to Singapore.

The **Japanese occupation,** while a mere 3½ years of Singapore's history, was a long and tortured period for its inhabitants. The Japanese staged huge massacres of Malay and Indian troops as well as Chinese believed to be anti-Japanese. British troops and supporters were marched to **Changi** in the eastern part of the island to be detained in miserable conditions. Many others were exported to work on Japanese rail and road projects in Burma and Thailand. Civilians lived in hunger and disease until the Japanese surrendered to Lord Louis Mountbatten, Supreme Allied Commander in Southeast Asia, on September 12, 1945. The museum and chapel at Changi, as well as the Surrender Chamber on Sentosa, illustrate with poignancy the horrors of the Occupation.

At the end of the war Singapore set out to put her affairs together. It became a Crown Colony in 1946, and eventually became part of the Federation of Malaya. But the people of Singapore desired self-rule. Amidst threats from the Communist Party of Malaya, groundwork was laid for a new constitution. In 1955, David Marshall was elected Singapore's first chief minister, but it was his successor, Lim Yew Hock, who successfully negotiated a Constitutional Agreement with London. Singapore became independent in 1959.

That year, during the first general election, the People's Action Party (PAP) won 53.4% of assembly votes, and **Lee Kuan Yew,** leader of the party, became the first prime minister. The PAP had risen to power through alliance with the communists, who were very powerful, but in 1961 the PAP split from all communist ties.

In 1963, Malayan prime minister Tunku Abdul Rahman and Lee Kuan Yew formed a merger of Malaya, Singapore, and Sarawak and Sabah on Borneo. In 1965 Singapore split from the newly formed Federation of Malaysia.

In the nearly 30 years that followed under the guidance of Prime Minister Lee, Singapore developed industrial relations, monetary policies, economic restructuring, public housing, armed forces, and political stability. In 1990, Lee stepped down as prime minister and was succeeded by Goh Chock Tong. Lee Kuan Yew, however, remains as senior minister.

Today, Singapore is recognized as an East Asian economic miracle, despite the setback of the economic crisis that began in mid-1997—a period in which Singapore has fared far better than many of her Asian neighbors due to prudent lending policies and swift government reaction to the crisis. In 1996, Singaporeans enjoyed a per capita GNP of S$35,220 (US$21,484). The GDP for 1997 was $96.3 billion with an annual growth rate of 7.8%.

## SINGAPORE'S PEOPLE & CULTURE

Estimates in 1996 put the population at 3,044,300, 77.3% of which is **Chinese.** The Chinese population is divided between dialect groups reflecting the many regions from which early immigrants migrated. Of the mix, the Hokkiens (from Fujian Province) are the largest group at 42% of the Chinese population, followed by the Teochews (from Guangdong Province), Cantonese (also from Guangdong), Hakkas (from central China), and finally the Hainanese (from Hainan Island), at 6%. Most are Buddhist combined with influences from Taoism and Confucianism.

**Malays** make up 14.1% of the population—very low, considering that the Malays were the original inhabitants of the island and Malaysia is just next door. Still, their culture has made its mark on society. Malay dishes are some of the nation's favorites, and the Malay language is one of the principle tongues spoken on the street (even the national anthem is sung in Malay). Malays are, by and large, Sunni Muslims, and are tolerant of other religions.

**Indians** were some of the earliest immigrants to Singapore, arriving with Raffles when he first landed in 1819. Today their population has reached 7.3% of the total. Most Indian immigrants originated in the Southern regions of India, and are derived from such ethnic groups as the Tamils, Malayalis, Punjabis, and Gujratis. The Indians are also divided between religious affiliation. While most are Hindu, other religious groups include Muslims, Christians, Sikhs, and Buddhists.

Other ethnic groups make up a mere 1.3% of the total population.

## 2 Planning a Trip to Singapore

In 1996, Singapore welcomed over seven million international visitors, each of whom stayed an average of 3.5 days. If this sounds like a profile of your planned stay, you'll want to make the most of your visit. Singapore, with its well-informed international tourism board offices, abundant on-line information, and state-of-the-art communications systems, makes it easy to plan the perfect trip. In this section I'll provide not only key information necessary to plan ahead, but also contacts and links to valuable sources of information to answer any questions you may have.

### VISITOR INFORMATION

The Singapore Tourism Board (STB) is the best place to start when planning your trip. Representative offices worldwide can provide information on festivals and holidays, new tourist attractions, and special offers, and can even help plan tours and activities. They'll be glad to mail information to those who inquire. The STB has an official Web site at **www.stb.com.sg** and sponsors the official New Asia–Singapore site at **www.newasia-singapore.com.**

### IN THE U.S.

**New York:** 590 Fifth Ave., 12th Floor, New York, NY 10036 (☎ **212/302-4861;** fax 212/302-4801). **Chicago:** Two Prudential Plaza, 180 North Stetson Ave., Suite 1450, Chicago, IL 60601 (☎ **312/938-1888;** fax 312/938-0086). **Los Angeles:** 8484 Wilshire Blvd., Suite 510, Beverly Hills, CA 90211 (☎ **213/852-1901;** fax 213/852-0129).

### IN CANADA

**Toronto:** The Standard Life Centre, 121 King St. West, Suite 1000, Toronto, Ontario, Canada M5H 3T9 (☎ **416/363-8898;** fax 416/363-5752).

### IN AUSTRALIA

**Perth:** 8th Floor, St. Georges Court, 16 St. Georges Terrace, Perth WA 6000, Australia (☎ **8/9325-8511;** fax 8/9221-3864). **Sydney:** Level 11, AWA Building, 47 York St., Sydney NSW 2000, Australia (☎ **2/9290-2888** or 2/9290-2882; fax 2/9290-2555).

### IN NEW ZEALAND

**Auckland:** 3rd Floor, 43 High St., Auckland, New Zealand (tel **9/358-1191;** fax 9/358-1196).

### IN THE UNITED KINGDOM

**London:** 1st Floor, Carrington House, 126–130 Regent St., London W1R 5FE, United Kingdom (☎ **171/437-0033;** fax 171/734-2191).

### IN SINGAPORE

Once you arrive in Singapore, you can stop at the local STB office at Tourism Court, 1 Orchard Spring Lane (☎ **65/736-6622;** fax 65/736-9423), just across from Trader's Hotel. There's also an STB Tourist Information Centre at 328 North Bridge Rd., no. 02–34 Raffles Hotel Arcade. Both are open from 8:30am to 7pm daily. There's a

toll-free tourist information hotline in Singapore at ☎ **1800/334-1335** or 1800/
334-1336.

## ENTRY REQUIREMENTS

To enter Singapore you'll need a valid passport. Visas are not necessary for citizens of
the United States, Canada, the United Kingdom, Australia, and New Zealand. Upon
entry, visitors from these countries will be issued a 30-day pass for a social visit only.
Visitors from other countries should contact the nearest Singapore overseas mission to
apply for an appropriate visa.

**To extend your stay,** apply at the Singapore Immigration Department at 10
Kallang Rd. in the SIR Building at the Lavender Street MRT (Mass Rapid Transit)
Station (☎ **65/391-6100**). The department is open Monday through Friday from
8am to 5pm and Saturday from 8am to 1pm. Detailed visa information can also be
obtained from the Internet at www.mha.gov.sg.sir.

**If you overstay your visa,** report to the Singapore Immigration Department office
immediately.

## CUSTOMS REGULATIONS

Singapore forbids import of the following items: firearms, firecrackers, and explosives;
cigarette lighters that look like firearms; endangered species and their by-products;
chewing tobacco; obscene articles, publications, videos, and computer software; reproductions of copyrighted materials; treasonable materials; and toy coins and currency
notes. There are no restrictions on the amount of real currency you can bring into Singapore. If you have any questions about what constitutes treasonable or obscene materials, direct inquiries to the **Customs Duty Office** at Singapore Changi Airport,
Terminal 1 (☎ **65/542-7058** or 65/545-9122) or Terminal 2 (☎ **65/543-0755** or
65/543-0754).

### THE TOURIST REFUND SCHEME

While Singapore attaches a 3% goods and services tax to all sales, as a tourist you can
reclaim the GST for items purchased during your trip if you spend more than S$300
(approximately US$183, at this writing). You can combine receipts of S$100 (US$61)
or more from participating shops (look for the Tax Free Shopping sticker) to come up
with the full amount. GST Claim Forms are available from participating retailers, to
be filed with receipts at the Tax Refund Counters at either of the Changi Airport
departure halls for cash on the spot. For more information contact the STB toll-free
at ☎ **800/334-1335** or 800/334-1336.

## MONEY

The local currency unit is the Singapore dollar, commonly referred to as the "Sing
dollar." Retail prices are marked as S$, a designation I've used throughout this chapter.
Notes are issued in denominations of S$1, $2, $5, $10, $20, $50, $100, $500, and
$1,000. Coins are issued in S1¢, 5¢, 10¢, 20¢, 50¢, and S$1. Singapore and Brunei
Darussalam have a currency interchangeability agreement, so Brunei currency is
accepted as equal to the Singapore dollar.

**CURRENCY EXCHANGE & RATES**    At the time of writing, exchange rates on
the Singapore dollar were as follows: US$1 = S$1.65, Canadian $1 = S$1.06, British
pound 1 = S$2.76, Australian $1 = S$1.05, New Zealand $1 = S$0.88.

While hotels and banks will perform currency exchanges, you'll get a better rate at
one of the many authorized money changers that can be found at major shopping
malls and shopping areas.

---

**Travel Tip**

For up-to-date **currency conversion rates,** visit CNN's Web site at www.cnn.com/ travel/currency.

---

Singapore has an abundance of 24-hour **automated-teller machines (ATMs).** Look for MasterCard/Cirrus or Visa/PLUS signs. You can use either your credit card for a cash advance or your bank's debit card to withdraw cash directly from your account at the day's exchange rate. Be sure you have your PIN number, whichever you use. The two most widely recognizable **traveler's checks** are American Express and Thomas Cook. They can be cashed at banks and hotels, but authorized money changers will always give you a better rate. Almost all major **credit cards**—American Express (AE), Diners Club (DC), Japanese Credit Bank (JCB), MasterCard (MC), and Visa (V)—are accepted at major hotels, restaurants, and shops. In shops, the better price is negotiated through cash purchases.

**TO REPORT LOST OR STOLEN CREDIT CARDS**   The number to call for **American Express** is ☎ **1800/732-2244. Diners Club** has a local number to report lost or stolen credit cards at ☎ **294-4222. MasterCard** has a toll-free Global Service Emergency Assistance for International Visitors hotline at ☎ **800/110-0113. Visa's** toll-free hotline is ☎ **1800/345-1345.**

## WHEN TO GO

**PEAK SEASON**   The busy season is from January to June. In the late summer months, business travel dies down, and in fall, even tourism drops off somewhat, making the season ripe for budget-minded visitors. These may be the best times to get a deal. Probably the worst time to negotiate will be between Christmas and the Chinese New Year.

**CLIMATE**   At approximately 82 miles (137km) north of the equator, you can count on hot and humid weather year-round. Temperatures remain uniform, with a daily average of 80.6°F (26.7°C). The daily average relative humidity is 84.4%. Rain falls year-round, and the annual rainfall is 94.08 inches (2,352mm).

The northeast monsoon occurs between December and March, when temperatures are slightly cooler, relatively speaking, than other times of the year. The heaviest rainfall occurs between November and January. The southwest monsoon falls between June and September, when temperatures are higher. July reports the lowest recorded average rainfall. In between monsoons, thunderstorms are frequent.

**PUBLIC HOLIDAYS**   There are 11 official public holidays: New Year's Day, Lunar New Year or Chinese New Year (2 days), Hari Raya Puasa, Good Friday, Labour Day, Hari Raya Haji, Vesak Day, National Day, Deepavali, and Christmas Day. On these days, expect government offices, banks, and some shops to be closed.

## HEALTH CONCERNS

In the heat and humidity, you should take a few precautions. *Drink plenty of water.* Singapore's tap water is potable. Tea, coffee, colas, and alcohol dehydrate the body and should never be substituted for water if you're thirsty.

Avoid overexposure to the sun. The heat may make you feel lethargic, but also be careful of air-conditioning. Moving in and out of air-conditioned buildings can leave you with a horrible summer cold.

You'll have no problems with the food in Singapore, other than the possible trouble from exposure to new ingredients. All fruits and vegetables should be thoroughly washed to rinse away any bacteria.

Singapore doesn't require that you have any **vaccinations** to enter the country, but strongly recommends immunization against diphtheria, tetanus, hepatitis A and B, and typhoid. While there's no risk of contracting malaria (the country's been declared malaria-free for decades by the World Health Organization), there is a similar deadly virus—**dengue fever**—that's carried by mosquitoes and has no immunization. Dengue symptoms include sudden fever and tiny red spotty rashes on the body. Your best protection is to wear insect repellent, especially if you are heading out to the zoo, bird park, or any of the gardens or nature preserves.

## GETTING THERE
### BY PLANE
For the best airfare deals, plan your trip for the low-volume season, which runs from September 1 to November 30. Between January 1 and May 31, you'll pay the highest fares. Plan your travel on weekdays only, and, if you can, plan to stay for at least 1 week. Also, if you have access to the Internet, there are a number of great sites that'll search out super fares for you (see chapter 3 and the appendix for more information). All flights listed are direct.

**FROM THE U.S.** **Singapore Airlines** (☎ 800/742-3333; www.singaporeair.com) has a daily flight from New York's JFK Airport (in partnership with Delta Airlines) and three flights weekly from Newark International; two daily flights from Los Angeles; and two daily flights from San Francisco (only one on Monday and Saturday). **United Airlines** (☎ 800/241-6522; www.ual.com) has daily flights from Los Angeles, San Francisco, and Seattle. **Northwest Airlines** (☎ 800/447-4747; www.nwa.com) has a daily afternoon flight from Minneapolis and two flights daily from Boston. **American Airlines** (☎ 800/433-7300; www.americanair.com) has two flights daily from Chicago, a daily from Los Angeles, and flights five times a week from San Francisco.

**FROM CANADA** **Singapore Airlines** (☎ 800/742-3333; www.singaporeair.com) has three flights weekly from Vancouver.

**FROM THE U.K.** **Singapore Airlines** (☎ 7470007 London or 4895768 Manchester; www.singaporeair.com) has two daily flights departing from London and flights five times a week departing from Manchester. **British Airways** (☎ 0345/222111; www.british-airways.com) has two daily flights from London. **Qantas Airways Ltd.** (☎ 0345/747767; www.qantas.com) has three flights daily from London.

**FROM AUSTRALIA** **Singapore Airlines** (☎ 131011; www.singaporeair.com) has twice-daily flights from Sydney and Perth; daily flights from Melbourne (two on Wednesday, Friday, and Sunday) and Brisbane; flights from Adelaide three times weekly; from Cairns three times weekly; and from Darwin once a week. **Qantas Airways Ltd.** (☎ 131211; www.qantas.com) has daily flights from Brisbane, Cairns, Darwin, and Melbourne, at least two flights daily from Sydney and Perth, and four flights weekly from Adelaide. **British Airways** (☎ 322/223-3123 Brisbane or 425-7711 Perth; www.british-airways.com) has daily flights from Brisbane and Perth.

**FROM NEW ZEALAND** **Singapore Airlines** (☎ 3032129 Auckland or 3668003 Christchurch; www.singaporeair.com) has daily flights from Auckland and Christchurch. **Air New Zealand** (☎ 0800/737000; www.airnewzealand.co.nz) has daily flights from Auckland and Christchurch.

### Getting into Town from the Airport
Most visitors to Singapore will land at **Changi International Airport** (flight information inquiries ☎ 1800/542-4422), which is located toward the far eastern corner of the island. The airport's two terminals have in-transit accommodations

---

**Travel Tip**

If you're passing through Singapore and are in transit at Changi Airport for 4 or more hours, the STB offers a **free sightseeing tour.** Go to their counter in the Terminal 1 Departure Hall to inquire.

---

(**Oberoi Services,** ☎ 65/542-3828; fax 65/545-8365. Rates: S$50–S$80/ US$30–US$49), restaurants, money changers and ATMs, car rental desks, a medical center (☎ 65/ 543-2223; open daily 8am to midnight), a business center (tel 65/543-0911; open daily 7am to 11pm), showers and saunas (S$5/US$3 and S$10/US$6, respectively), and tourist information. Local calls can be made for free from the Departure Lounge. There's also a hotel reservation service provided by the Singapore Hotel Association if you arrive and don't have a place to stay. They have counters in both airport terminals (☎ 65/505/0318; Terminal 1 hours: daily 7am to 11pm; Terminal 2 hours: Tuesday to Sunday 7am to 3am and Monday 7am to 11:30pm).

The city is easily accessible by public transportation. While there are **limousine taxi** counters inside the terminal, they'll charge S$35 (US$21.35) for a trip into the city. **City taxis** are just outside the Arrival Hall and cost only S$22 to S$25 (US$13.40–US$15.25) for the same trip (metered fare plus S$3 airport surcharge). The drive takes around 20 minutes. There's an **Airbus Shuttle** (☎ 65/542-1721) that takes you to many major hotels in the city. Check to see if your hotel is on the long list. The trip costs S$5 (US$3) and tickets can be purchased at the counter in the Arrival Hall. **Public bus** nos. 16 and 16E, whose stops are located in the basement level, will take you on a route to Orchard Road and Raffles City (in the Historic District). Bus nos. 24 and 34 will take you to Tanah Merah MRT (subway) station, from which you can access most major areas.

## BY TRAIN

The Keretapi Tanah Melayu Berhad railroad company runs express and local trains from **Malaysia to Singapore** four times daily. In Kuala Lumpur (KL), contact KTMB at ☎ 03/273-8000, or see their Web site at www.ktmb.com.my. The fare from KL is RM68 (US$25.85), RM34 (US$12.90), and RM19 (US$7.20) for first-, second-, and third-class travel, respectively. Further details on KTMB service are listed in the Malaysia chapter of this book. All trains let you off at the **Singapore Railway Station** (☎ 65/222-5165), on Keppel Road in Tanjong Pagar, not far from the city center. Money changing services are available in the station. A taxi into town is not expensive from here.

The **Eastern & Orient Express** (E&O) (Carlton Building, 90 Cecil St., no. 05–01, ☎ 65/323-4390), operates a luxury rail route between Bangkok and Singapore. Further details are provided in the Thailand section of this book.

## BY BUS

Buses to Singapore from Malaysia will let you off at either the **Ban Sen Terminal** at the corner of Queen Street and Arab Street in Kampong Glam or at the crossroads of Lavender Street and Kallang Bahru. Buses to Singapore depart from almost all cities in Malaysia. From Kuala Lumpur, buses depart from the Kuala Lumpur Railway Station (Plusliner/NICE, ☎ 03/272-2760, costs around RM50); Malacca Bus Terminal (Transnasional, ☎ 06/282-0687, RM15.10); and Johor Bharu's Tarkin Bus Terminal (Singapore-Johor Ekspress, ☎ 07/223-2276, RM2.40).

# MRT Transit Map

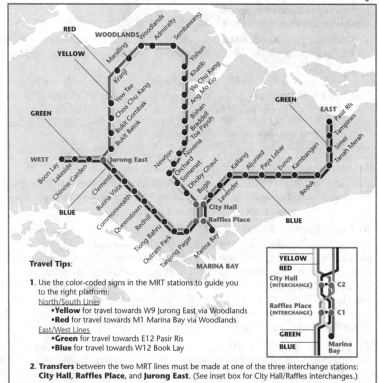

**Travel Tips:**

**1**. Use the color-coded signs in the MRT stations to guide you to the right platform:

North/South Lines
- **Yellow** for travel towards W9 Jurong East via Woodlands
- **Red** for travel towards M1 Marina Bay via Woodlands

East/West Lines
- **Green** for travel towards E12 Pasir Ris
- **Blue** for travel towards W12 Book Lay

**2**. **Transfers** between the two MRT lines must be made at one of the three interchange stations: **City Hall**, **Raffles Place**, and **Jurong East**. (See inset box for City Hall/Raffles interchanges.)

## BY FERRY

From the Johor Ferry Terminal in **Tanjung Belungkor** on the East coast of Malaysia (ferry terminal ☎ 07/251-7404) you can catch a FerryLink ferry four times daily and be in Singapore in 45 minutes. One-way fare for adults is MR15 (US$5.70). The ferry lets you off at Changi Ferry Terminal (no phone) on the east coast of Singapore. Taxis do not ply this route, so call a CityCab at ☎ 65/552-2222 to come fetch you. *Also note:* Changi Ferry Terminal does not have money-changing services. FerryLink's Singapore contact numbers are ☎ 65/545-3600; fax 65/545-5040.

From **Tioman Island** you can catch an Auto Batam Ferries and Tours ferry to Singapore at the Berjaya Jetty every day at 2:30pm. *Please note:* this service does not operate from mid-October to early March, due to the monsoon season. You're let off at Singapore's Tanah Merah Ferry Terminal, in the eastern part of the island. The terminal has money-changing facilities and a taxi queue outside. Auto Batam's contact in Singapore is ☎ 271-4866.

Tanah Merah Ferry Terminal is also home to companies that serve nearby Batam, a popular day trip, and Bintan, an Indonesian island resort area.

## GETTING AROUND

The many inexpensive mass transit options make getting around Singapore easy. While taxis always simplify the ground transportation dilemma, there is also the **Mass Rapid Transit (MRT)** subway service and city buses that span the city and outlying parts to help shuttle you around. I've also provided information on car rentals.

---

### Public Transportation Tips

Stored-fare **TransitLink fare cards** can be used on both the subway and the buses, and can be purchased at TransitLink offices in the MRT stations. Unused amounts are refundable.

The **Singapore Explorer** is a special deal for tourists. The 1-day bus pass is S\$5 (US\$3.15) and the 3-day pass is just S\$12 (US\$7.30), and both are good for unlimited trips. For more information, contact either of the two operating bus lines: **Singapore Bus Service** (SBS) (☎ **1800/287-2727**) or the **Trans-Island Bus Service** (TIBS) (☎ **1800/482-5433**).

---

Of course, if you're just strolling around the urban limits, many of the sights within the various neighborhoods are within walking distance, and indeed, some of the neighborhoods are only short walks from each other.

**BY MASS RAPID TRANSIT (MRT)**   The MRT is Singapore's subway system. It's cool, clean, safe, and reliable, and the four lines are color coded so you can find the train you're looking for. MRT operating hours are approximately 5:15am to 12:47am daily. Fares range from S60¢ to S\$1.50. Purchase refundable stored-value TransitLink cards at any MRT station. TransitLink also has an **MRT Tourist Souvenir Ticket** for S\$6 (US\$3.70). It's good for 120 days for trips up to S\$5.50 (the extra S50¢ is the deposit). For more information, call **Mass Rapid Transit** toll free at ☎ **1800/336-8900** (except Sunday and public holidays).

**BY BUS**   Singapore's bus system comprises an extensive web of routes that reach virtually everywhere on the island. First purchase a **TransitLink Guide** for S\$1.40 at the TransitLink office in any MRT station, at a bus interchange, or at selected bookstores around the city. It provides details for each route and stop, indicating connections with MRT stations and fares for each trip. All buses have a machine just to the right as you board. Tell the driver your destination and feed the machine either your TransitLink card or exact change, then push the button with the corresponding fare.

**BY TAXI**   Taxis are a very convenient and affordable way to get around Singapore, and since most drivers speak English, you'll find very few problems. In town, all of the shopping malls, hotels, and major buildings have taxi queues, which you're expected to use. Most destinations in the main parts of the island can be reached fairly inexpensively, while trips to the outlying attractions can cost between S\$10 and S\$15 (US\$6.10–US\$9.15) one-way. If you have difficulty finding a cab, you can book one for an extra charge of S\$3.20 (US\$1.95). The most popular taxicab companies are **CityCab** (☎ **65/553-3880**), **Comfort** (☎ **65/552-1111**), and **TIBS** (☎ **65/481-1211**).

All taxis charge the metered fare, which is S\$2.40 (US\$1.50) for the first kilometer and S10¢ for each additional 240 meters or 30 seconds of waiting. A S50¢ surcharge exists for peak-period fares outside the Central Business District (CBD) Monday to Friday 7:30am to 6:30pm and Saturday and the eve of public holidays 7:30am to 2pm, while inside the CBD the peak period surcharge is S\$1.50. Also, for rides between midnight and 6am, you'll be charged an extra 50% of your fare. Also beware, you may need to call a cab to fetch you between 5pm and 6pm each day, when the cabbies change shifts, and they're impossible to flag.

**BY CAR**   Singapore's public transportation systems are so extensive, efficient, and inexpensive that you shouldn't need a car to enjoy your stay. In fact, I don't advise it.

It is very expensive due to government taxation of motor vehicles, you have to drive on the left side of the road, all foreign drivers need a valid international driver's license, and you have to deal with confusing parking regulations. If you insist, however, **Avis** (☎ **65/543-8833**) and **Hertz** (☎ **65/542-5300**) have offices at Changi Airport. Both also offer **hourly rentals** of chauffeur-driven vehicles.

# Fast Facts: Singapore

**American Express**    The American Express office is located at no. 18–01/07 The Concourse at 300 Beach Rd. The direct line for travel services is ☎ **65/299-8133.** The 24-hour membership services hotline is ☎ 1800/732-2244. The 24-hour traveler's check refund hotline is ☎ 1800/616-1389.

**Business Hours**    **Shopping centers** are open Monday through Saturday from 10am to 8pm, and stay open until 10pm on some public holidays. **Banks** are open from 9:30am to 3pm Monday through Friday, and from 9 to 11am on Saturdays. **Restaurants** open at lunchtime from around 11am to 2:30pm and for dinner they re-open at around 6pm and take the last order sometime around 10pm. **Nightclubs** stay open until midnight on weekdays and until 2am on Fridays and Saturdays. **Government offices** are open from 9am to 5pm Monday through Friday and from 9am to 3pm on Saturdays. **Post offices** conduct business from 8:30am to 5pm on weekdays and from 8:30am to 1pm on Saturdays.

**Doctors & Dentists**    Most hotels have in-house doctors on call 24 hours a day. A visit to a private physician can cost anywhere between S$25 and S$100 (US$15.25–US$61). In the event of a medical emergency call ☎ **995** for an ambulance. Dental care in Singapore is excellent, and most procedures will cost less than they would at home. Emergency care is available at some hospitals. Check the Yellow Pages.

**Drug Laws**    In case you're one of the few on the planet who hasn't heard, Singapore executes convicted drug traffickers. Importing, selling, or using illegal narcotics is absolutely forbidden, and the law is strictly enforced. The death penalty applies for specific quantities of morphine, heroin, cocaine, marijuana, hashish, and opium.

**Electricity**    Standard electrical current is 220 volts, so if you're coming from the U.S. bring a converter or adapter for electronics. Some hotels have converters and plug adapters in-house for you to use.

**Embassies**    Foreign missions in Singapore are as follows: **United States,** 30 Hill St. (☎ **65/338-0251**); **Canada,** 80 Anson Rd., no. 14/15–00 IBM Towers (☎ **65/225-6363**); Australia, 25 Napier Rd. (☎ **65/737-9311**); **New Zealand,** 13 Nassim Rd. (☎ **65/235-9966**); **United Kingdom,** Tanglin Road (☎ **65/473-9333**).

**Emergencies**    For police dial ☎ **999.** For medical or fire emergencies call ☎ **995.**

**Hospitals**    If you need to seek emergency medical attention, go to either of the following centrally located private hospitals: **Mount Elizabeth Hospital Ltd.,** 3 Mount Elizabeth Road, near Orchard Road (☎ **65/737-2666**) or **Singapore General Hospital,** Outram Rd., in Chinatown (☎ **65/222-3322**). Medical care in Singapore is of superior quality. In fact, throngs of Asian neighbors make annual trips to Singapore for their physical examinations and other medical treatments. You can be assured of excellent care, should you need it.

**Internet/E-mail**   Surprisingly, Singapore is not as up on Internet cafes as other countries, so there are very few around. The best and most centrally located is **Cyberheart Café,** 442 Orchard Road, #B1-11 Orchard Hotel Arcard (☎ **65/735-8458**). Open daily from 11am to 11pm, they charge (US$3) per 15 minutes.

**Language**   The official languages are Malay, Chinese (Mandarin), Tamil, and English. Malay is the national language while English is the language for government operations, law, and major financial transactions. Most Singaporeans are at least bilingual, with many speaking one or more dialects of Chinese, English, and some Malay.

**Liquor Laws**   The legal age for alcohol purchase and consumption is 18 years. Public drunk-and-disorderly behavior is against the law and may snag you for up to S$1,000 (US$610) in fines for the first offense. There are strict drinking and driving laws.

**Police**   For emergencies, call ☎ **999.**

**Post Offices/Mail**   Most hotels have post services at the front counter. **Singapore Post** has centrally located offices at no. 04–15 Takashimaya Shopping Centre (☎ **65/738-6899**); Tang's department store at 320 Orchard Rd. no. 03–00 (☎ **65/738-5899**); World Trade Centre, 1 Maritime Square no. 01–41 (☎ **65/270-6899**); Chinatown Point, 133 New Bridge Rd. no. 02–42/43/44 (☎ **65/538-7899**); and Change Alley, 16 Collyer Quay no. 02–02 (☎ **65/538-6899**). Plus there are five branches at Changi International Airport. The going rate for international airmail letters to North America and Europe is S$1 for 20 grams plus S35¢ for each additional 10 grams. For international airmail service to Australia and New Zealand, the rate is S70¢ for 20 grams plus S30¢ for each additional 10 grams. Postcards and aerograms to all destinations are S50¢.

**Safety/Crime**   Singapore is a pretty safe place by any standards. There's very little violent crime, even late at night. If your children are missing, they probably aren't kidnapped, but are being consoled by a friendly passerby while they search for you. In recent years, some pickpocketing has been reported. The number to call for a **police emergency** is ☎ **999.**

**Taxes**   Many hotels and restaurants will advertise rates followed by "+++," which means an additional 3% goods and services tax (GST), 1% cess (a tax levied by the STB on all tourism-related activities), and 10% gratuity will be added to your bill. See the "Customs Regulations" section in this chapter for information on the GST Tourist Refund Scheme, which lets you recover the GST for some purchases

**Telephone & Fax**   Almost all hotels will send faxes locally and internationally for you and add the charge to your bill. **Public phones** are abundant and can be operated by coins or by phonecards, which can be purchased in increments of S$2, S$5, and S$10 values at post offices, provisioners shops, and some money changers. The charge for a local call from a coin phone is S10¢ for 3 minutes. Calls to numbers beginning with 1800 are toll free.

**International Direct Dialing** (IDD) is the long-distance service used by most hotels, businesses, and private residences in Singapore, with direct dialing to 218 countries.

Before you leave your home country, contact your long-distance provider to see if they offer a **long-distance calling card,** which will allow you to access their international operators and have your calls charged to your home phone bill at

## Telephone Dialing Info at a Glance

- **To place a call from your home country to Singapore:** Dial the international access code (011 in the U.S., 0011 in Australia, 0170 in New Zealand, or 00 in the U.K.), plus the country code (65), plus the 7-digit phone number (for example, 011 + 65/000-0000). For hotels, I've listed international toll-free numbers where applicable in individual reviews.
- **To place a call within Singapore:** Dial the 7-digit number. The "65" prefix need not be used. Toll-free numbers in Singapore use the standard "1-800" prefix.
- **To place a direct international call from Singapore,** dial the international access code (001 for direct dial, 004 for operator-assisted calls) plus the country code, the area or city code, and the number (for example, to call the U.S., you'd dial 001 + 01 + 000/000-0000).
- **To reach the international operator:** Dial ☎ 104.
- **To call Malaysia from Singapore via an operator:** Dial ☎ 109.
- **To call Malaysia from Singapore direct:** Dial ☎ 020 plus the city code and the number (for example, 020 + 3/000-0000). The two countries have a trunk line connecting them, to save money on both sides. There is no need to dial the country code for calls to Malaysia.
- **To call AT&T direct:** Call ☎ **800/011-1111;** for MCI, call ☎ **800-011-2112;** and for Sprint, call ☎ **800/017-7177.**
- **International country codes** are as follows: Australia 61, Burma 95, Cambodia 855, Canada 1, Hong Kong 852, Indonesia 62, Laos 856, Malaysia 60, New Zealand 64, the Philippines 63, Thailand 66, U.K. 44, U.S. 1, Vietnam 84.
- For **telephone directory assistance,** dial ☎ **100.**

their rates. Singapore has some of the lowest international call rates in the world, but unfortunately, hotels charge a huge surcharge for these calls.

See the "Telephone Info: Dialing to & from Singapore" box in this section for more information.

**Time Zone**   Singapore Standard Time is 8 hours ahead of Greenwich Mean Time (GMT). For the current time within Singapore, call ☎ **1711.**

**Tipping**   Tipping is discouraged at hotels, at bars, and in taxis. Basically, the deal here is not to tip. A gratuity is automatically added to guest checks.

**Toilets/Rest Rooms**   Rest rooms are easy to find in Singapore and most of the time they are clean.

**Water**   Tap water in Singapore passes World Health Organization standards and is potable.

## 3  Accommodations

As any traveler who's been to Singapore will attest, hotel rooms in this city are hardly inexpensive. Between the business community's demand for luxury and the inflated Singaporean real estate market, room prices tend to be high. Of course, this means that budget accommodations are not a high priority on the island.

# Urban Singapore Accommodations & Dining

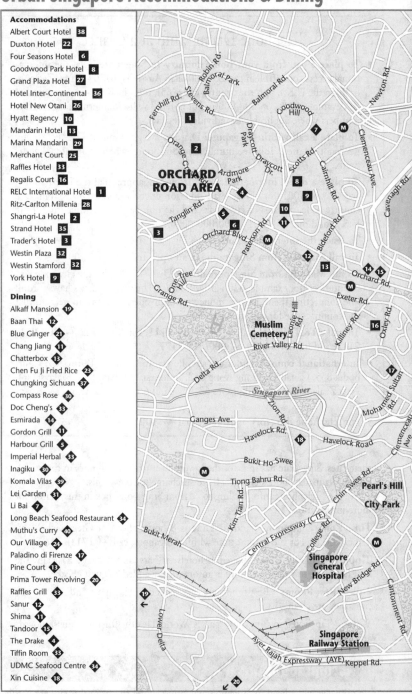

## Accommodations
Albert Court Hotel 38
Duxton Hotel 22
Four Seasons Hotel 6
Goodwood Park Hotel 8
Grand Plaza Hotel 27
Hotel Inter-Continental 36
Hotel New Otani 26
Hyatt Regency 10
Mandarin Hotel 13
Marina Mandarin 29
Merchant Court 25
Raffles Hotel 33
Regalis Court 16
RELC International Hotel 1
Ritz-Carlton Millenia 28
Shangri-La Hotel 2
Strand Hotel 35
Trader's Hotel 3
Westin Plaza 32
Westin Stamford 32
York Hotel 9

## Dining
Alkaff Mansion 19
Baan Thai 12
Blue Ginger 21
Chang Jiang 11
Chatterbox 13
Chen Fu Ji Fried Rice 23
Chungking Sichuan 37
Compass Rose 30
Doc Cheng's 33
Esmirada 14
Gordon Grill 11
Harbour Grill 5
Imperial Herbal 33
Inagiku 30
Komala Vilas 39
Lei Garden 31
Li Bai 7
Long Beach Seafood Restaurant 34
Muthu's Curry 40
Our Village 24
Paladino di Firenze 17
Pine Court 13
Prima Tower Revolving 20
Raffles Grill 33
Sanur 12
Shima 11
Tandoor 15
The Drake 4
Tiffin Room 33
UDMC Seafood Centre 34
Xin Cuisine 18

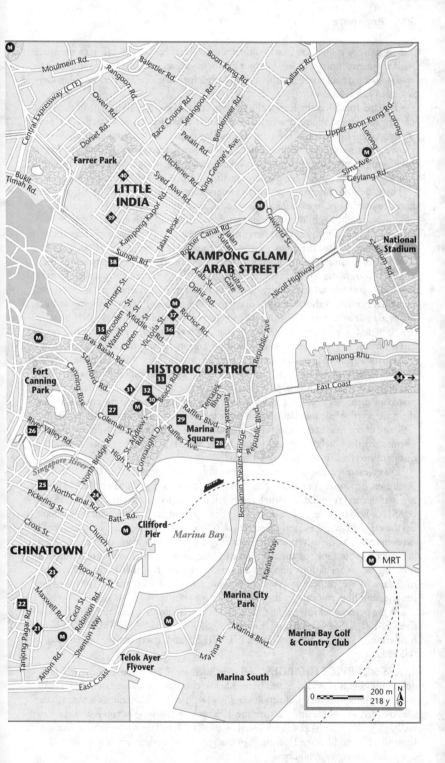

Singapore is a small city, and public transportation means you can stay anywhere within the city limits and still be close to where you want to go. Still, you may wish to stay in a particular neighborhood. The hotels listed are divided between neighborhoods to help you decide.

**Orchard Road** has the largest cluster of hotels in the city, and is right in the heart of Singaporean shopping mania. The **Historic District** has hotels that are near museums and sights, while those in **Marina Bay** center more around Suntec City, the giant convention and exhibition center located there. **Chinatown** and **Tanjong Pagar** have some lovely boutique hotels in quaint back streets, and **Shenton Way** has a couple of high-rise places for the convenience of people doing business in the area.

There are also different types of accommodations in the city. While Singapore is home to many large international chain hotels, new boutique hotels have sprung up in old pre-war buildings in quaint neighborhoods. While budget hotels have very limited facilities and interior stylings that never made it much past 1979, you can always expect a clean room. Par for the course, many of the guests in these places are backpackers. The budget accommodations listed here are places decent enough for any standards.

Unless you choose one of the extreme budget hotels, there are some standard features you can expect to find everywhere. While no hotels offer a courtesy car or limousine, many have **courtesy shuttles** to popular parts of town. Security key cards are catching on, as are in-room safes. You'll also see in-house movies and sometimes CNN on your TV, as well as a nifty interactive service that lets you check on your hotel bill, order room service, and get general information on Singapore with the touch of a button. Voice mail is gaining popularity, and fax services can always be provided upon request. You'll find most places have adequate fitness center facilities, almost all of which offer a range of massage treatments. Pools tend to be on the small side, and Jacuzzis are often placed in men's and women's locker rooms, making it impossible for couples to use them together. While tour desks are in some lobbies, car-rental desks are rare.

Many of the finest **restaurants** in Singapore are located in hotels, whether they are operated by the hotel directly or just inhabiting rented space. In each hotel review, the distinguished restaurants have been noted.

Let's talk money. **Rates** for double rooms range from as low as S$80 (US$50) at the Strand on Bencoolen (a famous backpacker's strip) to as high as S$650 (US$411), a night at the exclusive Raffles Hotel. Average rooms are usually in the S$200 to S$300 (US$126–US$189) range, but keep in mind that although all prices listed in this book are the official rates, they rarely represent what you'll actually pay. In fact, you should *never* have to pay the advertised rate in a Singapore hotel, as many offer special rates just after a renovation, or for reservations made through the Internet or through a travel agent, or for visitors booking long-term stays or stays that begin and end on weekdays. When you call for your reservation, always ask what special rates they are running and how you can get the lowest price for your room.

For the purposes of this guide, we've divided hotels into the categories **Very Expensive,** S$400 (US$244) and up; **Expensive,** S$300 to S$400 (US$183–US$244); **Moderate,** S$200 to S$300 (US$122–US$183); and **Inexpensive,** under S$200 (US$122).

**TAXES & SERVICE CHARGES**    All rates listed are in Singapore dollars, with U.S. dollar equivalents provided as well (remember to check the exchange rates when you're planning, though, as they will almost certainly be different). Most rates do not include the so-called **+++ taxes** and charges: the 10% service charge, 3% goods and services tax (GST), and 1% cess (a 1% tax levied by the STB on all tourism-related activities). Keep these in mind when figuring your budget. Some budget hotels will quote discount rates inclusive of all taxes.

# The Shophouses of Singapore

The shophouses that line many of Singapore's streets are perhaps the architectural feature travelers find most memorable about this city. These rowhouses were southern Asia's answer to urban commercial and residential buildings through the early 1800s and into the first half of the 20th century. Their design was perfect. Ground floors were occupied by shops or coffeehouses, while the upper floors were homes—an ideal situation for mom-and-pop operations. The rows of uniform buildings fit perfectly within the grid of the city streets, while inside air shafts and vents let air and sunlight circulate throughout. Out front, many of the shophouses featured ornately decorated facades, while the "five-foot-ways" (covered sidewalks) formed by the shophouses' projecting second stories shielded pedestrians from sun and rain.

In recent years, as part of the Urban Restoration Authority's renewal plans, rows of old shophouses and buildings in ethnic areas like Chinatown and Tanjong Pagar have been restored and transformed into small, lovely **boutique hotels.** Places like Albert Court Hotel, the Duxton, and the Royal Peacock are beautiful examples of local flavor turned into elegant accommodations. While these places can put you closer to the heart of Singapore, they do have their drawbacks: Both the hotels and their rooms are small, for one, and, due to lack of space and building codes, they're unable to provide facilities like swimming pools, Jacuzzis, or fitness centers.

**THE BUSY SEASON**    The busy season is from January to around June. In the late summer months, business travel dies down and hotels try to make up for drooping occupancy rates by going after the leisure market. In fall, even tourism drops off somewhat, making the season ripe for budget-minded visitors. These may be the best times to get a deal. Probably the worst time to negotiate will be between Christmas and the Chinese New Year, when folks travel on holiday and to see their families.

**MAKING RESERVATIONS ON THE GROUND**    If you are not able to make a reservation prior to your trip, there is a **reservation service** available at Changi International Airport. The Singapore Hotel Association operates desks in both Terminals 1 and 2, with reservation services based upon room availability for many hotels. Discounts for these arrangements are sometimes as high as 30%. The desks are open daily from 7:30am to 11:30pm.

## HISTORIC DISTRICT
### VERY EXPENSIVE

**Raffles Hotel.** 1 Beach Rd., Singapore 189673. ☎ **800/525-4800** from the U.S. and Canada, 008/251-958 from Australia, 0800/441098 from New Zealand, 0800/964470 from the U.K., or 65/337-1886. Fax 65/339-7650. www.slh.com/slh/. 104 suites. A/C MINIBAR TV TEL. S$650–S$6,000 (US$396–US$3,660) suite. AE, DC, JCB, MC, V. Near City Hall MRT.

Raffles Hotel has been legendary since its establishment in 1887. Named after Singapore's first British colonial administrator, Sir Stamford Raffles, it was founded by the Armenian Sarkies brothers. By the early 1900s it became a mecca for celebrities like Charlie Chaplin and Douglas Fairbanks, writers like Somerset Maugham and Noel Coward, and various sundry kings, sultans, and politicians. In 1987, Raffles Hotel was declared a landmark and restored to its early-20th-century splendor, with 14-foot molded and be-fanned ceilings; grand arches; tile, teak and marble floors; Oriental carpets; and period furnishings. Outside, the facade of the main building was similarly restored, complete with the elegant cast-iron portico and the verandas that encircle the upper stories.

Raffles is a "suite only" hotel: In each, you enter past the living and dining area with its Oriental carpets and reproduction furniture, then pass through louvered doors into the bedroom with its four-poster bed and beautiful armoire, ceiling fan twirling high above. It is a colonial fantasy come true.

The Raffles Hotel shopping arcade was designed in architectural harmony with the original design and houses a theater playhouse, Raffles Culinary Academy, the Raffles Hotel Museum, and 65 exclusive boutiques. Outstanding restaurants and bars include the Tiffin Room, Raffles Grill, and Doc Cheng's (all reviewed in the restaurants section), and the Bar and Billiards Room and Long Bar. Hotel services include an airport limousine and 24-hour room valet and concierge. Facilities include in-room VCRs with video rental, small outdoor pool (open 24 hours), 24-hour business center, and 24-hour fitness center with Jacuzzi, sauna, steam, and massage.

## EXPENSIVE

**The Grand Plaza Hotel.** 10 Coleman St., Singapore 179809. ☎ **800/44-UTELL** from the U.S. and Canada, or 65/336-3456. Fax 65/339-9311. E-mail: gph@pacific.net.sg. 338 units. A/C MINIBAR TV TEL. S$300–S$320 (US$183–US$195) double; S$360–S$380 (US$220–US$232) club; S$600–S$1,200 (US$366–US$732) suite. AE, DC, JCB, MC, V. 5-minute walk to City Hall MRT.

The Grand Plaza was built on top of (and incorporating) 2 blocks of prewar shop-houses, and you can see hints of shophouse detail throughout the lobby. Guest rooms are of average size, have considerable closet space, and sport sharp Italian contemporary furniture in natural tones, with homey touches like snuggly comforters on all the beds.

The hotel's Saint Gregory Marine Spa is Singapore's largest and most exclusive spa. There are 20 private treatment rooms where you can enjoy hydrotherapy baths, jet showers, hot and cold Jacuzzis, steam baths, sauna, facial and body treatments, and massage therapies. Other facilities include a small outdoor pool from which you can see the steeple of the Armenian Church across the street, a beauty salon, and a small shopping arcade.

**Hotel Inter-Continental Singapore.** 80 Middle Rd., Singapore 188966 (near Bugis Junction). ☎ **65/338-7600.** Fax 65/338-7366. 406 units. A/C MINIBAR TV TEL. S$410 (US$250) double; S$720–S$3,800 (US$439–US$2,318) suite. AE, DC, JCB, MC, V. Bugis MRT.

The government let Inter-Continental build a hotel in this spot with one ironclad stipulation: The hotel chain had to retain the original shophouses on the block and incorporate them into the hotel design. Reinforcing the foundation, Hotel Inter-Continental built up from there, giving touches of old architectural style to the lobby, lounge, and other public areas on the bottom floors while imbuing it with the feel of a modern hotel. The second and third floors have "Shophouse Rooms" styled with such Peranakan trappings as carved hardwood furnishings and floral linens, and with homey touches like potted plants and carpets over wooden floors. Guest rooms on higher levels are large, with formal European styling and large luxurious bathrooms. Although the pool area has a terrible view, the space is beautifully landscaped, with a wooden deck and comfortable lounge chairs. The hotel also has a rooftop garden, 24-hour health club, outdoor Jacuzzi, sauna, car-rental desk, and tour desk.

**Marina Mandarin Singapore.** 6 Raffles Blvd., Marina Square, Singapore 039594. ☎ **65/338-3388.** Fax 65/339-4977. www.marina-mandarin.com.sg. 575 units. S$360–S$420 (US$220–US$256) double; S$600–S$3,000 (US$366–US$1,830) suite. AE, DC, JCB, MC, V. 10-minute walk to City Hall MRT.

There are a few hotels in the Marina Bay area built around the atrium concept, and of them, this one is the loveliest. The atrium lobby opens up to ceiling skylights 21 stories above, guest corridor balconies hung with plants line the sides, and in the center hangs a glistening metal mobile sculpture in red and gold. One of the most surprising details is the melodic chirping of caged songbirds, which fills the open space every morning.

The rooms are equally impressive: large and cool, with two desk spaces and standard balconies. Try to get the Marina view—you won't be sorry.

Hotel facilities include a large outdoor pool; a fitness center with aerobics and massage, Jacuzzi, sauna, and steam room; a 24-hour business center; a squash court; two outside tennis courts; a putting green; a beauty salon; and a number of boutiques.

✪ **The Ritz-Carlton Millenia Singapore.** 7 Raffles Ave., Singapore 039799. ☎ **800/ 241-3333** from the U.S. and Canada, or 65/337-8888. Fax 65/338-0001. www. ritzcarlton.com. 610 units. A/C MINIBAR TV TEL. S$430 (US$262) double; S$1,350 (US$823) suite. AE, DC, JCB, MC, V. 10-minute walk to City Hall MRT.

Touted as the ultimate in Singapore luxury hotels, the Ritz-Carlton Millenia is just that, but you have to love ultra-modern design. The space-age lobby is like a science museum, and off to the right is a giant open space with elegant contemporary seating areas under a greenhouse skylight. All rooms have views of either Kallang Bay or the more majestic Marina Bay. Even the bathrooms have views, as the huge tubs are placed under octagonal picture windows so you can gaze as you bathe. Guest rooms here are about 25% larger than most five-star rooms elsewhere. There's room for lovely seating areas, big two-poster beds, and full walk-in closets.

Twenty-four-hour maid service is available, and facilities include voice mail; a health club with aerobics, massage, sauna, steam, hot and cold plunge pools, and spa cuisine; an outdoor tennis court; a beauty salon; and a gift shop. The hotel pool is a gorgeous 82-foot (25m) Greco-Roman monster done in streaks of shimmering blue tile. At the far end is a Jacuzzi tucked beneath a cascading waterfall.

## MODERATE

✪ **Albert Court Hotel.** 180 Albert St., Singapore 189971. ☎ **65/339-3939.** Fax 65/339-3252. www.fareast.com.sg/hotels. 136 units. S$210–S$230 (US$128–US$140) double; S$290 (US$177) suite. AE, DC, JCB, MC, V. 5-minute walk to Bugis MRT.

The Albert Court was first conceived as part of the Urban Renewal Authority's master plan to revitalize this block, which involved the restoration of two rows of prewar shophouses. The eight-story boutique hotel that emerged once the dust settled has all the Western comforts but has retained the charm of its shophouse roots. Decorators placed local Peranakan touches everywhere, from the carved teak panels in traditional floral design to the antique china cups used for tea service in the rooms.

The rooms are small, though the ones at the ends of the corridors are slightly larger. Details like the teak molding, floral batik bedspreads, bathroom tiles in bright Peranakan colors, and old-time brass electrical switches give this place true local charm and distinction. Secretarial services are available.

**Hotel New Otani Singapore.** 177A River Valley Rd., Singapore 179031. ☎ **800/ 421-8795** from the U.S. and Canada, 800/273-2294 from California, or 65/338-3333. Fax 65/339-2854. www.newotani.co.jp/index-e.htm. 408 units. A/C MINIBAR TV TEL. S$280–S$320 (US$171–US$195) double; S$600–S$800 (US$366–US$488) suite. AE, DC, JCB, MC, V. Far from MRT stations.

The Hotel New Otani sits along the Singapore River just next to Clarke Quay (a popular spot for nightlife, dining, and shopping) and a stroll away from the Historic District. At night, you have access to nearby Boat Quay bars and restaurants. The hotel was renovated in 1993, and recent additions (to all rooms) include multimedia PCs with Microsoft Office and tourist information. All rooms have small balconies letting onto unique views of the river, the financial district, Fort Canning Park, and China-town, and the standard rooms have large luxurious bathrooms like those in more deluxe accommodations. Facilities include a large outdoor pool and a fitness center with aerobics, a Jacuzzi, sauna, facials, and massage (you can even get a massage pool-side). The hotel runs daily shuttle service to Orchard Road, Shenton Way, and Marina Square, and each guest receives free Singapore Trolley passes and a free river cruise.

✪ **The Westin Stamford & Westin Plaza.** 2 Stamford Rd., Singapore 178882. ☎ **800/228-3000** from the U.S. and Canada, 008/803849 from Australia (Sydney 2/2903664), 0800/441737 from New Zealand, 0800/282565 from the U.K., or 65/338-8585. Fax 65/338-2862. www.asia-online.com/westin. E-mail: westin1@signet.com.sg. 2,062 units. A/C MINIBAR TV TEL. Westin Stamford: S$340–S$360 (US$207–US$220) double; S$680 (US$415) suite. Westin Plaza: S$360–S$380 (US$220–US$232) double; S$420 (US$256) club; S$700–S$1,000 (US$427–US$610) suite. AE, DC, JCB, MC, V. City Centre MRT.

The combined Westin Stamford and Westin Plaza hotels are a giant complex com-prising 2,062 combined guest rooms, the Raffles City Convention Centre, and 14 food and beverage outlets, all sitting directly atop the Raffles City Shopping Complex and City Hall MRT station. Both hotels opened in 1986, and ever since, the Westin Stamford has been in the Guinness Book of World Records as the tallest hotel in the world. Its 70 floors measure in at 735 feet (226m). Guest rooms have balconies and, as you'd guess, some pretty spectacular views. The rooms themselves are slightly larger than average. Westin also has weekend promotional rates. Facilities include a large out-door pool with lifeguard; 24-hour fitness center with aerobics, Jacuzzi, sauna, and steam room; six outdoor tennis courts; two squash courts; and table tennis. The excel-lent Compass Rose restaurant is perched right at the top of the hotel, offering stun-ning views in addition to some mighty scrumptious meals.

### INEXPENSIVE

**Strand Hotel.** 25 Bencoolen St., Singapore 189619. ☎ **65/338-1866.** Fax 65/338-1330. 130 units. A/C TV TEL. S$65–S$100 (US$40–US$61) double. No credit cards. 10-minute walk to City Hall MRT.

The Strand is by far the best of the inexpensive places in this area. The lobby is far nicer than you'd expect, and you get a clean and neat room. Although there are some hints that you really are staying in a budget hotel—older decor and uncoordinated furniture sets, for instance—they provide some little niceties, like hotel stationery. The no-frills bathrooms are clean and adequate. There are no tea- and coffee-making facilities, but there is 24-hour room service and a cafe on the premises. Free parking is available.

## CHINATOWN
### EXPENSIVE

**The Duxton.** 83 Duxton Rd., Singapore 089540. ☎ **800/882-3383** from the U.S. and Canada, 800/251664 from Australia, 800/446110 from New Zealand, or 65/227-7678. Fax 65/227-1232. www.integra.fr/relaischateaux/duxton. E-mail duxton@singnet.com.sg. 49 units. A/C MINIBAR TV TEL. S$240–S$330 (US$146–US$201) double; S$400 (US$244) suite. Rates include full English breakfast. AE, DC, JCB, MC, V. 5-minute walk to Tanjong Pagar MRT.

The Duxton was one of the first hotels to experiment with the boutique hotel concept, transforming their shophouse structure into a small hotel and doing it with an elegance that's earned them a place in the worldwide Relais & Chateau luxury hotel group. From the outside, the place has old-world charm equal to any lamplit European cobblestone street, and once you step inside you'll find a sophisticated and romantic little place, done entirely in turn-of-the-century styling that includes reproduction Chippendale furniture and pen-and-ink Audubon-style drawings. Rooms tend to be smaller than in conventional hotels, but they've succeeded in creating spaces that feel airy and open. Of course, regulations and space do not allow for pools or fitness centers, but you do get complimentary chocolates, fruit basket, mineral water, and shoe-shine services, and a free shuttle to Shenton Way and Orchard Road. Secretarial services are available.

✪ **Merchant Court Hotel.** 20 Merchant Rd., Singapore 058281. ☎ **800/637-7200** from the U.S. and Canada; 800/655-147 from Australia; 800/442-519 from New Zealand; 800/252-840 from the U.K.; or 65/337-2288. Fax 65/334-0606. www.raffles.com/ril. 476 units. A/C MINIBAR TV TEL. S$305–S$365 (US$186–US$223) double; S$810–S$1,500 (US$494–US$915) suite. AE, DC, JCB, MC, V. 10-minute walk to Raffles Place MRT.

Merchant Court is a very popular hotel for its location, convenience, and atmosphere. Situated on the Singapore River, the hotel has easy access to Clarke Quay and Boat Quay, which means you'll be able to take good advantage of the many entertainments and dining experiences of the area. Convenience is provided by a self-service launderette, drink and snack vending machines on each floor, and unstocked minibar fridge, so you can buy your own. Further convenience will be added when the city opens the Clarke Quay MRT stop in late 1999. The hotel touts itself as a city hotel with a resort feel, with landscaped pool area (with a view of the river) and cool, airy guest rooms. Facilities include in-house movies and a health spa and fitness center with sauna, steam, massage, and Jacuzzi.

### INEXPENSIVE

**Chinatown Hotel.** 12–16 Teck Lim Rd., Singapore 088388. ☎ **65/326-6766.** Fax 65/367-8695. 42 units. A/C TV TEL. S$155–S$180 (US$95–US$110) double. AE, DC, MC, V. 5-minute walk to Outram MRT.

Chinatown Hotel definitely has its pros and cons, but for clean rooms, friendly service, and a good rate, it's one of my favorites. Because this is a boutique hotel with limited space, the rooms, though modern and well maintained, are tiny, and the bathrooms are just a showerhead in the wall as you stand in front of the sink. Some rooms have no windows, so specify when you make reservations if you're fond of natural light. The hotel has one movie channel on the TVs and no facilities to speak of, not even coffee and tea service in the rooms, but there's free coffee, tea, and toast in the lobby. Larger hotels will charge higher rates so you can enjoy the luxury of a pool, fitness center, and multiple food and beverage outlets, but if you're in town to get out and see Singapore, it's nice to know you won't pay for things you'll never use. Besides, the folks at the front counter will always remember your name and are very professional without being impersonal.

## ORCHARD ROAD
### EXPENSIVE

✪ **Four Seasons Hotel Singapore.** 190 Orchard Rd., Singapore 248646. ☎ **800/332-3442** from the U.S. and Canada, or 65/734-1110. Fax 65/733-0682. www.fshr.com. 154 units. A/C MINIBAR TV TEL. S$435–S$490 (US$265–US$299) double; S$570–S$620 (US$348–US$378) club; S$750–S$4,400 (US$457–US$2,684) suite. AE, DC, JCB, MC, V. 5-minute walk to Orchard MRT.

A lot of upmarket hotels will try to convince you that staying with them is like visiting a wealthy friend. Four Seasons actually delivers. The guest rooms are very spacious and inviting, and even the standard rooms have creature comforts you'd expect from a suite, such as complimentary fruit, terry cloth bathrobes and slippers, CD and laser disc players, and an extensive complimentary laser disc and CD library that the concierge is just waiting to deliver to your room. The Italian marble bathrooms have double vanities, deep tubs, bidets, and surround speakers from the TV and stereo. Did I mention remote control drapes? Consider a standard room here before a suite in a less expensive hotel. You won't regret it.

In addition to business packages, Four Seasons also offers special shopping, spa, and tennis packages. The fitness center has a state-of-the-art gymnasium with TV monitors, videos, tape players and CD/LD players, a Virtual Reality Bike, aerobics, sauna, steam rooms, massage, facials, body wraps and aromatherapy treatments, and a staff of fitness professionals. Want more? How about a flotation tank and a Mind Gear Syncro-Energiser (a brain relaxer that uses pulsing lights), a billiards room, and an OptiGolf Indoor Pro-Golf System. Two indoor, air-conditioned tennis courts and two outdoor courts are staffed with a resident professional tennis coach to provide instruction or play a game. There are two pools: a 57-foot (20m) lap pool and a rooftop sundeck pool, both with adjacent Jacuzzis.

**Goodwood Park Hotel.** 22 Scotts Rd., Singapore 228221. ☎ **65/737-7411.** Fax 65/732-8558. 235 units. A/C MINIBAR TV TEL. S$425–S$465 double; S$615–S$650 (US$375–US$396) poolside suite, S$888–S$3,000 (US$542–US$1,830) suite. AE, DC, JCB, MC, V. 5-min. walk to Orchard MRT.

The Goodwood Park Hotel is a national landmark. Built in 1900 and designed in the manner of castles along the Rhine, it served as the Teutonia Club, a social club for the German community, before becoming the Goodwood Park Hotel in 1929. During World War II, high-ranking Japanese military used it as a residence, and 3 years later it served as a British War Crimes Court before reverting back to a hotel. Over the years the hotel has expanded from 60 rooms to 235, and has hosted a long list of international celebrities and dignitaries.

For the money, there are more luxurious facilities, but while most hotels have bigger and better business and fitness centers (Goodwood has *the* smallest fitness center), only Raffles Hotel can rival Goodwood Park's historic significance. The poolside suites off the Mayfair Pool are the best rooms in the house, offering direct access to the small Mayfair Pool with its lush Balinese-style landscaping. There are also suites off the main pool, which is much larger but offers little privacy from the lobby and surrounding restaurants.

Restaurants on premises include Chang Jiang, Gordon Grill, and Shima (all reviewed under "Dining," below).

**Hyatt Regency Singapore.** 10–12 Scotts Rd., Singapore 228211. ☎ **800/228-9000** from the U.S., or 65/738-1234. Fax 65/732-1696. www.hyatt.com. 693 units. S$350–S$460 (US$213–US$281) double; S$500–S$2,500 (US$305–US$1,525) suite. Near Orchard MRT.

Despite its fantastic location, this hotel was doing pretty poorly until they had a feng shui master come in and evaluate it for redecorating. Since then, the hotel has enjoyed some of the highest occupancy rates in town. Feng shui or not, the new decor is modern, sleek, and sophisticated, an elegant combination of polished black marble and deep wood. Quiet corridors with great artwork lead to bright guest rooms distinguished by small glass-enclosed alcoves looking over the hotel gardens. Bathrooms are large, with lots of marble counter space. All rooms have voice mail and data ports.

Two lush tropical gardens decorate the hotel, with rock formations, flowers, and a total of 16 waterfalls. Tucked inside the gardens is the swimming pool. There's also a children's slide pool, two floodlit tennis courts, and an air-conditioned badminton court. The fitness center has modern equipment, TV monitors, landscaped Jacuzzi, sauna and steam room areas, aerobics classes, and massage and beauty treatments.

**Mandarin Singapore.** 333 Orchard Rd., Singapore 238867. ☎ **800/380-9957** from the U.S. and Canada, or 65/737-4411. Fax 65/235-6688. www.commerceasia.com/mandarin. 1,235 units. A/C MINIBAR TV TEL. S$380 (US$232) double; S$400 (US$244) club; S$500–S$900 (US$305–US$549) suite. AE, DC, JCB, MC, V and Air Plus. Near Orchard MRT.

Smack in the center of Orchard Road is the Mandarin Hotel, a two-tower complex. The 39-story Main Tower opened in 1973, and with the opening of the South Wing 10 years later the number of rooms expanded to 1,200. True to its name, the hotel is decorated in Chinese style, from the huge lobby mural of the "87 Taoist Immortals" to the black-and-red Ming-design carpet murals and black lacquer-style guest room entrances. The South Wing is predominantly for leisure travelers, who have access to the tower from the side of the hotel off Orchard Road. The guest rooms here are slightly smaller and furnished with Chinese-style dark wood modular units. Hotel facilities include one outdoor tennis court, one squash court, a midsize outdoor pool, a shopping arcade, and a large fitness center with aerobics, Jacuzzi, sauna, and steam.

○ **Shangri-La Hotel.** 22 Orange Grove Rd., Singapore 258350. ☎ **800/942-5050** from the U.S. and Canada, 800/222448 from Australia, 0800/442179 from New Zealand, or 65/737-3644. Fax 65/733-7220. www.shangri-la.com. 879 units. A/C MINIBAR TV TEL. S$345 (US$210) Tower double; S$460 (US$281) Garden double; S$490 (US$299) Garden deluxe; S$495 (US$302) Horizon Club; S$495 (US$302) Valley double; S$525 (US$320) Valley deluxe; S$600–S$3,200 (US$366–US$1,952) suite. All published rates include free round-trip limo service to the airport, breakfast, laundry, and dry cleaning. AE, DC, JCB, MC, V. 10-min. walk to Orchard MRT.

Because it's an older hotel, the Shangri-La has the luxury of space, which it takes advantage of by providing strolling gardens, a putting course, and an outdoor pool paradise that are great diversions from the city's hustle and bustle. Maybe that's why visiting VIPs like George Bush, Benazir Bhutto, and Nelson Mandela have all stayed here.

The hotel has three wings: The Tower Wing is the oldest, but has undergone extensive modernizations to upgrade and enlarge the rooms. The Garden Wing has bougainvillea-laden balconies, half of which overlook the tropical atrium with its cascading waterfall and exotic plants. The exclusive Valley Wing has a private entrance and very spacious rooms, and is linked to the main tower by a sky bridge that looks out over the hotel's 15 acres of landscaped lawns, fruit trees, and flowers. Rooms in all wings have interactive TV, and fax machines are available on request. Facilities include two pools (one large outdoor and one small heated indoor); four tennis courts; two squash courts; and a fitness center with hot and cold Jacuzzis, steam, sauna, and massage. Sports equipment rentals are available. Xanadu, a disco, is located in the basement, and there's a fine restaurant, Latour, located in the rear of the lobby.

## MODERATE

**Regalis Court.** 64 Lloyd Rd., Singapore 239113. ☎ **65/734-7117.** Fax 65/736-1651. 43 units. A/C TV TEL. S$145–S$165 (US$88–US$101) double. AE DC JCB MC V. 10-min. walk from Somerset MRT.

For a bit of local charm at an affordable price, Regalis Court is a favorite. Centrally located just a 10-minute walk from Orchard Road, this charming old bungalow has been restored beautifully and outfitted with Peranakan-inspired touches. Everything here will make you feel as if you're staying in a quaint guesthouse rather than a hotel, from the open-air lobby (under the porte cochere) and corridors to the guest rooms, which have comforting touches like teakwood furnishings, textile wall hangings, Oriental throws over wooden floors, and bamboo blinds to keep out the sun. Although guest rooms are slightly smaller than conventional rooms, they are still quite comfortable. Facilities are few; however, a continental breakfast is standard with the room rate. They also offer laundry services, a steam room, and car hire.

☺ **Traders Hotel Singapore.** 1A Cuscaden Rd., Singapore 249716. ☎ **800/ 942-5050** from the U.S. and Canada, 800/222448 from Australia, 0800/442179 from New Zealand, or 65/738-2222. Fax 65/831-4314. www.shangri-la.com. 543 units. A/C TV TEL. S$265–S$310 (US$162–US$189) double; S$345 (US$210) club; S$540 (US$329) studio apt, S$725 (US$442) 2-bedroom family apt; S$540–S$1,000 (US$329–US$610) suite. AE, DC, JCB, MC, V. 10-min. walk to Orchard MRT.

A spin-off of Shangri-La (see above), Traders advertises itself as a "value-for-money" hotel, and is a fantastic bargain for leisure travelers. Rooms have an empty fridge that can be stocked from the supermarket next door (show your room card key at nearby Tanglin Mall for discounts from many of the shops); there are spanking-clean self-service launderette facilities with ironing boards on six floors; and there are vending machines and ice machines. They even provide a hospitality lounge for guests to use after check-out, with seating areas, work spaces with data ports, card phones, safe-deposit boxes, vending machines, and a shower.

Guest rooms are smaller than average, but feature child-size sofa beds and large drawers for storage. The large, landscaped pool area has a great poolside alfresco cafe, Ah Hoi's Kitchen, serving up tasty Chinese dishes at reasonable prices. Hotel facilities include a data port in each room and a fitness center with outdoor Jacuzzi, sauna, steam, massage, and facial services. Services include voice mail, free shuttle service to Orchard Road, Shangri-La Hotel, Shangri-La Rasa Sentosa Resort, Suntec City, and Shenton Way business district. (Taking advantage of the Rasa Sentosa Shuttle may save you admission to Sentosa Island.) Be sure to ask about promotion rates when you book your room. If you plan to stay longer than 2 weeks, they have a long-stay program that offers discount meals, laundry and business center services, and half-price launderette tokens.

**York Hotel Singapore.** 21 Mount Elizabeth, Singapore 228516. ☎ **800/221023** from Australia, 0800/899517 from the U.K, or 65/737-0511. Fax 65/732-1217. 406 units. A/C MINIBAR TV TEL. S$265–S$285 (US$162–US$174) double; S$285 (US$174) cabana, S$400 (US$244) split-level cabana; S$430–S$910 (US$262–US$555) suite. AE, DC, JCB, MC, V. 10-min. walk to Orchard MRT.

A little off the beaten track, this small hotel can boast a very professional and courteous staff (and spiffy "Have a Nice Day" carpets in the elevators!), but it doesn't offer all the facilities of the higher-profile hotels in this category. The hotel attracts a lot of tour groups, mostly Japanese, which probably accounts for the constant cigarette smoke drifting through the lobby from people standing around waiting for buses. The rooms are a bland decor of older-style, white-painted furniture, but the deluxe rooms are very spacious and some of the views of surrounding trees are quite nice. Bathrooms throughout are downright huge. Cabana rooms look out to a pool and sundeck decorated with giant palms. Despite surrounding buildings, it doesn't feel claustrophobic, as do some of the more centrally situated hotels. There's a Jacuzzi, but the business center is tiny and there's no fitness center at all. Guests in single-occupancy rooms are often upgraded to doubles.

## INEXPENSIVE

☺ **RELC International Hotel.** RELC Building, 30 Orange Grove Rd., Singapore 258352. ☎ **65/737-9044.** Fax 65/733-9976. www.hotel-web.com. E-mail: relcih@ singnet.com.sg. 128 units. A/C TV TEL. S$132–S$142 (US$81–US$87) double; S$152–S$180 (US$93–US$110) suite. Rates include American breakfast for 2. DC, JCB, MC, V. 10-min. walk to Orchard MRT.

My money is on the RELC because, for the rate, they give you more added value than just prime location. Close to the Shangri-La (see above), it's only a 10-minute walk to Orchard Road, and its facilities are generally more comfortable and useful than those of hotels that charge up to S$100 more for their rooms. There are four types of rooms here—superior twin, executive twin, Hollywood queen, and alcove suite—but no matter what the size, none ever feels cluttered, close, or cramped. Rooms have balconies, TVs with two movie channels, and a fridge with free juice boxes and snacks. Bathrooms are large, with full-length tub shower and hair dryers standard. Between the higher range rooms, I'd choose the Hollywood queen over the alcove suite—its decor is better and it can sleep a family very comfortably. The "superior" rooms don't have tea- and coffee-making facilities, but all rates include daily American breakfast for two. A self-service launderette is available.

## 4  Dining

Recent figures say Singapore has over 2,000 eating establishments, so you'll never be at a loss for a place to go. In this section, I'll begin by providing a brief overview of the main types of traditional cuisine to help you decide. The restaurants I've chosen for review in this section offer a crosscut of cuisine and price ranges, and were selected for superb quality and authenticity of dishes. Beyond this list, you're sure to discover favorites of your own without having to look too far.

A good place to start is right in your hotel, which probably has quite a few restaurants. In fact, many of Singapore's best restaurants are in its hotels. Shopping malls have everything from food courts with local fast food to mid-priced and upmarket establishments. Western fast-food outlets—McDonald's, Dunkin' Donuts, or Starbucks—are always easy to find, and local coffee shops and small home-cookin' mom-and-pop joints are down every back street. Then there are **hawker centers,** where, under one roof, the meal choices go on and on.

**CHINESE CUISINE**    The large Chinese population in Singapore makes this obviously the most common type of food you'll find, but China's a big place, and its size is reflected in its many different tastes, ingredients, and preparation styles. **Cantonese-style** food is what you usually find in the West. Your stir-fries, wontons, and sweet-and-sour sauces all come from this southern region of China. Typical preparation involves quick stir-frying in light oil, or steaming for tender meats and crisp, flavorful vegetables. These are topped off with light sauces that are sometimes sweet. The Cantonese are also responsible for **dim sum** (or "tim sum," as you'll sometimes see it written around Singapore). Meaning "little hearts," dim sum is a variety of deep-fried or steamed buns, spring rolls, dumplings, meatballs, spare ribs, and a host of other tasty treats. It's a favorite in Singapore, especially for lunch. In contrast to Cantonese is **Beijing-style** food, which comes to us from the north of China. Northern cuisine is the food of the emperors, and its rich garlic and bean-paste flavoring has just a touch of chili. **Shanghai-style** cuisine is similar to Beijing-style but tends to be more oily. Because of its proximity to the sea, Shanghai recipes also include more fish. **Sichuan-style** cuisine, second only to Cantonese in the West, also relies on the rich flavors of garlic, sesame oil, and bean paste, but is much heavier on the chilies. Sugar is also sometimes added to create tangy sauces. Some dishes can really pack a punch, but there are many Sichuan dishes that are not spicy. Another regional variation, **Hunan-style food,** is also renowned for its fiery spice, and can be distinguished from Sichuan-

### How Do I Get There?

See the **Urban Singapore Accommodations & Dining map** on page 388 for locations of all restaurants in this section.

style by its darker sauces. **Teochew-style** cuisine uses fish as its main ingredient, and is also known for its light soups. Many dishes are steamed, and in fact **steamboat,** which is a popular poolside menu item in hotels, gets its origins from this style. Although the **Hokkiens** are the most prevalent dialect group in Singapore, their style of cuisine rarely makes it to restaurant tables, basically because it's simple and homely. If Hokkien food is simple and homely, **Hakka** food is the homeliest of the homely. Flavored with glutinous rice wine, many dishes feature tofu and minced seafood and meats. Hakkas are also known for not wasting any animal body part—not exactly a good mesh with haute cuisine.

New Asia cuisine, also called "Fusion Food," combines Eastern and Western ingredients and cooking styles for a whole new eating experience.

**MALAY CUISINE**    Malay cuisine combines Indonesian and Thai flavors, blending ginger, turmeric, chilies, lemongrass, and dried shrimp paste to make unique curries. Heavy on coconut milk and peanuts, Malay food can at times be on the sweet side.

The ultimate Malay dish in Singapore is **satay,** sweet barbecued meat kebabs dipped in chili peanut sauce.

**PERANAKAN CUISINE**    Peranakan cuisine came out of the Straits-born Chinese community and combines such mainland Chinese ingredients as noodles and oyster sauces with local Malay flavors of coconut milk and peanuts.

**INDIAN CUISINE    Southern Indian food** is a superhot blend of spices in a coconut milk base. Rice is the staple, along with thin breads such as prata and dosai, which are good for curling into shovels to scoop up drippy curries. Vegetarian dishes are abundant, a result of Hindu-mandated vegetarianism, and use lots of chickpeas and lentils in curry and chili gravies.

**Banana leaf restaurants,** surely the most interesting way to experience southern Indian food in Singapore, serve up meals on banana leaves cut like place mats. It's very informal. Spoons and forks are provided, but if you want to act local and use your hands, remember to use your right hand only (see tips on etiquette in chapter 2), and don't forget to wash up before and after at the tap.

**Northern Indian food** combines yogurts and creams with a milder, more delicate blend of herbs and chilies than is found in its southern neighbor. It's served most often with breads like fluffy naans and flat chepatis. Marinated meats like chicken or fish, cooked in the tandoor clay oven, is always the highlight of a northern Indian meal.

Northern Indian restaurants are more upmarket and expensive than the southern ones.

**SEAFOOD**    One cannot describe Singaporean food without mentioning the abundance of fresh seafoods of all kinds. But most important is the uniquely Singaporean **chili crab,** chopped and smothered in a thick tangy chili sauce. **Pepper crabs** and **black pepper crayfish** are also a thrill. Instead of chili sauce, these shellfish are served in a thick black-pepper-and-soy sauce.

**FRUITS**    A walk through a wet market at any time of year will show you just what wonders the tropics can produce. Varieties of banana, fresh coconut, papaya, mango, and pineapple are just a few of the fresh and juicy fruits available year-round, but Southeast Asia has an amazing selection of exotic and almost unimaginable fruits. From the light and juicy **star fruit** to the red and hairy (but sweet and tasty) **rambutan,** they are all worthy of a try, either whole or juiced. But the fruit to sample—the veritable King of Fruits—is the **durian,** a large, green, spiky fruit which, when cut open, smells worse than old tennis shoes. The "best" ones are in season every June, when Singaporeans go wild over them.

## TIPS ON DINING

Of course, in any foreign land, the exotic cuisine isn't the only thing that keeps you guessing. Lucky for you, the following tips will make dining no problem.

Most restaurants keep **opening hours** for lunch as early as 11am, but close around 2:30pm to give them a chance to set up for dinner. Where closing times are listed, that is the time when the last order is taken. Some restaurants, especially more upscale ones, may require that **reservations** be made up to a couple days in advance. Reservations are always recommended for Friday, Saturday, and Sunday lunch and dinner. Because Singapore is so hot, the **dress code** at most nicer restaurants is "dress casual" (meaning a shirt and slacks for men and a dress or skirt/slacks and top for women). Where listed, formal attire is required.

With so many restaurant choices, **prices** for meals can vary greatly. **Lunch** at a hawker center can be as cheap as S$3.50 (US$2.15), while many places have set-price buffet lunches, but these can be as high as S$45 (US$27.45). Also watch for advertised specials for tim sum or Indian buffets, which can be great bargains. In this chapter, prices for Western restaurants list the range for standard entrees, and prices for Chinese restaurants list the range for small dishes intended for two. As a guideline, following are the relative **costs for dinner** for one in each category of restaurant. At a very expensive restaurant, you can expect to pay as much as S$145 (US$88.45) per person. The more expensive cuisines are Western and Japanese, but a full-course Cantonese dinner can be up to S$125 to S$150 (US$76–US$91.50) per person. At an expensive restaurant, dinner can be between S$50 and S$80 (US$30.50–US$49) per person, while at a moderate restaurant, dinner can be as low as S$25 (US$15.25) and as high as S$50 (US$30.50). Some inexpensive dinners are under S$5 (US$3) at hawker stalls, and up to around S$15 (US$9.15) for one if you eat at local restaurants.

**Tipping** your waiter is not a custom. Restaurants always add a gratuity to the bill.

Many restaurants carry fine selections of international **wines.** However, these bottles are heavily taxed. A bottle of wine with dinner starts at around S$50 (US$30.50) and a single glass runs between S$10 and S$25 (US$6.10–US$15.25), depending on the wine and the restaurant.

## HISTORIC DISTRICT
### Very Expensive

**Inagiku.** The Westin Plaza, 2 Stamford Rd. ☎ **65/431-5305.** Reservations recommended. Set lunch starts at S$35 (US$21.35), set dinners from S$100 (US$61). AE, DC, JCB, MC, V. Daily noon–2:30pm and 6:30–10:30pm. JAPANESE.

At Inagiku, not only will you have excellent Japanese food that gets top marks for ingredients, preparation, and presentation, but you'll get service that's second to none. In delicately lighted and subtle decor, you can enjoy house favorites like sashimi, Kobe beef, tempura, and teppanyaki. In addition to sake, they also have a good selection of wines. Dress smart casual.

✪ **Raffles Grill.** Raffles Hotel, 1 Beach Rd. ☎ **65/331-1611.** Reservations required. Entrees S$42–S$52 (US$25.60–US$31.70); set dinners from S$120 (US$73.20) per person. AE, DC, JCB, MC, V. Mon–Fri noon–2pm and 7–10pm; Sat–Sun 7–10pm. Closed public holidays. FRENCH.

Dining in the Old Dame of Singapore achieves a level of sophistication unmatched by any other five-star restaurant. Three set dinners allow you to select from the à la carte menu dishes like grilled tenderloin of U.S. beef and pan-roasted filet of sea bream. The most requested dish since the restaurant's opening has been the Raffles mixed grill of lamb, veal, and beef. The 400-label wine list (going back to 1890 vintages) could be a history lesson. Dress formal.

## EXPENSIVE

**Compass Rose.** The Westin Stamford, 2 Stamford Rd., Level 70. ☎ **65/338-8585.** Reservations required. Buffet lunch S$22 (US$13.40); dinner entrees S$24–S$29 (US$14.65–US$17.70). AE, DC, JCB, MC, V. Daily noon–2:30pm and 6:30–10:30pm. CONTINENTAL.

From the top of the Westin Stamford, the tallest hotel in the world, you can see out past the marina to Malaysia and Indonesia—and the restaurant's three-tier design means every table has a view. Lunch is an extensive buffet display of fresh seafood prepared in a host of international recipes. Dinner is à la carte, with dishes inspired by lighter tastes and low-fat recipes, such as seafood with lemon thyme. Dress smart casual.

✪ **Lei Garden.** 30 Victoria St., no. 01–24 Chijmes. ☎ **65/339-3822.** Reservations required. Small dishes S$28–S$60 (US$17–US$36.60). AE, DC, JCB, MC, V. Daily 11:30am–2:15pm and 6–10pm. Second branch at Boulevard Hotel, 200 Orchard Blvd. (☎ 65/235-8122). CANTONESE.

The elegance created by the light tones of this restaurant is enhanced by the view of the Chijmes courtyard (see description under "Attractions"). A small selection of French and Chinese wines is available. Dress smart casual.

**Paladino di Firenze.** 7 Mohamed Sultan Rd. (off River Valley Rd.). ☎ **65/738-0917.** Reservations required. Entrees S$38–S$56 (US$23.20–US$34.15). AE, DC, JCB, MC, V. Daily noon–2:30pm and 7–10:30pm. NORTHERN ITALIAN.

Located in a quaint restored shophouse, this place has lighting and decor that spell true romance. The northern Italian cuisine on the constantly upgraded menu is equally inspiring. Their latest specialty is osso buco, veal shank in a rich dark sauce. Other house favorites are marked with asterisks on the menu. They also have a large selection of wines to choose from. Dress smart casual.

**Tiffin Room.** Raffles Hotel, 1 Beach Rd. ☎ **65/337-1886.** Reservations recommended. All meals served buffet style. Breakfast S$30 (US$18.30); lunch S$35 (US$21.35); high tea S$25 (US$15.25); dinner S$45 (US$27.45). AE, DC, JCB, MC, V. 7:30–10am, noon–2pm, 3:30–5pm (high tea), and 7–10pm. INDIAN/TIFFIN CURRY.

Tiffin curry came from India and is named after the three-tiered container that Indian workers would use to carry their lunch. The Brits changed the recipes a bit so they weren't as spicy, and the cuisine that evolved is what you'll find served here. A buffet lets you select from a variety of curries, carved meats, homemade chutneys, and Indian breads. The restaurant carries the trademark Raffles elegance throughout its decor. Dress smart casual.

## MODERATE

**Chungking Sichuan Restaurant.** 200 Victoria St., no. 02–53/54 Parco Bugis Junction. ☎ **65/337-9915** or 65/337-9920. Reservations recommended. Small dishes from S$18–S$48 (US$11–US$29.30). AE, DC, JCB, MC, V. Mon–Fri 11am–2:30pm and 6–10:30pm; Sat–Sun and public holidays 11:15am–4:30pm and 6:15–10:30pm. SICHUAN/CANTONESE.

Chungking put aside the typical black lacquer and red lantern look for a fresh, bright ambiance, with large picture windows providing views of the shophouse streets below. The menu features dishes that blend Cantonese and spicy Sichuan. The Sichuan smoked duck is a perennial favorite, either a half or full bird, smoked with Chinese tea leaves and herbs in a sweet black sauce. Chungking has an impressive selection of wines. Dress smart casual.

**Doc Cheng's.** Raffles Hotel Arcade no. 02–20, Level 2. ☎ **65/331-1761.** Reservations recommended. Entrees S$23.50–S$29.50 (US$14.35–US$18). AE, DC, MC, V. Mon–Fri noon–2pm and 7–10pm; Sat–Sun 7–10pm. NEW ASIA.

Doc Cheng's concept of "restorative foods" is based on the Eat, Drink and be Merry philosophy rather than medicinal beliefs. As a result, the restaurant serves up "trans-ethnic" dishes smothered in tongue-in-cheek humor. The menu is ever changing, but the specials at the time of printing included Sichuan yellowfin and ravioli with scallops. The house wine is a Riesling from Raffles' own vineyard, with others to choose from.

**Imperial Herbal.** Metropole Hotel, 3rd Floor, 41 Seah St. (near Raffles Hotel). ☎ **65/337-0491** or 65/331-5112. Reservations necessary. Small dishes S$14–S$40 (US$8.50–US$24.40). AE, DC, JCB, MC, V. Daily 11:30am–2:30pm and 6:30–10:30pm. HERBAL.

Imperial Herbal's resident herbalist is a trained physician who will "prescribe" herbal remedies for what ails you and have the kitchen add them to your meal. What's more, quite a few locals come regularly for the food's curative powers. For a traveler, it makes for a pretty unique experience, and, surprisingly, the dishes turn out superb. If all this isn't wild enough for you, order the scorpion. The wine list includes panax ginseng deer penis wine. Go for it.

## INEXPENSIVE

✪ **Our Village.** 46 Boat Quay (take elevator to 5th floor). ☎ **65/538-3058.** Reservations recommended on weekends. Entrees S$9–S$19.90 (US$5.50–US$12.15). AE, DC, MC, V. Mon–Fri 11:30am–2pm and 6:30–10:30pm; Sat–Sun 6:30–10:30pm. NORTHERN INDIAN.

With its antique white walls stuccoed in delicate and exotic patterns and glistening with tiny silver mirrors, you'll feel like you're in fairyland. Each dish comes from a traditional homecooking recipe and is handmade from specially selected imported and local ingredients. There are vegetarian selections as well as meats (no beef or pork) prepared in luscious gravies or in the tandoor oven.

# CHINATOWN
## MODERATE

✪ **Blue Ginger.** 97 Tanjong Pagar Rd. ☎ **65/222-3928.** Reservations required for lunch, recommended for dinner. Entrees S$6.50–S$22.80 (US$4–US$14). AE, MC, V. Daily 11:30am–3pm and 6:30–11pm. PERANAKAN.

By and large, Malay and Peranakan cooking are reserved for home-cooked meals, meaning restaurants are not as plentiful—and where they do exist, they are very informal. Not so at Blue Ginger. Snuggled in a shophouse, the decor combines clean and neat lines of contemporary styling. The cuisine is Peranakan from traditional recipes, like the Ayam Panggang "Blue Ginger," really tender grilled boneless chicken thigh and drumstick with a mild coconut-milk sauce.

## INEXPENSIVE

**Chen Fu Ji Fried Rice.** 7 Erskine Rd. ☎ **65/323-0260.** Reservations not accepted. S$18–S$35 (US$11–US$21.25). No credit cards. Daily noon–2:30pm and 6–9:45pm. LOCAL CUISINE/FRIED RICE.

The decor is pure casual coffee shop, but the fried rice here is amazing. These people take loving care of each fluffy grain, frying the egg evenly throughout. The other ingredients are added abundantly, and there's no hint of oil. On the top is a crown of shredded crabmeat. Other dishes are served here to accompany, and their soups are also very good. This is the original branch; two newer branches are at Riverside Point and Suntec City Mall.

## LITTLE INDIA
### INEXPENSIVE

**Komala Vilas.** 12–14 Buffalo Rd. (temporary address; will soon be moving back to 76/78 Serangoon Rd.). ☎ **65/293-6980.** Reservations not accepted. Dosai S$2 (US$1.20); lunch for 2 S$10 (US$6.10). No credit cards. Daily 11:30am–3pm and 6:30–10:30pm. SOUTHERN INDIAN.

Komala Vilas is fast food in its finest hour—to sit here during a noisy lunch hour is to see all walks of life come through the doors. They serve delicious and satisfying southern-Indian–style vegetarian dishes, which have become legendary throughout the island. Order the dosai, a huge, thin pancake used to scoop up luscious and hearty gravies and curries. Best part is it's very inexpensive: two samosas, dosai, and an assortment of gravies for two is only S$8 (US$5) with tea.

✪ **Muthu's Curry Restaurant.** 76/78 Race Course Rd. ☎ **65/293-2389** or 65/293-7029. Reservations not accepted. Entrees S$3.50–S$6.50 (US$2.15–US$4); fish head curry from S$17 (US$10.40). AE, DC, JCB, MC, V. Daily 10am–10pm. SOUTHERN INDIAN.

Muthu's is like your neighbor's kitchen where the chairs don't match, but you know there's got to be a reason why folks from construction workers to business people flock here to eat: great food. The list of specialties includes crab masala, chicken biryani, and mutton curry, and fish cutlet and fried chicken are sold by the piece. Try the local favorite: fish head curry. In a huge portion of curry soup floats the fish head, its eye staring and teeth grinning.

## ORCHARD ROAD
### EXPENSIVE

**Chang Jiang.** Goodwood Park Hotel, 22 Scotts Rd. ☎ **65/730-1752** or 65/734-7188. Reservations recommended. Regular dishes feed 4 and range from S$20–S$28 (US$12.20–US$17). AE, DC, JCB, MC, V. Daily noon–2:30pm and 7–10:30pm. SHANGHAINESE.

The elegant Chang Jiang is a unique blend of East and West. While the cuisine is Chinese, the service is French Gueridon style, in which dishes are presented then taken to a side table to be portioned into individual servings. Sumptuous dishes include the tangy and crunchy crisp eel wuxi and the sweet batter-dipped prawns with sesame seed and salad sauce. The refined continental ambiance is accented by a view of the historic Goodwood Park Hotel's courtyard.

**Esmirada.** 180 Orchard Rd. no. 01–01, Peranakan Place. ☎ **65/735-3476.** Reservations recommended for dinner. Entrees S$24–S$42 (US$14.65–US$25.60); lunch and dinner weekend specials for 2 S$25 (US$15.25). AE, DC, MC, V. Daily 11am–midnight. MEDITERRANEAN.

This place revels in the joys of good food and drink, bringing laughter and fun to the traditional act of breaking bread. The menu is easy: There's one dish each from Italy, Spain, Greece, France, Yugoslavia, Portugal, and Morocco, and they never change. Huge portions are served family style, from big bowls of salad to shish kebab skewers hanging from a rack. Stucco walls, wrought-iron details, and terra-cotta floors create a homey Mediterranean feel.

**Gordon Grill.** Goodwood Park Hotel, 22 Scotts Rd. ☎ **65/730-1744** or 65/235-8637. Reservations required for dinner. Entrees S$35–S$45 (US$21.35–US$27.45). AE, DC, MC, V. Daily noon–2:30pm and 7–10:30pm. ENGLISH/SCOTTISH.

Gordon Grill wheels out a carving cart full of the most tender prime rib and sirloin you could imagine, cut to your desired thickness. The menu of traditional English and

Scottish fare includes house specialties like the (perfect) lobster bisque and the mixed seafood grill of lobster, garoupa (grouper), scallops, and prawns in a lemon butter sauce. The dining room is small but cozy, with dark tartan carpeting and portraits of stately Scotsmen. Formal dress.

**Harbour Grill.** Hilton International Singapore, 581 Orchard Rd. ☎ **65/730-3393.** Reservations recommended. Entrees S$28–S$48 (US$17.65–US$30.25). AE, DC, JCB, MC, V. Daily noon–2:30pm and 7–10:30pm. CONTINENTAL.

Grilled seafood and U.S. prime rib are perfectly prepared and served with attentive style in this award-winning restaurant. The Continental cuisine focuses on the natural freshness of ingredients rather than on creams and fat. For the main course, the prime rib is the best and most requested entree, and the rack of lamb melts in your mouth. The finishing kitchen is in the dining room, adding a sense of theater to the fine decor. Formal dress.

✪ **Li Bai.** Sheraton Towers, 39 Scotts Rd. ☎ **65/737-6888.** Reservations required. Entrees S$24–S$60 (US$14.65–US$36.60). AE, DC, JCB, MC, V. Daily noon–2:30pm and 6:30–10:30pm. CANTONESE.

Li Bai is very sleekly decorated in contemporary black and red lacquer, with huge vases of soft pussy willows adding an intriguing opulence. Guest chefs create a constantly evolving menu, so be sure to ask for their most recent creations. A great choice is the succulent boneless mango duck. Li Bai also has excellent shark's fin soup. The wine list is international, with many vintages to choose from.

✪ **Shima.** Goodwood Park Hotel, 22 Scotts Rd. ☎ **65/734-6281.** Reservations recommended. Dinner sets S$65–S$100 (US$39.65–US$61) per person. AE, DC, JCB, MC, V. Daily noon–2:30pm and 6:30–10:30pm. JAPANESE.

This large restaurant is made intimate with area lighting for each table, from the teppanyaki grill to the yakiniku barbecue. The menu is complete, and all dishes are excellent in both quality and preparation, from Japanese steamboat buffet to the best Kobe beef in Singapore. Special sets are featured, and the lunch menu is discounted quite a bit. Specify what you intend to eat when you make your reservations.

## MODERATE

**Baan Thai.** 391 Orchard Rd. no. 04–23, Ngee Ann City. ☎ **65/735-5562.** Reservations recommended. Entrees S$18–S$34 (US$11–US$20.75). AE, DC, JCB, MC, V. Daily 11:30am–2:30pm and 6:30–10:30pm. THAI.

Spotless and well lit, Baan Thai is fitted out with an exotic decor, from the giant Thai Buddha that greets you in the reception to dining nooks sectioned off with carved wooden screens. The phad Thai (fried rice noodles with prawn and chicken in a tamarind, chili, and peanut sauce) and the green curry gravy (combining coconut milk with lemongrass, lemon leaf, garlic, and green chili) are Thai favorites that this place prepares with delicious authenticity.

**The Drake.** Hotel Negara, 10 Claymore Rd. ☎ **65/737-0811.** Entrees S$12–S$33 (US$7.30–US$20.15). AE, DC, MC, V. Daily noon–10:30pm. BEIJING/INTERNATIONAL.

Imagine, if you will, a theme restaurant for duck, complete with hunting lodge stylings and waiters in red flannel. The menu completes the image, serving up duck in a host of international recipes, from deep-fried duck with Chinese wine in black sauce to French duck a l'orange surrounded with hearty mashed potatoes. The Traditional is Beijing duck with crispy skin that melts in your mouth and meat that's stir-fried with bean sprouts.

**Pine Court.** Mandarin Hotel, 333 Orchard Rd. (take the express elevator to the 35th floor). ☎ **65/831-6262** or 65/831-6263. Reservations recommended. Small dishes S$16–S$26 (US$9.75–US$15.85). AE, DC, MC, V. Daily noon–2:30pm and 7–10:30pm. CANTONESE/BEIJING/TEOCHEW.

Pine Court—stunningly decorated with lacy carved rosewood screens and clusters of delicate wood and paper lanterns—prepares Chinese dishes in a variety of regional styles, but the Peking duck is still everyone's favorite here. Another great dish is the specialty crispy roast chicken (whole or half), with the skin left on and seasoned with soya sauce.

✪ **Tandoor.** Holiday Inn Parkview, 11 Cavenagh Rd. ☎ **65/733-8333.** Reservations recommended. Entrees S$18.50–S$48 (US$11.30–US$29.30). AE, DC, JCB, MC, V. Daily noon–2:30pm and 7–10:30pm. NORTHERN INDIAN.

Which is better entertainment, the live music or the show kitchen? Tandoor is relaxing and friendly, and at the same time very elegant. Entrees prepared in their tandoor oven come out flavorful—the tandoori lobster is especially rich, but the chef's specialty is crab lababdar: crabmeat, onions, and tomato sautéed in a coconut gravy. Chefs keep a close eye on the spices to ensure the spice enhances the flavor rather than drowns it out.

### INEXPENSIVE

✪ **Chatterbox.** Mandarin Hotel, 333 Orchard Rd. ☎ **65/831-6288.** Reservations recommended for lunch and dinner. Entrees S$11–S$29 (US$6.70–US$17.70). AE, DC, JCB, MC, V. Daily 24 hours. LOCAL CUISINE.

If you'd like to try the local favorites but don't want to deal with street food, then Chatterbox is the place for you. Their Hainanese chicken rice is highly acclaimed, and other dishes—like nasi lemak, laksa, and carrot cake—are as close to the street as you can get. For a quick and tasty snack, order tahu goreng, deep-fried tofu in peanut chili sauce. This informal and lively coffee shop dishes out room service for the Mandarin Hotel and is open 24 hours a day.

**Sanur.** Ngee Ann City no. 04–16. ☎ **65/734-3434.** Reservations accepted only on weekdays. Be prepared to wait on weekends. Entrees S$6.50–S$32.95 (US$4–US$20). AE, DC, MC, V. Mon–Fri 11:30am–2:45pm and 5:45–10pm; Sat–Sun 11:30am–3:45pm and 5:30–10pm. MALAY/INDONESIAN.

Sanur is a family restaurant for folks who come to feast upon authentic and reasonably priced Indo-Malay food. The place can be bustling, and service is a bit rushed, but the food comes highly recommended by locals. Tahu Telor is the house specialty: fried bean curd cake with a chili sweet sauce nobody can imitate. The ayam goreng kampong is white meat chicken marinated in Sanur's own secret blend of spices, and while it's tasty, it's not hot.

## AROUND THE ISLAND
### EXPENSIVE

**Alkaff Mansion.** 10 Telok Blangah Green (off Henderson Rd.), Telok Blangah Hill Park. ☎ **65/278-6979.** Reservations recommended. Set rijsttafel menu S$65 (US$39.65) per person. AE, DC, JCB, MC, V. Daily noon–2:30pm, 2:45–5pm (tea), and 7pm–midnight. INDONESIAN.

Alkaff Mansion is one of the most richly ambient dinner settings in the city. Built by the wealthy Arab Alkaff family, the patios and great halls drip with old world charm. Dinner here is rijsttafel—home-style Indonesian fare influenced by Dutch tastes. A typical set dinner might include gado gado (an Indonesian salad with a sweet and mild peanut dressing), siakap masak asam turnis (fish in a tangy sauce); or crayfish in chili sauce. This is the only restaurant in Singapore that serves this cuisine.

## MODERATE

✪ **Long Beach Seafood Restaurant.** 1018 East Coast Pkwy. ☎ **65/323-2222.** Reservations recommended. Seafood is sold by weight according to seasonal prices. Most dishes S$9–S$16 (US$5.50–US$9.75). AE, DC, MC, V. Daily 5:50pm–1:30am. SEAFOOD.

They really pack 'em in at this place, which resembles a big indoor pavilion, complete with festive lights and the sounds of mighty feasting. This is one of the best places for fresh seafood of all kinds: fishes like garoupa (grouper), sea bass, marble goby, and kingfish, as well as prawns and crayfish. The chili crab here is good, but the house specialty is really the pepper crab, chopped and deliciously smothered in a thick concoction of black pepper and soya.

**Prima Tower.** 201 Keppel Rd. ☎ **65/272-8822.** Reservations required. 4 entrees for S$180 (US$110). AE, DC, MC, V. Daily 11am–2:30pm and 6:30–10:30pm. Closed Chinese New Year. BEIJING.

One of the main attractions is that the restaurant revolves, giving you an ever-changing view of the city from your table. The other main attraction is the food, which is Beijing-style Chinese. The best dish is the barbecued Peking duck, a house specialty since this restaurant opened 20 years ago. All of the noodles for the noodle dishes are prepared in-house using traditional recipes and techniques, which makes for some fresh dishes.

**Xin Cuisine.** Concorde Hotel, 317 Outram Rd. ☎ **65/732-3337.** Reservations recommended. Small dishes S$10–S$30 (US$6.10–US$18.30). AE, DC, JCB, MC, V. Daily noon–2:30pm and 6:30–10:30pm. HERBAL/CANTONESE.

A recent trend is to bring back the Chinese tradition of preparing foods that balance the body's yin and yang and restore energy. Xin (new) Cuisine transforms these concepts into light and flavorful creations, listed in a menu that's literally a book. The concentrated seafood soup with chicken and spinach is a light and delicious broth with chunks of meat and shredded spinach. The stewed Mongolian rack of lamb comes with buns to soak up the delicious sauce.

✪ **UDMC Seafood Centre.** Blk. 1202 East Coast Pkwy. Seafood dishes are charged by weight, with dishes from around S$12 (US$7.30). AE, DC, MC, V (some restaurants accept JCB). Daily 5pm–midnight. SEAFOOD.

Eight seafood restaurants are lined side by side in 2 blocks, their fronts open to the view of the sea outside. Dine on the famous local chili crab and pepper crab here, along with all sorts of squid, fish, and scallop dishes. Noodle dishes are also available, as are vegetable dishes and other meats. Have a nice stroll along the walkway and gaze out to the water while you decide which one to go for.

## HAWKER CENTERS

Hawker centers—large groupings of informal open-air food stalls—are Singapore's answer to fast food, and are the best way to sample every kind of Singaporean cuisine. The adventure begins when you walk in and stroll past each stall to see what's cooking. Order from whichever stall you feel, but take note, many centers are divided between Muslim halal and non-halal stalls. Once you find a seat, your food and drink will come to you. If it's crowded and you find a couple of free seats at an already occupied table, politely ask if they are taken and have a seat if they're free. You are expected to pay for your food upon delivery.

The most notorious hawker center in Singapore is **Newton,** which is located at Newton Circus, the intersection of Scotts Road, Newton Road, and Bukit Timah/Dunearn Road. It's commercialized and well trampled by tourists, but a good place to start.

# Cafe Society

In Singapore, traditions such as British high tea and the Chinese tea ceremony live side by side with a growing coffee culture. These popular hangouts are all over the city. Here are a few places to try.

- **For British High Tea:** Two fabulous places to take high tea in style are at **Raffles Bar & Billiard Room** at Raffles Hotel (1 Beach Rd.; ☎ **65/331-1746**) and **The Compass Rose Café** at the Westin Stamford (2 Stamford Rd.; ☎ **65/431-5707**).

- **For Chinese Tea:** There are a few places in Chinatown where tea is still as important today as it has always been in Chinese culture. The **Tea Village** (27–31 Erskine Rd.; ☎ **65/221-7825**) and **The Tea Chapter** (11A Neil Rd.; ☎ **65/226-1175**) offer tranquil respites from the day and cultural insight into Chinese tea appreciation.

- **Cafes:** True to what you'll find in the West, coffee at one of the many new coffee houses can set you back S$4 (US$2.45). Still, if you need your joe, good places to try are **The Coffee Club,** with branches in Takashimaya Shopping Centre (☎ **65/735-7368**) and Boat Quay (☎ **65/538-0061**); **Beans & Brew** at 230 Victoria St. no. B1–13 (☎ **65/337-8525**); or **The Coffee Connection,** with branches at Parco Bugis Junction (☎ **65/339-7758**) and Clarke Quay (☎ **65/336-1121**).

In Chinatown, a good starting-off point for the uninitiated is **Lau Pa Set Festival Village** (Telok Ayer Market), located at the corner of Raffles Way and Boon Tat Street. For a more authentic experience in Chinatown, try the unnamed center at the end of Amoy Street, or the one at the corner of Maxwell Road and South Bridge Road.

In the Historic District there's one behind Empress Place by the river that serves mostly Hainanese chicken rice, and another on Hill Street next to the Central Fire Station. Also look on Stamford Road between the National Museum and Armenian Street intersection.

In Little India, **Zhujiao Centre** is a nice-size hawker center. On Orchard Road, try **Cuppage Terrace,** just beyond the Centrepoint Shopping Centre. One place that's near and dear to Singaporeans, who have mostly been chased away by overcommercialization, is the **Satay Club** on Clarke Quay, off River Valley Road, which has been and still is the traditional place to have this local favorite.

# 5 Attractions

## THE HISTORIC DISTRICT

**Fort Canning Park.** Major entrances are from the Hill Street Food Centre, Percival Rd. (Drama Centre), Fort Canning Aquarium, National Library Carpark, and Canning Walk (behind Park Mall). Free admission. Dhoby Gaut or City Hall MRT.

When Stamford Raffles first navigated the Singapore River, he was already envisioning a port settlement, and had designs to build his own home atop the hill that is today this park. His home, a simple wooden structure (that stood where the lookout point is today), would serve as governor's residence for his successors until 1860, when **Fort Canning** was built to quiet the fearful Europeans' demands for a defense against invasion. It was demolished in 1907 and today the Fort Gate and Fort Wall are the only reminders that it was ever here. The Fort Gate is a deep stone structure, and behind its huge wooden door is a narrow staircase that leads to the roof of the structure.

There is a *keramat,* or **sacred grave,** in the park, which is believed—with much debate—to be the final resting place of Iskander Shah (also known as Para-meswara), an early ruler of Singapura. Many still come to pray beside the grave. Fort Canning was also the site of a **European cemetery.** To make improvements in the park, the graves were exhumed and the stones placed within the walls surrounding the outdoor performance field that slopes from the Music and Drama Society building.

Fort Canning Park is also home to **The Battle Box** (51 Canning Rise, ☎ 333-0519 (adults S$8/US$4.90; children S$5/US$3; Tuesday to Sunday 10am to 6pm), a World War II bunker museum telling the tale of Singapore's surrender to the Japanese.

**Singapore Philatelic Museum.** 23B Coleman St. ☎ **65/337-3888.** Admission S$2 (US$1.20). Tues–Sun 9am–4:30pm. Closed public holidays. Take the MRT to City Hall and walk toward Coleman St.

This building, constructed in 1895 to house the Methodist Book Room, recently underwent a S$7 million restoration and reopened as the Philatelic Museum in 1995. Exhibits include a fine collection of old stamps issued to commemorate historically important events, first day covers, antique printing plates, postal service memorabilia, and private collections.

✪ **Armenian Church.** 60 Hill St., across from the Grand Plaza Hotel.

No longer serving a much-diminished Armenian community, but lovingly maintained nevertheless, this chapel was the first permanent Christian church in Singapore. Designed by prolific architect George Coleman, it received most of its funding from the once-thriving Armenian community.

✪ **Asian Civilisations Museum.** 39 Armenian St. ☎ **65/332-3015.** Adults S$3 (US$1.85), children 6–16 and seniors S$1.50 (US$1). Tues–Sun 9am–5:30pm; except Wed 9am to 9pm. Free guided tours in English Tues–Fri 11am and 2pm, Sat–Sun 11am, 2pm, and 3pm.

Opened in 1997 and housed in the renovated Tao Nan School, this is the first branch of the Asian Civilisations Museum (the second is scheduled to open in 2000 in the Empress Place Building). Tao Nan (or ACM I) primarily focuses on the region's rich Chinese culture, displaying fine collections of jade, calligraphy, ceramics, furniture, and artworks, all offering visitors the chance to trace the archipelago's rich Chinese heritage. Changing exhibits in the temporary galleries represent the other Asian civilizations.

✪ **Singapore History Museum.** 93 Stamford Rd., across the street from Bras Basah Park. ☎ **65/375-2510.** National Heritage Board Web site www.museum.org.sg/ nhb.html. Adults S$3 (US$1.85), children and seniors S$1.50 (US$1). Tues–Sun 9am–5:30pm; except Wed 9am to 9pm. Free guided tours in English Tues–Fri 11am and 2pm, Sat–Sun 11am, 2pm, and 3pm.

Originally called Raffles Museum, the museum opened in 1887 as the first of its kind in Southeast Asia, housing a superb collection of natural history specimens and ethnographic displays. Renamed the National Museum in 1969, its collections went through a transformation, focusing on Singaporean history rather than that of the archipelago. Several years later, it became known as the Singapore History Museum. Twenty dioramas portray events from the settlement's early days to modern times. Included are tributes to Raffles and William Farquhar.

# Urban Singapore Attractions

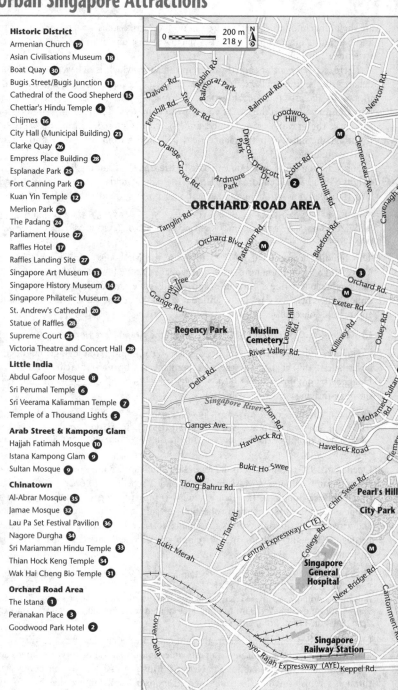

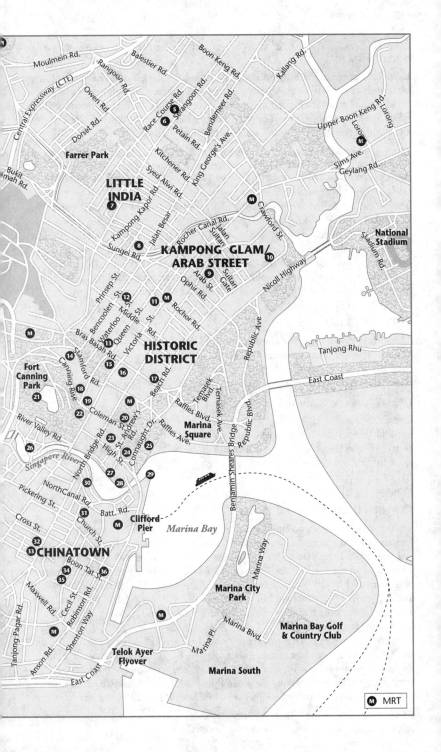

**Kuan Yin Temple.** Waterloo St., about 1½ blocks from Bras Basah Rd. Open to the public during the day.

Kuan Yin Temple is very busy on auspicious months of the Chinese calendar, as many locals believe that wishes made here come true. A temple devoted to the Taoist deity Kuan Yin, its most unique features are the fortune-telling sticks. Join the queue and follow the lead of those in front of you. Make a wish, and at the finish you will receive an interpretation of your fortune and the answer to your wish.

✪ **Singapore Art Museum.** 71 Bras Basah Rd. ☎ **65/332-3222.** www.museum.org. sg/nhb.html. Adults S$3 (US$1.85), children and seniors S$1.50 (US$1). Tues–Sun 9am–5:30pm; except Wed 9am to 9pm. Free guided tours in English Tues–Fri 11am and 2pm, Sat–Sun 11am, 2pm, and 3pm.

The Singapore Art Museum (SAM) was officially opened in 1996 and houses an impressive collection of over 3,000 pieces of art and sculpture, most of it by Singaporean and Malaysian artists, which are regularly rotated to make up special exhibits. The museum also displays a large collection of regional pieces, and showcases international exhibits regularly. Once a Catholic boys' school established in 1852, SAM has retained some visible reminders of its former occupants: Above the front door of the main building you can still see inscribed "St. Joseph's Institution."

**Cathedral of the Good Shepherd.** 4 Queen St., at the corner of Queen St. and Bras Basah Rd. Open to the public during the day.

This cathedral was Singapore's first permanent Catholic church. Built in the 1840s, it brought together many elements of a fractured parish—Portuguese, French, and Spanish—to worship under one roof. Designed in a Latin cross pattern, much of its architecture is reminiscent of London's St. Martin-In-The-Fields and St. Paul's.

**Chijmes (Convent of the Holy Infant Jesus).** 30 Victoria St.

The Convent of the Holy Infant Jesus, founded in 1854, was relocated to the suburbs in 1983, but its classrooms, living quarters, chapel, and large orphanage buildings remained. The Singapore government restored the buildings and converted them to space for fine restaurants, pubs, and shops, recognizing both the market value of the real estate and the architectural integrity of this colonial gem. The chapel is now a performance center.

✪ **Raffles Hotel.** 1 Beach Rd. ☎ **65/337-1886.**

Built in 1887 to accommodate the increasing upper-class trade, it was owned by the famous Armenian Sarkies, of Eastern and Oriental Hotel fame in Penang. In the twenties, the hotel was the place to see and be seen, and the crowded ballroom was jumping every night of the week. Raffles' guest book included famous authors like Somerset Maugham and Noel Coward. Later the hotel limped through the Great Depression and the Japanese Occupation, but real threats to its security didn't come until the 1970s, when new luxury hotels cropped up on Orchard Road, pushing the "grand old lady" to the back seat.

Its current owners recently restored the hotel using 1915 as a benchmark. Today, the hotel's restaurants and nightlife draw thousands of visitors daily to its open lobby, its theater playhouse, the Raffles Hotel Museum, and 65 exclusive boutiques. Its 15 restaurants and bars—especially the Tiffin Room and Raffles Grill (see restaurant section) are a wonder, as are its famous Bar and Billiards Room and Long Bar.

✪ **St. Andrew's Cathedral.** Coleman St., between North Bridge Rd. and St. Andrew's Rd., across from the Padang. Open during daylight hours.

Designed by prolific colonial architect George Coleman and erected on a site selected by Sir Stamford Raffles himself, St. Andrew's was the colonials' Anglican Church. Completed toward the end of the 1830s, its tower and spire were added several years later to accord the edifice more stature. By 1852, because of massive damage sustained from lightning strikes, the cathedral was deemed unsafe and was torn down. The cathedral that now stands on this site was completed in 1860. Of English Gothic Revival design, it's one of the few standing churches of this style in the region. The spire resembles the steeple of Salisbury Cathedral.

**The Padang & Surrounding Administrative Buildings.** Area between and around St. Andrews Rd. and Connaught Dr., just below Fort Canning Park.

In Raffles' Town Plan of 1822, he set aside this area of the settlement to house government offices and public areas. Its center was The Padang, a green around which government buildings were erected over the decades to follow. While most of these buildings are not open for public view, the STB can help organize tours of some parts of the buildings if you're really curious.

While today **The Padang** is mainly used for public and sporting events, in the 1940s it felt more forlorn footsteps when the invading Japanese detained the entire European community here before marching them 14 miles (22km) to Changi in the eastern part of the island.

**City Hall** (Municipal Building, St. Andrew's Rd., across from the Padang) has been a part of many historical events, including the surrender of the Japanese to Admiral Lord Louis Mountbatten in 1945. It was here that Singapore's first prime minister, Lee Kuan Yew, declared the country an independent nation. The **Supreme Court** (St. Andrew's Rd., across from the Padang) was completed in 1939. The sculptures across the front, executed by the Italian sculptor Cavaliere Rodolpho Nolli, represent Justice, Supplication, Thankfulness, Prosperity, and Abundance.

**Parliament House** (1 High St., at the south end of the Padang, next to the Supreme Court), built in 1826, is probably Singapore's oldest surviving structure. It originally housed government offices, and in 1953, following a major renovation, was renamed Parliament House. The bronze elephant just in front was a gift in 1872 from His Majesty Somdeth Phra Paraminda Maha Chulalongkorn (Rama V), Supreme King of Siam.

The **Victoria Theatre and Concert Hall** (9 Empress Place, at the southern end of the Padang (☎ 65/339-6120), was built in stages, its earliest part dating to 1862. It was the Town Hall until 1909, when it was converted to a theater. Since 1979 it has housed the Singapore Symphony Orchestra and various performance companies. Just outside the hall stands a sculpture of Sir Stamford Raffles that was erected on the Padang in 1887 and moved to its present position after getting in the way of one too many cricket matches.

Standing as a symbol of British colonial authority as travelers entered the Singapore River, the **Empress Place Building** (1 Empress Place, at the southern end of the Padang next to the Parliament Building) housed almost the entire government bureaucracy around the year 1905. It is currently being renovated as the second phase of the Asian Civilisations Museum.

**Raffles Landing Site.** North Boat Quay.

Standing on what is believed to be the site where Sir Stamford Raffles landed on January 29, 1819, the statue here was unveiled in 1972. It was made from plaster casts of the original 1887 figure located in front of the Victoria Theatre and Concert Hall.

## ALONG THE RIVER

The Singapore River had always been the heart of life in Singapore even before Raffles landed. Following a major cleanup project in the eighties, the river gained a new lease on life as a center of entertainment, food, and pubs day and night.

✪ **Boat Quay.** Located on the south bank of the Singapore River between Cavenagh Bridge and Elgin Bridge.

Known as "the belly of the carp" by the local Chinese because of its shape, this area was once notorious for its opium dens and coolie shops. Nowadays, thriving restaurants boast every cuisine imaginable and the rocking nightlife offers up a variety of sounds—jazz, rock, blues, Indian, and Caribe.

✪ **Clarke Quay.** River Valley Rd., west of Coleman Bridge.

In the 1880s, a pineapple cannery, iron foundry, and numerous warehouses made this area bustle. Today, with 60 restored warehouses and restaurants and a shopping section known as Clarke Quay Factory Stores, the Quay still hops. The **Clarke Quay Adventure Ride** (☎ **65/337-1680**) on the Singapore River provides a historical panorama of Singapore and its people. (Tickets are S$5/US$3 adults, S$3/US$1.85 children and seniors; open daily from 11am to 10:30pm.) On Thursdays and Fridays from 6:30 to 8:30pm, enthusiasts can catch a Chinese opera performance and makeup demonstration that is a treat to watch. Get up early on Sunday, and take in the flea market, which opens at 9am and lasts all day.

**Merlion Park.** South bank, at the mouth of the Singapore River, near the Anderson Bridge. Free admission. Daily 7am–10pm.

The Merlion is Singapore's half-lion, half-fish national symbol—the lion represents Singapore's roots as the "Lion City," while the fish represents Singapore's close ties to the sea. He spouts continuously every day from 10am to noon.

**Esplanade Park.** Connaught Dr., on the marina, running from the mouth of the Singapore River along the Padang to Raffles Ave. Open daily until midnight.

Esplanade Park and Queen Elizabeth Walk, two of the most famous parks in Singapore, were established in 1943 on land reclaimed from the sea. Several memorials are located here. The first is a fountain built in 1857 to honor **Tan Kim Seng,** who gave a great sum of money toward the building of a waterworks. Another monument, **the Cenotaph,** commemorates the 124 Singaporeans who died in World War I. On the reverse side, the names of those who died in World War II have been inscribed. The third prominent memorial is dedicated to **Major General Lim Bo Seng,** a Singaporean World War II hero.

**Chettiar's Hindu Temple.** 15 Tank Rd., close to the intersection of Clemenceau Ave. and River Valley Rd.

One of the richest and grandest of its kind in Southeast Asia, Chettiar's Hindu Temple is most famous for a **thoonganai maadam,** a statue of an elephant's backside in a seated position. The original temple was completed in 1860, restored in 1962, and practically rebuilt in 1984. Outside in the courtyard are statues of the wedding of Lord Muruga; his brother, Ganesh; another brother, Vishnu; and their father, Shiva; along with Brahma, the creator of all.

Used daily for worship, the temple is also the culmination point of Thaipusam, a celebration of thanks, and the Festival of Navarathiri.

# CHINATOWN/TANJONG PAGAR

**Wak Hai Cheng Bio Temple.** 30-B Phillip St., at the corner of Phillip St. and Church St.

Like most of Singapore's Chinese temples, Wak Hai Cheng Bio had its start as a simple wood-and-thatch shrine where sailors, when they got off their ships, would go to express their gratitude for sailing safely to their destination. Before the major land reclamation projects shifted the shoreline outward, the temple was close to the water's edge, and so it was named "Temple of the Calm Sea Built by the Guangzhou People." It's a Teochew temple, located in a part of Chinatown that was populated mostly by the Teochews.

**Nagore Durgha Shrine.** 140 Telok Ayer St., at the corner of Telok Ayer St. and Boon Tat St. ☎ **65/324-0021.**

Although this is a Muslim place of worship, it is not a mosque, but a shrine, built to commemorate a visit to the island by a Muslim holy man of the Chulia people (a very early immigrant group from India), who was traveling around Southeast Asia spreading the word of Indian Islam. There is controversy surrounding the dates that the shrine was built. The government, upon naming the Nagore Durgha a national monument, claimed it was built sometime in the 1820s. However, Nagoreallauddeen, who is the 15th descendant of the holy man for whom the shrine is named, claims it was built in 1815, 4 years before the arrival of Sir Stamford Raffles.

✪ **Thian Hock Keng Temple.** 158 Telok Ayer St., ½ block beyond Nagore Durgha Shrine.

Thian Hock Keng, the "Temple of Heavenly Bliss," is the oldest Chinese temple in Singapore. Before land reclamation, when the shoreline came right up to Telok Ayer Road, the first Chinese sailors landed here and immediately built a shrine, a small wood-and-thatch structure, to pray to the goddess Ma Po Cho, the Mother of Heavenly Sages, for allowing their voyage to be safely completed. The temple that stands today was built in 1841 over the shrine with funds from the Hokkien community. All of the building materials were imported from China, except for the gates, which came from Glasgow, Scotland, and the tiles on the facade, which are from Holland.

**Al-Abrar Mosque.** 192 Telok Ayer St., near the corner of Telok Ayer St. and Amoy St., near Thian Hock Keng Temple.

This mosque was originally erected as a thatched building in 1827. In the late 1980s, the mosque underwent major renovations that enlarged the mihrab and stripped away some of the ornamental qualities of the columns in the building. Little touches like the timber window panels and fanlight windows have been carried over into the new renovations.

**Lau Pa Set Festival Pavilion.** 18 Raffles Quay, located in the entire block flanked by Robinson Rd., Cross St., Shenton Way, and Boon Tat St.

Once the happy little hawker center known as Telok Ayer Market, it began life as a wet market. Now it's part hawker center, part Western fast-food outlets, and almost all tourist. The original was built in 1823, but after land reclamation in Telok Ayer Basin in 1879, the market was moved to its present home. The pavilion is constructed of 3,000 prefab cast-iron elements brought in from Europe.

✪ **Sri Mariamman Hindu Temple.** 244 South Bridge Rd., at the corner of South Bridge Rd. and Pagoda St.

As the oldest Hindu temple in Singapore, Sri Mariamman has been the central point of Hindu tradition and culture. In its early years, the temple housed new immigrants while they established themselves and also served as social center for the community. Today, the main celebration here is the Thimithi Festival in October/November.

The shrine is dedicated to the goddess Sri Mariamman, who is known for curing disease, but as is the case at all other Hindu temples, the entire pantheon of Hindu gods is present to be worshipped as well.

✪ **Jamae Mosque.** 18 South Bridge Rd., at the corner of South Bridge Rd. and Mosque St.

Jamae Mosque was built by the Chulias, Tamil Muslims who were some of the earlier immigrants to Singapore, and who had a very influential hold over Indian Muslim life centered in the Chinatown area. It was the Chulias who built not only this mosque, but Masjid Al-Abrar and the Nagore Durgha Shrine as well. Jamae Mosque dates back to 1827, but wasn't completed until the early 1830s. The mosque stands today almost exactly as it did then.

## LITTLE INDIA

**Abdul Gafoor Mosque.** 41 Dunlop St., between Perak Rd. and Jalan Besar.

Abdul Gafoor Mosque is actually a mosque complex consisting of the original mosque, a row of shophouses facing Dunlop Street, a prayer hall, and another row of houses ornamented with crescent moons and stars, facing the mosque. The original mosque, built in 1846, was called Masjid Al-Abrar, and is commemorated on a granite plaque above what could have been either the entrance gate or the mosque itself. It still stands, and even though it is badly dilapidated, it retains some of its original beauty.

✪ **Sri Veerama Kaliamman Temple.** On Serangoon Rd. at Veerasamy Rd. Open 8am–noon and 5:30–8:30pm.

This Hindu temple is primarily for the worship of Shiva's wife Kali, who destroys ignorance, maintains world order, and blesses those who strive for knowledge of God. Inside the temple in the main hall are three altars, the center one for Kali (depicted with 16 arms and wearing a necklace of human skulls) and two altars on either side for her two sons, Ganesh, the elephant god, and Murugan, the four-headed child god.

**Sri Perumal Temple.** 397 Serangoon Rd., ½ block past Perumal Rd. Best times to visit are between 7am and 11am or later, between 5pm and 7:30pm.

Sri Perumal Temple is devoted to the worship of Vishnu. As part of the Hindu trinity, Vishnu is the sustainer balancing out Brahma the creator and Shiva the destroyer. When the world is out of whack, he rushes to its aid, reincarnating himself to show humankind that there are always new directions for development.

The temple was built in 1855, and was most recently renovated in 1992. Thaipusam is the main festival celebrated here.

✪ **Temple of a Thousand Lights.** On Race Course Rd., 1 block past Perumal Rd. Open daily 7:30am–4:45pm.

Thai elements influence this temple, from the stupa roofline to the huge Buddha inside. On the right side of the altar are statues of baby boddhisattvas for whom worshippers leave candy and toys. Around the base of the altar are murals depicting scenes from the life of the Buddha as he searches for enlightenment. Behind the altar is a small doorway to a chamber. Inside is the Buddha, depicted at the end of his life, reclining beneath the Yellow Seraka tree. To the left of the hall is a wheel of fortune. For 50¢ you get one spin.

# ARAB STREET/KAMPONG GLAM

✪ **Sultan Mosque.** 3 Muscat St. Open daily 9am–1pm and 2–4pm. No visiting is allowed during mass congregation Fri 11:30am–2:30pm.

Though there are over 80 mosques on the island of Singapore, Sultan Mosque is the center of the Muslim community. This is the second Sultan Mosque to be built on this site. The first was built in 1826, partially funded by the East India Company as part of their agreement to leave Kampong Glam to Sultan Hussein and his family in return for sovereign rights to Singapore. The present mosque was built in 1928 and was funded by donations from the Muslim community. Interestingly, the mosque, with its Saracenic flavor of onion domes topped with crescent moons and stars, was designed by an Irish guy named Denis Santry.

Sultan Mosque, like other mosques, does not permit shorts, miniskirts, low necklines, or other revealing clothing to be worn inside. However, they do provide cloaks free of charge.

✪ **Istana Kampong Glam.** Located at the end of Sultan Gate, 1 block past the intersection of Sultan Gate, Bagdad St., and Pahang St. This is a private residence, so no entry is permitted.

The Istana Kampong Glam is the home of Singapore's former royal family. There's a fascinating controversy behind its current state of sad disrepair. In 1824, Sultan Hussein of Johor signed over his sovereign rights to Singapore in return for the Kampong Glam district. His son, Sultan Ali, built this "palace." Over time, as family fortunes dwindled, a decades-long dispute arose between Ali's descendants over estate rights. In the late 1890s, they went to court, where it was decided that no one had rights to the property, and the land reverted to the state. The family was allowed to remain in the house but lost the authority to improve the buildings of the compound. Any day now, Sultan Hussein's family will be given the royal boot and their palace will house Kampong Glam cultural exhibits. Now *there's* cultural appreciation for ya.

✪ **Hajjah Fatimah Mosque.** 4001 Beach Rd., past Jalan Sultan.

Hajjah Fatimah was a wealthy businesswoman from Malacca and something of a local socialite. She had originally built a home on this site, but after it had been robbed a couple times and later set fire to, she decided to build a mosque here and moved to another home. The minaret tower in the front was designed by an unknown European architect and could have been a copy of the original spire of St. Andrew's Cathedral. The tower leans a little, a fact that's much more noticeable from the inside. On the outside of the tower is a bleeding heart—an unexpected place to find such a downright Christian symbol.

# ORCHARD ROAD AREA

**The Istana and Sri Temasek.** Orchard Rd., between Claymore Rd. and Scotts Rd.

The Government House was built in 1859, after the construction of Fort Canning forced the governor's residence out of Fort Canning Park. With Singapore's independence, the building was renamed the Istana, becoming the official residence of the president of the Republic of Singapore. Used mainly for state and ceremonial occasions, the grounds are not generally open for visits.

✪ **Peranakan Place.** Located at the intersection of Emerald Hill and Orchard Rd.

The houses along Emerald Hill have all been renovated and the street has been closed to vehicular traffic. Now it's an alfresco cafe, landscaped with a veritable jungle of potted foliage and peopled by colorful tourists. But don't just blow it off as a tourist trap. Walk farther up the street to see the old private residences, which have been redone magnificently.

## THE WEST COAST

The attractions grouped in this section are on the west side of Singapore, beginning from the Singapore Botanic Gardens at the edge of the urban area all the way out to the Singapore Discovery Centre past Jurong.

A handy way to get around to some of the major attractions on the West Coast is the **West Coast Attractions Shuttle Service.** Buses operate from 8:30am to 6:30pm daily at a frequency of about 20 minutes. There are two bus loops, a red and a blue, which you can catch at either the Lakeside or Jurong East MRT stations for trips to the Chinese and Japanese Gardens, Ming Village, Singapore Science Centre, Omni Theatre, Tang Dynasty City, Jurong Crocodile Paradise, Jurong BirdPark, and Singapore Discovery Centre. Per trip it's between S70¢ and S$1.40 depending on where you're going, or S$2.50 (US$1.50) for a daily pass with unlimited rides.

✪ **Jurong BirdPark.** 2 Jurong Hill. ☎ **65/265-0022.** Adults S$10.30 (US$6.30), children under 12 S$4.12 (US$2.50); seniors S$7.21 (US$4.40). Mon–Fri 9am–6pm; Sat–Sun and public holidays 8am–6pm. MRT to Boon Lay Station, transfer to SBS nos. 194 or 251.

Jurong BirdPark has a collection of 8,000 birds from over 600 species, featuring Southeast Asian species and other colorful tropical beauties, some of them endangered. The over 49½ acres can be easily walked or, for a couple dollars extra, you can ride the panorail. The daily guided tours and regularly scheduled feeding times are enlightening. Two shows feature birds of prey acting out their natural instincts, and the **All-Star Birdshow** has birds that perform all sorts of silliness, including staged birdy misbehaviors. In the morning come for breakfast among hanging cages of chirping birds at the **Songbird Terrace.**

**Jurong Reptile Park.** 241 Jalan Ahmad Ibrahim. ☎ **65/261-8866.** Adults S$7 (US$4.30), children under 12 S$3.50 (US$2.15). Daily 9am–6pm. MRT to Boon Lay Station, transfer to SBS nos. 194 or 251.

Just next door to Jurong BirdPark is the newly refurbished Jurong Reptile Park, with over 2,500 crocs to see in action either in landscaped pens, in an enclosure for breeding, or in the underwater viewing areas. Featured attractions include regular feedings and photo opportunities with snakes.

**Haw Par Villa.** 262 Pasir Panjang Rd. ☎ **65/774-0300.** Adults S$5 (US$3), children S$2.50 (US$1.50). Daily 9am–6pm. MRT to Buona Vista and transfer to bus no. 200.

In 1935, brothers Haw Boon Haw and Haw Boon Par, the creators of Tiger Balm, took their fortune and opened Tiger Balm Gardens as a venue for teaching traditional Chinese values. They made over a thousand statues and life-size dioramas depicting Chinese legends and historic tales illustrating morality and Confucian beliefs. Many of these were gruesome and bloody and some of them were really entertaining. Unfortunately, in 1985, the grounds were converted into an amusement park and reopened as Haw Par Villa. Most of the statues and scenes were taken away and replaced with rides. They've since put back some of the old statues, some of which are a great backdrop for really kitschy vacation photos. There are also two theme rides: the Tales of China Boat Ride and the Wrath of the Water Gods Flume.

**Tang Dynasty City.** 2 Yuan Ching Rd. ☎ **65/261-1116.** Adults S$15.45 (US$9.40), children to 12 S$10.30 (US$6.30). Daily 10am–6:30pm. MRT to Lakeside, then transfer to SBS nos. 154 or 240.

This theme park re-creates Xian, the Chinese capital city during the Tang dynasty (A.D. 618–907), the "Golden Age" of Chinese history for great achievements in the sciences, architecture, religion, and the arts, and for trade along the Silk Road. The wax museum has over 100 historical Chinese figures, including animated figures of Sun Yat-Sen and Mao Zedong shouting propaganda. There are 2,000 reproduction terra-cotta warriors in an underground tomb display, plus Ghost Mansion, featuring Japanese-engineered illusions. Guides conduct tours daily.

⭐ **Chinese and Japanese Gardens.** Yuan Ching Rd. ☎ **65/265-5889.** Adults S$4.50 (US$2.75), children S$2 (US$1.20). Weekdays 9am–6pm daily. MRT to Chinese Garden or bus nos. 335, 180, and 154.

The gardens are situated on two islands in Jurong lake, reached by an overpass, and joined by the Bridge of Double Beauty. In the **Chinese Garden,** most of the area is dedicated to "Northern style" landscape architecture. The style of imperial gardens, the Northern style integrates brightly colored buildings with the surroundings to make up for northern China's absence of rich plant growth and natural scenery. The Garden of Beauty is in Suzhou style, representing the Southern style of landscape architecture. Southern gardens were built predominantly by scholars, poets, and men of wealth. Sometimes called Black-and-White gardens, these were smaller, with more fine detail, and featured more subdued colors as the plants and elements of the natural landscape gave them plenty to work with.

While the Chinese garden is more visually stimulating, the **Japanese Garden** is intended to evoke feeling. Marble-chip paths lead the way so that as you walk you can hear your own footsteps and meditate on the sound.

⭐ **Singapore Botanic Gardens.** Main entrance at corner of Cluny Rd. and Holland Rd. ☎ **1800/471-9933.** Free admission. Open daily 5am–midnight. National Orchid Garden: adults S$2 (US$1.20), children under 12 and seniors S$1 (US60¢). Daily 8:30am–6pm. MRT to Orchard. Take SBS nos. 7, 105, 106, 123, or 174 from Orchard Blvd.

The present Botanic Garden was founded in 1859 by a local horticulture society. It was an important contributor to regional economic development in the late 1800s when "Mad" Henry Ridley, then the garden's director, imported the first Brazilian rubber tree seedlings from Great Britain to this region. Carved out within the tropical setting are a rose garden, a sundial garden with pruned hedges, a banana plantation, and a spice garden. Sculptures by international artists are dotted around the area.

The **National Orchid Garden** is 7.4 acres of gorgeous orchids growing along landscaped walks. The English Garden features hybrids developed here and named after famous visitors to the garden—there's the Margaret Thatcher, the Benazir Bhutto, the Vaclav Havel, and more. The garden's Symphony Lake has an island bandshell for "Concert in the Park" performances by the local symphony and international entertainers. Call visitor services at ☎ **65/471-9933,** or 65/471-9934 for performance schedules.

**Singapore Discovery Centre.** 510 Upper Jurong Rd. ☎ **65/792-6188.** www.asianconnect. com/sdc. Adults S$9 (US$5.50), children under 12 S$5 (US$3); simulator ride S$4 (US$2.45); Shooting Gallery S$3 (US$1.85). Tues–Fri 9am–7pm; Sat–Sun and public holidays 9am–8pm. MRT to Boon Lay; transfer to SBS nos. 192 or 193.

This display of the latest military technology is a lot of fun, with hands-on exhibits that cannot be resisted. There are 19 interactive information kiosks, a virtual reality experience of parachuting from a plane, a fighter pilot motion simulator, and a computer-simulated combat firing range using real but decommissioned M16 rifles. The on-site IWERKS Theatre is a five-story IMAX projection.

**Ming Village.** 32 Pandan Rd. ☎ **65/265-7711.** Admission and guided tour free. Daily 9am–5:30pm. MRT to Clementi, then SBS no. 78. Ming Village offers a free Singapore Trolley shuttle from Paragon by Sogo on Orchard Rd. and from the Raffles Hotel bus stop at 9:20am and 9:30am respectively, and also at 10:30am and 10:40am.

Tour a pottery factory that employs traditional pottery-making techniques from the Ming and Qing dynasties and watch the process from mold-making, hand-throwing, and hand-painting to glazing each piece. After the tour, shop from their large selection of beautiful antique reproduction dishes, vases, urns, and more.

## THE NORTH

The northern part of Singapore contains most of the island's nature reserves and parks. Here's where you'll find the Singapore Zoological Gardens, in addition to some sights with historical and religious significance. Despite the presence of the **MRT** in the area, there is not any simple way to get from attraction to attraction with ease. Bus transfers to and from MRT stops is the way to go—or you could stick to taxicabs.

✪ **Bukit Timah Nature Reserve.** 177 Hindhede Dr. ☎ **1800/468-5736.** Free admission. Daily 8am–6pm. MRT to Newton, then TIBS bus no. 171 or SBS bus no. 182 to park entrance.

Bukit Timah Nature Reserve is pure primary rain forest. Believed to be as old as one million years, it's the only place on the island with vegetation that exists exactly as it was before the British settled here. The park covers over 202 acres of soaring canopy teeming with mammals and birds and a lush undergrowth with more bugs, butterflies, and reptiles than you can shake a vine at. Footpaths guide your way.

**Kranji War Memorial.** 9 Woodlands Rd., located in the very northern part of the island. MRT to Bugis. From Rochore Rd., take SBS no. 170.

Kranji Cemetery commemorates the men and women who fought and died in World War II. The Kranji War Cemetery is the site of 4,000 graves of servicemen, while the Singapore State Cemetery memorializes the names of over 20,000 who died and have no known graves. The memorial itself is designed to represent the three arms of the services.

✪ **Sungei Buloh Nature Park.** Neo Tiew Crescent. ☎ **65/793-7377.** Adults S$1 (US60¢); children under 12, students, and seniors S50¢ (US30¢). Mon–Fri 7:30am–7pm; Sat–Sun and public holidays 7am–7pm. MRT to Kranji, bus no. 925 to Kranji Reservoir Dam. Cross causeway to park entrance.

Located to the very north of the island, Sungei Buloh is devoted to the wetland habitat and mangrove forests that were once common to the region. The park, covering 218 acres, has constructed paths and boardwalks through tangles of mangroves, soupy marshes, grassy spots, and coconut groves. The most spectacular sight here is the birds, of which there are somewhere between 140 and 170 species in residence or just passing through for the winter.

**Siong Lim Temple.** 184-E Jalan Toa Payoh. Located in Toa Payoh New Town. Take MRT to Toa Payoh, then take a taxi.

One night in 1898, a Hokkien businessman and his son had the same dream—of a golden light shining from the West. The following day a ship arrived carrying a group of Hokkien Buddhist monks and nuns on their way from a pilgrimage to India. The businessman vowed to build a monastery if they would stay in Singapore. They did.

Laid out according to feng shui principles, Siong Lim's buildings include the Dharma Hall, a main prayer hall, and drum and bell towers. In the back is a shrine to Kuan Yin, Goddess of Mercy.

**Kong Meng San Phor Kark See Temple.** Bright Hill Dr. Located in the center of the island to the east of Bukit Panjang Nature Preserve. Bright Hill Dr. is off Ang Mo Kio Ave. Take MRT to Bishan, then take a taxi.

The largest and most modern religious complex on the island, this temple is comprised of prayer and meditation halls, a hospice, gardens, and a vegetarian restaurant. The largest building is the Chinese-style Hall of Great Compassion. There is also the octagonal Hall of Great Virtue and a towering pagoda. For S50¢ you can buy flower petals to place in a dish at the Buddha's feet.

**Mandai Orchid Garden.** Mandai Lake Rd., on the route to the Singapore Zoological Gardens. ☎ **65/269-0136.** Adults S$2 (US$1.20), children under 12 S50¢. Daily 8:30am–5:30pm. MRT to Ang Mo Kio and SBS no. 138.

Owned and operated by Singapore Orchids Pte. Ltd for breeding and cultivating hybrids for international export, the gardens double as an STB tourist attraction. Arranged in English garden style, varieties are separated in beds that are surrounded by a grassy lawn. On display is Singapore's national flower, the Venda Miss Joaquim, a natural hybrid in shades of light purple.

**✪ Singapore Zoological Gardens.** 80 Mandai Lake Rd., on the western edge of the Bukit Panjang Nature Reserve, on the Seletar Reservoir. ☎ **65/269-3411.** www.asian-connect.com/zoo. Adults S$10.30 (US$6.30), children under 12 S$4.60 (US$2.80). Discounts for seniors and handicapped. Daily 8:30am–6pm. MRT to Ang Mo Kio and take SBS no. 138.

They call themselves the Open Zoo because, rather than coop the animals in jailed enclosures, they let them roam freely in landscaped areas. Beasts of the world are kept where they're supposed to be through psychological restraints and physical barriers that are disguised behind waterfalls, vegetation, and moats. Guinea and pea fowl, Emperor tamarins, and other creatures are free-roaming and not shy; however, if you spot a water monitor or long-tailed macaque, know that they're not zoo residents—just locals looking for a free meal.

There are daily primate and reptile shows, as well as elephant and sea lion shows. The best show, however, is the 9am breakfast with an orangutan, who feasts on fruits, putting on a hilarious and very memorable show.

**✪ Night Safari.** Singapore Zoological Gardens, 80 Mandai Lake Rd., on the western edge of the Bukit Panjang Nature Reserve, on the Seletar Reservoir. ☎ **65/269-3411.** www.asianconnect.com/zoo/. Adults S$15.45 (US$9.40), children under 12 S$10.30 (US$6.30). Daily 7:30pm–midnight. Ticket sales close at 11pm. Entrance Plaza, restaurant, and fast-food outlet open from 6:30pm. MRT to Ang Mo Kio and take SBS no. 138.

Singapore brings you the world's first open-concept zoo for nocturnal animals. Here, as in the zoological gardens, animals live in landscaped areas, their barriers virtually unseen by visitors. These areas are dimly lit to create a moonlit effect, and a guided tram leads you through "regions" designed to resemble the Himalayan foothills, the jungles of Africa, and, naturally, Southeast Asia. Some of the free-range prairie animals come excitingly close to the tram. The 45-minute ride covers almost 2 miles (3½ km), and has regular stops to get off and have a rest or stroll along trails for closer views of smaller creatures.

**MacRitchie Nature Trail.** Central Catchment Nature Reserve. No phone. Free admission. From Orchard Rd. take bus no. 132 from the Orchard Parade Hotel. From Raffles City take bus no. 130. Get off at the bus stop near Little Sisters of the Poor. Next to Little Sisters of the Poor, follow the paved walkway, which turns into the trail.

The Central Catchment Nature Reserve is the largest reserve in Singapore, covering 5,000 acres, and is home to four of Singapore's reservoirs. There's one path for walking and jogging (no bicycles allowed) that stretches 1.8 miles (3km) and lets you out at the Singapore Island Country Club.

# THE EAST COAST

The East Coast is the region leading from the edge of Singapore's urban area to the tip of the east coast, at Changi Point. Eastern Singapore is home to the Changi International Airport, nearby Changi Prison with its chapel and museum, and the long stretch of East Coast Park along the shoreline. The **MRT** heads east in this region, but swerves northward at the end of the line. A popular **bus line** for east coast attractions not reached by MRT is the SBS no. 2, which takes you past many attractions.

**Malay Village.** 39 Geylang Serai, in the suburb of Geylang, an easy walk from the MRT station. ☎ **65/748-4700** or 65/740-8860. Adults S$10 (US$6.10), children S$7 (US$4.30). Daily 10am–10pm. MRT to Paya Lebar.

In 1985, Malay Village opened as a themed showcase of Malay culture. The Cultural Museum is a collection of artifacts from Malay life, which includes household items, musical instruments, and a replica of a wedding dais and traditional beaded ceremonial bed. "Kampung Days" lets you to walk through a kampung (village) house as it would have looked in the 1950s and 1960s. The village also has souvenir shops mixed with places that sell everything from antique knives to caged birds.

Two in-house groups perform **traditional Malaysian and Indonesian dances** in the late afternoons and evenings.

✪ **Changi Prison Chapel and Museum.** 20km Upper Changi Rd. North. ☎ **65/543-0893.** Free admission. Mon–Sat 10am–5pm. Closed public holidays. Changi Prison Chapel Sunday Service (all are welcome) 5:30–7pm. MRT to Tanah Merah station, then transfer to SBS no. 2.

Upon successful occupation of Singapore, the Japanese marched all British, Australian, and allied European prisoners to Changi by foot, where they lived in a prison camp suffering 3 years of overcrowding, disease, malnutrition, and beatings. In an effort to keep hope alive, the prisoners built a small chapel from wood and attap. Years later, at the request of former POWs and their families and friends, the government built this replica. The museum displays sketches by W. R. M. Haxworth and secret photos taken by George Aspinall—both men POWs who were imprisoned here.

**East Coast Park.** East Coast Pkwy. No phone. Free admission. MRT to Bedok, bus no. 31, or on Sun and public holidays bus no. 401.

East Coast Park is a narrow strip of reclaimed land, only 5.3 miles (8.5km) long, tucked in between the shoreline and East Coast Parkway. The beach is nothing more than a narrow lump of grainy sand sloping into yellow-green water with more seaweed than a sushi bar. However, paths for bicycling, in-line skating, walking, and jogging run the length of the park, and on Sundays you'll find kite flyers in the open grassy parts. The lagoon is the best place to start for bicycle and in-line skate rentals, canoeing, and windsurfing.

**Singapore Crocodilarium.** 730 East Coast Pkwy., running along East Coast Park. ☎ **65/447-3722.** Adults S$2 (US$1.20), children under 12 S$1 (US61¢). Daily 9am–5pm. MRT to Paya Lebar or Eunos and take a taxi.

Of the 1,800 crocodiles from Singapore, Africa, Louisiana, and Caiman (South Africa) who reside here, 500 are on display. A huge gift shop peddles crocodile products, which are made both in-house and imported from outside designers.

# SENTOSA ISLAND

In the 1880s, Sentosa was a hub of British military activity, with hilltop forts built to protect the harbor from sea invasion. Today, it has become a weekend getaway spot and Singapore's answer to Disneyland. If you want to get out of the city, the beaches are cooling and well stocked with activities. If you're into the museum scene, there are some very well-presented historical exhibits and nature showcases. If you want to keep the kids happy, there's a water park, theme parks, and amusement rides. If you're spending the day, there are numerous restaurants and a couple of food courts.

## GETTING THERE

Private cars are not allowed entry to the island, but there are more than a few ways to get to Sentosa. Admission to the island is S$5 (US$3) for adults and S$3 (US$1.85) for children. In the evenings it's reduced to S$3 (US$1.85) for adults and S$1.80 (US$1.10) for children. Tickets can be purchased from booths at the Mount Faber Cable Car Station, World Trade Centre Ferry Departure Hall, Cable Car Towers (next to the World Trade Centre), and Cable Car Plaza (on Sentosa); also at Sentosa Information Booth 4 (at the start of the causeway, opposite Kentucky Fried Chicken) and Sentosa Information Booth 3 (at the end of the causeway bridge, upon entering Sentosa).

**BY CABLE CAR**    Cable cars depart from the top of Mount Faber and from the World Trade Centre daily from 8:30am to 9pm at a cost of between S$5 and S$6.50 (US$3–$4) for adults, and S$3 (US$1.85) for children.

**BY FERRY**    The ferry departs from the World Trade Centre on weekdays from 9:30am to 9pm at 20-minute intervals, and on weekends and public holidays from 8:30am to 9pm at 15-minute intervals. The round-trip fare is S$1.30 (US80¢), and one-way is S80¢ (US50¢).

**BY BUS**    **SBS Leisure Pte. Ltd** operates bus service to and from Sentosa. Service A operates between 7:15am and 11:30pm daily from the World Trade Centre (WTC) Bus Terminal. Services C and M run from the Tiong Bahru MRT Station between 7:20am and 11:30pm daily. Service E has stops from Orchard Road to Raffles City, and operates from 10am to 10:45pm daily. Fares are paid to the driver and run from S$6 to S$7 (US$3.70–US$4.30) for adults and S$4 to S$5 (US$2.45–US$3) for children, which includes island admission.

**BY TAXI**    Taxis are only allowed to drop off and pick up passengers at the Beaufort Sentosa, Shangri-La's Rasa Sentosa Resort, and NTUC Sentosa Beach Resort. The taxi toll is S$3 (US$1.85) per entry from 7am to 10pm and is free from 10pm to 7am.

## GETTING AROUND

Once on Sentosa, a free monorail operates from 9am to 10pm daily at 10-minute intervals.

## SEEING THE SIGHTS

The attractions that you get free with your Sentosa admission are the **Fountain Gardens** and **Musical Fountain,** the **Enchanted Garden of Tembusu,** the **Dragon Trail Nature Walk,** and the **beaches.**

There are three beaches, **Siloso Beach** on the western end and **Central Beach** and **Tanjong Beach** on the eastern end, each dressed in tall coconut palms and flowering trees. At Central Beach, deck chairs, beach umbrellas, and a variety of water sports equipment like pedal boats, aquabikes, fun bugs, canoes, surfboards, and banana boats are available for hire at nominal charges. Bicycles are also available for hire at the bicycle kiosk at Siloso Beach. Shower and changing facilities, food kiosks, and snack bars are at rest stations.

Unless otherwise noted, the following attractions on Sentosa have separate admission charges.

**Asian Village.** ☎ **65/275-0338.** Free admission. Daily 10am–9pm. Adventure Asia daily 10am–7pm. Monorail stop 1.

Set around a tiny lake, three zones represent the cultural flavors of East, South, and Southeast Asia. In the back of the village is Adventure Asia, with 10 rides tucked inside a shady grove. Ten bucks (US$6.10) gets you unlimited rides.

**Maritime Museum.** ☎ **65/270-8855.** Free admission. Daily 10am–7pm. Closest to monorail stop 7, then walk along Gateway Ave.

From ship models to artifacts, sea charts, and photos, the museum tells the story of 14 centuries of maritime life, and the important connection of the sea to Singapore's history.

**Fantasy Island.** ☎ **65/275-1088.** Adults S$20 (US$12.20), children 3–12 S$12.50 (US$7.60). Daily 10am–7pm. Monorail stop 7.

Try out all kinds of water slides, water tunnels, surf rides, rapids, and a simulated lazy river running around the whole park. For the little ones, there are tree houses with water toys, special slides, and a kiddie pool. There are changing rooms, food outlets, and a first-aid team on duty.

**Cinemania.** ☎ **65/373-0159.** Adults S$10 (US$6.10), children S$6 (US$3.65). Daily 11am–8pm. Monorail stop 7.

Cinemania is a 3-D audiovisual ride with motion simulator. They rotate three films at a time from a library of 25 titles like *Cosmic Pinball, Desert Duel,* and *Runaway Train.*

**Sentosa Orchid Gardens.** ☎ **65/278-1940.** Adults S$2 (US$1.20), children S$1 (US60¢). Daily 9am–7pm. Monorail stop 1; the Orchid Garden is to the east of the Fountain Gardens.

The Sentosa Orchid Garden is mainly used as a venue for private parties, so you're better off at the National Orchid Garden at the Singapore Botanic Gardens or at Mandai Orchids to see the best collections.

**The Merlion.** ☎ **65/275-0388.** Adults S$3 (US$1.85), children S$2 (US$1.20). Daily 9am–10pm. Monorail stops 1 and 4.

Imagine, if you will, 12 towering stories of that half-lion, half-fish creature, the Merlion. Admission buys you an elevator ride to the ninth floor, where you can peer out the mouth, and to the top of its head for a 360° view of Singapore, Sentosa, and even Indonesia. Be at the Fountain Gardens at 7:30pm, 8:30pm, and 9:30pm nightly for the "Rise of the Merlion" show, where they light the thing up with 16,000 fiber-optic lights and shoot red lasers out its eyes.

**VolcanoLand.** ☎ **65/275-1828.** Adults S$10 (US$6.10), children under 12 S$6 (US$3.65). Daily 10am–7pm. Monorail stop 1 or 4.

The main attraction here is the ancient Central American "active volcano," a walk-through exhibit where you are taken on a journey to the center of the Earth with a mythological explorer and his Jules Verne–style robot buddy. Inside the "volcano" there's a multi-media show about the mysteries of life and the universe and a simulated volcano eruption.

○ **Images of Singapore.** ☎ **65/275-0388.** Adults S$5 (US$3), children S$3 (US$1.85). Daily 9am–9pm; last admission 8:30pm. Monorail stop 4.

# Sentosa Island Attractions

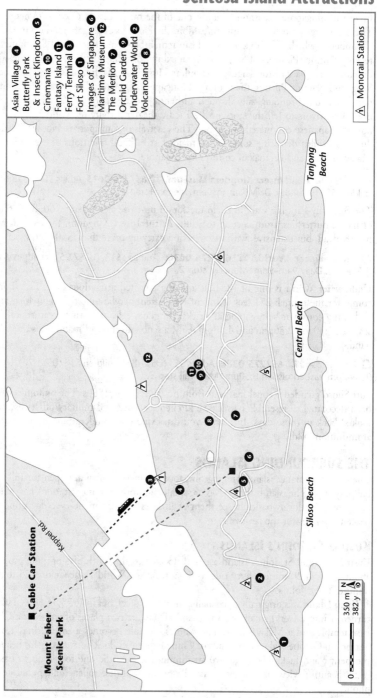

Asian Village **4**
Butterfly Park
& Insect Kingdom **5**
Cinemania **10**
Fantasy Island **11**
Ferry Terminal **3**
Fort Siloso **1**
Images of Singapore **6**
Maritime Museum **12**
The Merlion **7**
Orchid Garden **9**
Underwater World **2**
Volcanoland **8**

△ Monorail Stations

Cable Car Station

Mount Faber
Scenic Park

Keppel Rd.

Tanjong Beach

Central Beach

Siloso Beach

0   350 m
    382 y

Images of Singapore is without a doubt one of the main reasons to come to Sentosa. There are three parts to this museum/exhibit: the Pioneers of Singapore, the Surrender Chambers—which date back as far as I can remember—and Festivals of Singapore, a recent addition. Pioneers of Singapore is an exhibit of beautifully constructed life-size dioramas that place historic figures like Sultan Hussein, Sir Stamford Raffles, Tan Tock Seng, and Naraina Pillai in the context of Singapore's timeline. The Surrender Chambers leads you chronologically through authentic footage, photos, maps, and recordings of survivors to tell the story of the Pacific theater activity of World War II and how the Japanese conquered Singapore. The Festivals of Singapore is another life-size diorama exhibit depicting some of the major festivals and traditions of the Chinese, Malay, Indian, and Peranakan cultures in Singapore.

**Butterfly Park and Insect Kingdom Museum. ☎ 65/275-0013.** Adults S$6 (US$3.65), children S$3 (US$1.85). Daily 9am–6:30pm. Monorail stop 4.

The Butterfly Park is a walk-in enclosure for an up-close view of some 60 live species of native butterflies, from cocoon to adult. At the Insect Kingdom, the exhibits are mostly dead, but extensive, with its collection carrying more than 2,500 bugs.

**✪ Underwater World. ☎ 65/275-0030.** Adults S$13 (US$7.95), children S$7 (US$4.30). Daily 9am–9pm. Monorail stop 2.

Underwater World is one of the best and most visited attractions here. Everybody comes for the tunnel: 271 feet (83m) of transparent acrylic tube through which you glide on a conveyor belt, gaping at sharks, stingrays, eels, and other creatures of the sea. At 11:30am, 2:30pm, and 4:30pm daily, a scuba diver hops in and feeds them by hand.

**✪ Fort Siloso. ☎ 65/275-0388.** Adults S$3 (US$1.85), children S$2 (US$1.20). Daily 9am–7pm; last admission 6:30pm. Monorail stop 3.

Fort Siloso guarded Keppel Harbour from invasion in the 1880s. The buildings have been decorated to resemble barracks, a kitchen, laundry, and military offices as they looked back in those days. In places, you can explore the underground tunnels and ammunition holds.

## THE SURROUNDING ISLANDS

There are 60 smaller islands ringing Singapore, some of which are open for full- or half-day trips. The islands themselves are small and, for the most part, don't have a lot going on. The locals basically see them as little escapes from the everyday grind—peaceful respites for the family.

### KUSU & ST. JOHN'S ISLANDS

Kusu Island and St. John's Island are both located to the south of Singapore proper, about a 15- to 20-minute ferry ride to Kusu from the World Trade Centre, 25 to 30 minutes to St. John's.

**Kusu Island** was originally two small islands and a reef, but in 1975, reclaimed land turned it into a (very) small getaway island. There are two places of worship: a Chinese temple and a Malay shrine. The Chinese temple becomes a zoo during "Kusu Season" in October, when thousands of Chinese devotees flock here to pray for health, prosperity, and luck. There are two swimming lagoons (the one to the north has a really beautiful view of Singapore Island), picnic facilities, toilets, and public telephones.

Historically speaking, **St. John's Island** is an unlikely place for a day trip. As far back as 1874, this place was a quarantine for Chinese immigrants sick with cholera;

in the 1950s, it became a deportation holding center for Chinese Mafia thugs; and later it was a rehab center for opium addicts. Today you'll find a mosque, holiday camps, three lagoons, bungalows, a cafeteria, a huge playing field, and basketball.

**Ferries** leave at regular intervals and make a circular route, landing on both islands. Tickets are available from the desk at the back of the World Trade Centre. Adult tickets are S$6.20 (US$3.80) and tickets for children under 12 are S$3.10 (US$1.90). During October's "Kusu Season" the ferry departs from Clifford Pier.

## PULAU UBIN

Located off the northeast tip of Singapore, Pulau Ubin has industry (mining), some Malay kampungs, and trails throughout the island for hiking and mountain biking (rentals are available at the ferry pier). You can eat fresh seafood at a few restaurants, and there are public toilets. To get there, take bus no. 2 to Changi Village. Walk past the food court down to the water and find the ferry. There's no ticket booth, so you should just approach the captain and buy your ticket from him—it'll cost you about S$1.50 (US90¢).

# 6 Sports & Outdoor Activities

## GOLF

Like the rest of the world, Singapore is golf crazy. There are quite a few clubs, many of which are open for limited play by nonmembers. Greens fees range from S$60 to S$129 (US$37–US$79), with additional charges for caddies or trolleys. Bring your par certificate. Also, most hotel concierges will be glad to make arrangements for you, and this may be the best way to go.

Best bets are **Changi Golf Club,** 20 Netheravon Rd. (☎ **65/545-5133**); **Jurong Country Club,** 9 Science Centre Rd. (☎ **65/560-5655**); and **The Warren Golf Club,** 50 Folkestone Rd. no. 01–00 (☎ **65/777-6533**).

## WATER SPORTS

**BOAT RENTAL** Canoes, kayaks, and plastic Funyaks (banana boats) are available to rent at the beach at **Changi Village,** East Coast Parkway near the lagoon, and on **Sentosa Island's Central Beach,** where you can also rent pedal boats and aquabikes. Rental spots are open from around 9am to 6pm daily, and charge between S$6 and S$12 (US$3.65–US$7.30) per hour depending on what you rent. In Changi, try **American Unsinkable Kayak** on the beach (☎ **65/563-9015**). On Sentosa, try **Boathouse Watersports** at 60 Siloso Beach Walk (☎ **65/275-1053** or 65/275-0667). At East Coast Park, head for the lagoon, where there are a few outlets that can hook you up.

You'll find both **windsurfing** boards and **sailboats** for rent at the lagoon in **East Coast Park.** Most places are open from 9am to around 7pm daily. The charge for a board is S$20 (US$12.20) for 2 hours and for a sailboat is around S$20 for 1 hour. Deposits will be required. **Sailspirit,** 1210 East Coast Pkwy. (☎ **65/445-5108**), offers rentals only, while the **East Coast Sailing Centre,** 1210 East Coast Pkwy. (☎ **65/449-5118**), offers basic instruction as well as rental.

**WATERSKIING** The Kallang River has been the venue for international water-skiing tournaments. Contact the **Cowabunga Ski Centre,** Kallang Riverside Park, 10 Stadium Lane (☎ **65/344-8813**), where you can arrange lessons for adults and children and waterskiing by the hour or by the ride. The cost is anywhere from S$65 to S$85 (US$39.65–US$51.85) per hour. Open from about 9am to 5:30pm, but call ahead.

**SCUBA DIVING**   The locals are crazy about scuba diving, but are more likely to travel to Malaysia and other Southeast Asian destinations for good underwater adventures. The most common complaint is that the water surrounding Singapore is really silty—sometimes to the point where you can barely see your hand before your face. If you're still interested, the best place to try for a beginner certification course is at **Sea Dive,** 10 Jalan Serene, no. 02–115 (☎ **65/487-3178**), which also organizes diving trips and offers classes up to advanced levels. **Club Aquanaut,** 190 Clemenceau Ave., no. 05–33, Singapore Shopping Centre (☎ **65/334-3454**), also arranges diving trips.

## BICYCLE RENTAL

Bicycles are not for rent within the city limits, and traffic does not really allow for cycling on city streets, so sightseeing by bicycle is not recommended for city touring. At parks and beaches they can be rented from roughly 9am to 7pm for an average cost of S$5 (US$3) per hour.

**IN EAST COAST PARK**   You can rent bicycles at East Coast Park from **Ling Choo Hong** (☎ **65/449-7305**), near the hawker center at Carpark E; **SDK Recreation** (☎ **65/445-2969**), near McDonald's at Carpark C; or **Wimbledon Cafeteria & Bicycle Rental** (☎ **65/444-3928**), near the windsurfing rental places.

**ON SENTOSA**   On Sentosa, try **SDK Recreation** (☎ **65/272-8738**), located at Siloso Beach off Siloso Road. One favorite place for mountain-biking sorts of adventures is Pulau Ubin, off the northeast coast of Singapore. When you get off the ferry, there are a number of places to rent bikes.

## 7  Shopping

In Singapore, shopping is a sport—from the practiced glide through haute couture boutiques to skillful back-alley bargaining to win the best prices on Asian treasures. The shopping here is always exciting, with something to satiate every pro shopper's appetite.

**OPEN HOURS**   Shopping malls generally keep opening hours from 10am to 8pm daily, with some stores keeping shorter Sunday hours, and possibly longer hours on public holidays. Smaller shops are open from around 10am to 5pm Monday through Saturday, but are almost always closed on Sundays.

**PRICES**   Almost all of the stores in shopping malls have fixed prices. Sales are common, especially during the monthlong Great Singapore Sale in July. In the smaller shops and at street vendors, prices are never marked, and it will be expected that you bargain. It's a standard Asian routine, but it can be difficult at first for many westerners, who are accustomed to accepting fixed prices. See the tips on bargaining section in chapter 2 for pointers.

**TAXES**   When you shop in stores that display the blue **"Tax Free for Tourists"** logo, the government will refund the goods and services tax (GST) you pay on purchases totaling S$300 (US$183) or more. Refund forms are available in participating stores. Also, purchases of S$100 (US$61) or more can be combined to total S$300. Arrange the refund at the airport's Global Refund Counter when you leave, either in the form of a check via post or credit card refund. For complete details, call the hotline at ☎ **65/225-6238.**

   Changi International Airport has a large **duty-free** shop that carries tax-free cigarettes and liquor. There's also a chain of duty-free stores in Singapore called **DFS.**

Their main branch is at Millenia Walk, next to the Pan Pacific Hotel down by Marina Square (☎ 65/332-2118).

## ORCHARD ROAD

The focal point of shopping in Singapore is **Orchard Road,** a very long stretch of glitzy shopping malls packed with Western clothing stores, from designer wear to cheap chic, and many other mostly imported finds. You'll find the major department stores here, such as Robinson's, John Little, and Takashimaya—and also find that brand-name fashions are no less expensive than at home.

Some of the larger and more exciting malls to check out are **Centrepoint,** 176 Orchard Rd.; **Ngee Ann City/Takashimaya Shopping Centre,** 391 Orchard Rd.; **Specialists' Shopping Centre,** 277 Orchard Rd.; and **Wisma Atria,** 435 Orchard Rd. The **Hilton Shopping Gallery** (581 Orchard Rd.) deals only in exclusive top designer boutiques.

At **Far East Plaza** (14 Scotts Rd.) and **Lucky Plaza** (304 Orchard Rd.) there are some bargains to be had on electronics and camera equipment and luggage, among other things. But be wary of rip-off deals.

**Eyeglasses** are a surprising bargain in Singapore. A reputable outlet is **Capitol Optical** at no. 03–132, Far East Plaza (☎ 65/736-0365).

If you're in the mood for **jewels,** the most trusted dealer in Singapore is **Larry Jewelry (S) Pte. Ltd.,** Orchard Towers, Level 1, 400 Orchard Rd. (☎ 65/732-3222), but be prepared to drop a dime.

**Royal Selangor,** the famous Malaysian pewter manufacturer since 1885, has eight outlets in Singapore. The Orchard branch is at no. 02–40 Paragon by Sogo, 290 Orchard Rd. (☎ 65/235-6633).

The **Tanglin Shopping Centre** (Tanglin Rd., at the northern end of Orchard) is a treasure trove of antiques dealers and carpet shops. For the best selection of carpets visit **Hassan's Carpets,** no. 03–01/06 Tanglin Shopping Centre (☎ 65/737-5626).

## HISTORIC DISTRICT

While not as famous as Orchard Road, the Historic District has its share of shopping. One of the largest malls in the area is **Raffles City Shopping Centre** above the City Hall MRT station. For an up-market shopping adventure, I recommend the **Raffles Hotel Shopping Arcade,** at 328 North Bridge Rd.

Another big spot for shopping is the Marina Bay area. Malls such as **Marina Square** (6 Raffles Blvd.) and **Millenia Walk** (9 Raffles Blvd.) offer exciting shopping without all the crowds.

There's also a **night market at Bugis Street** (at the Bugis MRT stop next to Parco Bugis Junction Mall), where you'll find cheap chic clothing and accessories, CD-VDOs, some handicrafts, and all sorts of other finds.

## CHINATOWN

For shopping malls with a Chinese flair, go to **People's Park Complex** in Chinatown (1 Park Rd.) for Chinese goods and housewares, jade, and jewelry at good prices. Down Eu Tong Sen Street from People's Park Complex is **People's Park Centre** (101 Upper Cross St.). Look there for Yue Hua, an emporium for imported Chinese goods. Across the street from People's Park is the **Chinatown Complex,** with vendor stalls selling all sorts of inexpensive items, including souvenirs. For gold, visit **Pidemco Centre** (95 South Bridge Rd.), which is wall-to-wall jewelers.

The **Singapore Handicrafts Centre** (Chinatown Point; 133 New Bridge Rd.) will provide one-stop shopping with about 50 souvenir shops under one roof. Other handicraft shops can be found in Chinatown along Smith, Trengganu, and Pagoda streets. Here you can shop for Chinese handicrafts, art, curio items, and souvenirs (although not at the best prices). The **Zhen Lacquer Gallery** (1 Trengganu St.; ☎ 65/222-2718), **D'Art Station** (no. 65 Pagoda St.; ☎ 65/225-8307), **Chung Hwa Book Co.** (71 S. Bridge Rd.; ☎ 65/532-2045), and **Eng Tiang Huat** (284 River Valley Rd.; ☎ 65/734-3738), are shops to check out for everything from bird-cages to teapots, artist's chops to musical instruments.

There's also a small **flea market** in Chinatown on the corner of South Bridge Road and Cross Street, where you can pick up very odd items for bargains.

## ARAB STREET

Arab Street is a favorite for shoppers, and despite heavy tourism here, prices remain very reasonable. Be prepared to bargain for items like batik sarongs and crafts, brassware, silks, basketware, regional handicrafts (including some fabulous ethnic jewelry), and spices. For those who love to shop, Arab Street is a highly recommended jaunt.

Loose gemstones can also be a good find here. **Nam Hing Lin Kee Jewelry Pte. Ltd.,** 150 Arab St. (☎ 65/294-3623), and **Bril Diamonds Pte. Ltd.,** 123 Arab St. (☎ 65/291-2236), are both honest outlets.

## LITTLE INDIA

On Serangoon Road in Little India, you'll find gold in Western and Indian designs (with beautiful filigree work), northern and southern Indian-style fashions, watches, luggage, and Indian arts and handicrafts. At the corner of Serangoon Road and Hastings Road is the **Little India Arcade,** with 26 shops full of clothing and crafts.

A few shops along Serangoon Road in Little India have some fine **Indian silks.** The largest selection is at Little India's most famous department store, Mohd Mustapha & Samsuddin Co., Pte. Ltd., more commonly known as **Mustapha's,** 320 Serangoon Rd. (☎ 65/299-2603).

## OTHER AREAS

While shopping in town is easy, there are some interesting areas around the island that are only a taxi ride away, and can be equally as much fun as the more central places, if not more so.

To get an eyeful of some local and regional furnishings and objets d'art in antique Indonesian, Chinese, and Peranakan styles, take a taxi out to **Dempsey Road** and walk up the hill to the warehouses. Inside each warehouse is a dealer, with enticing names like **Asia Passion,** Blk. 13 no. 01–02 (☎ 65/473-1339); **Journey East Pte. Ltd.,** Blk. 13 no. 01–04 (☎ 65/473-1693); and **Eastern Discoveries,** Blk. 26 no. 01–04 (☎ 65/475-1814). There are over a dozen places here, each specializing in different wares. Mixed in with the antiques shops you'll also find at least a half dozen **carpet dealers.**

Also around the island are some good pottery factories. Antique reproductions are to be had at the showroom at **Ming Village,** 32 Pandan Rd. (☎ 65/265-7711). The ultimate in pottery shopping, however, is a place called **Thow Kwang Industry Pte. Ltd** but referred to by the locals as the "pottery jungle" for its rows upon rows of items. It's a taxi ride away at 85 Lorong Tawas off Jalan Bahar (☎ 65/265-5808).

Another good buy in Singapore is **crocodile products.** For selection and quality I recommend **Jurong Reptile Park,** 241 Jalan Ahmad Ibrahim (☎ 65/261-8866), and **Singapore Crocodilarium,** 730 East Coast Pkwy. (☎ 65/447-3722).

## 8  Singapore After Dark

Singapore nightlife offers up a wide range of exciting activities, whether you're in the mood for the symphony or a little jazz; whether you're looking for cultural dance performances or modern disco. The affluence of recent decades has inspired Singaporeans to spice up their evening leisure time with cafes, clubs, and pubs. And recent government campaigns have boosted the profile of the arts community, which offers up music and dance performances and modern theatrical productions. The STB is very involved in arts promotions this year, so stop by their office to learn about current runs.

**INFORMATION**  For updated information on what's going on, pick up a copy of the *Straits Times,* which lists events around town, as well as the *New Paper,* which lists musical performances by both local and international artists. Both of these papers also provide cinema listings and theater reviews.

**TELEPHONE BOOKINGS**  Telephone bookings for **Ticket Charge** events are through ☎ 65/296-2929, or stop by their locations at Centrepoint Shopping Centre, Tangs department store, or Wisma Atria shopping mall on Orchard Road. You can purchase tickets for **SISTIC** events by calling ☎ 65/348-5555 or visiting their outlets at Forum Shopping Centre, Parco Bugis Junction, Raffles City Shopping Centre, Specialist Shopping Centre, Takashimaya, and Victoria Concert Hall. These are also excellent places to learn about performances, or you can call the performance venues directly.

**OPEN HOURS**  Many **bars** keep opening hours in the late afternoon, a few as early as lunchtime. **Discos and entertainment clubs** usually open around 6pm, but generally don't get lively until 10 or 11pm. Closing time is at 1 or 2am on weekdays, 3am on weekends. **Theater and dance performances** can begin anywhere between 7:30 and 9pm.

**SAFETY**  You probably won't need to worry about your **safety** during the wee hours in most parts of the city, and even a single woman alone has little to worry about.

### THEATER, DANCE & MUSICAL PERFORMANCE

Singapore is no cultural backwater. Professional and amateur theater companies, dance troupes, opera companies, and musical groups offer a wide variety of not only Asian performances but Western as well. Broadway road shows such as *Cats, Phantom of the Opera,* and *Les Misérables* have played to sell-out audiences. Each of the three tenors—Domingo, Pavarotti, and Carreras—has played the town, and Yo Yo Ma brought down the house. Winton Marsalis, Tito Puente, and Michael Jackson have been equally as successful. The Merce Cunningham Dance Company and the Bolshoi Ballet have both graced the boards, and the New York Philharmonic, under the baton of maestro Zubin Mehta, thrilled Singaporeans and visitors alike.

International stars make up only a small portion of the performance scene, though. Singapore theater comprises four distinct language groups—English, Chinese, Malay, and Indian—and each maintains its own voice and culture. Some of the more acclaimed groups are the **Drama Centre** (☎ 65/336-0005), **The Necessary Stage** (☎ 65/733-2716), and **TheatreWorks** (☎ 65/338-4077).

The **Singapore Symphony Orchestra,** just 18 years old, gives concerts any jaded New Yorker or Londoner would find inspiring. They share their venue, Victoria Theatre and Concert Hall (☎ 65/339-6120), with other international and local performers, including musicals, festivals, and dance groups. Home-grown companies that regularly stage productions at the Victoria include **The People's Association Indian Orchestra** (☎ 65/440-9353), the **Indian Fine Arts Society Orchestra** (☎ 65/270-0722), and the **Nanyang Academy of Fine Arts Chinese Orchestra** (☎ 65/338-9176).

Around town, impromptu stages feature irregularly scheduled performances of traditional entertainments. **Wayangs (Chinese operas)** are loud, gaudy, and fun to watch. Gongs and drums herald the lavishly costumed, heavily made-up actors, who perform favorite Chinese tales in the original language. For a regularly scheduled Chinese Opera performance, head for Clarke Quay every Wednesday and Friday night at 7:45pm. Performed by the **Chinese Theatre Circle,** other shows are staged in the afternoons and evenings at their teahouse (5 Smith St., ☎ 65/323-4862).

Other cultural performances can be found at **ASEAN Night** at the Mandarin Hotel, Orchard Road (☎ 65/737-4411), with a dinner show featuring traditional music and dance from Singapore, Indonesia, Thailand, Malaysia, Brunei, and the Philippines. Also check out **Instant Asia** at the Singa Inn Seafood Restaurant, 920 East Coast Pkwy. (☎ 65/345-1111), for a dinner show of Indian, Malay, and Chinese dance.

Around town, you'll also find both **modern and traditional dance performances** from a number of local troupes. **Apsaras Arts** (☎ 65/339-7197) is an Indian classical dance troupe; the **Dance Ensemble Singapore** (☎ 65/334-7192) performs traditional Chinese dance; and the **Singapore Dance Theatre Ltd.** (☎ 65/338-0611) mounts classical as well as neo-classical productions. Call for performance schedules and venue information.

## DISCOS, CLUBS & BARS

Because of the government's added tariff, alcoholic beverage prices are high everywhere, whether in a hotel bar or a neighborhood pub. "House pour" drinks (generics) are S$10 and S$13 (US$6.10–US$8). A glass of house wine will cost between S$10 and S$15 (US$6.10–US$9.15), depending on if it's a red or a white. Local draft beer (Tiger, brewed in Singapore) is on average S$10 (US$6.10). Almost every bar and club has a happy hour before 7:30pm and discounts can be up to 50% off for house pours and drafts.

Most of the disco and entertainment clubs charge steep covers, but they will usually include one drink. You'll also find ladies' nights at the larger clubs.

Many clubs will require smart casual attire. Feel free to be trendy, but stay away from shorts, T-shirts, sneakers, and torn jeans. Be forewarned that you may be turned away if not properly dressed.

### ORCHARD ROAD

Orchard Road is a large center for Singapore nightlife. If you're looking for a good bar, **Brannigans,** at the Hyatt Regency, 10–12 Scotts Rd. (☎ 65/730-7107), is an old standard. A popular hangout for Singaporeans, expatriates, and tourists, it offers a live band and fun atmosphere that ensure this place is packed nightly. Irish bars are also favored here. One of the best is **Muddy Murphys,** no. B1–01/01–06 Orchard Hotel Shopping Arcade, 442 Orchard Rd. (☎ 65/735-0400), with Irish music and ambiance. And for a bar with a Southeast Asian feel to it, I recommend **No. 5,** 5 Emerald Hill, Peranakan Place (☎ 65/732-0818). In the restored shophouse, the dark teakwood and Oriental carpets add to a charm that has made this place a favorite for expats.

The Singapore scene has recently welcomed some excellent **wine bars.** Visit **Que Pasa,** 7 Emerald Hill, Peranakan Place (☎ **65/235-6626**), for a glass of good wine in a lively setting. And for a fine assortment of cigars (with cognacs available), visit **The Havana Club,** in the lobby level of the Marriott Hotel, 320 Orchard Rd. (☎ **65/ 834-1088**). It's Singapore's first cigar bar.

On the disco front, **Fabrice's,** in the Marriott Hotel basement, 320 Orchard Rd. (☎ **65/738-8887**), plays a wide assortment of worldbeat music and features live music from international bands. **Neo Pharaohs,** 56 Cairnhill Rd. (☎ 65/736-3098), is a disco fashioned in Moroccan style where you're sure not to hear any techno. There's no sign, so look for the shophouse with the gargoyles and red lantern on the porch. For a more traditional disco, **Xanadu,** in the Shangri-La Hotel, Orange Grove Rd. (☎ **65/737-3644**), is a sophisticated place, with more danceable old songs and some very friendly people.

## THE HISTORIC DISTRICT

The Historic District has some of the most unique nightspots in the city, and it's the home of Singapore's most famous bar, the **Long Bar,** in the Raffles Hotel Arcade, Raffles Hotel, 1 Beach Rd. (☎ **65/337-1886**). Birthplace of the Singapore Sling, the Long Bar still draws crowds like it did back in the 1920s and '30s. Raffles Hotel is also home to the historic **Raffles Bar & Billiards** (☎ **65/331-1746**), which, in addition to its rich elegance and colonial charm, features live jazz. For the real jazz aficionados, there's **Somerset's Bar,** Level 3 Raffles City Shopping Centre, 2 Stamford Rd. (☎ **65/ 431-5332**), a sophisticated lounge venue for nightly live performances by international jazz musicians.

There are some other variations on traditional bars in this area that are worth checking out. **The Next Page,** 15 Mohamed Sultan Rd. (☎ **65/235-6967**), is a happening place in an old shophouse decorated in tongue-in-cheek Chinese style. **The Fat Frog,** 45 Armenian St., behind the Substation (☎ **65/338-6201**), is a hangout for local artists. A bulletin board provides details of current and upcoming exhibits and performances.

There are some lovely **wine bars** in the historic district that are quiet getaways from the usual club scene. **Bonne Sante,** no. 01–13 The Gallery, Chijmes, 30 Victoria St. (☎ **65/338-1801**), serves wine from around the world in a very elegant setting, while **The Corner at 18,** 18 Mohamed Sultan Rd. (☎ **65/737-1518**), is a more casual bar with a menu selection of good accompanying snacks.

**Bugis Street** is home to Singapore's last remaining cabaret acts. The **Boom Boom Room,** no. 02–04 New Bugis St. (☎ **65/339-8187**), has nightly variety shows featuring Singapore's finest drag queens.

If you're not sure where you'd like to end up, **Mohamed Sultan Road** has a string of bars, each a little different than the next, in old restored shophouses. It can make for a fun evening of "hopping."

## ALONG THE RIVER

At night, **Clarke Quay** and **Boat Quay** are charged up with bars and restaurants to suit all tastes in food and entertainment. Take a stroll along Boat Quay to see what strikes your fancy. Places that are well worth a look-see are **Harry's Quayside,** 28 Boat Quay (☎ **65/538-3029**), Singapore's favorite jazz bar, and **Brewerkz,** no. 02–07 Riverside Point, 30 Merchant Rd. (☎ **65/438-7438**), an excellent microbrewery with an equally excellent lunch and dinner menu.

## CHINATOWN

While Chinatown isn't the most active in terms of nightclubs and bars, there are some interesting things happening. **JJ Mahoney,** 58 Duxton Rd. (☎ 65/225-6225), is a very nice bar with live music and a friendly atmosphere, and **Beaujolais,** 1 Ann Siang Hill (☎ 65/224-2227), has affordable wines in a sweet remodeled shophouse.

# Malaysia  9

*By Jennifer Eveland*

Compared with spicy Thailand to the north and cosmopolitan Singapore to the south, Malaysia is a relative secret to many from the West, and most travelers to Southeast Asia skip over it, opting for more heavily traversed routes.

Boy, are they missing out. Those who venture here wander through streets awash with international influences from colonial times and trek through mysterious rain forests and caves, often without another tourist in sight. They relax peacefully under palms on lazy white beaches that fade into blue, blue waters. They spy the bright colors of batik sarongs hanging to dry in the breeze. They hear the melodic drone of the Muslim call to prayer seeping from exotic mosques. They taste culinary masterpieces served in modest local shops—from Malay with its deep mellow spices to succulent seafood punctuated by brilliant chilies. In Malaysia I'm always thrilled to witness life without the distracting glare of the tourism industry, and I leave impressed by how accessible Malaysia is to outsiders while remaining true to its heritage.

Malaysia just doesn't get the tourism press it deserves, but it's not because foreign travelers aren't welcome. True, the Malaysian Tourism Board has almost no international advertising campaign—and you'll be hard pressed to get any useful information out of them—but everyone from government officials in Kuala Lumpur to boat hands in Penang, seems delighted to see the smiling face of a traveler who has discovered just how beautiful their country is.

This chapter covers the major destinations of both Peninsular Malaysia and East Malaysia (Malaysian Borneo). We begin with the country's capital, **Kuala Lumpur,** then tour the peninsula's west coast—the cities of **Johor Bahru** and **Malacca** (Meleka); the hill resorts at **Cameron** and **Genting Highlands;** and the popular island of **Penang.** Next I'll take you up the east coast of the peninsula, through resort areas such as **Desaru, Kuantan,** and **Cherating,** the small and charming **Tioman Island,** all the way north to the culturally stimulating cities of **Kuala Terengganu** and **Kota Bharu.** Our coverage will also include **Taman Negara,** peninsular Malaysia's largest national forest. Finally, we cross the South China Sea to the island of Borneo, where the Malaysian states of **Sarawak** and **Sabah** feature Malaysia's most impressive forests as well as unique and diverse cultures.

# Peninsular Malaysia

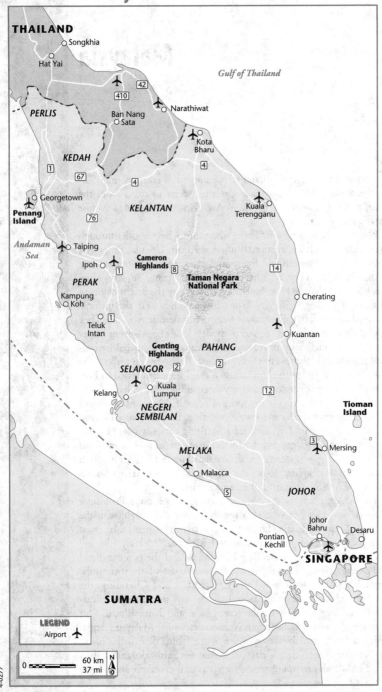

**THAILAND**

Songkhia

Hat Yai

*Gulf of Thailand*

42

410

*PERLIS*

Ban Nang
Sata

Narathiwat

*KEDAH*

Kota
Bharu

1

67

4

4

Georgetown

*KELANTAN*

76

**Penang
Island**

Kuala
Terengganu

*Andaman
Sea*

Taiping

Ipoh

1

**Cameron
Highlands**

8

**Taman Negara
National Park**

14

*PERAK*

Cherating

Kampung
Koh

1

Teluk
Intan

Kuantan

**Genting
Highlands**

*PAHANG*

2

*SELANGOR*

2

Kuala
Lumpur

Kelang

12

*NEGERI
SEMBILAN*

**Tioman
Island**

3

Mersing

*MELAKA*

Malacca

5

*JOHOR*

Johor
Bahru

Desaru

Pontian
Kechil

**SINGAPORE**

**SUMATRA**

| LEGEND |
| Airport ✈ |

0 ⸺ 60 km
37 mi

N

436

4-0277

## 1 Getting to Know Malaysia

### THE LAY OF THE LAND

Malaysia's territory covers peninsular Malaysia and two states on the island of **Borneo**—Sabah and Sarawak—approximately 150 miles (240km) east across the South China Sea. All 13 of its states total 202,020 square miles (336,700 sq. km) of land. Of this area, **Peninsular Malaysia** makes up about 134,680 square miles (465,000 sq. km) and contains 11 of Malaysia's 13 states: Kedah, Perlis, Penang, and Perak are in the northwest; Kelantan and Terengganu are in the northeast; Selangor, Negeri Sembilan, and Melaka are about midway down the peninsula on the western side; Pahang, along the east coast, sprawls inward to cover most of the central area (which is mostly forest preserve); and Johor covers the entire southern tip from east to west. Kuala Lumpur, the nation's capital, appears on a map to be located in the center of the state of Selangor, but it is actually a federal district similar to Washington, D.C., in the United States.

Peninsular Malaysia shares its north border with Thailand. In the south, just over the Strait of Johor, is Singapore, connected by two vehicular causeways. On Borneo, Sarawak and Sabah neighbor Indonesia's Kalimantan. In a tiny nook on the Sarawak coast is the oil-rich Sultanate of Brunei Darussalam.

The major cities of the peninsula are more or less along the coasts. Many were built on old trade or mining settlements, and lie near one of Malaysia's many rivers.

Over 70% of Malaysia is covered with tropical evergreen forest, estimated to be some of the oldest in the world. Its diverse terrain allows for a range of forest types, such as montane forests, sparsely wooded tangles at higher elevations; lowland forests, the dense tropical jungle type; mangrove forests along the waters' edge; and peat swamp forest along the waterways. On the peninsula, there are three national forests: Taman Negara (or "National Forest") and Kenong Rimba Park, both inland, and Endau Rompin National Park, located toward the southern end of the peninsula. Each of these parks has its own world to explore, whether you prefer quiet nature walks to observe wildlife or hearty adventures like white-water rafting, mountain climbing, spelunking, and jungle trekking. Similarly, the many national forests of Sabah and Sarawak provide a multitude of memorable experiences, which can include brushes with the indigenous peoples of the forests.

Peninsular Malaysia is surrounded by the South China Sea on the east coast and the Strait of Malacca on the west. The peninsula's east coast has a living coral reef, good waters, and gorgeous tropical beaches, and its more southerly parts have beach resort areas. By way of contrast, the surf in southern portions of the Strait of Malacca is choppy and cloudy from shipping traffic, and is hardly ideal for diving or for the perfect Bali Hai vacation. But once you get as far north as Penang, the waters become beautiful again. The sea coast of Sabah and Sarawak has numerous resort areas, and is also ideal for scuba diving. In fact, one of the world's top 10 dive sites is located at Sipadan in Sabah.

## MALAYSIA TODAY

The Malaysia of today is a peaceful nation of many races and ethnicities. The last national census, collected in 1991, placed the population at roughly 17.5 million. Today it's closer to 20 million. Of this number, Bumiputeras are the most numerous ethnic group, broadly speaking. Bumiputeras are those with cultural affinities indigenous to the region and to one another. Technically, this group includes people of the aboriginal groups native to the peninsula—the *orang asli* ("original people"), Malays, and other Malay-related groups, more specifically the ethnic groups found in Sabah and Sarawak such as the Iban, Bidayuh, Melanu, and Kadazan, to name a few. A smaller segment of the population is non-Bumiputera groups such as the Chinese, Indians, Arabs, and Eurasians, most of whom are descended from settlers who came to the region in the past 150 years. It is important to know the difference between the Bumiputera and non-Bumiputera groups to understand Malaysian politics, which favors the former group in every policy. During colonial rule, foreign powers and business people, mainly British, Chinese, and Indian, controlled the government and economy. Since independence, the Malaysian government has attempted to level the playing field for the Bumiputera groups, with questionable success and fairness, to promote a more equitable distribution of wealth and its benefits. Despite ethnic divisions, each group is considered no less Malaysian.

The state religion is **Islam,** with almost all ethnic Malays following Allah and the word of the Prophet Mohammed in the Koran. Islam is reflected in almost every element of the Malaysian lifestyle. In every town, the mosque is the center of life, restaurants serve halal food prepared according to strict Muslim dietary laws, and every hotel room has an arrow on the ceiling to indicate the direction of Mecca. Islam will most likely affect your travel plans in some way. For instance, liquor laws are more stringent than in neighboring nations, business hours can seem very odd in certain parts of the country, and you probably won't feel too comfortable walking around in a tank top and short shorts (which are verboten in traditionally modest and conservative Islamic dress codes).

As for the non-Muslim, life goes on under the government's very serious policy to protect freedom of religion. In multicultural towns such as Georgetown (Penang) or Malacca, you're likely to find churches, mosques, and Buddhist and Hindu temples almost side by side. Many of the *orang asli* tribes and indigenous groups of Sabah and Sarawak practice a religion based upon the presence of a spirit world on earth. While we're on the topic of religion, it is vital to note that despite its "freedom of religion" policy, Malaysia is very anti-Zionist. The local newspapers report anti-Semitic news almost daily, and Israel is the only country in the world to which Malaysia will not allow its citizens to travel. If you carry an Israeli passport, you will need to consult your embassy before considering travel to Malaysia. Jewish people from other countries who still wish to visit are advised to not advertise their religion and culture.

Until the Asian Economic Crisis that began in July 1997, Malaysia was one of the rising stars of the East Asian Miracle, its economy built upon the manufacturing sector in electronics and rubber products, as well as on agriculture and mining. Exports in raw rubber and timber also add to the coffers. At press time, however, Malaysia's gross domestic product had been hit hard by the regional economic crisis, and was estimated to be -8.6%.

The government is headed by a prime minister, a post that for the past 17 years has been held by YAB Dato' Seri Dr. Mahathir Bin Mohamad. Dr. Mahathir has been both criticized and praised for his unique efforts to solve his country's economic troubles. When the ringgit, Malaysia's currency, plummeted in mid-1997, Mahathir chose to ignore IMF advice for economic and debt restructuring—a prescient move, as in later months that advice revealed itself to have been rather bad. The most recent economic reports show that Malaysia, while still hit hard by the crisis, could very well be the nation to bounce back most strongly.

In September 1998 Dr. Mahathir's administration came under international scrutiny when he ousted his deputy prime minister, YAB Dato' Seri Anwar Bin Ibrahim, for alleged sexual misconduct and corruption. There were brief moments of civil unrest in the nation's capital as the population began to suspect that the charges were invented by Dr. Mahathir to ruin Anwar's political career. Demonstrations grew in frequency and numbers during the course of Anwar's trial, but Malaysians have conducted protests in a very peaceful manner to date.

The trial, which was ongoing at the time of writing, prompted some political change in Malaysia. While putting pressure on the media for accurate coverage, citizens called for more political transparency and accountability. As political opposition parties have seen their support base increase, Dr. Mahathir has been campaigning in the hopes that his popularity won't fade before the next election in April 2000.

## A LOOK AT THE PAST

If Malaysia can trace its success to one element, it would be geographic location. Placed strategically at a major crossroads between the Eastern and Western worlds and enforced by the north-east and south-west monsoons, Malaya (as it was known at the time) was the ideal center for east-west trade activities. The development of indigenous Malays is credited to their relationship with the sea, while centuries of outside influences shaped their culture.

The earliest inhabitants of the peninsula were the *orang asli,* who are believed to have migrated from China and Tibet as far back as 5,000 years ago. The first Malays were established by 1000 B.C., migrating not only to Malaya, but also throughout the entire Indonesian archipelago, including Sumatra and Borneo. They brought with them knowledge of agriculture and metalwork as well as beliefs in a spirit world (attitudes that are still practiced by many groups today).

Malaysia's earliest trading contacts were established by the first century B.C. with China and India. India proved most influential, impacting local culture with Buddhist and Hindu beliefs—evidenced today in the Malay language, literature, and many customs.

Recorded history didn't exist until the Malay Annals of the 17th century. These tell the story of **Parameswara,** also known as **Iskander Shah,** ruler of Temasek (Singapore), who was forced to flee to Malacca around 1400 A.D. He set up a trading port and, taking advantage of the favorable geographic location, led the port to world-renowned financial success. Malacca grew in population and prosperity, attracting Chinese, Indian, and Arab traders.

With Arabs and Muslim Indians came Islam, and Iskander Shah's son, who took leadership of Malacca after his father's death, is credited as the first Malay to convert to Islam. The rule of Malacca was transformed into a sultanate, and the word of Islam won converts in not only Malaya, but also throughout Borneo and the Indonesian archipelago. Today the people of this region are very proud to be Muslim by conversion rather than by conquest.

Malacca's success was noted on the world stage, and in 1511 the **Portuguese** decided they wanted a piece of the action. They conquered the city in 30 days, chased the sultanate south to Johor, built a fortress that forestalled any trouble from the populace, and set up Christian missionaries. The Portuguese stuck around until 1641, when the Dutch came to town, looking to expand their trading power in the region. For the record, after Malacca's fall to the Portuguese, its success plummeted and was never regained, even as of today.

The British came around in the late 1700s, when Francis Light of the British East India Company landed on the island of Penang and cut a deal with the Sultan of Kedah to cede the island to the British. By 1805, Penang had become the seat of British authority in Southeast Asia, but the establishment served less as a trading cash cow and more as political leverage in the race to beat out the Dutch for control of the Southeast Asian trade routes. In 1824, the British and Dutch finally signed a treaty dividing Southeast Asia. The British would have Malaya and the Dutch, Indonesia. Dutch-ruled Malacca was traded with British-ruled Bencoolen in Sumatra. In 1826, the British East India Company formed the Straits Settlements, uniting Penang, Malacca, and Singapore under Penang's control. In 1867, power over the Straits Settlements shifted from the British East India Company to British colonial rule in London.

The Anglo-Dutch treaty never provided for the island of Borneo. The Dutch unofficially controlled Kalimantan, but the areas to the northwest were generally under the rule of the Sultan of Brunei. Sabah was ceded for an annual sum to the British North Borneo Company and ruled by London until the Japanese invaded. In 1839, Englishman James Brooke arrived in Sarawak. The Sultan of Brunei had been having a hard time with warring factions in this territory, and was happy to hand over control of it to Brooke. In 1841, after winning allies and subjugating enemies, Brooke became the Raja of Sarawak, building his capital in Kuching.

Meanwhile, back on the peninsula, **Kuala Lumpur** sprang to life in 1857 as a settlement at the confluence of the Klang and Gombak rivers, about 21 miles (35km) inland from the west coast. Tin miners from India, China, and other parts of Malaya had came inland to prospect and set up a trading post, which flourished to such an extent that 40 years later, in 1896, Kuala Lumpur became the capital of the British Malayan territory.

In 1941, the Japanese conquered Malaysia en route to Singapore. Life for Malays during the 4-year occupation was a constant and almost unbearable struggle to survive hunger, disease, and separation from the world.

After the war, when the British sought to reclaim their colonial sovereignty over Malaya, they found the people thoroughly fed up with foreign rule. The resulting struggle for independence served to unite Malay and non-Malay residents throughout the country. By the time the British agreed to Malayan independence, the states were already united. On August 31, 1957, Malaya was cut loose, and Kuala Lumpur became its official capital. For a brief moment in the early 1960s, the peninsula was united with Singapore and the Borneo states of Sabah and Sarawak. Singapore left the federation in 1965, and "Malaysia" continued on its own path.

## MALAYSIAN CULTURE

The mix of cultural influences in Malaysia is the result of centuries of trade and immigration with the outside world, particularly with Arab nations, China, and India. Early groups of incoming foreigners brought wealth from around the world, their own unique cultural heritages, and Islam. Furthermore, once imported, each culture remained largely intact; that is, none have truly been homogenized. Traditional temples and churches exist side by side with mosques.

Likewise, **traditional art forms** of various cultures are still practiced in Malaysia, most notably in the areas of dance and performance art. Chinese opera, Indian dance, and Malay martial arts are all very popular cultural activities. Silat, originating from a martial arts form (and still practiced as such by many), is a dance performed by men and women. Religious and cultural festivals are open for everyone to appreciate and enjoy. Unique arts and traditions of indigenous people distinguish Sabah and Sarawak from the rest of the country.

Traditional **Malaysian music** is very similar to Indonesian music. Heavy on rhythms, its constant drum beats underneath the light repetitive melodies of the stringed gamelan (no relation at all to the Indonesian metallophone gamelan, with its gongs and xylophones) will entrance you with its simple beauty.

### CUISINE

Malaysian food seems to get its origins from India's rich curries and to be influenced by Thailand's herbs and spices. You'll find delicious blends of coconut milk and curry, shrimp paste and chilies, accented by exotic flavors of galangal (similar to turmeric), lime, and lemongrass. Sometimes pungent, a few of the dishes have a deep flavor that is an acquired taste for Western palates. By and large, Malaysian food is delicious, but in multicultural Malaysia, so is Chinese food, Peranakan food, Indian food—the list goes on. The Chinese brought their own flavors from their points of origin in the regions of Southern China. Teochew, Cantonese, and Sichuan are all styles of Chinese cuisine you'll find throughout the country. Peranakan food is unique to Malacca, Penang, and Singapore. The Peranakans or "Straits Chinese" combined local ingredients with some traditional Chinese dishes to create an entirely new culinary form. And Indian food, both northern and southern, can be found in most every city, particularly in the western part of the peninsula. And, of course, you'll find gorgeous fresh seafood almost everywhere.

## 2  Planning a Trip to Malaysia

Malaysia is easily accessible to the rest of the world through its international airport in Kuala Lumpur. Or if you want to hop from another country in the region, daily flights to Malaysia's many smaller airports give you access to all parts of the country.

Also from within the region, there are a variety of ways to enter Malaysia: by car, bus, or train from Singapore or Thailand. In this section I'll run through your options and get you started.

### VISITOR INFORMATION

The **Malaysia Tourism Board (MTB)** can provide some information by way of pamphlets and advice prior to your trip, but keep in mind they are not yet as sophisticated as the Singapore Tourism Board. Much of the information they provide is vague, broad-stroke description with few concrete details that are useful for the traveler.

Overseas offices are located as follows:

### IN THE U.S.

**New York:** 595 Madison Ave., Suite 1800, New York, NY 10022 (☎ 212/754-1113; fax 212/754-1116). **Los Angeles:** 818 W. 7th St., Suite 804, Los Angeles, CA 90017 (☎ 213/689-9702; fax 213/689-1530).

### IN CANADA

**Vancouver:** 830 Burrard St., Vancouver, B.C., Canada V6Z 2K4 (☎ 604/689-8804; fax 604/689-8899).

### IN AUSTRALIA

**Sydney:** 65 York St., Sydney, NSW 2000, Australia (☎ 02/299-4441; fax 02/262-2026). **Perth:** 56 William St., Perth, WA 6000, Australia (☎ 09/481-0400; fax 09/321-1421).

### IN THE U.K.

**London:** 57 Trafalgar Square, London, WC2N 5DU, U.K. (☎ 071/930-7932; fax 071/930-9015).

### IN MALAYSIA

Within Malaysia, the headquarters of the MTB are in Kuala Lumpur at 17–19 Floor, Menara Dato' Onn, Putra World Trade Centre, 45 Jalan Tun Ismail, 50480 Kuala Lumpur (☎ 03/293-5188). For MTB offices in other cities, refer to individual city listings. The official Web site of the Malaysia Tourism Board is http://tourism.gov.my.

### ENTRY REQUIREMENTS

To enter the country you must have a valid passport. Citizens of the United States do not need visas for tourism and business visits. Citizens of Canada, Australia, New Zealand, and the U.K. do not require a visa for tourism or business visits not exceeding 1 month.

If you are traveling from an area infected with yellow fever, you will be required to show proof of yellow fever vaccination. Contact your nearest MTB office to research the specific areas that fall into this category.

### CUSTOMS REGULATIONS

You can enter Malaysia with 1 liter of hard alcohol and one carton of cigarettes. Currency-wise, you are not supposed to bring in more than RM10,000 (US$2,631), and

**Travel Tip**

For up-to-date **currency conversion rates,** visit CNN's Web site at www.cnn.com/travel/currency.

you're not supposed to leave with more than RM5,000 (US$1,315). Due to recent controls on currency speculation, the government is keeping an eye on every ringgit. Upon entry you will be required to claim all of your currency, ringgit or otherwise, and all traveler's checks. When you leave you'll be asked for a tally once again.

Prohibited items include firearms and ammunition, daggers and knives, and pornographic materials. Be advised that, similar to Singapore, Malaysia enforces a very strict drug abuse policy that includes death to convicted drug traffickers.

## MONEY

Malaysia's currency is the Malaysian ringgit. It's also commonly referred to as the Malaysian dollar, but prices are marked as RM (a designation I've used throughout this book). Notes are issued in denominations of RM1, RM2, RM5, RM10, RM20, RM50, RM100, RM500, and RM1,000. One ringgit is equal to 100 sen. Coins come in denominations of 1, 5, 10, 20, and 50 sen, and there's also a 1-ringgit coin.

**CURRENCY EXCHANGE & RATES**    Following the dramatic decline in the value of its currency during the Southeast Asian financial crisis, the Malaysian government has sought to stabilize the ringgit to ward off currency speculation. At the time of writing, exchange rates were RM3.8 to US$1.

Currency can be changed at banks and hotels, but you'll get a more favorable rate if you go to one of the money changers that seem to be everywhere; in shopping centers, in little lanes, and in small stores—just look for signs. They're often men in tiny booths with a lit display on the wall behind them showing the exchange rate. All major currencies are generally accepted, and there is never a problem with the U.S. dollar.

**AUTOMATED-TELLER MACHINES (ATMs)**    Kuala Lumpur, Penang, and Johor Bahru have quite a few automatic-teller machines (ATMs) scattered around, but they're few and far between in the smaller towns. In addition, some ATMs do not accept credit cards or debit cards from your home bank. I have found that debit cards on the Mastercard/Cirrus or Visa/PLUS networks are almost always accepted at **Maybank,** with at least one location in every major town. Cash is dispensed in ringgit deducted from your account at the day's rate.

**TRAVELER'S CHECKS**    Generally, travelers to Malaysia will never go wrong with American Express and Thomas Cook traveler's checks, which can be cashed at banks, hotels, and licensed money changers. Unfortunately, they are often not accepted at smaller shops. Even in some big restaurants and department stores, many cashiers don't know how to process these checks, which might lead to a long and frustrating wait.

**CREDIT CARDS**    Credit cards are widely accepted at hotels and restaurants, and at many shops as well. Most popular are American Express, MasterCard, and Visa. Some banks may also be willing to advance cash against your credit card, but you have to ask around because this facility is not available everywhere.

**LOST/STOLEN CREDIT CARDS**    In Malaysia, to report a lost or stolen American Express card, contact the nearest **American Express** representative office (see individual city listings) or the head office in Kuala Lumpur (☎ **603/213-0000**).

MasterCard and Visa each have numbers that are toll-free from anywhere in the country. For **MasterCard** call ☎ **800-4594,** and for **Visa** ☎ **800-1066.**

## WHEN TO GO

**PEAK SEASON**    There are two peak seasons in Malaysia, one in winter and another in summer. The peak winter tourist season falls from the beginning of December to the end of January, covering the major winter holidays—Christmas, New Year's Day, Chinese New Year, and Hari Raya. Note that due to the monsoon at this time, the east coast of peninsular Malaysia is rainy and the waters are rough. Resort areas, especially Tioman, are deserted. Tourist traffic slows down from February through the end of May, then picks up again in June. The peak summer season falls in the months of June, July, and August, and can last into mid-September. After September it's quiet again until December. Both seasons experience approximately equal tourist traffic, but in summer months that traffic may ebb and flow.

**CLIMATE**    Climate considerations will play a role in your plans. If you plan to visit any of the east coast resort areas, the low season is between November and March, when the monsoon tides make the water too choppy for water sports and beach activities. On the west coast, the rainy season is from April through May, and again from October through November.

The temperature is basically static year-round. Daily averages are between 67°F and 90°F (21°C and 32°C). Temperatures in the hill resorts get a little cooler, averaging 67°F (21°C) during the day and 50°F (10°C) at night.

You will want to pack light, loose-fitting clothes, particularly those of natural fibers. **Women have additional clothing requirements,** as it can sometimes be uncomfortable walking through Muslim streets wearing a short skirt and sleeveless top. In many areas people *will* stare. The traditional dress for Good Muslim Women in Malaysia is that which covers the body, including the legs, arms, and head. And while many Malay women chose to continue this tradition (and with color and pizazz, I might add), those who do not are still perfectly acceptable within Malaysia's contemporary society. As a female traveler I pack slacks and jeans, long skirts and dresses (below the knee is fine), and loose fitting, short-sleeved cotton tops. In modern cities such as Kuala Lumpur, Johor Bahru, Malacca, Penang, and Kuching, I don't feel conspicuous in modest walking shorts, and at beach resorts I'm the first to throw on my bikini and head for the water. I always bring one lightweight long-sleeved blouse and a scarf large enough to cover my head—visits to mosques require it. If you get worried about what's appropriate, the best thing to do is to look around you and follow suit.

A tip for both male and female travelers is to wear shoes that are easily removed. Local custom asks that you remove your shoes before entering any place of worship or home.

**PUBLIC HOLIDAYS**    During Malaysia's official public holidays, expect government offices to be closed, as well as some shops and restaurants, depending on the ethnicity of the shop owner or restaurant owner. **Hari Raya Puasa** and **Chinese New Year** fall on the same dates, during which time Malaysia virtually shuts down for 3 days. Also count on public parks, shopping malls, and beaches to be more crowded, as locals will be taking advantage of their time off.

## HEALTH CONCERNS

The **tap water** in Kuala Lumpur is supposedly potable, but I don't recommend drinking it. Bottled water is inexpensive enough and readily available at convenience stores and food stalls.

# If It's Sunday, It Must Be . . . A Workday?

Malaysia's **work week** varies from state to state. In Kuala Lumpur, the southern states, and East Malaysia you can count on a standard work week, Monday through Friday. However, Fridays are the Muslim day of prayer, and while some places keep opening hours on Fridays, almost every place closes between the hours of noon and about 3pm so their employees can go to the mosque. In the northern states, especially Kelantan and Terengganu, the entire week is modified. It begins on Saturday and continues through Wednesday. Thursday and Friday are to these areas as Saturday and Sunday are to Westerners. This includes government offices, banks, shops, and museums. Many places will keep morning hours on Thursday.

**Food** prepared in hawker centers is generally safe to eat—I have yet to experience trouble and I'll eat almost anywhere. If you buy fresh fruit, wash it well with bottled water and carefully peel the skin off before eating it.

**Malaria** has not been a major threat in most parts of Malaysia, even Malaysian Borneo. **Dengue fever,** on the other hand, which is also carried by mosquitoes, remains a constant threat in most areas, especially rural parts. Dengue, if left untreated, can cause fatal internal hemorrhaging, so if you come down with a sudden fever or skin rash, consult a physician immediately. There are no prophylactic treatments for dengue. The best protection is to wear plenty of insect repellent. Choose a product that contains DEET or is specifically formulated to be effective in the tropics.

Malaysia requires that you present a health certificate if you're arriving in-country from yellow fever endemic zones.

## GETTING THERE
### BY PLANE

Malaysia has five international airports—at Kuala Lumpur, Penang, Langkawi, Kota Kinabalu and Kuching—and 14 domestic airports at locations that include Johor Bahru, Kota Bahru, Kuantan, and Kuala Terengganu. Specific airport information is listed with coverage of each city.

A Passenger Service Charge, or **airport departure tax,** is levied on all flights. The tax is RM5 (US$1.30) for domestic flights and RM40 (US$10.50) for international flights. These charges are usually included when you pay for your ticket.

**FROM THE U.S.**  Malaysia Airlines (☎ **800/552-9264**) flies at least once daily from Los Angeles to Kuala Lumpur, and three times a week from New York.

**FROM CANADA**  Malaysia Airlines (☎ **800/552-9264**) has a flight to KL twice a week from Vancouver.

**FROM THE U.K.**  Malaysia Airlines (☎ **0171/341-2020**) has at least two daily flights from London.

British Airways (☎ **0345/222111,** a local call from anywhere within the U.K.) departs London to KL daily, except on Mondays and Fridays.

**FROM AUSTRALIA**  Malaysia Airlines (☎ **02/132627**) flies at least once a day from Sydney, providing connection service from Melbourne. Qantas Airlines (☎ **02/131211**) provides service from Sydney to KL on Tuesday, Friday, and Saturday.

**FROM NEW ZEALAND**   Malaysia Airlines (☎ **09/373-2741**) has four flights weekly from Auckland and connecting service from Christchurch.

## BY TRAIN

**FROM SINGAPORE**   The Keretapi Tanah Melayu Berhad (KTM), Malaysia's rail system, runs express and local trains that connect the cities along the west coast of Malaysia, with stops in and between Johor Bahru, Kuala Lumpur, and Butterworth. Trains depart three times daily from the Singapore Railway Station (☎ **65/222-5165**), on Keppel Road in Tanjong Pagar, not far from the city center. Fares to Johor Bahru are S$10 (US$6.10) for second-class passage and S$6 (US$3.70) for third class for the half-hour journey (there's no first-class service on this train). Johor Bahru's train station is very centrally located at Jalan Campbell (☎ **07/223-3040**), and taxis are easy to find. Trains to Kuala Lumpur depart five times daily for fares from S$68 (US$41.60) for first class, S$34 (US$20.80) for second class, and S$19 (US$11.60) for third. The trip takes around 6 hours. The Kuala Lumpur Central Railway Station is on Jalan Hishamuddin (☎ **03/274-7435**), also centrally located, with a taxi queue. For Butterworth, the fare is S$127 (US$77.70) first class, S$60 (US$36.70) second class, and S$34 (US$20.80) third class. You will have to change trains in Kuala Lumpur. Please refer to the section on Penang for specific coverage about "getting there" options.

**FROM THAILAND**   KTM's international service departs from the Hua Lamphong Railway Station (☎ **02/223-7010** or 02/223-7020) in Bangkok, with operations to Hua Hin, Surat Thani, Nakhon Si Thammarat, and Hat Yai in Thailand's southern peninsula. The final stop in Malaysia is in Butterworth (Penang), so passage to KL will require you to catch a connecting train onward. The daily service departs at 3:15pm and takes approximately 22 hours from Bangkok to Butterworth. There is no first-class or third-class service on this train, only air-conditioned second class; upper berth goes for 940B, and lower is 1,010B.

   For a fascinating journey from Thailand, you can catch the **Eastern & Orient Express (E&O),** which operates a route between Bangkok, Kuala Lumpur, and Singapore. Traveling in the luxurious style for which the Orient Express is renowned, you'll finish the entire journey in about 42 hours. Compartments are classed as Sleeper (approximately RM3,120/S$2,000/US$1,248 per person double occupancy), State (RM4,395/S$2,790/US$1,758 per person double occupancy), and Presidential (RM8,175/S$5,190/US$3,270 per person double occupancy). All fares include meals on the train. Overseas reservations for the E&O Express can be made through a travel agent or, from the U.S. and Canada, call ☎ 800/524-2420, from Australia ☎ 3/9699-9766, from New Zealand ☎ 9/379-3708, and from the U.K. ☎ 171/805-5100. From Singapore, Malaysia, and Thailand, contact E&O in Singapore at ☎ **65/392-3500.**

## BY BUS

From Singapore, there are many bus routes to Malaysia from the bus terminal at the crossroads of Lavender Street and Kallang Bahru. Buses to Kuala Lumpur leave twice daily and cost S$17 (US$10.40). Contact Hasry Express (☎ **65/294-9306**). To Malacca, Hasry has two daily buses for S$11 (US$6.75).

## BY TAXI (FROM SINGAPORE)

At Queen Street the Singapore Johor Taxi Operators Association (☎ **65/296-7054**) can drive you to Johor Bahru for S$7 (US$4.30) per passenger.

## BY FERRY

Ferries are only convenient for travel to Desaru and Tioman Island in Malaysia. For specific information, please refer to each section in this chapter.

## BY CAR

For convenience, driving to Malaysia from Singapore can't be beat. You can go where you want to go, when you want to go, and without the hassle of public transportation—but it is quite expensive. Cars can be rented in Singapore (see Singapore chapter for details), then driven to and even dropped off in Malaysia. You must have an international driver's license.

# GETTING AROUND

The modernization of Malaysia has made travel here more convenient than ever, so whether it's by plane, train, bus, taxi, or self-driven car, traveling around the peninsula is easy. Malaysia Airlines has service to every major destination within the peninsula and East Malaysia. Buses have a massive web of routes between every city and town. Train service up the western coast provides even more options. And a very unique travel offering—the outstation taxi—is available to and from every city on the peninsula. All the options make it convenient enough for you to plan to hop from city to city and not waste too much precious vacation time. This chapter will help your logistical planning with tips on how to plan a trip with maximum holiday making and minimal frustration.

The first tip here is that people are always abbreviating Kuala Lumpur to "KL." OK, that's pretty obvious. But these people will abbreviate everything else they can get away with. JB is Johor Bahru. KB is Kota Bharu; KK, Kota Kinabalu. You get the picture. To make it easier for you, the only shortened version I've used in this chapter is KL.

By and large, all the modes of transportation between cities are reasonably comfortable. Air travel can be the most costly of the alternatives, followed by outstation taxis, then buses and trains.

## BY PLANE

Malaysia Airlines links from its hub in Kuala Lumpur (☎ 03/764-3000) to the cities of Johor Bahru (☎ 607/334-1001), Kota Bahru (☎ 609/744-7000), Kota Kinabalu (☎ 6088/213-555), Kuala Terengganu (☎ 609/622-1415), Kuantan (☎ 609/515-7055), Kuching (☎ 6082/246-622), Langkawi (☎ 604/966-6622), Penang (☎ 604/262-0011), and other smaller cities not covered in this chapter. The listed phone numbers are for Malaysia Airlines reservations offices in each city. Individual airport information is provided in individual sections on each city that follows. One-way domestic fares can average RM75 (US$19.75) to RM200 (US$52.65).

## BY TRAIN

The Keretapi Tanah Melayu Berhad (KTM) is Malaysia's railway system. Trains run from north to south between Bangkok and Singapore, with stops in between including Butterworth (Penang), Kuala Lumpur, and Johor Bahru. There is a second line that branches off this line at Gemas, midway between Johor Bahru and KL, and heads northeast to Tempas near Kota Bahru. Fares range from RM122 (US$32.10) for first-class passage between Johor Bahru and Butterworth, to RM64 (US$16.85) for first class between Johor Bahru and KL. Train station information is provided for each city beneath individual city headings in this chapter.

KTM has a good deal for students. For US$38, the ISSA Explorer Pass will get you anywhere in Malaysia, Thailand, and Singapore for a week (US$50 for 2 weeks,

US$60 for 3). The deal applies only to students under 30 who carry an ISIC International Student Identity Card, Go Card, or Youth Hostel Card. It's good for travel on second class only. Call Kuala Lumpur (☎ **03/442-4722** or fax 03/443-3707) for more information.

## By Bus

Malaysia's intercity coach system is extensive, reliable, and inexpensive. Buses depart several times daily for many destinations within the peninsula, and fares are charged according to the distance you travel. Air-conditioned express bus service (called Executive Coach service or Business Class) will cost you more, but since the fares are so inexpensive, it's well worth your while to spring the couple dollars extra for the comfort. It costs RM45 (US$11.85) for service from KL to Johor Bahru and to Kota Bharu. Individual bus services and bus terminal locations are listed in each city's subject heading. Note that bus terminals do not provide departure information. Information must be obtained from each independently run bus line.

## By Taxi

You can take taxis, called outstation taxis, between every city and state on the peninsula. Rates depend on the distance you plan to travel. They are fixed, and stated at the beginning of the trip, but many times can be bargained down. In Kuala Lumpur, go to the second level of the Pudu Raya Bus Terminal to find cabs that will take you outside the city. For taxis to destinations outside KL, call the Kuala Lumpur Outstation Taxi Service Station, 123 Jalan Sultan, KL (☎ **03/238-3525**). A taxi from KL to Malacca will cost you approximately RM100 (US$26.30), KL to Cameron Highlands RM150 (US$39.50), KL to Butterworth RM200 (US$52.65), KL to Johor Bahru RM200 (US$52.65). Outstation taxi stand locations are included under each individual city heading.

Also, within each of the smaller cities, feel free to negotiate with unmetered taxis for hourly, half-day, or daily rates. It's an excellent way to get around to see sights and shopping without transportation hassles. Hourly rates are anywhere from RM15 (US$3.95) to RM25 (US$6.60) per hour.

## By Car

As recently as the 1970s, there has been trouble with roadside crime—bandits stopping cars and holding up the travelers inside. Fortunately for drivers in Malaysia, this is a thing of the past. In the mid-1990s, Malaysia opened the North-South Highway, running from Bukit Kayu Hitam in the north on the Thai border and Johor Bahru at the southern tip of the peninsula. The highway (and the lack of bandits) has made travel along the west coast of Malaysia easy. There are rest areas with toilets, food outlets, and emergency telephones intervals along the way. There is also a toll that varies depending on the distance you're traveling.

Driving along the east coast of Malaysia is actually much more pleasant than driving along the west coast. The highway is narrower and older, but it takes you through oil palm and rubber plantations, and the essence of kampung Malaysia permeates throughout. As you near villages you'll often have to slow down and swerve past cows and goats, which are really quite oblivious to oncoming traffic. You have to get very close to honk at them before they move.

The speed limit on highways is 110 kilometers per hour. On the minor highways the limit ranges from 70 to 90 kilometers per hour. Do not speed, as there are traffic police strategically situated around certain bends.

Distances between major towns are: From KL to Johor Bahru, 368 kilometers (221 miles); from KL to Malacca, 144 kilometers (86 miles); from KL to Kuantan, 259 kilometers (155 miles); from KL to Butterworth, 369 kilometers (221 miles); from Johor Bahru to Malacca, 224 kilometers (134 miles); from Johor Bahru to Kuantan, 325 kilometers (195 miles); from Johor Bahru to Mersing, 134 kilometers (80 miles); from Johor Bahru to Butterworth, 737 kilometers (442 miles).

To rent a car in Malaysia, all you need is an International Driver's License. There are desks for major car-rental services at the international airports in Kuala Lumpur and Penang, and additional outlets throughout the country (see individual city sections for this information).

## TIPS ON ACCOMMODATIONS

For western peninsular Malaysia, peak months of the year for hotels are December, January, and February and July, August, and September. For the east coast the busy times are July, August, and September. You will need to make reservations well in advance to secure your room during these months.

**TAXES & SERVICE CHARGES**    All the nonbudget hotels charge 10% service charge and 5% government tax. As such, there is no need to tip. But bellhops still tend to be tipped at least RM2 (US50¢) and car jockeys or valets should be tipped at least RM4 (US$1.05) or more.

**HITCHHIKING**    It's not common among locals and I don't really think it's advisable for you either. The buses between cities are very affordable, so it's a much better idea to opt for those instead.

## TIPS ON DINING

I strongly recommend eating in a hawker stall when you can, especially in Penang, which is famous for its local cuisine.

Also, many Malaysians eat with their hands off banana leaves when they are having nasi padang or nasi kandar (rice with mixed dishes). This is absolutely acceptable. If you choose to follow suit, wash your hands first and try to use your right hand, as the left is considered unclean (traditionally, it's the hand used to wash after a visit to the toilet). While almost all of the food you encounter in a hawker center will be safe for eating, it is advisable to go for freshly cooked hot or soupy dishes. Don't risk the pre-cooked items.

Also, avoid having ice in your drink in the smaller towns, as it may come from a dubious water supply. If you ask for water, either make sure it's boiled or buy mineral water.

**TAXES & SERVICE CHARGES**    A 10% service charge and 5% government tax are levied in proper restaurants, but hawkers charge a flat price.

## TIPS ON SHOPPING

Shopping is a huge attraction for tourists in Malaysia. In addition to modern fashions and electronics, there are great local handicrafts. In each city section, I've listed some great places to go for local shopping.

For handicrafts, prices can vary. There are many handicraft centers, such as Karyaneka, with outlets in cities all over the country, where goods can be priced a bit higher but where you are assured of good quality. Alternatively, you could hunt out bargains in markets and at roadside stores in little towns, which can be much more fun.

Batik is one of the most popular arts in Malaysia, and the fabric can be purchased just about anywhere in the country. Batik can be fashioned into outfits and scarves or can be purchased as sarongs. Another beautiful Malaysian textile craft is songket weaving. These beautiful cloths are woven with metallic threads. Sometimes songket is fashioned into modern clothing, but usually it is sold in sarongs.

Traditional wood carvings have become popular collectors' items. Carvings by *orang asli* groups in peninsular Malaysia and by the indigenous tribes of Sabah and Sarawak have traditional uses in households or ceremonial purposes to cast off evil spirits and cure illness, and have become well sought-after by tourists.

Malaysia's pewter products are famous. Selangor Pewter is the brand that seems to have the most outlets and representation. You can get anything from a picture frame to a mug.

Silver designs are very refined, and jewelry and fine home items are still made by local artisans, especially in the northern parts of the peninsula. In addition, craft items such as *wayang kulit* (shadow puppets) and *wau* (colorful Malay kites) make great gifts and souvenirs.

## Fast Facts: Malaysia

**American Express**   See individual city sections for offices.

**Business Hours**   **Banks** are open from 10am to 2pm Monday through Friday and 9:30 to 11:30am on Saturday. **Government offices** are open from 8am to 12:45pm and 2 to 4:15pm Monday through Friday and from 8am to 12:45pm on Saturday. **Smaller shops** like provision stores may open as early as 6 or 6:30am and close as late as 9pm, especially those near the wet markets. Many such stores are closed on Saturday evenings and Sunday afternoons and are busiest before lunch. Other shops are open 9:30am to 7pm. **Department stores and shops in malls** tend to open later, about 10:30am or 11am till 8:30 or 9pm throughout the week. Bars, except for those in Penang and the seedier bars in Johor Bahru, must close at 1am.

**Dentists & Doctors**   Consultation and treatment fees vary greatly depending on whether the practitioner you have visited operates from a private or public clinic. Your best bet is at a private medical center if your ailment appears serious. These are often expensive but being virtual mini-hospitals, they have the latest equipment. If you just have a flu, it's quite safe to go to a normal MD. The fee at a private center would range from RM20 to RM45 (US$5.30 to US$11.85). Call ☎ **999** for emergencies.

**Drug Laws**   As in Singapore, the death sentence is mandatory for drug trafficking (defined as being in possession of more than 15 grams of heroin or morphine, 200 grams of marijuana or hashish, or 40 grams of cocaine). For lesser quantities you'll be thrown in jail for a very long time and flogged with a cane.

**Electricity**   The voltage used in Malaysia is 220-240V at 50 cycles. The three-point square plugs are used. Buy an adapter if you plan to bring any appliances. Many larger hotels can provide adapters upon request.

**Internet/E-mail**   Service is available to almost all of the nation, and I have found Internet cafes in the most surprisingly remote places. While the major international hotels will have access for their guests in the business center, charges can be very steep. Still, most locally operated hotels do not offer this service for their guests. For each city I have listed at least one alternative, usually for a very inexpensive hourly cost of RM5 (US$1.30) to RM10 (US$2.65).

**Language**   The national language is Bahasa Malaysia, although English is widely spoken. Chinese dialects and Tamil are also spoken.

# Telephone Dialing Info at a Glance

- **To place a call from your home country to Malaysia:** Dial the international access code (011 in the U.S., 0011 in Australia, 0170 in New Zealand, 00 in the U.K.), plus the country code (60), plus the Malaysia area code (Cameron Highlands 5, Desaru 7, Genting Highlands 9, Johor Bahru 7, Kuala Lumpur 3, Kuala Terengganu 9, Kota Bharu 9, Kota Kinabalu 88, Kuantan 9, Kuching 82, Langkawi 4, Malacca 6, Mersing 7, Penang 4, Tioman 9), followed by the six- or seven-digit phone number (for example, from the U.S. to Kuala Lumpur, you'd dial 011 + 60 + 3 + 000-0000).

- **To place a call within Malaysia:** You must use area codes if calling between states. Note that for calls within the country, area codes are preceded by a zero (i.e., Cameron Highlands 05, Desaru 07, Genting Highlands 09, Johor Bahru 07, Kuala Lumpur 03, Kuala Terengganu 09, Kota Bharu 09, Kota Kinabalu 088, Kuantan 09, Kuching 082, Langkawi 04, Malacca 06, Mersing 07, Penang 04, Tioman 09).

- **To place a direct international call from Malaysia:** Dial the international access code (001), plus the country code of the place you are dialing, plus the area/city code, plus the residential number of the other party.

- **To reach the international operator:** Dial ☎ 108.

- **International country codes** are as follows: Australia 61, Burma 95, Cambodia 855, Canada 1, Hong Kong 852, Indonesia 62, Laos 856, New Zealand 64, the Philippines 63, Singapore 65, Thailand 66, U.K. 44, U.S. 1, Vietnam 84.

**Liquor Laws**    Liquor is sold in pubs and supermarkets in all big cities, or in provision stores. You'll hardly find any sold at Tioman though, so bring your own if you're headed there and wish to imbibe. A recent ruling requires pubs and other nightspots to officially close by 1am.

**Newspapers & Magazines**    English-language papers the *New Straits Times, The Star, The Sun,* and *The Edge* can be bought in hotel lobbies and magazine stands. Of the local magazines, *Day & Night* has great listings and local "what's happening" information for travelers.

**Post Offices/Mail**    Post office locations in each city covered are provided in each section. Overseas airmail postage rates are as follows: RM.50 (US15¢) for postcards and RM1.50 (US40¢) for a 100-gram letter.

**Safety/Crime**    While you'll find occasional news reports about house robberies in the countryside, there's not a whole lot of crime going on, especially crime that would impact your trip. There's very little crime against tourists like pickpocketing and purse slashing. Still, hotels without in-room safes will keep valuables in the hotel safe for you. Be careful when traveling on overnight trains and buses. Keep your valuables close to you as you sleep.

**Taxes**    Hotels add a 5% government tax to all hotel rates, plus an additional 10% service charge. Larger restaurants also figure the same 5% tax into your bill, plus a 10% service charge, whereas small coffee shops and hawker stalls don't charge anything above the cost of the meal. While most tourist goods (such as crafts, camera equipment, sports equipment, and cosmetics, and select small electronic items) are tax-free, a small, scaled tax is issued on various other goods such as clothing, shoes, and accessories that you'd buy in the larger shopping malls and department stores.

**Telephones & Faxes**    Most hotels have International Direct Dialing service and will charge extra for calls made using the service.

Local calls can be made from **public phones** using coins or phonecards. Half the public phones (the coin ones) don't seem to work in Malaysia, though they'll happily eat your money. Among those that do work, one point of confusion stems from the fact that some phones take only 20 sen or 50 sen coins while others take 10 sen coins. Those that take the larger coins usually have an option for follow-on calls. If you've only spoken a short time and need to make another call, don't hang up after the first call; instead, just press the follow-on button and you can make another local call.

**Phonecards** can be purchased at convenience stores for stored value amounts. While these cards are much more handy than coins, there are three companies providing coin phone service in Malaysia. Telekom, represented by blue phone boxes, is the most reliable one I've found, and locations are more abundant than those of the two others.

International calls can be made from phones that use cards, or from a telecom office.

See the "Telephone Info: Dialing to & from Malaysia" box in this section for more information.

**Television**    Guests in larger hotels can get satellite channels such as HBO, Star TV, or CNN. Internet cafes are becoming popular in the big cities, allowing you to access the major American news networks through the Internet. Local TV station TV3 shows English-language comedies, movies, and documentaries.

**Time**    Malaysia is 8 hours ahead of Greenwich Mean Time, 16 hours ahead of U.S. Pacific Standard Time, 13 hours ahead of Eastern Standard Time, and 2 hours behind Sydney. It is in the same time zone as Singapore. There is no daylight saving time.

**Tipping**    People don't tip, except to bellhops and car jockeys. For these, an amount not less than RM4 is okay.

**Toilets**    To find a public toilet, ask for the *tandas*. In Malay, *lelaki* is male and *perempuan* is female. Be prepared for pay toilets. Coin collectors sit outside almost every public facility, taking RM20 per person, RM30 if you want paper. Once inside, you'll find it obvious that the money doesn't go for cleaning crews.

**Water**    Water in Kuala Lumpur is supposed to be potable, but most locals boil the water before drinking it—and if that's not a tip-off, I don't know what is. Elsewhere, just be safe and drink mineral water. It costs RM2 to RM2.50 (US50¢ to US65¢) for a 1-liter bottle.

# 3  Kuala Lumpur

Kuala Lumpur (or KL as it is commonly known) is more often than not a traveler's point of entry to Malaysia. As the capital it is the most modern and developed city in the country, with contemporary high-rises and world-class hotels, glitzy shopping malls and international cuisine. Kuala Lumpur is also a modern capital because it wasn't until recent decades that Malaysia selected this place to be its seat of government and center of commerce.

# Kuala Lumpur

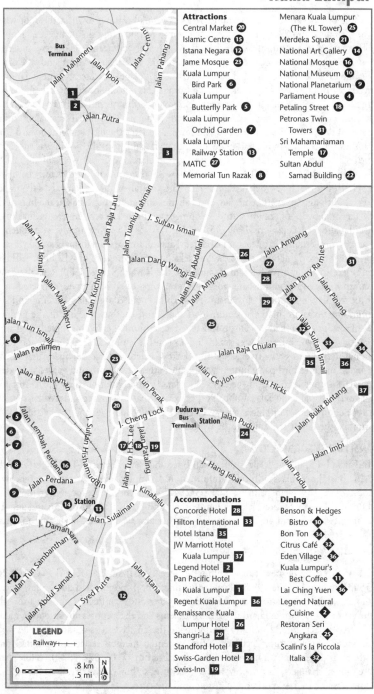

**Attractions**

| | |
|---|---|
| Central Market | 20 |
| Islamic Centre | 15 |
| Istana Negara | 12 |
| Jame Mosque | 23 |
| Kuala Lumpur Bird Park | 6 |
| Kuala Lumpur Butterfly Park | 5 |
| Kuala Lumpur Orchid Garden | 7 |
| Kuala Lumpur Railway Station | 13 |
| MATIC | 27 |
| Memorial Tun Razak | 8 |
| Menara Kuala Lumpur (The KL Tower) | 25 |
| Merdeka Square | 21 |
| National Art Gallery | 14 |
| National Mosque | 16 |
| National Museum | 10 |
| National Planetarium | 9 |
| Parliament House | 4 |
| Petaling Street | 18 |
| Petronas Twin Towers | 31 |
| Sri Mahamariaman Temple | 17 |
| Sultan Abdul Samad Building | 22 |

**Accommodations**

| | |
|---|---|
| Concorde Hotel | 28 |
| Hilton International | 33 |
| Hotel Istana | 35 |
| JW Marriott Hotel Kuala Lumpur | 37 |
| Legend Hotel | 2 |
| Pan Pacific Hotel Kuala Lumpur | 1 |
| Regent Kuala Lumpur | 36 |
| Renaissance Kuala Lumpur Hotel | 26 |
| Shangri-La | 29 |
| Standford Hotel | 3 |
| Swiss-Garden Hotel | 24 |
| Swiss-Inn | 19 |

**Dining**

| | |
|---|---|
| Benson & Hedges Bistro | 30 |
| Bon Ton | 34 |
| Citrus Café | 32 |
| Eden Village | 36 |
| Kuala Lumpur's Best Coffee | 11 |
| Lai Ching Yuen | 36 |
| Legend Natural Cuisine | 2 |
| Restoran Seri Angkara | 25 |
| Scalini's la Piccola Italia | 32 |

**LEGEND**

Railway +++

0 — .8 km
.5 mi

N

The city began sometime around 1857 as a small mining town at the spot where the Gombak and Klang rivers meet, where the Masjid Jame sits in the center of the city. Fueled by tin mining in the nearby Klang river valley, the town grew under the business interests of local Malay Raja Abdullah, a British resident and a Chinese headman (Kapitan China). The industry and village attracted Chinese laborers, Malays from nearby villages, and Indian immigrants who followed the British. And as the town grew, colonial buildings that housed local administrative offices were erected around Merdeka Square, close to Masjid Jame and bounded by Jalan Sultan Hishamuddin and Jalan Kuching. The town, and later the city, spread outward from this center. But life in KL had many difficult starts and stops then—tin was subject to price fluctuations, the Chinese were involved in clan "wars," but worst of all, malaria was killing thousands. Still, in the late 1800s, KL overcame its hurdles to become the capital of the State of Selangor and later the capital of the Federated Malay States (Perak, Selangor, Negeri Sembilan, and Pahang) and got its big break as the hub of the Malayan network of rail lines. Its development continued to accelerate, save for during the Japanese Occupation (1942–45), and it was in 1957 with newly won independence from Britain that Malaysia declared Kuala Lumpur its national capital.

Today the original city center at Merdeka Square is the core of KL's history. Buildings like the Sultan Abdul Samad Building, the Royal Selangor Club, and the Kuala Lumpur Railway Station are gorgeous examples of British style peppered with Moorish flavor. South of this area is KL's Chinatown. Along Jalan Petaling and surrounding areas are markets, shops, food stalls, and the bustling life of the Chinese community. There's also a Little India in KL, around the area occupied by Masjid Jame, where you'll find flower stalls, Indian Muslim and Malay costumes, and traditional items. Across the river you'll find Lake Gardens, a large sanctuary that houses Kuala Lumpur's bird park, butterfly park, and other attractions and gardens. Modern Kuala Lumpur is rooted in the city's "Golden Triangle," bounded by Jalan Ampang, Jalan Tun Razak, and Jalan Imbi. It's this section that is home to most of KL's hotels, office complexes, shopping malls, and sights like the KL Tower and the Petronas Twin Towers, the tallest buildings in the world.

## VISITOR INFORMATION

In Kuala Lumpur, the Malaysia Tourism Board has several offices. The largest is at the MATIC, the Malaysia Tourist Information Complex (see "Attractions," below), located on 109 Jalan Ampang (☎ **03/254-3929**); another is located at the Kuala Lumpur Railway Station, Jalan Sultan Hishamuddin (☎ **03/274-6063**); and another is at the Putra World Trade Centre, Level 2, Menara Dato 'Onn, 45 Jalan Tun Ismail (☎ **03/441-1295**).

## GETTING THERE

**BY PLANE**  The new Kuala Lumpur International Airport (KLIA) (☎ **03/826-5503**) opened in June 1998. Although its first 2 or 3 months had quite a few operational problems such as misdirected baggage and confusing sign boards, the government has worked hard to fix the problems and the airport runs smoothly today. Located in Sepang, 32 miles (53km) outside the city, KLIA is a huge complex with business centers, dining facilities, a fitness center, medical services, shopping, post offices, and an airport hotel operated by Pan Pacific (☎ **03/878-7333**). While there are money changers, they are few and far between, so hop on the first line you see, and don't assume there's another one just around the corner.

From KLIA, domestic flights can be taken to almost every major city in the country.

There are several options to town from the airport. There's a 24-hour express bus service that takes you as far as the Tun Razak Hockey Stadium. The Luxury Coach

(RM25) departs every 15 minutes, and the Semi Luxury (RM18) every hour. City taxis are not permitted to pick up fares from the airport, but from the Stadium you can take a taxi to the city. Airport Limousines operate round the clock. Coupons must be purchased at the arrival concourse for Premier Service (Mercedes–RM88) or Budget Service (Malaysian built Proton–RM65).

**BY BUS**   There's more than one bus terminal in Kuala Lumpur, and it can be somewhat confusing. The main bus terminal, Puduraya Bus Terminal, is on Jalan Pudu right in the center of town—literally. Buses heading in and out of the station block traffic along already congested city streets, spewing noxious gasses. The terminal itself is hot, filthy, and noisy; the heavy metal boom box wars between the provision shops is amusing for about 30 seconds. This terminal deals with bus routes to all over the country, but more specifically to areas on the west coast from north to south. Buses to Penang or Malacca will leave from here. I personally think Puduraya is a mess to be avoided at all costs. It is a well-kept secret that many business class and executive coaches to Penang, Johor Bahru, and Singapore depart peacefully from the KL Railway Station. A far saner alternative.

The other main terminals are the Putra Bus Terminal on Jalan Tun Ismail just across from the Putra World Trade Centre; and the Pekililing terminal on Jalan Ipoh, also not far from Putra WTC. Both terminals deal primarily with buses to East Coast cities such as Kota Bharu, Kuala Terengganu, and Kuantan.

The bus terminals have no telephone numbers in their own right. Inquiries must be made directly to individual bus companies.

**BY TAXI**   The outstation taxi stand in Kuala Lumpur is located at Puduraya Bus Terminal on Jalan Pudu. Call ☎ **03/232-6504** for booking to any city on the peninsula. Fares will run you about RM200 (US$52.65) to Cameron Highlands, RM130 (US$34.20) to Malacca, RM200 (US$52.65) to Johor Bahru, and RM250 (US$65.80) to Penang and to Kuantan. These taxis can pick you up at your hotel for an additional RM10 (US$2.65).

## Fast Facts: Kuala Lumpur

**Banks/Currency Exchange**   Banks are located all over the city. Other currency exchanges are concentrated around Jalan Hang Lekir.

**Internet/E-mail**   Internet cafes around town include Kafe Sibir Identity, on the 3rd floor of The Mall Shopping Center on Jalan Putra, next to the Legend Hotel, and Masterworld Surfnet Cafe, 23 Jalan Petaling, 2nd floor, across the street from Kota Raya shopping center.

**Post Office/Mail**   The general post office is on Jalan Sultan Hishamuddin (☎ 03/274-1122).

### GETTING AROUND

Kuala Lumpur is a prime example of a city that was not planned, per se, from a master graph of streets. Rather, because of its beginnings as an outpost, it grew as it needed to, expanding outward and swallowing up suburbs. The result is a tangled web of streets too narrow to support the traffic of a capital city. Cars and buses weave through one-way lanes, with countless motorbikes sneaking in and out, sometimes in the opposite direction of traffic or up on the sidewalks. Expect traffic jams in the morning rush between 6 and 9am, and again between 4 and 7pm. At other times, taxis are a convenient way of getting around, as the LRT (commuter railway) doesn't hit areas most frequented by tourists, and buses are hot and crowded with some very confusing routes. Walking can also be frustrating. Many sidewalks are in poor condition, with buckled tiles and gaping gutters. The heat can be prohibitive as well. However, areas within the colonial heart of the city, Chinatown, Little India, and some areas in the Golden Triangle are within walking distance of each other.

**BY TAXI**   Taxis around town can be waved down by the side of the road, or can be caught at taxi stands outside shopping complexes or hotels. The metered fare is RM1.50 (US40¢) for the first kilometer and an additional 10 sen for each 200 meters after that. Between midnight and 6am you'll be charged an extra 50% of the total fare. If you call ahead for a cab, there's an extra charge of RM1 (US25¢). Government regulations have made it compulsory for cabbies to charge the metered fare, but some still try to fix a price, which is invariably higher than what the metered fare would be.

   To request a cab pickup, call KL Hotline Cab at ☎ **03/255-3399.**

**BY BUS**   There are regular city buses and minibuses to take you around the city. The fare is 20 sen (US5¢) for the first kilometer and 5 sen for each additional kilometer. Know, however, that the buses in Kuala Lumpur are not dependable. You can wait at a stop for a long time only to find when the bus arrives that it's hot and packed so full that passengers seem to be hanging out every window. It's not the most relaxing way to get around.

**BY RAIL**   The LRT, or Light Rail Transit, has opened its first phase in Kuala Lumpur. It covers a 7.4-mile (12km) circuit, with 13 stops between Sultan Ismail and Ampang. The cost is 75 sen (US20¢) between stations, the longest ride costing RM2.95 (US80¢). Tickets are purchased at LRT stations. Stored value cards can be purchased in increments of RM20 (US$5.30) and RM50 (US$13.15). The system operates from 6am to midnight daily, with trains every 5 to 10 minutes.

**ON FOOT**   The heat and humidity can make walking between attractions pretty uncomfortable. However, sometimes the traffic is so unbearable that you'll get where you're going much faster by strapping on your tennis shoes and hiking it.

## ACCOMMODATIONS

There are dozens of hotels in Kuala Lumpur, most of them within city limits—an especially large number of them in the Golden Triangle area. Other hotels listed in this chapter are located in the Chinatown area, within walking distance of plenty of shopping attractions and nightlife.

### VERY EXPENSIVE

✪ **The Regent Kuala Lumpur.** 160 Jalan Bukit Bintang, 55100 Kuala Lumpur. ☎ **800/545-4000** from the U.S. and Canada, 800/022-800 from Australia, 0800/440-800 from New Zealand, 0800/282-245 from the U.K., or 03/241-8000. Fax 03/242-1441. 468 units. A/C MINIBAR TV TEL. RM500–RM570 (US$132–US$150) double; RM670–RM2,100 (US$176–US$553) suite. AE, DC, JCB, MC, V.

Of the five-star properties in Kuala Lumpur, nobody delivers first class accommodations with the finesse of The Regent. The lobby and guest rooms are contemporary and elegant, without a single sacrifice to comfort. Touches like soft armchairs and cozy comforters in each room will make you want to check in and never leave, and the large marble bathrooms will make you feel like a million bucks even on a bad hair day. The outdoor pool is a palm-lined freeform escape, and the fitness center is state-of-the-art, with sauna, steam, spa, and Jacuzzi.

**Renaissance Kuala Lumpur Hotel.** Corner of Jalan Sultan Ismail and Jalan Ampang, 50450 Kuala Lumpur. ☎ **800/HOTELS1** from the U.S. and Canada, 02/251-8484 from Sydney, 800/222431 from elsewhere in Australia, 0800/441111 from New Zealand, 0800/181738 from the U.K., 800/7272 toll free in Malaysia, or 03/262-2233. Fax 03/263-1122. 400 units. A/C MINIBAR TV TEL. RM535 (US$141) double, RM755 (US$199) club double; from RM855 (US$225) suite. AE, DC, JCB, MC, V.

The Renaissance is definitely geared to satisfying the needs of very discriminating travelers, and has become a very elegant address in KL. The lobby is a huge oval colonnade with a domed ceiling and massive marble columns rising from the sides of a geometric star burst on the floor. You could be walking into a futuristic version of Washington, D.C.'s Capitol Building. The guest rooms have an equally "official" feel to them—very bold and impressive, and completely European in style. In fact, you'll never know you're in Malaysia. Facilities include a very large free-form outdoor pool with beautiful landscaped terraces. The fitness center is one of the largest I've seen—and one of the most active, attracting private members from outside the hotel. It also has Jacuzzi and sauna. Other facilities include two outdoor tennis courts, a launderette, and a shopping arcade.

## EXPENSIVE

**Hotel Istana.** 73 Jalan Raja Chulan, 50200 Kuala Lumpur. ☎ **800/883-380** or 03/241-9988. Fax 03/244-0111. 593 units. A/C MINIBAR TV TEL. RM460–RM510 (US$121–US$134) double; RM650–RM850 (US$171–US$223) executive club; RM950 (US$250) suite. AE, DC, JCB, MC, V.

Fashioned after a Malay palace, Hotel Istana is rich with Moorish architectural elements, and songket weaving patterns are featured in decor elements throughout. The guest rooms have Malaysian touches like handwoven carpets and upholstery in local fabric designs, capturing the exotic flavor of the culture without sacrificing modern comfort and convenience. Located on Jalan Raja Chulan, Istana is in a favorable Golden Triangle location, with walking to shopping and some of the sights in that area. Ask about big rate discounts in the summer months. Facilities include a large outdoor pool in a landscaped courtyard, a fitness center with Jacuzzi and sauna, two outdoor tennis courts, a launderette, and a shopping arcade.

**JW Marriott Hotel Kuala Lumpur.** 183 Jalan Bukit Bintang, 55100 Kuala Lumpur. ☎ **800/228-9290** from the U.S. and Canada, 02/299-1614 from Sydney, 800/251259 from elsewhere in Australia, 0800/221222 from the U.K., or 03/925-9000. Fax 03/925-7000. 552 units. A/C MINIBAR TV TEL. RM490 double (US$128), RM590 (US$155) executive double; RM750 (US$197) suite. AE, DC, JCB, MC, V.

Opened in July 1997, the Marriott is still one of the newest hotels in town. The smallish lobby area still allows for a very dramatic entrance, complete with wrought iron filigree and marble. Modern styling in the guest rooms is sleek, in deep greens and reds. The decor is European in flavor with plush carpeting, large desks, and a leather executive chair for great work space. The staff is very motivated and enthusiastic. Another great plus—the hotel neighbors some of the most upmarket and trendy shopping complexes in the city. Facilities include a large outdoor pool; a very modern fitness center with Jacuzzi, sauna and spa; one outdoor tennis court; use of a nearby golf course; and a shopping arcade.

✪ **Kuala Lumpur Hilton International.** Jalan Sultan Ismail, 50250 Kuala Lumpur. ☎ **800/445-8667** from the U.S. and Canada, 800/222-255 from Australia (Sydney 02/9209-5209), 0800/448-002 from New Zealand. www.hilton.com. 577 units. A/C MINIBAR TV TEL. RM483–RM563 (US$127–US$148) double; RM684 (US$180) executive double; RM598–RM4,715 (US$157–US$1,240) suites. AE, DC, JCB, MC, V.

The Hilton opened in 1973, making it one of the leaders in world-class hotels in Kuala Lumpur. Situated on Jalan Sultan Ismail, it's in the middle of the business and shopping heart of the city. The hotel is set back from the road, stately and quiet, giving guests a bit of peace and quiet. The guest rooms are very spacious, with separate dressing areas, a sitting area, and nice desk space. City view rooms deliver fantastically on what they promise. Facilities include a small outdoor pool (with a view of the Petronas Twin Towers) and a popular fitness center with massage, sauna, steam, and facials. There's also a shopping arcade.

**The Pan Pacific Hotel Kuala Lumpur.** Jalan Putra, P.O. Box 11468, 50746 Kuala Lumpur. ☎ **800/327-8585** from the U.S. and Canada, 02/923-37888 from Sydney, 800/625959 from elsewhere in Australia, 800/8555 toll free within Malaysia, or 03/442-5555. Fax 03/441-7236. 565 units. A/C MINIBAR TV TEL. RM420–RM440 (US$110–US$115) double. AE, DC, JCB, MC, V.

One thing you'll love about staying at the Pan Pacific is the view from the glass elevator as you drift up to your floor. The atrium lobby inside is bright and airy and filled with the scent of jasmine, and the hotel staff handles the demands of its international clientele with courtesy and professionalism. The rooms are spacious and stately. Sunken windows with lattice work frame each view. Facilities include a mid-sized outdoor pool, fitness center with Jacuzzi and sauna, and squash and tennis courts.

✪ **The Shangri-La Hotel Kuala Lumpur.** 11 Jalan Sultan Ismail, 50250 Kuala Lumpur. ☎ **800/942-5050** from the U.S. and Canada, 800/222/448 from Australia (02/926202588 Sydney), 0800/442-179 from New Zealand, or 03/230-1514. Fax 03/230-1514. 681 units. A/C MINIBAR TV TEL. US$157–US$164 double; US$234–US$353 executive club rooms; US$411–US$1,343 suite. AE, DC, JCB, MC, V.

I don't know how they do it, but Shangri-La can always take what could easily be a dull building in a busy city and turn it into a resort-style garden oasis. Their property in KL is no different. With attention paid to landscaping and greenery, the hotel is one of the more attractive places to stay in town. The guest rooms are large with cooling colors and nice views of the city. Also recently renovated are the outdoor pool area and the fitness center (with totally new equipment). Other facilities include a travel office and a shopping arcade.

## MODERATE

✪ **Concorde Hotel Kuala Lumpur.** 2 Jalan Sultan Ismail, 50250 Kuala Lumpur. ☎ **03/244-2200.** Fax 03/244-1628. 610 units. A/C MINIBAR TV TEL. RM220–RM460 (US$58–US$121) double; RM600–RM3,000 (US$158–US$789) suite. AE, DC, JCB, MC, V.

Jalan Sultan Ismail is the address for the big names in hotels, like Shangri-La and Hilton, but tucked alongside the giants is The Concorde, a very reasonably priced choice. What's best about staying here is that you don't sacrifice amenities and services for the lower cost. Although rooms are not as large as those in the major hotels, they're well outfitted in an up-to-date style that can compete with the best of them. Choose Concorde if you'd like location and comfort for less. It also has a small outdoor pool facing a fitness center. A well-equipped business center adds additional value.

**The Legend Hotel.** Putra Place, 100 Jalan Putra, 50350 Kuala Lumpur. ☎ **800/637-7200** from the U.S., 1800/655147 from Australia, 0800/25-28-40 from the U.K., or 03/442-9888. Fax 03/443-0700. 400 units. A/C MINIBAR TV TEL. RM360–RM390 (US$95–US$102) double; RM480 (US$126) legend crest; RM680 (US$179) executive suite. AE, DC, JCB, MC, V.

Lovely marble in earthy tones creates a luxurious atmosphere in the Legend's public space, which is enhanced with Chinese touches such as carved wood furniture and terra-cotta warrior statues—and since the lobby is located nine stories above street level, there's not the usual commotion in it. Guest rooms are spacious, and all overlook the city, but ask to face the Twin Towers for the best view. Also, the less expensive rooms seem to have the nicest decor—with soft tones and modern touches. The Crest rooms are rather strange—mine had a bright pink frilly bed cover. Facilities

include an outdoor pool, fitness center with Jacuzzi and sauna, squash courts, a launderette, and a shopping arcade.

✪ **Swiss-Garden Hotel.** 117 Jalan Pudu, 55100 Kuala Lumpur. ☎ **800/3093** (toll-free
Malaysia) or 03/241-3333. Fax 03/241-5555. www.sgihotels.com.my. 326 units. A/C
MINIBAR TV TEL. RM300–RM350 (US$79–US$92) double; RM410–RM550 (US$108–US$145)
suite. AE, DC, JCB, MC, V.

For mid-range prices, Swiss-Garden offers reliable comfort, good location, and afford-
ability that attracts many leisure travelers to its doors. It also knows how to make you
feel right at home, with a friendly staff (the concierge is on the ball) and a hotel lobby
bar that actually gets patronized—by travelers having cool cocktails at the end of a
busy day of sightseeing. The guest rooms are simply furnished, but are neat and comfortable. Swiss-Garden is just walking distance from KL's lively Chinatown district,
and close to the Puduraya bus station. Facilities include an outdoor pool and a gym.

### INEXPENSIVE

**Stanford Hotel.** 449 Jalan Tuanku Abdul Rahman, 50100 Kuala Lumpur. ☎ **03/291-9833.**
Fax 03/291-3103. 168 units. A/C TV TEL. RM166–RM235 (US$44–US$62) double. AE, MC, V.

A good alternative for the budget-conscious traveler is the Stanford Hotel. The lobby
feels like a mini-version of a more upmarket hotel lobby, and with new carpeting in
the corridors and guest rooms, fresh paint, and refurbished furnishings and bathrooms, the place provides accommodations that are good value for your money. Some
of the rooms even have lovely views of the Petronas Twin Towers. Discounted rates as
low as RM100 (US$28.60) can be had if you ask about promotions. Facilities are thin,
with only a small business center and a coffee house with decent local dishes.

**Swiss-Inn.** 62 Jalan Sultan, 50000 Kuala Lumpur. ☎ **03/232-3333.** Fax 03/201-6699.
www.sgihotels.com.my. 110 units. A/C TV TEL. RM130 (US$34) standard; RM145 (US$38)
superior; RM160 (US$42) deluxe. AE, DC, JCB, MC, V.

You can't beat the Swiss-Inn for comfortable and modern accommodations in Kuala
Lumpur. Tucked away in the heart of Chinatown, just beyond this hotel's small lobby
is the action of the street markets and hawkers. The place is small and offers almost
no facilities, but the compact rooms are clean and adequate. Best yet, discounts here
can bring the rates down under RM100 (US$28.60) (beware, lower category rooms
have no windows). Make sure you reserve your room early, because this place runs
high occupancy year-round. The hotel offers in-house movies and has a 24-hour sidewalk coffee house. Guests have access to the Swiss-Garden Hotel's fitness center.

## DINING

Kuala Lumpur, like Singapore, is very cosmopolitan. Here you'll find not only delicious and exotic cuisine, but some pretty trendy settings.

**Benson & Hedges Bistro.** Ground floor, Life Centre, Jalan Sultan Ismail. ☎ **03/264-4426.**
Reservations not accepted. Entrees RM13.50–RM35 (US$3.55–US$9.20). AE, DC, MC, V. Daily
7–10am for breakfast, 11am–3pm lunch; Sun–Thurs dinner 6pm–midnight, Fri–Sat 6pm–2am.
TEX MEX/AMERICAN.

The latest in trendy hangouts, this bistro is part coffee bar and part restaurant, decorated in contemporary style, with mood lighting glistening off bronze coffee bean dis-
pensers. While it's not a place for a special night out, it is an excellent choice for a
quick bite in a fun and laid-back atmosphere. Staff is dressed in black, with casual and
hip attitudes. Good entrees are the chicken piccata, roast duck lasagna, or blackened
rack of lamb. Reservations are not accepted, and on the weekends the wait can be long,
partly because no one will ever rush you to get you out. In short: Be there early.

⭐ **Bon Ton.** No. 7 Jalan Kia Peng. ☎ **03/241-3611.** Reservations recommended. Entrees RM20–RM55 (US$5.25–US$14.50). Set meals RM40–RM101 (US$10.55–US$26.60). AE, DC, MC, V. Lunch Mon–Fri noon–2:30pm. Dinner daily 6–10:30pm. ASIAN MIX.

Let me tell you about my favorite restaurant in Kuala Lumpur. First, Bon Ton has an incredible atmosphere. In a 1930s bungalow that was once a school, the place winds through room after room, its walls painted in bright hues and furnished with an assortment of mixed and matched teak tables, chairs, and antiques. Second, the menu is fabulous. While à la carte is available, Bon Ton puts together theme set meals. You have 12 to chose from—Nonya, Malacca Portuguese, Traditional Malay, even vegetarian. They're all brilliant.

**Citrus Café.** 19 Jalan Sultan Ismail. ☎ **03/242-5188.** Entrees RM24–RM46 (US$6.30–US$12.10). AE, DC, JCB, MC, V. Daily: lunch noon–2:30pm; dinner 6–10:30pm. ASIAN MIX.

This place has become very popular with the yuppie international set—locals, expatriates, and tourists alike. The theme is Asia, contemporary style. It's reflected in the decor, music, and cuisine, which ranges from Malay to Thai to Japanese, with some Western elements thrown in too. The dining room, sushi bar, and terrace cafe are sparse and minimal. Dishes like the rotisserie chicken and the special sushi rolls are served in portions to share at your table.

⭐ **Eden Village.** 260 Jalan Raja Chulan. ☎ **03/241-4027.** Reservations recommended. Entrees RM18–RM100 (US$4.75–US$26.30) and up. AE, MC, V. Daily noon–3pm and 7pm to midnight, except lunch on Sunday. SEAFOOD.

Uniquely designed inside and out to resemble a Malay house, Eden Village has great local atmosphere. Waitresses are clad in traditional sarong kebaya, and serve up popular dishes like braised shark's fin in a clay pot with crabmeat and roe; and the Kingdom of the Sea, a half lobster baked with prawns, crab, and cuttlefish. The terrace seating is the best in the house.

⭐ **Lai Ching Yuen.** The Regent Kuala Lumpur, 160 Jalan Bukit Bintang. ☎ **03/249-4250.** Reservations recommended. Entrees RM26–RM32. AE, DC, JCB, MC, V. Lunch noon–2:30pm; dinner 6:30–10:30pm daily. CANTONESE.

In the Regent's signature elegant style, dining is truly fine at Lai Ching Yuen. With delicacies like shark's fin, bird's nest, abalone, and barbecue specialties, the menu is extensive. A lunchtime dim sum and set lunch menu are also excellent. Each dish is presented as a piece of art. The restaurant is large and sectioned with etched glass panels. Gorgeous accents are added with modern Chinese art and silver and jade table settings.

**Legend Natural Cuisine.** The Legend Hotel and Apartments, 100 Jalan Putra. ☎ **03/442-9888.** Reservations recommended for lunch and dinner; required for high tea. Entrees RM28–RM50; set dinner RM60. AE, DC, JCB, MC, V. Daily 6:30am–1am. INTERNATIONAL.

Natural Cuisine's menu is selected by dieticians, its dishes incorporating organically grown produce and calorie conscious recipes with a mind toward health awareness. Off the Legend Hotel's lobby, the restaurant is spacious and cozy, and the food is so good you'll never know it's healthy. It's easy to forget about dieting when you're traveling, but Legend's Natural Cuisine makes it incredibly easy to stick to one. Try the barbecued lamb kebab sautéed in garlic and sherry. The roasted garlic soup is an unbelievably good appetizer.

**Restoran Seri Angkasa.** Jalan Punchak, off Jalan P. Ramlee. ☎ **03/208-5055.** Reservations recommended. Lunch buffet RM55 (US$14.50); dinner buffet RM70 (US$18.40). AE, DC, MC, V. Daily: lunch noon–2:30pm; high tea 3:30–5:30pm; dinner 6:30–11pm. MALAYSIAN.

At the top of the Menara KL (KL Tower) is Restoran Seri Angkasa, a revolving restaurant with the best view in the city. Better still, it's a great way to try all the Malay, Chinese, and Indian inspired local dishes at a convenient buffet, with a chance to taste just about everything you have room for—like nasi goreng, clay-pot noodles, or beef rendang.

✪ **Scalini's la Piccola Italia.** 19 Jalan Sultan Ismail. ☎ **03/245-3211.** Reservations recommended. Entrees RM26–RM58 (US$6.85–US$15.25). AE, DC, MC, V. Sun–Thurs noon–2:30pm and 6–10:30pm, Fri noon–2:30pm and 6–11pm, Sat 6–11pm. ITALIAN.

Four chefs from Italy create the dishes that make Scalini's a favorite among KL locals and expatriates. From a very extensive menu you can select pasta, pesce, and carni, as well as a large selection of pizzas. The specials are superb and change all the time. Some of the best dishes are salmon with creamed asparagus sauce, and ravioli with goat cheese and zucchini. Scalini's has a large wine selection (that is actually part of the romantic decor) with labels from California, Australia, New Zealand, France, and, of course, Italy.

## ATTRACTIONS

Most of Kuala Lumpur's historic sights are located in the area around Merdeka Square/Jalan Hishamuddin, while many of the gardens, parks, and museums are out at Lake Gardens. Taxi fare between the two areas will run you about RM5 (US$1.30).

✪ **Central Market.** Jalan Benteng. ☎ **03/274-6542.** Daily 10am–10pm. Shops until 8pm.

The original Central Market, built in 1936, used to be a wet market, but the place is now a cultural center (air-conditioned!) for local artists and craftspeople selling antiques, crafts, and curios. It is a fantastic place for buying Malaysian crafts and souvenirs, with two floors of shops to chose from. The Central Market also stages evening performances (at 7:45pm) of Malay martial arts, Indian classical dance, or Chinese orchestra. Call the number above for performance information.

**Kuala Lumpur Railway Station.** Jalan Sultan Hishamuddin. ☎ **03/274-9422.** Daily 7:30am–10:30pm.

Built in 1910, the KL Railway Station is a beautiful example of Moorish architecture.

✪ **National Museum (Muzim Negara).** Jalan Damansara. ☎ **03/282-6255.** Admission RM1 (US25¢). Sat–Thurs 9am–6pm, Fri 9am–noon and 3–6pm.

Located at Lake Gardens, the museum has over 1,000 items of historic, cultural, and traditional significance, including art, weapons, musical instruments, and costumes.

**National Art Gallery.** Jalan Sultan Hishamuddin (across from the KL Railway Station). ☎ **03/230-0157.** Free admission. Sat–Thurs 10am–6pm, Fri 10am–noon and 3–6pm.

The building that now houses the National Art Gallery was built as the Majestic Hotel in 1932 and has been restored to display contemporary works by Malaysian artists. There are international exhibits as well.

**National Mosque (Masjid Negara).** Jalan Sultan Hishamuddin (near the KL Railway Station).

Built in a modern design, the most distinguishing features of the mosque are its 243-foot (73m) minaret and the umbrella-shaped roof, which is said to symbolize a newly independent Malaysia's aspirations for the future. Could be true, as the place was built in 1965.

**Sultan Abdul Samad Building.** Jalan Raja.

In 1897 this exotic building was designed by Regent Alfred John Bidwell, a colonial architect responsible for many of the buildings in Singapore. He chose a style called

"Muhammadan" or "Neo-saracenic," which combines Indian Muslim architecture with Gothic and other Western elements. Built to house government administrative offices, today it is the home of Malaysia's Supreme and High Courts.

**Merdeka Square.** Jalan Raja.

Surrounded by colonial architecture with an exotic local flair, the square is a large field that was once the site of British social and sporting events. These days, Malaysia holds its spectacular Independence Day celebrations on the field, which is home to the world's tallest flagpole, standing at 330 feet (100m).

**National Planetarium.** Lake Gardens. ☎ **03/273-5484.** Admission to exhibition hall RM10 (US$2.65), extra charges for screenings. Sat–Thurs 10am–7pm, Fri 10am–noon and 2:30–7pm.

The National Planetarium has a Space Hall with touch screen interactive computers and hands-on experiments, a Viewing Gallery with binoculars for a panoramic view of the city, and an Ancient Observatory Park with models of Chinese and Indian astronomy systems. The Space Theatre has two different outer space shows.

✪ **Jame Mosque (Masjid Jame).** Jalan Tun Terak.

The first settlers landed in Kuala Lumpur at the spot where the Gombak and Klang rivers meet, and in 1909 a mosque was built here. Styled after an Indian Muslim design, it is one of the oldest mosques in the city.

**Petronas Twin Towers.** Kuala Lumpur City Centre.

After 5 years of planning and building, Petronas Twin Towers has been completed. Standing at a whopping 1,482 feet (451.9m) above street level, the towers are the tallest buildings in the world. From the outside, the structures are designed with the kind of geometric patterns common to Islamic architecture, and on levels 41 and 42 the two towers are linked by a bridge. Opened just after the regional economic crisis, the towers' combined 88 floors are half empty—not because tourists aren't allowed in to look around, but because they can't rent the space.

**Islamic Centre.** Jalan Perdana. ☎ **03/274-9333.** Daily 7:30am–4:45pm; except Friday 7:30am–12:15pm and 2:30–4:45pm.

The seat of Islamic learning in Kuala Lumpur, the center has displays of Islamic texts, artifacts, porcelain, and weaponry.

**Istana Negara.** Jalan Negara.

Closed to the public, this is the official residence of the king. You can peek through the gates at the *istana* (palace) and its lovely grounds.

✪ **Menara Kuala Lumpur (The KL Tower).** Bukit Nanas. ☎ **03/208-5448.** Adult RM8 (US$2.10); child RM3 (US80¢). Daily 10am–10pm.

Standing 1,389 feet (421m) tall, this concrete structure is the third tallest tower in the world, and the views from the top reach to the far corners of the city and beyond. At the top, the glass windows are fashioned after the Shah Mosque in Isfahan, Iran.

**MATIC (Malaysia Tourist Information Complex).** Jalan Ampang. ☎ **03/264-3929.** Daily 9am–6pm.

At MATIC you'll find an exhibit hall, tourist information services for Kuala Lumpur and Malaysia, and other travel-planning services. On Tuesdays, Thursdays, Saturdays, and Sundays, there are cultural shows at 3:30pm. Shows are RM2 (US50¢) for adults, RM1 (US25¢) for children.

**Kuala Lumpur Lake Gardens (Taman Tasik Perdana).** Enter via Jalan Parliament. Free admission. Daily 9am–6pm.

Built around an artificial lake, the 229-acre (91.6-hectare) park has plenty of space for jogging and rowing, and has a playground for the kids. It's the most popular park in Kuala Lumpur.

**Kuala Lumpur Orchid Garden.** Jalan Perdana. ☎ **03/291-6011.** Adults RM5 (US$1.30), children RM2 (US50¢). Daily 9am–6pm.

This garden has a collection of over 800 orchid species from Malaysia, and also contains thousands of international varieties.

**Kuala Lumpur Bird Park.** Jalan Perdana. ☎ **03/291-6011.** Adults RM3 (US80¢), children RM1 (US25¢). Daily 9am–5pm.

Nestled in beautifully landscaped gardens, the bird park has over 2,000 birds within its 8 acres (3.2 hectares).

**Kuala Lumpur Butterfly Park.** Jalan Cenderasari. ☎ **03/293-4799.** Adults RM4 (US$1.05), children RM2 (US50¢). Daily 9am–6pm.

Over 6,000 butterflies belonging to 120 species make their home in this park, which has been landscaped with more than 15,000 plants to simulate the butterflies' natural rain forest environment. There are also other small animals and an insect museum.

**Memorial Tun Razak.** Jalan Perdana. ☎ **03/291-2111.** Free admission. Tues–Thurs and Sat–Sun 9am–6pm, Fri 9am–noon and 3–6pm.

Tun Razak was Malaysia's second prime minister, and this museum is filled with his personal and official memorabilia.

**Parliament House.** Jalan Parliament. Parliament sessions are not open to the public.

In the Lake Gardens area, the Parliament House is a modern building housing the country's administrative offices, which were once in the Sultan Abdul Samad Building at Merdeka Square.

**Sri Mahamariaman Temple.** Jalan Bandar.

At the time of writing, the temple was getting a face-lift (Hindu temples must renovate every 12 years), so by the time you arrive it should be wearing a fresh face. It's a beautiful temple tucked away in a narrow street in KL's Chinatown area and was built by Thambusamy Pillai, a pillar of old KL's Indian community. This temple is the starting place of Kuala Lumpur's Thaipusam Festival.

✪ **Petaling Street.**

This is the center of KL's Chinatown district. By day, stroll past hawker stalls, dim sum shops, wet markets, and all sorts of shops, from pawn shops to coffin makers. At night, from the hawkers' sidewalk cafes, you can watch the street life bustle by.

# SPORTS & THE OUTDOORS
## GOLF

People from all over Asia flock to Malaysia for its golf courses, many of which are excellent standard courses designed by pros. For a good time, call **Royal Selangor Golf Club,** P.O. Box 11051, 50734 Kuala Lumpur (☎ **03/984-8433;** fax 03/985-3939); **Kelab Golf Perkhidmatan Awam,** Bukit Kiara, off Jalan Damansara, 6000 Kuala Lumpur (☎ **03/757-5310;** fax 03/757-7821); or **Kuala Lumpur Golf & Country Club,** 10 Jalan 1/70D off Jalan Bukit Kiara, 6000 Kuala Lumpur (☎ **03/253-1111;** fax 03/253-3393).

## SHOPPING

Kuala Lumpur is a truly great place to shop. In recent years, mall after mall has risen from city lots, filled with hundreds of retail outlets selling everything from haute couture to cheap chic clothing, electronic goods, jewelry, and arts and crafts. The major shopping malls are located in the area around Jalan Bukit Bintang and Jalan Sultan Ismail. There are also a few malls along Jalan Ampang.

A good place for handicrafts is the huge **Central Market** on Jalan Benteng (☎ **03/274-6542**). There you'll find local artists and craftspeople selling their wares in the heart of town. It's also a good place to find Malaysian handicrafts from other regions of the country.

Another favorite shopping haunt in KL is **Chinatown,** along Petaling Street. Day and night, it's a great place to wander and bargain for clothing and accessories (love those DKNY and D&G knock-offs!), and to search for cultural treasures from China, India, and Burma.

**Pasar malam** ("night markets") are very popular evening activities in KL. Whole blocks are taken up with these brightly lit and bustling markets packed with stalls selling everything you can dream of. They are likely to pop up anywhere in the city. Two good bets for catching one: Go to Jalan Haji Taib after dark until 10pm. On Saturday nights, head for Jalan Tuanku Abdul Rahman.

## NIGHTLIFE

There's nightlife to spare in KL, from fashionable lounges to sprawling discos to pubs perfect for lounging. Basically, you can expect to pay about RM11 to RM17 (US$2.90–US$4.45) for a pint of beer, depending on what and where you order. While quite a few pubs are open for lunch, most clubs won't open until about 6pm or 7pm. These places must all close by 1am, so don't plan on staying out too late. Nearly all have a happy hour, usually between 5pm and 7:30pm or 7pm, when drink discounts apply to draft beers and "house pour" (lower shelf) mixed drinks. Generally, you're expected to wear dress casual clothing for these places, but avoid old jeans and tennis shoes, and very revealing outfits.

While there are some very good places in Kuala Lumpur, the true nightlife spot is in a place called **Bangsar,** just outside the city limits. It's 2 or 3 blocks of bars, cafes, and restaurants that cater to a variety of tastes. Every taxi driver knows where it is. Get in and ask to go to Jalan Telawi Tiga in Bangsar, and once there it's very easy to catch a cab back to town. Begin at **The Roof** (☎ **03/282-7168**), a three-story open air-cafe/bar that looks like a crazy Louisiana cathouse (you really can't miss it). From there you can try **Big Willy's** (☎ **03/283-1136**), a lively sports bar; **Echo** (☎ **03/248-3022**) for some funky dance music; **Grappa** (☎ **03/287-0080**), a sophisticated wine bar; or **Finnegan's** (☎ **03/284-0187**), obviously an Irish bar. And that's only the beginning.

Back in Kuala Lumpur, there are some very good bars and pubs that I'd recommend. **Bier Keller** (ground floor, Menara Haw Par, Jalan Sultan Ismail; ☎ **03/201-3313**) serves German beers in tankards and traditional German cuisine such as sauerkraut and beer bread. **Delaney's** (ground floor, Park Royal Hotel, Jalan Sultan Ismail; ☎ **03/241-5195**) has a good selection of draft beers.

For a little live music with your drinks, the **Hard Rock Cafe** (Wisma Concorde, Jalan Sultan Ismail next to Concorde Hotel; ☎ **03/244-4152**) is a lot of fun. Bands play nightly for a crowd of locals, tourists, and expatriates who take their parties very seriously.

While many of the larger dance clubs in the city cater to a young clientele, a good choice for a more upscale dance party head for **Modesto's** (Rohas Berkasa, Jalan P. Ramlee; ☎ **03/381-1998**).

## 4  Johor Bahru

Johor Bahru, the capital of the state of Johor, is at the southern tip of the Malaysian peninsula, where Malaysia's North-South Highway comes to its southern terminus. Since it's just over the causeway from Singapore, a very short jump by car, bus, or train, it's a popular point of entry to Malaysia. Johor Bahru, or "JB," is not the most fascinating destination in Malaysia, but for a quick day visit from Singapore or as a stopover en route to other Malaysian destinations, it offers some good shopping, sight-seeing, and dining.

Johor's early beginnings were very closely entwined with nearby Malacca's. The Portuguese and Dutch, who each had their eye on the successful city-port, used Johor—the Portuguese pummeled the place to get to Malacca in 1511, and in 1641, the Dutch formed a strategic alliance with Johor to overthrow the Portuguese. In an ironic twist, Malacca's success did not continue under the Portuguese or the Dutch. In fact, by the 1700s, favorable rights bestowed upon Johor turned the state into a powerful threat to Malacca's trade. Eventually the envious Dutch attacked Johor, driving its leaders to establish a capital on the island of Riau, just south of the peninsula.

Under the successful administration of the Temenggong and Bendahara families (ministerial agents for the Sultanate), Riau grew into a very successful entry port. But conflict between the two families led to the assassination of the Sultan. The city was weakened, as the Malays believed the Sultan to be the last direct descendent of Raja Iskander Zul-karnain, Alexander the Great, and his passing left a great void. This fragile state left the city vulnerable to the Bugis, who came to settle to escape conflict in their home in southern Sulawesi. The Bugis, master navigators and skilled traders with countless allies, catapulted Riau's status ever higher, but in meddling with affairs of the leadership won few supporters among the local Malays. By 1721, the Bugis were ruling under a puppet Sultan, yet intermarriage secured the Bugis' bloodline that many Malays carry with them to this day.

In 1757 the Malays once again aligned themselves with the Dutch to overthrow the Bugis, and by 1760 all foreign-born Bugis were expelled. However, the economic success of Riau waned in the decades to follow. The Bugis-controlled sultan was deposed, and the Dutch appointed one of his sons, Abdul Rahman, as his successor.

It was Temmenggong Ibrahim, under that Sultan Abdul Rahman, who signed a treaty in 1819 with Sir Stamford Raffles, allowing the British East India Company to set up shop on Singapore. During the 1800s Singapore's success greatly overshadowed Riau's former glory. In the mid-1800s, under Sultan Abu Bakar (who was raised and educated in Singapore), Johor became an administerial extension of Singapore. In 1866 Johor Bahru was named the state capital, and it was developed with a Western-style government. Hence, today Abu Bakar is known as the "Father of Modern Johor." Finally, in 1914 Johor was placed under the Federated States of Malaya. The sultan lost his power, except to perform ceremonial duties. For example, his successors could retain the official yellow costume of the Sultanate. To this day yellow is a color forbidden for anyone (including you) to wear, especially at the Sultan's favorite golf courses. The present sultan is His Majesty Sultan Iskander, who has held the title since 1981.

### VISITOR INFORMATION

The Malaysia Tourism Board office in Johor Bahru is at **The Johor Tourist Information Centre (JOTIC),** centrally located on Jalan Ayer Molek, on the second floor of the JOTIC center (☎ **07/224-2000**). Information is available not only for Johor Bahru, but for the state of Johor as well.

## GETTING THERE

**BY CAR**   If you arrive by car via the causeway, you will clear the immigration checkpoint (☎ 07/223-5007) upon entering the Malaysia side.

**BY BUS**   Buses to and from other parts of Malaysia are based at the Larkin Bus Terminal off Jalan Garuda in the northern part of the city. Taxis are available at the Terminal to take you to the city. The easiest way to catch a bus from KL is at the KL Railway Station. **Plusliner/NICE** (☎ 03/272-2760) runs service twice daily for RM40 (US$10.55). The trip takes just under 6 hours. Most all other cities in Malaysia have service to Johor Bahru. Consult each city section for bus terminal information. From Singapore, the **Singapore-Johor Express** (☎ 65/292-8149) operates every 10 minutes between 6:30am and 11:30pm from the Ban Sen Terminal at Queen Street near Arab Street. The cost for the half-hour trip is S$2.10 (US$1.30).

If you're looking to depart Johor Bahru via bus, contact one of the following companies at Larkin for route information: **Transnasional** (☎ 07/224-5182); or **Plusliner/NICE** (☎ 07/222-1316).

**BY TRAIN**   The **Keretapi Tanah Melayu Berhad** (KTM) trains arrive and depart from the Johor Bahru Railway Station at Jalan Tun Abdul Razak, opposite Merlin Tower (☎ 07/223-3040). Catch trains from KL's Railway station (☎ 03/274-7435) five times daily for RM18 to RM64 (US$4.75–US$16.85), depending on the class you travel. From the **Singapore Railway Station** (☎ 65/222-5165), on Keppel Road in Tanjong Pagar, the short trip is S$6 to S$10 (US$3.70–US$6.10).

**BY PLANE**   The **Senai Airport,** 30 to 40 minutes outside the city (☎ 07/599-4500), has regular flights to and from major cities in Malaysia and also from Singapore. The airport tax is RM20 (US$8) for international flights and RM5 (US$2) for domestic. For reservations on **Malaysian Airlines** flights call ☎ 07/334-1003 in Johor Bahru. A taxi from the airport to the city center will run you RM25 (US$13.15) per person. There's also **Hertz** (☎ 07/223-7520) and **National** (☎ 07/223-0503) counters for car rentals. A shuttle to the airport operates from the Malaysia Airline office at Plaza Pelangi on Jalan Kuning for only RM4 (US$1.05). For the record, I did not detect any money changing facilities at the airport.

**BY TAXI**   The Outstation taxi stand is located at Larkin Bus Terminal. The taxis can bring you to Johor Bahru from any major city on the peninsula. From KL's Puduraya Bus Terminal (Outstation Taxi ☎ 03/232-6504) the cost is about RM200 (US$52.65). For taxi stands in other cities please refer to each city's section. For taxi hiring from Johor Bahru call ☎ 07/223-4494. For an extra RM10 (US$2.65) they'll pick you up at your hotel.

## GETTING AROUND

As in Kuala Lumpur, taxis charge a metered fare, RM1.50 (US40¢) for the first kilometer and an additional 10 sen for each 200 meters after that. Between midnight and 6am you'll be charged an extra 50% of the total fare. For taxi pickup there's an extra RM1 (US25¢) charge. Call **Comfort** at ☎ 07/332-2852.

# Fast Facts: Johor Bahru

**American Express**   The Amex office is located at Mayflower Acme Tours, Wisma Tan Chong, 27a 2/F, Jalan Tun Abdul Razak (☎ 07/224-1357).

**Banks/Currency Exchange**   Major banks are located in the city center, and money changers at shopping malls and at JOTIC.

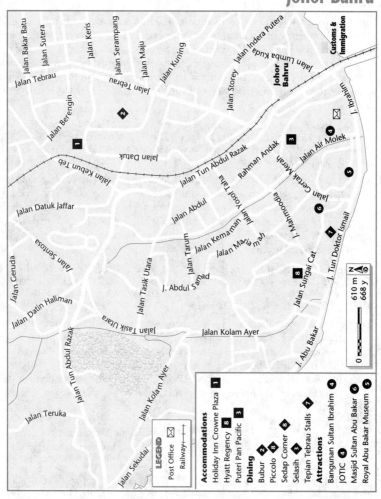

**Internet/E-mail**   The closest reliable Internet cafe can be found at Pelangi Leisure Mall on Level 2 (☎ 07/335-3757). Rates are RM10 (US$2.65)/hour.

**Post Office/Mail**   The main post office is on Jalan Dato Onn (☎ 07/223-2555) just around the corner from JOTIC.

## ACCOMMODATIONS

Several international chains have accommodations in JB. Most are intended for the business set, but holiday travelers will find the accommodations very comfortable.

**The Holiday Inn Crowne Plaza.** Jalan Dato Sulaiman, Century Garden, 80990 Johor Bahru, Johor. ☎ **800/465-4329** from the U.S. and Canada, 800/221066 from Australia, 0800/442222 from New Zealand, 0800/987121 from the U.K., or 07/332-3800. Fax 07/331-8884. 350 units. A/C MINIBAR TV TEL. RM185 double; RM550 suite. AE, DC, JCB, MC, V.

While this hotel is not within walking distance from the city center, it was the first five-star business class hotel in Johor Bahru, and is larger than the other hotels in the city. It is comfortable and not overly formal, with furniture wrapped in traditional fabrics, wood-paneling details, and marble floors in the lobby. VCRs are available upon request, with RM15 (US$3.95) video rentals. Services include airport shuttle and valet service. Facilities include a midsize outdoor pool; fitness center with sauna, steam bath, and massage; one squash court; and a business center; and there is a shopping complex attached. Recent deals offered by the hotel include a 50% discount off the suite rate.

✪ **The Hyatt Regency.** Jalan Sungai Chat, P.O. Box 222, 80720 Johor Bahru, Johor. ☎ **800/233-1234** or ☎ 07/222-1234. Fax 07/223-2718. 400 units. A/C MINIBAR TV TEL. RM420–RM480 (US$110–US$126) double; RM500–RM600 (US$131–US$158) Executive Floor; RM800 (US$210) and way up for suite. AE, DC, JCB, MC, V.

The Hyatt is near the City Square but likes to fancy itself a city resort, focusing on landscaped gardens and greenery around the premises—the private lagoon-style pool, with gardens seen from the glass windows of the main lobby, is surely spectacular. The deluxe rooms are located better than the others, with views of Singapore and fabulous sunsets. Facilities include a fitness center with sauna, Jacuzzi, and massage; two tennis courts; and a business center. Discount packages are available.

**The Puteri Pan Pacific.** "The Kotaraya," P.O. Box 293, 80730 Johor Bahru, Johor. ☎ **07/223-3333**, or 800/8533 toll free in Malaysia. Fax 07/223-6622. 460 units. A/C MINIBAR TV TEL. RM350–RM450 double (US$92–US$118); RM500–RM1,600 (US$132–US$421) suite. AE, DC, JCB, MC, V.

The good news about the Puteri is it's located in the heart of the city, near attractions and shopping. The bad news is it is a very busy hotel and human traffic makes it noisy and somewhat on the run-down side. Nevertheless, little traditional touches to the decor make the Pan Pacific unique. Be sure to ask about special discounts, which can bring the price down as low as RM120 (US$32)! Facilities include an outdoor pool, tennis and squash courts, fitness center, saunas, steam room, and business center.

## DINING

The majority of fine dining in Johor Bahru is in the hotels. Outside the hotels you can sample some great local cuisine, both Malay and Chinese, and wonderful seafood from the city's hawker stalls.

**Bubur.** 191 Jalan Harimau, Century Garden. ☎ **07/335-5891.** Reservations held for a half-hour only. Entrees RM7–RM12 (US$1.85–US$3.15). AE, MC, V. Daily 11am–5am except 4 days into the Chinese New Year. TAIWAN CHINESE.

For fast, inexpensive eats you can even order to take away, try this place. It's a family restaurant, so it can get pretty lively. The staff is quick and attentive without being imposing. Best dishes are the traditional braised pork in soya sauce and the grilled pomfret (a type of fish) in black bean sauce.

✪ **Piccolo.** Hyatt Regency, Jalan Sungai Chat. ☎ **07/222-1234.** Entrees RM20–RM58 (US$5.25–US$15.25). AE, DC, JCB, MC, V. Daily 11:30am–2:30pm and 6:30–10:30pm. ITALIAN.

Perhaps the most popular restaurant for the expatriate community in Johor Bahru, Piccolo's lush lagoon-style poolside ambiance has a very tropical and relaxed feel. Under the timber awning, the high ceiling and bamboo chick blinds make for romantic terrace dining. The antipasti are wonderful, as are dishes like chicken with shrimp and spinach. The grilled seafood is outstanding.

**Sedap Corner.** 11 Jalan Abdul Samad. ☎ **07/224-6566.** Reservations recommended. Entrees RM4.50–RM24 (US$1.20–US$6.30); most dishes no more than RM6/US$1.58. No credit cards. Daily 9am–9:45pm. THAI/CHINESE/MALAY.

Sedap Corner is very popular with the locals. It's dressed down in metal chairs and Formica-top tables, with a coffee shop feel. Local dishes like sambal sabah, otak otak, and fish head curry are house specials, and you don't have to worry about them being too spicy.

✪ **Selasih.** The Puteri Pan Pacific, "The Kotaraya." ☎ **07/223-3333**, ext. 3151. Reservations recommended. Buffet lunch RM25 (US$6.60); buffet dinner RM35 (US$9.20). AE, DC, JCB, MC, V. Daily 11:30am–2:30pm and 6:30–10:30pm. MALAY.

For a broad-range sampling of Malaysian cuisine, try Selasih, which has a daily buffet spread of more than 70 items featuring regional dishes from all over the country. Each night, the dinner buffet is accompanied by traditional Malay music and dance performances. Seniors over 55 receive a 50% discount and children under 12 pay only RM1 (US25¢) for each year of their ages.

## HAWKER CENTERS
✪ The Tepian Tebrau Stalls in Jalan Skudai (along the sea front) and the stalls near the Central Market offer cheap local eats in hawker-center style. The dish that puts Johor Bahru on the map, ikan bakar, barbecued fish with chilies, is out of this world at the Tepian Tebrau stalls.

# ATTRACTIONS
The sights in Johor Bahru are few, but there are some interesting museums and a beautiful istana and mosque. It's a fabulous place to stay for a day, especially if it's a day trip from Singapore, but to stay longer may be stretching the point.

✪ **Royal Abu Bakar Museum.** Grand Palace, Johor. Jalan Tun Dr Ismail. ☎ **07/223-0555**. Adults US$7; children under 12 US$3. Sat–Thurs 9am–5pm.

Also called the Istana Besar, this gorgeous royal palace was built by Sultan Abu Bakar in 1866. Today it houses the royal collection of international treasures, costumes, historical documents, fine art from the family collection, and relics of the Sultanate.

**Bangunan Sultan Ibrahim (State Secretariat Building).** Jalan Abdul Ibrahim.

The saracenic flavor of this building makes it feel older than it truly is. Built in 1940, today it houses the State Secretariat.

**Masjid Sultan Abu Bakar.** Jalan Masjid.

This mosque was commissioned by Sultan Ibrahim in 1890 after the death of his father, Sultan Abu Bakar. It took 8 years and RM400,000 to build. It is one of the most beautiful mosques in Malaysia—at least from the outside. The inside? I can't tell you. I showed up in "Good Muslim Woman" clothing, took off my shoes and crept up to the outer area (where I know women are allowed) and a Haji flew out of an office and shooed me off in a flurry. He asked if I was Muslim, I said no, and he said I wasn't allowed in. When I reported this to the tourism office at JOTIC, they thought I was nuts, and said anyone with proper attire could enter the appropriate sections. Let me know if you get in.

# SPORTS & THE OUTDOORS
In addition to its cities and towns, Johor also has some beautiful nature to take in, which is doubly good if you have only a short time to see Malaysia and can't afford to travel north to some of the larger national parks.

Johor Endau Rompin National Park is about 293 square miles (488 sq. km) of lowland forest. There's camping in four sites and jungle trekking through 16 miles (26km) of trails and rivers to see diverse tropical plant species, colorful birds, and wild animals.

The best way to get to Kluang is to take an outstation taxi from Johor Bharu (for booking call ☎ 07/223-4494) to the park entrance visitor's center at a cost of around RM60. For more information, contact the National Parks (Johor) Corporation, JKR 475, Bukit Timbalan, Johor Bahru (☎ 07/223-7471). It's advised that you obtain an entry permit in advance of your visit.

The **Waterfalls at Lombong,** near Kota Tinggi, measuring about 112 feet (34m) high, are about 34 miles (56km) northeast of Johor Bahru. You can cool off in the pools below the falls and enjoy the area's chalets, camping facilities, restaurant, and food stalls. An outstation taxi will also take you to the falls, which are a little off the track on your way east to Desaru. The cost would also be around RM60.

## GOLF

Johor is a favorite destination for golf enthusiasts. The Royal Johor Country Club and Pulai Springs Country Club are just outside Johor Bahru and offer a range of country club facilities, while other courses require a bit more traveling time but offer resort-style accommodations. Your options are **Royal Johor Country Club,** 3211 Jalan Larkin, 80200 Johor Bahru, Johor (☎ **07/223-3322;** fax 07/224-0729); **Palm Resort Golf & Country Club,** Jalan Persiaran Golf off Jalan Jumbo, 81250 Senai, Johor (☎ **07/599-6222;** fax 07/599-6001); **Tanjung Puteri Golf & Country Club,** Pasir Gudang, 81700 Johor Bahru, Johor (☎ **07/251-3533;** fax 07/251-3466); and **Pulai Springs Country Club,** 64 Jalan Padi Satu, Bandar Baru Uda, 81200 Johor Bahru, Johor (☎ **07/520-7222;** fax 07/520-7999).

Greens fees will vary from weekends to weekdays and depend on whether you're a guest or just visiting for the day. You'll pay anywhere between RM50 and RM250 (US$13.15 and US$65.80). *One note of caution:* If you play in Johor, especially at the Royal Johor Country Club, don't wear yellow. It is the official color of the Sultan, and is worn only by him when he visits the courses.

## SHOPPING

The **Johor Craftown Handicraft Centre** (☎ **236-7346**) at 36 Jalan Skudai off Jalan Abu Bakar has, in addition to a collection of local crafts, demonstration performances of handicrafts techniques. **Johorcraft** (☎ **07/883-6393**), at Lot 2135, 231/2 m.s. Jalan Johor Bahru and Kota Tinggi, is another handicraft center. **JOTIC** (☎ **07/ 224-2000**), 2 Jalan Ayer Molek, is a shopping mall with tourist information, cultural performances, exhibits, demonstrations of crafts, and restaurants.

## 5 Malacca

While the destinations on the east coast are ideal for resort-style beach getaways, the cities on the west coast are perfect for vacations filled with culture and history—and Malacca is one of the best places to start. The attraction here is the city's cultural heritage, around which a substantial tourism industry has grown. If you're visiting, a little knowledge of this history will help you understand and appreciate all there is to see.

Malacca was founded around 1400 by Parameswara, called Iskander Shah in the Malay Annals. After he was chased from Palembang in southern Sumatra by invading Javanese, he set up a kingdom in Singapore (Temasek), and after being overthrown by invaders at Temasek, he ran up the west coast of the Malay peninsula to Malacca, where he settled and established a port city. The site was an ideal midpoint in the east-west trade route and was in a favorable spot to take advantage of the two monsoons that dominated shipping routes. Malacca soon drew the attention of the Chinese, and the city maintained very close relations with the mainland as a trading partner and a political ally. The Javanese were also eager to trade in Malacca, as were Muslim merchants. After Parameswara's death in 1414, his son, Mahkota Iskander Shah, converted to Islam and became the first Sultan of Malacca. The word of Islam quickly spread throughout the local population.

During the 15th century, Malacca was ruled by a succession of wise sultans who expanded the wealth and stability of the economy, built up the administration's coffers, extended the sultanate to the far reaches of the Malay peninsula, Singapore, and parts of northern Sumatra, and thwarted repeated attacks by the Siamese. The success of the empire was drawing international attention.

The Portuguese were one of the powers eyeing the port and formulating plans to dominate the east-west trade route, establish the naval supremacy of Portugal, and promote Christianity in the region. In 1511, they struck, and conquered Malacca in a battle that lasted only a month. It is believed the local Malaccans had become accustomed to the comforts of affluence and turned soft and vulnerable. After it was defeated, the sultanate fled to Johor, where it reestablished the seat of Malay power. Malacca would never again be ruled by a sultan. The Portuguese looted the city and sent its riches off to Lisbon.

The Portuguese were also the first of a chain of ruling foreign powers who would struggle in vain to retain the early economic success of the city. The foreign conquerers had a major strike against them: Their Christianity alienated the locals and repelled Muslim traders. The city quickly became nothing more than a sleepy outpost.

In 1641, the Dutch, with the help of Johor, conquered Malacca and controlled the city until 1795. Again, the Dutch were unsuccessful in rebuilding the glory of past prosperity in Malacca, and the city continued to sleep.

In 1795, the Dutch traded Malacca to the British in return for Bencoolen in Sumatra, being far more concerned with their Indonesian interests anyway. Malacca became a permanent British settlement in 1811, but by this time it had become so poor and alienated that it was impossible to bring it back to life.

The final blow came in 1941, when the city fell under Japanese occupation for 4 years. It wasn't until 1957 that Malacca, along with the rest of Malaysia, gained full independence.

## VISITOR INFORMATION

Surprisingly, there is no Malaysia Tourism Board office in Malacca, but there is a **Malacca Tourism Association** office in the Town Square (☎ **06/283-6538**).

## GETTING THERE

There is an airport in Malacca that is serviced by Pelangi Air, but due to decreased travel, Pelangi only has routes between Malacca and Sumatra. The airport is nearly asleep. And while Malacca doesn't have a proper train station, the KTM stops at Tampin (☎ **06/411-034**), 23.75 miles (38km) north of the city. It's not the most convenient way in and out of Malacca, but if you'd like more information, you can call the **Malacca Railway Office** at ☎ **06/282-3091.** Following are more convenient routes.

**BY BUS**    From Singapore, contact **Malacca-Singapore Express** at ☎ **65/293-5915.** The trip is about 4½ hours and costs S$11 (US$6.70). From Johor Bahru's Larkin Bus Terminal **Jebat Ekspress** (☎ **07/223-3712**) has seven daily buses at a cost of RM9 (US$2.35). From KL's Puduraya Bus Terminal on Jalan Pudu, **Transnasional** (☎ **230-5044**) has hourly buses between 8am and 10pm for RM6.80 (US$1.80).

The bus station in Malacca is at Jalan Kilang, within the city. Taxis are easy to find from here.

**BY TAXI**    Outstation taxis can bring you here from any major city, including Johor Bahru (about RM120) and Kuala Lumpur (RM130). Taxi reservation numbers are listed in each city's section. The outstation taxi stand in Malacca is at the bus terminal on Jalan Kilang. There's no number for reservations.

## GETTING AROUND

Most of the historic sights around the town square are well within walking distance. For other trips taxis are the most convenient way around, but are at times difficult to find. They're also not as clearly marked as in KL or Johor Bahru. They are also not metered, so be prepared to bargain. Basically, no matter what you do, you'll always be charged a higher rate than a local. Tourists are almost always quoted RM10 (US$2.65) for local trips. Malaysians pay RM5. You should bargain for a price somewhere in between. Trips to Ayer Keroh will cost about RM20 (US$5.25).

Trishaws are all over the historic areas of town, and in Malacca they're renowned for being very, very garishly decorated (which adds to the fun!). Negotiate for hourly rates of about RM15 (US$3.95).

# Fast Facts: Malacca

**Banks/Currency Exchange**   Major banks are located in the historic center of town, with a couple along Jalan Putra.

**Internet/E-mail**   The nearest Internet cafe is not very centrally located. High Speed Siber Café (no. 22, Ground Floor, Taman Malinja on Bukit Bahru; ☎ 06/283-8797) has access for RM4 (US$1.05)/hour.

**Post Office/Mail**   The most convenient post office location is on Jalan Laksamana (☎ 06/284-8440).

## ACCOMMODATIONS

Malacca is not very large, and most of the places to stay are well within walking distance of attractions, shopping, and restaurants.

**Century Mahkota Hotel Melaka.** Jalan Merdeka, 75000 Malacca. ☎ **800/536-7361** from the U.S., or 06/281-2828. Fax 06/281-2323. 617 units. A/C MINIBAR TV TEL. RM300 (US$79) double; RM350–RM1,500 (US$92–US$395) suite. AE, DC, JCB, MC, V.

Located along the waterfront, the hotel is walking distance from sightseeing, historical areas, shopping, and commercial centers. It's a suite hotel that's better for families, and while it's not luxurious, its rooms are more like holiday apartments. The views are of either the pools, the shopping mall across the street, or the muddy reclaimed seafront. Facilities include two outdoor pools, a fitness center with sauna and massage, tennis and squash courts, mini golf, a game room, a children's playground, access to nearby golf, and a business center. It's across the street from the largest shopping mall in Malacca.

✪ **Heeren House.** 1 Jalan Tun Tan Cheng Lock, 75200 Malacca. ☎ **06/281-4241.** Fax 06/281-4239. 7 units. A/C TV TEL. Sun–Thurs RM139 (US$33) double; RM239 (US$63) suite. Fri–Sat RM149 (US$39) double; RM249 (US$65) suite. No credit cards.

This is the place to stay in Malacca for a taste of the local culture. Started by a local family, the guesthouse is a renovated 100-year-old building furnished in traditional Peranakan and colonial style and located right in the heart of historical European Malacca. All the bedrooms have views of the Malacca River, and outside the front door of the hotel is a winding stretch of old buildings housing antique shops. Just walk out and wander. The rooms on the higher floors are somewhat larger. Laundry service is available, and there's a cafe and gift shop on the premises.

# Malacca

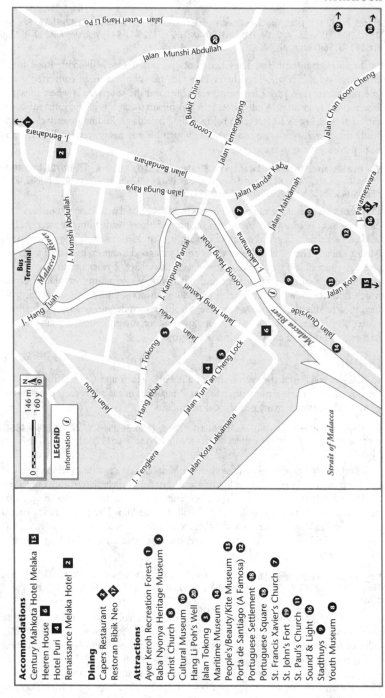

**Accommodations**
Century Mahkota Hotel Melaka **15**
Heeren House **6**
Hotel Puri **4**
Renaissance Melaka Hotel **2**

**Dining**
Capers Restaurant **2**
Restoran Bibik Neo **17**

**Attractions**
Ayer Keroh Recreation Forest **1**
Baba Nyonya Heritage Museum **5**
Christ Church **8**
Cultural Museum **10**
Hang Li Poh's Well **20**
Jalan Tokong **3**
Maritime Museum **14**
People's/Beauty/Kite Museum **13**
Porta de Santiago (A Famosa) **12**
Portuguese Settlement **18**
Portuguese Square **18**
St. Francis Xavier's Church **7**
St. John's Fort **19**
St. Paul's Church **11**
Sound & Light **16**
Stadthuys **9**
Youth Museum **8**

473

**Hotel Puri.** 118 Jalan Tun Tan Cheng Lock, 75200 Malacca. ☎ **06/282-5588.** Fax 06/281-5588. 50 units. A/C TV TEL. RM100–RM160 (US$26–US$42) double; RM200–RM250 (US$53–US$66) suite. AE, MC, V.

In the olden days, Jalan Tun Tan Cheng Lock was known as "Millionaire Row" for all the wealthy families who lived here. This old "mansion" has been converted into a guesthouse, its tiled parlor has become a lobby, and the courtyard is where breakfast is served each morning. While Hotel Puri isn't big on space, it is big on value (discount rates can be as low as RM68 (US$18) including breakfast). Rooms are very clean, and while not overly stylish, are comfortable enough for any weary traveler. Friendly and responsive staff add to the appeal.

✪ **Renaissance Melaka Hotel.** Jalan Bendahara, 75100 Malacca. ☎ **06/284-8888** in Malaysia, or 800/601-1882 from Singapore. Fax 06/284-9269. 316 units. A/C MINIBAR TV TEL. RM437 double; RM495–RM782 suite. AE, JCB, MC, V.

Renaissance is one of the more posh hotels in Malacca, and according to business travelers, the most reliable place for quality accommodations. Aside from the pieces of Peranakan porcelain and art in the public areas, you could almost believe you weren't in Malacca at all. The hotel is, however, situated in a good location, but you'll still need a taxi to most of the sights. Renovations were completed 2 years ago to upgrade the guest rooms, which are fairly large and filled with Western comforts. Don't expect much from the views, as the hotel is in a more business-minded part of the city. No historical landmarks to gaze upon here. Facilities include an outdoor pool; fitness center with massage, sauna, and steam; two indoor squash courts; a tour operator desk; and a beauty salon. Golf is located nearby.

## DINING

In Malacca you'll find the typical mix of authentic Malay and Chinese food, and as the city was the major settling place for the Peranakans in Malaysia, their unique style of food is featured in many of the local restaurants.

✪ **Capers Restaurant.** Renaissance Melaka Hotel, Jalan Bendahara. ☎ **06/284-8888.** Reservations recommended. Entrees RM20–RM48 (US$5.25–US$12.65). AE, DC, MC, V. Mon–Sat 6:30–10:30pm. CONTINENTAL.

This is the only fine-dining establishment in Malacca at the moment, which means it is quite formal and pricey. Warm lighting and crystal and silver flatware are only a few of the many details that add to the elegant and romantic atmosphere. The signature dishes come from the char grill, like the grilled tenderloin. The pan-fried sea bass is served quite artfully in a ginger and dill sauce over bok choy and potatoes. Their wine list is large and international, including Portuguese selections, in keeping with the Malacca theme.

**Portuguese Settlement.** Jalan d'Albuquerque off Jalan Ujon Pasir. No phone. Dinner from RM15–RM20 (US$3.95–US$5.25) per person. Open nightly from 6pm onward. No credit cards.

For a taste of Portuguese Malacca, head down to the Portuguese Settlement where open air food stalls by the water sell an assortment of dishes inspired by these former colonial rulers. Many dishes in the offering are fresh seafood. Saturday nights are best when, at 8pm, there's a cultural show with music and dancing.

A good recommendation for a quick bite at lunch or dinner if you're strolling in the historical area is the long string of open air food stalls along Jalan Merdeka, just between Mahkota Plaza Shopping and Warrior Square. **Mama Fatso's** is especially good for Chinese-style seafood and Malay sambal curry. A good meal will run you about RM35 to RM40 (US$9.20–US$10.55) per person. And believe me, it's a good meal.

✪  **Restoran Bibik Neo.** No. 6, ground floor, Jalan Merdeka, Taman Melaka Raya. ☎ **06/281-7054.** Reservations recommended. Entrees RM5–RM15 (US$1.30–US$3.95). AE, DC, MC, V. Daily 11am–3pm and 6–10pm. PERANAKAN.

For a taste of the local cuisine, the traditional Nyonya food here is delicious and very reasonably priced. And while the restaurant isn't exactly tops in terms of decor, be assured that the food here is excellent and authentic. Ikan assam with eggplant is a mild fish curry that's very rich and tasty. I always go for the otak-otak, pounded fish and spices baked in a banana leaf. Theirs is highly recommended.

# ATTRACTIONS

To really understand what you're seeing in Malacca you have to understand a bit about the history, so be sure to read the introduction above. Most of the really great historical places are on either side of the Malacca River. Start at Stadthuys (the old town hall) and you'll see most of Malacca pretty quickly.

## MUSEUMS

✪  **The Museums of History & Ethnography and The Museum of Literature.** Stadthuys. Located at the circle intersection of Jalan Quayside, Jalan Laksamana, and Jalan Chan Koon Cheng. ☎ **06/282-6526.** Admission RM2 (US50¢) adult, RM.50 (US15¢) child. Sat–Thurs 9am–6pm, Fri 9am–12:45pm and 2:45–6pm.

The Stadthuys Town Hall was built by the Dutch in 1650, and it's now home to the Malacca Ethnographical and Historical Museum, which displays customs and traditions of all the peoples of Malacca, and takes you through the rich history of this city. Behind Stadthuys, the Museum of Literature includes old historical accounts and local legends. Admission price is for both exhibits.

**The Peoples Museum, The Museum of Beauty, The Kite Museum, & the Governor of Melaka's Gallery.** Kota Road. ☎ **06/282-6526.** Admission RM2 (US50¢) adult, RM.50 (US15¢) child. Sat–Thurs 9am–6pm, Fri 9am–12:45pm and 2:45–6pm.

This strange collection of displays is housed under one roof. The Peoples Museum is the story of development in Malacca. The Museum of Beauty is a look at cultural differences of beauty throughout time and around the world. The Kite Museum features the traditions of making and flying *wau* in Malaysia, and the governor's personal collection is on exhibit at the Governor's Gallery.

**The Maritime Museum and the Royal Malaysian Navy Museum.** Quayside Road. ☎ **06/282-6526.** Admission RM2 (US50¢) adult, RM.50 (US15¢) child. Sat–Thurs 9am–6pm, Fri 9am–12:45pm and 2:45–6pm.

These two museums are located across the street from one another but share admission fees. The Maritime Museum is in a 16th-century Portuguese ship, with exhibits dedicated to Malacca's history with the sea. The Navy Museum is a modern display of Malaysia's less-pleasant relationship with the sea.

**The Youth Museums and Art Gallery.** Laksamana Road. ☎ **06/282-6526.** Admission RM2 (US50¢) adult, RM.50 (US15¢) child. Sat–Thurs 9am–6pm, Fri 9am–12:45pm and 2:45–6pm.

In the old General Post office are these displays dedicated to Malaysia's youth organizations and to the nation's finest artists. An unusual combination.

✪  **The Cultural Museum.** Kota Road, next to Porta de Santiago. ☎ **06/282-6526.** Admission RM1.50 (US40¢) adult, RM.50 (US15¢) child. Sat–Thurs 9am–6pm, Fri 9am–12:45pm and 2:45–6pm.

A replica of the former palace of Sultan Mansur Syah (1456–1477), this museum was rebuilt according to historical descriptions to house a fine collection of cultural artifacts such as clothing, weaponry, and royal items.

✪ **Baba Nyonya Heritage Museum.** 48/50 Jalan Tun Tan Cheng Lock. Admission RM7 (US$1.85) adult, RM4 (US$1.05) child. Sat–Wed 10am–12:30pm and 2–4:30pm, Thurs 9am–noon.

Called Millionaire's Row, Jalan Tun Ten Cheng Lock is lined with row houses that were built by the Dutch and later bought by wealthy Peranakans; the architectural style reflects their East-meets-West lifestyle. The Baba Nyonya Heritage Museum sits at nos. 48 and 50 as a museum of Peranakan heritage. The entrance fee includes a guided tour.

## HISTORICAL SITES

**Sound & Light.** Warrior Square, Jalan Kota. ☎ **06/282-6526.** Admission RM5 (US$1.30) adult, RM2 (US50¢) child. Shows nightly at 9:30pm.

The Museums Department has developed a light and sound show at the Warrior Square, the large field in the historical center of the city, which narrates the story of Malacca's early history, lighting up the historical buildings in the area for added punch. This is a good activity when you first arrive to help you get your historical bearings.

✪ **Porta de Santiago (A Famosa).** Located on Jalan Kota, at the intersection of Jalan Parameswara.

Once the site of a Portuguese fortress called A Famosa, all that remains today of the fortress is the entrance gate, which was saved from demolition by Sir Stamford Raffles. When the British East India Company demolished the place, Raffles realized the arch's historical value and saved it. The fort was built in 1512, but the inscription above the arch, "Anno 1607," marks the date when the Dutch overthrew the Portuguese.

**Hang Li Poh's Well.** Located off Jalan Laksamana Cheng Ho (Jalan Panjang).

Also called "Sultan's Well," Hang Li Poh's Well was built in 1495 to commemorate the marriage of Chinese Princess Hang Li Poh to Sultan Mansor Shah. It is now a wishing well, and folks say that if you toss a coin in, you'll someday return to Malacca.

**St. John's Fort.** Located off Lorong Bukit Senjuang.

The fort, built by the Dutch in the late 18th century, sits on top of St. John's Hill. Funny how the cannons point inland, huh? At the time, threats to the city came from land. It was named after a Portuguese church to St. John the Baptist, which originally occupied the site.

**St. Paul's Church.** Located behind Porta de Santiago.

The church was built by the Portuguese in 1521, but when the Dutch came in, they made it part of A Famosa, converting the altar into a cannon mount. The open tomb inside was once the resting place of St. Francis Xavier, a missionary who spread Catholicism throughout Southeast Asia, and whose remains were later moved to Goa.

**St. Francis Xavier's Church.** Located on Jalan Laksamana.

This church was built in 1849 and dedicated to St. Francis Xavier, a Jesuit who brought Catholicism to Malacca and other parts of Southeast Asia.

**Christ Church.** Located on Jalan Laksamana.

The Dutch built this place in 1753 as a Dutch Reform Church, and its architectural details include such wonders as ceiling beams cut from a single tree and a Last Supper glazed tile motif above the altar. It was later consecrated as an Anglican church, and mass is still performed today in English, Chinese, and Tamil.

**Portuguese Settlement and Portuguese Square.**

Located down Jalan d'Albuquerque off Jalan Ujon Pasir in the southern part of the city is the Portuguese Settlement, an enclave once designated for Portuguese settlers after their conquer of Malacca in 1511. Some elements of their presence remain in the Lisbon-style architecture. Later, in 1920, the area was a Eurasian neighborhood. In the center of the settlement, Portuguese Square is a modern attraction with Portuguese restaurants, handicrafts, souvenirs, and cultural shows. It was built in 1985 in an architectural style to reflect the surrounding flavor of Portugal.

✪ **Jalan Tokong.**

Not far from Jalan Tun Tan Cheng Lock is Jalan Tokong, called the "Street of Harmony" by the locals because it has three coexisting places of worship: the Kampong Kling Mosque, the Cheng Hoon Teng Temple, and the Sri Poyyatha Vinayar Moorthi Temple.

## OTHER ATTRACTIONS
**Ayer Keroh Recreational Forest.**

Outside of Malacca are the 500 acres (202 hectares) of forest that make up Ayer Keroh. Many attractions have been built here, and they can be fun. A taxi from Malacca will run you about RM20 (US$5.25). See the **Reptile Park** (☎ 06/231-9136), admission RM4 (US$1.05) adult, RM2 (US50¢) child, open daily 9am to 6pm; the **Butterfly & Reptile Sanctuary** (☎ 06/232-0033), admission RM5 (US$1.30) adult, RM3 (US80¢) child, open daily 8:30am to 5:30pm; **The Malacca Zoo** (☎ 06/232-4053), admission RM3 (US80¢) adult, RM1 (US25¢) child, open daily 9am to 6pm; and the **Taman Mini Malaysia/Mini ASEAN** (☎ 06/231-6087), admission RM5 (US$1.30) adult, RM2 (US50¢) child, open daily 9am to 5pm.

## SHOPPING
Antique hunting has been a major draw to Malacca for decades now. Distinct Peranakan and teakwood furniture, porcelain, and household items fetch quite a price these days, due to a steady increase in demand for these rare treasures. The area down and around **Jalan Tun Tan Cheng Lok** sports many little antique shops that are filled with as many gorgeous items as any local museum. Whether you're buying or just looking, it's a fun way to spend an afternoon.

Modern shopping malls are sprouting up in Malacca, the biggest being the **Mahkota Parade** on Jalan Merdeka, just south of the field (Warrior Square) in the historic district. Two hundred retail stores sell everything from books to clothing.

For crafts, start at **Karyaneka** (☎ 06/284-3270) on Jalan Laksamana close to the Town Square. If you travel down Laksamana you'll find all sorts of small crafts and souvenir shops.

There's also a daily **flea market** on the north end of the field (Warrior Square) just in the historic district. Try your bargaining skills here for batiks, baskets, regional crafts, and souvenirs.

## 6  Genting Highlands

Genting Highlands is a hill resort called the "City of Entertainment." It's more or less Malaysia's answer to Las Vegas, complete with bright lights (that can be seen from Kuala Lumpur) and gambling. And while most come here to gamble, there's a wide range of other activities, although most of them seem to serve the purpose of entertaining the kids while you bet their college funds on Black 19. Still, nestled in the cool mountains above the capital city, it's a hop from town and a fun diversion from all that *culture!*

### VISITOR INFORMATION

The Genting Highlands Resort is owned and operated by Resorts World Berhad, who'll be glad to provide you with any further information. For hotel reservations, call ☎ **03/262-3555.** For inquiries, dial toll-free within Malaysia (☎ **800/888-2288**). Their fax is 03/261-6611. You can also visit their central office at Wisma Genting on Jalan Sultan Ismail in KL.

### GETTING THERE

The resort has its own bus service from Kuala Lumpur. **Genting Highlands Transport** operates buses every half-hour from 6:30am to 9pm daily from the Pekeliling Bus Terminal on Jalan Ipoh. The cost for one-way is RM2.60 (US70¢) and the trip takes 1 hour. The bus lets you off at the foot of the hill, where you take the cable car to the top for RM3. For bus information, call ☎ **03/441-0173**.

   You can also get there by hiring an outstation taxi. The cost is RM40 (US$10.55) and can be arranged by calling the Puduraya outstation taxi stand at ☎ **03/232-6504.**

## ACCOMMODATIONS

There are four hotels of varying prices within the resort. Rates vary depending on whether it's the low season, shoulder season, peak season, or super peak. The calendar changes each year, but basically weekends are peak, as well as the last week in November through the end of December. Super peak times are around Christmas, the calendar New Year, and Chinese New Year, with a few other days dotted over the summer. With the above exceptions, weekdays are generally low season.

**Genting Hotel.** Genting Highlands 69000, Pahang Darul Makmur. ☎ **03/211-1118.** Fax 03/211-1888. 700 units. A/C MINIBAR TV TEL. Low RM160 (US$42); shoulder RM210 (US$55); peak RM260 (US$68); super peak RM350 (US$92) double. AE, MC, V.

Genting Hotel is a newer property in the resort complex, and is linked directly to the casino. Promotional rates can be as low as RM97 (US$25) for low period weekdays.

**Highlands Hotel.** Genting Highlands 69000, Pahang Darul Makmur. ☎ **03/211-1118.** Fax 03/211-1888. 875 units. A/C MINIBAR TV TEL. Low RM160 (US$42); shoulder RM210 (US$55); peak RM260 (US$68); super peak RM350 (US$92) double. AE, MC, V.

Highlands Hotel is linked directly to the casino. Promotional rates in this hotel are very rare.

**Resort Hotel.** Genting Highlands 69000, Pahang Darul Makmur. ☎ **03/211-1118.** Fax 03/211-1888. 800 units. A/C MINIBAR TV TEL. Low RM120 (US$31); shoulder RM160 (US$42); peak RM220 (US$58); super peak RM310 (US$81) double. AE, MC, V.

Resort Hotel is comparable to the Theme Park Hotel below, but it's a little newer and the double occupancy rooms all have two double beds and standing showers only.

**Theme Park Hotel.** Genting Highlands 69000, Pahang Darul Makmur. ☎ **03/211-1118.** Fax 03/211-1888. 440 units. A/C MINIBAR TV TEL. Low RM110 (US$29); shoulder RM150 (US$39); peak RM190 (US$50); super peak RM210 (US$55) double. AE, MC, V.

The Theme Park Hotel is a little less expensive than the others, primarily because it's a little older and you must walk outside to reach the casino. Promotional rates during the week can be as low as RM62 (US$16) for up to three people in one room.

## DINING & ENTERTAINMENT

Genting doesn't stop at the casinos when it comes to nightlife. International entertainers perform pop concerts, and the theaters put on everything from lion dance competitions to Wild West shows to magic extravaganzas. The Genting International Showroom hosts a dinner and show package. With tickets starting from RM40 (US$10.55), you can have a buffet dinner at one of the resort's many restaurants and afterwards head to the show. For RM71 (US$18.70), you can dine at The Peak Restaurant & Lounge, Genting's fine dining restaurant on the 17th floor of the Genting Hotel (the price includes the show as well).

## ATTRACTIONS

Gambling, gambling, and more gambling. The resort casino is open 24 hours. Entry is RM200 (US$52.65) whether you're a guest at the resort or just visiting for the day. By the way, you must be at least 21 years old to enter the casino. Inside it's a gambler's paradise, with all the games you'd care to wager a bet on, including blackjack, roulette, and baccarat.

For outdoor excitement, the resort has an outdoor pond with boats and a horse ranch with riding for all levels of experience. For somewhat less excitement (but better photo ops), the **cable car ride** down the mountain from the resort offers aerial views of the Malaysian jungle. A one-way fare is RM3 (US80¢) for adults, RM1.50 (US40¢) for children; hours are Sunday to Thursday 8am to 7:30pm and Friday to Saturday 8am to 8:30pm. Additional facilities include a bowling alley and an indoor heated pool.

For children, there's the huge **Genting Theme Park** (☎ 03/211-1118, ext. 58240). There is free admission to the Indoor & Outdoor Theme Parks. For attractions, purchase either a ride card for RM10 (US$2.65) or a one-day unlimited-ride pass for RM48 adult (US$12.65), RM43 (US$11.30) child. Outdoor Theme Park hours are Monday to Friday 10am to 6:45pm, Saturday to Sunday 8am to 7:45pm; Indoor Theme Park daily 9am to 2am.

The park is huge, covering 100,000 square feet, and is mostly rides, plus many Western fast-food eating outlets, games, and other attractions. The Outdoor Theme Park has four roller coasters, flume rides, and a balloon ride. The Indoor Theme Park has a Space Odyssey roller coaster and a motion simulator. Don't miss the Disco Bumper Cars!

For a break from the tables, head for the fairway. The **Awana Golf and Country Club** (☎ 03/211-3025; fax 03/211-3535) is the premier course in Genting.

## 7  Cameron Highlands

Although Cameron Highlands is in Pahang, it is most often accessed via Kuala Lumpur. Located in the hills, Cameron Highlands has a cool climate, which makes it the perfect place for luxury resorts tailored to weekend getaways by Malaysians, Singaporeans, and international travelers.

The climate is also very conducive to agriculture. After the area's discovery by British surveyor William Cameron in 1885, the major crop here became tea, which is still grown today. There is even a tea factory you can visit to see how tea leaves are processed. The area's lovely gardens supply cities from KL to Singapore with vegetables, flowers, and fruit year-round. As you go up into the highlands, you can see the farmland on terraces in beautiful patterns along the sides of the hills. Among the favorites here are the strawberries, which can be eaten fresh or transformed into yummy desserts in the local restaurants. At the many commercial flower nurseries you can see chrysanthemums, fuchsias, and roses growing on the terraces. Rose gardens are prominent here.

**Ringlet** is the first town you see as you travel up the highlands. It is the main agricultural center. Travel farther up the elevation to **Tanah Rata,** the major tourism town in the Highlands, where you'll find chalets, cottages, and bungalows. The town basically consists of shops along one side of the main street (Jalan Sultan Ahmad Shah) and food stalls and the bus terminal on the other. **Brinchang,** at 5,029 feet (1,524m) above sea level, is the highest town, surrounding a market square where there are shops, Tudor inns, rose gardens, and a Buddhist temple.

Temperatures in the Cameron Highlands average 70°F (21°C) during the day and 50°F (10°C) at night. There are paths for lovely treks though the countryside and to peaks of surrounding mountains. Two waterfalls, the Robinson Falls and Parit Falls, have pools at their feet where you can have a swim.

## VISITOR INFORMATION

There are no Visitor Information Services here. They've been closed for a very long time, and have no immediate plans for reopening.

## Fast Facts: Cameron Highlands

**Banks/Currency Exchange** You'll find banks with ATMs and money changing services in Tanah Rata.

**Post Office/Mail** The local post office is also in Tanah Rata (☎ 05/491-1051).

## GETTING THERE

Kurnia Bistari Express Bus (☎ **05/491-2978**) operates between Kuala Lumpur and Tanah Rata four times daily for RM10.10 (US$2.65) one-way. It also provides service to and from Penang two times daily for RM14.10 (US$3.70). The bus terminal is in the center of town along the main drag. Just next to it is the taxi stand. It's a two-horse town; you can't miss either of them.

Outstation taxis from KL will cost RM200 (US$52.65) for the trip. Call ☎ **03/232-6504** for booking. For trips from Cameron Highlands, call ☎ **05/491-2355.** FYI: Taxis are cheaper on the way back because they don't have to climb the mountains.

## GETTING AROUND

Walking in each town is a snap because the places are so small, but they're far apart, and a walk between them could take up much time. There are local buses that ply at odd times between them for around RM3 (US80¢). Or you could pick up one of the ancient, unmarked taxis and cruise between town for RM4 (US$1.05).

## ACCOMMODATIONS

**☼ The Cool Point Hotel.** 891 Persiaran Dayang Endah, 39000 Tanah Rata, Cameron Highlands, Pahang Darul Makmur. ☎ **05/491-4914.** Fax 05/491-4070. 47 units. A/C TV TEL. Off-season RM90–RM140 (US$24–US$37) double. Peak season RM125–RM180 (US$33–US$47) double. MC, V.

Cool Point has an outstanding location—a 2-minute walk to Tanah Rata. While the modern building has some Tudor-like styling on the outside, the rooms inside are pretty standard, but the place is very clean. Make sure you book your room early. This place is always a sell out. Cool Point also has a restaurant serving local and Western dishes.

**☼ The Smokehouse Hotel.** Tanah Rata, Cameron Highlands, Pahang Darul Makmur. ☎ **05/491-1215.** Fax 05/491-1214. 13 units. TEL. RM360–RM680 (US$95–US$179) suite. AE, DC, MC, V.

Situated between Tanah Rata and Brinchang is a gorgeous Tudor mansion with lush gardens outside and a stunning old world ambiance inside. Built in 1937 as a country house in the heyday of colonial British getaways, the conversion into a hotel has kept the place happily in the 1930s. Guest suites have four poster beds and antique furnishings, and are stocked with plush amenities. The hotel encourages guests to play golf at the neighboring course, sit for afternoon tea with strawberry confections, or trek along nearby paths (for which they'll provide a picnic basket). It's all a bizarre escape from Malaysia, but an extremely charming one.

## DINING

For fine dining in a restaurant, the continental cuisine at **The Smokehouse Hotel** (☎ **05/491-1215**) is really your only option. And although it's pricey, it's top rate. As for a more local experience, there's an al fresco **food court** along the Main Street in Tanah Rata that serves excellent Indo-Malay and Western dishes for breakfast, lunch, and dinner at unbeatable prices.

Also along Main Street are cafes that are good for dinner but seem even more popular for cold afternoon beers.

## ATTRACTIONS

Most of the sights can be seen in a day, but it's difficult to plan your time well. In Cameron Highlands, I recommend trying one of the sightseeing outfits in either Brinchang or Tanah Rata. **C.S. Travel & Tours** (47 Main Rd., Tanah Rata, ☎ **05/491-1200,** fax 05/491-2390) is a highly reputable agency. They'll plan half-day tours for RM15 (US$3.95) or full days for up to RM80 (US$21). You're required to pay admission to each attraction yourself. They also provide trekking and overnight camping tours in the surrounding hills with local trail guides. Treks are RM25 (US$6.60), camping RM120 (US$31.60). Bookings are requested at least 1 day in advance. Also, pretty much every hotel can arrange these services for you.

On your average tour you'll see the Boh tea plantation and factory, flower nurseries, rose gardens, strawberry farms, butterfly farms, and the Sam Poh Buddhist Temple.

## GOLF

If you want to hit some balls, **Padang Golf** (Main Road between Tanah Rata and Brinchang; ☎ **05/491-1126**) has 18 holes, with greens fees around RM63 (US$16.60). They also provide club rentals, caddies, shoes, and trolleys.

# 8 Penang

Penang is unique in Malaysia because, for all intents and purposes, Penang has it all. Tioman Island may have beaches and nature, but it has no shopping or historical sights to speak of. And while Malacca has historical sights and museums, it hasn't a good beach for miles. Similarly, while KL has shopping, nightlife, and attractions, it also has no beach resorts. Penang has all of it: beaches, history, diverse culture, shopping, food. You name it, it has it. If you only have a short time to visit Malaysia but want to take in as wide an experience as you can, Penang is your place.

Penang gets its name from the areca (or betel nut, as it is more commonly referred), a plant that is chewed habitually in the East. In the 15th century it was a quiet place populated by small Malay communities, attracting the interest of some southern Indian betel merchants. By the time Francis Light, an agent for the British East India Company, arrived in 1786, the island was already on the maps of European, Indian, and Chinese traders. Light landed on the northeast part of the island where he began a settlement after an agreement with the Sultan of Kedah, on the mainland. He called the town Georgetown, after George III. To gain the help of local inhabitants for clearing the spot, he shot a cannon load of coins into the jungle.

Georgetown became Britain's principal post in Malaya, attracting traders and settlers from all over the world. Europeans, Arabs, northern and southern Indians, southern Chinese and Malays from the mainland and Sumatra flocked to the port. But it was never extremely profitable for England, especially when in 1819 Sir Stamford Raffles founded a new trading post in Singapore. Penang couldn't keep up with the new port's success.

In 1826 Penang, along with Malacca and Singapore, became the Straits Settlements, and Penang was narrowly declared the seat of government over the other two. Finally in 1832, Singapore stole its thunder when authority shifted there. In the late 1800s Penang got a big break. Tin mines and rubber plantations on mainland Malaya were booming, and with the opening of the railway between KL and Butterworth (the town on the mainland just opposite the island), Penang once again thrived. Singapore firms scrambled to open offices in Butterworth.

The Great Depression hit Penang hard. So did the Japanese Occupation from 1941 to 1945. The island had been badly bombed. But since Malaysia's independence in 1957, Penang has had relatively good financial success.

Today the state of Penang is made up of the island and a small strip of land on the Malaysian mainland. Georgetown is the seat of government for the state. Penang Island is 171 square miles (285 sq. km) and has a population of a little more than one million. Surprisingly, the population is mostly Chinese (59%), followed by Malays (32%) and Indians (7%).

## VISITOR INFORMATION

The main **MTB** office is located at no. 10 Jalan Tun Syed Sheh Barakbah (☎ **04/261-9067**), just across from the clock tower by Fort Cornwallis. There's another information center at **Penang International Airport** (☎ **04/643-0501**), and an additional branch on the third level at **KOMTAR** on Jalan Penang (☎ **04/261-4461**).

## GETTING THERE

**BY PLANE**   Penang International Airport (☎ **04/643-0373**) has direct flights from Singapore about seven times daily (Singapore Airlines ☎ **65/223-8888;** Malaysia Airlines ☎ **65/336-6777**). From KL, Malaysia Airlines has no fewer than five flights daily (☎ **03/764-3000**). The airport is 12 miles (20km) from the city. To get into

# Penang Island

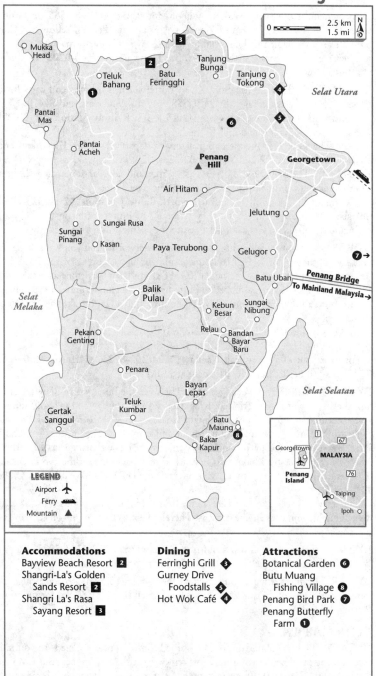

0 —— 2.5 km
—— 1.5 mi

N

*Selat Utara*

Mukka Head

Teluk Bahang ❶

**2** Batu Feringghi

Tanjung Bunga

Tanjung Tokong ❹

❺

Pantai Mas

Pantai Acheh

❻

**Penang Hill** ▲

Georgetown

Air Hitam

Jelutung

Sungai Rusa

Sungai Pinang

Kasan

Paya Terubong

Gelugor

❼ →

Batu Uban

**Penang Bridge**

**To Mainland Malaysia →**

Balik Pulau

*Selat Melaka*

Kebun Besar

Sungai Nibung

Pekan Genting

Relau

Bandan Bayar Baru

Penara

Bayan Lepas

*Selat Selatan*

Gertak Sanggul

Teluk Kumbar

Batu Maung

Bakar Kapur

❽

### LEGEND
Airport ✈
Ferry ⚓
Mountain ▲

Georgetown ✈ **MALAYSIA**

|1|

|67|

Penang Island

|76|

Taiping ✈

Ipoh

## Accommodations
Bayview Beach Resort **2**
Shangri-La's Golden
   Sands Resort **2**
Shangri La's Rasa
   Sayang Resort **3**

## Dining
Ferringhi Grill ❸
Gurney Drive
   Foodstalls ❺
Hot Wok Café ❹

## Attractions
Botanical Garden ❻
Butu Muang
   Fishing Village ❽
Penang Bird Park ❼
Penang Butterfly
   Farm ❶

town, you must purchase fixed-rate coupons for taxis—RM19 (US$5) to George-town; RM28 (US$7.35) to Batu Feringgi. There's also the **Penang Yellow Bus Company** bus no. 83, which will take you to Weld Quay in Georgetown.

There's also car rentals at the airport. See **Hertz** (☎ **04/643-0208**) or **Budget** (☎ **04/643-6025**).

**BY TRAIN**    By rail, the trip from KL to Butterworth is 6 hours and costs RM67 (US$17.65) first-class passage, RM34 (US$8.95) for second class, and RM19 (US$5) for third class. Four trains leave daily. Call the **KL Railway Station** (☎ **03/274-7435**) for schedule information.

From Thailand, KTM's international service departs from the **Hua Lamphong Railway Station** (☎ 02/223-7010 or 02/223-7020) in Bangkok, with operation to Butterworth. The daily service departs at 3:15pm and takes approximately 22 hours from Bangkok to Butterworth. See "Getting There by Train."

The train will let you off at the **Butterworth Railway Station** (☎ 04/323-7962), on Jalan Bagan Dalam (near the ferry terminal) in Butterworth, on the Malaysian mainland. From there, you can take a taxi to the island or head for the ferry.

**BY BUS**    Many buses will bring you only to Butterworth, so if you want the trip to take you all the way onto the island, make sure you buy a ticket that specifically says Penang. These buses will let you out at **KOMTAR** on Jalan Gladstone across from the Shangri-La Hotel. If you're dropped in Butterworth at the bus terminal on Jalan Bagan Dalam (next to the ferry terminal), you'll need to grab a taxi or take the ferry to the island.

In KL, **Plusliner/NICE** (☎ 03/272-2760) departs from the KL Train Station six times daily. The fare is RM40 (US$10.65) for the 4½-hour trip.

For buses out of Penang, call **Naeila** (☎ **04/262-8723**) or **Hosni** ☎ **04/261-7746**). They'll depart from the basement at KOMTAR.

**BY FERRY**    The ferry to Penang is nestled between the Butterworth Railway Station and the Butterworth bus terminal. It operates 24 hours a day and takes 20 minutes from pier to pier. From 6am to midnight ferries leave every 10 minutes. From midnight to 1:20am, boats run every half-hour and from 1:20 to 6am, they run hourly. Purchase your passage by dropping 60 sen (US15¢) exact change in the turnstile (there's a change booth if you don't have it). Fare is paid only on the trip to Penang. The return is free. The ferry lets you off at **Pengalan Weld** (Weld Quay; ☎ 04/210-2363).

The ferry will also take cars. Fares range from RM4 to RM8 (US$1.05–US$2.10), depending on your car's engine capacity. There's an extra charge of 40 sen (US10¢) per passenger.

**BY TAXI**    The outstation taxi stand is in Butterworth (☎ **04/323-2045**). Fares to Butterworth from KL will be about RM250 (US$65.80).

**BY CAR**    If you're driving you can cross the 8-mile (13.5km) Penang Bridge, the longest bridge in Southeast Asia. All cars are charged RM7 (US$1.85) for the trip to Penang. It's free on the return.

## GETTING AROUND

**BY TAXI**    Taxis are abundant, but be warned they do not use meters, so you must agree on the price before you ride. Most trips within the city are between RM3 and RM6 (US80¢–US$1.60). If you're staying out at the Batu Feringgi beach resort area, expect taxis to town to run RM20 (US$5.25); RM30 (US$7.90) at night. The ride is about 15 or 20 minutes but can take 30 during rush hour.

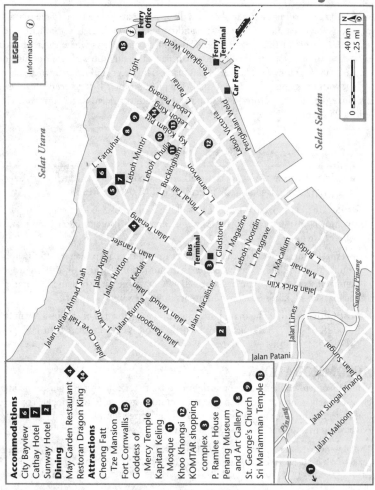

# Georgetown

**LEGEND**
*i* Information

N

.40 km
.25 mi
0

*Selat Utara*

*Selat Selatan*

Ferry Office
Ferry Terminal
Car Ferry

L. Light
Lebuh Penang
L. pantai
Pengkalan Weld
Lebuh Victoria
Pengkalan Weld

L. Farquhar
Kg. Kolam Pitt
Lebuh King
Lebuh Muntri
Lebuh Chulia
L. Pintal Tali
L. Buckingham
L. Canavon
L. Canarvon

Jalan Penang

Bus Terminal
J. Gladstone
J. Magazine
Lebuh Noordin
L. Presgrave
L. Macallum
L. Bridge

Jalan Transfer

Jalan Sultan Ahmad Shah
Jalan Clove Hall
J. Larut
Jalan Argyll
Jalan Hutton
Jalan Kedah
Jalan Yahudi
Jalan Burma
Jalan Rangoon
Jalan Macalister

Jalan Brick Kiln
L. Macnair

Jalan Lines

Jalan Patani

Jalan Sungai Pinang
Jalan Sungai
Sungai Pinang
Pinang
Jalan Sungai Pinang
Jalan Makloom

**Accommodations**
City Bayview 6
Cathay Hotel 7
Sunway Hotel 2

**Dining**
May Garden Restaurant 4
Restoran Dragon King 14

**Attractions**
Cheong Fatt
Tze Mansion 5
Fort Cornwallis 15
Goddess of
Mercy Temple 10
Kapitan Keling
Mosque 11
Khoo Khongsi 12
KOMTAR shopping
complex 3
P. Ramlee House 1
Penang Museum
and Art Gallery 8
St. George's Church 9
Sri Mariamman Temple 13

**BY BUS** Buses also run all over the island and are well used by tourists, who don't want to spring RM20 every time they want to go to the beach. The most popular route is the **Hin Bus Co. (Blue Bus) no. 93**, which operates every 10 minutes between Pengkalan Weld (Weld Quay) in Georgetown and the beach resorts at Batu Feringgi. It makes stops at KOMTAR Shopping Plaza and also at the ferry terminal. Fare is RM1 (US26¢). Give your money to the nice ticket person on board.

**CAR RENTAL** Hertz has an office in Georgetown at 38 Farquhar St. (☎ 04/263-5914).

**BY BICYCLE & MOTORCYCLE** Along Batu Feringgi, bicycles and motorcycles are available for rent.

**BY TRISHAW** In Georgetown, it's possible to find some trishaw action for about RM15 (US$3.95) an hour. It's fun and I recommend it for traveling between sights, at least for an hour or two.

**ON FOOT**   I think everyone should walk at least part of the time to see the sights of Georgetown, because between each landmark and exhibit there's so much more to see. A taxi, even a trishaw, will whisk you right by back alleys where elderly haircutters set up al fresco shops, the bicycle repairman sits fixing tubes in front of his store, and a Chinese granny fans herself in the shade. The streets of Georgetown are stimulating, with the sights of old trades still being plied on these living streets, the noise of everyday life, and the exotic smells of an old Southeast Asian port. Give yourself at least a day here.

## Fast Facts: Penang

**American Express**   Amex has an office in Georgetown at Mayflower Acme Tours, Tan Chong Building, 274 Victoria St. (☎ 04/262-6196).

**Banks/Currency Exchange**   The banking center of Georgetown is in the downtown area (close to Fort Cornwallis) on Leboh Pantai, Leboh Union, and Leboh Downing.

**Internet/E-mail**   Most of the cafes are geared to the backpacker set. On Leboh Chulia, the Rainforest Cafe is better than most, and if you walk the length of Chulia, it seems every shop has squeezed a PC on some back shelf and is charging backpackers all kinds of money to use it. Buyer beware.

**Post Office/Mail**   The main post office in Georgetown is on Leboh Downing (☎ 04/261-9222). Another convenient location is out on Jalan Batu Feringgi (☎ 04/881-2555).

## ACCOMMODATIONS

While Georgetown has many hotels right in the city for convenient sightseeing, many choose to stay at one of the beach resorts 30 minutes away at Batu Feringgi. Trips back and forth can be a bother (regardless of the resorts' free shuttle services), but if you're not staying in a resort, most of the finer beaches are off limits.

**The Bayview Beach Resort.** Batu Feringgi Beach, 11100 Penang. ☎ **04/881-2123.** Fax 04/881-2140. 366 units. A/C MINIBAR TV TEL. RM390 (US$103) hill-view double; RM470 (US$124) sea-view double; RM654 (US$172) hill-view suite; RM862 (US$227) sea-view double. AE, DC, JCB, MC, V.

Located right on Batu Feringgi Beach, the Bayview is a relaxing resort with all the conveniences you look for in a large international hotel. The feel of the place is spacious and airy, an ambiance carried into the rooms—the standard double room, for instance, is quite large. Rooms facing the road have views of the neighboring condominium complex, and can be noisy. Get the sea view so you can take advantage of your balcony. Facilities include an outdoor pool, squash and tennis courts, billiards, table tennis, and a fitness center with Jacuzzi, sauna, and steam. Cycling, parasailing, waterskiing, sailing, windsurfing, canoeing, and boat trips to beachside barbecues and fishing spots are all available. Recent discount packages offer 50% discounts off all categories of rooms.

**Cathay Hotel.** No. 15 Leith St., Georgetown 10200, Penang. ☎ **04/262-6271.** Fax 04/263-9300. 37 units. TV. RM57.50 (US$15) without A/C, RM69 (US$18) with A/C. No credit cards.

Cathay comes highly recommended for its location and price. Within walking distance of the city attractions, it's definitely a budget place, but it has a charming faded elegance. Housed in a traditional Chinese prewar mansion, nice touches include high ceilings, mosaic tile and wood floors, and whitewashed walls. The decor features Chinese lanterns and ceiling fans. You won't find a budget hotel with more style and respectability. The only real faults are the small, old bathrooms and the lack of room or laundry services.

✪ **The City Bayview Hotel, Penang.** 25–A Farquhar St., Georgetown, 10200 Penang. ☎ **800/8854** or 04/263-3161. Fax 04/263-4124. 176 units. A/C MINIBAR TV TEL. RM138 (US$36) double. AE, DC, MC, V.

Situated on Farquhar Street, City Bayview has a convenient location for visitors who want to take in the historic and cultural sights of Georgetown. A new wing has been opened featuring large guest rooms that have style and amenities that bring the hotel up to date (before this it hadn't seen renovation since 1975!). Suites are still under renovation, and the old wing will be updated, probably before the end of 1999. The price listed above is a promotional rate, as no rack rate had been established at the time of writing.

**Shangri-La's Golden Sands Resort.** Batu Feringgi Beach, 11100 Penang, ☎ **800/942-5050** from the U.S. and Canada, 800/222448 from Australia, 0800/442179 from New Zealand, or 04/881-1911. Fax 04/881-1880. www.shangri-la.com. 395 units. A/C MINIBAR TV TEL. RM300–RM490 (US$79–US$129) double; RM750 (US$197) suite. AE, DC, JCB, MC, V.

Rasa Sayang's little sister property is located just next door. A newer resort, it is priced lower than the Rasa Sayang, so it attracts more families. The beach, pool area, and public spaces fill up fast in the morning, and folks are occupied all day with beach sports like parasailing and jet skiing, and pool games. For the younger set, a kids' club keeps small ones busy while mom and dad do "boring stuff." Rooms are large with full amenities, and the higher priced categories have views of the pool and sea. Better still, guests here can use the facilities at Rasa Sayang.

✪ **Shangri-La's Rasa Sayang Resort.** Batu Feringgi Beach, 11100 Penang. ☎ **800/942-5050** from the U.S. and Canada, 800/222448 from Australia, 0800/442179 from New Zealand, or 04/881-1811. Fax 04/881-1984. www.shangri-la.com. 515 units. RM370 (US$97) double, RM470 (US$124) deluxe sea-facing double; RM520 (US$137) deluxe garden/patio rm; from RM850 (US$224) suite. AE, DC, JCB, MC, V.

Of all the beachfront resorts on Penang, Rasa Sayang is the finest. It has been here the longest of any resort, celebrating its 25-year anniversary in 1998, so it had the first pick of beachfront property and plenty of space to create lush gardens and pool areas. Get a room looking over the pool area, and your private balcony will be facing the picturesque palm-lined beach. The free-form pool is sprawled amidst tropical landscaping and cafes, and the rest of the grounds have strolling gardens that are romantically illuminated in the evenings. The hotel is both elegant and relaxed, with Malay-style decor in the public areas and rooms. You'll also appreciate the good seafood restaurants nearby. Facilities include an outdoor pool, fitness center, mini–putting green, and table tennis. Guests have access to nearby tennis courts, sailing, boating, and waterskiing. Make sure to ask about the incredible bargain packages.

**Sunway Hotel.** 33 New Lane, Georgetown, 10400 Penang. ☎ **04/229-9988.** Fax 04/228-8899. 262 units. A/C MINIBAR TV TEL. RM330 (US$87) double; RM470 (US$124) suite. Ask about discounts as low as 170RM (US$45) for double rooms. Rates include American breakfast. AE, DC, MC, V.

The Sunway is centrally located in Georgetown, near the KOMTAR shopping complex and the Penang Museum. Built in 1994, the hotel is warm and elegant, with marble details and a new and modern feel to the open spaces. The rooms are fresh and spacious, and rooms on all sides have views of the city. Facilities include an outdoor pool and a fitness center with Jacuzzi. The hotel can arrange tennis, squash, and sauna at nearby facilities.

## DINING

⭐ **Feringgi Grill.** Shangri-La's Rasa Sayang Resort, Batu Feringgi Beach. ☎ **04/881-1811.** Reservations recommended. Entree RM49.50 (US$13.05)–RM68 (US$17.90). Open daily 7–10:30pm. CONTINENTAL.

The Feringgi Grill is comparable to any five-star hotel grill anywhere. From the dreamy lobster bisque to the carving cart of perfectly grilled top quality meats flown in from all over the world, you'll be living the good life with each bite. A good wine selection will help revive you when you think you've died and gone to heaven. And don't even mention the desserts—the whole cart should be sent straight to hell. Feringgi is perfect for a romantic dinner, or a change from all that char koay teow you've been eating in town.

⭐ **Hot Wok Café.** 125–D Desa Tanjung, Jalan Tanjung. ☎ **04/899-0858.** Reservations recommended for weekends. Entrees RM9–RM15 (US$2.35–US$3.95). AE, DC, MC, V. Daily 11am–3pm and 6–11pm. PERANAKAN.

This place is the number one recommended Peranakan restaurant in the city, and small wonder: The food is great and the atmosphere is fabulous. Filled with local treasures such as wooden lattice work, wooden lanterns, carved Peranakan cabinets, tapestries, and carved wood panels, the decor will make you want to just sit back, relax, and take in sights you'd only ever see in a Peranakan home. Their curry capitan, a famous local dish, is curry chicken stuffed with potatoes, with a thick delicious coconut-based gravy. They also do a mean perut ikan—fish intestine with roe and vegetable—it's the house specialty.

⭐ **May Garden Restaurant.** 70 Jalan Penang. ☎ **04/261-6806.** Reservations recommended. Entrees start at RM8 (US$2.10). Seafood is priced by kg weight. AE, DC, MC, V. Noon–3pm and 6–10:30pm. CANTONESE.

This is a top Cantonese restaurant in Georgetown, and while it's noisy and not too big on ambiance, it has excellent food. But how many Chinese do *you* know who go to places for ambiance? It's the food that counts! Outstanding dishes include the tofu and broccoli topped with sea snail slices or the fresh steamed live prawns. They also have suckling pig and Peking duck. Don't agree to all the daily specials or you'll pay a fortune.

**Ocean Green.** 48F Jalan Sultan Ahmad Shah. ☎ **04/226-2681.** Reservations recommended. Entrees starting from RM12 (US$3.15); seafood priced according to market value. Open daily 9am–11pm. AE, MC, V. SEAFOOD.

I can't rave enough about Ocean Green. If the beautiful sea view and ocean breezes don't make you weep with joy, the food certainly will. A long list of fresh seafood is prepared steamed or fried, with your choice of chili, black bean, sweet and sour, or curry sauces. On the advice of a local food expert, I tried the lobster thermidor, expensive but divine, and the chicken wings stuffed with minced chicken, prawns, and gravy.

**Restoran Dragon King.** 99 Leboh Bishop. ☎ **04/261-8035.** Entrees RM8–RM20 (US$2.10–US$5.25). No credit cards. Daily 11am–3pm and 6–10pm. PERANAKAN.

Penang is famous around the world for delicious local Peranakan dishes, and Dragon King is a good place to sample the local cuisine at its finest. It was opened 20 years ago by a group of local teachers who wanted to revive the traditional dishes cooked by their mothers. Decor-wise, the place is nothing to shout about—just a coffee shop with tile floors and folding chairs—but all the curries are hand-blended to perfection. Their curry capitan will make you weep with joy, it's so rich. But come early for the otak-otak, or it might sell out. While Dragon King is hopping at lunchtime, dinner is quiet.

## FOOD STALL DINING

No section on Penang dining would be complete without full coverage of the local food stall scene, which is famous. Any dish you've had in Malaysia, Singapore, even southern Thailand—Penang hawkers can do it better. I had slimy char koay teow in Singapore and swore off the stuff forever. After being forced to try it in Penang (where the fried flat noodles and seafood are a specialty dish), I was completely addicted. Penang may be attractive for many things; history, culture, nature—but it is loved for its food.

**Gurney Drive Food Stalls,** towards the water just down from the intersection with Jalan Kelawai, is the biggest and most popular hawker center. It has all kinds of food, including local dishes with every influence: Chinese, Malay, Indian. In addition to the above mentioned char koay teow, there's char bee hoon, a fried thin rice noodle, laksa (fish soup with noodles), murtabak (a sort of curry mutton burrito), oh chien (oyster omelet with chili dip), and rojak (a spicy fruit and seafood salad).

After you've eaten your way through Gurney Drive, you can try the stalls on **Jalan Burmah** near the Lai Lai Supermarket.

## ATTRACTIONS
### IN GEORGETOWN

✪ **Fort Cornwallis.** Lebuhraya Light. ☎ **04/262-9461.** Admission RM1 (US26¢) adult, RM.50 (US13¢) child. Daily 8am–7pm.

Fort Cornwallis is built on the site where Capt. Francis Light, founder of Penang, first landed in 1786. The fort was first built in 1793, but this site was an unlikely spot from which to defend the city from invasion. In 1810 it was rebuilt in an attempt to make up for initial strategic planning errors. In the shape of a star, the only actual buildings still standing are the outer walls, a gunpowder magazine, and a small Christian chapel. The magazine houses an exhibit of old photos and historical accounts of the old fort.

✪ **Cheong Fatt Tze Mansion.** Lebuhraya Leith. ☎ **04/261-0076.** Admission RM10 (US$2.65) adults and children. Guided tours Mon, Wed, Fri and Sat at 11am only.

Cheong Fatt Tze (1840–1917), once dubbed "China's Rockefeller" by *The New York Times,* built a vast commercial empire in Southeast Asia, first in Indonesia, then Singapore. He came to Penang in 1890 and continued his success, giving some of his spoils to build schools throughout the region. His mansion, where he lived with his eight wives, was built between 1896 and 1904. Inside are lavish adornments—stained glass, crown mouldings, gilded wood-carved doors, ceramic ornaments—and seven staircases.

✪ **Khoo Khongsi.** Leburaya Cannon. ☎ **604/261-4609.** Free admission. Daily 9am–5pm.

The Chinese who migrated to Southeast Asia formed clan associations in their new homes. Based on common heritage, these social groups formed the core of Chinese life in the new homelands. The Khoo clan, who immigrated from Hokkien Province in China, acquired this spot in 1851 and set to work building row houses, administrative buildings, and a clan temple around a large square. The temple here now was actually built in 1906 after a fire destroyed its predecessor. It was believed the original was too ornate, provoking the wrath of the gods. One look at the current temple, a Chinese baroque masterpiece, and you'll wonder how that could possibly be. Come here in August for Chinese operas.

**P. Ramlee House.** Jalan P. Ramlee. No phone. Free admission. Daily 9am–5pm.

This is the house where legendary Malaysian performer P. Ramlee (1928–1973) was born and raised. The life of this prolific actor, director, singer, composer, and prominent figurehead of Malaysian film industry is remembered in a gallery at this house. Photos from his life and personal memorabilia offer a glimpse of local culture even those who've never heard of him can appreciate.

⭐ **Penang Museum and Art Gallery.** Leburaya Farquahar. ☎ **04/261-3144.** Free admission. Open Sat–Thurs 9am–5pm.

The historical society has put together this marvelous collection of ethnological and historical findings from Penang, tracing the port's history and diverse cultures through time. It's filled with paintings, photos, costumes, and antiques among much more, all presented with fascinating facts and trivia. Upstairs is an art gallery. Originally the Penang Free School, the building was built in two phases, the first half in 1896 and the second in 1906. Only half of the building remains; the other was bombed to the ground in World War II. It's a favorite stop on a sightseeing itinerary—it's *air-conditioned!*

**Kapitan Keling Mosque.** Jalan Masjid Kapitan Keling (Leboh Pitt).

Captain Light donated a large parcel of land on this spot for the settlement's large Indian Muslim community to build a mosque and graveyard. The leader of the community, known as Kapitan Keling (or Kling, which ironically was once a racial slur against Indians in the region), built a brick mosque here. Later in 1801, he imported builders and materials from India for a new, brilliant mosque. Expansions in the 1900s topped the mosque with stunning domes and turrets, adding extensions and new roofs.

**Goddess of Mercy Temple.** Leboh Pitt.

Dedicated jointly to the Goddess of Mercy, Kuan Yin, and Ma Po Cho, the patron saint of sea travelers, this is the oldest Chinese temple in Penang. On the 19th of each second, sixth, and ninth month of the lunar calendar, Kuan Yin is celebrated with Chinese operas and puppet shows.

**St. George's Church.** Farquhar Street.

Built by Reverend R.S. Hutchins, also responsible for the Free School next door, home of the Penang Museum, and Captain Robert N. Smith, whose paintings hang in the museum, this church was completed in 1818. While the outside is almost as it was then, the contents were completely looted during World War II. All that remains are the font and the bishop's chair.

**Sri Mariamman Temple.** Leburaya Queen.

This Hindu temple was built in 1833 by a Chettiar and received a major face-lift in 1978 with the help of Madras sculptors. The Hindu Navarithri festival is held here, whereby devotees parade Sri Mariamman, a Hindu goddess worshipped for her powers to cure disease, through the streets in a night procession. It is also the starting point of the Taipusam Festival, which leads to a temple on Jalan Waterfall.

## OUTSIDE GEORGETOWN

**Batu Muang Fishing Village.** Southeast tip of Penang.

If it's a local fishing village you'd like to see, here's a good one. This village is special for its shrine to Admiral Cheng Ho, the early Chinese sea adventurer.

⭐ **Botanical Garden.** ☎ **604/228-6248.** Free admission. Daily 5am–8pm.

Covering 70 acres (30 hectares) of landscaped grounds, this botanic garden was established by the British in 1884. The grounds are perfect for a shady walk, and a ton of fun if you love monkeys. They're crawling all over the place and will think nothing of stepping forward for a peanut (which you can buy beneath the DO NOT FEED THE MONKEYS sign). Also in the gardens are a jogging track and kiddie park.

**Penang Butterfly Farm.** Jalan Teluk Bahang. ☎ **04/881-1253.** Adults RM5 (US$1.30), children RM2 (US50¢); free for children under five. Mon–Fri 9am–5pm, Sat–Sun 9am–6pm.

The Penang Butterfly Farm, located toward the northwest corner of the island, is the largest in the world. On its 2-acre (0.8-hectare) landscaped grounds there are over 4,000 flying butterflies from 120 species. At 10am and 3pm, there are informative butterfly shows. Don't forget the insect exhibit—there are about 2,000 or so bugs.

✪ **Penang Hill.**

Covered with jungle growth and 20 nature trails, the hill is great for trekking. Or, you can go to Ayer Hitam, a town in the central part of Penang, and take the funicular railway to the top. The **Keretapi Bukit Bendera** (☎ **04/828-3262**) operates from 6:30am to 10:30pm weekdays and until midnight on weekends, sending trains up and down the hill every half-hour. It costs RM4 (US$1.05) for adults and RM2 (US50¢) for children. If you prefer the trek, go to the "Moon Gate" at the entrance to Botanical Gardens for a 9-mile (5.5km), 3-hour hike to the summit.

**Penang Bird Park.** Jalan Teluk, Seberang Jaya. ☎ **04/399-1899.** Adults RM3 (US80¢), children RM1 (US25¢). Daily 9am–7pm.

The Bird Park is not on Penang Island, but on the mainland part of Penang state. The 5-acre (2-hectare) park is home to some 200 bird species from Malaysia and around the world.

## SHOPPING

The first place anyone here will recommend for shopping is **KOMTAR.** Short for "Kompleks Tun Abdul Razak," it is the largest shopping complex in Penang, a full 65 stories of clothing shops, restaurants, and a couple of large department stores. There's a **duty free shop** on the 57th floor. On the third floor is a **tourist information center.**

Good shopping finds in Penang are batik, pewter products, locally produced curio items, paintings, antiques, pottery, and jewelry. If you care to walk the streets in search of finds, there are a few streets in Georgetown that are the hub of shopping activity. In the city center, the area around Jalan Penang, Lebuhraya Campbell, Lebuhraya Kapitan Keling, Lebuhraya Chulia, and Lebuhraya Pantai is near the Sri Mariamman Temple, the Penang Museum, the Kapitan Keling Mosque, and other sites of historic interest. Here you'll find everything from local crafts to souvenirs and fashion, and maybe even a bargain or two. Most of these shops are open from 10am to 10pm daily.

Out at **Batu Feringgi,** the main road turns into a fun night bazaar every evening just at dark. During the day, there are also some good shops for batik and souvenirs.

## NIGHTLIFE

Clubs in Penang stay open a little later than in the rest of Malaysia, and some even stay open until 3am on the weekends.

If you're looking for a bar that's a little out of the ordinary, visit **20 Leith Street** (11–A Lebuh Leith; ☎ 04/261-6301). Located in an old 1930s house, the place has seating areas fitted with traditional antique furniture in each room of the house. Possibly the most notorious bar in Penang is the **Hong Kong Bar** (371 Lebuh Chulia; ☎ 04/261-9796). This bar opened in 1920 and was a regular hangout for military personnel based in Butterworth. It has an extraordinary archive of photos of the servicemen who have patronized the place throughout the years, plus a collection of medals, plaques, and buoys from ships.

For dancing, the resorts in Batu Feringgi have the better discos. **Borsalino** (Penang Park Royal, 1 Batu Ferringhi Beach; ☎ **04/881-1133, ext. 8844**) is popular with upbeat dance music and slick disco decor. Much of the clientele seems to remember when disco meant doing the hustle. **Zulu's Seaside Paradise** (Paradise Tanjung Bungah; ☎ **04/890-8808**) is a world-beat dance club, spinning African, reggae and other danceable international music.

**Hard Life Café** (363 Lebuh Chulia; ☎ **04/262-1740**) is an interesting alternative hangout. Decorated with Rasta paraphernalia, the place fills up with backpackers, who sometimes aren't as laid back as Mr. Marley would hope they'd be. Still, it's fun to check out the books where guests comment on their favorite (or least favorite) travel haunts in Southeast Asia.

## 9  Desaru

Desaru is an odd place. If it weren't for the resorts here, it probably wouldn't be a place at all. A large arch appears over the road as you approach, welcoming you to the resort town, while just outside there's not much to speak of. Situated along 10 miles (17km) of sandy beach on the South China Sea, this collection of six resorts and campgrounds has become a very popular vacation spot. Its claim to fame? It's close to Singapore, which means the great majority (up to 90%) of folks who come are Singaporeans or expatriates on weekend getaways for beaches and golf. With this in mind, plan on a trip to Desaru from Monday through Thursday (and not during a public holiday). Weekends are jam packed and not very conducive to relaxation. Still, in all, Desaru has a far way to go before it's overdeveloped.

Once in Desaru, you'll probably stay within your resort most of the time. All have pools and beachfronts with varieties of water sports. The staff at the front desks can arrange golf for you at the local course.

## GETTING THERE

**BY CAR**  You can reach Desaru over well-laid roads by car from Johor Bahru.

**BY FERRY**  From the Changi Ferry Terminal on the east coast of Singapore, FerryLink (☎ 65/545-3600; fax 65/545-5040) departs daily at 8:15am, 11:15am, 2:15pm, and 5:15pm. The trip is S$19 (US$11.60) one-way and S$26 (US$15.90) round-trip. Children are S$11.50 (US$7) and S$16 (US$9.80) respectively. The trip is a slow and peaceful 45 minutes to the jetty at Tanjong Belungkor (☎ 07/251-7404). From here you can pre-arrange shuttle service with your resort, or for RM40 (US$10.55) with A/C or RM25 (US$6.60) without you can go it alone with one of the outstation taxis that wait outside the jetty building. The ride takes a half hour.

**BY TAXI**  Outstation taxis from Johor Bahru can deliver you to Desaru for about RM100 (US$26.30). For booking, call ☎ 07/223-4494. The number to call for outstation taxis from Desaru is ☎ 07/823-6916. They can take you to Kota Tinggi (see "Sports & The Outdoors" in the Johor Bahru section, earlier in this chapter) for RM50 (US$13.15) or to Mersing for RM150 (US$39.45).

## GETTING AROUND & GETTING ANYTHING ELSE

The resorts at Desaru are self-contained, with restaurants and activities—including golf and nature treks. Should you require other services, the front desk of any resort can help you out.

# ACCOMMODATIONS

✪ **Desaru Golden Beach Hotel.** P.O. Box 50, Tanjung Penawar, 81907 Kota Tinggi, Johor. ☎ 07/822-1101. Fax 07/822-1480. 57 units, 115 villas. AC MINIBAR TV TEL. Weekdays RM150–RM200 (US$39–US$53) double; RM350 (US$92) suite; RM170 (US$45) villa; RM370 (US$97) villa suite. Weekends RM220–RM280 (US$58–US$74) double; RM420 (US$110) suite; RM240 (US$63) villa; RM450 (US$118) villa suite. AE, DC, JCB, MC, V.

Desaru Golden Beach Resort is casual and comfortable, with a tropical open-air concept lobby with a high timbered ceiling to allow for cool breezes. The standard rooms face the parking area and garden, while the superior rooms face the sea and are assigned on a first-come, first-served basis. The villas are like small apartments, and their balconies have plenty of space for sitting with a cool drink. And while their privacy is nice, one feature I don't like is that the villas have carpeting, which makes the rooms feel warm. The double rooms off the lobby feel cooler and fresher with clean tiled floors. Dining options are a seafood restaurant and another offering local dishes. Facilities include a large outdoor lagoon pool, access to the fitness center at Desaru Perdana Beach Resort, a Jacuzzi, two outdoor tennis courts, water sports equipment, and bicycle rental.

The main attraction here besides the beach is golfing. Greens fees for hotel guests are RM70 (US$18) on weekdays and RM110 (US$29) on weekends. The resort complex has 45 holes, not including the 18-hole signature Robert Trent Jones Jr. course.

**Desaru Perdana Beach Resort.** P.O. Box 29, Bandar Penawar, 81900 Kota Tinggi, Johor. ☎ **07/822-2222.** Fax 07/822-2223. 229 units. Weekdays: RM 290 (US$76) double; RM546–RM900 (US$134–US$237) suite. Weekends: RM350 (US$92.10) double; RM750–RM1,200 (US$197–US$316) suite. AE, DC, MC, V.

Desaru Perdana Beach Resort is an upmarket resort, attracting more varied international guests (especially Japanese). It's newer than the others, so the architectural styling has a more modern distinction. The Bali-style open air lobby has a paneled ceiling and high wooden beams. Guestrooms are also very up-to-date, with new furnishings in Western styles and all the amenities. Perdana, unlike the older Golden Beach, fills huge blocks of buildings, which on the outside look like condominiums, while Golden Beach is smaller and a little more spread out. Perdana's has three restaurants (Japanese, Chinese, and Continental) and a bar with live entertainment nightly. Facilities include a large outdoor pool, small fitness center, Jacuzzi, sauna, tennis courts, water sports equipment, and souvenir shop.

# DESARU OUTDOORS

It goes without saying that many visitors come for the golf. Guests at any of the resorts can arrange golf through their resort's front desk. The **Desaru Golf & Country Club,** P.O. Box 57, Tanjung Penawar, 81907 Kota Tinggi, Johor (☎ **07/822-2333;** fax 07/822-1855), has 45 holes and an 18-hole Robert Trent Jones Jr. course. Greens fees for 18 holes on weekends and public holidays are RM150 (US$39.45) and RM90 (US$24) Monday through Friday. Club rentals, shoes, trolleys, and buggies are available for rent, and caddy fees range from RM12 (US$3.15) for a trainee to RM20 (US$5.25) for the best they've got. Be sure to confirm your reservation 2 weeks beforehand.

Beach activities include parasailing and windsurfing (with instruction), canoeing, jet skiing, waterskiing, fishing (including night fishing), snorkeling, and speedboat rides. The resorts can also arrange hikes in the nearby jungle, horseback riding, go-karts, tennis, volleyball and other activities.

## 10 Mersing

Mersing is not so much a destination in itself, but more a jump-off point for ferries to the islands on the East Coast of Malaysia, such as Tioman. Nobody really stays in Mersing unless they've missed the boat—literally. There are a couple of good seafood restaurants in town, but otherwise it's just a small, relaxed fishing town.

### GETTING THERE

The main focal point of the city is the **R&R Plaza,** by the main jetty to Tioman. The bus terminal is here, just behind the food stalls (which are great to graze as you wait for a ferry or bus). In front of these are the offices where you book the ferry or speed-boats to Tioman. Outside of R&R are taxis—some local, some outstation, none metered. Local trips are about RM5 (US$1.30).

Outstation taxis to other cities are also available at R&R Plaza. Expect to pay RM140 (US$37) for Kuantan, and RM120 (US$31.60) for Johor Bahru.

**BY BUS**   **Transnasional** has two daily buses from KL's Putra Bus Terminal opposite the Putra World Trade Center. Call ☎ **03/442-8945.** The trip to Mersing will cost RM16.60 (US$4.35). Johor Bahru's Larkin Terminal Transnasional (☎ **07/224-5182**) has quite a few buses that stop in Mersing on their way up the east coast. Fares are around RM10.10 (US$2.65).

For outgoing bus information, call Transnasional (☎ 07/799-3155) or **Johora Express** (☎ **07/799-5227**).

## ACCOMMODATIONS

Mersing has no world-class accommodations or resorts. The places you'll find here are basic accommodations for those just passin' through.

**Mersing Inn.** 38 Jalan Ismail, next to the Parkson supermarket, 86800, Mersing, Johor. ☎ **07/799-2288.** Fax 07/799-1919. 40 units. RM65 double (US$17). MC.

The rooms here are small but clean, but some do not have air-conditioning, so be sure to specify. Others don't have televisions or telephones. There are private baths for each room, however.

✪ **Timotel.** 839 Jalan Endau, 86800, Mersing, Johor. ☎ **07/799-5888.** Fax 07/799-5333. 50 units. AC MINIBAR TV TEL. RM120–RM140 (US$31–US$37) double; RM240–RM270 (US$63–US$71) suite. AE, MC.

This hotel, one of the newest and most pleasant in Mersing, has clean and neat rooms and modern conveniences like room and laundry services. The hotel provides free transfers to and from the jetty. There's a fitness center, and bicycle rental can be arranged.

## DINING

Like the hotels in Mersing, none of the restaurants are particularly "fine." There is, however, some pretty good seafood to be eaten here, if you don't mind a really low-key and colloquial dining experience. Neither of the places below has a phone, and if they did they probably wouldn't use them for silly things like taking reservations. Just head on down and find a table.

**Ee lo Restoran.** Jalan Abu Bakar, next to the roundabout beside the newspaper shop. No phone. Meals RM5–RM10 (US$1.30–US$2.65). No credit cards. Daily 9am to 10pm.

Here is the best place to eat while waiting for your boat. About a 5-minute walk from R&R Plaza, this coffee shop has menu items like mee hoon and kuay teow, Hainan chicken rice, and all sorts of seafood and vegetable dishes. The steamed prawns are succulent, and Ee lo serves an unusual dish—stir-fried vegetables in milk—which is quite tasty.

**Mersing Seafood Restaurant.** Jalan Ismail, next to the Shell station. No phone. Noodle dishes RM3 (US80¢) and up; other dishes RM10 (US$2.65) and up. M/C. Daily 12:30pm–midnight. CHINESE/SEAFOOD.

You won't need a reservation here, even though it gets crowded on weekends. The service is lousy and the place is a little grubby, but the food is so good nobody seems to care. It's also air-conditioned. Prices will range according to season. Some great dishes to try are the deep-fried squid stuffed with salted egg yolk, the bamboo or asparagus clams fried in chili sauce, or the sautéed garlic prawns.

## 11  Tioman Island

Tioman Island is by far the most popular destination on Malaysia's east coast. Although it's in the state of Pahang, Tioman's mainland gateway, Mersing, is in Johor. The island is only 23.4 miles (39km) long and 7.2 miles (12km) wide, with sandy beaches, clear water with sea life and coral reefs, and jungle mountain-trekking trails with streams and waterfalls. So idyllic is the setting that Tioman was the location for the 1950s Hollywood film *South Pacific.*

Despite heavy tourist traffic, Tioman has retained much of its tropical island charm, perhaps by virtue of the fact that few large hotels have been built on it. However, some parts are becoming very commercial, particularly Kampung Tekek, which is where you arrive at either the main jetty or the airport. A paved stretch of road runs up the west coast, between Tekek and Berjaya Tioman Beach Resort (the only true resort on the island), and this area is more built up than the rest of the island. "Built up" is really a relative term; trust me, it's a one-horse town. If you trek overland from Tekek to the east coast, you'll find beaches that are more peaceful and serene.

Activity is spread throughout the *kampungs* (villages) along the shores of the island. Each of these places has some sort of accommodation facilities, most of them very basic chalets, with some access to canteens or restaurants. In addition to Tekek, the other kampungs include Air Batang (also called ABC), Salang, Paya, Genting, and the only kampung on the eastern shore, Juara.

There is a small local population on the island living in the kampungs, but at almost any given time there are more tourists, mainly from Singapore and other parts of Malaysia, than locals. Most come for the scuba and beaches, but from November through February you won't find many tourists. Monsoon tides make Tioman impossible to access by ferry, and not the most perfect vacation in the tropical balmies.

### GETTING THERE

**BY PLANE**    Flights to Tioman originate from Singapore, Kuala Lumpur, and Kuantan. **Pelangi's** KL office is at 18th Floor, Technology Resources Tower, 161B Jalan Ampang (☎ **03/262-4446,** fax 03/262-4515). They service Tioman four times daily. A round-trip ticket is about RM282 (US$74). There's a daily flight from **Kuantan,** Sultan Ahmad Shah Airport (☎ **09/538-1177,** fax 09/538-1713) for a cost of around RM158 (US$41.60) round-trip. Pelangi also has two dailies from Singapore's Seletar Airport (not Changi International) at a cost of S$230 (US$140.65). Their ticketing and information office in Singapore is c/o Malaysia Airlines, 190 Clemenceau Ave. no. 02–09, Singapore Shopping Centre (☎ **65/336/6777**).

The airport in Tioman is in Kampung Tekek, where you'll also find the main jetty. The ticketing office is on the second floor of the complex across from the jetty just

---

### Tioman Travel Tips

If you have not already acquired a good **mosquito repellent,** do so before heading to Tioman. You'll need something with DEET. Tioman mosquitoes are hungry. If you plan to stay in one of the smaller chalet places, you might want to invest in a mosquito net. Also, bring a **flashlight** to help you get around after sunset.

---

next door to the airport. The number for inquiries is ☎ **09/419-1301.** If you're staying at Berjaya Tioman, a shuttle will fetch you; however, if you plan to stay elsewhere, you're on your own. See "Getting Around," below.

**BY FERRY**    There are 10 speedboats that ply the waters to and from Tioman. Book passage on one of them from the many booking agents huddled around the dock near the R&R Plaza. They're basically all the same, each reserving trips on the same boats. Boats leave Mersing Jetty at intervals that depend on the tide. The trip takes around 1½ hours and can cost between RM20 and RM25 (US$5.25–US$6.60), depending on the power of the boat you hire. The last boat leaves for Tioman between 5pm and 6pm every evening. If you miss this boat, you're stuck in Mersing for the night. If you're not sure when you want to leave and don't want to purchase round-trip, just show up at the jetty in Tekek before 8am. You can buy a ticket then and catch the boat.

From Singapore, **Auto Batam Ferries & Tours** (☎ **65/524-7105**) operates a daily ferry from the Tanah Merah Ferry Terminal for S$90 (US$55). The ferry takes you to Berjaya Tioman, which is also where the ferry to Singapore departs daily.

## GETTING AROUND

The lay of the land looks like this: On the west side of the island are most of the kampungs. Tekek is about midway from north to south. It's the only kampung with a paved road, which is only a few kilometers long. North of Tekek is Kampung Air Batang, and north of that is Salang. Both of these kampungs have paved walking paths, connecting them with Tekek and with each other. The path from ABC to Tekek is lighted at night. A hike between kampungs is about 30 to 40 minutes.

South of Tekek is the Berjaya Tioman Resort, and south of that are kampungs Paya and Genting. Neither Paya nor Genting is accessible via walking path. I haven't covered either of them because, frankly, I don't recommend you stay there. The main snorkel, dive, and fishing operators, as well as the better places to eat, are in other kampungs. And while Paya and Genting are secluded, the beaches there are not particularly good. So while most of the touting in Mersing is for accommodations in Paya and Genting, beware. I've seen plenty of travelers take up these offers, only to change kampungs within a day or two.

If you really want seclusion, head for Juara, the only kampung on the eastern side of the island. The beach is also the island's finest, but be prepared for provision of only the most minimal of human necessities. Juara is connected with Tekek by a hiking trail over the hills in the center of the island. While the locals can make the trip in just over an hour, most of us will need two.

The most popular mode of transport between kampungs is water taxi. Each village has a jetty—you can pay your fare either at tour offices located near the foot of the pier, or pay the captain directly. The taxis stop operating past nightfall, so make sure you get home before 6 or 7pm. A few sample fares: from Tekek to ABC is RM12 (US$3.15) per person, to Salang RM20 (US$5.25), to Juara RM60 (US$15.80). Also,

# Tioman Island

**LEGEND**
Airport ✈
Footpath – – –
Mountain ▲

Pulau Tulai

Kampung Salang

Kampung Penuba

Kampung Air Batang

Kampung Dungun

Kampung Tekek

Pulau Rengis

← Ferry to Mersing

■ Berjaya Tioman Beach Resort

Kampung Bunut

Kampung Juara

Kampung Paya

Kampung Genting

Kampung Nipah

Bukit Batu Sirau ▲

Bukit Simukut ▲

Mukut Waterfalls ■

Kampung Mukut

Kampung Asah

0    4.5 km
     2.8 mi

N

4-0279

these guys don't like to shuttle around only one person, so if there's only one of you, be prepared to pay double.

Note that water taxis usually don't hang around Juara. If you're looking to get back to civilization by boat, you either have to get lucky with a supplies delivery boat or wait for a taxi to make a drop off (which can be days). Otherwise, there's a daily sea bus at 3pm that can take you to the other kampungs.

If you're making the hike between Tekek and Juara, make sure you leave no later than 4pm to allow time to make it before dark.

In Tekek, where paved roads allow, many locals have motorbikes, and some will scoot you someplace for anywhere between RM5 and RM10 (US$1.30–US$2.65).

## Fast Facts: Tioman Island

**Banks/Currency Exchange**   There are money changers who accept traveler's checks in Tekek at the airport and by the jetty and at Berjaya Tioman Resort. Other places will take traveler's checks, and some of the smaller accommodations now accept them as payment. The best idea for a better rate is to cash them at a bank on the mainland before you go.

**Internet/E-mail**    The only Internet access on Tioman is in ABC—one terminal at Bamboo Hill at the north end of the beach for RM5 (US$1.30) per hour (when it's working).

**Telephones**    There are public phones at Tekek, ABC, and Salang, which you can use with Telekom phonecards bought on the island. Most guest houses have nothing more than cellular phones that they will allow guests to use—at a price.

## ACCOMMODATIONS

Unless you stay at the Best Western Berjaya Tioman Beach Resort, expect to be roughing it. For some travelers, the Berjaya Tioman, with its wonderful modern conveniences, is what it takes to make a tropical island experience relaxing. Your shower is always warm, you can order food to your room, and you can arrange any activity through the concierge in the lobby. For others, though, real relaxation comes from an escape from modern distractions. The small chalets in the kampungs have very minimal facilities and few or no conveniences such as hot showers and telephones. Why would you want to stay in them? Because they're simple, quiet, close to the beach, and less touristy than the resort. You will also have to trek around to find dining options, as few of these places have canteens. Yes, you sacrifice a lot, but the peaceful nature of the island is a more idyllic experience when you stay at a chalet. Be warned, however, that touts at the jetty in Mersing will offer you all sorts of really, really cheap accommodations, many of which are so rustic they're beyond Robinson Crusoe. Those I've listed under "The Kampungs," below, are all on the inhabitable side of rustic.

✪ **Best Western Berjaya Tioman Beach Resort.** Tioman Island, Pahang Darul Makmur. ☎ 09/419-1000. Fax 09/419-1718. 380 units. AC MINIBAR TV TEL. Mar–Oct RM245 (US$64) standard rm; RM340–RM430 (US$89–US$113) chalets; RM500–RM1,200 (US$131–US$316) suite. Nov–Feb RM195 (US$51) standard rm; RM265–RM345 (US$70–US$91) chalet; RM400–RM720 (US$105–US$189) suite. AE, DC, MC, V.

Berjaya Tioman is the only true resort, in the Western sense, on the island, and provides all the conveniences you'd expect from a chain hotel. For modern comforts and golf, this is the place to be, but be prepared for Tourist Central. A range of sports opportunities and facilities are offered, including scuba diving, windsurfing, sailing, fishing, snorkeling, canoeing, glass-bottom boat rides, horseback riding, four tennis courts, swimming pools, spa pool, water slide, children's playground, 18-hole international championship standard golf course with pro shop, jungle treks, slot machines and video games, billiards, and boat trips to nearby islands.

Services include complimentary airport transfers, foreign currency exchange, and laundry services. There are four restaurants and a bar on the premises.

## DINING

You won't find fantastic food on the island. Most cuisine consists of simple sandwiches and local food. There are inexpensive provision shops here and there. Beer is available in Tekek and Salang, and at Nazri's Place, a restaurant in the very southern part of ABC.

## THE KAMPUNGS
### KAMPUNG TEKEK

Kampung Tekek is the center of life on Tioman, which means it's the busiest, and while there are small accommodations here—as well as some convenience stores (open from 7am to 11pm), souvenir shops, and restaurants—you're better off in one of the other kampungs. The best eating is to the side of the main jetty, where you'll find open-air seafood stalls selling soups, noodle dishes, and seafood and vegetable dishes, at very inexpensive prices.

Just beyond the stalls is the office for **Dive Asia** (☎ **09/419-1337**). Daily dives usually hit two or three spots: Chebeh Island, Malang rocks, and Labas Island. With equipment rentals an excursion costs about RM230 (US$60.55). Night dives to Pirate Reef are about RM120 (US$35.60). Also offered are PADI courses starting at RM795 (US$209). Dive Asia accepts MC and V. Mask and snorkel equipment rentals are RM20 (US$5.25) per day. There is also a Dive Asia branch at Salang.

## KAMPUNG ABC

This village lines a long rocky beach that is not the best for swimming in spots, but ABC is very laid-back and comfortable in other ways. Chalets line the pathway along the beach, where you'll find small shady picnic areas and hammocks to swing in. While ABC is well populated by travelers, the people here tend to be more relaxed.

The nicest place to stay is **Air Batang Beach Cabanas,** Kampung Air Batang, 86800 Mersing (☎ **011/333-486** or 07/799-5405; fax 07/799-5405.) Creeping up the side of the hill, many with views of the sea, these chalets are the largest and newest in the kampung. Rates go from RM120 (US$31.60) for A/C and RM70 (US$18.40) without. All cabins have private toilets with cold shower. Cash is accepted, but not credit cards or traveler's checks.

Really the only place to eat here is Nazri's place in the south end of the beach, which serves breakfast, lunch, and fish or chicken barbecue dinner daily.

**B&J Diving Centre** (☎ **011/419-1218**) has a branch along the path. They charge RM160 (US$42.10) for two dives in 1 day, usually to nearby Chebeh and Sapoy. They also have PADI courses and accept MC and V. Daily snorkeling rentals are RM20 (US$5.25).

## KAMPUNG SALANG

This kampung is a happening spot. Snuggled in a big cove of lovely beach and blue water, the village has relatively more conveniences for visitors, such as a choice of eating places serving continental and local seafood dishes for a song, a few bars, money changers, convenience stores, and places to make international calls. It is not a metropolis by any standard, though, and accommodations remain basic.

Both **B&J** (☎ **011/419-5555**) and **Dive Asia** (☎ **011/716-783**) have offices in Salang. See above locations for prices and services.

A good place to stay is **Salang Indah Resorts,** Kampung Salang, Tioman (☎ **011/730-230** or 09/419-5015; fax: 09/419-5024). Choices of rooms vary from longhouse rooms with community toilets at RM25 to RM80 (US$6.60–US$21.05), to hillside chalets at RM40 (US$10.55) to air-conditioned chalets, rooms, or bungalows at RM160, RM180, or RM200 (US$42, US$47 or US$53). The showers all use cold water, though.

## KAMPUNG JUARA

Juara is where to go if you really want to get away from it all. A gorgeous cove of crystal blue waters and wide clean sand make for the best beach on the island. Come here expecting to rough it, though. Most of the chalets here are terrible, some only slightly more accommodating than dog houses. There are no phones, only one TV, one place to eat (The Happy Café, which has the one TV and a few small convenience store items), and no air-con anywhere. But I still found a quite decent place to stay. On the north end of the beach is **Juara Bay Village Resort,** with 20 rooms that go for RM30 (US$8) for hill views and RM40 (US$10) for sea views. Don't even dream of using a credit card here. Each room has a fan and private bath, and they're all good sized and clean. The best in the village, for sure. To make a reservation, call the owner's brother, Haji Bakar Yaacob, in KL at (☎ **03/981-6122**). Otherwise just show up and try your luck.

## TIOMAN OUTDOORS

After you're waterlogged, you can trek the trail from Tekek to Juara, and some of the paths along the west coast. The hike across the island will take around 2 hours. Bring water and mosquito repellent, and don't try it unless you are reasonably fit.

At the southern part of the island are Bukit Batu Sirau and Bukit Simukut, "The Famous Twin Peaks," and closer to the water near Kampung Mukut are the Mukut Waterfalls. There are two smallish pools for taking a dip. Some regular trails exist, but it's inadvisable to venture too far from them because the forest gets dense and it can be tough to find your way back. Negotiate with water taxis to bring you down and pick you up.

## 12 Kuantan

Kuantan is the capital of Pahang Darul Makmur, the largest state in Malaysia, covering about 22,475 square miles (35,960 sq. km). Travelers come to Pahang for the beautiful beaches, which stretch all the way up the East Coast, and for inland jungle forests that promise adventures in trekking, climbing, and river rafting. Much of Taman Negara, Malaysia's national forest preserve, is in this state, although most people access the forest via Kuala Lumpur. Kuantan, although it's the capital, doesn't have the feel of a big city. If you're staying at the beach at Telok Chempedak, 3.1 miles (5km) north of Kuantan, the atmosphere is even more relaxed.

### VISITOR INFORMATION

There is a Tourist Information Centre (☎ **09/617-1007**) located on Jalan Penjara in the center of town. Staff here are exceptionally helpful and good at answering inquiries.

### GETTING THERE

**BY AIR**   Malaysia Airlines has eight daily flights from KL. For reservations, call ☎ **03/764-3000.** Flights arrive at the Sultan Ahmad Shah Airport (☎ **09/538-1177).** Just outside the airport is a taxi stand that can take you to Kuantan for RM25 (US$6.60), or to Cherating for RM60 (US$15.80).

**BY BUS**   Bus routes service Kuantan from all parts of the peninsula. If you're coming from KL, **Transnasional** (☎ **03/442-8945**) at Putra Bus Terminal, opposite from the Putra World Trade Centre, has nine daily buses for RM12.20 (US$3.20). The trip takes about 5 hours. **Hosni Ekspres,** also at Putra Terminal (☎ **03/445-6684**) has business class coaches in the evenings for RM31.20 (US$8.20). From Mersing, **Transnasional/Naelia** (☎ **07/799-3155**) has an afternoon business class coach to Kuantan for RM12 (US$3.15). From Kuala Terengganu, Transnasional has two daily buses to Kuantan for RM8.10 (US$2.15).

The bus terminal in Kuantan is in **Kompleks Makmur.** Taxis at the stand just outside the terminal can take you to town for RM10 (US$2.65).

For buses from Kuantan to other destinations, call **Transnasional** at ☎ **09/515-6740** or **Hosni Ekspres** at ☎ **09/515-6128.**

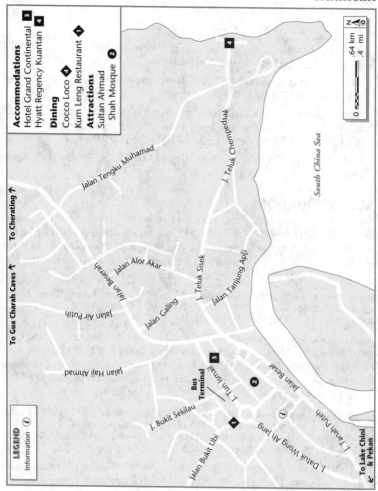

**Accommodations**
Hotel Grand Continental ③
Hyatt Regency Kuantan ④

**Dining**
Cocco Loco ④
Kum Leng Restaurant ①

**Attractions**
Sultan Ahmad
Shah Mosque ②

South China Sea

To Cherating ↑

To Gua Charah Caves ↑

To Lake Chini & Pekan ↓

Jalan Tengku Muhamad

J. Teluk Chempedsak

Jalan Alor Akar

Jalan Besrah

Jalan Air Putih

J. Teluk Sisek

Jalan Tanjung Apli

Jalan Galing

Jalan Haji Ahmad

Bus Terminal

J. Tun Ismail

Jalan Besar

J. Bukit Sekilau

Jalan Bukit Ubi

J. Datuk Wong Ah Jang

J. Tanah Puteh

**LEGEND**
Information ⓘ

**BY TAXI** Outstation taxis from KL (☎ **03/232-6504**) will cost RM250 (US$65.80). From Johor Bahru, the fare will be about RM150 (US$39.45), and from Mersing, RM100 (US$26.30). For outstation taxi booking from Kuantan, call ☎ **09/513-6950**. The stand is at the bus terminal.

## GETTING AROUND

The areas in the town's center are nice for walking. Otherwise stick with taxis, which can be waved down from any street. If you need to arrange for a pickup, call the taxi stand at the bus terminal at ☎ **09/513-4478**. There's also a stand behind the Tourist Information Centre where you'll be sure to find a cab in a pinch. Taxis here are not metered, so you must negotiate the fare before you set out. This is a good deal when you want to hire someone for a few hours to take you around the city. Rates are from RM15 (US$3.95) per hour.

Use taxis to travel to areas of interest outside the city that are covered later in this section.

# Fast Facts: Kuantan

**American Express**   The Amex office is at Mayflower Acme Tours, Tan Chong Building, Jalan Beserah (☎ 09/513-1866).

**Banks/Currency Exchange**   Most of the banks are located appropriately along Jalan Bank, near the State Mosque.

**Internet/E-mail**   For a good Internet cafe, go to Kompleks Makmur at the shopping mall adjacent to the bus terminal. Smart Tech Computer Centre (☎ 09/517-1721) has Internet access for RM4 (US$1.05)/hour.

**Post Office/Mail**   The central post office (☎ 09/552-1078) is near the State Mosque on Jalan Haji Abdul Aziz.

## ACCOMMODATIONS

Kuantan is not a very large place, and most of those who holiday here prefer to stay just a little farther north, in Cherating, which is more established as a resort destination. If staying in Kuantan is important to you, though, the Hotel Grand Continental is a fine, centrally located place. Near the beach at Telok Chempedak, the Hyatt Regency is as romantic and relaxing as any place at Cherating.

**Hotel Grand Continental.** Jalan Gambut, 25000 Kuantan, Pahang Darul Makmur. ☎ **09/515-8888.** Fax 09/515-9999. 202 units. AC MINIBAR TV TEL. RM212 (US$56) double, RM575 (US$151) suite. AE, DC, JCB, MC, V.

Located in the heart of Kuantan, this hotel is near the central mosque. Grand Continental is a simple three-star hotel, with new and adequate facilities that are somewhat reminiscent of the seventies. The front view of the bridge and river is more pleasant than the view in the rear rooms. Promotional rates can be as low as RM160 (US$42) a night. There's a fitness center, pool, and shops on the premises.

✪ **Hyatt Regency Kuantan.** Telok Chempedak, 25050 Kuantan, Pahang. ☎ **800/233-1234** from the U.S., or 800/8181 or 09/566-1234 in Malaysia. Fax 09/567-7577. 336 units. AC MINIBAR TV TEL. RM320–RM365 (US$84–US$96) double; RM430–RM525 (US$113–US$138) club; RM710–RM2,000 (US$187–US$526) suite. AE, DC, JCB, MC, V.

The Hyatt Regency is a beach resort on Telok Chempedak, about 10 minutes outside of Kuantan proper. The long stretch of sandy beach bordering it is perfect for relaxation and fun, and in the evening the crashing waves are the perfect romantic backdrop. Hyatt has built a five-star resort here, and it is five-star in every sense—from outstanding facilities to large well-appointed rooms. Higher prices are of course for rooms with sea views. Facilities include two outdoor swimming pools (one a more active family frolic spot while the other is quiet and calm), three lighted tennis courts, two squash courts, table tennis, darts, volleyball, and a water sports center with windsurfing, sailing, waterskiing, and jet skis. The hotel is near locations for golf, jogging, and jungle hikes.

## DINING

There are seafood and local food in Kuantan, but like the other smaller destinations in Malaysia, you'll be hard-pressed to find fine dining outside of the larger hotels. The best evening activities are centered around the beach area at Telok Chempedak.

**Cocco Loco Bistro & Bar.** Hyatt Regency Kuantan, Telok Chempedak. ☎ **09/566-1234,** ext. 7700. Reservations recommended. Entrees RM20–RM48 (US$5.25–US$12.65). AE, DC, JCB, MC, V. Daily noon–2:30pm; 6–10:30pm. ITALIAN.

For a little fine dining in Kuantan, your best bet is at the Hyatt's Italian restaurant, Cocco Loco. Local seafood like sea bass and prawns is transformed into beautiful entrees, with light sauces and the freshest ingredients. They have a good wine list with many international labels. If you arrive early, you can still see the ocean from huge glass windows. However, even after dark, Cocco Loco has a beautiful atmosphere enhanced by romantic lights, terra-cotta floors and bright table linens.

**Kum Leng Restoran.** E-897/899/901 Jalan Bukit Ubi, Kuantan. ☎ **09/513-4446.** Seafood priced according to seasonal availability; other dishes can be as low as RM5 (US$1.30) for fried tofu or as high as RM100 (US$26.30) for shark's fin. No credit cards. Daily 11:30am–2:30pm and 5:30–10:30pm. CANTONESE.

Kum Leng is probably one of the top restaurants in Kuantan. A bit cramped, it's always doing a good business but there's rarely a wait. Try the fried chicken with dry chili topped with onions and cashew nuts, or the fried chili prawns with shells. They're very fresh and not too spicy.

## ATTRACTIONS

Kuantan can really be seen in a day. While there are some fun crafts places, the place is not exactly a hotbed of culture.

The main attraction in town is the huge State Mosque, which is quite beautiful inside and out, with a distinct dome, minarets, and stained glass. Late afternoon is the best time to see it, when the light really shines through the glass.

Also in the city, you can have a nice walk down Jalan Besar, sampling local delicacies sold on the street and shopping in the smaller craft and souvenir shops. Visit **HM Batik & Handicraft** at (45 N–1, Bangunan LKNP, Jalan Besar ☎ **09/552-8477**) and **Kedai Mat Jais B. Talib** (45N–8, Bangunan LKNP, Jalan Besar ☎ **09/555-2860**) for good selections of batiks and crafts.

**Batik RM** has a showroom on Jalan Besar (2-C Medan Pelancung ☎ **09/514-2008**), but the showroom out on Jalan Tanah Puteh (☎ **09/513-9631**) is much more fun. Tours around the back allow you to watch the waxing and dyeing processes. Their showroom has some great batik fashions—more stylish than so much of the batik clothing that you find in the markets.

### ATTRACTIONS OUTSIDE KUANTAN

Pahang is home to peninsular Malaysia's most stunning forests. With Kuantan as your starting point, it's easy to jump to these spots for a day or half-day trip.

**Gua Charah caves** are about 15.6 miles (25km) outside of Kuantan. Also called Pancing caves (they're located at a town called Pancing), one of the caves in the network is a temple, home to a huge reclining Buddha. It is said that the monk caretaker, who has been growing very old, is having difficulty finding another monk who will take over his duties at the caves. An outstation taxi can take you there for RM80 (US$21).

Also fun is **Lake Chini,** 12 freshwater lakes that have local legends that rival Loch Ness. They say that there once was an ancient Khmer city at the site of the lakes, but it is now buried deep under the water, protected by monsters. Some have tried to find both city and monsters, but have come up with nothing. Boats are there to take you across the lake to an *orang asli* kampung to see the native way of life. Lake Chini is 38 miles (60km) southwest of Kuantan, and an outstation taxi can bring you for RM80 (US$21).

Just south of Kuantan is **Pekan,** which for history and culture buffs is far more interesting then Kuantan. Pekan is called the "Royal City" because it is where the

Sultan of Pahang resides in a beautiful Malay-style istana. The **State Museum** on Jalan Sultan Ahmad has displays depicting the history of Pahang and its royal family, as well as sunken treasures from old Chinese junks. Outstation taxis to Pekan are RM20 (US$5.25).

## GOLF

The **Royal Pahang Golf Club** is near Kuantan's beach resort area on Jalan Teluk Chempedak (☎ **09/567-5811;** fax 09/567-1170).

## 13  Cherating

Because Kuantan is such a small town, some travelers coming through these parts choose to stay 28 miles (47km) north in Cherating. This area supports a few international class resorts along the beautiful beachfront of the South China Sea. Funny thing: Compared to Kuantan, the town of Cherating has even fewer things to do, and guests tend not to stray too far from their resort. Self-contained units, the resorts each offer a few dining choices, arrange all the water-sports facilities and outdoor activities you have time for, and can even provide transport to and from Kuantan if you need to see a little "big city life." Resorts can also arrange trips through the mangroves up the Cherating River in a hired bumboat, and trips to crafts shops and cultural shows. A little more than 6.8 miles (11km) north of Cherating is Chendor Beach, one of the peninsula's special beaches where giant leatherback turtles lay their eggs from May to October.

## ACCOMMODATIONS

**Best Western Ombak Beach Resort.** Lot 2466, Mukin Sungai Karang, 26080 Kuantan, Pahang Darul Makmur. ☎ **09/581-9166.** Fax 09/581-9433. 30 units. A/C MINIBAR TV TEL. RM140 (US$56) double. AE, DC, MC, V.

The bad news is this resort only has 30 rooms; the good news is that they're spread out over 3 acres (1.2 hectares) of property, and each has its own terrace and carport. The resort atmosphere is perfect for lying about the beach, swimming in the pool, or enjoying a campfire barbecue. Facilities include an outdoor pool, children's pool, game room, water sports center, table tennis, and volleyball, and there's a souvenir gift shop on the premises. Try to bargain your room to as low as RM90 (US$24).

**Holiday Villa Cherating.** Lot 1303, Mukin Sungai Karang, 26080 Kuantan, Pahang Darul Makmur. ☎ **09/581-9500.** Fax 09/581-9178. 150 units. A/C MINIBAR TV TEL. RM110–RM190 (US$29–US$50) double; RM230–RM295 (US$60–US$78) suite. AE, DC, JCB, MC, V.

What a resort! This 10-acre (4-hectare) coastline property has three different wings to choose from: The Capital Wing houses modern amenities similar to any international-class hotel, while the Village Wing and the Palace Wing have chalets, longhouses, and istanas. The 13 Village Wing chalets are each decorated in the style of one of the 13 Malay states, and its kampung feel makes it perfect for unwinding. The chalets in both wings range from simple two-bedroom accommodations, to a Sarawak longhouse with 10 guest rooms and private balconies, to a replica of the Istana Lama Sri Menanti in Negeri Sembilan.

Facilities include two outdoor pools, two outdoor spa pools, a children's wading pool, a game room, three outdoor tennis courts, two indoor badminton courts, a fitness center, sauna, massage, a beauty parlor, and a water sports center (with windsurfing, beach surfing, catamaran, sailing, parasailing, scuba diving, jet scooters, canoeing, and boating). Also available are sightseeing tours, island excursions, fishing, and golfing.

# 14  Taman Negara National Park

**Taman Negara** is Malaysia's national park, covering 1,085,750 acres (434,300 hectares) of primary rain forest estimated to be as old as 130 million years, and encompassing within its borders Gunung Tahan, peninsular Malaysia's highest peak at 2,392 feet (2,187m) above sea level.

Prepare to see lush vegetation and rare orchids (up to 250 bird species) and maybe, if you're lucky, some barking deer, tapir, elephants, tigers, leopards, and rhinos. As for primates, there are long-tailed macaques, leaf monkeys, gibbons, and more. Malaysia has taken the preservation of this forest seriously since the early part of the century, so Taman Negara showcases efforts to keep this land in as pristine a state as possible while still allowing humans to appreciate the splendor.

There are outdoor activities for any level of adventurer. Short jungle walks to observe nature are lovely, but then so are the hard-core 9-day treks or climbs up Gunung Tahan. There are also overnight trips to night hides where you can observe animals up close. The jungle canopy walk is the longest in the world, and at 83 feet (25m) above ground, the view is spectacular. There are also rivers for rafting and swimming, fishing spots, and a couple of caves. For information, call the Kuala Tahan Office, Taman Negara Resort, Kuala Tahan, Jerantut, 27000 Pahang (☎ **609/263-500;** fax 609/261-5000).

## GETTING THERE

The entrance to the park is at **Kuala Tembeling,** which can be reached in 3 hours by road from Kuala Lumpur. By far the easiest way to visit the national park is through a **travel operator,** who will arrange your transport to the park, accommodation, meals, and activities. Taman Negara Resort (see below) is the largest operator, with a few others providing excellent packages as well.

**BY TAXI**   Outstation taxis from **Puduraya Bus Terminal** (☎ 03/232-6504), will cost about RM200 (US$52.65) to the park entrance. From there you must venture upstream 2 hours by boat to the Taman Negara Resort (below).

**BY TRAIN**   The **KTM** also travels to this area, making stops in Jerantut, from where you can also enter the park. From Johor Bahru, call KTM at (☎ **07/223-3040**). Budget your fare at RM38 (US$10) for second-class passage.

## ACCOMMODATIONS

**Nusa Camp.** Kuala Lumpur Office: Malaysia Tourist Information Centre (MATIC), 109 Jalan Ampang, ☎ **03/262-7682;** fax 03/262-7682. Kuala Tembeling Office: No 5 Jalan Jetty Taman Negara, ☎ 09/266-3043. Jerantut Office: 16 Jalan Diwangsa, Bandar Baru ☎ 09/266-2369; fax 09/266-4369.

Nusa Camp will send you to the park, put you up in their own kampung house, chalet or hostel accommodations, and guide your activities for you. Package deals are great at 3 days/2 nights, complete with activities for between RM255 to RM360 (US$67–US$92) per person. The 4-day/3-night deal is RM395 to RM532 (US$104–US$140) per person. Lower rates are for hostel accommodations, while the higher ones are for Malay houses and cottages. You can also go à la carte, with room charges at RM80 (US$21) for a Malay house and RM10 (US$3) for a hostel dorm. You then pay extra for each activity—RM50 (US$13.15) for water rafting; RM50 for night fishing; etc. The cafeteria serves set breakfast, lunch, and dinner for RM6, RM9 and RM18 (US$1.60, US$2.35, US$4.75) respectively.

**Taman Negara Resort.** Kuala Tahan Office, Taman Negara Resort, Kuala Tahan, Jerantut, 27000 Pahang. ☎ **09/266-3500.** Fax 09/266-1500. (Or contact Kuala Lumpur Sales Office,

2nd floor, Istana Hotel, Jalan Raja Chulan, 50250 Kuala Lumpur; ☎ 03/245-5585; fax 03/245-5430.)

Taman Negara Resort, well established in the business of hosting visitors to the park, organizes trips for 3 days and 2 nights or for 4 days and 3 nights, as well as an à la carte deal where you pay for lodging and activities separately. Accommodations come in many styles: a bungalow suite for families (RM600 or US$158 per night); chalet and chalet suite good for couples (RM216 or US$57 and RM300 or US$79, respectively); standard guest house rooms in a motel-style longhouse (RM165 or US$43 per night); and dormitory hostels for budget travelers (RM40.25 or US$11 per night). Their explorer package runs RM482 (US$127) per person for 3 days and 2 nights, or RM775 (US$204) per person for 4 days and 3 nights. Explorer visitors check into the chalets, which are air-conditioned with attached bathroom. Activities include treks to the canopy walkway, night jungle walks, boat trips to waterfalls for swimming, and river rafting. Shuttle transfers from KL (4 hours) are an extra RM50 (US$13) per person, and the boat trip to the resort is either RM38 (US$10) for the 3-hour traditional wooden boat or RM60 (US$16) for the 1-hour speedboat.

## 15 Kuala Terengganu

The capital of the state of Terengganu, Kuala Terengganu, has far more exciting activities to offer a visitor than its southern capital neighbor, Kuantan. And yet, many travelers to Malaysia often skip this part of the country for the more beaten paths. So why should you consider coming here? **Malaysian crafts.** Kuala Terengganu has the best cottage industries for Malaysian crafts—better than anywhere else on the peninsula. Terengganu artisans specialize in everything from boat building to kite making, and it is here that you can see it all happen.

Kuala Terengganu is small and easy to navigate, clustered around a port at the mouth of the Terengganu River. Many livelihoods revolve around the sea, so most of the activity, even today, focuses on the areas closest to the jetties. Life here is slow-paced and comfortable, and very Muslim, owing to its proximity to orthodox Muslim Kelantan in the north. It is a sedate town, so don't come here for the nightlife. As opposed to its west coast contemporaries, this city is mostly Malay (about 90%), so it's here that you see Malay culture in a more pure form, without fewer outside influences.

The local business week is from Saturday to Wednesday, so be prepared for that when you plan your time here. Also important to know: Terengganu is a dry state. Alcoholic beverages cannot be purchased in stores, and there is only one bar in town, at the Primula Parkroyal Resort (listed below). Chinese restaurants are also permitted to sell beer to diners.

### VISITOR INFORMATION

The Tourism Information Centre is on Jalan Sultan Zainal Abidin just next to the post office and across from the central market. The number there is ☎ **09/622-1553.**

### GETTING THERE

**BY AIR**  Malaysia Airlines has five daily flights from KL to Kuala Terengganu's Sultan Mahmud Airport. The reservations number in KL is ☎ **03/764-3000.** For airport information, call ☎ **09/666-4204.** For Malaysian Airlines bookings from Kuala Terengganu, call ☎ **09/622-1415.**

From the airport, a taxi to town is about RM15 (US$3.95).

**BY BUS**  The MPKT Bus Terminal is located on Jalan Sultan Zainal Abidin next to the water. For buses from KL, at the Putra Bus Terminal opposite the Putra World Trade Centre, Transnasional (☎ **03/442-8945**) has a morning bus for RM21.70 (US$5.70). **Hosni Ekspres** operates a business class coach twice daily for RM31.20 (US$8.20). The trip time is 8 hours. From Kuantan, call **Transnasional** at ☎ **09/515-6740**. There are two daily buses that make the 3-hour journey. It costs RM8.90 (US$2.35).

For buses out of Kuala Terengganu, call Transnasional at ☎ **09/623-8384**.

**BY TAXI**  Outstation taxis from Kuantan will cost RM90 (US$23.70). Call ☎ **09/513-4478** for booking. From Kota Bharu, taxis will be around RM80 (US$21.05). The number for the taxi stand there is ☎ **09/748-1386**.

Outstation taxi bookings from Kuala Terengganu can be arranged by calling ☎ **09/622-1581**.

## GETTING AROUND

While you can stroll around the downtown areas with ease, many of the bigger attractions will require a taxi. To call and arrange for a car, dial ☎ **09/622-1581**, or arrange it through your hotel concierge. It's a good idea to hire these guys for a half or whole day, so you can go around to places and not worry how you'll get back. Rates will be around RM15 (US$3.95) per hour.

## Fast Facts: Kuala Terengganu

**Banks/Currency Exchange**  Most banks are on Jalan Sultan Ismail.

**Post Office/Mail**  The main post office is on Jalan Sultan Zainal Abidin (☎ 09/622-7555), next to the Tourist Information Centre.

## ACCOMMODATIONS

✪ **The Aryani Resort.** Jalan Rhu Tapai–Merang, 21010 Setiu, Terengganu, Malaysia. ☎ **09/624-1111** or 09/624-4489; fax 09/624-8007. 20 units. MINIBAR TV TEL. RM440–RM539 (US$116–US$142) double, RM688 (US$181) modern suite; RM935 (US$246) heritage suite. AE, DC, JCB, MC, V.

Two and a half years ago, Raja Dato' Bahrin Shah Raja Ahmad (a most royal name), opened his dream resort. Raja Bahrin, an internationally celebrated architect, had previously designed the State Museum, and wished to translate the beautiful lines of Terengganu style into a special resort. The resulting Aryani is stunning—organic, stimulating, unique, and best of all, peaceful. In a rural 9-acre spot by the sea, the rooms are private bungalows situated like a village. Inside, each is masterfully decorated to suit both traditional style and modern comfort. The Heritage Suite wins the prize—a 100-year-old timber palace, restored and rebuilt on the site, it is appointed with fine antiques. The design of the outdoor pool is practically an optical illusion, and the spa (for massage and beauty treatments) is in its own Malay house. The resort's rural location has both a plus and a minus: plus—it's secluded, minus—it's 45 minutes from Kuala Terengganu. The resort can also arrange boat trips, tours to town, and golfing.

✪ **Primula Parkroyal Kuala Terengganu.** Jalan Persinggahan, P.O. Box 43, 20904, Kuala Terengganu, Terengganu Darul Iman, Malaysia. ☎ **800/835-7742** from the U.S. and Canada, 800/363-300 from Australia (Sydney 02/9935-8313), 0800/801-111 New Zealand, or 09/622-2100 or 09/623-3722. Fax 09/623-3360. 249 units. A/C MINIBAR TV TEL.

> # Terengganu's Wild Side
>
> While the state of Terengganu has its share of natural inland areas, the best nature here is found in the state's **marine parks** (see "Terengganu's Outdoors," below).
>
> A visit to **Redang Island** provides glimpses of an underwater heaven of marine life and coral. And Terengganu's beaches, in addition to being great for sunbathing, have something else to recommend them: **leatherback turtles,** which have been coming ashore to bury their eggs for centuries. Terengganu has a sanctuary to help the babies hatch and get on with their lives free from poachers.

RM220–RM250 (US$58–US$66) double; RM400–RM700 (US$105–US$184) suite. AE, DC, MC, V.

A top pick for accommodations in Kuala Terengganu is the Parkroyal. The first resort to open in this area, it commands the best section of beach the city has to offer and still is very close to the downtown area. It has full resort facilities, which include three excellent restaurants and the only bar in the city (perhaps even in the state). Make sure you get a room facing the sea, the view is dreamy. Other facilities include an outdoor pool with grassy lawns, water-sports facilities, a lobby shop, and a kid's club.

## DINING

**Ocean.** Lot 2679 Jalan Sultan Janah Apitin (by the waterfront). ☎ **09/623-9154.** Reservations not accepted. RM10–RM25 (US$2.65–US$6.60); seafood sold according to market prices. Open daily noon–2:30pm and 5:30pm–midnight. MC, V. CHINESE/SEAFOOD.

One of the most celebrated seafood restaurants in town, Ocean prepares tender prawns, light pomfret, and juicy crab in local and Chinese recipes that are very good. Don't count on much from the al fresco decor. The place looks more or less like a warehouse, to be honest, but the views of the sea help. So does the beer, which Ocean is permitted to serve.

**Pelangi Grill.** Primula Parkroyal, Jalan Persinggahan. ☎ **09/622-2100.** Reservations not necessary. RM10–RM24. Opens at noon to AE, DC, JCB, MC, V. LOCAL/CONTINENTAL.

In an open-air lanai facing the sea and the resort's gardens, this delightful multi-level outdoor cafe is good for either family meals or romantic dinners. The main level is set for standard menu items, which includes the house specialties, sizzling dishes of prawn or beef, plus pizzas and a great assortment of local and Western entrees. The lower patio is set for steamboat, a fondue-style dinner where you place chunks of fish and meats into boiling broth at your table. A small assortment of international wines is available.

## ATTRACTIONS

✪ **Central Market.** Jalan Sultan Zainal Abidin.

Open daily from very early until about 7pm, the central market is a huge maze of shops selling every craft made in the region. There's basket weaving for everything from place mats to beach mats. Batik comes in sarongs (with some very unique patterns), ready-made clothing, and household linens. Songet, beautiful fabric woven with gold and silver threads, is sold by the piece or sarong. Brassware pots, candlesticks, and curio items are piled high and glistening. Every handicraft item you can think of is here, waiting for you to bargain and bring it home. And when you're done,

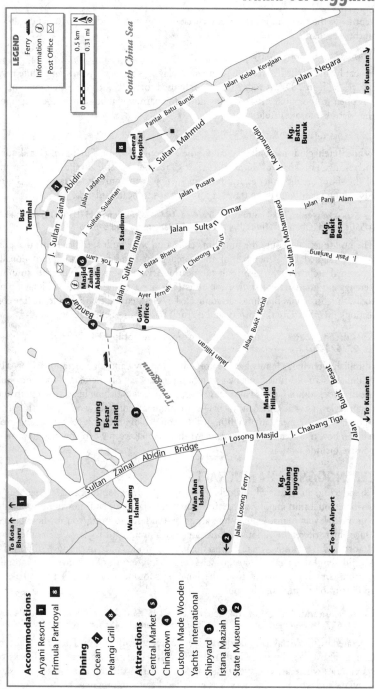

# Kuala Terengganu

**LEGEND**
- Ferry
- Information ⓘ
- Post Office ⊠

0 0.5 km
0.31 mi

*South China Sea*

Jalan Negara

To Kuantan →

Jalan Kelab Kerajaan

Jalan Panji Alam

Kg. Batu Buruk

Kg. Bukit Besar

J. Pasir Panjang

J. Kamaruddin

J. Sultan Mohammed

Pantai Batu Buruk

J. Sultan Mahmud

**8** General Hospital

Jalan Pusara

Jalan Ladang

J. Sultan Sulaiman

**7** J. Sultan Zainal Abidin

Bus Terminal

Stadium

Jalan Sultan Omar

J. Batas Bharu

J. Cherong Lanjut

**6** J. Tok Lam

⊠

ⓘ **Masjid Zainal Abidin**

**5**

Jalan Sultan Ismail

Ayer Jerneh

J. Bandar

**4**

Govt. Office

Jalan Bukit Kechil

Jalan Bukit Besar

Jalan Hiliran

Terengganu

Masjid Hiliran

Duyung Besar Island **3**

Jalan Bukit Besar

To Kuantan ↓

Sultan Zainal Abidin Bridge

J. Losong Masjid J. Chabang Tiga

Jalan Bukit Besat

Wan Embung Island

Wan Man Island

Kg. Kubang Buyong

← To the Airport

To Kota Bharu ← **1**

Jalan Losong Ferry

**2**

---

**Accommodations**
Aryani Resort **1**
Primula Parkroyal **8**

**Dining**
Ocean **7**
Pelangi Grill **8**

**Attractions**
Central Market **5**
Chinatown **4**
Custom Made Wooden
Yachts International
Shipyard **3**
Istana Maziah **6**
State Museum **2**

venture to the back of the market and check out the produce, dried goods, and seafood in the wet market.

**Istana Maziah, Jalan Masji.**

Probably one of the least ornate istanas in Malaysia, this lovely yellow and white royal palace, built in 1897, is today mainly only used for state and royal ceremonies. It is not open to the public. Tucked away down the narrow winding street is its neighbor, the Masjid (mosque) Abidin.

**Chinatown.** Jalan Bandar.

While Terengganu has only a small Chinese population, its Chinatown is still quite interesting. This street of shophouses close to the water is still alive, only today many of the shops are art galleries and boutiques, showcasing only the finest regional arts. Also along Jalan Bandar are travel agents for trips to nearby islands.

✪ **State Museum.** Bukit Losong. ☎ **09/622-1444.** Admission RM5 (US$1.30) adult; RM2 (US50¢) child. Open Sat–Thurs 10am–6pm; Fri 10am–noon and 3–6pm.

The buildings that house the museum's collection were built specifically for this purpose. Designed by a member of the Terengganu royal family, an internationally renowned architect who also built the nearby Aryani resort, it reflects the stunning Terengganu architectural style. Atop stilts (16—it's a tradition) with a high sloping roofs, the three main buildings are connected by elevated walkways. Inside are fine collections that illustrate the history and cultural traditions of the state.

✪ **Custom Made Wooden Yachts International Shipyard.** 3592 Duyong Besar, ☎ **09/623-2072.**

Abdullah bin Muda's family has been building ships by hand for generations. Now Mr. Abdullah is an old-timer, but he gets around, balancing on the planks that surround the dry-docked hulls of his latest masterpieces. He makes fishing boats in Western and Asian styles, as well as luxury yachts—all handmade, all from wood. But while Mr. Abdullah doesn't speak any English, he'll let you explore them on your own, and even tell you how much money he's getting for them. You'll weep when you hear how inexpensive his fine work is.

## TERENGGANU'S HANDICRAFTS

**Chendering,** an industrial town about 40 minutes' drive south of Kuala Terengganu, is where you'll find major handicraft production—factories and showrooms of batiks and other lovely items. Plan to hire a taxi by the hour to bring you to these places. Once you're there, the various factories are only 5 minutes' drive from each other, and almost all drivers know where to find them. Also, while you're in the area, stop by the **Masjid Tengku Tengah Zahara,** which is only 5 km outside of the town. The mosque is more commonly referred to as the Floating Mosque, as it is built in a lake and appears to be floating on the top.

✪ **Terengganu Craft Cultural Centre.** Lot 2195 Kawasan Perindustrian Chendering. ☎ **09/617-1033.** Open Sat–Wed 8am–5pm, Thurs 8am–12:45pm, closed Fri.

Operated by the Malaysian Handicraft Development Corporation, The Craft Cultural Center, also called Budaya Craft, not only sells handicrafts, but also has blocks of warehouses where artisans create the work. See batik painting, brass casting, basket weaving, and wood carving as well as other local crafts in progress.

**Suteramas.** Zkawasan Perindustrian Chendering. ☎ **09/617-1355.** Free admission. Open Sat–Wed 9am–5pm, Thurs 9am–12:45pm, closed Fri.

Suteramas specializes in batik painting on fine quality silks. At this, their factory show-room, you can buy their latest creations or just watch them being made. Not only do they dye the cloth, they make it from their own worm stock.

**Noor Arfa.** Lot 1048 K Kawasan Perindustrian Chendering. ☎ **09/617-5700.** Open Sat–Wed 8am–5pm, Thurs 8am–12:45, closed Fri. AE, MC, V.

Noor Arfa is Malaysia's largest producer of hand-painted batik. This former cottage industry business now employs 200 workers to create ready-to-wear fashions that are esteemed as designer labels throughout the country. There's also a shop in town at Aked Mara, A3 Jalan Sultan Zainal Abidin (☎ **09/623-5173**).

## TERENGGANU'S OUTDOORS

If you are in Terengganu between May and August, you've arrived just in time to see the baby leatherback turtles. For hundreds of years, possibly more, giant leatherback turtles have come to the shore here by the thousands. The females crawl to the beaches where they dig holes in which to lay their eggs. Sixty days later, the small turtles hatch and scurry for the water. In recent decades, the turtles have had trouble carrying out their ritual. Development and poaching have placed severe hardships on the popula-tion. Of the babies that are hatched, many never make it to the deep sea. At the Department of Fisheries of the State of Terengganu (Taman Perikanan Chendering, ☎ **09/884-4169**) there is a sanctuary that collects the eggs from the beaches, incu-bates them in hatcheries and sets the babies free. They welcome visitors to their exhibits about turtles and the sanctuary's activities, and to midnight watches to see mothers lay eggs and babies hatch. These activities are free of charge.

The first marine park in Malaysia, the **Terengganu Marine Park,** is situated around the nine islands of the Redang archipelago, 28 miles (45km) northeast of Kuala Terengganu and 17 miles (27km) out to sea. Sporting the best coral reefs and dive con-ditions off peninsular Malaysia, the park attracts divers with its many excellent sites. The largest of the islands is Pulau Redang (Redang Island), where most people stay in resorts on overnight diving excursions. Begin with an hour's drive to the northern jetty town of Merang (not to be confused with Marang, which is in the south), followed by an overwater trip to any one of the islands for scuba, snorkeling, and swimming.

One of the best resorts in Redang is the **Coral Redang Island Resort.** They have 40 detached and semi-detached bungalows and standard rooms on idyllic gardens next to the beach. At the resort is Eco Diving, specializing in everything from beginner PADI courses to boat dives and night dives, with equipment rental as well. The resort also has snorkeling gear. Contact Coral Redang at 137A, 1st Floor, Jalan Sultan Zainal Abidin (☎ **09/623-6200;** fax **09/623-6300**).

## 16  Kota Bharu

In the north-east corner of peninsular Malaysia, bordering Thailand, is the state of **Kelantan.** Few tourists head this far north up the east coast, but it's an fascinating journey for those interested in seeing Malaysia as it might have been without so many foreign influences. The state is populated mostly by Malays and Bumiputeras, with only tiny factions of Chinese and Indian residents, and almost no traces of British colonialism. Not surprisingly, Kelantan is the heart of traditional Islam in modern Malaysia. While the government in KL constructs social policies based upon a more open and tolerant Islam, religious and government leaders in Kelantan can be counted on for putting forth a strong Muslim ideal where they feel they may have influence. Indeed, the state has the only minister that is not a member of Dr. Mahathir's leading UMNO party.

Kelantan owes its character to the mountain range that runs north to south through the interior, slicing the peninsula in half. Isolated from other Malay areas, Kelantan for most of its history was aligned with Siam, which didn't care one way or another how Kelantan ran its territory. Cut off from the trade traffic on the other side of the mountains, Kelantan, and to some extent its southern neighbor Terengganu, had sufficient peace of mind to form its own Islamic bureaucracy, judicial system, and societal institutions, emphasizing Muslim standards of scholarship and learning. Trade in gold, mined from the interior, provided for business with Chinese and Thais, but Europeans, their mouths watering for the mineral wealth, were not welcome.

Well, Kelantan couldn't keep away the British in 1900. Not only were the Brits interested in all that gold, but they were also interested in keeping the region free from French and German interests. Arguments were fought and agreements made between London and Siam, and eventually Kelantan came under British rule. Several peasant uprisings disturbed the peace, and the Muslim elite in the cities took to developing their own modern knowledge in hopes of overcoming their Christian infiltrators. We all know how the story eventually ends.

**Kota Bharu,** the state capital, is the heart of the region. The area is rich in Malay cultural heritage, as evidenced in the continuing interest in arts like *silat* (Malay martial arts), *wayang kulit* (puppetry), *gasing* (top-spinning), and *wau* (kite flying). For the record, you won't find too much traditional music or dance, as women are forbidden from entertaining in public. Also beware that the state has strict laws controlling the sale of alcoholic beverages, which cannot be purchased in stores, hotels, or most restaurants. You will not find a single bar. Chinese restaurants, however, are permitted to sell beer to their patrons, but will probably not allow you to take any away.

## Visitor Information
You'll find the Kelantan Tourist Information Centre at Jalan Sultan Ibrahim (☎ **09/748-5534**).

## Getting There
**BY AIR**    From KL, Malaysia Airlines flies seven times daily. Call ☎ **03/746-3000** for reservations. You'll land at Kota Bharu's Sultan Ismail Petra Airport (☎ **09/773-7000**) about 20 minutes outside the city. A taxi shouldn't be any more than RM25 (US$6.60). The Malaysia Airlines office in town is at Ground Floor, Kompleks Yakin, Jalan Gajah Mati (☎ **09/744-7000**).

**BY TRAIN**    The KTM runs a line through the center of the peninsula all the way to the Thai border. The Wakaf Bharu station is closest to the city, and taxis are available, or you can take local bus nos. 19 or 27. For train information in KL, call ☎ **03/442-4722.**

**BY BUS**    Kota Bahru's bus terminal is at Jalan Padang Garong off Jalan Doktor. Buses bring you here from all corners of the peninsula. From KL, call Transnasional at Putra Bus Terminal (☎ **03/442-8945**). They've got two dailies at a cost of around RM25 (US$6.60). From Kuala Terengganu's bus terminal, Transnasional (☎ **09/623-8384**) has six buses daily for RM7.50 (US$2). To find out about buses out of Kota Bharu, call ☎ **09/748-2807.** The taxi stand is just across the street, and you may be hounded by all sorts of gypsy cabs; they're not proper taxi drivers but will take you places to make some extra cash. They're basically honest.

**BY TAXI**    The local taxi stand across from the bus terminal also acts as the outstation taxi stand. To reserve a car, the number is ☎ **09/748-1386.** Taxis from Kuala Terengganu run about RM80 (US$21).

# Kota Bharu

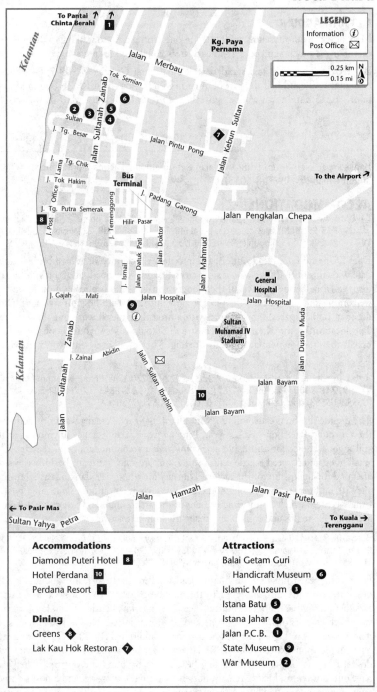

**LEGEND**
Information ⓘ
Post Office ✉

Kelantan

To Pantai Chinta Berahi ↑ ↑ 1
Kg. Paya Pernama

Jalan Merbau

Tok Semian

Jalan Sultanah Zainab

6
2 3 5
Sultan 4
J. Tg. Besar

Jalan Pintu Pong
7

J. Tg. Chik
J. Office Lama
J. Tok Hakim

Jalan Kebun Sultan

To the Airport ↗

J. Tg. Putra Semerak
8 J. Post

Bus Terminal

J. Temenggong

J. Padang Garong

Hilir Pasar

Jalan Pengkalan Chepa

J. Ismail

Jalan Datuk Pati

Jalan Doktor

Jalan Mahmud

J. Gajah Mati

Jalan Hospital

General Hospital

9 ⓘ

Jalan Hospital

Sultan Muhamad IV Stadium

Jalan Dusun Muda

Sultanah Zainab

J. Zainal Abidin

Jalan Sultan Ibrahim

✉

10

Jalan Bayam

Jalan Bayam

Kelantan

← To Pasir Mas

Jalan Hamzah

Jalan Pasir Puteh

Sultan Yahya Petra

To Kuala → Terengganu

0.25 km
0.15 mi
N

---

**Accommodations**
Diamond Puteri Hotel 8
Hotel Perdana 10
Perdana Resort 1

**Dining**
Greens 8
Lak Kau Hok Restoran 7

**Attractions**
Balai Getam Guri
  Handicraft Museum 6
Islamic Museum 3
Istana Batu 5
Istana Jahar 4
Jalan P.C.B. 1
State Museum 9
War Museum 2

## GETTING AROUND

Most of the major museums are located in one central area, so walking to them is very easy. For the beach and cottage industry areas you'll need to hire a taxi.

**BY TAXI**   The main taxi stand is at Jalan Padang Garong, ☎ **09/748-1386** for booking. Daily and half-day rates can be negotiated for about RM15 (US$3.95) per hour. Trips around town will be between RM5 (US$1.30) and RM10 (US$2.65).

# Fast Facts: Kota Bharu

Banks are at Jalan Pitum Pong and Jalan Kebun Sultan. The main post office is at Jalan Sultan Ismail (☎ **09/748-4033**).

## ACCOMMODATIONS

✪ **Diamond Puteri Hotel.** Jalan Post Office Lama, 1500 Kota Bharu, Kelantan, Malaysia. ☎ **09/743-9988**, KL sales office 03/413-0448. Fax 09/743-8388. 311 units. A/C MINIBAR TV TEL. RM220 (US$58) double; RM650–RM950 (US$171–US$250) suite. AE, DC, MC, V.

Does Diamond Puteri lead Kota Bharu into the next century, or at least bring it up to date with this one? Either way, it's the city's first five-star hotel, and as it's shiny and new, you'll be happy to have all the modern conveniences it offers. Guest rooms are welcoming and bright. Still, the place is a bit untried—with hesitant staff and sparse decor in public spaces, but I'm sure with a little time they'll work out the wrinkles. The location by the Kelantan River isn't the fabulous view you'd hope for, which makes the outdoor pool area not as inviting. They also have a fitness center with a sauna.

**Hotel Perdana.** Jalan Mahmood, P.O. Box 222, 15720 Kota Bharu, Kelantan, Malaysia. ☎ **09/748-5000.** Fax 09/744-7621. 178 units. A/C MINIBAR TV TEL. RM200–RM220 (US$52–US$58) double; RM600–RM750 (US$158–US$197) suite.

The premier business class hotel in Kota Bharu for years, Perdana was unrivaled until the Diamond Puteri opened last year. Perdana won't seem as fancy anymore, but it's still a good choice for affordable and comfortable accommodations in the city. The small guest rooms need a little refurbishing, but are spic and span. Besides, the rates are good for the quality of the facility. Unusual for a hotel, Perdana boasts a bowling alley (!), and more conventional hotel facilities such as an outdoor swimming pool, a fitness center (which is not exactly state-of-the-art), sauna, and steam bath. Sports activities like tennis and squash also make the hotel attractive.

**Perdana Resort.** Jalan Kuala Pa'Amat, Pantai Cahaya Bulan, P.O. Box 121, 15710 Kota Bharu, Kelantan, Malaysia. ☎ **09/774-4000.** Fax 09/774-4980. 117 units. A/C MINIBAR TV TEL. RM150–RM210 (US$39–US$55) chalet. AE, DC, MC, V.

For a little beach fun in Kota Bharu, head for Perdana Resort, just about the only beach resort in the area, and perhaps the only beach where you can wear a Western-style bathing suit and not feel out of place. The individual chalets make for great privacy, each with its own porch outside and bathroom inside. They're also spacious, so if you want to put in an extra bed or two for an additional RM30 (US$8), you'll still have ample room to get around. Perdana will arrange whatever beach activity you desire, from paddleboats to canoeing, beach volleyball, and fishing trips. They also have outdoor tennis, bicycle rentals, horseback riding, kite flying, and a host of other amusements to keep you busy. When you can't take anymore, collapse in the giant free form pool.

# DINING

**Greens.** Diamond Puteri Hotel, Jalan Post Office Lama. ☎ **09/743-9988.** Reservations not necessary. Prices RM10–RM38. AE, DC, MC, V. Daily 7am–midnight. WESTERN/LOCAL.

Set in a simple cafe style, Greens has yet to grow into its surroundings in the new Diamond Puteri Hotel. Serving as the coffee shop for the hotel, it is open from early in the morning till late at night and features a wide range of dishes. Choose from familiar Western favorites, or try their specialty local Kelantanese selections (which are the best dishes), such as ayam perchik—chicken in a coconut and fish stock gravy, a favorite in these parts.

**Lak Kau Hok Restoran.** 2959 Jalan Kebun Sultan. ☎ **09/748-3762.** Reservations not necessary. RM8–RM25 (US$2.10–US$6.60). Daily 11am–2:30pm and 6–10pm. No credit cards. CHINESE/SEAFOOD.

Kota Bharu isn't all that boring a town at night. Head down to Chinatown's Jalan Kebun Sultan where the streets get lively. Walk past glowing restaurants, hawker stalls, and friends out for a chat and a stroll, and when you reach the little house that is Lak Kau Hok, head inside. The smells of garlic and chilies will seduce you from the moment you enter, and after specialties like steamed garlic prawns and steamed fish Teochew style, with vegetables and mushrooms sautéed in a rich gravy, you'll be very happy you came. Did I mention they serve beer?

# ATTRACTIONS

Centered around the ✪ **Padang Merdeka** at the end of Jalan Hilir Kota are five of the most significant sights in Kota Bharu, run by the Kelantan State Museum Corporation. For information on any of these places, call ☎ **744-4666.** All are open daily 8:30am to 4:45pm and are closed Fridays.

At the **Istana Jahar,** adults RM3 (US80¢), children RM1.50 (US40¢), Kelantan traditional costumes, antiques, and musical instruments are displayed in context to their usage in royal ceremonies. **Istana Batu,** adults RM2 (US50¢), children RM1 (US25¢), takes you through a photographic journey of Kelantan's royal family, and a peek at their lifestyle through the past 200 years. The **Balai Getam Guri** handicraft museum, adults RM1 (US25¢), children RM.50 (US15¢), showcases the finest in Kelantanese textiles, basketry, embroidery, batik printing, and silversmithing. You'll also be able to buy crafts in the shops within the compound. The **Islamic Museum (Muzium Islam),** adults RM1 (US25¢), children RM.50 (US15¢), teaches everything you might want to know about Islam in this state, with a focus on Islamic arts and Kelantan's role in spreading Islam in the region. Finally there is the **War Museum (Bank Kerapu),** adults RM2 (US50¢), children RM1 (US25¢), which tells the story of Kelantan during World War II in a 1912 bank building that survived the invasion.

✪ **State Museum (Muzium Negeri).** Jalan Hospital. ☎ **09/744-4666.** Adults RM2 (US50¢), children RM1 (US25¢). Open daily 8:30am–4:45pm; closed Fridays.

It's been a long time since this old building served as the colonial land office, but in 1990 major renovations gave it a new life. Now the Kelantan Art Gallery, including ceramics, traditional musical instrument, and cultural pastimes exhibits, grace its halls.

# SHOPPING

For great local handicrafts shopping, visitors to Kelantan need go no further than **Jalan P.C.B.,** the road that leads to P.C.B. beach from Kota Bharu's Chinatown area. Hire a taxi and stop at every roadside factory, showroom, shop, and crafts house (the place crawls with them!) and you'll satisfy every shopping itch that needs scratching.

Some wonderful places to try are **Wisma Songket Kampung Penambang,** Jalan P.C.B. (☎ **09/744-7757**) for songket cloth and clothing, and to see the ladies weaving the fine cloth. The local kite man, **Haji Wan Hussen bin Haji Ibrahim,** makes and sells kites out of his home (328–A Kampong Redong Tikat, Jalan P.C.B. (☎ **09/744-0462**) and will invite you in for a look. He'll pack them sturdy so you can airmail them home. Also, **Pantas Songet & Batik Manufacturer** (Kampung Penambang, Jalan P.C.B. ☎ **09/744-1616**) has a nice selection of batik clothing and sarongs, plus some pieces of songket cloth.

In town, if you'd like to buy some silver, good (and inexpensive) filigree jewelry collections and silver housewares are to be had at **Mohamed Salleh & Sons** (1260B Jalan Sultanah Zainab, ☎ **09/748-3401**) and K.B. Permai (5406–C Jalan Sultanah Zainab, ☎ **09/748-5661**).

In the small but lively Chinatown area look for **A. Zahari Antik at 3953-B Jalan Kebin Sultan** (☎ **09/744-3548**) where you can shop for old treasures like *keris* (Malay daggers with wavy blades—he has a great selection) as well as pottery, carvings, and brass.

Finally, for a little local shopping experience, check out the giant **Pasar Besar** wet market on Jalan Parit Dalam. Behind the produce and fish stands are shops for cheap bargains.

## 17 Introducing East Malaysia

Borneo for the past two centuries has been the epitome of adventure travel. While bustling ports like Penang, Malacca, and Singapore attracted early travelers with stars in their eyes, Borneo attracted those with adventure in their hearts. Today, the island still draws visitors who seek new and unusual experiences, and few leave disappointed. Rivers meander through dense tropical rain forests, beaches stretch for miles, and caves snake out longer than any in the world. All sorts of creatures you'd never imagine live in the rain forest: deer the size of housecats, owls only 6 inches tall, the odd probiscus monkey—and the orangutan, whose only other natural home is Sumatra. It's also home to the largest flower in the world, the Rafflesia, spanning up to about 3 feet (1m) wide. Small wonder this place has special interest for scientists and researchers the world round.

The people of Borneo can be credited for most of the alluring tales of early travels. The exotically adorned tribes of warring headhunters and pirates of yesteryear, some of whom still live lifestyles little changed (OK, so headhunting and pirating are now illegal), today share their mysterious cultures and colorful traditions openly with outsiders.

Add to all of this the fabulous tale of the White Raja of Sarawak, Sir James Brooke, whose family ruled the state for just over a hundred years, and you have a land filled with allure, mystery, and romance unlike any other.

Malaysia, Brunei Darussalam, and Indonesia have divided the island. Indonesia claims Kalimantan to the south and east, and the Malaysian states of Sarawak and Sabah lie to the north and northwest. The small sultanate of Brunei is nestled between the two Malaysian states on the western coastline.

## 18 Sarawak

Tropical rain forest accounts for over 70% of Sarawak's total land mass, providing homes for not only exotic species of plants and animals, but for the different ethnic groups who are indigenous to the area. With over 10 national parks and four wildlife preserves, Malaysia shows its commitment to conserving the delicate balance of life

# Sarawak & Sabah's National Parks

here, while allowing small gateways for travelers to appreciate Sarawak's natural wonders. A network of rivers connects the inland areas to the rest of the world, and a boat trip to visit tribal communities and trek into caves and jungles can prove to be the most memorable attraction going.

The indigenous peoples of Sarawak make up over half the state's population. Early explorers and settlers referred to these people with the catch-all term "Dyaks," which didn't account for the variations between the more than 25 different ethnicities. Of these groups, the Iban are the largest, with over 30% of the population of the state. A nomadic people by tradition, the Ibans were once located all over the region, existing on agriculture, hunting and fishing. They were also notorious warriors who would behead enemies—a practice now outlawed but which has retained its cultural significance. The Ibans not only fought with other tribes, but within their own separate tribal units.

The next largest group, the Bidayuh, live peacefully in the hills. Their **longhouse communities** are the most accessible to tourist visits from Kuching. The Melanu are a coastal people who excel in fishing and boatbuilding. Finally, the Orang Ulu is an association of smaller tribes mostly in the northern parts of the state. Tribes like the Kayah, Kenyah, Kelabit, and Penan, while culturally separate entities, formed an umbrella organization to loosely govern all groups and provide representation. These groups are perhaps the least accessible to outsiders.

The indigenous people who still stay in the forest live in longhouse communities, many of which are open for visitors. Most travelers access these places with the help of local tour operators, who have trips that last from an overnight excursion to a week-long adventure. While some tours take you to well-trampled villages for the standard "gawk at the funny costumes" trips, many operators can take you to more remote places to meet people in an environment of cultural learning with a sensitivity that is appreciated by all involved. A few adventuresome souls travel solo into these areas, but I recommend that you stick with an operator. I don't care much for visitors who pop in unexpectedly, and I can't imagine why people in one of these villages wouldn't feel the same way.

Every visitor to Sarawak starts out from **Kuching,** the capital city. With a population of some 400,000 people, it's small, but oddly cosmopolitan. In addition to local tribes who gave up forest living, the city has large populations of Malays, Chinese, Indians, and Europeans, most of who migrated in the last two centuries. Sitting at the mouth of the Kuching River, most of your trips inland will originate from this point. But before you head off for the river, check out the many delights of this mysterious colonial kingdom.

Sarawak was introduced to the Western world by **James Brooke,** an English adventurer who in 1839 came to Southeast Asia to follow in the footsteps of his idol, Sir Stamford Raffles. Like Raffles' Singapore, there was a region waiting for Brooke to settle and start a bustling community. His wanderings brought him to Borneo, where he was introduced to the sultan of Brunei. The sultan was deeply troubled by warring tribes to the south of his kingdom, who were in constant revolt, sometimes to the point of pirating ships to Brunei's port. Brooke provided the solution, initiating a campaign to befriend some of the warring tribes, uniting them to conquer the others. Within a short amount of time the tribes were calmed. The sultan, delighted by Brooke, ceded Kuching to him for a small annual fee. In 1841, James Brooke became raja and set about claiming the land that is now Sarawak.

Raja Sir James Brooke became a colonial legend. He was known as "The White Raja of Sarawak," and his family ruled the territory and its people with a firm but compassionate hand. Tribal leaders were appointed to leadership and administrative positions within his government and militia, and by and large the Brookes were highly respected by the populations they led. However, Brooke was a bit of a renegade, turning his nose up at London's attempts to include Sarawak under the crown. He took no money from the British and closed the doors to British commercial interests in Sarawak. Instead he dealt in local trade and trade with Singapore. Still, Kuching was understood to be a British holding, but the city never flourished as did other British ports in Southeast Asia.

After his death in 1868, Raja James Brooke was succeeded by his nephew, Charles Brooke. In 1917 his son, Vyner Brooke, became the last ruling Raja until World War II, when the territory was conquered by invading Japanese. After the war, Raja Vyner Brooke returned briefly, but the territory became a crown colony in 1946. After Malaya was granted independence by Britain, Prime Minister Tunku Abdul Rahman formed Malaysia in 1963, uniting peninsular Malaya with Singapore, Sarawak, and Sabah. Singapore departed from the union two years later, but Sarawak and Sabah remained.

# KUCHING

The perfect introduction to Sarawak begins in its capital. Kuching's museums, cultural exhibits, and historical attractions will help you form an overview of the history, people, and natural wonders of the state. In Kuching your introduction to Sarawak will be comfortable and fun; culture by day and good food and fun by night. Kuching, meaning "cat" in Malay, also has a wonderful sense of humor, featuring monuments and exhibits to its feline mascot on almost every corner.

# Kuching

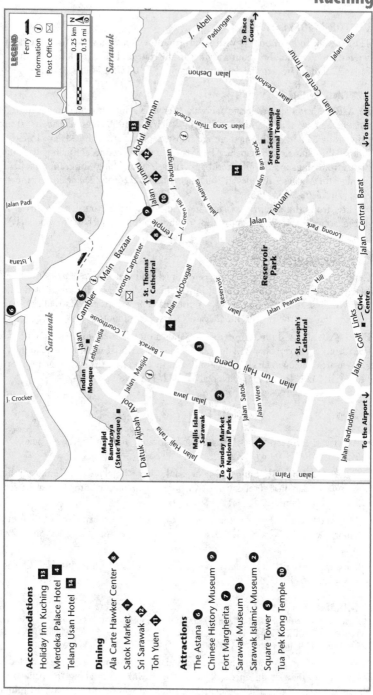

**Accommodations**
Holiday Inn Kuching **13**
Merdeka Palace Hotel **4**
Telang Usan Hotel **14**

**Dining**
Ala Carte Hawker Center **8**
Satok Market **7**
Sri Sarawak **12**
Toh Yuen **11**

**Attractions**
The Astana **6**
Chinese History Museum **9**
Fort Margherita **7**
Sarawak Museum **3**
Sarawak Islamic Museum **2**
Square Tower **5**
Tua Pek Kong Temple **10**

## VISITOR INFORMATION

The Sarawak Tourism Board's **Visitor Information Centre** has literature and staff that can answer any question about activities in the state and city. You'll find them at the Padang Merdeka next to the Sarawak Museum (☎ 082/423-600).

## GETTING THERE

**BY AIR**  Almost all travelers to Sarawak enter via Kuching International Airport, just outside the city. Malaysia Airlines (in KL ☎ 03/746-3000) flies here about 10 times daily from KL. In addition, there are nonstop flights from the Malaysian cities of Johor Bahru and Kota Kinabalu. Malaysia Airlines also connects Kuching with direct flights from Singapore, Bandar Seri Bagawan in Brunei, Hong Kong, and Manila. The number for Malaysia Airlines in Kuching is ☎ **082/246-622.** For airport information, call ☎ **082/454-255.**

**Taxis from the airport** use coupons that you purchase outside the arrival hall. Priced according to zones, most trips to the central parts of town will be RM16 (US$4.20).

## GETTING AROUND

Centered around a padang, or large ceremonial field, Kuching resembles many other Malaysian cities. Buildings of beautiful colonial style rise on the edges of the field; many of these today house Sarawak's museums. The main sights, as well as the Chinatown area and the river front, are easily accessible on foot.

**BY TAXI**  Taxis do not use meters, and most rides around town cost RM6 (US$1.60). Taxis can be waved down from the side of the road, or if you're in the Chinatown area, the main taxi stand is near Gambier Road near the end of the India Street Pedestrian Mall. To call for a taxi, dial ☎ **082/348-898.**

# Fast Facts: Kuching

**American Express**  The Amex office is located at Cph Travel Agencies, 70 Padungan Rd., ☎ 082/242-289.

**Banks/Currency Exchange**  Major banks have branches on Tunku Abdul Rahman Road near Holiday Inn Kuching, or in the downtown area around Khoo Hun Yeang Road.

**Internet/E-mail**  For a good Internet cafe try Cyber City (No. 46 Ground Floor Block D, ☎ 082/428-318) just behind Riverside Complex Shopping Mall.

**Post Office/Mail**  The central post office is on Jalan Tun Abang Haji Openg (☎ 082/245-952).

## ACCOMMODATIONS

**Holiday Inn Kuching.** P.O. Box 2362, Jalan Tunku Abdul Rahman, 93100 Kuching, Sarawak, Malaysia. ☎ **082/423-111.** Fax 082/426-169. 305 units. A/C MINIBAR TV TEL. RM360–RM385 double; suites RM635 and up. AE, DC, JCB, MC V.

Holiday Inn offers Western-style accommodations at a moderate price, and you'll appreciate its location in an excellent part of town. It sits along the bank of the Kuching River, so to get to the main riverside area you need only stroll 10 minutes past some of the city's unique historical and cultural sights, shopping, and good places to dine. Catering to a diverse group of leisure travelers and business people, the hotel has spacious, modern, and comfortable rooms, and while there are few bells and whistles, you won't want for convenience. The outdoor swimming pool and excellent fitness center facility will help you unwind, and the small shopping arcade has one of the best collections of books on Sarawak that can be found in the city.

✪ **Merdeka Palace Hotel.** Jalan Tun Abang Haji Openg, 93000 Kuching, Sarawak, Malaysia. ☎ **082/258-000.** Fax 082/425-400. 214 units. A/C MINIBAR TV TEL. RM380–RM410 (US$100–US$108) double; RM800–RM3,000 (US$210–US$789) suite. AE, DC, JCB, MC, V.

Towering over the Padang Merdeka in the center of town is the Merdeka Palace, practically a landmark in its own right (as soon as you see the easily distinguishable tower, you'll always know where you are). This is one of the most fashionable addresses in the city, for guests as well as banquets and functions. Its reputation for elegance is justified, from the large marble lobby to the mezzanine shopping arcade stuffed with designer tenants. Large rooms come dressed in European-inspired furnishings and fabrics. Try to get a view of the padang, as the less expensive rooms face the car park. The rooftop outdoor swimming pool is small, but the fully equipped fitness center has sauna and steam rooms, plus massage.

✪ **Telang Usan Hotel.** Ban Hock Road, P.O. Box 1579, 93732 Kuching, Sarawak, Malaysia. ☎ **082/415-588.** Fax 082/245-316. 66 units, A/C TV TEL. RM120–RM200 (US$32–US$53) double. AE, DC, JCB, MC, V.

While in Kuching I like to stay at the Telang Usan Hotel. It's not as flashy as some of the other places, but it's a fantastic bargain for a good room. Most guests here are leisure travelers, and in fact, many are repeat offenders, returning to this hotel with each visit. The small public areas sport murals in local Iban style, revealing the origin of the hotel's owner and operator. While rooms are small and decor is not completely up to date, they're spotless. Some rooms have only standing showers, so be sure to specify when making your reservation if a long bath is important to you. The coffee shop serves local and Western food from 7am to midnight, and the higher-category rooms have minibars.

## DINING

✪ **Sri Sarawak.** Crowne Plaza Riverside Kuching, Jalan Tunku Abdul Rahman, ☎ **082/247-777.** Reservations not necessary. Open noon–2:30pm, 6–10:30pm daily. Entrees RM8 to RM22 (US$2.10–US$5.80). AE, DC, JCB, MC, V. MALAY.

Sri Sarawak is the only place to find Malay food in a fine dining establishment. The restaurant occupies the 18th floor of the Crowne Plaza hotel, with views all around to the city below. The friendly and helpful staff is more than happy to help you navigate the menu, which includes Sarawak specialties such as umai, raw fish marinated in lime juice with onion, ginger, and chili.

**Toh Yuen.** Kuching Hilton, Jalan Tunku Abdul Rahman. ☎ 082/248-200. Reservations recommended on weekends. Open 11:30am–2:30pm, 6:30–10:30pm. RM14–RM48 (US$3.70–US$12.65). AE, DC, JCB, MC, V. CHINESE.

One of the premier Chinese restaurants in Kuching, Toh Yueh serves excellently prepared dishes that are as pleasing to the eye as they are to the palette. Chef's specialties like butter prawns melt in your mouth, as do any of the many bean curd selections and crunchy vegetable dishes. Call ahead for special promotions for weekend lunch and dinner, which can be surprisingly low priced.

### Hawker Centers

In addition to conventional restaurants, Kuching's food stalls are a culinary adventure at affordable prices. A good centrally located hawker center is at **Ala Carte** on Lebuh Temple. It's indoor and air conditioned. Also try the food stalls at

**Satok Market** out at Jalan Satok for excellent Malay, Chinese, and Sarawakian cuisine.

## ATTRACTIONS

✪ **Sarawak Museum.** Jalan Tun Haji Openg. ☎ **082/244-232.** Free admission. Open Sat–Thurs 9am–5pm, Fri 9am–12:45pm and 3–5pm.

Two branches, one old and one new, display exhibits of the natural history, indigenous peoples, and culture of Sarawak, and the state's colonial and modern history. The two branches are connected by an overhead walkway above Jalan Tun Haji Openg. The wildlife exhibit is a bit musty, but the arts and artifacts in the other sections are well tended. A tiny aquarium sits neglected behind the old branch, but the gardens here are lovely.

**Sarawak Islamic Museum.** Jalan P. Ramlee. ☎ **082/244-232.** Free admission. Open Sat–Thurs 9am–5pm, Fri 9am–12:45pm and 3–5pm.

A splendid array of Muslim artifacts here depicts the history of Islam and its spread to Southeast Asia. Local customs and history are also highlighted in this quiet and serene museum. While women are not required to cover their heads, respectable attire that covers the legs and arms is requested.

**Square Tower.** Jalan Gambier near the riverfront.

The tower, built in 1879, served as a prison camp, but today the waterfront real estate is better served by a tourist information center. The square tower is also a prime starting place for a stroll along the riverside. Here's where you'll find out about cultural performances and exhibitions held at the waterfront. You can also call ☎ **082/426-093** for performance schedules.

✪ **The Astana and Fort Margherita.**

At the waterfront by the Square Tower you'll find water taxis to take you across the river to see these two reminders of the white Rajas of Sarawak. The Astana, built in 1870 by Raja Charles Brooke, the second raja of Sarawak, is the official residence of the governor of Sarawak. It is not open to the public but visitors may still walk in the gardens. The best view of the Astana, however is from the water.

Raja Charles Brooke's wife, Ranee Margaret, gave her name to this fort, which was erected in 1870 to protect the city of Kuching. Inside the great castlelike building is a police museum, the most interesting sights of which are the depictions of criminal punishment.

**Chinese History Museum.** Corner of Main Bazaar and Jalan Tunku Abdul Rahman. No telephone. Free admission. Open daily 9am–5pm.

Built in 1912, this old Chinese Chamber of Commerce Building is the perfect venue for a museum that traces the history of Chinese communities in Sarawak. Though small, it's centrally located and a convenient stop while you're in the area.

**Tua Pek Kong Temple.** Junction of Jalan Tunku Abdul Rahman and Jalan Padungan.

At a main crossroads near the river stands the oldest Chinese temple in Sarawak. While officially it is dated at 1876, most locals acknowledge the true date of its beginnings as 1843. It's still lively in form and spirit, with colorful dragons tumbling along the walls and wafts of incense filling the air.

**Main Bazaar.** Along the river.

Main Bazaar, the major thoroughfare along the river, is home to Kuching's antiques and handicraft shops. If you're walking along the river, a little time in these shops is like a walk through a traditional handicrafts art gallery. You'll also find souvenir shops and some nice t-shirt silkscreeners.

✪ **Sarawak Cultural Village.** Kampung Budaya Sarawak, Pantai Damai, Santubong. ☎ **082/846-411.** Adults RM45 (US$11.85), children RM22.50 (US$5.90). Open daily 9am–5pm.

What appears to be a contrived theme park turns out to be a really fun place to learn about Sarawak's indigenous people. Built around a lagoon, the park re-creates the various styles of longhouse dwellings of each of the major tribes. Inside each house are representative members of each tribe displaying cultural artifacts and performing music, teaching dart blowing and showing off carving talents. Give yourself plenty of time to stick around and talk with the people, who are recruited from villages inland and love to tell stories about their homes and traditions. Performers dance and display costumes at 11:30am and 4:30pm daily. A shuttle bus leaves at regular intervals from the Holiday Inn Kuching on Jalan Abell.

## TOURING LOCAL CULTURE

When you come to Sarawak everyone will tell you that you must take a trip to witness **life in a longhouse.** It is perhaps one of the most unique experiences you'll have, and is a lot easier to arrange than it sounds. Many good tour operators in Kuching take visitors out to longhouse communities, where guests are invited to stay for 1 or more nights. You'll eat local food, experience daily culture, and view traditional pastimes and ceremonies. On longer tours you may stop at more than one village to get a cross-cultural comparison of two or more different tribes. Good tour operators to speak to about arranging a trip are **Borneo Adventure,** 55 Main Bazaar (☎ **082/245-175,** fax 082/422-626); and Telang Usan Travel & Tours, Ban Hock Road (☎ **082/236-945,** fax 082/236-589). These agencies can also arrange trips into Sarawak's national parks.

## TOURING SARAWAK'S NATIONAL PARKS

Before planning any trip into the national parks, travelers must contact the **National Parks Booking Office** at the Visitors Information Center next to the Sarawak Museum (☎ **082/248-088,** fax 082/256-301). You will need to acquire permission to enter any park, and will be advised on accommodations, transportation, park safety, and regulations.

**Bako National Park,** established in 1957, is Sarawak's oldest National Park. An area of 6,820 acres (2,728 hectares) combines mangrove forest, lowland jungle, and high plains covered in scrub. Throughout the park you'll see the pitcher plant and other strange carnivorous plants, plus long-tailed macaques, monitor lizards, bearded pigs, and the unique probiscus monkey. Because the park is only 22 miles (37km) from Kuching, trips here are extremely convenient.

A new project, the **Matang Wildlife Centre,** about an hour outside of Kuching, gives endangered wildlife a home, provides researchers with insight into wildlife conservation, and educates visitors about the animals and their habitat. For day trips, no parks permission is required.

**Gunung Gading National Park,** about a 2-hour drive west of Kuching, sprawls 10,265 acres (4,106 hectares) over rugged mountains to beautiful beach spots along the coast. Day-trippers and overnighters come to get a glimpse of the Rafflesia, the largest flower in the world. The flowers are short-lived and temperamental, but the National parks office will let you know if there are any in bloom.

**Gunung Mulu National Park** provides an amazing adventure with its astounding underground network of caves. The park claims the world's largest cave passage (Deer Cave), the world's largest natural chamber (Sararwak Chamber), and Southeast Asia's longest cave (Clearwater Cave). No fewer than 18 caves offer explorers trips of varying degrees of difficulty, from simple treks with minimal gear to technically difficult caves that require specialized equipment and skills. Above ground is 326 square miles (544 sq. km) of primary rain forest, peat swamps, and mountainous forests teeming with mammals, birds, and unusual insects. Located in the north of Sarawak, Mulu is very close to the Brunei border.

**Niah National Park,** while interesting to nature buffs, is more fascinating for those interested in archaeology. From 1954 to 1967 explorers excavated a prehistoric site dating as far back as 40,000 years that was continuously occupied until some 2,000 years ago. The **Niah Great Cave** revealed sharp stone implements, pottery vessels, and animal and botanical remains. Near the mouth of the cave is a burial ground dating from Paleolithic times. The Painted Cave is a magnificent gallery of mystical cave paintings and coffins that were buried here between A.D. 1 and A.D. 780. While a visit to the park requires parks permission, further information on the excavation sites can be obtained from the Sarawak Museum, ☎ **082/244-232,** fax 082/246-680.

# Bali & Lombok

*by Mary Herczog*

First of all, Bali is not in the South Pacific. It's actually nestled between the Java Sea and Indian Ocean. And while its residents do wear sarongs part of the time, they're considered somewhat formal wear—not a bit like Dorothy Lamour.

In other words, Bali is not the stuff of Hollywood movies or Michener novels. But don't fret—it's every bit as romantic and fantastic as you've imagined. This is a pocket-sized island, so small you can practically drive from one end to the other in 2 or 3 hours. And yet the culture is completely unique to this extraordinary place, a culture so rich, so layered, that expats who have lived here 20 years say with a sigh, "The longer I stay, the less I understand it." What you find will depend largely on what you put into the search. My experience may not be your experience, and any "facts" contained here about Balinese culture, ritual, and religion may differ somewhat from what you encounter.

Bali affords many delights for practically any tourist agenda. You can shop till you drop, swim and sun, climb to holy sites, visit villages largely untouched by time, and eat extremely well. You can be a conventional, conservative beach resort tourist living the high life on a rich person's budget; or get down and dirty Euro-hippie style, spending US$10 a day for food and lodging for two. You can travel all over the island, or you can settle down in Ubud and watch the days turn into weeks.

So what should you do? A little of everything, with an emphasis on spending whatever time you can with the Balinese. To come here and never leave the beach and a Western-style luxury hotel would be a sin. Stay a couple days in that fancy hotel, but stay a couple more in a basic losmen or homestay—rooms or bungalows let out by ordinary people, which cost just a few dollars a night, including breakfast. Forget about what comforts you may have traded in (though in some cases, not nearly as many as you might think) and take some time to get to know your hosts; chances are you are living in more or less their backyard. The Balinese are a very friendly people, and are usually pleased when tourists take the time to get acquainted. If their English is good enough (and in most tourist areas, it is), you can learn a great deal from them. Another highly recommended way to dip into the culture is to join in on temple ceremonies. Celebration and ceremony are integral parts of everyday Balinese life, and not a day goes by without a temple ceremony somewhere on the island.

# Bali

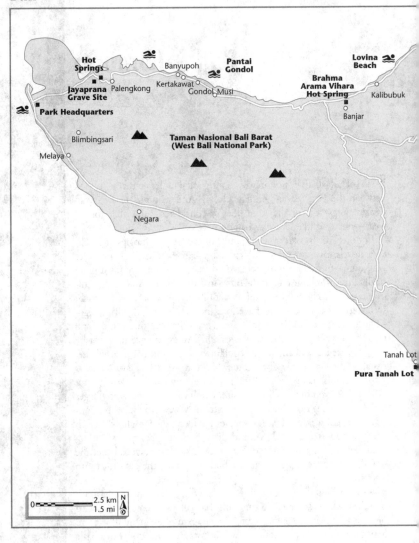

## BALI TODAY

As with any undiscovered paradise that isn't so undiscovered any more, Bali buffs mourn the loss of the island's innocence. But Bali has always been a magnet for tourists and expats, and if its economy is now almost solely based on tourism (and rice), well, at least they have one.

But to say that it's changed is only telling part of the truth. Sure, 25 years ago there were virtually no hotels on Kuta Beach. 25 years ago, there was no electricity in Ubud, and now there are at least three cybercafes. Peddlers ("touts") and hustlers have grown in numbers and aggressiveness, determined to take advantage of the walking wallets that are American, European, and Australian visitors. And yet, the essential Bali has not changed. The Balinese ritualized way of life remains precisely as it always has been.

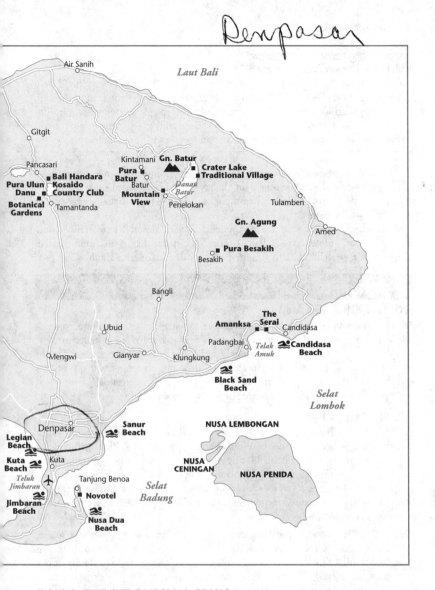

Air Sanih

*Laut Bali*

Gitgit

Pancasari

Pura Ulun Danu

Bali Handara Kosaido Country Club

Botanical Gardens

Tamantanda

Kintamani

Pura Batur

Batur

Mountain View

Gn. Batur

*Danau Batur*

Penelokan

Crater Lake

Traditional Village

Tulamben

Amed

Gn. Agung

Pura Besakih

Besakih

Bangli

Ubud

Amanksa

The Serai

Candidasa

Padangbai

*Telak Amuk*

Candidasa Beach

Mengwi

Gianyar

Klungkung

Black Sand Beach

*Selat Lombok*

Denpasar

Sanur Beach

NUSA LEMBONGAN

Legian Beach

Kuta Beach

Kuta

*Teluk Jimbaran*

Tanjung Benoa

*Selat Badung*

NUSA CENINGAN

NUSA PENIDA

Novotel

Jimbaran Beach

Nusa Dua Beach

# BALI & THE INDONESIAN CRISIS

The riots and protests that erupted in Indonesia in 1998 were the result of 3 decades of military rule and struggles to bring the world's fourth most populous country into the modern global economy. Chafing under the virtual dictatorship of President Suharto, the Indonesians finally revolted, with demonstrations turning into riots that made headlines around the world. Post-Suharto attempts at democratization have proven predictably troubled and the political situation remains in flux.

With its tourist-based economy and Hindu religion, Bali has remained largely unaffected by the tumultuous and unpredictable economic and social problems recently wracking the rest of the country. (Indeed, during the riots, the U.S. State Department told all tourists to come home immediately. Those on Bali, by and large, looked

To learn more about Bali, I cannot recommend Fred Eisenman's two-volume *Bali: Sekala & Niskala* (Periplus Editions) highly enough. It can be obtained in the U.S. or throughout Bali, particularly in Ubud. Eisenman spends part of the year in Jimbaran, and his writing about all aspects of Balinese culture—society, religion, tradition, art, and so on—is lovingly detailed, and most readable and accessible.

around, saw everything was normal, and stayed put.) However, some tourists have stayed away out of fear, while others simply have found it harder to get there, thanks to decreased flights (particularly when the state airline, Garuda, ceased being able to offer international flights).

At press time, matters were still too unpredictable and unstable to offer any strong opinions about Indonesia's—or Bali's—future. I can say that at the moment Bali remains a safe, peaceful place to visit, despite any other Indonesian troubles.

# 1 Getting to Know Bali

## THE LAY OF THE LAND

Bali may be a small island, but it doesn't lack in topographic variety. How accommodating of it to have something for every taste. The island is divided in half, east/west, by a volcanic mountain chain, and scored length-wise by deep river gorges. (Thanks to these, most traffic on the island has to be north-south, though a few major bridges have helped.) You can find photo-ready terraced colonial rice paddies, white sand beaches with clear blue aqua water, mountain lakes, forests, and more.

### THE REGIONS IN BRIEF

**THE SOUTH**   This is the most populous part of the island and the most heavily touristed, largely because of the beautiful beaches and coral reefs that surround the peninsula at the bottom of the island. It is also the most commercial and arguably the least scenic part of the island, flat and beachlike. **Kuta** is a highly trafficked tourist destination, most desirable if you like to surf or enjoy a Tijuana-type atmosphere. **Nusa Dua** is a resort manufactured for tourists, more laid back but also more sterile, while **Sanur** is roughly a cross between the two.

**THE CENTER**   Between the commercialization and build-up and the more sparse, flat landscape adjacent to the beaches, it's a shock to leave the south for the engaging village of **Ubud,** where the topography gives way to verdant greenery and hilly (if not outright mountainous) countryside. In my opinion—and probably only the most single-minded beach fan will disagree—this is the most beautiful area of Bali, with rice paddies, lush vegetation, and charming little villages. Nonetheless, in its own low-key way, the Center is every bit as commercial as the South; many of the communities are geared toward nothing but selling crafts to tourists, and Ubud itself full of touts seeking to make a buck off the hordes of visitors. But given the setting, you mind it less.

**THE EAST**   From the landmark **Gunung Agung,** the volcano that is the heart and center of Bali and its people, to the beaches along the coast, this may be the region that offers the most appealing diversity. You'll find terrific snorkeling and diving at **Candi Dasa** and nearby locations, without the intense level of commercialization found in the South. Inland, mountain lovers and climbers will find much to please them in the Gunung Agung region (complete with Besakih, the most important temple in Bali).

**THE NORTH**   Here the mountains and beaches virtually collide (expect a steep, twisting, turning ride to get to the coastline), and the climate is dry. Volcanic mountain lakes provide marvelous vistas, and surprisingly chilly temperatures at night. The black sand beaches of **Lovina** attract many visitors fleeing the hustle and bustle of Kuta, but the place manages to remain relatively relaxed and mellow.

**THE WEST**   This is a relatively undeveloped part of Bali, with a mountainous terrain mostly given over to the **Bali Barat National Park.** The few attractions for tourists in the area include the famous temple of **Tanah Lot,** the big **Sangeh Monkey Forest,** and the fabulous coral reef at **Pemutan** (usually done as a day diving or snorkel trip from Lovina or Candi Dasa). A Javanese influence can be felt here in everything from religion (with a stronger Muslim presence) to food. Though its charms are less immediate than those of other parts of Bali (and its few main roads fiercely crowded), the West does offer a less tourist-intensive experience of the island.

## A LOOK AT THE PAST

In just the last half century, Bali has been surrounded by remarkable change and turmoil—the birth of an independent Indonesia and its attempts to modernize, a bloody coup that brought about strong-arm military rule and, in the late '90s, violent protests, religious conflicts, and economic upheavals bringing a tentative return to democracy. Yet somehow, little of that seems to have touched Bali directly. The island goes on at its own pace.

The first indication that Bali is charmed as well as charming may have come at the time of the very first contact from the West, when, in 1588, a Portuguese ship seeking spice trade hit a reef and sank. Survivors who reached the shore were treated well but forbidden to leave. Nine years later, when three Dutch sailors landed to scout the island, only one returned—the other two were so charmed by the island that they stayed.

Perhaps the island itself exerts some power over visitors. As distinct as Balinese life is, its people and culture originated elsewhere. Evidence of settlement goes back to the Neolithic period of around 3000 B.C. Chinese–rooted culture made its way to the island around 800 B.C. By about A.D. 900, Buddhist and Hindu peoples had migrated from India and Southeast Asia, and for several hundred years rule of Bali alternated between home and conquerors from Java. In 1343 the Hindu **Majapahit kingdom of East Java** imposed its religious and social structure on the island, but that kingdom's reach soon began to erode in the face of a growth of the Islamic religion, and in 1515 the core of the Majapahit hierarchy fled to Bali, cementing the island's Javanese-originated culture. Somehow Bali remained Hindu as Islam swept to domination of all the surrounding islands. It experienced a flowering of art and culture still called the Golden Age, which gradually faded as the royal family fell into decline and regional ruling factions fragmented Balinese life.

The first real Western presence was established in 1601 when a Dutch contingent came to set up formal relations, and a trade agreement was established. Various other attempts to expand relations were largely rebuffed—even as the Dutch East India Company expanded throughout the area—save for the shipping of Balinese slaves to Dutch and French merchants. In the era of Napoleon, Holland's East Indian holdings passed first to the French, then to the British, who returned them to the Dutch in the peace agreement following Napoleon's Waterloo defeat in 1815. The regional presence of Sir Thomas Stamford Raffles (see chapter 8) led to several military skirmishes and the removal of the slave trade from the control of local rajas, and compromised the Balinese's willingness to deal with foreigners.

## Your First Purchase

Buy a sarong and sash as soon as you get to Bali and make it a rule to never go anywhere without it. You never know what passing parade you might want to join, and having this emergency kit means gaining entrance to some fascinating events. You'll also need them to tour temples and for cover-up on the beach.

Your sarong and sash can be of any fabric, but you may as well go ahead and get something nice. Expect to pay from Rp20,000 to 30,000 (as of this writing), depending on the quality of the cloth. Cheaper sarongs (for beachwear) are usually ordinary rayon tie-dye. More beautiful (and expensive) sarongs are made of ikat, endek, or batik fabric. Ikat is formed by a complicated process of binding and dyeing the warp threads before weaving them with the weft threads. Endek has the weft threads dyed. Batik uses wax to form patterns on the fabric which is revealed after the dyeing process. Ikat and batik come from other parts of Indonesia, whereas double ikat and endek are made on Bali. The fabric for sale in most tourist locales isn't that fine (and is usually rayon, despite claims that it's cotton), but is still fairly beautiful.

The modern era of internationalism was initiated in the 1830s by Danish trader Mads Lange, who operated directly with the rajas and bypassed the Dutch completely. That didn't sit well with the Dutch, and after several years of tension and shows of force on both sides, the Balinese formally recognized Dutch sovereignty. For several decades Dutch rule remained uneasy but strong—especially in the North, where its trade administration was based. Cultural tension was manifested most dramatically in resistance to the Dutch edict ending the practice of suttee, the ritual practice in which widows would throw themselves on their late husband's funeral pyres.

Perhaps the most dramatic and tragic event in Balinese history came in 1906 when, under a Dutch blockade at Badung precipitated by the looting of a wrecked Chinese trading vessel, natives found themselves in a desperate situation. With Dutch troops landing at Sanur and moving in through Denpasar, the Balinese lost any sense of hope and, to the horror of the Dutch, marched directly into open fire in a mass suicide. A similar scene was repeated in 1908, and Dutch control of Bali was total by 1909.

Over the next couple of decades, a steady stream of European settlers and visitors came—doctors and teachers at first, followed by the first tourists, artists, and cultural explorers. By the 1930s, Bali's reputation as a magical paradise was spreading rapidly, and such figures as anthropologist Margaret Mead, artist Walter Spies, and Canadian composer Colin McPhee became the island's most prominent proselytizers.

**World War II** saw an exodus of foreigners with the arrival of Japanese troops. For Indonesians, it was a time of both strain under the brief Japanese occupation and revelation in light of the damage done to Dutch control. Shortly after the end of the war in 1945, Nationalist Party founder **Sukarno,** a thorn in the side of the Dutch since the '20s, announced a declaration of Indonesian independence and was named president. The Dutch fought the movement, but withdrew under international pressure in 1949, allowing the creation of the Republic of Indonesia. Inevitably, perhaps, economic and social uncertainties undermined the democracy, and after just 10 years, parliament was dissolved and a new "guided democracy" was installed.

Bali was hit very hard by the economic problems, and maintained at best an uneasy relation with Jakarta, which wasn't helped by its Hindu status in the Islamic nation.

Sukarno's reign ended in 1965 when army major-general **Suharto** seized control in the wake of a supposed—and highly suspect—failed Communist coup. Bloody conflicts continued for several years and as many as 100,000 Balinese were killed, some as suspected Communists, others because of their Chinese heritage. Suharto officially became Indonesia's second president in 1968.

Increased tourism to Bali in the '60s and '70s helped increase its special position in Indonesia, and has given it something of a protected status. A steadily increasing influx of Australian surfers drawn by the waves at Kuta and spiritual seekers attracted to Ubud made tourism in Bali one of the few sources of stability in the Indonesian economy, and stimulated the eventual and continuing development of the island as an upscale resort destination.

The tourist presence also helped bring about some relaxation of censorship restrictions as the Suharto regime courted Western ties. But each step forward was followed by a step or two back, and freedoms gained on paper were often revoked once exercised. In 1997, massive student protests and international pressure forced Suharto to resign. A new move toward democracy continues, but has proven shaky. In the spring of 1998, the rupiah crashed, along with most of the rest of the Southeast Asian economy. At the same time, violence erupted in villages on Java, Sumatra, and other islands as tensions between Indonesians and ethnic Chinese came to a head. In a wave of paranoia and superstition, villagers brutally beat and killed people they believed to be sorcerers. At the same time, longstanding governmental battles to repress local leadership and rebellion on the island of East Timor continued.

Bali has suffered a great deal in the wake of this social and economic turmoil, with tourist traffic diminishing amid fears of violence and economic strife. In reality, Bali has seen virtually no conflict, continuing on at its own peaceful pace. Politics came home there with the fall 1998 convention of a break-away democratic party led by Megawati Sukarnoputri, the daughter of first president Sukarno, held in a field near Sanur. The island was festooned with the party's red banners and bull symbol and the buzz among the local youth, excited by Bali's potential role in a new Indonesia, was palpable. What shape that new direction for the nation may take remains uncertain, as does Bali's ultimate position in it. Whatever happens, there is little to suggest that the island's charms will be diminished.

## CEREMONY & CELEBRATION: BALI'S PEOPLE & CULTURE
### RELIGION

The Balinese are a deeply spiritual people and their religion is seamlessly incorporated into every facet of their day-to-day existence. Over 90% of the population is **Hindu,** with the minority made up of Muslims, Buddhists, and Christians. Balinese Hinduism is related to, but different from, Hinduism as practiced in India. Indeed, Balinese Hinduism has incorporated elements of Buddhism. There are no formal prayers, and the complexities of the Hindu teachings are usually left to the priests. Instead, the Balinese focus on pleasing God through aesthetic rituals and ceremonies.

There is one Supreme Being in Bali Hinduism. Since there can be no physical representation of this Being, it is symbolized in temples and shrines by an empty throne. The Supreme God has other godly manifestations, though, which is why Hinduism is erroneously seen as polytheistic. The three main forms are Brahma the Creator, Shiva the Destroyer, and Vishnu the Preserver. Their symbolic colors—red, white, and black, respectively—turn up over and over again in celebrations.

Balinese Hindus believe in dharma and adharma, order and disorder, and the need for balance between them. There can be no good without evil. Disease is as much a part of life as health; it's when disease takes over that disorder reigns. To achieve harmony, the forces of good must be saluted with offerings, while the forces of bad must be appeased.

The classic notions of karma, reincarnation, and enlightenment are also found here. One's behavior contributes to one's karma: Accumulate enough cosmic brownie points, and you will achieve enlightenment and be liberated from the cycle of life, death, rebirth. Another important concept is that of animism, or the belief that all things have a spirit and are alive. The stone statues that represent gods are not gods themselves, but they do have a spirit and are considered alive, as are all trees, plants, water—you name it. You will see daily offerings made to the river, the stone gods by your hotel or at a bridge, or in someone's car. This belief makes Bali seem totally alive. Contrast it with Lombok, which like the rest of Indonesia is predominantly Muslim, and you'll see how less vital it seems.

Add to this Bali's complex system of rituals, which govern every facet of life from birth to death. There is always some kind of ceremony, great and small, going on somewhere. Every morning, the Balinese place little offerings, delicate boxes made of leaves containing bits of rice, small flowers, and incense, in various places, to thank the gods and make the day go well. You will see these all over the streets, where they get stepped on or eaten by dogs—because once anything has been offered to the gods, its worth is spent and it is discarded. The amount of effort that goes into these elaborate but ultimately disposable offerings is astonishing.

Beyond these small daily offerings there are the ceremonies. Temple anniversary celebrations, tooth filings, cremations—every day, all over Bali, something is happening. The Tourism Board puts out a pamphlet listing the biggest ceremonies, but family events happen constantly. Particularly in a place like Ubud, something will be going on just about every day you are there. See that parade of gorgeously dressed Balinese, with towering offerings of fruit and flowers meticulously arranged in complex patterns balanced precariously on their heads, marching along to rhythmic music? They are on their way to a ceremony of some sort. Follow them. Really—it's okay, even expected. As long as you are respectful, the locals enjoy it when tourists come to watch. What does respectful mean? Well, first of all, it means proper dress. You need not be as glammed up as the Balinese, who will be bedecked in elaborate sarong outfits of the most fantastic cloth (the makeup of the outfits changes depending on what is being celebrated), but you must be wearing a sarong and sash yourself, and your arms should be covered to at least the elbow.

## Temples

Every village must have at least one temple, but one temple is really three: the *pura puseh,* the main central temple, dedicated to Vishnu; the *pura desa,* the everyday temple dedicated to Brahma; and the *pura dalem,* the temple of the dead, dedicated to Shiva. Add to these the small temples or shrines found in nearly every home, hotel, and restaurant, and all the little shrines along the road and riversides, and you have an island with an enormous number of temples—over 20,000, in fact.

Consequently, temples lose their ability to thrill rather early on, particularly since, to Western eyes, they aren't all that magnificent. These aren't the glittering piles of sequins you find in Thailand, but rather open-air constructions of brick and stone (and not even that many statues). One looks pretty much exactly like the next, with subtle differences of course, until you get to the north, where temples are festooned in elaborate, fanciful carvings.

Once inside a temple, you need not stick to the back wall, though you might prefer to start out that way. More often than not, the locals will pull you to the front so you can see what's going on, and even encourage you to take pictures. (But don't do so unless given permission.) If you are lucky, you might be asked to partake of some

Balinese coffee or even a meal. Ask someone to explain what you're seeing—don't be shy. If they don't want to talk, or can't speak English, they may well find someone who can. Often it's a ceremony honoring an anniversary of the temple you are in (held at 6- and 12-month marks).

## CELEBRATIONS

The big three events in Bali are tooth filings, weddings, and cremations. **Tooth filing** is a rite of maturation, wherein the sharp front teeth, especially the canines, are filed down smooth (the idea being to differentiate humans from the animals.) This can happen at any age, even after death, but is most often done to adolescents, who by that age have already been through the nearly dozen rituals that marked their first few days on the planet. Believe it or not, it's quite fun to watch the participants grimace through this rite of passage, then smile in a mirror afterward, admiring their new set of adult choppers. (The Balinese will be grinning like crazy.) **Weddings** are self explanatory but colorful events. But it's at cremations where the Balinese pull out all the stops.

**Cremation** is the only way a soul can be freed of its earthly self and travel to its next incarnation (or to enlightenment). Death is a joyous occasion in Bali, full of floats and fanfare that can resemble a Mardi Gras parade. Complicated towers (the higher the caste, the higher the tower—limited only by power lines) hold the body, carried aloft by cheering men, who turn the tower in circles to send the spirit to heaven, then take it to the burning ground. There the body is placed in receptacles resembling fabulous creatures (winged lions, bulls and so forth, again determined by caste), and set on fire. Sometimes the body won't burn quickly enough, and it is poked at, often mocked, to help free the spirit from its now-useless fleshy vessel and sent on its way. This is an extraordinarily beautiful and moving rite and marvelous to witness, even for Westerners whose view of death is so different from that of the Balinese. Cremations are expensive and so not as common as other ceremonies; sometimes, bodies have to be buried until such time (from a few months to many years) the family can afford the proper send-off. To share costs, they are also often group affairs. There are tours that take tourists to a cremation, which might be worth going on if it's your only shot at seeing one, but they can be somewhat embellished for the visitors.

Feel free to ask around about upcoming celebrations, but be sure to get confirmation from more than one person. If you are staying at a losmen, let your hosts know you would like to go to temple with them. Be aware, though, that Bali operates on "rubber time," which means a cremation scheduled for noon will happen promptly at 5pm. But hanging out has its own rewards. That's when you might get invited to dinner, or if nothing else, you get to listen to some music and observe real life in action. Compared to Western church-going, celebrations in Bali are very casual: women gossip, children play, and dogs wander temple grounds freely, snacking on offerings. A priest chants, people pray and then get up, and others take their places. The Balinese videotape and shoot photos. (You should not, unless someone tells you it's okay, but they probably will.) Again, they are generally most welcoming, provided you act with dignity and respect. Imagine being this receptive to a total stranger at a family funeral, and you have an idea of what kind of people the Balinese are.

## MUSIC & DANCE

Bali is "where musical sounds are as [much a] part of the atmosphere as the palm trees, the spicy smells and the charmingly beautiful people. The music is fantastically rich—melodically, rhythmically, texture (such orchestration!) and above all formally."

So wrote British composer Benjamin Britten to a friend while visiting Bali in January 1956. It was the sounds of the **gamelan**—the bright-sounding metal percussion

## Travel Tips: Dealing with Touts

This is the word for the persistent and ubiquitous hustlers who try to sell you everything from watches and sarongs to rides around the island. Be polite but firm and, for the most part, send them on their way. Buying something from one means you'll be swarmed by others offering exactly the same thing, and not taking "no" for an answer. They'll also try to latch themselves onto you as guides at tourist destinations, such as famous temples, where they also turn out in huge numbers to sell things. Even if you're already with an official guide, you aren't safe; there seems to be an unwritten code that guides can't interfere with their attempts to make a living.

ensembles that accompany just about every celebration and ceremony here—that turned Britten's head. And he was hardly the first major Western music figure to be infected. Claude Debussy was transfixed by gamelan music at a Java pavilion of the 1898 Paris Exposition—which is evident in such impressionist orchestral lynchpins as "La Mer." Canadian Colin McPhee lived outside of Ubud in the '30s, an experience recounted in his book *A House in Bali*. Lou Harrison has written for American variations of gamelan ensembles, and anyone hearing the music of Steve Reich or Philip Glass has, essentially, already had the gamelan experience.

But you don't have to be a trained musician to be transformed by the magic of Balinese music. It's everywhere, pouring from tapes played in shops and restaurants (though today you're just as likely to hear Bob Marley or Tracy Chapman in the bigger communities), accompanying both staged dance performances and temple festivals, weddings and tooth filings. The upscale hotels generally have two or three players chiming musical greetings to arrivals in the lobby.

The word *gong* is of Indonesian origin. Know that, and you've got a head start in understanding the archipelago's music—especially the vibrant Balinese brand. The gentler style featuring light sounds of metalophones and flute that you'll certainly hear played on tapes or CDs in many restaurants, shops and hotels is likely from Java or Sudan. It was from the courtly music of Java that Balinese gamelan evolved, the style and its tools brought to the island by fleeing Hindu royalty in the 16th century. That style remained until 1915, when in the north of Bali a movement bloomed for a distinctive sound called **kebyar,** which means lightning flash. Indeed, that's a terrific description of the style, notable for its sudden bursts of sound emerging from more tranquil lines.

And still today in the daily life of Bali, and even in many presentations made just for tourists, the local music of the gamelan and such vocal relatives as the **kecak (monkey chant)** is an essential feature. Every banjar has a gamelan (or at least, in poorer areas, access to one), with musicians not true professionals, but your workaday crew of drivers, farmers, shopkeepers, artisans, what have you.

Make no mistake: This is not folk music. It's highly structured, highly disciplined classical music, even more so (in the conventional Western sense) than Indian classical music. Though the music is not written, it is also not improvised, per se. That would be virtually impossible given the precision and intricacy of the musical mosaics produced, requiring years of study and practice.

As for dance, the most common in public performance are the **legong** and **barong dances,** intricate ballets presenting, as much Balinese art does, scenes from the *Mahabarata* or *Ramayama*. The latter, in particular, is highly entertaining, involving an evil witch, magic dragon, and men in a trance jabbing daggers at their own chests (how real the trance is probably depends on the setting). Many major hotels offer dance performances, and in Ubud at the central Palace and other locations there's one pretty much every night. Information can be had at the tourist center, but ask around and you might find a real (nontourist) performance taking place at an accessible village. Numerous tapes and CDs of these are available, some with the chanted/sung narration that accompanies performances, some just the music.

Ditto for the music of the wayang kulit—the **shadow puppet plays,** in which intricately cut leather figures are used to project images against a screen, again depicting a tale from one of the Hindu epics, all manipulated masterfully by a puppeteer who also does all the voices (often injecting news, gossip, topical humor and even crude jokes) to the accompaniment of a small gamelan ensemble.

The other major example of "traditional" music is the **kecak,** a very dramatic and visual a cappella piece featuring as many as 100 men depicting a saga of a monkey king and his warriors, featuring bursts of simian-styled chanting that gives the style its onomatapoeic name. Intriguingly, though, the kecak and to some extent the other generally seen performances are actually the invention of Westerners. In Balinese culture, where there's no distinction between sacred and secular, there is no real tradition of performance for performance's sake rather than for real ceremony. But in the '30s, artist Walter Spies, living in Bali, was asked to arrange some dance performances for a visiting filmmaker, and that was accomplished by using excerpts and pastiches of the true things. As tourism grew, the demand for such things grew as well, and today they are ubiquitous.

Gamelan isn't the only music you'll hear in Bali. An enticing brand of Indonesian pop, called **dangdut,** is a blend of Indian film music and Arabic pop. Sinewy and sexy, it has been used as a vehicle for topics that had generally been taboo.

## ARTS & CRAFTS

A tourist in Bali will see everything from profusely carved and decorated temples bedecked in shimmering fabrics, to winsome cat-shaped doorstops in faux-Appalachian folk style, to a perfect art-nouveau sideboard being carved under a bamboo rain cover. The volume and diversity of production on the island is stunning.

It is impossible to speak of Balinese art without speaking of Balinese culture as well. The rituals and celebrations that are a daily part of the Bali-Hindu religion and culture create a constant demand for traditional artwork. Even in the International Airport, Ngurah Rai, every doorway is decorated with the grotesque floral gargoyle called Karang Bhoma. Its purpose is not merely decorative, but to protect against evil influences. (Curious that it repeatedly appears over the doors tourists pass through as they enter Bali.) The novelty of baroque wedding cake decorative demons, dragons, and indecipherable deities will wear off even before you reach your hotel.

One reason there is so much art is that there are so many artists. The Balinese culture does not marginalize artistic activity the way Western cultures have. In fact, the rituals of Bali demand a level of aesthetic perfection that requires the average person to be able to recognize, if not create, beauty. The Balinese hold that their gods will only accept offerings that are aesthetically pleasing, from stone carvings to body posture (considered an offering like any other). A second reason for the preponderance of traditional art is that much of it is disposable. Elaborately decorated and carved coffins are cremated along with the deceased. And many other rituals render the objects used in them unusable a second time.

Climate plays a role in the arts as well. The humidity makes works of art decay rapidly, so that they require frequent replacement. This is particularly true of the very perishable palm ornaments and rice-paste sculptures, ikat weavings and carved masks used in sacred performances, but it is also true even of the stone and bricks of the

# Cultural Dos and Don'ts

The Balinese are by and large a friendly people, but not in an overt, big-gestured American way. Public display of emotions is frowned on. However, they are generally interested in visitors, and can ask probing questions, everything from "Where are you going?" to "Why don't you have any children?" (The Balinese love kids and feel sorry for those who have not reproduced.) This is not considered rudeness, but polite curiosity.

Touching the heads of children *is* considered rude. Also, affection can be shown in public between same-sex friends, but not between opposite sex partners, so polite visitors will confine physical caresses to their hotel room. Further, beach resort or not, this is not the place for nude or topless sunbathing, though that doesn't stop some tourists. Nor does the fact that the Balinese prefer their bodies to be mostly covered stop any number of tourists from parading around in swimsuits and skimpy clothes. It's okay in Kuta, but no matter how hot it gets, be polite and dress modestly elsewhere, except when on hotel grounds or at the beach. Billowing dresses or sarongs for men are perfect ways of staying modest and cool at the same time. Clothes—because they touch the body, which is dirty—are disgusting to the Balinese, so try not to leave yours drying outside your hotel room, or even on your hotel room furniture. Your maid won't say a word about it, but she won't like it any more than if you blew your nose on the furniture.

Finally, as in most other Southeast Asian countries, the left hand is traditionally reserved for sanitary actions (cleaning oneself after using the toilet, for example), so it is not used to eat with, or to gesture, or to offer anything.

---

temples themselves. The blue-gray tufa stone, called "paras" by the Balinese, absorbs water like a sponge and sprouts moss and fungi within a single rainy season. A 10-year-old shrine can look older than Angkor Wat, or the Pyramids.

For the collector interested in coming home with something representative of Bali, it is worth a brief enumeration of traditional art forms.

Traditional sculpture consists of **stone and wood carving** representing a variety of Balinese gods and guardians. Some of the wood carvings are used as temporary bodies for the gods to inhabit during rituals, others designate rank and are placed in the rafters of thatched living quarters. The area uphill of Ubud around Tegalalang, Pakadui, and Pujung specializes in wood carving. You can travel through entire villages inhabited by hundreds of half-finished eagle-faced Garudas. Of course, the next village might be full of slightly distorted Donald Ducks.

Stone statues, often frightening to look at, flank the gateways of palaces and temples, guarding against demonic forces. Stone is carved in Batubalan, Blabatuh, and Batuan, downhill from Ubud on the road to Sanur. Most is too large and heavy to transport, but small "replicas" of traditional forms are also produced. If you buy one, wrap it well, as Balinese stone is very brittle. A few statues are carved in hardened concrete, and some black lava stone sculptures are imported from Java, but being made of harder stone, these have far less detail.

**Masks** are another traditional sculptural form. They depict a wide range of characters used in both sacred and secular performances. Masks of the grotesque bug-eyed demoness Rangda are often seen hanging in garlands outside souvenir shops, seemingly bereft of any menace in their mass-produced multiplicity. But beware: The

Balinese hold that even a tourist mask may become inhabited if it possesses the proper qualities.

The features of heroes, heroines, villains, monsters, and clowns are fixed by ancient canons that allow for only limited interpretation. What that means is that they all tend to look alike. When looking at a cluster of 50 or so identical masks of Rama, hero of the Hindu *Ramayana* epic, it is difficult to visualize how his green serenity might look twelve thousand miles away on your wall. But sure enough, removed from the company of his legion of cloned companions, Rama is magnificent. Look for eyes that focus on a spot somewhere to the front of the mask. Turn it with your hand and watch the eyes to see if they convey a sense of seeing. Don't bother searching for antiques; they are well-faked and rare to boot—and probably haunted.

For those with an interest in two-dimensional art, there are the ancient stylized **paintings** of deities and the delicately carved "lontar" palm frond books, both still produced on the island. The center of this archaic painting style is now in the eastern territories of Bali near Klungklung. Perhaps the best example is seen in the painted ceiling of the Kerta Gosa in the town of Klungklung itself. Works of art in this Kamasan style are harder to find than the paintings, which have become one of the chief "modern" art forms of Bali.

Based in the Gianyar district in central Bali are several "schools" of wood carving and painting originating in a fortunate blend of Balinese and Western traditions. In the 1920s and '30s, and again in the late '50s and '60s, Balinese artists collaborated with foreign artists to create new styles that diverged from the traditional forms. Some of the foreign artists were expatriates who came to live on Bali for many years. **Walter Spies,** a German, and **Rudolf Bonnet,** a Dutchman, influenced Balinese art and artists in the pre–World War II years. Spies, patronized by the aristocratic Sukowati family, built a house on the site of the current Tjampuhan Hotel in Ubud that became a kind of ex-pat mecca in Bali. He has achieved mythic status as the prime mover of the modern Balinese art movement, helping create the now-famous kecak dance, the Pita Maha art society, and the Bali Museum in Denpasar. He is credited with inspiring a Balinese traditional painter, Anak Agung Gede Soberat, to work with scenes from daily life instead of mythology, thus initiating a new style of painting, and with guiding the development of the elongated sculptural style now so ubiquitous on Bali. His own paintings, at once meticulous and moody, are a fusion of cultural forms.

Despite the fertile contribution Spies and his followers brought to Bali, their fame unjustly overshadows the sources of their inspiration. Gusti Nyoman Lempad was already a master carver when, at Spies' suggestion, he turned to ink drawing and produced a half century of masterpieces. Ida Bagus Njana's various carving styles, from abstractly modified human forms to simple female studies, became style setters for the island. There are of course others by the score to be discovered by anyone with the determination to look.

Nowadays, the variety of painting styles available is as diverse as the artists producing them, and the profusion of choices can be hypnotic. Be patient, and be

## Getting Married in Bali

Tourists have come to love getting married on Bali (though the Balinese turn their noses up at it). If you want to get married legally on the island (as opposed to a simple vow renewal), you need to do some planning in advance. Contact **Bali Weddings International:** Jl. Padanggalak no. 4, Sanur (☎ 361-287516; fax 361-286262; e-mail: baliwed@denpasar.wasantara.net.id).

aesthetically demanding. You will find your masterpiece if you search. And remember, it's better to possess a small masterpiece than a large mediocrity.

## LANGUAGE

English is widely spoken throughout Bali, particularly in the major tourist areas. While not everyone is fluent, most of the people you will be dealing with will speak enough English that you can communicate with them. Many of the employees in the better hotels also speak other languages as well (I heard at least one switch from English to Italian to German with ease).

The Balinese speak both Indonesian and Balinese—the former when out in public, the latter at home. Aside from the tendency towards seemingly jawbreaking polysyllabic phrases, Indonesian is not that hard to learn—pronunciation is pretty straightforward and spelling is mostly phonetic. Balinese is much more complicated, not least because there are actually three levels of it—high, middle, and low—used depending on the class and authority of the person to whom you are speaking. Don't even try to learn it, but do worry about Indonesian—not because you need it, but because embarrassingly few tourists bother to even learn to say "Hello" or "Thank you" in their host country's language. People will be delighted that you took the time to learn how to exchange pleasantries. Besides, I've often noticed that *"Tidak, tremima kasih"* works better to get rid of a persistent tout than "No, thank you."

Often, you will be asked "Where are you going?" This is actually a routine, polite question that may not require an answer, but often it's a way of then asking if you need transport. If you don't, just say "Jalan jalan," which means "Just walking." And if they are truly insistent, to the point of huge annoyance, you can resort to "Pergi!" ("Go away!").

## 2  Planning a Trip to Bali

### VISITOR INFORMATION

Recently, the few Indonesian/Bali tourism offices outside of the country have been either shut down or incorporated into their nearest embassy/consulate. No matter; the information they gave was sketchy in terms of usefulness at best. There are other sources for getting what you need to know. The thick, multilingual *Visitor's Guide to Bali,* is a nice introduction to the island, full of information, annual events and even a mini-phone directory. Visit the Web site at **www.asiapages.com.sg** to find out how to obtain a copy.

The best Web site for information on accommodations, sight-seeing and just about everything else you can imagine is **Bali Paradise Online (www.bali-paradise.com).** It seems like it's run by the government, but it is not. They should have a calendar of events, including temple celebrations, but if not, you can write to the efficient **Badung Government Tourist Office** (Jl. Raya Kuta no. 2, Kuta, ☎ 361-756176). Another, less complete Web site is **Bali Online (www.indo.com),** which offers a less expansive range of the same information. Or you can try checking out **Bali Post,** whose Web site (**www.balipost.com**) has an English-language link providing recent news and hints. **Baliplus** offers informational pamplets (PT. Trijaya Dewata, P.O. Box 1148, Tuban, Dps, Bali; ☎ 361-297333; e-mail: Baliplus@denpasar.wasantara. net.id).

**IN BALI**   Try the Bali Government Tourist Information Center, Jl. Benasari 7, Legian Kuta, ☎ 361-754090. Better still is the Badung Government Tourist Office in Kuta (Jl. Raya Kuta no.2, ☎ 361-756176).

## ENTRY REQUIREMENTS

Visitors from the U.S., Australia, most of Europe, New Zealand, and Canada do not need visas. They will be given a stamp that allows them to stay for 60 days, provided they are entering the country through an officially designated gateway: Ngurah Rai Airport or the seaports of Padang Bai and Benoa. If you want to stay longer than 60 days, you must get a tourist or business visa before coming to Indonesia. Tourist visas are valid only for 4 weeks and can not be extended, while business visas can be extended for 6 months at Indonesian immigration offices.

## CUSTOMS REGULATIONS

Customs allows you to bring in, duty-free, 200 cigarettes or 50 cigars and 2 pounds of tobacco; cameras and film; 2 liters of alcohol; and perfume clearly intended for personal use. Forbidden are guns, weapons, narcotics, pornography (leave it at home if you're unsure how it's defined) and printed matter with Chinese characters. Plants and fresh fruit may also be confiscated.

## MONEY

Coins are available in denominations of Rp25, 50, 100, and even occasionally 5 and 10. Notes are Rp100, 500, 1000, 5000, 10,000, 20,000, and 50,000.

**CURRENCY EXCHANGE & RATES**   With the economic problems Indonesia is currently facing, Bali has become a bargain for tourists. In less than 2 years, Indonesia's currency, the **rupiah,** went from about 1,000 to the dollar to 10,000 and more. During recent trips, the exchange rate fluctuated wildly hour by hour. It is hard to say at press time precisely what things should cost—and so in many cases I have skipped price listings altogether. Even the prices listed (collected at rates that ranged from 6,000 to 10,000 rupiahs to the dollar) could be entirely different by the time you arrive. But no matter what the exchange rate, Bali is still going to be an inexpensive destination once you get there, particularly when it comes to food, souvenirs, and sightseeing.

Most major hotels offer **exchange services,** but their rates don't tend to be as good as those at the exchange places that proliferate on the street. These places are thick as flies, and you can go from one to the next in search of the best rate. (Hint: the first places you come across usually have the worst rates—this applies even at the exchange windows at the airport.) Be sure to double-check the math, even if you have to use their calculator (or bring your own small one, in case theirs is rigged), and count your cash *before* you leave. **ATMs** are becoming more common—there is at least one in most major tourist areas—and often give you a much better exchange rate. The same is true for **credit cards,** but their use is still mostly limited to major hotels, restaurants, and shops.

## WHEN TO GO

**PEAK SEASON**   The high tourist season is July and August, along with the weeks surrounding Christmas and New Year's, when prices are higher and tourist traffic considerably increased. Try to avoid these times, as well as February and March (given the increased heat and humidity).

**CLIMATE**   Bali is just below the equator, so the weather is more or less constant year-round (always some variation of hot and humid). A day is nearly always 12 hours long—from 6am to 6pm. The rainy season lasts from October to April, with nearly daily monsoons. The humidity is at its crushing worst during this period (there are times when you think you're breathing water) and the hottest months are February,

March, and April. Rain usually comes in short, violent bursts that often stop within an hour (though at night it can last a few hours). Temperatures are mostly in the 80s all year long. Sweaters are only necessary if you are staying up by the volcanos or mountains, where it can get nippy at night.

**PUBLIC HOLIDAYS**   Public holidays are New Year's Day (January 1), Idul Fitri (celebration of the end of Ramadan; late February), Nyepi (a major purification ritual and a time when Balinese are supposed to sit at home, silent; late March), Good Friday and Easter Sunday (late March/early April), Muslim New Year (mid-May), Indonesia Independence Day (August 17), Ascension Day of Mohammed (early December), and Christmas (December 25).

## HEALTH CONCERNS

**No inoculations are required,** but it's always a good idea to get shots for Hepatitis A, tetanus, polio, and typhoid. You might consult with your doctor or the CDC Web site if anything further is currently suggested. **Malaria** is not a concern in the tourist areas of Bali (indeed, the CDC has declared it malaria-free), only if you plan to be out in remote villages near rice paddies after dark. The anxious can take malaria pills, but be aware that the prevention is sometimes almost as bad as the disease. You probably should not pet strange dogs—there are many stray dogs in Bali, and nearly all of them have some kind of mange, or possibly rabies.

**You absolutely cannot drink the water on Bali,** but bottled water is cheap and readily available. Just about every hotel will supply you with a couple bottles or a jug of boiled water—remember to use it when brushing your teeth as well. Restaurants in tourist areas are used to supplying safe water, complete with ice made from boiled water, but if you want to be extra safe, ask for no ice, and *air minum* (drinking water). Salads, too, are generally safe in tourist areas. As always, you can help avoid "Bali belly" (the Indonesian version of Montezuma's Revenge) by sticking to foods that have been peeled or well cooked. When in doubt, you can also get meat-free dishes.

The greatest health concern on Bali is **dehydration,** which can easily sneak up on you. Be sure to drink plenty of liquids (beer does not count, as it also dehydrates), and get salt into your system regularly.

## GETTING THERE
### BY PLANE

**FROM THE U.S.**   As of press time, **China Air** (☎ 800/227-5118 in the U.S.) and **Eva Air** (☎ 800/695-1188), both through Taipei; **Singapore Air** (☎ 800/742-3333) through Singapore; and **Nippon** (☎ 800/235-9262) through Osaka fly to Bali from the U.S. with no obligatory overnight stay. Flights with overnight stays are available on **Thai Air (with United)** (☎ **800/241-6522**), **Continental** (☎ 800/231-0856), and **Cathay Pacific** (☎ 800/233-2742).

**What to Pack**

Given the heat and humidity, loose cotton clothing is essential in Bali. Though the Balinese do dress up, informality among foreigners has come to be expected. (See "Cultural Dos & Don'ts," above, about modesty in dress.) I suggest packing a minimal amount of clothing and buying more climate-appropriate wear once you get to Bali. You might also consider giving away all your clothes at the end of your stay, as Western clothes, even underwear, are luxury items for the Balinese. It's a nice thing to do and you'll have more room in your luggage for souvenirs.

## Travel Tip

When you leave Bali, there will be an **airport departure tax.** Ask your hotel for the current rate.

**FROM THE U.K.**   Bali is served from Europe by **British Air** (☎ 0345/222111), **Singapore Air** (☎ 7470007), **Thai Air** (☎ ), and **Air France** (☎ 0181/742-6600).

**FROM AUSTRALIA & NEW ZEALAND**   Flights from Australia and New Zealand can be booked through **Qantas** (☎ 131211).

### Getting to Your Destination from the Airport

**Ngurah Rai,** Bali's airport, is considered to be in Denpasar, but it's really 8 miles (13km) southwest. Given that, and how close you are to your real tourist destinations, there is probably no reason to ever go to Denpasar proper. Though it's not an unpleasant big city, it holds no real attractions for tourists. Instead, after changing a small amount of money from one of the exchange windows at the airport (check them all out—often the ones farthest down the row have the best rates), head outside and look for the **taxi window** counter near Customs. There are set rates to just about every major tourist area. You pay at this window and they will get your car for you. Do *not* use anyone who comes directly to you offering to give you a ride; they will charge considerably higher rates.

**BY CAR**   You can rent cars in Bali, but it's not recommended. Roads are not clearly marked—if marked at all—and even with a good map, there's a good chance you will get lost in the middle of nowhere. The Balinese are also wild drivers. Given how cheap and easy it is to get a tourist shuttle to most of the areas you want to go to, or to hire someone to drive you, it's best to avoid the headache. If you do decide to drive, just remember three things: (1) you will need an International Driver's License; (2) traffic is on the left hand side; (3) a honk from behind you means someone wants to pass, so move over; (4) the Balinese *always* have the right-of-way. Once they have gone by, then it's your turn.

**BY MOTORBIKE**   Motorbikes are even more dangerous than cars. You will see your share of bloody crashes (and how close do you think medical care is?) If you do decide to take the risk (and admittedly, it's a nice way to see the island), save them for remote areas where the traffic isn't so bad, and please be careful.

**BY PUBLIC TRANSPORTATION**   Blue and brown vans called *bemos* operate as buses in Bali. They work pretty well, in a sort of mysterious way. They have regular routes, but these aren't really written down. Just ask someone where the regular pickup is, and which bemo to take to get you where you want to go. Prices are also similarly secretive, and bemo drivers have no qualms about charging tourists lots more than locals. Ask one of the latter how much the ride really should cost. All things considered, bemos are better for short hops (around town, for example) than long distances, which may require many changes of vehicle.

Blue and yellow metered taxis run mostly in Kuta, though they can be hired to take you to nearby resorts like Nusa Dua and Sanur. Make sure they put their meter on, though.

**BY PRIVATE TRANSPORTATION**   There are two solid options for traveling around Bali, and both work quite well. Regular **tourist shuttles** run between all the major locales. These are reliable and cheap, though air-conditioned vehicles charge more. You can book them through a tourist office or your hotel, or just find one on your own—many stores will have signs advertising shuttle service. **Perama,** considered

# When Yes Means Yes . . . and No

It seems simple enough—you ask a transport guide if he can take you from point A to point B, and he says yes. You negotiate the price and 10 minutes later, after some uncertain turns and squinty looks, he pulls up in front of point Q. You realize that he had no idea where you wanted to go and was only guessing the whole way.

Welcome to one of the peculiarities of Balinese culture that, if you don't learn to navigate around it, could drive you nuts. The transport guide in question wasn't trying to scam you when he said he knew where you wanted to go. He simply didn't want to disappoint you with a negative answer. Balinese will do anything to avoid disappointing someone, even if it means not exactly telling the truth, and there seems to be no sense that taking someone on a wild goose chase will be a greater disappointment.

So what to do about it? First, don't take a condescending attitude. It's merely a cultural difference. But make sure that a driver (or shopkeeper, or whomever you've asked something) really understands and really means yes. Have a map or written directions to show, or at least ask the question several different ways until you're confident that you're going to get what you've asked for. Then sit back and enjoy the ride.

the most reliable operator, has offices in most tourist centers. The main office is in Kuta (☎ **361-751551**).

The other option is hiring a **transport guide.** You won't have any trouble finding one (avoiding them is the problem). In Ubud and other tourist spots, men cluster the streets, endlessly shouting, "Transport? Transport? Yes? Tomorrow? Yes?" Short or long distances, hire by the day, the hour or the week—just figure out exactly where you want to go, and what you think you would want to pay. (You may base an appropriate cost on what a taxi or shuttle would charge.) You have to bargain—you will know when they've gone as low as they can or want to, because they will probably refuse to drive you. If the one you've picked isn't going low enough, try somebody else. Be sure to write down your exact destination to avoid any possible misunderstanding. Also make it clear that you do not want to go to any crafts' place—generally, the guy will take you to someone who jacks up their price to pay for his cut.

**TOUR GUIDES**   Hiring a private tour guide can be more expensive than just using a transport guide off the street, but then again, you will get what you pay for. Trained professionals are rare in Bali—many a so-called "tour guide" doesn't have as good a command of English as you would like, nor as studied a sense of history. (Balinese don't always know much about their past.) So someone who can really illuminate matters for you, plus, ideally, tell you about their own experiences within the culture, is worth paying for. It doesn't matter where the office is located—they can pick you up

## A Note on Addresses and Phone Numbers

Street addresses in Bali can be somewhat sketchy. I've made every attempt to provide precise addresses here, but in smaller towns the address of a hotel or restaurant may simply be "on the main street." Don't worry: these places will be impossible to miss. As for phone numbers, if no phone number is listed for an establishment, chances are there's no phone.

and take you anywhere, your own itinerary or one they create for you. Expect to pay not only for the guide, but for a car and gas as well, all of which can run just over US$100 total for a day. Here are three I can recommend: **Santa Bali Tours and Travel,** Bali Beach Hotel, Sanur (☎ **361-288057,** 361-287628; fax 361-286825; e-mail: sedanartha@denpasar.wasantara.net.id). Ask for Guna. **Bali Taksu Tours & Travel,** Jl. Bypass Ngurah Rai 16, Sanur (☎ **361-288970;** fax 361-281627; e-mail: balitaksu@denpasar.wasantara.net.id). Ask for Made Suastika. **B.S.M. Tours & Travel,** Jl. Supratman G III/2, Denpasar (☎ **361-162704;** fax 361-162070).

## ACCOMMODATIONS

The range of hotel options in Bali is truly mind-boggling: from a US$5 a night (or less) bungalow with breakfast in the morning, to a US$900 a night villa with your own retinue of servants, and everything possible in between. There are those who think those US$900 a night places don't offer much more than their low-end cousins, and in some ways, they are right. Often all you gain (aside maybe from A/C) is increased and better frills. Think about that when booking a hotel. And don't stay every night in a Western chain. Sure, they offer applicable familiar comforts, and considerable consistency, but often they are almost entirely devoid of the local culture. Don't overlook **losmen/homestay locations,** where you often end up rubbing elbows with the proprietor's family (and dogs, chickens, and so on). Expect fans instead of A/C, and no hot water (but you'll probably prefer the cold). The good news is that many losmen have converted their squat toilets into the Western kind with a seat. In exchange, you'll get a bargain place to stay, often with a complete breakfast that leaves you full all afternoon, and a chance to observe some real Bali life.

Try a variety of hotels of varying quality and price, and instead of mourning lost creature comforts, consider what you gain in terms of local interaction and adventure. You will come home with a greater appreciation of the Balinese, and much better stories. Another option is to stay in a village—not just one on the fringes of, say, Ubud, but way off the beaten path. You can check with locals for suggestions, look for possibilities in the budget section of the **BaliOnline** service (**www.indo.com**), or call Guna at Santa Bali Travel (see "Tour Guides" under "Getting There," above) and ask him about the very comfortable homestay recently erected in his village.

Prices tend to fluctuate with the popularity of a region. Some of the most expensive choices are found on the ocean, and in ever-delightful, and thus ever-popular, Ubud. Moving off the main street, or out of the main action, you may find that prices drop astonishingly. One of the highest quality hotels on the island is located on Amed, a largely undeveloped fishing village 2 hours (part of it on a bumpy, unpaved dirt road) from Candi Dasa, the nearest built up community. The hotel costs a fraction of what a luxury hotel would elsewhere. But even on the outskirts of Ubud are some excellent options for ridiculously low prices. The remoteness, though, does make some guests feel too isolated—especially if you don't have a car.

**A NOTE ON PRICES**   Here's a big hint about how to further conquer high prices: The published rates are just that—the published rates. More than one hotel, after giving us their official rates, then said "now here's what we *really* charge", whereupon the price sometimes dropped by as much as half. The so-called "discounts" offered on the Internet on hotel Web sites are actually closer to the real price range. The brave of heart might want to only reserve their first night, and then just try and see what they can find once they get there. I noted many potential guests just showing up at some of the fanciest and most expensive hotels and demanding to know how the hotel would make it worth their while to stay. This won't always pan out—in high season, forget about it—but if you are looking for bargains—and possibly luxury as well—

making reservations in advance is not always the best for your budget. Besides, there are more losmen/homestays than you can count in Bali, and someone, somewhere, will have a room, for probably a heck of a lot cheaper than you think.

A final word about the rates: almost all the hotels charge what they call **plus plus**—a 21% government tax and service charge on top of the quoted rates. They also charge from US$15 to more than US$50 extra per room during high season (the 2 or 3 weeks around Christmas and New Year's, and July and August). Many places automatically include breakfast, but if you book through a travel agent (who might well get you a bargain price), they often negotiate meal plans into the room rate, which may or may not be to your advantage given how cheap restaurants outside the hotel will usually be.

## RESTAURANTS & DINING

Until recently, food in Bali was disappointing, because most of what was offered to tourists didn't reflect the genuine local cuisine. The fear was that Balinese and Indonesian food was too spicy or otherwise frightening for non-locals. That's changed somewhat, particularly in Ubud, where there has been an explosion of quality restaurants with an outstanding array of choices. You can get away without ever trying anything local, since just about every restaurant has part of its menu geared towards timid tourists, but I won't let you get away with it. Best of all, as long as you stay away from the largely pricey hotel restaurants, food in Bali is quite cheap, and local fare is always less expensive than European dishes. **Vegetarians** will also be quite happy, as many places have a veggie-only menu. And while the names of dishes will be the same from place to place, you might be surprised at how different the interpretations are.

Caution should always be exercised about food consumption, but greater care is taken in all the tourist areas; I ate uncooked green salads everywhere listed here and never experienced a problem. At all times, and particularly in tourist areas where most of the dining options run towards the aforementioned expensive hotel restaurants, or generic tourist-geared restaurants, I encourage you to try real **warungs.** Warung is actually the word for restaurant, and many places are called this, but authentic ones, mostly frequented by locals, are sort of little cafes—slightly grimy stores with just three or so seats for dining. Don't be put off by appearances; I've had some of my best meals in Bali at places like these, for literally pennies. If food prep concerns are an issue, order items fried (so to ensure thorough cooking) and without meat. Our standby is **nasi goreng** (fried rice), without meat, which is always prepared slightly differently, and always delicious.

Indonesian dishes you are most likely to encounter: **nasi goreng** (fried rice, usually topped with an egg); **mie goreng** (fried noodles); **nasi campur** (can be a plate of boiled rice with sides of meat and veggies, but often a sampler plate of different tasties offered by the restaurant, ranging from fish wrapped in banana leaves to deep-fried corn fritters); **ayam goreng** (fried chicken, often tough, scrawny birds); **gado gado** (salad with peanut sauce, served hot or cold); **satay** (small chunks of meat on skewers served with peanut sauce—more innovatively, the meat has been minced and spiced). **Padang food** (sold in little cafes called **rumah makan Padang**) is spicy tidbits (fried fish or chicken, various veggie dishes) piled up in dishes—you pick what you want or let them choose. They fill a plate for you and charge you by the amount; it's usually quite cheap.

Specifically Balinese food is harder to come by, mostly because the Balinese don't eat in warungs much, but rather at home, or at festivals. But the dishes are spectacular, particularly **babi guleng,** generally a feast of roasted suckling pig turned into several rich dishes, and **betutu bebek,** or smoked duck. Both need to be ordered a day in advance.

# SHOPPING

The shop-happy tourist will find a massive amount of arts and crafts available for purchase in Bali (see "Arts & Crafts," in section 1), and there's something for all budgets, from trinkets that cost pennies to paintings and furniture that can cost many thousands of dollars. Between fabrics, clothing, wood and stone carvings, paintings, and doodads of varying quality, it's a shopper's paradise. The important thing to remember is that everything runs the gamut; clothing can be high designer quality, or it can fall apart after two wearings; wood can be carved to order or mass-produced. Don't buy the first frame you see; you are likely to see thousands more.

Shopping in Bali is something like a mental contact sport. Only a few places have fixed prices; everywhere else, bargaining is the name of the game. It's simple, really. The seller offers the first price, which to a well-heeled rube sounds pretty good. In fact, it's often 10 times what the item is really worth. So the savvy then offer an amount substantially lower, whereupon the seller gasps, smiles, and shakes his head with dismay, but comes down a notch as a favor to you. The haggling continues, and sometimes you'll get fed up and leave, but they'll drag you back, offering to "make morning price just for you, for good luck." And so it goes until, ideally, you both reach a mutually satisfactory price.

These people are very good at what they do, and most of us are not, so the fainthearted give up early on and pay more than they need to. Here are some tips to remember:

1. If you start by countering with an amount that is half their original price, they've already won. Don't worry that your offer seems outrageously low; their price is outrageously high to begin with, and the melodramatic reaction is all part of the act.

2. Take your time to shop around, for a few days even, before you begin to actually shell out money, so that you know what's out there. Start with an easy item—a sarong for temple wear, for example. (As of this writing, sarongs were about Rp20,000 to Rp30,000, depending on the quality of the cloth.) Attempting to buy a sarong from a couple different sellers demonstrates that there is indeed ultimately a bottom line (at least, for tourists; Balinese will always pay less, and that's as it should be).

3. Don't hesitate to walk away if negotiations aren't going your way. Not only will there always be someone else to buy from, but this can sometimes be an effective bargaining tool. Suddenly, the price may drop dramatically. Or if you return the next day, they may be even more inclined to work with you. But remember, once you've agreed on a price, that means you've bought it. Reneging at that point is considered very rude.

4. Above all, relax. Someone will always have the item you wanted for less than you paid, or your friend will have gotten a better deal elsewhere. Often tourists get so caught up in negotiations, determined to get a bargain, that they fail to realize they are dickering over dimes. Remember, you can't get that item at home, and even if you can, how much more would you have to pay for it? (As an example, those flying wood creatures that are all over Ubud for about Rp40,000 will, in a certain New Orleans import shop, set you back US$40 to US$70.)

As mentioned above, the real name of the buying game in Bali, in terms of quality for value, is to commission something. This can be anything from a wood carving to a garment. The latter doesn't take as long, but in either case you must bring plenty of drawings or photos so that the creator will have a good blueprint to go by.

# Fast Facts: Bali

**American Express**   There is a branch in the Bali Beach Hotel in Sanur (☎ 361-288449).

**Business Hours**   Most places keep "daylight hours," which on the equator pretty much means 6am to 6pm. (Or a little later.)

**Doctors & Dentists**   Ask your hotel for a referral—many have a doctor on call. In Kuta, try the **Bali International Medical Centre** (Jl. Bypass Ngurah Rai No100X, ☎ 361-761263). It's open daily from 8am to midnight and sometimes will send someone to your hotel. There is a general hospital in Denpasar, but for any serious problems, go home as soon as possible for treatment. For dentists, ask your hotel for a referral.

**Drug Laws**   Though you may be offered hash and marijuana at every turn, Indonesia officially takes drug offenses very seriously, and you run the risk of getting busted readily (because, as a tourist, they rather assume you are using drugs) and languishing in jail for nine or more years.

**Electricity**   Currents may be either 110 volts, 50 AC or 220-240v, 50 AC.

**Embassies/Consulates   United States:** Jl. Segara Ayu 5, Sanur (☎ 361-288478); Jl. Hayam Wuruk no. 188, Denpasar (☎ 361-233605). **Australia:** Jl. Prof. Moch, Yamin 51, Denpasar (☎ 361-235092). **Canada:** Wisma Metropolitan I, 5th floor, Jl. Jen. Sudirman, Kav. 29, Jakarta (☎ 021-510709). **Great Britain:** Jl. Thamrin 75, Jakarta (☎ 021-330904).

**Emergencies**   The number for the police is 110, ambulance 118, fire 113.

**Hospitals**   There is a main hospital in Denpasaur, but for any serious ailment, get back to your own country as soon as you can or evacuate to Hong Kong, Singapore, KL, or Bangkok.

**Internet/E-mail**   Internet cafes are springing up all over Bali (and, realizing that the majority of travelers use Hotmail, have a direct link to same), but the connections can still be painfully slow, particularly early to mid-evening when everyone in Indonesia (so it seems) is checking their e-mail. Since the cafes charge by the minute, you can rack up quite a bill just trying to read your mail. Go at off hours and if the connection seems slow, sign off and come back again some other time. Many hotels also will let you use their Internet connection to read e-mail.

**Language**   The Balinese speak both Indonesian and Balinese—the former when out in public, the latter at home. English is widely spoken throughout Bali, particularly in the major tourist areas. While not everyone is fluent, most of the people you will be dealing with will speak enough English that you can communicate with them. (For more information, see "Language" earlier in this chapter.)

**Liquor Laws**   You won't find liquor in any Muslim restaurant, but you will find it otherwise readily available throughout Bali, particularly the potent rice spirit *arak* and, of course, Bali Hai beer.

**Police**   The phone number for the police is **110.**

**Post Office/Mail**   Your hotel can send mail for you, or you can go to the post office in Denpasar (Jalan Raya Puputan Renon, ☎ 361-223568). Other branches are in Kuta, Ubud, and Sanur. For big items, there are packing and shipping services in all major tourist areas. Cost is determined either by size or weight.

# Telephone Dialing Info at a Glance

- **To place a call from your home country to Bali,** dial the international access code (011 in the U.S., 0011 in Australia, 0170 in New Zealand, 00 in the U.K.), plus Indonesia's country code (62), plus the area code (361 for Kuta, Jimbaran, Nusa Dua, Sanur, and Ubud; 362 for Lovina; 363 for Candi Dasa; 370 for Lombok), followed by the six-digit phone number (for example, from the U.S. to Lovina, you'd dial 011 + 62 + 362 + 000000).

- **To place a call within Indonesia,** you must use area codes if calling between states. Note that for calls within the country, area codes are all preceded by a zero (i.e., Lovina 0362, Candi Dasa 0363, Lombok 0370, etc.).

- **To place a direct international call from Indonesia,** dial the international access code (001), plus the country code of the place you are dialing, plus the area code, plus the residential number of the other party.

- **To reach the international operator,** dial 102.

- **International country codes** are as follows: Australia 61, Burma 95, Cambodia 855, Canada 1, Hong Kong 852, Laos 856, Malaysia 60, New Zealand 64, the Philippines 63, Singapore 65, Thailand 66, U.K. 44, U.S. 1, Vietnam 84.

**Safety/Crime**   Bali is by and large a safe place to be, even after dark. Violent crime is rare. However, pickpockets are not, so you should exercise considerable caution by using a money belt, particularly in crowded tourist areas, and be careful not to flash large wads of cash (it's rude, besides). Many hotels offer safety deposit boxes, and it would be best to keep extra cash and other valuables in them. If nothing else, make sure your suitcase has a good lock on it. Even the best hotel can't always guarantee security for valuables left lying in plain sight.

**Taxes**   Most hotels and restaurants add a "plus plus" to the bill—a 10% and 11% combination of sales tax and service charge, for a total of 21%.

**Telephones**   As many hotels charge a great deal even for using your calling card, you are better off using **Wartels,** privately owned public phones. There's one in every tourist center, though some work better than others. Some also have Internet services.

**Time**   Bali is Greenwich Mean Time plus 8 hours, except during daylight saving time, which they do not observe. That's 13 hours ahead of Eastern standard time in the U.S., and 16 hours ahead of Pacific standard time.

**Tipping**   Tipping is not required, and not even encouraged. Most restaurants include a "service charge" in the "plus plus" added to the bill. If you feel you must tip when dining, just leave a very small amount. More often than not, the recipient will be surprised.

**Toilets**   Western style toilets with seats are becoming more common than the Asian squat variety, though cheap losmen/homestays and some less touristed public places still have the latter. Always carry some toilet paper with you or you may have to use your hand (the left one only, please) and the dip bucket available.

**Water**   Avoid tap water in Bali unless properly boiled. Bottled water is available everywhere and restaurants in tourist areas seem to use it as a matter of course, but you should always ask to be sure.

## 3 Kuta

Bob and Louise Koke, who built the first hotel in Kuta, around 1936, would be shocked to see the town today. Even as recently as 25 years ago, Kuta was still fairly undeveloped. Now it teems with tourists, mostly surfers and party-hearty types. Among the throngs are some of the most aggressive hucksters and touts in Bali, hawking overpriced, inferior wares. It's the Tijuana or Tangiers of Bali, and in its own way the energy has a strange attraction. Kuta is made up of narrow streets and alleys, with pedestrians crammed between honking, muffler-less cars and motorbikes and touts insisting that you buy a hat, wristwatch, or cologne. Walking the streets of Kuta is a hectic, cacophonous, wearying obstacle course, exciting and stimulating at first, but soon oppressive and maddening. The place has little to do with Bali, and unless you are a surfer, its appeal is limited. Families, and those with a low tolerance for chaos, might do better staying in Nusa Dua or Sanur, both of which are much lower key and yet still close enough for easy trips to Kuta for shopping or the bar and club scene.

### GETTING THERE

Kuta is virtually right next to the airport, so many, if not most, hotels offer free airport pick-up. There are also **taxis** galore, but be sure to take the official ones to get the set rates, usually one-tenth of what unofficial drivers will charge. As you exit the terminal, turn to your left and look for the window where you give your destination, pay your fare, and are assigned a cab.

### GETTING AROUND

Kuta is a big rectangle. The two main north-south streets are Jalan Pantai Kuta, running next to the ocean, and Jalan Legian. They are connected by Jalan Melasti at the top and bisected, sometimes in a crooked, meandering way, by Jalan Benesari, Poppies Gang I and II, and a few small alleys. You can easily **walk** all this, or take the reasonably priced blue and yellow **metered taxis** (but not the unofficial ones offered by touts). Kuta gradually becomes Legian and then Seminyak to the north—as you walk up Jalan Legian, you won't even notice where one ends and the other begins.

## Fast Facts: Kuta

**Banks/Currency Exchange**   There is an ATM in the Kuta Square shopping mall (about halfway down on the left). Money changers line the streets—pick the best rate you can find.

**Internet/E-mail   Graha Wisata,** Jl. Raya Legian no. 60, Kuta (☎ 361-756378). Internet only 8am to 1am. Offers money exchange, phones, airline tickets. R1,000 per minute for Internet. Bali Internet, Jalan Legian Kelod (in courtyard off the Hotel Restu Bali; ☎ 361-751251 ext. 800). 9am to 11pm. Small, but air conditioned! R1,000 per minute, 5-minute minimum. Cyber Cafe. Kuta Square Block C 18, Kuta (☎ 361-753330). This place has branches in Sanur, Nusa Dua, and Legian. R15,000 for 10-minute minimum. Additional 10 minutes R10,000.

# Kuta

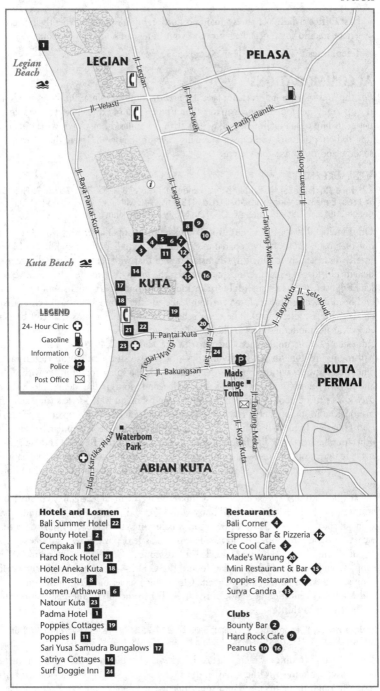

**Hotels and Losmen**
Bali Summer Hotel 22
Bounty Hotel 2
Cempaka II 5
Hard Rock Hotel 21
Hotel Aneka Kuta 18
Hotel Restu 8
Losmen Arthawan 6
Natour Kuta 23
Padma Hotel 1
Poppies Cottages 19
Poppies II 11
Sari Yusa Samudra Bungalows 17
Satriya Cottages 14
Surf Doggie Inn 24

**Restaurants**
Bali Corner 4
Espresso Bar & Pizzeria 12
Ice Cool Cafe 3
Made's Warung 20
Mini Restaurant & Bar 15
Poppies Restaurant 7
Surya Candra 13

**Clubs**
Bounty Bar 2
Hard Rock Cafe 9
Peanuts 10 16

**Post Office /Mail**   There is a main post office, but it's not conveniently located. There are also some postal agents, and your hotel can send mail for you.

**Telephones**   The area code in Kuta is 361.

## ACCOMMODATIONS

For the most part, hotels in Kuta lack the pizzazz found in Nusa Dua or even Ubud. If you really are looking for a luxury hotel/beach resort experience, you would do better in Nusa Dua or Jimbaran Bay (less than 3.1 miles/5 km away), where in addition to better options, you can also actually swim in the ocean. (Here the water is too shallow and the waves too violent.)

### VERY EXPENSIVE

✪ **Hard Rock Hotel.** Jl. Pantai, Banjar Pande Mas, Kuta, Bali. ☎ **361-761869.** Fax 361-761868. E-mail: bookings@hrbc-bali.co.id. 418 units. A/C MINIBAR TV TEL. US$160–US$170 double, US$325–US$725 suite. AE, DC, JCB, MC, V. Free parking.

On principle, I despise the Hard Rock Cafe's cultural imperialism and wouldn't eat at one on a bet. And so, fully prepared to extend that attitude to this hotel, instead I was utterly disarmed by its fanciful, whimsical design that while entirely un-Balinese is so delightful I forgot to care. Quickly move past the lobby (where the staff speaks excellent English), with its usual dubious memorabilia (once-used guitars, gold records), and head down brightly colored corridors labeled after different musical genres (psychedelic, blues, alternative). The color scheme extends into rooms that can best be called cabana moderne. They are light and airy, with a photo of an artist from the corridor genre, while unbleached cottons with the Hard Rock logo cover the bed. The bathrooms are done in playful geometrics—be sure to steal that cotton laundry bag. The fun continues with the pool—the largest in Bali, a sprawling monster with slides and its own beach (nonguests can use it for a fee, and rooms in the "deluxe block" have their own private pool). There's an outdoor living room, an MTV-style sitting area, an in-house radio station, and a recording studio where you can play out your own musician fantasies. Sure, rock blares 24/7 in the lobby, which has a popular bar, and in other public areas, but the fabulous kids' playroom—"Little Rock"—and that pool make it a great option for boomer families. This is not the place to stay if you want to experience even a modicum of Balinese culture, but it still is a model of modern hotel design.

Facilities and services include Kids Club, Karaoke Club, an extremely comfortable and well-stocked health club/spa, library with CDs and Internet access, Laundromat with jukebox, banquet and meeting rooms, ballroom, concierge, 24-hour room service, tour desk, gift shop, CD players, hair dryers, safe deposit boxes, and massage.

For dining, there's The Hard Rock Cafe of course; Gamelan, a 24 hour "coffee shop" serving traditional Indonesian food; HRBC Deli—yes, a New York–style deli; Canteen, an Asian noodle shop; Cabana Club, which serves burgers poolside at lunch and Mediterranean food at night; plus a lively bar in the lobby, another overlooking the beach, and a third poolside.

**Padma Hotel.** Jl. Padma no. 1, Legian, Bali. ☎ **361-752111.** Fax 361-752140. 403 units. A/C MINIBAR TV TEL. US$150–US$170 double. AE, DC, JCB, MC, V. Free parking.

This sprawling complex way up the beach in Legian has plenty of activities that make it attractive for families. Others may find it a bit out of the way from the heart of Kuta action (though there are shops and touts aplenty just outside the gate). Rooms have slightly better than average Bali furniture. Standard rooms, in a four-story high rise, have a balcony, but only deluxe rooms have good views. Family rooms open onto a patio and the garden, but all rooms have the same size bathroom. The pool is large and angular. There is a grassy place before you get to the actual beach that is kept tout-free for better beach enjoyment (which is still good only for surfing, not swimming). The many local culturally geared activities (egg painting, instrument demonstration) are admirable, but all that non–air-conditioned space means a long hot walk to any part of the complex.

Amenities include health club, Jacuzzi, sauna, tennis courts, water sports equipment, laundry, tour desk, beauty salon, concierge, 24-hour room service, dry cleaning, turndown, newspaper delivery on request, massage, and baby-sitting.

The seven restaurants—including Italian, Japanese, Indonesian, and a coffee shop—mean you won't have to leave the grounds to eat. There are also three bars.

## EXPENSIVE

**Bounty Hotel.** Poppies Gang II, Jl. Segara Batu Bolong no. 18, Kuta, Bali. ☎ **361-753030.** Fax 361-752121. 166 units. A/C MINIBAR TV TEL. US$93–US$175 double. AE, DC, MV, V. Free parking.

The biggest thing going on Poppies Gang II, the Bounty is clearly a party-down resort, but at least one that feels like it is in Bali. The rooms are decidedly Western-style (with familiar comforts like hair dryers), though they do have wood floors and are decorated with Balinese fabric. Standard rooms are slightly smaller than deluxe, with the wash basin in the room. Be careful—seemingly complimentary snacks left out for you are really from the minibar. The complex, arranged around an attractive pool, features stone carvings and red tile ornamentation. The hotel (always a good place to grab a cab) is positioned equal walking distance between the beach and the shopping on Legian, and the same people own the **Bounty Bar & Restaurant** over there, which is one of the area's most happening late night spots. That fact and the fliers advertising various party spots gives you an idea of the clientele.

Amenities are swimming pool, car rental, laundry, dry cleaning, sundries shop, safety deposit box, baby-sitting, secretarial service, 24-hour room service, games room, and tour desk.

**Natour Kuta.** Jl. Pantai Kuta no. 1, Kuta, Bali. ☎ **361-751361.** Fax 361-751362/753958. E-mail: nkbh@denpasar.wasantara.net.id. 137 units. A/C MINIBAR TV TEL. US$100–US$120 double. AE, DC, JCB, MC, V. Free parking.

The only hotel in Kuta that is right on the beach—and at a spot on the beach that while still not good for swimming is better for dipping up to your knees. If your other passion is shopping, being right next to Kuta Square and then Legian makes this the most perfectly situated hotel for you. Pleasant also is the butterfly-shaped pool on the way to the beach, which provides a nice spot for viewing the sunset. All this means you won't be spending too much time in the unimaginatively decorated long and narrow rooms—though try to get a third floor standard, which has an ocean view. Skip the more costly bungalows in back, which provide little more than some faux privacy or romance (even the bathrooms are the same size as standard). The beach access and pool may make this a good choice for families. Amenities include banquet facilities, conference room, tennis court, tour desk, travel agent, massage, baby-sitter, and in-house videos. For dining, there's a steak and seafood restaurant, coffee shop, and two bars, plus frequent buffet dinner shows.

## MODERATE

**Hotel Aneka Kuta.** Jl. Pantai Kuta, Kuta, Bali. ☎ **361-752067.** Fax 361-752892. E-mail: anekakuta@denpasar.wasantara.net.id. 60 units. A/C MINIBAR TEL. US$60–US$70 double with TV, US$80–US$200 suites. AE, MC, V. Free Parking.

This is a pretty complex of thatched villas, right across from the beach, down a long driveway which assures some peace and respite from beach bustle. It's a little more costly than its neighbor Sari Yasa, but it has a little more style and comfort as well, plus a nice pool. The rooms are sparely attractive, pulling up short before falling into the anonymous motel room trap. There's a pizza place right next door.

Amenities include a bar and restaurant, airport transfer, room service (until midnight), safety deposit boxes, massage, and laundry.

✪ **Poppies Cottages.** Poppies Lane I, Kuta, Bali. ☎ **361-751059.** Fax 361-752364. E-mail: info@bali.poppies.net. 20 units. (4 additional units at the older Poppies.) A/C MINIBAR TEL. US$85 double (US$30 double at other Poppies). AE, DC, MC, V. Free parking.

This is by far the best mid-range hotel in Kuta, with its individual thatched cottages set among gorgeous gardens abloom with a riot of bougainvillea. The small swimming pool, designed to look like a natural pond, complete with rock formations, is perhaps the prettiest in town, and is surrounded by many nooks for lounging. It's hard to leave such a spot for the madness of Kuta. The rooms, truth be told, aren't that special (despite a recent upgrade), but the open-air bathrooms are in marble, complete with a small sunken tub. An interesting touch is the Internet Cottage, where homesick guests can have their own e-mail address and Web page while in residence.

The original Poppies Cottages, a bit of a distance away, are less of a bargain, as the bungalows there badly need a face-lift (particularly the large but deeply drab bathrooms). They only look shabbier compared with similar places around town that give you more amenities (like A/C, telephone and an on-site pool) for around the same price. You can use the fabulous pool at the other Poppies, but it's a long, hot walk away.

For dining, there's the Poppies restaurant (see below) and a poolside bar. Amenities include free airport transfer, laundry, room service (until 11pm), baby-sitting, free newspaper, pool, and Jacuzzi.

## INEXPENSIVE

**Bali Summer Hotel.** Jl. Pantai Kuta no. 38, Kuta, Bali. ☎ **361-751503.** Fax 361-755637. 48 units. A/C TEL. US$40–US$60 double with TV and fridge. AE, DC, MC, V. Free parking.

Just a 2-minute walk from the beach, though it would be nice if the charms of the tree-filled courtyard carried over to the rooms. Standard rooms would benefit from having their somewhat chipped and worn furniture replaced and their musty smell thoroughly aired out. I won't even go into the horrors of the excessively pink bathroom. But they do have balconies and more amenities for the price. The deluxe rooms, which are split level and have their own patio, might be a better way to go. In any event, the whole package may be worthwhile—it's located on a busy shopping street but quiet inside, with a decent restaurant, smallish but nice pool, and that short walk to the beach. Amenities also include free airport transfer, safety deposit boxes, bar, and drugstore.

✪ **Hotel Restu Bali.** Jl. Raya Legian no. 113, Kuta, Bali. ☎ **361-751251.** Fax 361-751252. E-mail: restubali@denpasar.wasantara.net.id. 41 units. A/C TV TEL. US$35–US$55 double. Rates include breakfast. AE, JCB, MC, V. Free parking.

Technically, this is in Legian, but it's on the main shopping drag of Jalan Raya, which means you often end up wandering by here. It's about a 10-minute walk to the beach, but right in the middle of nighttime action. The deceptively simple small property is actually a long, narrow rabbit's warren of different tropical nooks and crannies. For all the hustle and bustle outside, it's unbelievably serene. Standard rooms have wicker furniture and stark but good bathrooms. The Puri Deluxe are bungalow style, with thatched roofs and woven mats covering the walls and private patios. Bathrooms are the same, but the sink is in the room. Two very nice swimming pools spill into gurgling fountain pools—some of which are right outside a handful of rooms, creating a noise that some might find soothing but others distracting. Amenities include safety deposit boxes, 24-hour room service, 24-hour restaurant, airport transfer, tour reservations, laundry, and welcome drink.

**Sari Yasa Samudia Bungalows.** Jl. Pantai Kuta, Kuta, Bali. ☎ **361-751562.** Fax 361-752948. 50 units. A/C TV TEL. US$23–US$40 double. Rates include breakfast. AE, MC, V. Free parking.

Located directly across from the beach, this may be the winner in terms of location combined with price—particularly if you can forgo air conditioning for a US$23 fan-only room. The so-called "superior" rooms in the new hotel building don't look like much and are smaller than the others, which are in traditional and aesthetically pleasing bungalows with gilt inlaid doors and wood carvings over portals. Superior rooms do have balconies that look down into the lush tropical garden or out at the beach for a glimpse of the famous Kuta sunset. Bathrooms are totally plain (or a hideous salmon). The staff speaks English well. Amenities include pool with swim-up bar, 24-hour room service, and small restaurant and bar.

**Satriya Cottages.** Poppies Lane II, Kuta, Bali. ☎ **361-758331.** Fax 361-752741. 47 units. A/C. US$28–US$48 double. Rates include breakfast. No credit cards. Free parking.

Conveniently located apart from the main beach bustle, but still less than a minute's walk away, this is a relatively new, pretty, Balinese-style hotel. The pavilion lobby sets the tone as you then move through a tropical garden with plenty of wood and stone carvings, while a waterfall fountain helps fill the swimming pool. Tile-roofed bungalows feature good-sized, if plainly decorated, bedrooms and simple bathrooms that are largely free of the ugly tile problem. Each also has a small private garden and patio plus front porch. Rooms in the hotel building lack these but gain a balcony. New rooms have a TV and fridge, while old rooms may not have hot water. Services include sauna and laundry.

## LOSMEN

**Cempaka II.** Poppies Gang II. ☎ **361-757750.** 7 units. Rp30,000. Rates include breakfast. No credit cards.

Very basic, but clean, and guests get a 15% discount at the adjoining laundry. Little porches overlook the spare courtyard. Rooms have fan, shower, and Western-style toilet.

**Losmen Arthawan.** Legian St. Poppies Gang II, Kuta, Bali. ☎ **361-752913.** Fax 361-758703. 43 units. Rp20,000–Rp30,000. Rates include breakfast. No credit cards.

Rooms, in villas or three-story blocks, are large and plain (bigger and newer for the more expensive ones), with hand-held showers and fans. The compound—a 5- to 10-minute walk to the beach—has a fish pond, a shrine, and many cats, and the owners speak adequate English.

**Surf Doggie Inn.** Jl. Bunisari 14, Kuta, Bali. ☎ **361-752381.** 20 units. Rp30,000–Rp70,000. Rates include breakfast.

Surfing stickers on the doorways and the relatively cheap price (not to mention the name) indicate the crowd catered to here. Not the finest of homestays—it's deceptively nice on the outside with a pretty temple pavilion in the center of the complex—though there are some attempts at decorating inside (purple walls, a Balinese mirror). Cheaper rooms are small and bottom-end basic—no fan, a hand shower, squat toilet. Pay more and get a bigger room with A/C or fan and a Western-style toilet.

# DINING

You won't be writing home about the food in Kuta. On one hand, the variety is stunning, thanks to all the homesick tourists who can't do without their German, Italian, and American favorites, and so if Indonesian food scares you (it shouldn't) you could easily avoid it during your entire stay. On the other hand—this is tourist food, and most places don't do anything all that well. There are only a couple of standouts, listed below. Besides these, if you absolutely must, there is the **Hard Rock Cafe,** which offers probably the best burger on the island (but I don't want to hear about it), and the two hotel restaurants directly across from the beach, which offer safe and solid, if unexciting, tourist specialties and fresh fish.

**Bali Corner.** Poppies Gang II. No phone. Reservations not accepted. Main courses Rp5,000–Rp8,000, fresh shrimp Rp10,000. Daily 8am–10pm. INTERNATIONAL.

The sign says "coffee shop" but it's really a cheerful warung whose cheap prices and international menu cater to the shirtless surfing crowd that congregates on Poppies Gang II. Chinese, Italian (pastas and pizzas), cheap steak, local favorites, and fish (small portions, deep fried and not the bargain it seems)—it's all very basic but also cheap. Stick closer to local fare with something like the chicken with coriander and curry, which comes with some nice veggies.

**Espresso Bar & Pizzeria.** Jl. Legian 83, Kuta. ☎ **361-752576.** Reservations not accepted. Main courses Rp4,900–Rp17,500. Daily 10am–1am. PIZZA, MEXICAN.

Pizza is the true international food, and it's interesting to see a local country's spin on this reliable item. Here, it's thin crust, light on the sauce, heavy on the cheese, with a variety of toppings (chicken, shrimp, veggies and . . . squid). Best of all, it's from a wood-fired brick oven! This spaghetti-Western themed place is just one of many restaurants serving pizza in Kuta, but one of the few that specialize in it. That, and the oven, does mean that you pay twice what you would in a warung. It also serves burgers, Mexican fare, and pasta. I say stick with the pizza; an individual 10-inch with various toppings runs about Rp16,000. Toss in a fancy ice cream dessert, banana fritters, espresso (including Italy's fab Illy coffee) or "Happy Soda" (cream and hyper-sweet syrup) and you've got a nice cheap snack or light meal, Western style.

**Ice Cool Cafe.** Poppies Gang II (opposite the Bounty Hotel), Kuta. Rp6,500 (scoops), Rp10,000 (shakes). Daily 8am–11pm. ICE CREAM.

This slightly larger than a sidewalk stand ice cream parlor claims to have the best ice cream in Bali—that may well be true. Certainly, places that offer scoops rather than premade bars are rare, and the selection of flavors here is fairly wide. Try a "thick shake" (as everywhere in Bali, if you get a regular shake, the consistency is like water) of fruit juice or a smoothie.

**Made's Warung.** Br. Pando Mas, Kuta. ☎ **316-755297.** Reservations not accepted. Main courses Rp12,000–Rp26,000. AE, MC, V (on orders of Rp80,000 or more). Daily 8am–12am. INDONESIAN.

A Kuta tradition that may serve what you think will be your best meal, until you eat much better Indonesian food elsewhere on the island. Still, this is a reliable, bustling, confusing open air warung on a noisy street, whose popularity means possibly sharing a table. Gado gado, satay (especially pork), and curries are all recommended, and you can get plenty of food (for a slightly light meal) for about US$2. Fun surprises on the menu include bagel and smoked marlin, tofu burgers, Caesar salad, and vegemite for an Aussie breakfast. They also have a large beverage selection, from iced coffee drinks to considerably potent booze (the menu warns you).

**Mini Restaurant & Bar.** Legian St., Kuta. ☎ **361-751651**. Reservations not accepted. Main courses Rp16,000–Rp22,000 (seafood by weight and somewhat higher). AE, MC, V. Daily 10am–noon. SEAFOOD.

One of two restaurants right next to each other that serve fresh fish out of a tank, this is the larger of the two—a cavernous, thatched-roof place. You choose your fish and preparation (steamed, barbecued, or fried). They—and I—recommend it fried, though the prices go up considerably. But a whole snapper runs about US$6 and easily serves two. Shellfish—enormous prawns and lobster—really hit the ceiling price-wise. Or go ahead and order the frog legs. Fish comes with choice of sauce: butter garlic (not that great, but the marinated onions are), sweet and sour, and soya. The menu offers many, many cocktails and some appealing frothy drinks. They do babi guleng combinations (with advance order), and also offer local, Chinese, and European dishes.

**Poppies Restaurant.** Poppies Cottages. Poppies Lane I, Kuta, Bali. ☎ **361-751059**. Reservations recommended. Men must wear shirts. Main courses Rp19,500–Rp37,000. AE, MC, V. Daily 8am–11pm. INDONESIAN.

Poppies is a veritable tradition thanks to its 25 years of serving Indonesian and not-so-Indonesian specialties. (If you need Italian or French-style pork, beef, and chicken, you will be happy here, but you will pay extra for it.) It's certainly the prettiest restaurant in town, with a garden setting, a mass of crawling vines overhead keeping the hot sun at bay, and babbling pools and waterfalls. Some feel the food has fallen off a bit in the last few years, but I was most satisfied with an outstanding ikan pepes—mashed fish cooked in a banana leaf (sort of a fish tamale) with nicely hot spices and served with an even spicier collection of vegetables they called "pickles." The mie goreng, loaded with shrimp and vegetables, also made us happy. Service is slow, but this is a good place to dawdle.

**Surya Candra.** Jl. Legian 83, Kuta. ☎ **361-752576**. Main courses Rp13,000–Rp23,000. DC, MC, V. Daily noon–midnight. SEAFOOD.

Exactly the same idea as the Mini Restaurant right next door—pick your fish victim out of the tank, tell them how you want it, sit, and eat. Those looking for more intimacy might prefer it here, since it is somewhat smaller than the inappropriately named Mini. Otherwise, why not have a progressive fish dinner and compare the two?

## OUTDOOR ACTIVITIES & WATER SPORTS

Obviously, **surfing** is number one in Kuta, as enthusiasts from all over are drawn to its stupendous breakers. You can't swing a dead cat here without hitting a surfer. Blame Bob Koke, who claims to have first brought the sport to Bali from Hawaii.

The best surfing is between March and July, though it's still good as late as October. Tubes Bar (see "Kuta After Dark" below) will have a list of tide charts and other important information, though the plethora of surf shops should be able to help you as well. The breaks along the beach all have their good points, but the legendary surf is the **Kuta Reef** (out from the southern end of the beach). You either have to paddle to get there (it takes about half an hour) or pay an outrigger at Jimbaran to take you.

Unfortunately, the same surf makes recreational **swimming** virtually impossible. The waves crash sharply in, and before them, the water barely covers the ankles. Even past the breakers, the current can be too strong. Pay close attention to swimming warnings and restrictions and be very careful if you do swim. Tanning and splashing to cool off are about all that's left to do. Few hotels in Kuta are right on the beach, and two beach chairs and umbrellas rent for Rp35,000 a day.

Other water sports are similarly disappointing—there is no good snorkeling or diving—any dive shop will send you to Sanur, Nusa Dua, or Candi Dasa. For better ocean swimming, and for parasailing, head to Jimbaran Bay, which is only a few kilometers away.

Another option is **Waterbom Park & Spa,** Jalan Kartika Plaza, Tuban, Kuta (☎ **361-755676**), just south of Kuta. A water park with slides, a lazy river, and spa facilities, it makes for an ideal family outing. Should your hotel not have a pool, you can pay for a day pass to the monster one at the **Hard Rock Hotel.** The biggest in Bali, it also has several large water slides, plus a faux beach.

## SHOPPING

With the touts constantly in your face, shopping in Kuta will seem mandatory. Certainly, you won't lack for quantity—but quality will have to wait until Ubud. Hucksters will constantly wave knockoff brand-name colognes, cheap hats, and dubious wristwatches at you. The streets (particularly Poppies Gang II) are lined with stalls offering tie-dyed sarongs, sarong skirts (with actual ties), shorts, and swimsuits. **Sarongs** are cheaper and nicer elsewhere, but then again, too nice in many cases to use as a swimsuit coverup, so if that's what you're looking for, here is the place to buy. In any event, given the hard sell, this might be the place to hone your bargaining skills— being cheated by a savvy Kuta salesperson is probably an essential Bali shopping rite of passage. There are regular fixed-price stores, but nothing you can't live without. Your serious shopping is better saved for Ubud.

**Kuta Square** is the place to go if you miss Western-style shopping—i.e., fixed prices and mall goods. On the first street right past the Natour Hotel is a shopping mall that could be called Brand Name Row, with Nike, Polo, and Armani stores, plus fast food places like McDonald's, KFC, and Round Table. There is also a CyberCafe here, and an ATM halfway down on the left.

The **ABC Bookstore,** Jl. Pantai Kuta no. 41E (☎ **361-752745**), offers used books with quite a few English language selections—mostly of the beach blanket variety undoubtedly left behind by tourists. A treasure does sneak in occasionally, however. Buy a book, bring it back when you are done, and get half price back. They're open from 10am to 9pm.

## KUTA AFTER DARK

Good heavens, is there nightlife in Kuta! So much, in fact, and so comparatively little elsewhere, you have to wonder if it all didn't just migrate over. Kuta nightlife doesn't even really kick in until after 11pm, and then it goes nearly until dawn—every night. In theory, each place has an individual atmosphere and attracts its own clientele, but unless you are a connoisseur, one nightclub or bar looks pretty much like the next. You can either find your own to call home or switch around, sampling everything Kuta has to offer.

Women should be aware of the Bali rent boys. These are young men who want nothing more than to attach themselves to a Western girlfriend, for a few days or a lifetime (who cares, as long as she pays the bills?). They aren't threatening, and can be quite handsome and attentive. Just know what you are getting into.

Kuta really rages (the verb of the moment) in December and January, when the spring break/frat party mentality that is always prevalent hits a fever pitch. If you aren't there then, you can always join the nonlegendary, twice weekly (Tuesday and Saturdays) Peanuts Pub Crawl, which picks up at several hotels and takes you to a few different nightspots, including both Peanuts I and II (both on Jalan Legian). By the time they return you to your hotel the next morning, don't expect to remember much of what you did the night before.

Or you could skip all that and do what the locals do: hang out by the food stalls on the beach on Friday and Saturday nights until midnight.

## CLUBS

Of course, there are many more, but here are some of the most high-profile clubs and best bets.

**Bounty Bar.** Jl. Legian. Daily 10pm–3am. No cover Sun–Fri (1 drink minimum), Rp10,000 Sat.

Here's where the tourists go to get ship-faced—it's built to look like a galleon, with a restaurant on the "deck" and a dance club below in the "hull," housing a bar and dance floor, with live bands some nights and deejays others. If it sounds cheesy, well, it is. But the club gets lively, with a young crowd. And on Tuesdays you can walk the plank. They've got a mini-bungee set-up from a board overhanging the dance floor.

**Hard Rock Cafe.** Jl. Raya Kuta. Occasional cover.

The most upscale place in town, and popular with locals as well as yuppie tourists. This is their new two-story location in the brand new Hard Rock Beach Club, and thanks to that atmosphere, it should be livelier than ever. Live bands play nightly starting around 11pm until at least 1am, but action can go on until dawn.

**Peanuts II.** Jl. Legian. Occasional cover.

Not the hottest game in town, except by reputation, but surrounded by other bars to get you oiled up before you head in. Either come specially for the rowdy pub crawl, or on other days come to avoid it.

## BARS

Again, there are too many bars to mention, but here are three to give you an idea of the variety available. You might also check out the bar in the lobby of the **Hard Rock Hotel,** which is a classy, lively place that often has live music as well.

**Macaroni Club.** Jl. Legian. ☎ **361-754662**.

It's really a pasta restaurant, but the nice lounge area up front turns into a hangout to listen to recorded jazz, sip beers or espresso, and watch the free show passing by in the noisy street.

**Paddy's Pub.** Jl. Legian, Kuta. ☎ **361-752363**.

Aussies flock to this tropical-themed "pub" (complete with faux palm trees), which gets quite noisy thanks to live music on Tuesdays and Fridays, karaoke, large beers for Rp7,000, and a happy hour that lasts from 8 to 11pm. The dance floor starts getting crowded around 10pm.

**Tubes Bar & Restaurant.** Poppies Gang II. ☎ **361-753510**. Daily noon–2am.

A beach movie setting ("Rock and surf is here") complete with a giant plaster wave with board, for photo op posing. Guess who they cater to? Movies are shown during the day and early evening, warming up the crowd for live music at night.

## DAY TRIPS FROM KUTA

The following destinations are easy day trips from either Kuta or Ubud. (Tanah Lot is somewhat closer to Kuta.) Tour companies often combine them as a package, or you can go through your hotel or your own transport guide.

**Tanah Lot.** 9.3 miles (15 km) west of Denpasar. Open during daylight hours. Admission Rp1,500.

Though it's not particularly near anything else, and not all that remarkable architecturally, Tanah Lot is a popular tourist destination, so expect possibly the biggest crowds you will encounter at a temple. Its popularity is due partly because of its ease as a day trip from Kuta, but also because of the undeniably spectacular setting, high on craggy bluffs overlooking the Java Sea. This is a truly magnificent example of how well temples in Bali are wedded to their locations, be they lakeside, mountainside, or seaside.

Tanah Lot is said to have been founded by a Brahmin priest in the 16th century. A rivalry with the local, established priest nearly led to his expulsion; instead, he meditated so hard he pushed Tanah Lot "out to sea," where it rests on an inlet that actually becomes an island at high tide. (The walk from the car park is not as long nor as steep as at many other sights, and there are no stairs.) Non-Hindus can't actually enter the temple, but have access to other parts of the complex, strung out across the rocks, and many of these afford a good view. The photo ops provided here are superb, though shutterbugs tend to spoil the meditative qualities of the place. Try to come close to sunset, when Tanah Lot is truly glorious. Skip the touristy snake cave; instead, if the tides allow, wade out to the part of the temple complex that's at your back when you reach the snake cave. It's beautiful and a much better use of time.

At press time, there are still plans to build an upscale hotel within sight of Tanah Lot—a controversial proposition, as it will hardly add to the beauty of the otherwise untouched place.

**Sangeh Monkey Forest.** 19 miles (31km) north of Denpasar. Daylight hours. Rp1,500.

The Sangeh Monkey Forest is much bigger than the somewhat more high-profile Monkey Forest in Ubud, with majestic trees and even more monkeys. So if you are simian fan, you should go (Sangeh is often combined with trips to Tanah Lot.) A personal "guide" will take you through the forest. It's an enjoyable walk, full of atmosphere thanks to the monkeys and the 17th-century temple they seem to guard. At the end, the guide will attempt to take you to his or her stall. The monkeys are even more wild and fearless than the ones in Ubud, which means fabulous closeups for photos, but it also means you must be careful not to bring any foodstuffs (they *will* find it on you, and none-too-gently) or any valuables, as they are larcenous beasts. You can also see huge fruit bats flying overhead like vultures. At the end, there is a stand where you can hold a tamed bat to admire its wingspan—touristy, of course (the point being to buy a photo), but it's a thrill to examine one of these beasts up close.

## 4 Jimbaran

Jimbaran is easily overlooked, because it's so small and because flashy Kuta is right next door. Accommodations come in only two sizes—super expensive and super inexpensive. Really, if you are going to stay here, it should be at the Four Seasons, which is the jewel in the Four Season crown and one of the great hotels of the world. But consider also just coming for the day, even if you are staying elsewhere—especially if you are staying in Kuta, which is less than 3.1 miles (5km) away. Jimbaran Bay curves to feature some of the purest sand and clearest water in Bali, protected enough so that the water is usually calm, with gentle waves. It's not suitable for surfing (though there is a famous break a ways out nearby), but perfect for swimming, not to mention windsurfing and the like. A fishing village still exists here, despite increasing development, and indeed, if you squint and cut out the hotels at the top and bottom of the curve, everything looks much like it did 20 or more years ago. There is a row of shacks that grill up cheap fresh fish all day long. Come for a swim and stay for lunch, when there are few people around (at night the places get flooded with the nearby hotel visitors, though candles flickering add romance).

### GETTING THERE

Jimbaran is on the road to Nusa Dua and so bemos go there frequently from Kuta and the airport. Cabs are also easy to grab at either location.

## GETTING AROUND

As Jimbaran really is just a few hotels, there are few other facilities. Consult your hotel for currency exchange, Internet access, postal service, and telephone service.

# ACCOMMODATIONS

✪ **Four Seasons at Jimbaran Bay.** Jimbaran 80361, Bali. ☎ **361-701010**. Fax 361-701020. www.fourseasons.com. 147 units. A/C MINIBAR TV TEL. 1-bedroom villa US$525. 2-bedroom and Royal villa US$1,200 and up. AE, DC, MC, V. Free parking.

Everything I say about foregoing luxury hotels in favor of real Bali experiences goes out the window when it comes to the Four Seasons. All I can do in my defense is mumble, "But it's pretty." It's more than that. In my opinion, this is *the* hotel of Bali, above even the Amandari in Ubud. This is what comes to mind when you think of a luxury resort, and yet it's so organic to its setting and so in harmony with its culture that you don't miss out (much) by staying here. Unlike the Western hotels of Nusa Dua, this could not exist anywhere else but Bali.

The Four Seasons' exquisitely landscaped grounds drape along a hillside that leads down to the bay. The layout is meant to suggest a series of Bali villages, with each set of accommodations like a traditional, multi-structure Bali home, within its own walled compound. A typical thatched villa consists of a good-sized bedroom, generous dressing room and large marbled bathroom with oversized tub, many thick towels and fancy amenities, his and her sinks, and both an indoor and outdoor garden shower (water comes out a bamboo pipe). There is an open-air sitting room decorated better than most of our living rooms at home, a little shrine, and best of all, your own private plunge pool. All this with a view of the blue sea. Posh? You bet. Each set of villas has its own staff ready to serve you or drive you around the expansive grounds in golf carts. The horizon pool matches the ocean it seems to blend into, and there are other small dipping and soaking pools. Staff waits to hand you towels, ice water, and icy sprays to keep the heat at bay. A library has quite a good collection of books and videos—each villa comes with a VCR. You can walk or be driven in a golf cart down to the beach, passing bales (open-air pavilions) and viewing spots down the way, to the luxe beach club, featuring all the same amenities as the pool. Who can begrudge the honeymooners who hole up here for days, rarely venturing to the outside world?

Amenities include 24-hour room service, CD players, VCRs, hair dryers, safes, turndown, laundry and dry cleaning, newspapers, library and lounge with books and videos, airport transfers, free transfer to Four Seasons Sayan (including packing on request), full service spa, tennis courts, fitness center, art gallery, boutique, meeting facilities, and tour desk.

Warung Mie and Taman Wantilan Restaurant each serve delicious Eastern and Western specialties, while PJ's down on the beach has pizza and seafood. The Pool Terrace Cafe sells snacks and sweets. Try afternoon tea or evening drinks in the gracious Terrace Bar and Lounge. There are frequent evening events, including weekly cocktail parties and dance programs.

## DINING

Jimbaran, with its row of **fish shacks** on the beach, is one of the best places to eat in Bali. You pick your fish, or just name the kind and approximate amount, they grill it and serve it with salad, dipping sauces, rice, and fruit for dessert. Lobster and giant prawns run about US$20 for two, but you will be just as well off with snapper; a whole grilled fish easily serves two and runs about Rp30,000 to Rp50,000. It's smokey, hot during the day, and completely delicious. Try any or all of the shacks—I did, and my favorite, with the best use of spices and grilling, was the last shack on the left (as you face the row), set back a little farther than the others. If you want s omething a little more conventional, try the Four Season's **PJ's,** between the fish shacks and the hotel, which serves pizza, seafood, and Mexican specialties.

## 5 Nusa Dua

Nusa Dua is probably the best spot in Bali for those who'd rather be in Hawaii. It's a string of giant hotels, each one bigger and more lavish and expensive than the next, a clean beach covered in golden mealy sand, and almost no local culture. True, the often disgusting frenzy of Kuta is missing, but the experience is entirely more sterile. Most of the hotels do provide as fine a beach resort experience as you could ask for, and the swimmable ocean and tout-free beaches make it stress-free and suitable for families, plus it's a scant half hour drive to Kuta for daytime shopping or nighttime activities. And as I said in the Kuta section, if you are going to spend your money on a fancy hotel, it's better to do so here, where there are more options, you can actually swim in the ocean, and the ambiance is calmer. Come for a couple days to ease into your vacation, but then move along to the real Bali.

### GETTING THERE

Couldn't be easier. Most hotels in Nusa Dua offer airport pickup, but you can find shuttles and cheap taxis both at the airport and in Kuta. (Be sure to take only the official blue and yellow taxis in Kuta.) Bemos from Denpasar go to Nusa Dua by way of Kuta and Jimbaran.

### GETTING AROUND

These big spreads make it so comfortable you don't want or even have to leave the grounds—but even the most starry-eyed honeymooner might want a break from expensive hotel meals. There isn't much to see other than the Galleria shopping mall and the village of Bulau, located on the other side of the massive gates that mark the entrance to the resort. Still, Bulau and the fishing village of Benoa at the north end of the peninsula are worth spending time in to get some Bali flavor. Getting around **on foot** can be a hot proposition on the main road, which runs parallel to the beach on the other side of the hotels. Walk along the beach instead (there's a paved walkway part of the way). **Don't take cabs,** which can take forever to get to your hotel, or your hotel's own transport, which, unless it's free, can cost 10 times as much as a cab. Better choices are the **local shuttle**—Rp2,000 per person (every 40 minutes) or the free **Galleria shuttle** (every 15 minutes); or just grab a **transport guide** off the street.

## Fast Facts: Nusa Dua

Everything you could possibly need is in the hotels.

**Banks/Currency Exchange**   Consult your hotel for currency exchange.

**Internet/E-mail**   There is a Wartel with Internet service in Bualu.

**Post Office/Mail**   There is a postal agent at the Galleria shopping center.

**Telephone**   The area code in Nusa Dua is 361.

## ACCOMMODATIONS
### VERY EXPENSIVE

**Nusa Dua Beach Hotel.** P.O. Box 1028, Denpasar, Bali. ☎ **361-771219**/771210. Fax 361-772617. E-mail: ndbhnet@indosat.net.id. 380 units. A/C MINIBAR TV TEL. US$200–US$350 double. Suites US$300–US$2,000. AE, DC, JCB, MC, V. Free parking.

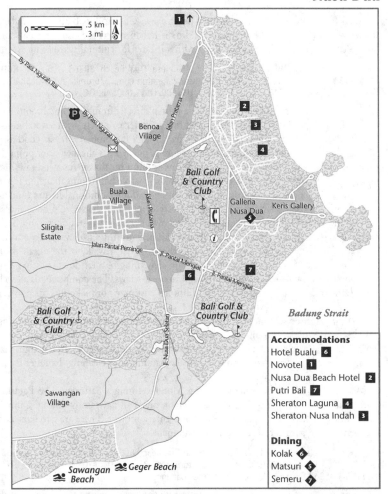

**Accommodations**
Hotel Bualu **6**
Novotel **1**
Nusa Dua Beach Hotel **2**
Putri Bali **7**
Sheraton Laguna **4**
Sheraton Nusa Indah **3**

**Dining**
Kolak **6**
Matsuri **5**
Semeru **7**

There are some things this hotel does very well, and it has a lot more local style than some of the other resorts. However, the bulk of the regular rooms—called Superior— are smaller and more ordinary (despite some Balinese art on the walls) than the price should warrant. The Deluxe and Palace rooms are bigger (although the Deluxe rooms still have no counter space by the sink), with Balinese fabric on the beds and, for the Palace rooms, CD and video players, wood carvings, Jacuzzi tubs, and free breakfast and afternoon tea. There are two swimming pools, a good-sized geometric one and a lagoon version right on the beach. The best amenity, though, is the exquisite spa. You can get a massage in the bright, open-air, thatched pavilion, then crash on a Bali-style bed set in a fountain of water. It's deeply romantic and relaxing. There is even a lap pool, should you have the strength. The gym, too, is well-equipped with all the right machines and free weights, nicely air-conditioned, with plenty of icy towels and fruit. Other amenities are hair dryers, safety deposit boxes, cable TV, 24-hour room service, medical clinic, shopping arcade, tour and travel office, bank, business center, water sports, business center, laundry, dry cleaning, tennis and squash courts, ballroom, and conference and banquet facilities.

Raja's Table offers Asian food with a beach view; Chess offers barbecue; Wedang Jahe is the hotel's top end restaurant; Sandro's is Italian. There are also three bars and a club offering evening programs, along with a theater for cultural performances.

**Sheraton Laguna Nusa Dua.** PO Box 77, Nusa Dua Beach 80363, Bali. ☎ **800/ 325-3535,** 361-771327. Fax 361-771326. www.sheraton.com. 276 units. A/C MINIBAR TV TEL. Rooms US$260–US$380 double. Suites US$500–US$1,000. AE, DC, MC, V.

There is something to be said for being able to step directly from your hotel room into the swimming pool—in this case, a serpentine monster complete with several sandy beaches, that winds its seemingly endless way through the property. It's as good as it sounds. Still, I actually don't like this hotel quite as much as its cheaper sister property next door, the Nusa Indah. The rooms are lavish but a bit flower-fussy, a brash and brassy, vaguely tropical decor. The huge wood and marble bathrooms make up for it, stocked with even more amenities than the ones next door. Additional luxury touches include in-room check-in (complete with fruity drinks and snacks), 24-hour butler service (no need for a coffeemaker), and your own personalized stationery and business cards to use while in residence. The housekeepers don't use trolleys, so quiet rules the day. The extensive grounds are so big, though, that a walk to the ocean is an endeavor. The additional swimming pools are something of a let down—only 58 of the rooms have swim-up access and none have ocean views. The pampering is all well and good—okay, *really* good—but the additional cost may not make this Sheraton as worthwhile as the one next door.

Facilities and services include 24-hour room service, unpacking and light pressing on check-in, cable TV, room safes, hair dryers, three swimming pools, water sports, tennis courts, fitness center, massage, daily activities, travel agent, airport transfers, business center, beauty salon, shopping arcade, laundry, dry cleaning, banquet facilities, and ballroom.

Mayang Sari offers Continental dining Monday through Saturday. The Poolside Terrace lets you snack until 11pm. Cafe Lagoon offers all-day family dining. Quinn's is a nautical nighttime pub complete with live entertainment. There are two bars, and frequent theme parties feature local entertainment.

✪ **Sheraton Nusa Indah.** P.O. Box 36, Nusa Dua Beach 80363, Bali. ☎ **800/325-3535,** 361-771906. Fax 361-771908. www.sheraton.com. 358 units. A/C MINIBAR TV TEL. US$195–US$240 double. AE, DC, MC, V. Free parking.

Short on character, but long on Western creature comforts, making for a most satisfying resort experience. The size is daunting—beginning with the airplane hangar–sized lobby (air-conditioned, which is rare in Bali), though a thatched pavilion bar warmed at night by candlelight helps bring it down to size, as does the attentive staff. Rooms have dark wood paneling and smooth parquet floors, with colorful local fabric on beds (which also have heavy down comforters—lush, but hardly necessary in this heat). Large marble bathrooms have a separate area for the toilet, and a sit-down shower or sunken tub. Standard rooms have a divider between the sitting area and the bedroom, while deluxe rooms are entirely open. Views are either of the garden or the pool; some rooms on higher floors have ocean views. Between the giant pool and the beach are open-air pavilions (*bales*) laid with cushions—perfect for serious all-day relaxing.

Amenities are 24-hour room service, hair dryers, safety deposit boxes, cable TV, baby-sitting, tour desk, business center, water sports, Garuda Airline office, car rental, beauty salon, boutiques, airport transfers, and welcome drink.

For dining, La Trattoria offers Italian food daily; you can have Japanese at Hamabe; Ikan, a beachfront Balinese restaurant is open for lunch and dinner; Le Bistro is open nightly for French food and live entertainment. There are also two bars and frequent theme dinners and buffets, with local entertainment.

## EXPENSIVE

**Hotel Bualu.** P.O. Box 6, Nusa Dua, Bali. ☎ **361-771310**/771311. Fax 361-771313. 50 units. A/C MINIBAR TV TEL. US$94–US$120 double. AE, DC, JCB, MC, V. Free parking.

The Hotel Bualu is what passes for a budget hotel in Nusa Dua. It was actually the first hotel to open in the resort (30 years ago), and if it's hard to live in the shadow of the mighty Hilton across the way, the marvelous, friendly staff more than make up for it. You don't get the bells and whistles of the big resorts here, but then again, you don't have to pay for them. They have their own private beach across the street, but feel free to use the beach chairs (and pools) of any of the bigger resorts as well. The rooms are fairly standard (though with a few surprising Bali touches), but bigger than you might expect, and the beds are comfortable. Additions such as a lovely children's playground, carriage rides around town, and pony rides on the beach make this good for families on a budget. Other amenities are room service until midnight, in-house movies, sundries shop, laundry, dry cleaning, concierge, tour and travel desk, baby-sitting, safety deposit box, and two swimming pools. There's also the excellent Kolak restaurant (see review below); Benoa (seafood and Continental cuisine); a bar; and live entertainment.

✪ **Novotel.** Jl. Pratama Tanjung Benoa, P.O. Box 39, Nusa Dua 80361, Bali. ☎ **361-772239.** Fax 361-772237. 192 units. A/C MINIBAR TV TEL. US$130–US$250 double. AE, DC, JCB, MC, V.

This is what a Bali hotel beach resort should be; it's the only hotel in Nusa Dua where you really feel like you're in Bali. Considerable creative thought went into the design, with sandstone, soft adobe patinas, thatched roofs, and carvings that form a unique space quite different from a generic tropical resort. It's gorgeous and very special. It's also way up at the northern end of the peninsula, removed from the rest of the tourist area—which could be an asset or a drawback. It does mean that right outside the grounds is the quite authentic fishing village of Benoa—a good trade-off, I think. The resort is on both sides of the main street—the more expensive ocean side has easier beach access, but the "garden" side is quieter. Up here, the ocean is much deeper and better for swimming. Rooms are big, bright, and airy, decorated in coconut wood and a minimalist Asian style that other hotels are beginning to copy. Better still, for the price, are the "Beach Cabanas," even bigger suites in semi-private bungalows (two per pavilion) complete with outdoor stone tubs—most of them honeymoon-worthy. The three swimming pools all have their own flair (including one with stone ledges for lounging on while stone heads spit cooling water on you), though none are very big. Amenities also include coffeemakers, hair dryers, laundry, dry cleaning, boutiques, 24-hour room service, concierge, tour desk, massage (poolside on request), baby-sitting, and airport transport. There's also a restaurant and coffee shop; three bars; and evening entertainment. Tons of activities (including aerobics, soccer, Balinese dance lessons, cooking classes, pool games, a kids' club with many goodies, and free tennis during the day) will keep you from feeling bored, but there is also a free shuttle down into Nusa Dua should you feel the need. But given that this is the best of both worlds—a terrific resort and real Bali right outside—it's hard to see that you would.

## DINING

If you've got the budget for it, you can eat very well in Nusa Dua. The problem is that most of the restaurants are in the hotels, and are priced accordingly—sky high in some cases, even by Western standards. And you are kind of trapped, particularly if the lazy days make you unwilling to stir very far. Options, should you be able to mobilize, include going to the Galleria, where there are a number of different cafes and restaurants—again, not the most bargain friendly, but better than the hotels—walking into town to find a warung, or better still, getting a ride up to Benoa, the fishing village on the north end of peninsula and eating at a warung there, where prices will be cheap and the fish fresh. Another solution is the supermarket in the Galleria, which offers cheap snacks and drinks, plus cereal and washed fruit, which could provide a budget alternative to pricey hotel breakfasts. Otherwise, here are some choices if you just don't want to stir very far.

✪ **Kolak Restaurant.** Hotel Bualu. ☎ **361-771310**/771311. Reservations suggested. Main courses Rp16,000–Rp38,000. AE, DC, JCB, MC, V. Daily 10am–11pm. INDONESIAN.

This is one hotel restaurant that is quite reasonable, and quite tasty. Located in the Hotel Bualu, the oldest hotel in Nusa Dua, Kolak offers authentic (in an upper middle–class way) Indonesian food, in little pavilions containing just four tables each, set around the swimming pool. Try the Rijstaffel, a sort of Indonesian sampler platter (Rp45,000 per person, with a two-person minimum). On a recent visit, it featured tahu telor (Indonesian omelet), empel pedas (fried beef in spicy sauce), pepes ikan (fish in banana leaves), bakewan tague (fishball soup), sate, dere udang (shrimp curry), gado gado, and a lot more. (No, I couldn't finish it all.) Most of it was spicy and all of it flavorful, except for the watered-down shrimp curry. Bigger appetites could try the Seafood Parade (Rp150,000), a platter of grilled whole fish, prawns, squid, lobster with veggies, fried rice, and mixed salad—two people could easily share without going hungry. They also offer an American breakfast for under US$4—considerably cheaper than at the other hotels.

**Matsuri Japanese.** Galleria, Nusa Dua, Bali. ☎ **361-772267.** Reservations suggested. Set meals US$10–US$17. AE, DC, JCB, MC, V. Daily 11am–11pm. JAPANESE.

Not the cheapest choice among the many cafes and such in the Galleria, but better than average Japanese food nonetheless. The set meals are quite large (the entree comes with appetizer, veggies, rice, miso soup, steamed egg with shrimp and chicken, pickles, and dessert) and two people could easily make a meal out of one, particularly if you throw in some sushi. (A 12-piece tuna roll, featuring butter-soft fish in larger portions than in the U.S., was US$3.) Try the ginger fried pork, thin strips of meat that look suspiciously like bacon (but taste nothing like it). It was delicious.

✪ **Semeru Rotisserie.** Putu Bali Hotel. ☎ **361-771020.** Reservations suggested. Main courses US$6.25–US$14. AE, MC, V. Daily 6–11pm. FRENCH.

This excellent French-influenced place is cheap for a gourmet hotel restaurant. Everything is beautifully presented and the staff is beautifully attentive. Veggies and dip are brought out to start, and if you have a starter (try the fresh asparagus with your choice of sauce), coconut sherbet follows to cleanse your palate. Lamb chops with fresh herbs were tender and juicy; pan-fried prawns in a turmeric sauce were plump and rich. Skip the disappointing cheese plate as you try the otherwise exquisite desserts, and leave room for the chocolate bonbons they serve as a finale.

## OUTDOOR ACTIVITIES & WATER SPORTS

The surf and swim situation here is the opposite of Kuta's. The surf is a considerable distance offshore, making swimming in the clear blue-green water most pleasant. At high tide, that is; it's not very deep to begin with, and at low tide the water can recede so much you can practically walk out to where the surf ought to be. This makes for interesting shell-gathering, at least. Jet skiing and windsurfing are also popular, but

## Tours

To find a travel agent or guide, try either the busy **Tunas Indonesian Tours & Travel** at Jl. D. Tamblingan 107 (☎ **361-288056**); or **Santa Bali Tours and Travel** at the Grand Bali Hotel (☎ **361-287628**).

dive excursions, all arranged by the hotels, will probably take you to areas closer to Sanur, or to Amed and Tambulen in the northeast.

Golf enthusiasts will be thrilled with the 18-hole championship course at the **Bali Golf and Country Club** (☎ **361-771791**). Covering 3 acres in the loveliest of settings across the street from the Galleria and the Hyatt, it looks like golf nirvana to these eyes. You'll pay for it though: greens fees are US$125.

## SHOPPING

You can get all the same goods as in Kuta (endless sarongs and the like) in the village of **Bualu.** Not far past the gates dividing the resort from the village are several collections of outdoor stalls, with somewhat less persistent salespeople than in Kuta, and cheaper goods.

Meanwhile, the **Galleria** gives you both Western-style shopping—in an outdoor mall that wouldn't look out of place in Palm Springs—and the ability to buy local crafts without hassle and bargaining. There is a Keris Department Store, foreign name brands like Versace and Benetton, and an American Express office. There's also a supermarket that stocks dry goods and many snack-worthy items.

## NUSA DUA AFTER DARK

Nightlife is strictly confined to the hotels, all of which offer bars and lounges—usually with some kind of music at night—and frequent Balinese dance and music programs, though these usually come as part of a costly buffet dinner package. (These are usually open-air, and you can get a partially obstructed but free show if you lurk around the edges.)

## 6 Sanur

Sanur is probably the perfect compromise between hectic, maddening Kuta and sterile Nusa Dua. It's not terribly threatening to the first-time Bali visitor, who may still be looking more for beach fun than anything else, but real life is still plenty in evidence here. It's also a manageable size, with Kuta-type shops, of slightly better quality and slightly less aggressive hustle, on the main streets. The beach is very nice, with better swimming than in Kuta and a paved walkway for promenading (though somewhat aggressive touts show up here, as do beggars, which is unusual for Bali).

### GETTING THERE

Many hotels offer airport pickup, and there are regular shuttles from Kuta and all other major tourist areas, as well as fixed-price priced cab rides from the airport. Bemos go from Denpasar's Tegal Station.

### GETTING AROUND

More than likely, your feet will handle most of your in-Sanur travel, either on the main roads or along the mostly paved beach walkway. **Bemos** do run up and down the main streets, and there are also metered taxis.

# Fast Facts: Sanur

**Banks/Currency Exchange**    Money changers are found along the streets of Sanur—be careful to double-check their math using their calculators and double-count the money they give you. There is an American Express office in the Grand Bali Beach Hotel.

**Internet/E-mail**    Santai Homestay on Jalan D. Tamblingan offers Internet access, in addition to accommodations and a bookstore.

**Telephone**    The area code in Sanur is 361.

## ACCOMMODATIONS

With the exception of the losmen, all the following are beach locations, generally set back quite a distance from the street (sometimes involving a spooky walk down a darkish lane at night).

### VERY EXPENSIVE

**Bali Hyatt.** Jl. Danau Tamblingan, Sanur, P.O. Box 392, Bali. ☎ **361-281234**. Fax 361-287693. www.hyatt.com. E-mail: bhyatt@dps.mega.net.id. 400 units. A/C MINIBAR TV TEL. US$170–US$225 double. Suites US$350 and up. AE, DC, JCB, MC, V. Free parking.

A massive property a short walk from the center of Sanur, this is high living, Western-style. The buildings date back to 1973 and show their age, as does, to a lesser extent, the inside decor. I like the bits of local crafts that show up in the bedrooms, but the marble bathrooms, with pretty fixtures, are much more interesting. Better are the more expensive Regency Club rooms, with Bali tile and wood, terraces with fans, complimentary breakfast, all-day coffee, evening cocktails, and newspapers. Even if it's not as innovative or fanciful as some newer offerings by other chains, the name brand is secure, and it might work well for families thanks to all the modern activities. The quite extensive though perhaps over-manicured grounds could be fun to get lost in, with two pools, including a large one with waterfalls, bridges, and other bits of interest. They have security on their beach, and a shuttle that goes to their property in Nusa Dua every 2 hours. Other amenities are 24-hour room service, safety deposit box, airport pickup, in-house doctor, baby-sitting, laundry, valet, tour and travel desks, shopping arcade, beauty salon, bank, post office, packing service, Jacuzzi, two tennis courts, volleyball court, water sports, jogging track, and children's activity center. A fancy new spa offers body treatments and massage.

For dining, Cupak Bistro and Wantilan Cafe offer different levels of Indonesian and Western cuisine; you can have Italian at Pizza Ria, Chinese at Telega Naga, and grilled specialties at Omang-Omang. There are three bars, including a piano bar and an espresso stop with live entertainment.

✪ **Tandjung Sari.** Jl. Danau Tamblingan no. 41, Sanur, Denpasar 80228, Bali. ☎ **361-288441**. Fax 361-287930. www.baliparadise.com/tandjungsairhotel. E-mail: tansri@dps.mega.net.id. 26 units. A/C MINIBAR TEL. US$160–US$275 double. Free parking.

Essentially the first boutique hotel in Bali, the Tandjung Sari opened in 1962 and was rewarded by a mention from Anaïs Nin in her diaries (as if there was anything she didn't write about in her diaries) who raved about the place's special, almost spiritual qualities. It's still a marvelous location, and from the walls out I wouldn't change a thing; it's a rabbit's warren of secret nooks and crannies, with stone statues, ponds, flowers, and surprises at every turn. But truth be told, the rooms—which are all in private, large and larger-sized thatched-roof bungalows, could use a quick face-lift to bring them up to date. All are constructed the traditional Balinese way, most with

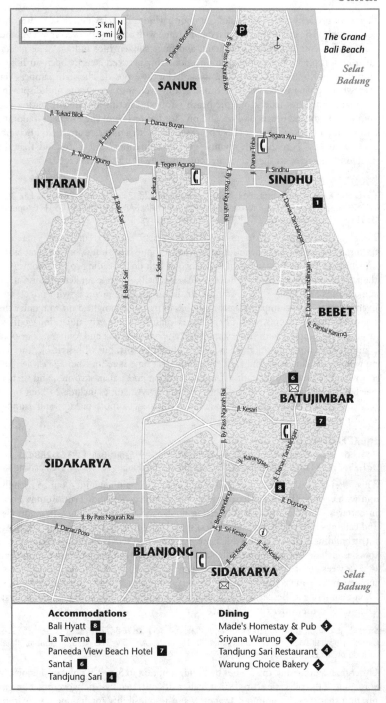

# Sanur

**The Grand Bali Beach**

*Selat Badung*

SANUR

INTARAN

SINDHU

BEBET

BATUJIMBAR

SIDAKARYA

BLANJONG

SIDAKARYA

*Selat Badung*

Jl. Danau Beratan
Jl. By Pass Ngurah Rai
Jl. Tukad Bilok
Jl. Danau Buyan
Jl. Segara Ayu
Jl. Intaran
Jl. Danau Toba
Jl. Sindhu
Jl. Tegen Agung
Jl. Tegen Agung
Jl. Sekura
Jl. Bali Sari
Jl. By Pass Ngurah Rai
Jl. Danau Tamblingan
Jl. Sekura
Jl. Bali Sari
Jl. Danau Tamblingan
Jl. Pantai Karang
Jl. Kesari
Jl. By Pass Ngurah Rai
Jl. Danau Tamblingan
Jl. Karangsari
Jl. Duyung
Jl. By Pass Ngurah Rai
Jl. Bengandang
Jl. Danau Poso
Jl. Sri Kesari
Jl. Sri Kesari
Jl. Sri Kesari

**Accommodations**
Bali Hyatt **8**
La Taverna **1**
Paneeda View Beach Hotel **7**
Santai **6**
Tandjung Sari **4**

**Dining**
Made's Homestay & Pub **3**
Sriyana Warung **2**
Tandjung Sari Restaurant **4**
Warung Choice Bakery **5**

their own private gardens and bales (outdoor pavilions for relaxing). Still, they're very comfortable. The bathrooms are just dandy, some with outdoor showers in yet another mini-garden complete with a fountain, and huge sunken tubs indoors. The rectangular pool is pretty, but sandwiched uncomfortably between a cushy open-air library and the very fine restaurant, so swimmers feel a bit exposed. The staff pampers you everywhere, giving you a welcome drink, settling you into your room and displaying the many amenities (check out the beach sarongs), offering turndown, getting you comfortable on the beach, and on and on. See the review of the excellent Tandjung Sari restaurant below. There is also a beachside bar with a nice cafe attached. I may not agree with Ms. Nin that the rooms "give off vibrations" but I do find that the Tangjung Sari remains the refuge she found it to be nearly 30 years ago.

## MODERATE

✪ **Hotel La Taverna.** P.O. Box 3040, Denpasar 80228, Bali. ☎ **361-288497.** Fax 361-287126. asiatravel.com/La Taverna. 34 units. A/C MINIBAR TEL. US$80–US$110 double; US$150–US$200 suites. AE, DC, JCB, MC, V. Free parking.

No bland European hotel room decor or apartment complex landscaping here. All rooms are full of exquisite details: carved wood antique furnishings, batik or ikat fabric on windows and beds, traditional carved wood Bali doors leading to bathrooms (but the tall should be warned—these doors are very small), separate sunken dressing areas, sunken tubs and so on. The rooms are small though (size increases with price), and in some cases a bit cramped. Claustrophobes in particular might want to request the ones with thatched roofs, which have higher ceilings. The pretty, quiet, foliage-filled grounds are complete with stone statues and a babbling brook and fountain. The pool is next to, but not right on, the beach. Not a luxury resort, but with style like this, it's no wonder the American ambassador to Indonesia stays here (in Room 31) when he's in town. The Beach Restaurant offers fresh seafood and Italian favorites, and there is one bar. Movies are shown in the lobby every night. Amenities include 24-hour room service, hair dryers, massage, baby-sitter, newspapers, airport pickup, and laundry service.

## INEXPENSIVE

**Peneeda View Beach Hotel.** Jl. Danu Tamblingan no. 89, Sanur, Bali. ☎ **361-288425.** Fax 361-286224. 44 units. A/C MINIBAR TEL. US$55–US$60 double. AE, MC, V. Free parking.

This hotel is a little worn at the edges, and lacking certain amenities, but so friendly, and with enough Bali/Asian flavor to lift it out of the generic hotel rut. Rooms are all in cottages—two rooms with connecting doors, with basic tile floors. Bali antiques and carvings help make them a little less spare than losmen. The two pools are apartment-building style, set amidst adequate gardens, and there is a private beach. Special touches include free afternoon coffee and tea poolside or in the lobby, free snorkeling once a week, four free mountain bikes (first come, first served), evening laser disc movies and live music, and an on-site bakery. Dine all day with an ocean view at the Nusa Lemobongan Beachside Restaurant, or have lunch at the Peneeda Poolside bar. Occasionally, they offer cultural dance evenings.

**Santai.** Jl. Danua Tamblingan 148, Sanur, Bali. ☎ **361-281684**/281685. Fax 361-287314. E-mail: pplhbali@denpasar.wasantara.net.id. 18 units. A/C TV TEL. US$27 double. Rates include breakfast. MC, V. Free parking.

Other than a homestay, this is your best budget option in Sanur, if only for the socially conscious, '60s collective attitude that fuels it. It's operated by a nongovernment organization that seeks to promote awareness and responsibility for Indonesia's environment. Homestay-style rooms are simple without being dreary, well maintained in a two-story building around a small pool, with low-end baths. Services include a health food restaurant, a combination Internet cafe and bookstore/library, a gift shop, a swimming pool, and conference room and business facilities—all of which give it facilities far above losmen.

## LOSMEN

**Made's Home Stay.** Jl. Danua Tamblingan 74 (across the street from La Taverna), Sanur, Bali. ☎ **361-288152.** Fax 361-288152. 15 units. A/C. US$20–US$25 double. Rates include breakfast. No credit cards.

A little pricey for something that bills itself as a "homestay," but it's very clean, all rooms have tubs, and there is a small pool. That, the attached pub, and the air conditioning may make the rate increase worth it. Carved wooden doors bright with red and gilt paint lead to rooms that have cute attempts at frilly bedclothes and the like—totally out of place, but charming.

## DINING

Dining in Sanur is, by and large, a dull proposition, with most of the non-hotel options consisting of generic tourist-oriented establishments offering bland fish and warung-typical dishes. (Such places are marked by their use of bamboo furniture and checked tablecloths.) There are a few decent options near the tourist path, and these are listed below.

✪ **Sriyana Warung.** Jl. D Tamblingan 70, Sanur 287792. Reservations not required. Main courses Rp6,500–Rp12,000 (*babi guleng* Rp40,000 for 2.) No credit cards. Daily 8am–"late." INDONESIAN.

Though it looks like one of the aforementioned tourist traps, I had several delightful (and one outstanding) meals here. This is precisely the kind of budget place to try out authentic Indonesian food, particularly if you are wary of the genuine roadside stand. The nasi goreng is served in generous portions, topped with chicken satay and a fried egg, and with a side of ayam goreng, for only Rp6,500. The nonalcoholic drinks were also quite good (one combo featured pineapple, orange, papaya, lemon, grenadine, and lemonade). And they offer good, reasonably priced American breakfasts. But best of all is the babi guleng feast: one suckling pig reduced to an enormous platter of spicy roast pig, fatty sausages, various deep-fried bits, soup, and more (including some vegetables for good measure). It was fiendishly good, and at that price sinfully cheap. Don't miss it.

✪ **Tandjung Sari Restaurant.** Jl. Danau Tamblingan no. 41 (in Tandjung Sari Hotel), Bali. ☎ **361-288441.** Reservations suggested. Main courses Rp22,000–Rp98,500. AE, MC, V. Daily 7pm–1am. INDONESIAN.

Generally, prominent hotel restaurants can be relied on for adequate food catering to the tastes of timid tourists and for higher-than-average prices. The excellent restaurant at the Tandjung Sari is an exception. It's open air, not too big, and you dine by the shimmering pool with the nearby waves crashing in your ears. The small menu doesn't look like much, but the portions are good-sized and quite tasty. I love the pork sate, which arrives on a small grill—simple, but perfectly cooked and with a lovely flavor—and the bebek betutu, a spicy duck, Bali-style, which should make your mouth very happy.

**Warung Choice Bakery.** Jl. D Tamblingan, Sanur. Main courses Rp6,500–Rp19,000. No credit cards. Daily 7am–10pm.

An example of the many rather ordinary warungs, though this one does have a bakery some have found worthy of note. The food sounded fine on the menu—Thai shrimp pumpkin in coconut and fresh basil cooked in coconut cream sauce, Angsohi fish with sweet and sour sauce, sautéed shrimp and veggies. It wasn't bad, just bland. Better was the fresh honeydew juice. If you haven't had good Bali food, you'd probably find it delicious, and so in that sense, this might not be a bad place to start.

## OUTDOOR ACTIVITIES & WATER SPORTS

Water sports are big in Sanur; most of the island's dive shops are based here. That's curious, as the local diving and snorkeling isn't all that good—experienced divers will probably end up taking day trips with dive masters to other locales. Snorkeling is either at a reef about a kilometer out to sea from the Bali Hyatt (you can wade out there at low tide), or a little farther offshore. But currents can often be strong, making the experience unpleasant and reducing visibility. Not that it matters, as neither the coral nor the fish are that extraordinary. Sanur is a decent place to dive for inexperienced divers or those looking to brush up on their skills, but soon you will probably want to try other options. Glass-bottom boat rides are also popular, as is a certain amount of sailing. Most hotels will hook you up with dive masters, or you can go directly to the operators (as some hotels do) such as **Bali Dive** on Sanur Beach (☎ 361-286520), though I found them a little disorganized, and their snorkeling equipment not in the best of shape (all the masks I used leaked).

Ocean swimming is a mixed bag; the water can be slightly rough at high tide, and too silty and shallow at low. Still, waves are usually nonexistent right at shore, so dipping at any time is possible. Surfing happens off shore, with inconsistent reefs 0.62 to 1.24 miles (1–3km) out in front of the Bali Hyatt and the Grand Bali Hotel.

Golfers may enjoy the easy nine-hole course at the **Grand Bali Beach Hotel** (☎ 361-288511, ext. 1388).

## SHOPPING ·

There are plenty of opportunities for bargaining here, with wares that land squarely between what's found in Kuta and the somewhat better merchandise of Ubud. You'll find shops along the Jalan Danau Tamblingan, and a market with many stalls just off the northern end of the beach (on the left after the giant lobster). The level of hucksterism can be just as annoying as in Kuta—be prepared to be virtually physically pulled into a stall—but there are somewhat fewer sellers and so the pressure feels slightly less intense. There is also an art market at the southeast corner of Jalan Pantai Sindu and Bypass Nigruah Rai. You might also check out the beautiful ikat and handwoven fabrics at **Nogo,** Jalan Danau Tamblingan 208 (☎ 361-28832).

## SANUR AFTER DARK

If your interpretation of nightlife is serious partying, drinking, and late hours, you are better off heading over to Kuta for the evening. The local hotels have bars, some of which can be interesting scenes, particularly the beachfront one at the **Tandjung Sari.** They also have regular Balinese entertainment, generally packaged as a show and dinner buffet, but the quality of these is better in Ubud, or even Kuta. There are some local hangouts along the main street, including **Mem'ries Musik Bar.** This is a rollicking place, with movies at 6:30 every night, and a live band afterwards. Consider also **Made's Pub,** located farther down the main street (see "Made's Home Stay," above).

## 7 Ubud

People tend to get all misty and/or mystical when talking about Ubud; this is both justified and not. The setting (lush and gorgeous, thanks to the rivers that cut through the region) and the vibe (mellower by far than Kuta or other beach communities) make it a natural attraction to arty types and New Age seekers. As with any such destination, though, it's prone to hype, shams, and zealots. Don't let that daunt you, though. It's easily sidestepped, leaving this charmed community an almost-certain highlight of any Bali trip, and a hard place to leave.

Don't expect to leave the tourist crowds behind when you come here—as I say, the place is hardly a secret—but they do seem less overwhelming. Even though it's as dependent on tourism as Kuta, and far from a typical Bali village, you still get a sense of a real town, with real life going on around you. And Ubud is surrounded by smaller villages, which become less and less tourist-oriented the farther you go.

Ubud is nestled among deep green gorges of jaw-dropping beauty. It is the richest region in Bali for art production, which is possibly why so many expat artists have made their homes here. The locals' commitment to spiritual life continues, and there always seems to be some ceremony or other going on. Ubud is also the closest thing going to a central Bali location; just about everything you might want to see is an easy day (or even half-day) trip from here, which makes it a good jumping-off point. About the only thing it doesn't have is a beach, but again, you can easily day-trip to Nusa Dua, Sanur, Candi Dasa, or Jimbaran for that. Consequently, unless you are a die-hard beach-goer, I think Ubud is the perfect base for the bulk of your trip.

Tourist exploitation does pop up first thing, however. The main roads of Ubud are lined with shops full of gewgaws. You will be accosted by countless young men urging you to buy tickets for that evening's dance performance, or asking the perennial question "Transport? Transport?". Mangy, bad-tempered dogs roam the streets.

But all this soon fades to a background white noise, as you begin to peel back that first layer and discover the real Balinese below it. The energy level is invigorating and inspiring, not draining and off-putting like it is in Kuta. Amidst all the tourist junk for sale you will find some high quality trinkets, or even real treasures. The food is some of the finest on the island. And the sheer beauty of the place—well, pretty soon you will understand why so many non-Balinese have come here for a visit and never left.

## GETTING THERE

Many hotels in the area offer hotel pickup, and taxis will come here from the airport. Bemos drop you in the center of town, while the tourist shuttles have their own stops, usually on one of the two main drags.

## GETTING AROUND

The sound that will be ringing in your ears and haunting your dreams for many days to come is, "Transport? Transport? Yes? Transport? Tomorrow? Yes?" This is the unending mantra of hopeful young men with **minivans,** ready to be hired by the trip, the hour, the day, or even the week. You don't really need them within the town. Ubud is small enough that **walking** is the preferred method of transportation, though admittedly there can be a fair amount of ground to cover. What's more, they'll overcharge you horribly for short distances. Use them only to get to sights outside of town. Hotels away from the main action generally provide regular **shuttles** into town. If you are staying at a losmen or other low-budget hotel without a shuttle, you can always grab a **bemo** (making sure not to get ripped off there either), or perhaps **rent a motorbike** if you're an experienced enough rider.

The layout of Ubud is slightly more complicated than the more or less one-road beach communities you may have encountered prior to coming here. The main street is the Jalan Raya, which runs east-west. Perpendicular to it is Monkey Forest Road, which runs north-south and does indeed end in a monkey forest. Parallel to Monkey Forest Road, to the east, is Jalan Hanoman. Intersecting these two roads, by the landmark football field, is Jalan Dewi Shinta. As Jalan Raya goes west, it crosses the

# Ubud

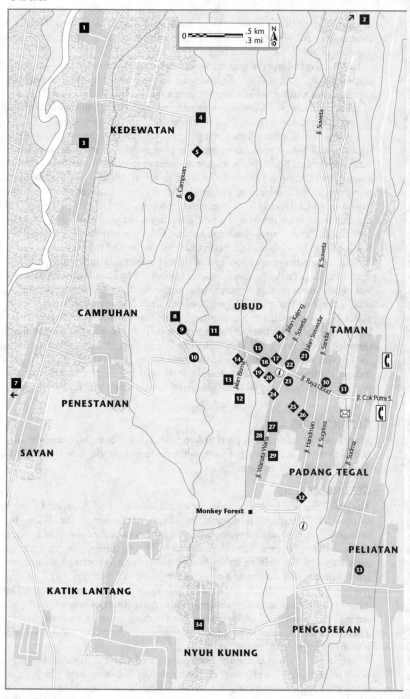

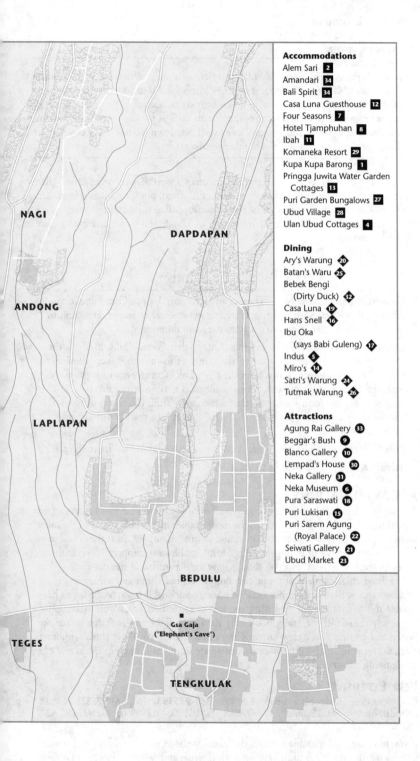

**Accommodations**
Alem Sari **2**
Amandari **34**
Bali Spirit **34**
Casa Luna Guesthouse **12**
Four Seasons **7**
Hotel Tjamphuhan **8**
Ibah **11**
Komaneka Resort **29**
Kupa Kupa Barong **1**
Pringga Juwita Water Garden
    Cottages **13**
Puri Garden Bungalows **27**
Ubud Village **28**
Ulan Ubud Cottages **4**

**Dining**
Ary's Warung **20**
Batan's Waru **25**
Bebek Bengi
    (Dirty Duck) **32**
Casa Luna **19**
Hans Snell **16**
Ibu Oka
    (says Babi Guleng) **17**
Indus **5**
Miro's **14**
Satri's Warung **24**
Tutmak Warung **26**

**Attractions**
Agung Rai Gallery **33**
Beggar's Bush **9**
Blanco Gallery **10**
Lempad's House **30**
Neka Gallery **31**
Neka Museum **6**
Pura Saraswati **18**
Puri Lukisan **15**
Puri Sarem Agung
    (Royal Palace) **22**
Seiwati Gallery **21**
Ubud Market **23**

NAGI

DAPDAPAN

ANDONG

LAPLAPAN

BEDULU

Gsa Gaja
("Elephant's Cave")

TEGES

TENGKULAK

---

**Tourist Info**

---

**Jalan Raya,** on the south side of the street, near the intersection with Monkey Forest Road (☎ 361-973285), is not the most helpful tourism office ever, but certainly friendly and a good place to go for touristy facts, such as times and places of dance programs, or to sign up for other events such as packages to see cremations, shuttles, and so forth. Tourist agencies exist all over town, each offering competitive prices for day trips and shuttles to other tourist areas.

---

Campuhan gorge, takes a hard right and becomes a north-south street called Jalan Raya Campuhan (this area is no longer technically Ubud, but Campuhan). It all runs together—indeed, the boundaries of several nearby villages, including Sayan, where the Four Seasons is located, meld into those of Ubud, and you won't even notice you've left town.

# Fast Facts: Ubud

**Banks/Currency Exchange**    There is an ATM next door to Casa Luna restaurant on Jalan Raya. Money changers are everywhere, and exchange rates seem to get better the farther away you get from the main intersection.

**Internet/E-mail**    The Roda Internet Cafe (Jalan Bisma) bills itself as the "Internet in a rice paddy." Closer to the center of town is the Jineng Business Center (Jalan Hanoman, across from the Dirty Duck), open 8am to 10pm daily, with the most computers and fastest modems. Or try a true cafe, Bali 3000 Internet Cafe, on Jalan Raya, past the market, away from the center of town. It has five computers that always seem to be full, but at least you can sip something while you wait.

**Post Office/Mail**    The post office is on the main road, but very far to the east.

**Telephone**    The area code in Ubud is 361.

## ACCOMMODATIONS

The sheer volume and variety of hotels in Ubud is amazing; here you really do find everything, from the top of the top to the most simple and humble. Some of the most interesting and lavish hotels in Bali are found in this region, but don't think you have to stay in one to have an indulgent time. Most Ubud losmen proprietors pride themselves on their breakfasts, and you should leave feeling stuffed in the morning.

I've listed an assortment of properties, both in central Ubud and some ways away. In most cases, the latter are either a calorie burning but doable walk, or the hotels have reliable shuttles into town. And what you lose in immediate access you make up for in scenery. Those in the know book only their first night and look for someplace better, and cheaper, once they arrive. There's little chance you'll get stuck without a place to rest your head—if nothing else, there are countless losmen in Ubud and the surrounding villages.

### VERY EXPENSIVE

✪ **Amandari.** Kedewatan, Ubud, Bali. ☎ **361-975333.** Fax 361-975335. E-mail: amandari@indosat.net. 29 units. A/C MINIBAR TEL. US$500–US$900 double. AE, DC, JCB, MC, V. Free parking.

If you have ample disposable income, this exquisite hotel is an excellent place to part with it. It's also the place to rub elbows with the rich and famous for whom nothing but the Amandari, and its pampering, will do. (Mick Jagger and Jerry Hall got married here). Laid out like the world's fanciest Balinese village, the rooms are all huge thatched stone cottage suites, full of delicate Balinese luxuries, each enclosed in its own walled compound. Some are two-story, and have their own private pool. Bathrooms are similarly generously sized, with many fluffy towels, a large shower inside and a tub outdoors. And the service—well, let's say you get what you pay for. It's all set on an eye-popping gorge, though the view is not as spectacular as the one over at the Kupa Kupa Barong hotel. However, its famous emerald green horizon pool (the water spills over the far edge), which mimics the exact color of the gorge, is marvelously engineered to blend seamlessly with the green beyond—it's the best pool in Ubud. And they even love children! Other amenities are hair dryers, CD player, cordless telephones, turndown, tennis court, gym, beauty salon, laundry, tour desk, 24-hour room service, newspapers, massage, complimentary baby-sitting, courtesy car, water sports, trekking, an excellent library, and shops. The one terrific restaurant has a bar and serves local and European favorites. There is a free shuttle to Ubud (the hotel is about a 15-minute drive away), but it's hard to imagine wanting to leave very often. If you can't afford to stay here, don't feel bad—neither can I. But let's meet up for lunch at the restaurant and admire that pool, okay?

✪ **Four Seasons Resort at Sayan.** Sayan, Ubud, Gianyar Bali 80571. ☎ **361-977577.** Fax 361-977588. www.fourseasons.com. 46 units. A/C MINIBAR TV TEL. Suites US$375–US$425; villas US$525 and up. AE, DC, MC, V.

This recently opened Four Seasons is an architectural wonder, a masterpiece of planning that takes full advantage of its extraordinary setting right on the River Ayung. It's incredibly posh, of course, though not intimidatingly so. To enter, you cross a long bridge leading into a pond that appears to rest in a bowl formed by its green surroundings, thus evoking the volcanic crater lakes found elsewhere on the island. You then descend a staircase and learn that, improbably, this pond rests on top of the lobby and the rest of the hotel. From here on out, the design is ultra-modern, yet not at the expense of Bali style. Rooms are either in two-story suites (bedroom below the sitting area), deluxe suites that are somehow even fancier, and high-end villas with private plunge pools. All the interiors are done in gleaming woods and natural fabrics and are full of precious local art and artifacts. Expect luxurious bathrooms (two to every suite/villa) with huge tubs, showers and dressing areas, and more thick towels than a linen shop. Every room has views of the deep green gorge and/or the river. The bi-level horizon pool (not as big as you might expect) follows the serpentine shape of the river, which you can also walk down to and dangle your feet in (it's a bit too rough to swim in). Pampering, of course, is at a maximum, and includes "seamless" transfer between here and the resort at Jimbaran Bay; they take care of everything, including, if you wish, your packing. Other amenities are 24-hour room service; hair dryers; safes; CD players; laundry; turndown; small, elegant library (with books and CDs); superior health club with three different temperature spas that overlook the river; massage and spa treatments; gift shop; meeting facilities; and tour desk.

There is a regular shuttle to Ubud, which is only about 10 minutes away, but as of this writing the last shuttle is at 3pm (this may change), which sort of strands you at the hotel, where the food is excellent, but expensive. There are two restaurants, the more formal Agung Terrace, and the more casual poolside Riverside Cafe, both of which serve nouvelle versions of Asian and Western favorites. There are also two bars. The hotel has regular weekly free entertainment, featuring local musicians and dancers—these serve as superior samplers of Balinese dance. If you are actually on a budget—which is hard to believe if you are staying here—or just want to have some local Sayan flavor, turn left immediately outside the hotel gates and walk down the street about five minutes to Cafe Sayan, at the Tamen Bebek homestay. It's a solidly good cafe where I had some terrific nasi goreng and mie goreng. I should note that the building of this hotel caused some controversy, as it took over a sacred bathing place for the local people. On the other hand, it also employs many people from the village of Sayan who would have had to move elsewhere for employment.

**Ibah.** Campuhan, Ubud, P.O. Box 193, Bali. ☎ **361-974466.** Fax 361-974467. www. bali-paradise.com. E-mail: ibah@denpasar.wasantara.net.id. 11 units. A/C TV TEL. US$215–US$275 double; US$385 and US$450 villas. AE, DC, JCB, MC, V. Free parking.

A fairly new resort on the tail edges of the main Ubud action, this is probably the most romantic hotel you'll find this close to town. It's a special combination of Indonesian style and Western comforts. The very big rooms have spare, clean lines that employ lots of wood and natural fabrics, including a four-poster canopy bed hung with mosquito netting. Good-sized bathrooms have either outdoor or wood floor showers. All rooms have spacious verandas or patios—you pay extra for a view of thatched roofs, trees and hills, but it might be worth it. One deluxe room has a tricky spiral staircase, while the Rose suite has a glimpse into the neighboring Gardenia suite bathroom (shouldn't reveal anything too intimate, but still). The grounds make good use of the hilly land, with all kinds of secret nooks and crannies, including a roughly heart-shaped swimming pool with two alcoves built into the walls next to it for cozy poolside tête à têtes. (The drawback is all the steep, potentially slippery stairs.) Spa and massage is in a lush wood and muslin-draped room, and there is a particularly sexy indoor Jacuzzi that turns the sacred into the profane by evoking a temple bath. Other amenities are 24-hour room service, saltwater swimming pool, laundry, CD players, turndown, art gallery, gift shop, free Ubud shuttle, complimentary afternoon tea, private tour guide, airport pickup, newspapers, massage, and baby-sitting. There is one restaurant and one bar.

**✪ Kupa Kupa Barong.** Kedewatan, Ubud, Bali. ☎ **361-975478.** Fax 361-975079. www. bali-paradise.com. E-mail: kupukupubarong@bali-paradise.com. 19 units. A/C MINIBAR TEL. US$335–US$405 double; US$699 suite. AE, DC, MC, V. Free parking.

The major selling point here is the view—so breathtaking it's hard to tear yourself away. The hotel is set on a deep green gorge with a river rushing far below, palm trees rising above rice fields—with a million dollar view like that, expensive rooms almost seem like a bargain. (Truth be told, some rooms have better views than others, but even the least impressive are extraordinary.) Deluxe bungalows are arranged in a straight line (bed, tub, sitting area), while everything in two-story luxury bungalows directly faces the windows, the better to take advantage of the main attraction. Wherever you end up will be comfortable and spacious, and you'll find yourself doing everything without looking down, so riveted will you be by the windows. The decor is plain—after all, what could compete?—but aesthetically pleasing. Bathrooms are in pieces—tub here, sink there, closet way over there—and this gives even more room, but not much counter space. Amenities include hair dryers, room service (until 10:30pm), turndown, massage, laundry, spa, boutique, and gallery. The two small pools are refreshing, but oddly they're the only areas that don't overlook the view. The long distance into town is minimized by free, reliable shuttle service every hour until 11pm. Guests with disabilities should request rooms near the entrance to avoid the many stairs. There's a highly praised restaurant, and one bar.

## EXPENSIVE

**Bali Spirit Hotel and Spa.** P.O. Box 189, Nyuh Kuning Village, Ubud 80571, Bali. ☎ **361-974013.** Fax 361-974012. www.bali-paradise.com/balispirit. E-mail: balispirit@denpasar.

wasnatari.net.id. 19 units. A/C TEL. US$95–US$135 double. Villas US$145 double. Rates include breakfast. AE, MC, V. Free parking.

Located considerably south of the main section of Ubud, this is a relatively reasonable alternative to the really high-end luxury hotels like the Amandari and Kupa Kupa Barong, largely thanks to the hillside setting overlooking a river gorge. The rooms are not as luxurious, but you wouldn't know that unless you compared them in person. As it is, they are comfortable, well-appointed and bigger than average, some with thatched roofs and Bali fabrics. The pool is a decent size, and there are traditional Balinese bathing pools in the holy river. There's a fine spa with a full range of services. That and the free chauffeured car to take you wherever you want to go "at a moment's notice" makes this a plenty pampering experience. Other amenities are hair dryers (available), safe deposit boxes, complimentary Ubud shuttle, airport transfers, babysitting and "youth escort," room service, laundry, dry cleaning, arrangements for all sorts of local activities and excursions, and gift shop. A two-level restaurant serves Western and Indonesian food. The pool bar is open 24 hours.

✪ **Komaneka Resort.** Monkey Forest Rd. ☎ **361-976090.** Fax 361-977140. E-mail: Komaneka@indosat.net.id. 17 units. A/C MINIBAR TEL. US$120–US$150 double. AE, DC, JCB, MC, V. Free parking.

This brand-new property is right on Monkey Forest Road, clean, modern, but still locally stylish, and the only one at this level in central Ubud. It's meant to be a modern luxury hotel, Bali style, but unlike other attempts, this doesn't look like suburban condos. Occupying a long, narrow space (flat and with downstairs rooms, which might make this a better choice for guests with disabilities), ending in a rectangular pool, guests are well away from street noise, with views of gardens and rice paddies. The rooms are done in natural woods and fabrics, and the beds are hung with cheese-cloth-like netting suspended from the ceiling. Deluxe rooms have deconstructed bathrooms that lack real walls but are still arranged for privacy. Suites are bigger and have cushioned window seats, with well-stocked bathrooms featuring big marble baths and showers with wood floors. Villas with private pool are being constructed. Services include 24-hour room service, laundry, dry cleaning, airport pickup, massage, shipping, and a small library.

## MODERATE

✪ **Alem Sari.** Keliki, Tromoi Pos 03, Kantor Pos Tegallalang, Gianyar 80561, Bali. ☎/fax **361-240308.** www.alamsari.com. E-mail: alamsari@indo.net.id. 10 units. A/C MINIBAR TEL. US$80 double; US$90 suite; US$150 family unit. AE, DC, JCB, MC, V. Free parking.

This is the very model of what a modern Bali hotel should be; its combination of comfort, social responsibility, setting, and price set a standard I sincerely hope other hotels will follow. Everything the Alem Sari does is with thought towards local economy, ecology, and culture. So all room furnishings, from wood furniture to brightly dyed fabrics, are entirely Indonesian made. (Try to get the room with the marvelous antique wood canopy bed.) They use solar heating and recycled paper, and waste disposal is done with a minimum of environmental impact. The only music you hear is live. They employ a large number of villagers from neighboring Keliki (known for its miniature painting), sell local wares in the hotel shop, and encourage guests to go into the village to view life there—a terrific change from the usual resort ivory tower. Not only are the rooms quite pretty, but there is a gorge view, complete with looming volcano, nearly as good as the one found at Kupa Kupa Barong, at a fraction of the price. (Admittedly, this one has a road cutting through it, and traffic noise intrudes.) The seclusion and opportunity for interaction with village life makes up for the 20-plus minute drive into Ubud. This remoteness does mean relying on the hotel for all services—they charge for transport to and from Ubud, but are fast and reliable. Cost-conscious guests might want to fill their room fridge with snacks and breakfast items.

There's an excellent Balinese-style restaurant and bar, which features live (and unamplified) Bali music at night. Amenities include safety deposit boxes, laundry, library, gift shop, swimming pool, baby-sitting, room service (until 11pm), turndown, transport to Ubud (Rp20,000 one-way), massage by pool (Rp15,000—much cheaper than at other hotels), crafts demonstrations, bike and car rental, transport to town (Rp20,000 one-way), and airport transfers.

**Hotel Tjamphuhan.** Jl. Raya Campuhan. P.O. Box 198, Ubud 80571, Bali. ☎ **361-975368.** Fax 361-975137. 64 units. US$60–US$106 double (with A/C). US$144 Walter Spies' house. Rates include breakfast. AE, MC, V. Free parking.

Built around the home of artist Walter Spies (in which you can stay), the Hotel Tjamphuhan doesn't quite have the range of services or the style that you would expect, but each room does have a wood statue of a man with an erection to absorb evil spirits away from the guests. It's still a nice location (though a 15-minute walk from central Ubud) with a pretty view of the gorge. "Raja" rooms, some of which have A/C, are large and plain, but not unpleasant, and can have a sweet view of hills and thatched roofs. Bathrooms are dull, with little sink space, but they do have tubs. "Agung" rooms are slightly smaller, with no view. Frankly, I think the extra money isn't worth it, unless you spend it on renting Spies' house. What's really pleasing are the grounds, which are full of stonework, plants, moss and—alas—steps, all leading down to the river. There are two very pretty pondlike pools, and one additional one with cold spring water, perfect for hot days (which is just about every day). A spa was being built as we went to press that should be high-toned and full-service. More rooms and a restaurant were also being added. There's room service until 11pm, airport pickup, and car rental.

**Pringga Juwita Water Garden Cottages.** Jl. Bisma, Ubud 80571, Bali. ☎ **361-975734.** Fax 361-975734. E-mail: pringga@dps.mega.net.id. 17 units. US$65–US$80 double. Rates include breakfast. JCB, MC, V. Free parking.

A popular small hotel heavy on the atmosphere thanks to the streams, lily ponds, and bubbling fountains that make the grounds more water than earth. Add plenty of stonework dripping with moss and you've got one lush place. Some people have complained about a smell of mold, while others find it perfection. (They spray for mosquitoes, by the way.) Deluxe rooms are two stories; downstairs is a totally open-air lounging area and open-air marble bathroom; up some treacherous stairs is the plainly decorated bedroom. It's rather like staying in the Swiss Family Robinson treehouse—and not for anyone with disabilities. Standard bedrooms, oddly, have a nicer decor. Amenities include some rooms with telephones (but only one, at US$150 double, with A/C), a small but pretty blue tiled pool, US$10 airport transfers, and free afternoon coffee and tea.

**Ubud Village Hotel.** Jl. Monkey Forest, Ubud, Bali. ☎ **361-975571**/974701. Fax 361-975069. 28 units. A/C MINIBAR TV TEL. US$60–US$90 double. Rates include breakfast. MC, V. Free parking.

This centrally located hotel attracts a loyal following, who know not to heed the official rates. Despite the Monkey Forest Road location, the pleasant local-style grounds (including a generic pool) are quiet. Rooms are called "cottages" but are all in the same building. They are large and bright, with tropical dull decor, and big private porches. Large open-air marble bathrooms have small sunken tubs and totally open showers. Services include a bar, a restaurant, and airport transfers.

**Ulun Ubud Cottages.** Sanggingan, Ubud, PO Box 3, Bali. ☎ **361-975024**, 975762. Fax 361-975524. 23 units. US$55–US$65. Rates include breakfast. MC, V. Free parking.

The limited number of amenities here (not even A/C) might scare some visitors off (particularly given the price), as might the somewhat remote location up near the Neka Museum, a long and potentially dangerous walk down a busy street that's not exactly conducive to pedestrians. But the staff is friendly, fun, and downright silly and speaks very good English. The owners live on the property—in fact, you pass through their kid-filled family compound to reach the actual hotel. All the rooms have wonderful views of the Campuhan gorge, ridge, rice paddies, and river, and all have thatched roofs and lots of carved wood detail work over doors and windows. The buildings and bungalows drape down the hillside to the river. (This, again, means potentially difficult stairs.) Rooms in bungalows are bigger and more expensive, with double beds, but frankly, the twins in the standards are nearly double size. Rooms are open at the top, but mosquito coils keep pests away. Baths are small but have tubs. The pool is disappointingly dull, but perched on a ridge so you aren't looking at the water anyway. You might do better in terms of creature comforts for the money, but you won't get this much style, flavor, or personality. There's a restaurant, room service until 10pm, and airport pickup.

## INEXPENSIVE

**Puri Garden Bungalows.** Monkey Forest Rd. ☎ **361-975395.** Fax 361-976188. 8 units. US$25 double. Rates include breakfast. MC, V.

Very much like a losmen, but a bit more upscale, so it's a good budget alternative. Rooms and baths (all clean and big enough not to be claustrophobic) are larger than in an average losmen. Rooms have bamboo on the walls and rushes on the floor, while bathrooms are nicely tiled. There's no A/C, only fans, but there is hot water. Second-story rooms have bathrooms down a steep flight of stairs, making middle-of-the-night calls of nature precarious. It's all arranged around a nice Buddha-adorned garden with fish ponds.

## LOSMEN

In addition to the ones below, there are literally dozens of losmen to chose from in Ubud. Just walk down Monkey Forest Road or the Jalan Hanoman, or better still, turn down any little alley or side street that cuts across them. Feel free to poke around until you find one that suits you—often there will be four or five within a few feet of each other. In addition, the **Ubud Sari Health Resort** (see "Pamper Yourself," below) has a couple of rooms that, while not the best accommodations offered, even by losmen status, do come with free use of sauna and other spa facilities and invitations for the morning yoga class.

**Badi House.** Jl. Dewi Sita, Maruti Lane, Ubud 80571, Bali. ☎ **361-973307.** 4 units. Rp25,000–30,000 double (fans and cold water only.) Rates include breakfast.

A pretty little compound off a small alley filled with places to stay. The family lives in the back, so you don't have to walk through their lives. The nice bungalows have decent beds and bamboo walls.

**Bella House.** Off Monkey Forest Rd., Ubud (first alley south of the football field across from the Pertiwi Bungalows). ☎ **361-975391.** 4 units. Rp60,000 double (all with hot water and fan). Rates include breakfast. No credit cards.

Clean and nice, with new tile and bamboo mat floors. The proprietor, Ketut Darmadi, speaks English well and is very friendly—almost as friendly as his little black puppy (by now a dog, presumably), Harley. Ketut's brother I Nyoman is an official tour guide, so they can arrange sightseeing for you with a higher level of quality.

⭐ **Casa Luna Guesthouse.** Jl. Raya, Ubud, Bali. ☎ **361-973283.** Fax 361-973282. www.bali-paradise.com/casaluna. E-mail: casaluna@bali-paradise.com. 6 units. Rp100,000 double. Rates include breakfast.

A step up from the typical losmen, with prices to match, but I think it's worth it. You are literally staying in the backyard (which, despite the mailing address, is actually on a dirt road, Jalan Bisma) of the people who bring you Casa Luna, Indus, and the Honeymoon Bakery, so boy do you get a good breakfast! (Frothy fruity drinks, thick, creamy homemade yogurt and fresh fruit, your choice of other goodies including thin green banana pancakes with coconut and cane syrup—I didn't need lunch.) Rooms are big enough (two to a bungalow), with small but lovely carved wooden canopy beds with mosquito netting, set in a charming garden overrun with plants, birds, pets, children, and treasures. This is also where they hold their cooking classes, which is mighty handy. The staff is far more attentive than any found at a luxury hotel—they can really spoil you.

**Esty's House.** Jl. Dewi Sita, Maruti Lane, Ubud. ☎ **361-977679.** 6 units. Rp35,000 double (cold water and fan only). Rates include breakfast. No credit cards.

A recently opened homestay, built specifically as such. It's very clean and comfortable, though the rooms are basic. Each room has an agreeable tiled patio sitting area in front. The owners, a congenial young couple, have a laundry (and gift shop) on the premises, which is awfully handy for grubby travelers.

**Kajeng Homestay.** Jl. Kajeng 29, Ubud, Bali. ☎ **361-975018.** 12 units. Rp45,000–Rp75,000 double. Rates include breakfast. No credit cards.

Just up from the main Ubud road, this losmen doesn't look like much upon entering, but it's surprisingly pretty in the back, with a big lily pond and quite a good view of the valley. Rooms are clean, with tile, and porches. Hot water only in the most expensive rooms, but all rooms have fans.

**Rice Paddy Bungalows.** Off Monkey Forest Rd. (at end of tiny alley about halfway down, just after Puri Garden Hotel). 6 units. Rp40,000–Rp60,000 double. Rates include breakfast.

A nice garden complex whose rooms have high ceilings, tiled floors, basic baths with Western toilets, and hand-held showers. Half the rooms are upstairs. Only two have hot water and another two have ceiling fans.

## DINING

Up until a couple of years ago, dining in Ubud was as disappointing as in most of the tourist regions where you had to rely on timid generic tourist-oriented warungs. But then an explosion happened, and now there is considerable choice, nearly all of it good. I predict that Ubud is where you will have your finest meals, the ones where good taste happily comes together with low costs. Don't rely on a hotel restaurant here—time is too short to try even all the dishes at Casa Luna and Satri's Warung, much less all the other restaurants. Vegetarians will be pleased to know that almost every menu in town has a separate, and delicious, section just for them. They might also try **Simpang Tigo** (where Jalan Hanoman begins to curve into Monkey Forest Road), a rumah makan Padang, where Rp5,000 will get you a plate full of carbs. Unless noted, reservations are not required at the restaurants below.

**Ary's Warung.** Main St. Main courses Rp25,500–Rp58,100 (duck, lamb, and salmon much higher—up to Rp120,000). No credit cards. Daily 7:30am–1am. INDONESIAN/EUROPEAN.

Ary's gourmet European and Indonesian specialties have many fans, but I love their honey ginger lime drink (with or without alcohol), which has helped us get through many a hot Bali day. (Consider also trying the honey mango mint, or banana lemon honey.) Ary's is particularly nice at night, when it's lit by candles and you can sit up on the second floor and watch the action in the busy street below, or bats catching bugs at the streetlights next to you. For appetizers, try the gazpacho, a generous bowl full of icy fresh flavor—perfect for a hot day—or the grilled goat cheese salad. Chicken crepes are surprisingly unmushy (crepes are tricky, and they do them right), stuffed with chicken, tomatoes, and leeks sautéed in garlic and white wine, with a creamy spinach sauce. Rendang Pedang is a West Sumatran beef dish simmered in coconut with local herbs—it's got a kick that sneaks up on you.

✪ **Batan's Waru.** Jl. Dewi Sita, Ubud. ☎ 361-977528. Main courses Rp10,500–Rp28,500. MC, V. Daily 8am–12am. INDONESIAN/EUROPEAN.

Everyone's new favorite Ubud dining spot, tucked away on the pleasant cross street just before the football field. It's particularly moody at night when they light up the street entrance with candles, though I could do without the sappy New Age music. A full menu with a number of traditional dishes beyond the usual suspects, and plenty of veggie options. For an appetizer, try urap pakis—wild fern tips with roasted coconut and spices. "Uncle Karaman's Humus" is spicy and comes with grilled pepper flat bread and tomato mint relish. Some swear by their nasi campur. I liked the tum ayam—chicken and paprika steamed in a banana leaf. They also do smoked duck and a babi guleng feast, with a day's advance order.

**Bebek Bengil/Dirty Duck.** Padang Tegel (at the end of the street as it hooks into Monkey Forest Rd.), Ubud, Bali. ☎ **361-975489.** Main courses Rp12,500–Rp28,500. MC, V. Daily 11am–11pm. INDONESIAN/EUROPEAN.

Yes, they serve duck here—the famous house specialty (no longer justifying its fame) is crispy duck stewed in Indonesian spices then deep fried. One serving is half a duck, ready to be torn to bits with your fingers. It's a bit dry, though the skin is delightfully fatty. Other poultry includes stuffed chicken (with shiitake, sprouts, and spinach). The menu also includes salads and well-stuffed, crunchy sandwiches. Grilled tuna salad with lemon cumin vinaigrette was light and healthy, and not overly dressed. There are veggie options, including a mushroom cashew pate appetizer.

✪ **Casa Luna.** Main St. ☎ 361-973282. Main courses Rp9,000–Rp33,000. No credit cards. Daily 8am–1am. ECLECTIC.

This innovative restaurant wouldn't be out of place in San Francisco—in fact, I know some dedicated Northern California foodies who dream of Casa Luna's chicken satay. One of the widest menus in Ubud, with dazzling versions of local cuisine and nouvelle food from pumpkin ravioli to Mediterranean tofu. It's all imaginative, fresh, and beautifully prepared. The big healthy salads make Californians happy, and the sandwiches feature the bakery's justly renowned bread. But despite their skill with Western dishes, you should really see how they are bringing Indonesian food into the modern era. Try the nasi campur or the ikan Bali and see how these traditional dishes fly. Try a health juice—fresh watermelon, cuke, and celery, or tomato and lemon basil, a frothy fresh juice, or my favorite, iced pinky red hibiscus blossom tea (like punch without the tooth-aching sweetness). Save room for dessert; the Casa Luna bakery made its rep a long time ago with killer brownies with ice cream and the Black Mischief cake. Or try an avocado shake. Since you won't be able to try everything, I bet you will end up eating here more than once.

**Hans Snell's.** Jl. Kajeng. ☎ **361-975699.** Main courses Rp9,000–Rp23,000. MC, V. Daily 9:30am–10pm. INDONESIAN.

An enjoyable walk up a cobblestone street and then a turn to the left (follow the signs) into a nice garden setting brings you to Hans Snell's. I know people who say they've eaten the best meal of their lives here, but I found the menu hit or miss. A decided hit was the opor ayam, a lightly smoked chicken simmered in coconut milk and spices that elicited cries of "Outstanding!" Skip, however, the really ordinary lemon chicken. Nothing is too spicy, but they will turn up the heat on request. Beware of waiters who might take advantage of slow nights and try to sell you crafts from their village (so they say).

**Ibu Oka (says Babi Guleng).** Jl. Suweta (across from the Palace, right before the Bambu restaurant). No credit cards. Open daily, no regular hours. BALINESE.

If you want to sample babi guleng, roast suckling pig, without the caloric commitment of the full feast, come here. Slightly better than a shack, right across from the Palace, you sit at low tables and get a paper plate full of spicy roast pig and crunchy pig parts, even spicier vegetables, and rice. Think of it as fast food, Bali style. Rp18,000 got us two orders of pig, two waters, and immense satisfaction. Pig may not be served on temple days.

**Indus.** Jl. Raya Sargingan, Campuhan, Ubud. ☎ **0812-380-2529** (cell phone). Dress "neat casual." No reservations. Main courses Rp14,000–Rp30,000. No credit cards. Daily 7:30am–11pm. ECLECTIC.

A brand new offering from the Casa Luna people, this eclectic restaurant is easily the most elegant in town. Don't let that scare you away, but do admire the graceful pillars, the use of marble, the lovely pale carved wood furniture, and the setting overlooking the Tjampuhan ridge. The view alone (not to mention the constant breeze wafting through) makes it worth the trip, but guests of the chic resorts up this way will be most grateful for something this good so close by. I went just as it was opening, and so some kinks were still being worked out, but I feel confident that by the time you read this they will be fully up to speed. Try such intriguing offerings as beetroot and feta empanadas, grilled calamari tostada, or some of the wraps and sandwiches—and don't overlook the spiced fish in banana leaves. Homemade ice creams include ginger, palm sugar, and black rice flavors, while the chocolate mocha tart nearly caused a riot when there wasn't enough to go around.

**Miro's.** Main Street, Ubud. ☎ **361-973314.** Reservations suggested. Main courses Rp11,500–Rp45,000. No credit cards. Daily 10am–10:30pm (except Saturday afternoon). INDONESIAN.

A wonderfully atmospheric restaurant, with an outdoor garden lit at night by oil lamps, and steps and ledges lined with white frangipani blossoms. The menu is geared towards gourmet versions of Balinese and Indonesian specialties, with a good vegetarian selection. Avocado chicken is poached in spicy coconut milk, with avocado slices and brown rice. Pancake Raja is a potato pancake with coconut chutney, yogurt, and cucumber raita. Pan-fried tuna can be disappointingly fishy. Fun drinks include lime and litchi nut coolers. There are just two drawbacks—large ants can wander freely on the table, and this can't be a good place when it rains.

✪ **Satri's Warung.** Monkey Forest Rd. (east side, 1-min. walk from Main Rd.—look for second yellow beer sign.) ☎ **361-973279.** Main courses Rp4,500–Rp9,500 (banana chicken for 2 Rp50,000.) Daily 8am–11pm. INDONESIAN/BALINESE.

When I want to torture myself, I think, "I could be eating banana chicken at Satri's right now." Hidden in a dirt-floored courtyard, off a twisting corridor, it's one of the finest warungs in all of Bali. The very friendly Satri serves her exceptionally good Indonesian food in generous portions—I know some vegetarians who ate here every single night for a month—but the reason to come, and dream about it afterward, is the banana chicken. Order it a day in advance, then feast on a whole chicken, marinated and glazed in a luscious sauce, succulent and falling off the bone, artfully arranged and served with heaping plates of equally delicious salad and cooked vegetables, and a large bowl of rice. Smoked duck is a similarly rapturous experience and must also be ordered a day in advance. (Top it off with fresh-squeezed lemonade.) Don't miss this restaurant, even if you don't have time for the chicken or duck. (But you'll make the time.)

✪ **Tutmak Warung Kopi.** Jl. Dewi Sita. ☎ **361-975754.** Reservations not required. Main courses Rp10,000–Rp30,000. No credit cards. Daily 9am–11pm.

Though it bills itself as a warung, this would be called a cafe anywhere else, complete with nouvelle cuisine and modern art on the walls. "Warung Kopi" actually means coffeehouse, and they claim to have the best coffee in Bali. (It's darn good.) Here, local cuisine is de-emphasized (though I do like their nasi campur) in favor of rich pastas, chicken Dijonaisse, grilled sausages, and "organic salads." I love the spicy chicken sandwich, on fat baguette bread, with a fresh salad on the side—not in the least Balinese, but a fine change of pace. Parents will be pleased with the kids' menu (about the only place that has one) including half sandwiches and similarly pint-sized portions. Kids—and parents—can then fill up on fancy desserts from lime and mango mousse to Orange Dream cake (the owner used to be a pastry chef).

## ATTRACTIONS

**Pura Saraswati.** Jl. Raya Ubud, Ubud. Daylight hours.

The royal family commissioned this temple and water garden, dedicated to the Hindu goddess of art and learning, at the end of the 19th century. The main shrine is covered in fine carvings, and the bale houses giant *barong* masks. The restaurant Cafe Lotus is situated at the front, on the main street, so that diners can look out over the lovely grounds.

**Puri Saren Agung, the Royal Palace.** Jl. Raya, Ubud. Daylight hours.

From the late 19th century to the mid-40s, this was the seat for the local ruler. It's a series of elegant and well-preserved pavilions, many of them decorated incongruously with colonial-era European furniture. Visitors are welcome to stroll around, though there are no signs indicating what you are looking at, so it palls quickly. Every night, dance performances are held in the courtyard, and it is by far the best and most dramatic setting for these in Ubud. Part of the complex functions as a hotel, which for atmosphere and central location can't be beat, but I found the staff, though not unfriendly, decidedly distracted and unhelpful. (Still, if the thought of Palace romance thrills you, call ☎ **361-975057,** or fax 361-975137.)

## MUSEUMS

Blame German artist Walter Spies, who arrived here in 1928, for Ubud's long relationship with artists. Well, with Western artists, since the Balinese are plenty artistic on their own, hence the many galleries in town. Unfortunately, tourists spend much of their time shopping for identical, often shoddy crafts, and ignore some of the extraordinary art on display in the local museums. There are two highly recommended museums in the vicinity; take the time to check one or both out. If nothing else, it's a crash course in Balinese art appreciation and will help you enormously should you

---

## Pamper Yourself

Have a massage. Most hotels offer massage and spa services, but at salons in Ubud you can get a 45-minute deep tissue massage (serious business that may leave you feeling bruised), a scrub with spices, a yogurt body mask, and a flower bath, all for about US$8. Milk baths, body peels, hair treatments, facials, mani-cures, and pedicures are all available at several locations around town (someone will hand you a flyer). At the **Milano Salon,** Monkey Forest Road (east side, south of the football field, ☎ **361-973488**), I had a milk bath for Rp60,000. You may also like the **Bodywork Center,** Jl. Hanoman 25 (☎ **361-975720**), or **Tri Madi Salon,** Jalan Bisma (☎ **361-977934**). Or head over to the **Ubud Sari Health Resort,** Jl. Kajeng 35 (☎ **361-974393**), where in addition to higher-priced spa and beauty salon services in a tranquil garden setting, they offer all sorts of healing treatments (chiropractic, high colonics, aromatherapy), all under the supervision of Dr. James Taylor (really), who has brought his (arguably dubious) New Age healing techniques to Bali with great success.

---

decide to upgrade from tacky souvenirs to more expensive purchases in the local gal-leries.

**Antonio Blanco's House and Art Gallery.** Jl. Campuhan, Ubud (just past the bridge). Admission Rp3,000. Daily daylight hours.

Antonio Blanco is a nutty guy, a Catalan expat artist who really loves topless Bali girls (including his wife, who is featured in many of his paintings) and himself, not neces-sarily in that order. He's often around and will strike up a conversation on a dime.

Decide for yourself whether his unabashed paintings are art, but don't miss his inspired multi-media pieces.

✪ **Neka Museum.** Jl. Raya Campuhan (about 10 minutes from central Ubud), Ubud. ☎ 361-975074/975034. Admission Rp5,000. Daily 9am–5pm.

This is the place to be introduced to Balinese art, and it's a lot more accessible than you might think. The museum was founded in 1982 by Suteja Neka, a former school-teacher and art patron. It's housed in several pavilions, the order and contents of which keep changing (signs and a guard will tell you where to go). The art comes with well-written, highly informative English-language labels, so there is no need to buy an expensive guide. Things to look for: In the second room of the first pavilion, which shows the four major schools of Balinese painting, I love the striking black and white "Pandawas in Disguise" and the acid flashback "Demonic Sacrifice." The Ubud-style paintings reflect various aspects of village life, and depict some scenes that—provided you've been getting out enough—should be very familiar to you. The artist Sonit seems to be a Balinese Gauguin, with his use of bold splashy colors. The two paint-ings collectively called "Mutual Attraction" (housed in the last pavilion) were put next to each other only after it was noticed that the man in one seemed to be admiring or leering after the woman in the other. Finally, in the photography archive, don't miss the black and white photos from the 1930s and 40s by Robert Koke, author of *Our Hotel in Bali,* and notice how very little has changed for the Balinese people in the last 5 or 6 decades. It's too bad more of this art isn't available in reproduction, but the Neka Museum does have a good book available to fill a bit of that void. Do look at the view of the Campuhan Gorge from the Smit Pavilion. It explains why so many artists, Western and Balinese, have been inspired here, and may well inspire you to take up painting yourself.

✪ **Puri Lukisan.** Jl. Raya Ubud, Ubud. ☎ 361-975136. Admission Rp5,000.

A major renovation has turned a formerly dilapidated display into something nearly on a par with the Neka Museum. Some feel it even exceeds its more prominent counterpart, thanks in part to the Puri Lukisan's gorgeous garden setting, complete with lily ponds, rice paddies, and maybe even a water buffalo. It was founded in 1956 by a prince of Ubud and a Dutch artist to help preserve the history and heritage of the changing Bali arts, particularly as they become ever-more corrupted by the ravenous tourist industry. There is an invaluable cross-section of styles to be seen here, paintings and sculptures that show the evolution of Balinese art, and a changing exhibit by young local artists.

✪ **Seniwati Galley of Art by Women.** Jl. Sriwedari 2B, Banjar Taman, Ubud. ☎ **361-975485.** Admission free. Daily 10am–5pm.

Like most museums, the Neka and the Puri Lukisan have a small ratio of female artists to male. This museum/gallery was founded to display often-overlooked art by women, and as a place for those who sometimes find themselves without a voice to express themselves. Both local and expat artists on are display, and some of the work is deeply powerful and moving. Besides fine art, the museum also includes pottery/ceramics, wood carving, and textiles. (I only wish there were more active displays of women creating these crafts—it would make a purchase more meaningful.) The permanent collection, special events showcase, gallery where art can be purchased, and various workshops help promote local female art and provide a place for an exchange of ideas, techniques, and information. They have a shop on Jalan Raya that sells high-quality crafts entirely made by village women.

## OUTDOOR ACTIVITIES & WATER SPORTS
### MONKEY FOREST

Yes, there is a monkey forest at the southern end of Monkey Forest Road. Towering trees cluster around to make a home for a troop of bad-tempered but endlessly photogenic primates, who swing from branches, cannonball into pools of water, engage in seemingly anthropomorphic activity, and generally delight photo-snapping visitors. Signs warn you not to feed them, while locals cluster beneath the signs selling you bananas and nuts for precisely that purpose. Do so if you must, but do not tease the critters, who are grumpy enough as it is—just hand them the food. Make sure you have no other food on you, as they will smell it. They also are known to snatch at dangling or glittering objects. There is a temple for the dead within the forest, and the track also leads to Nyuhkuning, a wood-carving village.

### BIRD WATCHING

Noted British birder Victor Mason leads bird-watching tours Tuesday, Friday, Saturday, and Sunday beginning at 9:30am from Victor's pub, the Beggar's Bush (at the Tjampuhan Bridge). It costs US$33, which includes water and lunch at Beggar's Bush after. Not too strenuous, it's suitable for all mobile ages, and Mason says you should see about 30 of the 100 or so varieties of birds in the area. (Birders I know point out that birds are most active and visible during the early morning and tend to be gone by 9:30am, so they doubt how many you might see. It's a nice walk anyway.) Bring binoculars if you can, though they should have a spare pair. Call **Bali Bird Walks** at ☎ **361-975009** for more details.

You can also go to the village of **Petulu,** northeast of Ubud, where every evening around 6pm countless white herons arrive to roost overnight in the trees. Local legend has it they are the reincarnated souls of the dead. To get there, take Tegalalang-Pujung road north from the T junction at the eastern edge of Ubud, go about 1½ km, turn left at the fork, then go another 1½ km.

## ELEPHANT RIDING

It may be called **Elephant Safari,** but the experience at ✪ **Elephant Safari Park,** Jalan By Pass Nigurah Rai, Pesanggaran (☎ 361-721480; fax 361-721481), is less safari and more elephant ride—but when was the last time you took one of those? The elephants, native to Sumatra, are beautifully cared for—indeed, elephant experts say these are the best-tended and most content they've ever seen. They live in a park that seems to be a model for ecologically and culturally minded attractions. The owners have worked carefully with locals from Pesanggaran, previously one of Bali's most remote and untouched villages, to make sure they have improved conditions, not destroyed local culture. (This means trying to find ways of reducing the sacred white cow population without killing them. Note their graves as you take your ride.) After learning some elephant facts (biology, care and feeding, threats, preservation), you can feed a pachyderm (they like sugar cane and yams). Then you are loaded two by two onto your beast (the guide sits on its neck), and off you go for a somewhat jostling, swaying trip through the nearby jungle. (It's not all that jungle-y, but who cares? You're riding an elephant.) Be sure to ask questions; guides are all knowledgeable about local flora, customs, and of course, elephants.

But only after the ride is over does the real fun begin: the optional elephant bath. This entails mounting an elephant bareback, arms about a guide's waist, and riding along as the animal slowly walks into a deep pool of (clean) river water. At the handler's command, the elephant rears up and plunges in to its knees, submerging you up to your chin. Shampoo is optional.

This may well have been the most fun I had in Bali. Bring your swimsuit (or not— I went in my clothes), hold on tight because you could fall off from laughing too hard, make sure someone other than a family member is taking your picture because they will surely screw it up as they laugh too hard, but don't miss this part of the excursion. Don't forget the words Bagus gajah (excellent elephant), and give that elephant a yam.

Safaris are US$39–US$56 adults, US$29–US$38 children. Family packages are available. The park is open daily, and reservations are recommended.

## RAFTING & TREKKING

Just west of Ubud is the Ayung River, where everyone comes for white-water rafting and kayaking. The rapids probably aren't that impressive for experienced rafters, but the scenery along the way is, with rice paddies, deep gorges, and photo-op waterfalls. The following two companies book 2-hour trips that include all equipment, hotel pickup, and lunch. Your hotel can also make the reservations.

**Bali Adventure Tours.** Jl. Bypass Ngurah Rai, Pesanggaran. ☎ **361-721480.** Fax 361-721481.

Packages may include the elephant safari described above, or other treks (jungle, nature reserves, rice paddies). The same people also book mountain cycling. White-water rafting (including transfers, instruction, equipment, and hot showers afterwards) is US$59 for adults, US$40 for children. Kayaking is US$58 per adult (no children).

✪ **Sobek.** Jl. Tirta Ening 9, By Pass Ngurah Rai, Sanur. ☎ 361-287059. Fax 361-289448.

This adventure outlet earns raves from customers for its professionalism and eye for details and comfort. Rafting (including transfers, lunch, changing facilities, and equipment) is US$68 for adults, US$45 for children under 12. They also offer kayaking, cycling, and trekking, plus package combos of everything.

## WALKING

By far, one of the most delightful activities in Ubud is walking. And I don't mean just past all those shops. Ubud is surrounded by fascinating villages, scenic rice paddies, gorges, and rivers, and there are roads and paths that lead to all of them. You can just wander, but I strongly urge you to buy a copy of the **Ubud Surroundings map,** available in bookstores, grocery stores and newsstands throughout town (particularly on the Jalan Raya). It shows all the roads and trails and gives suggestions on where to go and what to see. Try walking to the village of **Penestanan,** just west of the Campuhan Bridge. Ascend the stairs directly opposite the Hotel Tjampuhan (on Jalan Raya Campuhan) and follow the path over the river and through the woods (really), turning left at the crossroads with Penestanan's main street. This will eventually bring you back down a steep road that ends about where Jalan Raya Campuhan turns into Jalan Raya Ubud.

You can also try the most popular walk in Ubud (and certainly my favorite) the **Campuhan Ridge walk.** Follow the Jalan Raya downhill as it curves. Right before the bridge, past the Ibah on the right-hand side, there is a path that heads down from the road. When it forks, don't go towards the river, but scramble briefly uphill to the right, then follow the path. It will take you through a temple, then up a hill to follow along the gorge. It's a breathtaking vista of green rice paddies, sheer cliffs, and trees, and you may well have it to yourself, aside from a friendly local or two. The friend who first told me about this walk (saying it's his favorite in the world) suggested that you start at around 6am, walk for about an hour, then turn around and come back just in time for breakfast—well before the morning heat sets in. You can also keep going; the path leads through two tiny settlements. After the temple of the second one, the road forks. If you go left it leads you back down to the Campuhan road, about 0.62 miles (1km) above the Neka Museum (from there I suggest you catch a bemo or other transport, as the walk back to Ubud is a bit dicey with all the cars). If you go right you'll eventually arrive at the village of Keliki. From there, it's about a 2-hour walk to Ubud, though you can always go to the Hotel Alem Sari just outside Keliki for a meal and a ride back to town.

Or just grab any likely looking path or road and see where it goes. You won't have quite the sense of discovery and wonderment visitors did when Ubud and the surrounding villages were less built up, but the beauty remains undiminished.

## SHOPPING

Adding to its other delights, Ubud is Shopping Central. With a range from the tackiest, cheapest, mass-produced souvenirs to say-goodbye-to-the-college-fund priced art, you are likely to find something here to commemorate your trip. Do like friends of mine did and entirely decorate your house with Ubud crafts, carvings, and fabric. Or do like I do and get all your Christmas shopping done on a budget.

The amount of goods available can be overwhelming, particularly since many carry nearly identical items. Before buying anything, you might want to check out the **Ubud Market,** at the southeast corner of Monkey Forest Road and Jalan Raya Ubud (open during daylight hours). It's a real market, great noisy fun, with dozens of stalls selling goods intended for locals (check these out for bargains), produce, livestock, and the like, among the tourist kitsch. This is a good place to pick up a sarong and sash, if you haven't yet, or to start working on a more climate-appropriate wardrobe. It also functions somewhat as a wholesale market—many of the stores buy their goods here.

Bargaining can be a bit tougher here, owing to some really hard-nosed (but often quite charming) lady proprietors. You might well get better prices elsewhere, but at least you can get an idea of what to pay. If you arrive first thing in the morning you can try some of the snacks the ladies bring to sell.

For more shopping, just walk down **Monkey Forest Road, Jalan Raya Ubud**, and **Jalan Hanoman.** Shop after shop is filled with gorgeous sarongs, wood carvings, mobiles, various flying creatures, jewelry, incense, pottery, gaily colored–shirts, and so on. It's nearly all geared towards tourists, and you'll have to sort out the treasures from the dreck. In between are some shops with more legitimate merchandise, a few of which are noted below. All should be fixed price. Higher quality items—and higher prices—are found on Jalan Raya Ubud west of Monkey Forest Road.

Several nearby crafts villages seem to be entirely devoted to some kind of commercial production. **Mas,** on the bemo route to Ubud from the south, is the most prominent wood-carving village, but there is also **Tegalalang** to the north. **Batubulan,** to the south, specializes in stone carving, while **Celuk** is where you find silver jewelry. **Batuan** and **Keliki** are major art centers, with their own distinctive styles. The sheer amount of apparently identical goods for sale in these places can be bewildering, but if you have the patience you can find (or commission) treasures. All are accessible by bemo, though it can be a wearying trip involving several changes. Unfortunately, your other choice is a transport guide, who will certainly get a cut of the then probably inflated price of whatever you buy.

## ART GALLERIES

There are art galleries galore in Ubud; the following are just the most highly regarded or highest profile. Go take a look at what's on display at the Neka or the Puri Lukisan (see "Museums," above) to familiarize yourself with the different styles of art (and get an idea of what is good quality) before leaping into a purchase. Also consider patronizing the **Seniwati Gallery of Art by Women** (see "Museums," above), Jl. Sriwedari 2B.

**Agung Rai Fine Art Gallery,** Jalan Peliatan, Peliatan, open during daylight hours, is a highly regarded source for artwork, with a superior selection for all budgets. **Hans Snel's Gallery,** Jalan Kajeng, Ubud (open daily 8am–8pm), is owned by Dutch expat Snel, who moved to Bali and married his teenage model. Snel has worked in a variety of styles, most recently abstract compositions. The former home of Ubud's most significant artist, I Gusti Nyoman Lempad, **Lempad's House,** Jalan Raya, (open 8am–6pm), is unfortunately less a museum of his work (most of which is at the Neka Museum) than a gallery showcasing a group of painters calling themselves "Puri Lempad." Owned by the founder of the Neka Museum, **Neka Gallery,** Jalan Raya (open 8am–7pm), is more than reliable for good quality art in all price ranges. It includes artists from all over Indonesia.

## BOOKS

**Cintra Bookshop,** Dewi Sita Street (☎ **361-973295**), has used books well organized by language and some by category—even alphabetized! Opposite the post office, the ✪ **Ganesha Bookstore,** Jalan Raya (☎ **361-976339**), is an oasis for serious readers. Ganesha is delightfully low on Danielle Steele and high on a wide assortment of both new and used novels, classics and nonfiction in several languages, with a fine selection of Bali-related items. They also carry a small but strong selection of CDs and tapes, along with good Balinese crafts, especially musical instruments. Owner Ketut Yuliarsa keeps his own instruments in a loft upstairs, where he gives hands-on classes every Tuesday evening—a great way to learn a little about the local music, whether you're an experienced pro or a tin ear.

## CLOTHING

**Baingin,** on Jalan Hanoman, has an interesting selection of clothing and gifts. ✪ **Mutiarti Art,** with two locations on Jalan Raya, sells high-quality shirts with beautiful designs. Pelangi Design, **Monkey Forest Road** (☎ 361-973398), sells upscale Indonesian and Asian gifts and clothing.

## HOUSEHOLD ITEMS

Owned by the Casa Luna folks, and located on the corner of Jalan Raya and Jalan Bisma, **Casa Lina Homewares** has everything you need to decorate your house in Bali style, including gorgeous pillows, wall hangings, bed coverings, and kitchen ware.

# CLASSES

There are various ever-changing classes in art and dance instruction throughout Ubud—keep your eyes peeled for bulletin boards and other signs advertising them. Yoga is offered at the **Ubud Sari Health Spa** (see "Pamper Yourself," above). See above for information about the **Ganesha Bookstore**'s music classes.

✪ **Casa Luna Cooking School.** Jl. Raya. ☎ **361-973283.** Classes Monday 10am–2pm, Tuesday (market day) 8am–noon, Wednesday 10am–2pm. Rp100,000 per person. Book in advance.

Janet de Neefe runs this cooking school in the backyard of her lovely home, where she'll teach you how to cook just like she does—or close enough to impress your friends. Learn to make that fabulous spiced fish in banana leaves you raved about at Casa Luna restaurant, or the green pancakes she serves for breakfast at her homestay. On Tuesdays, you go to the Ubud market, buy what's there, and spontaneously turn it into something delicious. Best of all, there's a feast at the end!

**Meditation Shop.** Monkey Forest Road. ☎ **361-976206.**

Your New Age center, offering silent meditation hours and instruction in meditation (an interesting concept), along with metaphysical literature.

# UBUD AFTER DARK

Ubud isn't exactly hopping at night. Many of the restaurants, at least, are now staying open after 9pm, and many of them show laser disc movies nightly. Dinner, a movie, and a lingering drink or two, with or without alcohol, isn't a bad way to pass an evening. There are a couple of bars and clubs, two of which are listed below. You might also check out the action at Victor Mason's **Beggar's Bush** pub (see "Bird Watching," above).

## PERFORMANCES

There are usually several dance, music, and shadow puppet performances to choose from every night in Ubud, both at the **Palace** (the recommended location) and other nearby stages (when needed, transportation is included). Barong, legong, kecak, gamelan, abbreviated dance performances of the *Mahabarata* and *Ramayana*—it's all there for you to sample in various forms. If you have time for only one, a Barong performance at the Ubud Palace would be your best bet. Barong is highly visual, employing both acting and dance. It's both comedic and dramatic, and comes close to what Westerners would consider a traditional narrative, which also makes it suitable for children. Seeing a performance of anything at the Palace, where the stage is in the dramatic courtyard, is a treat in and of itself.

It's easy to learn what's on the performance agenda; boys will come up to you in the street every day trying to sell tickets for that evening's program. Or you can plan ahead by getting a schedule at the tourist office on Jalan Raya. You can purchase tickets at the venue in question, or indeed from the street boys. Check prices in advance, just in case. As of this writing, tickets were about Rp15,000–Rp20,000.

## BARS

**Jazz Cafe.** Jl. Sukma 2 (4 streets east of Monkey Forest Rd., just off main road). ☎ **361-976595.**

One of the few true nightspots in town, and a hot one at that, with live performances of surprisingly good jazz bands, including one that combines modern jazz with gamelan.

**Prasa Bar.** Jl. Kajeng 1.

A "cave bar" reminiscent of the inside of a temple, with movies and recorded music every night until late. You can also use it as a message center. There's a good atmosphere that seems less likely to get rowdy than the bars in Kuta.

# 8  Sights & Destinations Near Ubud

The following are sights that are either quite close to Ubud or can easily be done in a half-day trip, even in combination with other spots. (Though if you want to really linger, this will take up an entire day.) Some are quite popular on the tourist track and thus often incredibly crowded. If you go earlier in the day, both the crowds and the heat will be more bearable. Better still, don't just settle for the hot spots—many of the locations neglected by tourists make for far better viewing anyway. All locations will probably insist on a sarong and sash. Most will provide them for free, or for a small fee (less than Rp1,000), but you will look more stylish—not to mention polite—if you come with your own. There will be locals offering to be your guide at every site. You don't really need them, and their information may be highly suspect—but then again, they could be entertaining. Be sure, however, to negotiate a firm price ahead of time, and be prepared for them to insist at the end that that price was quite a bit higher than actually agreed upon.

There are **organized tours** that go to many, but not all, of these sights—check with the various tourist agencies in town to see if one or two fit the bill. Or you can grab one of those pesky **transport guides** and tell them for once that yes, you really do want transport. Believe it or not, they are reliable, being desperate for business, and if you negotiate a time and place they will show up. Have your itinerary clearly written down—nothing I have listed here is unusual, and any guide who acts even vaguely puzzled should not be hired. Decide in advance how much you want to spend for a day or half-day's worth of someone's time and gas. You will have to negotiate (chances are they will start quite high), and be sure to make it clear that you do not want to go to any shops (assuming you don't) and won't pay the full price if somehow you do accidentally end up at one. You might also ask your guide to tell you exactly where you are when he lets you off at a site, since there often aren't clear signs ("Hmm, is this Titra Empul or Yeh Pulu?"). And don't forget to tip at the end of the day (10% or so should be fine).

## BESAKIH

About 12 miles (20km) north of Klungkung. Daylight hours. Rp1,500.

The so-called "Mother Temple", the center of Bali Hinduism and the most important temple in Bali. Set on the slopes of the volcanic Gunung Agung, the highest mountain in Bali, with a grand and marvelous view, this is one of the top tourist sights.

I think this is wrong.

Okay, that's sacrilege, both in a religious and tourism sense, but here's my reasoning. First of all, and perhaps most importantly, if you are expecting to see the St. Peter's Basilica of Bali, forget it. Culturally, Besakih is monumentally significant, being the holiest temple in Bali, but architecturally, it's more like a big village church (to continue with the analogy from another religion and culture). Further, Besakih is not just one temple, but a series of temples in a compound. And non-Hindus are not allowed inside the walls of any of the temples. So the best a camera-toting tourist can hope for is a glimpse over a wall, or through an open door. There are no signs, markers, maps or information brochures anywhere (it is a working religious compound and not a museum or other tourist-oriented construction) and so even when you do see something, it's unlikely you will know what you are looking at. The touts are so insistent that it's almost worth paying one of them; even if their information is dubious, at least it's something. The view is wonderful when it isn't raining or threatening to rain, and clouds aren't entirely obscuring it. Add to this a very long, steepish walk up from the car park, and this becomes a less-than-rewarding experience.

A temple, after all, is a temple is a temple, at least in Bali, and while the divine nature of this one makes it worth considering, there are other, prettier and occasionally less crowded ones. (Including the by far prettier, second-most-sacred, Pura Ulun Batour nearby.) If you have the chance to see just one temple, this need not be it. Having said that, obviously, on a clear day you probably can see forever, and on a celebration day—and these are many—it is without question colorful and glorious. Sometimes a kind Hindu will let you into a temple area; we accompanied one woman who gave us offerings to make, and conducted an entire prayer ritual with us, complete with holy water and rice on forehead—special enough on its own, but in the most sacred place in Bali ever more so.

Besakih is the oldest and largest of Bali's roughly 20,000 temples. It may date back as far as the 8th or 10th centuries, but the first hard records of it come from the 14th and 15th centuries. There are 22 temples spread over about 2 miles (3km) in the complex, which was destroyed by an earthquake in 1917, and heavily damaged again in the 1963 eruption. It has since been well restored. The three main temples venerate the Hindu holy trinity. The **Pura Penataran Agung** (originally a funeral temple for the Gelgel kings dynasty and the island's central temple) is more or less in the center; it's the largest and is dedicated to Shiva. **Pura Batu Medog,** diagonal from Penataran Agung's upper left corner, is dedicated to Vishnu. **Pura Kiduling Kreteg,** off from the right upper Penataran Agung corner, is dedicated to Brahma. The notable feature of Penataran Agung is its giant stairway, lined by seven levels of carved figures, with characters on the right from the *Ramayana* and the ones on the left from the *Mahabarata.*

To best enjoy Besakih, try to arrive early in the morning, ahead of the busloads of tourists. Or come during the Bhata Turun Kabeh, a month-long festival celebrating the time the gods descend from the heavens to hang out in Besakih. It usually falls during March or April; check the calendar of festivals issued annually by the Bali government tourist office.

In passing, the little warungs among the shops lining the car park at the base of the hill are quite cheap and tasty.

## GUNUNG AGUNG

At 9,888 feet (3,014m), the tallest mountain in Bali, Gunung Agung is utterly sacred to the Balinese, who like to sleep with their heads facing it. The mountain is believed to have been created by the gods, and is the center of the world. It can be seen from most points (provided clouds aren't in the way) in east Bali.

Gunung Agung is the center of one of the greatest modern-day Bali disasters. In 1963, as plans were being made for the once-a-century ceremony Eka Dasa Rudra, the great ritual held to purify the entire island and to ensure good luck (which hadn't been held in several centuries, so no one thought it would matter that it was not the correct year for it), the long-dormant volcano began to rumble. The ceremony went ahead on March 8, even as ash rained down on the probably glum participants. The volcano erupted on March 17, pouring lava down and spewing poisonous gas. As many as 2,000 people were killed, and another 100,000 lost their homes. East Bali was a near total wreck and it took many years to rebuild, with scars still visible. As for the ceremony, it was held again in 1979—the year it should have been held in the first place—and this time went off without a hitch.

You can climb the now-quiet Gunung Agung, but it is a serious trek that absolutely calls for a guide (the trails are not well marked) and proper supplies. Most hotels can arrange for it, but figure you will have to start climbing in the middle of the night, or very early in the morning to make the top by sunrise.

## OTHER SIGHTS NEAR UBUD

**Goa Gajah/Elephant Cave.** About halfway between Ubud and Mas, approximately 1.2 miles (2km) to the east. Daylight hours. Rp1,100.

The mouth of this man-made cave doesn't quite look like an elephant, which makes the legend that that is how it got its name suspect. In any case, Goa Gajah was built in the 11th century, probably as a type of monk's cell. Inside the small, dark, and clammy cave are statues of Ganesha to the left (most definitely an elephant) and three phallic emblems of Siwa to the right. Outside to the left of the cave is a worn statue of a woman with children; she's both a Balinese folk heroine and a Buddhist goddess, so Goa Gajah seems to have been both Hindu and Buddhist. There is also a large rectangular bathing area, and just beyond it, steps leading to a pretty ravine, where there are some statues of Buddha.

✪ **Yeh Pulu.** 0.62 mile (1km) south of signs just east of Goa Gajah. Rp1,100. Daylight hours.

This is one of our favorite Bali sights, a row of bas-relief carvings in a rock face. It's pretty, simple, intriguing, and for some reason largely unvisited by tourists. You can actually walk to Yeh Pulu from Goa Gajah, but it's through some rice paddies, and you do need one of those guides to help you find it. If you arrive by car, after paying your fee you will have a medium-length walk through a rice field, past a bathing place on the left (don't turn in there or you may startle some naked bathers). The carvings date back at least 400 years, and while no one is exactly sure what the five panels depict, they do seem to tell the story of a hunt. Note the religious and cultural details on the figures, culminating with a statue of Ganesha. A slightly nutty older woman may bless you with holy water and ask for a donation. Go ahead and give it to her; we could all use an extra blessing.

**Pura Panti Pasek Gelgel/Pura Gunung Kawi.** Sebatu. About 5.6 miles (9km) northeast of Ubud. Rp1,500. Daylight hours.

On the grounds of these two pretty temples in the village of Sebatu you find lovely little bathing pools of holy water, fed by mountain springs. The place was undergoing renovation recently, even though it was already fairly well maintained. A priest occasionally offers guests (of which there aren't many non-Balinese) treats like rice balls with a cane syrup center. Take one and then have a dip in the pool, making sure you go to the appropriate gender section. (For the main Gunung Kawi, see below.)

✪ **Gunung Kawi.** 7.4 miles (12km) northeast of Ubud. Rp1,500. Daylight hours.

Hands down my favorite Bali sight, and inexplicably neglected by tourists. If I do my job right, that's going to change, but it will still be worth a look. Here you find the so-called "royal tombs" or *chandi*. Actually, no one knows what they really are—no ashes or bones were found inside, so they were probably memorials or cenotaphs, and the best guess is they were built to honor 11th-century King Udayana and his consorts and concubines. They are rare stone monuments, set deep in niches, all carved directly out of the mountain face (rather like Mount Rushmore). No identifying marks, aside from some cryptic faded writing, were found on them. To reach them, you walk down a steep flight of 300 steps (and yes, you'll have to walk back up), which brings you to a small gorge. Go to the left, and view the first set of tombs, which honor the King's minor wives. The second set, for the King and his favorite wives, are arguably even better. They're across the river, all the way through the temple complex; turn left and walk through the complex until you actually exit it, down some steps towards the river (note the cavelike monks cells carved out of the mountain along the way). The monolithic tombs stand silent and enigmatic, mysterious and awesome, in a lovely setting of green gorge and rushing river; you could probably spend hours just staring at them. A tenth tomb, possibly of an advisor, is back across the river, to your left through marshy rice paddies as you head towards the exit.

**Titra Empul.** About 500m north of Gunung Kawi turnoff. Rp1,500. Daylight hours.

The holy water of Titra Empul is considered the most sacred on Bali, and it is part of a ritual following recovery from a serious illness to come bathe here. The waters burble up in a clear cool blue from a black silt–bottomed rectangular pool; legend has it that a warrior pierced a stone here and let loose the healing liquid, which saved his poisoned army. There are separate bathing places for different body parts and different kinds of people, and along with the Balinese who come here there are usually hordes of jabbering tourists brought in by the busload. (Come in the early morning to miss the bulk of them.) Take a healing dip if you like, and notice the modern building on the clifftop to your right; it was used by Indonesian President Suharto or the Balinese governor, who liked to pick out the best looking of the naked local gals and summon them up for closer encounters.

## 9   Candi Dasa

A beach resort that almost entirely lacks a beach, Candi Dasa rests on the easternmost end of a large bay. Thanks to enthusiastic but overly rapid development, Candi Dasa's coral reefs were largely destroyed, leaving the beaches so exposed that the sand eroded away, replaced by nasty, foot-cutting coral. (Sea walls have been built as protection in the hopes that small beaches will start to form.) On the other hand, Candi Dasa is quieter and much more laid back than other beach areas (touts are forbidden), and the snorkeling and diving are excellent. It's easy enough to day trip from Ubud or Nusa Dua, but consider staying a night or two; not only do you want to go snorkeling or diving first thing in the morning, but the more mellow nighttime pace is a good way to recharge your batteries.

Another option nearby is the village of **Padangbai,** in the westernmost part of the bay, where you'll experience something closer to village life and gain easy access to the best snorkeling in the area, but lose some of the tourist infrastructure.

### GETTING THERE

There are shuttles from all major tourist areas to Candi Dasa, and most of the hotels offer airport pickup for a fee.

### GETTING AROUND

There isn't much to the town of Candi Dasa itself—just one road, parallel to the beach—so your feet will do you just fine. Hotels just outside the center (or farther in

---

**Tour Operators**

There are a number of tour offices on Candi Dasa's main street, including the reliable **Perama.**

---

the case of the Amankila and the Serai) generally offer regular **shuttles** into town, or, if you prefer, **motorbike** rental. **Bemos** also travel frequently up and down the main strip.

## Fast Facts: Candi Dasa

**Banks/Currency Exchange**   Money changers are all up and down the main street, offering competitive prices.

**Post Office/Mail**   Asri Shop on the main street offers postal services.

**Telephone**   Go to the Kupu Bali Hotel, on the main street. Candi Dasa's area code is 363.

## ACCOMMODATIONS

There are not quite as many accommodation choices in Candi Dasa as one might think, but between the high end, ultra-luxurious Amenkila and the several basic losmen, there is enough of a range to satisfy everyone. If you choose to stay in Padang-gbai, losmen are the only option. They're easy to find, and pretty much all the same.

### VERY EXPENSIVE

✪ **Amenkila.** Manggis. ☎ **361-771267** (reservations), 363-41333. Fax 361-771266 (reservations), 363-41555. 35 units. A/C MINIBAR TEL. US$500–US$700 double; US$1,500 2-bedroom suite. AE, DC, JCB, MC, V. Free parking.

This is the seaside cousin of the Ubud gorge–based Amandari, with another breathtaking view (this one of the ocean) and prices to match. The hotel is located somewhat outside of Candi Dasa and is too far to walk anywhere, but a shuttle can take you into town. (That is, if you ever decide to leave.) That the well-heeled guests rule here is evident from the gracious and hospitable service and the statues guarding the doors to the individual bungalows. Enjoy ruling over a large bungalow with a sleeping room dominated by a solid wood four-poster canopy bed, an enormous dressing area/ bathroom, and cushioned windows. (Prices are higher for ocean views and private pools.) An elegant, well-stocked library puts the pitiful shelves of weather-beaten volumes other hotels call their library to shame. There's a private beach—the only one in Candi Dasa with sand—and a breathtaking bi-level pool, whose water matches the color of the ocean it seems to spill into. Amenities include water sports, video arcade, laundry, dry cleaning, tour desk, 24-hour room service, newspaper, baby-sitting, CD players, hair dryers, turndown, massage, afternoon tea, gift shop. One restaurant serves breakfast and lunch; another serves dinner. There's also a bar.

### EXPENSIVE

✪ **Puri Bagus.** P.O. Box 129, Candi Dasa, Karangasem 80801, Bali. ☎ **363-41131.** Fax 363-41290. E-mail: pdcandi@denpasar.wasantara.net.id. 15 units. A/C MINIBAR TEL. US$95–US$130 double; US$200–US$300 villas. AE, DC, MC, V. Free parking.

A lengthy but doable walk from the center of town, this is a compromise between the high-priced Amenkila or Serai and the lesser hotels in Candi Dasa. Pretty and

# Candi Dasa

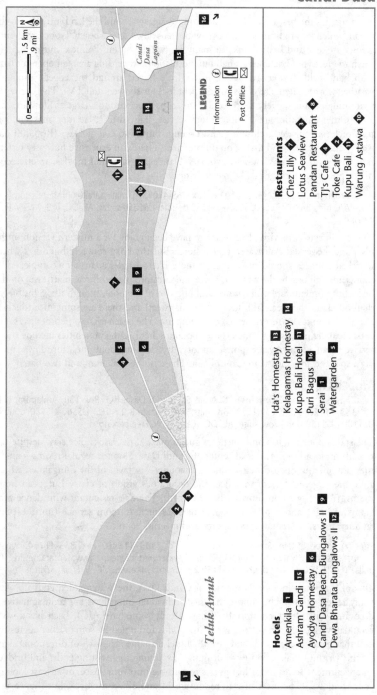

Teluk Amuk

*Candi Dasa Lagoon*

0   1.5 km
0   .9 mi

**LEGEND**

- ⓘ Information
- ☎ Phone
- ✉ Post Office

## Hotels

Amenkila **1**
Ashram Gandi **15**
Ayodya Homestay **6**
Candi Dasa Beach Bungalows II **9**
Dewa Bharata Bungalows II **12**
Ida's Homestay **13**
Kelapamas Homestay **14**
Kupa Bali Hotel **11**
Puri Bagus **16**
Serai **1**
Watergarden **5**

## Restaurants

Chez Lilly **7**
Lotus Seaview **3**
Pandan Restaurant **8**
TJ's Cafe **4**
Toke Cafe **2**
Kupu Bali **1**
Warung Astawa **10**

595

romantic, it's the best of its class. The grounds zigzag around the land jutting into the ocean, which laps right up to the edge, with steps down to the beach. Good-sized bungalows are airy and light thanks to many big windows, and Balinese music plays in them to greet you. Each has a small but clean and pretty sitting area, an open-air bath with hand-held showers (these are just a little frayed around the edges—probably weather-worn). There are plans to add pebble-floor showers and TVs. The U-shaped swimming pool has a very deep section for scuba practice and a large shallow area for kids. Other amenities are 24-hour room service, baby-sitting, laundry, massage, airport pickup, tour desk, climbing and cycling, shuttle to Candi Dasa (Rp5,000 one way), scuba lessons, and dive shop on premises. There's an expensive but tasty restaurant with a fine ocean view, and two bars. Dance programs and movies are offered at night, plus a full range of daily free activities.

**Serai.** Manggis, Bali. ☎ **363-41011.** Fax 363-41015. E-mail: serail@ghmhotels.com. 58 units. A/C MINIBAR TV TEL. US$130–US$155 double; US$250 suites. AE, DC, JCB, MC, V. Free parking.

This comfortable, newish place seems to have been going for a modern version of the lily pond–bedecked Bali water garden hotel. But the boxy concrete buildings where thatched cottages should make it look more like a singles apartment complex. The rooms are Bali beach–themed, attractive and comfortable (with real mattresses on the beds) but unmemorable. The same could be said of the pool, though it is a bit bigger than others in the area. Still, the staff seems sweet, and there are some nice touches, like afternoon tea and treats served on your patio. The beach even sometimes has sand. A particularly interesting bonus is the cooking school. Other amenities include room service (until 11pm), water sports, laundry, dry cleaning, boutiques, turndown, massage, spa, and free shuttle to Candi Dasa. There is one restaurant and two bars.

## MODERATE

**Candi Dasa Beach Bungalows II.** Main St., Candi Dasa. P.O. Box 130, Amlapura, Bali. ☎ **363-41126.** Fax 363-41537. 68 units. A/C MINIBAR TV TEL. US$60–US$80 double; US$100–US$150 bungalow/suite. AE, DC, JCB, MC, V. Free parking.

The staff's poor English and hustle of guests make this a last-choice stay, despite the beachfront location in the dead center of Candi Dasa. Skip the regular rooms—unless they are offering one of their frequent discounts—in favor of the bungalows, which are quite large, and seem to reflect the decorator's vision of classy European hotel rooms. (A semi-glamour now fairly well worn.) There's a restaurant with dance programs at night and a poolside bar. Amenities include room service (until 11pm), laundry, tours, car rental, water sports, and meeting rooms.

**Watergarden.** Main Street, Candi Dasa. ☎ **363-41540.** Fax 363-41164. www. bali-paradise.com/watergardenhotel. E-mail: watergarden@denpasar.wasantara.net.id. 14 units. TEL. US$70–US$80 double; US$150 2-bedroom suite. AE, MC, V. Free parking.

One of the better-looking properties in Candi Dasa, the Watergarden ends up with many repeat guests. The simple thatched individual bungalows are unimaginatively decorated, but plenty comfortable (though only some have A/C). Each has a wide veranda overlooking one of the many lily ponds (occupied by some rather aggressive koi) that bisect the grounds and give the hotel its name. The lack of directional signs (at this writing) makes finding your bungalow among the twisting paths and bridges an adventure. (Be ready for lost guests to bumble into your space, or at least look in your windows.) The most private rooms are 11 and 12, at the back, but they're also the farthest walk. Only deluxe rooms have A/C. Amenities are room service (until 11pm), safety deposit boxes in some rooms, laundry, water sports, tours, airport pickup, and gift shop. For dining, see the review of TJ's and bar below.

## INEXPENSIVE

**Ashram Gandhi Candi Dasa.** Main St., Candi Dasa. ☎ and fax **361-225145** (reservations)**; 363-41108.** 14 units. US$20–US$35 double. Only married couples can share rooms. Includes 3 vegetarian meals a day. 3-night minimum stay.

Yes, this is a real ashram, and they are serious about it. It's a truly unique experience to stay here, with a number of pros and cons. The pros: It's an ashram (recently featured in a travel article in the *New York Times*), and you are welcome to join in all daily activities including prayer routines, yoga, meditation, English classes, and cleaning (the place has to stay clean somehow), though it's not required. The vegetarian (naturally) meals are by all accounts quite good, and you can't beat the peaceful vibe. On the other hand, this is a commune—30 people live here full-time, and there is a kindergarten school on the grounds. Amenities are minimal—cold water and fan only (though it's not uncomfortable at all)—and they do prohibit smoking, alcohol, non-married couples sharing rooms, and nudity on their beach. However, it's a nice location, wrapping around the lagoon, with grazing cows and a well-stocked reading room (many books on religion). The outside walls of the buildings feature quotes from Gandhi ("Learn to be your own judge and you will be happy"). Guides are available for touring and day trips.

**Dewa Bharata Bungalows.** Main St., Candi Dasa. ☎ **363-41090.** Fax 363-41091. 24 units. US$25–US$35 double (with A/C). Rates include breakfast. Free parking.

A good budget choice if you're looking for something a step above a losmen. It's essentially the same idea in terms of rooms and furnishings, but with a slight upgrade in each. Bathrooms are clean, with showers only. Outside, the tiled pavilions have lots of Bali frills and are set amidst a manicured garden. There is a small pool (which you don't get at a losmen) that overlooks the beach and is particularly nice for a budget place.

**✪ Kupu Bali.** Main Street, Candi Dasa. ☎ 363-41532, 363-41256. Fax 363-41531. 20 units. A/C TEL. US$55 double; US$65 suite. JCB, MC, V. Free parking.

A great value for the price, the Kupu Bali is an extremely comfortable and well thought-out hotel that terraces up the hillside across from the ocean. The handsomely decorated individual bungalows flank stone stairways and a series of cascading ponds, all dotted with statues, benches, aviaries, and pavilions. It's crowned by an extremely pretty pool with an excellent view of the ocean and islands. There's room service (food until 10pm, drinks 24 hours), and an excellent restaurant (see below).

## LOSMEN

**Ayodya Homestay.** Main St., Candi Dasa. ☎ **363-41992.** 4 units. Rp35,000–Rp60,000. Rates include breakfast.

Since most of the bungalows here are rented by locals (only four are left for tourists), you won't be isolated in a tourist bubble from real Balinese. It's a cold-water and fan-only facility, with the baths totally open-air (no roofs)—but it's clean and nice, and right on the ocean. Inquire about staying here in the sundries store in front (you'll know it by the monkey chained to the tree). They offer car, motorbike, and bicycle rental and can arrange transport.

**Ida's Homestay.** Main St., Candi Dasa. ☎ and fax **363-41096.** 6 units. Rp50,000–Rp90,000 double. Rates include breakfast.

They've done a lot with a little in this popular homestay. Comfortable cottages on idyllic seaside grounds feature cold water and fan only. One cottage is two stories with an upstairs double bed and nice sitting area. There's a common room with a TV. It's simple but satisfactory.

**Kelapamas Homestay.** Main St., Candi Dasa. P.O. Box 103, Amlapura 80801, Bali. ☎ and fax **363-41947.** 24 units. Rp60,000–Rp200,000 (with A/C and bathtub) double. Rates include breakfast.

Thatched and bamboo cottages of varying sturdiness and comfort, arranged around well-maintained, grassy grounds. Expat artists on a small trust fund make this their home away from home. Prices go up with A/C and proximity to the ocean, but the ones directly facing the beach (which has a sheltered place for swimming) are probably worth the price increase. Unlike other losmen, they offer such amenities as a small restaurant, massage (Rp30,000 per hour), motorbike rental, and tour and snorkeling arrangements.

## DINING

It's not surprising that most of the better eating options in Candi Dasa are found in hotels. What is surprising is the lack of the kind of affordable fish places one finds in other beach areas. It's a shame, but there's an opportunity there for some enterprising expat.

**Chez Lilly.** Main St. Main courses Rp6,000–Rp17,000. No credit cards. Daily 8am–11pm. ECLECTIC/INDONESIAN.

Once a rather innovative, popular place, Chez Lilly has gone downhill quite a bit, and many of the formerly notable dishes have disappeared from the menu. Some odd dishes still pop up—like quiche and chicken paprika, aubergine tapas (fried, salty slices of Chinese eggplant served with dip), or honey peanut chicken (covered in a sauce remarkably like actual peanut butter). Prawns are massive, but so is the amount of coconut coating them. Slow service irritates until you catch those in the know visiting and chuckling away with the staff.

**Kubu Bali.** Kubu Bali Hotel. Reservations not required. Main courses Rp12,500–Rp35,000 (prawns higher). MC, V. Daily 9am–10pm. INDONESIAN/SEAFOOD.

This is possibly the nicest looking restaurant in town, with pavilions bedecked with elaborate chandeliers, arranged among ponds, and set with large marble tables. The big open kitchen (which helps ease fears about food sanitation) is at the entrance. It churns out a large menu, heavy on fish prepared all ways. You are better off having dessert at TJ's, however.

**Lotus Seaview.** Candi Dasa Beach. ☎ **363-41257.** Main courses Rp13,000–Rp33,000. AE, MC, V. Daily 8am–10pm. SEAFOOD/INDONESIAN.

Located at the nominal entrance to Candi Dasa, but a small walk from the center of things (take advantage of their free shuttle service), this branch of the Lotus restaurants offers slightly more interesting variations on the usual local fare—in other words, everything isn't deep fried. Choices include pastas, dishes "for meat lovers," or satay grilled on your table. The ocean setting, under Balinese pavilions, is utterly swell. Try the grilled fish satay, or the udang goreng, sautéed shrimp with garlic, tomatoes, onions, and Balinese veggies. Or drop in after snorkeling for pineapple, banana, and papaya mixed fruit—it's nearly as sweet as an ice cream shake. Whatever you do, don't miss the VERY dense chocolate mousse—a barely whipped pure chocolate concoction. Happy hours include a coffee and dessert special, and they serve high tea.

**Pandan Restaurant.** Candi Dasa Beach. ☎ **363-41541.** Reservations not required. Main courses Rp10,000–Rp50,000. No credit cards. Daily 8am–12am. SEAFOOD.

This place is right on the beach, with sand underfoot and the sound of waves crashing in your ears. It's too bad the seafood, though fresh, emphasizes deep frying, as do their Indonesian dishes. Grilled fresh fish, which is more expensive, comes with a garlic sauce. Usually "fresh fish" means tuna, but they do sometimes have snapper (coated in some mild chilies), which must be purchased whole but can easily feed two or more people.

**TJ's.** In the Watergarden Hotel, Main St., Candi Dasa. ☎ **363-41540.** Reservations not required. Main courses Rp10,000–Rp30,000. AE, MC, V. Daily 8am–midnight. INDONESIAN.

Considered the best restaurant in Candi Dasa, with prices to match. Still, the presentation is quite nice; note that satay comes on little grills with actual glowing embers. The bar is one of the few nighttime hangouts in town, even if the atmosphere is a little less Bali and a little more Tahiti/tropical island.

You could just come for dessert; try the moist Chocolate Ecstasy Cake, with little bits of orange peel—more interesting than the Wicked Chocolate Cake.

**Toke Cafe.** Main St., Candi Dasa. ☎ **363-41991.** Reservations not required. Main courses Rp7,000–Rp12,000. Daily 7am–11pm. INDONESIAN/EUROPEAN.

A perennially popular cafe with a large and mostly tasty menu that includes pasta, pizza, and even Indian food, plus a number of veggie alternatives. Surprises pop up on the appetizer menu—bruschetta, fried cheese, avocado and shrimp, guacamole. A dessert special is the "Toke Sweetheart"—fruit mixed with rum over ice cream. Live Balinese music 3 nights a week adds to the fun at this friendly place.

**Warung Astawa.** Main St., Candi Dasa. ☎ **363-41363.** Reservations not required. Main courses Rp6,000–Rp16,000. Daily 8am–11pm. INDONESIAN/CHINESE.

It's hard to find good breakfast places around Candi Dasa—probably because most people eat at their hotels—and many places wait until evening to bring out their dinner and buffet specials. But this little warung has won raves for its morning meal: pancakes, fruit salad, and tomato and cheese omelets all get a thumbs up. At night you can taste their spring rolls and shrimp cocktails while watching Balinese dancers.

## OUTDOOR ACTIVITIES & WATER SPORTS

Water sports are the main reason for coming to Candi Dasa, which boasts excellent diving and snorkeling. You can snorkel at two spots: The Blue Lagoon, at the western end of the bay, by Padangbai (about 40 minutes by outrigger boat), has otherworldly coral worthy of National Geographic, but somewhat fewer varieties of Day-Glo fish than the "little island" of Gili Mimpang, just a few minutes directly off the coast. Gili Mimpang's rougher waters may be better for divers than snorkelers, as are the small nearby islands of Gili Tepekong and Gili Biaha. Other good spots for diving are Padangbai; Amed, a bit north of Candi Dasa (which also has perhaps the best snorkeling on Bali); or Tulamben, considered one of the finest diving spots on the island. The sunken wreck of the USS *Liberty* has been offshore at Tulamben since World War II.

Snorkeling and diving trips can be arranged through your hotel, with one of several operators along the main road (a couple are listed below), or with someone you just meet on the beach (this could be the cheapest, but he may not have the right equipment.) For snorkeling, I booked through my hotel, which just used a local fisherman, but he was excellent—good equipment, plenty of safety precautions, and a strong knowledge of the area.

As for swimming, the water between the "beach" and the seawalls is shallow, but good for a dip; beyond the walls it can be too rough.

### DIVE SHOPS

The following shops can arrange diving trips around Candi Dasa or anywhere else in Bali, and most dive trips include equipment rental and lunch.

**Divelite.** Main St. (beach side), Candi Dasa. ☎ **363-41669.**

A new diving facility that seems superior to the other well-established operations, and certainly more confidence-inspiring than the street shacks. The manager is very friendly and helpful. They offer a full range of diving trips, from snorkeling to extensive excursions and diving instruction; they have low-season prices; and they host a party at the shop every day after the dive.

**Maoka Dive Center.** Main St., Candi Dasa. ☎ **363-41463.**

Offers a full range of diving options, from introductory dives and dive courses to trips out, which call for a minimum of two people. A 4-day program of instruction is US$265 per person.

## SHOPPING

Shopping isn't much to write home about in Candi Dasa, but the absence of hard-selling touts can come as a relief. The **Asri Shop,** opposite from the beach on the main street, is one exception, offering a cross section of decent goods at fixed prices. There are a couple bookstores in the area as well, including the **Candi Bookstore** on the main street, but most of what they offer is sun-faded used volumes.

## CANDI DASA AFTER DARK

Candi Dasa is pretty low-key at night, probably because most people come for the water sports and need to get to bed early for the best snorkeling and diving in the morning. The main beach road, opposite from the ocean, has several little bars and restaurants, most of which offer laser disc movies as entertainment at night. A few offer a bit more, and are listed below. Nightly dance programs are offered at the **Warung Candi Agung,** Main Street (☎ **363-41157**)—the price includes a buffet dinner and transport from your hotel. Tuesday through Friday at 9pm, the **Pandan Harum Stage** on Main Street offers Barong and Legong dance. Or you could just hang out with the adventurer types at **TJ's** bar, in the Watergarden Hotel.

**Legenda.** Main St., Candi Dasa.

Legenda calls itself a rock cafe, but it's really a reggae place, so either Bob Marley or live bands wail most evenings. It gets busier later in the evening.

**Candi Bagus Pub.** Main St., Candi Dasa.

A "sports bar"/pub that shows Australian soccer (sorry, football), and often draws full crowds for its movies.

## 10  Sights & Destinations Near Candi Dasa

### TO THE NORTH

**Amed.** 2 hours north of Candi Dasa.

The fishing village of Amed is an increasingly popular tourist destination, despite its relative inaccessibility—it's about 2 hours north of Candi Dasa, the last bit along a harsh dirt road. The snorkeling here is possibly the best in Bali. You can come here as a day trip from Candi Dasa (all the diving places offer trips), or even Ubud (it's easy to arrange land transport), but you might want to spend the night. Lodging options are limited to either losmen or the very posh **Hotel Indra Udhyana,** just outside of town. The latter offers luxuriant bungalows (around US$160 for a double) with balconies or verandas, air conditioning, TV, and telephones. I've heard even Princess Diana was a guest here. The hotel is at Amed Beach, Bunutan, P.O. Box 119, Jl. Katrangan no. 22, Karangasem 80852, Bali. The phone number is ☎ **361-241107;**

fax 361-234903; www.indo.com/hotels/indra-udhyana; e-mail: hiuamed@ indosat. net.id.

**Tenganan.** 5 miles (8km) north of Candi Dasa.

Tenganan is lauded as a well-preserved slice of Bali village life, with everything here much as it has been for centuries. In reality, once tourists started to come and villagers figured out what a cash cow they had on their hands, the place became uncomfortably like a theme park—call it Bali Land. Sure, cottages line the quaint, carless cobblestone streets, and traditions are still adhered to with a strictness found nowhere else on the island. And yes, this is the only place in Indonesia where they still make double ikat cloth. But you have to pay an enforced "donation" to enter, and once inside, it all seems plastic and commercial. It doesn't help that you are treated like a giant walking wallet, as stall after stall tries to attract you to identical wares. And how can the uninformed know if they are buying genuine, good quality ikat cloth anyway?

**Tirtagangga.** 12.4 miles (20km) north of Candi Dasa. Rp1,500. Daylight hours.

This Water Palace is hardly the most ancient site in Bali—it was built in 1947 by the last raja of the region, and partly demolished by both earthquake and volcanic eruption, which means that much of what you see is a modern restoration of something that wasn't that old to begin with. Still, the restoration was a good one, and if you like water as much as the raja did, you will enjoy the many fountains, water-spitting stone figures, and pools of this serene, parklike place. Be sure to bring your bathing suit; you can swim here for a small fee. At least one of the pools is well-maintained and on a hot day, you will regret not taking advantage of its cool waters. There is also a homestay on the premises.

## BETWEEN CANDI DASA AND UBUD

**Goa Lowah/Bat Cave.** 6.2 miles (10km) east of Klungkung. Rp1,500. Daylight hours.

A pretty little temple, a big snake, and bats—lots of bats. Some complain about the smell and mess (bats are an untidy bunch of flying rodents), but others (myself among them) find the scene too surreal and fascinating to care. It's like something right out of *The Jungle Book,* with the large python coiled around that ancient-appearing throne, just waiting for his next, easy meal, and countless squeaking bats hanging from the ceiling. The cave is said to be the mouth of a tunnel that reaches all the way to Gunung Agung and Besakih. Watch out for touts at the entrance offering you "free" necklaces; they will demand money for them when you leave.

**Klungkiung.** 16 miles (26km) southeast of Ubud.

More or less on the road to Candi Dasa from Ubud, Klungklung was the seat of the local raja until the last one died in 1965. It's a rather interesting, almost colonial-looking town, worth poking around a bit. Note the shops more or less across and catty corner from the parking lot across from the palace, where you can you can get gorgeous, elaborate real temple wear— as opposed to what you would normally buy in tourist areas.

**Taman Gili.** In Klungklung. Rp1,500. Daylight hours.

The Taman Gili gardens contain the only remnants of the Semara Pura Royal Palace, and are referred to as the Palace by guides. Very little remains of the palace, which was mostly destroyed by fighting in 1908, but two main buildings are set in the relaxing gardens. The **Kerta Gosa** is an open-air pavilion, once the Hall of Justice, notable for its famous painted ceiling, a nine-level mural showing scenes and characters featured in wayang puppet theater. The murals have been restored many times, and nothing remains of the original. Still, they are interesting and virtually unique. The paintings show all sorts of punishments in store for the wicked, and probably made the accused brought here for trial tremble. The **Bale Kambung**, a floating pavilion entirely surrounded by a moat, was reserved for tooth-filing ceremonies. Its ceiling, also gaily and elaborately painted, illustrates Balinese astronomy and folk tales. There is a museum on the property that lacks any explanatory aids, but within its virtual junk shop hodgepodge display are some fascinating items, including relics and photos of the royal family. Don't overlook (as if you could) that photo-op brick and stone gateway to the right of the Bale Kambung.

## BETWEEN CANDI DASA & LOVINA

**Gunung Batur and Lake Batur.** 38.4 miles (62km) north of Ubud.

Gunung Batur is the most sacred mountain in Bali after Gunung Agung. It's a beautiful sight thanks to the volcanic lake near its peak (the biggest in Bali), and the smoke that still pours from it. You can see lava tracks streaking down its side and villages built on or near them—an act of great faith, considering that its last eruption was 1926 (surely it must be feeling due again?). You can hike Batur, more easily than Agung, even without a guide, though having one can be handy.

The best place to view Lake Batur and the volcano is from **Penelokan,** a village on the lake crater rim, whose name means "Place to Look." It's a heck of a view, provided the weather cooperates (clouds are not conducive to vistas). You can improve your odds by arriving early in the morning.

That this is a scenic tourist spot has not been lost on the locals, and the most aggressive touts on the island will be here waiting for you. The word "no" is like a dog whistle; they can't hear it. Their phenomenally irritating and incredible persistence, and the small fee you have to pay even to enter Penelokan (around Rp1,500 per person) may make this a hassle you want to avoid. Then again, it's a beautiful volcanic crater—sure you want to miss it? (There is actually an alternative; see Pura Ulun Danu Batur review, below.)

**Pura Ulun Danu Batur.** 2.48 miles (4km) north of Penelokan.

This is the second most important temple in Bali after Besakih, and in my opinion, far more striking. As a bonus, it rests on the lip of the lake crater, so you have a peaceful way to get much of that fabulous view without the touts, who aren't permitted inside. (Though not only do you have to run a gauntlet of them to enter, lately they've set up camp between the temple and the rim and do try to call to you and get your attention.)

There are quite a few shrines within the temple complex (300 are ultimately planned), which is dedicated to the goddess of the crater lake, but the one that stands out is the 11-roofed meru (a pagoda-style shrine) in the inner courtyard.

**Lake Bratan and Pura Ulun Danu Bratan.** 30 miles (48km) north of Denpasar. Daylight hours. Rp1,500.

A beautiful lake set in a long-defunct volcanic crater whose serenity seems impossible to shatter—that is, unless you are here during tourist season, when the water is full of buzzing boats and the like. It's directly on the way to Lovina, and so worth stopping to look at, certainly for the temple, Pura Ulun Danu Batur. Dedicated to the water goddess, and an important directional temple, it's the one that shows up in all the guidebook photographs, with its meru set beautifully against a backdrop of water, almost appearing to float there. Truth be told, it photographs somewhat better than it looks in person, so photo op buffs will be the happiest for coming here. But anyone will be pleased with the pretty manicured grounds, not quite so cluttered with tourists as you might think, with a multi-level shrine to Buddha.

# 11 Lovina

Lovina Beach is a low-key tourist area, a good place to go to get away from crowds and noise. With some exceptions, however, the standard of accommodations and food go way down. That seems like a small price to pay when you engage in the excellent snorkeling available here. The black sand beaches unfortunately have far too many overly aggressive touts to make them suitable for much sunbathing (but at least it is a beach, unlike Candi Dasa). Otherwise, Lovina has largely avoided the commercialization of the other prominent tourist locales, which makes it an appealing destination for many an intrepid Bali traveler. Consider it the laid-back vacation from your vacation. Those touts do make strolling the beach somewhat of a hassle, but since you will be doubtless staying feet from the ocean, viewing the gorgeous sunset just means stepping right outside your room.

Lovina was given its name by Anak Agung Panji Tisna, the ruler of northern Bali, but the name now applies to a stretch of six small villages that blend together in a row along the ocean: Pemaron, Tukadmungga, Anturan, Kalibukbuk, Kaliasem, and Temukus. Kalibukbuk is where the main action is (along with most of the losmen), so staying at the western or easternmost villages ensures more quiet.

## GETTING THERE

Tourist shuttle buses to Lovina can be picked up in Kuta, Ubud and Candi Dasa. Bemos come through via Singaraja, but be sure to ask if they actually stop in Lovina, and where.

## GETTING AROUND

The main road (that's what it's called) runs parallel to the coast, with two tiny (and easily missed) side streets coming off it, in Kalibukbuk, to the ocean. **Jalan Bina Ria** is the western street and **Ketapang** is the eastern one. Most losmen and restaurants are found on these streets and alleys coming off them, with a few more along the main road. If you are staying right here, walking is not a problem (though as mentioned, walking along the beach can be a hassle), and motorbikes can be rented. Many of the hotels farther out have **shuttles** to this main area, but it's easy to grab any **bemo** that zips up and down along the main road. Just be sure you know where you want to be let off—they often don't speak much English.

## Fast Facts: Lovina

**Banks/Currency Exchange**   Money changers are along the main road (as are some banks), and the Jalan Bina Ria.

**Internet/E-mail**   Spice Cyber, located in a Spice Dive, a dive shop on Jalan Bina Ria, offers e-mail and fax service.

**Post Office/Mail**   There is no post office proper, but there are agents on the main road (or just hand your envelopes to your hotel to mail for you).

**Telephone**   On the main road west of Jalan Bina Ria. The area code for Lovina is 362.

## ACCOMMODATIONS

With two exceptions, the level of accommodations in Lovina are basic; for the most part, the luxury hotels have not yet invaded here. All properties are on the beach unless otherwise noted, though none have truly private beaches—leaving the hotel grounds for the sand means being suddenly surrounded by a swarm of touts who don't care that you've already booked a dolphin watching or snorkeling trip. (For some reason, these folks largely disappear near sunset, so a walk to and from town then is most enjoyable.)

## VERY EXPENSIVE

✪ **Damai Lovina Hotel.** Jl. Damai, Kayuputih Lovina, Singaraja, Bali. ☎ **44-331-48034** (from abroad), 362-41008. Fax 362-41009. www.damai.com. 8 units. A/C MINIBAR TEL. US$168–US$206. Rates include breakfast. MC, V. Free parking.

The motto of this hotel is "hard to find, hard to leave," and I can solemnly assure you that this is correct. Located way up the hill overlooking Lovina, what you lose in beach access, you gain in some of the finest accommodations in Bali. It's a nearly perfect little jewel of a place, the brainchild of a Danish ex-pat. Rooms are all villas, and they are all utterly beautiful, with gorgeous wood furniture, Balinese fabric on the furnishings, many windows, and a four-poster canopy bed draped with cheese cloth. More carved wood leads to the dressing areas and bathrooms, which have green stone outdoor showers, wood sinks and vanities, and amenities in glass bottles. Deluxe villas have a bigger bath and an outdoor Jacuzzi spa tub, and a sitting area with a low-set table with a sunken area for your feet. Some rooms have an ocean view. The grounds overlook a panorama of green hills and gorge and blue ocean—a spectacular view no matter where you look—with a small, lovely pool that seems to spill into the surroundings. For those worried about being so far (15–20 minutes) from the ocean, there's a free shuttle to the beach all day long. It's virtually the comfort and style of an Amendari at a fraction of the cost. Amenities include room service (until 10pm), hair dryers, massage, laundry, baby-sitting, water sports, area tours, and airport pickup. See the review below of the terrific Damai Restaurant, but note it's very expensive at night unless you have meals built into your room rates, so plan to go into Lovina for dinner most evenings (or stock your fridge with snacks). There's one small bar.

## EXPENSIVE

**Mas Lovina Cottages.** Jl. Raya Lovina, Kalibukbuk, Bali. ☎ **362-41237.** Fax 362-41236. 20 units. A/C MINIBAR TV. US$110–US$220. JCB, MC, V.

These "cottages" are actually two-story cabinlike structures, with two bedrooms that share a living room and kitchen area. The space is wonderful, and the bathrooms are big, with tubs, and nicely tiled, but the furniture is shabby and uncomfortable. It's nothing a good face-lift wouldn't fix, but at these prices it's probably not worth it except for families. Each half of the cottage (bedroom plus living room or kitchen, a rarity in Bali) can be rented separately, or you can take the entire structure. The pool is by far the largest in Lovina, and it's virtually right on the beach (though touts tend to hang over the walls, trying to get your attention). The same company owns the **Hotel Bali Danau Buyan,** at nearby Lake Buyan (Jalan Raya Bedugul, Pancasari, ☎ 362-21351), and it's basically the same layout and rates, but the location on a mountain location overlooking the lake provides a different, rather peaceful experience you might want to look into for a night.

Amenities include VCR, CD player, kitchen utensils, washing machines in cottages, pool, tennis court, putting green, airport pickup, free rides into Lovina, and water sports (though I had better luck arranging my own snorkeling/dolphin watching with touts on the beach). There is one restaurant and a bar.

✪ **Puri Bagus Lovina.** P.O. Box 225, Lovina, Singaraja, Bali. ☎ **362-21430.** Fax 362-22627. E-mail: pblovina@denpasar.wasantara.net.id. 40 units. A/C MINIBAR TV TEL. US$95–US$130 double; US$200–US$300 suites. AE, DC, JCB, MC, V. Free parking.

If you want luxury (or close to it) accommodations, without the isolation and lack of beach access that comes with the Damai, here is your other option. This is a splendid

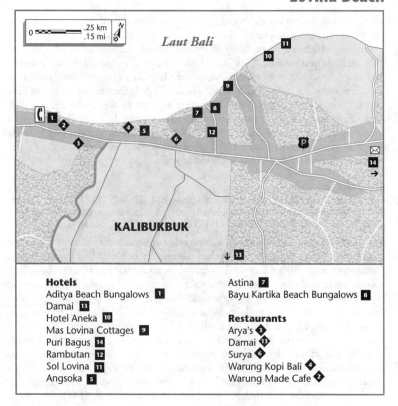

Laut Bali

KALIBUKBUK

**Hotels**
Aditya Beach Bungalows **1**
Damai **13**
Hotel Aneka **10**
Mas Lovina Cottages **9**
Puri Bagus **14**
Rambutan **12**
Sol Lovina **11**
Angsoka **5**

Astina **7**
Bayu Kartika Beach Bungalows **8**

**Restaurants**
Arya's **3**
Damai **13**
Surya **6**
Warung Kopi Bali **4**
Warung Made Cafe **2**

place (better than their property in Candi Dasa), decidedly high-end (but more afford-able than comparable Bali beach resorts), and imaginative without being funky like most Lovina hotels. Rooms, all in villas, are simple but elegant and comfortable, dec-orated with bits of Bali fabric and paintings. Prices vary according to the view (rice paddy, garden, or ocean), but they all have high thatched ceilings with glass at the top to keep the air in and the bugs out. Large bathrooms come with both indoor and out-door showers, and there are big verandas, some of which look right out to the sea. Suites will get you a private pool, CD player, and a basic tub, and some have kitchens. The landscaped grounds go right to the seawall (there is no beach but there are steps into the water), with several small cushioned bales overlooking the blue Java sea. A pretty blue amorphous pool also peers out at the ocean (sometimes you share the water with the hotel's four ducks). Facilities and services include water sports, bicycles, sight-seeing excursions, free shuttle to Lovina, 24-hour room service, car rental, sundries shop, boutique, laundry, safety deposit boxes, and massage. For dining, there's a small seafood restaurant with outdoor kitchen, and a second restaurant that serves Balinese items. There is a poolside bar. Occasional evening entertainment is offered.

**Sol Lovina.** Jl. Rayan Lovina, Lovina Beach, Bali. ☎ **362-41775.** Fax 362-41659. www. solmelia.es. E-mail: sollovina@singarajah.wasantara.net.id. 129 units. A/C MINIBAR TV TEL. US$90–US$107 double. US$250–US$300 villas. AE, DC, JCB, MC, V. Free parking.

This is a newish higher-end hotel in Lovina, and in that sense, it's welcome. But every-thing is just a bit too calculated, with deliberate, rather than organic, Bali touches. Exteriors and interiors try for harmony between Western and Balinese styles—and as nearly always, the result feels something like an apartment complex. Still, rooms start large and only get larger, and if the use of natural fabrics and woods tends to make everything a bit beige, it's certainly plenty comfortable. Bathrooms are also big, with tubs and an open section. "New" standards are not in cottages, but in a two-story building (the second story yields views of red tile roofs and mountains), with newer furniture and good bathrooms in gray granite. All offer generous amenities and closet space. Though generic, there's nothing wrong with any of this, and indeed, it's a lot better than many of the more shopworn accommodations in town. Other amenities are safety deposit boxes, baby-sitting, gym, massage, laundry, dry cleaning, tour and water sports, and airport pick up. There's one seafood restaurant, and one with Bali/international cuisine. A bar is offered as well.

## MODERATE

**Hotel Aneka Lovina.** Jl. Rayan Lovina, Singaraja, Bali. ☎ **362-41121,** 41122. Fax 362-41827. www.indo.com/hotels/aneka-lovina. E-mail: anki-lovina@denpasar.wasantara.net.id. 59 units. A/C MINIBAR TV TEL. US$55–US$75 double. JCB, MC, V. Free parking.

A typical mid-range Lovina Beach accommodation—not bad at all, just not all that memorable. Rooms here are in thatched cottages set in pretty Bali garden grounds (complete with a dolphin fountain). Standard rooms are boring, with tiny basic bathrooms, but second-story rooms offer nice views of green and thatch. Deluxe rooms are bigger, with carved wooden doors that lead to slightly less disappointing interiors—bamboo furniture, and bigger bathrooms, some with tubs. For size and less oppressive decor, these are a better deal. The small pool has a swim-up bar, and the waterfall-flanked stage offers occasional nighttime entertainment. There's one seafood restaurant and one offering the usual assortment of Indonesian and European fare. A pool bar and bars inside both restaurants occasionally provide nighttime entertainment. Amenities include room service (until 11pm), safety deposit boxes, pool, playground, water sports, laundry, tour desk, massage, and airport transfers (US$45).

## INEXPENSIVE

**Aditya Beach Bungalows.** P.O. Box 134, Singaraja 81101, Bali. ☎ **362-41059.** Fax 362-41342. 65 units. US$20–US$45 double. Rates include breakfast. AE, MC, V. Free parking.

This big property looks impressive from a distance (you can see it when out on the water snorkeling or dolphin watching), but it's really just an adequate budget choice. High-end rooms are big, clean, thatched and oceanfront, with slightly shabby furniture and slightly smelly bathrooms (sinks are actually in the rooms). They do have air conditioning and televisions. Oddly, the cheaper standard rooms in a two-story concrete block are somewhat nicer, with Bali fabric and less grim bathrooms. Skip the low-end, fan-only US$20 standard, which is very old. The swimming pool is nothing special, despite some spitting fountains. There's a restaurant that serves Indonesian, European and Chinese food. The bar serves "many kind drinks with qualified bartender." Amenities include safety deposit boxes, pool, laundry, taxi service, car rental, and water sports.

✪ **Rambutan Beach Cottages.** PO Box 195, Singaraja, Bali. ☎ **362-41388.** Fax 362-41057. E-mail:Rambutan@singaraja.wasantara.net.id. 18 units. US$15–US$40 double. Rates include breakfast. JCB, MC, V. Free parking.

By far the best budget option in Lovina. All rooms are in two-story red and white bungalows that are set among the prettiest tropical garden around. Budget rooms (US$15) are better than others in this price range, but better still are standards and superiors, with hot water and TVs (and A/C in superiors) and plenty of very nice Indonesian carved wood furniture and Bali fabrics. The rooms are big and bright, with funky-tiled, slightly shabby bathrooms. The pool looks like a small blue pond. There is a small children's area and a slightly run-down badminton court. The staff is friendly (and can arrange water sports and tours) and speaks decent English, and it's just a short walk to the beach. There's one Indonesian restaurant, with a buffet and dance entertainment every Wednesday and Sunday; also one bar.

## LOSMEN

**Angsoka.** Jl. Bina Ria, Lovina Beach, Bali. ☎ **362-41841.** Fax 362-41023. 38 units. Rp20,000–Rp150,000. Rates include breakfast. No credit cards.

A friendly place, with very clean and comfortable losmen style rooms. As the price goes up, so does the amount of space and the quality of the bathrooms, and you gain fans, showers, tubs and, finally, A/C. At these prices, spring for the latter. Some rooms are in small bungalows (which curiously have inferior bathrooms), and some come with high bamboo ceilings. There is a small pool and a tiny temple on the grounds.

**Astina Seaside Cottages.** P.O. Box 141, Singaraja, Bali. Lovina Beach (500m from main road), Kalibukbuk. ☎ **362-41187.** 16 units. Rp30,000–Rp50,000 double. Rates include breakfast. No credit cards.

A friendly losmen with all rooms in cottages or bungalows. The more you pay, the more you get: private baths, ceiling fans, even a welcome drink and fruit basket! The paint is chipped, but they do have carved wood beds. Cold water only. Grand plans include a swimming pool by the year 2000, and rooms for Rp75,000 with hot water and bathtubs. They can book dolphin watching and snorkeling trips.

**Bayu Kartika Beach Bungalows.** Jl. Ketapang, Kalibukbuk, Lovina Beach. ☎ **362-41055,** 41219. 24 rooms. Rp65,000–Rp150,000. Rates include breakfast. No credit cards.

Though more expensive than a regular losmen (as prices go higher, you gain A/C and hot water), this is a very popular place—travelers you would expect to find at higher-end locations proclaimed great satisfaction with the accommodations. Rooms are all duplex bungalows (some with garden baths), sprawled out in a large garden setting with ponds and fountain. The location, adjacent to the beach, can't be beat. Plans are to add more rooms, and a swimming pool (which may be ready by the time you read this). Phones and TV may also be added to some rooms. There's a small restaurant and bar overlooking the beach.

## DINING

With perhaps one exception, dining in Lovina is a pretty dull proposition. Most of the options, outside of hotels, are on the main street or on Jalan Bina Ria, which runs perpendicular from it to the beach. Wander the latter and pick a restaurant at random—it will be okay, but probably nothing special. (They do often offer dance programs and competing buffets spilling over with food.)

**Arya's @ Planet Lovina.** Jl. On the main road. ☎ **362-41797.** Reservations not required. Rp 6,500–Rp18,500. No credit cards. Daily 8:30AM–11PM. INDONESIAN.

The former Arya's, whose new name now spoofs Planet Hollywood, used to serve the best desserts in Lovina. Alas, these (including apple crumble, brownies and "Fruity Planet Surprise") have gone downhill, and the rest of the menu features merely adequate food (admittedly, in a pleasant enough atmosphere). It does have lots of cocktails, dessert coffee, and dubiously "healthy" drinks (orange, spinach, and ginger with milk, egg and honey—all in one glass).

✪ **Damai Restaurant.** Jl. Damai (in Hotel Damai), Kayuputih, Lovina. ☎ **362-41008.** Reservations suggested. Lunch main courses US$4.95–US$7.40, dinner set menu US$35. AE, MC, V. Daily 11am–3pm, 7–10pm. NOUVELLE INDONESIAN.

Apparently, the proprietor of the Damai is a foodie who imported his own gourmet chef. If you aren't staying here, do make the trip up the mountain. Skip the expensive (outrageously so by Bali standards) set dinner menu (you can't see the marvelous ocean/mountain view at night anyway), and come up for lunch. You will pay more than you would for an average Bali meal, but the same perfect, world-class meal back in the U.S. would cost at least four times as much. The menu is limited (perhaps only four entry choices, and two appetizers), but more than sufficient. Melt-in-the-mouth pan fried fish was topped with a heavenly creamy dill sauce. Fried chicken is really also pan-fried, served with a spicy ginger sauce. Chicken sate was more Chinese in flavor than Balinese. The presentation was modern, simple and elegant, with small portions, but the contents were rich, so the amounts proved just right. And if you really wish to spend more money, the many expensive bottles of wine can bring your bill up to staggering heights.

**Surya Restaurant & Bar.** Main Street, Kalibukbuk. Reservations not required. Main courses Rp6,500–Rp18,000. No credit cards. Daily 8am–10pm. SEAFOOD/INDONESIAN.

Surya is a popular and reliable local restaurant, well situated on the main drag, that serves everything a hungry traveler could want—brunch, seafood, local specialties, pizza, and a happy hour with a range of booze and mixed drinks.

**Warung Kopi Bali.** Jl. Binara, Singaraja. ☎ **362-41361.** Reservations not required. Main courses Rp5,900–18,900. No credit cards. Daily 8am–11pm. SEAFOOD/INDONESIAN.

Probably a bit better than the other tourist-oriented restaurants along the Jalan Bina Ria. They serve garlicked seafood kebabs, the notable flavors of pepes isi laut (marinated shrimp, tuna and veggies made with Balinese sauce all grilled together in a banana leaf) and the big, good value seafood basket that combines more garlicky tuna, sweet-and-sour shrimp, deep-fried squid, fries and rather nice vegetables. As at other places, you get a free shot and some tepid garlic bread at happy hour.

**Warung Made Cafe.** Jl. Main St. (right next to Aditya Hotel). ☎ **362-41239.** Reservations not required. Main courses Rp6,500–Rp16,500. No credit cards. Daily 8am–11pm. Indonesian.

A bit noisy because it's on the busy main street, but a nice menu of Bali, veggie (including several good salads), and seafood items. It's also an "ice cream parlor" as envisioned by Jimmy Buffet, offering concoctions with various flavors, sauces, and whipped cream. In addition to the usual suspects, try a papaya or avocado shake or a "Lovina Sunset" sundae. Don't ask what they all contain—the friendly staff speaks minimal English and can't really tell you. Continue to cool yourself down with their many sweet and lethal tropical cocktails (fruit juice and Bali brews figure heavily). A bulletin board has much info of interest to a traveler, and at night there is live music or "bring your own tape or CD."

## OUTDOOR ACTIVITIES & WATER SPORTS

The crystal-clear water, which is often as calm as glass, makes for some very fine **swimming**—though the dark sand can cloud the first several feet or even yards. But persist; not too far out you can actually **snorkel** without a guide, as coral begins rather close to shore. There aren't that many fish this close, but look for the cobalt blue starfish. There's better snorkeling on the reefs a few hundred yards away, but you'll need a guide with a boat. These reefs have been badly damaged over the years, but there are still a great variety of psychedelic fish, sometimes in impressive numbers. Be sure your guide brings some bread so you can feed the fish; being at the center of a cloud of tropical fish, all nibbling at your fingers, is a thrill. The reefs aren't significant enough for experienced divers, most of whom go to **Menjangan** or **Deer Island** to the west, or **Amed** and **Tulamben** to the east. Trips can be booked through dive shops in town. Snorkeling can be booked by just about any hotel or losmen, but frankly, many of the lesser-end hotels just flag someone down on the beach. You could do that on your own and get the same person for less money. (I was quite happy with the guy who operates boat no. 37 just east of the Mas Lovina.) The disadvantage is that these guys may not have very good, or enough, equipment; a dive shop should be able to guarantee better standards.

Finally, there is **dolphin watching,** for which Lovina is famous and for which I have mixed feelings. At about 5:30am every morning, dozens of boats go out full of tourists, to sit offshore and wait for the morning dolphin-feeding migration. This can involve a pretty long wait, which most of the time is rewarded by at least a few, and perhaps dozens of leaping dolphins. The way the boats chase the creatures so that their customers can get a good look is uncomfortably reminiscent of the touts on the beach chasing down hapless tourists. It's hard to say how the dolphins feel—they come back every morning, after all—but still. That said, I can also say that the moment your boat is surrounded by leaping, laughing Flippers may well be one of your grandest in Bali. Dolphin watching can be arranged by any hotel, or you can go flag down the same guy on the beach who took you snorkeling.

## DIVE SHOPS

**Baruna,** Main Road, Kalibukbuk (☎ 362-23775) offers snorkeling and dolphin watching. **Permai Dive Sports,** Permai Hotel, Panti Happy, Tukadmungga (perpendicular to main road, ☎ 362-23471) offers dive trips to Menjangan. **Spice Dive,** Jalan Rina Bia (☎ **362-41509**) offers a full range of diving facilities and excursions, as well as Internet service.

## SIGHTS NEAR LOVINA

All of these require transport, either your own (motorbike or car) or something you've arranged with a transport guide. Most hotels will also book day excursions.

**Gitgit Waterfall.** 6.8 miles (11km) south of Singaraja.

If you take the mountain roads through Bedugal and past Lakes Bratan, Buyan and Tambingan, you will pass by Gitgit waterfall on your way to Lovina. Park on one side of the street (whatever you do, don't eat at the restaurant there with its ghastly buffet), cross the road, pay a small donation (Rp600), and make your lengthy way down a twisty concrete path and stairs. Once past the many stalls, you'll come across a small temple and a thrilling 148-foot (45m) freefalling waterfall. Cool off in the pool at its base, and admire the considerable jungle foliage before making the hot climb back up.

**Brahma Vihara Asrama Buddhist Monastery.** 6.2 miles (10km) southwest of Lovina.

Built in 1970, this is the only Buddhist monastery in Bali. It attracts regular pilgrims (including, once, the Dalai Lama). It was severely damaged in the 1976 earthquake, but has been completely restored. It's brightly colored, with a fine gold Buddha statue, but truth be told, Zen students will find it of the most interest, while everyone else will only note how different the architecture is from Hindu temples.

**Air Panas Hot Springs.** 3.7 miles (6km) east of Lovina, or 1km from the monastery—turn left at the crossroads as you go downhill, then left at the next major crossroads, and from there follow the signs. Rp1,100. 8am–4pm.

These are some of the nicest and best-maintained hot springs on the island and generally not very crowded. Be sure to cover yourself with a sarong.

⭘ **Pura Bejai.** About 5 miles (8km) east of Singaraja, 656 feet (200m) up small road to north.

This small temple barely rates a mention in most guidebooks, but it's one of my all-time favorites, because of its unusual look. Festooned with a riot of carvings—demons, gods, monsters, animals, you name it—it gives you a good idea of how different the temples of the north are from the cookie-cutter ones of the south.

**Pura Dalem Jagaraga.** Main road above, 1,312 feet (400m) past the turning for Pura Bejai, 2.48 miles (4km) down.

About 1 kilometer to the north of the town of Jagaraga (where the Balinese fought a great battle against the Dutch in 1848) is a temple covered in editorializing comic strip–type panel carvings that show how simple village pursuits like kite flying and fishing were corrupted by the arrival of the Dutch. The favorite photo-op is on the right hand side: two Dutch men driving a Model T, being held up by a Balinese Clyde Barker.

✪ **Pura Meduwe Karang at Kubutambahan.** 7.4 miles (12km) east of Singarajah.

More extraordinary and unusual carvings characterize one of the largest temples in the north: figures from the *Ramayana,* soft porn, monkeys, village life, and most famously, a shorts-wearing bicyclist about to turn a dog-chased rat into roadkill. Folklore has it this is Dutch artist WOJ Nieuwenkamp.

⭘ **Air Saneh.** 3.7 miles (6km) from Kubutambahan. Rp500 (more if you want to swim.) 7am–7pm.

A freezing cold—oh, isn't that nice?—fresh water springs in a rock-lined natural swimming pool, set in pleasing gardens that overlook the sea. It's just enough off the beaten path so that it's often uncrowded (with the possible exception of school holidays and package tour days; weekdays seem best)—a delicious little secret I am blowing here. Don't be shy; bring your bathing suit and jump in. There are clean changing rooms.

# 12 Lombok

Some people talk of Lombok as being what Bali was 20 years ago—an unspoiled paradise just starting to be discovered by tourists. Well, yes and no. Lombok's wonderful beaches, reefs and volcanic slopes are relatively uncrowded and free of touristy distractions and tackiness. And though only 22 miles (35km) east of Bali, it's in many respects worlds away from its more renowned neighbor.

Geographically, the two islands are separated by a deep trench that marks the meeting point of the Asian and Australian tectonic plates, and scientists have theorized that as an explanation for the stark differences in their topography and climate. Lombok is significantly drier than Bali, especially in the south, where a vast expanse of gently rolling hills fans out from the island's lone looming volcano, **Gunung Rinjani,** culminating in spectacular, rocky shores and half-moon bays with brilliant white sands. It's less fertile than Bali and has thus been a poorer relation since long before Westerners sailed these waters.

Lombok is also culturally quite distinct from Bali, being Islamic rather than Hindu—though like Bali, where ancient animist beliefs still color the practice of religion, pre-Islamic elements left over from the ancient Sasak people influence Lombok's spiritual life. This element, though, is not as evident as in Bali—no endless parade of temple processions or sidewalks strewn with offerings, no ever-present ceremony and music. As such, Lombok is not as much a magnet for the kind of seekers who flock to Ubud.

# Lombok

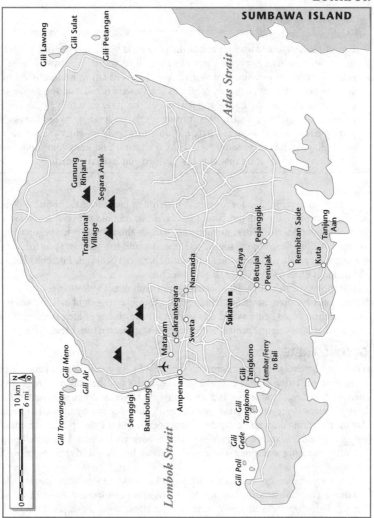

SUMBAWA ISLAND

Atlas Strait

Gili Lawang
Gili Sulat
Gili Petangan

Gunung Rinjani
Segara Anak

Traditional Village

Narmada
Cakrankegara
Mataram
Sweta
Sukaran ■

Praya
Betujai Penujak
Pejanggik

Rembitan Sade
Kuta
Tanjung Aan

Gili Tangkono
Lembar/Ferry to Bali

Senggigi
Batubolung
Ampenan

Gili Trawangan
Gili Meno
Gili Air

Gili Tangkono
Gili Gede
Gili Poli

Lombok Strait

10 km
6 mi
N

---

But the parade of daily life is no less fascinating, with carts drawn by small ponies (the most common mode of transportation on the island) or communal trucks loaded with perhaps 20 people going to or from town and market. **Temples and water gardens** offer quite pleasant sightseeing prospects, while the food—the name Lombok means chili pepper, so Sasak cooking has a kick—is every bit as rewarding as Balinese warung fare.

Art is not as prevalent here as on Bali, but crafts are a big attraction, particularly pottery and fine woven fabric—the intricate double-ikat cloth, where the threads are strung and dyed in pattern before being woven. **Crafts villages** are eager to show visitors how the wares are made.

Increasingly, visitors are swooping in via hydrofoil or small plane from Bali, drawn by the unspoiled beaches, the **snorkeling and diving** off the shores of Lombok and the nearby Gili Islands, and the stunning treks around the volcano. This puts the island at a crossroads. Eager to pick up on the spillover from Bali, Lombok has taken

---

### Beach Etiquette

Part of the reason to visit Lombok is the clear aqua water and the fine white sand of the beaches, many of which you can have all to yourself. But please note that while these bits of paradise tend to make you dress—or rather, undress—like Adam and Eve before the fall, remember that this is a Moslem island, and you should cover up once you are off the sand—and maybe even on it. Even if some locals are used to nearly nekkid tourists, that doesn't mean it's the polite thing to do. I'm not suggesting entire djellabahs or the like, nor does this apply to when you are on your hotel grounds. Just demonstrate a little local courtesy and keep your top on while sunbathing, and cover up that cute bikini when you leave the beach.

---

steps to court development for tourists. A plan for an international airport, to be built on land owned by the Suharto family, has been put on hold with Suharto's downfall and the economic crisis. But construction of state-of-the-art resorts has begun with the Novotel at Kuta Beach in the south, and adjacent land has been set aside for more of the same. As an alternative to the more rustic charms of Senggigi, Lombok's Kuta has the makings of an equivalent to Bali's Nusa Dua.

But there's the rub. If people are coming to Lombok as an alternative to Bali, what happens if development makes it more and more like its neighbor? The economic boost tourism could bring would do wonders for the quality of life here. But at what cost to the island's sights, people, and culture—its greatest natural resources?

### GETTING THERE

There are three ways to get to Lombok—by ferry, by hydrofoil, and by plane. If time is an issue, the latter is probably your best choice. It's not that much more expensive than the hydrofoil, and it means a 25-minute flight versus 2 hours. (The ferry is at least 4 hours.) If pressed for time, you can easily do a day trip by plane, and package day tours, designed around a typical tourist agenda (a little shopping, a little beach-going), are even available by hydrofoil. But if your goal is island exploration, particularly searching out those private white sand beaches, 1 day is probably not enough.

Any travel office on Bali can book your Lombok trip (try the always reliable **Parama**). They can arrange bus transfer packages too, so inquire about this if your hotel does not offer shuttle service at the harbor (most do at the airport).

**BY FERRY**   The ferry leaves Padang Bai (just south of Candi Dasa) twice a day, arriving about 4 hours later at Lempar.

**BY HYDROFOIL**   The Mabua Express departs twice a day from Benoa (just north of Nusa Dua) and arrives in Lempar about 2 hours later.

**BY PLANE**   **Merpati Nusantara** (☎ **361-263918** or 361-751374) and **Garuda National** (☎ **361-227825,** 361-772231, or 361-751179) fly nearly hourly to Lombok's **Selaparang Airport.** Note that later flights are often consolidated and/or canceled, so if you are making a day trip, you should double-check that your flight back is still running.

### GETTING AROUND

You have two choices of public transportation: **bemos** and **horse-drawn carts.** Given those options, even though traffic is nearly as chaotic as on Bali (and those horse-drawn carts just add to the mayhem), you might be better off **renting a car,** especially if you want to go exploring by yourself instead of on a hotel's planned day-tour. Your hotel can set you up with a rental, or you can get one at the airport when you arrive. **Motorbikes** are an attractive option, particularly for searching out private beaches, but if you don't already know how to ride one, this is not the place to learn. A simple—though admittedly more costly—option is to have your hotel arrange for a car and driver for you.

# Fast Facts: Lombok

**Banks/Currency Exchange**   There are banks in Matarama and throughout the main tourist areas are money changers.

**Internet/E-mail**   As of this writing, Internet cafes have not made it to Lombok but that may change by the time you get there.

**Post Office/Mail**   There are post offices in Mataram and one in the center of Senggiggi, but your hotel can also mail for you.

**Telephones**   There are several telephones in the center of Senggiggi.

## AMPENAN–MATARAM–CAKRANEGARA–SWETA

Together, these four towns, a few kilometers south of the airport, make up one sprawling mass that actually is far less oppressive and suffocating than you would expect from an Indonesian city. True tourist sights are few, but poking around here can be surprisingly interesting. Still, nearly all tourists quickly move on to more beach-appropriate locales, like Senggigi and Kuta.

## SENGGIGI

Senggigi, 7.4 miles (12 km) north of Mataram, is the main beach resort for Lombok and it is here most tourists end up. The beach isn't as outstanding as those found farther south, but it is here the main—okay, only (so far)—tourist infrastructure is set up, and so for that convenience, not to mention its better proximity to various Lombok sights, this may make it the best place for the causal visitor, particularly if you are planning only a short trip to Lombok.

If you have more time, I suggest going south to **Kuta,** to take advantage of the real attractions (in our opinion) of the island—but at an admitted loss of convenience, nightlife, and other things someone on vacation might consider a necessity. Water sports can be arranged by your hotel, or you can call **Baruna** (at the Senggigi Beach Hotel, ☎ **370-93210**) to arrange scuba diving, lessons, snorkeling trips, and windsurfing. There are dives right in front of the Senggigi Beach Hotel, but most dive trips take you to the Gili Islands. For shopping and other basic needs, the **Senggigi Square,** right across the street from the Sheraton, is a brightly colored, rather abstract mall (of original and whimsical enough architecture that it did not offend our sensibilities) that contains boutiques, gift shops, money changers, and a travel agent.

### ACCOMMODATIONS

With one exception, Lombok has a long way to go to catch up to the Bali hotel experience. Apart from the Novotel in Kuta (by far the best hotel on the island), all Western-style accommodations are in Senggigi, because few Western tourists venture beyond there. Otherwise, you have to make do with losmen, which are almost all extremely basic (think shack on the beach).

**Hotel Jayakarta.** Jl. Raya Senggigi Ampenana, Lombok. ☎ **370-930458**. Fax 370-93043. www.lombokisland.com. E-mail: jayakarta@mataram.wasantara.net.id. 76 units. A/C MINIBAR TV TEL. US$80–US$100 double; US$185 suites. AE, JCB, MC, V.

A bit outside town, which is probably why the rates are cheaper for essentially the same generic product. Textbook hotel rooms with typical tropical fabrics and bamboo furniture are in either two- or four-story blocks. (The four-story building is newer.) Bathrooms are done in a gray marble that comes off a bit cold and industrial, but they do have tubs. The swimming pool is adequate, and there are two additional kids' pools, including one with a mini beach. Plans are to add an additional 92 rooms by the beginning of 1999. Amenities include 24-hour room service, welcome drink, laundry, drugstore, massage, tour and travel desk, shuttle service to Lombok, fitness center, jogging track, and children's playground.

**Lombok Intan Laguna.** Jl. Raya Senggigi, Senggigi. P.O. Box 1049, Mataram 83125, Lombok. ☎ **370-93090.** Fax 370-93185. www.indo.com/hotels/bali_intan/laguna.html. E-mail: intan@mataram.wasantara.net.id. 121 units. A/C MINIBAR TV TEL. US$110–US$120 double; US$130–US$275 bungalows and suites. AE, DC, MC, V.

This sprawling full-service compound built around a lagoon comprises 50 bungalows, 32 garden cottages, and a 39-room "garden wing." Opened in 1989, it's already in the midst of an ongoing, and somewhat needed, face-lift. It seemed a bit plain when I visited, like a basic Western condo complex with a few superficial tropical Sasak touches, though not lacking in any standard amenities. A spacious, comfortable lobby pavilion has a nice, sociable feel, and the staff is friendly and attentive. It's also well-suited for families, with baby-sitting offered free of charge, and a particularly nice, large, meandering lagoon-type pool. A breakfast buffet is served, though not normally included with the room fee.

Amenities also include 24-hour room service, laundry, safety deposit boxes, shopping arcade, tour desk, car rental, airport transfers, drugstore, meeting and banquet facilities, two tennis courts, an adequate health club, massage, sauna, and water sports. The Laguna restaurant serves Indonesian and international dishes 24 hours a day. You can get Italian at the Harbor restaurant and drink at either the Sunset bar or Gili Lounge.

**Senggigi Beach Hotel.** Jl. Pantai Senggigi, Senggigi, P.O. Box 1001, Mataram 83010, Lombok. ☎ **370-693210/19.** Fax 370-693200. www.aerowisata.com/seng.html. E-mail: hsa@mataram.wasantara.net.id. 149 units. A/C MINIBAR TV TEL. US$130 double; US$160–US$250 bungalows. AE, DC, JCB, MC, V.

Located down an unprepossessing dirt lane, these equally unassuming accommodations get the job done in a comfortable but standard beach motel kind of way. Bungalows are slightly nicer, with somewhat bigger baths, and half of them have outdoor showers. (Guests here are also welcomed with a cake with their name on it.) Each bungalow houses two rooms and some have connecting doors, so this might be a good option for families. Kids might also like running around the quite large grounds. The pool is disappointingly unimaginative, but close to the beach. Amenities include coffeemakers, hair dryers and safety deposit boxes in bungalows only, 24-hour room service, baby-sitting, tennis court, laundry, dry cleaning, water sports and tour desk, and clinic. There are three restaurants—buffet at the Rinjani, Italian at Basilico Italian Pavilion, and seafood and Indonesian specialties at the candlelit Seahorse—and three bars. Frequent evening theme dinners are offered.

**Sheraton Sengiggi.** Jl. Raya Senggigi km 8, Senggigi, Lombok. ☎ **370-693333.** Fax 370-693140. www.sheratonitt.com. E-mail: sheraton@mataram.wasantara.net.id. 156 units. A/C MINIBAR TV TEL. US$150–US$170 double (deluxe rooms); US$350–US$400 suites. AE, DC, JCB, MC, V.

This is somewhat of a letdown compared to the Bali-based Sheratons. Sure, everything is plenty comfortable here: the highly efficient, helpful staff speaks excellent English;

the newly redone lobby is tropical elegant; and the ocean-side garden lines the seaside setting with a profusion of lush plants. But the rooms are in a rather boring Western style—though bright and cheerful, with good use of tropical colors and wood, and nice-sized bathrooms. It's just a bit dull, which is one thing you can't say about the Bali Sheratons. All rooms technically have an ocean view, but the rampant foliage can obscure it. The fine free-form pool with a water slide right through a giant's head is a step in the right direction. The beach is for hotel guests only, and a massage pavilion and a bright kids' playground are currently being built. Ask your travel agent or the hotel's booking office about their fine vacation getaway packages that add various bits of pampering to a few nights' getaway. Amenities are hair dryers, safes, coffeemakers, 24-hour room service, newspapers, baby-sitting, airport pickup, laundry, dry cleaning, tour desk, car rental, business center, water sports, and in-house clinic. There are three quite good restaurants (see review below of Kebun Anggrek) and two bars, one with a lovely view of the sunset. Every night they have a theme dinner.

## DINING

Restaurants in Senggigi are generally of fairly good quality, though none are all that special. The following are all in the same area on Jalan Raya, roughly in the center of Senggigi action, which makes it easy to start looking for nightlife after dinner. Consider also asking your hotel to help you find a genuine Sasak warung, so you can try some of their spicy, original dishes (I especially like the way they do fish). **Gili Masak** serves Indonesian, Chinese, and European food daily from 8am to 11pm (☎ 370-693105). Main courses run from Rp25,000 to Rp40,000 (MC, V). You can try Thai and seafood at **Naga Restaurant** (☎ 370-693101), open daily from 10am to 2:30pm and 5:30 to 10:30pm; main courses are Rp20,000 to Rp40,000. **The Princess of Lombok** (☎ 370-693011) serves a range of food that includes not just seafood and steaks, but chili, enchiladas, fajitas, and nachos. It's open daily from 7:30am to 11pm; main courses are Rp20,000 to Rp35,000 (no credit cards). **Taman Senggigi** (☎ 370-693842) offers more Indonesian and Western combinations. It's open daily from 7am to 11pm; main courses run Rp25,000 to Rp50,000 (MC and V). Finally, you can spend a bit more with some confidence up the road at the Sheraton's **Kebun Anggrek** (☎ 370-69333), which serves international cuisine daily from 5am to 11pm; main courses are Rp55,000 to Rp120,000.

## ATTRACTIONS

**Batu Bolong Temple.** 0.62 miles (1km) south of Senggigi (near the Jayakarta Hotel). Daylight hours.

There isn't much in the way of sights in Senggigi, but this temple, perched on a rocky ledge, should help fill that void. It's not so much historical as it is pretty, offering good views and photo ops. But that's enough, particularly if you find yourself going through temple withdrawal after Bali's profusion of them. Admire the hole in the rock where virgins were once sacrificed in the good old days—or at least, in someone's vivid imagination.

**Puri Mayura Water Palace.** Jl. Selaparang, Cakranegara. Rp1,500. Daylight hours.

Much as I hate to keep comparing poor Lombok unfavorably to Bali, this 18th-century water palace isn't nearly the dazzler that Tirtagangga is. It's more like the palace at Klungklung, with a floating bale (all that's left of the original structure, destroyed in 1894 by the Dutch) set in the middle of a good-sized artificial lake. Water pours from spouts, and it's pretty and peaceful, particularly in the bustling city, but it's no more than a nice rest stop.

## GILI ISLANDS

Just to the northwest of Lombok are the three small islands that offer some of the best snorkeling and diving in this area. Many tourists take day diving trips out to enjoy them, though each of the islands does offer overnight accommodations (mostly losmen). Unfortunately, the golden goose is slowly being strangled, as constant mooring, shell removal, and other commercial activities linked to the tourist trade are starting to destroy the reefs. The range of fish is impressive, however, though currents can be rough and visibility not what it should be. Snorkelers will be happy with spots right off the beaches at the north of **Gili Trawangan** and **Gili Meno,** and should probably skip going out into deeper water with the divers. **Gili Air** is the most accessible island, close to shore, while Gili Meno has better fish and brilliant blue coral, and is recommended for beginners. Gili Trawangan is the farthest away, but rewards you with the most reliably good diving. Dive shops in Senggigi and the local hotels will arrange trips out to the islands. The Barunas at the Sheraton and Sengiggi Beach hotels are reliable.

## KUTA

Not to be confused with the Bali Kuta—in fact, here is finally something Lombok has all over Bali. Actually, this Kuta, located 18.6 miles (30km) south of Mataram, is little more than a wide spot in the road. But across the road are some of the finest white sand beaches on the whole island. As of this writing, there are exactly two choices of accommodations: the quite fabulous Novotel resort and a losmen shack on the beach. That may change, and not necessarily for the better, if the developers have their way and turn this into Lombok's Nusa Dua, so go now. It's easy to find your own private beach—just get a ride from the Novotel, or take your own car or motorbike and head down the road a ways. There are plenty of beaches to go around, all with clear aqua blue waters and a sense, however false, that you are the first person to set foot on them. You aren't—so be careful with your belongings while swimming. Some of these beaches have self-appointed locals who will guard your possessions or rent you shade from the sun. It's petty larceny, but you might as well pay them to avoid an argument.

### ACCOMMODATIONS

✪ **Novotel Lombok.** Mandalika Resort Pantai Putri Nyale, Pujut Lombok Tengah, Nusa Tenggara Barat. ☎ **370-53333.** Fax 370-53555. www.lombokonline.com/novotel. E-mail: novotel@lombokonline.com. 108 units. A/C MINIBAR TV TEL. Deluxe rooms US$130–US$140 double. Bungalow and villas US$250–US$450 double. AE, DC, JCB, MC, V.

For now, the Novotel is hands down the best hotel on Lombok, and while it's perhaps not as superlative as its Nusa Dua counterpart, it's awfully close. It's also off the beaten tourist path; unlike the Bali Kuta, there is nothing—and I mean nothing—near here. (The hotel does offers excursions, and the guides/drivers for these can be exceptionally good.) The standard rooms, in sandstone blocks, are arranged around bungalows constructed to look like the distinctive Sasak villages you pass on the way to Kuta (see above). The bungalows offer more space, and have their own swimming pool (which smacks a bit of elitism, thanks to the way the property is laid out). Otherwise, all rooms are essentially the same, with simple but attractive natural fabrics and woods. The staff is superb, all genuinely friendly, and most speak excellent English. (At least one employee, who oversees the library/business center/tour desk, speaks multiple languages—I heard him converse in both Italian and German in the space of a few minutes.) The property is big and confusing enough to require a map at first, but blundering around will ultimately take you to an elevated horizon pool, plus a series of fountains you can splash in, all overlooking a pure white beach with lovely clear water and nothing else around to spoil the view of hills and sky. And all this within steps of all sorts of cushy comforts, from towels to icy bottles of water—just the right way to effect a romantic, luxurious getaway. Other facilities and services include 24-hour room service, hair dryers, massage, laundry, library with Internet hookup, boutiques, meeting rooms, kids' club, water sports, excursions, car rental, jogging track, playground, beach sports, and regular shuttle to nearby Tanjung Aan beach.

A disadvantage of staying here is that it's a long dark walk to any food outside the hotel. And while the offerings are superb, they are also expensive, so try to get a meal plan when booking. Empat Ikan offers upscale dining, but frankly, I had some of the best fish of my life, butter-soft and full of flavor, at their "coffee shop," Kafe Chilli, which also offers nightly buffets around varying international themes.

## TANJUNG SEGER, TANJUNG AAN & TANJUNG PEDAU BEACHES

These three beaches are among the most superb in this part of Lombok—but as a result, they have a higher profile and you will probably not be alone (though if it's not high season, other tourists in the area may confine themselves to the comfortable Novotel beach). All are located within 3 miles (5km) of the Novotel—you can ask there or at any shack along the road how to find them.

## REMBITAN & SADE

You can't miss the traditional Sasak villages of Rembitan and Sade 5 miles (8km) and 3.7 miles (6km) north of Kuta, respectively). Not only do you have to drive through them to get to Kuta, but their distinctive thatched huts, with unusual, almost whimsical peaked roofs, almost look like a community for elves—that is, if elves used dung in their building construction. This is the look, rightly or wrongly, that the Novotel is trying to copy with its own upscale hotel villas, but this has been the real thing for centuries. Sade is set up to receive visitors (and their donations), while Rembitan is less overtly commercial, though that may be changing. Regardless, since the nightly cost of those Novotel villas is probably more than a Rembitan inhabitant's annual income, it would be gracious to help support the inspiration and the real people who live there.

## GUNUNG RINJANI

The massive bulk of Indonesia's second highest mountain, a volcano, spreads across 40 miles (65km) of the north part of Lombok. Way up near the top—but actually still another day's climb from the peak—is the awe-inspiring crater lake **Segera Anak.** You can't see it unless you make that climb, but only the hardiest should attempt it—not to mention the cold night such an ascent forces you to spend near the summit. If "because it's there" is your motto, by all means try it, but you must have a guide and proper trek arranged for you (hotels in Senggigi and Kuta can do this). Once at the top, if the weather gods are kind, you can wave at Bali's Gunung Agung volcano. Try to not think about the fact that **Gunung Baru,** part of the chain of peaks that make up this area, exploded in 1994.

## CRAFTS VILLAGES

About 13.6 miles (22km) south of Sweta you'll find a group of villages, centered around Praya, that specialize in different types of crafts. There are other crafts villages on Lombok, but this particular center is right on the route to Kuta from the airport and Senggigi, and has become a regular stop on the tourist circuit. It's your call whether you actually want to stop here (though some guides either make it mandatory, or at least smooth-talk you into it). While it is educational to learn about the various crafts—the intricacies of ikat weaving, for example, are astonishing and the skills demonstrated by its makers humbling—the hard sell that can come at the end, when you are virtually turned upside down to shake the money out of your pockets, can be off-putting to say the least. You'll find ikat weaving in **Sukarara** and **Pejanggik,** rattan baskets in **Beleka,** and wood carving in **Sukaraja** and **Senanti.** My personal recommendation is the pottery in **Penunjak.** The village is part of the 10-year-old Lombok Craft Project, which seeks to raise the standard of living among the potter families, who have been practicing their craft since the 16th century. You've seen this stuff for sale in Bali and didn't know it (Lombok pottery is quite distinctive)—come buy it from the source and support a good cause.

## TAMAN NARMADA

This sprawling complex of terraces and lakes 6 miles (10km) east of Carkranegara seems to go on forever. It was built by an aging raja in the late 1700s, who supposedly modeled it on the lake at Gunung Rinjani; it does kind of look like it, if you squint. Like many sights on Lombok, it's not all that remarkable if you just breeze in for a quick look (though there is a rather sweet little temple to poke around in). Better you should bring your swimsuit and spend part of a day here—its parks make for pleasurable ambles and the water is fine for dipping, and more, as evidenced by the shrieking, naked local boys who splash around and cannonball off pedestals. It's open during daylight hours, and admission is Rp1,000.

# The Philippines 11

*By Michelle Fama*

Coconut and palm trees rooted like a backbone along white sand beaches, bowing to the warm clear blue waters. Rusted corrugated roofs piled on top of each other like a lopsided deck of cards. The entire spectrum of color swirling around you underwater as fish of all sizes and patterns come to investigate your oxygen bubbles. The huge gray mass of a caribou—rope tied through its flaring nostrils—parting thick brush as its young guide surfs its back through rice terraces. And a kaleidoscope of smiles from everyone, everywhere.

The archipelago of 7,107 islands and islets that makes up the Philippines will impress all your senses with its diversity and beauty. Its relaxed nature, colorful personality, friendly people, and inexhaustible activities are like dessert for the spirit. And the fact that there are so many islands means you'll find endless stretches of pristine beach to wrap yourself in secluded paradise whenever you please.

For many years the Philippines went unrecognized as a tourist destination, overshadowed by its more popular Southeast Asian neighbors like Bali and Thailand. Images of revolt and protest during the People Power campaign, the corruption and greed (and shoes) that typified the Marcos reign, and the devastating eruption of Mount Pinatubo tarnished its reputation even further. But tyrannical regimes slip away, scarred landscapes heal, and a new optimism has come to the country with 1998's centennial celebration of independence. Today, the Philippines is a country waiting to be explored, teeming with beauty and adventure.

The Philippines is a playground for active travelers, with fish-rich seas and lakes, caves, subterranean rivers, volcanic peaks complete with smoke, rain forests, subterranean rivers, and a diverse flora and fauna that will leave any mountain climber, trekker, caver, bird watcher or tree hugger more than satisfied. The country is also home to some of the most beautiful coral reefs in the world, and Japanese ships sunk not far offshore are there for the exploring.

For the urbanite who may feel intimidated by so much nature, Manila and Cebu offer all the modern conveniences, with international hotels, excellent shopping for every budget, and bars and discos at night. And tours and museums offer glimpses into Filipino history and culture.

## 1 Getting to Know the Philippines

### THE LAY OF THE LAND

The Philippines are southeast of Hong Kong and northeast of Indonesia, bordered on the west by the South China Sea and on the east by the Pacific Ocean. Borneo is only 15 miles (24km) from the country's southernmost point.

Philippine mythology tells of a quarrel between the sea and the sky. A giant bird seeking a dry place to rest and roost sparked the spat. The fierce ocean threw wet punches toward the sky with its mighty waves, and the sky threw down islands and rocks to calm the temper of the sea. The sky won as the sea retreated around the many islands and rocks. The bird found a home and the Philippine archipelago was born.

### THE ISLANDS IN BRIEF

The 7,107 islands and islets that make up the Philippine archipelago form a landmass about the same size as Italy. Its sprawling shape, with a coastline that extends more than 11,000 miles (17,742km), makes it seem much larger than it really is.

The country is divided into three main island groups: **Luzon, the Visayas,** and **Mindanao.** The northern island of Luzon (home of Manila), together with Mindoro and Palawan, is the largest of the three. The Visayan Islands form the central region and include Cebu, Bohol, Negros, Panay (with Boracay), Samar, and Leyte. Mindanao is the second largest island in the south and it contains the island chains of Camiguin, Basilan, and the Sulu islands.

The diversity of the islands and the varying experiences that each offers will cater to any traveler's needs. Are you a one-stop resort hound who likes all the creature comforts of island living at your fingertips? Try the resorts of **Boracay** or **Cebu's Mactan Island.** Both offer blindingly white-sand beaches, teeth-numbing cool fruit shakes to sip while you soak, and a funky, leisurely mood that will have even the most wound-up executives building sandcastles. Or are you a Teva-toting hiker whose idea of a vacation involves unpredictable, adrenaline-raising treks or diving hundreds of miles from shore? Consider **Palawan,** the "last frontier" of the Philippines. Palawan's exclusive resorts provide the best of both worlds for the traveler who likes a bit of pampering with his or her adventure. The islands of **Bohol** and **Mindoro** have excellent diving for both pros and novices. On Mindoro, the party vibe and friendly nature of Puerto Galera attract expatriates from Manila and locals alike. Bohol has an authentic mix of village life and pristine beaches, especially on Panglao island.

And finally, **Luzon,** the biggest island of the archipelago, is home to the cosmopolitan capital, Manila, and the small towns of the province along the Central Cordillera Mountains. In this mountainous region you'll find the Ifugao tribespeople and their miraculously cultivated Banaue rice terraces; the caving opportunities and burial caves of Sagada; and farther north, the Spanish-influenced historic town of Vigan, where horse-drawn carriages can trot you through the cobblestone streets.

### Travel Trivia: Philippine Volcanoes

Mount Apo on Mindanao is the highest of the Philippines' many peaks, at 9,695 feet (2,954m). Twenty-three volcanos on the islands are considered active. Four of the six most active volcanoes are on Luzon Island. These include Mt. Mayon (famous for its perfectly shaped cone), Taal Volcano, and Mt. Bulusan. The eruption of Mt. Pinatubo in 1991 spewed volcanic ash that circled the globe and caused dramatic sunsets all over the world.

# The Philippines

0 | 100 mi
160 km

N

*Luzon Strait*

**Itbayat**
**BATAN IS.**  **Batan**

*P A C I F I C*
*O C E A N*

*S O U T H*
*C H I N A*
*S E A*

**Calayan**  **Babuyan**
**Dalupiri**  **BABUYAN IS.**
**Fuga**  **Camiguin**

Laoag ○  **Cape Engaño**

Vigan ○

▲
○ **Baguio**

**LUZON**

○ Angeles
San Fernando ○  **POLILLO IS.**
○ Quezon City
○ Manila

*Manila*  ○ **San Pablo**

**Lubang Is.** Batangas ○  *Tayabas* **Catanduanes**
*Bay*  *Ragay Gulf*  *Lagonoy Gulf*
**Marinduque**  ○ **Legazpi**

**Mindoro**  *Sibuyan* **Burias**
*Sea*
*Tablas Strait*  **Sibuyan**  **Samar**
**CALAMIAN**  **Tablas**  **Masbate**
**GROUP**  *Visayan*
*Linapacan Strait*  *Sea*  *Samar Sea*

*Mindoro Strait*  **Cuyo Is.**  **Panay**  **Leyte**
○ Taytay  San Jose de  **Cebu**  *Leyte*
Buenavista ○  *Gulf*
*Palawan Passage*  **Dumaran**  *Panay Gulf*  *Camotes* **Dinagat**
Cebu ○  *Sea*  **Siargao**
○ Puerto Princesa  **Negros**  **Bohol**
**Palawan**  **Camiguin**  *Bohol*
*Sea*
**Siquijor**

*S U L U   S E A*

**Balabac**
*Balabac Strait*  **MINDANAO**
**Banggi**
*Illana*
*Bay*
**Mapin**  ▲
*Moro*  *Davao Gulf*
*Gulf*

**Pangutaran**  **Samales**
**Group**  **Group**
**MALAYSIA**  *SULU ARCHIPELAGO*  **Sarangani**
**Tapul**  **Balut**  **Kepalauan**
**Group**  **Nanusa**
**KEPALAUAN**
**TALAUD**  **Karakelong**

*C E L E B E S   S E A*

*Thus I left the Philippines. But the Philippines did not so easily leave me. For months, I could not get the country out of my head: it haunted me like a pretty, plaintive melody.*

—Pico Iyer, *Video Night in Kathmandu*

The destinations listed here are by no means all-inclusive. The Philippines are made up of over 7,000 islands, and it would be impossible for any one person or guide to cover them all. I welcome you to do a little exploring of your own.

## THE PHILIPPINES TODAY

The year 1998 marked the Philippines' centennial celebration, but amidst the revelry many took the occasion to ponder the state of the nation today, and what the future holds, particularly in light of the recent economic and political crisis that has swept through most of Asia.

President Fidel Ramos, whose 6-year rule ended in 1999, is widely credited for giving the country a rare taste of political stability and sustained growth in its economy, which has been able to withstand some of the worst ravages of the Asian financial crisis. In contrast to some other countries in the region, the Philippines' economy is projected to have modest growth, though still well below what had been predicted before the regional crisis struck.

The man who replaced Ramos as president (by the largest number of votes in any democratic election ever held in the Philippines), former film star Joseph Estrada, warned he would battle hard against the endemic corruption that is blamed for having stunted economic growth in the Philippines in the past. Many, especially the poor, were initially overwhelmingly supportive, and Estrada's early performance in office seemed to indicate that he could rise above his reputation as an intellectual lightweight with too many political debts to Marcos-era cronies.

That trust has diminished. The economy shrank by 0.5% last year, but the culprit turned out to be Mother Nature, in the form of poor harvests. El Niño was pulling agricultural production down, while La Niña was just around the corner to destroy the crops that survived the drought. More worrisome, concerns about Estrada have been born out. It seems that a series of government and legal decisions made recently has benefited the very Marcos-era cronies everyone was worried about. His leadership has been criticized as weak, one degree shy of lazy, and dependent on his somewhat fractious cabinet to make real his vague policy goals.

Another sticking point for the body politic of the country has been a violent civil war, centered in the southern island province of Mindanao. Since 1521, the Moro movement on Mindanao resisted Spanish and then American colonial rule, and conflict continued after Philippine independence. Muslim resentment in the region flared as a result of large-scale migrations of Christians from other Filipino regions, which reduced the Muslims to a minority on the island. Discrimination, land-occupation, and the destruction caused by Christian vigilantes fueled the movement's desire for a separate Islamic state.

The 1996 peace agreement between the Philippine government and the Moro National Liberation Front (MNLF), which supposedly marked an end to the MNLF's 26-year military struggle for autonomy, served to cover up rather than address the basic problems of economic, social, and religious disaffection felt by the Muslim south. The breakaway faction from the MNLF, the militant Moro Islamic Liberation

Front (MILF), disagreed with the deal and waged a guerrilla war against government troops for independence on the island. Kidnapping incidents and the peace and order in this area were making headlines throughout the international community and their secessionist program of political and military pressure on the government remains a key threat to stability in the Philippines.

In some areas, the outlook for the new millennium is much rosier. Agricultural growth is expected to resume, and local banks are among Asia's healthiest. Tourism will see a big boost, particularly on the island of Boracay, which President Estrada is determined to make the number-one tourist destination in the Asian region. Baguio, Tagatay, and Palawan are other destinations targeted by the administration's "Rediscovery" program for tourism. For small islands like Boracay, this could be a blessing or a curse, as complaints of it being overrun with tourism already have tainted its reputation as a getaway paradise.

## A LOOK AT THE PAST

The first inhabitants of the Philippines arrived as early as 300,000 years ago, probably migrating over a land bridge from the Asian mainland. The Negrito, a tribe located near Mt. Pinatubo, arrived 25,000 years ago, but were driven back by several waves of immigrants from modern-day Indonesia and Malaysia. In 1380, the Arab-taught Makdum arrived in the Sulu archipelago and established what became a powerful Islamic sphere of influence over the next hundred years.

When **Ferdinand Magellan** arrived in 1521 he claimed the archipelago for Spain, but twenty days later he was killed by the Cebuan chieftain, Lapu-Lapu. Another determined conquistador, Ruy Lopez de Villalobos, followed in 1543 and named the territory Filipinas, after the king of Spain. In 1565 the Spanish began to permanently occupy the territory, and by 1571 the entire country—except for the strictly Islamic Sulu archipelago—was under Spanish control.

The Spanish hold was challenged by outside forces, including the Dutch and the British. But it was the Filipinos themselves who ultimately started an independence movement. During the Spanish-American War in 1898, Filipinos fought on the side of the Americans, and when the Spanish were defeated, they thought they had achieved independence. But the U.S. purchased the islands from the Spanish for US$20 million. Before recognizing the Filipinos' desire for independence and ultimately letting go, the Americans introduced their system of schooling, government, democratic ideals, and improved sanitation. In 1935, Manuel L. Quezon was sworn in as the first president of the Philippine Commonwealth. But in 1942, Japan invaded the country, brutally interrupting the process of transition from colony to independent nation. Filipino and American troops, under the direction of **General Douglas MacArthur,** resisted Japan's advance until MacArthur was ordered by President Roosevelt to retreat. "I shall return," was MacArthur's famous promise, and after years of oppression, rebellion, and disarray under Japanese rule, MacArthur did return and seized control once again, in 1944. The Philippines achieved full independence again in 1946, and Manuel Roxas was sworn in as president of the Philippine Republic.

**Ferdinand Marcos** was elected president in 1965, and hopes ran high that he would be able to control the political and economic deterioration that had gripped the country since the end of the war. Instead, in 1972 he declared martial law, "to handle the economic crisis and the peace-and-order situation." He continued to rule virtually as a dictator until 1986, when communist and Muslim guerrillas attacked his regime, and he was accused of ballot-rigging and fraud. A snap election saw the opposition parties rally around **Corazon Aquino,** widow of a prominent opposition figure whose 1983 assassination had sparked massive anti-government protests. Cory Aquino initiated a program of nonviolent civil unrest that resulted in Marcos and his beauty-queen wife, Imelda, fleeing the country to Hawaii, where Marcos died in 1989.

Aquino re-established the democratic institutions of the country, but failed to tackle economic problems or win over the military or the powerful Filipino elite. U.S. influence in the country diminished following the 1991 Mt. Pinatubo eruption, which destroyed the United States Air Base, and after the Philippine Senate refused to ratify the lease on the Subic Bay Naval Station. Aquino survived seven coup attempts in 6 years and was succeeded by her Defense Minister, **Fidel Ramos,** in 1992. Finally, progress was starting to be seen and felt by the Filipino people and the international community. Ramos succeeded in revitalizing the economy, attracting foreign investment, and defusing long-running tensions with the Muslim National Liberation Front. In 1998 he was replaced by the Philippines' answer to Clint Eastwood, former actor Joseph Estrada.

## PHILIPPINE CULTURE

The Philippines are a cultural potpourri thanks to their long colonial history. The Indonesian and Malaysian background of the people has been infused with Chinese, Spanish, American, South American, and Asian influences, making for a culture and appearance uniquely Filipino.

### CUISINE

An eclectic mix of culinary delights awaits you in the Philippines. Don't just stick to the familiar Italian or French cuisines, but venture toward local delicacies like lapu-lapu fish, or the more adventurous Balut, a fertilized egg eaten semi-raw. The **seafood** is so much fresher (not to mention cheaper) than most places that even people who don't like fish may be converted. The **fruits** are amazing: Treat yourself to the familiar mangoes, papaya, avocado, and guava, and to lesser-known fruits like lanzones (beige clusters of fruit) and the smelly durian. For hard drinkers, Tanduay Rum is unbelievably cheap and popular here. You'll also find that bottled water is more costly than beer or soda.

### THE ARTS

The Philippines is marked by a vibrant, thriving artistic and cultural breadth that's among the most interesting in Southeast Asia, with diverse influences of Spanish, Chinese, Japanese, American, and Malaysian and Indonesian Islamic styles. Under the Marcos administration, the country's cultural heritage, traditions, and arts were revitalised. The National Museum, the National Library, the Metropolitan Museum of Manila, and many other, smaller exhibits contain collections of some of the best painting, sculpture, and literature the country has to offer. Out of this renewal also came the **Cultural Center of the Philippines** (CCP), based in Manila. The CCP hosts many national and international events, displays, and performances in its Folk Arts Theatre, Main Theatre, Manila Film Center, library, museum, and various small art galleries.

**Music** is everywhere in the Philippines—booming out of jeepneys, hotel lobbies, restaurants, street stalls, karaoke bars, and almost everywhere else. And they sure have their arms wrapped around love songs! You'll find popular rock as well as the indigenous sounds of exotic instruments like bamboo flutes, gongs, and wooden drums.

**Cinema** in the Philippines never really seems to get its head above water. The typical fare? Your cheap, low-budget horror or romance flick. Although these films attract their fair share of fans, you'll find the most popular movies are Hollywood's finest.

## RELIGION

The Spanish missionaries came, they saw, and they surely conquered, converting over 90 percent of the population to Christianity, of whom 80 percent are **Roman Catholic** and 6 percent are **Protestant.** About 4 percent of Filipinos belong to the **Philippine Independent Church,** also known as the Aglipay, an early 20th-century sect that is closely related to the Anglican and Episcopalian churches. In the south, on the island of Mindanao and along the Sulu archipelago, the Spanish were not so successful in anchoring Christian ideals.   About 5 percent of Filipinos, concentrated mostly in these areas, are **Muslim.**

## ETIQUETTE

The hospitality of the Filipinos is legendary in Southeast Asia. Seldom will you find a people who so enjoy the company of their Western visitors. More often than not guests in Filipino homes are offered the best seat at the dining table and almost always served the host's finest dish. Perhaps due to their long association with Spain, Filipinos are emotional and passionate about life, food, and fiestas in a way that seems more Latin than Asian.

In honoring their hospitality it is important to understand certain cultural differences. I wondered why people turned away when I gestured for them to come closer, only to find out that the hand movement that means "come here" to Westerners signifies "go away" in the Philippines. Other gestures to be aware of: A brief raising of the eyebrow is meant positively; one hisses and makes a kissing-type noise to get attention; and pursed lips point in a particular direction.

The Filipino attitude of *bahala na* (come what may) is a source of strength, but it often results in complacency. Just remember that you are in their country, where time is not of the essence, and relax. Filipino pride demands that once a confrontation begins, there is no backing down, so try to avoid talking politics, religion, or corruption. Filipinos are aware of the problems in their country but are not prepared to listen to foreign visitors pointing those problems out and voicing criticism. They love talking about their families though!

Here's a quick checklist of cultural dos and don'ts:

- Show respect to elders. Always greet any who are present.
- Take a taste of food when offered. It is customary to leave some food on the plate to show you've had enough.
- Don't be punctual for social meetings. Arrive at least 30 minutes late if you want to be really polite.
- It is customary to take off your shoes before entering a home.
- For women travelers, be prepared to answer the question "Do you have a companion?" or "Where is your companion?"
- For business travelers, punctuality is expected. And be sure not to leave home without your business cards, as Filipinos like to know who they are dealing with.

## LANGUAGE

The Philippines has nearly 2,000 regional languages scattered throughout its thousands of islands. The national language, however, is **Tagalog,** and though English is widely spoken, the Filipinos get a kick out of any foreigner who at least attempts some Tagalog.

**English** will get you by everywhere, but there is one quirk I want to point out: Filipinos answer positively to a negative question. So if you ask a taxi driver, "You don't know where you're going?" the reply will be "yes," which actually means "no." It can be quite confusing. In fact, Filipinos in general hate to say no, or "I don't know," preferring to beat around the bush or indulge in euphemisms. This can be frustrating when you want a straight answer or prompt service. Be patient and understanding and don't show an ugly tourist face by getting angry or confrontational.

The word "*ano,*" which you'll hear in almost any circumstance or setting, means something like "you know"; it's used to avoid specificity or to fill in gaps. Give yourself a few weeks here and you'll find the word creeping into your own vocabulary.

## USEFUL PHILIPPINE PHRASES

Most Filipinos speak at least three languages: Tagalog (the national language) and their own regional dialect are usually supplemented by American English and sometimes Spanish.

Although you will, in most cases, not need to use any Tagalog, the Filipinos get a real kick out of any attempt, botched or not. In Tagalog, *p* and *f* are often interchangeably pronounced and used. The written *p* can be pronounced as an *f.* You'll notice this even carries over into English (*Filipinas* pronounced *Pilipinas* and *food* pronounced *pood.*) Double vowels are pronounced separately, for example Ta-al Volcano. *I* is pronounced *ee*. The combination *ng* is pronunced "nang" and *mga* is pronounced "manga." Using *po* (masculine) or *ho* (feminine) signifies respect and should be used whenever talking with an older person. Basically the words are pronounced phonetically—how it looks is usually how it's pronounced.

**Greetings**

| | |
|---|---|
| Welcome | Mabuhay (Mah-*boo*-hih) |
| Good Morning | Magandang umaga (Mah-gahn-*dahng* oo-*mah*-gah) |
| Good Night | Magandang gabi |
| I'm Fine | Mabuti (Ma-boot-ee) |
| How are you? | Kumusta ka (Kuh-moos-tah ka) |

**Common Phrases**

| | |
|---|---|
| Please | Paki (*Pah*-kee) |
| Thank you | Salamat (Sah-*lah*-maht) |
| You're Welcome | Walang anuman (Wahl-*ahng* ah-noo-*mahn*) |
| What time is it? | Anong oras na ba? (A-nong *oh*-rahs nah bah?) |
| What is your name? | Anong pangalan mo? (pahng-*ahl*-ahn) |

**Handy Phrases**

| | |
|---|---|
| Where is the... | Nasaan ang... (Nah-su-*ahn* ahng...) |
| Toilet? | CR (comfort room)? |
| Bus/jeepney? | Bus/djipney sa? |
| Do you have A/C? | Mayroon bang air-condition? (May-oh-*oon* bahng air-condition?) |
| The bill, please | Akina ang kuwenta ko (AH-keenah *kwehn*-tuh koh) |
| How much is this? | Magkano ito? (ee-*toh*) |

**Handy Words**

| | |
|---|---|
| Water | Tubig (*too*-bihg) |
| Hot/Cold | Mainit/Malamig (Mah-*een*-iht/Mah-*luh*-mihg) |
| Here | Dito (Dee-*toh*) |
| Stop | Para (Pahr-*ah*) (used in vehicles) |
| Yes/No | Oo/Hindi (*Oh*-oh/Hihn-*dee*) |
| Today | Ngayong (Nigh-*oon*) |
| Tomorrow | Bukas (Boo-*kahs*) |

## 2  Planning a Trip to the Philippines

### VISITOR INFORMATION

The long arm of the Philippine Department of Tourism (DOT) reaches many potential overseas visitors through its branch offices, which will gladly provide brochures and booklets to help you plan your trip. Below is a listing of several DOT offices in the English-speaking world. You can also check out their Web site at **www.tourism.gov.ph.**

### IN THE U.S.

**New York:** Philippine Center, 556 5th Ave., New York, NY 10036 (☎ **212/575-7915;** fax 212/302-6759). **Los Angeles:** 3660 Wilshire Blvd., Ste. 285, Los Angeles, CA 90010 (☎ **213/487-4527;** fax 213/386-4063). **San Francisco:** 447 Sutter St., no. 507, San Francisco, CA 94108 (☎ **415/956-4060;** fax 415/956-2093).

### IN CANADA

**Toronto:** Philippine Consulate General, 151 Bloor St. West, Suite 365, Toronto, Ontario, Canada M5S 1S4 (☎ **416/922-7181;** fax 416/922-2638).

### IN AUSTRALIA

**Sydney:** Wynyard House, Suite 703, Level 7, 301 George St., Sydney 2000 (☎ **612/9299-6815** or 9299-6506; fax 612/9299-6817; e-mail: ptsydney@ozemail.com.au).

### IN THE U.K.

**London:** 17 Albermarle St., London W1Y 7HA (☎ **171/499-5652** or 499-5443; fax 171/499-5772).

### WEB SITES

- **www.philippine.org** (A great site for up-to-date information on airport transportation and pick-up, and information on the Philippines' various provinces.)
- **www.asiatravel.com** (This is a valuable resource with information on hotels throughout Asia, particularly resorts that offer promo rates.)
- **www.sino.net/asean/philippn.html** (Titled "Tourist Information," this Web site gives all the expected facts on visas, customs, weather, accommodations, and more.)

### ENTRY REQUIREMENTS

If you are staying up to 21 days, visas are not required, provided you have a valid passport and return tickets. If you wish to stay longer than 21 days, a visa for 59 days can

### Recommended Books

*A Short History of the Philippines* by Teodoro Agoncillo is a general introduction to the country's past. *The Philippines* and *Readings in Philippine History* by Horacio de la Costa are good reads if you're not keen on formal historical analysis. If you're looking for a good biography of Marcos, read *For Every Tree a Victory* by Hartzell Spence. Others include *In Our Image: America's Empire in the Philippines,* by Stanley Karnow; *Brownout on Breadfruit* by Timothy Mo; *Wonder Healers of the Philippines,* by Harold Sherman; and *Playing with Water: Alone on a Philippine Island* and *Ghosts of Manila,* both by James Hamilton-Paterson.

be purchased for US$25 from a Philippine embassy or consulate in your country or from the Immigration offices in Manila, Angeles, Cebu City, and San Fernando. Bring extra passport photos if you will be applying for a visa. If you plan an even longer stay, direct your visa inquiries to the Philippine embassy or consulate in your home country. For anyone interested in retiring in the Philippines, there is a **Philippine Retirement Authority,** 15th floor, Antel 2000, Corporate Center, 121 Valero St., Salcedo Village, Makati, Manila (☎ 2/751-9300 to 9303; e-mail: prama@info.com.ph).

## PHILIPPINE EMBASSY LOCATION

**In the U.S.:** 1600 Massachusetts Ave. NW, Washington, D.C. 20036 (☎ **202/ 467-9300**); also, Philippine Consulate, 56 5th Ave., 3rd floor, New York, NY 10036 (☎ **212/575-7915**).

**In Canada:** 130 Albert St., Ottawa, Ontario K104G5 (☎ **613/233-1121**).

**In Australia:** 1 Moonah Place, Yarralumla, ACT 2600 Canberra (☎ **06/273-2535**).

**In New Zealand:** 50 Hobson St., Thurndon, Wellington (☎ **04/472-9921**).

**In the U.K.:** 17 Albermarle St., London WIY 7HA (☎ **171/499-5443;** fax 171/ 499-5772).

## CUSTOMS REGULATIONS

Any amount over US$3,000 brought into the country must be declared. You are allowed to bring in 400 cigarettes or two tins of tobacco, and two bottles of alcoholic beverages not to exceed 1 liter each. When you leave the Philippines you have to pay a departure tax of P500 (US$20). If you are returning to the U.S., you may take back US$400 worth of goods purchased in the Philippines. Duty-free items include 200 cigarettes or 100 cigars (no Cuban cigars), a liter of alcohol, and most handicraft goods. Shells, coral, animals, or produce are not allowed.

## MONEY

The Philippine currency is the **peso.** It's divided into 100 centavos. Coins come in denominations of 1, 5, 10, and 25 centavos and 1 and 5 pesos. Banknotes are in denominations of 5, 10, 20, 50, 100, 500, and 1,000 pesos.

**CURRENCY EXCHANGE & RATES**   At the time I did my research, the exchange rate was 40.25 pesos to the U.S. dollar (see chapter 3 for conversions to other currencies; to obtain the latest conversions, go to CNN's web site at **www.cnn.com/travel/ currency**). In Manila, currency can be changed at banks (Monday through Friday from 9am to 3pm) and hotels, but for a more favorable rate try one of the money changers scattered throughout all major city centers and at the airport. All major currencies are accepted, but you will have more luck with U.S. dollars. In the smaller towns it will be more difficult to find a bank or hotel to exchange money, especially traveler's checks, so plan ahead and bring enough pesos with you along the routes less traveled. And load up on small bills like 10, 20, 50 and 100 peso notes, because more often than not hotels and taxis won't have change for large ones. The wad will weigh down your pocket but ultimately save you time and patience.

It seems the farther you get from Manila (or other larger cities) the lower the exchange rate you receive. One way around this is to pay for as much as you can with a credit card—the exchange rate is calculated based on your home country's exchange rate, not the local rate.

Several hundred bank branches throughout the country are equipped with **automated-teller machines.** Cirrus ATMs are more plentiful than PLUS and can be found at Citibank and Philippine National Bank branches throughout the country.

**Unionbank,** located in most of the big cities (Manila, Cebu, Davao), is affiliated with PLUS. ATM locator services are available through MasterCard/Cirrus and Visa/PLUS. Simply dial the operator, request an international collect call, and dial: **MasterCard/Cirrus** (☎ **314/275-6690**) or **Visa/PLUS** (☎ **410/581-7931**).

Most major **credit cards** (MasterCard, Visa, American Express, Diners Club, Japan Credit Bank) are widely accepted. Cash withdrawals can be made at any Equitable Bank branch with your Visa or MasterCard. You can get cash or traveler's checks with your American Express card at the **American Express** Bank in Manila, 6750 Ayala Ave., Makati (☎ **2/818-6731**).

**LOST/STOLEN CREDIT CARDS & TRAVELER'S CHECKS**    **MasterCard** has a toll-free Global Service Emergency Assistance for International Visitors hotline at ☎ **800/110-0113;** the international collect call number is ☎ **314/275-6690; Visa's** toll-free hotline is ☎ **800/345-1345,** or call collect at ☎ **410/581-7931.** The number to call for **American Express** is ☎ **800/732-2244.** The 24-hour traveler's check refund line for **American Express** is ☎ **800/738-3383;** for **Thomas Cook,** it's ☎ **800/223-7373.**

## WHEN TO GO

**PEAK SEASON**    Hot and dry, the period from March through May is considered the high season; prices will be higher for accommodations and transportation. For better bargains, consider the period from June to November (though these are much wetter months).

**CLIMATE**    Most activities like scuba-diving, snorkeling, fishing, and golfing can be enjoyed year-round. For warm, sunny days and balmy nights, the most pleasant time to visit the Philippines is from November to February (except along the Pacific coast, which can be wet at this time). Temperatures range from 20 to 28°C (68 to 82°F). March to May are the hottest months and the season for harvest festivals like Flores de Mayo. This is the dry season, ideal for a traveler planning to spend time at the beach. It's also considered the high season and prices will be higher for accommodations and transportation. You definitely have more bargaining power from June to November or so. The southwest monsoon brings on the rains from June to October, with July and August being the wettest months. If you're planning to head to the mountain provinces for hiking or caving during this season, expect roads to be muddy (sometimes impassable) and flights to these areas unpredictable. This is also the time when typhoons violently sweep through, although they are usually predicted far enough in advance to plan around them. Flexibility is the key if you arrive during this season. Ferries will be postponed at the first threat of a typhoon. With the arrival of El Niño and La Niña, seasons have been out of whack a bit; it's best to check ahead for the latest weather patterns.

**PUBLIC HOLIDAYS**    Businesses, banks, and government are closed on New Year's Day (Jan 1), Good Friday (the Friday before Easter), Araw ng Kagitingan (April 19), Labor Day (May 1), Independence Day (June 12), National Hero's Day (August 30), Bonifacio Day (Nov. 30), Christmas Day (Dec. 25), and Rizal Day (Dec. 31). All

---

### Carrying Money

As with any foreign country, the most sensible way to carry money, checks, tickets, and documents is in money belts or secret pockets. In other words, don't be flashy with your valuables.

Saints Day (Nov. 1) and Christmas Eve (Dec. 24) are not official holidays, but are usually treated as such.

Christmas is celebrated throughout the country, and major festivals such as Ati-Atihan, Sinulog, and Dinagyang take place in January. This makes late December to January a crowded time to visit, and getting around can be quite a push-and-shove experience.

## HEALTH CONCERNS

The two biggest threats to your health in the Philippines are heat and mosquitoes. Heat and humidity can hit you hard if you're not used to them, and can result in prickly heat, heat exhaustion, heat stroke, and fungal infections. Drink lots of fluids, especially water. And obviously, take it easy with the sun. I used SPF 20 and still came back with quite a deep tan, so protect yourself.

In a country comprised of over 7,000 islands, you are likely at some point to find yourself on a boat. Pack **motion-sickness medication** if you're susceptible. The tablets must be taken before setting sail—by the time you're feeling sick it's too late. Ginger is a natural preventative and is available in capsule form. And remember, keep your eye on the horizon for a stomach-calming reference point.

If you do become seriously ill, your hotel should be able to recommend a good place to go for treatment, or contact your embassy. Public facilities are below par here, so ask about the nearest private hospital.

### DIETARY PRECAUTIONS

They say the water is potable in Manila, but I recommend the very affordable bottled water, just in case. Purification tablets are also available in local drug stores. As with visiting any foreign country, there is always the inevitable bowel adjustment to new food, water, climate, and stress. Anti-diarrhea medicine may help, although in my experience it's best to flush whatever is in you out. Oral rehydration salts may help severe cases of dehydration brought on by diarrhea or intense heat.

### VACCINATIONS

Unless you have been to cholera or yellow-fever regions, no vaccinations are required. Tetanus shots are recommended for divers and snorkelers.

**Malaria,** carried by the nocturnal anopheles mosquito, and **dengue fever,** transmitted via the early morning mosquito, can be a problem within the archipelago. Most of the Philippines is malaria safe except for remote places on Palawan and Mindanao. Manila just recovered from an epidemic of dengue fever, which spreads quickly in such a densely populated place. There is no preventative for this; just try to avoid bites by using repellent (one thing you shouldn't forget to pack!). You may want to consult your doctor about malaria tablets, which are only suppressants, not preventatives. I strongly suggest bringing a hanging mosquito net or bivy sack, which pops up like a tent over any bed. Both are portable and durable and can be found at most outdoor supply stores or army/navy stores.

## GETTING THERE
### BY PLANE

Air travel is the only sure bet to get to the Philippines. There are no regular passenger ships to the country. A few cruise ships stop here, but not long enough to allow passengers much time to explore the country.

Manila's **Ninoy Aquino International Airport** is the main port of entry, followed by Cebu's **Mactan International Airport** (flights from Hong Kong, Singapore, Malaysia, and Japan).

> # The "Don't Leave Home Without 'Em" List
> Dramamine (motion-sickness tablets)
> Anti-diarrhea medicine
> Anti-bacterial cream
> Rain poncho/small umbrella
> A few trash bags to line your luggage
> Ziploc bags for everything and anything (wet clothes, shells, sand, etc.)
> Batteries (it's also a good idea to bring an extra camera battery)
> Film
> A warm fleece or sweater
> Bug repellent
> Sunscreen
> Water bottle
> Waterproof sandals
> Padlock and wire cable (comes in handy to lock your bag up and attach it to anything)

**FROM THE U.S. & CANADA**    Flying in from the U.S. or Canada will take you, including stopovers, about 24 hours from the East Coast, 14–18 hours from the West Coast. Bring your fluffy socks and lots of books for this long flight. You will lose at least 12 hours going, but when you return to the U.S. you will arrive before you left, thanks to that mysterious International Date Line. Airlines with service to Manila include: **Cathay Pacific** (☎ 800/233-2742); **Continental** (☎ 800/231-0856); **Japan Airlines** (☎ 800/525-3663); **Korean** (☎ 671/649-3301); **Northwest** (☎ 800/225-2525); **Philippine Airlines (PAL)** (☎ 800/435-9725); and **United** (☎ 800/241-6522).

Almost as fast as **Philippine Airlines** went out of business, it came back again, although with limited service. Check with them for promotional fares or updated routes. PAL has **Canadian offices** in Vancouver and Toronto, and Cathay Pacific offers regular flights between Vancouver and Manila, with a stopover in Hong Kong.

An increasingly popular way of traveling to Eastern destinations like Manila and Hong Kong is with courier airlines like DHL, Federal Express, Skypack, and TNT Courier. Your assignment as an air courier is easy. You'll travel coach class on regularly scheduled airlines accompanying air freight checked as passenger baggage. All you have to do is carry the freight documents and hand them over to the courier company representative at your destination. A Web site to check out with valuable information on courier flights is www.aircourier.org/whois.html.

**FROM THE U.K.**    **British Airways** (☎ 345/222-111; www.british-airways.com), **Philippine Airlines** (☎ 800/435-9725) and several European airlines fly from London to Manila. London is probably the bucket shop capital of the world. Bucket shops, for those who are not familiar with them, are travel agencies that offer discounted tickets released by airlines eager to fill seats, even if it means at a reduced profit. Magazines that feature ads for bucket shop deals in the U.K. are *Time Out, City Limits, LAM, Trailfinder, Australasian Express,* and specialized magazines like *The Geographical Magazine, Traveler, Wanderlust,* and *Business Traveler.*

---

**Travel Tip: Insurance for Active Pursuits**

If your itinerary includes diving, caving, kayaking, or other adrenaline-pumping activities, keep in mind that some policies won't cover them. Before setting off on your adventure, verify what kind of coverage you have under your current insurance policy. If you don't have a policy already, I strongly recommend picking up one. Coverage is very affordable, and it's better to be safe than sorry. (See chapter 3 for more information on travel insurance.)

---

**FROM AUSTRALIA**    Flying to Australia is quite expensive, but this can be side-stepped if you use Manila as a stopover to other European, North American, or Asian destinations. **PAL** (☎ **800/435-9725**) offers service to the continent. **Qantas Airlines** (☎ **131313**; www.qantas.com) flies from Melbourne, Adelaide, Brisbane, and Sydney. **Air Niugini** (☎ **612/92901544**) flies to Manila with a stopover in Port Moresby. **STA** (☎ **02/92121255** in Sydney) is one of the best discount agencies, with offices in Sydney, Perth, Melbourne, Adelaide, Canberra, Brisbane, and Hobart.

**FROM NEW ZEALAND    Thai Airways International** (☎ **65/224-2011**) offers the cheapest flights, via Bangkok. Because there are no direct flights from New Zealand to Manila, there are few bargains. Small student discounts may be available through **New Zealand Student Travel Services** (☎ **64/95256901**).

## GETTING AROUND
### BY PLANE

For the most part the domestic airlines run on a pretty reliable schedule. However, during peak seasons and holidays, many flights will be booked up, and during bad weather, services will obviously be delayed or cancelled. **PAL,** which until recently had the greatest number of flights and served the largest number of destinations, temporarily closed its doors after a long, bitter strike. After successful negotiations, services were restored, but have not yet completely returned to normal. As a result, businesses have suffered, tourism has been on the decline, and other airlines have been left to pick up the pieces. Navigating around the islands via plane is a more difficult task, as many areas are no longer serviced.

The popular **air pass,** which allowed travelers to island-hop to several destinations for a low price, hasn't been resurrected yet, but according to PAL management, it's only a matter of time. **Air Philippines** is also considering a similar bargain fare, so be sure to inquire.

Domestic air services covering regularly scheduled routes are operated by **Philippine Airlines** (☎ 2/816-6691), **Air Philippines** (☎ 2/843-7770), **Air Ads Inc.** (☎ 2/833-3264, 833-3278), **Asian Spirit** (☎ 2/840-3811 to 18), **Cebu Pacific** (☎ 2/636-4938 to 45), **Grand Air** (☎ 2/833-8080, 833-8090), and **Pacific Air** (☎ 2/812-1555, 812-1511). **A. Soriano Aviation** (☎ 2/834-0371) is a reliable charter company.

**Air Ads** and **Pacific Air** are your basic puddle jumpers and if you are fainthearted when it comes to sailing the skies and want to close your eyes and hold on to your stomach. Sample one-way fares from Manila are: Cebu, P1,688 (US$42.20); Caticlan/Boracay, P2,900 (US$72.50); Puerto Princessa/Palawan, P2,098 (US$52.45). (Round-trip fares are twice as much.) Obviously, these will just give you a rough idea of what you can expect to pay, and all prices are subject to change.

# Getting a Circle Pacific Fare

Certain airlines have come together to offer tickets that circle the globe, either originating from or stopping in the Philippines. PAL, Qantas, and American Airlines offer a ticket valid for up to 6 months that allows you to combine the United States, New Zealand, Australia, the Philippines, and other parts of Asia in one glorious loop with as many stopovers as you can fit in. **High Adventure Travel,** based out of San Francisco, offers good deals. Check out some sample tours and fares at their Web site, www.highadv.com, or call ☎ 800/350-1612.

## BY TAXI

In Manila, Cebu, and other major cities, taxis are everywhere, pretty reliable and very affordable. They are usually easy to flag down and most have air-conditioning. The question to ask before you take off is whether the meter works. Many drivers will have you believe their meters don't work and charge you much more than the trip should cost. They'll also try to charge more because of traffic. There's *always* traffic, so let them know you're not a sucker. The meter starts at P20 (US50¢) and increases at a very slow pace. In traffic the meter barely moves, so do tip the driver for his time and patience. Taxis that wait outside major hotels will charge you more than regular taxis; you may want to just stroll to the street and hail down a metered taxi.

## BY BUS

Buses are a great way to see the country. Most routes are no more than 10 hours, with some longer routes running on overnight schedules. You will be able to tell which buses are reputable by scanning them at the stations; avoid the ones with lopsided axles that are dirty with rust and dents. **Victory Liner** (☎ 2/361-1506) is one of the most dependable, comfortable, and safest companies. Other companies with service out of Manila are **Baliwag Transit** (points north, including Pampanga), ☎ 2/912-3343; **Dangwa** (points north including Baguio and Banaue); and **BLTB** (Batangas, Legazpi, Tagaytay and other points south of Manila).

Generally, buses are cheap, efficient (some complain too efficient—meaning too speedy), and fairly reliable, unless unpaved roads have been washed out or mud slides have occurred in the northern provinces. Seat reservations are not necessary. Tickets are purchased at designated counters in the terminal, or you can simply pay the conductor while en route. Ask about air-conditioning. Express buses (usually the air-conditioned ones) have fewer stops, and you can expect a pretty bad B movie or Chuckie horror flick. Your bags will be tossed on top and covered with a tarp, or if there's room you can store them above your seat. Don't worry about food: Street vendors will board the buses at several stops offering everything from Celine Dion cassettes to chewy pig skin. Generally this food is OK to eat, but use your judgment. There are also meal stops at local restaurants. It is common for tires to blow more than once over the course of a trip, but don't worry—the driver and his minions will have it changed before you know what happened.

## BY TRICYCLE

You will quickly get used to the sound and smell of the motorized and pedal tricycles (pedicabs) that jam the dusty or muddy streets in the provinces and small towns. They

---
**Travel Tip: Taxis**

---

When you go to the airport for a domestic flight, be sure to tell the taxi driver that you are leaving from the domestic airport, not the international airport.

---

carry two to three passengers in their sidecars, and one on the pillion behind the driver. You'll be surprised at the way these things can climb. Expect to pay anywhere from P5 to P20 (US15¢–US50¢) per person for "a special ride," meaning you will not be sharing the ride with any other passengers. Drivers rarely quote you the correct local rate, so it is best to check before boarding and then simply hand over the money at the end.

### BY TRAIN OR LIGHT RAIL TRANSIT

Nobody takes the train. It's that simple. The Philippine National Railway (PNR) is old, slow, rickety, unreliable, and seedy. In Manila, however, the Light Rail Transit (LRT) provides the most painless, carbon monoxide–free, traffic-less way to cross the city. (See "Getting Around" in the Manila section below.)

### BY BOAT

Ships, ferries, launches, pumpboats, and bancas are the main means of inter-island transport. Manila is the jump-off point to major provinces and cities; Cebu is the secondary link between the Visayas and Mindanao. Fares vary according to level of comfort, service, and regularity. Accommodations range from luxury cabin suites with private facilities to tarpaulin deck cots with disgusting toilets and salt water bucket showers. (Bring plenty of snack foods and toilet paper for these rides.) An air-conditioned cabin for four costs between P500 to P1,200 (US$12.50–US$30) per person, including meals, depending on the destination. Once again, the harbor in Manila is quite rowdy with activity and people. Be prepared to be hassled, coerced, and watched, and hold onto your bags.

You can book tickets through any travel agent or purchase them at the pier at the shipping lines' harbor offices. Two main lines include **Asuncion Shipping Lines,** Pier 2, North Harbor (☎ 2/204024), and **WG&A**, Pier 14 (☎ 2/894-3211 or 2/245-4061 through 2/245-4080; e-mail: reservations@wgasuperferry.com), one of the nicest and most reliable ferries, with service to Cebu, Negros, Palawan, Panay, and Mindanao. Tickets for all shipping lines can be obtained on the day of departure at the pier, but it is best to book at least two days in advance, especially during the peak months of December and January. Schedules are published in national dailies such as the *Philippine Daily Inquirer,* the *Business Daily,* and the *Manila Bulletin.* Motor launches service longer routes between smaller ports. Schedules are subject to delays, as the captain will wait for the boat to fill up before departing.

**Ferry boats** service medium to large outlying islands. These are small vessels where passengers sit on deck chairs for periods of travel lasting from about 30 minutes to 2 hours. Cebu has regular ferry boat departures for shorter routes such as Bohol, Dumaguete, and Dapitan, as well as longer routes for Surigao, Cabayan de Oro, and Zamboanga on Mindanao.

Note that there are numerous **ferry accidents** every year in the Philippines; one in September 1998 killed about 400 people, and caused legislatures to call for stricter regulations. Nevertheless, use your judgement. If you feel uncomfortable boarding a ferry that looks leaky, lopsided, and overcrowded, look for an alternative. And always locate the life vests as soon as you board.

# Philippine Pop Culture on Wheels:
# Getting Around by Jeepney

What do old Tom Cruise pictures from his *Risky Business* days, *Three's Company* posters, proverbial stickers, colored lights, cheerleaders' pom-poms, rosary beads, Christmas garland, iron horses, and chrome—lots of it—have in common? They all accessorize the king of the Philippine road, the ubiquitous jeepney. Your Philippines experience will not be complete without squeezing into or on top of one. When asked to describe the jeepney, I got many interesting replies. "A tin can meets a disco ball," one tourist said. "It's Elvis reincarnated," a proud driver boasted.

Created out of surplus U.S. army jeeps, no two jeepneys are ever alike. They're longer than the usual 4-person American jeep they are modeled after, seating up to 15 comfortably in the elongated metal cab. It's hip to hip on the long benches that face each other, and the comfortable 15 can turn into a very uncomfortable 30 passengers, especially in the rural areas, where jeepneys are less frequent.

To ride a jeepney you must have a good idea of the area you're traveling in. The jeepney services only a short distance; the route is written on the side. Ask the driver or another passenger for the best place to get off for your destination. And be prepared to jump out, as the jeepney will only slow down. The fare is a whopping 2.50 pesos (US6¢) for a 4-kilometer ride, plus an additional 50 centavos for each kilometer thereafter—definitely the cheapest ride in town. Do it once for the experience—once you've endured the heat, the perspiration, and the exhaust fumes (bring a handkerchief to cover your face) you've earned the right to air-conditioned taxis for the rest of your trip.

**Pumpboats** and **bancas** are motorized and nonmotorized outrigger boats that either ply short island crossings or run along the coast from port to port.

The latest addition to the sea-lanes are high-speed **catamarans** and **hydrofoils**— fast, comfortable, and clean. Cebu is the main port for these vessels, with routes to Visayan ports and to Northern Mindanao. Passage usually costs from P40 to P1,000 (US$10–US$25). Food and drinks can be purchased at a snack bar.

## BY CAR

You must have the patience of a saint to venture onto Manila's roads. The traffic is the worst I have ever seen, and sitting idle in all that carbon monoxide is not my idea of a healthy vacation. If you must, though, the familiar rental car agencies are here, where you can either rent a car to drive yourself (you must have an international driver's license or a valid license from your home country) or hire the services of a driver. Hiring a driver is the best way to go, a cheap luxury used by most expats and many Filipinos. Hired drivers know the roads and understand their rules (or lack thereof). They can negotiate with traffic police and can be a valuable source of information. In Manila call: **Avis** (☎ 2/734-5851); **Budget** (☎ 2/818-7363); **Dollar** (☎ 2/844-3120); or **Nissan Rent-A-Car** (desk at the airport; ☎ 2/816-1808), and they'll direct you to the closest location. Rental cars are also available in Baguio and other points on Luzon, Cebu, and Bohol.

## TIPS ON ACCOMMODATIONS

As with most of the Southeast Asian countries in this book, the currency crisis throughout the region has brought prices for accommodations spiraling downward. Always ask for seasonal discounts if you're traveling during the low season. If you plan on staying at the same place for a few days you should definitely ask for a reduced rate. At some of the smaller beach resorts you can get as much as 40% off the rack rate if bookings are slim.

## TIPS ON DINING

While exploring the familiar Italian or French cuisines, do venture toward the local delicacies like lapu-lapu fish, or, for the more adventurous, balut (a fertilized egg eaten semi-raw). Don't be scared of street stalls, which are the best way to taste local cooking and a good opportunity to meet the locals. These stalls are pretty safe, though, once again, use your common sense: If there's a cloud of flies around and the food is not warm, stay away. You can find fruits and local specialties like pork adobo at most stalls. Also, the seafood is so fresh, not to mention much cheaper than most places, that if you didn't particularly like fish, you just may become converted. And although it is not as widely eaten as in previous years, dog (or "aso") is still sold in some local markets, especially in northern Luzon. Don't worry, though: It's not disguised as any other meat, and the Filipinos do their best to hide it from us pro-pooch westerners.

## TIPS ON SHOPPING

Malls, malls, malls. You can find nearly anything in the many malls throughout Manila and other large cities. (See "Shopping" in the Manila section for specific listings and more tips.) Be prepared to bargain at markets—you should usually expect to pay no more than half the price asked for. Be cautious when buying shells: They are unique and quite beautiful but some are illegal to sell and forbidden to enter most countries.

## Fast Facts: The Philippines

**American Express**    In Manila, the American Express office is located in the Ace Building, corner of Rada and de la Rosa streets, Legazpi Village, Makati, Manila. It's open from 8:30am to 5pm weekdays, 8:30am to noon Saturdays. The direct line for travel services is ☎ **2/814-4770** to **73.** In Cebu, the office is in the PCI Bank Bldg., by the U.S. Consulate, Gorordo Avenue, 2nd floor (☎ 32/232-2970). It's open weekdays from 8:30am to 4pm, 8:30am to 11am Saturday. American Express's 24-hour traveler's check refund hotline is ☎ **800/738-3383.**

   **Thomas Cook** has an office at Skyland Plaza Building, in Manila (☎ **2/816-3701**); and on the ground floor of Metro Bank Plaza, Osmena Boulevard, in Cebu (☎ **32/219-229**).

**Bookstores**    In Manila, the **National Book Center** in Robinson's Mall, Ermita, has a current selection of best-selling books, magazines, and Filipino literature. They also have a wide selection of travel guides (should you happen to lose this one!). There are branches in Cebu City also.

**Business Hours**  Private and government offices are usually open from 8am to 5pm. Most shopping centers, stores, and supermarkets open at 10am and close at 7pm; during December, stores stay open until 10pm. Banks are open Monday through Friday from 9am to 3pm.

**Cameras and Film** There are many camera equipment shops in Manila. **One-Stop Photo Center** at SM Megamall (☎ **2/633-5041**) is in a convenient location, with another branch in the Shangri-la Plaza in Makati (☎ **2/632-1543**). Film is readily available everywhere at prices comparable to those in the West. Most malls have fast, inexpensive, and good-quality film developing. There are also photo labs for the photo enthusiast who wants more specialized developing; **New City Studio Photography** is one such lab, located at Robinson's Galleria, Ortigas Ave. (☎ **2/636-4891**).

**Doctors & Dentists**    I wouldn't recommend dental care outside of Manila. If you do need it, try **Dr. Jose Francisco,** National Life Insurance Bldg., Ayala Ave., Makati, Manila (☎ **2/810-0519**). Most procedures will cost less here than they would at home.

Most of the top hotels have a doctor on the premises available 24 hours a day. Otherwise, if you need emergency medical treatment, go to **Makati Medical Center** (☎ **2/815-9911**). (It's good enough for the president.) Treatment is inexpensive in the Philippines, and most medicines are available in cities, but usually under local brand names.

**Drug Laws**    Penalties are extremely strict for possession, use, or trafficking of illegal drugs in the Philippines. Convicted offenders can expect jail sentences, fines, or even the death penalty. This applies to possession of over 750g of marijuana, 50g of hashish, 200g of shabu (a methamphetamine, a.k.a speed), or 40g of heroin, cocaine, opium, or morphine.

**Earthquakes**    The Philippines is rocked by tremors and earthquakes quite often. If it feels like it's a big one, seek cover under tables, beds, or door frames to protect yourself from falling debris.

**Electricity**    The country's electric power is set at 220–240 volts AC; however, most hotels come equipped with outlets for devices that run on 110–120 volts. If you are not sure about an outlet's voltage be sure to ask first before using it, and ask your concierge if they have converters and plug adapters for you to use. Housekeeping at most big hotels can provide things like hair dryers and electric razors for you.

Power failures, called "brownouts," are very common in the Philippines, even in Manila. Pack a flashlight and maybe a candle or two. In the countryside or coastal towns, electricity is run off generators that usually have curfews of 10pm or 12am.

**Embassies**    The **U.S. Embassy** is located at Roxas Blvd., Manila (☎ **2/521-7116**). The **Canadian Embassy** is at Allied Bank Center, Ayala Avenue, Makati, Manila (☎ **2/810-8861**). The **Australian Embassy** is at Salustiana D Ty Tower, 104 Paseo de Roxas, Makati, Manila (☎ **2/817-7911**). The **New Zealand Embassy** is at Gammon Center Building, Alfaro St. Salcedo Village, Makati, Manila (☎ **2/818-0916**). The **Embassy of the U.K.** is at LV Locsin Building, Ayala Ave., Makati, Manila (☎ **2/810-8861**).

**Emergencies**    For police, dial **166.** For medical or fire emergencies, dial **7575.**

**Doctors/Hospitals**    In Manila, most hotels either have an in-house doctor available or can suggest a reputable doctor for whatever you may need. **Makati Medical Center** (☎ **2/815-9911**) is the best around. A few others are: **Saint Lukes Medical Center,** ☎ **2/722-0901; Cardinal Santos Medical Center,** ☎ **2/721-3361;** and **Medical City General Hospital,** ☎ **2/631-8626.**

# Inter-Island Travel Tips

- Airlines often change their flight schedules during peak months. Reconfirm your flights at least 2 days before the date of departure. Call your travel agent, the airline itself, or the concierge in your hotel for assistance.
- Domestic airlines require passengers to check in at least 45 minutes before departure time. Otherwise, they will release your seat in favor of wait-listed passengers. The airports are crowded and hectic during peak seasons, so come even earlier to cut down on stress and hassle.
- Airlines impose a "no-show" fee for reservations that have not been cancelled. If you have to cancel your flight, do so at least 2 days in advance.
- Avoid packed buses. It is impossible to hang on to those hand rails while you're being shoved and pushed from all sides.
- If you have to board a boat from the North Harbor in Manila, don't wear expensive jewelry, be extra careful with your belongings, and guard your bag with your life (hold it in front of you).
- You will be hassled to death at ports and piers; the swarms of people selling their services is unrelenting, and they don't take no for an answer. Wait for crowds to thin out at the pier before disembarking from the boat, so the hawkers will have already found their victims.
- Don't be surprised when you are asked to pay a small fee for "the porter," the nice old man you thought was simply volunteering to help you carry your bag to the airplane, boat, or taxi.

**Internet/E-mail** Internet cafes can be found throughout the Philippines, even in some pretty remote places. Wherever there are phone lines, you can bet someone is connected. Most of the bigger hotels in Manila and Cebu offer net access in their business centers, and some even have individual hook-up in the rooms.

**Language** Tagalog is the official language of the country, but English is widely spoken.

**Liquor Laws** The legal age for alcohol purchase and consumption is 18 years, although IDs are rarely checked. Bars and clubs don't stick to any official closing time, but it's generally 2–4am. (Most bar owners will stay open until the last customer leaves.) Don't worry about finishing that beer before you venture to the bar next door; it's common practice to BYOB to most places.

**Post Offices/Mail** Most tourist hotels offer postal services at the front counter. Post offices are open Monday to Friday from 8am to 5pm. Postcards cost P8 (US20¢), regardless of the destination. Airmail letters to North America and Europe cost P11 (US28¢), and to Australia and New Zealand, P10 (US25¢). Count on the mail to be slow. Courier companies in Manila include **DHL** (☎ 2/895-0511); **Federal Express** (☎ 2/833-3604); and **UPS** (☎ 2/832-1516).

**Police** The emergency services are pretty reliable in Manila. On remote islands such as Palawan, however, expect the grocer clerk to wear many hats (police chief, fire chief, judge, and doctor). These fellas may not be the most reliable or helpful of civil servants. For police emergencies, dial **166.**

**Safety/Crime** As in any country, theft, extortion, and assaults on tourists can probably be avoided with a little common sense and foresight. Like any other

## Telephone Dialing Info at a Glance

- **To place a call from your home country to the Philippines,** dial the international access code (011 in the U.S., 0011 in Australia, 0170 in New Zealand, or 00 in the U.K.), the country code (**63**), the city or area code (see below), and then the seven-digit phone number.

- **To place a call within the Philippines,** use the area code of the city you are trying to call, then simply dial the seven-digit number. In some cases, you will find only five-digit numbers. These old numbers still work but will soon be replaced. Some area codes are: Manila 2, Cebu 32, Bohol 38, Baguio 74, Batangas 43, Puerto Princessa 48, Boracay 36, and Puerto Galera 912.

- **To place a direct international call from the Philippines,** dial the international country code (for the U.S. and Canada 01, for Australia 61, for New Zealand 62, and for the U.K. 44), then the area or city code, then the number (for example, 01 + 212/999-9999).

- **International country codes** are as follows: Australia 61, Burma 95, Cambodia 855, Canada 1, Hong Kong 852, Indonesia 62, Laos 856, Malaysia 60, New Zealand 64, Singapore 65, Thailand 66, U.K. 44, U.S. 1, Vietnam 84.

place in the world, traps are lying in wait for the gullible. Almost everyone has caught wind of the kidnappings (mostly of Chinese businessmen) that occur here, which the country is seriously cracking down on. Obviously, if you are flaunting cash, wearing expensive jewelry, or leaving your room unlocked, you are asking for trouble. It is best to keep valuables and excess cash in your hotel's safe-deposit box until you need them. When walking around, keep your money, passports, and camera hidden. Consider wearing a money belt, or a small purse with the straps hidden under a shirt and tucked into your pants. (And ladies, the bra is still a viable option for money and ID.) Also, shoes tend to disappear on ferries, so if you kick your shoes off keep a watchful eye on them.

Manila isn't the safest place at night, so take a taxi if you have to go out. Rural towns tend to be poorly lit, so unless you have your flashlight, you will probably want to be inside anyway.

I strongly advise staying away from portions of **Mindanao,** particularly the southern islands of **Sulu** and **Jolo,** which are inhabited by rebels and pirates. The Philippine government and the Moro National Liberation Front (MNLF) signed a peace agreement in 1996 supposedly ending the MNLF's 24-year military struggle for autonomy in Mindanao. However, peace remains elusive following the rise of the militant Moro Islamic Liberation Front (MILF), which opposes the agreement. Best just to stay away.

**Taxes**   Visitors tend to get slammed at top hotels and resorts when it comes to taxes (most hotels set their own tax on food, lodging, and excursions); however, the official taxes are: hotel .75%; restaurants 10%; and sales or VAT (Value Added Tax) 1%.  Purchases usually indicate if VAT is included in price.

**Telephone & Faxes**   Phone service is good in the Philippines, and reception is incredibly clear. Phone booths come in two varieties: coin-operated and Fonkard Plus, for calls using prepaid cards, which are available at most major hotels and post offices. The cost for a local 3-minute call is around two pesos. Dial ☎ 114 for directory assistance.

Hotels charge a ridiculous rate for international calls, and there's usually a 10% surcharge. If you don't have a calling card already, I suggest you get one; the rates will be much cheaper. Almost all hotels will send local or international faxes and will add the charge to your bill.

**Time** Philippine Standard Time is 8 hours ahead of Greenwich Mean Time (GMT). International time differences will change during daylight savings, or summer time. Time differences during standard time are: U.S. East Coast: -13, U.S. West Coast: -16, London: -8, Darwin +1, Melbourne +2, Brisbane and Sydney: +3.

**Tipping** Tipping in restaurants and hotels is always optional. A tip is appreciated but there is no resentment when it is not given. Generally a 5% tip is sufficient. At finer restaurants, the service charge is usually included in the bill.

**Toilets** Bathrooms are called "comfort rooms," or the "CR." The low-down on the toilet is that some are downright alive and crawling while others are clean and comfortable. Be prepared for anything. In the countryside plumbing hasn't made its debut yet, so you will be introduced to the bucket toilet—a brightly colored bucket used to fill with water from a tap and then dumped down the toilet. You will also notice that most toilets, except for in the nice hotels, lack toilet seats. Why they take them off, I'm not sure, but I was told that women here actually stand up on the seat instead of sitting. Anyway, bring toilet paper with you.

**Water** They say the water is potable, but bottled water is so cheap and widely available that you should drink it instead just to be safe.

## 3 Manila

"Shapeless, confused—an unrelievedly twentieth century mess strung out along a reeking bay." OK, so James Hamilton-Paterson's description of Manila in his book *Playing with Water* is pretty accurate. It's hard for the first-time visitor to overlook the hovering pollution from the relentless traffic, the unfinished gray skyscrapers, or the overcrowded slums. There's no question that the city could use a face-lift. Still, the country's capital offers the full spectrum of sights, and pulsates with life at all hours. You can shop in sprawling malls in Makati or test your bargaining moxie at local markets. You can get a sense of Manila's colonial past inside the fortress walls of Intramuros, or stand on the vast lahar field created by Mount Pinatubo's devastating eruption only a short drive away. For most travelers a few days is plenty of time to spend in metro Manila before moving on to other sights in Luzon or farther afield.

### VISITOR INFORMATION

The **Department of Tourism** (DOT) has several regional offices. Stop by the tourist information desk when you arrive at the airport in Manila or Cebu City. The main branch of the DOT at Rizal Park has maps, brochures, and nifty computer print-outs for all the provinces with run-downs on accommodations, transportation, and attractions. Call ☎ 2/523-8411 or stop by between 8am and 5pm weekdays. There is also a **tourist assistance hotline** available 24 hours Monday through Saturday, ☎ 2/524-1660.

### GETTING THERE

See "Getting There" above, since you'll almost certainly be arriving by air from abroad.

In Manila, **airport taxis** (private companies that serve the airport) will be waiting to take you to any part of the city. Rates are usually fixed; to Makati, the upscale business district, or Ermita, the tourist area, expect to pay about P500 (US$12). This is much higher than regular taxis but more hassle-free, as you won't have to bargain with the driver or worry about his not using the meter or taking a roundabout route.

Regular, **metered taxis** are on the upper level of the airport. The ride should be between P70 and P100 (US$1.75 to US$2.50). Insist on the meter, and if they don't cooperate, just get another taxi.

Most of the major hotels in Manila provide an airport taxi service. If you have made reservations, your name will appear on a list that the dispatcher has handy, and he will signal for the taxi to take you to the hotel. The amount—usually from P450 to P600 (US$11.20–US$14)—will be charged to your bill. It's the most hassle-free way to go, especially when you are jet-lagged.

## GETTING AROUND

Manila is a sprawling city, with at least three separate skylines. Most newcomers find the city's disorganized, seemingly unplanned layout hard to navigate. But in the middle of this apparently shapeless sprawl are clearly defined centers, each with its own unique character.

South of the river, the oldest part of Manila, including **Intramuros,** is where most of the historical and cultural interest lies. **Rizal Park,** stretching from Taft Avenue down to Roxas Boulevard on the bay, lies just south of here in what might be termed the main city center.

South of Rizal Park is the tourist belt of **Ermita, Malate,** and **Pasay City,** with their hotels, restaurants, trendy cafes, handicraft shops, bookshops, airline offices, and travel agencies. **Remedios Circle** is a bohemian section of Malate where artists and musicians hang, sleep, and strum. Linking all these areas is **Roxas Boulevard,** running north and south along Manila Bay. Before World War II this was the most elegant boulevard in the city, with stuccoed white mansions and walled villas whose well-groomed gardens and lawns lined the beachfront. Now it's home to five-star bay-view hotels, the **Cultural Center Complex,** and the **Metropolitan Museum.**

Just to the east is the cosmopolitan financial hub of **Makati.** Home to Gucci stores, high-rise condominiums, office tower blocks, and top hotels, this is where the rich, the famous, the expat, and the powerful reside and relax. In nearby **Forbes Park** you'll find the Manila Polo Club and Manila Golf Club, along with a thriving nightlife scene.

First and foremost get yourself a good map of Manila. **"EZ" Maps** are sold at most hotels and newspaper stands throughout the city. Even if you take taxis everywhere, it's always a good idea to have an idea of where you are.

Secondly, don't expect to get around very fast. During rush hours it can take as long as 2 hours to travel a measly 4km. This is partly due to the lack of traffic signals and signs, which has cars creeping across intersections and doing all sorts of illegal things, including driving against oncoming traffic. Hard as it might be, understand that these folks have grown up with this madness and know how to navigate the roads. Believe it or not, there are actually few accidents in Manila.

**By Taxi**    This is the preferred way of getting around town. Aside from being cheap, taxis are AIR-CONDITIONED! They are everywhere, pretty safe, and easy to identify as most have a light indicator on top and writing on the side. Before you take off, make sure the meter is working. Drivers will convince you that it's broken only to charge you triple the usual fare. Meters start at P20 (US50¢) and inch up by increments of P1 (US3¢). You can spend an hour driving all the way across town and still only pay about P100 (US$2.50). Make sure to carry small bills, because drivers often don't have any change. You should leave a tip of 5 to 10%.

# Manila

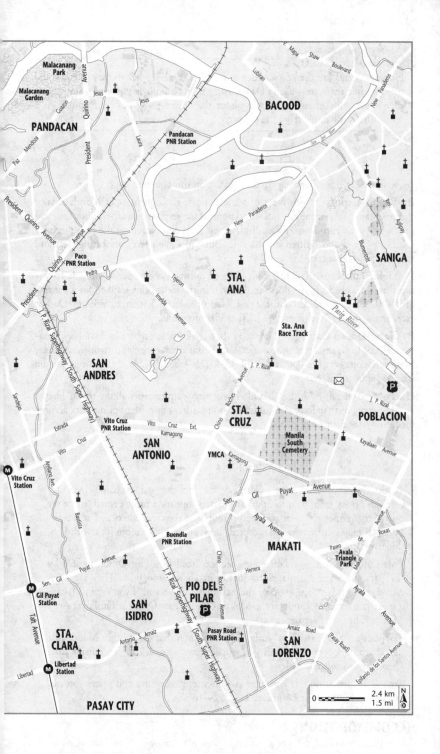

## Persona non grata

Finding Manila less than the Garden of Eden? Be careful what you say or you could wind up like the actress Claire Danes. After filming a movie in Manila, she reportedly made some offensive remarks about the city, causing quite an uproar. As a result, she was banned from the country.

**By Rental Car**　See "Getting Around" earlier in this chapter.

**By Bus & Jeepney**　Both types of vehicles pulse through most of Manila's major thoroughfares. Few of the city buses and none of the jeepneys are air-conditioned, and they're all pretty run-down. Buses display their final destination on the front; jeepney routes are fixed and written on the side. But unless you like suffocating heat and exhaust, just take a taxi.

**By Light Rail Transit (LRT)**　This elevated railway system speeds through 18 stations from Caloocan in the north to Baclaran in the south. Buy a token for a flat rate of P10 (US25¢) at staffed booths. The LRT is open from 5:30am to 9:30pm. Do not carry bulky loads while riding the LRT, as it is often full.

**By Horse-Drawn Carriage**　*Calesas,* as they are known, operate in Manila's Chinatown, Rizal Park, and Intramuros, and along Roxas Blvd. A romantic trot along Roxas Boulevard costs between P50 and P100 (US$1.25–US$2.50). As always, negotiate the fare before boarding one.

**On Foot**　You can do it, but Manila is not really a pleasant walking town. There's nothing very pretty to look at, and sidewalks are either nonexistent or not very accommodating to the floods of people.

## Fast Facts: Manila

**Banks/Currency Exchange**　Currency can be changed at banks (Monday through Friday from 9am to 3pm) and hotels, but for a more favorable rate try one of the money changers scattered throughout the city centers and at the airport. All major currencies are accepted, but you will have more luck with U.S. dollars.

**Post Office**　Most hotels offer mail service. Rizal Park Post Office, located by the park, near the Manila Hotel in Ermita, is not too busy. They are open Monday to Friday, 8am to 5pm, and Saturday until noon. If you are in Makati, a more convenient location is the Makati Central Post Office at Gil Puyat Ave., Makati. The hours are the same.

**Telephone**　See "Fast Facts" earlier in this chapter. For calls within Manila just dial the number. From a hotel you usually have to dial 9 for an outside line. Directory assistance is 114.

**Transit Information**　If you have any questions on routes and prices you can call the 24-hour tourist hotline at ☎ 2/524-1660.

## ACCOMMODATIONS

You can expect to find the whole gamut of accommodations within Manila. Most of the popular hotels in all price ranges are clean, comfortable, and safe. There are a few bad apples, but these are pretty obvious from appearances. Manila will be the only place in the country where you can find a variety of the reliable international chains like Holiday Inn, Shangri-La, and the Inter-Continental. Prices will be higher at these hotels than the more native-style accommodations at the beach destinations.

When choosing a neighborhood, Ermita and Malate are closest to the tourist areas and less congested with people and traffic than Makati. Nightlife is abundant here, and the city's countercultural and artistic community tends to congregate in this area. If business is your priority, Makati, Manila's business and financial district, is where you need to be. Stores, dining, and hotels are all top-notch in this area, but rush hours can be a nightmare.

## ERMITA/MALATE
### Very Expensive
**Manila Hotel.** One Rizal Park, 1099 Manila, Philippines. ☎ **800/9-MNL-HTL** or 2/527-0011. Fax 2/527-0022 to 24. www.manila-hotel.com.ph. 500 units. A/C MINIBAR TV TEL. P10,000–P12,000 (US$250–US$300) double; P13,000–P100,000 (US$325–US$2,500) suites. AE, DC, JCB, MC, V.

Manila Hotel has a story to tell. Without a doubt Manila's most famous hotel, for 7 decades it has stood as witness to the lives, loves, triumphs, and heartbreaks of a city. Since its opening in 1912, the hotel, nestled between the walled city of Intramuros and the famed Manila Bay, has hosted everyone from Ernest Hemingway to John F. Kennedy to Michael Jackson to the Beatles. General MacArthur lived here for 6 years, and you can stay in his re-created suite, although priority for this gorgeous, museum-like room goes to diplomats and presidents. Rooms exude a turn-of-the-century charm, with four-poster beds, old world fabrics and textures, and ceiling fans. Rooms in the 18-story wing, added in 1970, are less expensive than rooms in the original building. All the first-class amenities you would expect are here, but the height of luxury is in the Penthouse and Presidential suites, with their live-in butlers, indoor swimming pools, and helipads. The MacArthur Club is perfect for the executive traveler. Amenities are tennis courts, pool, putting green, 24-hour business center, health club, 24-hour room service, dry cleaning, laundry, newspaper delivery, baby-sitting, superior travel assistance center, and car/limo hire. The food is excellent at any of the hotel's 10 restaurants and bars, which include Japanese, Italian, and a steakhouse and seafood grill. (See Cowrie Grill under "Where to Eat" below.)

### Expensive
**The Pan Pacific.** M. Adriatico and Gen. Malvar St., Malate, Manila. ☎ **2/536-0788.** Fax 2/526-6503. 240 units. A/C MINIBAR TV TEL. P5,800–P7,000 (US$145–US$175) double; P9,200–P11,200 (US$230–US$280) suites. AE, DC, MC, V.

Because of its location outside of Makati, the Pan Pacific isn't in direct competition with its closest rivals, the Peninsula and the Shangri-la. Though of the three I prefer the Shangri-la, this is a very nice hotel. Spacious and technologically advanced, every room has personal computers on granite desks, fax/printers, and stereo systems. Double doors herald expansive mirrors reflecting Italian marble and sandblasted glass in the bathrooms. And while you are soaking in the bath you can watch TV through the remote-controlled sliding doors that link the bathroom with the bedroom. The elegant down duvet comforter is a nice touch.

The hotel boasts a large selection of fine dining restaurants, including the très chic Le Taxi for French food, and Sapporo Sam, whose chef has two passions in life: sumo wrestling and Japanese food. Amenities include 24-hour business center, 24-hour room service, outdoor pool and Jacuzzi, poolside bar, executive floor privileges for the business traveler, complimentary laundry service and suit pressing on arrival, covered parking, and butler service to all rooms.

## Moderate

**Bayview Park Hotel.** 1118 Roxas Boulevard, Ermita, Manila (corner of United Nations Avenue). ☎ **2/526-1555.** Fax 2/521-2674. Bayview@wpi.webquest.com. 275 units. A/C MINIBAR TV TEL. P6,000–P6,800 (US$150–US$170) double; P8,000–P12,000 (US$200–US$300) suites. AE, DC, MC, V.

Quality and value are why the Bayview is popular. Its location across from the U.S. embassy is prime, overlooking the bay and within easy walking distance of attractions. But you don't pay sky-high prices for it. The ambiance is classier and more personal than that of the neighboring Holiday Inn, thanks to renovations in 1994. They offer a range of corporate, bay-view, and executive suites; you'll enjoy the best views from the junior suite's corner room. All standard and superior rooms are equipped with gadgets like individual bed-side panel control, coffeemakers, and deposit boxes, and many rooms are interconnected for a large family or business gathering. The tranquil rooftop pool is far above the noise and traffic of the city, and the modest fitness center offers massage services. They also have a business center, conference center, limo service, and the **Giardino Cafe** for Asian and international delights.

✪ **Holiday Inn.** United Nations Avenue, Ermita, Manila. ☎ **800/465-4329** in the U.S. and Canada (800/553-888 in Australia, 800/442888 in New Zealand, 0800/897121 in the U.K.) or 2/526-1212. Fax 2/526-2552. 590 units. A/C MINIBAR TV TEL. P6,000–P7,200 (US$150–US$180) double; P12,000–P26,400 (US$300–US$660) suites. AE, DC, MC, V.

Perfect for tourists who don't need elegance and business facilities but still want first-class service, comfort, convenience, and uncompromising hospitality. The Holiday Inn gives you all that and a reliable name. The location is also ideal for checking out tourist spots like Rizal Park, Intramuros, and Robinson's Mall. Rooms are quiet and cozy, although there's nothing unique about the floral chain hotel decor. Holiday Inn wins the award for the most spirited hotel in Manila—every large festival is celebrated in their lobby with food, decoration, and entertainment. You can dine at the **Rotisserie** for good continental dishes and an extensive wine list, the **Pavilion Court** for Asian food, or **Cafe Coquilla** for buffet-style meals. The patisserie serves excellent pastries. There's a pool with sundeck, a fully equipped gym, a cordial business center, and a casino.

## Inexpensive

**Centrepoint Hotel.** 1430 A Mabini St., Ermita, Manila (near Robinson's Mall). ☎ **2/521-2751.** Fax 2/521-5331. 104 units. A/C MINIBAR TV TEL. P2,410–P2,880 (US$60–US$72) double. AE, DC, MC, V.

This is a good value in the heart of the tourist belt, near great bars, restaurants, and shopping. All rooms are carpeted and are pretty spacious for this price range. The staff is very knowledgeable and eager to please, and the continental fare at the restaurant is good. It's also where trips to Mindoro originate (see "Mindoro," below).

**Malate Pension.** 1771 M Adriatico St., Malate, Manila. ☎ **2/596-672.** Fax 2/597-119. 45 units and 48 dorm beds. P1,240–P1,520 (US$31–US$38) room with air-conditioning and private bath; P880 (US$22) room with fan and private bath; P520–P600 (US$13–US$15) room with fan and common bath; P240 (US$6) per person in dorm with fan. AE.

The cozy atmosphere and budget prices make this the most popular stop for backpackers and other travelers looking for a good bang for their buck. The rooms are clean, the sheets smell good, the water is hot, and the staff is super helpful and knowledgeable. The antiques in each room add a charming, warm touch. You'll even find a business center with e-mail. The restaurant and cafe are fine if you don't feel like wandering out at night.

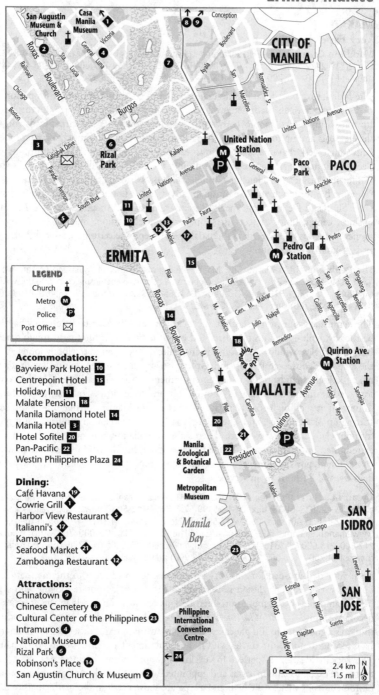

**LEGEND**
Church †
Metro Ⓜ
Police Ⓟ
Post Office ✉

**Accommodations:**
Bayview Park Hotel **10**
Centrepoint Hotel **15**
Holiday Inn **11**
Malate Pension **18**
Manila Diamond Hotel **14**
Manila Hotel **3**
Hotel Sofitel **20**
Pan-Pacific **22**
Westin Philippines Plaza **24**

**Dining:**
Café Havana **19**
Cowrie Grill **1**
Harbor View Restaurant **5**
Italianni's **17**
Kamayan **13**
Seafood Market **21**
Zamboanga Restaurant **12**

**Attractions:**
Chinatown **9**
Chinese Cemetery **8**
Cultural Center of the Philippines **23**
Intramuros **4**
National Museum **7**
Rizal Park **6**
Robinson's Place **14**
San Agustin Church & Museum **2**

648    The Philippines

# MAKATI
## Very Expensive
**Mandarin Oriental.** Paseo de Roxas and Makati Avenue, Makati, Manila. ☎ **2/750-8888.** Fax 2/817-2472. 464 units. A/C MINIBAR TV TEL. P11,800–P17,600 (US$295–US$440) double; P19,800–P51,200 (US$495–US$1,280) suites. AE, DC, JCB, MC, V.

The Mandarin fits its loyal business clientele like a good pair of shoes, with personalized service that treats them better than a stay at grandma's. Service separates this hotel from its competitors. Employees warmly welcome you and a red carpet leads you to the elevators and up to your room. The rooms are soothing, in muted, relaxing tones, with a huge desk that makes it easy to spread out your laptop and files. Bathrooms are sleek, in all marble and porcelain. For dining, there's Tivoli Grill for superb grills and California cuisine; Tin Hau for Chinese; The Brasserie for buffets and snacks; The Captains Bar for lunch and live music nightly; Clipper Lounge for Asian fare; and the Cake Shop and Deli for light meals, desserts, and snacks. Amenities include 24-hour business center, limo service, gift shop, florist, beauty salon, medical clinic, travel agency, gorgeous pool, health club, massage, golf, tennis, electronic safes, baby-sitting, and 24-hour room service.

**The Peninsula.** 1226 Makati City, Manila, Philippines (corner of Ayala and Makati Ave.). ☎ **2/810-3456.** Fax 2/815-4825. tpm@peninsula.com. www.peninsula.com. 500 units. A/C MINIBAR TV TEL. P10,600–P13,000 (US$265–US$325) double; P16,400–P108,000 (US$410–US$2,700) suite. AE, DC, JCB, MC, V.

The Peninsula is one of the classiest, most elegant hotels in Manila. It certainly has the best lobby, with enormous tapestries and bright natural light filtering through gracefully arched glass windows. A wide curving staircase takes you to the lobby lounge and the popular Conservatory Bar and Grill. The airy rooms are equipped with a fax machine and a handsome wooden entertainment center with a large TV. The comfortable bathrooms have separate shower, tub, and toilet areas. For dining, you'll feel important at such high-society palate pleasers as Old Manila, for fine dining; Spices, stirring up Asian cuisine; and The Lobby, for 24-hour food and live music, a hot spot for politicians and the social elite. There's also an Italian restaurant, a bar, and an à la carte buffet. Hotel amenities include L-shaped pool, health spa, business center, helicopter rental, gift shop, flower shop, cigar store, laundry and dry cleaning, newspaper delivery, and 24-hour room service.

**Shangri-La Hotel.** P.O. Box 4191, MCPO 1281, Makati, Manila (corner of Ayala and Makati aves). ☎ **2/813-8888;** fax 2/813-5499. ☎ **800/942-5050** in the U.S. and Canada (800/222-448 in Australia, 0800/442-5050 in New Zealand, 44 181/747-8485 in the U.K.). www.Shangri-La.com. 703 units. A/C MINIBAR TV TEL. P12,000 (US$300) deluxe; P12,600–P15,600 (US$315–US$390) executive; P15,600–P19,800 (US$390–US$495) horizon rooms; P54,200–P116,000 (US$1,355–US$2,900) presidential suites. AE, DC, MC, V.

Keep your tie buttoned for this very professional resort catering to the international business executive. The design is as varied as the diverse corporate moguls who stay here. Compared to the more pure-bred designs of other top hotels in the area, it's a decorative mutt—*Gone With the Wind* meets Malaysia. And for some reason they think it's a good idea to flip pancakes in the lobby. But in terms of service the Shangri-La is second to none, and carries with it the reputation of a premier Asian hotel chain. The Makati location is perfect for exclusive shopping and business dealings. The rooms are exceptionally spacious and appointed with coffeemaker, a convenient push-button control panel by the bed, and a separate shower stall in the marble bathroom. The suites are huge and luxurious, radiating a timeless ambience and making you feel like royalty. Amenities include tennis courts, large free-form pool, gym, health club, massage, newspaper delivery, same day laundry, complimentary shoe shine, parcel and

# Makati

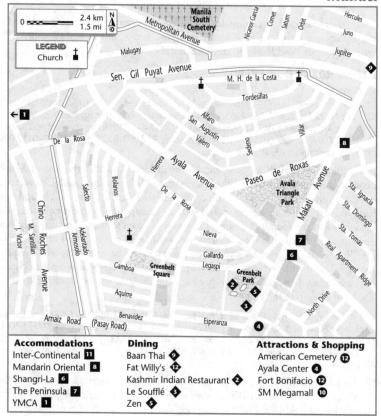

**Accommodations**
Inter-Continental **11**
Mandarin Oriental **8**
Shangri-La **6**
The Peninsula **7**
YMCA **1**

**Dining**
Baan Thai **9**
Fat Willy's **12**
Kashmir Indian Restaurant **2**
Le Soufflé **3**
Zen **5**

**Attractions & Shopping**
American Cemetery **12**
Ayala Center **4**
Fort Bonifacio **12**
SM Megamall **10**

postage service, travel agency, shopping arcade, and medical clinic. For dining, the Shangri-La is home to excellent restaurants featuring Eastern and Western cuisines, and also home to the city's current hot-spot disco, the **Zu** (see "Manila After Dark," below).

### Expensive

**Inter-Continental.** 1 Ayala Ave., Makati. Near Edsa. ☎ **2/815-9711.** Fax 2/817-1330. 343 units. A/C MINIBAR TV TEL. P10,400–P11,600 (US$260–US$290) double; P14,000–P100,000 (US$350–US$2,500) suite. AE, DC, MC, V.

The recently refurbished Inter-Continental is a pleasant oasis in the middle of the busy commercial district of Makati. Less expensive than other high-end hotels in this district, you still get attentive staff and a decent, secure room. Views are either of the commercial center, which is not bad at night, or, on the pool-side, of residential villages occupied by diplomats and expatriates. The pool is second only to the Shangri-La's, and they have a good gym and efficient 24-hour business center, 24-hour room service, newspaper delivery, laundry and dry cleaning, car hire, and travel agency. The Jeepney Coffee Shop and the Prince Albert are popular with politicians, and the Euphoria (see "Manila After Dark," below) is one of the more visited discos in Manila.

### Inexpensive

**YMCA.** 7 Dao St., San Antonio Village, Makati (near Makati Central Post Office). ☎ **2/899-6101.** Fax 2/899-6097. 30 units. P1,840 (US$46) double. A/C.

As you would expect from the Y, rooms are simple and clean, providing a roof over your head if nothing else. It's a great place to meet other travelers. They also offer cheap, dormitory-style accommodations, although it can be quite noisy and hard to sleep. Facilities include a pool, small gym, and tennis and basketball courts. The restaurant serves good local and continental dishes.

## ALONG ROXAS BOULEVARD
### Expensive

**Manila Diamond Hotel.** Roxas Boulevard at the corner of Dr. J Quintos St., Manila. ☎ **2/526-2211.** Fax 2/526-2255. Diamond@cnl.net. www.mindgate.com.ph/diamond. 500 units. A/C MINIBAR TV TEL. P9,600–P10,400 (US$240–US$260) superior singles and doubles; P10,800–P16,000 (US$270–US$400) deluxe; P12,000–P80,000 (US$300–US$2,000) executive floor suites. AE, DC, JCB, MC, V.

A 15-minute walk to Rizal Park, the Diamond Hotel straddles the best of Manila between the tourist district and the business center. It's popular with business executives and visiting Japanese. The lavish combination of black granite, marble, and opulent gold leaf creates an elegant early 1900s art deco/postmodern design throughout the lobby and the rooms. Beds are a fluffy nest of down feathers. The wide bay windows in all the rooms afford magnificent views of Manila Bay and the illuminated skyline. Rooms are equipped for fax and computer hookup. Amenities are well-equipped spa, curvy pool with waterfall, laundry and dry cleaning, 24-hour room service, and business center. Japanese and French cuisine are available on the top floor. There is also a coffee shop in the lobby.

**Hotel Sofitel.** 1990 Roxas Boulevard, P.O. Box 776, Manila. ☎ **800/221-4542** in U.S. and Canada (in Australia 800/642244, in New Zealand 800/444422, in the U.K. 44 71/724-1000) or 2/526-8588. Fax 2/524-2526. 500 units. A/C MINIBAR TV TEL. P7,200–P10,800 (US$180–US$270) double; P14,400–P24,800 (US$360–US$620) sunset and executive suites. AE, DC, MC, V.

Marble lobbies and towering tiers of concrete dominate the façade and interior of this mostly tourist-occupied hotel. The decor is Donald Trump meets the Jetsons, with a kitsch 24-carat gold-plated talking revolving door. All rooms are large, with spacious bathrooms, individual thermostat controls, and safety deposit. The cafe dishes up good food 24-hours a day. There's also a fitness center, currency exchange, medical clinic, gift shop, business center, 24-hour casino, laundry and dry cleaning, and babysitting. The Dip N' Sip swimming pool on the third floor overlooks the bay and the city.

## PASAY (NEAR THE AIRPORT)
### Very Expensive

✪ **Westin Philippines Plaza.** Cultural Center Complex, Roxas Blvd., Pasay City, Philippines. ☎ **2/551-5555.** Fax 2/551-5610. 670 units. A/C MINIBAR TV TEL. P12,000–P14,000 (US$300–US$350) double; P18,200–P125,120 (US$455–US$3,128) suites. AE, DC, JCB, MC, V.

The fabled sunsets of Manila are the backdrop to this resortlike hotel complex on the bay, which caters mostly to international business travelers who want to take advantage of its convenient location and vacationlike atmosphere. The huge pool curves around water slides and a poolside bar that hosts cultural performances and barbecues. You can also practice your swing at their putting green. Other amenities are a state-of-the-art health club, golf equipment rental, shopping arcade, 24-hour business center, 24-hour room service, newspaper delivery, turndown twice daily, 24-hour massage, and laundry and dry cleaning. The best views are from the "pool-view" rooms that overlook the bay. Service is excellent and rooms and bathrooms are spacious and first-class. There are several restaurants, a great bakery, a disco, and a bar with Guinness on tap. The hotel is located near the Cultural Center of the Philippines (CCP), so if you want easy access to entertainment without waiting hours in traffic, it's perfect.

## DINING

If you crave it, Manila's got it, whether you are looking for gourmet dining or a quick-and-cheap but tasty meal. There's plenty of that familiar, salty, greasy, American fast food to choose from here, including T.G.I. Friday's, Hard Rock Cafe, Fashion Cafe, Chilis, Benihana, McDonalds, Wendy's, Dominos, Pizza Hut, Shakey's, Kentucky Fried Chicken, Kenny Roger's Roasters, and Texas Chicken. I've listed some of the most popular, and tastier, restaurants, giving you a variety of ethnic tastes and types of atmosphere to choose from.

### ERMITA/MALATE

**Café Havana.** 1903 M. Adriatico (at Remedios St.), Malate. ☎ **2/521-8097.** Main courses P170–P220 (US$4.25–US$5.50). AE, DC, MC, V. Daily 11am–2am. CUBAN.

It's easy to spot this muy popular corner hacienda, with its windows that surround the entire façade. The airy inside is just as festive, with hardwood floors, pastel paintings, and interesting Cuban knickknacks decorating the bar and restaurant. At lunchtime, the scene turns corporate with the suit-and-tie type taking advantage of the lunch special. They have great pork sandwiches and tasty Cuban kebabs. Most entrees come with an accompaniment of Spanish rice and an array of dipping sauces, including hot spicy chilies.

Dinnertime finds an eclectic mix of people, and after dinner the bar gets pretty packed. Impromptu dancing is not uncommon at any hour, and even the waiters seem to always be moving their hips and clapping. It's kind of hard to keep still with the sensual beat of Latino music blasting from the speakers.

**Cowrie Grill.** Manila Hotel, One Rizal Park. ☎ **2/527-0011.** Main courses P500–P1,600 (US$12.50–US$40). AE, DC, MC, V. Noon–2:30pm, 7–11pm. STEAKHOUSE.

The Cowrie Grill offers the meat lover an international variety of steaks and grilled main courses. The choicest cuts of Australian and U.S meats—lamb, beef, veal, and game—are all available, as are grilled main courses cooked in a no-charcoal broiler. The cowrie-shell decor creates a graceful mood, and the partitioned tables make for a quiet, private evening to dine, relax, and while away the time.

**Harbor View Restaurant.** On Manila Bay, Gate A, South Boulevard, Rizal Park, Ermita. ☎ **2/524-1571.** Main courses P80–P500 (US$2–US$12.50). AE, MC, V. Daily 6am–midnight. FILIPINO/SEAFOOD.

This restaurant jutting out over the harbor is considered one of the most romantic spots in Manila. Watching the boats passing by, you feel like you are peacefully at sea, away from the hectic city. When the mercury drops, the breeze is relaxing, and you can dance to the tunes of Frank Sinatra and the other swingers playing over the sound system. The food ranges from your basic cheeseburger to the more exotic crab in ginger sauce, venison, and tuna steak. The mango salad is refreshing, with chopped green mangos, onion, and tomato seasoned with baboong sauce. It's a great place to sit alone, or quietly with your companion, and write postcards.

**Italianni's.** 2nd Level, Robinsons Place, Ermita, Manila. ☎ **2/536-7961.** (Or Greenbelt Ayala Center, Makati. ☎ **2/892-2897.**) Main courses P70–P250 (US$1.75–US$6.25). AE, DC, MC, V. Daily 11am–11pm. ITALIAN.

Italianni's is a casual place to have some great pasta while you enjoy the quiet and soothing atmosphere. The old black and white photos depicting life in the "old country" give an authentic, familiar feel to the place. Breads such as focaccia and pan de sal are baked fresh every day and sold for take-out. The pizza margherita is the best pizza I tasted in Manila. Salads complement your pasta orders and the iced teas and sodas are all you can drink. It's a great value, and you will definitely be full after eating their large portions. The mall location is very convenient, but the Makati location's unmistakable entrance reminds you of old Italy, with its yellow stucco façade and wood-paneled glass doors.

**Kamayan.** 523 Padre Faura cor. M. Adriatico, Ermita, Manila. ☎ **2/528-1723.** Main courses P100–P600 (US$2.50–US$15). Daily buffet P330 (US$8.25), 11am–2pm. AE, DC, MC, V. Daily 11am–11pm. FILIPINO.

According to folklore, eating with one's bare hands used to be seen as the ultimate pleasure, a way of celebrating the plentiful feast. You'll understand why at Kamayan, but for the squeamish, they do give you silverware. It's a rather touristy venue, but according to locals it's a must-stop for great-tasting Filipino food, and the atmosphere is better than that of nearby Zamboanga. Patrons and staff clap along to the serenading band. If you're feeling adventurous, order the Nilalang Bulalo (cow foot soup) or the enormous sweet and sour prawns. Portions are huge, service is almost overly attentive, and the atmosphere is fun and lively.

✪ **Kashmir.** Padre Faura, Ermita. ☎ **2/524-6851.** (A second location is in the Festejo Building, 816 Pasay Rd., Makati; ☎ 2/844-4924.) Main courses P250–P600 (US$6.25–US$15). AE, DC, JCB, MC, V. Daily 11am–11pm. INDIAN/MALAYSIAN.

With a variety of sauces ranging from tomato cream and butter, to coconut milk with spices, to spicy tandoori, it's no wonder Kashmir's cuisine ranks among the top five in the city with locals and expats alike. The space is small, dimly lit, and quiet; the food is anything but. There are plenty of vegetable main courses and rice specialties to choose from, and a sure palate pleaser is the Kesu Pullao, a subtle, saffron-seasoned rice dish. Most main courses come with an assortment of mango chutney, mint sauce, and a spicy crushed pickles-and-ginger dip. Those wary of spicy food might try the T-bone steaks and lamb chops in a milder mushroom sauce.

**Seafood Market.** Ambassador Hotel, Mabini St., Malate. ☎ **2/524-7756.** Entree with soup and salad P400–P800 (US$10–US$20). AE, DC, MC, V. SEAFOOD.

There is a method to this seafood madness. First, grab a cart or basket and pick out a fresh lobster, crab, lapu-lapu (a delicious local white fish related to the grouper), or one of the many other mouthwatering creatures on offer. Put it in a plastic bag, but wrap it tightly, as they get jumpy when they're out of the water. Then select how you want your fish prepared from a long list of options. Try the delicious sinigang ni hipon, which is a tamarind-based soup with prawns and loads of local vegetables, or the sweet and sour lapu-lapu.

**Zamboanga.** 1619 Macario Adriatico St., Ermita, Manila. ☎ **2/525-7638** or 521-9836. Reservations recommended during peak season. Main courses P80–P400 (US$2–US$10). AE, DC, MC, V. Daily 9am–11pm. FILIPINO/SEAFOOD.

The gifts of the sea are truly appreciated here, their flavor brought out with delicious Filipino sauces and spices. The menu will need interpretation, which only goes to show how authentic the dishes are here. The wait staff is very friendly and will gladly stand over you for as long as it takes until you are clear about what's what. The local specialty adobo is good, as is Fisherman's Delight, a delectable assortment of fresh oysters, crabs, shellfish, and crustaceans, steamed and delicately spiced. If seafood is not your thing, there are plenty of noodle, rice, and vegetarian dishes. All main courses come in a native basket lined with banana leaves. One word of caution: If you order the pig, you get the whole pig—head and all! At 8:30pm nightly, there is an hour-long traditional dance performance. For the record, David Hasselhoff ordered 20 pieces of prawn when he was here.

## MAKATI

**Baan Thai.** At the corner of Makati Avenue and Jupiter St., Bel Air I, Makati, Manila. ☎ **2/895-1666** or 1669. Main courses P75–P250 (US$1.90–US$6.25). AE, DC, MC, V. Daily 11am–11pm. THAI.

The home-cooked spicy Thai food at this popular restaurant won't burn your tongue or your pocket. The ingredients are fresh, and if not found locally are flown in straight from Bangkok. It's a small, casual, friendly spot where the wood-paneled walls and the Thai pictures create a nice backdrop to the exotic and contrasting tastes that are so distinctly Thai. As always, there's something for lemongrass lovers, ginger groupies, and satay suckers. Feel free to make special requests if you don't see what you want on the menu.

**Fat Willy's.** Unit A, The Fort, Bonifacio Center, Fort Bonifacio, Taguig. ☎ **2/555-1207.** Drinks P90–P150 (US$2.25–US$3.75) drinks; sandwiches and main courses P120–P260 (US$3–US$6.50). AE, DC, MC, V. Daily 11am–1am. DRINKS/CONTINENTAL.

This is a spirited, energetic, industrial-looking place where people come mostly for the large, creative drinks. Ask about their biggest beer—you won't be disappointed. The smoothies are the prettiest and the tastiest around, or try the iced cafe mocha complete with streams of whipped cream and Hershey's chocolate syrup. To the left of the bar is a wine cellar with hundreds of reds and whites. The psychedelic and colorful menu contributes good eats to accompany any drink, with a variety of sandwiches and pastas in large portions. The name Fat Willy's is explained, according to one waiter, by the fact that the British owner is "horizontally challenged."

✪ **Le Souffle.** 2nd Floor, Josephine Building, Makati Ave. at West Dr., Ayala Center, Makati. ☎ 2/812-3287. E-mail: souffle@l-manila.com.ph. Main courses P680–P1,200 (US$17–US$30). AE DC MC V. Daily 11am–2am. FRENCH/MEDITERRANEAN.

The name says it all—the soufflés here (especially the chocolate one) are to die for: rich with flavor, yet airy and light. The chef enjoys a good challenge and says his best dishes have been unique requests from guests. "If the ingredients are here, we will do our best!" The menu offers such unique dishes as grilled lapu-lapu in a warm tarragon/tomato vinaigrette and crispy vegetable julienne topped with sour cream and paprika. They believe one should eat as one wishes, so there is no distinction between appetizers and main courses. The atmosphere is just the right mix of sophistication and casualness. There's an excellent wine bar.

**Zen.** Glorietta 3, level 1 Ayala Center, Makati. ☎ **2/892-6851.** Main courses P230–P600 (US$5.75–US$15). AE, DC, MC, V. Sun–Thurs 11am–11pm; Fri and Sat 11am–midnight. JAPANESE/SUSHI.

At Zen you're guaranteed not only fresh and excellent Japanese food, but also service with a smile. You can sit at the simple sushi bar or at a table. The spicy tuna rolls are excellent—not so spicy that you can't taste the tuna. If sushi doesn't float your boat, there are plenty of noodle and curry dishes, as well as pork, chicken, beef, or seafood teriyakis.

## OUTSIDE THE CITY CENTER

**The Aviary Restaurant, Iguana Bar, Pet Museum Café, and Pet Park!** 233 Jose Abad Santos St., Little Baguio, San Juan (near Cardinal Santos Hospital). ☎ 2/726-4618. Main courses P320–P600 (US$8–US$15). AE DC MC V. Daily 7am–2am. INTERNATIONAL.

Any bar or restaurant can remind you of a zoo; the Aviary actually is one. You'll hear the grunts of lizards and the howls of silver-crested Australian cockatoos at this zany watering hole popular with artists and politicians. The owner couldn't quite decide whether he wanted to open a pub, a restaurant, or a zoo, so he combined the three into one. Antiques punctuate the stylish Spanish colonial decor. The bar offers a wide selection of beers and wines, while the restaurant serves up an eclectic mix of palate pleasers—thanks to Chef Ronald's schooling at the French Culinary Institute in New York. A must is the fondue bourguignonne—their version of beef fondue accompanied by a turnstile of six unique sauces. Don't be surprised to see a 9-foot albino boa constrictor hanging from the bar; he's with the owner.

**L'eau Vive in Asia.** 1499 Paz M. Guazon Ave. (formerly Otis), Paco, Manila. ☎ 2/563-8558 or 59. Reservations recommended. Main courses P250–P600 (US$6.25–US$15). AE, DC, MC, V. Daily 11am–3pm and 7–11pm. FRENCH.

This missionary settlement run by Carmelite nuns serves up authentic French cuisine, including frog legs in garlic butter and rabbit in white wine cream sauce. Not only is the food delicious, but it's beautifully arranged with complementary colors and textures. The lapu-lapu à la bouillabaisse is excellent, filled with shrimp and tomato in a delicate white wine cream sauce, and served with fettuccine noodles. The service is cordial and attentive (they are nuns, after all), and because the place is somewhat off the beaten track, in a rather run-down area, it's quiet and sometimes a little empty. To warm your heart and spirit, catch the 9:30pm prayer, when local street children kneel down in front of the garden courtyard and the statue of Mary and sing along to Ave Maria.

## ATTRACTIONS

There are plenty of guided tours available through most hotels. However, most of the sights below are easy to reach, and taxi drivers will be familiar with all of them.

### ERMITA/MALATE

**San Agustin Church and Museum.** Real and General Luna sts. (within the walls of Intramuros). Admission P40 (US$1). Daily 9am–5pm.

The Monastery was originally used as the living quarters, classroom, refectory, vestry, sacristy, library, and infirmary of the Augustinians. The church was ravaged by several wars, but was restored and turned into a museum in 1973, showcasing Filipino, Spanish, Chinese, and Mexican art, with an interesting collection of photos of 19th-century Manila.

**Casa Manila.** Real & General Luna sts. (right across from San Agustin Church). ☎ 2/496-793 or 2/483-275. Admission P15 adults, P5 students and children. Tues–Fri 9am–6pm (until 7pm Sat–Sun).

A perfect quick stop for anyone interested in period houses and architecture, Casa Manila embodies 19th-century design, with original adobe stones, European furnishings and decor, and Philippine weavings.

**Rizal Park.**

Just outside the walls of Intramuros, along Roxas Boulevard and United Nations Avenue, Rizal Park honors the nationalist hero who was executed here at dawn by the Spanish on December 30, 1898. Stroll around to see his bronze statue and the Japanese gardens, and stop in the Department of Tourism along the park, on TM Kalaw St. You might even catch a free Sunday concert or get a delicious mango shake at the nearby Manila Hotel.

## MAKATI

**The National Museum.** Padres Burgos St. (a short walk from Rizal Park). Mon–Sat 8:30am–noon and 1–5pm. ☎ **2/494-450.** Free admission.

Archaeological, ethnological, and natural history exhibits focus on Filipino culture and heritage. There's a section of the fossilized skullcap of Tabon Man, a prehistoric find from Palawan. For boat enthusiasts, check out the display in the museum's Maritime Heritage Gallery of seven native boats, carbon-dated to between 890 and 710 B.C.

## PASAY

**The Cultural Center of the Philippines.** CCP Complex, bay side of Roxas Blvd. ☎ **2/832-1135.**

A costly pet project of Imelda Marcos, the main building houses a 2,000-seat concert hall, a 400-seat theatre, an archaeological museum, a library, and the Contemporary Art Museum. Events and times are listed at the entrance to the complex. They can range from aboriginal dancing, to orchestra or dance performances, to seminars on the history of film, to a showing of Vietnamese water puppets.

## OUTSIDE THE CITY CENTER

**Chinatown.** Quintin Paredes and Ongpin sts.

Located in the old districts of San Nicolas and Binondo, you'll know you've entered Chinatown when you pass through the three Chinese-Philippine friendship arches called the Welcome Gates. You'll find Chinese herbal medicine, gold jewelry, silk embroideries, porcelain, preserved fruit and meat, and a variety of delicious fresh fruit. Grab a *hopia*, an interesting dumpling-like pastry, from any of the bakeries and eat it while sitting on a *calesa*, the horse-drawn carriages that frequent Chinatown.

✪ **The Chinese Cemetery.** North of Santa Cruz, along Aurora Ave. and Jose Abad Santos St.

This cemetery is more like a well-kept suburb. In fact, the dead are better off than the living inhabitants of the squatter towns surrounding it. Some house-size tombs are complete with mailboxes, air-conditioning, and even fax machines to make the afterlife as comfortable and convenient as life on earth was. Guides are recommended, as they have some fascinating tales to tell about the area, and it's easy to lose yourself in the many alleys that branch through the cemetery. Not to be missed.

**The American Cemetery.** Fort Bonifacio in Makati; 2km from where Ayala Ave. meets Edsa (Epifanio de los Santos Ave.).

If you find your spirit in need of a little green among the hustle and bustle of the concrete city, the American Cemetery is a perfect getaway. It's the largest American burial ground outside the U.S., with the graves of 17,000 soldiers who died in the

### Where to Tee off on Luzon

If you are interested in getting in a few rounds of golf, Manila and the surrounding area have plenty of courses to choose from. Some are for members only, but the following are open to tourists: **Aguinaldo Golf Club,** Quezon City (☎ 2/911-8142); **Fort Bonifacio Golf Club,** Fort Bonifacio, Makati (☎ 2/812-7521); **Philippine Navy Golf Club,** BNS Fort Bonifacio, Makati (☎ 2/819-2780); **Calatagan Golf Club,** Calatagan, Batangas (☎ 43/818-6961).

## Where to Find a Pharmacy

Most hotels stock the basics, like shampoo, toothpaste, aspirin, hairspray, and feminine products, in their gift shop. Otherwise, try **La Botica Inc.,** located in SM Megamall, ☎ 2/634-2222; **Emilene's Pharmacy Inc.,** at East Service Rd, ☎ 2/842-3186; or **Mercury Drug Corp,** in the Mercury Drug Corp Bldg., Quezon City, ☎ 2/911-5071.

Philippines and surrounding Pacific during World War II. There are beautiful tiled mosaic maps illustrating the historic battles inside the circular memorial.

# SHOPPING
## SHOPPING CENTERS
### Ermita & Malate
**Robinson's Place.** Along M. Adriatico St. in Ermita, next to Manila Midtown Hotel.

For unique antiques, knickknacks, jewelry, coins, and woodwork, go to **Yamasawa** on the third floor. **Hanuman Music and Crafts** offers a selection of hand drums with Philippine tribal designs and traditional rattan weaving. They also carry hand-sculpted pottery and bowls, incense, and New Age books and music.

**Harrison Plaza.** Between A. Mabini and M. Adriatico sts. in Malate.

This plaza has two major department stores under its roof: **Shoemart** (SM) and the upscale **Rustan's.** On the first floor is an antique shop called **Kabul.** On the second floor, **Fo Kuang Yuen** sells Chinese decorative objects, statues, and small samples of jewelry made of jade and other semi-precious stones. Check out the bargain stalls on the ground floor's center atrium for gift items.

### Makati
**Ayala Commercial Center.** Between Edsa, Ayala Ave., Makati Ave., and Pasay Rd.

This is a vast, sprawling complex, so use the convenient map displays or the user-friendly Automated Shoppers Guides (ASGs) located at the ends of hallways. **Island Spice** and **Pidro** offer tropical clothing, light cotton shirts, T-shirts, shorts, and sarongs. **The Museum Shop** and **Things** sell art reproductions, statues, and a few native souvenirs.

   For Filipino antiques go to **Goldcrest Square;** even if you don't intend to buy anything, it's still a great place to see how Spanish, Chinese, Japanese, and American influences have blended with tribal Filipino culture. At **Tesoro's** you'll find wearable native dresses as well as woven and embroidered items like place mats and tablecloths made from indigenous materials.

**SM Megamall.** Along Edsa Ave., near the Hotel Inter-Continental.

This is said to be the largest mall in the country, with 6 floors of shops and 12 cinemas. Stores like **Old Manila** and **Memory Lane** display Philippine-made furnishings, small antiques, and old books and jewelry. **Tahanan** is a good place to find modern basketwork. And have I mentioned shoes? Check out **Shoemart** department store. If the heat gets to you, there's an ice-skating rink.

**Shangri-La Plaza.** Right beside SM Megamall, bordered by Edsa Ave. and Shaw Blvd.

This exclusive mall is home to **Rustan's Department Store** and a range of high-end boutiques and stores. The main attraction here is an eight-story atrium with live trees and a musical fountain.

---

**A Few Shopping Tips**

- Look for the mall-wide sales, such as the midnight madness sales, and decide whether you want to join in or avoid the crush.
- You'll get better service if you dress up a bit—casual but nice. They take malls seriously here and rubber flip-flops will get you snubbed.
- When paying for sale items with a credit card, ask the clerk if a discount still applies; sometimes charges are excluded.
- Comfort rooms are pretty clean, but make sure to bring your own toilet paper.
- It is customary for store guards to collect your packages before you enter the store.
- Don't be annoyed if the store clerk follows you around; that's the way it is here.
- Plan your shopping in the early morning hours, as teenagers flock the malls after school.

---

## HANDICRAFTS/ANTIQUES

The oldest items available are Chinese ceramics excavated from early grave sites, some of them brought to the archipelago as early as the 10th century A.D. **Tahanan,** on the second floor of SM Megamall in Makati, has some high-priced exquisite blankets, pottery, and coffee and tea sets. A one-stop shop for antiques and wood furniture is on the fourth floor of SM Megamall, or at the Shangri-La Hotel's shopping arcade. **Silahi's Arts and Artifacts** along Real Street, in Intramuros, has three floors of ethnic crafts and some fine antiques. It's a convenient stop after visiting other sights in Intramuros like Casa Manila and San Agustin Church and Museum. **Balikbayan Handicrafts,** Arnaiz Avenue, Makati, is a good place to go for wood, bamboo, and wicker items, along with shell, stone, metal, pottery, paintings, and embroidery.

## OPEN MARKETS

No trip to Manila is complete without venturing to the open markets where local artists, weavers, sculptors, and the like spread their livelihood out for all to see. You will need bargaining moxie to get through the experience; if you don't have it, you'll soon learn.

**Central Market,** in Santa Cruz by Quezon Avenue, is a good place to go for fabrics and clothes. It's a fairly large sprawl and it's open every day, weather permitting. **Baclaran,** just off Roxas Boulevard, beside the Baclaran Church, has clothing and handicrafts.

## MANILA AFTER DARK

Anyone who thinks New York City is the only city that never sleeps has never been to Manila. Filipinos love to go out, and you'll be surprised at the variety of nightlife the city has to offer. The Malate/Ermita area has a bohemian, laid-back atmosphere, while Makati hosts more of a jet-setting scene.

## BARS

**Giraffe.** 6750 Ayala Ave., facing the Glorietta Circle, Makati.

In direct competition with Venezia (see below), Giraffe attracts the cocktail crowd of Manila's younger power people. Grab a seat at the trendy, circular bar, or take the spiral stairs to the balcony area above. The left side of the bar is where most gay patrons hang out. This place gets pretty packed and, as at Venezia, dress code is enforced.

**Heckle & Jeckle Café & Bar.** Ground floor, Villa Bldg., Jupiter St., corner of Makati Ave., Makati. ☎ **2/890-6904.** Daily 11am–4am.

Named after the two cartoon magpies, people come to this bar to play a game of pool or to listen to the live band every Thursday to Saturday. Come between 8 and 10pm to avail yourself of the P175 (US$4.30) drink-till-you-drop special. They also make a mean pizza, and cocktail lovers should try the *Heckle Special.*

**Jools.** 5043 P. Burgos St., Makati. ☎ **2/897-9097** or 9098. Cover charge of P150 (US$3.75). Drinks are about P90 (US$2.25), P220 (US$5.50), if you buy drinks for the ladies.

This is probably Manila's finest cabaret. Given the scantily clad women on stage, some would consider it a girly bar, but expats say they feel comfortable bringing their visiting parents or bosses here for a night of innocent entertainment. It really is quite a show, with lots of sequins, feathers, and great dancing, and nothing too graphic—a nice change from the regular sit-and-drink bars. (If real girly bars are what you're after, you'll find them along P. Burgos Street.)

**Prince of Wales Pub.** Basement, New Plaza Building, near the Greenbelt Center, Makati. ☎ **2/815-4274.**

This British-style pub is the friendliest in town and very popular among expatriates and tourists. If you're homesick, this might be the place to come. Perhaps have a dart game or two, or just head for the bar and start chatting. Aside from the usual British pub grub, P.O.W. serves Middle Eastern specialties like hummus, and the popular *mishman,* a spicy dish of shrimp, chicken, or beef on a bed of water cabbage and chili peppers. It goes great with a beer. Lunchtime here is more businesslike, but the atmosphere is still relaxed. Honorable mention goes to **Blarney Stone,** the only bar in town that has Guinness on tap! It's on the Upper Basement floor, Glass Tower Building, Palanca Jr. St., Legazpi Village, Makati (☎ **2/818-6541**).

✪ **Venezia Bar and Restaurant.** Ground Floor, Glorietta II, Ayala Center, Makati. ☎ **2/845-1732.**

What a scene. This is the posh place where Manila's jet set and local expats come to see and be seen. The huge L-shaped, fully-stocked bar is set in a Venetian-style, almost gothic decor. If the plushy art-nouveau bar chairs don't do it for you, have a seat at one of the tables. Dance to the funky beats, then kick up your feet and smoke a cigar while soaking in the trendiness all around you. Stylish clothes and shoes are required, and men must wear shirts with collars.

## LIVE MUSIC
**Conservatory.** Manila Peninsula Hotel, corner of Ayala and Makati aves. ☎ **2/810-3456.**

Come to the Conservatory for an elegant, relaxed evening of jazz and pop music. It's a good way to wind down after a hectic day or heavy dinner. Happy hour is from 7 to 8pm.

**Hard Rock Cafe.** Glorietta, Ayala Center, Makati. ☎ **2/893-4661.**

As at all Hard Rocks, you'll find a long line of tourists and locals waiting to get in here. You know what to expect: typical Hard Rock memorabilia, occasional live bands, both local and visiting, and loud music to pump that beef burger down your stomach.

**The Hobbit House.** Mabini St., Malate. Small cover after 8pm.

The most "novel" place to hear live folk music is this bar/pool hall/restaurant where all the waiters and waitresses are dwarves. They are more than happy to pose with you for a picture.

**Euphoria.** In the Hotel Inter-Continental, 1 Ayala Ave., Makati (near Edsa Ave.). ☎ **2/815-9711.**

**Zu.** At the Shangri-La Hotel, corner of Ayala and Makati aves.

These are two clubs in close competition. Zu is more popular, and you'll get a good show there from transvestites impersonating such icons as Madonna and Tina Turner. At both places bartenders do some cool tricks with bottles, and the staff is very friendly and affectionate. The crowd is mixed, ranging from the young and hip to married couples. At both clubs, closing time depends on you.

## MOVIES

If you missed the blockbusters everybody was talking about 6 or more months ago, you'll be able to do some catching up in the Philippines. It's a cheap way to pass the night, only setting you back P60 to P100 (US$1.50–US$2.50). One caveat though: Theaters are large, air-conditioned, and repeat the movie over and over, making them perfect places for overheated Filipinos to hang out, socialize, and even sleep. It can be quite frustrating to have people wandering in and out while you're trying to watch the movie. The best theaters are at the **Shangri-La Mall,** the **Galleria,** and the **MegaMall.**

## A DOSE OF CULTURE

At the **Maynila Restaurant** in the Manila Hotel, One Rizal Park (☎ 2/527-0111), you can watch **Philippine folk dancing** with dinner from 7 to 10pm Monday through Saturday. If it's theater you want, visit the **William J. Shaw Theater** in the Shangri-La Mall (☎ 2/633-4821) or the **Cultural Center of the Philippines** (CCP) on Roxas Boulevard (☎ 2/832-1125; see "Attractions," above).

# EXCURSIONS FROM MANILA

There are a number of day trips you can take within easy distance of Manila. Most of the destinations listed below are within 3 hours or less of the city, and can be booked through your hotel or a travel agency in Manila. Try **Baron Travel** (☎ 2/817-4926), with offices in major hotels such as the Holiday Inn and the Pan Pacific, and others scattered throughout the city.

## TAGAYTAY RIDGE TOUR/TAAL VOLCANO TREK

About a 1½-hour drive south of Manila lies the picturesque and scenic city of Tagaytay. Treat yourself to a panoramic view of the countryside, with its orchards, fruit stalls, and coconut plantations. Rising 2,250 feet (686m) above sea level, Tagaytay is cool and invigorating, and offers a majestic view of lush green mountain ranges as a backdrop to the calm blue waters of Taal Lake. Jutting out of the center of the lake is the "tiny but terrible" Taal Volcano, which stands on its own island amid landscapes of ash and cinder. Despite being one of the country's smallest volcanoes, it has been

### Cockfights

For an offbeat experience, check out the Sunday cockfights at the **Pasay Cockpit Arena,** located on Dolores Street off Roxas Boulevard, before you get to the airport in Pasay. Admission is P50 (US$1.25) and you can place bets if you wish. They run pretty much all day, but the area is pretty shabby, so I wouldn't venture there at night.

the site of many powerful eruptions. Scientists monitor the island closely for signs of impending eruptions, so you can safely hike or ride a pony to the island's many natural wonders, including the mysterious Crater Lake, with its famous "island in a lake on an island in a lake on an island." After trekking up the slope of the volcano you can swim in the warm lake and actually see smoke coming up from cracks in the earth. On the way back to Manila be sure to stop by the jeepney factory and the impressive bamboo organ.

## PAGSANJAN FALLS TOUR

If Pagsanjan gives you a sense of déjà vu, it's probably because you have seen it in such movies as *Apocalypse Now* or *Platoon.* Be prepared to board a native canoe steered by two boatmen and maneuvered upstream for about 7km through rocks and boulders, steep gorges, and tropical vegetation. Next, you'll scurry onto a bamboo raft that slides you under the curtainlike rush of the falls into a crystal cave. You will most definitely get wet. The adrenaline starts to pump when you hit the 14 small rapids downstream. Be sure to take along a waterproof bag for cameras and film. In the past many tourists complained about the *banqueros,* the boat operators who stop and refuse to take you any farther without a generous tip. Tourist authorities are now attempting to curb this behavior, but if it happens, resist the pressure and report it once you get back. It's best to hook up with a tour that includes round-trip transportation and lunch.

## ✪ CORREGIDOR

Twenty-six nautical miles (8m) west of Manila, just off the southern tip of the Bataan Peninsula, Corregidor is a must for the history buff. The island, dominated by huge limestone formations and nicknamed "the Rock," was the playground for pirates from Sulu and China and the scene of naval battles between the Spanish and the Dutch. But it is probably best remembered as the scene of a bloody battle that ended with the Americans retaking the island from the Japanese in 1945. In 1947, in an impressive turnover ceremony, the American flag was lowered at Topside Flagstaff for the last time and the flag of the Philippines was hoisted in its stead. You can walk most of the island to see memorials erected by the U.S. in honor of Filipino and U.S. soldiers, a seacoast gun, the mile-long barracks once used as the quarters for U.S. officers, and the Spanish lighthouse.

The *Sun Cruiser* departs for the island from the ferry terminal near the Cultural Center in Manila at 9am Monday through Friday, returning at 3pm. Saturday and Sunday departures are at 7:30am and 1:30pm, returning at 12:30pm and 5:30pm. The trip takes about an hour.

## ✪ MOUNT PINATUBO

The lahar fields created by the enormous 1991 eruption of Mount Pinatubo should not be missed. (See "The Best Outdoor Adventures" in chapter 1.) The lunar landscape is massive and eerie and you get a real sense of the devastation this volcano caused worldwide when it blew its top. The sulfuric ravines and rising smoke near the crater are enough to instill a healthy respect for Mother Nature in anybody. Hiking through the fields to the crater lake will take a day, and you can camp for the night at the lake. It's possible to do a round-trip hike in one day, but it will be exhausting and you'll be racing against the sun. Tours can be arranged through any travel agency; they'll provide tents and food for the overnight stay at the crater lake. A cheaper option is to go to Angeles City yourself and ask around for local tour operators. Try the **Woodland Park Resort Hotel,** MacArthur Highway, Pampanga (☎ 455/322-3529; e-mail: Woodland@mozcom.com).

## VILLA ESCUDERO, SAN PABLO CITY

Two hours south of Manila, at the boundary of Quezon Province, lies the quaint and historic Villa Escudero. The Villa is set amidst a pastoral grove of coconut palms, verdant fields, and mountains that will bring you back to the days of colonial plantation life. You can take a caribou-drawn cart ride to see demonstrations on the processing and use of coconuts, a cultural show, and the Escudero Museum, with its diverse collection ranging from silver altars to plastic spoons. Local folk singers will serenade you. It's a bit touristy, but still a good day trip. If you want to spend an evening at the villa, contact the booking office in Manila at ☎ 2/521-0830 or 8698.

# 4  Northern Luzon

The Central Cordilleras Mountain Range, home to the mountain provinces of Baguio, Bontoc, Sagada, and Banaue, is like a spine running up the back of Luzon. This part of the island is well worth a visit, offering you a change of scenery and climate and a cultural experience different from anything else you'll find on the archipelago. In many of these areas you can still see Ibaloi, Kankana-ey, Ifugao, Bontoc, Kalinga, Gaddang, and a few other tribes, generically known as Igorots, living and cultivating as they have for centuries. You can visit local markets and faith-healers in Baguio; hike, go caving, and explore the hanging coffins in Sagada; and see Banaue's famous rice terraces, or "stairway to the sky." To get the full experience of this region you should plan on spending about a week here.

## GETTING THERE

Manila is the jumping-off point for all points north. Road travel, by bus or rental car, is the best way to capture the flavor of this region. Some of the roads heading north through the mountains are more of an adventure than the destination itself. When mapping out your route, consider how much travel time you can or are willing to endure, and remember that the rainy season and typhoons can seriously impede ground travel.

**BY BUS**  Several companies ply the 6- or 7-hour trip from Manila to Northern Luzon: **Dangwa Tranco** (☎ 2/731-2859); **Philippine Rabbit** (☎ 2/361-4821); and **Victory Liner** (☎ 2/361-1506) all have air-conditioned buses that make several daily trips. It's P210 to Baguio; P136 to Sagada. The terminals of the individual bus companies are scattered throughout Manila, so call first, or ask a taxi driver if he knows how to reach a particular terminal. Most likely, he will.

**BY PLANE**  Air travel is a more costly option (roughly P1,200 round-trip). The flight from Manila into Loakan Airport, near **Baguio,** takes about 50 minutes; from there, you can take a rental car, bus, or jeepney to wherever you're going. Availability of flights depends on weather conditions. One woman told me that if the sun is shining the flights will leave. For schedules, call **Asian Spirit** at ☎ 2/840-3811. **Philippine Airlines** (☎ 2/816-6691) also offered daily flights before they went out of business and resurfaced again; at press time, service to the area had not resumed, but plans are in the works. **Pacific Air** (☎ 2/812-1555) offers more expensive charter flights.

## GETTING AROUND

Jeepneys and taxis provide transport in and around Baguio City. Some taxi drivers also lend their services as tour guides and do a pretty good job. You won't have to look very far for accommodations or transportation, as tour operators and hotel representatives will swarm you at the bus terminal, and there's a tourism information counter at the airport. Baguio City is the only place in the north to rent a car, with **Avis** on Harrison Road (☎ **74/442-4018**), and **Hertz** on Session Road (☎ **74/442-3045**). However, the roads are hard to navigate and can be scary, so I recommend taking jeepneys or buses when exploring this area. You'll be roughing it, but the experience will be a memorable one. In Sagada and Bontoc there are no taxis, only jeepneys and tricycles.

## BAGUIO

Probably remembered for the devastating earthquake that killed thousands and destroyed most of the mountain terraced city, Baguio has emerged from the rubble and remains a popular summer destination for Filipinos seeking to escape the heat. With its mountainside houses and winding roads, Baguio affords some amazing panoramic views. And it is much cooler here, at an elevation close to 5,000 feet (1,524m). You won't need air-conditioning.

**VISITOR INFORMATION** The **Department of Tourism** is on Governor Pack Road (☎ **74/442-6708**). It's open daily from 8am to noon and 1 to 5pm.

## Fast Facts: Baguio

**Banks/Currency Exchange** The Philippine National Bank on Session Road has money withdrawal machines and can exchange traveler's checks and currency.

**Internet/E-mail** CyberSpace (☎ 74/443-8730), at the Mt. Crest Hotel on Legarda Rd., offers e-mail and Internet access.

**Post Office/Mail** The local post office is located on Upper Session Road.

**Telephone** The area code is 74.

## ACCOMMODATIONS

**Concorde Hotel.** Europa Center, Legarda Rd., Baguio. ☎ 74/443-2058. Fax 74/443-2060/61. 139 units. TV TEL. P1,790–2,706 (US$44.75–US$67.65) double; P4,026–P4,488 (US$100.65–US$112.20) suite. AE, DC, MC, V.

This new establishment has the most unique architecture of any hotel in Baguio, with a peaceful, cozy feel, natural light, exposed brick, and curved stairways. The lobby area has a great atmosphere, with a garden cafe and a piano playing soothing tunes, topped by a high atrium. The unique artwork in the hall and lobby areas carries into the rooms, which are neat and clean, with wide-planked hardwood floors, but they have very small windows and no refrigerator. (Opt for the deluxe suite if you can.) The patio furniture is made out of logs and sticks—a nice touch that complements the all-natural ambiance the hotel has succeeded in achieving. Bathrooms have hot and cold showers but no soap or shampoo. Amenities include a beauty salon, convenience store, car rental, on-call doctor, laundry, safe-deposit boxes, boutique, travel agency, fitness center, business center, city tour, Chinese and Japanese restaurant, and a discotheque that's open until 3am.

**Hotel Supreme.** 113 Magsaysay Ave., Baguio. ☎ 74/443-2011 to 18. Fax 74/442-2855. E-mail: Supreme@burgos.slu.edu.ph. 59 units. A/C TV MINIBAR. P1,800 (US$45) double; P2,000 (US$50) suite. MC, V.

This centrally located hotel is the best in town when it comes to amenities. The lobby is nothing too grand, just a simple counter with a friendly staff. The good-size rooms are carpeted, and some have pool-side views, though mattresses are a bit on the stiff side. There is also a family deluxe room with a double bed, four single beds, and

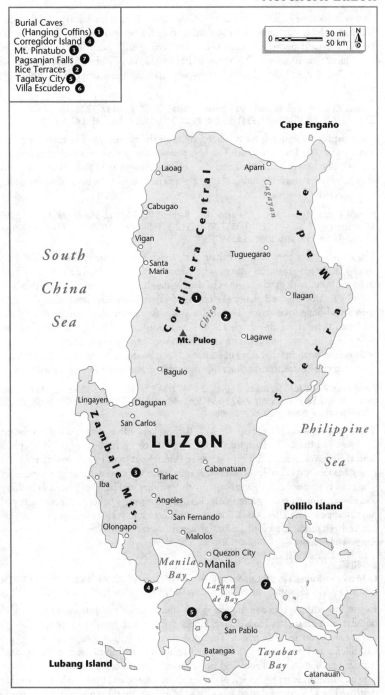

# Northern Luzon

Burial Caves
  (Hanging Coffins) **1**
Corregidor Island **4**
Mt. Pinatubo **3**
Pagsanjan Falls **7**
Rice Terraces **2**
Tagatay City **5**
Villa Escudero **6**

0     30 mi
0     50 km

N

Cape Engaño

Laoag

Aparri

*Cagayan*

Cabugao

Vigan

Tuguegarao

Santa
Maria

Ilagan

**1**

*Chico*

**2**

▲ Mt. Pulog

Lagawe

Baguio

Lingayen

Dagupan

San Carlos

*Philippine*

**LUZON**

*Sea*

Cabanatuan

**3**   Tarlac

Iba

Pollilo Island

Angeles

San Fernando

Olongapo

Malolos

Quezon City

*Manila*   Manila

*Bay*

**7**

*Laguna*
*de Bay*

**4**

**5**

**6**

San Pablo

Batangas

*Tayabas*

*Bay*

**Lubang Island**

Catanauan

*South*

*China*

*Sea*

*Cordillera Central*

*Sierra Madre*

*Zambale Mts.*

complete cooking facilities. You can get Chinese or Filipino food at Ivy's Grill or Cafe Palmero, which stay open until around 11pm. For after-dinner drinks try Orchid Bar. If the hard mattresses leave your back feeling stiff, head for the modest spa, with Jacuzzi and sauna. Other amenities include a gift shop, valet service, car rental, laundry and dry cleaning, mini-park and children's playground, and travel arrangements.

**Mount Crest Hotel.** Legarda Rd., corner Urbano St. ☎ **74/442-3324.** Fax 74/443-9273. 25 units. A/C TV. P1,400 (US$35) double; P2,000 (US$50) deluxe. AE, DC, MC, V.

Don't expect too much from this hotel right on the main drag. The rooms are clean and comfortable but very basic. The best thing about the place is the restaurant and internet cafe next door. The bar next door offers ballroom and live jazz bands, so noise may get to be a problem. You can ask for a quieter room in the back, if you're willing to sacrifice the front view.

**Prince Plaza Hotel.** No. 17 Legarda Rd., Baguio. ☎ **74/442-5082.** Fax 74/442-5093. 48 units. TV. P1,500–P1,700 (US$37.50–US$42.50) double; P3,000 (US$75) deluxe suite; P3,500 (US$87.50) apartment. AE, MC, V.

The lobby of this hotel near Burnham Park feels almost sanitary, decorated in shiny, almost lacquered grays and whites, with Mexican tile windows. The rooms are fairly large and neat, with excellent views of the highlands. All come with two double beds, large TVs, carpeting, and plenty of closet space. Bathrooms have hot and cold showers with a pull-out shower head. The Shabu Shabu Restaurant dishes up good local cuisine, and there is a coffee shop. The deluxe rooms are the best value, with balcony, living area, minibar, and separate standup shower and bathtub. There is a loud discotheque in the hotel that stays open until 11pm, so if you are an early sleeper it may drive you crazy. Amenities include massage services and room service until 10pm.

**Swagman Attic Inn.** 90 Abanao St. ☎ **74/442-5139.** Fax 74/442-9859. For Manila reservations to any Swagman's Inn, 2/523-8541. 20 units. TV TEL. P750 (US$18.75) single; P1,200 (US$30). MC, V. Near open-air markets.

This Australian-run place, popular with backpackers, offers decent accommodations for low-end prices. The Swagman name seems to be everywhere in the Philippines, with their travel agencies and inns scattered throughout most tourist destinations. The lobby conveniently doubles as a travel agency, and they'll even exchange your money. The cozy place feels like a guesthouse, with furniture and benches placed in hallways and carpet runners trailing the floors. Rooms are on the smaller size, decorated with neat aboriginal knickknacks. Bathrooms are functional, with hot-water showers. The bar and restaurant are excellent and at certain times of the year host pretty rowdy, Aussie-style events.

## DINING

**Café by the Ruins.** No. 25 Chuntug St., in front of City Hall. ☎ **74/442-4010.** P150–P250 (US$3.75–US$6.25) main courses. DC, MC, V. Daily 7am–10pm. BAKED GOODS/FILIPINO.

Exotic, tropical, and relaxed are the words that describe this interesting place that's popular with tourists and locals alike. Check out the fresh bread counter, if the aroma doesn't stop you in your tracks. The food here is delicious, ranging from regional Cordilleran to European; try the Chicken Palawan stewed in coconut milk and basil. A huge bamboo-thatched roof and rice-papered lanterns create a subtle twilit effect. The nominal ruins are what's left of the governor's home and garden that was partially destroyed by U.S. forces during World War I. You can see the remains of it among the arches and the adjoining vine-covered gazebo.

# Baguio City

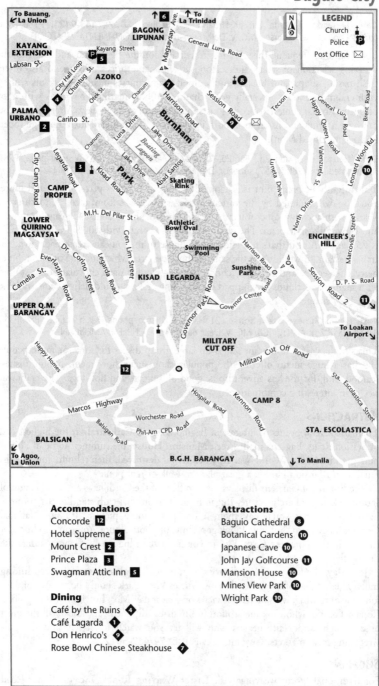

**Accommodations**
Concorde **12**
Hotel Supreme **6**
Mount Crest **2**
Prince Plaza **3**
Swagman Attic Inn **5**

**Dining**
Café by the Ruins **4**
Café Lagarda **1**
Don Henrico's **9**
Rose Bowl Chinese Steakhouse **7**

**Attractions**
Baguio Cathedral **8**
Botanical Gardens **10**
Japanese Cave **10**
John Jay Golfcourse **11**
Mansion House **10**
Mines View Park **10**
Wright Park **10**

**Café Legarda.** Legarda Rd. at Urbano St., Baguio. ☎ **74/443-9421.** P160–P480 (US$4–US$12) main courses. MC, V. Daily 6am–midnight. CONTINENTAL/SEAFOOD.

Local families frequent this relaxing restaurant for the live piano and the mouth-watering selection of steaks and seafood at reasonable prices. The menu also offers fresh pastas, soups, and breads, and seafood main courses including prawns stuffed with crabmeat and an especially good charbroiled blue marlin. They cook with a lot of butter, so the cholesterol conscious should ask them to go easy. After dinner you can have a drink and listen to smooth jazz upstairs at **Gimbals Music Lounge** (open 6pm–3am, closed Mon).

**Don Henrico's.** Session Rd., Baguio. ☎ **74/442-8802.** P120 (US$3) small pizza, P240 (US$6) medium, P280 (US$7) superior. DC, MC, V. Daily 10am–12am. ITALIAN.

This brightly lit pizza joint is a happening place that serves pizza, pasta, and more. You'll be overwhelmed by the variety of pizzas to choose from: taco, pesto chicken, Viking with anchovy, caper mushroom and tomato, and of course Chicago deep-dish and New York–style pizza. The classic hand-tossed pizza with 100% fresh mozzarella is very good. And if that's not enough to choose from, you can create your own. An Italian restaurant wouldn't be the same without desserts, which include tiramisu, blue-berry cheesecake, and my fave, choco mango—double dark chocolate cake stuffed with mango and clouds of whipped cream filling. Take-out and delivery are available for a 10% charge.

**Rose Bowl Chinese Steakhouse.** 21 Harrison St. No phone. Main courses P80–P350 (US$2–US$8.75). AE, DC, JCB, MC, V. Daily 6am–11pm. CHINESE/AMERICAN.

This simple, casual restaurant serves up large group dishes for three or more people and has a huge menu offering the popular chop suey, chow mein, noodle dishes, seafood, and, for the less adventurous, good ol' burgers and hot dogs. The crabmeat rice is an interesting combination.

## ATTRACTIONS

There are several points of interest in Baguio: **Baguio Cathedral,** at the highest end of Session Road, Baguio's main street; **Mansion House,** the summer home of Philippine presidents until World War II, when it was destroyed, then rebuilt; and **Wright Park,** near Mansion House, a great place to walk or rent ponies.

The **Botanical Gardens** displays the rich flora of the Cordilleras and a collection of Igorot folk art and architecture. Ifugao in their traditional garb stand at the entrance in the hopes that you'll pay them a few pesos for a picture. It's not National Geographic–worthy, but it will look good in your photo album. You can also hunt for treasure in the **Japanese Cave,** said to contain a stash hidden by General Yamashita during the war.

**John Jay,** the former U.S. military camp, is now a **golf** course with steep **hiking** trails. The lodging office has trail maps. **Mines View Park** should be the cap of your long day of touring, with incredible views on a clear day. Most hotels offer tour guides. Ronald Lozano, who took me around in his air-conditioned van, knows all the most obscure sights, the faith-healers who will let you watch for a fee, and the gut-wrenching meat markets. Give him a call at ☎ **74/442-5012.**

## SHOPPING

For traditional Igorot weavings visit **Easter Weaving Room, Inc.** on Easter Road (☎ **74/442-4972**), where downstairs you can watch the weavers manipulating the wooden machines to create all sorts of geometric patterns. **Ibay's Silver Shop,** on Easter Road (no phone), sells interesting charms, bracelets, and anything else made of silver, though prices are not as cheap as you would expect. In the back room you can see them melting down junk scrap silver and pouring it into bar molds. Finally, everyone's favorite spot in Baguio is the **city market,** on Magsaysay Avenue, where you'll find anything and everything traditional, hand-made, or edible. Be sure to hold on to your valuables while working your way through the market.

## ✪ SAGADA

No place could be more enchanting than this small village tucked away among green mountains and rice terraces—most people who come here find that it's one of the highlights of their trip. The mountain air is fresh and cool (pollution is still minimal), the people are friendly and laid-back, and the hiking opportunities are fantastic. Nature is alive and well here, since there is no commercial logging, and ancestral land is protected by the elders. An underground honeycomb of caves lies beneath the town. It is a traditional Ifugao practice to hang the wooden coffins of the dead in caves and along the tall limestone cliffs; these **hanging coffins** are a must-see for the benefit of your friends back home (see "Hiking & Caving," below).

### GETTING THERE

You have the choice of arriving via Banaue or Baguio City, depending on where you're coming from. For the **Manila-Banaue-Bontoc-Sagada** route (13–14 hours), a **Dangwa Tranco bus** leaves the Cubao terminal once a day at 7am for the 9-hour trip to Banaue. A daily jeepney leaves Banaue at 7:30am for the 2- to 3-hour ride to Bontoc. In Bontoc, jeepneys leave from outside Nellie's Eatery on Bontoc's main street several times a day for the 2-hour ride up to Sagada.

For the **Manila-Baguio-Sagada** route (12–13 hours): There are many bus companies that travel the popular direct route (6 hours) to Baguio, but **Victory Liner** leaves hourly and is air-conditioned and comfortable. From Baguio, several early morning **Lizardo** buses depart from the Dangwa Terminal starting at 6:30am. The trip to Sagada takes you along the scenically breathtaking Halsema Highway, also known as the Mountain Trail. The trip takes about 6 or 7 hours with stops for snacks and lunch.

### VISITOR INFORMATION

For maps and detailed information on the caves and trails, go to the very small **tourism window** in the Municipal Hall Building, which also houses the Sagada Environmental Guides Association (SEGA) Information Center. You can hire a guide here with a lamp for cave exploration.

### ACCOMMODATIONS

Don't come to Sagada expecting first-class accommodations and dining. Neither phones nor hot water heaters have found it here yet. Most showers will consist of a large bucket filled with water and a cup to spoon its cold contents over your body. What is so endearing about Sagada to most visitors is its natural, untouched spirit. What it lacks in amenities, it makes up for in charm. Family-owned guesthouses are the main source of accommodation, although a big hotel was recently built. Most will charge around P70 (US$1.75) per person for a room with a common bath; attached units with a private bath go for about P500 (US$12.50) per unit, up to P1,000 (US$25) for a self-contained cottage. Mattresses are nothing more than varying thicknesses of foam, and you will have to get used to the cockadoodle-doo alarm clocks.

**Masferre Café and Inn.** Past the Municipal Hall on the left. 7 units. P100 (US$2.50) per person. No credit cards.

Popular with the backpacking crowd, this place is very cozy and clean. Windows (in the rooms that have them) swing out like those in a country cottage. Rooms have two single beds, and there are two common baths in the inn. The proprietress is the widow of Eduardo Masferre, who spent his life documenting the mountain life of the Ifugao tribespeople. His beautiful black and white photographs are displayed in the dining area. The food is excellent.

**Olahbinan Resthouse.** Next to the Prime Hotel, down the stairs on your left. 11 units. P80–P150 (US$2–US$3.75) per room. No credit cards.

One of the larger guesthouses, Olahbinan has 11 comfortable and clean rooms, a restaurant with a fireplace, and an upstairs balcony with excellent views. They have running hot water.

**Sagada Guest House.** Up from the central bus stop. 15 units. P70–P200 (US$1.75–US$5). No credit cards.

Owned by the ex-mayor, Sagada Guest House will provide comfortable accommodations and a great meal in its cafe.

**Sagada Prime Hotel.** A 5-minute walk past the Municipal Hall on your left. 43 units. P600 (US$15) room with common bath; P1,000 (US$25) room with private bath. No credit cards.

This is Sagada's first official hotel, opened in March 1997. It offers spacious rooms and a large restaurant serving meals and drinks at reasonable prices. Always negotiate room rates during the low season.

**St. Joseph's Rest House.** Up the hill to the right as you come into town. 29 units. P60 (US$1.50) per person for dorm room; P100 (US$2.50) per person for double. No credit cards.

This cozy cottage was originally a convent. It was converted into Sagada's first guesthouse by St. Mary's Mission in the 1970s, and now it's managed by the Episcopal Diocese of the northern Philippines. The grounds are the most beautiful in town, with all sorts of manicured flowers and bushes in front and back. Rooms are small and quaint, with hot water showers. Noisier, dorm-style rooms are also available. Amenities include a large restaurant, a gift shop selling local crafts, and secured garage parking for anyone who may have rented a car for the journey here.

## DINING

In addition to the guesthouses, there are several cafes in town, offering a variety of choices at any time of the day or early evening. (Most close at 9pm.) It's customary in Sagada to reserve meals in advance. This may seem like an inconvenience, but realize that you are getting a home-cooked meal, and whatever you request has to be slaughtered. Next door to the Municipal Hall is **Shamrock Café,** providing breakfast, lunch, dinner, snacks, and nighttime guitar playing. Lots of tourists come here, so it's a good place to share information with other travelers. **The Log Cabin,** down the hill from Shamrock, will give you delicious European-style food, including lasagna and omelets. They have an excellent music selection. Masferre Inn and Country Café both have excellent local dishes as well as hamburgers, pancakes, and other European/American dishes.

## HIKING & CAVING

Wear biker shorts or grungy clothing that you don't mind getting dirty. You can wear hiking boots, but waterproof sandals are perfectly fine also. If you have rock-climbing shoes or diving booties that's even better.

   **Sumaging (Big Cave)** is the one most popular with tourists. It's a 40-minute walk from Sagada on the Suyo Road. When I say road, I mean a dirt path, which winds its way through the cozy villages and above beautiful rice terraces and rivers—it's gorgeous. You will spend about 3 hours inside the cave looking at Mother Nature's unusual limestone sculptures, creatively named the pig pen, giant's foot, pregnant woman, Romeo and Juliette, king's curtains, etc. The first part of the climb is slippery, partly due to the limestone, but also from the droppings of the squealing bats overhead. (Be prepared to get grimy.) The second part of the exploration is done barefoot, mostly over sandpaper-like calcium formations. This is where you will get wet and have the chance to wash the dung off your clothes. Toward the end you will have to navigate quite a confined, narrow space appropriately called "the tunnel," using a rope and lots of upper body strength. The claustrophobic should simply take a deep breath; the tunnel doesn't last longer than 2 minutes or so and then you're back in the huge dome-like space. It's great, adventurous fun, and you don't have to be too fit to do it—you're mostly climbing over rock on your hands and knees.

**Lumiang** is a 30-minute walk from Sagada on the way to the Big Cave, down a path to your left. This burial cave, where many old and a few newer coffins are stacked, is well worth a visit. You can see the coffins right at the entrance of the cave, without going inside. The bodies are still intact and the old, thin wooden covers to the coffins are not bolted on. You can see the bones still peacefully tucked in the fetal position. Do not remove anything from these sacred areas. A local elder told me about a tourist who took a bone or two and the next day fell and broke his leg. Believe what you will, but do respect the dead.

**Loko-ong (Crystal Cave)** has been closed for quite some time now thanks to tourists who raped it of its stalactites and stalagmites. It may be re-opening, so check when you arrive. It's for the more adventurous, involving more physical exertion and some rope climbing and swimming.

The paths that lead to **Echo Valley** are very overgrown, and you may find yourself wandering around in circles for hours. That's OK though, considering how beautiful the area surrounding the valley is. You'll walk through an old cemetery and past some hanging coffins and small burial caves along the way. You'll even see "death chairs," which were used to prop up the body during mourning periods. Echo Valley has beautiful views of limestone cliffs, some with coffins hanging from them. It's a nice place to sit, eat, and listen to your echo. There is a path that leads to the valley floor.

Set amidst rice terraces and only 25 minutes from town, **Bokong Waterfall** is a popular spot for both locals and visitors. The falls are small but spill into a deep pool—an ideal spot for a picnic or quick dip. Just past Sagada Weaving, take the cement steps to the left. Follow the path down to the river, cross over, and head upstream. **Bomod-ok** is a bigger waterfall, but farther away. To get there, you'll have to walk along the Banga-an Road for about an hour, then go down the cement steps just past the Banga-an Elementary School. Another hour's walk will take you down the path through the village of **Fidelisan** and some rice terraces to the waterfall.

Mt. Ampacao is the highest peak in Sagada, at 6,198 feet (1889m). You will need a lot of endurance for the 2-hour hike to the top. You can pick wild blueberries on the slopes, and from September to December it's on the flight path of migratory birds.

✪ **Mt. Polis** is in my opinion the best hike in the area. On its old Spanish trail are waterfalls, forests, villages, and great vistas. Start early in the morning with a water bottle and packed lunch for the 8-hour round-trip.

## SHOPPING

**R.J. Café and Crafts,** just past the Sagada Prime Hotel, sells artifacts, jewelry, T-shirts, pottery, and ethnic music tapes. For weaving and baskets try **Sagada Weaving** on the Bontoc Road. If you are here on Saturdays, don't miss the Saturday market, where you will get a dose of everything local.

# BANAUE

According to tribal mythology, the inhabitants of Banaue were descended from the deity Kabunyan. The name for the people who live in this region, Ifugao, comes from *ipugo,* meaning eaters of rice, a staple food said to have been a gift from the gods, as are the lands that the tribes hold sacred. The rice terraces were built as a tribute to the heavens in thanks for the sustaining food.

This myth is still alive and well in the way the lives of the modern Ifugao revolve around the land, rice, harvesting, and planting. Long before the Spaniards came upon their fertile lands, the Ifugaos were already farmers and miners living in communities, with a well-developed culture of their own. They carved paddies out of the rugged mountainsides, dammed them with stone and clay, and developed an ingenious system of irrigation to hold water in the fields even during the dry season. These **rice terraces,** the most well known of which are in Banaue, rise like stairways to Kabunyan's domain.

The famed Banaue Rice Terraces, the oldest of which date back from 1,000 to 2,000 years ago, are the best examples of a time-honored method of cultivating sloping land in mountainous regions. They are a sight to behold, reaching up to heights of 4,921 feet (1,500m); if stretched end to end, they would extend to over 12,400 miles (20,000km). It was a singular feat of engineering achieved by people equipped only with primitive tools and undying dedication.

## GETTING THERE

**BY BUS   Dangwa Tranco** has early morning daily buses leaving from Manila to Banaue, for about P130 (US$3.25) per person. The trip will take about 10 hours. If that seems like a torturously long ride, then I suggest breaking it up by spending some time along the way in Baguio (6 hours from Manila) and Sagada (7 hours from Baguio). From Sagada, it's a 2-hour trip to Bontoc, where you'll connect with a jeepney for another 2 hours to Banaue. It seems like a lot of traveling, and it is. Understand that the mountains in this region are very hard to navigate. But if you follow the route I just prescribed you will take in the most of the mountain province efficiently.

**BY PRIVATE CAR/TOUR**   The best way to see Banaue is by arranging a tour to include round-trip transport from Baguio and accommodations. Most hotels can arrange this for you. A sample tour for 4 days, 3 nights would be: First day, leave from Baguio to Sagada and spend the day exploring caves there with an overnight stay. Day two, depart Sagada early and arrive in Banaue shortly before noon, with check-in at the Banaue Hotel. The next day and a half, you may take advantage of organized walks, hikes, or a vehicle tour around the terraces. Then the return trip to Baguio. Rates for such a package tour are usually about US$250 per person, with a minimum of two persons. For this type of itinerary you can call **Swagman Travel** in Manila at ☎ **2/523-8541** to 45, or in Baguio at ☎ **74/442-5139.**

**BY PLANE   Philippine Airlines** (☎ **2/816-6691**) used to have flights to Cauayan in adjacent Isabela Province, where transport to Banaue is available. However, with the closing and subsequent reopening of the airline this service has yet to become active again. It is best to call the airline and inquire about possible service.

## ACCOMMODATIONS

**Banaue Hotel and Youth Hostel.** Just outside town, on the main road. ☎ **73/386-4087** to 88. Fax 73/386-4048. Manila reservations, ☎ 2/812-1984, 2/810-3655. Fax 2/812-1164. 60 units. A/C TEL. P300 (US$7.50) dorm bed; P1,500 (US$37.50) single; P2,000 (US$50) double. AE, DC, MC, V.

This is Banaue's only true hotel, a short walk to many hiking trails, with large rooms and private bathrooms with hot water. Views are gorgeous: each room has a balcony that overlooks the rice terraces, and the sunsets are even better. Rooms are decorated in those familiar '70s bright oranges, browns, and greens, but they are clean. The rustic, wide-open lobby is used for cultural performances in the evenings. The pool is a great way to wash off the heat and sweat from a day's hike, and after a swim, the restaurant and bar are perfect. Food is great here—it's one of the only really good restaurants in town (see "Dining," below). Other amenities include valet parking, tours, and laundry. The hotel is the only place to exchange money in town, though the rates aren't very good. During the low season, this place can feel like something out of *The Shining;* don't be surprised if you are the only one staying here.

## DINING

If you are planning on staying a few days in Banaue, you will obviously want some variety in your meals. Besides the Banaue Restaurant, local guesthouses have good fare for cheap prices. **Halfway Lodge,** on the road to Mayoyao, **Sanafe Lodge,** beside the bus stop and across from the market, and **Stairway Lodge,** near Halfway Lodge, all offer excellent local dishes.

**Banaue Restaurant.** The Banaue Hotel. Main courses P170–P250 (US$4.25–US$6.25). Daily 6am–10pm, with cultural show at 8:30pm, depending on the number of people. FILIPINO/INTERNATIONAL.

In keeping with the essence of Banaue, the dining area has excellent views of the terraces. Breakfast here is quite good and hearty, offering a variety of large omelets, huge pancakes, and homemade cinnamon buns. Choose from a selection of Western-style sandwiches for lunch, and for dinner try the Ifugao beef with tomato and ginger sauce. The meat will be fatty and not as nicely prepared as what you're used to; expect to bite into fat and get skin with it. If that prospect has suddenly turned you into a vegetarian, there are a few vegetable dishes, like chop suey and chow mein. After dinner, catch the touristy cultural show, where locals wearing traditional Ifugao garb demonstrate various war, marriage, courting, and healing rituals.

## HIKES AROUND BANAUE

Banaue is a hiker's dream. Hikes lasting from a few minutes to all day are all around you. You'll feel like yodeling along the paths that follow the high, cloud-skirted peaks, but panic may set in if you are afraid of heights. Transport to various trail entrances can be arranged through **Banaue Hotel.** The Department of Tourism, next to Sanafe Lodge, can provide **maps** of the area including hiking trails.

The **Village of Batad** is the most popular trek and will take you the whole day. You have to get transport for the 12-kilometer ride to the start of the trail. From there you will hike a strenuous 3 hours uphill for the first half; the second half is less steep. Local children at the halfway point sell a much-needed beverage to exhausted hikers. Be prepared for the over 2,000 cement steps! You will be sore after this hike, but the views from the Ifugao village are well worth it. The rice terraces resemble an amphitheater surrounding the tiny village. Beware of the locals and children trying to offer their services. They are used to tourists and are trying to optimize on the surge. Children will ask for money or candy and can be quite nasty. Just simply say no and continue your hike. You can choose to stay overnight in Batad (the **Hillside Inn,** overlooking the village, is popular) or trek back the way you came. Make sure you arrange for your transport to be waiting for you at the drop-off junction.

The **Village of Bang-an** is an alternative for those who aren't up for the strenuous hike to Batad. It's only 2 kilometers in from the junction leading to Batad. Just before sunset, you can see rainbows against the setting sun at the horizon.

**Tam-an village** is perfect for a late-night walk, just before sunset. Simply walk down the 240 steps from the Banaue Hotel's pool. It's supposedly a traditional Ifugao village, but you will find more corrugated metal roofs than stilted huts. Plenty of pigs, chickens, monkeys, and children, though. Villagers may ask you into their homes to show you their ancestor's bones, dragged up from the basement in a burlap sack. What would grandpa think if he knew curious Westerners were being charged as much as P150 (US$3.75) to see him?

**Guihob Natural Pool.** It's a 4-kilometer ride or a 45-minute hike from the town center. Pick up some sandwiches and bring your bathing suit for a numbing swim in the spring water that comes out of a small waterfall. You can also stop here on your way back from Batad, since it's on the way.

**Banaue Viewpoint** is great for the adventurous and photo-op seeking hiker. You'll scramble through rocks and balance on narrow, very high terraces. It should take you about an hour. You can take care of all your shopping and souvenir needs up here at the many stalls.

## VIGAN

Vigan is the best preserved Spanish town in the Philippines, practically a 17th-century time capsule. The Spanish conquistador Juan de Salcedo had his *encomienda* here. Narrow cobblestone streets are lined with old Castilan houses and baroque churches that have stood the ravages of time and modernization. Age-old street lamps light the path for *calesas,* horse-drawn carriages, which you can ride. To ensure Vigan's legacy, UNESCO has approved money for the redevelopment of the old town center.

### GETTING THERE

**BY BUS**   Commercial buses ply the 8-hour route from Manila to Vigan daily. **Philippine Rabbit** (☎ 2/363-0677), **Times Transit** (☎ 2/731-4180), and **Farinas Transit** (☎ 2/743-8582) all make the trip. From Baguoi, it's only a 3-hour ride, on **Times Transit.** The cost is about P170 (US$4.25) from Manila and P90 (US$2.25) from Baguio. Schedules change, so ask your hotel to check, or call the bus company for current schedules.

**BY PLANE**   The only flight option was **Philippine Airlines** (☎ 2/816-6691) to Laoag, then a 1-hour bus ride to Vigan. Once again, service to this area was suspended while PAL renewed its service, but you can check to see if the route has been reinstated.

### ACCOMMODATIONS

**R.F. Aniceto Mansion.** Plaza Burgos. ☎ **77/722-2383.** 11 units. P1,000 (US$25) single and double, air-conditioned with bath; P1,160 (US$29) triple; P1,280 (US$32) quad. MC, V.

A beautifully renovated and restored colonial home with most impressive antiques. Grandfather clocks, rod-iron chandeliers, and intricately carved furniture decorate the main areas, as well as the small but cozy rooms. Bathrooms are basic with hot and cold water. Café Florecita serves up good local cuisine and some Western-style dishes. Follow the red brick arches and the stone hallway to the stone well.

**Villa Angela Heritage.** Quirino Boulevard, Vigan. ☎ **77/722-2914**, 722-2755, 722-2756. 6 units. P800 (US$20) single or double without A/C; P1,600 (US$40) single or double with A/C. MC, V.

Old-world charm makes this quaint restored mansion a popular place to stay. Antiques decorate the small, cozy rooms, and the ever-smiling staff will make sure your stay is comfortable. Large groups are preferred, and they serve meals.

## DINING

Most hotels have restaurants that serve the local Ilocano cuisine and other Filipino dishes. Try **Cool Spot** in the Vigan Hotel off Quirino Boulevard; the restaurant is in a garden under a *nipa* pavilion. **Food stalls** surrounding Plaza Burgos off Burgos Street serve up tasty snacks and local food.

## ATTRACTIONS IN & AROUND VIGAN

You can hire a tricycle to take you to the locations on the outskirts of town. Jeepneys and minibuses have set routes that cover surrounding areas also.

For visitor information, **The Ilocos Sur Tourism Council** (☎ 77/722-2740, 722-2746) is in the Provincial Capitol Building along Quezon Avenue. The **City Tourism Council** (☎ 77/722-2466) is in the Vigan Municipal Building, also along Quezon Avenue.

Declared a national shrine, **Tirad Pass,** located in the municipality of Gregorio del Pilar, was the last stand of the Filipino Revolutionary Forces under General Emilio Aguinaldo. The battle of Tirad Pass was led by the youngest Filipino general, Gregorio del Pilar.

**Magsingal Church** on Liberation Boulevard was beautifully carved in 1827. The remains of two other churches lie behind this one. There is a museum in the ruins of the second church, but it's small and doesn't have a lot.

**Santa Maria Church,** in the town of Santa Maria, is a national landmark. It's located atop a hill reached through a stone stairway. The tiled church was built in 1769, and you may notice how the builders curved the tower to compensate for the tilt that was caused when the foundation fell during construction. The church was used as a fortress during the 1886 revolution.

**Pug-os Beach,** along Gomez Street in Cabugao, is about 30 minutes north of Vigan. The white-sand beach has resthouses and picnic sheds, and you can see the local fishermen hauling in their nets. It's great for photo-ops. You can hire a tricycle or take a jeepney from Vigan to the beach. About 10 minutes from Cabugao, at Salomague Port, you can buy fresh fish and have it cooked for you.

## 5 Southern Luzon/Legazpi

Easily distinguishable as the peninsula jutting east like an arm into the Pacific, Southern Luzon has an altogether different attitude from its northern brother. This part of the island is best known for the festering volcanos—Mt. Iriga, Mt. Bulusan, and, of course, the giant Mayon near Legazpi—that have left their distinctive scars on the landscape. Mayon spewed lava, ash, and steam into the atmosphere and down its slopes as recently as 1993. The region is also a convenient jumping-off point for travel to Mindoro and other Visayan islands.

A trip to **Legazpi,** the capital of Albay Province, can provide two of the most incredible adventures of a lifetime: trekking the formidable **Mayon Volcano,** considered the world's most beautiful and symmetrical volcano; and swimming with the gentle, giant **whale sharks** in the Donsol River. Other points of interest here include **St. Raphael Church,** where the altar is made out of Mayon's volcanic rock, and the **local market** that sells handicrafts. There is also snorkeling.

## GETTING THERE

**BY PLANE** **Philippine Airlines** (☎ 2/816-6691) has a daily flight at 10am that arrives at 11am. **Air Philippines** ☎ 2/843-7770 offers an 8:50am daily flight. Round-trip flights for either airline will cost you about P1,648 (US$41.20). But keep in mind that schedules and prices change often, so call to confirm.

**BY BUS**   Usually done as an overnight express for the 14-hour trip, **BLTB** (☎ 2/833-5501), **JB Bicol Express** (☎ 2/834-0927 or 0926), and **Philtranco** (☎ 2/833-5061) all make the trip from Manila for about P200 (US$5). Unless you are pinching pennies, I suggest you fly.

## GETTING AROUND

Jeepneys and tricycles offer public transport in and around Legazpi. Hotels can arrange transport to and from Mayon Volcano.

## VISITOR INFORMATION

Legazpi's tourist office can provide you with an update on Mayon's activity, facts on the whale sharks, and information on other things to see and do in the area. The **Department of Tourism office** is at Albay Freedom Park (☎ 5221/44-492 or 44-026; fax 455-050). Or try the **Legazpi City Tourism Council,** in City Hall.

## Fast Facts: Southern Luzon/Legazpi

**Banks/Currency Exchange**   Philippine National Bank and the Central Bank, along Rizal Street in Legazpi, offer money exchange.

## ACCOMMODATIONS

**Hotel La Trinidad.** Rizal St., Legazpi City. ☎ **5221/523-8054.** Fax 5221/521-1309. 14 units. A/C TV TEL. P1,000 (US$25) double, P2,000 (US$50) suite. MC, V.

Although this is the best hotel in Legazpi, it is still pretty standard. The main attraction is the convenient on-site cinema, which usually shows pretty old flicks, but it gives you something to do in the evening. Rooms are fairly large, and carpeted, and you can have music piped in if you wish. All rooms have private baths with hot and cold water. Amenities include airport transfer, shopping arcade, so-so restaurant, bar and cocktail lounge, car rental, tours, and swimming pool.

## DINING

You'll find many dining options simply by taking a stroll down Rizal or Penaranda streets. Two must-try local specialties are **laing,** a spicy mixture of shrimp and pork rolled in taro leaves and stewed in coconut milk, and the **Bicol express,** minced beef tartare with chili peppers—sure to waken up your taste buds and stomach. Try **Wayway Restaurant** on Penaranda for the latter.

You'll find Chinese food at **Pekinghouse Restaurant** on Penaranda Street and **Four Seasons** on Rizal Street (☎ 5221/243-354). **Sa Bay Bay,** on the beach before the city, serves up fresh fish and other seafood as well as European food. **My Brother's Place** on Rizal Street is popular with tourists and backpackers for the San Miguel beer and the live music.

## HIKING THE VOLCANOES: MAYON, MT. BULUSAN, & MT. IRIGA

The tourism office in Legazpi can organize the climb for you and provide a guide and porter. You can also contact the local Mayon Mountaineers Club through this office.

Don't forget to bring sunscreen, sunglasses, a warm fleece or sweater, a water bottle, a rain parka, and tweezers (for leeches).

### MAYON (7,943 FT.; 2,421M)

This is a fairly difficult climb, and you should be a seasoned hiker to attempt it. The first part of the climb is through razor-sharp *talahib* grass (definitely wear pants); the

# Swimming with Giants

From February to late May, the largest recorded gathering of **whale sharks** in the world venture to the surface of the calm water of the Donsol River, allowing snorkelers to swim safely alongside them. No one in the small town of Donsol near Legazpi knows why they come; some assume that the river carries nutrients the giant gentle mammals feed on. Whatever the reason, the whale shark's presence has lured curious tourists and locals alike to get a closer look by grabbing a snorkel and jumping alongside them.

Before the phenomenon was exploited for tourism, the whale sharks were being hunted, killed, and traded to a Taiwanese market, making enormous profits for otherwise desperate individuals in other parts of the Philippines. The town of Donsol, environmental groups, and even the president, succeeded in passing legislation banning these whale shark fisheries. To bring much-needed revenue to the town, and to keep world awareness focused on the well-being of the sharks, regulated access was allowed for tourists.

What seems like a blessing, however, could cause a backlash. With the surge in tourism, locals are cashing in and charging exorbitant amounts of money for boat rides, and fishermen are cooking up fish for the hungry day-trippers, creating garbage and pollution. Some believe the very efforts set forth to protect the delicate balance of the whale shark's environment may ultimately create so much disruption that it does more harm than good.

To book whale-watching tours, call **Scuba World** in Manila at ☎ **2/985-7805** or **2/8890-7805**. Bubbles from scuba gear make the sharks nervous, so only snorkeling is permitted. For more information on the whale sharks of Donsol, contact: **WWF Philippines** at ☎ **2/433-3220** to **22;** fax **2/426-3927;** e-mail kkp@mozcom.com.

second half is through a desert of rocks and boulders. The incline to the summit is pretty consistent, with the last portion requiring climbers to be roped together to avoid slipping on the loose cinders and lava. Gas masks or an improvised cotton mask should be used at the summit to protect yourself and your lungs from the hot, poisonous gases that are leaking out. Do make a stop at the volcanology station right at the start of the climb.

**How Much:** About P1,000 (US$25) per person for guide, porter, tent, and food.

**How Long:** A round-trip trek, including transport to and from Legazpi, should take you 3 days.

**When to Go:** The best time for ascents is from March to May.

**Things Not To Tell Your Loved Ones:** Dislodged rocks can cause an avalanche. The peak's surface is hollow, and a fall is not out of the question. Poisonous fumes are still emitted by the volcano. It's still very active and considered unpredictable.

**Soreness Factor:** Your knees and lower back will ache from the bouldering, and descending always makes your knees throb.

## MT. BULUSAN & MT. IRIGA

Bulusan (5,079 ft., 1,548m) is not too difficult, and Iriga (4,823 ft., 1,470m) just a long hike. Iriga appears like a giant in the midst of a forest. Declared a national park in 1935, it is made up of rain forest that harbors rare plants and animals. You will need bug spray for both volcanoes.

**How Much:** About P500 (US$12.50) per person for guide and food.

**How Long:** It's really up to you. For Mt. Bulusan, people usually arrange for a 3-day trek, camping along the way, but it's possible to do it in 2 days, taking time to see Crater Lake nearby. Mt. Iriga can be done in a day, usually requiring a 4-hour ascent.

**When to Go:** Any time of year, but keep a close ear out for any tropical storms or typhoons that may be brewing.

**Things Not to Tell Your Loved Ones:** Leeches are plentiful in the lush vegetation you'll be hiking through, so wear long pants, preferably light-weight hiking pants that dry quickly and allow ventilation.

# 6  Mindoro

The close proximity of the island of Mindoro to Manila makes it a favorite weekend retreat for urbanites who want to escape the city to an altogether different world. Rugged mountain ranges divide the island into two provinces, Oriental Mindoro to the east, and Occidental Mindoro to the west. There are tribes in the mountains, and plenty of hiking and incredible forest to see. But most visitors opt for the popular beach destinations in **Puerto Galera** on Mindoro's east side. You can visit Puerto Galera at any time of year, although you should be careful during typhoon season, from September to December. With the slightest threat of a typhoon, ferry services come to a halt, and you can find yourself stranded for a few days.

## GETTING THERE

**BY PLANE**   There are no flights to Puerto Galera. But if you really want to make a holiday out of it, you can hire a private helicopter for US$1,000 or a seaplane for US$350. Call ☎ **973/497-503** for more information.

**BY BUS & FERRY**   The trip is in two legs: from Manila to Batangas (2 hours), then across to Mindoro Island by boat or ferry (another 2 hours). A daily through-trip starts at 9am in front of the **Centrepoint Hotel,** Mabini St., Ermita, Manila (☎ **2/521-2751**). The air-conditioned bus takes you to Batangas City Pier just in time to catch the 2:30pm M/B *Si-Kat II* ferry. Book the P400 (US$10) combined ticket at the hotel.

Taxis in Manila will also take you to Batangas for about P1,000 (US$25). And other reliable ferry options are **Viva Shipping Lines,** which leaves Batangas at 8:30am, 10:20am, 12:30pm, 2:30pm, 5pm, and 7pm, for P60 (US$1.50), and **DSL Fastcraft M/V *Blue Eagle,*** which leaves at 11am, noon, 3:30pm, and 4:30pm, for P110 (US$2.75). The latter is the fastest ferry, taking about 1½ hours.

*Note:* Use your judgment before boarding a ferry. If it's floating crooked and dressed in rust, don't get on. If you arrive at the pier after the last ferry, usually after 5pm, you can hire a private *banca* to take you across to Mindoro for about P2,000 (US$50). You will be besieged by people offering their bancas who will insist that there are no more ferries, but don't take anybody's word for it. Seek out someone official or go to the terminal and ask to be sure. And hold onto your bags; the pier is a crazy place.

## GETTING AROUND

Once you arrive at Puerto Galera's pier you have three options to get to neighboring beaches and elsewhere on the island.

**BY JEEPNEY**   The trip from Puerto Galera to Sabang Beach takes 20 minutes, for P10 (US25¢). From Sabang you can walk to Big La Laguna or Small La Laguna Beach. Jeepneys to neighboring Talipanan take 35 minutes, for P20 (US50¢); to Aninuan, it's 20 minutes for P15 (US37¢); and to White Beach, it's 10 minutes, for P10 (US25¢).

---

**Travel Tip: Mayon for the Non-Hiker**

If hiking isn't your thing, Mayon and the area surrounding it offer plenty of other things to explore. You can visit ancient churches, swim at a coral islet, traverse recent lava flows, hike to falls, walk through caves, and see the remains of a community that stood in the wake of Mayon's 1814 eruption. Mayon is a bit camera shy, and hides behind clouds most of the time.

---

**BY TRICYCLE**   I'm not sure how they pedal the mostly uphill, pot-holed route, but they do. A "regular" trip to Sabang Beach with three or four people will cost P50 (US$1.25). Prices for a special trip (when you're the only one they take) will have to be negotiated.

**BY BANCA OR PUMPBOAT**   This is the best way to see the lay of the islands. You will be hassled by banca operators as you walk the beach, so finding one is no problem. And many hotels can arrange one for you. Here's a guideline of prices and times to various islands from the pier: San Antonio, 10 min, P60 (US$1.50); Coco Beach, 15 min, P80 (US$2); Big La Laguna, 18 min, P100 (US$2.50); Small La Laguna, 20 min, P120 (US$3); Sabang, 23 min, P150 (US$3.75); White Beach, 40 min, P450 (US$11.25); Talipanan, 60 min, P550 (US$13.75). The ultimate price depends on your bargaining savvy.

## VISITOR INFORMATION

There is no tourist office in Puerto Galera, but travel arrangements, questions, and maps can be obtained from **Swagmans Travel** at Sabang Beach, ☎ **912/347-6993,** or at their Small La Laguna Beach location, ☎ **912/306-6585.** You can also try the **tourist hotline** at ☎ **912/524-1728.** If you're planning in advance, the Tourism department has e-mail set up and can answer questions you send to **kit@puerto-galera.net.** Most resorts will have accurate, up-to-date information on what to see and do here and packages available.

# Fast Facts: Mindoro

---

**Banks/Currency Exchange**   There are lots of money changers along the pier in Puerto Galera. Swagman Travel will exchange cash and traveler's checks and make card advances. They have locations in Puerto Galera (☎ 912/ 319-9587), Sabang Beach (☎ 912/347-6993), and Small La Laguna Beach (☎ 912/306-6585).

**Doctors/Hospitals**   Provincial Hospital (☎ 43/288-4186); Palm Medical Clinic (☎ 912/352-9519); and Puerto Galera Lying in Clinic for pharmacy and lab services (☎ 912/352-9531) are all in Puerto Galera.

**Emergencies**   Dial ☎ 166 for the police. For serious emergencies requiring evacuation to a hospital, free helicopter air-lift service is provided by the Philippine Army Search and Rescue Squad. Contact any of the resorts and they will radio for you, or call ☎ 912/305-0652.

**Internet/E-Mail**   Asia Divers provides e-mail service (no Internet access) at both locations, on Sabang Beach and Small La Laguna Beach, between 8am and 5pm. They charge P50 (US$1.25) per 10 minutes of use. Replies will be printed out and left with the shop secretary for you to pick up. The Atlantis Resort Hotel (see below) also offers e-mail access.

**Police**   The Puerto Galera Police Station is at ☎ 973/800-168.

**Post Office/Mail**   The easiest place to drop off mail is at Swagman's Travel on Sabang Beach or at La Laguna Beach Club on Big La Laguna Beach (☎ 973/855-545).

**Telephone**   International and long-distance calls can be made at Swagman's Travel in Sabang Beach or at any of the bigger resorts like La Laguna Beach Club. Phone service in Puerto Galera is on cellular phones, which are not always reliable.

# PUERTO GALERA

Puerto Galera—or "PG," as expatriates and locals affectionately call their playground—plays host to incredible opportunities for diving and snorkeling, lounging at the beach, and rowdy nightlife, making it an easy one-shop stop to satisfy every mood.

## ACCOMMODATIONS

✪ **Coco Beach Resort.** Puerto Galera, Mindoro. ☎ **917/377-2115** or 917/890-1426. Booking: Roxas Blvd., Manila, 2/521-5260 or call the resort directly: 2/521-5260. Fax 2/526-6903. www.cocobeach.com. E-mail: cbrpsort@info.com.ph. 80 units. P1,520–P1,920 (US$38–US$48) double; P2,720 (US$68) suite. Includes round-trip transfers from Manila and buffet breakfasts. AE, DC, MC, V.

This resort doesn't have much in the way of comfortable amenities—it lacks hot water, A/C, and TV—but it's a charming Robinson Crusoe family getaway surrounded by tropical flora and fauna on a private island close to Puerto Galera, offering peace and privacy at an unbeatable price. Everything in the rooms is natural, from the bamboo poster bed with draped netting to the tribal artifacts. Bathrooms are large, covered with white tiles and plants, and some have walls built out of pieced-together coral. You get hanging hammocks in your bungalow terrace, which feels like a tree house. There are suspension bridges throughout the complex, which is a gardener's dreamscape filled with lilacs, orchids, azaleas, and other exotic flowers and plants all around you. There's an enormous lagoon-shaped pool and kiddie extension at the center of the "village," along with a tennis court, a golf course overlooking the harbor, and a shopping arcade. They offer picnics and seafood buffets on the beach and in their restaurant. It's a very popular vacation spot for German and Dutch families.

**Puerto Galera Resort Hotel.** Conception Street, Puerto Galera, Mindoro. (Right up from the wharf.) ☎ **43/442-0160** to 62. Booking: Ermita, Manila, 2/525-4641. Fax 2/522-2968. 40 units. A/C MINIBAR TV. P820 (US$20.50) per person includes double room and breakfast. V.

There's nothing to write home about regarding this hotel. It's a good place to stay if you have to on your way in or out of Mindoro because of its convenient location at the pier in Puerto Galera. You can't enjoy the beach here, but they do offer a free banca ride to the beach several times a day. Rooms are huge and comfortable, and bathrooms have running hot and cold water with a stone bathtub. There is a nice pool and a restaurant. Ask about package deals.

### Sabang Beach

✪ **Atlantis Resort Hotel.** Sabang Beach, Puerto Galera, Mindoro. ☎ **973/497-503** or 912/308-0672. www.vasia.com/atlantis. E-mail: Atlantis@vasia.com. 32 units. A/C MINIBAR TV. P1,400–P1,800 (US$35–US$45) double; P2,200–P3,800 (US$55–US$95) suites. AE, DC, MC, V.

This is said to be the best and most comfortable hotel in Puerto Galera. The contemporary Spanish-Mediterranean decor, with its terra-cotta tile and white stucco walls, make the place feel like a cross between a Greek isle and an amusement park. White bridges lead to separate castles peeking through the palm trees. They even have a "Flintstones House" for families with children. Each room looks sculpted, with curved stucco shelving units and beds that seem to be carved right out of the walls. The secluded suites, with private terrace, are exceptional. All rooms are airy, quiet, and clean. The tiled bathrooms are spacious, with pedestal sinks and separate shower rooms. Atlantis is in the heart of town, so a few shops and a dirt walkway separate you from the beach. If nightlife is your priority, you're where it all happens. There are a pool, billiards, five-star dive shop, e-mail and faxing, laundry, baby-sitting, beauty parlor, small fitness room, and massage—what a relief!

**Big Apple Dive Resort.** Sabang Beach, Puerto Galera, Mindoro. ☎ **912/308-1120.** E-mail: Big-apple@qinet.net. A/C TV. 21 units. P480–P1,400 (US$12–US$35) double. AE, DC, MC, V.

Located on the beach, close to the restaurants, this traditional-style resort is a popular place for European divers. Its advantage over the other budget dive resorts in the area is its billiard room and nice pool. Standard rooms just have a fan, while deluxe rooms offer air-conditioning, a double bed, and television, and some have kitchenettes. There's a nice pool and a restaurant.

### Small La Laguna

**El Galleon.** Small La Laguna, Puerto Galera, Mindoro. ☎ **973/865-252.** Fax 912/305-0652. E-mail: Elgaleon@mozcom.com. A/C. 25 units. P960 (US$24) standard; P1,520–P1,920 (US$38–US$48) deluxe. AE, DC, MC, V.

At El Galleon, built high along a cliff on the beach, you'll get excellent seaside breezes and views, but you'll have to endure many zigzagging steps to get up to your room. At least the rooms are equipped with intercoms, so you can make requests or have laundry and food delivered to you without having to make the long trip down. The setting is exotic, tropical, and festive. Rooms are cozy, with the bed set on a step-up platform and bay windows surrounding you. Built-in window seats and handmade tapestries create a rustic atmosphere. Some mattresses are springy and lumpy, while others are just right, so do the test before you choose your room. The triangular-shaped pool characterized by a huge palm tree is right next to the pavilion restaurant that dishes up excellent international cuisine. It's popular with divers, as its famous owner, Allan Nash, also owns Asia Divers and the Point Shooter Bar, a watering hole where everybody who's anybody parties.

**Portofino Resort.** Small La Laguna Beach, Puerto Galera, Mindoro. ☎ **973/776-704.** www.portofino.com.ph. E-mail: Resort@portofino.com.ph. 25 units. A/C TV TEL. P1,500 (US$37.50) deluxe studio, P3,500 (US$87.50) double suite. AE, DC, MC, V.

You'll feel like you are staying in a stylish apartment here at the haciendalike Portofino. Every unit is outfitted slightly differently, with fully equipped kitchens (microwave, toaster oven, coffeemaker, blender, dishes, mugs), tiled bathrooms, contemporary rattan beds, handmade batik prints, and stained glass windows in the foyer. Room no. 31 even has a Jacuzzi. You'll have incredible views of the beach and Verde Island across the bay. And if a view just doesn't do it for you, the beach is only a stone's throw away past the stone pool and waterfall. The clientele tends to include Filipino executives, embassy employees, and European families.

### Big La Laguna

**La Laguna Beach Club and Dive Center.** Big La Laguna Beach, Puerto Galera, Mindoro. ☎ **973/855-545.** Fax 973/878-409. www.epic.net/La Laguna. E-mail: La Laguna@llbc.com.ph. A/C MINIBAR. 30 units. P1,260–P1,620 (US$31.50–US$40.50) double; P1,800–P2,000 (US$45–US$50) family. AE, DC, MC, V.

This place doesn't quite live up to its reputation. You'd expect more after seeing the pool and the exterior, or eating in the restaurant. But the rooms are very basic and

# Puerto Galera Area

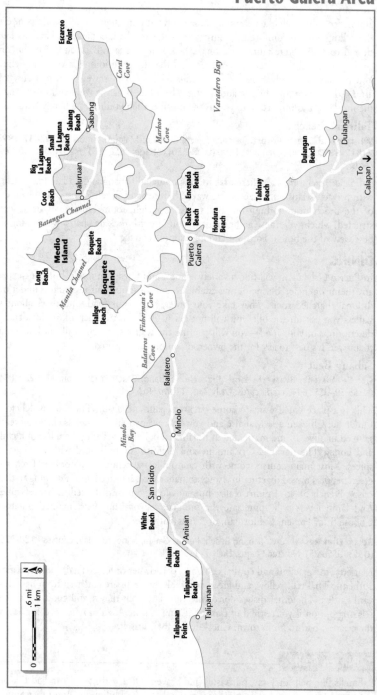

Escareo Point

Coral Cove

Varradero Bay

Sabang

Markoe Cove

Small La Laguna Beach

Sabang Beach

Big La Laguna Beach

Dalaruan

Coco Beach

Dulangan

Dulangan Beach

To Calapan

Batangas Channel

Encenada Beach

Tabinay Beach

Medio Island

Boquete Beach

Balete Beach

Hondura Beach

Manila Channel

Long Beach

Boquete Island

Puerto Galera

Halige Beach

Fisherman's Cove

Balateros Cove

Balatero

Minolo Bay

Minolo

San Isidro

White Beach

Aniuan

Aniuan Beach

Talipanan Beach

Talipanan Point

Talipanan

N

.6 mi
1 km

0

almost feel and smell like Grandma's basement, with dim light, small windows next to the ceiling, and uncomfortable, clingy sheets. It's too bad, because La Laguna's location, dive shop, and restaurant/bar on the beach are excellent. Bathrooms have hot and cold water in all rooms except cottages, and the air-conditioning is very, very chilly. You can also take advantage of international direct dial, travel confirmations, and arranged activities like hiking and diving. The white beach is wide and quiet, and if the inside isn't as important to you as the outside, then you may be happy here.

### Talipana Beach

**White Sand Beach Resort.** Talipana Beach. Booking: Malou E. Ambal, ☎ **2/817-1993, 2/817-6109.** 22 units, fan only. P500 (US$12.50) cottage; P650 (US$16.25) room. No credit cards.

Talipana Beach offers an alternative to the populated Sabang and La Laguna Beaches, with privacy, seclusion, and crashing waves. White Sand Beach Resort is at the far end of the beach near nothing but beauty. A new eight-room building is being constructed, which will house an open-air restaurant with rocking chairs overlooking the best view of the beach. For now, choose a simple cottage.

## DINING

In Puerto Galera you will find a variety of local and European foods, but don't expect any theme or enclosed, fine-dining establishments, just open-air restaurants under traditional thatched roofs. They take your order, serve your food, and that's about it. Unless you ask for the bill, you will not get it. And don't bother asking for detailed descriptions of your food—you will confuse the waitress and she will not know how to answer. It's best to ask for the owner, or simply be surprised.

### Sabang Beach

✪ **Le Bistrot Brasserie and Pizzeria.** Sabang Beach. Main courses P220–P340 (US$5.50–US$8). No credit cards. Daily 7am–11pm. FRENCH.

This is a place you'll want to come back to again and again. The food is delicious. Order the Chicken à la Maltaise and you will get two large boneless chicken breasts sautéed in olive oil and marinated in Kalamansi (a lime-like fruit grown locally), chili, and honey. The flavor is very unique and delicate, subtly spiced with homegrown spices. Most main courses come with ratatouille—zucchini, tomatoes, and red and green peppers mixed together in a spicy tomato sauce. It's excellent for dipping in their crispy French bread. I didn't realize how fun fondue is until I tried their beef cubes. And lamb lovers will appreciate the pungent leg of lamb with mashed potatoes. Choose from French, Californian, or Australian wine.

**Relax Thai Restaurant.** Sabang Beach, Puerto Galera, Mindoro. Main courses P120–P250 (US$3–US$6.25). No credit cards. Daily 7–11am. THAI.

Marietta, the gracious and cordial cook and part owner of Relax Thai, cooks the most authentic Thai red, yellow, and green curry; all the herbs are cut fresh from her backyard garden. The other dishes don't taste very Thai, but they're still good. It's a nice, relaxing option if you're tired of classic Filipino cuisine. It's also renowned for having the cleanest bathroom in town. Check it out for yourself.

### Durian Fruit

Smells like hell, they say, but tastes like heaven. Durian fruit reeks so bad that it's banned from many hotels and buses throughout the Philippines and other Southeast Asian countries. But partakers of this green, spiky Southeast Asian fruit swear by its thick, custard-like core. It's a must try!

**Ristorante de Franco.** Atlantis Resort, Sabang Beach. Main courses P250–P450 (US$6.25–US$11.25). AE, DC, MC, V. Daily 7am–11pm. SOUTHERN ITALIAN.

Franco is his name and Italian is his game. Atlantis resort's restaurant serves classic Italian cuisine, some of the best food on the beach. Appetizers include bruschetta or oven-baked eggplant with cheese. Choose from seafood specialties, homemade pastas with a variety of sauces, meat dishes, and homemade pizzas. The beef gives new meaning to "tender" loin—it's like butter. Called the "wool shed" by its Aussie visitors, the space is as rustic as a hangar, yet relaxing and quiet. They have a large drink menu including French and Italian wine and sangria. And for dessert, if you have room, try the crepes, zabaglione, or banana split. Franco will prepare any special requests not on the menu, with a money-back guarantee if you are less than satisfied. Mangia!

**Sunshine Coast Bar and Restaurant.** Sabang Beach, next to South Sea Divers. Main courses P80–P180 (US$2–US$4.50). No credit cards. Daily 6:30am–11pm. INTERNATIONAL.

This place is very popular with the locals for its varied offerings and cheap prices. Most tourists come for either the English, Japanese, Filipino, or American breakfast. Or, depending on what kind of evening you've had, try the frequently ordered "feeling shitty breakfast": coffee, Coke, and two cigarettes. What it lacks in atmosphere it makes up for with good humor.

**Tamarind Restaurant and Music Pub.** Sabang Beach. Main courses P120–P300 (US$3–US$7). MC, V. Daily 7am–midnight. FILIPINO.

Tamarind juice, tamarind fish, tamarind coffee, tamarind chicken—this place lives up to its name. The wooden menu and authentic bamboo furnishings set this local place apart from the rest. Sit inside the jungle of hanging, standing, and potted plants, or enjoy the ocean breezes on the beachfront terrace. (This is not recommended during high tide though.) The food is typical Filipino—nothing extraordinary, although the Tamarind fish special is good, seasoned with paprika, tomato, tamarind juice, and shrimp. And it's only place in Puerto Galera where I saw crab and lobster on the menu, but you have to give advance notice so they can fish it out for you. And if you feel like a cup of Joe, they have more than enough choices for any caffeine connoisseur.

### Small La Laguna Beach

**El Galleon Beach Resort Restaurant.** Small La Laguna Beach. P40–P300 (US$1–US$7.50) main courses. AE, MC, V accepted for amounts over P1,000 (US$20). Daily 6am–midnight. INTERNATIONAL.

The witty humor and honesty of the menu is typical of its Australian owner. This is a hub for divers, who chat away on their cell phones. The menu is broad, with slices of pizza, peel 'n' eat shrimp, cheese fondue, Filipino dishes, soups, even peanut butter-and-jelly sandwiches. With three days' notice you can have a goat. A must try on a typhoon day is the spicy tomato-based fish soup, loaded with lapu-lapu, parsley, and thyme.

**Full Moon Restaurant.** Small La Laguna Beach. ☎ **973/751-968.** Main courses P120–P280 (US$3–US$7). No credit cards. Daily 6:30am–midnight. FILIPINO.

The mighty meat pie lives and breathes here! And while you stuff your face with it, sit around the beachfront bar and listen to gossip of the goings-on around town by the "PG" regulars. No frills here, but they offer a large assortment of seafood, beef steaks, and ice cold beer. Try their homemade rye bread and the vegemite spread, which Aussies claim is to them what spinach is to Popeye. Monday nights, feast on a barbecue roast while watching a video.

**Portofino Resort.** Small La Laguna Beach. Main courses P180–P320 (US$4.50–US$8). MC, V (additional 8% fee when using credit cards). Daily 6am–midnight. STEAKS/MEXICAN.

It's worth getting a cheap drink here simply to be able to use the pool that overlooks the beach. The food is well worth a visit too. The recently completed restaurant and bar will make you feel like you've been transported to a cliff-side villa on the Mediterranean. Sit next to the lopo birds if the chatter doesn't annoy you and enjoy main courses like beef tenderloin or rib-eye steak, charcoal broiled to your liking and served with steamed vegetables, rice, or stuffed baked potatoes. They have a selection of sandwiches and Mexican-style platters, and ask about their daily specials. Portofino's claim to fame is their ice cream: Black Forest, rocky road, strawberry, and chunky mascapuno (nuts) are just a few you can choose from to make magnolia double Dutch sundaes, banana splits, or milk shakes.

### Big La Laguna Beach

**La Laguna Beach Club.** Big La Laguna Beach. P200–P450 (US$5–US$11.25) main courses. AE, DC, MC, V. Daily 6:30am–10pm. INTERNATIONAL.

For good eats and good reading at the same time, check out La Laguna's nine-page menu; it's a literary masterpiece. The main characters are the delicious seafood selections, like prawns with ginger, onion, chili, garlic, and rice. Follow along as the plot changes to spaghetti and pizza, then comes the gut-busting meat chapter. Feel free to request anything that's not on the menu. Service is prompt and the atmosphere is peaceful, especially by the pool. A warning to those who fear felines: They will beg and mew until some soft-hearted visitor drops a morsel, but they will scatter like flies as soon as you pick up a stone. Prices are a bit higher here than at other places.

## DIVING

The number of dive shops around Puerto Galera can be quite overwhelming. All have up-to-date equipment and are PADI recognized. This is a very popular place to learn how to dive, if that's your goal.

In **Small La Laguna Beach** there are **Action Divers,** ☎ 973/751-968 and **Asia Divers,** ☎ 973/782-094. In **Sabang Beach** there's the **Atlantic Dive Resort,** ☎ 912/308-0672; the **Big Apple Dive Resort,** ☎ 912/308-1120; **Capt'n Greggs Resort** ☎ 912/306-5267; **Cocktail Divers,** ☎ 912/306-5828; **Octopus Divers,** ☎ 912/313-4486; and **South Sea Divers,** ☎ 912/332-4286. And in **Big La Laguna,** there's the **La Laguna Dive Center,** ☎ 912/306-5622. All of these places pretty much offer the same prices and go to the same sights. Asia Divers, a national chain, is probably the best known.

## MINDORO AFTER DARK

**The Point Shooter Bar.** Small La Laguna Beach. ☎ **973/865-252.**

"Your body is an evil thing. It's got to be punished, so get to the Point!" So reads the warning posted here, and your life will indeed flash before you as you make your way through a five-shot sequence called the Walk of Life, each drink named after a troublesome rite of passage. First there's the Umbilical Cord, followed by the Afterbirth close behind. And if you've always wanted to forget the tortures of Puberty (though I guarantee Puberty will be harder to swallow this time around), you most certainly will after working your way through Mid-Life Crisis and the fifth and final shot, Stairway to Heaven. If you are still standing after this and the more difficult African Passage sequence, you will get a free T-shirt and your name on a plaque underneath your country. So if you don't do it for the sake of your stomach, do it for your fellow countrymen who gave their "lives" before you. Spontaneous bar dancing is not uncommon.

# 7  Cebu

The island of Cebu is located at the navel of the archipelago, making it the main hub for shipping destinations and flights to the central Visayan regions. The island's beautiful beaches, superb diving, and historical heritage continue to attract not only foreigners but also Filipino tourists looking for an easy getaway. It's also a short hop to Bohol and Boracay. Cebu Province is comprised of 167 islands, and the historic city of Cebu, the country's third largest city, is considered the regional center for the Visayas island group. Over the past few years Cebu City has undergone an economic transformation known as "Ceboom." But despite the surge in business and economy, the city has sustained a small-town flavor. And visitors flock to neighboring Mactan Island, just across the bridge, for a taste of its leisurely laid-back lifestyle, tropical resorts, and seaside lounging.

You will only need a day or two in Cebu City to see the sights and move on. If you're looking to stay in one place at an all-inclusive resort, then Mactan Island is perfect, although most of the beach here is private, making it difficult to walk from resort to resort. Moalboal, a short bus ride away from Cebu City, provides some of the best dive spots in the country.

## CEBU CITY/MACTAN ISLAND
### GETTING THERE

**BY PLANE**   The new **Mactan International Airport** is the nicest and cleanest in the country. **Cebu Pacific** (☎ 2/636-4938) offers seven daily flights from Manila, lasting just over an hour. **Philippine Airlines** (☎ 2/816-6691) has three daily flights and **Air Philippines** (☎ 2/843-7770) has five daily flights. A one-way ticket will cost you about P1,688 (US$42.20); it's twice as much for a round-trip. It is also possible to arrange your international ticket direct to Cebu. Check with your travel agent or with Philippines Airlines, which offers a program called "Cebu Express." Airport tax for international passengers in Cebu is P400 (US$10).

Getting to the city or to Mactan Island is simple. If you've booked a resort already, they will have transportation waiting for you. If not, there are a number of chauffeur driven–car rental desks inside the terminal. Rate sheets are posted at the desks; it will cost US$6 to US$8 to resorts along Mactan Island, and US$10 to US$12 to Cebu City. There are also shuttle buses at the airport that will take you to the Park Place Hotel in Cebu City for P100 (US$2.50). Taxis are also available and will try to charge you a large sum. If you can't find a driver willing to use the meter (even though they're required to by law), try to settle on a fixed rate in advance. This should be no more than P200 (US$5) to Cebu City, or P100 to P150 (US$2.50–US$3.75) to resorts on Mactan Island.

**BY BOAT**   WG&A SuperFerry (☎ 2/245-4061) makes daily trips to Cebu from Manila costing about P880 to P4,000 (US$22–US$100). Count on 21 to 22 hours.

### GETTING AROUND

**BY CAR**   Cebu's points of interest are spread out and can be a hassle to get to, especially if you are staying on Mactan Island, where taxis aren't easy to come by. Resorts have shuttle service, but if you want ultimate freedom consider renting a car. **Dollar Rent-A-Car** (☎ 32/254-7425, 8255, 8256); **Hertz Rent-A-Car** (☎ 32/254-5004, 5006); and **Guani Rent-A-Car** (☎ 32/253-5463) are all at the airport.

**BY TAXI**   Taxi meters start at P20 (US50¢) and increase P1 (US3¢) every 200 meters. Make sure to point to the meter if the driver conveniently forgets to put it on.

For longer trips a price should be negotiated in advance; you can reasonably expect to pay about P500 (US$12.50) for 5 hours. If you are taking a ferry to Bohol, or any other boat, keep in mind that taxis have to pay a P5 (US13¢) fee to get into the dock area.

**BY TRICYCLE**   In Cebu, taxis are a better option than tricycles. On Mactan Island, however, tricycles are the easiest way to get from resort to resort. Your hotel can arrange one for you.

## VISITOR INFORMATION

The **Department of Tourism** office is located at GMC Plaza Building, Cebu City, ☎ 32/254-2811. There is also a **tourist information counter** at Mactan International Airport, ☎ 32/340-2486 or locally, 340-2450. In case you are in need of any special services, the **U.S. Consulate** is in the PCI Building, 3rd floor, Gorordo Avenue, ☎ 32/231-1261. The **U.K. Consulate** is in Maria Louisa Park, ☎ 32/346-0525. (There are no consulates for Canada, Australia, or New Zealand in Cebu.)

## Fast Facts: Cebu City/Mactan Island

**Banks/Currency Exchange**   The Philippine National Bank on Osmena Boulevard, ☎ 32/253-1663; Standard Chartered Bank on Burgos Street, across from City Hall, ☎ 32/709-85; and Citibank, Osmena Boulevard, ☎ 32/255-9333, all can change traveler's checks and foreign currency. Most big resorts and hotels also have currency exchange, although at a less favorable rate. Banking hours are Monday to Friday 9am to 3pm. ATMs are open 24 hours. You'll find an American Express Office on the 2nd floor of the PCI Bank Building, on Gorordo Avenue (☎ 32/232-2970). It's open weekdays from 8:30am to 4pm and on Saturday from 8:30am to 11am. Thomas Cook (☎ 32/219-229) has an office at the ground floor of Metro Bank Plaza, Osmena Boulevard. It's open weekdays from 8:30am to 4pm and 8:30am to 11am on Saturday.

**Doctors/Hospitals**   Cebu Doctor's Hospital, Osmena Boulevard, near the Provincial Capitol Building (☎ 32/253-7511) is a reputable place to deal with any emergencies that may arise. They also have a decompression chamber. For any dental work contact Jose Vicente Araneta at ☎ 32/255-0229 from 9am to 6pm Monday to Saturday.

**Emergencies**   Dial ☎ 166 for the police. Cebu also has an emergency tourist assistance hotline to help you with any situations involving crime, theft, or illness. It's ☎ 32/254-4023.

**Internet/E-Mail**   The Ruftan Pension (☎ 32/79138) on Legaspi Street has an Internet cafe. They charge P30 (US75¢) an hour and are open from 8am to 10pm. Resorts on Mactan Island can provide e-mail service, but you won't be able to surf the Web.

**Police**   Cebu City Police Station (☎ 32/253-5636) is on Jose L. Briones Street; or Lapu-Lapu City Police (☎ 32/340-0250) is by the public market off S. Osmena Street on Mactan Island.

**Post Office/Mail**   The main post office in Cebu City is located in the Quezon Building, near Plaza Independencia (☎ 32/346-1851). On Mactan Island there is a post office by the Lapu-Lapu City Hall off A.C. Cortes Avenue. Most resorts on the island will post letters or postcards for you, which is much easier.

# Cebu City

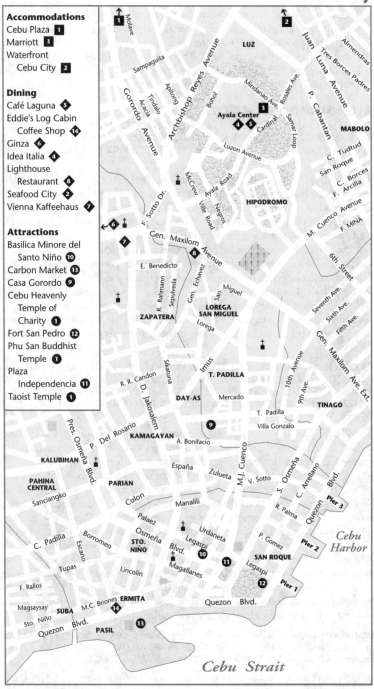

**Accommodations**
Cebu Plaza **1**
Marriott **3**
Waterfront
    Cebu City **2**

**Dining**
Café Laguna **5**
Eddie's Log Cabin
    Coffee Shop **14**
Ginza **6**
Idea Italia **4**
Lighthouse
    Restaurant **8**
Seafood City **2**
Vienna Kaffeehaus **7**

**Attractions**
Basilica Minore del
    Santo Niño **10**
Carbon Market **13**
Casa Gorordo **9**
Cebu Heavenly
    Temple of
    Charity **1**
Fort San Pedro **12**
Phu San Buddhist
    Temple **1**
Plaza
    Independencia **11**
Taoist Temple **1**

687

**Telephone**    You'll notice both five- and seven-digit numbers here. The five-digit numbers are part of the old system and will soon be completely replaced. Hotels are equipped with IDD (International Direct Dial) and NDD (National Direct Dial). Cebu's area code is 32. There are international phone boxes sprinkled throughout the city, or calls can be made at the Philippine Long Distance Telephone Company (PLDT) on Osmena Boulevard, ☎ 32/253-1961.

## ACCOMMODATIONS: CEBU CITY

**Cebu City Marriott.** Cebu Business Park, Cebu City. ☎ **32/232-6100.** Fax 32/232-6101. ☎ **800/888-2233.** Ccmhotel@mozcom.com. 303 units. A/C MINIBAR TV TEL. P5,200 (US$130) regular; P7,600 (US$190) business suite; P6,200–P10,200 (US$155–US$255) executive rooms. AE, DC, JCB, MC, V.

The first truly international hotel to establish itself in Cebu, the Marriott offers guests what no other hotel here can—a known quantity with excellent business facilities. The lobby feels like home, with muted tones, thick textures, and large treelike plants that make it a nice place to sit and read or to conduct meetings. Rooms offer all the first-class amenities you would expect: voice mail, modem hookup, individual climate control, hair dryer, iron and ironing board, coffeemaker, electronic safe, slippers, shoe rack, and almost anything else you can think of that the business traveler could need. Towels are extra-large and thick, and beds are very plush and comfortable, with down-feather pillows. The large photographs of beautiful flowers sprinkled throughout the rooms were taken by the owner. The Garden Café and Palm Lounge both offer live entertainment. Other amenities include fitness center, gift shop, baby-sitting, pool, meeting and banquet rooms, newspaper delivery, room service, car hire, and travel agency.

✪ **Cebu Plaza.** Nivel Hills, Lahug. ☎ **32/231-1231** to 59. Fax 32/231-2071. Manila reservations: ☎ 2/634-7505 to 08. Fax 2/634-7509. Cphres@cebu.webling.com. 385 units. A/C MINIBAR TV TEL. P5,400–P9,600 (US$135–US$240) double; P8,960–P17,480 (US$224–US$437) "Presidents Club" floors; P15,080–P44,000 (US$377–US$1,100) suites. AE, DC, JCB, MC, V.

The Plaza is Cebu City's most reputable hotel, superbly managed and staffed, with commanding views of the city (request a city-view room). It has a more relaxing, pleasurable feel than the business-oriented Marriott or the high-rolling Waterfront. The lobby is spacious and calm, with a subdued decor and two hallways that house a travel agency, gift shops, and a business center. The spacious rooms are a blend of East and West, with bamboo and wood-designed European furniture. Beds are comfortable and come with a lot of pillows. The rooms vary from standard to President's Penthouse, the latter offering complimentary breakfast, 6pm cocktails, and 24-hour butler service. The hotel houses the funky and popular Bai Discotheque and Pards Bar and Restaurant. Or you can belt out your best Tina Turner at the Karaoke bar. Other amenities include two pools overlooking the city, a playground with a kiddie pool, an 18-hole golf course, two tennis courts, a shooting range for air and rifle pistols, billiards, table tennis, and a jogging trail. The most valuable service is the complimentary taxi to top city restaurants, centers, and malls.

**Waterfront Cebu City.** 1 Waterfront Dr., Salinas Drive, Cebu City. ☎ **32/232-6888.** 564 units. A/C MINIBAR TV TEL. Fax 32/232-6880. P5,400 (US$135) superior; P8,800 (US$220) deluxe; P16,000–P40,000 (US$400–US$1,000) suites. AE, DC, JCB, MC, V.

As glitzy as Vegas, as glam as Versace, the newly opened Waterfront Cebu City is overwhelming. The pink castlelike façade sticks out like a sore thumb in the barren landscape that surrounds it, and the neo-classical lobby is likely to cause sensory overload. Once inside the huge and poorly planned hotel you'll feel lost. But the hotel's **Filipino**

**Casino** is one of Asia's largest, attracting high rollers from Hong Kong, Japan, and other nearby Asian countries. Rooms are in blocks—one has a French country garden motif, one (the casino block) takes a more gaudy approach, with black and gold Versace-style comforter, chair, and curtain patterns. Some rooms have windows, others don't. Some have extensions, while others have patios. Just let the desk know what you're looking for in a room and they'll accommodate you. Aesthetic objections aside, you will be comfortable here, and it's in a prime location near the financial district, shopping malls, and golf course. There are restaurants, including a lobby lounge, coffee house, Chinese, Japanese, Italian, and seafood restaurants, and of course casino dining. Other amenities are fitness center, kids' club, diving tour counter, travel agency, spa, beauty salon, business center and large meeting rooms, shopping arcade, limo service, baby-sitting, parking, newspaper delivery, and 24-hour room service.

## ACCOMMODATIONS: MACTAN ISLAND
### Very Expensive
**Plantation Bay.** Marigondon, Mactan Island. ☎ **32/340-5900.** Fax 32/340-5988. 188 units. A/C MINIBAR TV TEL. P9,200–P11,600 (US$230–US$290) singles and doubles; P11,600–P60,000 (US$290–US$1,500) suites. AE, MC, V.

Dubbed "the most distinctive resort to open this decade," Plantation Bay Mactan offers a slice of turn-of-the-century romance and Southern comfort. It has been admitted as a member of the Small Luxury Hotels of the World Association. But all honors aside, it truly is a quaint village that succeeds in balancing colonial plantation simplicity with beach resort luxury. About a third of the stunning landscape is water, including a man-made saltwater lagoon and the country's largest freshwater swimming pool. And spectacular waterfalls help maintain a sense of tranquility. All rooms pamper you with unique furnishings, original artwork, and marble bathrooms, and all have views. Try the presidential suite on for size. The restaurant overlooking the bay is very romantic, and serves fresh and tasty seafood. They also offer sunset dining on your private terrace. Amenities are room and butler service, laundry service, children's activities, and baby-sitting.

✪ **Shangri-La's Mactan Island Resort.** P.O. Box 86, Lapu-Lapu City, Mactan Island. ☎ 32/231-0288. Fax 32/231-1688. 546 units. A/C MINIBAR TV TEL. P6,200–P8,000 (US$155–US$200) superior double; P7,400–P11,000 (US$185–US$275) ocean-view double; P10,800–P66,000 (US$270–US$1,650) suites. AE, DC, JCB, MC, V.

For the best accommodations, best beach, and best food on Mactan, all fingers point to Shangri-La. In fact, it's one of the best hotels in the Philippines in terms of size, service, and splendor; since its opening in 1994 it remains the only international deluxe resort hotel in the country. All rooms have complete amenities and a private balcony. Bay-view rooms overlook the Bay of Cebu, while ocean-view rooms offer unrivaled views of the ocean, the beautiful multi-level pool, and the gardens. Terrace rooms are equipped with extra large private terraces that attract lots of sun. Bathrooms feature a basket of toiletries, jumbo towels, slippery and cool marble, and his and her bathrobes.

You will be overwhelmed by the dining options here. Everything is top notch, including the delectable seafood at the Cowrie Cove overlooking the ocean; the Pool Bar, for more seafood grilled next to your table; Asiatica, with a selection of Asian cuisines, including crispy pata (deep-fried pigs' feet); Shang Palace for good Chinese dishes; the Garden Patio for buffet and continental fare; and the Lobby Lounge for snacks.

The resort offers every toy and water sport your wilder side might have a craving for, and the scuba center is excellent. There's also newspaper delivery, 24-hour room service, a business center, turndown twice daily, and baby-sitting. If you pay full rack rates you get a complimentary breakfast for two (free for children under 6), free local calls, free laundry except dry cleaning, and late check-out.

## Expensive

**Cebu White Sands Beach Resort.** Maribago, Mactan Island. ☎ **32/340-5960.** Fax 32/340-5969. www.gsilink.com/user/wsands. E-mail: wsands@gsilink.com. 15 units. A/C MINIBAR TV TEL. P4,640–P5,480 (US$116–US$137) deluxe; P7,640–P8,480 (US$191–US$212) semi-suites; P16,000 (US$400) suites. AE, DC, JCB, MC, V.

This charming resort retains a turn-of-the-century ambience, with an antique collection the owners proudly display throughout the lobby and the rooms. Wood and capiz shell windows and wood dividers add to the unique atmosphere, making the resort one of the more quaint and personal on the island. All rooms are spacious and have quiet air-conditioning and private balconies, some overlooking the swimming pool among the sprawling landscaped garden. Bathrooms are large, with hot and cold showers. The semi-suite rooms are the most attractive, with a rod-iron and wicker bed draped with a sheer netting canopy that will make you feel like you're in Arabia. One room even has a Jacuzzi. The small beach has a bar. For fine dining try the Dona Estrella restaurant, or the poolside patio for coffee and snacks.

**Delta Philippine Dream.** Cebu Yacht Club, Lapu-Lapu City. ☎ **32/340-3084,** 3085. Fax 32/340-3083. 100 units (cabins). A/C MINIBAR. P3,200–P7,000 (US$80–US$175) per cabin. AE, DC, JCB, MC, V.

It's a hotel, casino, entertainment center, and boat all in one, permanently docked at the Cebu Yacht Club on the northwest shoreline of Mactan Island. The staterooms are smaller than the suites, but both have portal windows and a larger window, so natural light abounds. The variety of dining and entertainment options includes a sports bar, a sushi and noodle bar, an outdoor sky deck lounge, a karaoke lounge, a disco, and a branch of Roy Yamaguchi's famous chain of restaurants, Roy's, which showcases Pacific Rim and Euro-Asian cuisine. Try your luck on the slots or tables in the casino. The boat does sway, so if you are prone to seasickness I recommend sleeping on solid ground.

## Moderate

**Costabella Tropical Beach Hotel.** Buyong, Mactan Island. ☎ **32/253-0828.** Reservations: Cebu City, ☎ 32/231-4244, 2787, 3273. Fax 32/253-0563. 35 units. A/C MINIBAR TV TEL. P3,200–P3,960 (US$80–US$99) superior; P3,600–P4,000 (US$90–US$100) poolside; P4,600–P5,480 (US$115–US$137) deluxe poolside; P6,400–P7,200 (US$160–US$180) suites. AE, DC, JCB, MC, V.

You'll find cheaper prices and lots of promo rates at this Mediterranean-style villa. It's a bit understated in comparison to the other resorts nearby, but you'll still get all the comfortable amenities and excellent service. The beach area is larger than others, and the two swimming pools cater to both the serious swimmer and those who simply like to cool off or use the slide. Rooms are large, beds are thick and comfortable, and showers are just right. The superior rooms are farther back from the beach, so if beach views are a priority, request the suites. The staff is very attentive, and all the standard water activities and city tours are offered.

**Maribago Bluewater Beach Resort.** Mactan Island. ☎ **32/492-0100.** Fax 32/492-0128. Reservations: Malate, Manila, ☎ 2/525-1204. Fax 2/523-6567. Bluwater@mozcom.com. 78 units. A/C MINIBAR TV TEL. P3,200 (US$80) deluxe; P4,800 (US$120) family room; P6,000 (US$150) royal bungalow. AE, DC, JCB, MC, V.

After passing through the open-air pavilion lobby furnished with traditional rattan furniture, you cross a pond with starfish and white-tip reef sharks on one side and tropical fish on the other, then arrive at a fountain containing statues of the resort's signature seven dolphins. The beachfront rooms are authentic Philippines, down to

# Mactan Island

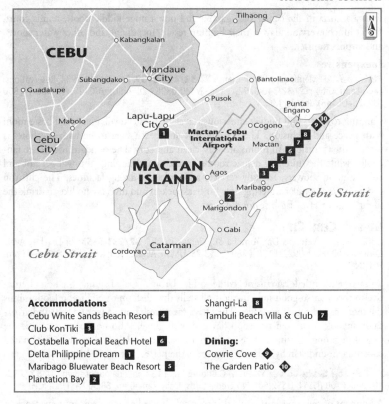

**Accommodations**

Cebu White Sands Beach Resort **4**
Club KonTiki **3**
Costabella Tropical Beach Hotel **6**
Delta Philippine Dream **1**
Maribago Bluewater Beach Resort **5**
Plantation Bay **2**

Shangri-La **8**
Tambuli Beach Villa & Club **7**

**Dining:**
Cowrie Cove **9**
The Garden Patio **10**

the bamboo hangers, fuzzy slippers, umbrellas, and custom paintings done by a worker at the resort. Shells decorate the rooms, which have large terraces with a cushioned bamboo hammock for lounging. Bathrooms are large, with loads of counter space. The bungalows are the best and most spacious option for families or for anyone who needs a lot of space and a homey feel. There are two curved pools. Aquasports include jet skiing, waterskiing, windsurfing, and more. The resort also has a shooting gallery, gym, sauna and whirlpool, billiards, badminton, volleyball, and tennis. Sunset Cove offers fresh seafood, Palmera Restaurant has indoor air-conditioned dining, and Allegro Café is open 24 hours.

**Tambuli Beach Villa and Club.** Mactan Island. ☎ **32/232-4811** to 19. Reservations: Cebu City, 32/254-0640. Fax 32/53097. www.tambuli.com. E-mail: Tambuli@mozcom.com. 114 units. A/C TV MINIBAR. Beach Club: P2,400–P3,400 (US$60–US$85) superior. Beach Villa: P3,200–P3,400 (US$80–US$85) deluxe. AE, DC, JCB, MC, V.

A branch of the Bohol Beach Club on Bohol Island, Tambuli resort is comprised of rooms within the beach club and larger cottages within the Beach Villa, both on the longest stretch of beach boasted by any of the resorts on this part of the island. This hotel is casual and comfortable, with a tropical open-air lobby with high timbered ceiling to allow for cool breezes. The rooms are basic, medium sized, and arranged in a row with the superior rooms commanding front-row views of the beach. During low tide you can walk from the standard rooms to the villa and use their more modern, updated facilities. The more contemporary, less native villas, which are nestled between palm trees and the beach, are newer than the beach club rooms, which were the first of their kind on the island. Facilities at both locations include three pools (one with a Jacuzzi in the center of a gazebo and one a huge kiddie pool), tennis court, buffet lunch every Sunday in their Filipino restaurant, diving and other water sports, and airport transfer.

### Inexpensive

**Club KonTiki.** Maribago, Mactan Island. ☎ **32/492-3189.** Fax 32/340-9934. Reservations: Lapu-Lapu City, ☎ 32/340-0292. Fax 32/340-0306. 26 units. A/C TV. P1,000–P1,800 (US$25–US$45) double. MC, V.

Catering to divers and budget conscious travelers, KonTiki will give you a basic room with peace and seclusion. There really isn't any beach here to be had; the hotel is located on a cliffside. All rooms are very clean and cozy. The standard rooms are fan-cooled while the suite and deluxe rooms have air-conditioning. You will get hot and cold running showers, friendly service, and excellent diving facilities. The cliff-top restaurant is a popular watering hole for backpackers and divers, who like to drink the night away or savor fresh seafood dishes.

## DINING: CEBU CITY

**Café Laguna.** Veterans Dr., Torralba St., Cebu City. ☎ **32/231-3553;** or Level 1, Ayala Center. ☎ 32/231-0922. P150–P280 (US$3.75–US$7). AE, DC, JCB, MC, V. Daily 9am–10pm. FILIPINO.

To savor authentic local cuisine, come to Lita Urbina's Café Laguna, the best alternative to those oh-so-good hole-in-the-wall stalls that dish up true Filipino food, minus the roosters and cats at your feet. They have great fresh lumpia (spring roll) and arroz-caldo manok, a chicken-rice soup flavored with ginger. Also not to be missed is the puto bungbong, glutinous rice steamed in bamboo tubes and served with grated coconuts. Sound starchy? The Pandan tea is the perfect accompaniment.

**Eddie's Log Cabin Coffee Shop.** M C Briones St., a 15-min. ride out of town. ☎ **32/723-40.** P40–P100 (US$1–US$2.50). No credit cards. Daily 7am–8pm. BREAKFAST/LUNCH.

A remnant of the American years, this cozy cafe has led an inconspicuous existence in the hills of Cebu since 1950. The place looks like the set of some John Wayne Western flick, with pictures of American presidents, old U.S. knickknacks, and posters covering the pine walls. If your favorite meal is breakfast, you'll love their hotcakes with thick maple syrup. No mix here, just a coveted house recipe that has hit the griddle for the last 45 years. The pancakes come thick and golden brown with a slab of bacon on the side.

**Ginza Japanese Restaurant.** Old Banilad Rd., Cebu City. ☎ **32/231-6019,** 231-4612. P400–P1,200 (US$10–US$30). AE, DC, JCB, MC, V. Daily 10am–2pm, 6–10pm. JAPANESE.

The owner of this exceptional 18-year-old dining establishment says her family has always had a fascination with Japanese food. The beat of a huge Japanese drum welcomes diners inside, where origami cranes suspended from the skylight hover above the authentic tatami, and you can watch the art of Japanese cooking in the glassed-in kitchen. For a hefty price, go for the "super boat," which sails to your table loaded down with fresh sushi and sashimi. Other Japanese offerings include the house specialty, head of parrot fish in a subtly spicy sauce, and vegetable tempura.

**Idea Italia.** Level 1, Ayala Center. ☎ **32/232-4292.** P180–P230 (US$4.50–US$5.75). AE, DC, JCB, MC, V. Daily 10am–9pm. SOUTHERN ITALIAN.

The most authentic Italian cuisine in Cebu, where jolly old Chef Alfredo, whose "hobby is the kitchen," will be happy to toss up the house specialty, tagliatelle with Parmesan, fresh tomato, and vegetables. Since the restaurant opened two years ago others have tried to copy them, but regulars insist that Idea Italia is the best. The nocciola ice cream is smooth, chunky, and tasty. Come for dinner, then catch a film at the neighboring cinema inside the mall.

**Lighthouse Restaurant.** Gaisano Country Mall, Cebu City. ☎ **32/781-26.** Main courses P200–P400 (US$5–US$10). AE, DC, JCB, MC, V. Daily 10:30am–2pm, 5:30–10:30pm. SEAFOOD/JAPANESE.

This popular Filipino restaurant keeps on evolving, so there's always something new to try. They have a large variety of seafood (the baked scallops come highly recommended), as well as Japanese and sushi main courses. The relaxed, fine-dining ambiance is enhanced by a string band composed of blind musicians.

**Seafood City.** JY Square, Salinas Dr. ☎ **32/213-793,** 213-795. Prices vary according to selection and weight. AE, DC, MC, V. Daily 11am–2pm, 6–10:30pm. SEAFOOD.

Cebu's closest thing to a seafood wharf, housed inside what appears to be the engine room of a ship. Select your prey from an array of seemingly every sea creature imaginable, including lobster, king-size prawns, crabs, squid, lapu-lapu, snapper, sole, blue marlin, and tuna. Then roll your grocery-style cart over to make your selection, from the freshest vegetables and fixings this side of the South China Sea. Tired yet? Not to worry, your final decision is easy—just choose how you want your food prepared from the dozens of suggestions listed on the menu. In a couple of minutes you will sit down to a finely prepared meal, as fresh as the flopping fish you held in your hands moments before. It can get crowded, so reservations are recommended.

**Vienna Kaffeehaus.** GF Wayne's Inn Hotel, ☎ **32/346-1459;** 2nd level SM City, ☎ 32/232-0691; GF City Park Inn, in front of Metro Ayala, ☎ 32/412-2364. Main courses P180–P220 (US$4.50–US$5.50). AE, DC, MC, V (only in GF Wayne's Inn Hotel location). Daily 6:30am–11pm. SWISS/GERMAN.

This popular place has lots of coffee and hot chocolate to wash down the overload of cakes. Original Vienna Eiscoffee, topped with vanilla ice cream and whipped cream, is a favorite. There are a lot of breakfast options, including blueberry pancakes. And for the not-so-cholesterol-conscious, there's the Austrian-fried meatloaf with onion sauce and hash browns. Oh, and don't forget the sausages. The SM location is the biggest; the City Park Inn version is the smallest, with only four tables; and the Wayne's Inn location is a favorite with travelers.

## DINING: MACTAN ISLAND

✪ **Cowrie Cove.** Oceanfront, Shangri-La's Mactan Island Resort. ☎ **32/231-0288.** Formal dress required. Main courses P320–P600 (US$8–US$15). AE, DC, JCB, MC, V. Daily 6–10pm. FILIPINO/SEAFOOD.

Life doesn't get much better than this, sitting under the stars with the sizzle of seafood jostling your taste buds awake. If the stars are too dizzying, sit under the huge canvas parasols on the wooden deck that juts out into the sea. Fresh catches might include blue marlin, grouper, lobster, prawns, or squid, and it's all grilled to perfection. Roving guitarists will serenade you with a varied repertoire including anything from a *Kundiman*, a local love song, to Jimmy Buffet's "Margaritaville." An experience not to be missed!

**The Garden Patio.** Shangri La's Mactan Island Resort. ☎ **32/231-0288.** P220–P440 (US$5.50–US$11). Daily 6am–11pm. AE, DC, JCB, MC, V. INTERNATIONAL.

There are no walls in this restaurant, just panels slid back for you to take in the view of rolling lawns and the bougainvillea in full bloom. The setting is perfect for breakfast, lunch, dinner, or snacks. Fresh fruit and freshly baked breads, pasta and salad bar, sushi and sashimi, noodles, curry, carvery, buffet. . . whew! You'll scream for their

---

**Travel Trivia: Aquatic Marriages**

Trade in the tux for a wet suit and tank and follow Father Ray to a unique matri-monial chapel below the sea off Pescador Island. He will marry you underwater for a small fee. Just ask at any dive shop, and don't forget the ring!

---

homemade ice cream: mango, avocado, jackfruit, or ube (purple yam), all dispensed from a sorbetero, the local old-fashioned ice-cream cart.

## SPORTS & OTHER OUTDOOR ACTIVITIES

**GOLF**    Cebu Country Club, on the outskirts of the city, about 5 minutes from Cebu Plaza (☎ 32/74-901, 74-905 or 74-813), has 18 holes on a relatively flat green. Weekday fees will run you about US$70; weekends are much higher, at US$120 a day. Caddy fees are US$9 and a set of clubs is US$12 per day.

**TENNIS**    The Cebu Plaza Hotel has tennis courts where nonguests can play.

**SCUBA DIVING**    Cebu has three main diving destinations to choose from: Mactan Island, Sogod on the northeast coast, and Moalboal in the southwest. The advantage of Mactan is that it is close by. A number of beach resorts offer diving courses, and there are also separate diving schools. Some good dive operators in Cebu and Mactan Island are Club Kontiki, on Maribago Beach, ☎ 32/86-555, 40-0292, 40-0310; Scotties Dive Center at Shangri La's Mactan Island Resort, ☎ 32/231-5060; and Seaquest in Cebu City, ☎ 32/210-2650. Moalboal, particularly Panagsama Beach, is an even more popular area for diving (see below).

## OTHER THINGS TO SEE & DO

Most of Cebu City and Mactan's sights can easily be seen in a half day on foot or by taxi; you can be eating dinner at the Cebu Plaza by sunset. Start at **Fort San Pedro** in Cebu City, which served as the first Spanish settlement in the Philippines. Since then it has been a stronghold for Filipino revolutionaries, a defense post, barracks for the U.S. army, a prison camp during the Japanese occupation, a city zoo, and now a small park. Entry is P15 (US40¢). Next to the fort is **Plaza Independencia,** where remnants of the cross left by Magellan and Fray Pedro Valderrama are on display in the gazebo. Across the street at the **Basilica Minore del Santo Nino,** dating from 1740, you can see the image of the Santo Niño thought to have been left by Magellan. Continue along Burgos Street for a few blocks and turn right at the fork, and you will see the **Casa Gorordo Museum and Art Gallery.** For photo buffs, the museum houses his-toric and cultural photos of old Cebu, as well as contemporary art and paintings. It's open Monday to Saturday from 9am to 5pm and there is a P24 (US60¢) fee. If you have important questions to be answered, head to the **Phu San Buddhist Temple** or the Taoist **Cebu Heavenly Temple of Charity,** where you'll see locals praying and seeking advice from prayer intercessors. From here, seek out the **Carbon Market,** via the city's main boulevard of Colon Street, for its warren of bazaars that can turn up some interesting bargains. Sample some of the region's famous mangoes, fresh or dried; otap, a crunchy sugar-coated biscuit; and turrones, a rolled wafer filled with peanut or cashew candy.

Mactan Island, a 20-minute drive away, is a world unto itself of beaches, resorts, and diving. Although most of the resorts occupy their own private beach here, you can pay a small fee, usually P200 (US$5), for a day's admittance, which usually includes use of the pool too. The **Mactan Shangri-La** has the best stretch of beach on Mactan Island, and the **Tambuli Beach Villa and Club** is also a nice place to relax.

## SHOPPING

Mactan Island is known for its custom-made guitars; try the street stalls in Abuno and Maribago if you're interested in taking one home with you. Shell collectors should check out **Jewel of the Sea,** STC Campus, General Maxilom Avenue in Cebu City (☎ **32/52-807**), where proceeds support Mother Teresa's legacy at the orphanage. For local artists' paintings and antiques, go to **Arthaus,** off Archbishop Reyes Street, in downtown Cebu City. And of course, you can find almost anything at any of the local malls in the city, such as **Gaisano's,** off Colon Street; **Robinson's,** off MacArthur Boulevard; and **Ayala Center,** off Gorordo Avenue.

## CEBU CITY & MACTAN ISLAND AFTER DARK

Compared to Manila, you'll find Cebu City a pretty lively place. **Bai Disco** in the Cebu Plaza Hotel is the most popular spot for jet-setting locals and expatriates to congregate. For bars, try **Prince William's Pub,** North Escario Street, and **Street Moritz,** off Gorordo Avenue, for a Euro pub atmosphere. **Tops,** on Busay Hill about 3 miles (5km) north of the Cebu Plaza Hotel, is popular with locals, offering splendid views of the city and distant islands. It's one of the more romantic spots, especially during sunset, and you can buy beer and sodas at the stalls. On Mactan Island, each resort offers its own nightlife. The **Shangri-La**'s nocturnal cornucopia will give you the most options, or if you're feeling lucky head for the **casino** at the Waterfront Hotel.

# MOALBOAL

Located about 56 miles (90km) south of Cebu City, on the other side of the island, the quaint town of Moalboal, along with tiny Panagsama Beach a short distance away, is a popular destination for budget travelers and serious divers looking to visit the world-class sites along Pescador Island and Santa Rosa. They're mostly small fishing villages, and the only thing for the traveler to do here is dive; it hasn't been a beach destination since a severe typhoon came through several years back. You can, however, hike to beautiful waterfalls, take day trips to White Beach, or horseback ride in the scenic countryside. Most resorts and restaurants are very basic and family-owned, with a friendly, congenial atmosphere. The villagers are the friendliest I've met, and it's a nice change from the coddled resort mode you may have just left.

## GETTING THERE

Non-air-conditioned buses leave every hour from the South Bus Terminal in Cebu City. They're hot, though, and not that comfortable to start with, so wait for the air-conditioned bus, which is supposed to leave every 1½ hours. They are not that dependable, so your best bet is to simply arrive at the terminal and see what you get. ABC, Autobus, Cetrasco, Philippine Eagle, SM Liner, and Villaneuva all make the trip to Moalboal. It takes about 3 hours and will cost you P40 (US$1). If you're going to Panagsama, let the driver know, and he will drop you off at the turnoff where tricycles are waiting to take you the bumpy 2km to the beach (P20 or US50¢).

Your other option is to arrange private transport from your resort or hotel in Cebu City or Mactan.

## ACCOMMODATIONS

Panagsama Beach has no world-class accommodations or resorts. The places you will find are basic, meant for those just passing through or for serious divers who just want a place to rest their head and equipment. You will get private bathrooms, and some places even have televisions and air-conditioning. Prices will range from US$10 to US$20 for the more primitive cottages to US$40 to US$60 for the more complete rooms.

**Sunshine Pensione House** (☎ 918/773-3021) offers small rooms—nothing glamorous. It's one of only two places here with a pool—a welcome escape from the heat, since there isn't really a beach. They have a dive shop and a good restaurant that serves Swiss food.

**Quo Vadis Beach Resort** (☎ 918/770-8684, 771-1853) will give you air-conditioning, hot water, and a minibar. Choose from native cottages or rooms, and enjoy their beautiful pool. The new seafood restaurant should be open by the time you read this; the menu looks excellent! It's definitely one of the better places here.

**Sumisid Lodge** (☎ 918/770-7986) has some air-conditioning rooms. There's no hot water, but the price includes three meals a day. The Lodge is one of two places that actually has a beach front. Don't get an attic room: quaint they may be, but heat rises! Seaquest dive shop is here.

**Hannah's Place** (☎ 918/771-3439) is very cute and has air-conditioning, hot water, private bath, and minibar. The beds aren't very comfortable (it's like hitting a dense piece of rotting wood), but the location, at the south end of the beach, makes it quieter than other places in the heart of the action. The restaurant here is very good, and the price includes breakfast.

The centrally located **Cabana Resort** (☎ 918/770-7599) is the closest thing you'll find to a real resort here. All major credit cards are accepted, and you get air-conditioning, television, and thick mattresses. It's situated in a private garden courtyard, so it's quiet and peaceful. Large rooms are uniquely decorated and have verandas. (Suites no. 1 and no. 7 are the biggest and the best.) The Italian restaurant is excellent.

## DINING

For such small towns, you'll get a pretty varied dining experience in Moalboal and Panagsama. Most places serve local cuisine in traditional open-air settings. Prices are cheap, ranging from US$2 to US$10 for a huge meal.

**Love's Bar and Restaurant** (open daily 6am to 10pm), at the far south end of the beach, is a pleasant place to sit and eat local cuisine. They can also organize picnic lunches and barbecues for day trips to White Beach or Kawasan Falls. **Visaya Bar and Pizza House** (open daily 7am to 11pm), in the middle of the beach, serves Swiss and German food and pizza. They have a variety to satisfy any taste, whether it's seafood, steaks, pasta, or zigeuner schnitzel. **The Last Filling Station** (7am to whenever) occupies a prime location right along the sea and the main path. It's a popular place not just for its lazy-dazy people watching, but for its pita sandwiches, macrobiotic selections, Thai dishes, and delicious pizza that's even better than Visaya's. The bar selections are excellent as well. **Hannah's Restaurant** (open daily 6am to 10pm) specializes in garlic dishes and international specialties. (Garlic lovers and their friends look out!) Check their daily specials, which include some variation of lamb chops, filet mignon with pepper sauce, and the catch of the day. All the way at the south end of the beach is an excellent place for Italian food: **Franceska's Place** (open daily 6:30pm to midnight). Laid-back 1940s music plays throughout the high-beamed native pavilion. It feels like a real restaurant, not the usual local place with a handwritten menu. The food takes a while to arrive, and they go heavy on the butter, but the homemade gnocchi, other pastas, and meat dishes are very good. The bar is stocked and they have billiard tables.

## SCUBA DIVING

There are seven dive shops on the tiny beach, offering similar prices and destinations. **Savedra Dive Center** (☎ 63/918-770-8193 and fax: 63/32-340-9935), which also has a shop on Alona Beach in Bohol, is excellent. Other shops include: **Visaya Divers,** ☎ 918/770-8684 or 771-1853; **Abyss Divers,** ☎ 918/773-3021; **Ocean Safari,**

☎ 918/772-1873; **Neptune Diving Unlimited,** ☎ 918/770-7951; **Seaquest Dive Center,** ☎ 32/346-9629; and **Nelson Scuba Diving School,** ☎ 918/773-3730. Prices are fixed among the competing shops: US$60 introductory dive, US$250 open water course, US$180 advanced open water course, US$260 rescue course, and US$600 dive master course. Single dives without courses are US$20 including gear or US$16 with your own gear.

   **The Sites**   The House Reef is close, and perfect for night dives. White Beach is more challenging, with wall dives, caves, and overhangs. Some say Pescador Island is the best site they've ever seen; its enormous mushroom rising off the sea bottom is rich with a variety of hard and soft corals. Big fish, including sharks, are often spotted here. And for a bit of intrigue, try Sunken Island, an underwater mountain rising from unknown depths. It's a tough dive due to strong currents, and if it weren't for the marker-buoy you wouldn't find it.

## OTHER ACTIVITIES

Horse trekking, river and rock climbing, volcano trekking, mountain biking, canoeing, and sailing can all be arranged through the newly opened ✪ **Planet Action Adventure** on Panagsama Beach ( ☎ 32/474-0024; e-mail: planet@solnets.net). Trips range from easy half-day activities to extended hardcore challenges, and can be custom-tailored to fit your level of adventure. It's a godsend if diving isn't your thing, giving you the chance to experience serious outdoor adventures while seeing the countryside and waterfalls of the island. Lunches are included in any excursion. You can also rent mountain bikes for independent discovery of the island, for about P200 (US$5) a day.

## 8  Bohol

Bohol Island, southeast of Cebu in the center of the Philippine archipelago, is "God's Little Paradise." Although it doesn't have as much to offer as some of the other island destinations here, Bohol's attractions are quite unique and varied. There are caves with stalagmite formations, natural parks, centuries-old churches, hanging bridges, waterfalls, and beautiful beaches. Bohol is also a diver's playground—its diverse marine life and coral reefs are rated among the best in the world. The people are the friendliest I've met, and you really get a true sense of what village life is like here.

### GETTING THERE

**BY PLANE**   Philippine Airlines ( ☎ 2/816-6691) offers a 2-hour daily flight from Manila to Tagbilaran, Bohol's capital, at 9:30am, for P1,688 (US$42) one-way. There is no outgoing service. Tricycles to the city center at Agora Market should cost P5 (US13¢) per person. Three people can fit if one doesn't mind straddling the bike. Tricycles to Alona Beach on Panglao Island should cost P150 to P200 (US$3.75–US$5) total for the ride. Otherwise, you can flag an air-conditioned taxi for about P300 (US$7.50) to Panglao Island. Taxis are generally not metered; you'll have to negotiate with the driver.

   Another option is to fly into Cebu City (see "Getting There," above), and take a taxi to the pier for the 2-hour ferry to Bohol. **Supercat** ( ☎ 32/232-3455 or 3183) leaves from Pier 4 at 7:15am and 11am for P150 (US$3.75); **Bullet Express** ( ☎ 32/255-1384) has departures from Pier 1 at 6am, 10am, and 3pm daily, for the same price. You can take a tricycle into town from the pier for about P5 per person, or even to Panglao Island, for about P100 (US$2.50), although it will take about an hour to get there. Taxis are quicker and will cost about P200 (US$5).

**BY BOAT**   **WG&A Superferry,** Pier 4 North Harbor, Manila ( ☎ 2/894-3211 or 893-2211), makes trips to Bohol twice a week for P600 (US$15). Superferry 5 leaves

Manila on Tuesdays at 7am (26 hours). Superferry 7 leaves Saturday at 7am (26 hours). You can get private cabins for a bit more, but the air-conditioning usually doesn't work, and cabins can be a bit stale-smelling and unpleasant. Bunks occupy the higher decks and come with padding if you wish.

## GETTING AROUND

**BY BUS**    Linking the main outlying towns to Tagbilaran are the St. Jude Bus Lines at the bus terminal on East Butalid Street. They cost about P20 (US50¢) for a 2-hour trip. Use your judgement when you select a bus at the station. If one looks rusty and rickety, than I suggest finding another one in the lot.

**BY RENTAL CAR**    Bohol Travel and Tours on Carlos P. Garcia Avenue in Tagbilaran (☎ 38/411-3840, 411-2984) can arrange a rental car and driver for you, for around P1,500 to P2,000 (US$37.50–US$50) a day.

**BY MOTORBIKE**    This is the best way to get around and see the island. An all-day rental will run you P600 (US$15) and can be arranged at **Bohol Travel and Tours** on Carlos P. Garcia Avenue in Tagbilaran (☎ **38/411-3840,** 411-2984). On Alona Beach, try **Sunshine Travel and Tours.** Ask for Jessie.

## VISITOR INFORMATION

There is no tourism office in Tagbilaran, but **Bohol Travel and Tours** (☎ **38/411-3840**) or **Sunshine Travel and Tours** (no phone) can arrange island tours and handle ticket bookings and confirmations, visa information, and accommodations.

# Fast Facts: Bohol

**Banks/Currency Exchange**    In Tagbilaran, Allied Bank and Philippine National Bank on Carlos P. Garcia Avenue will change cash and traveler's checks. PCI Bank at the city center has the only ATM and can give you cash on your MasterCard. On Panglao Island, the Alona Kew and Aquatica resorts on Alona Beach change cash and traveler's checks. Or try Patrick at Savedra & Great White Dive Shop (no phone).

**Doctors/Hospitals**    Ramiro Hospital (☎ 38/411-3515) and Tabilaran Community Hospital (☎ 38/411-3324) are small but decent facilities. Otherwise, Cebu City is your best bet.

**Emergencies**    Dial ☎ 166 for police, ☎ 161 for fire, and ☎ 32/340-5643 for rescue helicopter. A decompression chamber is located at Camp Lapu-Lapu in Cebu City, ☎ 32/310-709.

**Post Office/Mail**    In Tagbilaran it's on JS Torralba Street, near the town hall. Panglao town also has a small post office. Most hotels can post letters and post cards for you.

**Telephone**    Tagbilaran: The Philippine Long Distance Telephone Company (PLDT) on Noli Me Tangere Street offers fax and long distance service. On Panglao Island there are only cell phones. Overseas and local calls can be placed at the Alona Kew Resort and most of the dive shops. The area code is 38.

## PANGLAO ISLAND

Why stay in the city when a bridge connects you to beautiful Panglao Island, only 45 minutes away? It's a quaint, quiet, safe beach destination that affords an opportunity to see true Filipino life in the nearby villages. The serene, sleepy **Alona Beach** is the

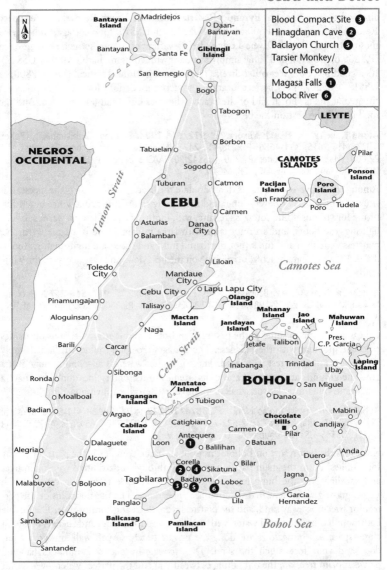

# Cebu and Bohol

Blood Compact Site ❸
Hinagdanan Cave ❷
Baclayon Church ❺
Tarsier Monkey/
  Corela Forest ❹
Magasa Falls ❶
Loboc River ❻

**LEYTE**

**NEGROS OCCIDENTAL**

*Tanon Strait*

**CEBU**

**CAMOTES ISLANDS**

*Camotes Sea*

**BOHOL**

**Chocolate Hills**

*Cebu Strait*

*Bohol Sea*

N

Bantayan Island — Madridejos
Daan-Bantayan
Bantayan — Santa Fe
Gibitngil Island
San Remegio
Bogo
Tabogon
Borbon
Tabuelan
Sogod
Catmon
Tuburan
Carmen
Asturias
Danao City
Balamban
Liloan
Toledo City
Mandaue City
Cebu City — Lapu Lapu City
Pinamungajan
Talisay — Olango Island
Aloguinsan
Naga — Mactan Island
Barili
Carcar
Ronda
Sibonga
Moalboal
Badian
Argao
Alegria
Dalaguete
Alcoy
Malabuyoc
Boljoon
Samboan
Oslob
Santander

Pilar
Ponson Island
Pacijan Island
Poro Island
San Francisco
Poro — Tudela
Mahanay Island
Jao Island
Mahuwan / Island
Jandayan Island
Jetafe
Talibon
Pres. C.P. Garcia
Inabanga
Trinidad
Ubay
Laping Island
Mantatao Island
San Miguel
Pangangan Island
Tubigon
Danao
Cabilao Island
Catigbian
Mabini
Antequera
Carmen
Pilar
Candijay
Loon
Balilihan
Batuan
Corella
Sikatuna
Bilar
Duero
Anda
Tagbilaran
Baclayon — Loboc
Jagna
Panglao
Lila
Garcia Hernandez
Balicasag Island
Pamilacan Island

❶ ❷ ❸ ❹ ❺ ❻

place to stay, with its long stretches of white sand and world-class diving opportunities around the many surrounding islands. Alona Beach has yet to be overrun with tourists and shooter bars, and it's probably the loveliest beach around after Boracay. Sea urchins make swimming and wading through the water difficult, though.

See "Getting There" above for information on getting to the island by taxi or tricycle from the airport or the pier.

## ACCOMMODATIONS

Along Alona Beach are numerous native-style resorts that all offer comfortable, convenient cottages, and most have restaurants. Don't expect hot water or air-conditioning, though. **Pyramid Resort, Alonaville Beach Resort,** and **Aquatica Resort** all charge about P500 to P600 (US$12.50–US$15) for a cottage, and provide mosquito nets. **Bohol Divers Lodge** offers a variety of rooms, some air-conditioned (P2,200 or US$55), and some simply standard with common bath (P480 or US$12). It's a good place to meet other divers. The charming **Alona Tropical** (P680–P800, or US$17–US$20) offers perfect location and accommodations for a budget price. It's situated at the far north end of the beach, where it's quiet and less crowded. And the food here is the best on the beach.

**Alona Kew White Beach Resort.** ☎ **912/516-2904.** Booking: Tagbilaran City, Bohol, ☎ 38/411-2615, 411-4686. Fax 38/411-2471. Alonakew@mozcom.com. 35 units. A/C. P2,000 (US$50) A/C suite; P1,700 (US$42.50) A/C superior; P750–P900 (US$18.75–US$22.50) fan rooms. AE, DC, JCB, MC, V.

Among the native-style cottages that populate the beach, Alona Kew is the nicest. It is situated in the heart of everything, and is the only resort that actually has beach furniture for your use. The cottages are cute, with mother-of-pearl lamps, warm subdued lighting, tile floors, and a vanity table with large mirror. There is a large wardrobe, mattresses are firm and thick (not the foam kind), and sheets are high-quality. Rooms 8, 10, 12, and 14 are beachfront, giving you the best views and easy access to the white sand.

**Balicasag Dive Resort.** Balicasag Island, Panglao, Bohol. ☎ **912/516-2675.** Booking: Makati, Manila, ☎ 2/812-1984. Fax 2/812-1164. 20 units. P2,880 (US$72) double. AE, DC, JCB, MC, V.

Balicasag is home to some of the best reefs in Bohol, and it attracts serious divers. It's especially popular with the Japanese. The cottages are comfortable but basic, simply giving you a place to rest your head. There is no hot water or air-conditioning, just a fan. The grounds are beautiful and quiet, thanks to its solitary location. They have a restaurant, billiard table, volleyball, and, of course, excellent diving facilities.

**Bohol Beach Club.** Panglao Island. ☎ **38/411-5222** to 24. Fax 38/411-5226. Booking: UN Avenue, Ermita, Manila, ☎ 2/522-2301 to 03. Fax 2/522-2304. 65 units. A/C MINIBAR TV TEL. US$65–US$100 double. AE, DC, JCB, MC, V.

Known as the best resort on Bohol, this popular beach complex is the perfect getaway for families. From the main pavilion, you walk through a path lined with palm trees and spotlights to the bungalows. All the traditional-style rooms are covered with *Cogon* grass, giving them that deserted isle appearance. The tile floors inside are perfect for sweeping away sand, and the mattresses are thick and comfortable. The marble bathroom has hot and cold water, with excellent water pressure, and there is plenty of closet space. All bungalows are along the private beach, so you walk out your front door and your feet touch the sand. The strategically placed hammocks hanging between palm trees are the only thing between you and the perfect water—watch out for sea urchins though. Enjoy a massage, swim, or the Jacuzzi after playing tennis or eating from their buffet or Peammila ("good taste") Bar.

**✪ Jul Resort.** Panglao Island. ☎ **38/411-4999.** Fax 38/411-2697. 7 units. A/C MINIBAR TV. P1,700 (US$42.50) A/C cottage, P700 (US$17.50) non-A/C cottage, P3,500 (US$87.50) for 5-bedroom main house. AE, MC, V.

A jewel called Jul on a cliff by the sea, this hotel is located about 15 minutes from Alona Beach, away from the huddle of the resorts. Its unique sparkle would only tarnish the competition. You'll notice a gradual metamorphosis as you drive here—from paved road, to red clay, to tall grass and fields of corn, until you finally arrive at the quiet sea. The main house is perfect for large groups, with its kitchen, stereo system, rustic charm, and five spacious bedrooms, each with a double bed. The cottages have that *Miami Vice* feel, decorated in pinks and lavenders. If you know your antiques, you'll be surprised at the incredible pieces that seem to be there for everyday use—a flower vase, a rocking chair, the relaxing *butaka* seats on the porch. Lifted from the matriarch's private collection, they stand as reminders of the breezy trade that went on between the island and dynastic China. Bathrooms are quite luxurious, with step-up tub and bay window. Tables come set with coffee and tea. The resort won't keep you distracted with beach toys like water skis, but there is a gorgeous, airy reading room saturated with natural light and a collection that includes the complete works of Nostradamus and Shakespeare. You get a lot of personal attention from the staff. They'll run errands for you, cook, serve, and tell you stories. You can even drop by the kitchen and watch the cook, or cook up something yourself. In the evenings relax on the sundeck overlooking the gardens and sea, or walk down the wooden stairs to the beach. As one guest put it, "If God was on earth, he would live here."

**Kalipayan Beach Resort**. Danao, Panglao Island. ☎ **38/411-3060.** Fax 38/411-3615. Meridian@mozcom.com. 18 units. A/C. P1,400 (US$35), includes breakfast. AE, DC, JCB, MC, V.

If you want to be on Alona Beach but away from the main drag, this newly opened bed-and-breakfast is your best bet. Situated up on a cliff at the south end of the beach, the not-yet-finished Kalipayan is well on its way to becoming a cozy, complete resort. The landscape is still quite barren, but it has plenty of potential and space, not to mention a great cliff-side pool. The cottages, neatly arranged in a row, are spacious and clean. Decor is basic, a little generic, and the fluorescent lights aren't so nice. The family-style rooms are larger and can accommodate a double and two twin beds. There are a restaurant, room service, laundry (with machines), and pressing. The hotel offers diving through the Atlantic Dive Shop, island tours, and transportation transfers. Every Monday there is an acoustic band—folk rock of sorts—in the restaurant. And to add a touch of nostalgia, the owners decided to leave up the 30-year-old cliff-side tree house where the family used to come and vacation. I suggested putting up telescopes to bring the stars a bit closer—we'll see!

**TGH Casa Nova Garden**. Danao, Panglao Island. ☎ **38/198111.** 11 units (one with A/C). P1,000 (US$25) family room, P450–P500 (US$11.25–US$12.50) ordinary, P600–P800 (US$15–US$20) standard. No credit cards.

This cute, colorful resort is located behind the Kalipayan Resort, set back from the beach among goats, chickens, and traditional-style houses. It's a 5- to 10-minute walk to the beach, and the only real reasons to stay here over the more convenient beach locations are the pool and overgrown tennis court. All the rooms are clean and quiet and have private bathrooms with no hot water. If you can wake the staff up, they will show you to the billiard table and serve you some food from the restaurant.

## DINING

**Alona Kew Restaurant**. Alona Beach. Main courses P150–P500 (US$3.75–US$12.50). AE, DC, JCB, MC, V with a minimum purchase of P500 (US$12.50). Daily 6am–10pm. FIL-IPINO/INTERNATIONAL.

More expensive than most places here, Alona Kew's open-air bamboo pavilion—decorated with conch shells galore—dishes up hearty portions of steamed crabs, sizzling gambas (shrimps), and other seafood. You can select your own fresh fish from the tank and they will prepare it however you wish. There are tons of sizzling platters here, from squid to tenderloin tips. They also have a variety of sauces like lemon butter, chili-tomato, Thousand Island, and their mother-in-law sauce, a spicy, sour, vinegar and soy combination.

**Alona Seaside.** Alona Beach. Main courses P70–P185 (US$1.75–US$4.63). No credit cards. Daily 6am–midnight. FILIPINO.

You can't beat the prices at this local beachfront joint. Select from fish, curries, adobo, and menudo dishes. It's a good, simple place with fast service.

✪ **Alona Tropical.** Alona Beach. P90–P280 (US$2.25–US$7) main courses. No credit cards. Daily 5:30am–midnight. INTERNATIONAL.

What a gorgeous spot! From the southern part of the beach, walk the path that winds through rows of curvaceous palm trees along the white-sand beach; you'll find the Alona Tropical Restaurant in a native-style cabana right on the beach. The menu offers all the familiar fare, but it is by far the best on the beach. This is obvious when you see the crowd that develops after 7pm. Try the grilled chicken breast, or the pork chop with onions and a cucumber-tomato salad in a sweet vinaigrette. Down it with some wine or a fruit shake, and top it all off with a banana split.

**Bohol Divers Lodge.** Alona Beach. P80–P400 (US$2–US$10) main courses. AE, DC, JCB, MC, V. (Give them an hour or two's notice if you plan on using your card.) Daily 6am–midnight. FILIPINO/INTERNATIONAL/FRENCH.

Most visitors give this place two thumbs up for service, food, and the view from the second floor open-air terrace. Locals and tourists rave about the Filipino food and mixed seafood sizzler platter. Its claim to fame, though, is the imported Australian beef, so tender you don't even need a knife!

**Flying Dog and Kamalig.** Alona Beach. P70–P200 (US$1.75–US$5) main courses. No credit cards. Daily 6am–midnight. GERMAN/ITALIAN.

These two neighboring restaurants get the award for best personality. The art and pictures are entertaining and the food, German or Italian, is good and varied. You'll get good German beer at the Flying Dog and a tasty dish of pasta at the Kamalig. Get an outside table in the shared space and enjoy both at the same time!

## DIVING

Simply walk the stretch of beach and take your pick from the seven dive shops here (prices are the same). **Savedra Great White Dive Shop** is friendly and fun. Their outings tend to have fewer people than at **Atlantis Dive Center,** which seems to cater to large groups of Germans. Balicasag Island, with its impressive corals, house morays, and larger fish, is only 20 minutes from Alona Beach by pumpboat. Another popular site is Pamilican Island, with shallow caves and sea turtles.

## SHOPPING

You can't leave Bohol without a traditional basket made from nito, bamboo, sig-id, and other vines in **Antequera,** north of Tagbilaran. Have a taxi take you there. Sunday is the perfect day to go—it's market day, so come early to get your pick of the better items. You can also find shops selling baskets in Tagbilaran, though with less variety.

In Panglao, you will no doubt see women selling shells on the beach and in small boats while you dive. These are unique-looking, deep-sea shells, and make excellent gifts. You should pay about half of their first offer.

## CHOCOLATE HILLS

Located 55km from Tagbilaran City is a landscape of Chocolate. Chocolate Hills that is. Scoop after scoop, or hill after hill, stretches to the horizon as far as the eye can see. It's quite a surreal landscape, and the most famous attraction in Bohol.

Some believe the hills are limestone formations that lie atop impermeable clay. Two more interesting explanations come in the form of legends. The first tells of two giants who got into a brawl, throwing stones and sand at each other. The "battlefield," as locals call it, became the hills. The other involves a giant named Arogo whose heart was broken after his mortal lover died; the hills are said to be his tears.

A climb up 213 steps will lead you to an observation deck where you get a 360° view of the uniform hills. It's especially magnificent at sunrise or sunset.

## GETTING THERE

The best way to see Chocolate Hills and the rest of the island's sights all in 1 day is through an arranged tour. Bohol Travel and Tours in Tagbilaran (☎ 38/411-3840) and Sunshine Tours and Travel on Alona Beach (no phone) can arrange an air-conditioned car for you. Expect to pay about P1,500 (US$37.50). Along the way you'll see Baclayon Church, the Blood Compact Site, Loboc River, the Tarsier monkey, and waterfalls via boat ride (see "Attractions" below). The Hills are the last stop.

**BY MOTORBIKE**    See "Getting Around" above. The roads are not smooth, however, so be prepared for soreness and for changing a tire or two!

**BY BUS    St. Jude Bus Lines** go directly to the Hills. Buses leave almost hourly for Carmen from Tagbilaran's bus terminal on East Butalid Street. It's P20 (US50¢) for the 2-hour trip. Tell the driver you want Chocolate Hills and you will be dropped off at the turn-off, where you can either walk 1km uphill to the Chocolate Hills Complex, or pay P10 (US25¢) per person for a motorbike lift.

## ACCOMMODATIONS

The Chocolate Hills Complex is the only place to stay in the area. Unfortunately, it's a run-down, cobwebbed, chipped-paint, picked-foam mattress mess! You're better off doing a day tour, seeing the Hills, and returning to Tagbilaran or Panglao Island for the night. If you must stay here, do so at your own risk. Solo female travelers should be extra careful: It's never very full, doors are not very secure—and let's not even get into the peephole I discovered. The pool is the best thing going for it. The restaurant is pretty good for lunch or dinner and has a terrace with great views.

## ATTRACTIONS

The best way to get to these places is to hire a car. A round-trip tour will take a day and you can stop as you please at sites along the way. The bus route toward Chocolate Hills follows the road most of these sites are on, but you obviously have less control over when and where you stop.

**Bohol Museum.** A. Hontanosas St., Tagbilaran. Open daily 9am–5pm (closed noon–1:30pm).

Once the home of President Carlos P. Garcia (the fourth president of the Philippines) and his family, this museum gives you a feel for what Bohol was, is, and will be. On display are memorabilia, relics, and samples of the island's flora and fauna.

**Blood Compact Site.** 10-min. ride by tricycle or taxi from Tagbilaran.

In 1565 native chieftain Datu Sikatuna forged a blood compact here with Spaniard Miguel Lopez de Legaspi to foster friendly relations between their two nations. It's considered the first treaty of friendship between the native people and the Spaniards in the Philippines.

**Hinagdanan Cave.** 4 miles (6km) from Tagbilaran.

A 20-minute ride by bus or jeepney, the cave is an eerie underworld of stalactites and stalagmites that form sculptures in the underground pool. You can go caving and swim in the pool.

**Baclayon Church.** Baclayon, 4 miles (7km) from Tagbilaran City. P10 (US25¢) per person, Mon–Sat 8am–5pm, Sun 9am–5pm.

Built by the Jesuits in 1595, this is the oldest stone church in the country. The massive edifice still retains its centuries-old design. Painted murals and relics from the 16th century can be seen inside. The convent houses a museum where old urns, chalices, and other relics are preserved.

**Tarsier Monkey.** In the forest of Corela, 6 miles (10km) from Tagbilaran.

The Tarsius Syrichta is the world's smallest primate, measuring 4 to 5 inches, with a tail longer than its body. Its big brown eyes, large hairless ears, and long claws—not to mention its ability to rotate its head nearly 360° and leap like a frog—make this quite a unique animal. They are on display at the edge of the forest off the main road toward Chocolate Hills. In their open cage they are free to climb the trees or eat crickets off your arm.

**Magasa Falls.** Antequera, 12 miles (20km) from Tagbilaran.

A 45-minute ride by bus or jeepney, these falls are about 25 feet tall, with verdant forest as the scenic backdrop to the placid waters.

**Loboc River.** In the small town of Loay.

Take a motorized pumpboat from the bamboo hanging bridge in Loay, snaking your way through the serene waters and palm-fringed banks. The hour-long ride ends at Busay Falls, where you can jump in for a swim.

**Balicasag Island.** 45 minutes by pumpboat from Alona Beach.

More beautiful beaches abound here, not to mention excellent scuba. The island is a Coast Guard reservation, and its surrounding waters are declared a fish sanctuary. It's a great day trip: Hire a boat for about P1,000 (US$25) for the day, catch some fish, and have a picnic on the island. Any of the resorts will be able to arrange boat hire.

# 9 Boracay

Boracay is most people's idea of paradise—talcum powder–white beaches; crystal-clear, warm shallow waters; brilliant sunsets; swaying palm trees; tropical sunshine; peerless blue skies; and colorful fruits and flowers. It is the Philippines' best known and best loved island. Considered a well-kept secret by wandering backpackers when it was first discovered, the remote deserted isle has now become a full-service stop for droves of tourists all wanting a piece of paradise. Some complain that the island has lost its innocence and prefer more remote locations on Palawan. But Boracay remains so pristine and beautiful that it's hard to turn your back on. You'll find most of the resorts, restaurants, bars, and shops on White Beach, a 2-mile (3.5km) stretch of cool, silky sand. Vendors comb the beach between all three boat stations selling shells, jewelry, fruit, sunglasses, and hour-long massages. Take to the hills on a motor scooter, jet ski along the calm surf, dive the reefs, or put your hat over your head and prop yourself up against a palm tree with a good, long book.

## GETTING THERE

**BY PLANE**   The fastest way to get to Boracay is to fly the tiny planes of **Asian Spirit** or **Pacific Air,** which will cost about P3,160 (US$79) one-way from Manila. The 1-hour flight takes you to Caticlan Airport, where the terminal is a nipa hut. The airport is a short motorized tricycle ride (P30, or US75¢) away from Caticlan port. From the port, it's a 15-minute boat ride (P15, or US40¢) to boat station no. 2, midway along White Beach. **Air Philippines** offers a cheaper flight, but a more involved,

# Boracay Island

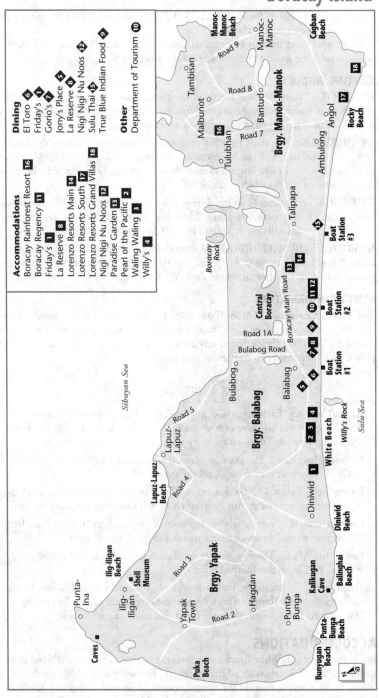

**Dining**
El Toro **6**
Friday's **1**
Gorio's **7**
Jony's Place **5**
La Reserve **8**
Nigi Nigi Nu Noos **12**
Sulu Thai **15**
True Blue Indian Food **9**

**Other**
Department of Tourism **10**

**Accommodations**
Boracay Rainforest Resort **16**
Boracay Regency **11**
Friday's **1**
La Reserve **8**
Lorenzo Resorts Main **14**
Lorenzo Resorts South **17**
Lorenzo Resorts Grand Villas **18**
Nigi Nigi Nu Noos **12**
Paradise Garden **13**
Pearl of the Pacific **2**
Waling Waling **3**
Willy's **4**

705

longer route to Kalibo, for P1,970 (US$49.25). From Kalibo it's a 90-minute bus journey to Caticlan port, P150 (US$3.75).

Don't wear good trousers or shoes on the way to Boracay, because you'll have to wade through the water getting on and off the outrigger boats.

## GETTING AROUND

**ON FOOT**    White Beach is where all the shops, resorts, and restaurants are, and everything is within walking distance. Walking from boat station no. 1 all the way through to boat station no. 4 will take you about an hour.

**BY TRICYCLE**    You won't have any problem finding a tricycle during the day, but at night they are hard to come by. Tricycles will normally charge P10 (US25¢) for any point along White Beach, but as a tourist you will most likely be charged a bit more. Always agree on the price before taking off.

**BY BANCA**    For island hopping, diving, snorkeling, or exploring by sea, you can rent a banca almost anywhere along White Beach, or make arrangements through your resort. Rentals will cost you about P700 (US$17.50) for a half day.

**BY BICYCLE OR MOTORBIKE**    A motorbike for island exploration will cost you about P200 (US$5) an hour; bikes will cost P80 (US$2) per hour. You can arrange rentals from your resort or anywhere along White Beach.

## VISITOR INFORMATION

**The Tourist Center** (☎ 36/288-3704, 3705) located near boat station no. 2 is a one-stop shop where you can confirm travel arrangements, exchange money, post letters, receive packages, use their telecom services and fax machines, or shop in their shopping arcade. They are open daily from 9am to 6pm.

## Fast Facts: Boracay

**Banks/Currency Exchange**    Go to the Tourist Center or most resorts. The Tourist Center will also give cash advances on credit cards for a 7.5% fee. Rates will not be very good in Boracay, so try to bring enough pesos with you.

**Doctors/Hospitals**    The Boracay Medical Clinic and Drugstore (☎ 36/288-3147) is along boat station no. 2, off the main road.

**Emergencies/Police** ☎ 166. For serious illness or injury, the 505 Rescue Helicopter is in full operation. Any hotel or resort will be able to contact it for you.

**Internet/E-mail**    Some hotels will send e-mail for you. Nigi Nigi Nu Noos (see "Accommodations," below) has an Internet cafe, with one computer.

**Post Office/Mail**    There's a small post office in Balabag near boat station no. 2, but your best bet is the Tourist Office.

**Telephone**    The area code for Boracay is 36. International and national calls can be made at the Tourist Office's Telecom desk, open daily from 9am to 10pm. Many resorts also have international direct dial at the reception desk.

## ACCOMMODATIONS

Accommodations on White Beach range from the rustic and basic to high-end native-style cottages and hotels with all the amenities. The wider and whiter north end of White Beach is where most of the upscale resorts are located. Prices vary seasonally: They peak in mid-December to the first week of January, Chinese New Year, and Easter (reservations are a must during these times), and are lowest from June to October 31.

## Expensive

**Friday's Resort.** Far north end of White Beach. Bookings: 8741 Paseo De Roxas, Makati, Manila. ☎ **2/750-4488** or 750-8459. Fax 2/750-8457. fridays@boracay.webquest.com. 35 units. A/C MINIBAR TV TEL. P4,000–P6,400 (US$100–US$160) deluxe; P4,800–P7,200 (US$120–US$180) premier. AE, DC, JCB, MC, V.

Friday's cottages are situated on the finest part of the talcum-powder white-sand beach. Although simple and native—with walls of woven bamboo ribbons and framed mats, thatched roofs and wooden floors—it boasts air-conditioning, tiled baths, and direct-dial phones. Verandas outside overlook the beach, face the freshwater pool, or are nestled among the tree tops. The restaurant is one of the best on Boracay. (See "Dining" below.) A plethora of leisure activities are offered, including paddleboats, windsurfing, jet skis, island tours, volleyball, and mountain biking. You are right next door to Red Coral Diving School, which is convenient for anyone considering a course. For indoor enthusiasts there are a video library and game room with billiards, darts, and table tennis.

**Pearl of the Pacific Beach Resort.** Balabag, White Beach. ☎ **36/288-3962.** Fax 36/288-3220. Bookings: Quezon City, Manila, ☎ 2/924-4480. Fax 2/924-4482. 56 units. A/C MINIBAR TV TEL, except standard rooms. P2,880–P6,200 (US$97–US$155) standard; P4,680–P7,000 (US$117–US$175) deluxe; P5,280–P16,800 (US$132–US$420) suites. AE, DC, JCB, MC, V.

The well-appointed rooms of this contemporary resort blend in naturally with the sprawling hills and slopes along White Beach. The design is the most original of all the resorts here; the furnishings were created by a famous Filipino designer and radiate relaxation, using neutral colors, textures, and shapes. Choose from beach-level rooms or hillside cottages, connected to the main pavilion by a funky zigzag industrial metal bridge. The cottages were under renovation when I was there, but the suites are very nice, with seaward views. Each suite is two levels; the beds and bathroom are on the top level, and a few steps down takes you to the living room, where two people can sleep on the sofas. The rod iron poster beds are plush and comfortable, and the bathrooms are large, with separate shower and bath, a scale, and unfinished wooden wardrobes with sliding doors. If you find yourself on the hillside and feeling a little lazy, a van can escort you down to the beach. There's fun and sports galore here, as with most resorts in the area. Just inquire at the desk. At the Princesa Rita Restaurant, you can enjoy the international cuisine and beach views in an alfresco whitewashed space with soft wood lighting and piped-in music. The Principe Alberto Bar makes cool and smooth fruit shakes.

**✪ Waling Waling Beach Hotel.** Balabag, White Beach. ☎ **36/288-5555** to 60. Fax 36/288-4555. Bookings: Manila, 2/ 724-2089, 727-7493. Fax 2/721-4927. 23 units. AC MINIBAR TV TEL. P3,600–P4,000 (US$90–US$100) standard; P4,000–P5,600 (US$100–US$140) deluxe; P5,600–P8,000 (US$140–US$200) suites. AE, DC, JCB, MC, V.

What stands out about this place is that every room's private terrace looks out onto White Beach. You're directly on a peaceful part of the beach but only a stone's throw away from the action. Unlike the traditional nipa cottage style of so many other resorts here, the Mediterranean-style façade and interior will make you feel at home, with large, spacious rooms, thick mattresses, dresser drawers, and large TVs. The wooden lounge chairs and side tables are perfect for sunbathing, sipping a mango shake, or flagging down a passing masseuse. Be sure to inquire about special promo rates—excellent bargains. Amenities include laundry service, room service, and airport transfers. The friendly staff can arrange water sports and island activities. The restaurant and bar are great for hanging out, and the seafood is fresh and terrific, especially the jumbo stuffed prawns. They can also arrange for a seafood barbecue on the beach for a group.

**Willy's Beach Resort.** Balabag, White Beach. ☎ **36/288-3151,** 3395. Fax 36/288-3016. 40 units. A/C MINIBAR TV TEL. P4,600–P5,400 (US$115–US$135) single or double. AE, MC, DC, V, JCB.

Right across from Boracay's most photographed landmark, Willy's Rock, is Willy's Beach Resort, an impressive Mediterranean-style villa shaded by lofty coconut and palm trees. Compared to Friday's, Pearl of the Pacific, and Waling Waling Resorts, which offer similar amenities in this neck of the beach, Willy's gives you the best value. The decor is basic, with foam mattresses. All rooms have hot showers and French doors that open onto terraces surrounding the sandy, shaded courtyard and restaurant. Breakfast is included in the price and is quite good. The palm thatched roof hangs out quite far, so if you are a natural light enthusiast, you may find the rooms a bit dark and too artificially lit. Breakfast is included in the room rates and the open air court-yard facing the beach is a nice place to take it. The popular beach bar offers happy hour between 5pm and 7pm. There are also room service, turndown twice daily, laundry, arranged tours, and complimentary transport to the airport.

## MODERATE

**Boracay Regency Beach Resort.** Balabag, Boracay. ☎ **36/288-6111.** Fax 36/288-6777. regency@iloilo.net. 43 units. A/C MINIBAR TV TEL. P3,500 (US$87.50) superior; P4,000 (US$100) deluxe; P4,900 (US$122.50) family room; P6,000 (US$150) suite. Price includes breakfast for 2. AE, DC, JCB, MC, V.

A lot of individual features set this newest and most modern resort apart from similar resorts like Pearl of the Pacific, Waling Waling, and Lorenzo. It's the only place with a pool on the front beach, using fresh water from a natural underground spring on the property. No more salty showers! This place isn't part of the Regency that we all know, though it does look and feel like a chain hotel. All rooms are nicely lit, furnished with dark wood and bamboo. The deluxe rooms are a bit bigger than the standard supe-riors, and you can soak in their bathtubs. The terraces off each room face the pool. Services include island-hopping and boat tours, ticket confirmations, laundry and pressing, safe-deposit boxes, currency exchange, and room service, and they are in the process of building a gym and a beach bar.

**La Reserve Resort and Hotel.** Akland, Boracay. ☎ **36/288-3020.** Fax 36/288-3017. lare-serv@pny-fmail@webquest.com. 7 units. A/C MINIBAR TV. June–Nov P2,000–P4,000 (US$50–US$100) bungalow; Dec–May P3,200–P7,200 (US$80–US$180). AE, DC, MC, V.

Each of these creatively painted bungalows can fit up to 3 people, and some have an upstairs, which make it an ideal place for a small family. You don't need a magazine or newspaper in these bathrooms—the huge oil paintings that cover the ceiling will transport you into space or 10,000 leagues under the sea. The wallpaper in each room is hand-painted too. There is hot water, and the location, near boat station 1, is directly on the beach where all the action takes place.

**Lorenzo Resorts: Main, South and Grand Villas.** Bookings: Quezon City, Manila. ☎ **2/928-0719,** 926-3958. Fax 62/926-1726. www.boracay-lorenzo.com. E-mail: reserva-tions@boracay-lorenzo.com. A/C MINIBAR TV TEL. P2,080–P3,080 (US$52–US$77) double; P2,000–P8,800 (US$50–US$220) 1- and 2-bedroom villas. AE, DC, MC, V.

Each of the three Lorenzo properties offers guests comfortable accommodations, and no matter which one you choose, you can use any of the resorts' facilities. **Lorenzo Main** is located in the heart of White Beach and can be a bit loud. It's near the beach within a garden; the rooms, in wooden cottages with nipa roofing, are clean and tra-ditionally decorated. There are two swimming pools, a game room, a disco, and a Fil-ipino restaurant. **Lorenzo Grand Villas,** the newest of the family, is situated at the far south end of the island on a cliff that commands beautiful views of the passage between Boracay and Panay. It's bright and designed with a whimsical seaside motif that leaves you feeling peaceful and energized. The landscape is extravagant, with a pool, Asian-style ponds with fish, and the sound of chimes lingering throughout. This is the best place for families, although access to the beach involves cliff-side stairways. There are a pool and restaurant. **Lorenzo South** is probably the most convenient; it is not as loud as Lorenzo Main and not as far away as Lorenzo Villas, where transportation can be a problem. The beachfront here is secluded and the snorkeling is excellent. All rooms have a balcony facing the beach, and the suite has a Jacuzzi.

**Paradise Garden Resort Hotel.** Manggayad, Boracay. ☎ **36/288-3411.** Fax 36/288-3557. 52 units. A/C TV MINIBAR. P3,200–P4,400 (US$80–US$110) deluxe; P4,000–P5,400 (US$100–US$135) VIP; P4,600–P48,000 (US$115–US$1,200) suites. AE, DC, MC, V.

Set a bit back from the beach, this mansionlike hotel in boat station no. 3 has the most extravagant two-floor royal suite, with pillars, a huge private terrace, two floors, glass paneled French doors, and unmatched personal service. But even if you aren't lucky enough to be able to afford that suite, you will still be comfortable in the other spacious rooms, with hot water, air-conditioning, private terraces, and a courtyard swimming pool set in a beautiful tropical garden. They also have a golf putting green and golf cart rentals.

## INEXPENSIVE

**Boracay Rainforest Resort.** Malay, Aklan, Boracay. ☎ **36/621-1772.** 4 units. A/C MINIBAR. P1,200 (US$30) deluxe; P2,500 (US$62.50) A/C suite. AE, DC, JCB, MC, V.

If you want to be away from the strip of resorts and have a truly personal, independent, unique vacation, this is the place—here it's just you and the rhythm of nature. Popular with stressed execs, weary urbanites, and honeymooners, the eco-conscious hideaway resort is tucked away in the middle of an ancient tropical rain forest, on a mountain overlooking a small private white-sand beach that faces the Sibuyan Sea. All cottages look like your dream childhood tree house, mounted on top of cliffs, with spectacular views from wrap-around verandas of the sea and distant islands. The rooms are well-equipped, with CD/radio, refrigerator, bathroom (no hot water), desk, queen-size bed, alarm clock, coffeemaker, and intercom to the main house where the restaurant is located. There's an outdoor bamboo bed nook, where you can snuggle up with huge oversized pillows. Transportation can be a problem, but they can provide a tricycle or their big, hummerlike vehicle. You'll have to do some daily hiking through the forest path to get to the junction for pickup.

**Nigi Nigi Nu Noos.** Manggayad, Boracay. Boat station no. 2. ☎ **36/288-3101.** Fax 36/288-3112. niginigi@pworld.net.ph. 22 units. A/C TEL. P1,000 (US$25) fan rm cottage; P2,000 (US$50) air-conditioned cottage; P3,200 (US$80) apt. Breakfast included, and 7th night is free. AE, DC, MC, V.

The name is so catchy, you'll find yourself repeating it for years to come. The excellent Asian restaurant, funky art masks, and cone-shaped pagoda-style cottages will also leave an impression. It's a truly native experience, with comfortable accommodations tucked in the middle of White Beach, where you can shop and eat easily. The interiors are decorated with native materials like woven palm leafs, rattan grasses, cocoa bark, tropical hardwoods, and bamboo, but with the convenience of European-style bathrooms. There's also an Internet cafe (with only one computer), a souvenir shop, and a festive, popular bar.

## DINING

Boracay is a culinary melting pot. The cuisine is as diverse as the nationalities of its visitors: French, German, Swiss, Italian, Indian, Japanese, and Thai are all here side by side with native cuisine and scrumptious seafood. And don't go home without sampling from the rainbow of fruit shakes.

**El Toro.** Boat station no. 2. ☎ **36/373-6288.** Main courses P60–P395 (US$1.50–US$9.87). AE, MC, V. Daily 5:30am–11pm. SPANISH.

What a lovely place to sit. Stucco walls, stone pillars, and wood moldings around the swing windows create a breezy Mediterranean mood. The specialty of the house is the paella sangria, fresh mixed seafood combined with saffron rice and Spanish seasonings, served with sangria. The menu also has local favorites, pastas, burgers, and tacos. Feel like a whole roasted pig? Give them 24-hour notice and you're in for a gut-busting feast.

**Friday's Resort.** Far north end of White Beach. Main courses P120–P320 (US$3–US$8). AE, DC, JCB, MC, V. Daily 6am–midnight. INTERNATIONAL.

One of the best places on the beach for Filipino favorites and seafood, Friday's offers a casual, open-air dining experience. It's especially popular with European families. The service is excellent, and the dishes are artistically presented. You can choose continental standbys like pasta al pesto after your chef's salad, or the more adventurous Japanese sashimi or Indian tandoori. The bar concocts refreshing tropical shakes and carries an impressive wine list. In the evenings they offer "The Beach Grill," a selection of fresh seafood and meats laid out on the beach during sunset. This place is pricier than most, especially the shakes—P90 (US$2.25), compared to P40 (US$1) elsewhere!

**Gorio's Restaurant.** Boat station no. 2, next to Aquarius Dive Shop. ☎ **36/288-3132.** Main courses P120–P170 (US$3–US$4.25). AE, DC, JCB, MC, V (7% surcharge added for credit cards). Daily 8am–10pm. FRENCH/ITALIAN.

You've probably noticed the women pulling and stretching noodles all day—they're preparing Gorio's fresh, homemade tagliatelle. That's the Italian part; the French contribution is the much sought-after crepes. "Islander," made of fresh mango, banana, pineapple, vanilla ice cream, and chocolate sauce, is the winner, and the first runner-up for most people is the "Fire Ball," with mixed fresh fruits flambéed in rum. Inquire about the catch of the day and ask for unsweetened iced tea, or you're in for an instant cavity.

**Jony's Place.** Aklan, off the main road in boat station no. 1. ☎ **36/288-6119.** Main courses P120–P240 (US$3–US$6). No credit cards. Daily 7am–11pm. MEXICAN.

You won't have to run for the border here in Boracay, just to Jony's Place. Seating is outside on the sandy floor, where hanging lanterns light up the night. Choose à la carte chicken or beef tacos, enchiladas, burritos, or flautos, a fried burrito. Combo platters add spicy Mexican rice and beans. The mango daiquiri is perfect for cooling the brow and the tongue. They also deliver.

✪ **La Reserve.** Boat station no. 2. ☎ **36/288-3020.** P160–P1,600 (US$4–US$40). (The high end is for caviar.) AE, DC, JCB, MC, V. Daily 7am–11pm. CLASSIC FRENCH.

This is fine dining with sand at your feet, palm leaves brushing against your hair, and the sea breeze at your back. Every bit of the pricey meals is worth it. You can sit in the garden or in the alfresco interior while you enjoy stuffed crab, caviar, T-bone steaks, or tanguegue fish with mango sauce. The dishes, though truly rich, are all prepared and presented in a light nouvelle cuisine style that goes easy on the stomach. And no meal is complete without a good glass of wine; the owner prides himself on his collection of 5,000 bottles. Prices range from US$15 a bottle to—gulp—US$1,320! Desserts tend to be rich, gooey, and caloric. After all this gastronomic love-making, light up one of their Havana cigars.

**Nigi Nigi Nu Noos.** Boat station no. 2. ☎ **36/288-3101.** Main courses P80–P200 (US$2–US$5). Cash only. 2-for-1 happy hour 5–7pm (local beers and mixed drinks). Daily 7am–midnight. THAI/CHINESE.

There's that name again. The mellow exotic birds, giant carved masks, and sea breezes make you feel like you're on the island of Dr. Moreau. The place is always packed with a cool crowd eating in the open-air restaurant, drinking at the beach-side bar, or melting to jazz in the jazz and blues area. Ginger is favored in the cooking, and they offer the most eclectic mix of meat preparations I've seen on the island: beef with ginger, Burmese chicken with coconut milk, and honey lemon glazed chicken. Stay and daydream or play a game of backgammon after your meal.

**Sulu Thai.** Boat Station no. 3. ☎ **36/288-3400.** P80–P190 (US$2–US$4.75) main courses. Cash only. Daily 7am–10pm. THAI.

This is a great place for people-watching on the "beach expressway." It's nothing much to look at (hardly the height of elegant dining) but they serve great Thai food. The menu is heavy with crab, fish, meat, rice, egg, soup, and noodle dishes. The sautéed mixed seafood with basil leaves is cooked perfectly, with snappy shrimp, chewy squid, and succulent crab. Word on the beach is that this is better than Siam Thai Restaurant farther up the beach.

**True Blue Indian Food.** Malay, in boat station 2 on the main walkway. ☎ **36/288-3142.** Main courses P105–P295 (US$2.63–US$7.37). Cash only. Daily 9am–noon, 6–11:30pm. NORTHERN INDIAN.

Bring the candles and incense and sharpen your yoga skills for this excellent Indian restaurant. You'll be taking your shoes off and sitting on oversized floor pillows on the top floor wooden terrace, where rice paper lamps cast distorted shadows and create a subdued atmosphere. The menu is equally satisfying, with spicy chicken, meat, and vegetarian dishes; tandoori; masala; and the usual unleavened bread dishes like chapati. Funky, spiritual world music plays in the background.

## SPORTS & OUTDOOR ACTIVITIES
### HITTING THE BEACHES
Only 11 miles (7km) long and 0.5 mile (1km) wide at its narrowest point, Boracay's beaches are all around you. The popular **White Beach** is where all the action is, including massage vendors who comb the beach and shallow waters. The north end of White Beach is very scenic and less congested.

**Diniwid Beach,** at the far north end of White Beach, is peaceful, although the waters don't seem as clear as at White Beach.

### SCUBA DIVING
The clear sea off Boracay—you can see 100 feet (30m) or more through the water—offers a variety of sites, including walls, bat caves, coral formations, and tidal surges. The sealife is abundant, including sharks, barracuda, tuna, sturgeon, pennant coral fish, sweetlips, jacks, large eagle rays, sea snakes, barrel sponges, lapu-lapu, and lionfish. Most sites are only a few minutes off shore, so you can go for a dive in the morning and be eating lunch by noon. For experienced divers, Boracay may be a disappointment—the coral isn't as abundant or beautiful as at Palawan or Bohol.

There are about 20 scuba schools on this small island, so you can imagine the competition. All offer the same prices, about US$25 for one dive, and US$275 to US$300 for an open water course. **Red Coral Diving School** (☎ **36/288-3486**), near Friday's Resort, comes highly recommended. Miguel (or "Mike") is excellent, and you'll feel safe and informed since he is a member of the Philippine Coast Guard and president of the Boracay Scuba Divers Association.

---

**Travel Trivia**

---

Because the sand in Boracay is white (there's no quartz, feldspar, or manganite in it) it never gets hot, so you won't have to worry about burning your feet on the beach.

---

## SNORKELING

Snorkeling is good at Lapuz-Lapuz, Ilig-Iligan, Crocodile Island, and Yapak. If you didn't bring gear, you can rent it from any dive shop, or at your resort.

**Tribal Adventure Tours,** located at Sandcastles Resort on boat station no. 1 (☎ 36/288-3207, fax 36/288-3449), offer eco-friendly, tailor-made kayaking, trekking, mountain biking, and caving tours in and around Boracay. They don't stick to any set itinerary, and will be happy to create a package for you combining any or all of these activities.

## JET SKIS & WATER SKIS

Most resorts can arrange these activities for you. Also check with the Tourist Office.

## HORSEBACK RIDING

Saddle up at **Boracay Horse Riding Stables,** located past Friday's Resort heading north. They charge about P350 (US$8.75) for a 1-hour ride with guide through the hills and mountains of the more rural villages of Boracay. Bring water, as it can get very hot.

## TENNIS & GOLF

**Tirol and Tirol Resort,** next to the tourist office, will rent out rackets and balls for about P150 (US$3.75) for an hour's play. **Fairways and Bluewater Resort Golf and Country Club,** north of White Beach, has an 18-hole par 72 Graham Marsh–designed golf course. It's normally for members only, but occasionally it's open to nonmembers—check with your resort to find out. A tricycle can take you there.

## SHOPPING

If the many vendors that wander the beaches don't have what you want, check out the selection of souvenirs, carvings, T-shirts, and sarongs at the **Talipapa Flea Market** at the southern end of boat station 2. Another excellent shop along the main strip in boat station 2 is **NoyJinji,** where a husband and wife team sell unique hand-painted shirts, postcards, and world music recordings.

## BORACAY AFTER DARK

Dance the night away at one of the island's discos, all located on White Beach: **Beachcomber** (boat station no. 1), **Bazura** (boat station no. 2), or **Sulo Bar** (boat station no. 3). **Moondogs** (boat station no. 1) offers a commemorative T-shirt to anyone still standing after 15 shots, and your name gets added to a plaque. **Titay Main Garden Theater Restaurant and Bar** (boat station no. 3) hosts performances of ethnic dance and music. You'll need to take a tricycle to get here.

## 10  Palawan

Time has stood still on Palawan. The island has managed to preserve its fascinatingly natural habitat over the centuries, and today it's considered the country's last frontier. Situated southwest of Mindoro and north of Malaysia's Sabah Island, Palawan is the country's fifth-largest island, with only half of 1% of its population. More than a thousand islands and islets make up Palawan's territory, making the province an ideal

# Palawan Island

Mindoro Strait

Busuanga

Coron

**Calamanian**

**Group**

*South*

*China*

Linapacan Strait

Linapacan

El Nido

Taytay

*Sea*

San Vincente

**Dumaran**

Roxas

Puerto Princesa

Aborlan

Narra

*Palawan*

Quezon

*Passage*

Rizal

Brooke's Point

*Sulu Sea*

Batarasa

**Balabac**

*Balabac Strait*

0   30 mi
50 km

N

breeding ground for diversity; monkeys, squirrels, bear cats, and zebras all thrive here, as do wild tropical plants and corals.

Palawan's human population is just as diverse. Through the years, the province has attracted peoples of all backgrounds, and it is said that today's Palawenos are a mix of 81 different cultural groups. Even Europeans, especially Swiss and Germans, have been attracted to this quiet province. What is it about Palawan that has drawn so many outsiders? The fine weather? The temperate sea? Or its almost magical powers of making time stand still? This is where you'll find the country's most exclusive beach resorts perched on their own private island, explore one of the world's best diving sites, navigate the world's longest underground river, and feel a sense of youthful, curious adventure.

## GETTING THERE

**BY PLANE   Air Philippines** (☎ 2/843-7770) has a daily flight that leaves Manila at 11:30am and arrives in Puerto Princesa at 12:40pm. A round-trip fare will cost you about P4,000 (US$100). **Philippine Airlines** (☎ 2/816-6691) offers daily flights at 1:35pm, arriving in Puerto Princesa at 2:45pm. Fares are about the same. **Air Ads** (☎ 2/833-3264) and **Asian Spirit** (☎ 2/840-3811 to 3814) fly the Manila–Coron (in northern Palawan) route daily in a small prop plane, for about P2,000 (US$50) one-way. See also "Getting There" under El Nido, below.

**BY BOAT   WG&A SuperFerry,** Pier 4, North Harbor, Manila (☎ 2/894-3211), makes two trips a week to Puerto Princesa from Manila; the trip takes about 24 hours. This is the most reliable, clean, and comfortable sea travel in the country; accommodations range from economy class to your own private cabin with air-conditioning. Approximate fare is P549 (US$13.70). **Asuncion Line,** 3038 Jose Abad Santos, Tondo, Manila (☎ 2/245-2830 or 711-3743), sails to Coron three times a week (22 hours). Accommodations will cost about P350 (US$8.75). It makes a longer, 28-hour journey to El Nido twice a week, which costs about P400 (US$10). The ship isn't in the best condition, though. You can also take a 2-hour bus ride from Manila to Batangas and hop aboard **Viva Shipping Lines** from there. It leaves three times a week for Coron, costs about the same as Asuncion, and is in better shape.

## GETTING AROUND

**BY TRICYCLE/MOTORBIKE**   In Puerto Princesa, El Nido, and Coron, tricycles are the main mode of transport. The long lines of motorized tricycles popping, backfiring, and smoking their way down the unpaved roads are quite a sight. Expect to pay around P2 (US5¢) per kilometer. Tricycles around town can be flagged down along the side of the roads just about anywhere. The exhaust can be choking, so I advise bringing a bandanna to help filter out the fumes. Don't take these for long distances if you're short on time.

**BY BANCA**   The quickest and most scenic way of getting around Palawan is by hired pumpboat, or *banca.* The sea is often more reliable than land, and a banca ride is usually a highlight of the Palawan experience. You'll find them along the beaches. Price varies depending on the destination and the boat operator (once again, you have to bargain). They do tend to rob you because transport is so unpredictable and hard to arrange throughout Palawan. But if you are traveling with more than one person it's less heavy on your pocket.

**BY JEEPNEY**   These are usually crowded and bad for your back, especially on the unpaved roads throughout Palawan. If you're adventurous or crazy enough to take a jeepney from Puerto Princesa to El Nido, be prepared for a sore back and to arrive covered with "Palawan powder."

**BY RENTAL CAR**    Rental cars are available in Puerto Princesa, but you might have to mortgage your home to afford one. The roads are impossible to navigate without knowing the route. Even if you hire a driver, tires will blow, and you won't be able to go faster than 30 miles an hour on the erupting, bumpy roads. If you're still not convinced, **Puerto Travel and Tours** in Puerto Princesa (☎ **48/433-4652**) offers car hire to any point in Palawan, including the Underground River, Port Barton, Taytay, and El Nido. They are usually chauffeured. Another option is **Sierra Rent-a-Car** at ☎ **48/433-8113,** 8423, 6949.

## VISITOR INFORMATION

The **City Tourism Office,** to the right as you exit the airport in Puerto Princesa (☎ **48/433-2983**), can offer you information, mostly on Puerto Princesa. There is also a **tourist information counter** at the arrival terminal in the airport. It's open daily until planes leave. For more island-wide information, check the **Provisional Tourist Office** (☎ **48/433-2968**) on the ground floor of the Capitol building complex on Rizal Avenue.

# Fast Facts: Palawan

**Banks/Currency Exchange**    All banks in Palawan will ask to see your passport and a copy of purchase receipts for traveler's checks. Make sure you have these items or you won't be able to get money. (There are no ATMs.) Philippine National Bank on the corner of Rizal Avenue and Valencia Street, Puerto Princessa (☎ 48/433-2321) is open Monday to Friday 9am to 3pm. In Sabang (Underground River), El Nido, and Coron, it will be very difficult to exchange money anywhere but at the resorts, whose rates are usually not as good as the banks'.

**Doctors/Hospitals**    The private Adventist Hospital (☎ 48/433-2156) is located on San Pedro Street in Puerto Princesa.

**Emergencies**    The emergency police assistance number is ☎ 166.

**Internet/E-mail**    Trattoria Inn (see "Accommodations," below) offers Internet and e-mail access.

**Police**    Puerto Princesa's Police Station (☎ 48/433-2818 or 433-2101) is on Peneyra Road. Outside of Puerto Princesa, you can get assistance from the local Municipal Hall. Just ask someone where it is.

**Post Office**    Most towns have post offices, but mail will arrive faster if you send it from Puerto Princesa or Manila.

**Telephone**    The area code for Puerto Princessa is 48. You can make international and local calls from most hotels in Puerto Princessa, and at Piltel on Roxas Street or RCPI on Rizal Avenue, both phone service providers. Other parts of Palawan either don't have phone service or are serviced by cellular phones. If you need to make a call in these areas, check with a local dive shop.

# PUERTO PRINCESSA
## ACCOMMODATIONS

**Asia World.** National Rd., Puerto Princesa. ☎ **48/433-2212.** Fax 48/433-2111. For bookings: 15th Floor, AIC Center, Manila, ☎ 2/242-6546, 6547, 6551. Fax 2/242-6550. 109 units. A/C MINIBAR TV. P5,600–P6,400 (US$140–US$160) standard; P6,400–P7,200 (US$160–US$180) superior; P10,000–P80,000 (US$250–US$2,000) suites. AE, DC, JCB, MC, V.

Ideally located about 2 miles (3km) out of town, and away from the noisy tricycles, Asia World is the only place in town that feels like a real hotel. The lobby is a relaxed, dimly lit space with a contemporary feel and decor. You pay more for the resort feel and amenities than for the unextraordinary rooms. They do have nice, dark hardwood floors and overlook the bay through the sliding carved wood window covers. Windows are large, allowing lots of natural light in. The first thing you'll notice in the bathroom is the gigantic mirror, then the extra-large towels and complimentary slippers. The hotel's pool is large and outlined by palm trees. And after a swim or workout in the gym, you can soothe those nerves and muscles in the sauna and Jacuzzi. Other amenities include two tennis courts, business center, 24-hour room service, tours, gift shop, massage, baby-sitter, and money exchange. See "Dining" below for restaurants. The hotel has changed management many times, and presently seems to be struggling.

**Casalinda Tourist Inn and Restaurant.** Trinidad Road, Rizal Avenue, Puerto Princesa. ☎ **48/433-2606.** Fax 48/433-2309. 12 units. A/C TEL. P750 (US$18.75) double. No credit cards.

This is the best place in town if you just want to sleep or hang out. The peace and quiet of its off-road location helps create a relaxed, island mood, as does the tropical courtyard lined with palm and banana trees. Rooms are not as equipped as at the Trattoria Inn, but they have large windows, and the funky lamps handmade in Palawan add a unique charm. (They're not for sale; I already asked.) Mattresses are the not-so-firm 5-inch foam type that are almost inescapable in Palawan. You'll have a private bath but no hot water. An American, Pat Murray, and his Filipina wife, Gina, own the place, and are always around if you have any needs or questions.

**Trattoria Inn and Swiss Bistro.** 353 Rizal Ave., Puerto Princesa (right on the main road). ☎ **48/433-2719,** 433-4985. Fax 48/433-8171. www.palawan.net/trattori/palawan.html. E-mail: trattori@pal-onl.com. 17 units. A/C TV TEL. P270–P350 (US$6.75–US$8.75) double with common bath; P490–P580 (US$12.25–US$14.50) double with air and semi-private bath; P750 (US$18.75) double with air and private bath. AE, DC, MC, V.

Imagine Gilligan's hut with e-mail. Remarkably, this native-style inn with *sawali* thatched walls is in the process of providing guests individual Internet hook-up capabilities in each room, in case you brought your laptop. Between that, the excellent bistro, and the helpful, knowledgeable travel agency, you get first-class service and convenience here on a shoestring budget. The rooms are festive, with fishy shower curtains, rattan bed frames, and the familiar flip-flops for your use. The only disadvantage is the noise from the main road, which may cause light sleepers some aggravation. The gracious owner, Claudio Schoch from Switzerland, will make sure you are comfortable and familiar with the area and your travel options. Conveniently, he owns an excellent resort near the underground river in Sabang, and will gladly arrange a stay there for you. The popular garden-side bar comes complete with a hanging bell, if you are feeling generous and want to hoof a round for the entire bar. See also "Dining" below.

## DINING

**Asia World.** Puerto Princesa. ☎ **48/433-2212.** Prices vary at the different restaurants but range from P180–P210 (US$4.50–US$5.25) for local dishes, and P250–P380 (US$6.25–US$9.50) for grilled steaks. AE, DC, JCB, MC, V. Daily 6am–midnight. JAPANESE/CHINESE.

A culinary mix of Japanese, Chinese, and international dishes awaits at Asia World Hotel's restaurants. It's a one-stop dining experience. Choose Tagpuan Garden Grill for tasty steaks and seafood, Seven Dragon for Chinese, or Yoko for Japanese. Scoop yourself some homemade ice cream at the lobby lounge. After dinner and dessert head to Musikahan, where live bands perform nightly and you can sing along with Videoke.

## Puerto Princesa's Wine & Cheese Club

You'll be surprised at the places you can find a chunk of Brie and a glass of chablis. In Puerto Princesa, I was surprised to discover a local wine and cheese club that meets monthly. Plates of over 30 imported cheeses, breads, and six different wines made an impressive spread for expatriates and well-to-do locals who gather to "not talk business—just to see each other and enjoy the varieties," as one organizer explained. If you are interested, contact Claudio or Aida at Trattoria Inn, ☎ **48/433-2719** or 433-4983. There is a fee of P500 (US$12.50).

If you want to dance, Obsession Disco hosts nightly ballroom dancing lessons complete with instructors and music from the king of swing, Old Blue Eyes himself.

**Ka Lui.** Rizal Avenue, Puerto Princesa. ☎ **48/433-2580.** Main courses P250–P320 (US$3.25–US$8). No credit cards. Daily 7am–10pm. FILIPINO.

Ka Lui offers the most atmosphere in town—its native nipa and bamboo design doesn't let you forget you're in another world. After taking off your shoes, situate yourself on the *abaca* sand sacks, where you will be served excellent local dishes and seafood. There are plenty of vegetable dishes here. My favorite feature is the group of children who play local instruments like bamboo flutes and harps and maracas made from flame-tree seeds.

**Trattoria Inn and Swiss Bistro.** 353 Rizal Ave., Puerto Princesa. ☎ **48/433-2719,** 433-4985. Breakfast P140–P170 (US$3.50–US$4.25); dinner P180–P270 (US$4.50–US$6.75). AE, DC, MC, V. Daily 6am–midnight. FILIPINO/INTERNATIONAL.

This small bistro has excellent pizza and international breakfasts, and entrees like lasagna or schnitzel. And of course it's the only place around where you can get good cheese. Sit inside at a cozy table, at the bar, or outside in the tropical garden. It's a popular gathering place for locals, backpackers, and expatriates in the area, and can be a valuable place to get information and advice and to share travel tales. A television airs a cable sports channel.

## ATTRACTIONS

You can arrange for a tricycle to take you to most of these sights for about P200 (US$5) for a half day, or P400 (US$10) full day.

**Iwahig Prison.** About 15½ miles (25km) south of Puerto Princesa.

This prison established during the American regime is a unique concept in rehabilitation. About 1,700 inmates live on the landscaped grounds (some even with their families) among orchards, coconuts, rice, and other crops. If it weren't for the tangerine-colored shirts of the workers in the fields, Iwahig would resemble a tranquil farm rather than a hard-knock prison whose convicts have committed the most serious of offenses. The prisoners have free range of the farm and are allowed to earn an income by working at some of the handicraft stores around the farm.

You can visit the farm and interact with the prisoners if you wish. When I went I had a long, interesting talk with a prisoner who, in between bumming cigarettes, kept insisting that he was charged with robbery first, then murder. I don't recommend female travelers going alone.

If you don't want to take a tricycle, a jeepney leaves at 9:30am from Valencia Street in Puerto Princesa and returns at 1:30pm. It shouldn't cost you more than P10 (US25¢) each way.

**Crocodile Farming Institute.** Halfway between Puerto Princesa and Iwahig Penal Colony. Mon–Fri 1:15–4:15pm, Sat 9am–noon and 1–4pm.

If you're intrigued by crocodiles, you can visit a breeding farm about 30km away from Puerto Princesa where the prehistoric beasts are raised and observed for conservation purposes. Feeding time—Monday and Thursday afternoons —is a particularly good time to go.

**Tubbataha Reef.** 113 miles (182km) southeast of Puerto Princesa, in the Sulu Sea.

Without a doubt, Tubbataha Reef is the best dive site in the Philippines. It's only reached by a live-aboard boat. The entire Tubbataha Reef was protected as a national marine park in 1988. Most divers head to the larger, isolated north reef, which plunges to a sheer vertical wall over a hundred feet deep. Shovel-nose rays, leopard sharks, giant manta rays, and reef sharks are among the full-time residents, with even larger fish occasionally turning up from the deep. **ScubaWorld Dive Shop** offers 5- to 6-day outings on their live-aboard, the M/V *Explorer,* a 130-foot boat with a 24-person capacity in 12 cabins. Contact their Manila office at ☎ **2/895-3551,** 890-7805, 890-7807; fax 2/890-8982. March to June, when the monsoon winds cease, is the best season to dive. Trips average about US$150 to US$200 per person per day. You have to book months in advance for these trips, as they fill up quickly.

# ST. PAUL SUBTERRANEAN RIVER NATIONAL PARK (THE UNDERGROUND RIVER)

This park is a unique and fascinating part of the island. The 2.5-mile (4km) Monkey Trail, or the more difficult 4-mile (7km) Jungle Trail, is the best way to get to the river. You will hike through beautiful forest, on wooden walkways along the white-sand beach, up cliff-side stairways and down the gorge to the river. Bring binoculars to see the monkeys, monitor lizards, Philippine cockatoos, and white-bellied sea eagles and other rare birds. After you put on a hard hat and bright orange vest, your guide will direct the kayak through the mouth of the underground river for the fascinating 1-mile (1.5km) journey past stalagmite and stalactite sculptures. Some have names, like God's Highway, the Candle, and the Holy Family. The guides will point out others along the way, as you marvel at the formations and try to dodge flying bats.

## GETTING THERE

Before entering the park you must secure an entry permit, which you can get at the **St. Paul Subterranean River National Park Office,** on Manalo Street in Puerto Princesa (☎ **48/433-2409**) for P150 (US$3.75) adults, P75 (US$1.87) ages 13 to 17, or P50 (US$1.25) ages 6 to 12. The price includes boat and guide. You can also purchase the permit at the park's entrance in Sabang.

You'll be overwhelmed by transport options in Puerto Princesa, but I'll make it very simple for you. **Go Palawan Travel and Tours** at the Trattoria Inn on Rizal Avenue (☎ **48/433-4570,** 433-9344) offers the cheapest, most comfortable, and reliable means of getting to Sabang and the underground river. They provide a nice, air-conditioned van for P250 (US$6.25) per person, which leaves (depending on demand) daily at 7:30am for the 3-hour bumpy ride. It will drop you directly at the Park Information Office, where permits can be secured if you haven't already done so. From there, pumpboats (included in your permit fee of P150 (US$3.75)) can take you the 20 minutes to the cave, or you can start on your way to the **Monkey Trail** or the **Jungle Trail** to go there by foot.

If you are making it a day trip only, the van leaves to go back to Puerto Princesa promptly at 3:30pm. If you want to stay overnight, **Go Palawan** can radio to

Panaguman Resort, which will have a boat waiting at the cave to take you the 10 minutes to the resort.

## ACCOMMODATIONS

**St. Paul National Park, Central Park Station Camping Facilities.** Book at National Park Office in Puerto Princesa (☎ 48/433-2409). P100 (US$2.50) per person, bungalow; P50 (US$1.25) per person, tent.

You have to bring your own supplies if you want to camp here, although they provide tents. You'll be roughing it in the bungalows, but it's worth it to hear the sounds of the night. Cooking facilities are available.

**Panaguman Beach Resort.** No phone, only radio transmission. Book through: Trattoria Inn, Rizal Ave., Puerto Princesa, ☎ 48/433-2719 or 433-4985. Fax 48/433-8171. P500 (US$12.50) room with common bath, P1,500 (US$37.50) double bungalow. No credit cards, unless you book in Puerto Princesa.

"Harmonious and peaceful" is how patrons describe this family-style resort, who agreed that this was exactly what they envisioned as "getting away from everything." Nestled in a private bend in the river, Panaguman's small native resort in the middle of nowhere is the perfect place to relax. There's nothing else to do. Your only obligation is to catch sunrise or sunset off the terrace or on the small beach just out front. The attic rooms share a common bath and are quite cozy, with screened windows and wooden slatted blinds. The cottages have a private bath with cold water only, mosquito nets, towels, and sleeping sheets.

The lobby, with its domed bamboo construction, is the perfect place to shuffle in your slippers, grab a pen, and sit at the family-style table to write, meet travelers, listen to music, or try some of the delicious Filipino main courses on the menu. The only thing missing is a fireplace. If the resort is full enough they will offer nightly buffets. There are kayaks, games like Monopoly, backgammon, and chess, and hand-me-down books you can rent for a small fee.

## TAYTAY

The main reason for coming to Taytay is to enjoy the beautiful white-sand beaches and the pampering of its main resort, **Club Noah Isabelle.** If you are not looking for a resort getaway, you can skip this and head straight to El Nido.

## GETTING THERE

From Puerto Princesa, the bus trip takes 7 to 8 hours. Royal Express makes daily departures at 8pm and midnight for P150 (US$3.75) per person. If you arrive in the middle of the night they'll let you sleep on the bus, or you can see if there's a taxi waiting to take you to the resort. Contact **Club Noah Isabelle** for the latest travel information, as transport in this area is unpredictable.

## ACCOMMODATIONS

**Club Noah Isabelle.** Located on its own island. Booking: 2/F Basic Petroleum Bldg., C. Palanca Jr. St., Legaspi Village, Makati, Manila, ☎ 2/810-7291 to 93. Fax 2/818-2640. www.clubnoah.com.ph. E-mail: clubnoah@I-manila.com.ph. 30 units. A/C. Regular season: P5,360 (US$134) per adult, P3,300 (US$82.50) per child 3–12; peak season: P7,400 (US$185) per adult, P3,700 (US$92.50) per child. Rates include all activities and meals. AE, DC, MC, V.

The name Isabelle is derived from an old Spanish fort in Taytay. Puerto de Sta. Isabel, named in honor of Queen Isabela II of Spain, was built to provide a refuge from 18th-century pirates for the local townspeople. Today, Club Noah Isabelle provides a different kind of refuge—peace and tranquility from the stress of the 20th century.

Hidden in a cove behind huge limestone formations, Club Noah's stilted cabanas are perched out over the water, with verandas that face the sea. There is nothing better than dozing off to the gentle lapping of the sea underneath you. The cabanas are cozy and comfortable, and all are equipped with hot water. Hair dryers are also available. Out of all the top beach resorts in the Philippines, Club Noah is probably the most dedicated to eco-tourism and harmonizing with its natural surroundings—you can explore rejuvenated coral reefs here, or bird watch (binoculars are available). For the active they offer waterskiing, kayaking, beach volleyball, fishing, river cruises, caving, and excellent diving packages. All this and three meals a day are included in the rate, making this a popular family destination.

# EL NIDO

Many say El Nido is the place to go for a true Philippine adventure, in what is considered "the last frontier" of the country. The people here, although eager to share their communities, watch warily as tourism soars. El Nido embodies purity and a simple beauty uniquely its own, with lazy sunsets and towering limestone formations punctuating docile clear waters that teem with marine life. With lush forests, caves, lagoons, and shipwrecks to explore, there's always something to do here.

## GETTING THERE

**BY PLANE**    The easiest way to get to El Nido is by plane from Manila. **A. Soriano Aviation** (☎ **2/804-0760**) has small twice-daily chartered flights to El Nido, at 7:30am and 3:30pm. This service is usually reserved for visitors staying at the resorts around El Nido, but in low season extra seats are usually available. A one-way fare is about P4,600 (US$115). You can check on availability of seats at **Ten Knots Office** (known as the White House) in El Nido town (no phone).

**BY BANCA**    From Sabang, at the same place where you get dropped off for the Underground River, you can find local boat owners who will make the 7-hour trip to El Nido on their small pumpboat for about P5,000 (US$125). It works out well if you can divide that amount between four or five people. Of course, you can always try to negotiate a lower price. It's a beautiful ride along the white beaches on the South China Sea.

**BY BUS**    You'll be roughing it if you do the Puerto Princesa route to El Nido by land. Expect 10 hours of bumpy, tire-busting, packed travel. Buses usually leave early in the morning from Malvar Street. The cost is about P140 (US$3.50).

## GETTING AROUND

If you are staying at one of the resorts in El Nido, you will have access to kayaks and boats that can take you from island to island. They will also arrange for transport to and from the small **Dio Airport.** El Nido town is small, and you can get around easily by foot, although there are tricycles.

## VISITOR INFORMATION

There is a **tourist office** in El Nido town (next to the post office on Calle Real Road) that can assist you with resort accommodations if you haven't already made arrangements. There are no phone lines in El Nido, only cellular phones. Bring enough pesos with you, as there is no place outside of the resorts to exchange money.

## ACCOMMODATIONS

Prices at the following resorts are all-inclusive, covering three meals a day and all water activities except dives.

✪ **Dolarog Resort.** 53–13 El Nido, Palawan. Fax all inquiries to Edo Flisi at ☎ **48/433-4892.** 6 units. P1,500 (US$37.50) cottage. No credit cards.

# Pamilican Island & the Amanpulo Resort

You can't do much better than **Amanpulo** here in the Philippines: It's the best of the best. A paradise retreat for the rich and famous, the sophisticated Amanpulo, meaning "peaceful island," gives its guests so much serenity and privacy that you wouldn't even know it if Robert de Niro was next door. (Rumor has it that he is a regular.) The cottages, called *casitas*, are spaciously arranged on the beach, perched on hillsides or set between treetops. If you really want the best (of the best of the best), request casita 39 or 40, which has its own private beach. All casitas feature a stately king-size bed, two window divans, a huge bathroom with tub, separate shower, and a dressing room large enough to accommodate Imelda Marcos herself. A private terrace surrounds the front of each casita, and you'll get your very own personal motorized cart so you can tour the island at your own pace and leisure. All rooms have laser disc players and natural, hushed lighting accentuated with natural white and wood-textured furniture. Fresh flowers are placed throughout your casita daily. The beauty of this paradise will take your breath away and it won't be easy to go back to the real world.

Aside from the beautiful pool, facilities and services include tennis courts, a library, an art gallery, walking tracks, and in-room massage. The surrounding waters provide a wide variety of marine life and dive sites. You have your choice of sailing (jet skis, lasers, and windsurfing), rowing, fishing, snorkeling, and scuba diving. Dive courses are overpriced here, going for about US$500 for a 4-day open water course. The air-conditioned restaurant overlooks the pool, with views of the island and surrounding sea. The beach club serves light snacks and refreshments throughout the day.

**BOOKING**    P.O. Box 456 Pasay Tramo Post Office, Pasay City, Manila. ☎ 2/532-4040. Fax 2/532-4044. 40 units. A/C MINIBAR TV TEL. June 1 to October 31: P18,000 (US$450), treetop casitas; P20,000 (US$500) beach and hillside casitas; P22,000 (US$550) hillside casita 39 and 40. Prices increase about US$100 during the regular season, November 1 to May 31. AE, DC, MC, V.

**GETTING THERE**    Flights from Manila will take you to the resort's private airstrip daily at 1:30pm. This is the only way to get here. A round-trip, on **A. Soriano Aviation Charter Flights** (☎ 2/834-0371), will cost you US$275 per adult. Be sure to call the resort for reservations and any schedule changes.

This is a secret just waiting to be discovered. If you don't want to spend hundreds at the big resorts in the area, but still crave a hut on a private secluded island with breathtaking views of the stars, sunsets, and rock formations, than Dolarog is for you. Owned by the mild-mannered Italian Edo and his Filipina wife, Dolarog's immaculate native cottages sit up on a beautifully manicured green lawn slightly above the small white-sand beach. Each cottage is large and comes with two double beds, mosquito net, and huge sliding shutters. The bathrooms are in Italian marble with all-new European fixtures. There is no hot water or air-conditioning, but that shouldn't dissuade you from this small piece of paradise. If the offerings here—family-style dining, island hopping, airport transfers, paddleboats, windsurfing, and diving equipment— become overwhelming, just relax on the hammocks or stroll the beautiful landscape. Open up the window shutters, become familiar with the local lizard's croak, keep track of the shooting stars, and enjoy the serenity.

⭐ **Lagen Island Resort.** Reservations: 2nd floor, Builders Center Building, 170 Salcedo St., Legaspi Village, Makati, Manila, ☎ 2/894-5644. Fax 63 2/810-3620. E-mail: elnido@mail-station.net. 51 units. A/C MINIBAR TV TEL. P8,600–P9,600 (US$215–US$240) Forest Rooms; P9,200–P10,200 (US$230–US$255) Beachfront Water Cottages; P9,800–P10,800 (US$245–US$270) Forest Suites. AE, DC, JCB, MC, V.

What a resort! Set within a pristine bay, in a rain forest surrounded by sheer limestone cliffs, Lagen's stilted cottages give its guests every bit of first-class comfort and convenience while creating a unique and memorable stay. Built in 1997 to replace a resort that burned down on a nearby island, Lagen is three times larger and more romantic than its neighbor Miniloc, and less expensive than Amanpulo. The place exudes relaxation and calm, which even the most high-strung exec or couple won't be able to resist. The only difference among the various types of accommodations is location and view. You can expect the same amenities: individually controlled temperature, stereo system with CD player, VCRs upon request, and even handy umbrellas. I recommend a beachfront cottage for the best views and that unique experience of being up on stilts. Each cottage or room is furnished with indigenous Filipino materials; in fact, only two trees were cut down to build the resort, proving its concern and respect for the natural surroundings. Each cottage or room has a veranda with protruding balcony seats, reminiscent of the Philippine "banguerra," which is traditionally built adjacent to the kitchen seat for drip-drying dishes. The dining area overlooks the pool and ocean. They also host sunset dinners on a boat, and you can arrange picnics on a deserted isle. The menu has incredible options to suit your moods. Amenities include 25-meter swimming pool, library with games and children's entertainment, garden chapel, boutique, clinic, small nature trails, bird watching, game area with billiard tables, darts, and table tennis. All marine sports are at your disposal, including excellent diving facilities. Services include laundry, baby-sitting, room service, turndown twice daily, and nightly entertainment.

**Malapacao Island.** El Nido 5313, Palawan. Fax 48/433-4892. Manila reservations, ☎ 2/828-5330. For walk-ins go to the booking office in El Nido town. E-mail: leeann@pal-onl.com. P1,600–P2,160 (US$40–US$54) cottage; P2,800–P3,000 (US$70–US$75) during peak season (Dec 20–Jan 8; 2 weeks before Easter). Discounts are available if not fully booked. No credit cards.

Lovers of nature need look no further than this harmonious eco-conscious resort situated in a cove among El Nido's Bacuit Bay Marine Sanctuary. No meat-eating or smoking allowed. The simple, airy cottages with private bath are meant for couples, and are not designed with total privacy in mind—here, it's communal living with one's fellow human being and nature. The only source of power comes from solar panels. Hikes to waterfalls, mountain climbing, snorkeling, island hopping, and other activities can all be arranged. But your favorite activities will be gastronomic. They use homegrown spices and herbs to create spicy Asian dinners served on a common table, family-style. Everything here is homemade, and lunches rely on the fresh catch of the day. The Malapacao special curry with coconut milk and homemade mango chutney is heavenly. It's a true modern-day Garden of Eden—you almost expect to see people walking around in loincloths.

**Miniloc Island Resort.** Miniloc Island, El Nido. Reservations: 170 Salcedo St., Legaspi Village, Makati, Manila. ☎ 2/894-5644. Fax 2/810-3620. E-mail: elnido@mailstation.net. 31 units. A/C MINIBAR TEL. P7,680 (US$192) per person, cottage; P7,000 (US$175) per person, sea-view rooms. AE, DC, MC, V.

Miniloc Resort caters to the active traveler, as opposed to the more romantic setting you'll find at Lagen Resort. Accommodations are the same: Stilted waterfront cottages tucked in front of cliffs. With all the activities at your disposal, though, you'll hardly be in your cottage. A mountain trail brings you into the forest, where you'll see tropical birds, playful monkeys, and large monitor lizards. Just around the corner from the resort, through a crack in the mountain barely large enough for your kayak to pass through, is a clear, shallow interior lagoon. (It's a perfect hideaway for frisky couples.) Windsurfing, snorkeling, aqua bike, and water skis are available at their Marine Sports Activity Center and are included in your room rate. They even have a fish feeding station at their pier. The staff is "very accommodating and organized," as one patron put it. From the good-night chocolates placed on your pillow to the good-bye serenade, you will be taken care of and energized here.

## DINING

All resorts offer complete meal packages with your stay. However, if you venture to El Nido town, check out **Mac Mac's** on Calle Hama Road for excellent Filipino and international dishes. It's small, dark, hot, and run-down, but so is everything else in town. It's a great place to meet other travelers and talk diving. Lobsters are plentiful in the waters around El Nido, and you can get a huge one for dirt-cheap. At Mac Mac's you can request a lobster feast in the morning, and by dinnertime Max, the proclaimed best chef in El Nido, will have it and the delicious accompaniments ready. Also try **Virgies Eatery** around the corner for excellent homestyle Filipino cuisine. (The food will be different every day.)

## OUTDOOR ACTIVITIES

**DIVING & SNORKELING**    When you tell someone you are going diving in the Philippines, the next question is "Have you gone to El Nido?" The area is known for some of the best diving spots in the country, although many have walked away discouraged and disgusted by the scars and destruction that dynamite and cyanide fishing have caused to some of the reefs in the area. If you don't already have your certification, the El Nido Resorts (Miniloc and Lagen) and other nearby smaller resorts, like Dolarog, can arrange for instruction, dives, and snorkeling.

In El Nido town, **Mac Mac's Dive Shop** (on Calle Hama Road), operated by Max from Austria and James from the U.S., will show you great dives for a good price, and even park the boat on an island and grill fresh tuna and lapu-lapu. Be sure to let them know what kind of dive you are looking for—slow and in-depth, or quick, covering more distance and coral. Prices are P1600 (US$40) for two dives or an intro dive, and P500 (US$12) for snorkeling, including lunch and equipment rental.

**ISLAND HOPPING**    Spend a day on a pumpboat exploring El Nido's towering black limestone and marble cliffs and tiny white-sand beaches like Turtle Beach. Resorts can arrange this for you—in fact it's usually included in the price. Or try **Mac Mac's Dive Shop** in town (see above) or **El Nido Boutique,** on Palmera Street. For half-day tours, prices are about P600 (US$15) for the boat hire.

**MOUNTAIN BIKE**    Rentals are available at **El Nido Boutique** in town, for P30 (US75¢) per hour or P150 (US$3.75) per day.

## CORON

Diving is really the only reason to come to Coron, on the large island of Busuanga northeast of El Nido. The town itself is ugly and dirty, but at the bottom of the sea off its shores you can explore the hulls, masts, and decks of 14 Japanese wrecks, each with its own character and story. This, plus the chance to dive in freaky geothermal lakes (where the temperature changes every 10 feet and the different temperature layers have different colors) could mean the diving experience of a lifetime for the experienced or novice diver.

## GETTING THERE

**BY PLANE    Air Ads** (☎ 2/833-3264, 3278) and **Pacific Air** (☎ 2/812-1555, 1511) have daily flights to the tiny airport outside Coron. Expect to pay about P4,000 (US$100) round-trip. Several resorts like Club Paradise or Sangat Island Reserve offer airport transfers. Otherwise, you can take a jeepney for the 45-minute trip to Coron town for about P75 (US$1.87). If you're coming from El Nido you can charter a flight (around P4,400, or US$110, per person one way) by inquiring at "The White House" in El Nido town (see "Getting There" under El Nido, above).

## ACCOMMODATIONS

**Club Paradise.** Dimakya Island. Bookings: Celery Rd., FTI Complex, Taguig, Manila, ☎ **2/838-4956** to 63. Fax 2/838-4422. E-mail: clubpara@pworld.net.ph. 40 units. P6,000–P10,000 (US$150–US$250) native cottage. Includes all meals, an introductory dive, and full use of all the sports facilities. AE, DC, MC, V.

Located on Dimakya Island, about an hour and a half north of Coron, Club Paradise is a good choice if you are action-seeking but not just concentrating on diving. The native-style nipa huts are comfortable, with verandas and tiled bathrooms. They're tucked within tall palm trees that frame a shallow cove, which is ideal for swimming. There are a nice seaside lounge, pool, game room, and tennis court. For the water enthusiast there are fishing, diving, snorkeling, and island-hopping tours. The resort offers competitive packages during the low season.

**Sangat Island Reserve.** Sangat Island, Coron Bay, North Palawan. Manila booking, ☎ **2/526-1295.** Fax 2/525-8041. 8 units. Diver package: P4,000 (US$100) deluxe cottage, all meals, and 2 dives per day; non-diver package: P2,800 (US$70) per day with all meals. No credit cards.

This beautiful family-owned resort has the best location if you are planning to dive the wrecks, most of which are only a few minutes' boat ride away. Sangat Island has long been a traditional hunting ground for the Tagbanua tribe. It was recently declared a wildlife reserve, and the surrounding waters a marine sanctuary. Your stay here will be spent in a large cottage right on the beach overlooking the beautiful clear water and the distinctive rock formation that acts as the resort's centerpiece. Cottages are double occupancy, with screened windows and a huge closet area—perfect for storing bags and diving equipment. Bathrooms have everything but hot water. All furnishings are made locally by the Tagbanua people. In fact, the entire resort blends into the surrounding wilderness, creating a natural, peaceful mood. There isn't much else to do here but dive or take a breezy, easy stroll among the papaya, mango, or banana trees. The delicious meals are served buffet style and are made from island-grown ingredients.

## DIVING

All the dive shops in town specialize in the wrecks. But you are sure to have the best time with Mike and Chris, the proprietors of the newly opened **ScubaVenture Dive Shop** (no phone). They are very knowledgeable and good at explaining the characteristics of each wreck and the best way to explore them. You can even see detailed pictures and layouts of the wrecks on their Web page. (It's not live yet, but they will gladly show you what they have so far.) The shop is a great place to hang out. It looks more like a trendy cafe than a dive shop, and for entertainment you can watch evening movies on their hi-tech audiovideo system or enjoy a free round of drinks at the bar. Prices are fixed among all the dive shops at P1,500 (US$37.50) for two dives. Other dive shops in the area are **Dive Right** (☎ 45/892-0332; fax 63 2/526-6065) and **Discovery Divers** (no phone; fax ☎ 2/922-9750).

# Difficult Destinations: Cambodia & Myanmar (Burma)

**12**

In preparing this guide, we were confronted with problematic political realities in Cambodia and Myanmar—realities that made us question the advisability of sending readers there. These questions were only compounded when an author originally assigned to write coverage of Myanmar found that the country's borders had essentially been closed following the conviction of a group of Americans for pro-democracy actions in late 1998.

For this reason, we present this chapter, which will introduce you to these two troubled countries, provide some background on their histories, cultures, and political situations, and suggest resources and tour operators the intrepid traveler can contact for aid in planning a trip.

## 1 Cambodia

*By Stacy Lu*

Once upon a time, almost two millennia ago, a powerful people known as the Khmer ruled over much of present day Southeast Asia, including parts of what is now eastern Thailand, southern Vietnam, and Laos. Theirs was a kingdom that seems to have been created in a dream, full of wondrous temples, magnificent cities rising from steamy jungles, and glorious gods.

After fighting many wars of attrition through the ages, however, the Khmer kingdom's size was chiseled away considerably. Remaining is what we know today as Cambodia, a tiny land half the size of Germany.

And the name Cambodia hardly evokes thoughts of ancient glories. To those of us born in the late 20th century, especially in the West, Cambodia suggests instead a history of oppression, civil war, genocide, drug running, and coups d'etat, the most recent in July of 1997. Constant political turbulence and the presence of gun-toting rebels, bandits, land mines, and unexploded bombs have given the country a reputation as one of the world's most dangerous places to travel, rather than a repository of man-made and natural wonders.

Yet Cambodia's beauty and history are still there to be explored. First and foremost there is **Angkor Wat,** a monumental Hindu temple breathtaking both in its beauty and historical significance. It is but a part of the former lost city of Angkor, which tells the story of a civilization in its crumbling roads, buildings, and ornate bas-reliefs that decorate hundreds of feet of crumbling temple walls. There is **Phnom Penh,** the capital, tatty but charming, with crumbling French colonial architecture and a splendid palace.

Cambodia is also resplendent with natural gifts; the **Mekong River** winds its way down from Laos to almost bisect the country vertically. Its **Tonle Sap,** or Great Lake, is Southeast Asia's largest lake and is surrounded by fertile lowlands. White-sand beaches line its southwest coast.

The Cambodian people of today have their own rich culture. Eight-five percent of the population is Khmer, with the remaining 15% Vietnamese and Chinese. Oddly, given their horrific history, Cambodians are strongly religious; 95% of the population of 11.5 million are Theravadan Buddhists, Buddhism having taken over as the country's dominant religion at the beginning of the 13th century. (A Hindu-Buddhist mix predominated previously.)

At this writing, it looks as if Cambodia's assets may finally be able to get their due attention. Since the formation of a new coalition government in November of 1998, relative peace has descended. Tour groups are coming back, as are independent travelers, though both usually follow a circumscribed itinerary.

While Cambodia is not yet risk-free and a trip will entail following safety precautions to the letter (see below), this land's marvels will be well worth your effort.

## A TURBULENT POLITICAL PAST

Cambodia has been populated by people of the Mon-Khmer ethnic group, who probably migrated from the north as far back as 1,000 B.C. It was part of the kingdom of Funan, a Southeast Asian empire that also extended into Laos and Vietnam, to the sixth century, when it was briefly absorbed into a rebel nation called Chenla. It then evolved into its glorious Angkorian period in the eighth century, from which sprung many of Cambodia's treasures, most notably the lost city of Angkor.

By the late 12th century, however, the Angkor kingdom began a decline, marked by internal rebellions and culminating in a loss to the Kingdom of Siam in 1431. Vietnam jousted with Siam and also had a hand in controlling the kingdom to some degree beginning in the early 17th century. The French took over completely in 1863, followed by Japanese, then the French again. Cambodia finally regained independence in 1953 under the leadership of **Prince Norodom Sihanouk.**

Vietnamese communist outposts in the country, however, drew the country into the Vietnam War, and it was heavily bombed by American forces in the late 1960s. A U.S.-backed military coup followed in 1970, but in 1975 the infamous **Khmer Rouge,** led by the tyrannical Pol Pot, took over Cambodia, renamed it Kampuchea, and established a totalitarian regime in the name of communism. Opposition—even imaginary opposition—was brutally crushed, resulting in the death of over two million Cambodians. The civil and Vietnam wars decimated Cambodian infrastructure. It became, and still is, one of the world's poorest nations, with a mainly agrarian economy and a literacy rate of about 35%.

In response to Khmer Rouge infractions in its country, Vietnam invaded Cambodia in 1978 and occupied it with a small number of troops until 1989, installing a puppet regime led by Hun Sen as prime minister. When Vietnam departed, the United Nations stepped in and engineered a fragile coalition government between the Sihanouk and Hun Sen factions. There was never full agreement, however, and Hun Sen took over in a violent 1997 coup. The Khmer Rouge subsequently waned in power and its former leader, Pol Pot, died in 1998.

In November of 1998, as this book was written, a new coalition government was formed leading to relative political peace. Cambodia is now leaning toward war crimes

trials for Khmer Rouge perpetrators, but it still has not decided how to confront its vicious and bloody past and move forward.

## ATTRACTIONS

Except for hard-core independent travelers, most people come to Cambodia to see the ruins of the ancient city of **Angkor,** capital of the Khmer kingdom from 802 until 1295, and its several historical and wondrous temple complexes. Four days there will suffice (though many do it in fewer), with perhaps 2 or 3 days in the capital, **Phnom Penh.** There are comfortable and even fine accommodations in both the capital and **Siem Reap,** the city closest to Angkor.

### ANGKOR WAT

A sandstone and laterite temple complex, Angkor Wat is one of the world's marvels, the largest religious monument ever constructed. Unknown to the world until French naturalist Henri Mahout discovered it in 1861 by literally stumbling over it, the area of Angkor existed for centuries only as a myth—a wondrous city (or cities to be exact), its exact location in the Cambodian jungle unknown.

The wat is a central tower surrounded by four smaller towers, standing in a rectangle of about 2,800 by 3,800 feet (850 by 1,000 meters) and surrounded by a moat. Built under King Suryavarman II in the 12th century, these spectral towers seem to rise from the earth's undergrowth, and are a magnificent celebration of Hinduism and of the god Vishnu. Angkor Wat is decorated by the longest bas-relief in the world, carvings depicting the customs and culture of the Khmer people, Hindu epics like the

*Ramayana,* and the life of King Suryavarman. The mesmerizing figures are fashioned in a bold, curvaceous style, the figures seeming to leap off the stone wall.

There is still more in the Angkor complex, which covers 60 square miles and carries the remains of passageways, moats, temples, and palaces that represent centuries of building in the capital. **Angkor Thom,** which means "the great city" in Khmer, is famed for its fantastic 148-foot (45m) central temple, **Bayon.** A Buddhist temple built under a later king, Jayavarman VII, the Bayon nevertheless follows the Hindu cosmology concept of architecture as a metaphor for the natural world. It has four huge stone faces, with one facing out, keeping watch, at each compass point. Bayon is also surrounded by two long walls with bas-relief scenes of legendary and historical events, probably painted and gilded originally. There are fifty-one smaller towers surrounding Bayon, each with four faces of its own.

## PHNOM PENH

Phnom Penh is a town with a lengthy history, having been founded in the mid-14th century by the Khmers as a monastery and replacing Angkor Thom a century later as the country's capital. It is historically and currently a port city at the confluence of three rivers: the Mekong, Tonle Sap, and Bassac. Perhaps the city's most momentous moment was actually when it lay vacant: Following an eviction order from Pol Pot, almost all of Phnom Penh's residents moved to the countryside in 1975, to return under the authority of Vietnamese troops in 1979.

Today, Phnom Penh's 1.4 million people live in a world of semi-chaos. Prostitution, drugs, and banditry of all sorts proliferate, incongruous among the motorbikes, rickshaws, and remnants of French colonial structures. As well as soaking up the local color, as it were, you'll actually find much to see of historic interest in Phnom Penh. Its **Royal Palace** is a stone showpiece of classical Khmer architecture, decorated with bold, curvaceous motifs including the *garuda,* a mythic Hindu bird. The **Silver Pagoda** on the palace grounds, its floors covered with 5,000 blocks of silver weighing more than 6 tons, is another fascinating attraction. It houses a 17th-century Buddha made of Baccarat crystal, and another made almost entirely of gold and decorated with almost 10,000 diamonds.

Throughout the city you'll see the faded glory of aged **French colonial architecture.** There are also four notable *wats,* religious temples with resident monks.

Of more grisly interest is the Tuol Sleng, or **Museum of Genocide,** a schoolhouse-turned-prison where up to 20,000 victims of Pol Pot's excesses were tortured before being led to the Cheoung Ek, otherwise known as the killing fields, about 10 miles from Phnom Penh. There is a glass tower memorial on the spot, erected in 1988 and filled with tens of thousands of skulls arranged by age and sex.

## PLANNING A TRIP TO CAMBODIA
### VISITOR INFORMATION

You'll find a wealth of information (government-approved but of undetermined origin) at **www.cambodia-web.net.** A privately run information site offers excellent background information at **www.cambodia.org.** The Cambodian embassy to the U.S. sponsors **www.embassy.org/cambodia.** Area specialist **Diethelm Travel** also does a good job at **www.diethelm-travel.com** or **www.asiatour.com.**

### ENTRY REQUIREMENTS

All visitors are required to carry a passport and visa. A 1-month visa can be had at the Phnom Penh or Siem Reap airports for US$20. Bring two passport photos for your application.

## CAMBODIAN EMBASSY LOCATIONS

**In the U.S.:** 4500 16th St. NW, Washington, D.C. 20011 (☎ **202/726-7742;** fax 202/726-8381).

**In Australia:** no. 5 Canterbury CR, Deankin, ACT 2600, Canberra (☎ **61-6/273-1259**).

**In France:** no. 4, Rue Adolphe Yvon 75016, Paris (☎ **33-1/4503-4720;** fax 4503-4740).

## SAFETY

At the time this was written, the U.S. Department of State (DOS) had removed Cambodia from its list of countries Americans should avoid. Check with the proper authorities in your home country before your departure, however.

**GENERAL SAFETY**    The days of the Khmer Rouge taking backpackers hostage have passed. Today, general lawlessness poses the biggest threat to visitors and locals alike. **Banditry** is rampant in rural areas and in Phnom Penh after dark, with tourists an easy target for mugging and purse snatching. While some travelers report seeing or hearing nothing at all untoward, others tell tales of children roaming the streets of the capital with submachine guns.

**DRUGS**    As Cambodia is one of the world's biggest producers of cannabis—not to mention heroin, amphetamines, and other substances—petty producers abound, as do petty skirmishes. You may be tempted to buy or sample substances offered, but if caught you may face a lengthy jail sentence, which is guaranteed to be uncomfortable. Also, you'll want to be in full control of your faculties here at all times, and to avoid the unsavory characters who conduct such business.

**MEDICAL SAFETY & EVACUATION INSURANCE**    A word here about the Cambodian medical system, which is rudimentary at best and nonexistent at worst. Make sure that you have medical coverage for overseas travel, and that it includes emergency evacuation. For details on purchasing insurance, see chapter 3.

**SAFETY TIPS**    Now that you're properly frightened, here's the good news: The tourism route here is very well developed, and operators know exactly when and where to go. Follow their instructions. If you're going it alone, below are some straightforward safety measures recommended by the DOS that should lead to a trouble-free visit:

- Sporadic political violence is not uncommon, so avoid political gatherings or demonstrations, and avoid the vicinity of government buildings, which may betray themselves by the presence of armed guards.
- Travel only by air or hydrofoil to Siem Reap, avoiding regular boats and speedboats, which rarely take safety precautions. Once in Siem Reap, stay in the city or near the temple complexes.
- Stay inside after dark in Phnom Penh.
- If you're traveling by road outside of urban areas, go only between the hours of 8am and 4pm.
- Land mines and unexploded ordnance can be found in rural areas in Cambodia, but especially in Battambang, Banteay Meanchey, Pursat, Siem Reap, and Kampong Thom provinces. If by some chance you find yourself in these areas, don't walk in heavily forested spots or in dry rice paddies without a local guide. Areas around small bridges on secondary roads are particularly dangerous.

**FOREIGN EMBASSIES IN CAMBODIA**    Should you encounter problems during your visit, go to your embassy. Addresses for embassies in Phnom Penh: **U.S.,**

no. 27 EO Street 240 (☎ **023/426-436** or 023/426-438; fax 023/426-437); **Canada,** Villa 9, Senei Vinnavaut Oum (☎ **023/426-001;** fax 023/211-389); **Australia** (also serves New Zealanders), Villa 9-11, Street 254 (☎ **023/426-002;** fax 023/426-003); and **U.K.,** no. 26 Street 75, (☎ **023/427-124** or 023/427-125).

## GETTING THERE
### WORKING WITH A TOUR OPERATOR

There are at least three good reasons to go to Cambodia on a guided tour with an experienced operator: (1) your itinerary is likely not to be adventurous; (2) without a guide, you'd miss the finer details of what you're seeing (unless you're an expert on Cambodian history); (3) going with a group is safer. Even if you travel independently, you may want to sign up with a local tour operator (like Diethelm, below) once you're there.

A few well-known tour operators:

- **The Global Spectrum.** 1901 Pennsylvania Ave. NW, Washington, DC 20006 (☎ **800/419-4446** or 202/293-2065; fax 202/296-0815; e-mail: gspectrum@ idsonline.com).

- **Latitudes, Expeditions East.** 870 Market St., Suite 482 San Francisco, CA 94102 (☎ **800/580-4883** or 415/398-0458; fax 415/680-1522; e-mail info@ weblatitudes.com).

- **Himalayan Travel, Inc.** 110 Prospect St., Stamford, CT (☎ **800/225-2380;** fax 203/359-3669; e-mail worldadv@netaxis.com).

- **Mountain Travel-Sobek.** 6420 Fairmount Ave., El Cerrito, CA 94530. (☎ **888/687-6235** or 510/527-8100; fax 510-525-7710; e-mail info@mtsobek. com). Australian Sales Office ☎ 02/9264-5710; fax 02/9267-3074. E-mail adventure@africatravel.com.au. European Sales Office ☎ 44-1-49/444-8901; fax 44-1-49/446-5526; e-mail sales@mtsobekeu.com; Web site www.mtsobek. com/.

- ✪ **Intrepid Small Group Adventures.** P.O. Box 2781, Fitzroy, D.C. Victoria, Australia (☎ **3/9743-2626;** fax 3/9419-4426; e-mail info@intrepidtravel.com.au. www.intrepidtravel.com.au/). Highly recommended.

- **Diethelm Travel,** No. 65, Street 240, P.O. Box 99, Phnom Penh, Cambodia (☎ **23/219-151;** fax 23/219-150; e-mail: dtc@gncomtext.com). In Siem Reap: House No. 4, Road No. 6, Krum no. 1, Sangkat no. 2, Phum Taphul, Siem Reap, Cambodia (☎ 63/963-524; fax 63/963-694). In Bangkok: 140/1 Wireless Rd., Kian Gwan Building 2, Bangkok 10330, Thailand (☎ 66-2/255-9150; fax 66-2/256-0248; e-mail: dto@dto.co.th).

### GETTING THERE INDEPENDENTLY

If you choose to travel to Cambodia independently, by all means go by plane for maximum safety. You are almost guaranteed to connect in Bangkok. From there, you can currently fly to Phnom Penh or directly to Siem Reap, though there are rumors that the government will discontinue the latter to promote tourism to the capital.

## 2 Myanmar (Burma)

*By George Spelvin*

Consider the travel pioneers of the 19th and early 20th century. Boarding steamships instead of planes, these men and women pushed the limits of comfort in exchange for the romance of destinations little known to the rest of the world. They wanted to be inspired by people with ways of life untouched by the hands of modern ruin. They wanted to be charmed by mysterious customs and awed by magnificent sights. Some sought escape from civilization. Some desired thrilling adventures in dangerous lands. Others went in search of spiritual answers. Many went simply because no person—at least of their nationality—had been there before.

Nowadays such experiences are becoming increasingly difficult to find. The entire world has been mapped, and many previously unspoiled destinations now disappoint travelers who show up to find Coca-Cola billboards being erected near picturesque beaches, or local people trading colorful traditional attire for American Levi's. Mystical oriental harbors have been replaced by steel and glass cityscapes. And for the real traveler, nothing can shatter an experience like the arrival of a busload of gawking tourists.

Not so in Myanmar (formerly Burma), which seduces travelers with the promise of adventure and beauty unspoiled by the trampling hordes of Western feet. Yangon (Rangoon), the nation's capital, still resembles a postcard from the 1950s. Ancient and serene temples rise from the morning mist, uncluttered by souvenir tents and idling tour buses. Local people still stop and gaze curiously at strangers passing through. Adventure lurks in the forests and hills.

Unfortunately, the preservation of this pristine portrait has cost the Burmese people dearly. Since 1962, Myanmar has been under the strangling grip of a military junta whose "Burmese Way of Socialism" closed the country to the outside world and ground its economy to near collapse. The Burmese people struggle to survive amidst poverty, political oppression, and revolutionary violence.

So what's an interested traveler to do? On one side, the State Law and Order Restoration Council (SLORC), the ruling elite, opens its arms to foreign visitors, luring them with smiles and welcoming them to spend foreign money—money it hopes will help mask the problems of a nation it has so sadly neglected. On the other side, nongovernmental organizations that support Myanmar's pro-democracy movement are raising the call to world travelers, urging them to avoid travel to Myanmar and thus prevent the SLORC from obtaining the hard currency and global legitimacy it needs to survive.

If you yearn for an adventurous travel experience, Myanmar can satisfy your expectations. With the proper preparations, you can enjoy this hidden corner of the world with relative security, and with current and accurate information you can minimize your contributions to the damages caused by the current regime. Please travel wisely.

## BURMA YESTERDAY, MYANMAR TODAY

Myanmar sits in the northwest corner of Southeast Asia, sharing borders with Thailand, Laos, China, Tibet, India, and Bangladesh. The northern regions rise and plunge with the foothills of the Himalaya mountain range. It is here that streams originate, converging in low-lying plains to form the Ayeyarwady (Irrawaddy) River. The river bisects the country before branching out into deltas, flowing southward through Myanmar's tropical southern landscape to the Andaman Sea.

The people are divided into over 67 unique ethnic groups. Descended from people who migrated in waves from central Asia, Tibet, and southern China, the many races that developed over the centuries battled each other constantly, and in some cases still do so today. The majority of the population is **Bamar,** the race of the ruling elite. Most of the other races are divisions of hill tribe peoples who share similar cultures with the people of northern Thailand and Southern China.

**Theravada Buddhism** is the country's ruling religion, having drifted to the country from its origins in Sri Lanka. Prior to Buddhism, the people of Burma practiced as many different forms of animism—the worship of spirit and nature gods—as there were tribes. Today, although a profound majority of the population is Buddhist, animism is still alive and well in the northern regions.

Buddhism's influence has a far-reaching influence on the people of Myanmar. Theravada, the most orthodox of Buddhist tracts, follows strictly the teachings of the Lord Buddha. Many men and boys enter the monkhood (if only for a short time); life is conservative; and the artistic tradition of Sri Lankan Buddhism abounds, from Myanmar's many breathtaking temples to a multitude of fascinating Buddha images.

Myanmar is rich in natural resources, including rubies and other gemstones mined in the north, and teak trees, desirable for their fine hardwood lumber. Its fertile soils yield bountiful rice crops, but unfortunately, Myanmar's biggest claim to agricultural fame is the opium poppy. Hill tribe farmers in the north depend on poppies for survival, as their sale brings more money than other subsistence crops. Farmers sell the crops to manufacturers who produce and distribute the opium and heroin derivatives globally. Much of the true wealth gained by the sale is diverted to tribal rebel groups for the purchase of weapons in the fight for independence from Myanmar's ruling military junta.

## HISTORY & POLITICAL TURBULENCE

Prior to the Anglo-Burmese wars, which ended in 1886, Burma had been a monarchy since the 11th century. British colonialism put the country on the world map, but failed to protect it from the invading Japanese in World War II. In 1946, following the Japanese surrender, Burma became an independent state, and a fledgling democracy began under the courageous leadership of **Aung San,** an independence hero who was able to unite Burma's many ethnic groups to form a single nation. Unfortunately, the following year, Aung San was killed in a coup. To this day, he remains a national hero, his image plastered on almost every wall in the country.

The following 15 years were wrought with domestic chaos until General Ne Win took hold of the reins. He filled government positions with high-ranking military officials, which gave rise to the all-powerful Revolutionary Council. Under a socialist decree, privatization was banished, the military ruled all affairs (including those social and economic), and the country was virtually closed to the outside world.

Since then, there have been many challenges to Ne Win's government, most of which were initiated by the country's many different ethnic minority groups. The most threatening challenge came in 1988, following a brief and rare period of relative political openness, when people began to collect and speak openly about their human rights and democracy. In September of that year, the army retaliated with a brutal sweep, killing as many as 10,000 people. It was this massacre that drove the government to form the **State Law and Order Restoration Council (SLORC),** and inspired a young intellectual, **Aung San Suu Kyi,** daughter of independence leader Aung San, to become head of the opposition party, the pro-democracy National League for Democracy (NLD).

General elections were held in 1990, and despite the political imprisonment of Ms. Suu Kyi, the NLD won 82% of the votes. The SLORC chose to ignore the expressed wishes of the Burmese people and remained in power, imprisoning many NLD figures.

Today, Ms. Suu Kyi remains under house arrest in Myanmar's capital. She is recognized globally as the voice of democracy for the people of Burma, who suffer under strict SLORC oppression policies. In early 1999 the International Labour Organization (ILO) pointed a finger at the SLORC as a leading abuser of basic labor rights, and shortly after, a report to the United Nations Human Rights Commission (UNHCR) stated that human rights violations were on the rise, with the government

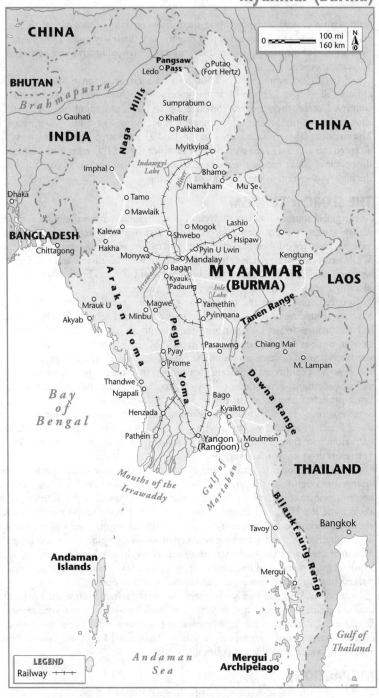

# Myanmar (Burma)

CHINA

BHUTAN

*Brahmaputra*

Naga Hills

Pangsaw Pass
Ledo

Putao (Fort Hertz)

Sumprabum

Gauhati

Khafitr
Pakkhan

INDIA

CHINA

Myitkyina

Imphal

*Indawgyi Lake*

Bhamo

Namkham
Mu Se

Dhaka

Tamo

Mawlaik

*River*

Lashio

Kalewa

Mogok

Shwebo

Hsipaw

BANGLADESH

Hakha

Pyin U Lwin

Chittagong

Monywa

Mandalay

Kengtung

LAOS

Bagan

MYANMAR
(BURMA)

Kyauk-
Padaung

Mrauk U

Magwe

*Inle Lake*

Tanen Range

Arakan Yoma

Minbu

Yamethin

Akyab

Pyinmana

*Irrawaddy*

Chiang Mai

M. Lampan

Pegu Yoma

Pasauwng

*Bay
of
Bengal*

Pyay

Prome

Dawna Range

Thandwe

Ngapali

Bago

Henzada

Kyaikto

Pathein

Yangon
(Rangoon)

Moulmein

THAILAND

*Mouths of the
Irrawaddy*

*Gulf of
Martaban*

Bilauktaung Range

Tavoy

Bangkok

Andaman
Islands

Mergui

*Gulf of
Thailand*

*Andaman
Sea*

Mergui
Archipelago

0   100 mi
    160 km

N

intimidating citizens and preventing them from exercising fundamental rights. An exiled opposition group has stated that recently in a single day up to 270 citizens had been accused of threatening national security and sentenced to anywhere between 7 to 52 years in prison.

In March 1999, when Aung San Suu Kyi's husband, Englishman Michael Aris, fell critically ill with cancer, the Myanmar government refused him a visa to enter the country. Instead, they tried to convince her to leave, promising her that she'd be allowed to return. In fear of permanent exile, Aung San Suu Syi remained in Myanmar, and her husband died in England shortly after. The global press has accepted this as proof of the cruel manner in which the SLORC regards its people, and the people of Myanmar see the incident as yet another reason to hold Ms. Suu Kyi in the highest of esteem as the true soul of the nation.

## THE SLORC & TOURISM

As the global tourism industry grows and grows, leading some economists to predict it may one day account for the largest global exchange of currency, many countries have begun to regard their history, nature, and culture as valuable sources of revenue. While many Southeast Asian nations have bought into this theory, and consequently welcome over a million travelers annually, Myanmar has yet to break 100,000 visitors in a single year—a fact that frustrates the government.

To encourage tourism and increase the government's military power, the SLORC has been rebuilding its infrastructure, primarily roads and railways. But because they lack the finances to pay for labor costs, the government has conscripted Burmese citizens to work as forced labor. Reports in the BBC have described Myanmar as "one vast labour camp," a description that the *New York Times, Daily Telegraph,* and *Financial Times* have confirmed with scenes of prisoners in chains, working under harsh and violent conditions, many times collapsing from beatings and heat exhaustion. Such labor projects increased dramatically when the SLORC declared 1996 as "Visit Myanmar Year." The BBC reported cruel labor practices during the restoration of the Royal Palace in Mandalay in preparation for 1996. A northern Burmese stated, "Ten years from now Burma won't be the same. It'll only be for the army and tourists. . . . Foreigners don't know what we're going through for this tourism year."

The SLORC hopes to attract foreign money through high-priced package tours arranged through foreign operators. The foreign operators seem legitimate enough; however, nongovernmental organizations such as the Open Society Institute's Burma Project and the UK-based Burma Action Group state that the government receives enormous kickbacks for such tour operations. All tours are planned with the blessing of the government, and stick to main corridors—giving visitors only the image of Myanmar the government wants them to see. A few luxury hotels provide modern comforts for travelers, and more are popping up each day. Naturally, the government pockets huge sums for allowing these upmarket hotels to operate.

In response, Aung San Suu Kyi has urged tourists to refrain from visiting Myanmar until a legitimate government has been established. The international community of Burmese pro-democracy nongovernmental organizations work tirelessly to educate potential tourists of the horrors of the current regime and how their visits will only support it, both financially and politically.

## ATTRACTIONS

Despite international concern regarding tourism, many will chose to visit Myanmar, and understandably so. With little debate, it is a country of astounding beauty, the most famous and exquisite sight being the **Shwedagon Pagoda** in Yangon. The construction of the pagoda remains a mystery, hidden in many local legends; however, recorded history suggests it predates the 11th century. The huge Sri Lankan–influenced, bell-shaped pagoda rises above the cityscape, a vision of glistening gold—8,688 precious solid gold plates, bejeweled in a huge fortune of diamonds, rubies, sapphires, and other gems. Inside, the stupa enshrines eight hairs from the Lord Buddha; outside, within the temple walls, is a small city of pagodas, temples, shrines, and astrological pillars.

Yangon also retains the charm of an exotic British outpost. A walk down city streets is a sensory assault of exotic city planning, with tropical colonial architecture interlaced with Burmese temples, markets, and shops.

And then there's **Bagan,** a riverside city containing over two thousand pagodas, located up the Ayeyerwady just south of Mandalay. Rivaling Cambodia's Angkor Wat, these 11th-century temples stretch as far as the eye can see, and are a stunning image of ancient Buddhist expression and a testimony to the wealth of a once mighty kingdom.

Just north of Bagan, **Mandalay** is the most visited city in Myanmar next to Yangon. The main attraction is the **Royal Palace,** a perfect square enclosed in walls over 2 kilometers in length on each side. Surrounded by a moat, the walled palace is open to the public through special guided tours that visit only the Lion's Room, where the royal throne was located, and the palace museum.

# PLANNING A TRIP TO MYANMAR
## VISITOR INFORMATION

While the government has no agency to handle tourism promotion, limited information on tour operators and attractions is available through Myanmar consulates worldwide. While planned tours are unarguably the most convenient way to see Myanmar, nongovernmental organizations are suggesting a "backpacker" route for those who are really interested in seeing "the true Burma." They urge foreign visitors to patronize family-run guest houses and restaurants, and use transportation that supports local people to ensure that your money stays out of the hands of the government and finds its way to the people who truly need it.

The best place to start is by contacting the **Burma Action Group** at Collins Studios, Collins Yard, Islington Green, London N1 2XU (☎ **71/359-7679,** fax 71/354-3987). They produce a booklet, *Burma: The Alternative Guide,* which provides a detailed account of why you should *not* visit Myanmar, but they can also give you practical advice for planning your journey. The Burma Project at the **Open Society Institute,** 400 W. 59th St., 4th Fl., New York, NY 10019 (☎ **212/548-0632;** fax 212/548-4655; www.soros.org/burma), can also provide information that will be useful in planning your trip, such as suggested places to stay and visit and safety issues that may prevent you from being harassed by government bureaucrats (the number-one complaint of visitors to Myanmar), or from wandering into dangerous regions.

## ENTRY REQUIREMENTS

Myanmar consulates issue visas for stays of up to 4 weeks. Be warned: They may refuse your application if they suspect you represent a media firm or a pro-democracy or human rights organization. Look like a tourist.

## MYANMAR EMBASSY LOCATIONS

**In the U.S.:** Myanmar Embassy, 2300 S St. NW, Washington, D.C. 20008 (☎ **202/332-9045**); Permanent Mission of Myanmar to the United Nations, 10 E. 77th St., New York, NY 10021 (☎ **212/535-1310**).

**In the U.K.:** 19A Charles St., London W1X 8ER (☎ **0171/629-6966**).

**In Australia:** 22 Arkana St., Yarralumla, Canberra A.C.T. 2600 (☎ **6102/627-33811**).

**In Canada:** 85 Range Rd., Suite 902–903, Sandringhan, Ottawa, Ontario (☎ **613/232-6434**).

There is no Myanmar representation in New Zealand.

## SAFETY

It is highly recommended that you check with your home country's overseas travel departments or with the United States Department of State to be warned of travel advisories and current affairs that may affect your trip.

**FOREIGN EMBASSIES IN MYANMAR**   Many countries will strongly urge that you keep in touch with your native consulate within Myanmar upon arrival and throughout your stay. In the event of an emergency, you'll be thankful that they have your travel itinerary on hand. International representatives in Myanmar are as follows: **U.S.,** 581 Merchant Rd. (☎ 951/282-055); **U.K.,** 80 Strand Rd. (☎ 951/295-300); **Australia,** 88 Strand Rd. (☎ **951/251-797**). There is no presence for New Zealand or Canada in Myanmar at this time.

**MEDICAL SAFETY & EVACUATION INSURANCE**   It is highly recommended that you obtain emergency evacuation insurance coverage for the length of your stay, in addition to your health insurance policy. A good evac plan will get you out of the country in situations that pose political danger, will help you secure adequate legal assistance should you be unfortunate enough to need it, and will transport you to the nearest reputable medical facility in the event of a health emergency.

## GETTING THERE & GETTING AROUND

Travelers will almost always enter Myanmar by plane, most likely in Yangon via Bangkok, or Mandalay via Chiang Mai in northern Thailand. Upon arrival, you will be required to purchase no less than US$300 worth of local currency—a great trick on the government's part to make sure you spend.

Once in Myanmar, public transportation between cities is conveniently provided by the Singapore-backed Air Mandalay, which operates between most major cities, and a rail system that will take you from Yangon to Mandalay and beyond. Buses ply between cities, as well as riverboats for stunning tours of the Ayeyerwady and its sights.

There are a few luxury hotels in Yangon, most notably **The Strand Hotel,** 92 Strand Rd. (☎ **951/243-377,** fax 951/289-880). Built at the turn of the century, the Strand is a gorgeous monument to British colonial opulence, and the only really elegant address in the country. Mandalay and Bagan also have tourist class hotels with modern comforts.

# Appendix: Airlines Serving Southeast Asia

**Air Canada**   800/776-3000 in the U.S.; 800/555-1212 in Canada for local number; www.aircanada.ca

**Air France**   800/237-2747 in the U.S.; 514/847-1106 in Canada; 0181/742-6600 in the U.K.; 02/9321-1000 in Australia; 068/725-8800 in New Zealand; www.airfrance.com

**A. Soriano Aviation**   2/834-0371 in the Philippines

**Air New Zealand**   800/262-1234 in the U.S.; 800/663-5494 in English and 800/799-5494 in French in Canada; 0181/600-7600 in the U.K.; 0800/737000 in New Zealand; 13 2476 in Australia; www.airnewzealand.co.nz

**Air Niugini**   612/92901544 in Australia

**Air Philippines**   2/843-7770 in the Philippines

**Air Ads Inc**.   2/833-3264 or 2/833-3278 in the Philippines

**All Nippon Airways**   800/235-9262 in the U.S. and Canada

**American Airlines**   800/433-7300 in the U.S.; www.americanair.com

**Asian Spirit**   2/840-3811 in the Philippines

**British Airways**   800/247-9297 in the U.S. and Canada; 0345/222111 in the U.K.; 02/9258-3300 in Australia; 09/366-3200 in New Zealand; www.british-airways.com

**Canadian Airlines International**   800/665-1177 in Canada and the U.S.; 1300/655767 in Australia; www.cdnair.com

**Cathay Pacific**   800/233-2742 in the U.S.; 0171/747-8888 in the U.K.; 131747 in Australia; www.cathaypacific.com

**Cebu Pacific**   2/636-4938 in the Philippines

**China Airlines**   800/227-5118 in the U.S.; www.china-airlines.com

**Continental**   800/231-0856 or 800/525-0280 in the U.S.; 800/776-464 in the U.K.; www.continental.com

**EVA Air**   800/695-1188 in the U.S.; 44/171-3808300 in the U.K.; 61/2-221-7055 in Australia; 64/9-358-2885 in New Zealand

**Grand Air**   2/833-8080 or 2/833-8090 in the Philippines

**Japan Airlines**   800/525-3663 in the U.S.; www.japanair.com

**KLM Royal Dutch Airlines**   800/374-7747 in the U.S.; 514/939-4040 in Canada (Montreal) or 416/204-5100 (Toronto); 0990/750-9900 in the U.K.; 02/9231-6333 in Australia; 09/309-1782 in New Zealand; www. klm.nl

**Korean Air**   671/649-3301 in Korea; 800/438-5000 in the U.S.

**Malaysia Airlines**   800/552-9264 in the U.S. and Canada; 0171/341-2020 in the U.K; 02/132627 in Australia; 09/373-2741 in New Zealand; 65/336-6777 in Malaysia; www.malaysaiair.com

**Northwest Airlines**   800/447-4747 or 800/225-2525 in the U.S.; 0990-561000 in the U.K.; 008-221-714 in Australia; www.nwa.com

**Orient Express**   053/818092 in Chiang Mai, Thailand; 079/200071 in Surat Thani, Thailand

**Pacific Air**   2/812-1555 or 2/812-1511 in the Philippines

**Philippine Airlines**   800/435-9725 in the U.S.; 649/379-8522 in New Zealand; 2/816-6691 in the Philippines; www.philippineair.com

**Qantas Airways Ltd.**   800/227-4500 in the U.S. and Canada; 0345/747767 in the U.K.; in Australia call 02/131313 for domestic flights and 131211 for international; 0800/808-767 in New Zealand; www.quantas.com

**Singapore Airlines**   800/742-3333 in the U.S. and Canada; 0181/7470007 in the U.K.; 131011 in Australia; in New Zealand, call 3032129 in Auckland and 3368003 in Christchurch; www.singaporeair.com

**Thai Airways International**   800/426-5204 in the U.S.; 1800/651-960; 02/280-0070 in Bangkok; 65/224-2011 in New Zealand; www.thaiair.com

**United Airlines**   800/241-6522 in the U.S. and Canada; ; 131777 in Australia; www.ual.com

**Virgin Atlantic**   800/862-8621 in the U.S. and Canada; 01293/747-747 in the U.K.; 02/9352-6199 in Australia; www.fly.virgin.com

**Key to Abbreviations**

| | |
|---|---|
| BL=Bali | MC=Macau |
| BM=Burma | MA=Malaysia |
| CB=Cambodia | PH=Philippines |
| HK=Hong Kong | SP=Singapore |
| LS=Laos | TL=Thailand |
| LB=Lombok | VN=Vietnam |

Page numbers in *italics* refer to maps.

Index

Index

Index

## FROMMER'S® DOLLAR-A-DAY GUIDES

Australia from $50 a Day
California from $60 a Day
Caribbean from $70 a Day
England from $70 a Day
Europe from $60 a Day
Florida from $60 a Day

Hawaii from $70 a Day
Ireland from $50 a Day
Israel from $45 a Day
Italy from $70 a Day
London from $85 a Day
New York from $80 a Day

New Zealand from $50 a Day
Paris from $85 a Day
San Francisco from $60 a Day
Washington, D.C.,
  from $60 a Day

## FROMMER'S® PORTABLE GUIDES

Acapulco, Ixtapa &
  Zihuatanejo
Alaska Cruises & Ports of Call
Bahamas
Baja & Los Cabos
Berlin
California Wine Country
Charleston & Savannah
Chicago

Dublin
Hawaii: The Big Island
Las Vegas
London
Maine Coast
Maui
New Orleans
New York City
Paris

Puerto Vallarta, Manzanillo
  & Guadalajara
San Diego
San Francisco
Sydney
Tampa & St. Petersburg
Venice
Washington, D.C.

## FROMMER'S® NATIONAL PARK GUIDES

Family Vacations in the
  National Parks
Grand Canyon

National Parks of the
  American West
Rocky Mountain

Yellowstone & Grand Teton
Yosemite & Sequoia/
  Kings Canyon
Zion & Bryce Canyon

## FROMMER'S® GREAT OUTDOOR GUIDES

New England
Northern California

Southern California & Baja
Washington & Oregon

## FROMMER'S® MEMORABLE WALKS

Chicago
London

New York
Paris

San Francisco
Washington D.C.

## FROMMER'S® IRREVERENT GUIDES

Amsterdam
Boston
Chicago
Las Vegas

London
Los Angeles
Manhattan

New Orleans
Paris
San Francisco

Seattle & Portland
Vancouver
Walt Disney World
Washington, D.C.

## FROMMER'S® BEST-LOVED DRIVING TOURS

America
Britain
California

Florida
France
Germany

Ireland
Italy
New England

Scotland
Spain
Western Europe

# WHEREVER YOU TRAVEL, *H*ELP IS NEVER FAR AWAY.

From planning your trip to providing travel assistance along the way, American Express® Travel Service Offices are always there to help you do more.

## *Southeast Asia*

### CAMBODIA
Diethelm Travel Cambodia (R)
No. 65 Street 240
Phnom Penh
(855) (23) 219151, 911271

### INDONESIA
Pacto Ltd. Tours & Travel (R)
Galleria Nusa Dua
Shop A5, Unit 1-3-5
Bali
(62) (361) 773334

Pacto Ltd. Tours & Travel (R)
Jl. Taman Kemang II Blok D2/4
Jakarta
(62) (21) 7196550

### MALAYSIA
Mayflower/American Express Travel Service (R)
18th Floor, The Weld
Jalan Raja Chulan
Kuala Lumpur
(60) (3) 2130007

### SINGAPORE
American Express International, Inc.
300 Beach Road
The Concourse, 18/F
Singapore
(65) 2998133

### HONG KONG
American Express Travel Service
25 Kimberley Road, 1st Floor
Tsimshatsui
Kowloon
(852) 27327327

### MACAU
International Express (Exchanger) Ltd. (R)
23B Rua de St. Paulo, R/C
Macau
(853) 363262

### PHILIPPINES
Adventure International Tours Inc. (R)
1810 A. Mabini St. Malate
Manila
(63) (2) 52868406-08

### THAILAND
Sea Tours Company Ltd. (R)
Suite 88-92, 8th Floor Payatai Plaza
128 Phyathai Road, Rajthavee
Bangkok
(66) (2) 2165934-36, 2165783-93

Sea Tours Company Ltd. (R)
95/4 Phuket Road
Muang District
Phuket
(66) (76) 218417/8

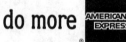

**do more** AMERICAN EXPRESS

**Travel**

www.americanexpress.com/travel

**American Express Travel Service Offices are found in central locations throughout Southeast Asia.**

Listings are valid as of July 1999. (R)=Representative Office.
Not all services available at all locations. © 1999 American Express.